Contagion and the State in Europe, 1830–1930

This book explains the historical reasons for the divergence in public health policies adopted in Britain, France, Germany and Sweden, and the spectrum of responses to the threat of contagious diseases such as cholera, smallpox and syphilis. In particular the book examines the link between politics and prevention. Did the varying political regimes influence the styles of precaution adopted? Or was it, as Peter Baldwin argues, a matter of more basic differences between nations, above all their geographic placement in the epidemiological trajectory of contagion, that helped shape their responses and their basic assumptions about the respective claims of the sick and of society, and fundamental political decisions for and against different styles of statutory intervention? Thus the book seeks to use medical history to illuminate broader questions of the development of statutory intervention and the comparative and divergent evolution of the modern state in Europe.

PETER BALDWIN is Professor of History at the University of California, Los Angeles. He is the author of *The Politics of Social Solidarity: Class Bases of the European Welfare State* (1990). His book *Disease and Democracy: The Industrialized World Faces AIDS* (University of California Press, 2005), takes the story told here into the present.

CONTAGION
AND THE STATE
IN EUROPE, 1830–1930

PETER BALDWIN

CAMBRIDGE
UNIVERSITY PRESS

CAMBRIDGE UNIVERSITY PRESS
Cambridge, New York, Melbourne, Madrid, Cape Town, Singapore, São Paulo

Cambridge University Press
The Edinburgh Building, Cambridge CB2 2RU, UK

Published in the United States of America by Cambridge University Press, New York

www.cambridge.org
Information on this title: www.cambridge.org/9780521616287

First published 1999
First paperback edition 2005

Printed in the United Kingdom at the University Press, Cambridge

A catalogue record for this book is available from the British Library

ISBN-13 978-0-521-642880 hardback
ISBN-10 0-521-642884 hardback
ISBN-13 978-0-521-616287 paperback
ISBN-10 0-521-61628X paperback

For Dagmar

Contents

Acknowledgments

The wherewithal for the archival and other peregrinations required to carry a comparative project like this to fruition, not to mention the release time from teaching obligations that made it the work of years rather than decades, I owe to many sources: the History Departments of Harvard University and UCLA, the William F. Milton Fund of the Harvard Medical School, the German Marshall Fund, the Center for German and European Studies at Berkeley, the Alexander von Humboldt Stiftung, the Council on Research of the Academic Senate and the International Studies and Overseas Programs, both of UCLA, and the National Institutes of Health.

I have also been helped by many research assistants over the years: David Durant, Laurel Davis, Andrea Kohler, Amy Sueoshi, Sara Ghafari, Sumithra Rajashekara, Gloria Saliba and above all the tireless Kristin Leaf.

For hibernation, refuge, archive-related crashing and other hospitality, I am indebted to Hildebrand Machleidt, Katharina George, Elisabeth Grosse-Venhaus, Elisabeth Lux and Frank Oehring, all of Berlin, Andrew Paulson in Paris, Julie Marriott in London, Morten Vest and Lisbeth Holten in Copenhagen, Marianne Öberg in Stockholm, Peter and Renate Stange in St. Augustin.

For readings and assistance far beyond and above the demands of residual scholarly solidarity, I am very grateful to: Christopher Hamlin, who showed how supple and nuanced one could be in thinking about public health and who will probably still be disappointed at the rough and ready categories I have brought to bear; Peter Hennock, whose interests and mine seem to travel along sufficiently parallel tracks that I have followed him over the years from one form of statutory intervention to another; Robert Jütte, who alerted me to much of the most recent German literature; Philippa Levine, who guided me around many a syphilitic pitfall, historically speaking; Lion Murard and Patrick

Zylberman, joint authors of the single most magisterial work in public health history; Roy Porter, the colossus who bestrides medical history like none other; Lutz Sauerteig, author of an excellent comparative study of VD prophylaxis in Germany; and Jan Sundin, who helped me navigate the (for outsiders) tricky shoals of Nordic social development.

Others on whom I have been able to count for much-needed advice and counsel include: John Baldwin, Jenny Jochens, Yvonne Johansson, Elizabeth Lunbeck, Peter Mandler, Charles Maier, Claus Offe, Dorothy Porter, Gerhard A. Ritter, Aron Rodrigue and Hans-Ulrich Wehler. Heiner Ganssmann graciously helped facilitate two stays in Berlin. William Davies, at Cambridge University Press, did not blanch at the prospect of yet another big book on a boring topic and for that I am thankful. Richard Weinstein was the one who mercifully made possible that rarity among dual-career academic households: a combination of work and family, sans commute. My many fellow historians at UCLA have shown me that collegiality and size, both of department and surrounding metropolis, are not necessarily at odds. For the intellectual home they have given me, I am very grateful.

It is a common lament of acknowledgments that the work involved in the opus at hand has come at the expense of the author's family, whose forgiveness is therefore sought. (How many neglected children these libraries represent!) I would like to think that my wife and I have been partners in all things, large and small, and that, rather than a tradeoff between work and family, the benefits, and not just the burdens, have been mutual. The dedication acknowledges my greatest debt in this respect.

Abbreviations

AGM	*Archives générales de médecine*
AK	Andra Kammaran
ALR	Allgemeines Landrecht für die Preussischen Staaten, 1794
Amts-Blatt	*Amts-Blatt der Königlichen Regierung zu Potsdam und der Stadt Berlin*
AN	Archives nationales
Anhang zur Gesetz-Sammlung	*Anhang zur Gesetz-Sammlung für die Königlichen Preussischen Staaten*
Annales	*Annales d'hygiène publique et de médecine légale*
ASA	*Annalen der Staatsarzneikunde*
BA	Bundesarchiv
Berichte	*Berichte der Cholera-Kommission des Deutschen Reiches* (6 Hefte, Berlin, 1875–79)
Berlinische Nachrichten	*Berlinische Nachrichten von Staats- und gelehrten Sachen*
BFMCR	*British and Foreign Medico-Chirurgical Review*
BGB	Bürgerliches Gesetzbuch
BHM	*Bulletin of the History of Medicine*
Bihang	*Bihang till [Samtlige] Riks-Ståndens Protocoll, Bihang till Riksdagens protokoll*
Bihang till Post	*Bihang till Post- och Inrikes-Tidningar*
Bilagor till Borgare	*Bilagor till Protocoll hållna hos vällofige Borgare-Ståndet*
BJVD	*British Journal of Venereal Diseases*
BMJ	*British Medical Journal*
Bonde	*Hederwärda Bonde-Ståndets Protocoller*
Borgare	*Protocoll hållna hos vällofige Borgare-Ståndet*
Bulletin	*Bulletin de l'Académie [royale] de médecine*

Cholera-Zeitung	*Cholera-Zeitung, herausgegeben von den Ärzten Königsbergs*
Cobbett's	*Cobbett's Parliamentary Debates*
Comptes rendus	*Comptes rendus des séances de l'Académie des sciences*
Conférence 1851	Ministère des affaires étrangères, *Procès-verbaux de la Conférence sanitaire internationale ouverte à Paris le 27 juillet 1851* (Paris, 1852)
Conférence 1859	Ministère des affaires étrangères, *Protocoles de la Conférence sanitaire internationale ouverte à Paris le 9 avril 1859* (Paris, 1859)
Conférence 1866	*Procès-verbaux de la Conférence sanitaire internationale ouverte à Constantinople le 13 février 1866* (Constantinople, 1866)
Conférence 1874	*Procès-verbaux de la Conférence sanitaire internationale ouverte à Vienne le 1 juillet 1874* (Vienna, 1874)
Conference 1881	*Proceedings of the International Sanitary Conference Provided for by Joint Resolution of the Senate and House of Representatives in the Early Part of 1881* (Washington, DC, 1881)
Conférence 1885	*Protocoles et procès-verbaux de la Conférence sanitaire internationale de Rome inaugurée le 20 mai 1885* (Rome, 1885)
Conférence 1892	*Protocoles et procès-verbaux de la Conférence sanitaire internationale de Venise inaugurée le 5 janvier 1892* (Rome, 1892)
Conférence 1893	*Protocoles et procès-verbaux de la Conférence sanitaire internationale de Dresde 11 mars–15 avril 1893* (Dresden, 1893)
Conférence 1894	*Conférence sanitaire internationale de Paris, 7 février–3 avril 1894* (Paris, 1894)
Conférence 1897	Ministère des affaires étrangères, *Conférence sanitaire internationale de Venise, 16 février–19 mars 1897* (Rome, 1897)
Conférence 1903	*Conférence sanitaire internationale de Paris, 10 octobre–3 décembre 1903* (Paris, 1904)

Conférence 1911	Ministère des affaires étrangerès, *Conférence sanitaire internationale de Paris, 7 novembre 1911–17 janvier 1912* (Paris, 1912)
CP	Confidential Paper
CSP	Code de la santé publique
DGBG	Deutsche Gesellschaft zur Bekämpfung der Geschlechtskrankheiten
DORA	Defence of the Realm Act
DVöG	*Deutsche Vierteljahrsschrift für öffentliche Gesundheitspflege*
DZSA	*Deutsche Zeitschrift für die Staatsarzneikunde* (Erlangen)
EMSJ	*Edinburgh Medical and Surgical Journal*
FK	Första Kammaran
FO	Foreign Office
Förhandlingar	*Förhandlingar vid Svenska Läkare-Sällskapets sammankomster*
Gesetz-Sammlung	*Gesetz-Sammlung für die Königlichen Preussischen Staaten*
GHMC	*Gazette hebdomadaire de médecine et de chirurgie*
GStA	Geheimes Staatsarchiv Preussischer Kulturbesitz
JHM	*Journal of the History of Medicine*
JO	*Journal officiel*
LGB	Local Government Board
LMG	*London Medical Gazette*
Mémoires	*Mémoires de l'Académie royale de médecine, Mémoires de l'Académie impériale de médecine*
Mitteilungen	*Mitteilungen der Deutschen Gesellschaft zur Bekämpfung der Geschlechtskrankheiten*
MTG	*Medical Times and Gazette*
NCCVD	National Council for Combatting Venereal Diseases
Post	*Post- och Inrikes-Tidningar*
PP	*Parliamentary Papers*
Preste	*Högvördiga Preste-Ståndets Protokoll*
PRO	Public Record Office
RA	Riksarkivet, Stockholm

RD prot	*Riksdagens protokoll*
Recueil	*Recueil des travaux du Comité consultatif d'hygiène publique de France et des actes officiels de l'administration sanitaire*
Riddorskapet och Adeln	*Protocoll hållna hos Högloflige Ridderskapet och Adeln*
RmdI	Reichsministerium des Innern
RT	Reichstag
Sammlung	*Sammlung der von den Regierungen der Deutschen Bundesstaaten ergangenen Verordnungen und Instructionen wegen Verhütung und Behandlung der asiatischen Brechruhr (Cholera morbus)* (Frankfurt am Main, August 1831–March 1832: 9 pamphlets, continuously paginated)
SB	Reichstag, *Stenographische Berichte der Verhandlungen*
SFPSM	Société française de prophylaxie sanitaire et morale
SFS	*Svensk Författnings-Samling*
SPVD	Society for the Prevention of Venereal Disease
Staats-Zeitung	*Allgemeine Preussische Staats-Zeitung*
Stabi	Staatsbibliothek Preussischer Kulturbesitz
Upsala Läkareförening	*Upsala Läkareförenings förhandlingar*
VD	venereal disease
Verhandlungen	*Verhandlungen der physikalisch-medicinischen Gesellschaft zu Königsberg über die Cholera*
Veröffentlichungen	*Veröffentlichungen des Kaiserlichen Gesundheitsamtes*
ZBGK	*Zeitschrift für die Bekämpfung der Geschlechtskrankheiten*

CHAPTER I

Preventive variations

"One foot in the brothel, the other in the hospital," goes the old saying, as applicable centuries ago as today. A universal for all mortals, disease is also an artifact of history. Patients racked by the fastigium of illness will take little comfort from the insight that they are suffering from a historical construct with only contingent objective reality, but scholars have found the multiplicity and mutability of illness irresistible.[1] This diversity of signification attached to disease itself holds equally for the means employed to prevent and contain its spread. Why such precautions, the prophylactic strategies adopted in hopes of avoiding or ameliorating the ravages of epidemics, have varied dramatically among nations even though, in biological terms, the problem faced by each has been much the same is the question in search of an answer. Medical history is the immediate subject, but the ultimate purposes of this study extend beyond the precisely scientific. Since at least the era of absolutism, preventing and dealing with contagious and epidemic disease have together been one of the major tasks of states.[2] When Cicero advised rulers to consider the *salus populi* as the highest law, he was thinking more of military security than sewers, but his dictum was soon to be interpreted as

---

[1] Charles Rosenberg and Janet Golden, eds., *Framing Disease: Studies in Cultural History* (New Brunswick, 1992); Jens Lachmund and Gunnar Stollberg, eds., *The Social Construction of Illness: Illness and Medical Knowledge in Past and Present* (Stuttgart, 1992); Keith Wailoo, *Drawing Blood: Technology and Disease Identity in Twentieth-Century America* (Baltimore, 1997); Paula A. Treichler, "AIDS, Homophobia, and Biomedical Discourse: An Epidemic of Signification," in Douglas Crimp, ed., *AIDS: Cultural Analysis, Cultural Activism* (Cambridge, 1988), p. 69; Joseph Margolis, "The Concept of Disease," *Journal of Medicine and Philosophy*, 1, 3 (September 1976); Peter Conrad and Joseph W. Schneider, *Deviance and Medicalization: From Badness to Sickness* (St. Louis, 1980), ch. 2. A truly untenable version, either trivial or false, is that of Andrew Cunningham, "Transforming Plague: The Laboratory and the Identity of Infectious Disease," in Cunningham and Perry Williams, eds., *The Laboratory Revolution in Medicine* (Cambridge, 1992), pp. 238–44.

[2] George Rosen, *From Medical Police to Social Medicine* (New York, 1974), pp. 120ff.; Abram de Swaan, *In Care of the State: Health Care, Education and Welfare in Europe and the USA in the Modern Era* (New York, 1988), ch. 4; Marianne Rodenstein, *"Mehr Licht, mehr Luft": Gesundheitskonzepte im Städtebau seit 1750* (Frankfurt, 1988), pp. 35–40.

a reference to the public health. Such protection is in many ways a classic public good, demanding a communal decision to require tickets of potential free riders: the quarantine evader whose personal convenience bodes collective catastrophe; the unvaccinated who, themselves benefiting from herd immunity, refuse to contribute to it; the tubercular who, failing to complete their prescribed medical regimen, spread an ever more resistant and virulent strain of bacillus. The dilemmas raised counterpose the rights of the individual to autonomy and freedom and the claims of the community to protection against the potential calamity threatened by its infectious members. They cast up the basic problem of reconciling individual and community in the most fundamental, pressing and unavoidable of terms.

An examination of the historical evolution of preventive techniques against contagious disease and their variation among nations therefore seeks to use public health to illuminate broader issues of state intervention. Taking epidemic control as its example, the question posed concerns the reasons for national differences not just in terms of hygiene, but also in broader realms of statutory intervention and control. In particular, the problem concerns the direction in which causality has worked. That political culture, a style of governance, the nature of a particular national state would leave their mark on the tactics applied to disease control seems intuitively obvious. The more interesting question concerns the extent to which, in fact, the dilemmas thrown up by the threat of epidemics were experiences that shaped and changed the style of statutory intervention. To mangle Clausewitz yet again, was prophylaxis a continuation of politics with other means or were politics shaped by the imperatives of prevention? What are the sources of the political traditions that are so often themselves invoked as final historical causes of variation between nations?

THE EPISTEMOLOGY OF EPIDEMICS

Sketched with a thumbnail, the history of understanding contagious disease has unfolded in a field of polar tension. On the one hand, certain illnesses (ophthalmia, smallpox, syphilis, phthisis and plague) have long been recognized as contagious, transmitted directly between humans, via touch or over short distances through the air, sometimes through the intermediation of objects or animals. The idea that disease can be communicated directly between humans was held already by the ancient Egyptians and Jews. The Book of Leviticus detailed rules for isolating lepers and the concept of contagion became widely recognized in the Latin west with the acceptance of the Old Testament as a holy book of Christianity. In the early sixteenth century Fracastoro elaborated ideas of contagiousness for plague, smallpox, measles, tuberculosis, rabies and syphilis.[3]

On the other hand, a localist school of thought has long preached that disease, rather than spreading contagiously from one place to another, arose independently in each from various indigenous circumstances. The conditions in question have varied over the development of this strain of analysis with the emphasis shifting, broadly speaking, from natural to humanmade factors. Hippocrates and Galen formulated a miasmatic concept of disease involving an epidemic constitution of the atmosphere, corrupted by climatic, seasonal and astronomical influences. During the seventeenth century, Sydenham argued that epidemics were started by changes in the air resulting from emanations either from the earth's core or out in the universe. While such causes were largely beyond human influence, by the middle of the eighteenth century other environmental factors began to attract attention, ones that were potentially controllable. Miasmas arising from swamps and stagnant waters, filthy and crowded living conditions and the putrefaction of organic matter were all considered conspirators in the production of fevers.[4] But since, even given such general causes (whether exotic or environmental), not everyone was affected, another factor seemed necessary to explain why only some succumbed in epidemic circumstances: an individual predisposition that could be aggravated by fatigue, diet, habits, emotional strain and the like. With long historical precedence, immunology is the modern version of accounting for why, even given uniform contact with the sources of illness, morbidity varies individually.[5] The basic building blocks of etiological argument, from which in varying combinations conceptions of disease causation are constructed, have thus long been in place: a focus on environmental causes of various sorts, a recognition of the role played by individual predisposition and

[3] Charles-Edward Amory Winslow, *The Conquest of Epidemic Disease* (Princeton, 1944), pp. 73–74; Sven-Ove Arvidsson, "Epidemiologiska teorier under 1800-talets koleraepidemier," *Nordisk medicinhistorisk årsbok* (1971), p. 181; William Bulloch, *The History of Bacteriology* (London, 1938), p. 4; Robert P. Hudson, *Disease and Its Control* (Westport, 1983), p. 143; Harry Wain, *A History of Preventive Medicine* (Springfield, 1970), pp. 50, 96.

[4] James C. Riley, *The Eighteenth-Century Campaign to Avoid Disease* (New York, 1987), pp. ix–x, xv; Margaret Pelling, *Cholera, Fever and English Medicine 1825–1865* (Oxford, 1978), p. 18.

[5] Antoinette Stettler, "Die Vorstellungen von Ansteckung und Abwehr: Zur Geschichte der Immunitätslehre bis zur Zeit von Louis Pasteur," *Gesnerus*, 29 (1972).

an acknowledgment that at least certain diseases were contagious, transmitted from person to person, sometimes through the intermediation of
objects or, as later recognized, other animals.[6]

In terms of preventive strategy, different etiologies had, broadly
speaking, various implications. A view of disease as spread by contagion
sought above all to break chains of transmission, interrupting the circulation of carriers by means of cordons, quarantines and sequestration.
These were the techniques that we may generally call quarantinist, classically employed against leprosy, whose victims became the ultimate epidemiological outcasts. In German, the very name of the disease, *Aussatz*,
indicates the social fate of its victims, set, as they were, outside the
normal life of the community. For localists, in contrast, disease was best
prevented by removing or correcting its environmental causes. As long
as these were still seen as primarily atmospheric, climatic or astronomical, little could be accomplished. Once, however, the pertinent conditions had been narrowed to humanmade and individual factors in the
proximate surroundings, something might be done about them.
Localists sought to drain stagnant water, separate humans from their
filth and excrement, build better housing, plan more hygienic cities,
provide healthy food and warm clothing, encourage individuals to
change their predisposing habits. Where the sun does not penetrate, as
the old Persian proverb had it, the physician is a frequent visitor. Do not
fixate on germs, Newman cautioned in 1930. "The essential thing is the
healthy and resistant body of man, and the maintenance of his harmonious functioning in relation to Nature and his environment, and in relation to human society."[7] In a broad sense we may call the prophylaxis
associated with this social version of a localist etiology an environmental or sanitationist approach, an attempt to ameliorate the surrounding
circumstances seen as causing illness. Where quarantinism sought to
control people, as one observer has succinctly put it, environmentalism
took aim at property.[8]

Individual predisposition, in turn, played a role in both preventive
approaches, explaining why it was that any particular individual succumbed to disease, whether caused by a transmitted something or by
the effect of local noxiousness. In sum, however, predisposing factors

---

[6] Winslow, *Conquest of Epidemic Disease*, pp. 73–74, 181; Charles E. Rosenberg, *Explaining Epidemics and Other Studies in the History of Medicine* (Cambridge, 1992), pp. 294–96.

[7] George Newman, *Health and Social Evolution* (London, 1931), p. 115.

[8] Gerry Kearns, "Private Property and Public Health Reform in England 1830–1870," *Social Science and Medicine*, 26, 1 (1988), p. 188.

were of greater concern to environmentalists than quarantinists. Since
the latter were concerned above all with breaking chains of transmission, the precise reason for the infectiousness of the victim in question,
whether predisposed or not, was largely irrelevant for the precautions
to be imposed. For the former, in contrast, attacking predisposing
factors was an element of prevention. Some of these (deficient housing,
impoverished diet, the stress and strain of market competition) could be
ameliorated through the broad, communal social reform that preoccu-
pied sanitationists. Others, however (bad habits, excess and immodera-
tion, especially in matters sexual and dietary), were elements that
required an individual change in behavior. The hope of effecting such
modifications elicited the hectoring and moralizing side of sanitationist
efforts, the ambitions to impose the standards of personal hygiene and
moderate behavior characteristic of middle-class public health officials
not only down the social scale, on lower classes feared as uncouth and
insalubrious, but also upwards, on aristocrats often regarded as sexually
promiscuous, gustatorially insatiable and morally suspect. From this
preoccupation with individual predisposition sprang the Janus face of
an environmentalist approach to disease, tergiversating between public
and private goods: its socially reforming concern to assure even the
poorest of basic sanitary infrastructure and decent living conditions; its
socially controlling interest in making the circumspect and hygienic
habits of the urban middle classes the standard to which all could be
held.[9]

Like quarantinist techniques of disease prevention, an environmentalist approach too sports a venerable pedigree. The ancient Jews had
been the first to develop not only the rules of contagionist prophylaxis
detailed in Leviticus, but had also formulated other pertinent aspects of
public hygiene: a weekly day of rest, protection of the food and water
supply, concern with abnormal discharges of the genitals and more
general bodily cleanliness, including perhaps (if one is willing to attribute also functional motives to religious rituals) circumcision. Hippocrates
at Athens attempted to burn miasma out of the air by lighting pyres. The
Romans built sewers and laid on water with an accomplishment that
would take centuries to replicate. English regulations requiring the salubrity of the urban environment date from the late thirteenth century.
The plague of the following century prompted renewed cleansings of

---

[9] Some of the most subtle and nuanced analysis in this respect is to be found in Christopher
Hamlin, *Public Health and Social Justice in the Age of Chadwick: Britain, 1800–1854* (Cambridge, 1998),
pp. 201–13 and passim.

public spaces, prohibitions on emptying cesspools and keeping pigs.[10] Starting in the fifteenth century, waste removal, sewerage and cleansing became part of a concerted public health program in central and northern Italy; indeed in Florence regulations on street cleaning and other sanitary measures were two centuries older. The Venetians had strictures governing a panoply of public health eventualities, from food to filth.[11] Environmentalist public works (draining land, street paving, sewerage) continued in a sustained fashion during the middle of the eighteenth century in other European nations. As a coherent current of public health, such attempts to improve local, and especially urban, conditions took root with the Enlightenment and then especially in the early nineteenth century, starting in France with the theories of Villermé.[12] In Germany, prominent sanitationists included Virchow and later Pettenkofer. As in so many things, while the French may have taken the intellectual lead, in practical terms they lagged and the baton was grasped by the British who, toward the middle of the century, began the process of urban improvement and hygienic reform that realized in its classic sense an environmentalist approach to epidemic disease. Drainage, sewerage, water filtration, zoning laws to separate work from residence and production from recreation, building codes to ensure sweetness and light, fresh air and elbow room: all were techniques brought to perfection in Britain during this period.[13] Under the leadership of Chadwick, Southwood Smith, John Simon and colleagues, a radical strain of environmentalist ideology evolved here that, attributing most disease to unpropitious local conditions, held out the possibility

[10] George Newman, *The Rise of Preventive Medicine* (Oxford, 1932), pp. 47–49; Arthur Newsholme, *Evolution of Preventive Medicine* (Baltimore, 1927), p. 57; John Simon, *English Sanitary Institutions* (London, 1890), p. 39; Karl Sudhoff, *Skizzen* (Leipzig, 1921), pp. 151–53; Jean-Noël Biraben, *Les hommes et la peste en France et dans les pays européens et méditerranéens* (Mouton, 1976), v. II, pp. 104, 178–79; Robert S. Gottfried, "Plague, Public Health and Medicine in Late Medieval England," in Neithart Bulst and Robert Delort, eds., *Maladies et société (XIIe–XVIIIe siècles)* (Paris, 1989), pp. 348–59.

[11] Carlo M. Cipolla, *Miasmas and Disease: Public Health and the Environment in the Pre-Industrial Age* (New Haven, 1992), pp. 6–7; Carlo M. Cipolla, *Public Health and the Medical Profession in the Renaissance* (Cambridge, 1976), pp. 34–35; Ann G. Carmichael, *Plague and the Poor in Renaissance Florence* (Cambridge, 1986), pp. 96–97; Ernst Rodenwaldt, *Die Gesundheitsgesetzgebung des Magistrato della sanità Venedigs, 1486–1550* (Heidelberg, 1956).

[12] Riley, *Eighteenth-Century Campaign*, p. 102; Erwin H. Ackerknecht, "Hygiene in France, 1815–1848," *BHM*, 22, 2 (March–April 1948), p. 141; Ann F. La Berge, *Mission and Method: The Early Nineteenth-Century French Public Health Movement* (Cambridge, 1992), pp. 96–97; John M. Eyler, *Victorian Social Medicine: The Ideas and Methods of William Farr* (Baltimore, 1979), p. 7; Laurence Brockliss and Colin Jones, *The Medical World of Early Modern France* (Oxford, 1997), pp. 750–60.

[13] As emblematic of a vast literature, see Anthony S. Wohl, *Endangered Lives: Public Health in Victorian Britain* (London, 1983).

that the problems of public health could, with one prolonged herculean effort, be solved simultaneously and in much the same way as those of poverty and general social iniquity: through the rebuilding of the urban environment as a well-planned, -plumbed, -lit and -ventilated city, by means of improvements in the living conditions of the poor.

The quarantinist approach, in the meantime, did not pass away in the face of this totalizing utopian sanitary vision. While certain illnesses were generally conceded to be transmissible, doubts voiced early in the nineteenth century concerning plague and yellow fever acquired critical mass when, in the 1830s, the cholera epidemics ravaging western Europe did not appear to spread solely by means of personal contact. During the heyday of an environmentalist stance (at midcentury in France, in Britain with Chadwick, Germany under Pettenkoferian sway) contagionism was seen as an outmoded, oldfashioned and conservative approach to disease that denied its obvious causes in filth and squalor, preferring to lock victims in lazarettos rather than improve their living conditions. But far from vanishing, contagionism celebrated a triumphant return with the bacteriological revolution at the end of the century when Pasteur, Koch and others vindicated the insight that much disease, caused by specific microorganisms, was often transmitted among humans and that, whatever the effects of predisposing factors, however detrimental filth and unfortunate poverty, certain illnesses spread independently of social and local circumstances, requiring therefore precautions other than the mop and bucket full of soapy water and good intentions wielded by the sanitationists.

A strictly binary view of either etiology (localism vs. contagionism) or prophylaxis (sanitationism vs. quarantinism) would, however, be a distortion. These three basic building blocks of epidemiological theory (local factors, whether natural or social, individual predisposition and contagion) were multiply and mutually permeable.[14] Miasmas could be regarded as localist, contagionist or both, seen as emanations produced by environmental causes, other times as the vehicle by which disease spread from one place to another.[15] The fact that physicians attending

---

[14] Christopher Hamlin, "Predisposing Causes and Public Health in Early Nineteenth-Century Medical Thought," *Social History of Medicine*, 5, 1 (April 1992), pp. 46–49.

[15] In the late eighteenth century, for example, VD, clearly recognized as transmissible from person to person, was thought to be carried by micro-miasmas from one set of genitals to the next: Johann Valentin Müller, *Praktisches Handbuch der medicinischen Galanteriekrankheiten* (Marburg, 1788), pp. 29–31, 67. Yellow fever in the 1860s was regarded as imported, but not contagious, as arising from a specific miasma, not generally from filth or fouled air: William Coleman, *Yellow Fever in the North: The Methods of Early Epidemiology* (Madison, 1987), pp. 23, 55.

the ill were also stricken with typhus, as Virchow reasoned in 1848, could equally well prove that the disease was of local origin (doctor and patient afflicted by the same factors) as show that it was contagious.[16] Individual predisposition was a factor of interest both to localists and contagionists, explaining in either scheme why not everyone succumbed even in the worst of epidemics. Nor was bacteriology, which disproved the fundamental assumption of the most fervent sanitationist creed, that epidemic disease arose of virgin birth each time anew, irreconcilable with other devoutly held localist beliefs. Bacteriology showed environmentalists in what respect they had been right, how it was that filth, though not a cause per se of disease, might favor its multiplication and spread, why in fact it was right to locate the outhouse far from the well.[17] Bacteriologists and sanitationists could readily agree that unhygienic conditions promoted the spread of disease, even though the latter saw filth itself as the generator of disease, the former regarding it mediately as a condition favorable to propagating the microorganisms ultimately responsible for illness.[18] If hygienic reform eliminated malevolent microorganisms, as with Koch's insistence on water filtration to solve Hamburg's cholera problem, then sanitarians and contagionists were in perfect harmony. Dietary excess could be a predisposing factor in both views, whether because of a general weakening of resistance for sanitationists or a neutralizing of the stomach acidity necessary to kill microorganisms for their opponents.[19] Overcrowding was an insalubrious condition, much lamented by environmentalists, which bacteriologists had reasons consistent with their etiological position (ease of vector transfer) to regard as conducive to the spread of disease.[20] Promiscuity, all could agree, was a factor in the dissemination of venereal disease, although only some thought it also a cause. Both sides could favor removing cholera victims from their abode, whether the reasoning was to prevent germs from spreading or to allow noxious domestic atmospheres to dissipate. Both considered disinfection, fumigation and cleansing effective prophylaxis, either because the contagium was thus destroyed or because putrefac-

[16] Rudolf Virchow, *Collected Essays on Public Health and Epidemiology* (Canton, 1985), v. I, pp. 276–78, 340–41.

[17] Hudson, *Disease and Its Control*, p. 188; Wolfgang Locher, "Pettenkofer and Epidemiology: Erroneous Concepts – Beneficial Results," in Yosio Kawakita et al., eds., *History of Epidemiology* (Tokyo, 1993).

[18] *Sanitary Record*, 1 (26 September 1874), pp. 229–31; Carl Barriés, *Die Cholera morbus* (Hamburg, 1831), pp. 68–69, 238ff. [19] *Hygiea*, 55, 6 (June 1893), pp. 609–23.

[20] As Richard Thorne Thorne pointed out for smallpox: *First Report of the Royal Commission Appointed to Inquire into the Subject of Vaccination* (C.-5845) (London, 1889), QQ 764, 770.

tion and pestilential emanations were neutralized.[21] Both could advocate isolation of the ill, either to break chains of transmission, or as a kind of purification of the population.[22]

Environmentalists were often willing to concede that diseases originally arising from local causes (and even the most ardent contagionist without an intergalactic approach had to admit that all must ultimately have started somewhere for reasons other than importation) might attain a degree of virulence rendering them transmissible.[23] Localism and contagionism were regarded by many as compatible.[24] Disease might arise locally, but could then be transmitted; whatever its origin, contagious illness often struck differentially depending on predisposing factors. Infectionism and contingent contagionism were terms used for such formulations of the interdependence of contagion and local factors.[25] Contagionism and localism were thus two poles in a field of intellectual tension within which any individual position took its stance. While absolute contagionists and localists, convinced quarantinists and sanitationists, could be found, most observers fell somewhere between the extremes. Nonetheless, without reifying the concepts and anachronistically fixing in time concepts that have never, of course, stood outside the flux of historical development, it remains the case that a crucial distinction persists over the *longue durée* of western thinking about diseases and their causes that can and should not be effaced by attempts to render nuanced and more subtle otherwise overly stark dichotomies. Just as the myths of Hygeia and Asclepius, the ideals of prevention and cure, the approaches of "ecology" and "engineering," have identified two polar medical ambitions over centuries, so too a closely related distinction has been drawn, etiologically speaking, between a focus on the environmental background of epidemic disease and its transmissibility among humans; prophylactically, between attempts to ameliorate toxic surroundings and limiting contagious spread.[26] The remedy, says the

[21] R. J. Morris, *Cholera 1832: The Social Response to an Epidemic* (New York, 1976), p. 174.

[22] Lloyd G. Stevenson, "Science down the Drain: On the Hostility of Certain Sanitarians to Animal Experimentation, Bacteriology and Immunology," *BHM*, 29, 1 (January–February 1955), p. 9.

[23] *Gazette médicale de Paris*, 3, 15 (1832), p. 155; 3, 74 (1832), p. 516; Rudolph Wagner, *Die weltgeschichtliche Entwicklung der epidemischen und contagiösen Krankheiten und die Gesetze ihrer Verbreitung* (Würzburg, 1826), p. 10; Martha L. Hildreth, *Doctors, Bureaucrats, and Public Health in France, 1888–1902* (New York, 1987), pp. 114–17; Hamlin, "Predisposing Causes and Public Health," p. 47.

[24] L. Pappenheim, *Handbuch der Sanitäts-Polizei* (2nd edn.; Berlin, 1870), v. II, p. 154; Hermann Eulenberg, ed., *Handbuch des öffentlichen Gesundheitswesens* (Berlin, 1881), v. I, p. 511; *PP* 1866 (3645) xxxiii, p. 455. [25] Hudson, *Disease and Its Control*, p. 142.

[26] Rene Dubos, *Mirage of Health* (New York, 1959), ch. 5; John Powles, "On the Limitations of Modern Medicine," *Science, Medicine and Man*, 1 (1973), p. 25.

physician in Brieux's *Damaged Goods*, speaking of tuberculosis and summing up the dichotomy, is to pay decent wages and tear down substandard housing, but instead workers are advised not to spit.

THE POLITICS OF PUBLIC HEALTH

How to prevent and protect against contagious disease is a problem that invokes some of the most fundamental and perduring dilemmas in the contradiction between individual rights and the demands of society, between (most starkly) the claim to personal corporeal integrity and the authority of the community to ensure the health of its members.[27] To what extent may society protect itself against individuals whose misfortune to be stricken with a transmissible ailment poses a threat to others? Contagious disease has accordingly raised issues that go beyond the epidemiological to become political. The spirit of partisanship, as one early observer of cholera put it, burns with almost the same ferocity on topics medical as political, while others extended the comparison even to the ticklish realm of theology.[28]

One might be forgiven for considering the prevention of contagious disease a question of medical technique. Faced with a biologically identical problem, each nation could be expected to resort to similar preventive measures, ones dictated by the state of etiological knowledge. In fact, variations in prophylactic strategies employed by different nations have been remarkably pronounced. Before the bacteriological revolution this was perhaps less surprising. With no single accepted scientific guide to follow, nations were free to choose preventive tactics according to other criteria. But such divergences persisted, indeed in many respects sharpened, during the era when, scientifically speaking, general agreement had been wrought on the etiological bases of at least the classic contagious diseases.

For the early phases of cholera (up to the 1850s), for example, the extremes were defined by, on the one hand, the strict quarantinist practices (sealing borders, isolating travelers, sequestering the sick and generally seeking to break chains of transmission in much the way traditionally employed against the plague) imposed in Russia, Austria and Prussia and, on the other, the sanitationist approach eventually adopted in Britain and, for the time being, France (allowing unrestricted movement of

---

[27] Jean-Marie Auby, *Le droit de la santé* (Paris, 1981), p. 24.
[28] Bisset Hawkins, *History of the Epidemic Spasmodic Cholera of Russia* (London, 1831), p. 154; *Westminster Review*, 2 (1825), pp. 135–36.

goods and travelers, but seeking instead to render salubrious the filthy circumstances still considered the main cause of this and other epidemic diseases). Even once the cause of cholera became known, the bacteriological revolution having leveled the playing field of knowledge, stark differences in approach persisted. By the 1890s, however, the nations facing off in prophylactic contest had shifted to ally the Germans with the British, together opposing the French who had in the meantime hoisted the banner of quarantinism, now insisting on strict measures to be imposed at the epidemiological bottleneck in the Middle East.

With the other diseases under the glass here, differences in national preventive strategies were even more clearcut. For smallpox, the extremes varied between the compulsory system of universal vaccination and revaccination of all citizens imposed in Germany, eventually France and, for a while, Sweden and the British government's inability to maintain similarly strict measures in the face of widespread protest, its adoption instead of a purely voluntary approach. For syphilis, the contrast was triangular, among (1) the regulation of prostitution found in France and Germany that was considered sufficient to control VD, (2) the British policy (once the Contagious Disease Acts, a form of regulationism, had been repealed in the late 1880s) of largely ignoring the problem of prostitution and instead applying the principles of voluntary treatment to such illness and (3) the Scandinavian solution of ending regulation, but in turn obliging all infected citizens to undergo compulsory treatment, threatening those who refused with forced hospitalization. Even in our own day of scientific globalization, precautions used against the AIDS epidemic have varied dramatically among nations, with the extremes represented by the hyperquarantinism (testing all foreigners and returning nationals for HIV, quarantining seropositives) of nations like Cuba, China and Iran, at one end, and the benign laissez-faire approach (providing medical care and education, but otherwise rattling few prophylactic sabers) of the Dutch and British at the other.

Why have different states adopted such divergent prophylactic strategies in the face of similar epidemiological problems? Variations in national temperament, habit and custom have been proposed – a plausible, but unsatisfying answer in its vague generality.[29] One of the most

---

[29] John Cross, *A History of the Variolous Epidemic which occurred in Norwich in the Year 1819, and destroyed 530 Individuals, with an Estimate of the Protection afforded by Vaccination* (London, 1820), p. 220; *Bulletin de la Société de médecine publique et d'hygiène professionnelle*, 2 (1879), pp. 328–34; *Wiener Medizinische Presse*, 10 (1869), col. 1129; Pierre Darmon, *La longue traque de la variole: Les pionniers de la médecine préventive* (Paris, 1986), p. 383; Claude Quétel, *History of Syphilis* (Baltimore, 1990), p. 7.

powerful explanations suggests a close connection between a nation's political system and culture and the approach it takes to contagious disease, a correlation, in other words, between politics and prophylaxis. Erwin Ackerknecht formulated this idea most notably, arguing that sanitary cordons, quarantines, sequestration and other measures of the sort traditionally marshaled against contagious disease, which necessarily impinged on the individual's autonomy, giving priority to the interests of the community and the state, were most likely to be favored by absolutist, autocratic or conservative regimes.[30] In contrast, more liberal, democratic systems, reluctant to interfere with individual freedom, sought less intrusive strategies, usually some variety of environmentalism, or, in default, preferred to forego preventive interventions altogether. Economically speaking, the contrast was between commercial and trading interests, hoping to avoid quarantinist restrictions, and the mercantilist state bureaucracies for whom free trade and private profitability were but secondary considerations to be weighed against the nation's demographic, military and public health concerns. Because, during the first half of the nineteenth century, the scientific weight was too equally balanced between both sides of the argument for a clear intellectual preponderance in any one direction, other factors – social, economic and political – tilted the scales in each nation for or against a quarantinist approach.

In Ackerknecht's scheme, etiology, prophylaxis and politics were elegantly and powerfully correlated with each other. An autocratic ideology favored a view of epidemic diseases as contagious and consequently applied quarantinist tactics. Liberals, in contrast, approached the issue from some variety of localist perspective, especially concerned with social problems (poor waste removal, drainage, tainted water, noxious vapors, inadequate housing), and sought to prevent disease by correcting deficiencies of the environment through hygienic reform. Quarantinism, in this view, was authoritarian and interventionist in a drastic and imposing sense, legitimating the state's right to infringe on its subjects' liberties by invoking a higher good, posing a zero-sum tradeoff between individual and public weals. Sanitationism, in contrast, suited the desires of liberal polities not to interfere unnecessarily in the life of the individual, offering an approach to disease prevention that not only left civil

---

[30] Erwin H. Ackerknecht, "Anticontagionism Between 1821 and 1867," *BHM*, 22, 5 (September–October 1948); Erwin H. Ackerknecht, *Medicine at the Paris Hospital 1794–1848* (Baltimore, 1967), pp. 156–57. He was following the cue given by Sigerist who distinguished broadly between absolutist and liberal styles of public health: Henry E. Sigerist, *Civilization and Disease* (Ithaca, 1944), p. 91.

society comparatively unhampered, but also identified the best means of prophylaxis as social and hygienic reform. Because of this elegant fit between political system and public health, the choice of preventive strategy was dictated – so the implication of Ackerknecht's argument – at least as much by politics as biology. It was not the nature of the disease which specified how it would be prevented and limited, but the kind of political regime under epidemic attack.

At its most messianic, environmentalism rose from a merely prophylactic technique to become part of a complete worldview, a belief that filth, disease and sin were but various manifestations of the same maleficent principle. In social terms its precepts dictated a total program of thoroughgoing reform. It was not filth or overcrowding, as in a narrow Chadwickian accounting, which caused or predisposed to disease, but poverty in the broadest sense (long hours, exhausting labor, low wages and the dingy routine following in their train) that, grinding down the health of the poorest, left them susceptible to affliction. Whereas a narrowly sanitationist approach offered technical solutions to disease prevention – drainage, ventilation, sewerage and the like – its broader formulation would rest satisfied with nothing less than reform on a scale promising the poor social and therefore epidemiological circumstances comparable to the middle and upper classes: fresh air, unadulterated food, potable water, dwellings of light, cleanliness and space.[31] Hygienic reform thus held out the opportunity not only of checking the spread of (what were considered to be) filth diseases, but also, in the long run, of improving the lives of those who had suffered most from industrial urbanization. Virchow formulated this mutual inflection of social and sanitary reform in his slogan, "Medicine is a social science and politics nothing but medicine on a grand scale." Free and unlimited democracy was his remedy for epidemic disease.[32] G. B. Shaw espoused a view that combined sanitation and socialism, measures to improve the circumstances of the worst-off rather than technical stopgap interventions by a professional medical caste to patch up the status quo.[33] In international terms, an environmentalist approach

---

[31] Stevenson, "Science down the Drain," pp. 2ff.; B. L. Hutchins, *The Public Health Agitation 1833–1848* (London, 1909), p. 84; A. J. Youngson, *The Scientific Revolution in Victorian Medicine* (New York, 1979), p. 22; La Berge, *Mission and Method*, pp. 96–97; John V. Pickstone, "Dearth, Dirt and Fever Epidemics: Rewriting the History of British 'Public Health,' 1780–1850," in Terence Ranger and Paul Slack, eds., *Epidemics and Ideas* (Cambridge, 1992), p. 126; Hamlin, *Public Health and Social Justice*, pp. 186–87.

[32] Rosen, *From Medical Police*, p. 62; Virchow, *Collected Essays*, v. I, pp. 307–15.

[33] Roger Boxill, *Shaw and the Doctors* (New York, 1969), p. 66.

promised to unite nations, superseding distinctions drawn by quarantinists between the sources and the victims of infection, between healthy and filthy countries. With the gradual spread of the principles of public hygiene back to the Orient, where they had originated in the first place, the human family would no longer be divided by fears of contagion into mutually antagonistic epidemiological blocs.[34] As a measure of this total and comprehensive vision espoused by environmentalism at its loftiest, one may take its all-or-nothing view of reducing mortality in what was known as the "displacement theory."[35] Attempts at reducing the damage due to any particular disease (vaccination for smallpox was among the best-rehearsed examples) were futile since, even if effective, other ailments would fill the gap, the vaccinated carried off instead by, say, typhoid or measles.[36] Unless all diseases were prevented simultaneously through hygienic reform, measures targeted at specific illnesses were pointless. What counted was the overall mortality rate, not of this or that ailment.[37] By attacking fundamentally unhealthy living conditions, all (or at least many) diseases would be prevented. Sanitationism in its heyday was thus a totalizing, unified view of etiology and prophylaxis, standing in stark contrast to the contagionist and eventually bacteriological approach that regarded each ailment as having its own particular cause, specific cure and form of prevention, however much generally squalid circumstances might favor transmission and sickness.

From the environmentalist vantage, hygienic reform involved no costly tradeoffs between the interests of the individual and the community, both standing to gain from such improvements. This wholly benign sanitationist self-image was captured by John Hamett, friend of the British consul at Danzig[38] during the first cholera epidemic, who thought that the disease, caused through atmospheric contamination,

---

[34] *Conférence 1851*, 39, pp. 9–14.

[35] Bernhard J. Stern, *Should We Be Vaccinated? A Survey of the Controversy in Its Historical and Scientific Aspects* (New York, 1927), p. 51.

[36] William Tebb, *Compulsory Vaccination in England: With Incidental References to Foreign States* (London, 1884), pp. 61–62; *Vaccination Inquirer and Health Review*, 7, 78 (September 1885), p. 95; *Hansard*, 1871, v. 208, col. 1715; 1883, v. 280, col. 992; *La médecine contemporaine* 21 (1880), pp. 147–52; P. A. Siljeström, *A Momentous Education Question for the Consideration of Parents and Others Who Desire the Well-Being of the Rising Generation* (London, 1882), pp. 10–17; *Förhandlingar* (1908), p. 226; Jno. Pickering, *Anti-Vaccination: The Statistics of the Medical Officers to the Leeds Small-Pox Hospital Exposed and Refuted* (Leeds, 1876), pp. 32–34.

[37] William White, *The Story of a Great Delusion* (London, 1885), pp. xxxiv, 450–51; *Bihang*, 1885, 1 Saml., 2 Afd., v. 2/13, no. 79.

[38] In the interest of avoiding anachronism, generally speaking, place names used by the contemporary sources are employed here.

was best counteracted by cleaning the homes of the poor, keeping victims warm and providing timely medical assistance – in other words, in a phrase that immortalizes the fuzziest sort of sanitationism, preventing cholera "by comfort, consequent cheerfulness, cleanliness, dryness, and ventilation."[39] Quarantinists, in contrast, prided themselves on being hardnosed realists. They did not oppose social and hygienic reform, but considered such matters distinct from the more immediately pressing issue of checking the ravages of contagious disease. Citizens could be spared the worst effects of epidemics without first having to rebuild the urban environment; effective prophylaxis was possible without the inevitable delay and expense of major social reform. Pasteur himself put the position most baldly with his claim, "whatever the poverty, never will it breed disease."[40] Quarantinists were generally willing to concede that unhygienic living conditions fostered the spread of illness and were not, in the sense of the sanitationists' withering caricature, a filthy party. But since such diseases were conveyed by contagion, filth was not the immediate problem. It may be an exaggeration to claim that general urban salubrity is without significance, as one quarantinist put it with respect to cholera, but it is common knowledge that some of the cleanest cities are hard hit while dirty ones are spared.[41] Mortality from epidemic disease and insanitary circumstances were only mediately connected. Much more urgent than improving urban living conditions, and an attainable goal to boot, was to impose cordoning, quarantining, notification, isolation, disinfection and similar precautions that made up the quarantinist palette of remedies. That this involved some limitation of personal liberties was no secret, but the public good was seen to far outweigh the restrictions thereby imposed on individual citizens.

ETIOLOGICAL DUALITIES

Ackerknecht's own formulation of a prophylactic dichotomy between conservative quarantinism and liberal sanitationism was little more than a suggestion. He has, moreover, been justly criticized for an overly manichean division, on the question of nineteenth-century cholera etiology,

[39] John Hamett, *The Substance of the Official Medical Reports upon the epidemic called Cholera, which prevailed among the poor at Dantzick, between the end of May and the first part of September, 1831* (London, 1832), p. 189.
[40] Paul Weindling, ed., *International Health Organisations and Movements, 1918–1939* (Cambridge, 1995), p. 253. The equivalent claim by Koch is quoted in Georges Vigarello, *Le sain et le malsain* (Paris, 1993), p. 257. [41] Paul Bert, *Le choléra: Lettres au "Tagblatt" de Vienne* (Paris, 1884), p. 19.

into contagionists and localists.[42] Nonetheless, if we pass from the narrow issue of etiology to the broader one of basic and perduring differences in public health strategies, his fundamental idea of a connection between political ideology and preventive tactics has proven enormously fruitful, widely accepted and, indeed, often implicitly assumed by many observers. Even though British medical opinion may not have been divided into camps of contagionists and miasmatists as resolutely at war with each other as Ackerknecht believed, it is still the case, and by far the more interesting issue for a comparative view, that Britain as a whole took a preventive public health approach more informed by anticontagionist assumptions than was true on the continent. More importantly from the vantage of this book, however diffuse the etiological dualities may in fact have been, the prophylactic juxtapositions, seen at the level of broad national strategies, were much more crisply binary: quarantinism vs. sanitationism, compulsory vs. voluntary vaccination, regulation of prostitution vs. alternate techniques.[43] Ackerknecht's idea of the causes of such divergence has had an impact for reasons that, not justified by his own intellectual investment, rests on a knack for bringing to the fore political correlations of a deeper and enduring conceptual dichotomy between localist and contagionist approaches to disease. If this split has not been quite a Lovejoyian unit idea, it has informed thinking about disease and its prevention for centuries.

At its broadest, this etiological distinction separates, on the one hand, a view of disease as an imbalance between humans and the environment whose prevention requires a reequilibriation from an understanding, on the other, of illness as the outcome of a specific external attack on the

---

[42] Pelling, *Cholera, Fever and English Medicine*, pp. 295–310; Margaret Pelling, "The Reality of Anticontagionism: Theories of Epidemic Disease in the Early Nineteenth Century," *Society for the Social History of Medicine: Bulletin*, 17 (1976), pp. 5–7; Roger Cooter, "Anticontagionism and History's Medical Record," in Peter Wright and Andrew Treacher, eds., *The Problem of Medical Knowledge* (Edinburgh, 1982), pp. 87–93; La Berge, *Mission and Method*, pp. 95–98; Roy Porter, "Cleaning up the Great Wen: Public Health in Eighteenth-Century London," in W. F. Bynum and Roy Porter, eds., *Living and Dying in London* (London, 1991), pp. 70–71; Coleman, *Yellow Fever in the North*, pp. 187–94; Hamlin, "Predisposing Causes and Public Health," p. 46; John B. Blake, "Yellow Fever in Eighteenth-Century America," *Bulletin of the New York Academy of Medicine*, 2/44, 6 (June 1968), pp. 680–82; Michael Dorrmann, "'Das asiatische Ungeheuer': Die Cholera im 19. Jahrhundert," in Hans Wilderotter and Michael Dorrmann, eds., *Das grosse Sterben: Seuchen machen Geschichte* (Berlin, 1995), p. 215; Michael Stolberg, *Die Cholera im Grossherzogtum Toskana* (Landsberg, 1995), p. 51; Hamlin, *Public Health and Social Justice*, pp. 62–66.

[43] Antagonism between clearly articulated sanitationist and contagionist positions seems to have been a constant of nineteenth-century public health development in the United States: John Duffy, *The Sanitarians: A History of American Public Health* (Urbana, 1990), pp. 108, 129, 166, 206; Howard Markel, *Quarantine! East European Jewish Immigrants and the New York City Epidemics of 1892* (Baltimore, 1997), pp. 154–58.

autonomous integrity of the body which, if not preventable (by vaccination) or curable through various targeted medical manipulations, can at least be rendered innocuous, from the community's point of view, by ensuring that the victim does not infect others. In the first instance, disease is an imbalance that can be righted or avoided only by reinstating the original harmony. In its older theological version, one that continues in good health, illness is divine punishment for moral or theological transgression, rectified by ending the behavior that had merited retribution in the first place.[44] The Bible mentions leprosy and plague as instances of such punishment and it was common to include prayer and repentance among the tactics used in hopes of avoiding or mitigating illness. During the plagues of the sixteenth century, however, theology and science had begun pursuing different avenues of explanation and London clergy were officially enjoined from preaching a supernatural approach to a disease officially understood to be infectious and all too worldly.[45] By the time of yellow fever and cholera in the early nineteenth century, the moral element had faded for the classic contagious ailments, while it has remained strong for sexually transmitted diseases, from syphilis to AIDS.

In the secularized version of this theory, disease was a disharmony between humans and the natural world, with filth substituting for sin and sewerage replacing atonement. In some variants, disease was itself the act of reestablishing harmony, the means by which the body was repaired.[46] Smallpox, for example, was still regarded in the late eighteenth century as an act of cleansing by which poisons were expelled through special glands intended for this purpose.[47] Such noxious effluvia were an inherent part of the human condition, a form of epidemiological original sin. In this disequilibrium view, cure and any other form of targeted preventive manipulations were suspect. Cure was an attempt to circumvent

[44] Wolf von Siebenthal, *Krankheit als Folge der Sünde* (Hannover, n.d. [1950]); Walther Riese, *The Conception of Disease* (New York, 1953), pp. 14–19; Keith Thomas, "Health and Morality in Early Modern England," in Allan M. Brandt and Paul Rozin, eds., *Morality and Health* (New York, 1997), p. 16.

[45] Owsei Temkin, *The Double Face of Janus* (Baltimore, 1977), p. 458; Paul Slack, *The Impact of Plague in Tudor and Stuart England* (London, 1985), p. 29; L. Fabian Hirst, *The Conquest of Plague* (Oxford, 1953), p. 15.

[46] Florence Nightingale, *Notes on Nursing* (Edinburgh, 1980), p. 1; Owsei Temkin, "The Scientific Approach to Disease: Specific Entity and Individual Sickness," in A. C. Crombie, ed., *Scientific Change* (London, 1963), p. 632; Rosenberg, *Explaining Epidemics*, p. 94.

[47] Christian August Struve, *Anleitung zur Kenntniss und Impfung der Kuhpocken* (Breslau, 1802), p. 84; "Belehrung über ansteckende Krankheiten," *Anhang zur Gesetz-Sammlung*, 1835, Beilage B zu No. 27 gehörig, pp. 26–27; Otto Lentz and H. A. Gins, eds., *Handbuch der Pockenbekämpfung und Impfung* (Berlin, 1927), p. 673.

reharmonization, while true recuperation came from the body itself and, at most, needed to be encouraged and stimulated. Cures could not be attacks from without, injections of foreign substances, administerings of drugs or any of the other violations of basic bodily integrity inflicted by allopathic medicine. Curing VD, to take an extreme example of this approach, was an invitation to continue the illicit behavior that had brought on disease in the first place and threatened, if anything, to make matters worse.[48] At its core, an environmental approach saw humans and nature in fundamental harmony, while their opponents regarded nature as sufficiently malevolent to attack the human body with illness, leaving it open to legitimate countermeasures with the marshaled armamentarium of orthodox allopathic biomedicine.[49] A belief in such harmony is clear with Rousseau and other anti-Enlightenment ideologues who sought to prevent the illnesses of civilization, prompted by the strains and contradictions of modern life, by returning to allegedly natural conditions. But even Chadwickian sanitationists, believing that civilization promoted health, thought that humankind was, through hygienic behavior, solving problems it had brought upon itself through unregulated urban industrial life, not correcting faults in nature itself.[50]

Seen in terms of this etiological dichotomy there is a unity to the techniques employed to prevent and contain the diseases under the glass here. Quarantinism applied to cholera, vaccination to smallpox, the regulation of prostitution in hopes of stemming syphilis: all were specific manipulations dictated by the precepts of allopathic biomedicine, involving violations of the freedom and bodily integrity of those feared as infectious, subordinating the (afflicted) individual to the interests of the community.[51] The same holds, in our own day, for the classic tech-

---

[48] It meant bringing on a moral syphilization of society that would have more devastating consequences than the merely bodily variety, as the German abolitionist Katarina Scheven argued: Ed. Jeanselme, *Traité de la syphilis* (Paris, 1931), v. I, p. 378.

[49] L. Belitski, *Gegen Impfung und Impfzwang* (Nordhausen, 1869), pp. 2–3. Homeopathy, in this dichotomy, is thus an attempt to brook a fundamental contradiction, unwilling to believe wholly in nature's ability to correct imbalances under its own steam without some allopathic prompting, but able to argue that the basic immorality of human tinkering with natural processes could be excused if the doses administered were in fact so dilute as to be, from the orthodox point of view, nonexistent. Because of its willingness to employ medicine, however dilutedly, homeopathy was rejected by most diehard believers in "natural" cures: Karl E. Rothschuh, *Naturheilbewegung, Reformbewegung, Alternativbewegung* (Stuttgart, 1983), pp. 100–02.

[50] Carl Haffter, "Die Entstehung des Begriffs der Zivilisationskrankheiten," *Gesnerus*, 36, 3/4 (1979), pp. 228–29; William Coleman, *Death Is a Social Disease: Public Health and Political Economy in Early Industrial France* (Madison, 1982), pp. 284–92. The contribution of civilization to disease is the leitmotif of Kenneth F. Kiple, ed., *Plague, Pox and Pestilence* (London, 1997).

[51] Analogies among quarantinism, vaccination and regulation were drawn by contemporaries in

niques of contagious disease prophylaxis that, when deployed against AIDS, have been called the contain-and-control strategy or hard line.[52] Conversely, the environmentalist side of this division seeks, often by means of broad social reform, to correct the supposedly underlying general causes of disease. Sanitationism was a widely popular technique applied to cholera up through the last decades of the nineteenth century. End the social iniquities that condemned the poor to miserable, unhealthy and crowded circumstances and epidemics would resolve themselves. Similar ideas held also for other classic contagious diseases. "The plague," as the Medical Officer of Health for Kensington put it at the height of the bacteriological age, "can find no permanent home among a wellfed community living clean lives in clean surroundings."[53] Many took a comparable approach to smallpox, convinced that hygiene promised to eliminate the disease or at least render it benign.[54] Diseases, as one prominent sanitationist antivaccinator put it, were often the result of an empty stomach, a naked back or a domicile without comfort. The solution was not to be found in antidotes and specifics, through prisons, penalties, police, asylums, lazarettos and dispensaries. If all classes lived in healthy conditions and were alike sober, industrious, temperate and cleanly, epidemics would be eradicated.[55]

For syphilis, a similarly environmentalist faith in the coincidence of social and hygienic reform has held. It was common in the seventeenth century to regard the disease as the outcome of poverty and poor living conditions, amenable therefore to their amelioration.[56] In the nineteenth century, such an environmentalist approach was broadened. Since prostitution was believed to spring from artificial social circumstances (late marriage, commodification of women, unrestricted male sexual access,

the nineteenth century: Mary Spongberg, *Feminizing Venereal Disease: The Body of the Prostitute in Nineteenth-Century Medical Discourse* (New York, 1997), p. 57; Judith R. Walkowitz, *Prostitution and Victorian Society: Women, Class and the State* (Cambridge, 1980), pp. 43–44. In our own day, some AIDS libertarians are also antivaccinators: Richard A. Mohr, "AIDS, Gays, and State Coercion," *Bioethics*, 1, 1 (1987), p. 48.

[52] David L. Kirp and Ronald Bayer, "The Second Decade of AIDS: The End of Exceptionalism?," in Kirp and Bayer, eds., *AIDS in the Industrialized Democracies* (New Brunswick, 1992); Birgit Westphal Christensen et al., *AIDS Prævention og kontrol i Norden* (Stockholm, 1988), p. 66.

[53] *Sanitary Record*, 19 (5 March 1897), p. 200.

[54] *Die Cholera. Ihre Verhütung und Heilung: Von einem erfahrenen Ärzte* (Hannover, 1885), p. iv; *SB*, 1882/83, Akst. 164, pp. 578–79.

[55] Jno. Pickering, *Which? Sanitation and Sanatory Remedies, or Vaccination and the Drug Treatment?* (London, 1892), pp. 84–85, 143.

[56] Annemarie Kinzelbach, "'Böse Blattern' oder 'Franzosenkrankheit': Syphiliskonzept, Kranke und die Genese des Krankenhauses in oberdeutschen Reichsstädten der frühen Neuzeit," in Martin Dinges and Thomas Schlich, eds., *Neue Wege in der Seuchengeschichte* (Stuttgart, 1995), p. 51.

instinctual overstimulation), both the demand for and supply of mercenary sex could be reduced. On the former side, male prenuptial continence, earlier marriages and subsequent monogamy promised to lessen demand, while improved living conditions, greater employment possibilities, expanded educational opportunities and higher wages for women held out the prospect of drying up the supply. The point, as one observer put it, was to remove the cause of irregular intercourse and its attendant VD, to teach the young to live cleanly, morally and chastely. Seeking to prevent the effects of VD without removing the cause was (in an analogy that spoke to the faith in prevention at the heart of the environmentalist enterprise regardless of the disease at issue) no more scientific than treating tonsillitis due to sewer-gas by swabbing throats and prescribing formamint tablets rather than renewing the drains.[57] An environmentalist approach to syphilis envisioned a reformed society where sexual and social practices had been brought into harmony and (depending on the vantage) either chastity and monogamy had equilibrated demand and legitimate supply at a low level or, in the free-love version, natural copulation unhindered by the constraints of marriage, family or convention had dried up the demand for mercenary sex, although, in this case, not necessarily solving the problem of VD spread through consensual, non-commercial but promiscuous relations. An environmentalist approach continues even today in good health among those who question or minimize the role of the HIV as the (single) cause of AIDS, focusing instead on the effects of poor nutrition, bad sanitation, "environmental insults," compromised immune systems due to drug abuse, sperm overload or other illness, depression, poor access to medical care and other alleged cofactors of the epidemic as a way of applying a social analysis to what virologists insist is a purely microbiological problem.[58]

---

[57] *Nineteenth Century*, 82 (July–December 1917), p. 1052; *ZBGK*, 8, 2 (1908), pp. 51–57.

[58] Meredeth Turshen, "Is AIDS Primarily a Sexually Transmitted Disease?," in Nadine Job-Spira et al., eds., *Santé publique et maladies à transmission sexuelle* (Montrouge, 1990), p. 347; Michel Jossay and Yves Donadieu, *Le SIDA* (Paris, 1987), pp. 167–79; Rolf Rosenbrock, "The Role of Policy in Effective Prevention and Education," in Dorothee Friedrich and Wolfgang Heckmann, eds., *Aids in Europe: The Behavioural Aspect* (Berlin, 1995), v. V, pp. 25–26; Rolf Rosenbrock, "Aids-Prävention und die Aufgaben der Sozialwissenschaften," in Rosenbrock and Andreas Salmen, eds., *Aids-Prävention* (Berlin, 1990), p. 18; Gene M. Shearer and Ursula Hurtenbach, "Is Sperm Immunosuppressive in Male Homosexuals and Vasectomized Men?," *Immunology Today*, 3, 6 (1982), pp. 153–54; G. M. Shearer and A. S. Rabson, "Semen and AIDS," *Nature*, 308, 5956 (15 March 1984), p. 230; Henri H. Mollaret, "The Socio-Ecological Interpretation of the Appearance of Really New Infections," in Charles Mérieux, ed., *SIDA: Épidémies et sociétés* (n.p., 1987), p. 112; Treichler, "AIDS, Homophobia, and Biomedical Discourse", pp. 53–54; J. A. Sonnabend, "The Etiology of AIDS," *AIDS Research*, 1, 1 (1983), p. 9; Peter H. Duesberg, *Infectious AIDS: Have We Been Misled?* (Berkeley, 1995), pp. 328–33,

In our own era, the concept of social medicine, begun in the previous century, has continued a broadly environmentalist approach.[59] Even at the height of bacteriology's prestige, during the 1890s, a concern had been voiced for the social background against which disease, however immediately and necessarily caused by microorganisms, however preventable by hygienic habits, ebbed and flowed.[60] The Pasteurian variant of bacteriology, in any case, allowed for environmental influences in its conception of the varying virulence of microorganisms.[61] The discovery that many more were infected with the tubercle bacillus than actually suffered symptoms of consumption, and in general the issue of asymptomatic carriers, implied that, because omnipresent, microorganisms (however necessary) were not sufficient causes and shifted attention back to the cofactors, both social and individual, required for fullblown clinical cases.[62] The development of immunology has displaced interest from predatory microorganisms to the human body's (often socially determined) ability to resist them.[63] Contemporary social medicine accentuates the limits of therapeutic intervention, focusing instead on the environmental, psychological and social conditions behind both disease itself and its spread and incidence. Attention has been trained on the worrisome prevalence of differences in morbidity and mortality

539; Peter Duesberg, ed., *AIDS: Virus- or Drug-Induced?* (Dordrecht, 1996), pp. 71, 78, 179; Peter Duesberg, *Inventing the AIDS Virus* (Washington, DC, 1996), chs. 7, 8, pp. 595–96; Robert S. Root-Bernstein, *Rethinking AIDS: The Tragic Cost of Premature Consensus* (New York, 1993), pp. 26–30, ch. 10.

[59] Howard Waitzkin, "The Social Origins of Illness: A Neglected History," *International Journal of Health Sciences*, 11, 1 (1981), pp. 77–103; Claudine Herzlich and Janine Pierret, *Malades d'hier, malades d'aujourd'hui* (Paris, 1984), pp. 154–55; Milton Terris, "The Changing Relationships of Epidemiology and Society," *Journal of Public Health Policy*, 6, 1 (1985), pp. 23–24.

[60] Rosen, *From Medical Police*, p. 95; Sally Smith Hughes, *The Virus: A History of the Concept* (London, 1977), pp. 21–22; Paul Weindling, "Scientific Elites and Laboratory Organisation in Fin-de-Siécle Paris and Berlin," in Cunningham and Williams, *Laboratory Revolution in Medicine*, pp. 171–72; Owsei Temkin, "Studien zum 'Sinn'-Begriff in der Medizin," *Kyklos*, 2 (1929), pp. 97–98.

[61] John Andrew Mendelsohn, "Cultures of Bacteriology: Formation and Transformation of a Science in France and Germany, 1870–1914" (Ph.D. diss., Princeton University, 1996), pp. 234–63, ch. 8.

[62] Alfons Labisch, "'Hygiene ist Moral – Moral ist Hygiene': Soziale Disziplinierung durch Ärzte und Medizin," in Christoph Sachsse and Florian Tennstedt, eds., *Soziale Sicherheit und soziale Disziplinierung* (Frankfurt am Main, 1986), p. 278; Nancy Tomes, "Moralizing the Microbe: The Germ Theory and the Moral Construction of Behavior in the Late Nineteenth-Century Antituberculosis Movement," in Brandt and Rozin, *Morality and Health*, pp. 276–77.

[63] Anne Marie Moulin, *Le dernier langage de la médecine: Histoire de l'immunologie de Pasteur au Sida* (Paris, 1991); Paul U. Unschuld, "The Conceptual Determination (Überformung) of Individual and Collective Experiences of Illness," in Caroline Currer and Meg Stacey, eds., *Concepts of Health, Illness and Disease: A Comparative Perspective* (Leamington Spa, 1986), pp. 67–68; Emily Martin, *Flexible Bodies: Tracking Immunity in American Culture – From the Days of Polio to the Age of AIDS* (Boston, 1994).

among social classes, even in the era when access to medical attention has, in principle, become increasingly democratized. Now concentrating less on personal hygiene, basic sanitary conveniences and other material factors that can today be taken for granted, social medicine is concerned instead with pollution, education levels, unemployment, job insecurity, income distribution, social cohesion and such more generally social issues.[64] In its most extreme form, concerned with multiple chemical sensitivity (MCS), it sees itself as a revival of a miasmatic theory of environmentally caused disease with its radical political solution of thoroughgoing reform, rather than standard biomedical intervention, as the solution.[65]

At the same time, an environmentalist approach has changed from its nineteenth-century heyday. In certain ways, environmentalism has edged out the traditional quarantinist means of prevention. With the decline of the classic contagious diseases as dangerous killers and the increasing importance instead of illnesses against which the most effective prophylaxis (still) appears to involve modification of habits, lifestyle and environmental factors (cancer, heart disease, stroke), public health has in large measure abandoned the inherited quarantinist techniques, seeking instead to alter behavior to encourage healthier, less disease-prone lives. In this respect, social medicine has become less social than it used to be. Thanks to the achievements of the heroic era of sanitary reform, with the broad provision of basic hygienic living conditions, and undergirded by the insights of bacteriology and virology that have facilitated more targeted means of preventing transmission, public health has become an increasingly individualized, less collective

---

[64] Malcolm Morris, *The Story of English Public Health* (London, 1919), pp. 133–34; Sol Levine and Abraham M. Lilienfeld, eds., *Epidemiology and Health Policy* (New York, 1987), p. 3; Richard Wilkinson, *Unhealthy Societies: The Afflictions of Inequality* (London, 1996); Vicente Navarro, *Crisis, Health and Medicine* (New York, 1986), pp. 36ff., 143ff.; Daniel M. Fox, "AIDS and the American Health Polity: The History and Prospects of a Crisis of Authority," *Milbank Quarterly*, 64, suppl. 1 (1986), pp. 12–13; Claudine Herzlich, *Health and Illness: A Social Psychological Analysis* (London, 1973), pp. 23–27; Klaus Hurrelmann, *Sozialisation und Gesundheit: Somatische, psychische und soziale Risikofaktoren im Lebenslauf* (Weinheim, 1988); Richard Smith, *Unemployment and Health* (Oxford, 1987); Mel Bartley, *Authorities and Partisans: The Debate on Unemployment and Health* (Edinburgh, 1992); Andreas Mielck, ed., *Krankheit und soziale Ungleichheit* (Opladen, 1994); Finn Diderichsen et al., eds., *Klass och ohälsa* (n.p., 1991); Ralf Schwarzer and Anja Leppin, *Sozialer Rückhalt und Gesundheit* (Göttingen, 1989).

[65] Steve Kroll-Smith and H. Hugh Floyd, *Bodies in Protest: Environmental Illness and the Struggle over Medical Illness* (New York, 1997), pp. 1–2; Deborah Lupton, *The Imperative of Health: Public Health and the Regulated Body* (London, 1995), p. 50; Meredith Minkler, "Health Education, Health Promotion and the Open Society: An Historical Perspective," *Health Education Quarterly*, 16, 1 (1989), pp. 24–25; Bryan S. Turner, *Regulating Bodies* (London, 1992), pp. 130–31.

endeavor.[66] The microenvironmentalism of a focus on individual habits has increased in relative importance as battles over the macroenvironmentalism of the nineteenth-century concern with communal infrastructure have been won. Even as the "socialism of the microbe" ushered in by bacteriology revealed the increasing interdependence of modern society, with germs largely indifferent to social status, the precautions now advocated were more likely to focus on individual behavior than on collectively improving the condition of the endangered.[67] Whereas earlier, only the rich could afford the luxuries of corporeal grooming, personal hygiene and the sanitary necessities of health in proximate urban conditions, the habits and wherewithal that have allowed individuals to assume greater responsibility for the collective wellbeing have cascaded in an ever-swelling stream down the social scale. *Homo hygienicus* has become a common species.[68]

The growing prevalence of chronic ailments has shifted the aim of public health from the physical environment to the habits of individuals in recognition that private acts have social consequences.[69] Knowledge of the specific etiology and pathways of disease has allowed prevention to be targeted at groups subject to particular risk. To avoid tuberculosis epidemics, as one enthusiastic American bacteriologist calculated, the living conditions of all citizens need not be improved when instead active cases could be prevented from infecting others.[70] Because of this individualized focus, social medicine is less unambiguously identified with reformist and democratic political currents than were its predecessors in the past century. One approach to the question of individual predisposition that

---

[66] Paul Starr, *The Social Transformation of American Medicine* (New York, 1982), pp. 189–91; David Armstrong, *Political Anatomy of the Body* (Cambridge, 1983), pp. 10–11; Christopher Lawrence, *Medicine in the Making of Modern Britain, 1700–1920* (London, 1994), pp. 73–74.

[67] Pierre Rosanvallon, *L'état en France de 1789 à nos jours* (Paris, 1990), pp. 130–31; Charles Nicolle, *Naissance, vie et mort des maladies infectieuses* (Paris, 1930), pp. 13–16; Tomes, "Moralizing the Microbe," p. 284.

[68] Alfons Labisch, *Homo Hygienicus: Gesundheit und Medizin in der Neuzeit* (Frankfurt, 1992); Johan Goudsblom, "Public Health and the Civilizing Process," *Milbank Quarterly*, 64, 2 (1986), pp. 185–86.

[69] Ronald Bayer, "AIDS, Power and Reason," *Milbank Quarterly*, 64, suppl. 1 (1986), p. 171; Charles Rosenberg, "Banishing Risk: Continuity and Change in the Moral Management of Disease," in Brandt and Rozin, *Morality and Health*, p. 37.

[70] Elizabeth Fee and Dorothy Porter, "Public Health, Preventive Medicine, and Professionalization: Britain and the United States in the Nineteenth Century," in Fee and Roy M. Acheson, eds., *A History of Education in Public Health* (Oxford, 1991), p. 35. Charles V. Chapin, Health Commissioner of Providence, Rhode Island, was exemplary for American circumstances in this displacement of sanitation by bacteriology: Judith Walzer Leavitt, *Typhoid Mary: Captive to the Public's Health* (Boston, 1996), pp. 23–25.

sought answers in the genetic endowment of the ill found solutions in the eugenic and eventually racialist movements of the 1930s and forties and has been damned accordingly.[71] In other respects, critics have attacked what they see as the tendency of this approach to blame the victim, foisting responsibility for illness on the patient's lifestyle while ignoring the larger social context within which individual choices are made.[72] Having achieved much of the basic sanitary infrastructure that was the object of contention in the past century, and with the classic contagious diseases believed to be a thing of the past, environmentalism has come to focus instead more exclusively on the question of individual predisposition, with the attendant micromanagement and often moralizing tone of such endeavors.[73]

THE ACKERKNECHTIAN PAST

Ackerknecht may have given the most coherent modern exposition of this sense that nations have chosen prophylactic strategies in line with their political proclivities – for reasons, in other words, that have as much to do with their own nature as with the epidemic faced. But the general theme, that different approaches to contagious disease corresponded roughly to political ideology, has long been a leitmotif of epidemiological debate, not only concerning the illnesses (cholera, smallpox, syphilis) under consideration here, but also reaching back to the plague and yellow fever and continuing into our own day with AIDS. Ackerknecht's argument is one formulation of a more general political interpretation of disease prophylaxis that identifies two basic approaches, quarantin-

---

[71] Weindling, *International Health Organisations*, p. 136; Dorothy Porter and Roy Porter, "What Was Social Medicine? An Historiographical Essay," *Journal of Historical Sociology*, 1, 1 (March 1988), pp. 98–102; Greta Jones, *Social Hygiene in Twentieth-Century Britain* (London, 1986), pp. 5–7; Dorothy Porter, ed., *Social Medicine and Medical Sociology in the Twentieth Century* (Amsterdam, 1997), pp. 10–11.

[72] Dorothy Nelkin and Sander L. Gilman, "Placing Blame for Devastating Disease," in Arien Mack, ed., *In Time of Plague* (New York, 1991), pp. 48–52; "The Lifestyle Approach to Prevention," *Journal of Public Health Policy*, 1, 1 (March 1980), pp. 6–9; Robert Crawford, "You Are Dangerous to Your Health: The Ideology and Politics of Victim Blaming," *International Journal of Health Services*, 7, 4 (1977), pp. 671–74.

[73] The dangers in contemporary life to health held out in the opening paragraphs of the Lalonde report indicate the shift in priorities and the moralizing undertone at work: "environmental pollution, city living, habits of indolence, the abuse of alcohol, tobacco and drugs, and eating patterns which put the pleasing of the senses above the needs of the human body" (Marc Lalonde, *A New Perspective on the Health of Canadians* [Ottawa, 1974], p. 5). See generally the essays in Brandt and Rozin, *Morality and Health*.

ism and sanitation, or (in the words of Richard Thorne Thorne, Medical Officer of Health to the Local Government Board) restriction and salubrity, seeking, in turn, to excavate their roots in the various emphases attached by different political systems to individual or communal rights.[74]

Faced for the first time with cholera in the early nineteenth century, anticontagionists and sanitationists from Moscow to London viewed quarantinism as an unwarranted violation of individual freedom and needless to boot. Most charitably, they portrayed it as a throwback to a primitive age, a policy adequate perhaps for a less civilized and enlightened, more authoritarian society, but no longer justified at current levels of European social evolution.[75] All nations were susceptible to a heroically whiggish public health teleology that portrayed a sanitationist approach as the natural complement to civilization. While cordons and quarantines were barbaric and oldfashioned, sanitationism was the prophylactic method appropriate to a nation placed, like France, at the acme of civilization.[76] At the most general level, cholera was seen as affecting the nations of Europe less drastically than Asia because of the greater freedom, wealth and civilization it encountered along its westerly peregrination toward "the Focus of civilization and comforts," as one British observer described his own country.[77] The further west one moved, the better organized and prophylactically equipped the state, the less extreme the divide between rich and poor, the more propitious the condition of the lower classes, the better able they were to withstand the

[74] PRO, FO 83/1277, British Delegation to the Dresden Conference, no. 5, 29 March 1893; R. Thorne Thorne, "On Sea-Borne Cholera: British Measures of Prevention v. European Measures of Restriction," *BMJ*, 2 (13 August 1887).

[75] F. C. M. Markus, *Rapport sur le choléra-morbus de Moscou* (Moscow, 1832), pp. 202–03; *Hamburgisches Magazin der auslandischen Literatur der gesammten Heilkunde*, 23 (1832), p. 42; *PP* 1871 (c. 408-1) xix, 29, p. li; Kenneth F. Kiple, ed., *The Cambridge World History of Human Disease* (Cambridge, 1993), p. 648.

[76] *Annales*, 9, 1 (1833), p. 55; Delagrange, *Mémoire contre le choléra d'asie, la peste d'orient et les fléaux dits contagieux ou diversement transmissibles* (Paris, 1850), pp. 25–27, 67; J. Bouillaud, *Traité pratique, théorique et statistique du choléra-morbus de Paris* (Paris, 1832), p. 290; P. A. Enault, *Choléra-morbus: Conseils hygiéniques a suivre pour s'en préserver* (Paris, 1831), pp. 9–10; *Rapport sur le choléra-morbus, lu à l'Academie royale de médecine, en séance générale, les 26 et 30 juillet 1831* (Paris, 1831), p. 137; *Journal des Débats*, 3 April 1832, p. 2; *Gazette médicale de Paris*, 3, 72 (1832), p. 500; 2, 39 (1831), p. 333; François Delaporte, *Disease and Civilization: The Cholera in Paris, 1832* (Cambridge, MA, 1986), pp. 16–20.

[77] *An Enquiry into the Disease Called Cholera Morbus* (London, 1833), p. 49; C. D. Skogman, *Anmärkningar om karantäns-anstalter framställde vid præsidii nedläggande uti Kongl. Vetenskaps-Academien den 4 april 1832* (Stockholm, 1832), pp. 13–14; Charles C. F. Greville, *The Greville Memoirs* (2nd edn.; London, 1874), v. II, pp. 287–88; Brigitta Schader, *Die Cholera in der deutschen Literatur* (Gräfelfing, 1985), pp. 63–65; Charles Rosenberg, *The Cholera Years* (Chicago, 1962), pp. 15–16.

epidemic.[78] "It is not quarantines, but the rule of law and a chicken in every pot that cholera will respect," as a German put it.[79]

More pointedly, sanitationists saw in quarantinism the expression of authoritarian instincts among Europe's least popularly based regimes. A Scotsman worried lest such precautions be the Trojan horse by which public health become an excuse for incursions into private liberties, ultimately despotism. Having witnessed the mail opened, examined, fumigated and resealed in a quarantine station on the Austrian frontier, he warned that such lazarettos were the one spot on earth wholly beyond the control of public opinion.[80] One observer associated quarantinism with "the gigantic military organization of Russia – the rigorous military despotism of Prussia – and the all-searching police of Austria, with their walled towns, and guards and gates."[81] Another drew a clear association between quarantinism and its adoption by "fanatical Popes and despotic governments, to dissolve refractory councils, or to repress the rising spirit of a nation."[82] Quarantinist precautions were necessarily arbitrary and capricious, giving governments extensive means of coercion and mischief and needlessly enhancing the powers of administrative bureaucracies.[83] Pettenkofer drew an explicit analogy between epidemiology and

---

[78] *EMSJ*, 58 (July 1831), p. 119; F. W. Becker, *Letters on the Cholera in Prussia: Letter I to John Thomson, MD, FRS* (London, 1832), p. 41; J. C. Röttger, *Kritik der Cholera nach physikalischen Gründen* (Halle, 1832), pp. 8–9; *Die Cholera morbus, oder ostindische Brechruhr: Eine für Jedermann fassliche Zusammenstellung des Wichtigsten aus den vorzüglichsten, bisher über diese Krankheit erschienenen Schriften* (Tübingen, 1831), pp. 69–70; M. Kalisch, *Zur Lösung der Ansteckungs- und Heilbarkeitsfrage der Cholera* (Berlin, 1831), p. 8; *Rathgeber für alle, welche sich gegen die Cholera morbus schützen wollen* (6th edn.; Breslau, 1831), p. 28; *Bemerkungen über die Furcht vor der herschenden Brechruhr* (Leipzig, 1831), pp. v–vi; J. N. Edlem von Meyer, *Einige neue Beobachtungen über das Wesen der Cholera Morbus aus der Erfahrung geschöpft* (Vienna, 1831), pp. 4–5.

[79] Friedrich Schnurrer, *Die Cholera morbus, ihre Verbreitung, ihre Zufälle, die versuchten Heilmethoden, ihre Eigenthümlichkeiten und die im Grossen dagegen anzuwendenden Mittel* (Stuttgart, 1831), p. 75.

[80] John Bowring, *Observations on the Oriental Plague and on Quarantines, as a Means of Arresting its Progress* (Edinburgh, 1838), p. 12.

[81] William Fergusson, *Letters upon Cholera Morbus* (London, 1832), pp. 11–12. Quarantinism was the conservative position, as Thorne Thorne put it from the Dresden Sanitary Conference: PRO, FO 83/1277, British Delegation, acct. no. 5, 29 March 1893.

[82] John Webster, *An Essay on Epidemic Cholera* (London, 1832), pp. 102–03; George Hamilton Bell, *Letter to Sir Henry Halford . . . on the Tendency of the proposed Regulations for Cholera . . .* (Edinburgh, 1831), p. 6; Emanuel Pochmann, *Die Cholerapilz-Massregeln von Prof. Robert Koch mit ihren Irrthümern und Gefahren und das Cholera-Elend in Hamburg* (Linz a/d Donau, 1892), p. 45; Coleman, *Yellow Fever in the North*, p. 44.

[83] Charles Maclean, *Evils of the Quarantine Laws and Non-Existance of Pestilential Contagion* (London, 1824), p. 249; *London Medical and Surgical Journal* 7 (1835), pp. 699–702; Gavin Milroy, *The Cholera Not to Be Arrested by Quarantine* (London, 1847), pp. 32–35; White, *The Evils of Quarantine Laws and Non-Existence of Pestilential Contagion* (London, 1837); *LMG*, n.s., 3 (1846), p. 202; *Journal of Public Health*, 2 (1849), pp. 15–16; *Transactions of the National Association for the Promotion of Social Science* (1862), p. 871; Ambroise Tardieu, *Dictionnaire d'hygiène publique et de salubrité* (Paris, 1852), v. II, p. 301; C. R. Meers, *Notice sur la nature et le traitement du choléra asiatique* (Maastricht, 1875), p. 6.

politics: quarantines and cordons, like censorship, attempted the hopeless task of excluding a spore, whether biological or intellectual, that once inevitably smuggled in would multiply and spread.[84]

Conversely, quarantinists complained that their position was regarded as an "old prejudice, hastily and heedlessly adopted," in contrast to sanitationism which better fit the "liberal spirit" of the day.[85] The Central Board of Health in London, initially a seat of convinced quarantinism, was accused by its foes of being the "juntas of this metropolis."[86] The association between quarantinism and political reaction was cemented in France when the Restoration government used the military guarding the sanitary cordon drawn against the yellow fever in Catalonia in 1821 as the nucleus of the army that invaded Spain two years later, deposing the republic and reinstating a Bourbon on the throne.[87] Sanitationism, in contrast, concerned itself with the plight of the poor, seeking prevention through social reform, and was regarded as one of the many blessings of the Revolution. Thanks to the overthrow of tyranny in '89, average citizens now conducted themselves so as to avoid disease, drinking and smoking only in moderation.[88] Cholera did not exist in republics, one contemporary bravely theorized, since there all citizens were comfortably well fed, housed and clothed.[89]

In national terms, the British were generally regarded, and certainly saw themselves, as the strongest supporters of a sanitationist approach during the cholera era, while the continental autocracies were quarantinists.[90] Among the German states, Prussia was often portrayed as the

[84] Max von Pettenkofer, *Über Cholera mit Berücksichtigung der jüngsten Choleraepidemie in Hamburg* (Munich 1892), pp. 31–32.

[85] William MacMichael, *Is the Cholera Spasmodica of India a Contagious Disease?* (London, 1831), pp. 3–4.   [86] *London Medical and Surgical Journal*, 2, 46 (1832), p. 632.

[87] Delagrange, *Mémoire contre le choléra*, pp. 25–27, 67: much as sanitary cordons of Prussian and Austrian troops on the Polish borders in the winter of 1770/71 were used both to hamper spread of the plague and as an exercise for the partition of that nation in 1771; Georg Sticker, *Abhandlungen aus der Seuchengeschichte und Seuchenlehre* (Giessen, 1908), v. I/1, p. 258.

[88] M. Le Baron Larrey, *Mémoire sur le choléra-morbus* (Paris, 1831), p. 32; although he also thought that in monarchical Britain the rules of hygiene were even better observed.

[89] George D. Sussman, "From Yellow Fever to Cholera: A Study of French Government Policy, Medical Professionalism and Popular Movements in the Epidemic Crises of the Restoration and the July Monarchy" (Ph.D. diss., Yale University, 1971), p. 345. Alibert thought that certain skin diseases arose from tyranny: Ackerknecht, *Medicine at the Paris Hospital*, p. 156. Thomas Jefferson held similar views on the connection between good political systems and public health: Rosen, *From Medical Police*, pp. 246–58.

[90] J. A. Gläser, *Gemeinverständliche Anticontagionistische Betrachtungen bei Gelegenheit der letzten Cholera-Epidemie in Hamburg 1892* (Hamburg, 1893), p. 50; Friedrich Wolter, *Das Auftreten der Cholera in Hamburg in dem Zeitraume von 1831–1893 mit besonderer Berücksichtigung der Epidemie des Jahres 1892* (Munich, 1898), pp. 168–72; *Der Choleralärm in Europa 1884* (Hannover, 1884), p. 138; Ferdinand Hueppe, *Die Cholera-Epidemie in Hamburg 1892* (Berlin, 1893), p. 100.

archquarantinist, while others, as various as Bavaria and Hamburg, were seen as more prophylactically liberal.[91] Britain, much as Ackerknecht would have it, was regarded by contemporaries during the nineteenth century as sanitationist because its working class would not brook drastic statutory intervention and because trading interests resisted quarantinism's interference in commercial liberty.[92] More nebulously, the British spirit of individual liberty was considered resistant to such restrictions on personal freedom.[93] In such national accountings, the French generally placed somewhere between the sanitationist British and the quarantinist autocracies. On the one hand, they regarded much German legislation as dictatorial, although a certain grudging respect for the efficiency and effectiveness of their transrhinean neighbors was often part of the mix.[94] On the other, they were often astounded to discover that nations, such as the British, the Dutch or the Americans, renowned for their concern with personal liberties, were nonetheless willing to impose measures far more interventionist than anything they had accomplished.[95]

In much the same way, as will be shown later in detail, compulsory smallpox vaccination was regarded by its opponents as a violation of personal liberty and those nations which ended such precautions, above all Britain, were hailed as defenders of individual rights against the overweening pretensions of public health authorities. For the regulation of prostitution and attempts to control syphilis, the contrasts were, if any-

---

[91] *Hygiea*, 10, 8 (August 1848), p. 494; C. J. Le Viseur, *Über die Cholera und die erfolgreichste Kur derselben* (2nd edn.; Posen, 1868), pp. 7–8; Aloys Martin, ed., *Haupt-Bericht über die Cholera-Epidemie des Jahres 1854 im Königreiche Bayern* (Munich, 1857), pp. 426, 429; Gläser, *Gemeinverständliche Anticontagionistische Betrachtungen*, pp. 45–50; *Die Misserfolge der Staatsmedicin und ihre Opfer in Hamburg* (Hagen i. W., [1892]), p. 12; *Die Cholera. Ihre Verhütung und Heilung*, pp. iv–vii.

[92] Imagine a city like Manchester or London with its factory workers and then try to impose quarantines on their houses. Who would want to be a constable there?: Albert Sachs, ed., *Tagebuch über das Verhalten der bösartigen Cholera in Berlin* (Berlin, 14 September–31 December 1831), pp. 236–37.

[93] Becker, *Letters on the Cholera in Prussia*, p. 48; Sachs, *Tagebuch*, p. 312; *Hansard*, 1831, v. 9, cols. 310–14; *EMSJ*, 109 (October 1831), p. 415; Gilbert Blane, *Warning to the British Public Against the Alarming Approach of the Indian Cholera* (London, October 1831), p. 2.

[94] *Bulletin*, 3, 55 (1906), p. 68; Bert, *Le choléra*, pp. 14–20.

[95] Chartier, Laennec and Lapeyre, "Rapport sur l'isolement des malades atteints d'affections contagieuses présenté au Conseil de santé des hospices civils de Nantes," *Rapport sur les travaux du Conseil central d'hygiène publique et de salubrité de la ville de Nantes et du département de la Loire-Inférieure* (1880), pp. 98–100; *JO*, Sénat, Débat, 21 May 1901, p. 664; 30 January 1902, p. 87; *Moniteur universel*, 172, 20 June 1868, p. 887; Alfred Fillassier, *De la détermination des pouvoirs publics en matière d'hygiène* (2nd edn.; Paris, 1902), p. 402; *Bulletin de la Société de médecine publique et d'hygiène professionnelle*, 2 (1879), pp. 328–30; Sachs, *Tagebuch*, p. 34; Henri Monod, *La santé publique* (Paris, 1904), p. 8; André Latrille, *Les difficultés d'application de la loi du 15 février 1902 relative à la protection de la santé publique* (Bordeaux, 1944), p. 144; Aquilino Morelle, *La défaite de la santé publique* (Paris, 1996), pp. 266–69.

thing, even starker, with divisions drawn between the conservatism of the inscription system and the liberalism of its abolition. In a classically Ackerknechtian sense, regulation too was a political, not just a prophylactic issue.[96] In Britain and Scandinavia, among those countries which abandoned regulation early, native political instinct was seen as unable to accept such continued violation of prostitutes' civil rights, however much the system may have suited allegedly despotic nations.[97] Even Acton, among the most important English proponents of regulation, recognized that a fullscale system on the continental model would be repugnant to the political sentiments of Britain, a nation incapable of paternal government that "boasts itself to be the peculiar home of freedom."[98] Conversely, in the continental nations where regulation continued, the argument was that, since the higher good of public health took precedence, the system, far from being a violation of civil liberties, was a hygienic measure targeted at the potentially dangerous, much as quarantines imposed restrictions on travelers for the benefit of the common weal.[99]

Modern historians too have followed the lead indicated by such early observers and then formulated in one version by Ackerknecht, the idea of divergent prophylactic strategies that corresponded to different political instincts. The history of public health has undergone a chastening reconsideration of the grand teleological accounts once offered by scholars such as George Rosen, where evolving scientific knowledge lit the path for increasingly powerful and effective statutory efforts to improve overall salubrity. Whether through McKeown's attempts to demonstrate

[96] *Journal des maladies cutanées et syphilitiques*, 14, 10 (October 1902), p. 773; XVIIth International Congress of Medicine, London 1913, Section XIII, *Dermatology and Syphilography* (London, 1913), p. 55; Käthe Schirmacher, *The Modern Woman's Rights Movement* (New York, 1912), p. 179.

[97] William Osler, *The Principles and Practice of Medicine* (8th edn.; New York, 1919), p. 278; anon., *The Greatest of Our Social Evils: Prostitution* (London, 1857), pp. 1, 306–11; Dubois-Havenith, ed., *Conférence internationale pour la prophylaxie de la syphilis et des maladies vénériennes: Enquêtes sur l'état de la prostitution et la fréquence de la syphilis et des maladies vénériennes dans les différents pays* (Brussels, 1899), v. I, pt. 2, p. 10; Louis Deck, *Syphilis et réglementation de la prostitution en Angleterre et aux Indes* (Paris, 1898), pp. 11–12; Louis Fiaux, *La prostitution réglementée et les pouvoirs publics dans les principaux états des deux-mondes* (Paris, 1902), p. xxxiv; *Förhandlingar*, 1912, p. 393; H. Mireur, *La syphilis et la prostitution* (2nd edn.; Paris, 1888), pp. 4–6; L. Reuss, *La prostitution au point de vue de l'hygiène et de l'administration en France et a l'étranger* (Paris, 1889), pp. 481–82, 592.

[98] William Acton, *Prostitution, Considered in Its Moral, Social, and Sanitary Aspects, in London and Other Large Cities and Garrison Towns* (2nd edn.; London, 1870), pp. 160, 204–06, 217, 221. Similar points of view are found in *Annales*, 3/15 (1886), p. 517; Félix Regnault, *L'évolution de la prostitution* (Paris, n.d. [1906?]), p. 105.

[99] Dubois-Havenith, ed., *Conférence internationale pour la prophylaxie de la syphilis et des maladies vénériennes: Compte rendu des séances* (Brussels, 1900), p. 33.

the inconsequentiality of much public health effort, through those of Foucault and battalions of social control theorists, seeking to unmask governmental repression, class oppression and the imposition of bourgeois norms on the unwilling poor in the guise of what earlier observers in their naive neo-Eliasian fashion had regarded as the spread of civilized behavior, or through the maw of racialism into which the initially progressive ambitions of eugenicism had been dragged, public health has long been unable to claim the status of a universally accepted good in any simple fashion.[100] The focus here, in contrast, is not on the overall direction of public health, teleological or meandering as it may be, but on political interpretations of different strategies internal to the development of prevention against contagious disease.

Historians, writing of measures imposed against the first European epidemics of cholera, have described the contagionist etiology of the disease and its attendant quarantinist precautions as a "ruling-class doctrine," the platform of strong interventionist government and, more generally, as "the assertion of the superior claim of the public good over private property and personal liberty."[101] Watts calls the quarantinist policies first elaborated in Italy against the plague the "Ideology of Order," an authoritarian set of interventions that disrupted the everyday lives of citizens.[102] Rosen as well as other more contemporary observers accept Ackerknecht's suggestion that contagionism and quarantinism corresponded to authoritarian political instincts, miasmatism and sanitationism to liberal.[103] Sussman, an expert on yellow fever and

[100] Deftly outlined in Dorothy Porter, "Introduction," in Dorothy Porter, ed., *The History of Public Health and the Modern State* (Amsterdam, 1994), pp. 2–3.

[101] Morris, *Cholera 1832*, pp. 183–84; Norman Howard-Jones, "Prelude to Modern Preventive Medicine," in N. F. Stanley and R. A. Joske, eds., *Changing Disease Patterns and Human Behavior* (London, 1980), p. 70; C. Fraser Brockington, *Public Health in the Nineteenth Century* (Edinburgh, 1965), p. 71; Christian Barthel, *Medizinische Polizey und medizinische Aufklärung: Aspekte des öffentlichen Gesundheitsdiskurses im 18. Jahrhundert* (Frankfurt, 1989), pp. 60–63; Deborah Lupton, *Medicine as Culture: Illness, Disease and the Body in Western Societies* (London, 1994), pp. 30–31.

[102] Sheldon Watts, *Epidemics and History: Disease, Power and Imperialism* (New Haven, 1997), pp. 16–17.

[103] George Rosen, *A History of Public Health* (expanded edn.; Baltimore, 1993), p. 266; Hildreth, *Doctors, Bureaucrats, and Public Health*, p. 110; David M. Vess, *Medical Revolution in France, 1789–1796* (Gainesville, 1975), p. 145; Asa Briggs, "Cholera and Society in the Nineteenth Century," *Past and Present*, 19 (April 1961), p. 83; Barbara Dettke, *Die asiatische Hydra: Die Cholera von 1830/31 in Berlin und den preussischen Provinzen Posen, Preussen und Schlesien* (Berlin, 1995), pp. 13, 24–25, 301; Thomas Stamm-Kuhlmann, "Die Cholera von 1831: Herausforderungen an Wissenschaft und staatliche Verwaltung," *Sudhoffs Archiv*, 73, 2 (1989), p. 188; Rodenstein, *"Mehr Licht, mehr Luft"*, pp. 56–58; Richard S. Ross, "The Prussian Administrative Response to the First Cholera Epidemic in Prussia in 1831" (Ph.D. diss., Boston College, 1991), pp. 264–65; Olivier Faure, *Histoire sociale de la médecine* (Paris, 1994), pp. 115, 143–44; Esteban Rodríguez Ocaña, "La dependencia social de un comportamiento científico: Los médicos españoles y el cólera de 1833–1835," *Dynamis*, 1 (1981), pp. 102–03;

cholera in France, follows Ackerknecht without remorse, drawing exact and unwavering parallels between matters medical and political. The restored monarchies of the early nineteenth century were contagionist in their etiology, quarantinist in prevention and authoritarian in politics. Their opponents, in turn, were the liberals and commercial Interests, the united supporters of a free exchange of goods and ideas who favored a sanitationist approach.[104] Mitchell draws a similar contrast between France and Germany that is wholly in thrall to an oldfashioned teutonic *Sonderweg*: the French were liberals and therefore unwilling to impose statutorily interventionist prophylaxis, while the Germans had no such compunctions.[105] Evans, in his massive account of cholera in Hamburg, draws a stark contrast between the interventionist, quarantinist policies engineered by Koch in Berlin and imposed by late absolutist and "military-bureaucratic" Prussia on a recalcitrant Hamburg, more interested in taking a liberal, laissez-faire approach in harmony with its Anglophilic inclinations.[106] Labisch and Tennstedt, dwelling on the difference between local and national health policy, portray the quarantinist poli-

Hamlin, *Public Health and Social Justice*, pp. 4, 113. Also basically accepting Ackerknecht's contention that anticontagionism was economically liberal, although less certain that it was also politically so, is Catherine J. Kudlick, *Cholera in Post-Revolutionary Paris* (Berkeley, 1996), pp. 78–81. A similar division exists between the only moderately quarantinist approach to leprosy in "enlightened" Norway and the hyperquarantinism of "imperialist" nations, fearful that the disease would spread to the colonialist homelands: Zachary Gussow, *Leprosy, Racism and Public Health: Social Policy in Chronic Disease Control* (Boulder, 1989), chs. 4, 5.

[104] Sussman, "From Yellow Fever to Cholera," pp. 43, 184, 222–23. Heavily informed by Ackerknechtian assumptions are also: Léon-François Hoffmann, *La peste à Barcelone* (Princeton, 1964), ch. 3; Martin S. Pernick, "Politics, Parties and Pestilence: Epidemic Yellow Fever in Philadelphia and the Rise of the First Party System," in Judith Walzer Leavitt and Ronald L. Numbers, eds., *Sickness and Health in America* (2nd edn.; Madison, 1985); Gerd Göckenjan, *Kurieren und Staat machen: Gesundheit und Medizin in der bürgerlichen Welt* (Frankfurt, 1985), pp. 112–14; Oleg P. Schepin and Waldemar V. Yermakov, *International Quarantine* (Madison, CT, 1991), pp. 73, 113. Kearns distinguishes between environmentalist and quarantinist approaches to public health, but seems willing, although the argument is nebulous, to attribute the possibility of subordinating individual rights also to the former: Gerry Kearns, "Zivilis or Hygaeia: Urban Public Health and the Epidemiological Transition," in Richard Lawton, ed., *The Rise and Fall of Great Cities* (London, 1989), pp. 120–22.

[105] Allan Mitchell, "Bourgeois Liberalism and Public Health: A Franco-German Comparison," in Jürgen Kocka and Allan Mitchell, eds., *Bourgeois Society in Nineteenth-Century Europe* (Oxford, 1993); Allan Mitchell, *The Divided Path: The German Influence on Social Reform in France After 1870* (Chapel Hill, 1991), pp. 46, 63, 66, 87, 127–32. Similar assumptions that political ideology is transparently reflected in health care policies informs Donald W. Light and Alexander Schuller, eds., *Political Values and Health Care: The German Experience* (Cambridge, 1986), pp. 10–18; Matthew Ramsey, "The Politics of Professional Monopoly in Nineteenth-Century Medicine: The French Model and Its Rivals," in Gerald L. Geison, ed., *Professions and the French State, 1700–1900* (Philadelphia, 1984), pp. 231–32.

[106] Richard J. Evans, *Death in Hamburg: Society and Politics in the Cholera Years 1830–1910* (Oxford, 1987), pp. 219–20, 242, 258, 264 and passim.

cies of the Prussian state as autocratic, while the efforts of municipalities
to improve urban living conditions spoke to the concerns of liberals and
merchants.[107] Mendelsohn shifts the Ackerknechtian distinction, repli-
cating what is in essence the contagionist/sanitationist split now within
the field of bacteriology itself. He distinguishes the Pasteurian approach,
placing microbes in a broad environmental context, from the German
school's insistence that they be understood independently of their surroundings, and draws a parallel between Koch's bacteriological campaign against typhoid and Schlieffen's military bulwarks – both offering
antidemocratic, "police state," conservative and technocratic solutions
to problems of national defense, rejecting the need for social reform
when instead the enemy, whether germs or Gauls, could be targeted.[108]
Even the magisterial work of Murard and Zylberman repeats the tired
saw of Germany, land of public health compulsion, with liberal Britain
as its counterfoil and France hovering in between.[109] In a less immediately political sense, Ackerknechtian dichotomies inform the division
between the individualized preventive strategies (quarantine, isolation)
adopted by the mercantilist, bureaucratic German and Swedish states
and the sanitary impulse aimed not at the patient, but the environment,
pursued in liberal Britain.[110] Others have, more generally, accepted the
Ackerknechtian contention that not etiology alone, but political and economic concerns colored medical and prophylactic views.[111] An environmentalist concern with the social background of disease is (much as

---

[107] Alfons Labisch, with Florian Tennstedt, *Gesellschaftliche Bedingungen öffentlicher Gesundheitsvorsorge*
(Frankfurt, 1990), pp. 88–90, 119–20; Alfons Labisch and Florian Tennstedt, *Der Weg zum "Gesetz über
die Vereinheitlichung des Gesundheitswesens" vom 3. Juli 1934* (Düsseldorf, 1985), pp. 122–23; Gottfried,
"Plague, Public Health and Medicine in Late Medieval England," pp. 350, 365.

[108] Mendelsohn, "Cultures of Bacteriology," pp. 560–63, 596–600, 623.

[109] Lion Murard and Patrick Zylberman, *L'hygiène dans la république: La santé publique en France, ou
l'utopie contrariée (1870–1918)* (Paris, 1996), p. 8. They are, however, careful to insist on the administrative fragmentation of the nation: pp. 148–54.

[110] Gerard Kearns et al., "The Interaction of Political and Economic Factors in the Management of Urban Public Health," in Marie C. Nelson and John Rogers, eds., *Urbanisation and the
Epidemiologic Transition* (Uppsala, 1989), pp. 34–35; W. F. Bynum, *Science and the Practice of Medicine in
the Nineteenth Century* (Cambridge, 1994), pp. 56, 59.

[111] Chantal Beauchamp, *Delivrez-nous du mal: Epidémies, endémies, médecine et hygiène au XIXe siècle
dans l'Indre, l'Indre-Loire et le Loir-et-Cher* (n.p., 1990), pp. 91–92; Vera Boltho-Massarelli and
Michael O'Boyle, "Droits de l'homme et santé publique, une nouvelle alliance," in Eric Heilmann,
ed., *Sida et libertés: La régulation d'une épidemie dans un état de droit* (n.p., 1991), p. 43; Anne Marie Moulin,
"Révolutions médicales et révolutions politiques en Egypte (1865–1917)," *Revue du monde musulman
et de la méditerranée*, 52–53 (1989); Stolberg, *Cholera im Grossherzogtum Toskana*, pp. 62–64; A. A.
MacLaren, "Bourgeois Ideology and Victorian Philanthropy: The Contradictions of Cholera," in
MacLaren, ed., *Social Class in Scotland* (Edinburgh, n.d.), pp. 46–49; Stephen J. Kunitz, "The
Historical Roots and Ideological Functions of Disease Concepts in Three Primary Care
Specialities," *BHM*, 57, 3 (1983); Jürgen Diedrich, "Zwist der Könige," in Antje Kelm and
Heidemarie Grahl, eds., *Der blaue Tod: Die Cholera in Hamburg 1892* (Hamburg, 1992), p. 58; S. Ryan

Ackerknecht would have formulated it had he been concerned with the twentieth and not an earlier century) often considered characteristic of the left, while the individualization of modern medicine is regarded as a conservative conceit of "bourgeois epidemiology."[112] Bacteriology is routinely identified as a conservative doctrine that shifted the blame for disease from social conditions to microbes, requiring only limited statutory intervention rather than the wholescale change implicit in an environmentalist approach.[113] In the most extreme statements, bacteriology and its attendant prophylactic measures are the techniques of police control in imperial states.[114] Behind such linkages lies, of course, an awareness of the bacteriologically inspired imagery of interwar racialist thought and especially the analogies drawn by Nazi ideology between pestilential microbes and Jews.[115]

For smallpox, a similar dichotomy has been posed between liberal nations which repealed compulsory vaccination and conservative regimes, insistent on the greater good of herd immunity.[116] On the regulation of

Johansson, "Food for Thought: Rhetoric and Reality in Modern Mortality History," *Historical Methods*, 27, 3 (Summer 1994), p. 117.

[112] Lesley Doyal with Imogen Pennell, *The Political Economy of Health* (London, 1979), pp. 31–35; Evan Stark, "The Epidemic as Social Event," *International Journal of Health Services*, 7, 4 (1977), p. 697; Simon Szreter, *Fertility, Class and Gender in Britain, 1860–1940* (Cambridge, 1996), pp. 86–89, 187–88, 235–36.

[113] Jack D. Ellis, *The Physician-Legislators of France: Medicine and Politics in the Early Third Republic, 1870–1914* (Cambridge, 1990), p. 179; Meredeth Turshen, *The Politics of Public Health* (New Brunswick, 1989), pp. 20–22; Labisch, *Homo Hygienicus*, pp. 132–34; Labisch, "Hygiene ist Moral," pp. 276–77; Paul Weindling, *Health, Race and German Politics Between National Unification and Nazism, 1870–1945* (Cambridge, 1989), pp. 158–62; Zygmunt Bauman, *Modernity and the Holocaust* (Ithaca, 1989), pp. 70–71; Barbara Bromberger et al., *Medizin, Faschismus und Widerstand* (2nd edn.; Frankfurt, 1990), pp. 64–65; Jane Lewis, "Public Health Doctors and AIDS as a Public Health Issue," in Virginia Berridge and Philip Strong, eds., *AIDS and Contemporary History* (Cambridge, 1993), pp. 44–45; Janet McKee, "Holistic Health and the Critique of Western Medicine," *Social Science and Medicine*, 26, 8 (1988), p. 777; Rolf Å. Gustafsson, *Traditionernas ok: Den svenska hälso- och sjukvårdens organisering i historie-sociologiskt perspektiv* (Stockholm, 1987), pp. 308–09.

[114] Theodore M. Brown, "J. P. Frank's 'Medical Police' and Its Significance for Medicalization in America," in Marten W. de Vries et al., eds., *The Use and Abuse of Medicine* (New York, 1982), p. 216. [115] Saul Friedländer, *Nazi Germany and the Jews* (New York, 1997), v. I, p. 100.

[116] R. M. MacLeod, "Law, Medicine and Public Opinion: The Resistance to Compulsory Health Legislation 1870–1907," *Public Law*, Summer/Autumn 1967, p. 211; Marie Clark Nelson and John Rogers, "The Right to Die? Anti-Vaccination Activity and the 1874 Smallpox Epidemic in Stockholm," *Social History of Medicine*, 5, 3 (December 1992), p. 386; Evans, *Death in Hamburg*, pp. 219–20; J. R. Smith, *The Speckled Monster: Smallpox in England, 1670–1970, with Particular Reference to Essex* (Chelmsford, 1987), p. 175; Mitchell, "Bourgeois Liberalism and Public Health," pp. 355–57; Eberhard Wolff, "Medikalkultur und Modernisierung: Über die Industrialisierung des Gesundheitsverhaltens durch die Pockenschutzimpfung und deren Grenzen im 19. Jahrhundert," in Michael Dauskardt and Helge Gerndt, eds., *Der industrialisierte Mensch* (Hagen, 1993), p. 198; Frederick F. Cartwright, *A Social History of Medicine* (London, 1977), pp. 89–90; Eberhard Wolff, "Prävention, Impfzwang und die Rolle der Medizinethnologie," *Curare*, 14, 1–2 (1991), p. 87. Frevert, in contrast, argues that it was the Prussian state's inability and unwillingness to ram vaccination down its subjects' throats that here delayed compulsion: Ute Frevert, *Krankheit als politisches Problem 1770–1880* (Göttingen, 1984), pp. 73–74.

prostitution modern historians have also found themselves in debt to Ackerknecht, accepting the abolitionist claim that inscription was the venereal expression of authoritarianism.[117] Evans gets himself into an Ackerknechtian conceptual gnarl in his insistence on upholding simultaneously the beliefs that regulationism was autocratic and yet that Hamburg (despite its hyperregulationist system) was the liberal foil to autocratic Prussia.[118] Criminalizing sex by the VD-infected and other techniques proposed by reformers as alternatives to regulation, including the possibility of compulsory biomedical treatment, have been branded as authoritarian, indeed totalitarian.[119] Finally, for AIDS a similar dichotomy persists in the argument that traditional coercive methods of contagious disease control (medical surveillance, isolation and quarantine) were the inclination of conservative governments, while more progressive ones have preferred education and other voluntary means of persuading citizens to alter their behavior in less risky directions.[120] Most broadly

---

[117] Alain Corbin, *Women for Hire: Prostitution and Sexuality in France After 1850* (Cambridge, MA, 1990), p. 256; Paul Weindling with Ursula Slevogt, *Alfred Blaschko (1858–1922) and the Problem of Sexually Transmitted Diseases in Imperial and Weimar Germany: A Bibliography* (Oxford, 1992), p. 7; Weindling, *Health, Race and German Politics*, p. 158; Mary Gibson, *Prostitution and the State in Italy, 1860–1915* (New Brunswick, 1986), pp. 62–63; Laurie Bernstein, *Sonia's Daughters: Prostitutes and Their Regulation in Imperial Russia* (Berkeley, 1995), pp. 17, 295; Anita Ulrich, "Ärzte und Sexualität – am Beispiel der Prostitution," in Alfons Labisch and Reinhard Spree, eds., *Medizinische Deutungsmacht im sozialen Wandel* (Bonn, 1989), pp. 224–26; Paul Weindling, "The Politics of International Co-ordination to Combat Sexually Transmitted Diseases, 1900–1980s," in Berridge and Strong, *AIDS and Contemporary History*, p. 103; Jean-Pierre Machelon, *La république contre les libertés? Les restrictions aux libertés publiques de 1879 à 1914* (Paris, 1976), pp. 194–98, 234–35.

[118] His claim that, in Hamburg, regulationism was a way of resisting the Prussian demand to abolish official brothels clearly will not do: the authoritarian solution would thus become liberal resistance to the Prussian autocrats who, inconveniently, were pursuing a liberal quasi-abolitionist line (Richard J. Evans, "Prostitution, State and Society in Imperial Germany," *Past and Present*, 70 [February 1976], pp. 110–11). For a similar example, see Amy Hackett, "The German Women's Movement and Suffrage, 1890–1914: A Study of National Feminism," in Robert J. Bezucha, ed., *Modern European Social History* (Lexington, 1972), p. 355.

[119] Richard J. Evans, *The Feminist Movement in Germany 1894–1933* (London, 1976), p. 169; Barbara Greven-Aschoff, *Die bürgerliche Frauenbewegung in Deutschland 1894–1933* (Göttingen, 1981), p. 234; Weindling, *Health, Race and German Politics*, p. 345; Lutz Sauerteig, "Salvarsan und der 'ärztliche Polizeistaat': Syphilistherapie im Streit zwischen Ärzten, pharmazeutischer Industrie, Gesundheitsverwaltung und Naturheilverbänden (1910–1927)," in Martin Dinges, ed., *Medizinkritische Bewegungen im Deutschen Reich (c. 1870–c. 1933)* (Stuttgart, 1996).

[120] Günter Frankenberg, *AIDS-Bekämpfung im Rechtsstaat* (Baden-Baden, 1988), pp. 14, 26; Roland Czada and Heidi Friedrich-Czada, "Aids als politisches Konfliktfeld und Verwaltungsproblem," in Rosenbrock and Salmen, *Aids-Prävention*, p. 257; Uta Gerhardt, "Zur Effektivität der konkurrierenden Programme der AIDS-Kontrolle," in Bernd Schünemann and Gerd Pfeiffer, eds., *Die Rechtsprobleme von AIDS* (Baden-Baden, 1988), p. 76; Douglas A. Feldman, "Conclusion," in Feldman, ed., *Global AIDS Policy* (Westport, 1994), p. 239; Mohr, "AIDS, Gays, and State Coercion," p. 49; Roy Porter, "History Says No to the Policeman's Response to AIDS," *BMJ*, 293, 6562 (1986), p. 1590; Roy Porter, "Plague and Panic," *New Society* (12 December 1986), p. 13; Felix Herzog, "Das Strafrecht im Kampf gegen 'Aids-Desperados,'" in Ernst Burkel, ed., *Der AIDS-Komplex: Dimensionen einer*

Ackerknecht's connection of prophylaxis to politics has been generalized in the claim that preventive policies are but the expression of hidden ideological agendas.[121]

What we may call the Ackerknechtian position, the claim that prophylaxis is a continuation of politics, is thus a powerful and elegant argument that continues in enviable historiographical health, seeking to explain why different nations have adopted divergent preventive strategies even though faced with the same biological problem. Public health measures, as one recent observer sums the matter up, unquestionably carried political implications.[122] At least two issues should therefore be kept in mind as we examine the reaction of the German states, Sweden, Britain and France to the successive problems of cholera, smallpox and syphilis during the long nineteenth century. First, do the Ackerknechtian correlations hold? Did the concatenation of contagionism–quarantinism–authoritarianism, on the one hand, and localism–sanitationism–liberalism, on the other, cluster with sufficient consistency that we may say these various elements (etiological, prophylactic and political) have been historically congruent? If not, then how do we best explain the spectrum of prophylactic divergence? How might one amend or supplement a political interpretation of this most politicized aspect of public health and statutory intervention?

Second comes a broader problem that carries us beyond medical history to the wider arena of state formation and the comparative development of statutory interventionism. To the extent that there are correlations here, what can we say about the direction of causality? The Ackerknechtian position implies that politics have influenced etiological conceptions and prophylaxis. Knowledge is once again gleefully exposed as but the handmaiden of power. But what if we pose the problem the other way around? The nineteenth century was a crucially formative

Bedrohung (Frankfurt, 1988), p. 343; Daniel Defert, "Epidemics and Democracy," in Mérieux, *SIDA*, pp. 161–62; Larry O. Gostin, "Public Health Strategies for Confronting AIDS: Legislative and Regulatory Policy in the United States," *Journal of the AMA*, 261, 11 (17 March 1989), p. 1621. For a more general connection between politics and prophylaxis for AIDS, see Maria Paalman, "Epidemic Control through Prevention," in Alan F. Fleming et al., *The Global Impact of AIDS* (New York, 1988), p. 216; Karl Otto Hondrich, "Risikosteuerung durch Nichtwissen," in Burkel, *AIDS-Komplex*, p. 135; Patrick Wachsmann, "Le sida ou la gestion de la peur par l'état de droit," in Heilmann, *Sida et libertés*, pp. 102–03.

[121] Sylvia Noble Tesh, *Hidden Arguments: Political Ideology and Disease Prevention Policy* (New Brunswick, 1988), ch. 1 and passim. A similar belief, that approaches to disease generally are the outcome of divergent worldviews among social subcultures, informs Mary Douglas, *Risk and Blame* (London, 1992), ch. 6.

[122] Matthew Ramsey, "Public Health in France," in Dorothy Porter, *History of Public Health*, p. 58.

period in the development of public health strategies, during which European nations – starting from a broadly equivalent common situation – diverged significantly. All began the century as quarantinists, their prophylactic strategies largely determined by the experience of the plague a century earlier. At most, the British had begun to strike out on their own during the early eighteenth century by reversing positions on the plague to abandon quarantines when it threatened from Marseilles in the 1720s and by not applying similar tactics against the yellow fever at home, although in the Mediterranean dependencies precautions were as draconian as anywhere. It was therefore during the nineteenth century, beginning with cholera, that these nations began differing in prophylactic terms, eventually reaching points of maximum distance starting at midcentury with the radical sanitationism of the Chadwickian Board of Health in one corner and, occupying the other, the tempered, but still fairly classic, quarantinism of Prussia; with compulsory smallpox vaccination enforced in Germany and eventually France, while abandoned in Britain and Sweden; with the regulation of prostitutes in force on the continent, abolished across the Channel and in the Nordic countries. So which came first, political proclivities or prophylactic agenda? And which determined the other? Did politics shape preventive strategies, or prophylactic imperative help mold political regime and shape ideological traditions?

CHAPTER 2

Enter cholera

From the perspective of eagle-eyed retrospection it is clear that when, during the early 1820s in Russia and then in western Europe a decade later, cholera first arrived in Europe, no one had any idea what had struck. Here was a disease that hit with astonishing ferocity, terrifying like only the plague and yellow fever before it, making its way from its origins in India by leaps and bounds along the main routes of commercial intercourse in an imprecise, yet identifiably northwesterly movement. And yet, it was a disease whose fundamental nature was long to remain concealed from even the most ardently attentive observers, a disease, as one German put it, "die wir wol nennen, aber nicht kennen."[1]

Ignorant of cholera's basic characteristics, medical expertise betrayed its helplessness in a luxuriant polymorphousness of preventive recommendations and cures, ranging from the harmless (steambaths, veils, fresh water, acupuncture, rubbings) to the gruesome: dousings with ice water, rectal injections of turpentine, extraction via pumps of inhaled miasma from the innards, cauterization of the stomach skin with boiling water and endless bleedings, which in the dehydration of the disease and its attendant coagulation, meant that blood had to be practically squeezed from the veins when it could be extruded at all.[2] That homeopaths seized the opportunity to press their cause at least did

---

[1] B. W. Beck, *Was ist bei der anhaltenden Cholera zu lassen oder zu thun?* (Berlin, 1837), p. 1; Christoph Johann Heinrich Elsner, *Über die Cholera: Ein Versuch dieselbe zu deuten* (Königsberg, 1831), p. iv.

[2] Johann Ludwig Casper, *Die Behandlung der asiatischen Cholera durch Anwendung der Kälte: Physiologisch begründet, und nach Erfahrungen am Krankenbette dargestellt* (Berlin, 1832), pp. 30–35; *AGM*, 27 (1831), pp. 133, 267; Carl Ferdinand Kleinert, ed., *Cholera orientalis: Extrablatt zum allgemeinen Repertorium der gesammten deutschen medizinisch-chirurgischen Journalistik*, 2, 33 (Leipzig, 1831), p. 513; M. Oertel, *L'eau fraiche, spécifique infaillible contre le choléra* (Paris, 1831); M. Oertel, *Die indische Cholera einzig und allein durch kaltes Wasser vertilgbar* (Nuremberg, 1831); Sven-Ove Arvidsson, "Koleran i Sverige 1834," *Medicinhistorisk årsbok* (1967), pp. 144–45; Norman Howard-Jones, "Cholera Therapy in the Nineteenth Century," *JHM*, 27 (October 1972).

little harm.[3] Dr. Strack of Augsburg, convinced that different cloths and colors absorbed varying quantities of miasma, recommended white linen over black silk for the worried vain.[4] In the absence of effective remedies and given the Babel of competing and contradictory medical opinions, the authority of academically trained and officially certified physicians was shaken.[5] In this vacuum, the quacks hawked their wares, from cholera wines, liquors, chocolates and cakes, through cholera fumigation powder, tobacco and essences to cholera footwear – something for every orifice and appendage.[6] Among the most successful was the shoemaker Haamann, of Heubude near Danzig. Shortly before the first epidemic, he had treated diarrhea and cramps with an infusion of herbs, fortified by generous admixtures of spirits. With cholera delivering a torrent of similar symptoms, his medicine soon had Danzigers pilgrimmaging in his direction, adding a note of carnival to the otherwise somber atmosphere, making Haamann's fortune and lining the pockets of Heubude's restauranteurs.[7]

It was not for lack of attention and effort that few results were forthcoming. The literature on the first cholera epidemic of the early 1830s alone is overwhelming. One observer diagnosed a veritable bibliocholera – an ailment he classified as acutely contagious, whatever the case with its subject.[8] The most hotly debated issue in this vast corpus,

[3] Leipziger Localverein homöopathischer Ärzte, ed., *Cholera, Homöopathik und Medicinalbehörde in Berührung* (Leipzig, 1831), pp. 3–4; Röhl, *Bestätigte Heilung der Cholera durch homöopathische Arzneien* (Eisleben, 1831); Samuel Hahnemann, *Sendschreiben über die Heilung der Cholera und die Sicherung vor Ansteckung am Krankenbette* (Berlin, 1831); *Berliner Cholera Zeitung*, ed. Johann Ludwig Casper (1831), pp. 155, 172–73, 196ff.

[4] J. A. F. Ozanam, *Histoire médicale générale et particulière des maladies épidémiques, contagieuses et épizootiques, qui ont régné en Europe depuis les temps les plus reculés jusqu'a nos jours* (2nd edn.; Paris, 1835), v. II, pp. 303–04.

[5] *Schlesische Cholera-Zeitung* (1831–32), pp. 35–37; [Bogislav Konrad] Krüger-Hansen, *Curbilder, mit Bezug auf Cholera* (Rostock, 1831), pp. vi–vii; Albert Sachs, *Betrachtungen über die unter dem 31. Januar 1832 erlassene Instruction durch welche das in Betreff der asiatischen Cholera im Preussischen Staate zu beobachtende Verfahren festgesetzt wird* (Berlin, 1832), pp. 18–19; M. Kalisch, *Zur Lösung der Ansteckungs- und Heilbarkeitsfrage der Cholera* (Berlin, 1831), p. 28 and passim; [Eucharius F. C. Oertel], *Medicinische Böcke von Ärzten welche sich für infallible Herren über Leben und Tod halten in der Cholera geschossen* (Bocksdorf, [1832]).

[6] Lichtwerden, *Menschenrettung, oder die sichersten und einzigsten Mittel gegen die Cholera* (Berlin, 1831), p. 3; Michael Durey, *The First Spasmodic Cholera Epidemic in York, 1832* (York, 1974), p. 17; O. v. Hovorka and A. Kronfeld, *Vergleichende Volksmedizin* (Stuttgart, 1909), v. II, pp. 304–05.

[7] *Geschichte der Cholera in Danzig im Jahre 1831* (n.p., n.d.), pp. 21–26; E. Bangssel, *Der Schuhmacher Haamann in Heubude und seine Wundertropfen wider die Cholera* (Danzig, 1831).

[8] Friedr. Alexander Simon, Jr., *Die indische Brechruhr oder Cholera morbus* (Hamburg, 1831), p. vii; Leviseur, *Praktische Mittheilungen zur Diagnose, Prognose u. Cur der epidemischen Cholera* (Bromberg, 1832), p. iii; *Hansard*, 1846, v. 88, col. 227.

as his lament indicates, concerned cholera's transmissibility. Since the nature of the preventive measures to be taken by governments eager to protect their subjects hinged in large measure on the answer, the question clamored for resolution. During the 1830s, however, medical opinion was wholly at odds over the issue, and basic questions of distinguishing contagious from other diseases remained wide open. Even illnesses whose infectiousness had long been acknowledged by many were still considered the product of local causes by important observers. In Britain, thanks to the provocations of Charles Maclean, an itinerant physician interested in fevers, the nature of the plague was seriously disputed during the 1820s.[9] Similar arguments over both plague and yellow fever raged in France.[10] The single most sustained body of literature on cholera available during the first European epidemic came from British doctors in India. Although some have suggested that their testimony gave the British an edge in dealing with the disease, tilting them toward an anticontagionist approach, this experience was influential elsewhere as well.[11] Moreover, the Indian physicians were far from unanimous in their conclusions and, while most rejected contagionism, there remained significant exceptions.[12] Once the disease threatened to hit home during the summer of 1831, some of these former anticontagionists had second

[9] William Macmichael, *A Brief Sketch of the Progress of Opinion upon the Subject of Contagion* (London, 1825), pp. 5–7, 28–31; *Quarterly Review*, 27 (1822), pp. 524–53; 33 (1825), pp. 218–57; *London Medical Repository*, n.s., 3 (1825), pp. 390–95; *Medico-Chirurgical Review*, 6, 19 (1 January 1825), pp. 18–21; *Westminster Review*, 3 (1825), pp. 135–67; *British and Foreign Medical Review*, 16 (October 1843), pp. 289–91.

[10] *Conférence 1851*, 21, pp. 5–6; *ASA*, 3 (1838), p. 134; Jaehnichen, *Quelques réflexions sur le choléra-morbus* (Moscow, 1831), pp. 8–9, 118; *Gazette médicale de Paris*, 2, 20 (1831), pp. 169–72; Joseph Adams, *An Inquiry into the Laws of Different Epidemic Diseases* (London, 1809), p. 20; *Annales*, 27 (1842), pp. 454–73; Erwin H. Ackerknecht, "Anticontagionism Between 1821 and 1867," *BHM*, 22, 5 (September–October 1948), pp. 572–73, 584; Claire Salomon-Bayet et al., *Pasteur et la révolution pastorienne* (Paris, 1986), p. 97; Daniel Panzac, *Quarantaines et lazarets: L'Europe et la peste d'orient* (Aix-en-Provence, 1986), pp. 102–08.

[11] Michael Durey, *The Return of the Plague: British Society and the Cholera 1831–1832* (Dublin, 1979), pp. 109–10; *Staats-Zeitung*, 275 (4 October 1831), p. 1515; E. F. G. Herbst, *Untersuchung über die Verbreitungsart der asiatischen Cholera* (Göttingen, 1832), pp. 2, 86; Christian Friedrich Harless, *Die Indische Cholera nach allen ihren Beziehungen, geschichtlich, pathologisch-diagnostisch, therapeutisch und als Gegenstand der Staats- und Sanitäts-Polizei dargestellt* (Braunschweig, 1831), p. v; Simon, *Die indische Brechruhr*, pp. 220ff.; J. R. Lichtenstädt, *Die asiatische Cholera in Russland in den Jahren 1829 und 1830: Nach russischen amtlichen Quellen bearbeitet* (Berlin, 1831), p. xiii; *Hamburgisches Magazin der auslandischen Literatur der gesammten Heilkunde*, 23 (1832), pp. 9–10; *LMG*, 11 (1833), pp. 356–61.

[12] Reginald Orton, *An Essay on the Epidemic Cholera of India* (London, 1831); Whitelaw Ainslie, *Observations on the Cholera Morbus of India* (London, 1825), p. 20; W. White, *Treatise on Cholera Morbus* (London, 1834), p. 34; H. W. Buek, *Die Verbreitungsweise der epidemischen Cholera, mit besonderer Beziehung auf den Streit über die Contagiosität derselben* (Halle, 1832), pp. 7ff.; Mark Harrison, *Public Health in British India: Anglo-Indian Preventive Medicine 1859–1914* (Cambridge, 1994), pp. 102–05.

thoughts and such tergiversations were exploited elsewhere by those wishing to argue the opposing position.[13]

Faced with the predations of an unknown and devastating disease and bolstered only by the ambiguous and self-contradictory opinions of medical men, the authorities responsible for taking precautions in the nations of central and western Europe were understandably tempted by an approach analogous in its logic to Pascal's ontological wager. Given that cholera might be either contagious or not, they decided to assume the worst, hoping to be pleasantly surprised. As an anonymous Briton put it, "To consider it as contagious can do little harm, even should it not be so – but if it be contagious, not so to consider it must be fatal."[14]

Assuming cholera to be contagious and spread by contact directly between humans, by means of objects or across short distances through the air meant to apply the same sorts of measures that had been trained in the past against other diseases generally recognized as transmissible, most recently yellow fever, but above all the plague. Seeking precedents and examples to emulate, the authorities could turn to the techniques applied in the past as well as to the contemporary experience of nations where such diseases remained common. In Turkey, for example, resident Europeans had sought to spare themselves the plague by imposing strict sequestration from the outside world, in some cases going so far as to isolate each member of the household, allowing meals in common only so long as each kept to separate sections of the dining room, marked on the floor with chalk and extending to the table at the center, denuded for this purpose of any covering.[15] More influential, however, was domestic historical precedence. Like generals facing the last war, public health authorities, bereft of unambiguous scientific knowledge to the contrary, at first fought cholera in terms of the plague as it had been dealt with during the epidemics, most recently, of the eighteenth century.[16] This

[13] PRO, PC1/106, "Evidence of Medical Practitioners in India taken before the Board of Health"; *Papers Relative to the Disease called Cholera Spasmodica in India, Now Prevailing in the North of Europe* (London, 1831); Kleinert, *Cholera orientalis,* 2, 21–40 (1831), pp. 443–48.

[14] *Directions to Plain People as a Guide for Their Conduct in the Cholera* (London, 1831), p. 5.

[15] Friedrich Hempel, *Kurzer Bericht über die öffentlichen und privaten Schutz-Maassregeln, welche in den Jahren 1812–1814 in der Türkei und in Russland gegen Ansteckung durch die Orientalische Pest mit unzweifelhaftem Erfolge angewendet worden sind, in Rücksicht auf die Hemmung der Cholera zum Besten der Hospitäler zu Danzig* (Hamburg, 1831), p. 5; C. G. Ehrenberg, *Ein Wort zur Zeit: Erfahrungen über die Pest im Orient und über verständige Vorkehrungen bei Pest-Ansteckung zur Nutzanwendung bei der Cholera* (Berlin, 1831), pp. 3–17, 27; Franz Freiherr von Hallberg zu Broich, *Einige Erfahrungen bei ansteckenden Krankheiten, zur Bekämpfung der Cholera* (Jülich, 1831), pp. 4–5. For a general study, see Daniel Panzac, *La peste dans l'empire ottoman, 1700–1850* (Louvain, 1985), pp. 312–16.

[16] *Staats-Zeitung,* 283 (12 October 1831), p. 1548; Ragnhild Münch, *Gesundheitswesen im 18. und 19. Jahrhundert: Das Berliner Beispiel* (Berlin, 1995), p. 57.

implied a two-pronged approach: first, local causes were mitigated by cleansing public spaces and lowering individual predisposition through correct diet and habits. Secondly, it meant wheeling out the full arsenal of quarantinist measures: cordoning national boundaries; sequestering infected areas, identifying, reporting and isolating the ill; disinfecting, fumigating and cleansing goods and travelers; imposing special burial procedures.[17] The Austrians had the particular advantage of experience with quarantinist techniques gained from the permanent thousand-mile sanitary cordon that, since the eighteenth century, had aimed to keep at bay the plague among their Ottoman neighbors.[18] Against this background of common etiological ignorance and heated controversy as to cholera's characteristics, the nations of central and western Europe responded initially along common lines, assuming the disease to be contagious and imposing traditional measures of quarantinist prevention.

THE AUTOCRACIES RESPOND

The autocratic nations of east-central Europe – Russia, Austria-Hungary and Prussia – intervened decisively and drastically to protect themselves. By geographical happenstance the first to be threatened by cholera's northwesterly march, they were forced to act largely in the absence of foreign precedence or example. In Prussia the authorities had no firm opinion on the nature of the disease in November 1830 when Russia was struck. Several teams of medical men, dispatched there in hopes of dispelling doubts, reported back in December that, in all likelihood contagious, cholera required corresponding measures to prevent its import. Three sorts of reasons inclined the authorities toward a contagionist view: (1) the logical argument that, found in a variety of climates and local circumstances, the disease could not be caused by such factors alone; (2) the significant body of medical opinion that regarded it as such; (3) the Russian government's actions which showed that it shared this approach. As a final consideration, the war between

[17] On measures against the plague, see Georg Sticker, *Abhandlungen aus der Seuchengeschichte und Seuchenlehre* (Giessen, 1912), v. II, p. 286; Jean-Noël Biraben, *Les hommes et la peste en France et dans les pays européens et méditerranéens* (Mouton, 1976), v. II, ch. 6B; Panzac, *Quarantaines et lazarets*, chs. 2, 3.

[18] *Staats-Zeitung*, 275 (4 October 1831), p. 1516; Gunther E. Rothenberg, "The Austrian Sanitary Cordon and the Control of the Bubonic Plague: 1710–1871," *JHM*, 28, 1 (January 1973), pp. 16–19; Erna Lesky, "Die österreichische Pestfront an der k.k. Militärgrenze," *Saeculum*, 8 (1957), pp. 102–05; Gunther Erich Rothenberg, *The Austrian Military Border in Croatia, 1522–1747* (Urbana, 1960); Gunther E. Rothenberg, *The Military Border in Croatia 1740–1811* (Chicago, 1966); Markus Mattmüller, *Bevölkerungsgeschichte der Schweiz* (Basel, 1987), v. I, p. 239.

Poland and Russia meant that circumstances on Prussia's borders were likely to foster the spread of disease and caution was called for.[19] By the turn of the year, the Prussians had therefore decided to treat cholera as though conveyable through personal contact. A few months later the possibility of transmission also through objects was added and goods and merchandise were now also subject to the same measures of quarantine and disinfection as travelers.[20]

Having made up their collective mind, the Prussian authorities were in a position to promulgate regulations.[21] An Immediat-Kommission, responsible for enforcing protective measures and authorized to act independently of the usual governmental machinery, was established and regulations, issued in April 1831, were implemented once cholera had arrived in Warsaw the following month. A sense of the ambitions for a clearly delineated and crisply hierarchical structure of preventive response entertained by the autocratic regimes can be gleaned from the machinery of prophylaxis erected by the Prussians. Once the disease had penetrated the country, commissions of police and medical personnel were to carry out sanitary measures. These were to be established in a clear chain of command, with local commissions meeting daily and reporting weekly to district committees which, in turn, were to ensure that rules from Berlin were obeyed in even the remotest locality. The district committees, in turn, answered to the departmental authorities, they to the provincial governor and he to the Immediat-Kommission. A similar sense of meticulous hierarchy informed the measures issued for Berlin. Here, a local sanitary committee, established in June 1831, was to prevent the import of disease, preparing arrangements in case such precautions failed. To know for sure whether cholera had arrived, the first case reported was to be thoroughly confirmed. Any physician in the presence of a possible victim was to consult two certified colleagues and report the case only if all, or at least two, agreed in their diagnosis, or if one nonetheless persisted in his opinion. The account sent to the sanitary commission was to give the details of such deliberations, signed by

[19] *Cholera-Archiv mit Benutzung amtlicher Quellen*, ed. J. C. Albers et al., 1 (1832), pp. 3–9, 15–17; "Bekanntmachung," *Staats-Zeitung*, 138 (19 May 1831); "Über die Cholera," *Beilage zu den Berlinische Nachrichten*, 105 (6 May 1831).
[20] *Amtliche Belehrung über die gegen die ansteckende oder asiatische Cholera anzuwendenden Schutzmaassregeln und ersten Hülfsleistungen* (Berlin, 1831), pp. 3–8; *Sammlung*, pp. 22–23, 26.
[21] Richly detailed accounts are in Richard S. Ross, "The Prussian Administrative Response to the First Cholera Epidemic in Prussia in 1831" (Ph.D. diss., Boston College, 1991), ch. 3; Barbara Dettke, *Die asiatische Hydra: Die Cholera von 1830/31 in Berlin und den preussischen Provinzen Posen, Preussen und Schlesien* (Berlin, 1995), ch. 4.

all three physicians, with a duplicate copy sent to the all-Berlin Sanitary Committee.[22]

With well-ordered administrative structures of the sort exemplified by the Prussian in place, on paper at least, the autocracies were in a position to take what seemed to be decisive, thorough and consequent action against cholera. In each, various, but broadly similar, measures were implemented as part of their initial response to the epidemic.

Cordons at the national borders were the first line of defense. When, in 1823, cholera threatened to enter Russia through Astrakhan, St. Petersburg sent troops to prevent the access of potentially infected travelers and goods. In 1829 when disease struck at Orenburg, Kazan was almost entirely sealed off, with neither people, animals nor goods allowed in on pain of death.[23] With the epidemic before Moscow in September 1830, no effort was spared in sequestering the city: a military cordon was drawn, the approaching roads dug up, bridges and ferries destroyed, the city sealed at all but four entrances. After the Emperor visited his second city in October, the cordon was tightened, guards multiplied and heavily armed, spaced within visual contact of each other and fortified with cannon. Any who sought to breach the line were to be arrested, tried before a military tribunal and executed on the spot.[24] In Austria, a triple military cordon was drawn along the borders of Galicia, Bukovina and Bessarabia, with infected areas strictly isolated.[25] Along Prussia's eastern borders with Russia and Poland an immense military cordon was drawn, some two hundred miles long and enforced by the efforts of 60,000 troops.[26] Toward Poland, it boasted triple lines of defense. Outermost came a line of wooden thatched huts, each occupied by six soldiers and a petty officer,

---

[22] *Sammlung*, pp. 43, 45; *Berlinische Nachrichten*, 131 (8 June 1831); *Amts-Blatt*, 24 (17 June 1831), pp. 101–03; *Verordnung über das Verfahren bei der Annäherung und dem Ausbruche der Cholera in Berlin* (n.p., n.d.), p. 19.

[23] [Carl Trafvenfelt], *Sammandrag af Läkares åsigter och erfarenhet af den Epidemiska Choleran uti Asien och Europa* (Stockholm, 1832), v. III, pp. 17–28; Buek, *Verbreitungsweise*, pp. 20–21; Lichtenstädt, *Cholera in Russland*, pp. 31–32, 44; Victor Adolf Riecke, *Mittheilungen über die morgenländische Brechruhr* (Stuttgart, 1831), v. I, p. 110.

[24] G. Swederus, *Cholera morbus: Uppkomst, härjningar, kurmethod och preservativ, efter Skrifter utgifna i Tyskland och Moskwa år 1831* (Stockholm, 1831), p. 34; Riecke, *Mittheilungen*, v. III, p. 77–78; Roderick E. McGrew, *Russia and the Cholera 1823–1832* (Madison, 1965), pp. 78–81.

[25] Buek, *Verbreitungsweise*, pp. 72–74; *Sammlung*, pp. 4–5; Joseph Johann Knolz, *Darstellung der Brechruhr-Epidemie in der k.k. Haupt- und Residenzstadt Wien, wie auch auf dem flachen Lande in Oesterreich unter der Enns, in den Jahren 1831 und 1832, nebst den dagegen getroffenen Sanitäts-polizeylichen Vorkehrungen* (Vienna, 1834), p. 227; Sticker, *Abhandlungen aus der Seuchengeschichte*, v. II, p. 286.

[26] Johann Carl Friedrich Ollenroth, *Die asiatische Cholera im Regierungs-Bezirk Bromberg während des Jahres 1831* (Bromberg, 1832), p. 4; Auguste Gerardin and Paul Gaimard, *Du choléra-morbus en Russie, en Prusse et en Autriche, pendant les années 1831 et 1832* (2nd edn.; Paris, 1832), p. 78; *Sammlung*, pp. 22–23.

spaced evenly at intervals of one-fifteenth of a mile.[27] Cavalry patrols formed the second line of defense, and infantry units from nearby villages, dispatched intermittently according to need, brought up the prophylactic rear. Similar arrangements were in place along Prussia's Baltic coast, with the beaches guarded and batteries erected to ensure that ships obeyed instructions.[28]

Cordons rarely aimed to cut off all intercourse, but to restrict exchange to controlled points at which travelers and goods could be inspected, quarantined and disinfected before passing. In Russia and Austria, quarantine stations were a ubiquitous feature of cordons.[29] In Prussia, the meticulous detail characteristic of Berlin's regulations also applied. Travelers seeking to enter from Poland could cross at one of twelve stations, undergoing regimens of varying duration, depending on their place of origin.[30] The stations were located on the outskirts of towns, surrounded by deep trenches and guarded to prevent any contact with neighboring residents. During their stay, travelers bathed repeatedly, in water fortified with soap or chloride of lime, and were fumigated with nitric acid. Itinerants considered likely to be especially filthy (journeymen and Jewish peddlers, for instance) could undergo a more thorough cleansing, with their clothing soaked for several days. Nonlavable vestments, especially furs, and paper goods were to be fumigated and aired, all other objects washed with water, vinegar or chloride of lime solutions. Unusually old or filthy possessions (furs, bedding and the like) could be subject to an extending cleansing or rejected altogether. Upon completion of quarantine, travelers were issued a certificate of discharge, with separate papers for the draught animals of those who had arrived by carriage.

---

[27] By comparison, on one of the longest modern cordons, the US–Mexican border, the number of agents was doubled in 1993 to one every quarter of a mile: *Economist,* 16 March 1996, p. 27.

[28] Harless, *Indische Cholera,* pp. 711–12; Karl Christian Hille, *Beobachtungen über die asiatische Cholera, gesammelt auf einer nach Warschau im Auftrage der K.S. Landesregierung unternommenen Reise* (Leipzig, 1831), pp. 122–23; *Sammlung,* pp. 23–29, 69.

[29] J. A. E. Schmidt and Joh. Christ. Aug. Clarus, ed., *Sammlung Kaiserlich Russischer Verordnungen zur Verhütung und Unterdrückung der Cholera* (Leipzig, 1831), pp. 1–2, 14–19, 68ff.; *Instruction für die Sanitäts-Behörden, und für das bei den Contumaz-Anstalten verwendete Personale, zum Behufe die Gränzen der k.k. österreichischen Staaten vor dem Einbruche der im kaiserlich-russischen Reiche herrschenden epidemischen Brechruhr (cholera morbus) zu sichern, und im möglichen Falle des Eindringens, ihre Verbreitung zu hemmen* (Hannover, 1831), pp. 3–10, 26–27; Knolz, *Darstellung der Brechruhr-Epidemie,* pp. 221–24.

[30] *Sammlung,* pp. 23–29, 65–69; A. P. Wilhelmi, *Die bewährtesten und auf Autoritäten gegründeten Heilmethoden und Arznei-Vorschriften über die bis jetzt bekannt gewordenen verschiedenen Hauptformen der Cholera, oder das Wissenswürdigste über die sogenannte epidemische asiatische Brechruhr* (Leipzig, 1831), pp. 224–33.

Goods, in turn, underwent extensive procedures: they were unpacked, aired on special latticework platforms, fumigated and, if necessary, immersed in running water and scrubbed. Shorthaired animals were washed once, with repeated baths for the hirsute. When cholera was present immediately across the frontier, sheep and lambs were allowed in only after shearing, dogs and poultry not at all. For shipments of specie across international borders special rules applied. Small, dirty and potentially contagious coins were not permitted through the mails, but other currency could be sent if packed correctly. Upon arrival in the quarantine stations, packets of money, wrapped in sturdy paper and encased in oilcloth, were washed with black or green soap and a brush or sponge. At its final destination, currency was unpacked while submerged in soapy water, counted while wet and laid to dry on a cloth which, in turn, was immersed in a chloride of lime solution, also used for the hands of the counters. Letters had their own particular regimen: fumigated in a special tripartite container where, in epistolary purgatory, they suffered for five minutes, they were removed, repeatedly punctured with an awl, sometimes slit up the side, fumigated again and finally burnished with the official sanitary stamp and sent on their way.[31]

In order to lessen restrictions on communication and trade, a system of health certificates was employed. Travelers able to prove that they had passed only through uninfected areas could enter Prussia after an attenuated quarantine. The certificates were to show not only whence they came and how, but to furnish a detailed list of accompanying goods, their weight and how packed. Travel passes had to be endorsed each evening by the local Prussian legation or consulate, duly furnished with signature and official seal, and provide information on local health conditions. Once cholera had struck Danzig, in June 1831, Berlin imposed a complicated system of documents required of all travelers (military and civil servants on official business excepted) regardless of whether they were normally obliged to bear passports or not. Not even animals, required in August to possess their own health certificates, were exempted. Infected localities were forbidden to issue travel papers, whether of the human or bestial variety, thus preventing their inhabitants from journeying abroad.[32]

---

[31] *Sammlung*, pp. 65ff., 82–86, 89f., 103–05; *Berlinische Nachrichten*, 189 (15 August 1831). For background, see K. F. Meyer, "Historical Notes on Disinfected Mail," *Journal of Nervous and Mental Disease*, 116, 6 (December 1952), pp. 523–54.

[32] *Sammlung*, pp. 23–29, 45, 90–93; *Amts-Blatt*, 34 (26 August 1831), Beilage; 24 (17 June 1831), pp. 102–03; 27 (8 July 1831), pp. 130–32.

FIGHTING CHOLERA AT HOME

If disease managed to penetrate such defenses, new measures were to
take effect. To ensure accurate knowledge of the extent of the epidemic,
all cases were to be reported at once. In Russia and Austria, notification
of disease was required on pain of severe punishment. In Prussia,
heads of families were to report all cases of illness or unexpected death;
in Berlin, houseowners accounted daily for the condition of resident
patients to the local sanitary commission first thing in the morning, but
no later than 9 a.m.[33] Special hospitals were established for the cholera
ill which, given the state of medical knowledge, were more effective in
ameliorating housing problems than curing disease. Those who could
were to be isolated and cared for at home, with the hospitals reserved for
the poor with cramped or insalubrious accommodations.[34] In Vienna,
as many as seventeen hospitals with beds for 3,200 were provided; in
Warsaw, Jews had their own establishment. In Berlin the smallpox lazaretto in the Kirschallee did duty for cholera, while five other hospitals
were opened to provide gratis for patients who could not remain at home
and four served the military.[35]

The most controversial question in this respect was whether the
stricken could be forced to enter hospitals against their will. Because of
the poorhouse stigma attached to them, intensified by the anxiety
attached to cholera in general and brought to the boil by the eminently
reasonable consideration that an institution replete with the (possibly)
contagiously ill held few prospects of a cure, fear and dread of hospitalization was widespread. The authorities, for their part, based much of
their hope to contain cholera's spread on isolating its victims. Voluntary
hospitalization promised little in limiting the epidemic, compulsory
sequestration broached the threat of popular resentment and the
outcome was a prophylactic Hobson's choice. In November 1831, the
Russian police in Tambov rounded up cholera patients for transport to
the hospitals, seizing all who appeared suspicious, stripping them, dosing
them with calomel and opium, immersing them in hot baths and beating
the recalcitrant into submission. Two days of such drastic interventions,

---

[33] *Instruction für die Sanitäts-Behörden*, pp. 3–10, 26–27; Jaehnichen, *Quelques réflexions*, pp. i–iii;
Verordnung über das Verfahren, p. 22.
[34] *Verordnung über das Verfahren*, p. 24; Maria Petzold, "Die Cholera in Berlin unter besonderer
Berücksichtigung sozialmedizinischer und städtehygienischer Gesichtspunkte" (MD diss., Freie
Universität Berlin, 1974), p. 29.
[35] W. Sander, *Die asiatische Cholera in Wien beobachtet* (Munich, 1832), p. 104; [Trafvenfelt],
Sammandrag af Läkares åsigter, v. III, pp. 154–55; *Berliner Cholera Zeitung* (1831), pp. 91–93.

which gave new depth to the old cliché about remedies worse than the ailment, led to protests and eventually riots and similar unrest was sparked in St. Petersburg. But Russian policy was nothing if not inconsistent. In Reval, the authorities, faced with widespread refusal to enter the hospital, allowed the ill to remain at home, managing to defuse resentment.[36] To the west, tactics were not quite as severe. In Poland, the Central Sanitary Committee merely recommended removal of the sick who lacked care at home. Nor in Austria does compulsion seem to have been involved.[37]

In Prussia the evidence on compulsion is ambiguous. From some sources, it appears that physicians of the sanitary commissions had the authority to decide the fate of patients, ordering the removal of those living in squalid circumstances. In Berlin, certain categories of people (fragile individuals living alone and orphaned children) who could not be cared for properly at home were to be hospitalized and in Danzig the first victims were sent to the lazaretto because their homes were too small and dirty to allow medical treatment.[38] But other sources, in contrast, imply that compulsion was not an arrow in the authorities' quiver. If cholera victims did not have sufficient space at home, the physician was to convince them to be removed, but apparently wielded no authority beyond his powers of persuasion. One observer claimed that the Prussian regulations had never allowed for compulsory hospitalization, which, he insisted, would have offended public sentiment, provoking widespread dissatisfaction. Another testified that many, even among the poorer classes, were not removed and that the prejudice against cholera hospitals was even stronger in Prussia than in Britain.[39] When, in fact, removals did occur, the customary lovingly detailed instructions applied. Patients were carefully wrapped in blankets with a hot water bottle on their stomachs, placed in a hamper on a leather-covered straw mattress and transported by a two-horse, spring-suspended wagon, accompanied by four bearers in black glazed linen, patent leather hats and gloves,

[36] McGrew, *Russia and the Cholera*, pp. 50–51, 69ff., 108–15; Riecke, *Mittheilungen*, v. III, pp. 174–75; Gerardin and Gaimard, *Du choléra-morbus en Russie*, pp. 6–7.

[37] Brierre de Boismont, *Relation historique et médicale du choléra-morbus de Pologne* (Brussels, 1832), pp. 169–74; Knolz, *Darstellung der Brechruhr-Epidemie*, pp. 240–41.

[38] *Amts-Blatt*, 35 (2 September 1831), p. 192; *Verordnung über das Verfahren*, pp. 24, 39; *Sammlung*, pp. 46–48; GStA, 84a/4178, Königl. Pr. Gouvernement und Polizei-Präsidium hiesiger Haupt- und Residenz-Stadt, "Publikandum," Königsberg, 23 July 1831.

[39] *Archiv für medizinische Erfahrung* (1831), pp. 319–21; Johann Wendt, *Über die asiatische Cholera bei ihrem Übertritte in Schlesiens südöstliche Gränzen: Ein Sendschreiben an seine Amtsgenossen in der Provinz* (Breslau, 1831), pp. 36–38; F. W. Becker, *Letters on the Cholera in Prussia: Letter I to John Thomson, MD, FRS* (London, 1832), p. 50.

escorted, in turn, by a policeman and a two guards, each keeping a distance of at least five paces.[40]

Isolation or sequestration of the ill was among the more drastic of possible measures. The St. Petersburg authorities recommended sequestration already when cholera struck in 1823 and in Austria the first regulations followed suit.[41] In Prussia, once a single case had been detected and an area declared infected, no one was permitted to leave without undergoing quarantine. All houses with an illness or death were to be isolated, even those from which the afflicted had been removed. In Berlin, other residents who had already left were brought back and sequestered as well, while in Danzig those who returned to discover families stricken in their absence were forbidden to rejoin them. To seal off infected houses renters were to surrender their house keys, guards, armed with cudgels, were posted, and sometimes a string was suspended around the house to indicate the perimeter of sequestration.[42] In Danzig, large crosses were painted on doors and staffs topped with a thatch of straw planted at the outer gates were quickly dubbed Plague Trees by local wags. In Liegnitz windows and doors were nailed shut, although in some cases use of a rope allowed doors to be opened a foot or so.[43] The sequestered whose condition improved were subject to full quarantines, as were recovered patients and their caretakers and physicians. In the sickrooms exacting cleanliness was to be observed, tainted substances removed, especially excreta, fresh air assured and daily fumigations undertaken. Before the isolation of a house could be lifted, it had to be cleaned, fumigated and disinfected, the walls scraped down and whitewashed, the floors, windows and doors repeatedly washed with lye or a chloride of lime solution and the entire structure aired out for a fortnight. Structures not worth the effort could be burnt down.[44]

If the disease showed itself in several houses or a neighborhood, the entire area was to be isolated and the sequestered provided with all necessities. An elaborate ritual of contact avoidance governed relations

---

[40] Allerhöchstverordnetes Gesundheits-Comité für Berlin, *Vorläufige Bestimmungen für den Fall des Ausbruchs der Cholera in Berlin*, 28 June 1831, copy in GStA, Preussisches Justizministerium, 84a/4178; *Verordnung über das Verfahren*, pp. 40–41; *Berliner Cholera Zeitung* (1831), pp. 91–93.

[41] Lichtenstädt, *Cholera in Russland*, pp. 15–16; Riecke, *Mittheilungen*, v. I, pp. 147–48; Schmidt and Clarus, *Sammlung Kaiserlich Russischer Verordnungen*, pp. 14–19; *Instruction für die Sanitäts-Behörden*, pp. 3–10, 26–27; Knolz, *Darstellung der Brechruhr-Epidemie*, pp. 240–41.

[42] *Sammlung*, p. 45; *Verordnung über das Verfahren*, pp. 24, 31; Allerhöchstverordnetes Gesundheits-Comité, *Vorläufige Bestimmungen*; *Verhandlungen* (1831), p. 3.

[43] Eduard Bangssel, *Erinnerungsbuch für Alle, welche im Jahre 1831 die Gefahr der Cholera-Epidemie in Danzig mit einander getheilt haben* (Danzig, 1832), p. 38; *Cholera-Archiv*, 3 (1833), p. 397.

[44] *Sammlung*, pp. 23–29, 51–52, 54.

between the isolated and their caretakers. Shopping requests were to be shouted at a great distance, monies to pay for supplies was deposited on a table outside the house, paper currency as such, coins in a bowl of vinegar. The caretaker, in turn, retrieved the bills and any shopping lists with a tong, fumigated them and threw them into a special sack, and scooped out the coins with a spoon. When he returned, the procedure was acted out again in reverse, the food placed in containers (meat thrown into one filled with water) before withdrawing to avoid any direct contact. The authorities were to ensure that crucial activities normally undertaken by the sequestered would continue. An isolated victim whose work was necessary for the wellbeing of the community could be required to leave, undergoing disinfection or quarantine. If cholera spread widely, entire areas could be sealed off by the military, sometimes with a double cordon. Inside, all places of public assembly – schools, the-aters, inns – were closed and soldiers employed to prevent crowding at shops. A general house quarantine could be imposed with no one allowed to leave home except by permission, guards posted on all streets and physicians to inspect each inhabitant daily.[45] Sequestering animals presented problems, their obedience to authority being notoriously spotty. In Prussia, cats, dogs and other pets were to be killed, and poultry had its wings trimmed. In Danzig, Dr. Barchewitz, an opponent of qua-rantine and other harsh measures, insisted that consistency required extending such precautions also to birds and insects and indeed, in Liegnitz, flies in sickrooms were to be killed. Such epidemiological micromanagement prompted ridicule, accusations of pedantry and even orations in defense of flies. In Austria, animals fared slightly better: dogs were to be killed, poultry enclosed, birds scared off by musket shots, but larger animals in sequestered houses were merely to be washed and brought to pasture.[46]

The authorities also sought to influence the individual behavior of their subjects, preventing contact between the infected and the well. The Prussians encouraged the healthy to avoid afflicted or suspected areas, persons and things. Restrict social intercourse even with those whose only sin was being unable to prove that they had sidestepped all contact with disease, they advised. Without abandoning customary patterns of sociability, isolate yourselves and your families from strangers. In

---

[45] *Sammlung*, pp. 23–29, 48, 50–51; *Amts-Blatt*, 24 (17 June 1831), p. 105; *Verordnung über das Verfahren*, pp. 36–39.
[46] *Sammlung*, pp. 46–47; *Geschichte der Cholera in Danzig*, p. 27; *Cholera-Archiv*, 3 (1833), p. 398; Knolz, *Darstellung der Brechruhr-Epidemie*, p. 251.

crowded houses, act with reserve toward your fellow occupants and pay attention to the comings and goings of servants and apprentices. When going out, bypass large gatherings, avoid frequented areas and contact with others, keeping cats and dogs at bay with a walking stick. Be careful in using public conveniences of any sort, washing hands and face frequently. Exit into the fresh air once you have transacted your business and otherwise stay at home.[47] Buying food also required caution. Vegetables, fruit and bread demanded no particular attention, but meat should be dunked in water before handling. Letters and other papers received from strangers were first to be fumigated, money stirred with a spoon in a pot of vinegar. Those necessarily in communication with the ill (physicians, ministers and the like) should at least avoid direct contact and follow special rules: never visit on an empty stomach, but only after a stimulating drink (coffee, tea, wine or liqueur), and chew ginger, calamus, orange peel or peppermint cookies, or smoke tobacco while in the sickroom, taking care to spit out the accumulated saliva. Do not visit patients if you feel ill yourself, if you have been up all night, if you are drunk or overly warm or cold or if you have just experienced strong emotions. Wear an outer garment of waxed cloth, hold your breath while in the immediate proximity of the ill and avoid their exhalations. Salve the hands with rose pomade before actually touching them. Upon leaving a sickroom, wash hands and face in a chlorine solution and gargle with a mixture of vinegar or red wine and water, blow your nose, comb your hair, change your clothes and take at least one warm bath weekly.[48]

As an extra precaution, disinfection was also popular. In Russia, where chlorine was the substance of choice, its gas was developed in living and bedrooms; furniture, food and money was rubbed with chloride of lime; breastplates, gloves, hats and coats were lined with it; sacks and bottles of it were held to the mouth. In Moscow, those in contact with the ill were advised to wash their entire bodies or at least their hands, foreheads and behind their ears with chloride of lime or

[47] Friedrich Ludwig Kreysig, *Versuch einer leichtfasslichen und ausführlichen Belehrung über die rechten Mittel, durch welche ein Jeder die Cholera von sich meistens abwenden, oder auch grösstentheils selbst heilen könne* (Dresden, 1831), p. 19.

[48] *Amts-Blatt*, 24 (17 June 1831), p. 109; K. F. Burdach, *Belehrung für Nichtärzte über die Verhütung der Cholera: Im Auftrage der Sanitätskommission zu Königsberg verfasst* (Königsberg, 1831), p. 17; *Amtliche Belehrung*, pp. 15–26; *Sammlung*, pp. 59–60; *Anweisung zu dem die Zerstörung des Ansteckungsstoffes der Cholera bezweckenden Reinigungsverfahren (Desinfectionsverfahren)* (n.p., n.d.); Dyrsen, *Kurzgefasste Anweisung die orientalische Cholera zu verhüten, zu erkennen und zu behandeln, für Nichtärzte, insbesondere aber für die Bewohner des flachen Landes im Livländischen Gouvernement* (Riga, 1831), p. 18; *Anhang zur Gesetz-Sammlung*, 1835, Beilage B zu No. 27 gehörig, p. 10.

vinegar.[49] Vinegar was the preferred remedy in Prussia, where inhabitants were told to carry a bottle to sniff in the vicinity of suspicious places. To reduce the number of potentially contagious objects, lessening the burden of cleaning and disinfecting them later, Prussians were exhorted to pack away all objects not in daily use, officially sealing the boxes and trunks, to be opened only after the epidemic.[50] To such individually focused instructions came more general efforts to prevent the spread of cholera by controlling the movements and behavior of subjects. In hopes of preventing miasmas, church services in Russia were to be held in the open, inhabitants were in general to be prevented from congregating in public and a 7 p.m. curfew was imposed. In Poland crowding in taverns and cafés was prohibited; in Austria, schools, inns, bars and shops could be closed. In Berlin, unnecessary congregation was prevented, with guards posted in commercial districts, and schools, theaters and bars closed if necessary.[51]

The fear of contagion prompted the autocracies to impose regulations on their subjects even after death. The bodies of victims were to be interred only according to precise instructions that often represented a stark and much resented departure from custom and precedence. Burials were to be held promptly after death, sometimes on the same day, with the funeral procession graced by little religious ritual and few, if any, mourners and scheduled for early morning or late night to minimize contact with bystanders. Quarantined and sequestered while alive, cholera victims were also isolated in death, their bodies buried in separate cemeteries or at least in distinct, and often walled-in, areas of existing graveyards. Funeral rituals were also altered. In Russia, relatives were forbidden to kiss or otherwise touch the corpse during the ceremony, which was, in any case, conducted graveside rather than in the church. In Poland, the authorities advised against viewing the body, while in Berlin, the usual custom of washing, shaving and dressing corpses was prohibited, the victims encoffinated as they had expired. The graves were to be especially deep, at least six feet, or with a corresponding layer of extra soil piled on top, the corpses covered with lime, and some accounts report bodies buried naked without coffins in mass graves. In Austria, the

[49] *Post*, 257 (5 November 1830); Burdach, *Belehrung für Nichtärzte*, pp. 10–11. For a general view, see Rudolph Brandes, *Über das Chlor, seine Verbindungen und die Anwendung derselben, besonders bei ansteckenden Krankheiten, als luftreinigende und desinficirende Mittel, so wie auch in der Ökonomie und Technik* (Lemgo, 1831).

[50] *Amtliche Belehrung*, pp. 15–26; *Sammlung*, pp. 46, 59–60.

[51] Schmidt and Clarus, *Sammlung Kaiserlich Russischer Verordnungen*, pp. 13–19; Brierre de Boismont, *Relation historique*, pp. 169–74; Knolz, *Darstellung der Brechruhr-Epidemie*, pp. 225, 251; *Instruction für die Sanitäts-Behörden*, p. 11; *Verordnung über das Verfahren*, p. 21.

dead were not to be disinterred for fifty years. In Prussia, attendants wore patent leather gauntlets to the elbows and avoided touching the corpses with bare hands. Gravediggers lived in special rooms at the cemetery, forbidden to leave, guarded and disinfected after each burial. Families of the deceased were allowed to visit the graves upon application to the authorities, but unrestricted public access was forbidden.[52]

To enforce such precautions, the autocracies backed up their decrees with the threat of stiff punishments. Travelers who ignored the challenges of Prussian soldiers patrolling the border cordons could be shot on sight. Later, such orders were moderated so that only those actually attempting to cross the line running between guard houses would be fired upon. Nonetheless, the public was warned that even the slightest resistance might provoke fire, although another version suggested that only determined obstreperousness would be met with official violence.[53] Those seeking to evade military patrols or who fled quarantine stations risked charges of damaging the nation, with punishments of imprisonment up to ten years or even death.[54] Aiding others to violate quarantine regulations (housing or transporting strangers without proper documents or failing to report violations) also merited punishment. Stealing items from quarantine stations, hospitals or sealed houses was treated as a capital offense if transmission ensued. Failure to report illness or suspicious deaths and burials without medical permission might lead to jail. Trials and sentencing could be expedited, with no more than three days to pass before the handing down of punishment. Civil servants employed in prevention who broke the law would be severely punished, not excluding death.[55]

---

[52] Brierre de Boismont, *Relation historique*, pp. 169–74; *Berliner Cholera Zeitung* (1831), p. 245; Schmidt and Clarus, *Sammlung Kaiserlich Russischer Verordnungen*, pp. 14–19, 28, 44; Knolz, *Darstellung der Brechruhr-Epidemie*, pp. 240–41, 251; *Sammlung*, pp. 54–55; *Verordnung über das Verfahren*, pp. 43–46; Albert Sachs, ed., *Tagebuch über das Verhalten der bösartigen Cholera in Berlin* (Berlin, 14 September–31 December 1831), p. 276; *Verhandlungen* (1831), pp. 4–5.

[53] Hille, *Beobachtungen*, p. 123; *Berlinische Nachrichten*, 108 (10 May 1831); 208 (6 September 1831); 130 (7 June 1831).

[54] In contradiction to this, however, was the punishment threatened in a dual-language (German/Polish) overview of the measures taken in Posen. Here, those who managed to sneak across the cordons were subject to nothing more draconian than twenty days' jail, which was the length of time they would have spent in quarantine anyway had they gone the official route: *Kurze Übersicht des Seitens des Königl. Preussischen Staates zur Abwendung der durch die asiatische Cholera drohenden Gefahr erlassenen Verordnungen* (Posen, 1831), p. 6.

[55] *Kurze Übersicht*, p. 12; *Gesetz-Sammlung*, 1831, 8/1290, pp. 61–64. To what extent the regulations were strictly enforced is, not surprisingly, harder to determine than what the letter of the law sought to impose. The accounts that mention violations of cordons and regulations generally indicate that such actions were the exception and that the law was largely followed: *Cholera-Archiv*, 3 (1833), pp. 162, 398; *Berlinische Nachrichten*, 130 (7 June 1831).

SANITATIONISM

The autocracies did not, however, take a contagionist and quarantinist approach to the exclusion of all others. Cordons, quarantines and sequestration did, to be sure, predominate among their precautions, but attempts to deal with the possibly local causes of cholera were also important. Most simply, the authorities saw no reason why a concern with local predisposing factors should lessen the force of their conclusion that cholera was contagious. No disease was unmitigatedly infectious in the sense that all who came within its ambit were unfailingly smitten. Clearly, cholera's progress could be encouraged or retarded by local circumstances, whether individual habits or environmental conditions, without it thereby being any less contagious or susceptible to quarantinist policies.[56] The official Prussian position affirmed cholera's transmissibility while also insisting that individuals could lessen or increase their predisposition to it.[57] Such predisposing factors ranged from the personal through the social to the natural. They included individual dietary and hygienic habits, states of mind, insanitary and crowded living circumstances and atmospheric conditions. Some of these were under the control of the individual, some of society, some of the Almighty alone, and modifying the first two sorts held out hopes of tempering the incidence and severity of epidemics. From the outset, therefore, medical and official advice encouraged the public to correct the predisposing factors over which it had a say, issuing a stream of pamphlets that promoted a regular, moderated, temperate mode of life as the most reliable defense, if far from the best revenge.

Be careful of sudden changes in temperature, potential cholera victims were warned, do not sleep in the open, stay inside at night. Avoid noxious emanations, whether produced by overcrowding or decomposition. If your living quarters are overcrowded, at least keep them clean. Wash your rooms weekly, scouring the walls with straw. Throw open your windows several times a day for fresh air, but not, of course, to the extent of catching draughts. Keep your body clean, taking warm baths and avoiding cold ablutions in streams, ponds or the ocean. For the

---

[56] *Kurze Anweisung zur Erkenntniss und Heilung der Cholera* (Berlin, 1831), pp. 10–11; *Sammlung*, pp. 23, 26; *Amtliche Belehrung*, pp. 3–8; Harless, *Indische Cholera*, pp. 331–33; *Die Erkenntniss und die Behandlung der nach Deutschland verschleppten asiatischen Cholera: Zum Gebrauch für Civil- und Militär-Ärzte und Wundärzte nach den besten Quellen zusammengestellt* (Dresden, 1831), pp. 16–17; *Belehrung über die asiatische Cholera für Nichtärzte: Auf allerhöchsten Befehl in dem Königreiche Sachsen bekannt gemacht* (Dresden, 1831), pp. 22–25; *Instruction für die Sanitäts-Behörden*, p. 9. [57] *Staats-Zeitung*, 138 (19 May 1831); *Kurze Übersicht*, p. 14.

Russians special rules on steambaths warned against going out into the air directly afterwards and certainly not naked, while Berliners were exhorted to wash hands and face several times a day.[58] Never go out on an empty stomach in the mornings.[59] Dress in warm and dry clothes, avoiding linen, and change immediately if wet. Chills, especially of the stomach, were dangerous. Keep your feet warm and dry, never go out at night unless properly attired. Change your clothes often, especially underwear and bedding. Abdominal belts were highly recommended, especially for those unable to afford a complete set of flannel clothing. In Stettin, the sanitary commission distributed them to the poor and in Danzig everyone wore one, while some went further, dressing in furs and even entering drawing rooms without first removing their hats.[60] Undue exertion was to be avoided; indeed in Berlin it was official advice that citizens refrain from hard work, both physical and mental. But moderate amounts of physical activity – an hour of daily walks or horserides in fresh air, for example – were recommended.[61]

The underlying assumption behind such recommendations concerned the prophylactic virtues of regular habits and a simple life. Their customary routines should not, Danzigers were advised, be changed in response to the disease. Even bad and otherwise predisposing habits were better persisted in for the sake of continuity than precipitously altered in mid-epidemic.[62] Equanimity and calm should be maintained; productive work and sociability were healthy distractions.[63] Regular

[58] Schmidt and Clarus, *Sammlung Kaiserlich Russischer Verordnungen*, pp. 6–13; Riecke, *Mittheilungen*, v. I, pp. 165–74; *Amts-Blatt*, 24 (17 June 1831), pp. 107–09; *Unterricht, wie Nichtärzte die asiatische Cholera verhüten, erkennen und behandeln sollen, zum Nutzen der gebildeten Landbewohner bekannt gemacht von dem Königlichen Schleswig-Holsteinschen Sanitätscollegium in Kiel* (Kiel, 1831), pp. 5–7; *Sammlung*, p. 58; Dyrsen, *Kurzgefasste Anweisung*, p. 4; *Berlinische Nachrichten*, 211 (9 September 1831).

[59] *Gründliche und fassliche Anweisung für den Bürger und Landmann zur Verhütung der Ansteckung durch die Cholera und zur Erhaltung der Gesundheit beim Herannahen dieser Krankheit* (Dresden, 1831), pp. 18–21; *Allgemein fassliche Anweisung zur Erkennung, Verhütung und Heilung der asiatischen Cholera, nebst Andeutungen über die Gefahr derselben im Allgemeinen, zur Belehrung und Beruhigung der Nichtärzte herausgegeben von einem praktischen Arzte* (Leipzig, 1831), p. 25; Brierre de Boismont, *Relation historique*, pp. 169–74.

[60] *Unterricht, wie Nichtärzte die asiatische Cholera verhüten*, pp. 8–9; *Sammlung*, p. 58; Patrice Bourdelais and Jean-Yves Raulot, *Une peur bleue: Histoire du choléra en France 1832–1854* (Paris, 1987), p. 238; *Berlinische Nachrichten*, 135 (13 June 1831); *Geschichte der Cholera in Danzig*, p. 36.

[61] *Amts-Blatt*, 24 (17 June 1831), pp. 107–09; Riecke, *Mittheilungen*, v. I, pp. 168ff.; Bisset Hawkins, *History of the Epidemic Spasmodic Cholera of Russia* (London, 1831), pp. 3–5; McGrew, *Russia and the Cholera*, p. 165; *Sammlung*, p. 56; *Anhang zur Gesetz-Sammlung*, 1835, Beilage B zu No. 27 gehörig, p. 9.

[62] Ernst Barchewitz, *Die Behandlung der Cholera in ihren verschiedenen Perioden und Graden* (Danzig, 1831), p. 6; *Sammlung*, p. 56.

[63] *Unterricht, wie Nichtärzte die asiatische Cholera verhüten*, pp. 5–7; *Belehrung über die asiatische Cholera für Nichtärzte*, pp. 27–28; *Ansprache ans Publicum, zunächst der Herzogthümer Schleswig und Holstein über die epi-*

sleeping habits were important, while nightowls could expect the worst.[64] Meals taken at the same time each day allowed the body to digest with a certain predictability. Moderation in all things was the highest good while overindulging in food or drink was to court perdition.[65] Excessive thinking and intellectual activity was detrimental to the same degree that a moderate amount was propitious. Frequent sexual intercourse was among the most worrying habits, often followed immediately by an attack, and explained why newly married couples occasionally succumbed on their wedding night.[66]

The dietary advice was mouthwatering, with official instructions recommending elaborate lists of food and drink, including detailed accounts of which wines in what quantities were acceptable. Most alarming were the indigestible foods likely to aggravate or even provoke attacks of cholera: greasy pastries, elles, carp, salmon, smoked fish, fatty geese and ducks, sharp cheese, hardboiled eggs – all were strictly off-limits, as were raw vegetables and fruits in general, but especially apples, plums, melons, watermelons, mushrooms, turnips, beans, yellow peas, cabbage, rapes, salads and cucumbers.[67] Old cheese was dangerous, especially at night. Recommended instead were fresh and healthy foods, moderately spiced with pepper, horseradish and mustard, especially tender meats such as veal, mutton, poultry, venison, and beef, as well as flour, rice, semolina, groats and potatoes. As an exception to the ban on raw fruit, ripe cherries, strawberries or raspberries, with a bit of rum or wine, were considered harmless. As for drink, easily fermentable liquids

demische Cholera vom königl. Schleswig-Holsteinischen Sanitätscollegium zu Kiel (Kiel, 1831), p. 6; *Anweisung wie man bei etwa eintretender asiatischer Cholera seine Gesundheit erhalten, die Krankheit erkennen, und der Ansteckung und Weiterverbreitung vorbeugen kann: Bekannt gemacht durch die oberste Sanitäts-Kommission zu Cassel* (Cassel, 1831), pp. 5–6.

[65] *Sammlung*, pp. 56–57; *Instruction für die Sanitäts-Behörden*, pp. 10–11; J. R. Lichtenstädt, *Rathschläge an das Publikum zur Verhütung und Heilung der herrschenden asiatischen Cholera* (Berlin, 1831), pp. 15–16; *Die Cholera morbus, eine allgemein fassliche und belehrende Abhandlung über das Entstehen und die Verbreitung derselben, deren Symptome, wie auch Vorbauungsmaasregeln, um sich beim Ausbruche der Krankheit gegen dieselbe zu schützen* (Breslau, 1831), pp. 12–15.

[65] J. Ennemoser, *Was ist die Cholera und wie kann man sich vor ihr sicher verwahren?* (Bonn, 1831), p. 43; A. v. Pohl, *Über die Cholera oder Brech-Ruhr und deren Behandlung und Verhütung für Nicht-Ärzte* (Moscow, 1831), p. 40; *Instruction für die Sanitäts-Behörden*, p. 11.

[66] Ernst Barchewitz, *Über die Cholera: Nach eigener Beobachtung in Russland und Preussen* (Danzig, 1832), p. 56; Pulst, *Cholera im Königreich Polen* (Breslau, 1831), p. 25; Moritz Hasper, *Die epidemische Cholera oder die Brechruhr* (Leipzig, 1831), pp. 30–31; *Die Erkenntniss und die Behandlung*, p. 17.

[67] *Anweisung wie man bei etwa eintretender asiatischer Cholera seine Gesundheit erhalten*, pp. 9–11; *Amts-Blatt*, 24 (17 June 1831), pp. 107–09; Riecke, *Mittheilungen*, v. I, pp. 168ff.; Hawkins, *History*, pp. 3–5; Hille, *Beobachtungen*, pp. 13–18; *Unterricht, wie Nichtärzte die asiatische Cholera verhüten*, pp. 5–7; *Belehrung über die asiatische Cholera für Nichtärzte*, pp. 27–28.

were to be avoided (sour beer and milk) and, of course, excessive quantities of alcohol. Instead, bitter infusions were recommended, good wines (Medoc, aged dry Hungarian) or spirits spiced with caraway, aniseed, calamus, Seville oranges or juniper berries. Sometimes beverages were sorted by social class: red wine for the well-off, bitter vermouth or curaçao brandy for the poorer, brown ale boiled with caraway and mixed with sugar and nutmeg for the beer drinkers. In Schleswig-Holstein, cold water mixed with cumin brandy was the drink of choice for laborers in the fields, but in Prussia the peasant was warned against cold beverages after working in the sun.[68]

Finally, proceeding from the stomach to the soul, it was believed that states of mind influenced receptivity to disease. Official opinion took it for granted that the spirit was crucial to maintaining bodily health and that a mental equilibrium out of kilter was an important predisposing condition.[69] Strong depressive emotions were to be avoided, however difficult in epidemic circumstances, while pleasant ones promised to strengthen the body's resistance.[70] Time and again, activities that improved the mood, keeping one distracted and content, were recommended. The fear of the disease itself, choleraphobia, was widely considered a dangerous factor.[71] Whether the poor or rich were more afflicted by such anxiety remained, in contrast, a matter of dispute.[72] The sight of a patient, the attendants, bearers, transport hamper or

[68] Barchewitz, *Behandlung der Cholera*, p. 7; Lichtenstädt, *Cholera in Russland*, p. 29; *Sammlung*, pp. 57–58; *Unterricht, wie Nichtärzte die asiatische Cholera verhüten*, pp. 5–7; *Amts-Blatt*, 29 (22 July 1831), p. 146.

[69] *Sammlung*, p. 56. On body–mind connections in nineteenth-century medicine, see Biraben, *Les hommes et la peste*, v. II, p. 37; Charles E. Rosenberg, *Explaining Epidemics and Other Studies in the History of Medicine* (Cambridge, 1992), ch. 4.

[70] Schmidt and Clarus, *Sammlung Kaiserlich Russischer Verordnungen*, pp. 6–13; Riecke, *Mittheilungen*, v. I, pp. 165–74; Barchewitz, *Über die Cholera*, p. 56; Pulst, *Cholera im Königreich Polen*, p. 25; Hasper, *Cholera*, pp. 30–31; *Die Erkenntniss und die Behandlung*, p. 17.

[71] *Berliner Cholera Zeitung* (1831), p. 286; Lichtenstädt, *Rathschläge*, p. 15; J. Ch. v. Loder, *Über die Cholera-Krankheit: Ein Sendschreiben* (Königsberg, 1831), pp. 13–14; Anton Friedrich Fischer, *Es wird Tag! Deutschland darf die herrschende Brechruhr (Cholera) nicht als Pest und Contagion betrachten: Ein Wort an die hohen Staatsbeamten Deutschlands und zur Beruhigung des Publikums* (Erfurt, 1832), p. 7; *Verhandlungen*, 1 (1832), pp. 373–75; *Cholera-Zeitung* (1832), pp. 38, 94; Wilhelm Cohnstein, *Trost- und Beruhigungsgründe für die durch das Herannahen der Cholera aufgeschreckten Gemüther* (Glogau, 1831), pp. 4–5; *(Allgemeine Cholera-Zeitung)*, 2 (1832), p. 136; Barchewitz, *Behandlung der Cholera*, pp. 9–10; *Magazin für die gesammte Heilkunde*, 42 (1834), pp. 104–06; *Post*, 267 (17 November 1830); Carl Mayer, *Skizze einiger Erfahrungen und Bemerkungen über die Cholera-Epidemie zu St. Petersburg* (St. Petersburg, 1832), p. 61; *Sammlung*, p. 59; [Trafvenfelt], *Sammandrag af Läkares åsigter*, v. II, pp. 24–34.

[72] *Cholera-Archiv*, 2 (1832), p. 278; *Staats-Zeitung*, 283 (12 October 1831), p. 1548; Friedrich Schnurrer, *Die Cholera morbus, ihre Verbreitung, ihre Zufälle, die versuchten Heilmethoden, ihre Eigenthümlichkeiten und die im Grossen dagegen anzuwendenden Mittel* (Stuttgart, 1831), p. 75; Hartung, *Die Cholera-Epidemie in Aachen* (Aachen, 1833), pp. 79–80.

hearse was potentially dangerous and seeing someone vomit could easily elicit a similar reaction in the observer.[73] Cases caused by fear alone, *Angst-Cholera*, were reported, although denied by the Prussian government. Needless worries were sought dispelled by having physicians use other designations for the disease on death certificates so as not to alarm the survivors.[74]

Because of this widespread belief that predisposing factors played an epidemiological role, the authorities never pursued a onesidedly quarantinist approach. Besides exhorting their subjects to change habits and customs, the autocracies also pursued collectively sanitationist measures, most obviously various forms of rudimentary urban hygiene. In Russia, little seems to have been undertaken in this respect, although the St. Petersburg Medical Council warned against overcrowded living quarters. One visionary military doctor recommended less densely populated accommodations, but could think of no better solution than removing excess inhabitants from the cities in order to make conditions more palatable for important people like the troops and civil servants.[75] In Poland, the Central Sanitary Committee recommended police visits to the homes of the poor and of Jews to discourage overcrowding. In Vienna various ameliorations were set in motion during the epidemic: cleaning courtyards, clearing drains and cesspools, inspecting drinking water.[76] In Prussia, the local sanitary commissions were instructed to cleanse streets and public spaces on a daily basis, removing putrid and decomposing matter and keeping the gutters in working condition. A primitive sort of industrial sanitation was also on occasion attempted, as in the case of a yarn wash which, for polluting a local stream, was closed down. Regulations dealt with the health and sanitation of food. Cleanliness within individual residences was also the responsibility of the local cholera commissions, enforced, if necessary, with threats of

---

[73] Barchewitz, *Über die Cholera*, p. 56; *Die asiatische Cholera in der Stadt Magdeburg 1831–1832: Geschichtlich und ärztlich dargestellt nach amtlichen Nachrichten auf höhere Veranlassung* (Magdeburg, 1832), p. 48; Barchewitz, *Behandlung der Cholera*, p. 8.

[74] E. Housselle, "Gutachten über die Häusersperre," in *Vorläufige Nachricht von des Herrn Dr. Leviseur, Kreisphysicus im Regierungsbezirk Bromberg, glücklicher Methode gegen die Cholera* (Kiel, 1831), p. 20; Sachs, *Tagebuch*, p. 165; *Cholera-Archiv*, 1 (1832), p. 22; *Über die Furcht vor der herrschenden Brechruhr, zugleich enthaltend eine wissenschaftlich begründete Vorstellung an die oberpolizeilichen und Gesundheitsbehörden zu Beruhigung des Publikums* (Leipzig, 1831); Knolz, *Darstellung der Brechruhr-Epidemie*, pp. 362–63.

[75] Lichtenstädt, *Cholera in Russland*, pp. 15–16; Riecke, *Mittheilungen*, v. I, pp. 147–48; Tilesius v. T., *Über die Cholera und die kräftigsten Mittel dagegen, nebst Vorschlag eines grossen Ableitungsmittels, um die Krankheit in der Geburt zu ersticken* (Nuremberg, 1830), pp. 129–31.

[76] Brierre de Boismont, *Relation historique*, pp. 169–74; Knolz, *Darstellung der Brechruhr-Epidemie*, pp. 239–40, 303–05; *Instruction für die Sanitäts-Behörden*, pp. 3–10, 26–27.

legal sanction.[77] Individuals were advised to keep their living quarters immaculate, cleaning latrines, removing middings, draining marshy ground and sleeping in the upper stories beyond reach of putrid exhalations.[78]

The poor, widely agreed to be especially susceptible to disease, either because of their insalubrious living conditions, poor nourishment or unfortunate habits, were the object of particular attention. In Berlin, poor relief authorities were to ensure that recipients observed cleanliness in all respects, inspecting their homes, reporting overcrowding, instructing the inhabitants on sanitary precautions and exhorting them to adjust their habits accordingly. Since excess of any sort, especially strong drink, enhanced susceptibility, local sanitary commissions were to admonish those whose public behavior betrayed such influences, with recalcitrants reported for suitable punishment. That quarantine and other regulations gave the authorities control over the presence and hygienic deportment of vagabonds, beggars, peddlers, journeymen and the like was regarded as a virtue.[79] More benign attempts were also made to improve the health of the popular classes. Medicines and food were distributed gratis and various means sought of keeping the poor employed. In Vienna and Berlin foreign workers and artisans were banished to reduce competition on the labor market. Factories and workshops sought to keep running despite the epidemic, asking only that each morning workers present certification from the local sanitary commission that their homes were free of cholera. Many of the otherwise unemployed were able to find work thanks to the epidemic, taking up positions as attendants, bearers, guards, messengers and the like. The authorities were also willing to bend sanitary regulations in hopes of maintaining production and work and instituted public works projects to soak up the

[77] *Archiv für medizinische Erfahrung*, 1 (1832), pp. 41–54; Schmidt and Clarus, *Sammlung Kaiserlich Russischer Verordnungen*, pp. 13–14; Brierre de Boismont, *Relation historique*, pp. 169–74; *Sammlung*, p. 44.

[78] *Amts-Blatt*, 29 (22 July 1831), p. 146; 24 (17 June 1831), pp. 107–09; *Verordnung über das Verfahren*, pp. 10–11, 13; *Unterricht, wie Nichtärzte die asiatische Cholera verhüten*, pp. 5–7; *Anweisung wie man bei etwa eintretender asiatischer Cholera seine Gesundheit erhalten*, p. 7; Carl Brockmüller, *Ansichten über die herrschende Cholera, Vergleiche derselben mit dem Wechselfieber und Beweise, dass dieselbe so wenig ansteckend ist, noch werden kann, als das Wechselfieber* (Jülich, 1832), pp. 36–39.

[79] Joh. Christ. Aug. Clarus, *Ansichten eines Vereins praktischer Ärzte in Leipzig über die Verbreitung der asiatischen Cholera auf doppeltem Wege* (Leipzig, 1831), p. 12; Carl Barriés, *Ein Wort zu seiner Zeit. Was ist in der jetzigen Lage Deutschlands nothwendig die Cholera abzuwenden, ohne dass der Handel dadurch gesperrt wird: Rathschläge für Regierungen, Orts-Obrigkeiten und für jeden einzelnen Privatmann* (Hamburg, 1831), p. 29; *Sammlung*, pp. 179–82; *Berliner Cholera Zeitung* (1831), p. 284; *Amts-Blatt*, 32 (12 August 1831), p. 164; 36 (9 September 1831), Beilage, pp. 7–8; Brierre de Boismont, *Relation historique*, p. 118; *Verordnung über das Verfahren*, pp. 10–11, 13.

unemployed.[80] Finally and most ethereally, the authorities attempted to improve everyday conditions in hopes of raising their subjects' spirits and strengthening resistance. In Berlin, pleasurable pursuits being considered crucial, theaters and other amusements were not shut. Schools and churches remained open, while the beginning of the autumn university semester in 1831 was merely postponed until November. Because tobacco was thought to protect against disease, smoking (previously forbidden as unworthy of a great and dignified metropolis) was exceptionally permitted on public streets and in the Tiergarten. In Vienna, the royal theaters performed shows with proceeds earmarked for the poor.[81]

THE AUTHORITIES RELENT

As earlier with the plague, the autocracies thus took two parallel tacks to cholera, one localist and quasi-sanitationist, the other quarantinist. And yet, in terms of the detail of the regulations, the ambition of the project and the efforts expended, the quarantinist approach predominated. Localist efforts were largely limited to exhortations for change in individual habits and mores, with some incipient attempts to improve public hygiene. The quarantinist approach, in contrast, mobilized vast efforts, requiring drastic interventions. Such, at least, was the theory. Whether, in practice, anything remotely resembling the hierarchical, efficient, seamless web of quarantinist prophylaxis of the authorities' ambitions was ever put in place is an entirely different question. At least two sorts of factors conspired to prevent the full implementation of their preventive strategies as first conceived and, instead, to moderate the severity of the measures initially promulgated. The first concerns the practical difficulties of execution, the resistance among their subjects to measures that violated ingrained habit and venerable custom, the impossibility of enforcing administratively rational, but utopian precautions. The second deals with the learning process through which the authorities passed, the gradual realization that the initial measures,

[80] Schmidt and Clarus, *Sammlung Kaiserlich Russischer Verordnungen*, pp. 6–19; Riecke, *Mittheilungen*, v. I, pp. 165–74; Hille, *Beobachtungen*, p. 21; *Verordnung über das Verfahren*, pp. 21, 38; *Berlinische Nachrichten*, 136 (14 June 1831); 208 (6 September 1831); Carl Zeller, *Die epidemische Cholera beobachtet in Wien und Brünn im Herbste 1831* (Tübingen, 1832), pp. 126–27, 130; *Sammlung*, pp. 200–01; *Berliner Cholera Zeitung* (1831), pp. 131–33.

[81] Zitterland, ed., *Cholera-Zeitung* [Aachen], 6 (18 October 1831), p. 43; *Berliner Cholera Zeitung* (1831), pp. 141–43; *Berlinische Nachrichten*, 136 (14 June 1831); H. Scoutetten, *Relation historique et médicale de l'épidémie de choléra qui a régné à Berlin en 1831* (Paris, 1832), p. 7; Knolz, *Darstellung der Brechruhr-Epidemie*, pp. 239–40, 303–08.

even if implemented as planned, would have offered little protection and the conclusion drawn that change was necessary.

Besides representing drastic incursions into whatever realm of privacy and individual rights may be said to have existed in these nations during the early nineteenth century, many of the regulations promulgated also ran at odds to inherited popular custom and sparked resistance.[82] The insistence that victims be buried at once, for example, conflicted with the practice of laying bodies in state and the legal requirement that the dead not be interred until it was certain that they had in fact expired.[83] This, in turn, was linked not only to religious precepts but also to a widespread fear of being buried alive that was especially understandable in an age when the physician's ability to distinguish the comatose quick from the truly dead did not exceed that of the lay person by more than a degree of experience.[84] It was normal in Berlin, for example, for corpses to remain unburied until the onset of putrefaction, a practice the cholera regulations now sought to overturn.[85] In hopes of overcoming objections to speedy interments, the authorities proposed various means of making certain that only the truly deceased were buried. In Vienna, the cholera dead were left in bed for six hours, after which a doctor dripped burning sealing wax on their stomachs or applied redhot irons to the soles of their feet to ascertain that they were no longer among the living. In Prussia, no body was to be buried until inspected by a sanitary commission physician, although the motive here was also to prevent cholera deaths from being concealed.[86]

On cemeteries, objections were raised to undifferentiated cholera

---

[82] Popular objections to cholera regulations among the European lower classes during the 1830s were strikingly similar to those advanced by Indians against British colonial plague regulations at the end of the century: fears of poisoning, anger at disrespect for the dead, distrust of the medical examiners, fear of compulsory isolation and hospitalization (David Arnold, *Colonizing the Body: State Medicine and Epidemic Disease in Nineteenth-Century India* [Berkeley, 1993], pp. 211–26, 233–39). Whatever its other significance, this parallel tends to undermine Arnold's claim that the Indians were rejecting "western" colonializing medicine, at least no more than such practice was also rejected in the west.

[83] In Prussia, bodies were not buried (ALR, II, 11, §§474–76) until it was absolutely certain that they were dead.

[84] *Schlesische Cholera-Zeitung* (1831–32), pp. 124–25; Sachs, *Tagebuch*, p. 276; Sachs, *Betrachtungen*, pp. 2ff.; *Geschichte der Cholera in Danzig*, pp. 15–16; Bangssel, *Erinnerungsbuch für Alle*, p. 47; *Systematische Übersicht der Veranstaltungen gegen die Cholera in den Herzogthümern Schleswig, Holstein und Lauenburg* (Kiel, n.d. [1831/32]), pp. 11–12; Alfons Fischer, *Geschichte des deutschen Gesundheitswesens* (Berlin, 1933), v. II, pp. 226–29. On similar fears in Britain, see Stephen Brougham, *On Cholera: A Treatise, Practical and Theoretical on the Nature of This Disease* (London, 1834), p. 69.

[85] *Medicinischer Argos*, 1 (1839), p. 317; Sachs, *Tagebuch*, p. 276; *AGM*, 28 (1832), pp. 281–82.

[86] Bernard Röser and Aloys Urban, eds., *Berichte bayerischer Ärzte über Cholera Morbus*, Erste Abtheilung (Munich, 1832), p. 55; *Sammlung*, pp. 23–29, 44–45.

graveyards that failed to respect religious differences. The poor, eager for a respectable burial regardless of why they had perished, resented the possibility of being buried apart from their families like criminals, suicides and plague victims. In Danzig the cholera dead were at first buried together regardless of religion in unconsecrated and unenclosed ground. In deference to concerns at such practices, the authorities in Berlin established two cholera cemeteries, duly consecrated in the Protestant and Catholic faiths, while Jewish victims were buried in a special cholera graveyard next to the usual Jewish cemetery. In Cracow, Jews were allowed to continue burying their dead in the customary manner despite regulations to the contrary, carrying them to the cemetery only covered, not encoffinated.[87] Many of the regulations which offended popular sensibilities seemed calculated to degrade the dead: special graves, burials without the requisite dignity, handling of the cadavers with metal hooks and, above all, disinfection with lime. Women in Königsberg claimed to prefer suicide to cremation with lime. The poor resented such precautions as affecting them particularly, since, as with removals to the hospital, the well-off were able to avoid the worst consequences of what society required for the protection of all.[88] The same sense of injustice at being singled out was prompted among the common people by the dissections sometimes undertaken on cholera cadavers at the hospitals. The authorities responded by emphasizing the propriety with which they were conducted and the decent burials accorded the remains. In Russia, dissections were forbidden in deference to popular sentiment, except at the General Military Hospital and then only in case of doubt as to the cause of death.[89]

Another factor in public discontent was the geography of contagionist and correspondingly quarantinist attitudes. It was a common opinion that quarantinism was an approach best adapted to rural and small-town conditions. Here, in the epidemiologically transparent circumstances of individual family homes, low population densities and

[87] Friedrich Dörne, *Dr. Louis Stromeyer zu Danzig in Ost-Preussen: Ein Beitrag zur Geschichte der Cholera-Contagionisten* (Altenburg, 1832), p. 11; Sachs, *Tagebuch*, pp. 175–81; *Geschichte der Cholera in Danzig*, pp. 15–16; Bangssel, *Erinnerungsbuch für Alle*, p. 45; *Berliner Cholera Zeitung* (Berlin, 1831), pp. 91–93; *Verordnung über das Verfahren*, pp. 43–46; [Trafvenfelt], *Sammandrag af Läkares åsigter*, v. III, pp. 41–42.

[88] [Bogislav Konrad] Krüger-Hansen, *Zweiter Nachtrag zu den Curbildern, mit Bezug auf Cholera* (Rostock, 1831), p. 16; *Geschichte der Cholera in Danzig*, pp. 15–16; *Schlesische Cholera-Zeitung* (1831–32), pp. 31–32; *Sammlung*, pp. 54–55; *Verhandlungen* (1831), pp. 4–5; Dettke, *Die asiatische Hydra*, pp. 287–91.

[89] Sachs, *Tagebuch*, pp. 175–81; *Berliner Cholera Zeitung*, p. 103; *Supplement to the EMSJ* (February 1832), p. clxiii. For similar themes in Britain, see Ruth Richardson, *Death, Dissection and the Destitute* (London, 1987).

neighborly familiarity, the course of disease transmission could be traced with precision from one person or household to the next. Moreover, the quarantinist precautions taken on the basis of a contagionist etiology fit circumstances in the countryside snugly since, better able to provision themselves independently than urban dwellers, rural denizens could more easily be sequestered.[90] Rural towns were less likely to be damaged in their commercial relations than large cities and could better withstand the rigors of cordons and quarantines.[91] Anticontagionism, in contrast, was considered an ideology suited to big cities with their complex internal relations that obscured the pathways of infection.[92] It was also commonly remarked that quarantinism was favored by the wealthy, able to ride out a resulting period of economic inactivity while the poor earned their bread day to day. The well-off supported quarantinist policies in hopes of being spared disease while the worse-off knew all too well what they stood to suffer in terms of economic hardship.[93] Given the choice between cholera and free trade, on the one hand, and no disease, but a trade embargo on the other, one observer bet that the poor would chose the epidemiological over the economic disaster. Better, as the old saying had it, to fall into the hands of God than those of humans.[94]

By imposing measures that were unrelenting in their insistence that contagion should be fought first and foremost with cordons, quarantines and sequestration, measures bespeaking a belief that even hamfisted means were justified to protect the public health at the expense of the individual weal, the authorities provoked indignation and resentment among the poorest and most urban of their subjects. Popular unrest, riot and rebellion were the fruit. In Saratov in Russia the ill from the poorer classes were roughly removed to the hospital by police searching house to house. Such behavior marled the soil for a bumper crop of unrests that was harvested most abundantly in Moscow, St. Petersburg,

---

[90] This was a general conception, found in all nations: *Staats-Zeitung*, Beilage zu No. 285, 14 October 1831, pp. 1557–59; *Cholera-Archiv*, 2 (1832), p. 264; 3 (1833), p. 235; *(Allgemeine Cholera-Zeitung)*, 2 (1832), p. 281; Becker, *Letters on the Cholera*, p. 21; *Schlesische Cholera-Zeitung* (1831–32), pp. 139–40, 143; D. M. Moir, *Proofs of the Contagion of Malignant Cholera* (Edinburgh, 1832), p. 70; Jacques Piquemal, "Le choléra de 1832 en France et la pensée médicale," *Thales*, 10 (1959), pp. 52–53; François Delaporte, *Disease and Civilization: The Cholera in Paris, 1832* (Cambridge, MA, 1986), pp. 169ff., 175–76; Chantal Beauchamp, *Délivrez-nous du mal: Épidémies, endémies, médecine et hygiène au XIXe siècle dans l'Indre, l'Indre-et-Loire et le Loir-et-Cher* (n.p., 1990), pp. 133–34; *Annales*, 2/25 (1866), p. 343; Charles-Edward Amory Winslow, *The Conquest of Epidemic Disease* (Princeton, 1944), p. 282.
[91] *Cholera-Archiv*, 1 (1832), p. 286; Kreysig, *Versuch einer leichtfasslichen und ausführlichen Belehrung*, p. 20.
[92] *Heidelberger Klinische Annalen*, 8 (1832), pp. 154–55; *(Allgemeine Cholera-Zeitung)*, 2 (1832), p. 281.
[93] *Verhandlungen*, 1 (1832), pp. 335–40, 344; *Cholera-Zeitung* (1832), pp. 91–92; Housselle, "Gutachten über die Häusersperre," p. 22.
[94] Fischer, *Es wird Tag!*, p. 22; *Conférence 1874*, p. 157; *Verhandlungen* (1831), p. 9.

Novgorod, Pest, Königsberg, Posen and Stettin.[95] Among the first disturbances caused by strict precautions, especially sequestration and compulsory hospitalization, were those of Witegra where, in July 1831, a mob
rose, destroyed hospitals, broke open sealed houses, tore down cholera
signs and set patients free. In St. Petersburg, popular protests at forcible
removals escalated into attacks on hospitals to liberate patients. Similar
unrest erupted in Novgorod and in New Ladoga the quarantine institutions were destroyed.[96] In Neidenburg, the local sanitary commission,
seeking to prohibit sour beer, was rewarded for its efforts by the brewers'
refusal to pursue their craft at all. Carpenters would not make coffins
and were persuaded to build beds for the hospital only after the police
supplied them with wood and sent constables to force the issue. In
Königsberg, the poor refused to believe that cholera was contagious or
that it required extraordinary measures. Prophylactic regulations were
regarded as a means of harassing the lowest classes, cordoning off the
city as but an excuse to raise prices, sequestration a way of rendering the
victims unemployed, destitute and hungry. Secret removals to the hospital, isolation of the ill, surreptitious burials after nightfall: all suggested
motives other than the public weal and the conclusion that cholera was
but a scare and the official precautions in fact intended to despatch the
poor through poison and hunger.[97] Indeed, Königsberg provided the
clearest expression of the belief, also common in unrests elsewhere, that
cholera was a conspiracy by the wealthy and mighty to thin the ranks of
the otherwise ungovernable masses.[98]

Not surprisingly, more specific scapegoats were also sought for the
misery of cholera and its prophylaxis. Jews and Jesuits were occasionally mentioned along with the rich and the government authorities as
forces and vectors behind the disease, but physicians were especially
singled out for opprobrium and physical attack as that group most obviously implicated. Doctors were regarded as allies of the authorities,
united in cahoots to oppress and, in the worst cases, to poison the lower
classes. Physicians, so the accusation ran, sought to increase their power

[95] Huber, *Rettung von der Cholera: Tagebuch aus Saratow vom 10ten bis 31sten August 1830* (Dessau, 1831),
pp. 6–9; Harless, *Indische Cholera*, p. 716; Buek, *Verbreitungsweise*, pp. 52–53.

[96] Buek, *Verbreitungsweise*, pp. 51–52; Riecke, *Mittheilungen*, v. III, pp. 174–75; McGrew, *Russia and
the Cholera*, pp. 50–51.

[97] *Cholera-Zeitung* (1832), pp. 92–93, 102–03.

[98] *Cholera-Zeitung* (1832), p. 9; *Verhandlungen*, I (1832), pp. 335–40, 344. For similar fears in Berlin
and St Petersburg, see PRO, PC1/101, Board of Health, minutes, 19 September 1831, Chad to
Viscount Palmerston, 11 September 1831; Charles C. F. Greville, *The Greville Memoirs* (2nd edn.;
London, 1874), v. II, p. 193.

by exaggerating cholera's dangers, thus making themselves indispensable. In Braunsberg it was believed that they were poisoning the poor at the behest of the authorities, rewarded for their efforts with four Gulden per death. In the wildest conspiracy fantasies, current especially in St. Petersburg, foreign physicians were part of an international plot directed from London to apply the same techniques first tried out in British India of eliminating the lower classes, who had become too numerous to be conveniently governed.[99]

The secrecy and isolation surrounding cholera hospitals did little to alleviate popular fears of what physicians were up to. So current and convincing were rumors in Breslau of inmates being poisoned or tortured that one hospital publicized the names and addresses of two cured patients in hopes that their testimony would bear witness to the selfless efforts of the attending physicians. In Bromberg, the public believed that patients were asphyxiated with sulfur fumes or that poisonous medicines were administered. The precipitous death of the victims (fit as a fiddle in the morning, a corpse on the slab by nightfall), the blue-black hue of their bodies, the caustic substances used to fumigate and disinfect – all seemed to confirm such fears.[100] In Königsberg, where a doctor had administered phosphorescent ether, witnesses were convinced that the patient had been killed by burning medicine. In Danzig, the lazaretto was built on the Holm, an island in the harbor, from which, the locals were convinced, no one ever returned. The guards, it was whispered, were issued live ammunition and vast quantities of unslaked lime had been shipped over for the open burial trenches. Mighty clouds of smoke rose daily from the Holm and when the flames were visible on the mainland, the residents remarked that corpses were being cremated and that doubtless some were only apparently dead.[101] Because of such fears, people caught on the streets of St. Petersburg carrying bottles of vinegar or packets of chlorine powder were attacked as poisoners and physicians were pursued and killed. In Reval, the fear of poisoning led many to refuse all forms of aid, including distributions of food. In Breslau, Dr. Wendt, known as a contagionist, had his windows broken by a mob.

[99] *Allgemein fassliche Anweisung*, p. 6; *AGM*, 27 (1831), pp. 558–59; Bangssel, *Erinnerungsbuch für Alle*, pp. 4–5; Fischer, *Es wird Tag!*, p. 22; *Cholera-Archiv*, 3 (1833), pp. 225–26; PRO, PC1/101, Board of Health, minutes, 19 September 1831, Chad to Viscount Palmerston, 11 September 1831; Greville, *Memoirs*, v. II, p. 193.

[100] *Schlesische Cholera-Zeitung* (1831–32), pp. 31–32; *Die asiatische Cholera in der Stadt Magdeburg*, p. 4; Housselle, "Gutachten über die Häusersperre," p. 21; Ollenroth, *Asiatische Cholera*, pp. 18–19; August Vetter, *Beleuchtung des Sendschreibens die Cholera betreffend, des Präsidenten Herrn Dr. Rust an den Freiherrn Alexander von Humboldt* (Berlin, 1832), pp. 42–43.

[101] *Verhandlungen*, 1 (1832), p. 342; *Cholera-Zeitung* (1832), p. 9; *Geschichte der Cholera in Danzig*, pp. 15–16; Bangssel, *Erinnerungsbuch für Alle*, pp. 46–47.

Around Danzig, there were villages where doctors could not work without police protection and in one case, Ohra, even this did not suffice, forcing the authorities to retreat and leave the place to its fate.[102] In Königsberg, physicians were attacked: one managed to flee, another was beaten and several saw their carriages stoned. An apothecary in the suburbs was set upon and destroyed, weapons were secured and police headquarters stormed. The uproar lasted several hours until the militia could restore order and in the aftermath some physicians refused to attend patients in fear of their lives. At the end of July 1831 some hundred Königsbergers were arrested in connection with cholera unrests, only – the jails full – to be released.[103] The untenable proposition, as one observer put it, that cholera could be contained by quarantinist measures had managed to accomplish the impossible: tumult in Prussia.[104]

THE WATERS CLOUD

The poor and the laboring classes were not, however, alone in objecting to quarantinist measures. On at least one crucial point they were supported by those whose living was made from commerce and trade: while cordon, quarantine and sequestration policies might be advisable from a prophylactic perspective, economically they were a disaster. Mercantile and commercial interests objected to the authorities' initial tactics, arguing that cholera was not transmissible and did not require such procedures, that the disease could not, whatever the case, be thus contained, or (their final fallback position) that, however advisable in theory such precautions might be, in reality they promised a remedy worse than the affliction.[105] Nor were the government authorities immune to such considerations. Dampening economic activity through prophylactic restrictions meant not only more poverty to alleviate, but also a decline in tax receipts and, in any case, such precautions did not come cheap.[106] Prussia's initial measures early in 1831 would, if implemented to the letter,

---

[102] Riecke, *Mittheilungen*, v. III, pp. 174–75; Gerardin and Gaimard, *Du choléra-morbus*, pp. 6–7; Buek, *Verbreitungsweise*, pp. 51–52, 68; *Verhandlungen*, 1 (1832), p. 448.

[103] Krüger-Hansen, *Zweiter Nachtrag*, pp. 14–16; *Verhandlungen*, 1 (1832), pp. 335–40, 342–44; Dettke, *Die asiatische Hydra*, pp. 134–40; GStA, Rep 84a, 4178, Bekanntmachungen from the Criminal-Senat des Königl. Oberlandes-Gerichts, 29 July 1831.   [104] *Cholera-Zeitung* (1832), pp. 102–03.

[105] Friedrich Alexander Simon, Jr., *Weg mit den Kordons! quand meme . . . der epidemisch-miasmatische Charakter der indischen Brechruhr, ein grober Verstoss gegen die Geschichte ihres Zuges von Dschissore in Mittelindien nach dem tiefen Keller in Hamburg* (Hamburg, 1832), p. 44; *Staats-Zeitung*, 283 (12 October 1831), p. 1548; *Cholera-Archiv*, 2 (1832) p. 274; Ross, "Prussian Administrative Response," pp. 171–73.

[106] In France, this was one of Chervin's main arguments against quarantinism: *Annales*, 10, 1 (1833), p. 222; Delaporte, *Disease and Civilization*, pp. 141–42.

have consumed vast resources. For the central government, there was the employment of thousands of soldiers on the cordons; for local administrations, the expense of quarantine stations and hospitals, medicine and food for the ill and sequestered.[107] In Elbing two hundred workers were employed merely to seal off and provision sequestered houses, while in Bromberg 407 out of a total population of 6,683 souls were quarantined. Isolating 285 dwellings in Danzig in July 1831 obliged the municipality to maintain 1,076 residents at its expense. Because quarantines shut businesses, 170 artisans had to be fed and, when the theater closed, twenty-seven actors were added to the rosters of those maintained from the public purse.[108]

Such considerations – fear of provoking popular disturbances, pressure from commercial interests and the states' own ambivalent position, hamstrung as they were between concern for the public weal and their inability to disregard the costs thereof – helped convince the autocracies to moderate the rigor of the initial regulations. Already during the winter of 1829–30 the Russian government reviewed quarantine policies to relax the most economically damaging. In Moscow, pressure from commercial interests helped ease medical opinion away from contagionism. Merchants here insisted that, if transmissible at all, cholera was communicated only by personal contact, never by goods or merchandise.[109] The Medical Council of Moscow let itself be convinced partly by the influence of Dr. F. C. M. Markus, who maintained close ties to the local merchant community, that cholera had not been imported by persons or goods, that it had arisen for local reasons and that quarantines and cordons were useless. The government, in turn, was persuaded to exempt from quarantine goods entering Moscow from infected areas, excluding only the accompanying carriers and horses.[110] In much the same way, considerations of the expense of qua-

---

[107] Heinrich Georg Schäfer, "Staatliche Abwehrmassnahmen gegen die Cholera in der Rheinprovinz während der Seuchenzüge des 19. Jahrhunderts, dargestellt am Beispiel der Stadt Aachen" (MD diss., Technische Hochschule Aachen, 1978), p. 20. For similar considerations later in Bavaria, see Wolfgang Locher, "Pettenkofer and Epidemiology: Erroneous Concepts – Beneficial Results," in Yosio Kawakita et al., eds., *History of Epidemiology* (Tokyo, 1993), pp. 97–98.

[108] *Cholera-Zeitung* (1832), p. 101; *Verhandlungen*, 1 (1832), pp. 439, 443–44; *Cholera-Archiv*, 3 (1833), pp. 107–11; Ollenroth, *Asiatische Cholera*, pp. 10, 22; Dettke, *Die asiatische Hydra*, pp. 108–09.

[109] PRO, PC1/4395/pt. 1, Heytesbury to the Earl of Aberdeen, 20 October 1830; Hawkins, *History*, pp. 280–86; *Supplement to the EMSJ* (February 1832), pp. cxxiv–cxxix; *PP* 1831 (49) xvii, pp. 12–14; Brüggemann, *Über die Cholera: Einige Worte zur Beruhigung über die Möglichkeit und die Grösse der Gefahr* (Leipzig, 1831), pp. 10–11; McGrew, *Russia and the Cholera*, p. 49.

[110] F. C. M. Markus, *Rapport sur le choléra-morbus de Moscou* (Moscow, 1832), pp. 176–77, 188, 209–10; *Hamburgisches Magazin der ausländischen Literatur der gesammten Heilkunde*, 23 (1832), p. 18; *LMG,*

rantinist measures and their pernicious effect on trade and taxability figured large in the Austrian emperor's decision to moderate policies during the autumn of 1831.[111] In Gumbinnen, a Prussian district on the Polish border, strict procedures were moderated in December 1831 for simple lack of the funds necessary for a full-blown quarantinist approach. Such ameliorations of the initially draconian quarantinist approach were now appreciated as interfering less with commerce and trade.[112]

But even had the authorities wished to, they could not have implemented their initial regulations in all their extravagant detail. Another factor in the decision to relent on the severity of the first measures was the extent to which (ignoring for the moment the question of cost) their reach exceeded their grasp. The restrictions prescribed were so extensive and complex, requiring so powerful an administrative machinery, that they were in effect unworkable. Testimony to the authorities' inability to live up to their own ambitions is legion. St. Petersburg undermined its own powers through the unhappy initial choice of an antagonistic and ineffective emissary, Count Zakrevskii. But even the most able administrator would have faced daunting tasks in the Slavic vastness. Russia's administrative districts were so large and lacking in the military personnel necessary for effective cordons that, when the sequestering of whole provinces was discussed, the outcome was most likely to have been nothing more adventurous than an interruption of communication along the main roads.[113] In Poland the chaotic circumstances of war with the Russians encouraged an anticontagionist line that required less immediate enforcement of costly measures and many of the recommended precautions were, in any case, never put into effect.[114] Even in Prussia, where official ambition and administrative reality were most proximate, the problems of implementation were overwhelming. Alexandre Moreau de

---

11 (1833), p. 358; F. C. M. Markus, *Pensée sur le choléra-morbus* (Moscow, 1831); Buek, *Verbreitungsweise*, p. 37.

[111] *Haude- und Spener-Zeitung*, 232 (4 October 1831), copy in the Stadtarchiv Berlin, 01-02GB/257; Knolz, *Darstellung der Brechruhr-Epidemie*, pp. 230–33. For a similar argument, see Johannes Wimmer, *Gesundheit, Krankheit und Tod im Zeitalter der Aufklärung: Fallstudien aus den habsburgischen Erbländern* (Vienna, 1991), pp. 114–15.

[112] *Cholera-Archiv*, 3 (1833), pp. 107–11; *Einiges über die Cholera: Ein Sendschreiben des Präsidenten Dr. Rust an Se. Excellenz den Königl. Preussischen wirklichen Geheimen Rath und Kammerherrn, Freyh. Alex. v. Humboldt in Paris* (Berlin, 1832), p. 5.

[113] McGrew, *Russia and the Cholera*, pp. 15, 61–63; Riecke, *Mittheilungen*, v. I, pp. 156, 166–67; v. III, pp. 77–79, 173.

[114] *Verhandlungen* (1831), p. 103; Carl Julius Wilhelm Paul Remer, *Beobachtungen über die epidemische Cholera gesammelt in Folge einer in amtlichem Auftrage gemachten Reise nach Warschau, und mit höheren Orts eingeholter Genehmigung herausgegeben* (Breslau, 1831), p. 57.

Jonnès, a prominent French contagionist and spokesman for restrictive measures in his own country, claimed that the Prussian regulations, "si etendu, si rigide, si minutieux," existed only on paper.[115] An exaggeration, spiced by national rivalry, his remark nonetheless grasped the gist of the problem. Cordons were more like sieves than dams, especially when they sought to seal national borders that in commercial and personal terms scarcely existed. Near Bromberg, for example, along the Polish border, the cordon was easy to pass. When the crops were high, sneaking across the fields, especially at night, was child's play.[116] Cordons here were also hampered by the arbitrariness of the Prussian–Polish border. In Posen, for example, it cut through crowded neighborhoods, haphazardly separating houses from their gardens. In an area where inhabitants on both sides spoke the same language, enjoying close relations, it was all but impossible to impose any real separation. Smugglers pushed their way across the cordons, sometimes by stealth, sometimes brazenly in the face of the sentries' fire. At Strizalkovo, where Brierre de Boismont, reporting on Poland for the French, underwent quarantine, he heard sentries firing on smugglers throughout the night.[117] The Russo-Polish war also defeated attempts to cut off relations between Prussia and Poland, indeed set at odds with each other Prussia's foreign and quarantine policies. The Prussians, although officially neutral in the conflict, in fact permitted provisioning of the Russian armies from Prussian territory, especially Königsberg and Danzig.[118]

The sealing-off of infected dwellings was equally riddled with holes. In Danzig, the sanitary commission admitted that the guards posted at infected houses were simply incapable of ensuring that no one entered or left. Here sequestration was commonly regarded as a joke, since almost every house had an unguarded back door.[119] A bordello, sealed off along with its clientele, managed to preserve its guests' reputations by smuggling them out through a hidden egress. In another case, the widow of a wealthy cholera victim, wishing to avoid the rigors of the official regulations and to bury her husband in the usual manner, cut a deal with the wife of a poor man who had perished of innocent causes. The

---

[115] PRO, PC1/108, Moreau de Jonnès to Pym, 17 September 1831; 21 September 1831.

[116] Ollenroth, *Asiatische Cholera*, p. 17; Dettke, *Die asiatische Hydra*, pp. 113–14.

[117] Brierre de Boismont, *Relation historique*, p. 115; *Supplement to the EMSJ* (February 1832), p. ccxvi; *(Allgemeine Cholera-Zeitung)*, 2 (1832), pp. 276–77.

[118] J.-A. Buet, *Histoire générale du choléra-morbus, depuis 1817 jusqu'en août 1831* (Paris, 1831), p. 34; Simon, *Weg mit den Kordons!*, pp. 30–34; *Verhandlungen*, 1 (1832), p. 331; *Cholera-Archiv*, 3 (1833), pp. 112, 161; Greville, *Memoirs*, v. II, p. 157.

[119] *Verhandlungen*, 1 (1832), pp. 438–39; Ollenroth, *Asiatische Cholera*, pp. 48–49; Dörne, *Dr. Louis Stromeyer*, p. 13; Bruno Valentin, "Cholera-Briefe," *Sudhoffs Archiv*, 37, 3/4 (November 1953), p. 420.

corpses switched, the poor woman (suitably rewarded) was sequestered; with the cadavers switched once again, the rich man's remains were buried in the style to which his wife thought him entitled: cholera bouffe. In other cases, the tone was uglier. In Kiev, a cobbler's apprentice nursing a grudge sought to have his master's house sealed off by getting drunk and, through copious vomiting, simulating the symptoms of cholera. Instead (so cautioned this admonitionary tale) he actually caught the disease and died.[120]

MEDICINE RECONSIDERS

Most important among the causes encouraging the authorities to reconsider their initial regulations was the shift in opinion on cholera and its precautions that followed in the train of accumulating experience, a seachange traceable in both lay and medical circles. With all due account of the numerous exceptions to this rule, it remains true that, on balance, greater familiarity with cholera encouraged a tempered notion of its contagiousness and a reevaluation of the measures likely to limit its spread. At the least, as in Prussia, initial certainties that cholera was directly transmissible gave way to fierce dispute over the nature of the disease and how to counter it.

Medical opinion evolved through several stages. During the teens and twenties when Europe was still virgin epidemiological territory, the evidence of the Indian physicians spoke for localist assumptions. Once cholera had arrived in Europe during the 1820s, however, the Russian authorities and much medical opinion began to consider it contagious. Many took their cue from the French contagionist Moreau de Jonnès, who based his conclusions on reports from French doctors on Bourbon.[121] The contagionism of the St. Petersburg Central Medical Council was influenced by Dr. Lichtenstädt who argued that, while cholera may have been miasmatic and arisen from local causes in India, by the time it got to Russia its character had changed.[122] Local

---

[120] *Geschichte der Cholera in Danzig*, pp. 36–37; A. L. Köstler, *Anweisung sich gegen die epidemische Cholera zu schützen, und dieselbe bey ihrem Beginn zweckmässig zu behandeln* (Vienna, 1831), pp. 8–9; *Cholera-Zeitung* (1832), p. 96.

[121] *Instruction für die Sanitäts-Behörden*, pp. 25–26; *Bemerkungen über die Furcht vor der herschenden Brechruhr, zugleich enthaltend eine wissenschaftlich begründete Vorstellung an die oberpolizeilichen und Gesundheitsbehörden zu Beruhigung des Publikums* (Leipzig, 1831), p. v; Buek, *Verbreitungsweise*, p. 17; Jaehnichen, *Quelques réflexions*, pp. 10–11, 21.

[122] *Cholera-Zeitung* (1832), p. 24. In other writings, however, he seemed to be hedging his bets, not taking sides. See Lichtenstädt and Seydlitz, eds., *Mittheilungen über die Cholera-Epidemie in St. Petersburg im Sommer 1831, von praktischen Ärzten daselbst herausgegeben und redigirt* (St. Petersburg, 1831), pp. 54–55; McGrew, *Russia and the Cholera*, p. 22.

physicians here, especially those from the epidemiological front lines who had met the disease face to face tended, in contrast, to be noncontagionists, persisting despite the grudging need to toe the line from St. Petersburg. Jaehnichen, member of the Moscow Temporary Medical Council, was convinced that cholera was not contagious and doubted the transmissibility of even the plague. In Tiflis, physicians were such convinced noncontagionists that they encouraged the inhabitants to disperse into the surrounding countryside.[123] Such opinions began to gain ground as cholera spread into the big cities. First to volteface were the Moscow physicians. While they were generally contagionists before having had any direct experience of the disease, their minds changed with increased familiarity.[124] In St. Petersburg, their colleagues followed this cue, although never quite as unanimously as to the south.[125]

After 1831, once cholera had arrived in the German-speaking lands, the simple certainties of the first phase evaporated. In Austria, medical opinion moved quickly away from contagionism once experience was won and the hardships of the attendant regulations became evident.[126] In Prussia, where opinion was equally divided between contagionists and their opponents, etiological hand-to-hand combat raged.[127] The diehard contagionists continued to believe that the exhalations, excreta and other effluvia of the stricken imparted the disease.[128] Anticontagionists countered with heroic feats of personal risk-taking (foreshadowing and often putting to shame Pettenkofer's later imbibitions) to demonstrate that cholera was not transmissible through imme-

[123] Buek, *Verbreitungsweise*, pp. 20–21, 26–27; Lichtenstädt, *Cholera in Russland*, pp. 29, 36ff., 63ff., but also pp. 90ff.; Jos. Herm. Schmidt, *Physiologie der Cholera* (Berlin, 1832), pp. 167–68; Riecke, *Mittheilungen*, v. II, pp. 43–44; *Gazette médicale de Paris*, 2, 20 (1831), pp. 169–72; *EMSJ*, 58 (July 1831), p. 140.

[124] Buek, *Verbreitungsweise*, pp. 32–33; *PP* 1831 (49) xvii, pp. 3, 8–9; B. Zoubkoff, *Observations faites sur le cholera morbus dans le quartier de la Yakimanka à Moscou, en 1830* (Moscow, 1831), p. 15.

[125] *Staats-Zeitung*, Beilage zu No. 285, 14 October 1831, pp. 1557–59; Lichtenstädt and Seydlitz, *Mittheilungen*, pp. 124–25, 95–102, 154–55; *Berliner Cholera Zeitung* (1831), pp. 51–53; [Paul] Horaninow, *Beitrag zur Geschichte und Behandlung der epidemischen Cholera* (St. Petersburg, 1832), pp. 12–13; *LMG*, 9 (1832), pp. 792–93; *Cholera-Archiv*, 1 (1832), p. 2; J. G. Lindgren, *Der epidemische Brechdurchfall, beobachtet zu Nishni-Nowgorod* (Dorpat, 1831), pp. 30–33; [Trafvenfelst], *Sammandrag af Läkares åsigter*, v. II, pp. 35–41.

[126] Knolz, *Darstellung der Brechruhr-Epidemie*, pp. 234–35; Egon Schmitz-Cliever, "Die Anschauungen vom Wesen der Cholera bei den Aachener Epidemien 1832–1866," *Sudhoffs Archiv*, 36, 4 (December 1952), p. 262.

[127] By far the most detailed account of the spectrum of opinion is Buek, *Verbreitungsweise*, sect. 1. Buek himself was a miasmaticist anticontagionist from Hamburg. See also H. W. Buek, *Die bisherige Verbreitung der jetzt besonders in Russland herrschenden Cholera, erläutert durch eine Karte und eine dieselbe erklärende kurze Geschichte dieser Epidemie* (Hamburg, 1831), pp. 24–26.

[128] *Kurze Anweisung zur Erkenntnis und Heilung der Cholera*, pp. 10–12; *Anweisung zur Erhaltung der Gesundheit und Verhütung der Ansteckung bei etwa eintretender Cholera-Epidemie* (revised edn.; Berlin, 1831), pp. 8–9; *Cholera-Archiv*, 1 (1832), pp. 236, 333.

diate contact. A military physician named Koch sought to prove the disease uncontagious by doing his damnedest to catch it: keeping his naked hands under the covers on the bodies of his patients and inhaling their breath, performing autopsies on cadavers so fresh that their stomachs and chest cavities steamed when split open, thrusting his hands deep into their bodies, rinsing afterwards only with water, lying naked in bed with the ill and the dying.[129] Between the outliers, much medical opinion preferred to avoid clearcut distinctions between contagionism and localism, happily content with the peaceful coexistence of individual predisposition, environmental influences and transmission.[130]

There were also debates over cholera beyond the confines of the medical community – a general and ongoing discussion of appropriate responses that the historian might court anachronism by calling public opinion were it not that terms to this effect were used by contemporaries themselves.[131] In Austria, the authorities invoked public opinion as the force that, assuming contagiousness, demanded strict measures. Conversely, once public opinion here was convinced that cordons and quarantines were worse than the disease, official policy shifted, now favoring their abolition.[132] In Prussia public opinion favored cordons and quarantines before cholera had struck, only to reject them once their effect had become apparent.[133] Opponents of cordons and sequestration here hammered home a few primary points: quarantinist measures

---

[129] Sachs, *Tagebuch*, pp. 45–47; *Cholera-Archiv*, 1 (1832), pp. 20–21. For similar examples from other nations, see *Supplement to the EMSJ* (February 1832), p. cxxxvii; Casimir Allibert et al., *Rapport lu a l'Académie royale de médecine, et remis a M. le Ministre du Commerce et des Travaux publics* . . . (Paris, 1832), pp. 64–65; Buek, *Verbreitungsweise*, p. 31; Horaninow, *Behandlung der epidemischen Cholera*, p. 13; [Trafvenfelt], *Sammandrag af Läkares åsigter*, v. III, p. 36; Brierre de Boismont, *Relation historique*, p. 93; *AGM*, 26 (1831), pp. 274, 437–38; *Supplement to the EMSJ* (February 1832), p. xi; Delaporte, *Disease and Civilization*, p. 165.

[130] Johann Adolph Schubert, *Heilung und Verhütung der Cholera morbus* (Leipzig, 1830), pp. 19ff.; Tilesius v. T., *Über die Cholera*, pp. 72–73; Clarus, *Ansichten eines Vereins*; Hartung, *Cholera-Epidemie in Aachen*, pp. 68–69; *(Allgemeine Cholera-Zeitung)*, 2 (1832), pp. 133–34; *Mittheilungen über die ostindische Cholera zunächst für die Ärzte und Wundärzte Kurhessens: Herausgegeben von den ärztlichen Mitgliedern der obersten Sanitäts-Kommission* (Cassel, 1831), pp. 59–60; *Magazin für die gesammte Heilkunde*, 42 (1834), pp. 69–70; Ludwig Wilhelm Sachs, *Die Cholera: Nach eigenen Beobachtungen in der Epidemie zu Königsberg im Jahre 1831 nosologisch und therapeutisch dargestellt* (Königsberg, 1832), pp. 110–11; Dyrsen, *Kurzgefasste Anweisung*, pp. 19–20; Barchewitz, *Über die Cholera*, p. 52.

[131] Buek, *Verbreitungsweise*, pp. 2–3; Ollenroth, *Asiatische Cholera*, pp. 48–49; *Geschichte der Cholera in Danzig*, pp. 30–31; *Berliner Cholera Zeitung* (1831), pp. 179–83, 207–08; *Schlesische Cholera-Zeitung* (1831–32), p. 70. For Sweden, see *Preste*, 1834, v. 10, p. 84; *Ridderskapet och Adeln*, 1834–35, v. 12, pp. 357–61. For Britain, see Greville, *Memoirs*, v. II, pp. 156–57, 278.

[132] Gerardin and Gaimard, *Du choléra-morbus*, p. 268; Knolz, *Darstellung der Brechruhr-Epidemie*, pp. 237–38.

[133] John Hamett, *The Substance of the Official Medical Reports upon the Epidemic Called Cholera, Which Prevailed Among the Poor at Dantzick, Between the End of May and the First Part of September, 1831* (London, 1832), p. 95; Brigitta Schader, *Die Cholera in der deutschen Literatur* (Gräfelfing, 1985), pp. 47–51.

were selfcontradictory and impractical. Fear of the consequences meant that the sick hid their affliction rather than seeking aid. Strict sequestration was simply not feasible. Even ignoring the inevitable illegal circumventions, there remained all manner of exceptions: doctors, priests, sanitary inspectors, legal personnel and the like, all of whom had legitimate reasons for contact with the ill. Once the diagnosis had been rendered, patients often dashed out to enjoy their last moments of freedom, inform acquaintances or collect necessities, spreading the disease farther than had there been no sequestration in the first place.[134] Because quarantinism held out unfulfillable hopes of protection, it lulled society into an illusion of security. Fear of sequestration needlessly magnified anxieties, hindering convalescence.[135] By provoking resistance, such policies undermined respect for authority, disturbed the peace and weakened society. Quarantinism violated elemental rules of human sociability, tearing families apart, rending the bonds of nature, giving vent to expressions of crass egotism and discouraging the healthy from helping the ill.[136] Most generally, quarantinist policies with their infringement of personal freedom betrayed an official disrespect for individual rights.[137]

Proponents of quarantinism returned fire with equal force: incidental problems with the system should not be allowed to obscure its overall advantages. Naturally it was expensive, but certainly cheaper, in a global social accounting, than the cost of medical aid, production foregone because of illness and death, maintenance of the victims' survivors and the other expenses incurred in the absence of precautionary measures, not to mention the price of a fullblown epidemic. In any case, alternative means of prevention also did not come cheap and often hampered trade and production.[138] Quarantinist policies also benefited the poor, for many of whom sequestration or quarantine actually raised their standard of living or at least provided for them at the public

---

[134] Sachs, *Tagebuch*, pp. 159–61; *Verhandlungen* (1831), pp. 2, 4–5; 1 (1832), pp. 433, 436, 439–40; *Cholera-Zeitung* (1832), pp. 93ff.; *Berliner Cholera Zeitung* (1831), pp. 31–32; Housselle, "Gutachten über die Häusersperre," pp. 18–20.

[135] *Berliner Cholera Zeitung* (1831), pp. 179–83, 207–08; *Schlesische Cholera-Zeitung* (1831–32), p. 70; K. F. Burdach, *Historisch-statistische Studien über die Cholera-Epidemie vom Jahre 1831 in der Provinz Preussen, insbesondere in Ostpreussen* (Königsberg, 1832), p. 37; *Bemerkungen über die Furcht*, pp. 39–40.

[136] Gottfried Christian Reich, *Die Cholera in Berlin mit Andeutungen zu ihrer sichern Abwehrung und Heilung* (Berlin, 1831), p. 137; *Verhandlungen* (1831), p. 3; 1 (1832), pp. 433–36; *Cholera-Zeitung* (1832), pp. 93ff., 101–03; *(Allgemeine Cholera-Zeitung)*, 1 (1831), pp. 187f.

[137] *Moskau und Petersburg beim Ausbruch der Cholera morbus. Blätter aus dem Tagebuch eines Reisenden: Mit Bemerkungen über die bisher gemachten Erfahrungen von dieser Krankheit von Dr. Theodor Zschokke* (Aarau, 1832), p. 86; Sachs, *Tagebuch*, p. 164.

[138] *Cholera-Archiv*, 3 (1833), pp. 417–18; 2 (1832), pp. 384–85; *(Allgemeine Cholera-Zeitung)*, 2 (1832), pp. 275, 279.

expense.[139] The sharpened controls inherent in such policies also had the advantage of lessening the incidence of crime and vagabondage.[140] More overarching than such nuts-and-bolts arguments, however, was the Pascallian logic at the heart of the quarantinist project: whatever cholera's true nature, in the absence of reliable knowledge the authorities should assume and prepare for the worst. If they turned out to have been mistaken, some unnecessary precautions would have been the worst consequence. Had they, in contrast, been right and yet not sought to keep the disease at bay, horror threatened.[141]

Opinion on the appropriate prophylactic strategy differed, of course, between the two camps. The quarantinist position was clear, while the sanitationists were the ones groping toward new solutions to an old problem. Their maximalist program called for hygienic and healthy living conditions for all. Not cordons and quarantines, as the physicians of Riga blithely concluded in the summer of 1831, but good food, clean housing, warm clothing.[142] Short of thus rebuilding the world, solving the problem of social inequity in order to head off an epidemic, there were various more easily attainable intermediate solutions that differed from the standard quarantinist approach. Most modestly, distributing barley soup, wool stockings, blankets, hot water bottles and a few ounces of roasted coffee beans to the poor was thought to do the trick. Disinfecting rather than sequestering patients would limit the spread of disease; purification institutions and well-ventilated hospitals should replace quarantines.[143] Rather than isolating patients in lazarettos, doctors ought to visit them at home, in accustomed surroundings and convivial company.

Such opposition between divergent prophylactic strategies extended beyond public health and into politics. In Russia, links between contagionism, quarantinism and autocracy on the one side, between localism,

---

[139] *Berliner Cholera Zeitung* (1831), pp. 42, 155, 179–83, 242–44; *Cholera-Archiv*, 3 (1833), pp. 397, 417; 2 (1832), pp. 367–68; *Geschichte der Cholera in Danzig*, p. 19; Sachs, *Tagebuch*, p. 336; Thomas Stamm-Kuhlmann, "Die Cholera von 1831: Herausforderungen an Wissenschaft und staatliche Verwaltung," *Sudhoffs Archiv*, 73, 2 (1989), p. 183; Ross, "Prussian Administrative Response," p. 164.

[140] *Cholera-Archiv*, 2 (1832), p. 181.

[141] *Cholera-Archiv*, 2 (1832), pp. 383–84; Carl Heinrich Ebermaier, *Erfahrungen und Ansichten über die Erkenntniss und Behandlung des asiatischen Brechdurchfalls* (Düsseldorf, 1832), p. 106; Sachs, *Tagebuch*, p. 66; [Trafvenfelt], *Sammandrag af Läkares åsigter*, v. I, p. 61.

[142] [Trafvenfelt], *Sammandrag af Läkares åsigter*, v. II, pp. 24–34.

[143] Fischer, *Es wird Tag!*, pp. 13–14; *Berliner Cholera Zeitung* (1831), pp. 179–83, 207–08; *Schlesische Cholera-Zeitung* (1831–32), p. 70; Housselle, "Gutachten über die Häusersperre," p. 24; D. A. Gebel, *Aphorismen über die Brechruhr, nebst Angabe ihrer Heilung, Vorbeugung und sonstigen polizeilichen Maassregeln* (Liegnitz, 1831), p. 19. Others, however, went further to argue that disinfection and cleansing were as useless as quarantine, since, if there was no contagium, what was the point of trying to destroy it?: Ollenroth, *Asiatische Cholera*, p. 52.

sanitationism and liberalism on the other, were not closely or uniformly tied.[144] In Prussia, however, Ackerknechtianism *avant la lettre* reigned and the political battlelines were as clearly drawn as those of the epidemiological dispute. The localists accused their opponents of autocratic leanings, in thrall to what the main sanitationist periodical in Berlin dubbed the absolutist–contagionist theory.[145] A non-Prussian observing the general dispute classified the sanitationists as the left, the quarantinists the right, the former supported by most of the popular classes and free traders.[146] Anticontagionists portrayed themselves as opposition figures in terms of Prussian politics. Albert Sachs, a prominent Berlin sanitationist, described himself as an *Antizwänger*, opposed to the compulsory aspects of quarantinism and accordingly punished for his views, the authorities having attempted (unsuccessfully in the event) to censor his periodical.[147] Quarantinists were portrayed by their opponents as those already in power, seeking to enhance their authority. Prominent and established members of the medical profession tended to be quarantinists, while lower-ranking physicians disagreed. The same sort of division between high and low could also, it was claimed, be observed among civil servants.[148] The quarantinists, in turn, attacked their opponents as undermining the state's authority while they themselves pursued the common good against sectional and often egotistic interests.[149] Two themes predominated. First, narrow group and individual concerns should of necessity be sacrificed for the public good, sometimes phrased as that of the state.[150] The second identified the enemies of quarantinism as those factional interests with a stake in trade and commerce. Occasionally the Jews, whom neither cordons nor quarantines could prevent from trading, were singled out, with Polish Jews especially considered better at sneaking across the borders than Prussian guards at stopping them.[151] But far more frequently, the enemy in this respect was identified generically as the middle and commercial classes, the trading interests whose self-serving ambitions subordinated the

[144] McGrew, *Russia and the Cholera*, p. 49.   [145] Sachs, *Tagebuch*, p. 82.

[146] *Heidelberger Klinische Annalen*, 8 (1832), pp. 154–55. Others claimed journalists and writers as well for this side: *Cholera-Archiv*, 2 (1832), p. 380.

[147] Ebermaier, *Erfahrungen und Ansichten*, p. 106; Sachs, *Tagebuch*, pp. 353, 370; Dettke, *Die asiatische Hydra*, pp. 199–200.

[148] Petzold, "Cholera in Berlin," p. 8; *(Allgemeine Cholera-Zeitung)*, 2 (1832), p. 132; Sachs, *Betrachtungen*, pp. 18–24; *Cholera-Archiv*, 2 (1832), p. 380.   [149] *Cholera orientalis*, 2, 21–40 (1831), p. 444.

[150] K. F. H. Marx, *Die Erkenntnis, Verhütung und Heilung der ansteckenden Cholera* (Karlsruhe, 1831), pp. 271–72.

[151] *Cholera-Archiv*, 2 (1832), p. 237; Schmidt, *Physiologie der Cholera*, p. 179; Dettke, *Die asiatische Hydra*, pp. 114–15.

common epidemiological good to their own striving for unfettered commercial exchange.[152]

THE FRONT LINES

In this heated politico-epidemiological debate one set of antiquarantinist opinions that weighed heavily with the authorities, in this case in Berlin, was the attitude taken along the borders of the realm in those communities first faced with cholera. Asked to bear not only the initial epidemic onslaught, but also the weight of precautions, these were the first areas to suffer the weaknesses of the central authorities' policies, becoming the forcing ground of change in the quarantinist position. Despite scattered doubts, quarantinism remained a strong contender in the eastern border regions, both in medical and official circles.[153] Stralsund, in eastern Prussia, held off cholera altogether (until November 1832 at least), the authorities crediting their quarantinist policies with this happy outcome; Liegnitz maintained restrictive tactics unabated even as other communities were relaxing theirs; and the Silesian authorities took a similar approach.[154] At the same time, a sanitationist approach was also well represented. In Bromberg, experience of the ease and impunity with which the military cordon had been breached, coupled with the absence of cholera locally, prompted doubts as to its contagiousness. In Posen, the sanitary commission was unable to win public opinion for sequestration of infected localities – an unsurprising result, perhaps, considering that the Lord Lieutenant himself, Flottwell, believed that quarantines did more harm than good.[155] The progress of the epidemic was to strengthen the hand of such skeptics.

---

[152] *Cholera-Archiv*, 3 (1833), pp. 419–22; 2 (1832), pp. 57, 83, 398; *Gründliche und fassliche Anweisung für den Bürger und Landmann zur Verhütung der Ansteckung durch die Cholera und zur Erhaltung der Gesundheit beim Herannahen dieser Krankheit* (Dresden, 1831), p. 12. See also *Gesetz-Sammlung*, 1835, 27/1678, pp. 260–62.

[153] *Hypothese über die Cholera-Morbus. Nach Ansichten des allgemeinen Natur-Lebens: Auf Verlangen und zum Besten des Pommerensdorfer Schul- und Kirchen-Wesens herausgegeben* (Stettin, 1832), p. 11; Adolph Schnitzer, *Die Cholera contagiosa beobachtet auf einer in Folge höheren Auftrages in Galizien während der Monate Mai, Juni und Juli, und im Beuthner Kreise in Oberschlesien im August gemachten Reise* (Breslau, 1831); *Cholera-Archiv*, 2 (1832), pp. 277ff.; 3 (1833), pp. 226–27; *Rathgeber für alle, welche sich gegen die Cholera morbus schützen wollen* (6th edn.; Breslau, 1831), pp. 27–28; *Berliner Cholera Zeitung* (1831), pp. 164–67.

[154] *Cholera-Archiv*, 3 (1833), pp. 246ff., 298–302, 413–15; *Schlesische Cholera-Zeitung* (1831–32), pp. 139–40, 217–21.

[155] *Cholera-Archiv*, 1 (1832), p. 19; 2 (1832), pp. 273–75; *Schlesische Cholera-Zeitung* (1831–32), pp. 92–93; Ollenroth, *Asiatische Cholera*, pp. 17, 21; *Cholera-Zeitung* (1832), pp. 69–70, 96–97; *Berliner Cholera Zeitung* (1831), pp. 156–57.

The most revealing cases of opinion and policy on the epidemiological front lines came from the two Baltic ports of Danzig and Königsberg, both of which switched from a strict quarantinist approach to its opposite in rapid succession. Initial measures here did not differ from the contagionism that was official policy at first throughout Prussia. Danzig had entrusted its defense to the cordon along the Polish border. When, at the end of May 1831, cholera nonetheless struck home as the first place on Prussian soil, the ensuing measures were especially strict in hopes of compensating for such initial laxity. In order to contain the disease, Danzig was surrounded by a military cordon, becoming the only large city isolated for any substantial time.[156] Measures familiar from the general Prussian regulations were implemented in both cities. Commerce suffered accordingly and, as one observer put it, on the exchanges the only trade was in opinions for and against contagiousness.[157] Thanks to the hardships that followed, official and medical opinion here soon took an antiquarantinist turn. Local physicians tended to view contagionism skeptically, believing that cholera arose from chills and inappropriate gratifications.[158] An important factor weakening the contagionist position in Danzig was the presence of Dr. Barchewitz, one of the official Prussian observers in Russia who passed through on his return from Moscow, remaining from July to November 1831. Unafraid of contact with the illness, he condemned sequestration and helped persuade the merchant community, the authorities and public opinion to reject quarantinism.[159]

With Danzig mobilized against quarantinism, changes followed. Barchewitz was instrumental in returning the lazaretto from the Holm and opening a cholera cemetery on the Stolzenberg where families could secure an individual, marked grave for their dead. More far-reaching changes, however, required Berlin's imprimatur, or at least collusion, and local officials in both cities, impelled by the shift in public opinion, were now ready to plead their case on high.[160] The familiar arguments on

---

[156] *Geschichte der Cholera in Danzig*, pp. 5–6; *Cholera-Archiv*, 2 (1832), pp. 131ff.; Buek, *Verbreitungsweise*, p. 58.   [157] *Verhandlungen*, 1 (1832), pp. 424–54; *Geschichte der Cholera in Danzig*, pp. 10–12.
[158] Hamett, *Substance of the Official Medical Reports*, p. 71; Sachs, *Die Cholera*, pp. 110–11; *Die Cholera-Krankheit in Danzig* (Danzig, 1831), pp. 6–7, 17; *Verhandlungen* (1831), pp. 10–35; 1 (1832), p. 437; *Cholera-Zeitung* (1832), pp. 92–93; Bangssel, *Erinnerungsbuch für Alle*, p. 119; Ross, "Prussian Administrative Response," ch. 4.
[159] *Geschichte der Cholera in Danzig*, pp. 26–27, 29–31; *Cholera-Zeitung* (1832), p. 27; Barchewitz, *Über die Cholera*, pp. 30, 33, 61; *Verhandlungen*, 1 (1832), pp. 424–54; Bangssel, *Erinnerungsbuch für Alle*, p. 69. He had much the same effect in Königsberg: Sachs, *Die Cholera*, p. 119.
[160] Hamett, *Substance of the Official Medical Reports*, p. 91; *Verhandlungen* (1831), p. 7; 1 (1832), pp. 341–42; Gerardin and Gaimard, *Du choléra-morbus*, pp. 254–55; *Cholera-Zeitung* (1832), p. 92.

quarantinism's inherent impractibility were put through their paces by the Danzig sanitary commission, but most important for this commercial port were economic considerations. Over 1,000 sequestered citizens were maintained at municipal expense, poverty was rampant, food prices ascendant, trade and commerce declining, the legal machinery had ground to a halt. In the countryside, sequestration was all but impossible to impose. During the harvest every able-bodied person was needed in the fields and local officials, though entrusted with enforcing quarantine in the villages, were more interested in securing willing hands to bring in the crops. Quarantinist measures brought only ruin and misery. It would, so ran the conclusion, be less of a catastrophe were in fact a third of Danzig's inhabitants to perish, since at least the rest would be well-off.[161] Instead, the sanitary commission sought moderation in Berlin's approach: an end to cordons imposed on the city or its infected parts, to the sequestration of entire houses and to the incineration of bedding and clothing. At work during the day, the laboring classes returned home only to sleep and therefore lived in crowded circumstances. Sealing off an entire house because of one victim threatened to hurt many others. Since most working families shared one bed, committing it to the flames after a single illness condemned the others to the floor. Modifications were proposed: merely cleansing the dwellings of the ill, not sequestering the healthy housemates of the stricken, isolating the diseased, in any case, for only ten days. If sealing-off was unavoidable, then at least it should be only the victim's apartment, not the entire building. Fresh bedding should be given the ill, lest they otherwise refuse to part with the old.[162]

In Königsberg, the local allergy to quarantinism had at least two sources: history and timing. Königsberg's municipal memory of the strict regulations imposed by the Prussian Plague Edict of 1708 was still vivid. It is unclear that the city had been any more harshly treated than others in this respect, but here the hyperquarantinism of the plague precautions had sparked successful protests, in particular a sermon by a local clergyman in the early winter of 1708 in which was advanced the daring proposition that the gallows should be used not for violators of the official restrictions, but for the authorities who had managed to kill more people with their strictures than the epidemic itself. This protest (the sermon had been confiscated, but the clergyman was left untouched

---

[161] *Verhandlungen*, 1 (1832), pp. 439–40, 448–49; *Cholera-Zeitung* (1832), p. 96; *(Allgemeine Cholera-Zeitung)*, 1 (1831), p. 181; *Heidelberger Klinische Annalen*, 8 (1832), p. 128.
[162] *Verhandlungen*, 1 (1832), pp. 424–54.

and shortly thereafter cordons against the city had been lifted) had apparently become a sufficiently important chapter of Königsberger mythology to be recalled when similar measures were imposed against cholera.[163] The outcome was that here too local authorities moderated the quarantinism handed down from Berlin. To appease public anxieties medical personnel and undertakers were identified by a sign on their sleeves, but no longer required to suit up with oilcloth in the plague manner. Lengthy sequestrations of infected houses were scaled back to two days and, with physician consent, the ill could be treated at home rather than hospitalized. Burials were permitted in the customary way, although still only in late evenings or early mornings. Those interred at the public expense went to special cholera graveyards, but others whose families met the costs had a choice. Only those in direct contact with the ill were restricted in their movements.[164] The late timing of the epidemic was also to Königberg's advantage. Having instituted harsh measures early on and yet been spared the disease until the end of July 1831, after Danzig and other cities, the popular classes had long reached the limits of their patience once the illness finally hit and they took to the streets in protest. By the time the Königsbergers appealed to Berlin in July, the central powers had themselves begun to see their point. Already on 25 July, two days after the epidemic struck Königsberg, the governor of the province of Prussia, Theodor von Schön, a committed anticontagionist himself, permitted unrestricted access to the city. The following day, a royal proclamation conceded that internal cordons had proven useless and that the fear and anxiety encouraged by quarantinist tactics only worsened the situation. Houses were no longer to be sealed off, the ill could remain at home if treatment were available and burials might, at the family's request, take place in the usual graveyards.[165]

VOLTEFACE

For such reasons – primarily the practical obstacles of imposing a rigidly quarantinist system and changing opinions on the nature of the disease that made such policies seem unreasonable and ineffective, but also, of course, because by this point the epidemic was burning itself out – the

[163] *Verhandlungen*, I (1832), pp. 321–26, 335–40, 344.

[164] *Verhandlungen* (1831), pp. 1–9, iv–vi; I (1832), pp. 340–41; G. Hirsch, *Über die Contagiosität der Cholera: Bemerkungen zu dem Sendschreiben des Herrn Präsidenten Dr. Rust an A. v. Humboldt* (Königsberg, 1832), p. 21; *Cholera-Zeitung* (1832), p. 93.

[165] *Cholera-Zeitung* (1832), p. 92; Stamm-Kuhlmann, "Die Cholera von 1831," pp. 181–82; Ross, "Prussian Administrative Response," pp. 128–37.

autocracies modified their initial approach. Quarantinism in the strictest sense turned out to be an internally contradictory, economically unsustainable and politically unenforceable policy. In Russia, the Emperor ordered an end to cordons and quarantines in July 1831. Reaction in Poland was colored by the war against its neighbor. Although cholera had entered well in advance of enemy troops, the authorities had propaganda interests in presenting the disease as part of the Russian onslaught, indeed as an attempt to exterminate the Polish people. The government, wishing to portray cholera as contagious, therefore at first implemented the appropriate measures. On the other hand, the Polish medical authorities, quickly convinced of the contrary, ended by recommending only fearlessness and tranquility, without seeking to restrict communication or otherwise impose quarantinist precautions.[166] In Austria the turnabout was swift. During the autumn of 1831 the Emperor and his officials, partly prompted by Baron Stifft, the court's first physician, decided that quarantinism had proven unaffordable and unworkable and ended the most stringent policies. Sequestration of dwellings was replaced in September with a policy of thorough cleansing. Quarantine at the cordon between Hungary and the Austrian territories was reduced from twenty to ten days, to five in October and finally eliminated altogether. The military cordon from the Prussian–Silesian border to the Donau ended and only the usual border formalities were enforced, and the Sanitary Commission and other administrative cholera organs were decommissioned. Special cholera burials were suspended, martial law at the remaining cordons ended, the death penalty for their violation lifted and punishments turned over to the criminal courts.[167]

In Prussia, the volteface in official approaches came first to the eastern regions, Danzig and Königsberg most notably, but also, for example, in Breslau, Gumbinnen and Elbing.[168] In Berlin, too, the tune was changing, but the turnabout tempo was slower. Public opinion here was quick

---

[166] Riecke, *Mittheilungen*, v. III, p. 176; McGrew, *Russia and the Cholera*, p. 100; Hille, *Beobachtungen*, pp. 1–3, 13–16; Hawkins, *History*, pp. 273–75; Henry Gaulter, *The Origin and Progress of the Malignant Cholera in Manchester* (London, 1833), pp. 20–21; Buek, *Verbreitungsweise*, pp. 43–45; Ollenroth, *Asiatische Cholera*, p. 17; Brierre de Boismont, *Relation historique*, pp. 169–74.

[167] Gerardin and Gaimard, *Du choléra-morbus*, p. 271; *Haude- und Spener-Zeitung*, 232 (4 October 1831), copy in the Landesarchiv Berlin, 01-02GB/257; Buek, *Verbreitungsweise*, pp. 69–74; Zeller, *Die epidemische Cholera*, pp. 128–29; Sander, *Die asiatische Cholera in Wien*, p. 103; Knolz, *Darstellung der Brechruhr-Epidemie*, pp. 229–33.

[168] *Cholera-Archiv*, 3 (1833), pp. 107–11; Göppert et al., *Die asiatische Cholera in Breslau während der Monate October, November, December 1831* (Breslau, 1832), p. 91; Buek, *Verbreitungsweise*, p. 59; Dettke, *Die asiatische Hydra*, ch. 6.

to oppose quarantinism, but the influence of prominent contagionist physicians and the officials whose reputations were staked on the success of promulgated policies did not ebb as quickly.[169] The first changes were ambiguous. Some represented a real scaling back of the initial precautions; others were more a redeployment than redirection. Regulations on sequestering houses were eased already in August, allowing isolation to be limited to the patient's living quarters or even the sickroom alone. From November, sequestration was imposed only so long as the patient remained in the building and, once removed, until the dwelling and its contents had been cleansed. Families and other contacts of the ill who would earlier have been hospitalized now underwent only a ten-day quarantine at home, followed by the usual disinfection procedures; the other inhabitants of an infected house were subject only to cleansing and fumigation of their persons and possessions. In September, the authorities clarified their position on hospitalization, explaining that it was strictly voluntary and that patients could remain at home to the extent possible. Burials were now allowed in normal cemeteries if possible without danger to the public health, especially in graveyards distant from densely populated areas.[170]

Faith in the power of cordons remained, in contrast, more durable. By the beginning of August, it had become clear to the Prussian Cholera Commission that even strict military cordons had failed and were consuming resources with so voracious an appetite that local cordons, as required by the earlier instructions, would no longer be feasible. In order to protect the western provinces, triage was now practiced on the east. A fallback position was adopted, splitting the country in two, with a sanitary cordon to the west of the easternmost provinces. Travelers passing west were subject to the same restrictions as those earlier at Prussia's eastern frontier, with the shoot-to-kill orders for transgressors now strengthened in their language. In September, however, the same procedure had to be repeated once again along a new fallback line following the Elbe, Spree, Neisse and upper Oder rivers when, undaunted, cholera appeared further to the west, striking Berlin in late August. The Prussians had thus established at least three military cordons, each bristling with the attendant epidemic-arresting

---

[169] Sachs, *Tagebuch*, pp. 189–93; Buek, *Verbreitungsweise*, pp. 64–65; Dettke, *Die asiatische Hydra*, ch. 7; Ross, "Prussian Administrative Response," ch. 6.

[170] *Amts-Blatt*, 44 (4 November 1831), pp. 301–03; 35 (2 September 1831), pp. 191–93; *Die asiatische Cholera in der Stadt Magdeburg*, p. 6; *Sammlung*, pp. 109–10; "Bekanntmachungen," *Berlinische Nachrichten*, 213 (12 September 1831).

apparatus, yet each failing to halt the epidemic.[171] It was at this point that a new approach was sought.

During August and September, the regulations of the first hour were dismantled. Experience with the disease and the necessities of economic life, one royal proclamation announced, demanded amelioration. Strict quarantinism had harmed commerce and trade, threatening livelihoods with effects worse than the disease itself. In any case, it was impossible to tie up so many troops given the approach of autumn (and presumably the harvest) and a new strategy was needed. Quarantines were to be shortened and local communities given more responsibility for their own protection.[172] Localities could seek security by limiting intercourse with infected regions if, but not entirely as, they wished. To prevent checks on internal communication, they were no longer allowed to prevent travelers from passing in transit, although they could still forbid them from staying. Uninfected areas could not seal themselves off, but had to rest content with the protection afforded by the system of health and travel documents. Only entire provinces that were as yet unstricken were allowed to sever contact with their neighbors, but even here, customary crossborder traffic was allowed up to three miles on the healthy side. A less stringent and costly set of general regulations to restrict contact and the spread of disease was implemented. The military cordons were largely ended, except for the internal one protecting the westernmost and still uninfected provinces and one along the outer border of Silesia. On Prussia's external frontiers, the quarantine stations remained with periods reduced to five days, but those inside the country were shut. To the east of the new internal sanitary cordon, attempts to isolate infected areas were abandoned as unfeasible, replaced instead by extending the system of health attests and passports.[173]

A loosening of quarantine and disinfection regulations for goods also followed in September. Experience had shown that transmission by means of objects was rare and cleansing effective. To free up commercial relations, only certain goods (used clothing and bedding, rags, feathers, animal hair, furs and the like) required disinfection. Quarantine officials were instructed to temper their zeal for the public health with

---

[171] *Sammlung*, pp. 105–12, 482–83; Ollenroth, *Asiatische Cholera*, p. 18; *Amts-Blatt*, 35 (2 September 1831), p. 189. [172] *Amts-Blatt*, 37 (16 September 1831), pp. 219–21.

[173] *Sammlung*, pp. 105–11. Stralsund continued to isolate itself at its own expense: *Cholera-Archiv*, 3 (1833), pp. 246ff. See also *Amts-Blatt*, 37 (16 September 1831), pp. 221–23; *Einiges über die Cholera*, pp. 3–4; "Bekanntmachung," from the Immediat-Commmission, 12 September 1831, copy in GStA, 84a/4179.

mercantile considerations and not ruin goods in the process of purifying them, fumigating furs, for example, rather than soaking them in water. In other instances, only the packing material needed cleaning. In early November the disinfection of most goods was ended and only clothing, bedding and other effects actually used by cholera patients required thorough cleansing before reuse. Schools could now be opened so long as only children from uninfected homes attended, pupils arrived clean and were, if possible, also washed at school; instruction was shortened daily by two hours and the young scholars spared strenuous work.[174] By November the change in official position was being given voice by articles in the Prussian *Staats-Zeitung*, including ones by Hufeland, the royal physician, claiming that cholera, produced by local causes, was not contagious and that the earlier precautions had been largely worthless.[175] Within Berlin itself, the same sort of moderating influences had an effect. Contaminated houses were no longer emblazoned with warning signs; only the ill, not all inhabitants of infected houses, were sequestered; civilian caretakers replaced soldiers to guard sealed-off dwellings; the dead and ill were transported in ways that approximated the normal; quarantines were shortened to five days; procedures for death certificates and coroner's inquests were simplified to lessen the temptation of concealment. To prevent increases in food prices, Berlin was not cut off by cordons from its hinterland.[176]

By November 1831 most of the initial quarantinist precautions had thus been abolished or ameliorated. The French observers en route from St. Petersburg to Berlin encountered no quarantinist obstacles and found local medical opinion unanimous in its rejection of cordons. At the turn of the year, the Prussian king ended punishments for violation of cholera regulations, pardoned those already sentenced and closed ongoing investigations; the Cholera Commission was dissolved in February.[177] In January 1832, a Royal Instruction made official the lessons drawn by the authorities from their experience with cholera.[178]

---

[174] *Amts-Blatt*, 38 (23 September 1831), pp. 235–37; 44 (4 November 1831), pp. 301–05; Ollenroth, *Asiatische Cholera*, p. 19.

[175] *Staats-Zeitung*, 275 (4 October 1831), pp. 1515ff.; 307 (5 November 1831), pp. 1647–48. See also Sachs, *Tagebuch*, pp. 82–84; C. W. H., "Ein Wort an meine lieben Mitbürger über die Ansteckung der Cholera und die beste Verhütung derselben," *Berlinische Nachrichten*, 213 (12 September 1831); *Cholera-Zeitung* (1832), pp. 74–75.

[176] *Berliner Cholera Zeitung* (1831), pp. 131–33; *Verordnung über das Verfahren*, pp. 29–30; *Die asiatische Cholera in der Stadt Magdeburg*, p. 6.

[177] *Gazette médicale de Paris*, 2, 52 (1831), pp. 437–38; Ollenroth, *Asiatische Cholera*, p. 20; *Amts-Blatt*, 52 (30 December 1831), pp. 382–83; *Berliner Intelligenz-Blatt*, 42 (18 February 1832).

[178] *Gesetz-Sammlung*, 1832, 5/1343, pp. 43–55.

Local authorities were now to decide when to take precautions, including in the measures at their disposal a broad array of sanitationist techniques: ameliorating unhealthy local conditions and providing nourishing food and warm clothing. They were to build hospitals and arrange for separate burial grounds (but only if this was deemed necessary in the first place). On the stricter side, it remained a requirement to report all cholera-related cases of illness and death and forbidden to bury such corpses without a physician's permission. Once cholera had struck, passports and legitimation papers would be issued only to the healthy. Public amusements and other places of congregation, excepting churches, could be shut; truancy laws were to be strictly enforced, but schools not to be closed without pressing reason. This time commercial interests won more consideration. Weekly markets could be closed, but annual fairs only at the request of the provincial governor and on instructions of the relevant ministry. Removals to hospitals were to hinge on the possibility of care at home, but as a general rule no patient was to be transported against the will of the head of the family, whose wishes could be overridden only by decision of the local sanitary commission itself.

Moderation also won the day when it came to sequestration. In the countryside and spacious homes, isolation of an entire house could be attempted; elsewhere only the sickroom needed to be sealed off. Healthy members of the family could come and go after disinfection. Burials were to occur only after the customary waiting period unless a doctor certified that haste was of the essence. The usual cemeteries could be used if they were safely situated; otherwise special graveyards were required, partitioned by religion and consecrated accordingly. No limitations on the movement of goods, letters or currency were imposed, except to forbid the import for sale of used clothing and bedding from areas stricken within the previous two months. Such changes indicated the Prussian authorities' response to their first experience with cholera. Promulgated were measures that still struck the most ardent antiquarantinist as insufficient in their rollback, ones which remained vague enough in their formulation to allow the bureaucracy room for maneuver, but which nonetheless represented a major step away from Berlin's initial attitude.[179] Each of the autocracies had thus drastically changed its initial plans to deal with cholera within months of its first appearance.

[179] Sachs, *Betrachtungen*, p. 2; Ross, "Prussian Administrative Response," pp. 262–67.

THE LEARNING CURVE

There was one major factor in the response to cholera among European nations, beginning already with the autocracies, that was largely independent of their political regime. Since transmissible largely by human carrier, the disease followed routes of commercial intercourse and along these tracks the initially afflicted served as laboratory rats for the nations lucky enough to be spared for the moment. An accumulation of experience snowballed across Europe in a broad movement from east to west; a learning curve was traced, with those further along taking their cue from mistakes committed by the firstlings. Other than past and possibly similar diseases, the main source of information guiding the European states in their precautionary attempts was the news each derived from the others. Because of cholera's generally westward movement (from Russia, through Poland, Austria-Hungary, the German states, hopskotching to Britain and from there to France, with peripheral Sweden struck only in 1834) the nations of the arrière-garde benefited from the experiments undertaken at great cost by their easterly neighbors.

Russia's initial decision in favor of strict quarantinism was at first thought to form the mold for the rest of Europe and, indeed, in the beginning its lead was followed by Austria and Prussia.[180] It soon became clear, however, that the information from here was contradictory at best. Russian medical opinion, as well as the reports sent back by foreign observers, conveyed hopelessly mixed signals.[181] Much of it advised at most a moderated form of quarantinism. In Galicia, cholera was considered uncontagious because the Russian sanitary authorities had pronounced it so and, in Warsaw, the Central Medical Committee used Russian precedents as authority for similar conclusions in April 1831. From Poland, in turn, came the news that cholera was only weakly contagious, dependent on particular circumstances and predispositions, but equally that it was directly transmissible like the plague.[182] In Danzig,

---

[180] *EMSJ*, 58 (July 1831), p. 120; Buek, *Verbreitungsweise*, pp. 24–25; Lichtenstädt, *Cholera in Russland*, pp. iv–v, 151, 218; Lichtenstädt, *Rathschläge*, p. 12; *Instruction für die Sanitäts-Behörden*, pp. 3–10, 26–27.

[181] V. Loder, *Cholera-Krankheit*, pp. 3–4, 14; v. Loder, *Zusätze zu seiner Schrift über die Cholera-Krankheit* (Königsberg, 1831); Theodor Friedrich Baltz, *Meinungen über die Entstehung, das Wesen und die Möglichkeit einer Verhütung der sogenannten Cholera* (Berlin, 1832), p. 4; *Über die Cholera: Auszug aus einem amtlichen Berichte des königl. preuss. Regierungs- und Medicinal-Raths Dr. Albers* (n.p., dated Moscow, 9/21 March 1831), pp. 8–13; Riecke, *Mittheilungen*, v. III, pp. 105, 109; Buek, *Verbreitungsweise*, pp. 38–39; *Cholera orientalis*, 1, 1-20 (1832), p. 87; *Moskau und Petersburg beim Ausbruch*, pp. 5–7, 19–23, 50–53.

[182] *Berliner Cholera Zeitung* (1831), pp. 282–87; Hahnemann, *Sendschreiben über die Heilung der Cholera*, p. 7; Hille, *Beobachtungen*, pp. 16–18; Pulst, *Cholera im Königreich Polen*, p. 24; *Zeitschrift über die Staatsarzneikunde*, 22 (1831), p. 195.

local opinion was heavily influenced by Polish and Russian experiences, mediated through the antiquarantinism of Dr. Barchewitz, and Königsberg and the rest of Germany, in turn, learned from Danzig.[183] In Prussia generally the moderating influence of the lessons drawn further east was evident.[184] With such ambiguous opinions, precedence and authority could be found for almost any position desired. Nevertheless, the general trend of experience pointed away from the strict quarantinism of the initial measures. Indeed, observers in all nations advanced as something of a general rule the proposition that a belief in cholera's contagiousness and thence quarantinism was inversely proportional to the degree of experience with the disease.[185] As a Viennese physician confided to a Parisian colleague, "Seen from afar, this disease is a monster; up close, it is less frightening."[186]

This learning curve continued as the epidemic proceeded westwards from Austria and Prussia into the other German states. Those further to the south and west reacted differently from their eastern neighbors for two reasons: first and most obviously, the simple fact of geographic distance from the immediate source of infection and a faith in the protection offered by the Prussian and Austrian precautions.[187] In Saxony, the authorities initially relied on the Prussian and Austrian cordons, establishing none themselves and stipulating only that travelers have undergone quarantine outside the kingdom or have been underway for twenty days since crossing infected territory.[188] In Bavaria similar measures were instituted for travelers from Russia, Poland and Galicia, while from Austria and Bohemia they were allowed to enter the kingdom with fewer formalities, but still only at border crossings with customs offices and only with official passes and Austrian health attests. In Württemberg travelers and goods across Bavaria from eastern Europe and, later, also Prussia were admitted only with the appropriate papers

[183] *Verhandlungen* (1831), pp. iv–vi, 1–35, 102–04. Danzig presented itself as "the painful cholera school for civilized Europe": *Geschichte der Cholera in Danzig*, pp. 5, 17–19.

[184] *Staats-Zeitung*, Beilage zu No. 285 (14 October 1831), pp. 1557–59; Burdach, *Historisch-statistische Studien*, pp. 13–14.

[185] *Cholera-Zeitung* (1832), p. 26; Buek, *Verbreitungsweise*, pp. 29–30; Krüger-Hansen, *Zweiter Nachtrag*, p. 14; Sticker, *Abhandlungen aus der Seuchengeschichte*, v. II, p. 287; [Trafvenfelt], *Sammandrag af Läkares åsigter*, v. I, pp. 4–6, 31, 185; *Svenska Läkaresällskapets Handlingar*, 1 (1837), p. 331; *PP* 1849 (1070) xxiv, p. 21; Aladane de Lalibarde, *Etudes sur le choléra épidémique: Sa nature et son traitement* (Paris, 1851), pp. 56–58. [186] *Gazette médicale de Paris*, 3, 15 (1832), p. 155.

[187] *Systematische Übersicht*, p. 4.

[188] *Sammlung*, pp. 118–19. The Leipzig fair, attracting visitors from afar, also gave Saxons reasons not to exclude or detain travelers: [S. J. Callerholm], *Några ord om kolera, spärrningar och krämare-intresse* (Stockholm, 1853), p. 16.

from the Bavarian or Austrian authorities. Baden and Mecklenburg-Schwerin felt equally little need to take their own precautions, insisting instead that travelers have undergone the procedures of their eastern neighbors.[189] When, in the autumn of 1831, Austria and Prussia moderated their tactics, their westerly neighbors, still beholden to contagionist orthodoxies and aghast at such a cavalier approach, scrambled to replicate these precautions. In Saxony, Bavaria, Hannover, Mecklenburg, Hamburg and Lübeck, the authorities were now prepared to reestablish the quarantinist guard let slip by the Prussians.[190] Baden, in turn, faced two fronts. Here, the ameliorating effect of distance from the eastern sources of infection was undermined by the threat posed in the meantime from other directions and in July 1831 the focus on travelers and goods from the north and east was replaced by stricter quarantines and disinfections for entrants from all neighboring countries.[191] Distance from the epidemiological front lines thus served to moderate measures taken by the more westerly states, but, once the disease approached, this simple sense of security evaporated and quarantinism was tried out also here.

The other factor influencing the precautions adopted in the German states at one remove from the trenches of epidemic attack was the effect of accumulated experience. It would certainly be misleading to present a constant and inexorable decline of quarantinism as areas behind the lines profited from the hardwon knowledge of the epidemiological avantgarde. As in Prussia and Austria, strict quarantinism coexisted with retreat from such measures in a patchwork quilt of official response. Quarantinist precautions were imposed throughout the rest of Germany at one time or another.[192] In Mecklenburg-Schwerin, instructions concerning infected ships were as lengthy, detailed and draconian as any elaborated by the Prussians, while punishments in Anhalt-Dessau were as harsh. The Saxons at first adopted regulations similar to the Prussian and often followed their example verbatim, although without quite the same penchant for minute detail.[193] Lübeck sealed itself off

---

[189] *Sammlung*, pp. 114–17, 177–79, 189, 194–96; *Amts-Blatt*, 32 (12 August 1831), p. 164.

[190] Simon, *Weg mit den Kordons!*, pp. 39ff.; Simon, *Die indische Brechruhr*, ch. 5; *Die morgenländische Brechruhr (Cholera morbus), von der Sanitäts-Commission in Lübeck bekannt gemacht* (Lübeck, 1831), pp. 3–4; *Sammlung*, p. 118; Buek, *Verbreitungsweise*, pp. 75–76.

[191] *Sammlung*, pp. 198–200, 202–04; Francisca Loetz, *Vom Kranken zum Patienten: "Medikalisierung" und medizinische Vergesellschaftung am Beispiel Badens 1750–1850* (Stuttgart, 1993), pp. 160–61.

[192] And of course there was quarantinist medical opinion: Georg Freiherrn von Wedekind, *Über die Cholera im Allgemeinen und die asiatische Cholera insbesondere* (Frankfurt am Main, 1831), pp. 47f.

[193] *Belehrung über die asiatische Cholera*, pp. 25–27, 39; *Sammlung*, pp. 137–50, 333–53, 479–81.

from the outside world with armed guards, cordons and quarantines, shifted the cemetery outside the city and closed taverns in the surrounding countryside. Illegal cordon crossers risked being shot, patients without permanent abode could be hospitalized against their will and, indeed, the Prussians themselves complained that the Lübeckers' measures were exaggerated.[194] In Württemberg, travelers were quarantined and fumigated daily, their effects cleansed and aired, their horses scrubbed. In Schleswig-Holstein, quarantine stations were to be established, the coasts patrolled, health certificates required of overland travelers, imported goods inspected, the ill sequestered or hospitalized and public institutions closed. Once the Prussian sanitary cordon along the Oder had been breached, the duchies established their own, turning it also against Hamburg and Lübeck after they had succumbed.[195] In certain cases the fact that the disease had first swept through neighboring states presented the followers with novel problems. Journeymen banished from Austria and Prussia, for example, threatened to disseminate the very contagion they had been exiled to avoid. In consequence, Saxony, Baden and Braunschweig imposed various restrictions on their entry, when not forbidding it outright.[196]

And yet, even at their strictest, the measures taken elsewhere in Germany profited from the experience of their eastern neighbors. Saxon medical opinion was reputed to be less contagionist thanks to lessons learned from the east. The authorities of Schleswig-Holstein worried that rigid precautions had provoked rebellion in the east, feared public unrest and were prepared to clamp down, posting sufficient military power in the cities or organizing a citizens' militia. But along with the stick came carrots. Churches were not to be closed at a time when religious consolation was important; school teachers and ministers were to help spread the word about the disease; a sufficient supply of physicians was to be ensured, especially in the countryside, by dispatching the younger ones from Kiel. In Koblenz, the authorities drew the lesson from the experience of Danzig, Königsberg, Posen and Magdeburg that strict

---

[194] E. Cordes, *Die Cholera in Lübeck* (Lübeck, 1861), p. 53; Dietrich Helm, *Die Cholera in Lübeck* (Neumünster, 1979), pp. 14–19.

[195] *Sammlung*, pp. 184–88; *Instruktion für die Ärzte der Herzogthümer Schleswig und Holstein über das Verfahren bei einem Ausbruche der epidemischen Cholera in den Herzogthümern, von königl. Schleswig-Holsteinischen Sanitätscollegium zu Kiel* (Kiel, 1831), pp. 3, 8–9; *Ansprache ans Publicum*, p. 7; *Systematische Übersicht*, pp. 1–5, 6–11; *Unterricht, wie Nichtärzte*, pp. 7–9.

[196] *Sammlung*, pp. 153–55, 200–01; *Amts-Blatt*, 34 (26 August 1831), pp. 179–81; Anneliese Gerbert, *Öffentliche Gesundheitspflege und staatliches Medizinalwesen in den Städten Braunschweig und Wolfenbüttel im 19. Jahrhundert* (Braunschweig, 1983), p. 105.

sequestering had encouraged concealment and provoked resistance. In Cassel, the ill were to be isolated, but allowed to remain at home. Saxony permitted the sort of flexibility in sequestering patients at home already in July that the Prussians accepted only a month or so later and, where to the east the military was ordered out to prevent such situations, Saxons were merely warned against crowding at food stores.[197] As the southern and western German states issued instructions on cholera, the combined effects of geographical remove and the learning curve became increasingly evident. In Bavaria (spared cholera until 1836) medical opinion was decidedly anticontagionist, recommending instead general sanitary measures: engineering and excavating to prevent flooding, draining standing water, removing nuisances, establishing hospitals.[198] Aachen, though under Prussian administration, had shaken off any quarantinist inclinations by the time cholera arrived and medical opinion was sanitationist. The initial Prussian regulations were much disliked here where, like the rest of the Rhineland, manufacture, industry and trade dominated the economy. Quarantines and even the system of health attests and legitimation cards were considered vexatious and exemptions granted for most daily circulation across the borders. In Braunschweig, the conclusion that isolating the city was costly and ultimately impractical was quickly drawn.[199]

In Hamburg, northwestern outpost of the German Confederation, medical and official opinion was largely antiquarantinist and few internal precautionary measures were taken. No districts were sealed off, infected houses were not marked and dwellings of the dead were disinfected only at first.[200] Nonetheless, in other respects, measures here followed patterns familiar from elsewhere. Public houses were shut; domestic animals loose in the streets were killed; the dead were buried quickly and (except for those with family plots) separately; foreign arti-

[197] *(Allgemeine Cholera-Zeitung)*, 1 (1831), pp. 179ff.; *Systematische Übersicht*, pp. 6–13; Alexander Stollenwerk, "Die Cholera im Regierungsbezirk Koblenz," *Jahrbuch für westdeutsche Landesgeschichte*, 5 (1979), p. 247; *Anweisung wie man*, pp. 16–17, 20; *Sammlung*, pp. 137ff.

[198] Sander, *Die asiatische Cholera in Wien*, pp. 100–04; Georg Kaltenbrunner, *Über die Verbreitung der Cholera Morbus und den Erfolg der dagegen in den k. preussischen und k.k. österreichischen Staaten ergriffenen Massregeln* (Munich, 1832), pp. 175, 197, 204.

[199] Hartung, *Die Cholera-Epidemie in Aachen*, pp. 74–78; *Heidelberger Klinische Annalen*, 8 (1832), pp. 154–55; Schäfer, "Staatliche Abwehrmassnahmen," p. 30; Gerbert, *Öffentliche Gesundheitspflege*, pp. 122–26.

[200] Richard J. Evans, *Death in Hamburg: Society and Politics in the Cholera Years 1830–1910* (Oxford, 1987), p. 233; Woldemar Nissen, *Über die Ursachen der Cholera, nebst Vorschlägen zur Bekämpfung derselben* (Altona, 1831), pp. 23–24; Buek, *Verbreitungsweise*, pp. 70–71; K. G. Zimmermann, *Die Cholera-Epidemie in Hamburg während des Herbstes 1831* (Hamburg, 1831), pp. 4–5.

sans, beggars and vagabonds were expelled. The ill who could not be cared for at home might be removed to the hospital on official orders.[201] Nor were external measures unusual. Hamburg's position as a trading city and its powerful merchant class made it averse to quarantines and other measures that interrupted commerce. A trade embargo, as one observer put it, was worse than cholera itself. But at the same time, faced with British threats to quarantine its ships in the absence of precautions, Hamburg established cordons on the North Sea and the Elbe, later, when the Prussians loosened their regulations, joining Saxony and Hannover in instituting strict measures against travelers from the east. Until October 1831, when the outbreak of cholera in Hamburg rendered such measures superfluous, quarantine was established at Cuxhaven at the mouth of the Elbe and a guard ship at Geesthacht took charge of vessels that had not already been quarantined elsewhere. Mounted guards throughout Hamburg territory challenged anyone who appeared not to be a local and at the city gates police investigated all foreign travelers, admitting only the healthy or already quarantined. To ease conditions for commerce, ships that had undergone the Prussian quarantine at Sacrow could pass without further ado.[202] Hamburg's actions thus did not differ appreciably from those of other German states outside Prussia. Like these, it relied heavily on the protection offered by the cordons and quarantines thrown up by its easterly neighbors and, like these, it took fewer internal precautions than had the Prussians at first. As in other German states, most of the quarantinist measures anxiously imposed at the outset of the epidemic had been lifted by early 1832.[203]

EVER WESTWARD: LEARNING TO BE LIBERAL

From the Baltic, cholera moved to Britain, thence to Ireland, the Netherlands and France, eventually to Sweden. Following its path westward allows a further disentangling of those aspects of the official reaction that were due to domestic political arrangements from those caused by the gradual Europe-wide accumulation of experience. Consider

[201] Friedrich Wolter, *Das Auftreten der Cholera in Hamburg in dem Zeitraume von 1831–1893 mit besonderer Berücksichtigung der Epidemie des Jahres 1892* (Munich, 1898), p. 220.
[202] Barriés, *Ein Wort zu seiner Zeit*, p. v; Buek, *Verbreitungsweise*, pp. 75–76; PRO, PC1/4395/pt. 1, "Mandat. Gegeben in Unserer Raths-Versammlung, Hamburg am 21 September 1831"; Zimmermann, *Cholera-Epidemie in Hamburg*, pp. 14–16, 26; Simon, *Weg mit den Kordons!*, p. 40.
[203] Evans, *Death in Hamburg*, pp. 245–47; Wolter, *Das Auftreten der Cholera in Hamburg*, p. 241.

three nations with different political systems, yet all faced alike with the same epidemic predator: Sweden with among the most representative assemblies in Europe, France of the bourgeois quasi-constitutional monarchy and Britain under a newly elected Whig government in the throes of agitation over the Reform Bill. The first doubt to clear from the table is whether these nations were capable of imposing harshly quarantinist measures and willing to do so if necessary. That they were we know because, in fact, at least two of them had done so in the years immediately preceding the first cholera epidemic. Plague was a distant horror by the early nineteenth century, but yellow fever had only recently provoked official responses that drew on the institutional memory of the black death. Both Sweden and France had instituted quarantinist measures against yellow fever that they could have emulated when the turn came to cholera.

In Sweden, a new quarantine law was promulgated in 1806, in the last years of the quasi-absolutist regime, remaining in effect through the first cholera epidemic. Since salt required for its herring industry was imported mainly from southern Spain and as trade with North America was picking up during this period, yellow fever from these locales was a worry. The 1806 law, largely continuing that of 1770, was as strict as such measures came.[204] All ships from infected parts were to be quarantined at the permanent station built for these purposes two years earlier at Känsö near Gothenburg on the west coast.[205] Detailed instructions governed the procedure by which arriving vessels' documents were to be disinfected, immersed in the sea and fumigated before inspection by the authorities. Ships that failed to dock at Känsö, or sought to sneak by, had their descriptions relayed throughout the coastal districts and read aloud from the pulpits of local churches in hopes of sighting and hindering any attempts to dock. Every three miles along the shoreline an overseer was appointed to prevent ships from landing without quarantine, while along the west coast patrol ships ensured that none slipped by unnoticed. Local residents, warned to avoid contact with passengers or crew rescued from foundering ships, were instead to provide survivors with an empty and isolated house as refuge; cargo washed ashore was be left untouched.

[204] P. Dubb, "Om den Svenska Qvarantaines-Anstalten på Känsö," *Kongl. Vetenskaps Academiens Handlingar*, 1818, p. 29; Sven-Ove Arvidsson, *De svenska koleraepidemierna: En epidemiografisk studie* (Stockholm, 1972), p. 106; Lars Öberg, *Känsö karantänsinrättning 1804–1933* (Gothenburg, 1968), pp. 35ff.; Rolf Bergman, "De epidemiska sjukdomarna och deras bekämpande," in Wolfram Kock, ed., *Medicinalväsendet i Sverige, 1813–1962* (Stockholm, 1963), p. 368.

[205] "Kongl. Maj:ts Nådiga Quarantains-Förordning," *Kongl. Förordningar*, 1806.

Captains of ships departing Känsö without permission could be fined, but executed if plague-like illness was transmitted as a result, and the same held for passengers and crew. Lying about the epidemiological state of his ship could land a captain in jail for a decade. Those who concealed plague-like illness on board, their provenance from a diseased port or the presence of infectious goods or passengers could be put to death.[206] Physicians were obliged to report cases of fever to the Quarantine Commission in Gothenburg. Similar regulations applied to travelers coming overland from Norway to the west.

Procedures at Känsö were no less draconian.[207] Those who died onboard were to be buried at sea; if an entire crew perished in quarantine, its ship was to be set ablaze and sunk. Food and necessities were supplied by attendants in protective garments of waxed linen who might be executed for stealing the effects of their charges. Patients brought off a ship were washed with vinegar and had their hair shorn. Conveyed to the lazaretto, they were raised by lift into a bathing room without being touched and submerged fully clothed; their garments were then removed with hooks and cutting instruments. Sickrooms were fumigated thrice daily before each meal and detailed instructions governed the cleansing of possibly infected goods. Regulations in 1813 concerning transmissible diseases in general continued this contagionist approach. Clergymen were to report cases of illness, warnings were issued from the pulpits and contact between healthy and infected prevented. Public gatherings were discouraged and potentially infected clothing was not to be resold without prior cleansing.[208] Corpses were to be interred immediately at the first sign of putrefaction, burials conducted with little ceremony, and few mourners and separate cemeteries could be prescribed if necessary.[209]

In France, too, cholera was preceded by strict precautions imposed against yellow fever. The epidemic in Spain in 1819 and especially the

---

[206] Equally detailed and draconian procedures had been published the previous year for procedures on board ship during epidemics: *Kongl. Quarantaine Commissionens Underrättelse för Svenske Skeppare, om hvad de böra iakttaga så väl på Utrikes orter som vid återkomsten til Svenska hamnar* (Gothenburg, 8 January 1805), pp. 1–13.

[207] "Kongl. Maj:ts Nådiga Reglemente för Quarantains-Inrättningen på Känsö," *Kongl. Förordningar*, 1807. Details are in Dubb, "Om den Svenska Qvarantaines-Anstalten"; *Rapport sur l'établissement de quarantaine à Känsö* (Stockholm, 1819).

[208] "Kongl. Maj:ts Nådiga Circulaire Til Samtelige Landshöfdingarne Och Consistorierne, Om Hvad iakttagas bör i afseende på Smittosamma Sjukdomar," 25 August 1813, *Kongl. Förordningar*, 1813.

[209] *Underrättelse Om Hwad iakttagas bör til förekommande af smittosamma Sjukdomars och Farsoters utbredande* (Stockholm, 1813), §§8–10.

outbreak in 1821 at Barcelona, uncomfortably close to the border, obliged the Restoration monarchy to forge a sanitary response. Assuming that yellow fever should be treated much as the plague in the early eighteenth century, Paris instructed prefects along the Pyrenees in September 1819, once Cadiz had been struck, to keep watch over travelers from Spain, especially beggars and vagrants. Mendicants were rounded up and sent back, the import of wool was forbidden and letters from Spain were fumigated. A sanitary cordon was established, manned eventually in the summer of 1822 by almost 30,000 troops. The border to Spain was closed at all but three points, equipped with lazarettos where travelers from uninfected areas underwent quarantine up to the traditional forty days, while those from infected localities were refused admission at all.[210] Penalties for violating sanitary measures had an impressive bark, whatever their actual bite. Animals and goods illegally introduced to France were destroyed without compensation and violators of the cordon were to be "repulsed by main force." Those who had managed to avoid quarantine could be forced to undergo its regimen or arrested and prosecuted under prerevolutionary edicts which foresaw harsh penalties, including death, although capital punishments were in practice commuted. Fairs and markets were proscribed, as was the circulation of peddlers within five leagues of the cordon.[211]

Out of the contagionist assumptions applied here to yellow fever came the sanitary law of 3 March 1822 which vested the government with power to establish sanitary cordons. All who imported pestilential disease were threatened with death, while those who knowingly failed to report symptoms could be jailed for three months and fined, and physicians lost their licenses.[212] Two levels of quarantine (observation and strict) were distinguished to govern the admission of ships and a system of bills of health (foul, suspect, clean) classified them according to the state of the port of origin.[213] The 1822 law was thus firmly based on quarantinist premises and closely linked in the view of those who resisted its passage in the Chamber with the Restoration and its political complex-

[210] *Moniteur universel*, 273 (30 September 1821), pp. 1373–74.

[211] George D. Sussman, "From Yellow Fever to Cholera: A Study of French Government Policy, Medical Professionalism and Popular Movements in the Epidemic Crises of the Restoration and the July Monarchy" (Ph.D. diss., Yale University, 1971), pp. 57–61, 74–75, 97–105.

[212] *Annales*, 6 (1831), pp. 424–25. A detailed account of the law and its supplementing ordinance of 7 August 1822 can be found in F.-G. Boisseau, *Traité du choléra-morbus, considéré sous le rapport médical et administratif* (Paris, 1832), pp. 293–372.

[213] *Moniteur universel*, 223 (11 August 1822), pp. 1189–91. See also Ordinance of 20 March 1822, arts. 32–34, *Annales*, 6, 2 (1831), pp. 450–73.

ion. Critics complained that it granted extraordinary powers over the individual, allowing the government to suspend fundamental rights guaranteed by the Charter. Even more baldly conservative were its foreign policy implications. Not only did the Restoration government favor quarantinist tactics, it also used the military cordon drawn against the fever as the means to meddle in Spanish politics, mobilizing soldiers massed on the border as the army of intervention to restore in 1823 the Bourbon king, thus associating quarantinism and antirepublicanism indelibly in the French mind.[214]

While Sweden and France had marshaled strict quarantinist tactics against yellow fever during the 1820s and were in a position, had they desired, to impose similar measures against cholera, Britain was in this respect the odd nation out, having liberalized such practices on the eve of this most recent epidemic. To quarantines the English had come comparatively late, not until the sixteenth century, although Scotland, with its important Baltic trade, had started earlier. Nor, in physical terms, was British quarantine particularly impressive. Compared to the great lazarettos of Pisa, Venice, Genoa and Marseilles, the British were pennypinchers, preferring temporary expedients like sheds or the floating hulks of old men-of-war.[215] Nonetheless, as late as the early eighteenth century, the authorities remained empowered to take drastic measures. Faced with an outbreak of plague, the king could order quarantines and establish lazarettos, throw up internal cordons and put violators to death. Masters of vessels could be executed if they concealed information about the state of their ships and any who refused to enter quarantine from a ship could be compelled to by "any kind of violence" and were also subject to capital punishment. The ill could be removed from their homes, citizens could be ordered to keep watch on ships in quarantine and infected goods could be burnt.[216] In the early 1720s, once it became clear that the threat of the plague currently devastating Provence would not materialize, a reaction against the harshly quarantinist measures adopted as a precaution in 1721 set in. In the face of opposition from merchants and opponents of the Walpole administration, a more moderate

---

[214] Sussman, "From Yellow Fever to Cholera," pp. 7–10, 175–81; Léon-François Hoffmann, *La peste à Barcelone* (Princeton, 1964), ch. 3; Peter Sahlins, *Boundaries: The Making of France and Spain in the Pyrenees* (Berkeley, 1989), pp. 204–07.

[215] J. C. McDonald, "The History of Quarantine in Britain During the 19th Century," *BHM*, 25 (1951), pp. 22–24.

[216] E. A. Carson, "The Customs Quarantine Service," *Mariner's Mirror*, 64 (1978), pp. 63–64; Charles F. Mullett, "A Century of English Quarantine (1709–1825)," *BHM*, 23, 6 (November–December 1949), pp. 530–31.

policy was adopted.[217] At midcentury, however, the right of the authorities to impose quarantines on ships with force if necessary was reaffirmed, along with the death penalty for various violations, and at the turn of the eighteenth century quarantine measures were extended from the plague to all contagious diseases.[218] To the extent that quarantine was not practiced at home, the British relied on precautions imposed abroad. During the eighteenth century, ships from the east were required to perform quarantine in the Mediterranean before arrival in the motherland and many goods imported had in fact undergone such procedures.[219]

During the nineteenth century, it was in Britain's dependencies that quarantinist tactics were most drastically applied. When Valetta was attacked by the plague in 1813, Sir Thomas Maitland ordered a cordon drawn around the city, with violators shot.[220] In 1804, despite the best quarantinist efforts, yellow fever decimated the population of Gibraltar. At home, the College of Physicians favored quarantine along with sequestration of patients and a strict enforcement of sanitary cordons. The Central Board of Health, briefly established in this period, formulated an approach to epidemic disease that remained firmly contagionist. Should yellow fever threaten Britain, measures recommended, in addition to maritime quarantine, included having physicians in coastal regions report strangers or arrivants with suspicious fevers and, if the disease actually entered, placing infected localities under quasi-martial law with troops employed to cut contact between the sick and well. In London and larger trading towns, patients were to be sequestered in single detached houses. Medical attendants, duly instructed in the best manner of isolating the sick, were to stand ready for dispatch to any part of the country. Sequestration, disinfection, fumigation and cleansing were seen as the best means of countering plague and other contagious diseases.[221]

But it was also at this time, with quarantinism still in favor, that the

[217] Alfred James Henderson, *London and the National Government, 1721–1742* (Durham, NC, 1945), pp. 35–39, 53–54; Paul Slack, *The Impact of Plague in Tudor and Stuart England* (London, 1985), pp. 331–33.

[218] Leon Radzinowicz, *A History of English Criminal Law* (London, 1948), v. I, pp. 625–26; Mullett, "English Quarantine," pp. 532–34; Carson, "Customs Quarantine Service," pp. 65–66.

[219] John Baldry, "The Ottoman Quarantine Station on Kamaran Island 1882–1914," *Studies in the History of Medicine*, 2, 1/2 (March–June 1978), p. 9; Sticker, *Abhandlungen aus der Seuchengeschichte*, v. I/2, p. 311; J. M. Eager, *The Early History of Quarantine: Origin of Sanitary Measures Directed Against Yellow Fever* (Washington, DC, 1903), pp. 23–24.

[220] Sherston Baker, *The Laws Relating to Quarantine* (London, 1879), p. 15.

[221] C. Fraser Brockington, *Public Health in the Nineteenth Century* (Edinburgh, 1965), ch. 1.

debate began which would eventually shift things in a different direction. The authorities, backed by established medical opinion, retained their faith in quarantines.[222] Their opponents, tracing most disease to local causes, rejected such measures as unnecessary and economically harmful. Chief among the noncontagionists was Charles Maclean, an itinerant servant of the East India Company and medical polymath who had devoted much of his life to arguing the nontransmissibility of all pestilential disease. He was a man of uncommon persistence whose conviction that the plague was noncontagious survived even his own illness, caught in Constantinople in the Greek Pest Hospital where he was staying in hopes of proving his point. Maclean's arguments portrayed contagionism and quarantinism as both moral and economic failures. Ethically, contagionism was prompted by self-love, avarice and ambition. Each nation refused to accept that disease had local and indigenous origins, preferring instead to blame others for its import. Contagionism encouraged moral breakdown and an abandonment of the ill, which especially afflicted the poor, bereft of resources for their sustenance. Quarantine was immoral in sacrificing one part of the population in hopes of rescuing another. Since the goal was to remove the ill from noxious atmospheres, shutting them up in the especially concentrated pestilential air of quarantine stations was little short of authorized murder.[223] Maclean's role as spokesman for commercial interests that, during the Napoleonic wars, began to find the old quarantine regulations overly restrictive added economic motives to the moral. Cotton importers, who had begun shipping from Egypt in the 1820s, feared competition from the French and resented the delays and extra expenses imposed by such precautions (estimated by Maclean at half of total freight costs), were among the strongest opponents of quarantine.[224]

Pressed in the Commons by the Liberal MP John Smith and the Radical John Cam Hobhouse, Maclean's views prompted a series of investigations into epidemic disease and its prevention.[225] In 1824, an official committee saw no reason to doubt the contagiousness of illnesses

[222] Margaret Pelling, *Cholera, Fever and English Medicine 1825–1865* (Oxford, 1978), p. 27.

[223] Charles Maclean, *Results of an Investigation, Respecting Epidemic and Pestilential Diseases; Including Researches in the Levant Concerning the Plague* (London, 1817), v. I, pp. 274–75, 424–25, 429; Charles Maclean, *Evils of the Quarantine Laws and Non-Existance of Pestilential Contagion* (London, 1824), pp. 236–37; *Fraser's Magazine for Town and Country*, 47 (1853), p. 79.

[224] Charles Maclean, *Observations on Quarantine* (Liverpool, 1824), p. 33; R. J. Morris, *Cholera 1832: The Social Response to an Epidemic* (New York, 1976), p. 24; McDonald, "Quarantine in Britain," p. 26.

[225] Pelling, *Cholera, Fever and English Medicine*, pp. 27–28; Michael Durey, *The Return of the Plague: British Society and the Cholera 1831–1832* (Dublin, 1979), p. 13.

such as plague and cholera, but concluded nonetheless that the quarantine system could be improved. Commercial considerations were becoming increasingly weighty. As practiced, quarantine threatened to hobble Britain's ability to compete against the Netherlands, with its laxer precautions, and dimmed British hopes of becoming a place of transit or deposit for Mediterranean produce and the supply of the continent. Much silk, for example, was shipped overland from Italian ports in order to avoid the charges and delays of British quarantine. Goods shipped from the Levant to England via Holland arrived quicker and cheaper than directly. Despite the concerns of medical men that leaving such decisions to commercial interests meant abandoning all protection against transmissible disease, the committee agreed that quarantine should be reformed to lessen economic disincentives.[226] In 1825, a new quarantine law ameliorated existing procedures.[227] Rather than abolishing quarantine, as sought by Maclean and company, it made the system more flexible, granting the Privy Council discretionary powers in matters prophylactic. It still remained possible to use "any kind of necessary force" to prevent the quarantined from exiting before their appointed time, but in other respects moderation was the order of the day. Where the old regulations had stipulated precise periods of quarantine for ships from certain ports, the council could now determine its duration. Strictures were also ameliorated, most notably in abolishing the death penalty for violations.[228]

It would, however, be misleading to portray Britain as off the scale of European events in this respect, as the land of liberalism and free trade that drew the epidemiologically logical consequences, abandoning the last vestiges of the quarantinism inherited from its plague regulations. Debates similar to that provoked by Maclean rattled etiological cages in France as well, fought out in this case over yellow fever. Nicolas Chervin, a physician and convinced noncontagionist who had worked extensively on the disease in Spain and the Americas, sought in 1825 to have the Chamber suspend the 1822 law. The Academy of Medicine reported favorably on Chervin's ideas two years later. Between its interventions in Spain in 1823 and attempts during the same period to reorganize the Paris Faculty of Medicine, the Restoration government had rapidly been losing allies among physicians and the Academy's decision to support Chervin reflected a larger turnabout in medical opinion

---

[226] *PP* 1824 (417) vi, pp. 3–4, 6–11, 21, 94–95.   [227] 6 George IV, c. 78.
[228] Durey, *Return of the Plague*, p. 9; Mullett, "English Quarantine," p. 538.

against contagionism, quarantinism and the Restoration.[229] A report on the yellow fever epidemic at Gibraltar in 1828, coauthored by Chervin, helped shift opinion even further toward a noncontagionist approach. During the early 1830s, Chervin continued pestering the government to investigate cholera and plague in the same anticontagionist spirit, garnering support from the Academies of Medicine and Science, both of which were offended that the government had based its sanitary policies on the advice of experts, like Moreau de Jonnès, who were not medical men and whose quarantinist approach they rejected.[230] Commercial interests in France tended, as in Britain, to reject a strict application of quarantine, but the situation here was complicated by geographical peculiarities.[231] The Atlantic and Channel ports supported a rollback in precautionary measures, but the Mediterranean cities, Marseilles and Toulon especially, with their closer and more immediate contacts with the Levant, feared the plague, had vested institutional and economic stakes in quarantine and saw no good reason to drop their guard. Marseilles, moreover, still had control of its own quarantine procedures, whereas the Atlantic ports, like Le Havre, smarted under regulations issued from Paris. The Atlantic cities wished for more local autonomy in matters sanitary, while the southern ports sought to strengthen central control over quarantine practice in hopes of minimizing local variations that threatened to undermine the stringency of regulations in one place through the leniency of its neighbors.[232]

Even in Britain, it would be misleading to portray commercial interests as uniformly opposed to quarantines. Contagion and quarantine were double-edged issues. Besides the obvious necessity of weighing the respective interests of public and economic health, narrower mercantile interests were not arrayed without exception on one side of the issue. The import and export trades had opposing stakes in the matter. During discussion of Maclean's arguments in the 1820s, some MPs were concerned lest Britain's trading partners abroad gain the impression that

---

[229] Sussman, "From Yellow Fever to Cholera," pp. 149–52; Ackerknecht, "Anticontagionism Between 1821 and 1867," pp. 572–73; Salomon-Bayet, *Pasteur et la révolution pastorienne*, pp. 97–98; Ann F. La Berge, *Mission and Method: The Early Nineteenth-Century French Public Health Movement* (Cambridge, 1992), pp. 90–94; Erwin H. Ackerknecht, *Medicine at the Paris Hospital 1794–1848* (Baltimore, 1967), p. 158; Jacques Léonard, "La restauration et la profession médicale," in Jean-Pierre Goubert, ed., *La médicalisation de la société française 1770–1830* (Waterloo, Ontario, 1982), pp. 73–74.

[230] *Annales*, 10, 1 (1833), p. 213; *AGM*, 2nd ser., 1 (1833), pp. 608–09; William Coleman, *Yellow Fever in the North: The Methods of Early Epidemiology* (Madison, 1987), ch. 2.

[231] M. J. Mavidal and M. E. Laurent, eds., *Archives parlementaires de 1787 à 1860* (Paris, 1888), v. II/69, pp. 591–93. [232] Sussman, "From Yellow Fever to Cholera," pp. 24–25, 31–33.

quarantines were to be abolished and slap restrictions on shipping. An appearance of indifference to quarantine, William Huskisson, President of the Board of Trade, feared, might hurt commercial ties. The government made it clear that its reason for maintaining a contagionist approach was to support British shipping, recently hurt in the Mediterranean by rumors that the nation was about to change its policies. Commercial interests found Maclean and other radical antiquarantinists useful in keeping up pressure to moderate restrictions, but would probably not have supported him in a full abolition of such precautions.[233] The same mixed motives continued into the cholera era. Merchant and commercial circles objected to more stringent quarantinist measures than necessary, heartened to learn that much medical opinion considered the disease not contagious.[234] Shipowners complained that the cost of quarantine should, as the price of public health, be borne by the nation as a whole, not just one group. Joseph Hume argued their case in the Commons with the claim that cordons and quarantines "add famine to pestilence, and aggravate tenfold the evils of both."[235] The story is well known of how the commercial interests of Sunderland, which through widespread ownership of the means of transport included much of local society, pressured physicians to withdraw their first and accurate reports of cholera's arrival and later to undercount the number of cases, lest London otherwise attempt to isolate the disease in the city.[236] Others argued that, with its important manufacturing base, Britain could not afford the imposition of strict quarantines.[237] But at the same time, the ambiguity of commercial interests was also evident once cholera had struck. The government was

[233] Mullett, "English Quarantine," pp. 542–43; McDonald, "Quarantine in Britain," p. 27; *Fraser's Magazine for Town and Country*, 47 (1853), pp. 80–81.

[234] "Poulett Thomson, who is a trader as well as Privy Councillor, is very much disgusted in his former capacity at the measures he is obliged to concur in in his latter": Greville, *Memoirs*, v. II, pp. 152, 224. Generally, see James Kennedy, *The History of the Contagious Cholera* (London, 1831), pp. 252–53.

[235] PRO, PC1/4385, 4 August 1831, Letter from the Treasury with Petition from Ship Owners of Kincardine; *Hansard*, Commons, 1832, v. 10, col. 268.

[236] Morris, *Cholera 1832*, pp. 44ff.; Durey, *Return of the Plague*, pp. 143ff.; Norman Longmate, *King Cholera* (London, 1966), ch. 4; William Ainsworth, *Observations on the Pestilential Cholera (Asphyxia pestilenta), as It Appeared at Sunderland in the Months of November and December, 1831 and on the Measures Taken for Its Prevention and Cure* (London, 1832), pp. 23ff. But see also S. T. Miller, "Cholera in Sunderland 1831–1832," *Journal of Regional and Local Studies*, 3, 1 (1983), pp. 12–17. The Board of Health knew exactly what was going on from its emissary in Sunderland, Robert Daun: PRO, HO 31/17, Daun to the Board, 9 November 1831, Board of Health, minutes, 12 November 1831; Daun to the Board, 15 November 1831, Board of Health minutes, 15 November 1831. For similar situations in Manchester and Liverpool, see J. Delpech, *Étude du choléra-morbus en Angleterre et en Écosse* (Paris, 1832), pp. 145–48.   [237] *Quarterly Review*, 46 (1831), p. 266; Durey, *Return of the Plague*, p. 23.

reluctant to publicize the extent of the disease (engaging in heroic feats of circumlocutive hairsplitting to avoid admitting its presence) lest Britain's trading partners impose sanctions on its ships.[238] Nonetheless, it also realized that other nations would inflict yet harsher measures if they suspected that Britain was giving vessels clean bills of health despite the presence of sickness.[239] The mercantile interests of certain towns did not oppose quarantine as such, seeking only to limit it to the minimum necessary and shift its costs to the community at large. In other cases, merchants were concerned that cholera not spread among their workers and supported quarantine regulations.[240]

Such, then, was the situation when cholera struck: institutional memories of plague regulations from the previous century, renewed attempts in this spirit to deal with yellow fever, incipient doubts within medical circles as to contagiousness in general, encouraged by the desire among commercial interests to moderate oldfashioned quarantinism. In each case, the Pascallian logic of the predicament authorities found themselves in prevailed and with it at first a quarantinist approach.

FIRST ATTEMPTS

Sweden faced the advancing cholera in 1831 equipped with the quarantine law of 1806. Distant from the well-trod epidemic pathways of central Europe and surrounded on much of three sides by water, its concern was first and foremost to prevent the import of contagion by ship. The Känsö station having been located on the west coast, with plague and yellow fever in mind, to intercept traffic from the Mediterranean, the east was unprotected from the threat of cholera across the Baltic and a string of quarantine stations was now established here.[241] Quarantine was required of ships from infected ports and various goods were forbidden from import.[242] Vessels turned away as infected were to be prevented, with force if necessary, from contact with

---

[238] *Hansard*, Commons, 1832, v. 14, col. 520.

[239] *Hansard*, Commons, 1832, v. 10, cols. 691–92; Durey, *Return of the Plague*, p. 10.

[240] P. Swan, "Cholera in Hull," *Journal of Regional and Local Studies*, 3, 1 (1983), p. 8; Morris, *Cholera 1832*, p. 29.

[241] RA, Medicinalväsendet, v. 5, Karantän, "Beskrifning öfver Känsö"; *Rapport sur l'établissement de Quarantaine*, p. 5; Öberg, *Känsö karantänsinrättning*, pp. 28–29; *SFS*, 1831/16, pp. 94–95.

[242] *SFS*, 1831/17, pp. 97–98; 1831/21, pp. 114–15; 1831/32, pp. 233–35; *Post*, 128 (7 June 1831); 139 (20 June 1831); 143 (25 June 1831); 146 (29 June 1831); Buek, *Verbreitungsweise*, p. 77; Brita Zacke, *Koleraepidemien i Stockholm 1834* (Stockholm, 1971), p. 20.

the shore. To add muscle, three cannon barges were mustered between Svindesund and Kullen on the west coast to intercept ships and the military guarded all landing docks and ports. Fifty Hussars and 330 infantry to relay messages were posted along the west coast, while signal stations were erected on mountain tops. No boat was to land without being observed.[243]

In July 1831, having watched the epidemic make its way across much of Europe, the Swedish authorities, still convinced that cholera was directly transmissible, promulgated measures to take effect once it struck home. In most respects, they followed the Prussian lead, with a slightly less draconian tone than Berlin's initial regulations, but an equal penchant for detail.[244] Hospitals were to be provided for paupers and those who could not be cared for at home, but as in Germany it was unclear whether recalcitrants were to be compulsorily removed.[245] During transports, the bearers were to rest only where the street was wide enough for traffic to pass upwind. Once recuperated and released, patients on their way home were to avoid all contact with the healthy, alerting others of their condition by distinctive clothing. Burials were to occur early or late in the day at special cemeteries, with restricted processions and mourners wearing the same identifying marks as released hospital patients, with deep graves and common interments unless the family could afford otherwise, with lime sprinkled on the casket. If there were more than one priest, duties should be divided so that he who performed cholera burials not be responsible for normal rituals of the healthy. Churches in isolated areas could be attended only by the healthy and were to be fumigated before and after services. Schools and administrative offices were closed, markets, auctions and other public assemblies forbidden. Infected houses were to be sealed off and marked, with instructions on animals and packing superfluous clothes familiar from Prussia. The Swedes were stingier than the Prussians when it came to provisioning and only the sequestered who could not work at tasks assigned by the sanitary authorities were to be supplied at the public expense. The healthy residents of infected houses could leave only after two weeks of quarantine and entire areas might be sealed off by military cordons. Against transgressors, the Swedes were only slightly more merciful than the Prussians.

[243] *Sammandrag ur Gällande Författningar och Föreskrifter af hwad iagttagas bör till förekommande af Utrikes härjande Farsoters inträngande i Riket* (Stockholm, 1831), pp. 5, 9; Öberg, *Känsö karantänsinrättning*, pp. 92–93.   [244] *SFS*, 1831/30.

[245] Not just the poor, but – space permitting – also the higher classes were to be allowed to seek refuge in the hospitals: RA, Äldre Kommittee, v. 689, no. 266, 20 June 1831.

Local sanitary committees could levy fines, with the upper limit determined individually in serious cases. The sequestered who violently sought to escape were to be repelled by force, and the guards were permitted to kill them. Transgressors of cordons were, along with their contacts, to be resequestered and held liable for the costs of provisioning and damages to those who, as a consequence, also had to be isolated. Animals and goods illegally transported across cordons were to be cleansed and sold.

In Britain, the initial official reaction was also based on contagionist assumptions. Like the western German states, the British at first relied on foreign protective efforts to shield them. They compelled Hamburg to impose quarantines, threatening otherwise to take measures against shipping from the Hanseatic and other Baltic ports, and put similar pressure on Sweden. In the early summer of 1831, with cholera in Riga, quarantines were established at home.[246] Seeking medical legitimacy for its actions, the government asked the Royal College of Physicians for an assessment and was assured that cholera was infectious, could be transmitted by goods and required quarantine.[247] When the government shortly thereafter established a Central Board of Health to advise the Privy Council on cholera, however, it got more than it had bargained for. Having sought a degree of quarantinism that promised to exclude cholera while not restricting trade and commerce more than necessary, what the government now heard was an extreme position.[248] The Board's first measures (fourteen-day quarantine and elaborate procedures for airing and drying goods) were largely an application of inherited plague regulations. Unwilling to act against the organ it had just created, the Privy Council was forced at first to acquiesce in its instructions.[249]

The Board overstepped the tolerable, however, when in late June it recommended strict quarantinist precautions to be taken within the

---

[246] *PP* 1831 (49) xvii, p. 15; Buek, *Verbreitungsweise*, pp. 75–77; Morris, *Cholera 1832*, p. 24; Swan, "Cholera in Hull," pp. 6–7; Öberg, *Känsö karantänsinrättning*, p. 91.

[247] *PP* 1831 (49) xvii, pp. 15–19; Greville, *Memoirs*, v. II, p. 151; Morris, *Cholera 1832*, p. 25; Durey, *Return of the Plague*, p. 11. Halford's report, in the name of the Royal College of Physicians, to the Privy Council, 15 June 1831, in fact said that cholera in Russia was communicable from one person to another, but doubted that it could be transmitted by merchandise. In the absence of better knowledge, however, it recommended quarantine for goods coming from infected places: PRO, MH 98/1, Halford to Privy Council, 15 June 1831; Henry Halford, Turner, Macmichael, Hawkins, untitled report, 9 June 1831.

[248] PRO, MH 98/1, Greville to Halford, 16 June 1831; Halford to Greville, 18 June 1831; Durey, *Return of the Plague*, pp. 12–15; Brockington, *Public Health in the Nineteenth Century*, ch. 2; Morris, *Cholera 1832*, pp. 26–29. [249] Greville, *Memoirs*, v. II, pp. 154–57.

country. Internal cordons it considered but rejected as impracticable in favor of a policy of sequestering the first cases of cholera and separating sick from healthy. To this end, it proposed an unprecedented system of local boards of health to ferret out and treat early cases. Once found, "expurgators," who lived apart from the general public, would be sent in and patients removed under police or military guard on special conveyances to lazarettos. Military guards around hospitals and isolation houses were to allow sequestration of the sick or suspected. All contacts were to be taken to isolation houses, preferably close to the lazaretto, and barriers erected before such institutions would allow deliveries without communication. After the first onslaught of epidemic had passed, the better-off classes could be accommodated at their expense in airy and detached houses, but otherwise the same strict rules should apply to them as to the poor. The expurgators were to purify infected houses, burning rags, cordage, paper and old clothing without (apparently) any compensation to the owner, boiling and washing clothing and furniture in strong lye, pouring chloride of lime down the drains and privies, scrubbing the walls with hot lime, followed by a week-long airing of the rooms. The dead were to be buried in the immediate vicinity of the isolation houses, not in normal cemeteries. In York, the sorts of burial procedures familiar from the continent were practiced: quick interments (twelve hours after death), abbreviated ceremonies graveside, quicklime in the coffins.[250] Various monetary rewards were promised for detection of cases and fines threatened for concealment. The Board of Health realized that such measures would harm commerce and do violence to the ordinary spirit of social intercourse, especially if families had to be split, but concluded that, faced with such a mortal threat, "private feelings must give way to the public safety, and the state has a right to expect from its subjects an acquiescence in means of indispensable General Policy."[251]

    In France the initial official reaction was equally contagionist. The French had first encountered cholera simultaneously with yellow fever. In 1819, as the Restoration was formulating its plans against the fever, cholera struck in the Indian Ocean at Mauritius, a British possession. On the neighboring French island of Bourbon, despite strict quaran-

[250] Margaret C. Barnet, "The 1832 Cholera Epidemic in York," *Medical History*, 16, 1 (January 1972), pp. 29, 32; Morris, *Cholera 1832*, pp. 104–05.
[251] PRO, PC1/101, Board of Health, minutes, 11 July 1831; also MH 98/1, "Report" 10 July 1831; Brockington, *Public Health in the Nineteenth Century*, pp. 69–71; Morris, *Cholera 1832*, pp. 31–32; Durey, *Return of the Plague*, pp. 15–16.

tine, the disease invaded, St. Denis was abandoned by many of its inhabitants and surrounded by a military cordon. To protect the homeland, Marseilles imposed a thirty-day quarantine on ships from the island and the Ministry of the Interior ordered the same for other ports. From local physicians' accounts, P. F. Keraudren and Moreau de Jonnès concluded that cholera was contagious. Moreau de Jonnès wrote a series of reports on the disease in the Indian Ocean during the early 1820s and was later to win a hearing for his contagionist conclusions when the disease appeared in Europe.[252] When cholera began to spread from eastern Europe, the French government dispatched observers in March 1831 and sought the counsel of its Academy of Medicine. The disease advancing more swiftly than the machinery of official advice, however, it was forced to act before hearing the experts. Proceeding on the conclusions drawn from Bourbon, the authorities now took a quarantinist approach. In June and July 1831, measures imposed at the frontiers were familiar from elsewhere. Cholera was to be considered generally, if not invariably, contagious. Ships from the Baltic were subject to quarantine of three to twenty-five days depending on their bill of health, with Russian vessels due for the maximum. At Calais the sanitary commission proposed quarantining all ships from the north, mounting a cannon at the tip of the east jetty to ensure compliance. In August, the twenty northeastern border departments established quarantines for travelers and the purification of effects, restricting the import of certain goods.[253] As the September fair in Frankfurt approached, the French closed the eastern border near the city except at six customs posts equipped with quarantine and purification procedures, imposing stays of five to twenty days. In September 1831, all letters from Germany were being punctured and soaked in vinegar, a procedure which subjected the mails to a (by modern postal standards) miraculously short delay of only twenty-four hours. Later that month, sanitary cordons were established in all military districts. In November, with cholera in Sunderland and thus looming from the west as well, new ordinances restricted the ports of

---

[252] F. E. Foderé, *Recherches historiques et critiques sur la nature, les causes et le traitement du choléra-morbus* (Paris, 1831), pp. 290–93; Sussman, "From Yellow Fever to Cholera," p. 214; Buek, *Verbreitungsweise*, pp. 16–17.

[253] *AGM*, 26 (1831), p. 444; 27 (1831), p. 277; *Gazette médicale de Paris*, 2, 27 (1831), pp. 233–34; *Moniteur universel*, 184 (3 July 1831), p. 1168; 231 (19 August 1831), p. 1419; 233 (21 August 1831), p. 1435; *Dictionnaire encyclopédique des sciences médicales* (Paris, 1874), v. III/1, pp. 49–51; Jacques Léonard, *Les officiers de santé de la marine française de 1814 à 1835* (Paris, 1967), p. 247; Sussman, "From Yellow Fever to Cholera," p. 218.

entry open to British ships, prescribing quarantines.[254] In February 1832, a five-day observation quarantine was ordered for ships from the Thames. At Boulogne-sur-Mer, the municipal authorities sought to make such restrictions as pleasant as possible, with elegant barracks constructed on the quays and a large well-furnished house, only recently inhabited by the king of Württemberg, converted into a temporary lazaretto.[255]

LESSONS FROM ABROAD

Despite their initially quarantinist approaches, Sweden, Britain and France, unlike the autocracies, had the advantage of foreign experience, a favorable placement along the learning curve. Geographical isolation gave the Swedes extra time, until 1834, for contemplation before encountering cholera. They were meticulous collectors of the fruits of their neighbors' experience, publishing an exhaustive summary of foreign opinion and subsidizing the translation of pertinent works from Russia and Germany.[256] The lesson eventually drawn was that cholera sprang largely from local causes and that, in any case, whatever its nature, the quarantinist approach taken at first in the east had done more harm than good. The first news from Russia in late 1830 was the usual opinions seen elsewhere. From the Swedish ambassador in St. Petersburg came optimistic hopes that cordons would keep cholera, currently in Moscow, from the capital.[257] But once the disease had penetrated even St. Petersburg, two Swedish physicians reporting thence changed the tune: however helpful in excluding the disease cordons and quarantines might be, once it had broached the outer defenses, sealing off individual houses was of little use. By October 1831, one of these physicians, writing from the lazaretto at Gisslinge, was fully convinced that the disease could not be transmitted by personal contact and that the best prevention was good sanitation.[258] Barchewitz, who had worked to convert Danzig and

---

[254] *Moniteur universel*, 239 (27 August 1831), p. 1463; Henri Monod, *Le choléra (Histoire d'une épidémie – Finistère, 1885–1886)* (Paris, 1892), p. 600; *Berlinische Nachrichten*, 211 (9 September 1831); Delaporte, *Disease and Civilization*, p. 25.

[255] *Moniteur universel*, 47 (16 February 1832), p. 459; 67 (7 March 1832), p. 662.

[256] [Trafvenfelt], *Sammandrag af Läkares åsigter*; Sven-Ove Arvidsson, "Epidemiologiska teorier under 1800-talets koleraepidemier," *Nordisk medicinhistorisk årsbok* (1971), p. 183.

[257] *Årsberättelse om Svenska Läkare-Sällskapets arbeten*, 1830, pp. 121–22; *Post*, 257 (5 November 1830); N. O. Schagerström, *Korrt Underrättelse om Cholera* (Helsingborg, 1831), p. 4; Swederus, *Cholera morbus*, pp. 36–43, 120; Zacke, *Koleraepidemien*, p. 18.

[258] *Bihang till Post* (6 September 1831); *Post*, 171 (28 July 1831); Zacke, *Koleraepidemien*, pp. 29–30; [Trafvenfelt], *Sammandrag af Läkares åsigter*, v. II, pp. 12–13, 126–31; v. III, pp. 30ff.

Königsberg from quarantinism, worked similar magic in Sweden.[259] A Swede publishing in St. Petersburg argued that the world owed Russia a debt for having suffered under strict quarantinist regulations, thereby demonstrating their uselessness.[260]

Swedish medical opinion was colored by such lessons. Most physicians believed in the importance of predisposing factors and few if any were strict contagionists.[261] Their contribution to etiology lay in adding to the list of predisposing causes compiled throughout the world a melancholic sanguine temperament and strong hemorrhoidal disposition.[262] Trafvenfelt, editor of a massive anthology of foreign opinion, concluded that cholera required both a miasmatic atmosphere and individual predisposition for transmission and that, in any case, it was not contagious like the plague.[263] By 1834, when cholera finally struck Sweden, most physicians had joined the antiquarantinist camp, many taking a decidedly sanitationist approach.[264] At the same time, it did not escape notice that Sweden had avoided the epidemic until long after the rest of Europe.[265] Many were willing to believe that this good fortune was not just a divine partiality for northerners or the advantages of geographic peripherality, but owed something to the precautions imposed on shipping and travelers. They were therefore ready to accept cordons and quarantines at the nation's borders, although drawing the line at sequestration and sealing off individual houses within the country.[266]

In Britain, as elsewhere, opinion on the nature of cholera and the course of prevention implied was conflicting. The initial reports from

[259] Bangssel, *Erinnerungsbuch für Alle*, p. 98; [Trafvenfelt], *Sammandrag af Läkares åsigter*, v. I, pp. 56–57; *Bihang till Post* (21 June 1831), copy in RA, Karantänskommissionen, 580b, Skrivelser till Kungl. Maj:t, 1831, no. 659.

[260] Carl von Haartman, *Tankar om choleran* (St. Petersburg, 1832), pp. 26–27.

[261] Cederschjöld was the closest the Swedes had to a contagionist physician and his approach was contingent: P. G. Cederschjöld, *Om cholera* (Stockholm, 1831), pp. 4–6; *Tidskrift för läkare och pharmaceuter*, 12 (December 1834), pp. 493–94; J. A. Engeström, *Anvisning på skyddsmedel mot smittosamma sjukdomar i allmänhet och mot farsoten cholera* (Lund, 1831).

[262] [Trafvenfelt], *Sammandrag af Läkares åsigter*, v. I, p. 107. Otherwise advice on avoiding cholera was strictly standard-issue: *Årsberättelse om Svenska Läkare-Sällskapets arbeten*, 1831, pp. 50–51.

[263] [Trafvenfelt], *Sammandrag af Läkares åsigter*, v. I, pp. 4–6, 31, 185; v. III, p. 114.

[264] Arvidsson, *De svenska koleraepidemierna*, p. 100; Arvidsson, "Epidemiologiska teorier," p. 185; *Post*, 204 (4 September 1834); *Svenska Läkare-Sällskapets nya handlingar*, 1 (1837), p. 331; Arwid. Henr. Florman, *Underrättelse om bruket af de mest bepröfvade Preservativer och Botemedel, mot den nu i Europa grasserande Cholera-Sjukdomen* (Lund, 1831); J. Ouchterlony and A. E. Setterblad, *Anteckningar öfver den epidemiska, asiatiska Choleran* (Stockholm, 1832), pp. 75–76.

[265] In March 1834, a prayer prematurely thanking God for sparing the country was read aloud from pulpits. Once the disease had hit in August, another prayer of a humbler tone followed: *SFS*, 1834/4, pp. 1–2; 1834/18.

[266] [Trafvenfelt], *Sammandrag af Läkares åsigter*, v. I, pp. 185–86; Ouchterlony and Setterblad, *Anteckningar*, pp. 3–9, 75–76.

Russia and elsewhere in the east pointed in various directions. Drs. William Russell and David Barry, dispatched to St. Petersburg, thought it contagious. Dr. Walker, a St. Petersburg physician consulted by the Privy Council, prudently refused to come down firmly on one side or the other, considering it unable to be transmitted by goods, but probably from person to person.[267] The *Edinburgh Medical and Surgical Journal* at first drew contingently contagionist conclusions from the Russian news, while reports collected by the government offered a melange of similar opinion. Becker, a Prussian physician reporting from Berlin, considered cholera contagious, but also that, once introduced, it poisoned the atmosphere, turning it miasmatic. George William Lefevre, on the other hand, reported his noncontagionist conclusions from St. Petersburg and John Hamett and the British consul in Danzig, Alexander Gibsone, were both infected by that city's tradition of noncontagionism.[268]

Medical opinion at home was even more variegated, at least at the outset. On the one hand, there were the noncontagionists among physicians with Indian experience and whatever opinion in this vein had survived the plague debates of the 1820s.[269] On the other, the historical analogy of the plague remained powerful in Britain, fortunate as it was in having been spared any major epidemics since 1665. Thanks to this fortuitous epidemiological virginity, the quarantinist approach inherited from plague legislation remained untested, having been neither discredited nor modified. The Royal College of Physicians was contagionist in part because its opinions were locked fast at the level of knowledge current a century earlier.[270] Except for its East India members, the Edinburgh Board of Health was contingently contagionist.[271] The range of other medical opinion ran the gamut.[272] But as elsewhere, increasing

[267] PRO, PC1/2660, Letter of instruction, C. C. Greville to Dr. Russell, 17 June 1831; Hawkins, *History*, pp. 247ff. Walker's reports are reprinted in *PP* 1831 (49) xvii. The originals are in PRO, PC1/106.

[268] *EMSJ*, 58 (July 1831), pp. 118ff.; *PP* 1831 (49) xvii, p. 9; Becker, *Letters on the Cholera*; George William Lefevre, *Observations on the Nature and Treatment of the Cholera Morbus Now Prevailing Epidemically in St. Petersburg* (London, 1831), pp. 32–33; PRO, PC1/106, John Hamett to C. C. Greville, 2 September 1831; Hamett, *Substance of the Official Medical Reports*, pp. 87ff.

[269] *Instruction für die Sanitäts-Behörden*, pp. 3, 24.

[270] Durey, *Return of the Plague*, p. 108. On the other hand, noncontagionists on the plague may have been encouraged by the lack of any direct experience: Slack, *Impact of Plague*, p. 330.

[271] *Report of the Edinburgh Board of Health*, 16 November 1831; *Supplement to the EMSJ* (February 1832), pp. cclxvi–cclxix.

[272] Contagionists included James Butler Kell, *The Appearance of Cholera at Sunderland in 1831; With Some Account of That Disease* (Edinburgh, 1834), pp. vii, 18; William MacMichael, *Is the Cholera Spasmodica of India a Contagious Disease?* (London, 1831), pp. 3–4; W. Haslewood and W. Mordey, *History and Medical Treatment of Cholera, as It Appeared in Sunderland in 1831* (London, 1832), pp. 141–49; James Copland, *Of Pestilential Cholera: Its Nature, Prevention and Curative Treatment* (London, 1832), pp.

experience with the disease impelled many observers away from contagionism and toward a sanitationist approach.[273] Among anticontagionists, opinion varied little from the continental mold: quarantinism was
immoral, rending asunder the natural bonds of kin and society. Overly
drastic interventions were likely to prompt evasion, defeating their
own purpose. The proper solution was warm clothing, nourishing food,
personal hygiene, tidy dwellings, serenity of mind. Personal failings,
debauchery and immorality were regarded as predisposing factors.[274] To
a sanitationist approach, the British added little not already developed
at greater length on the continent. Among the culinary novelties in
advice on avoiding predisposition was the recommendation of roast
rather than boiled meat, among practical measures the suggestion of
removing duties on soap to encourage cleanliness among the lower
classes. Flannel belts were also popular, with over seven thousand distributed in Exeter alone during the 1832 epidemic.[275] Britain too benefited
from an advanced placement along the geoepidemiological learning
curve. The government clearly had no desire to provoke the sorts of disturbances that had accompanied harshly quarantinist measures to the
east. Foreign precedence was invoked against precautions that had
shown themselves impracticable and useless.[276] Even British contagionists tended to reject sanitary cordons which sought to isolate an area otherwise in lively communication with its surroundings.[277]

France, in turn, also profited from its position toward the pinnacle of
the epidemic pyramid of experience. News from eastern and central
Europe was contradictory and, to clear matters up, the government

99–101; D. M. Moir, *Practical Observations on Malignant Cholera as That Disease Is Now Exhibiting Itself in Scotland* (Edinburgh, 1832); D. M. Moir, *Proofs of the Contagion of Malignant Cholera* (Edinburgh, 1832). For noncontagionists, see Brougham, *On Cholera*, p. 6; Gaulter, *Origin and Progress*; George Hamilton Bell, *Treatise on Cholera Asphyxia* (2nd edn.; Edinburgh, 1832); W. Reid Clanny, *Hyperanthraxis; or, the Cholera of Sunderland* (London, 1832), pp. 87, 101–05.

[273] Arvidsson, "Epidemiologiska teorier," p. 182; Morris, *Cholera 1832*, pp. 180–81.

[274] Brougham, *On Cholera*, pp. 70–71; White, *Treatise on Cholera Morbus*, p. 1; [James Gillkrest], *Lettters on the Cholera Morbus* (London, 1831), p. 42; George Hamilton Bell, *Letter to Sir Henry Halford . . . on the Tendency of the proposed Regulations for Cholera . . .* (Edinburgh, 1831), p. 6; *London Medical and Surgical Journal*, 1 (1832), pp. 118–23; T. M. Greenhow, *Cholera: Its Non-Contagious Nature and the Best Means of Arresting Its Progress* (Newcastle, 1831), pp. 4–5; *Hansard*, Commons, 1832, v. 10, col. 268; William Fergusson, *Letters upon Cholera Morbus* (London, 1832), pp. 10–11.

[275] *Lancet*, 2 (1831–32), p. 653; *Hansard*, Commons, 1831, v. 8, col. 901; W. Hobson, *World Health and History* (Bristol, 1963), p. 82.

[276] PRO, PC1/4395 pt 1, Board of Health to Gilbert Blane, 4 October 1831; *Hansard*, Commons, 1831, v. 9, cols. 310–14; Durey, *Return of the Plague*, p. 21; *Supplement to the EMSJ* (February 1832), pp. cclxv, ccxvi–ccxvii; Greenhow, *Cholera*, pp. 10–11; Fergusson, *Letters*, p. 11; *Official Correspondence on the Subject of Spasmodic Cholera in Ireland* (Dublin, 1832), Appendix, p. 10.

[277] Ainsworth, *Observations on the Pestilential Cholera*, p. 99; Copland, *Of Pestilential Cholera*, pp. 99–101.

dipatched observers.[278] The team to Russia made its leisurely way through Germany, idling away a few pleasant hours at Weimar in chat with Goethe about the Madrepore islands, proceeded through Denmark, Sweden and Finland, finally to arrive in St. Petersburg whence it reported back in September in a noncontagionist vein: overly strict measures provoked hostility and had not hindered cholera. Sanitary cordons might be effective on the French borders, but isolation and sequestration within cities and forcible removals of the ill were techniques unlikely to work at home.[279] The Polish team stressed the noncontagious nature of the disease, encouraging the French government to rely instead on sanitation and urban renewal.[280] The embassy in Russia reported that cholera was both contagious and not and that, while external cordons might work to delay an epidemic, internal cordons and quarantines were merely vexatious. From other observers in Prussia and elsewhere came similar rejections of strict quarantinism.[281] Reporting from England, in turn, one observer concluded that cholera was contagious, but that, while external cordons and quarantines were not effective, individual isolation was. Others, including Magendie, considered it untransmissible.[282]

Contagionist opinions, or at least the willingness to entertain the possibility of cholera's transmissibility, could of course be found in France.[283] Ozanam, in his exhaustive work on epidemic disease, relied

[278] Is contagious: *AGM*, 25 (1831), p. 423. Is not: *AGM*, 25 (1831), pp. 433–34, 438–39; 26 (1831), p. 274; 28 (1832), pp. 134, 280; *Gazette médicale de Paris*, 2, 20 (1831), pp. 169–70. Won't really say: Sophianopoulo, *Relation des épidémies du choléra-morbus observées en Hongrie, Moldavie, Gallicie, et a Vienne en Autriche, dans les années 1831 et 1832* (Paris, 1832), pp. 4–5, 157. Confused: *Gazette médicale de Paris*, 2, 10 (1831), pp. 85–87.

[279] Gerardin and Gaimard, *Du choléra-morbus*, pp. vii–ix, 6–13. The British took a very dim view of the report's empirical basis: *LMG*, 11 (1833), pp. 356–61.

[280] Allibert, *Rapport lu*, pp. 119–20; Casimir Allibert et al., *Rapport de la commission medicale envoyée en Pologne, par M. le Ministre du Commerce et des Travaux publics, pour étudier le choléra-morbus* (Paris, 1832), pp. 86–93. For other anticontagionist opinion sent back from Poland, see F. Foy, *Du choléra-morbus de Pologne* (Paris, 1832), pp. 134–43; Buek, *Verbreitungsweise*, pp. 46–47; Brierre de Boismont, *Relation historique*, pp. 110ff., 121; *Supplement to the EMSJ* (February 1832), p. ccxv; *Gazette médicale de Paris*, 2, 40 (1831), pp. 337–40.

[281] *Observations sur le choléra-morbus, recueilliés et publiées par l'ambassade de France en Russie* (Paris, 1831), pp. 7–17; Scoutetten, *Relation historique*; M. B. Mojon, *Conjectures sur la nature du miasme producteur du choléra asiatique* (Paris, 1833), pp. 20–21; *Gazette médicale de Paris*, 2, 44 (1831), pp. 372–73.

[282] Delpech, *Etude du choléra-morbus en Angleterre*, pp. 151, 274; Halma-Grand, *Relation du choléra-morbus épidémique de Londres* (Paris, 1832), pp. 140–43; *Gazette médicale de Paris*, 3, 53 (1832), p. 383. When he reported from Sunderland in December 1831, however, Magendie offered no opinion one way or the other: *Gazette médicale de Paris*, 2, 52 (1831), p. 444.

[283] B. Brassier, *Considérations sur le choléra-morbus des Indes* (Strasbourg, 1831), p. 17; L. P. Aug. Gauthier, *Rapport sur le Choléra-Morbus fait a la Société de médecine de Lyon* (Lyons, 1831), pp. 69, 90; L. J. M. Robert, *Lettre a M. de Tourguenef . . . sur le choléra-morbus de l'Inde* (Marseille, 1831); Foderé,

on observers in Russia and Poland for his conclusion that cholera traveled atmospherically and was therefore harder to contain than diseases like the plague, spread by human contact. His prophylactic recommendations, however, were much the same as for plague and yellow fever: personal and urban hygiene, sequestration of the ill and fumigation of sickrooms, although whether cordons and quarantines were also necessary for cholera was unclear.[284] Moreau de Jonnès, on whose advice the government had based its initial precautions, was the most notorious of the contagionists. In the Academy of Science, he fought a pitched battle with Magendie who thought that, given etiological ignorance, no prophylaxis other than the general rules of hygiene was possible.[285] Despite the persistence of contagionist views, however, the opposing position was coming to dominate medical opinion.[286] Most Parisian physicians were noncontagionists, it was noted in July 1832, remaining steadfast once cholera had hit home. Quarantinism they dismissed as useless, if not harmful, preferring to see the resources thus squandered used on behalf of the poor.[287] Broussais considered cholera an inflammation of the intestines and thus at worst infectious, but not contagious, and in any case dependent on predisposing factors. Alas for his reputation, he applied his cure (a combination of leeches and bleedings) with such enthusiasm that many of his patients succumbed and his was the misfortune of having thus treated one of the epidemic's most illustrious victims, Casimir Périer, whose death served only to call further attention

Recherches historiques; *Le traitement domestique et les préservatifs du choléra oriental* (Paris, 1831); J.-N. Guilbert, *Moyens à opposer au choléra pestilentiel* (Paris, 1832); J.-C.-A. Récamier, *Recherches sur le traitement du choléra-morbus* (Paris, 1832), pp. 51–52; Larrey, *Mémoire sur le choléra-morbus* (Paris, 1831), p. 35; H. M. J. Desruelles, *Précis physiologique du choléra-morbus* (Paris, 1831), p. 69; *Gazette médicale de Paris*, 3, 37 (1832), p. 282.

[284] Ozanam, *Histoire médicale générale*, v. II, pp. 252–54, 266; v. IV, pp. 63–73.

[285] Moreau de Jonnès, *Rapport au conseil supérieur de santé sur le choléra-morbus pestilentiel* (Paris, 1831), p. 122. He liked the measures taken by the Swedes and recommended them to the Conseil supérieur de santé: PRO, PC1/108, Moreau de Jonnès to W. Bathurst, n.d., but probably December 1831; *Gazette médicale de Paris*, 3, 50 (1832), p. 363; 3, 53 (1832), p. 383; *AGM*, 28 (1832), pp. 431–32. Generally, see M. F. Magendie, *Leçons sur le choléra-morbus, faites au Collége de France* (Paris, 1832).

[286] La Berge, *Mission and Method*, pp. 67–69, 91–94, 185–86; Erwin H. Ackerknecht, "Hygiene in France, 1815–1848," *BHM*, 22, 2 (March–April 1948); Sussman, "From Yellow Fever to Cholera," p. 183; Ange-Pierre Leca, *Et le choléra s'abattit sur Paris 1832* (Paris, 1982), p. 140; Piquemal, "Le choléra de 1832," p. 49; Bourdelais and Raulot, *Une peur bleue*, pp. 70–72.

[287] *Gazette médicale de Paris*, 3, 64 (1832), p. 454; *Moniteur universel*, 92 (1 April 1832), p. 939; 99 (8 April 1832), p. 1002; 123 (2 May 1832), p. 1152; A.-T. Chrestien, *Etude du choléra-morbus, à l'usage des gens du monde* (Montpellier, 1835), pp. 53–54; Scoutetten, *Histoire médicale et topographique du choléra-morbus* (Metz, 1831), pp. 67–73; *Journal de médecine et de chirurgie pratiques*, 111 (1832), pp. 241–45; Stanislas Sandras, *Du choléra épidémique observé en Pologne, en Allemagne et en France* (Paris, 1832), pp. 94–95; Félix Maréchal, *Rapport statistique et médical sur l'épidémie de choléra qui a régné à Metz et dans le département de la Moselle en 1832* (Metz, 1839), p. 35; Boisseau, *Traité du choléra-morbus*, pp. 287–89.

to Broussais's dismal success rate.[288] Unsurprisingly, Chervin found no reason to change his position when it came to cholera.[289] The Academy of Medicine was outraged that the government did not await its reports before acting, that it had assumed contagiousness and, perhaps worst, that it had relied on the advice of Moreau de Jonnès, a military man, not a doctor, whose conclusions were based on secondhand information rather than personal experience.[290] When it finally did venture an opinion, the Academy took a moderate position: cholera might be transmissible by humans, although even here it was skeptical, but certainly not through goods. It also followed the general consensus that quarantines and cordons, though possibly effective at the frontiers, would be harmful within the country, hampering economic activity and increasing misery.[291] In other respects, opinions were broadly similar to those elsewhere. Environmental factors – stagnant water and putrefaction, insalubrious dwellings – were considered important. Predisposing elements were crucial, whether individual or social.[292] Recommendations on personal behavior were much the same as elsewhere: open the windows, change your underwear, avoid extremes in temperature, activ-

[288] *Moniteur universel*, 112 (21 April 1832), pp. 1104–05; *Examen de la doctrine physiologique appliquée à l'étude et au traitement du choléra-morbus, suivie de l'histoire de la maladie de M. Casimir Périer; par les rédacteurs principaux de la "Gazette médicale de Paris"* (Paris, n.d. [1832]); *Gazette médicale de Paris*, 3, 23; 3, 24 and 3, 26 (1832); *Journal des Débats* (19 May 1832), pp. 1–2; Bourdelais and Raulot, *Une peur bleue*, pp. 139–40.

[289] *Gazette médicale de Paris*, 3, 31 (1832), p. 240; *Journal universel et hebdomadaire de médécine et de chirurgie pratiques et des institutions médicales*, 12 (1833), pp. 84–90.

[290] *AGM*, 26 (1831), p. 273; 27 (1831), p. 277. For similar complaints, see Scoutetten, *Histoire médicale*, pp. 67–68; Jaehnichen, *Quelques réflexions*, pp. 6–7. Moreau de Jonnès's opinion on the Academy's report returned the favor in similarly invective coin: PRO, PC1/108, Moreau de Jonnès to William Pym, 1 December 1831. His reputation has since been rehabilitated by modern scholars who consider him the most perspicacious of contemporary observers: Bourdelais and Raulot, *Une peur bleue*, p. 47; Jean Théodoridès, *Des miasmes aux virus: Histoire des maladies infectieuses* (Paris, 1991), p. 117. In July, medical amour propre was offended anew when it was announced that none of the ten new members with which the Conseil supérieur de santé had been expanded were medical men: *AGM*, 27 (1831), p. 278.

[291] *Rapport sur le choléra-morbus, lu à l'Academie royale de médecine, en séance générale, les 26 et 30 Juillet 1831* (Paris, 1831), pp. 142–44, 161–69; *AGM*, 26 (1831), pp. 428–34; *Journal des Débats* (18 February 1832), p. 4; *Gazette médicale de Paris*, 2, 42 (1831), pp. 351–52. After discussion, the report ended up saying that cholera was essentially epidemic, but that in certain circumstances it could be spread by people: *AGM*, 26 (1831), p. 576; *Gazette médicale de Paris*, 2, 33 (1831), pp. 285–86.

[292] *Mémoires*, 3 (1833), p. 391; A. N. Gendrin, *Monographie du choléra-morbus epidémique de Paris* (Paris, 1832); E. L. Jourdain, *Conseils hygiéniques pour se préserver du choléra-morbus* (Colmar, 1832), pp. 3–5; Desruelles, *Précis physiologique*, p. 11; Boisseau, *Traité du choléra-morbus*, pp. 160–66; Trolliet, Polinière et Bottex, *Rapport sur le Choléra-Morbus* (Lyons, 1832), pp. 42, 51; Sandras, *Du choléra*, p. 93; Robert, *Lettre*, p. 21; L. A. Gosse, *Rapport sur l'épidémie de choléra en Prusse, en Russie et en Pologne* (Geneva, 1833), p. 328; J. R. L. de Kerckhove dit de Kirckhoff, *Considérations sur la nature et le traitement du choléra-morbus* (Anvers, 1833), pp. 202–03; *Gazette médicale de Paris*, 3, 58 (1832), p. 416; 3, 106 (1832), pp. 727–32; Delaporte, *Disease and Civilization*, pp. 31, 69–70.

ity and nourishment. The one novelty here was that the reign of the flannel belt seems to have met its geographical limit, a border marked by the observation that such vestments – a recommendation from northern Europe – made sense in France only during the winter.[293]

CONCLUSIONS ARE DRAWN

With the tide of experience and opinion making matters difficult for strict quarantinism, the Swedish authorities altered course. The July regulations were attacked as needlessly alarming and harmful to trade and culture. The king himself was said to be unhappy with them and may have worried about possible unrest. The Collegium Medicum reported difficulties with treating and removing the ill as well as associated disturbances and criminality.[294] Changes followed. For travelers quarantine was cut from thirty days to eight and ships were relieved of various strictures imposed earlier. Measures whose harshness threatened to impede their objectives were moderated. The 1806 law required, for example, the destruction of illegally imported goods. Fearing that this would instead encourage concealment and transmission, they were now merely to be cleansed, with incineration as but the choice of last resort.[295] The need for change was becoming increasingly obvious and a committee was established to revise precautions. Although discussions were not noted in detail, its records show that those members whose rejection of internal cordons and quarantines eventually won out based their view on foreign experience and the apparent uselessness of such measures abroad.[296] The new regulations,

[293] P. A. Enault, *Choléra-morbus: Conseils hygiéniques a suivre pour s'en préserver* (Paris, 1831), pp. 12–13; *Instruction populaire sur le choléra-morbus et rapport fait a l'Intendance sanitaire du département du Bas-Rhin par son Comité médical, et publié par cette intendance* (n.p., n.d. [1832]), pp. 10–11; *Annales*, 6 (1831), pp. 438–39; Cayol, *Instruction pratique sur le régime et le traitement du choléra-morbus épidémique au printemps de 1832* (Paris, 1832); *AGM*, 29 (1832), pp. 122–40; *Moniteur universel*, 51 (20 February 1832), pp. 497–98; 90 (30 March 1832), pp. 911–12; Trolliet et al., *Rapport*, pp. 52–53. On the other hand, belts apparently remained popular: *Moniteur universel*, 196 (15 July 1831), p. 1216; 51 (20 February 1832), pp. 497–98; *Gazette médicale de Paris*, 3, 55 (1832), p. 390.

[294] RA, Skrivelser till Kungl. Maj:t, Collegium medicum, 1834, v. 62, no. 397; Zacke, *Koleraepidemien i Stockholm*, pp. 30–31.

[295] *SFS*, 1831/21, pp. 115–16; 1831/36, pp. 249–50; 1831/49, pp. 329–30. Other moderations in quarantine regulations for ships arriving in Sweden were instituted in 1832–34: *Bidrag till allmänhetens upplysning i frågan om spärrnings- och karantäns-anstalterna mot koleran* (Stockholm, 1854), pp. 89–91; *SFS*, 1832/9, pp. 85–95; 1833/1, pp. 1–10; 1834/6.

[296] RA, ÅK 690, De under H.K.H. Kronprinsens ordförandeskap utsedde Committerade att föreslå erforderliga jämkningar uti K.K. den 9 Juli 1831 ang. åtgärder i händelse Cholerafarsoten yppades inom Riket, minutes, 5 September 1831; *Bidrag till allmänhetens upplysning*, pp. 53–54.

in November 1831, once again followed the Prussians, this time in their retreat from strict quarantinism.[297] Cordons and quarantines on Sweden's borders, still judged useful, were left in place, but similar measures within the country were no longer compulsory for travelers overland, although remaining in effect on the inland waterways, and surveillance was still allowed of itinerants and travelers. The practice of removals to hospitals was now clarified to make explicit the need for the patient's or his master's permission.[298] Sequestration was moderated by allowing free access to sickrooms, requiring only that visitors cleanse themselves before leaving.

Cholera did not hit Sweden until the summer of 1834, but even with the beast at the door, the antiquarantinist trend was too powerful simply to be reversed. In February, the principle of inspecting all foreign ships and quarantining the dangerous, nailed fast in 1806, was reaffirmed for cholera.[299] But for measures at home, the tone was more moderate. The medical authorities kept up pressure on the government to resist the temptation of tightening measures, it having been shown elsewhere that quarantinism offered little respite. The Ministry of Commerce, predictably enough, agreed with such conclusions and even the Quarantine Commission opposed internal quarantines along the roads.[300] In the Estates, the issue was debated vituperatively, with representatives from regions not yet infected standing on their right to self-protection, pitted against those who lamented the inconveniences and restrictions brought in the train of internal quarantines. One horror story concerned a farmer near Stockholm who was effectively locked in his home when neighbors tore up a bridge along one egress and posted guards along another.[301] It is hard to make much of divisions among the Chambers, except to note that, although both sides were represented in each camp, the Nobles, Clergy and Peasants were generally in agreement on the harm and cost of quarantinism, arguing for sanitationist policies instead, while many among the Burghers were convinced that external cordons had spared Sweden the disease earlier and that internal quaran-

---

[297] *SFS*, 1831/51, pp. 337–56.

[298] Although there remains some question whether patients were actually hospitalized against their will; Zacke has found two cases of this happening: Zacke, *Koleraepidemien i Stockholm*, pp. 32–33, 99–100.   [299] *SFS* 1834/6, §§5–6.

[300] RA, Skrivelser till Kungl. Maj:t, Collegium Medicum, 1833, v. 60, no. 16; 1834, v. 62, nos. 397, 507; Skrivelser till Kungl. Maj:t, Kommerskollegium, 1834, v. 469, no. 506, 9 September 1834; *Post*, 210 (11 September 1834).

[301] *Bihang*, 1834–35, v. 10/1, no. 125; 1834–35, v. 8, no. 115; *Ridderskapet och Adeln*, 1834–35, v. 12, pp. 357–61; v. 13, pp. 151–52; *Borgare*, 1834–35, v. 5, pp. 570, 574; *Ridderskapet och Adeln*, 1834–35, v. 13, pp. 38–56.

tines still had a role to play.[302] The consideration behind the Burghers' support of quarantines seems to have been that public opinion demanded the right of localities to protect themselves, with unrest otherwise a threat.[303] Those provinces already infected divided on whether to continue quarantines while the still-spared favored them.[304] Other geoepidemiologically influenced regional disputes over quarantinism pitted seaports, which saw no reason why they alone should pay for guarding the nation, against the hinterland, in agreement that quarantines were a cost of doing business for trading concerns.[305] The provinces and the countryside were regarded as more worried about the onset of cholera than the cities and more concerned to maintain cordons and quarantines.[306]

Despite the advice of its ministries and of three Chambers, the government sided with the Burgher Estate, reaffirming its policy of eliminating cordons on the major roads, but allowing localities to isolate themselves at their own expense.[307] Towns were permitted to exclude potentially infectious travelers from remaining, but not from passing through, nor could visitors from infected areas be denied lodging. Connections with the surrounding countryside were not to be severed, but markets could be relocated to suburban areas. If a town so wished and bore the costs, ships on the inland waterways could be inspected and possibly quarantined. Stockholm imposed a ten-day observation quarantine on travelers from infected areas. Örebro, surrounded by disease, preserved itself by felling logs across the roads to block access. Other

---

[302] *Bihang*, 1834–35, v. 10/1, no. 125; *Ridderskapet och Adeln*, 1834–35, v. 13, pp. 90, 156; *Bonde*, 1834, v. 6, pp. 497–99; *Borgare*, 1834–35, v. 5, pp. 557–58. From the Clergy came some of the most extensive arguments against quarantinism: *Preste*, 1834, v. 10, pp. 57–76. On the position of the Burghers, see *Borgare*, 1834–35, v. 5, pp. 562–65; *Bonde*, 1834, v. 7, pp. 44–45; *Preste*, 1835, v. 16, p. 286. Among the Peasants, there were worries that they would be excluded from buying medicine and visiting physicians if cordons were allowed: *Bonde*, 1834, v. 6, p. 502; *Preste*, 1834, v. 10, pp. 57–76. For dissenting opinions, see *Bonde*, 1834, v. 7, pp. 76–77; *Bidrag till allmänhetens upplysning*, pp. 58–77.

[303] *Borgare*, 1834–35, v. 5, pp. 560–62, 568–69, 572–74.

[304] Zacke, *Koleraepidemien i Stockholm*, pp. 67–69; *Bihang*, 1834–35, v. 8, no. 145; *Ridderskapet och Adeln*, 1834–35, v. 18, p. 72; *Bonde*, 1834, v. 6, pp. 500, 504.

[305] *Borgare*, 1834, v. 1, pp. 361–64; *Borgare*, Bilagor, 1834, no. 61, pp. 202–05; no. 79, pp. 243–44; no. 83, pp. 249–50; no. 110, pp. 320–21. This was an issue that remained contentious and raised hackles in the coastal communities that were forced to bear quarantine costs in the interests of the nation's health: *Borgare*, 1847–48, iv, pp. 386–89; *Bihang*, 1847–48, iv, 2, no. 73; *SFS*, 1850/25; 1850/53; *Bihang*, 1853–54, viii, no. 85; 1853–54, 10, 1, v. 1, no. 84.

[306] *Preste*, 1834, v. 10, pp. 84, 139–40. Besides the force of public opinion, the authorities may have worried that abolishing internal quarantines in the autumn of 1834, just after Stockholm had finally been attacked, would be seen by the provinces as a sign that the capital's health was their main concern: Zacke, *Koleraepidemien i Stockholm*, pp. 65–67; *SFS*, 1834/22.

[307] *Bihang*, 1834–35, v. 8, no. 115; Arvidsson, *De svenska koleraepidemierna*, p. 110; Zacke, *Koleraepidemien i Stockholm*, p. 64.

localities went even further, as in Falun where all gatherings, not just at taverns and inns, but also in private, were strictly forbidden on pain of fines.[308]

The outcome of Sweden's first experience with cholera was thus a more attenuated form of quarantinism than the full-blown measures initially foreseen. The motives behind this partial retreat were similar to those found in Germany. Trading interests had an influence, although, with the Burgher Estate backing quarantinism, the effect was ambiguous at best. The southern regions that, as the first victims, had already found prevention worse than the disease helped moderate quarantinist tendencies. The sheer topography of the region also worked against a quarantinist approach, with the ratio of inhabitants to acreage sufficiently disproportionate that the task of cordoning off so sparsely inhabited a nation appeared hopeless.[309] Most important for Sweden's ability to retreat from strict quarantinism, however, was its placement along the learning curve. The late arrival of the epidemic meant that the virtue of such restrictions had lost the attractions they had held in the frontline mentality of the autocracies of east-central Europe.[310]

Nor, in Britain, were the initially strict regulations maintained for long. Sentiment in Parliament did not favor a quarantinist approach. Warburton, the member for Bridgeport, stood practically alone in its favor, arguing in October 1831, with cholera in Hamburg, that cordons be drawn around infected districts.[311] The Privy Council, unwilling to accept the Central Board's strictly quarantinist recommendations, yet unable to reject them out of hand, neglected them benignly. It promised to circulate the Board's regulations as long as they were not contrary to law, full knowing that various of its provisions (especially forcible removal of the ill) could not, according to the terms of the 1825 Quarantine Act, be enforced until an infectious disease had been officially declared to exist in the country.[312] The Council juggled various interests. Commercial circles objected to more stringently quarantinist measures than necessary. In the opposite corner, much public opinion and that of many medical men looked to the government for firm meas-

---

[308] *SFS*, 1834/28; 1834/22; Arvidsson, *De svenska koleraepidemierna*, p. 110; *Borgare*, 1834–35, v. 5, p. 562; *Bidrag till allmänhetens upplysning*, p. 78. For other measures, see *SFS*, 1834/19.

[309] *Preste*, 1835, v. 16, p. 287.

[310] It was not the influence of the merchants who rejected quarantines that was decisive, said Professor Engeström, a member of the Clergy, but the experience of Russia, Prussia and Austria, where cholera had spread regardless of strict measures: *Preste*, 1835, v. 16, p. 287.

[311] *Hansard*, Commons, 1831, v. 8, col. 900; v. 9, cols. 308–09; 1832, v. 10, cols. 267–68.

[312] PRO, PC1/101, C. C. Greville to Dr. Seymour, 8 August 1831.

ures of prevention. Physicians urged the authorities to discount the claims of merchants, favoring the public weal over private gain. "A little commercial inconvenience is a small price to pay for the chance of immunity."[313] The government happily pounced on disagreements among physicians on the nature of cholera as an excuse not to invoke drastic interventions. The Council had no desire to impose measures that would bring troops into working-class districts or otherwise raise the specter of confrontation. The situation was already tense, the Reform Bill having just cleared its second reading in the Commons a few days before presentation of the Board's quarantinist recommendations. Cholera disturbances and riots of the sort familiar from the continent had broken out sporadically. The information being received by the Council about the disease increasingly cut against the grain of the Board's conclusions and, in any case, the lesson it drew from experience abroad was that cordons and internal quarantines had provoked agitation among the poor.[314]

The epidemic, however, would not sit still for the convenience of the Council. By October, when cholera struck Hamburg, decisive action and at least a semblance of official unity were required. Under likely pressure from the Council, the Board now submitted revised and more broadly acceptable regulations which did away with frightening terminology like expurgators and lazarettos, making no mention of forcible removal. The ill were to be voluntarily transferred to special isolation houses, with a conspicuous sign ("Sick") identifying their dwellings as quarantined in case of refusal. The inhabitants of infected houses were not at liberty to move about or communicate with others until after purification. Burials remained unchanged. Caretakers of the ill were to live apart from the rest of the community, families in quarantined houses to avoid all unnecessary communication with the public, their food and necessities conveyed without contact. Convalescents and their contacts were kept under observation for twenty days, cases of disease reported immediately to the local board. All intercourse with infected towns and the neighboring countryside was to be prevented by the best means within the magistrates' power. In one respect the new regulations struck a more drastic note. Were the disease ever to appear in Britain "in a terrific way," it might be necessary to draw troops or a strong body of the police around infected areas to cut off all contact with the surrounding countryside. Fifteen-day quarantines

---

[313] *EMSJ*, 58 (July 1831), p. 144.
[314] *Hansard*, Commons, 1831, v. 9, cols. 310–14; Richardson, *Death, Dissection and the Destitute*, pp. 223–30; Durey, *Return of the Plague*, pp. 16–17; *Gazette médicale de Paris*, 2, 52 (1831), p. 444.

were imposed on all ships from Sunderland in November and a ten-day quarantine on Newcastle after it was hit.[315] In Scotland, the authorities were more willing to enforce strict measures. Police stationed on the highways turned back beggars and vagrants seeking to stay in Edinburgh, keeping those in transit under observation, and visits to town from the surrounding countryside were discouraged. Fumigation and cleansing of houses and possessions followed, with the destruction of worn-out objects, replaced by the Board. The ill poor were hospitalized using every means other than outright force and contacts were also removed to temporary quarters under police charge for eight to ten days. Physicians were expected to report all cases of disease daily.[316]

In November with cholera at home, in Sunderland, the Privy Council toppled its own Board, transferring its functions to a new Board, established at the Council and manned by more experienced and workaday physicians, including Russell and Barry who had seen the disease in Russia. Where the old Board had favored coercive measures of the sort familiar from the continent, the new one put its faith in persuasion. Russell and Barry, witnesses to the failure of Russian techniques of compulsion and the ensuing riots, considered the British even less willing to accept such measures. Inspectors were now to carry out daily house-to-house visits, reporting on nuisances, deficiencies of food, clothing and bedding among the poor, ventilation of living quarters, space, habits of hygiene and temperance.[317] In York, for example, extensive cleansings of public spaces and private residences were undertaken, with teams of visitors inspecting all streets and most houses at a minimum every other day and physicians reporting new cases every morning. All measures of coercion were now frowned upon and instead, "good sense and good feeling" were relied on to undergird quarantine and isolation.[318] In December came regulations requiring rapid and streamlined burials with special precautions. Quarantine was not mentioned and a sanitationist approach was now given greater voice. The local community was urged to attend especially to the poor, assuring them a decent diet and warm clothing, or at least flannel belts and woolen stockings. In February 1832, with London invaded, the Board recommended its now familiar combination

---

[315] *Lancet*, 1 (1831–32), pp. 158–60; Brockington, *Public Health in the Nineteenth Century*, pp. 112–16; Longmate, *King Cholera*, pp. 29–30; Durey, *Return of the Plague*, pp. 19–20, 147.

[316] *Supplement to the EMSJ* (February 1832), pp. cclxvi–cclxix; *Report of the Edinburgh Board of Health*, 16 November 1831.

[317] A procedure from France that the British admired in 1831: *LMG*, 9 (1832), pp. 158–62.

[318] Barnet, "The 1832 Cholera Epidemic in York," pp. 27–31, 38; Durey, *First Spasmodic Cholera Epidemic*, p. 4; Morris, *Cholera 1832*, pp. 32–35; Durey, *Return of the Plague*, p. 25.

of sanitationist and moderately quarantinist precautions: whitewashing houses, cleaning streets, removing nuisances, setting up hospitals and isolating the ill. Theaters and public amusements were closed at the height of the epidemic. Vagrants were driven from towns or incarcerated, but other forms of communication left largely unimpeded; markets, fairs and festivals were regarded suspiciously, but allowed to continue.[319]

A major obstacle to an effective response was that the 1825 Quarantine Act did not permit precautions until the disease had actually struck and been officially declared to exist, thus by definition largely ruling out preventive action. Financing was equally a problem since the government could not order poor rates, the main source of local revenue, to be levied for public health measures.[320] Frustrated by such limitations, the government sought greater powers for the Privy Council and a cholera bill was passed in mid-February giving Councillors powers to implement measures for prevention, relief to the sick and speedy interments, all backed by the threat of fines.[321] The financing problem was solved in allowing the Council to require local overseers or Guardians of the Poor to pay for expenses incurred by the Board out of monies raised in the usual way. Over its objections, the government was forced by proposals in Parliament from both Radicals and Tories to accept having the Privy Council reimburse individual parishes for expenses they could not otherwise cover. In this way local Boards were provided with guaranteed financing only weeks before the epidemic broke out in full force and the central government accepted a large measure of responsibility for dealing with the disease.[322]

In terms of removing cholera victims from their homes, the British were scarcely distinguishable from their continental neighbors. The first Central Board of Health apparently assumed the possibility of compulsorily removing patients once the disease had struck.[323] In December 1831, the new moderate Board's regulations directed that, since space, cleanliness and pure air were the best means to recovery, patients should

---

[319] Durey, *Return of the Plague*, p. 149; Morris, *Cholera 1832*, pp. 35, 71, 103, 117–18; *PP* 1831–32 (155) xxvi, p. 479.

[320] *PP* 1831–32 (155) xxvi, pp. 10–11; Durey, *Return of the Plague*, pp. 5, 21–22, 84–85; Durey, *First Spasmodic Cholera Epidemic*, pp. 5–6, 18–19. [321] *PP* 1831–32 (153) i, 323.

[322] Longmate, *King Cholera*, p. 89; Morris, *Cholera 1832*, pp. 72–73; Durey, *Return of the Plague*, pp. 98–99, 204; *Hansard*, Commons, 1832, v. 10, cols. 337–38.

[323] Before cholera had officially been declared to exist, the Board admitted, the 1825 Quarantine Act forbade forced removals and such actions would, in any case, be "an unwarrantable attack on the Liberty of the Subject, and expose Persons and Property to great inconvenience." But what happened thereafter was another matter, although here left unspoken: PRO, PC1/4395 pt 1, Board of Health to Gilbert Blane, 4 October 1831.

be isolated in their own homes or otherwise "be induced to submit to an immediate removal" to an isolation building. In Edinburgh in 1832, the indigent and, in cases of serious overcrowding, also their neighbors were removed from their homes to houses of refuge and observed until their dwellings had been fumigated and cleansed.[324] In March 1832, the Privy Council enhanced the possibility of removals. Victims could voluntarily be evacuated to a hospital, but the Boards could also cause to be placed in a house of observation anyone who, in the opinion of two physicians, should be removed from communication with the infected or from crowded situations, with no mention of consent. By August, however, the Central Board had softened its stance. It now strongly deprecated all coercive measures of the sort proven useless on the continent. Providing medical care through public charitable institutions held out the most promising inducement to the ill to acknowledge that they were stricken and to separate voluntarily from their families.[325]

By the time cholera made its way to France at the beginning of 1832, the government, medical authorities and public opinion had, broadly speaking, reached a consensus on dealing with the epidemic. The Academy of Medicine and much medical opinion considered quarantines and sanitary cordons at the borders useful, but advised against similar precautions internally, recommending instead measures of public and private hygiene.[326] It did not take long for the government to adjust its position accordingly. In September 1831, it still insisted on a strict quarantinist approach. Wary of alienating medical opinion, it took no firm position on the nature of cholera, circumspectly noting that its tendency to follow trade and travel suggested transmissibility. Other nations had acted on the premise of contagion and the government refused to abandon the security of measures based even on a theory that might prove to be wrong. France could not refuse to emulate what *les états policés* had undertaken. Already a fortnight later, however, the force of precedence was weakening. Even strictly enforced cordons had not saved Moscow, St. Petersburg or Berlin, it was noted, but at the same time, certain circumstances, especially large agglomerations of people, could apparently render cholera contagious.[327]

---

[324] *PP* 1849 (1115) xxiv, pp. 107–08; *Supplement to the EMSJ* (February 1832), pp. cclxvi–cclxix; Morris, *Cholera 1832*, pp. 35, 103; Hilary Marland, *Medicine and Society in Wakefield and Huddersfield 1780–1870* (Cambridge, 1987), p. 43.

[325] *PP* 1831–32 (258) xxvi, p. 490; *Lancet*, 2 (1831–32), pp. 652–53.

[326] *Annales*, 6 (1831), pp. 429, 433; Delaporte, *Disease and Civilization*, pp. 24, 141–42; Beauchamp, *Delivrez-nous du mal*, pp. 88–89.

[327] Mavidal and Laurent, *Archives parlementaires*, v. II/69, pp. 456, 591–93.

The precautions implemented were in fact guided largely by the consensus of pursuing quarantinism only at the borders, sanitationism at home. Travelers and goods from abroad were quarantined and cleansed while domestic regulations took a more purely environmentalist approach, with recommendations for isolation and sequestration largely ignored.[328] Policy at home in fact amounted to last-minute stopgap measures of local sanitation. Cleanliness of dwellings was regarded as the best preservative. In August 1831 the Parisian police ordered the formation of district health commissions to implement improvements in local hygiene. Dwellings were inspected for insalubrity and owners reminded of regulations in such matters. Observers inspected public gathering places, warehouses, storage yards and private residences, regulated noxious or dangerous industries, checked sewage connections, wells, cesspools, latrines and outhouses. Letters indicating the necessary repairs were to be sent to owners, with legal proceedings the eventual result of inaction. Neighborhood sanitary commissions visited insalubrious locations, seeking to persuade citizens in positions of authority that they, in turn, should convince workers of the virtues of hygiene, enlisting their efforts to clean the city.[329] In the Luxembourg quarter alone, 924 properties were visited within two months; unhealthy conditions were reported in more than 400 and over 200 reports were sent to the prefect of police. Extra street sweepings were ordered, fountains ran continuously, houseowners were invited to whitewash their interiors, flushing sinks and basins with solutions of chloride, and prefects in the provinces were instructed to follow the Parisian example. In Toulon, streets were cleansed daily and the authorities granted extensive rights to enter private residences in pursuit of insalubrity, with recalcitrance reported to the mayor. In Metz, local authorities ordered the whitewashing of houses known to be centers of infection. Paganini's offer of a concert for the benefit of the poor in Paris was graciously accepted.[330]

Once cholera had arrived in Paris, aid stations were established in each neighborhood, medical personnel and bearers were to treat the ill

---

[328] *Rapport sur la marche et les effets du choléra-morbus dans Paris* (Paris, 1834), pp. 13–14; *Mémoires de M. Gisquet, ancien Préfet de police* (Paris, 1840), v. I, pp. 429–30; Delaporte, *Disease and Civilization*, pp. 26–27.

[329] *Mémoires de M. Gisquet*, v. I, pp. 433–34; Mavidal and Laurent, *Archives parlementaires*, v. II/69, p. 456; *Rapport sur la marche*, pp. 15–18; *AGM*, 27 (1831), pp. 279–82; Sussman, "From Yellow Fever to Cholera," pp. 232–37; Delaporte, *Disease and Civilization*, pp. 28–29.

[330] *Mémoires de M. Gisquet*, v. I, pp. 422–24; *Moniteur universel*, 90 (30 March 1832), p. 911; 93 (2 April 1832), p. 949; A. Dominique, *Le choléra à Toulon* (Toulon, 1885), pp. 8–10; Maréchal, *Rapport statistique et médical sur l'épidémie de choléra*, p. 7; *Journal des Débats* (13 April 1832), p. 2.

at home or remove them to hospitals, their dwellings purified with chloride solutions. Physicians, houseowners and tenants were obliged to report cases immediately to the police. Only those patients who could not be treated in their own dwellings were to be hospitalized and there seems to have been no question of forcing the unwilling, it being the prefect of police's opinion that patients were best cared for at home.[331] As in the more easterly nations, many among the poor refused hospitalization in fear that they were being singled out for medical poisoning.[332] The General Council of Hospitals opened all hospitals to cholera patients, but also sought to isolate them in separate wards, forbidding communication with them and refusing admission to family and friends. The bodies of the deceased were not allowed to lie in state in the church, nor delivered to their families, and could be removed if necessary less than twenty-four hours after death. As in other nations, however, such initially strict precautions were quickly abandoned under the pressure of events.[333]

Both autocratic and more liberal nations thus followed the dictates of the Pascallian logic of their predicament, assuming the worst in the face of an unknown but possibly devastating eventuality. All nations under the glass here began quarantinist only to conclude that such strict interventions were unenforceable and unnecessary. In each the popular masses resisted prophylactic dictates in contradiction to their customs, sometimes favoring but often rejecting quarantinist measures. In each, trading and commercial interests had mixed motives, while exerting a generally moderating force on the strictness of precautions imposed. In all the initial pretensions of the central authorities to control the response from the capital quickly gave way to a delegation of power and initiative out to the localities. Where they differed was in the rapidity and extent of the rollback. The liberal nations, relying on the lessons drawn from the frontline experience of their neighbors in east-central Europe, were able to pull back quicker and further. The fact that they were also the ones favorably placed along the geoepidemiological learning curve was no coincidence. Sweden was in this sense slightly anomalous, with

---

[331] *Mémoires de M. Gisquet*, v. I, pp. 435–36. Although there was at least one case of a man alone in a garret lying amidst his own vomit and feces who was removed despite his protestations: Sussman, "From Yellow Fever to Cholera," pp. 269–70.

[332] AN, F⁷ 9734ᴬ, Préfecture de l'Indre, 2ᵉ Bureau, to the Minister of the Interior, Chateauroux, 20 June 1832; Sussman, "From Yellow Fever to Cholera," pp. 276ff., 282ff.; Delaporte, *Disease and Civilization*, p. 55.

[333] M. Blondel, *Rapport sur les épidémies cholériques de 1832 et de 1849, dans les établissements dépendant de l'administration générale de l'assistance publique de la ville de Paris* (Paris, 1850), pp. 46–47.

two extra years to contemplate the lessons of the epidemic and yet willing to follow the Prussian lead in only partially retracting its quarantinist approach.

Even the autocracies drastically changed their initial plans to deal with cholera within months of its appearance. Such an ability to wheel the policy machinery around within a surprisingly small radius undermines the Ackerknechtian claim of an inherent fit between political regime and public health strategy, with the autocracies naturally tending toward quarantinism. In fact, a contradictory argument might be made with equal plausibility: despite their interventionist bluster and bluff, the autocracies were those regimes which were least able to sustain measures that impinged on their subjects' liberties. Lacking the popular legitimacy that supported more liberal regimes, they were ultimately weaker in their ability to demand sacrifices of their citizens. Each precautionary measure had to be cautiously calibrated for fear of provoking resistance, with swift policy changes following threats and fears of popular unrest, sometimes outright rebellion.

This was the point made by Moreau de Jonnès, the French quarantinist who observed transrhinean developments with the caustic conviction that the Germans had overdone an approach that was basically correct. The Prussians and the Austrians, he thought, fearing insurrection more than cholera, were in fact dependent on popular whim for the precautions they could implement. Starting out with a harshly interventionist approach, they were forced by the threat of dissatisfaction to change their tune. But precisely such erratic behavior, precipitously abandoning the measures that were at first enforced with threats of death, switching abruptly from strict to a more moderated form of quarantinism – such tergiversations undermined their authority. Because these governments appeared incapable of steering a steady prophylactic course, many of their subjects were given cause to believe that cholera and its attendant precautions were a conspiracy against the poor, making a mockery of whatever benevolent intentions the authorities could hope to claim.[334]

Though it underestimates the prophylactic vacillation found in common across all nations, whatever their political stripe, Moreau de Jonnès's argument has the advantage of not taking at face value the autocracies' own evaluations of their ability to intervene against cholera,

[334] PRO, PC1/108, Moreau de Jonnès to Pym, 9 October 1831; 17 September 1831; 21 September 1831.

a belief that Ackerknecht implicitly accepts, and instead punctures the myth of decisive autocratic power. But even though he turns Ackerknecht's reasoning on its head, like him, Moreau de Jonnès presupposed a close tie between a political regime and its strategies of preventive intervention. The truth of that is one of the issues that remains to be examined. Moreover, to the extent that there is such a connection between politics and prophylaxis, the interesting question is: which caused what? Did political instinct determine preventive response, or was it pride of place along the learning curve that, allowing Britain and France to be prophylactically insouciant, also helped cement their political liberalism? It is to an untangling of these different strands that we must now turn, as cholera became a repeat visitor in Europe during the nineteenth century.

CHAPTER 3

Cholera comes of age

The first wave of cholera had broken unexpectedly over Europe, pro-voking at first reactions that were little more than the application of lessons learnt from past attacks of pestilential disease. Already during this first pandemic, however, it became clear that inherited quarantin-ist strategies would not necessarily prove effective this time. Examining their own experience and that of their predecessors, each nation under-went an epidemiological learning process that undercut the standing of quarantinism. In cholera's second phase, the half-century from the late 1830s up through Koch's discovery of the comma bacillus as the disease's cause and the gradual acceptance in official circles of its pre-ventive implications during the late 1880s and early nineties, a similar process of experimentation, trial, error and the accumulation of expe-rience continued. This increase in knowledge, though commonly shared among all nations, did not, however, lead in any automatic sense to uniform prophylactic strategies. States continued to take divergent approaches to cholera and other contagious diseases; indeed it may well have been that differences in national preventive tactics increased. Why, given a shared and increasingly accepted basis of knowledge, different tacks to a common problem persisted, is the question in need of an answer.

In the decades following the first epidemic, medical opinion remain-ed largely unformed, while public health authorities continued the retreat from their initially strict quarantinism. As it became increas-ingly clear that cholera was not as directly contagious as the plague, as experience showed that the medical personnel in closest contact were not necessarily more afflicted than others, that its incidence varied by class, season, region, neighborhood and person, the evidence seemed to mount that something other than a contagium was at work, that local factors or predisposing causes associated either with the individ-ual, the locality or both, were equally part of and perhaps indeed the whole story. Contagionism ceded ground to a variety of localist approaches.[1]

In the German states, much medical opinion considered the ongoing dispute between contagionists and their opponents undecided, often simply because sufficient knowledge was lacking.[2] From the failure of cordons and similar restrictive measures others concluded that quarantinism was untenable.[3] That cholera might share the characteristics of different diseases or that it was not classifiable according to the inherited dichotomy was a widespread view.[4] Miasmatists and other localists of every stripe found their ranks swelling and theirs was often considered the dominant opinion.[5] Largely because of the failure of their methods to ward off the disease, contagionists were now on the defensive. A few clung tenaciously to inherited certainties; others merely lamented the declining fortunes of their position.[6] Most, however, moderated the strict position initially adopted, now advocating instead measures that offered adequate protection while causing as little offense as possible: limiting quarantines or replacing them with other measures, sequester-

[1] *Monatsblatt für öffentliche Gesundheitspflege*, 17, 6 (1894), pp. 89–90; Lorenz von Stein, *Handbuch der Verwaltungslehre* (2nd edn.; Stuttgart, 1876), pp. 170–71.

[2] *(Allgemeine Cholera-Zeitung)*, 5, 101 (22 August 1832), cols. 65–71; H. W. Buek, *Die Verbreitungsweise der epidemischen Cholera, mit besonderer Beziehung auf den Streit über die Contagiosität derselben* (Halle, 1832), p. 3; Moritz Bruck, *Das Wesen und die Behandlung der asiatischen Cholera* (Berlin, 1841), p. v; Karl Julius Wilhelm Paul Remer and Ludwig Ad. Neugebauer, *Die asiatische Cholera, ihre Behandlung und die Mittel sich gegen sie zu verwahren* (Görlitz, 1848), p. ix.

[3] Ernst August Ludwig Hübener, *Die Lehre von der Ansteckung, mit besonderer Beziehung auf die sanitätspolizeiliche Seite derselben* (Leipzig, 1842), p. 320; C. J. Le Viseur, *Über die Cholera und die erfolgreichste Kur derselben* (2nd edn.; Posen, 1868), pp. 7–8.

[4] Moritz Ernst Adolph Naumann, *Grundzüge der Contagienlehre* (Bonn, 1833), pp. 12–18; *ASA*, 3 (1838), pp. 135–36; Karl Christian Anton, *Die bewährtesten Heilformeln für die epidemische Cholera* (Leipzig, 1849); *DZSA*, 3 (1855), pp. 11–13; n.F., 8 (1856), pp. 3–4; *Vierteljahrsschrift für gerichtliche und öffentliche Medicin*, 5 (1854), pp. 288–89; E. Cordes, *Die Cholera in Lübeck* (Lübeck, 1861), pp. 9–10, 60; *Medicinisches Correspondenz-Blatt des Württembergischen ärztlichen Vereins*, 48, 19 (10 July 1877), p. 145; William Bulloch, *The History of Bacteriology* (London, 1938), p. 164.

[5] E. H. C. Kölpin, *Skizze der Seuchen-Lehre* (Stettin, 1838), pp. 7–9, 36; *Cholera Orientalis*, 4, 61-80 (1833), pp. 1039–40; G. Ludwig Dieterich, *Beobachtung und Behandlung des wandernden Brechdurchfalles in München* (Nuremberg, 1837), pp. 44–45; Anton, *Heilformeln*, pp. 58–59; Otto Behr, *Die Cholera in Deutschland* (Leipzig, 1848), pp. 5–13; G. F. Stiemer, *Die Cholera: Ihre Ätiologie und Pathogenese, Ihre Prophylaxe und Therapie* (Königsberg, 1858), pp. 234–35, 240–41; C. J. Heidler, *Die Schutzmittel gegen die Cholera mit Rücksicht auf ein ursächliches Luftinfusorium und dessen nicht-contagiöse Natur* (Prague, 1854); Fr. Oesterlen, *Choleragift und Pettenkofer* (Tübingen, 1868); Fr. Schneider, *Verbreitung und Wanderung der Cholera* (Tübingen, 1877), pp. 34–41; G. Honert, *Die Cholera und ihre Ursache* (2nd edn.; Iserlohn, 1885), p. 1; Remer and Neugebauer, *Die asiatische Cholera*, pp. 51–52; *Allgemeine Zeitung für Chirurgie, innere Heilkunde und ihre Hülfswissenschaften*, 48 (26 November 1843), p. 389.

[6] *Medicinische Zeitung* (Berlin), 20, 1 (1851), pp. 1–2; Carl Axmann, *Die indische Cholera und das Ganglien-Nervensystem nebst Bemerkungen über die Verhütung der Cholera* (Erfurt, 1867), pp. 46–47; Hübener, *Lehre von der Ansteckung*, pp. vii–x; [Franz] Pruner-Bey, *Die Weltseuche Cholera oder die Polizei der Natur* (Erlangen, 1851), pp. 57–60; Julius Wilbrand, *Die Desinfection im Grossen bei Cholera-Epidemien* (2nd edn.; Hildesheim, 1873), p. 123.

ing the ill in a less drastic manner.[7] In Sweden, similar ambiguity reigned. Anticontagionism was strongly represented, the 1834 epidemic having taught some the lesson that cholera was not directly transmissible. In Gothenburg at midcentury, most physicians went further to conclude that the disease had arisen spontaneously from local circumstances and an all-Nordic scientific congress in 1851 was heavily dominated by antiquarantinists. Old-fashioned miasmatists abounded among doctors and especially in the Swedish Physicians' Association.[8] But so did contagionists who thought cholera spread by personal contact.[9] Many adopted the halfway position of contingent contagionism.[10]

While the movement away from the contagionism and quarantinism of the first phase was hesitant and ambiguous in Germany and Sweden, French and British opinion inclined more clearly in this direction. In France, both medical and official views, having been strongly anticontagionist already during the 1830s, tended in the aftermath of the epidemic to be almost unanimously converted. At midcentury, the lesson widely drawn was that quarantinism was of little avail compared to measures aimed at local causes.[11] Official preventive instructions insisted on the safety of normal contact with the ill, while analysis of the Paris

[7] Franz Brefeld, *Die endliche Austilgung der asiatischen Cholera* (Breslau, 1854), pp. 48, 55ff.; *Magazin für die gesammte Heilkunde*, 43, 2 (1835), pp. 316–20, 334, 340–46; *Medicinische Zeitung* (Berlin), 21, 36 (8 September 1852), pp. 169–71; Mecklenburg, *Was vermag die Sanitäts-Polizei gegen die Cholera?* (Berlin, 1854), pp. 29–31; August Hirsch, *Über die Verhütung und Bekämpfung der Volkskrankheiten mit spezieller Beziehung auf die Cholera* (Berlin, 1875).

[8] *Hygiea*, 10, 2 (February 1848), p. 97; H. I. Carlson, *Iakttagelser om Choleran under epidemien i Göteborg 1850* (Gothenburg, 1851), p. 42; Lars Öberg, *Göteborgs Läkarsällskap: En historik* (Gothenburg, 1983), pp. 120–21; *Bidrag till allmänhetens upplysning i frågan om spärrnings- och karantäns-anstalterna mot koleran* (Stockholm, 1854), p. 44; Gust. von Düben, *Om karantäner och spärrningar mot kolera, enligt svensk erfarenhet* (Stockholm, 1854), pp. 35–38; Hilding Bergstrand, *Svenska Läkaresällskapet 150 år: Dess tillkomst och utveckling* (Lund, 1958), pp. 188, 196–97, 200–01; F. Lennmalm, *Svenska Läkaresällskapets historia 1808–1908* (Stockholm, 1908), pp. 288–89; *Post*, 242 (17 October 1850).

[9] Fr. Th. Berg, *Sammandrag af officiella rapporter om Cholerafarsoten i Sverge år 1850* (Stockholm, 1851), p. 340; [Georg Swederus], *Till Svenska Läkaresällskapet, från En af Allmänheten (Om Koleran)* (Stockholm, 1850), pp. 9–12; *Hygiea*, 18, 1 (January 1856), p. 23; 10, 8 (August 1848), p. 494; 11, 1 (January 1849), p. 4.

[10] A. Timoleon Wistrand, *Kort skildring af Sveriges tredje kolera-epidemi i jemförelse med andra samtidigt gängse farsoters härjningar* (Stockholm, 1855), pp. 83–85; L. A. Soldin, *Åtgärder, egnade att i betydlig mån skydda såväl kommuner som enskilda mot asiatisk kolera* (Gothenburg, 1855), pp. 8–13; [Ewerlöf], *Några ord om den sednaste Cholera-epidemien med hufvudsakligt afseende på Svenska Quarantaine-väsendet* (Copenhagen, 1854), pp. 3–5; *Bidrag till allmänhetens upplysning*, p. 18.

[11] Aladane de Lalibarde, *Etudes sur le choléra épidémique: Sa nature et son traitement* (Paris, 1851), pp. 56–58; C. Rousset, *Traité du choléra-morbus de 1849* (Paris, 1851), pp. 10–13, 124–25; Martinenq, *Choléra de Toulon* (Toulon, 1848), pp. 35–38; Ambroise Tardieu, *Du choléra épidémique* (Paris, 1849), pp. 188–93; Tardieu, *Dictionnaire d'hygiène publique et de salubrité* (Paris, 1852), v. I, p. 301; Félix Maréchal, *Rapport statistique et médical sur l'épidémie de choléra qui a régné à Metz et dans le département de la Moselle en 1832* (Metz, 1839), p. 35; *Moniteur universel*, 102 (12 April 1849), pp. 1331–32.

epidemic in 1849 emphasized social and hygienic factors behind cholera's spread, advocating sanitary improvements.[12] Contagionists were correspondingly thin on the ground.[13] The doctrine was rejected as alarmist and egotistical, frightening the masses and undercutting efforts to care for the sick.[14] During the 1840s, Chervin continued his relentless attack on the whole notion of contagion and its attendant quarantinism and the plague was tirelessly debated in this context at the Academy of Medicine.[15] Early in the decade, Aubert-Roche called for a rollback of maritime quarantine. The report in 1846 of a committee, appointed by the Academy and chaired by Prus, to examine the plague emphasized local predisposing factors, questioning the extremes to which quarantine had been taken.[16] The 1848 revolution intervened before much could be done to implement such antiquarantinist sentiments, but two years later the French began to make good on their ambitions by calling the first International Sanitary Conference in hopes of regularizing and reducing the quarantines imposed at Mediterranean ports and, more generally, reconciling the liberty of communication, commerce and trade with the dictates of public health.[17]

While the French had thus fully abjured contagionism by midcentury, it was in Britain that the move away from quarantinism and toward a fullblown sanitationist position went furthest. Anticontagionism and antiquarantinism here became firmly entrenched, although far from uniformly shared along the full gamut of medical thought. Much opinion on cholera and other epidemic diseases had become heavily anticontagionist after the thirties and remained so during the following decades. The debate on the plague sparked by Maclean continued into the forties, with the Indian doctors trotted out once again and quaran-

---

[12] *Moniteur universel*, 91 (1 April 1849), p. 1168; 113 (23 April 1849), pp. 1497–98; *Annales*, 2/1 (1854), p. 95; *Mémoires*, 17 (1853), p. 383.

[13] An isolated example is Delagrange, *Mémoire contre le choléra d'asie, la peste d'orient et les fléaux dits contagieux ou diversement transmissibles* (Paris, 1850), p. 5.

[14] Amédée Latour, "A propos du cholera de l'Angleterre," *L'union médicale*, 7, 111 (17 September 1853); J.-F. Sérée, *Traité sur la nature, le siége et le traitement du cholera* (Pau, 1865), p. 126; *Bulletin*, 14 (1848–49), p. 824.

[15] *Bulletin*, 6 (1840–41), pp. 532–33, 664–65, 787–94; 7 (1841–42), pp. 60, 307ff., 429ff.; *L'union médicale*, 7, 72 (18 June 1853), p. 285; *Moniteur universel*, 20 June 1843, p. 1566; *Lancet*, 1 (1844), pp. 20–23; Ilza Veith, "Plague and Politics," *BHM*, 28, 5 (September–October 1954), p. 409.

[16] *Annales*, 33 (1845), pp. 240–43; *Moniteur universel*, 171 (20 June 1843), p. 1566; *Bulletin*, 9 (1843–44), pp. 200–12; *Rapport à l'Académie royale de médecine sur la peste et les quarantaines fait, au nom d'une commission, par M. le Dr Prus* (Paris, 1846).

[17] Although the government shortened quarantine periods and established a system of public health inspectors in foreign ports in 1847 as a result of the Prus report: George Weisz, *The Medical Mandarins: The French Academy of Medicine in the Nineteenth and Early Twentieth Centuries* (New York, 1995), p. 77; *Conférence 1851*, 2, p. 3; 7, annexe; 11, pp. 5–12.

tinism attacked as harmful to trade, prosperity and happiness.[18] It was at the General Board of Health under Chadwick and Southwood Smith during the 1840s, however, that sanitationism was not only elaborated in its classic terms, but also for a period became official policy, nailing fast a localist approach to disease etiology and prevention that would set British strategies at variance with those pursued on the continent.[19] Cholera, in the Board's view, was the product not of something imported, but of morbid atmospheric constitutions, brought forth most generally by filth and the putrid emanations of decomposing organic matter.[20] Since its source could invariably be traced back to a neglect of hygienic precautions, keeping it out by means of quarantines was therefore like Milton's man who thought to "pound up" the crows by shutting his park gates.[21]

Sanitationism, in its all-explaining Chadwickian version, was more than just an account of disease etiology. At its broadest, it was a totalizing worldview resting on certain presuppositions concerning the balance of nature and the role of illness and disease in the divine harmony of the universe.[22] Epidemics were nature's revenge on those who neglected its laws, as John Sutherland put it in a remarkably succinct and lucid statement of the essentials of the sanitationist position at the 1851 International Sanitary Conference.[23] Disease was the outcome of a disequilibrium in the natural harmony, the preventible result of filth and putrefaction. To such a single unified cause of disease there corresponded a monolithic view of illness itself. Sanitationist etiology glossed over distinctions among epidemic ailments, classified for its purposes

[18] *Mémoires*, 28 (1867–68), p. 176; *British and Foreign Medical Review*, 16 (October 1843), pp. 289–91; Gavin Milroy, *Quarantine as It Is, and as It Ought to Be* (London, 1859), pp. 4–7; *PP* 1849 (1070) xxiv, pp. 125–26; 1854–55 (1869) xlv, pp. 76–77; J. Gillkrest, *Cholera Gleanings* (Gibraltar, 1848), pp. 2–15; *London Medical and Surgical Journal*, 7 (1835), pp. 699–702; *LMG*, n.s., 3 (1846), pp. 201–03; Gavin Milroy, *The Cholera Not to Be Arrested by Quarantine* (London, 1847), pp. 32–35; White, *The Evils of Quarantine Laws and Non-Existence of Pestilential Contagion* (London, 1837); *Medical Times*, n.s., 3 (1851), pp. 100–01; *Journal of Public Health*, 2 (1849), pp. 15–16.

[19] Margaret Pelling, *Cholera, Fever and English Medicine 1825–1865* (Oxford, 1978), pp. 36–39; W. M. Frazer, *A History of English Public Health 1834–1939* (London, 1950), pp. 38–39.

[20] PRO, FO 881/299, "Letter from the General Board of Health respecting the spread of Cholera in this Country, and the inutility of Quarantine Regulations for preventing its introduction," 1 December 1848; *PP* 1850 (1273) xxi, 3, pp. 45–58; *Hansard*, Lords, 1848, v. 101, col. 614.

[21] PRO, MH 5/1, General Board of Health, minutes, 26 April 1849; *BFMCR*, 5, 9–10 (January 1850), pp. 223–25; *PP* 1852 (1473) xx, p. 3; *Edinburgh Review*, 96 (1852), p. 408; William Fergusson, *Letters upon Cholera Morbus* (London, 1832), pp. 10–11.

[22] Lloyd G. Stevenson, "Science down the Drain: On the Hostility of Certain Sanitarians to Animal Experimentation, Bacteriology and Immunology," *BHM*, 29, 1 (January–February 1955); Gerry Kearns, "Private Property and Public Health Reform in England 1830–1870," *Social Science and Medicine*, 26, 1 (1988), pp. 188–89, 196. [23] *Conférence 1851*, 39, pp. 9–14.

unifiedly as filth diseases or fevers. Influenza, yellow fever, plague, typhus and cholera – all were individual variations of illnesses caused by insalubrious conditions. Stench generally indicated the presence of putrid material dangerous to health and, in this still innocently protoindustrial era, the malodorous decomposition of organic matter was considered less innocuous than more visible industrial pollution.[24] Discounting both the general atmospheric causes that had earlier been an important analytical category for comprehending epidemic disease and the influence of individual predisposing factors, Chadwickian sanitationists focused on the hygienic misconditions of squalid urban surroundings. While fevers would be prevented outright by sanitation, other diseases, even the undeniably transmissible, could at least be moderated in this fashion. Prophylactically, sanitationism implied that prevention was better than cure and that measures affecting society as a whole were more effective than those targeted at individuals, either in hopes of treating them post facto or of preventing transmission by sequestering the ill.[25] Breaking chains of transmission, the heart of the quarantinist approach, paled in effectiveness compared to attacking the root of disease through general sanitary reform, providing potable water and breathable air, removing filth, detritus and excrement, ensuring decent, spacious, well-lit and ventilated housing. The distinction still drawn in other nations between measures imposed within the country and those taken at its borders against arriving vessels and travelers blurred in the sanitationist view. The same hygienic measures applied to the urban environment were also to be enforced at sea and, with shipshape vessels, disease would be excluded without resort to quarantines. Ultimately all nations would become immune to epidemic diseases through sanitationist reform, rendering superfluous any sort of precautions against their import.[26]

Sanitationism was a remarkably consistent and unified vision that combined social reform and public hygiene in a seamless whole. All epidemic diseases were to be prevented, or at least ameliorated, in one fell swoop while at the same time social problems were addressed that, in the

[24] Pelling, *Cholera, Fever and English Medicine*, pp. 46–49 and passim; Charles E. Rosenberg, *Explaining Epidemics and Other Studies in the History of Medicine* (Cambridge, 1992), pp. 93–94; *PP* 1850 (1273) xxi, 3, pp. 45–58; *Conférence 1851*, 29, annexe 1, annexe 1 to annexe 1; John M. Eyler, *Victorian Social Medicine: The Ideas and Methods of William Farr* (Baltimore, 1979), p. 102; James C. Riley, *The Eighteenth-Century Campaign to Avoid Disease* (New York, 1987), p. 111.

[25] *PP* 1886 (4873) xxxi, 763, pp. 107–09.

[26] PRO, MH 5/1, General Board of Health, minutes, 23 April 1849, 25 May 1849; *PP* 1849 (1070) xxiv, pp. 100–01; 18 & 19 Vict. c. 116, s. 11; William Baly and William W. Gull, *Reports on Epidemic Cholera Drawn up at the Desire of the Cholera Committee of the Royal College of Physicians* (London, 1854), pp. 214–32; *Conférence 1851*, 39, pp. 9–14.

quarantinist view, were tangential to epidemiological considerations. Housing reform and disease prevention, for example, went hand in hand, part and parcel of the same grand vision of a society that through its concern with public health also improved the lives of its poorest. Hygienic reforms providing all with potable water and efficient waste removal and social change to ensure the poorest what had formerly been a middle-class standard of dwelling and diet: such was the sanitationists' modest prescription for preventing epidemic disease. Best of all, sanitationism was a self-sustaining program of reform that not only improved matters for all, but paid for itself. In the short term, the excrement and offal removed from cities would fertilize and boost the productivity of surrounding farmland.[27] Over the long haul, the cost of bad hygienic conditions was expected to outstrip that of ameliorating them. The national interest in terms other than the narrowly pecuniary was also served by sanitation. Healthy living conditions promised to produce contented workers, able-bodied recruits, fertile parents. The social expense of early mortality and shortened work lives would be lessened, the criminality associated with poor living conditions reduced. Ultimately, hygiene promised to elevate public morality, with decent housing prompting improvements in working-class habits, clothing, furniture, taste and morale. Hygiene, as the French caricatured the British view, was indeed civilization.[28]

But if sanitationism was official policy at the Board, it did not reign unchallenged. A large minority of medical opinion remained contagionist, with the Royal College of Physicians, for example, in 1848 admitting a role for human intercourse in cholera's spread.[29] The extremity of the Board's position brought it into conflict with those who continued to regard certain diseases, including cholera, as transmissible. The contagionists saw the Board under Chadwick and Southwood Smith dominated by nonphysicians with little medical expertise. Chadwick in turn dismissed such opponents as more interested in curing than preventing disease and ignorant of the nuts and bolts of sanitary science.[30] In 1848, when the Board issued its most dogmatically sanitationist pronouncement yet, suggesting that medical expertise prevented an appreciation of

[27] Although this point was controversial: see Christopher Hamlin, "Providence and Putrefaction: Victorian Sanitarians and the Natural Theology of Health and Disease," *Victorian Studies*, 28, 3 (Spring 1985), pp. 381–411.   [28] *Conférence 1851*, 39, pp. 9–14.

[29] Baly and Gull, *Reports on Epidemic Cholera*, pp. 214–32.

[30] R. A. Lewis, *Edwin Chadwick and the Public Health Movement 1832–1854* (London, 1952), pp. 191–94; Michael Durey, *The Return of the Plague: British Society and the Cholera 1831–1832* (Dublin, 1979), p. 208.

its insights and attacking physicians who continued to regard cholera as contagious and quarantines useful, the medical community lashed back.[31] This was the report, full of "zymotic gibberish," which convinced its opponents that the Board was (in the words of the *Lancet*) "wedded to a theory."[32] In 1854, prompted also by the Chadwickian Board's centralizing ambitions, the Commons mounted a counterattack, replacing its members with more moderate officials. Yet despite this correction in course from an extreme to a more tempered form of public hygiene, the basic approach taken by the British authorities was more distinctively sanitationist than any mustered on the continent.

LEARNING FROM THE THIRTIES

This chastened approach to cholera that followed the first epidemic – moderation, even a denial, of quarantinist instincts on the continent, forays into sanitationism in Britain – was reflected in official policy. In 1835, Prussia drew its conclusions from the epidemic in the first general regulation on contagious disease to reveal a softening of, though hardly a full retreat from, the strict quarantinism of the early thirties.[33] Cholera was still thought to be spread through contagion, but it was now ranked below other diseases (VD, smallpox and typhus) in the virulence of its infectiveness and the precautions marshaled against it were moderated.[34] Sanitation played a greater role than earlier, with commissions to be established in all cities to mitigate insalubrious conditions. In other respects, the 1835 regulation made official the moderated quarantinism adopted in the autumn of 1831: crowds dispersed, public institutions other than churches and schools closed, markets suspended or restricted, limitations on travel, removal of the ill to hospitals, but not generally against the wishes of the family head, partial sequesterings of infected houses, bodies interred in the usual graveyards if harmless, otherwise in special confessionally consecrated cemeteries, sealed coffins, deep

[31] *PP* 1849 (1070) xxiv, p. 20.
[32] Pelling, *Cholera, Fever and English Medicine*, pp. 63–65, 74–75; J. C. McDonald, "The History of Quarantine in Britain During the 19th Century," *BHM*, 25 (1951), pp. 32–33; John Simon, *English Sanitary Institutions* (London, 1890), pp. 225–26.
[33] *Gesetz-Sammlung*, 1835, 27/1678, pp. 239–86; Richard S. Ross, "The Prussian Administrative Response to the First Cholera Epidemic in Prussia in 1831" (Ph.D. diss, Boston College, 1991), pp. 207–11. This remained in effect until replaced by the Prussian law on contagious diseases of 1905: Schmedding and Engels, *Die Gesetze betreffend Bekämpfung übertragbarer Krankheiten* (2nd edn.; Münster, 1929), pp. 20, 196.
[34] "Belehrung über ansteckende Krankheiten," *Anhang zur Gesetz-Sammlung*, 1835, Beilage B zu No. 27 gehörig, pp. 2–4.

graves, no wakes. Punishments were reduced from jail and possibly death in the initial measures to fines.[35] Ships from infected areas were subject to a mere four-day observation quarantine, except in harbors themselves stricken, which could dispense with this.

If Prussia tacked in a moderately quarantinist direction, Bavaria set sail for different shores altogether. Spared the disease until 1836, it was their favorable geoepidemiological position that allowed the Bavarians to avoid deploying the full arsenal of quarantinism. The first regulations in 1831 had largely followed the Prussian lead, but in 1836, once it had become clear how little such an approach had helped, the Bavarians struck out in a sanitationist direction.[36] It was in Mittenwald, near Garmisch-Partenkirchen, that the new techniques of public hygiene later generalized throughout Bavaria were first tried.[37] Soup and clothing were distributed to the needy, the streets cleansed, food inspected. A collective once-daily ringing of the bells for all deceased substituted for what would otherwise have been a constant and disconcerting tintinnabulation. The main innovation, however, was the medical visitations. Working on the premise that fullblown cholera was often preceded by initial diarrhea and could best be cured if treated early, the ambition was to provide even the poorest with treatment at the onset of symptoms. Ten young physicians were dispatched to Mittenwald to assist the two already present, each responsible for some twenty houses, visiting all daily to seek out cases of diarrhea, prescribe dietary strictures and offer the appropriate therapy.

The regulations promulgated shortly thereafter for all of Bavaria in September 1836 followed the example set here.[38] Even if cholera were contagious, a quarantinist approach, these concluded, had been burdensome and impractical, doing more harm than good by upsetting the population. Instead, measures to promote cleanliness were now emphasized, inspecting food, disinfecting excrement and cleansing lavatories, drains and sewers. Bars and restaurants, the scene of potential dietary excesses, were to close at their appointed hours, but inns would not be shut for fear of provoking unrest, nor should markets and fairs be prohibited unless

---

[35] Maria Petzold, "Die Cholera in Berlin unter besonderer Berücksichtigung sozialmedizinischer und städtehygienischer Gesichtspunkte" (MD diss., Freie Universität Berlin, 1974), p. 92.

[36] Aloys Martin, ed., *Haupt-Bericht über die Cholera-Epidemie des Jahres 1854 im Königreiche Bayern* (Munich, 1857), pp. 838–40; Max von Pettenkofer, *Über Cholera mit Berücksichtigung der jüngsten Choleraepidemie in Hamburg* (Munich, 1892), pp. 36–37.

[37] Karl Pfeufer, *Bericht über die Cholera-Epidemie in Mittenwald* (Munich, 1837).

[38] *ASA*, 3, 1 (1838), pp. 235–47; Freymuth, *Giebt es ein praktisch bewährtes Schutzmittel gegen die Cholera? Versuch zur Rettung der Haus-zu-Hausbesuch?* (Berlin, 1875), pp. 2–6.

the local inhabitants so desired. Families were never to be removed against their will – an unjustifiable administrative intervention – but empty housing should be made available to relieve overcrowding. The schools were to remain open, with parents deciding whether to send their children. The deceased were to be viewed promptly after death, but burials otherwise conducted as usual. A concern for timely medical intervention also prompted imitation of the house-to-house visits tried in Mittenwald, with physicians attending families once or twice daily, checking for early symptoms and providing food, fuel, bedding and clothing as required.[39]

Germany's other states positioned themselves between Prussia's moderated quarantinism and Bavarian sanitationism. Baden ended obligatory hospitalization of the ill in 1836.[40] Many localities threw up their hands when cholera reappeared in the revolutionary year 1848, making few if any attempts to contain the epidemic. The experts could not agree on its nature, one observer lamented, and after the failures of the 1830s, the authorities had simply thrown in the towel. The officials of Aachen, concluding that cholera was noncontagious and hoping to avoid added expenses and statutory interference amidst political turmoil, forswore sequestration, establishing neither quarantines nor a cholera hospital. In Lübeck, cordons were declared useless and few were undertaken; in Düsseldorf, earlier regulations were moderated.[41] As elsewhere, the authorities in Hamburg strove to avoid anything that might arouse popular fears, whether public notices calling attention to cholera before its arrival or quarantinist measures thereafter. Quarantines and cordons had not worked in the 1830s, an observer who formulated the consensus in Germany at midcentury argued, and now, with political upheaval and economic downturn, they would be even more disastrous. At best some commonsense precautions should suffice: permitting fairs and markets, but not vulgar amusements and nocturnal carousing. Closing public theaters would rightly be seen as a blow to personal freedom and, while large performances should be discouraged, garden concerts on warm, sunny days were unobjectionable.

[39] Martin, *Haupt-Bericht*, pp. 856–57; Freymuth, *Giebt es ein praktisch bewährtes Schutzmittel*, pp. 10–11.
[40] Francisca Loetz, *Vom Kranken zum Patienten: "Medikalisierung" und medizinische Vergesellschaftung am Beispiel Badens 1750–1850* (Stuttgart, 1993), p. 166.
[41] Brefeld, *Die endliche Austilgung*, pp. 4–5; Egon Schmitz-Cliever, "Die Anschauungen vom Wesen der Cholera bei den Aachener Epidemien 1832–1866," *Sudhoffs Archiv*, 36, 4 (December 1952), pp. 264–65, 273–74; Georg Fliescher, *Die Choleraepidemien in Düsseldorf* (Düsseldorf, 1977), pp. 15–16; Dietrich Helm, *Die Cholera in Lübeck* (Neumünster, 1979), p. 30; Cordes, *Die Cholera in Lübeck*, pp. 7–8, 53.

Public balls and masquerades were precluded, bars to close early, but schools and churches kept open.[42]

In this dichotomy between the moderated quarantinism of Prussia and the incipient sanitationism of Bavaria, Sweden hewed to the Prussian side, toeing the quarantinist line well into midcentury and only hesitantly abandoning it. In the years following the 1834 epidemic, precautions were at first relaxed. In 1838, quarantines for foreign ships were cut to five days and, in 1840, the inspections required of vessels by the 1834 legislation were abolished.[43] This trend away from restrictive measures slowed, however, in the forties. Despite objections that Sweden's continued quarantinist approach marked it as culturally inferior and out of step with the prophylactic reconsideration underway elsewhere in Europe, the government pressed ahead in the old spirit.[44] When cholera struck Russia in 1847, ships from there and Finland were once again subject to inspections and, if victims were found onboard, quarantine. Health certificates were subsequently required of all ships from Russia and Finland, with five-day observation quarantines for those without, even in the absence of illness onboard. Once cholera had arrived in St. Petersburg, quarantine stations were again established on Sweden's east coast and a separate quarantine commission in Stockholm added to Gothenburg's. Such precautions were then extended to vessels from any infected region and all were required to document the epidemiological state of their port of origin, with the suspected quarantined, and all others inspected before contact with Swedish soil, cleansed and fumigated. To underline the seriousness of the matter, two gun-sloops were ordered out in July 1848, one to Malmö, the other to Helsingborg, strengthening the coastal fortifications.[45]

Similar measures were also instituted against all voyagers from abroad, who now had to carry health attests. If cholera erupted in neighboring countries, entry was restricted to certain crossing points and in the worst case all communication could be severed except for the mail and by royal permission. Travelers from infected places were inspected: those en route for at least ten days since the last contact and who were

---

[42] Richard J. Evans, *Death in Hamburg: Society and Politics in the Cholera Years 1830–1910* (Oxford, 1987), pp. 250–51; Friedrich Wolter, *Das Auftreten der Cholera in Hamburg in dem Zeitraume von 1831–1893 mit besonderer Berücksichtigung der Epidemie des Jahres 1892* (Munich, 1898), pp. 259–61; Anton, *Heilformeln*, pp. 118–23.   [43] *SFS*, 1840/10, pp. 1–2; 1834/6, §§5–6.

[44] Von Düben, *Om karantäner*, p. 52; Klas Linroth, *Om folksjukdomarnes uppkomst och utbredning* (Stockholm, 1884), p. 78; Carlson, *Iakttagelser om Choleran*, p. 41; *Bidrag till allmänhetens upplysning*, pp. 12–13; *Conférence 1866*, 37, annexe, p. 3.

[45] *SFS*, 1847/34; 1847/35; 1847/37; 1847/38; Berg, *Sammandrag af officiella rapporter*, p. 15.

healthy could continue after cleansing their clothing; others were quarantined. In 1850, with cholera in Malmö in southern Sweden, ships
thence were subject to quarantine as though arriving from abroad.
During this epidemic, many (in some districts most) local communities
made use of the right to seal themselves off, taking precautions against
travelers and ships. Christianstad, for example, sequestered itself,
posting guards at the city gates, building a quarantine station, levying
fines for unlawful entry and subjecting possibly infected goods to an
extensive purification regimen. Some towns refused travelers admission,
requiring them to seek lodging outside, where they were visited by the
quarantine commission. In others they were permitted in during the day
only to conduct their business. Elsewhere travelers were escorted
through town preceded by a banner proclaiming, "Beware of contagion," and in one case such precautions were carried out even though
the distinguished visitors were a drove of oxen.[46] Patients were still being
removed to hospitals.[47] Although such local quarantinist measures
tended to diminish in the years after midcentury, being maintained primarily in remote rural areas, they still stood in contrast to the sanitationist approach now being tried out elsewhere.[48]

At midcentury, debate over these issues erupted in the Estates with
proposals to modify the official quarantinist approach. The Burghers,
now reversing their earlier position, proposed an end to the right of
localities to seal themselves off, seeking instead uniform regulations
across the country that would lessen the prevalence and severity of internal cordons and quarantines and free the circulation of travelers. In their
place medical care should be assured once epidemics had struck, along
with measures to ensure cleanliness, warm clothing and good food for
the poor. While the pertinent committee considered quarantines for
foreign ships still useful, it agreed that similar precautions should not be
imposed domestically. The Nobles, Peasants and Burghers approved, but

---

[46] *SFS*, 1848/1; 1850/44; 1850/59; 1853/37; Berg, *Sammandrag af officiella rapporter*, pp. 17–18, 343,
364; *Hygiea*, 14, 3 (March 1852), p. 136; *Bidrag till allmänhetens upplysning*, pp. 36, 100; *Borgare*, 1853–54,
v. 1, p. 184.

[47] To judge from the concerns of the Sundhets-Collegium that transports were often harmful
and patients would be better off treated at home: "Kongl. Sundhets-Collegii Circulär till
Konungens Befallningshafwande i Riket, rörande Cholera-sjukwården," 26 August 1850, copy in
Riksdagsbiblioteket, Stockholm. This circular is also excerpted in A. Hilarion Wistrand, ed.,
Författningar angående medicinal-väsendet i Sverige (Stockholm, 1860), pp. 588–90; *Förhandlingar*, 1866, pp.
170–71; 1867, pp. 31, 34.

[48] A. Timoleon Wistrand, *Kort skildring*, pp. 6–7, 86; A. Timoleon Wistrand, *Sundhets-Collegii underdåniga berättelse om kolerafarsoten i Sverige år 1853* (Stockholm, 1855), p. 371; *Hygiea*, 18, 1 (January 1856),
p. 24.

the Clergy had doubts, preferring to maintain localities' allegedly natural right to protect themselves.[49] The outcome in 1854 was that external quarantines against ships from abroad were shortened to five days, while for internal precautions a compromise was struck. All agreed that a welter of different measures was a nuisance, but also that each locality had a prerogative to protect itself. In the end, the right to bar travelers from infected areas was revoked along with all internal cordons, but localities were permitted, at their own expense, to inspect ships, hospitalize ill visitors and isolate vessels for two days, cleansing them and any potentially infectious cargo. Three years later, measures allowed the authorities to keep an eye on suspicious itinerants, provide medical care to sick wayfarers and prevent their contact with local inhabitants.[50]

With one important exception, practice in France during this period followed medical opinion in its antiquarantinist bent. In 1847 quarantines were shortened and, under certain circumstances, abolished altogether for ships from Turkey and Egypt when those countries were free of epidemic disease. In 1848 no quarantines were imposed and open communication was maintained with countries struck by cholera. The sanitary decree of 1853 sought uncontroversially to walk the line between competing interests. At home, the Second Republic established councils of public hygiene in each district, responsible for domestic cleanliness, measures against contagious disease, distribution of medicine to the poor, sanitation in the workplace, schools, hospitals and prisons. Precautions implemented in Toulon in 1849 betrayed little quarantinist influence: inspecting slaughterhouses, not selling pork and cured meats, postponing the start of the school year, providing treatment stations and ambulances, ending the ringing of church bells and other public signs of mourning, creating a council of public hygiene. In 1854 in Gy, the impoverished were provided decent food and a hospital opened in a poor neighborhood, but otherwise nothing of a quarantinist bent appears to have been implemented.[51] The exception to this antiquarantinist tendency in French opinion and practice was the approach

---

[49] *Bihang*, 1853–54, viii, no. 85, pp. 1–2; viii, no. 102; x/1, v. 1, no. 84; *Bonde*, 1853–54, v, p. 92; *Ridderskapet och Adeln*, 1853–54, vii, pp. 473ff.; *Preste*, 1853–54, iv, pp. 478–90.

[50] *Hygiea*, 17, 1 (January 1855), pp. 44–52; 17, 2 (February 1855), pp. 118–27; *SFS*, 1854/51; 1854/54; 1857/69.

[51] Sherston Baker, *The Laws Relating to Quarantine* (London, 1879), p. 413; *Moniteur universel*, 209 (28 July 1850), p. 2591; 356 (21 December 1848), p. 3629; William Coleman, *Yellow Fever in the North: The Methods of Early Epidemiology* (Madison, 1987), pp. 93–94; A. Dominique, *Le choléra á Toulon* (Toulon, 1885), pp. 54–55; P. Al. Niobey, *Histoire médicale du choléra-morbus épidémique qui a régné, en 1854, dans la ville de Gy (Haute-Saône)* (Paris, 1858), pp. 23–26.

taken along the Mediterranean coast and especially at Marseilles. Backed by the 1822 law and its delegation of such powers to the local level, the Intendance sanitaire of Marseilles had implemented strictly quarantinist practices. Its quarantine regulations issued in 1835 formalized the techniques already in use and were subsequently adopted by other Mediterranean ports. Concerned mainly with the plague and fearful of its extreme transmissibility, these stipulated such precautions as keeping the ill under guard in strict isolation, having patients open their own buboes to spare physicians any physical contact and conducting medical examinations with a telescope at a distance of twelve meters.[52]

The sanitationism of the General Board of Health and a Chadwickian approach to disease in general left its mark on the prophylactic measures implemented in Britain during the decades after the first epidemic. General sanitary improvement, though the ideal solution, was at best a longterm goal. In the meantime, other sorts of measures were required and here the Board's sanitationist attitude hardly dictated a hands-off approach. As staunchly as the quarantinists, although for different reasons, the Chadwickians sought to remove the ill from their dwellings. If cholera struck overcrowded rooms, the Medical Officer of Health could remove either the patient or the other occupants, with the Guardians required to provide alternate accommodation. With a cholera death in cramped circumstances, either the corpse or the survivors were to be removed.[53] Because the Board regarded noxious atmospheres and overcrowding as dangerous factors, it recommended removing still unstricken family members to houses of refuge.[54] Such reverse sequestrations of the healthy were implemented in certain places considered irremediably filthy (Wolverhampton and Mevagissey, a small fishing village in Cornwall), where the inhabitants were evacuated from their homes to tents borrowed from the army. In Bristol, the police turned out sixty-four residents from an insalubrious lodging house. In 1854 at Newcastle upon Tyne the authorities met resistance until they

[52] *Rapport à l'Académie royale de médecine . . . par M. le Dr. Prus*, pp. 204–07, 220–22; Georg Sticker, *Abhandlungen aus der Seuchengeschichte und Seuchenlehre* (Giessen, 1912), v. I/2, pp. 334–35, 343–44.

[53] *PP* 1849 (1115) xxiv, pp. 95–96; *MTG*, 7 (1853), pp. 354–55; *PP* 1850 (1274) xxi, 185, p. 131. The Board was careful to point out, however, that it was enforcing removal of corpses without thereby subscribing to a contagious view of cholera: PRO, MH 5/1, General Board of Health, minutes, 19 January 1849.

[54] *PP* 1849 (1115) xxiv, pp. 108–09; Norman Longmate, *King Cholera* (London, 1966), p. 161; *PP* 1847–48 (917) li, pp. 7, 44–45. See also PRO, MH 113/9, LGB, "General Memorandum on the Proceedings which are advisable in Places attacked or threatened by Epidemic Disease," April 1888, p. 2.

began pitching the sort of tent used by publicans at fairs, equipped with plank flooring.[55]

Even more directly interventionist were the house-to-house visitations recommended by the Board.[56] A new tactic in the preventive arsenal, such inspections were based on the idea that the main thrust of a cholera attack was preceded by prodromal diarrhea, during which phase medical intervention could still prevent the worst.[57] Because symptoms often struck the sufferers as trivial, self-reporting was unreliable, and frequent, regular surveillance of the dwellings of the poor therefore necessary.[58] During visitations medical inspectors questioned inhabitants as to the condition of their bowels and other matters not normally the subject of interchange between the state and its subjects. Visitors spent from two to seven minutes per case and estimated a quota of anywhere from 72 to 1,000 families daily. The numbers visited and the meticulous detail in which the alleged effects of such inspections were recorded are remarkable compared to the epidemiological interventions undertaken in any other nation during this period.[59] In 1848, in the most crowded localities of the largest cities, some 130,000 infected people were discovered with premonitory diarrhea. In London in 1848, 44,000 were visited and a similar number in Newcastle during the epidemic of 1854.[60] In addition to their intestinal inquiries, inspectors also exerted influence to remove families from infected houses and patients to hospitals. They were to

[55] *Sanitary Record*, n.s., 3 (1881), pp. 270–71; *PP* 1849 (1115) xxiv, p. 108; Benjamin Ward Richardson, *The Health of Nations* (London, 1887), v. II, pp. 227–28; *PP* 1850 (1273) xxi, 3, p. 125; *PP* 1854 (1818) xxxv, p. 10.

[56] Sanitary inspections were a technique whose precedence was contested among nations. The French claimed visitations as their idea, the Bavarians were among the first in 1836 actually to implement them and the British, having tried them out in 1831–32, were the first to institute them on a large scale in 1848: Patrice Bourdelais, "Présentation," in Jean-Pierre Bardet et al., eds., *Peurs et terreurs face à la contagion* (Paris, 1988), p. 35; *L'union médicale*, 7, 121 (11 October 1853), p. 477; 7, 136 (15 November 1853), p. 541; Tardieu, *Dictionnaire d'hygiène publique*, v. III, pp. 594–95; *Annales*, 2/1 (1854), pp. 85–86; *GHMC*, 1, 5 (4 November 1853), p. 53; 2, 2 (1865), pp. 650–51; *Moniteur universel*, 113 (23 April 1849), pp. 1497–98; 259 (15 September 1864), pp. 1140–41; *Revue médicale française et étrangère*, 2 (31 October 1853), pp. 449–50; G. Danet, *Des infiniment petits rencontrés chez les cholériques* (Paris 1873), p. 83.

[57] Premonitory symptoms had been identified first during the 1832 epidemic, but had widespread practical consequences only in 1848: *Sanitary Record*, n.s., 3 (1881), p. 272; *PP* 1849 (1115) xxiv, pp. 74, 80; *PP* 1854–55 (255) xlv, 18; *PP* 1849 (1070) xxiv, pp. 10–13; Pelling, *Cholera, Fever and English Medicine*, pp. 51–52; Simon, *English Sanitary Institutions*, pp. 173–75, 218; Tardieu, *Dictionnaire d'hygiène publique*, v. I, p. 297; *Annales*, 2/41 (1874), pp. 17, 20.

[58] *PP* 1849 (1115) xxiv, p. 9; *PP* 1850 (1273) xxi, 3, p. 95; PRO, FO 881/331, "Statement explanatory of the Preventive Measures adopted in Great Britain by the General Board of Health in 1848 and 1849, with the view of arresting the progress of Epidemic Cholera," p. 1.

[59] *PP* 1850 (1275) xxi, 365, p. 534; *PP* 1854 (1837) lxi, 109.

[60] *PP* 1850 (1273) xxi, 3, pp. 140–43; *PP* 1854–55 (1893) xlv, 69, p. 124; *PP* 1854 (1768) xxxv, 1, pp. 8–9.

check for decomposing organic matter and cleanse filthy dwellings. To reinforce such visitations, heads of families, schoolmasters and employers were to examine daily, either for themselves or through an agent, every person in their employ for loose bowels.[61]

To supplement such measures, good hygienic conditions were to be ensured in public spaces and filthy private dwellings – the "abodes of sluttishness – the forerunner of disease."[62] In 1846, the Nuisances Removal Act gave Guardians of the Poor in rural areas the authority to have dwellings cleansed, whitewashed and purified, nuisances removed, undertaking such actions themselves in cases of refusal. Two years later, Guardians were granted further powers to remove nuisances, with the right to enter private property if noxious matter or a death by contagious disease were suspected.[63] The Board of Health's regulations for the 1848 epidemic included daily scourings of all streets, courts and alleys declared dangerous by the Medical Officer. Dungheaps in mews and stables were to be carted off daily; owners were to remove nuisances on their properties and fumigation with chlorine gas was a possibility. The Medical Officer could enter lodging houses, requiring them to be ventilated and cleaned. In 1853, he was allowed to inspect houses recently the scene of disease to check on their cleanliness and other predisposing factors.[64]

In 1848, the sanitationist approach was given its overarching legislative incarnation in the Public Health Act, establishing the General Board of Health to help bring every region up to the hygienic standards of the healthiest.[65] A panoply of sanitary issues were here regulated: sewers and their maintenance, building codes to equip new housing with water, drains and privies, street cleansing, industrial hygiene, urban land use zoning. Against contagious disease, houses could be cleansed or whitewashed by order of the Board, local authorities could provide facilities for removal of corpses, burials were no longer permitted within or underneath any church. The Nuisances Removal and Disease Prevention Act of 1855 formalized the process of sanitation for places other than London.[66] Inspectors of Nuisances were appointed, entitled to enter private premises without notice during working hours if they suspected the presence of nuisances and empowered to make orders

---

[61] *PP* 1850 (1274) xxi, 185, p. 53; *PP* 1849 (1115) xxiv, pp. 79–80.

[62] *MTG*, 7 (1853), pp. 355–56.   [63] 9 & 10 Vict. c. 96; 11 & 12 Vict. c. 123.

[64] *PP* 1849 (1115) xxiv, pp. 83ff., 97–98, 102–05; *MTG*, 7 (1853), pp. 354–56.

[65] 11 & 12 Vict. c. 63.

[66] 18 & 19 Vict. c. 121; Royston Lambert, *Sir John Simon 1816–1904 and English Social Administration* (London, 1963), p. 226.

for the abatement, discontinuance and prohibition of threats to public hygiene. Local authorities could require houseowners to provide sufficient privy accommodation, drainage and ventilation, to whitewash, cleanse or disinfect their premises, drain pools, ditches and gutters, and to undertake and pay for structural work to remedy sanitary defects. They might prohibit the use of an irremediably insanitary house for human habitation and fines could be levied against those who permitted overcrowded conditions.[67]

THE NEW TURN OF THE SIXTIES

The 1860s and seventies saw a gradual change to a new approach: not a return to quarantinism, but a rejection of the simple sanitationism of midcentury and the development of a new variant of quarantinism, one based on accumulating experience with cholera. Despite the work of Snow, Budd, Pettenkofer and others, there were not yet scientific breakthroughs of the caliber to come during the 1880s with Koch's discovery of the microbial causes of cholera – work, in other words, whose scientific merits would eventually oblige the adoption of measures congruent with its principles. Rather, a growing consensus gradually emerged on how to prevent and limit the spread of cholera, a coalescence of opinion based on the fruits of hardwon practical experience harvested by customs, colonial and public health officials. Medical opinion, having initially favored contagionism, was impelled by the disappointments of the 1830s toward various forms of localism by midcentury. Official measures, in contrast, were more variegated, differing significantly among nations. Prussia and Sweden remained most faithful to the tenets of quarantinism; Britain headed off in a sanitationist direction, laying the basis for the ambitious program of urban renewal and public hygiene that would occupy it for the following half-century; France struck a sanitationist pose while accomplishing less of practical significance in these respects. Nonetheless, all nations clearly distanced themselves from the strict quarantinism of the thirties to adopt a more moderate position. This drift away from quarantinism was now halted, stabilized and even reversed after the middle of the century with the development of a form of neoquarantinism.

Behind this shift lay the powerfully formative experience of the 1865

---

[67] In the 1866 Sanitary Act, repeated convictions for such offenses could result in closing of the house: 29 & 30 Vict. c. 90, s. 36.

epidemic which revealed the extent to which cholera was imported to
Europe from the Orient and, in particular, the role played in this
diffusion by religious pilgrimages. The threat now identified was posed
by the Muslim faithful who journeyed from all over the Middle and Far
East to Mecca, thence to disperse home once again.[68] Combined with
the recent introduction of steamships across the Mediterranean and
along the Red Sea routes of pilgrimage from Egypt, as well as the
gradual development of railroads, the result of this religiously systolic
movement of the observant through Mecca had been an unprecedent-
edly rapid dissemination of cholera. The impending opening of the
Suez Canal, still four years off, promised only to make matters worse. In
1865, cholera arrived in the Hejaz with pilgrims from Java and
Singapore, where it was epidemic, passing through the Suez to Egypt.
From Alexandria, whence 35,000 people fled within a few weeks of
the outbreak, the ports of the Mediterranean and the rest of Europe
were infected. Finally, within six months, a ship from Marseilles to
Guadaloupe continuing on to New York introduced the disease to the
new world. Covering the distance from India to Europe had earlier taken
five to six years, but this time, traveling by steamship, cholera was on the
road for only two.[69] However much local circumstances might hinder or
promote its spread, cholera was ultimately imported: this was the conclusion drawn by many after 1865. The contagionists' fears seem to have
been confirmed and, yet, the very circumstances that now assisted
cholera's spread (increased and more rapid travel, trade and communication) also meant that the old means of containing its dissemination
would no longer work. Thanks to their speed, steamships would have
to remain longer in quarantine upon arrival. With the swelling legions
of travelers and the ever vaster agglomerations of goods in transit,
quarantines undertaken in the traditional sense of isolating potentially
infectious persons and objects until the uneventful passage of an incubation period had proven them harmless would have to be expanded on
an impossibly heroic scale. Oldfashioned quarantine was becoming
increasingly unworkable in the age of mass transportation, however
effective in theory it might have remained.[70]

[68] *Annales*, 2/30 (1868), pp. 5–7; *Moniteur universel*, 280 (7 October 1865), p. 1297; 300 (27 October 1865), p. 1358; *Recueil*, 25 (1895), p. 395; PRO, FO 78/2005, Earl Cowley to Earl Russell, 9 October 1865, no. 1092.

[69] Neville M. Goodman, *International Health Organizations and Their Work* (2nd edn.; Edinburgh, 1971), p. 5; *Conférence 1866*, 37, annexe, pp. 12–13; Erwin H. Ackerknecht, *History and Geography of Important Diseases* (New York, 1965), p. 28.

[70] Although it was also argued in defense of overland quarantine that the development of rail-

In response to this dilemma there developed a school of neoquarantinist thought and practice that, while accepting the transmissibility of cholera and other epidemic diseases, sought new means of hindering their import. Inspection in search of cholera's victims and their symptoms (revision, as the system was sometimes called), notification of disease to the authorities, isolation of the ill, medical surveillance of travelers, sometimes observation quarantines for ships, disinfection of persons, goods, vessels and dwellings: these now became the main tenets of neoquarantinist prophylaxis. The approach remained quarantinist in assuming cholera's basic infectiousness and seeking to block its transmission between humans. At the same time, it accepted that quarantine in the old sense was impracticable and unrealizable. In essence, it sought to shift the means of cutting chains of transmission from the lazaretto out into society at large, through surveilling the potentially infected, identifying the ill and imposing the necessary measures of disinfection and sequestration to render them harmless.[71] Not only did neoquarantinism promise to be more effective than traditional measures, it also held out the possibility of overcoming the inherited Hobson's choice between the virtues of free communication and the dictates of public health. The new techniques of inspection, isolation and disinfection promised to reconcile those erstwhile enemies, public hygiene and safety in one corner, trade, commerce and unrestricted peregrination in the other.[72] By inspecting passengers, only those who were infectious would be held back and ships would not be detained longer than necessary for surveillance and purification. Through disinfection, vessels, goods and travelers could be rendered harmless while lessening the bother and commercial distress of quarantine.[73] Purifying the dwellings of the ill would substitute for more far-reaching sequestrations of houses, neighborhoods or entire towns.

Disinfection and isolation are often considered, along with quarantine, among the "classic contagionist methods."[74] Such techniques rested on

---

roads, by concentrating travelers at a few border crossings, in theory made sanitary cordons more effective than in the age when travel had been more Brownian in its motions: *Annales*, 3/2 (1879), p. 544.   [71] Paul Bert, *Le choléra: Lettres au "Tagblatt" de Vienne* (Paris, 1884), pp. 14–20.

[72] Trolard, *De la prophylaxie des maladies exotiques, importables et transmissibles* (Alger, 1891), pp. 3–4; A. Proust, *La défense de l'Europe contre le choléra* (Paris, 1892), pp. 415–19; *JO*, 28, 20 (21 January 1896), pp. 357–58.

[73] *Sanitary Record*, 10 (14 February 1879), pp. 98–99; *Annales*, 3/14 (1885), p. 154; *JO*, 16, 298 (29 October 1884), p. 5684.

[74] Evans, *Death in Hamburg*, p. 490; "Reichsseuchengesetz und Diktatur der Medizin," *Gr. Lichtenfelder Wegweiser*, 8 (17 February 1893); BA, R86/946, v. 2, 1974/93, "Petition gegen den Entwurf eines Gesetzes, betr. die Bekämpfung gemeingefährlicher Krankheiten."

the assumption that there was a contagium (as yet unknown) conveyed by people and goods that could be destroyed by disinfection or rendered harmless by sequestration of the infectious. Nonetheless, disinfection was also a measure advocated by sanitationists. In the future, when public hygiene had been perfected, with waste properly disposed of, filth not accumulating to putrefy and overcrowding not concentrating dangerous bodily exhalations, disinfection would no longer be necessary. But, in the short term, it was a way of neutralizing the harmful effects of decomposing organic matter and noxious vapors, a means of achieving the goals of sanitary reform before having implemented flawless public hygiene. Disinfection was the poor person's sanitation, a shortcut to the same ends that did not involve the massive outlays for new infrastructure required by thoroughgoing hygienic reform. From the sanitationist perspective, disinfection hindered putrefaction; from the quarantinist's, it destroyed the contagium. For different reasons both could agree on at least one of the main tenets of neoquarantinism.[75] Neoquarantinism thus did not stand in as diametrical opposition to sanitationism as its traditional predecessor. Sanitationists and neoquarantinists could agree on some of the preventive techniques to be applied against contagious disease: inspection, cleansing and disinfection. Conversely, no one, however diehard their quarantinism, rejected the need for improved public sanitation. The question was rather the order of immediate priorities. The maximum sanitationist program implied change on a revolutionary scale, granting to the poor living conditions already largely achieved by the well-off. It was this element of the utopian that galvanized neoquarantinists. Attainable improvements in the fortunes of the poor, as both Prussian and French delegates put it at the International Sanitary Conference in 1866, would never give them the same circumstances as the fortunate. Widening the streets, improving drains and the like was not enough. Spacious and airy dwellings, good food, rigorous cleanliness – in short, the circumstances of a comfortably well-off life – were equally necessary and reform of such ambition was not a realistic prophylactic strategy. Heroic sanitary reform, if not impossible, could at best be accomplished over many years at great cost. In the long term, hygienic improvement was the answer to cholera and other epidemic disease, the French argued at the 1894 Sanitary Conference. Not disinfection, not even prevention, but salubrity should be the final word in public hygiene. But such meas-

[75] *Conférence 1874*, pp. 67–74; Martinenq, *Appendice au choléra de Toulon de 1835* (Grasse, 1866), pp. 50–53; Carl Barriés, *Relation über die Natur der asiatischen Cholera* (Hamburg, 1832), pp. 63–64; Freymuth, *Giebt es ein praktisch bewährtes Schutzmittel*, p. 62.

ures could not be hurried and in the meantime more immediate steps were required to stem the spread of epidemic illness.[76] Social reform, in other words, could not plausibly substitute for disease prevention except in the most expansive view.

THE AMBIGUITIES OF NEOQUARANTINISM

In Germany, the new halfway position, suspended awkwardly between a recognition that cholera and other epidemic diseases were in fact contagious and an acknowledgment that the old prophylactic strategies were nonetheless failures, was associated above all with Pettenkofer. Pettenkofer was one of the most remarkable, versatile, eccentric, persuasive, stubborn and ultimately tragic figures in the history of epidemiology. He elaborated a theory of vast influence that straddled the localist/contagionist dispute inherited from the 1830s. A cholera epidemic, so his argument ran, depended on the interaction of three factors, X, Y and Z: the specific germ, the local and seasonal preconditions required to transform it into the actual cause of an epidemic and the individual predisposition that explained why anyone in particular succumbed.[77] Among the local factors, most important was the nature of the ground, with porous soil, replete with water and fecal contamination, crucial for the development of cholera.[78] Because dependent on the import of a germ, cholera was transmissible; because the germ alone was insufficient to cause an epidemic, cholera was not (unmediatedly) contagious. The distinction separating these two terms lay at the heart of Pettenkofer's ability to sidestep any binary decision between localism and contagionism. Because of this etiological trapeze act, he has often been misunderstood. Some have taken him to be an outright sanitationist, a kind of Bavarian Chadwick.[79]

---

[76] Wolff, *Bericht über die Cholera-Epidemie des Jahres 1866 in Quedlinburg, vom Standpunkte der öffentlichen Gesundheitspflege* (Quedlinburg, 1867), p. 69; *Conférence 1866*, 26, pp. 4–6; *Conférence 1894*, pp. 6–7, 9, 199; Monod, *La santé publique* (Paris, 1904), p. 78. They are conditions, as the British delegates to the 1866 Conference put it, "which cannot be created in a moment – they can only be the work of time": PRO, FO 78/2006, p. 400.

[77] Max Pettenkofer, *Untersuchungen und Beobachtungen über die Verbreitungsart der Cholera nebst Betrachtungen über Massregeln, derselben Einhalt zu thun* (Munich, 1855), pp. 247–49; Pettenkofer, *Über Cholera*, p. 4; Pettenkofer, *Cholera: How to Prevent and Resist It* (London, 1875), p. 26.

[78] On this, he had been influenced by the British India physicians: W. Rimpau, *Die Entstehung von Pettenkofers Bodentheorie und die Münchner Choleraepidemie vom Jahre 1854* (Berlin, 1935), pp. 13, 34, 37. This focus on the soil had been foreshadowed by A. N. Gendrin, *Monographie du choléra-morbus épidémique de Paris* (Paris, 1832), pp. 287–88.

[79] Jean-Pierre Goubert, *The Conquest of Water: The Advent of Health in the Industrial Age* (Cambridge, 1989), p. 61; Bruno Latour, *The Pasteurization of France* (Cambridge, MA, 1988), p. 23; Rene Dubos, *Mirage of Health* (New York, 1959), p. 125.

From a strict localist point of view, in contrast, insisting on the necessity of an imported germ made Pettenkofer a contagionist, however contingently.[80]

Pettenkofer's balancing act took various forms during his long and polymorphous career. At first, he recommended disinfection in order to render harmless the cholera germ in its victims' excrement. Quarantine, however, he rejected – not as mistaken, but impractical. In theory epidemics could be prevented by excluding all Xs, but in reality even quarantining all travelers could not hinder the entrance of every germ. From this position of quasi-contagionism Pettenkofer then shifted his emphasis from the imported germ to the local factors that allegedly render it dangerous. In the late 1860s he concluded that excrement was harmless, since otherwise medical attendants would have succumbed in droves, and disinfection therefore unnecessary. Instead, affecting predisposing local conditions became important and sanitary improvements such as drainage, water purification and street asphaltation the solution.[81] Given his comfortable position squarely astraddle the localist/contagionist distinction, it is perhaps not surprising that, when Koch introduced the comma bacillus in 1884, Pettenkofer felt little pressure to revise his own thoughts on the matter. Happy to accept Koch's vibrio as his factor X, he continued to insist that, without the further influence of Y and Z, epidemics would not arise.[82] The main point of contention between Kochians and Pettenkoferians thus concerned whether the germ alone (along with an individual predisposition) produced cholera or whether local and seasonal factors were also required.

Pettenkofer's influence in Germany was immense. His ability to shift attention from medical policing to public hygiene in the 1850s and his appointment to the first professorship in that subject in Munich in 1865

---

[80] Th. Ackermann, *Die Choleraepidemie des Jahres 1859 im Grossherzogthum Mecklenburg-Schwerin* (Rostock, 1860), p. 142; A. Bernhardi, Sr., *Die Cholera-Epidemie zu Eilenburg im Sommer 1866* (Eilenburg, 1867), pp. 4, 6; Ernst Delbrück, *Bericht über die Cholera-Epidemie des Jahres 1855 in der Strafanstalt zu Halle, in Halle, und im Saalkreise* (Halle, 1856), pp. 8–9; Oesterlen, *Choleragift und Pettenkofer*, pp. 1–2, 111–12; Emanuel Pochmann, *Die Cholerapilz-Massregeln von Prof. Robert Koch mit ihren Irrthümern und Gefahren und das Cholera-Elend in Hamburg* (Linz a/d Donau, 1892), pp. 34, 43; *GHMC*, 2, 2 (1865), pp. 679–82, 709–16.

[81] Pettenkofer, *Untersuchungen und Beobachtungen*, p. 290; Edgar Erskine Hume, "Max von Pettenkofer's Theory of the Etiology of Cholera, Typhoid Fever and Other Intestinal Diseases," *Annals of Medical History*, 7, 4 (Winter 1925), pp. 331, 337; Friedrich Küchenmeister, *Handbuch der Lehre von der Verbreitung der Cholera und von den Schutzmaassregeln gegen sie* (Erlangen, 1872), pp. 5–6, 28–29; *Berichte*, Heft 2, p. 3; Heft 4, p. v; *Archiv für Hygiene*, 18 (1893), pp. 131–32; Peter Münch, *Stadthygiene im 19. und 20. Jahrhundert* (Göttingen, 1993), p. 132.

[82] Max von Pettenkofer, *Choleraexplosionen und Trinkwasser* (Munich 1894), p. 5; *Archiv für Hygiene*, 18 (1893), p. 117; *DVöG*, 27 (1895), p. 159.

marked the institutionalization of a German strain of sanitationism first associated with Virchow.[83] His strife with Koch and bacteriology has often been portrayed as one between northern and southern Germany, of Bavarian resistance to the hegemony of ascendant Prussia in the newly established Empire.[84] If so, it was a debate in which it is hard to identify a clear victor, one in which Pettenkofer exerted as much influence as Koch, his generally sanitationist approach eventually embraced to great effect in the Empire. During the years immediately preceding the unification, his theories had been sharply criticized in Prussia. The Prussian delegates to the International Sanitary Conference in 1866, at which Bavaria was not represented, took a strictly quarantinist approach.[85] But by the 1874 Conference, Pettenkofer was a member of the German delegation, his influence was ascendant and a much more sanitationist tack was being pursued.[86] In 1873, the German Cholera Commission, headed by Pettenkofer, demonstrated the effect of this new emphasis. Cholera had unquestionably been imported from Russia and Austria, it concluded, but at the same time, other factors, both local and individual, explained why it spread, especially affecting some places and people. Cholera, thus dependent on local conditions, was not a directly contagious disease and maritime quarantines made little sense until it was known exactly what it was whose import was to be prevented.[87] By the 1880s, Pettenkofer and his antiquarantinist allies

[83] Paul Weindling, *Health, Race and German Politics Between National Unification and Nazism, 1870–1945* (Cambridge, 1989), p. 157.

[84] *Eira*, 9, 5 (1885), p. 152; *SB*, 1892/93, 21 April 1893, p. 1957B; Preussischer Medizinalbeamten-Verein, *Verhandlungen*, 10 (1893), pp. 8–9, 45; *DVöG*, 27 (1895), p. 159; *Annales de l'Institut Pasteur*, 4 (1890), pp. 299ff.; "Reichsseuchengesetz und Diktatur der Medizin," *Gr. Lichtenfelder Wegweiser*, 7 (10 February 1893); "Das Reichsseuchengesetz," *Berliner Tageblatt*, 65 (4 February 1893); *Münchner neueste Nachrichten*, 135 (23 March 1893); "Das Reichs-Seuchen-Gesetz und die bayerische Medizinal-verwaltung," *Augsburger Abendzeitung*, 57 (26 February 1893), Zweites Blatt.

[85] Bernhardi, *Die Cholera-Epidemie*, pp. 4–6; Wilbrand, *Die Desinfection*, pp. 101–03; Ernst Delbrück, *Bericht über die Cholera-Epidemie des Jahres 1866 in Halle, in der Straf-Anstalt zu Halle und im Saalkreise* (Halle, 1867), pp. 36–38; Rudolf Virchow, *Collected Essays on Public Health and Epidemiology* (Canton, 1985), v. I, pp. 197–204; *Conférence 1866*, 6, pp. 6–7; 26, pp. 4–6.

[86] *Conférence 1874*, pp. 28–29, 112–13; Norman Howard-Jones, *The Scientific Background of the International Sanitary Conferences 1851–1938* (Geneva, 1975), p. 38; August Hirsch, *Handbuch der historisch-geographischen Pathologie* (Erlangen, 1860), v. I, pp. 134–41.

[87] *Berichte*, Heft 1 (2nd edn.), pp. 21–25; Heft 6 (Berlin, 1879), pp. 308–10, 312. For similar views, see H. Zeroni, *Das Auftreten der Cholera in den Provinzen Posen und Preussen im Jahre 1873: Eine Besprechung des Reiseberichts des Herrn Prof. Dr. A. Hirsch über diese Epidemie* (Mannheim, 1874), pp. 1–3, 10–11. And, yet, Pettenkofer's influence should not be dated strictly from the Empire. The official report on the epidemic of 1866 in Berlin demonstrates acceptance of his basic ideas: E. H. Müller, *Die Cholera-Epidemie zu Berlin im Jahre 1866: Amtlicher Bericht erstattet im Auftrage der königlichen Sanitäts-Commission* (Berlin, 1867), pp. 1, 51–53; *Amts-Blatt der Königlichen Regierung zu Marienwerder*, 35 (29 August 1866), pp. 230–31 (copy in GStA, A181/10524).

were regarded from across the Rhine as the dominant opinion in Germany and even in the nineties, at the highpoint of Koch's influence, Pettenkoferian arguments were still current in medical circles.[88]

In France opinion moved dramatically away from the sanitationism of midcentury, shifting the country in the opposite direction as Germany under Pettenkofer's spell. During the 1860s, the anticontagionist stance of official and medical circles had begun to weaken.[89] Contagionism rebounded. By the 1854 epidemic, the balance had tipped in its favor and by 1865 it clearly predominated.[90] Even opponents admitted that it was sweeping the field, holding the rising generation of physicians in its sway.[91] As always the middle, contingently contagionist, position was also widely adopted.[92] This was the position now accepted in 1867 by the once so anticontagionist Academy of Medicine. In 1871, the Comité consultatif d'hygiène publique joined it in agreement that both the import of germs and local conditions were necessary for an epidemic.[93] Although antiquarantinists were still holding forth in scientific fora in the 1880s and nineties, prominent public health officials were now firmly quarantinist, cautiously accepting Koch's bacillus as the likely cause of cholera from the very beginning.[94]

---

[88] *Annales*, 3/10 (1883), pp. 474–75; Howard-Jones, *Scientific Background*, p. 75. After his suicide in 1901, Pettenkofer's position continued to be upheld by his students, especially in Rudolf Emmerich, *Max Pettenkofers Bodenlehre der Cholera Indica* (Munich, 1910).

[89] Continuing anticontagionist views are represented in *L'union médicale*, 7, 14 (3 February 1853), p. 54; J.-P. Bonnafont, *Le choléra et le congrès sanitaire diplomatique international* (Paris, 1866), pp. 17, 23; Em. Rebold, *Moyens simples et faciles de combattre le choléra asiatique, la peste et la fièvre jaune* (Paris, 1865), p. 3; Rézard de Wouves, *Du choléra: Preuves de sa non-contagion* (Paris, 1868), pp. 47ff.; Bruck, *Le choléra ou la peste noire* (Paris, 1867), pp. vi–vii, 430–35.

[90] *GHMC*, 2, 2 (1865), pp. 679–82, 709–16; 25, 3 (22 June 1866), pp. 399–400; Sirus Pirondi and Augustin Fabre, *Etude sommaire sur l'importation du choléra et les moyens de la prévenir* (Marseilles, 1865), pp. 12, 39, 59–60; V. Seux, *Encore quelques mots sur la contagion du choléra épidémique* (Marseilles, 1867), pp. 5–7, 87–91; *Mémoires*, 30 (1871–73), pp. 347–48, 354–55, 400, 415; *Recueil*, 5 (1876), p. 44.

[91] *Journal de médécine et de chirurgie pratiques*, 37 (1866), pp. 193–94; *Gazette médicale de Paris*, 3, 21 (1866), pp. 150–52; Jules Girette, *La civilisation et le choléra* (Paris, 1867), pp. ii, 2, 29, 213ff.; G.-P. Stanski, *Contagion du choléra devant les corps savants* (Paris, 1874), pp. ii–7; *Le choléra n'est ni transmissible, ni contagieux: Etude critique et pratique par un rationaliste* (Paris, 1885), pp. viii–ix.

[92] Niçaise, *Etude sur le choléra* (Paris, 1868), pp. 33–39; *Mémoires*, 28 (1867–68), pp. 69, 104, 161–64; *Bulletin*, 34 (1869), pp. 279–80; Duboué, *Traitement prophylactique et curatif du choléra asiatique* (Paris, 1885), pp. 2–5; Danet, *Des infiniment petits*, pp. ii–vii, 81–85.

[93] *Mémoires*, 28 (1867–68), pp. 60, 161–70; *Recueil*, 3 (1874), pp. 316–28; Martha L. Hildreth, *Doctors, Bureaucrats, and Public Health in France, 1888–1902* (New York, 1987), pp. 114–17. On the violent debates between contagionists and localists in the Academy during the following years, see *Bulletin*, 36 (1871), pp. 605–06, 689–90; 2, 2 (1873), pp. 796ff., 801; 2, 3 (1874), pp. 321–40; 2, 4 (1875), p. 476; H. Mireur, *Etude historique et pratique sur la prophylaxie et le traitement du choléra basée sur les observations fournies par l'épidémie de Marseille (1884)* (Paris, 1884), pp. 5–6.

[94] *Annales*, 3/12 (1884), pp. 351–68; 3/13 (1885), p. 239; 3/15 (1886), p. 472; *Bulletin*, 2, 13 (1884), pp. 961–62, 968, 993 and passim; 3, 28 (1892), pp. 527–43.

Even in the British citadel of anticontagionism things changed, the official sanitationism of midcentury gradually dissipating. Snow's first writings on the aqueous transmission of cholera in 1849 were not conclusive, but his dramatic experiment in 1853 with the Broad Street pump strongly suggested that the disease spread through contaminated drinking water.[95] The Board of Health stuck to its view of cholera as the product of decomposing organic matter. In 1854, it grudgingly accepted a role for drinking water, not in the Snowian sense that the specific cause of disease was transmitted hydraulically, but only in the general sanitationist understanding that water contaminated by decaying matter was a predisposing factor, much like tainted air. Some sort of widespread atmospheric cause was still believed to lie at the root of cholera.[96] But starting in the mid-1850s, a note of contagionism began to corrupt the hitherto pure atmosphere of official British sanitationism. The cumulating effect of Snow's arguments constituted a major attack on the Board's position. Snow agreed that domestic sanitary arrangements, not quarantines and cordons, were the appropriate prophylaxis, but such measures had to be calibrated to the actual mode of transmission rather than taking blunderbuss aim at every distasteful metropolitan odor. The Board's insistence that cholera was not communicable, he argued, had in fact helped increase the mortality of the latest epidemic and some of its sanitary improvements were downright dangerous. The policy of draining cesspools, for example, meant that an even greater volume of feces (sped to its destination by Chadwick's misguided policy of flushing sewers) was ejected daily into the Thames and from there into Londoners' libations. Snow's own prophylactic recommendations included avoiding contaminated water, encouraging habits of personal hygiene among the poor, strict cleanliness for contacts, separating the healthy from the sick and removing patients if they had no place but the sickroom in which to take their meals.[97] Such finetuning of the means of avoiding contact with the discharges of the ill was clearly not social reform on the heroic scale dear to the Chadwickians. But from Snow's vantage, knowledge of the specific mechanism of

[95] Margaret Pelling, "The Reality of Anticontagionism: Theories of Epidemic Disease in the Early Nineteenth Century," *Society for the Social History of Medicine: Bulletin*, 17 (1976), pp. 5–7. An early adumbration of concerns with water supply, recommending boiling to prevent cholera, is *Heidelberger Klinische Annalen*, 8 (1832), p. 150.

[96] *PP* 1854–55 (1980) xxi, 1, pp. 46–48, 57; *PP* 1854–55 (1989) xlv, 1, pp. 5–7; Christopher Hamlin, *A Science of Impurity: Water Analysis in Nineteenth-Century Britain* (Berkeley, 1990), pp. 105–07; Wolfgang Locher, "Pettenkofer and Epidemiology: Erroneous Concepts – Beneficial Results," in Yosio Kawakita et al., eds., *History of Epidemiology* (Tokyo, 1993), pp. 111–12.

[97] *Medical Times*, 3 (1851), pp. 559–62, 610–12.

transmission allowed more effective precautions than did the vague, well-intentioned, but impossibly longterm and hopelessly ambitious hygienic harangues of the sanitationists. Because cholera was conveyed through a specific aqueous contamination, not just impure water as a general predisposing factor, it could be avoided as easily as the itch. "Every man may be his own quarantine officer," as he put it, "and go about during an epidemic among the sick almost as if no epidemic were present."[98] The weakness of Snow's position, however, was his inability to identify the entity that carried cholera through the water supply. His Broad Street pump experiment therefore lacked the resonance at the time that it would acquire in retrospect, although it did help discredit the radical miasmatism of the Board.[99]

Although the new Board after 1854 remained largely faithful to a miasmatic approach, elsewhere opinion shifted away from purebred sanitationism. In 1855, doubts were prominently voiced as to one of the Board's central premises, that offense to the olfactory sense and danger to health were much the same thing, Chadwick's infamous axiom, "all smell is disease." The Great Stench of 1858, when the Thames' role as London's cloaca maximus was illustrated to pungent effect but with no increase in mortality, would eventually provide illustration of Budd's claim that filth and foul smells were not the cause of fevers.[100] Starting in the late 1850s and early sixties, the opinion that cholera could, under certain circumstances, be transmitted and that it did not arise out of insanitary conditions alone was, as elsewhere, increasingly heard.[101] In India, long a hotbed of noncontagionism, the Special Commission on Cholera of 1861 accepted that a specific cholera germ was disseminated through human intercourse. During the 1866 epidemic, Snow's argu-

---

[98] *MTG*, 11 (1855), pp. 31–35, 84–88.

[99] R. J. Morris, *Cholera 1832: The Social Response to an Epidemic* (New York, 1976), p. 209; Kathleen Jones, *The Making of Social Policy in Britain 1830–1990* (London, 1991), p. 40; Frazer, *History of English Public Health*, pp. 64–65.

[100] *PP* 1854–55 (82) xlv, 227; *PP* 1854–55 (1893) xlv, 69, pp. 40–48; *PP* 1850 (1273) xxi, 3, pp. 57–72; *Hansard*, 1855, v. 139, cols. 449–50; Christopher Lawrence, "Sanitary Reformers and the Medical Profession in Victorian England," in Teizo Ogawa, ed., *Public Health* (Tokyo, 1981), p. 149; George Rosen, "Disease, Debility, and Death," in H. J. Dyos and Michael Wolff, eds., *The Victorian City* (London 1973), v. II, pp. 637–38; Charles-Edward Amory Winslow, *The Conquest of Epidemic Disease* (Princeton, 1944), p. 288.

[101] C. Macnamara, *A Treatise on Asiatic Cholera* (London, 1870), pp. 328–29, 463; Richard Hassall, *Cholera: Its Nature and Treatment* (London, 1854), pp. 6–15; Henry Wentworth Acland, *Memoir on the Cholera at Oxford in the Year 1854, with Considerations Suggested by the Epidemic* (London, 1856), pp. 73–74, 83; Alexander Bryson, *On the Infectious Origin and Propagation of Cholera* (London, 1851), pp. iii–iv, 5, 47. On the general shift to early forms of germ theory during the 1860s, see J. K. Crellin, "The Dawn of Germ Theory: Particles, Infection and Biology," in F. N. L. Poynter, ed., *Medicine and Science in the 1860s* (London, 1968), pp. 57–76.

ments were bolstered when William Farr at the Registrar-General's office demonstrated that most cholera deaths were concentrated among customers of one particular water company.[102] This shift away from strict sanitationism was emblematized, starting in the mid-1860s, by the work of John Simon, Medical Officer of Health first to the City, then the government, who was able harmonize new germ theories of the Snowian sort with inherited localist views. While insisting on cholera's transmissibility, Simon and his associates also thought that only under certain predisposing circumstances, among which filth and insalubrity ranked high, would it achieve epidemic proportions.[103] Hampering its dissemination thus involved sanitary reform, but at the same time accepting transmissibility put Simon in support of measures that, though occasionally practiced by the old Board, were not at the core of its sanitationist vision: removing and hospitalizing the infected, transferring bodies to mortuaries, disinfecting articles and conveyances, preventing the ill from appearing in public or using public transportation.

NEOQUARANTINISM TAKES HOLD

Despite their sanitationist reputation and practice, the British in fact refused to choose absolutely between the two approaches at loggerheads in the battle of prophylactic strategies. Their approach to public health remained two-pronged. At its core lay the nation's massive infrastructural investments devoted to improving sewerage, laying on water, disposing of waste, building better-lit and -ventilated, less crowded housing. Such efforts were embodied in a vast corpus of legislation, including the 1872 Public Health Act which sought to guarantee, as Lyon Playfair put it, the right of each Briton to pure air, water and soil, entrusting the authorities with significant new powers to this end.[104] Besides improving public health conditions in general, sanitary reform

---

[102] H. W. Bellew, *The History of Cholera in India from 1862 to 1881* (London, 1885), pp. 4–9, 772ff.; W. Luckin, "The Final Catastrophe: Cholera in London, 1866," *Medical History*, 21, 1 (January 1977), pp. 32–41; John M. Eyler, "William Farr on the Cholera: The Sanitarian's Disease Theory and the Statistician's Method," *Journal of the History of Medicine and Allied Sciences*, 28, 2 (April 1973).

[103] *PP* 1866 (3645) xxxiii, p. 459; Winslow, *Conquest of Epidemic Disease*, p. 264; Lambert, *John Simon*, pp. 368–69; Pelling, *Cholera, Fever and English Medicine*, pp. 295–96. However, Simon did at times hew close to the old Chadwickian view of cholera as but one instance of a general category of filth-caused fevers: *PP* 1875 (1370) xl, 143, p. 9; Arthur Newsholme, *The Story of Modern Preventive Medicine* (Baltimore, 1929), pp. 83–84; L. Fabian Hirst, *The Conquest of Plague* (Oxford, 1953), pp. 87–89.

[104] *Lancet*, 71, 2 (1 July 1893), pp. 50–51; *BMJ*, 2 (13 August 1887), pp. 339–40; PRO, FO 881/5424, FO CP 5424, April 1887, no. 35; *Hansard*, 1872, v. 209, cols. 860–61.

also promised eventually to prevent contagious disease. The true
defenses against epidemics, in this view, lay not in precautions imposed
along the coast, but in hygienic measures taken throughout the
country.[105] Such reforms, the subject of a large literature that needs no
rehearsal here, form the backdrop against which techniques more narrowly focused on contagious disease were deployed.[106]

For, of course, sanitary reform could not be all, at least not in the short
run. Such efforts took time to be implemented, while in the interim the
authorities recognized that, pace the Chadwickians, some diseases, in
fact imported from abroad, might best be halted by preventing their
ingress.[107] One element of this second aspect to British public health
strategies was the simple continuation of traditional quarantinist techniques during the period before sufficient sanitary progress had allowed
the external guard to be lowered. The British did not abandon the
protection of quarantine until they felt secure behind the bulwark of
their hygienic reforms.[108] During the 1840s, ships from the Orient
with unclean bills of health underwent two days of quarantine at
Southampton, Falmouth and Liverpool. In the sixties, quarantines were
still imposed and cholera-stricken vessels were isolated for three days and
inspected, and the ill sequestered.[109] The British delegates to the 1866
Constantinople Sanitary Conference reported back enthusiastically
in favor of quarantinist measures.[110] During the summer of 1871,
Sunderland and Seaham took steps to place infected ships in strict quarantine. In 1879, fearing plague, the Privy Council invoked the
Quarantine Act of 1825 to detain a Swedish ship, the Prima, en route
from Russia with a cargo of rags, but only until it had been fumigated
and disinfected. In 1885, ships from Spain and other cholera-suspected
places entering the Bristol Channel were brought into quarantine for
inspection, their ill transferred to a lazaretto built for this purpose on an

[105] *PP* 1886 (4873) xxxi, 763, pp. viii–ix; *PP* 1894 (8215) xxxvii, 667, p. v.

[106] The state of the art is represented by Anthony Wohl, *Endangered Lives: Public Health in Victorian Britain* (London, 1983).

[107] *Conférence 1874*, pp. 440–44; PRO, MH 113/5, LGB, "Precautions against the Infection of Cholera," 5 July 1873, p. 2.

[108] A date put at 1884 by the sharpsighted and Anglophilic observer, Henri Monod, Director of Public Hygiene at the French Interior Ministry: *Lancet*, 1 (9 January 1892), p. 111.

[109] *Lancet*, 1 (1844), pp. 20–23; *Mémoires*, 12 (1846), p. 555; *Berliner klinische Wochenschrift*, 10, 42 (1873), p. 505. In 1865 and 1866, thirteen and seven ships, respectively, were quarantined: *PP* 1867 (423) lxiv, p. 619. During the same period, the British were indignantly denying rumors spread in France that quarantines were imposed on ships from cholera-stricken ports abroad: PRO, FO 97/217, International Sanitary Conference, no. 83, 2 November 1859.

[110] PRO, FO 78/2006, p. 266, British Cholera Commissioners to the Earl of Clarendon, 25 May 1866.

island, and the import of rags was forbidden.[111] By this point, however, quarantine was employed so seldom that when, in 1886, a ship possibly stricken with yellow fever appeared off Dover and when, three years later, the Neva was ordered into quarantine at Southampton for the same reason, it was generally unknown that yellow fever and the plague remained quarantinable diseases under purview of the Privy Council.[112] In 1892 the Port Medical Officers of Health were still willing to consider seriously the worth of quarantine, although by now only to reject it. Finally, with the Public Health Act of 1896, quarantine was ended once and for all.[113]

More interesting than any diminishingly important continuation of traditional quarantinism, however, was the development in Britain of neoquarantinist techniques, which, dealing with diseases other than cholera as well, here achieved their earliest and most notable successes during the late 1860s and early seventies, becoming known in the process as the English system.[114] The neoquarantinist principles of inspection, isolation, disinfection and surveillance had been foreshadowed by Gavin Milroy already in the early 1860s. Heading a committee to investigate quarantine appointed in 1858 by the National Association for the Promotion of Social Science, he concluded two years later that medical inspection and disinfection of ships should replace traditional techniques. The new approach aimed to issue vessels bills of health reflecting their epidemiological state upon arrival, not the condition of the port of departure.[115] Ships with clean bills of health would be admitted at once to free pratique, while on others, the sick would be hospitalized, but the healthy not detained. Inspection was thus to replace, or at least moderate, quarantine by targeting efforts at those who were demonstrably sick, rather than all travelers from an infected origin. Implementation of

---

[111] *Lancet* (12 August 1871), p. 226; *Sanitary Record*, 10 (21 March 1879), p. 187; 1 (26 September 1874), p. 231; n.s., 7, 83 (15 May 1886), p. 543; *Recueil*, 4 (1875), pp. 250–55; *Veröffentlichungen*, 9, 2 (28 July 1885), p. 36.
[112] *Sanitary Record*, n.s., 8, 90 (15 December 1886), p. 264; *Practitioner*, 43 (July–December 1889), pp. 67–69; PRO, FO 881/6401*, R. Thorne Thorne, "Disease Prevention in England," 7 June 1893, p. 2.   [113] *Sanitary Record*, n.s., 14, 178 (15 February 1893), p. 395; 59 & 60 Vict. c. 19.
[114] Simon, *English Sanitary Institutions*, pp. 303, 314; Hirst, *Conquest of Plague*, p. 384; J. C. McDonald, "The History of Quarantine in Britain during the 19th Century," *BHM*, 25 (1951), pp. 35–36; Anne Hardy, "Cholera, Quarantine and the English Preventive System, 1850–1895," *Medical History*, 37, 3 (July 1993); Anne Hardy, "Public Health and the Expert: The London Medical Officers of Health," in Roy MacLeod, ed., *Government and Expertise: Specialists, Administrators and Professionals, 1860–1919* (Cambridge, 1988), pp. 135–36.
[115] C. W. Hutt, *International Hygiene* (London, 1927), p. 4. This was a matter of concern to Britain especially since otherwise ships from India would inevitably carry foul bills of health: MH 19/239, Thorne Thorne, untitled report, 23 November 1893.

Milroy's proposals began in the late sixties. The 1866 Sanitary Act allowed nuisance authorities to hospitalize infected travelers arriving by ship. In 1872, the Port Sanitary Authorities were created and endowed with greater powers to act against communicable diseases than their colleagues on shore.[116] The following year, ships were required to undergo medical inspection, the sick removed, the dead buried at sea, clothing, bedding and other articles disinfected or destroyed. Persons suffering suspicious symptoms could be detained up to two days, but once having undergone this regimen, the healthy were at liberty to disembark and the ship granted free pratique. The Public Health Act 1875 continued compulsory removals of the infectiously ill from ships, permitting port sanitary authorities to make regulations for obligatory notification and isolation of contagious diseases and for disinfection.[117] In 1883, such neoquarantinist techniques were reinforced with a system of medical surveillance. Healthy passengers, permitted to land after inspection, now had to provide names and destinations and were visited for five consecutive days to check for possible symptoms. As of 1896, they were to notify the authorities within forty-eight hours if arriving somewhere other than indicated and it was explicitly forbidden to give fictitious names or addresses, although there seem to have been no penalties for violation.[118]

While such measures sought to prevent the import of disease in the first place, others aimed at limiting its spread after arrival. These included: continuing the system of house-to-house visitations to check for premonitory cholera symptoms, disinfecting soiled linen and removing the inhabitants of infected dwellings. Special fever and isolation hospitals were created starting in the 1860s, encouraged by legislation in 1893, and many sanitary authorities provided such services free to the poor, some even reimbursing lost wages for the sequestered. Eventually, by the early 1880s, isolation in hospitals was made available also to non-paupers unable to remain safely at home.[119] Compulsory isolation of the

---

[116] *MTG*, 2 (4 April 1874), p. 385; 29 & 30 Vict. c. 90, ss. 29–30; 35 & 36 Vict. c. 79, s. 20; Hardy, "Cholera, Quarantine," pp. 256–58.

[117] *London Gazette*, 23999 (18 July 1873), pp. 3408–09; *Lancet* (26 July 1873), p. 121; *Conférence 1874*, pp. 445–49; *DVöG*, 9 (1877), pp. 749–52; 38 & 39 Vict. c. 55, s. 125; Anne Hardy, "Smallpox in London: Factors in the Decline of the Disease in the Nineteenth Century," *Medical History*, 27, 2 (April 1993), pp. 124–26.

[118] *PP* 1886 (4873) xxxi, 763, pp. 102–05; PRO, FO 881/6401*, R. Thorne Thorne, "Disease Prevention in England," 7 June 1893; *Conférence 1897*, pp. 48ff.; Arthur Whitelegge and George Newman, *Hygiene and Public Health* (12th edn.; London, 1911), pp. 524–25.

[119] *PP* 1867–68 (4072) xxxvii, 1, pp. x–xii, lxxxv; 45 & 46 Vict. c. 35, s. 7; *Practitioner*, 22 (1879), p. 145; *Sanitary Record*, 5 (2 December 1876), p. 362; 6 (20 January 1877), p. 42; 6 (27 January 1877), p. 57; 19 (5 February 1897), p. 109; *Journal of the Sanitary Institute*, 17, 1 (April 1896), p. 44; Jeanne L.

ill, so ticklish an issue on the continent, quickly passed into law in allegedly liberalist Britain. The 1866 Sanitary Act allowed mandatory removals to hospitals of the ill without adequate accommodation at home. In
the early seventies informal methods were employed to enforce isolation.
In Bristol, for example, the Medical Officer dealing with typhus in
lodging houses would frighten away the other inhabitants in order to
sequester the infected. The Sanitary Law Amendment Act of 1874 fined
those refusing to be removed.[120] The 1875 Public Health Act allowed
local authorities to threaten fines in order to compel hospitalization of
the infected without adequate accommodation, including residents of
common lodging houses.[121] Certain local authorities were now granted
particular powers in such respects. As of 1876 Huddersfield could hospitalize those without proper accommodation, Greenock (1877) could
remove healthy residents of infected dwellings to reception houses, while
Bradford, in 1881, and Warrington adopted their local acts to allow compulsory removal of contagious disease victims.[122]

Isolation was taken seriously enough that special legislation detailed
the means to be used in conveying patients. In 1860, local authorities
were allowed to provide special carriages for transporting victims from
their homes. The 1866 Sanitary and the 1875 Public Health Acts threatened any diseased person using public conveyances with fines and compensation of the owner for purification and losses.[123] Disinfection was
taken equally seriously. Owners were required to cleanse and disinfect
their houses and contents. Local authorities could require the destruction of bedding, clothing or other infected articles, compensating for
such loss, and passing along in any manner such objects without first disinfecting them was an offense. Owners of public conveyances were to

Brand, *Doctors and the State: The British Medical Profession and Government Action in Public Health, 1870–1912*
(Baltimore, 1965), p. 51; John M. Eyler, *Sir Arthur Newsholme and State Medicine, 1885–1935* (Cambridge,
1997), p. 107; 56 & 57 Vict. c. 68; *Hansard*, 1893, v. 9, col. 1549.

[120] 29 & 30 Vict. c. 90, s. 26; *Transactions of the National Association for the Promotion of Social Science*,
1870, p. 409; 37 & 38 Vict. c. 89, s. 51; Albert Palmberg, *A Treatise on Public Health* (London, 1895),
pp. 146ff.

[121] 38 & 39 Vict. c. 55, s. 124; *Sanitary Record*, n.s., 8, 88 (15 October 1886), p. 160. This was continued in the 1936 Public Health Act: 26 Geo. 5 & 1 Edw. 8 c. 49, ss. 168–69.

[122] *BMJ*, 1 (14 February 1880), pp. 259–60; *PP* 1882 (164) lvii, 587, pp. 18, 46–48. In Birkenhead,
for example, a police order was granted to remove a child with scarlatina whose mother, though
claiming that he was isolated at home, in fact let him play in public: *Sanitary Record*, n.s., 15, 200 (30
September 1893), p. 177; Eyler, *Arthur Newsholme and State Medicine*, p. 104.

[123] 23 & 24 Vict. c. 77, s. 12; *PP* 1863 (41) ii, 1; *Hansard*, 1863, v. 169, cols. 1590–95; 29 & 30 Vict.
c. 90, ss. 24–25; 38 and 39 Vict. c. 55, ss. 123, 126. In 1891 employees of the Prince of Wales Theatre
were fined 40s and costs for having sent off one of their colleagues suffering from scarlatina in a
hackney carriage: *Sanitary Record*, n.s., 12, 143 (15 May 1891), p. 583.

cleanse them after transporting the infected. Fines awaited those who rented out rooms or houses formerly occupied by the ill without first disinfecting them, and owners who lied about the presence during the previous six weeks of a diseased inhabitant risked jail. Institutions to provide for the free disinfection of contaminated items were authorized.[124] Thanks to the 1866 and 1875 acts, local authorities had the power of entry on private property during epidemics. They could remove corpses in overcrowded dwellings to a mortuary and order burials within certain time limits. In 1877, Greenock received increased powers of entry for Medical Officers, prohibited the sale of milk from infected farms and penalized attendance at school of potentially infected children. Even more dramatic, victims of contagious disease themselves were now targeted with criminal liability for the possible consequences of their condition, making it an offense for the infected to put others at risk. Patients or their guardians could be fined for willfully appearing in public without proper precautions or for entering any public conveyance without giving warning of their condition.[125]

Finally, as part of this neoquarantinist system, reporting contagious disease to the authorities was mandated. During the 1848 cholera epidemic, a rudimentary sort of notification had been introduced with the requirement that not only deaths, but also daily lists of persons stricken, compiled by the Guardians, were to be sent to the General Board of Health. The 1875 Public Health Act insisted that keepers of common lodging houses report cases of fever and infectious disease. Starting in the late seventies, various local acts required notification.[126] Under the so-called dual system, these often obliged, on pain of fines, not only the attending physician, but also, in his absence, those responsible for the patient, the head of family, other inhabitants of the dwelling or even the ill themselves. Despite various problems with physicians who feared losing patients or resented the subsequent interference of the Medical Officer of Health, doctors welcomed the fees paid for each certificate of

---

[124] 29 & 30 Vict. c. 90, ss. 22–23; 38 & 39 Vict. c. 55, ss. 120–22, 128–29; PRO MH 113/5, LGB, "Precautions against the Infection of Cholera," 5 July 1873, p. 2; MH 113/9, LGB, "General Memorandum on the Proceedings which are advisable in Places attacked or threatened by Epidemic Disease," April 1888, p. 1; *Sanitary Record*, n.s., 8, 90 (15 December 1886), p. 268.

[125] 29 & 30 Vict. c. 90, ss. 27–28, 38; 38 & 39 Vict. c. 55, s. 126; *BMJ*, 1 (14 February 1880), pp. 259–60.

[126] *PP* 1849 (1115) xxiv, pp. 95–96; *MTG*, 7 (1853), pp. 354–55; 38 & 39 Vict. c. 55, s. 84; *BMJ*, 1 (14 February 1880), pp. 259–60; *Sanitary Record*, 7 (2 November 1877), pp. 287–88; n.s., 14, 170 (15 October 1892), p. 202; John C. McVail, *Half a Century of Small-Pox and Vaccination* (Edinburgh, n.d. [1919]), p. 48.

disease and such acts became increasingly popular.[127] After failed attempts during the early eighties, a national law in 1889 introduced notification to any district that so chose.[128] So successful was this that by the early nineties, some five-sixths of the population of England and Wales had been brought under compulsory notification. The law allowed Medical Officers to prosecute a wide variety of citizens, from a lodging-house operator in Leith who, having neglected to give notice of a case of measles, was fined two pounds and deprived of his license for three years, to a mother who failed to report her children's scarlet fever and endangered the public by taking them out in a perambulator, fined four pounds. One zealous Medical Office hired a detective to follow an ambulance calling at a private residence and, when it headed for the fever hospital, brought charges against the passengers for having failed to report the case.[129] In 1899 notification was required throughout the country.[130]

Although neoquarantinism was often called the English system, the British were hardly alone in treading new prophylactic ground. A similar switch to techniques of inspection, notification, isolation and disinfection took place on the continent. In Germany the influence of Pettenkofer and the gradual decline of oldfashioned quarantinism led to a new phase of preventive strategy during the epidemics of the 1860s and seventies. Central to Pettenkofer's view was the transformation of the cholera germ in soil fouled by excrement. To avoid such epidemic mutation, regulations now governed the removal of bodily wastes from dwellings, seeking to prevent fecal contamination by requiring watertight containers. Measures from the 1860s, inspired by Pettenkoferian concerns to neutralize the cholera germ, prescribed widespread disinfection. Cesspools, sewers and drains were to be cleansed and flushed with water, latrines disinfected. Toilets likely to be used by visitors from stricken origins, especially in railway station restaurants, were to be disinfected frequently,

---

[127] *PP* 1882 (164) lvii, 587, pp. 7–14; PRO, MH 23/1, Town Clerk, Borough of Huddersfield, to LGB, 31 October 1878; Edward Sergeant, *The Compulsory Registration of Infectious Disease with Especial Reference to its Practical Working in the Borough of Bolton* (Bolton, 1878); *Sanitary Record*, n.s., 8, 88 (15 October 1886), pp. 151–57; n.s., 8, 90 (15 December 1886), p. 277; *Transactions of the Seventh International Congress of Hygiene and Demography*, London 1891 (London, 1892), v. IX, pp. 166–67.

[128] 52 & 53 Vict. c. 72; *PP* 1881 (229) ii, 367; *PP* 1882 (52) ii, 509; *PP* 1883 (100) vi, 285; *PP* 1884 (303) ii, 35; *Hansard*, 1883, v. 280, cols. 1650–52; *PP* 1889 (293) iii, 269; Dorothy E. Watkins, "The English Revolution in Social Medicine, 1889–1911" (Ph.D. diss, University of London, 1984), pp. 214–17.

[129] *Sanitary Record*, n.s., 14, 170 (15 October 1892), p. 202; n.s., 14, 178 (15 February 1893), p. 412; n.s., 12, 138 (15 December 1890), p. 316; n.s., 17, 297 (9 August 1895), p. 135. Attempts to extend the 1889 act can be found in: *PP* 1894 (209) iv, 621; *PP* 1899 (111) v, 253.   [130] 62 & 63 Vict. c. 8.

including each time a traveler used them in a suspicious manner. During epidemics, excretions were to be collected in special containers, disinfected and removed, the clothing, bedding and other effects of the ill disinfected.[131] In Bavaria cleansings of sewers and latrines had been required already in 1836 and now, at midcentury, disinfections were expanded to include the living quarters and effects of the ill. In the early seventies Munich restaurants, theaters, barracks and railroad stations were ordered to disinfect their toilets and cesspools during the summer months; in 1873 a compulsory disinfection of all toilets and fumigation of sickrooms were introduced.[132] Restaurant and bar owners in Augsburg were to discourage their guests from relieving themselves on the sidewalks and, in any case, to scrub outside their establishments daily with a mixture of carbolic acid. In Dresden, the homes, effects, toilets and house sewers of the cholera dead were disinfected. Fumigations and disinfections of clothing, bedding and similar effects were common. In Augsburg sickrooms were fumigated, and this was repeated three days later; only after ten to twenty days did the police return the house keys to their inhabitants.[133]

In Cologne, at first unable to persuade the authorities to undertake disinfections of lavatories and the like, a local public health committee assumed such responsibilities at its own expense until the police were finally brought to do so in 1867. Elsewhere the authorities discovered that simply ordering citizens to disinfect their toilets, even when materials were provided free or cheaply and fines threatened, was not effective.

---

[131] Martin, *Haupt-Bericht*, pp. 892–96; *DVöG*, 16 (1884), pp. 140–44; Helm, *Cholera in Lübeck*, pp. 50–51; Wolff, *Bericht*, pp. 73–74, 81–86; W. Griesinger, Max v. Pettenkofer and C. A. Wunderlich, *Cholera-Regulativ* (Munich, 1866), pp. 16–17; Robert Bolz, *Die Cholera auf dem badischen Kriegsschauplätze im Sommer 1866* (Karlsruhe, 1867), pp. 51–52; *Ärztliche Mitteilungen aus Baden*, 27, 19 (24 September 1873), pp. 155–59; Anneliese Gerbert, *Öffentliche Gesundheitspflege und staatliches Medizinalwesen in den Städten Braunschweig und Wolfenbüttel im 19. Jahrhundert* (Braunschweig, 1983), p. 135; Marianne Pagel, *Gesundheit und Hygiene: Zur Sozialgeschichte Lüneburgs im 19. Jahrhundert* (Hannover, 1992), pp. 91–92.

[132] *ASA*, 3, 1 (1838), pp. 235–47; M. Frank, *Die Cholera-Epidemie in München in dem Jahre 1873/74, nach amtlichen Quellen dargestellt* (Munich, 1875), pp. 46, 54–55, 83, 283–84; Martin, *Haupt-Bericht*, pp. 775, 819–20; Wilbrand, *Die Desinfection*, pp. 127–32; Carl Friedrich Majer, *General-Bericht über die Cholera-Epidemieen im Königreiche Bayern während der Jahre 1873 und 1874* (Munich, 1877), p. 10.

[133] L. Fikentscher, *Die Cholera asiatica zu Augsburg 1873/74 vom sanitätspolizeilichen Standpunkte aus geschildert* (Augsburg, 1874), pp. 18–20, 36; *DVöG*, 17 (1885), pp. 610–14; Gustav Warnatz, *Die asiatische Cholera des Jahres 1866 im K.S. Regierungsbezirke Dresden* (Leipzig, 1868), pp. 40–43; Friedr. Aug. Mühlhäuser, *Über Epidemieen und Cholera insbesondere über Cholera in Speier 1873* (Mannheim, 1875), pp. 87–88; Carl Julius Büttner, *Die Cholera Asiatica, deren Ursachen, Behandlung und Verhütung auf Grund der während der 1866er Epidemie in der Seidau bei Budissin gemachten Erfahrungen* (Leipzig, 1868), p. 170; Carl Richard Lotze, *Die Choleraepidemie von 1866 in Stötteritz bei Leipzig* (Leipzig, 1867), p. 5; Wilbrand, *Die Desinfection*, p. 103.

Despite various legal complications, therefore, in certain states they undertook such measures directly. In Zwickau the town council ordered the disinfection of all toilets in November 1865, hiring thirteen workers who swabbed away for seven weeks. Leipzig was one of the first major cities to carry out a planned and compulsory disinfection by municipal workers. The city having been divided into 100 districts, successive floors of all houses were disinfected each day, starting on Sundays with the first. In Dresden in 1873, a team of forty-eight workers under police supervision went house to house disinfecting all toilets and cesspools, a special squad tackling dwellings with especially impressive accumulations of filth, thus cleansing the entire city once a week.[134] Prussia belied its reputation as a place where the authorities took the initiative in such respects. In Berlin in 1866 the sanitary commission sought to have them disinfect directly, but the police refused, skeptical that such precautions were in fact effective, diffident in the face of organizing such measures in a large city, hesitant at the lack of authority to impose taxes for these purposes. Instead, measures were to be carried out by property owners and only in default by the government. The poor, however, could bring their bedding for disinfection at no charge on Friday afternoons and in 1873 their dwellings were purified at the public expense. Special disinfective procedures were instituted in 1871 for unhospitalized patients: evacuations to be steeped in carbolic acid, spaces adjacent to the sickroom fumigated several times daily with chlorine, the floors sprayed with carbolic acid, followed by a general ventilation. Clothing, bedding and other effects were to be doused with carbolic acid and then boiled, worthless objects burned, corpses sprinkled with acid or chlorine.[135]

The question of hospitalizing patients remained as delicate as ever. Regulations rarely allowed obligatory removal, but in fact compulsion was occasionally practiced informally.[136] In Bavaria, sequestration was viewed skeptically and not rigorously enforced. The issue arose in

[134] Comité für öffentliche Gesundheitspflege in Köln, *Bericht über die zweite Cholera-Epidemie des Jahres 1867 in Köln* (Cologne, 1868), pp. 28–52; Rudolf Günther, *Die indische Cholera in Sachsen im Jahre 1865* (Leipzig, 1866), pp. 115–16; Wolff, *Bericht*, pp. 64–68, 81–86; Thomas, ed., *Verhandlungen der Cholera-Konferenz in Weimar am 28. und 29. April 1867* (Munich, 1867), pp. 36–37; *Berichte*, Heft 3, pp. 94–95.

[135] Thomas, *Verhandlungen der Cholera-Konferenz*, pp. 72–77; Müller, *Cholera-Epidemie zu Berlin 1866*, pp. 14–15, 60–63, 146–47; Küchenmeister, *Handbuch*, pp. 214–15; E. H. Müller, *Cholera-Epidemie zu Berlin im Jahre 1873: Amtlicher Bericht* (Berlin, 1874), pp. 53–55; Wolter, *Das Auftreten der Cholera*, p. 311; Albert Guttstadt, *Deutschlands Gesundheitswesen* (Leipzig, 1891), v. II, p. 131.

[136] Ute Frevert, *Krankheit als politisches Problem 1770–1880* (Göttingen, 1984), p. 68; Palmberg, *Treatise on Public Health*, p. 369. The testimony is often ambiguous: Mühlhäuser, *Über Epidemieen und Cholera*, pp. 87–88.

Munich when house-to-house visitations in 1854 brought to light cases that would have benefited from removal. Although physicians were encouraged to persuade patients to be hospitalized, their permission remained essential. In Baden in 1873, patients were, if possible, to be removed to special isolation quarters. In Augsburg it was considered prudent to isolate the first cholera cases in the barracks of the hospital and physicians were to persuade them accordingly. In Dresden, large numbers of patients unable to be cared for at home accumulated in the municipal hospital and compulsory evacuations were apparently carried out.[137] In Berlin in 1866, with the Charité replete with the casualties of Bismarck's wars, four cholera lazarettos were established. The ill were not to be removed without permission of the family head, but if he refused despite the physician's insistence, the district head was to bring his influence to bear, with the threat of being reported to the sanitary commission held out in cases of persistent recalcitrance. Once the epidemic struck, the tone of instructions became shriller, although still stopping short of direct compulsion.[138] Removing the well from the noxious atmosphere of contaminated dwellings, the British "tenting-out" system, was also employed. In Munich during the 1880s evacuating healthy occupants of stricken buildings was allowed and in Augsburg family members of patients were sequestered. In Speyer some 200 people were evacuated in 1873, their dwellings cleansed and disinfected. In Magdeburg, a notoriously filthy house was evacuated by force and sealed. The same, although accompanied by much protest, happened to a compound of barracks housing the homeless, who were now shifted to tents outside the city. In hard-hit and crowded dwellings in Dresden, physicians sought to convince the inhabitants to move to the evacuation station where they were medically inspected thrice daily, and those with symptoms were to be removed to the cholera barracks. In Prussia, strongly infected houses were evacuated and their use was permitted again only after disinfection.[139]

---

[137] Martin, *Haupt-Bericht*, pp. 858–60; *Ärztliche Mittheilungen aus Baden*, 27, 19 (24 September 1873), pp. 155–59; Fikentscher, *Cholera asiatica zu Augsburg*, pp. 18–20, 26; Majer, *General-Bericht*, p. 56; Warnatz, *Asiatische Cholera*, pp. 40–43; Frank, *Cholera-Epidemie in München*, pp. 68–69. Other evidence speaks only of attempting to persuade the ill to be removed: *Berichte*, Heft 3, pp. 91–92.

[138] Müller, *Cholera-Epidemie zu Berlin 1866*, pp. 146–47, 150–51; Küchenmeister, *Handbuch*, p. 214; *Berichte*, Heft 6, p. 112.

[139] *DVöG*, 16 (1884), pp. 140–44; Fikentscher, *Cholera asiatica zu Augsburg*, pp. 18–20; Joseph Heine, *Die epidemische Cholera in ihren elementaren Lebenseigenschaften und in ihrer physiologischen Behandlungsmethode aus der grossen Epidemie von Speyer 1873* (Würzburg, 1874), pp. 42–47; Majer, *General-Bericht*, p. 41; Gähde, *Die Cholera in Magdeburg* (Braunschweig, 1875), pp. 25–28; *Berichte*, Heft 3, pp. 91–92; Heft 6, p. 112.

The switch to neoquarantinism with its emphasis on inspection and disinfection can also be seen in precautions taken at the borders. The Prussians imposed neoquarantinist prophylaxis on shippers from the east who plied the inland waterways. In 1866, the authorities disinfected all vessels traveling upstream past the Plötzensee sluice. During three months in the late summer of 1873, over 4,000 ships and 11,000 persons were inspected and disinfected on the inland waterways near Berlin.[140] Raftsmen entering Prussia and Posen in 1873 were inspected and, if they proved ill, the strictures of the 1835 regulation on contagious disease were enforced. Once cases of cholera had been detected, an inspection station was established at Schilno and timber raftsmen were subject to five days of quarantine. This throwback to an oldfashioned approach soon had to be abandoned, however, because the numbers of shippers proved unmanageable and strictures were being circumvented by paying off the raftsmen downstream from the station and then proceeding overland. Quarantines were therefore replaced by a series of inspection stations at which crews were examined, corpses buried, the sick hospitalized, but vessels otherwise allowed to pass. To prevent raftsmen from spreading disease on their way home overland, employers were to provide special trains, subsequently disinfected. As of July, all arriving raftsmen were fumigated with chlorine gas for ten minutes in boxes enclosing them up to their necks.[141]

The Swedes clove more faithfully to traditional precautions than their neighbors and neoquarantinism was introduced only hesitantly and late. While other Scandinavian nations had introduced the revision system already during the late 1860s, Sweden did not follow suit until the following decade. In 1875 quarantines were moderated with inspections and isolation. Healthy passengers on infected ships could land while the vessel, crew and the ill were isolated, the dead were removed and the effects of the sick and sometimes the entire ship disinfected.[142] Within the country oldfashioned quarantinism was also reformed. Measures implemented by local communities were no longer needlessly to obstruct circulation within the kingdom.

---

[140] Müller, *Cholera-Epidemie zu Berlin 1866*, pp. 60–63; Müller, *Cholera-Epidemie zu Berlin 1873*, p. 15. Almost 7,000 persons were inspected and disinfected on the Weichsel: [Woldemar] Berg, *Die Cholera, eine ansteckende Volksseuche, der Import und die Verbreitung derselben im Kreise Marienburg vom Jahre 1873* (Marienburg, 1874), p. 4.

[141] *Berichte*, Heft 1 (2nd edn.), pp. 44–46; *Medicinisches Correspondenz-Blatt des Württembergischen ärztlichen Vereins*, 47, 22 (10 August 1877), p. 171.

[142] *Förhandlingar*, 1866, pp. 166–69; 1868, pp. 162–65; 1897, p. 225; *Conférence 1874*, p. 135; *SFS*, 1875/21; Bergstrand, *Svenska Läkaresällskapet*, p. 208; *Upsala Läkareförening*, 13, 1 (1877–78), pp. 11–12.

Sequestration was strictly enforced, following what the Swedes took to be the British precedent. The ill were to be compulsorily hospitalized unless able to be cared for in separate marked rooms at home or if evacuation would endanger their health. Once patients had either died or recuperated, their living quarters and clothing were disinfected. Local authorities willing to bear the expense could evacuate unhealthy or infected houses or restrict the number of inhabitants in certain dwellings. Corpses were to be disinfected and surrounded by fresh spruce twigs in the coffin.[143] Nonetheless, despite such nods in the direction of preventive reform, oldfashioned quarantinism remained in vigorous health in Sweden, as can be seen from the reaction to the threat of plague during the late 1870s. Overland travel from infected nations was now shut off altogether; ships thence were to dock at the quarantine stations where possibly infected vessels underwent two weeks of isolation, with various classes of goods subject to differing regimens of prohibition and purification. In 1883 with cholera in Egypt, quarantine in the oldfashioned sense of isolating all from an infected area to see who might succumb was applied once again and ships from Egyptian or Turkish ports were to land at Känsö. Two years later similar regulations were extended equally to ships from elsewhere.[144]

In France, lip service was paid to the principles of neoquarantinism, but less was accomplished. Official instructions in 1871 on cholera judged restrictions on maritime traffic difficult, impracticable on circulation overland, and focused instead on the danger of contact with choleraic evacuations, recommending pure water, inspected food and disinfected latrines. During the early 1870s high-ranking French officials were still recommending quarantine. By mid-decade, however, a compromise had been found in a variant on the revision system. In 1876, following the precedent set already in the early sixties for yellow fever, a new set of maritime sanitary measures imposed observation quarantines on ships suspected of disease and strict quarantine, involving landing passengers and discharging cargo, on those with cholera actually

---

[143] *SFS* 1874/68, §§13, 29, 32, 36; 1875/21, §22; *Hygiea*, 37, 3 (March 1875), p. 178; 37, 11 (November 1875), p. 641; A. Kullberg, ed., *Författningar m.m. angående medicinalväsendet i Sverige, omfattande tiden från och med år 1860 till och med år 1876* (Stockholm, 1877), pp. 538–45; Aug. Hæffner, ed., *Lexikon öfver nu gällande författningar, m.m., rörande kolera* (Gothenburg, 1894), p. 33.

[144] *Hygiea*, 41, 2 (February 1879), pp. 130–40; 41, 4 (April 1879), pp. 265–77; 41, 5 (May 1879), pp. 329–33; *SFS*, 1879/28; 1885/37; Sven-Ove Arvidsson, *De svenska koleraepidemierna: En epidemiografisk studie* (Stockholm, 1972), p. 108.

onboard.[145] Although this meant that not every ship had the full force of traditional quarantine imposed, the principle at the heart of the revision system (that the healthy be allowed to pass, only the ill retained) was not yet followed. At the same time, however, quarantines were shortened.[146] Off to a slow start, the French continued to follow the neoquarantinist trend with less alacrity or consequence than their neighbors. Well into the 1880s and nineties, disinfection was still being discussed as a technique gradually gaining favor as a means of supplementing and moderating quarantine. In 1884, Adrien Proust, the tireless Inspector General of French epidemic prophylaxis and father of Marcel, recommended a combination of quarantine for passengers from infected places and disinfection of their soiled effects. At the 1885 Rome Sanitary Conference, the French delegates came out, with the fervor of recent converts, behind the new techniques of sanitary management (disinfections, cleansings, inspections of passengers, isolation of the ill) onboard ships from the Orient that would allow them to land in Europe without quarantine. By the late eighties, vessels at Marseilles were being inspected and, if in satisfactory hygienic condition, allowed to pass rather than uniformly subjected to quarantine. Yet, as late as 1896, while healthy passengers on ships with clean bills of health and those suspected of infection were allowed to disembark, subject to surveillance, uninfected travelers on cholera-stricken vessels were still liable to five days' observation quarantine.[147]

While the French implemented a variant of neoquarantinist measures externally in their ports, little was done within the country and even those few measures were taken late. The sorts of sanitary reforms familiar from Britain came in fits and starts with grand renovation projects such as Haussmann's. But even more modest interventions in the neoquarantinist spirit were most notable for their absence. The system of isolation and disinfection was still being discussed in the 1870s and early eighties as a new trend in prophylaxis, found especially in Britain. In Marseilles municipal authorities reverted to (admittedly fruitless) calls for a sanitary

---

[145] *Recueil*, 3 (1874), pp. 316–28; 4 (1875), pp. 250–55; 5 (1876), pp. 4–24; Coleman, *Yellow Fever in the North*, pp. 104–05.

[146] Proust, *La défense de l'Europe*, pp. 399–404; Henri Monod, *Le choléra (Histoire d'une épidémie – Finistère, 1885–1886)* (Paris, 1892), pp. 615–16; *Medical Record*, 43, 1 (1893), p. 1.

[147] *JO*, 17, 185 (9 July 1885), pp. 3523–24; Proust, *La défense de l'Europe*, pp. 25–26; Trolard, *De la prophylaxie*, p. 11; *JO*, 16, 298 (29 October 1884), pp. 5682–84; *Annales*, 3/16 (1886), pp. 419–20; *Conférence 1885*, pp. 124, 131–35, 151; A. Proust, *L'orientation nouvelle de la politique sanitaire* (Paris, 1896), pp. 271–75; *JO*, 28, 20 (21 January 1896), pp. 360–61.

cordon against Toulon when cholera struck in 1884. Isolation of disease victims was not commonly practiced, although advocated by many and admired in other nations, again Britain especially.[148] But such techniques, especially sequestration, were also viewed skeptically. Recommendations that the poor be isolated in hospitals and barracks during epidemics prompted worries that such measures would degenerate into the compulsory removal of patients.[149] Such measures were accordingly adopted slowly and hesitantly. In Toulon in 1884 the sanitary commission, wishing to evacuate residents of and disinfect dwellings with a cholera death, were able to cleanse, but found the cost of lodging inhabitants elsewhere prohibitive. In the Finistère in 1885–86 the authorities had only partial success trying to convince 2,000 visiting fishermen to prevent overcrowding by moving into military tents erected for the purpose.[150] But slowly the tide changed. In Lille in 1886, a sanitary commission sought to evacuate insalubrious buildings and possibly also their neighbors during cholera epidemics. During the 1884 epidemic in the Seine, cholera patients were removed in special wagons, and their dwellings were fumigated. The Paris police organized a special squad to disinfect the rooms of dead or hospitalized victims and one dwelling, a hovel beyond salvation, was instead burned to the ground. In 1888, Paris began building stations for special wagons to remove the infectious and, by the nineties, disinfections were well organized and in full swing.[151]

In all of these nations a requirement to report contagious disease had been enforced during the first cholera epidemic. Like Britain, the continental countries now also continued and formalized notification as part of the neoquarantinist emphasis on identifying in order to isolate cases.[152] In Germany, many localities had introduced such strictures

---

[148] *Bulletin*, 2, 6 (1877), pp. 447–49; *Annales*, 3/10 (1883), p. 357; Frank M. Snowden, *Naples in the Time of Cholera, 1884–1911* (Cambridge, 1995), p. 64; Chartier, Laennec and Lapeyre, "Rapport sur l'isolement des malades atteints d'affections contagieuses présenté au Conseil de santé des hospices civils de Nantes," *Rapport sur les travaux du Conseil central d'hygiène publique et de salubrité de la ville de Nantes et du département de la Loire-Inférieure* (1880), pp. 98–100, 105; *Annales*, 2/49 (1878), pp. 267–69; 3/5 (1881), pp. 550–51; 3/15 (1886), pp. 219–29; A. Proust, *Le choléra: Etiologie et prophylaxie* (Paris, 1883), pp. 45, 200; L.-H. Thoinot, *Histoire de l'épidémie cholérique en 1884* (Paris, 1886), pp. 173–75, 246–49, 353; *Mémoires*, 17 (1853), p. 383.

[149] Mireur, *Etude historique*, pp. 156, 159; *Bulletin de la Société de médecine publique et d'hygiène professionnelle*, 2 (1879), pp. 328–30.

[150] Dominique, *Le choléra a Toulon*, p. 116; Monod, *Le choléra*, pp. 87–88; Monod, *La santé publique*, p. 48.

[151] *Bulletin médical du Nord*, n.s., 7 (1886), pp. 224–26; *Veröffentlichungen*, 9, 2 (7 July 1885), pp. 5–6; *BMJ*, 2 (23 August 1884), p. 381; Monod, *La santé publique*, p. 76; *Annales*, 3/19 (1888), p. 282; 3/26 (1891), pp. 305ff. The 1902 law, although relying heavily on disinfection, nonetheless made no use of isolation: Jean Humbert, *Du role de l'administration en matière de prophylaxie des maladies épidémiques* (Paris, 1911), pp. 181–83.   [152] *Conférence 1893*, p. 79.

during the nineteenth century: requiring smallpox to be reported in Anspach in 1807, Berlin in 1810, Lübeck in 1823; broadening this to other disease as well in 1862 in Bavaria, 1877 in Cassel, 1881 in Baden, 1890 in Saxony.[153] In Prussia decrees from the late eighteenth century required reporting by physicians and clergy. The 1835 regulation obliged heads of families, clergy, innkeepers and physicians to report, but in 1845 this was limited to medical personnel. Hamburg had required not just physicians but every citizen to report cases already in 1818. In 1836, when finally faced with cholera, Munich physicians were to report all cases.[154] During the middle years of the century, many localities required reporting of cholera by both physicians and family members. In 1892, those without a reporting requirement were to introduce one and, in Prussia, this was expanded to cover also suspected cases, including every instance of diarrhea with vomiting, except in children under two.[155] Official physicians were allowed to inspect and perform autopsies on corpses to determine the presence of disease. The Contagious Disease Law of 1900 required reporting both actual and suspected cases, although the Prussian version removed the latter in fear of overreporting.[156] In Stockholm, physicians were required to report all cholera-like fatal cases starting in 1850. Notification was subsequently generalized to the nation in 1874–75, required of both physicians and clergy and, in 1919, also heads of families.[157] In France, notification of cholera, plague and yellow fever was called for in the 1822 law, in various local legislation and a law of 3 March

[153] John Cross, *A History of the Variolous Epidemic Which Occurred in Norwich in the Year 1819, and Destroyed 530 Individuals, with an Estimate of the Protection Afforded by Vaccination* (London, 1820), pp. 245–46; F. L. Augustin, *Die Königlich Preussische Medicinalverfassung* (Potsdam, 1818), v. I, pp. 175–76; Regulativ über das Verfahren beim Ausbruche der Menschenblattern, 15 October 1823, in BA, Reichskanzleramt, 14.01/999; *Recueil*, 23 (1893), pp. 170–71; *DVöG*, 17 (1885), pp. 605–06.

[154] Augustin, *Preussische Medicinalverfassung*, v. I, pp. 35–36; Franz Brefeld, *Die endliche Austilgung der asiatischen Cholera* (Breslau, 1854), p. 64; Fliescher, *Die Choleraepidemien in Düsseldorf*, pp. 15–16; Guttstadt, *Deutschlands Gesundheitswesen*, v. II, p. 92; Franz Xaver Kopp, *Generalbericht über die Cholera-Epidemie in München einschlüssig der Vorstadt Au im Jahre 1836/37* (Munich, 1837), pp. 59–60.

[155] Gähde, *Cholera in Magdeburg*, pp. 25–28; Bolz, *Cholera auf dem badischen Kriegsschauplatze*, pp. 56–57; *Ärztliche Mittheilungen aus Baden*, 27, 19 (24 September 1873), pp. 155–59; Wolff, *Bericht*, pp. 81–86; Müller, *Cholera-Epidemie zu Berlin 1866*, pp. 60–63; *Der amtliche Erlass, betreffend Massnahmen gegen die Choleragefahr: Vom 19. August 1893* (Königsberg, 1893), pp. 3–5; Prussia, Haus der Abgeordneten, *Anlagen zu den Stenographischen Berichten*, 1892/93, Akst. 76, pp. 2067, 2095, 2106.

[156] *SB*, 1892/93, Akst. 172, p. 916; *Anweisung zur Bekämpfung der Cholera. (Festgestellt in der Sitzung des Bundesrats vom 28. Januar 1904): Amtliche Ausgabe* (Berlin, 1905), pp. 7–10; Wilhelm Markull, *Die Gesetze betreffend die Bekämpfung übertragbarer Krankheiten* (Berlin, 1906), p. 2; Martin Kirchner, *Die gesetzlichen Grundlagen der Seuchenbekämpfung im Deutschen Reiche unter besonderer Berücksichtigung Preussens* (Jena, 1907), pp. 32–33.

[157] "Kongl. Sundhets-Collegii Cirkulär till samtlige i Stockholm anställde eller praktiserande Läkare," 26 August 1850, copy in Riksdagsbiblioteket, Stockholm; *SFS*, 1851/17; 1875/21, §21; 1874/68, §33; *Betänkande med förslag till hälsovårdsstadga för riket och epidemistadga* (Stockholm, 1915), pp. 131ff.; *SFS* 1919/443, §2.

1882. The procedure was not brought up to date, however, until 1892 with the law on the practice of medicine and then continued in the 1902 public health law. Although attempts were made to follow the broader British example that both physicians and family members report, the requirement was limited to medical professionals.[158]

Neoquarantinism thus meant substituting inspections and medical surveillance of symptomless passengers for quarantines, cleansing and disinfecting the ill, their effects and dwellings in order to shorten the duration or need for sequestration. In other respects, however, many of the practices familiar from the 1830s continued through the century. Public institutions, amusements and gatherings were closed or limited. In 1873 Munich made the ultimate sacrifice and canceled Oktoberfest, while dances and iceskating were regarded with suspicion as probable venues of dietary excess and chills.[159] The dead were still feared as dangerous, corpses removed and buried promptly, elaborate and well-attended funerals prevented.[160] Infected houses were marked.

KOCH AND THE NINETIES

Koch's (re)discovery of the comma bacillus in 1883 as the cause of cholera was part of the bacteriological revolution of the late nineteenth century, a quantum leap in knowledge based on Pasteur's pioneering work and later to reap further results as the microorganisms responsible for other contagious diseases were identified. In etiological terms, Koch's breakthrough settled finally the chronically festering dispute between contagionists and localists by proving that, whatever predisposing factors might help disease spread, without the import of a specific microorgan-

---

[158] *Recueil*, 21 (1891), pp. 406–07; 23 (1893), pp. 170–72, 548; Alfred Fillassier, *De la détermination des pouvoirs publics en matière d'hygiène* (2nd edn.; Paris, 1902), p. 169; Jacques Léonard, *La France médicale: Médecins et malades au XIXe siècle* (n.p., 1978), p. 77; Hildreth, *Doctors, Bureaucrats, and Public Health*, pp. 196–98; *JO*, 25, 354 (30 December 1893), pp. 6173–75; Ann-Louise Shapiro, "Private Rights, Public Interest, and Professional Jurisdiction: The French Public Health Law of 1902," *BHM*, 54, 1 (Spring 1980), p. 20; Mosny, *La protection de la santé publique* (Paris, 1904), p. 21; *Annales*, 3/31 (1894), pp. 182–89; 3/16 (1886), p. 468; *Mémoires*, 34 (1884), pp. clviii–clix. In 1908 and 1914, this was changed to include the heads of families and those who cared for or lodged the ill: *JO*, 40, 255 (19 September 1908), pp. 6493–94.

[159] Mühlhäuser, *Über Epidemieen und Cholera*, pp. 87–88; Gähde, *Cholera in Magdeburg*, pp. 25–28; Bolz, *Cholera auf dem badischen Kriegsschauplatze*, pp. 58–59; *Recueil*, 3 (1874), pp. 316–28; Proust, *La défense de l'Europe*, pp. 429–30; Mireur, *Etude historique*, pp. 162–63; *SFS*, 1874/68; 1875/21; *Conférence 1866*, 24, annexe; Wilbrand, *Die Desinfection*, p. 147; Frank, *Cholera-Epidemie in München*, pp. 66, 72, 75, 95–97; Fikentscher, *Cholera asiatica zu Augsburg*, pp. 18–20.

[160] Heine, *Die epidemische Cholera*, pp. 42–47; Majer, *General-Bericht*, p. 41; Gähde, *Cholera in Magdeburg*, pp. 25–28; Wolff, *Bericht über die Cholera-Epidemie*, pp. 81–86; Proust, *La défense de l'Europe*, pp. 429–36; *Hygiea*, 37, 11 (November 1875), p. 641; Kullberg, *Forfattningar*, pp. 538–45.

ism, cholera would not arise. In prophylactic terms, however, his conclusions had a much more tempered influence. Koch's discoveries and the changes in official precautions based thereon did not represent a rollback of sanitationist efforts, much less a return to traditional quarantinism. The march away from a simple form of localism and sanitationism had set off already decades earlier and Koch prompted but a shift in the emphasis of an already existing neoquarantinist approach that dated back at least two decades before the comma bacillus – a sharpening of the focus, but no fundamental alteration, of the tenets of neoquarantinist prophylaxis.[161] Knowledge of the specific means by which cholera was transmitted meant that the techniques of inspection, isolation and disinfection could be made more effective, but these procedures had been elaborated and adopted long before the comma bacillus had made its debut on the epidemiological stage.

Take disinfection, one of the main strings in the Kochian bow, as an example. Disinfection, fumigation and other methods of destroying the contagium, far from being a novelty of the 1880s and nineties, had been tried during the Middle Ages on the plague, retried again in the 1830s for cholera, only then to be reintroduced in a more systematic manner with the development of neoquarantinism in the late 1860s.[162] The problem with disinfection in the pre-bacteriological era was, of course, that, shooting in the dark, no one had any idea of what they were seeking to destroy, nor therefore how to do so. It was consequently impossible to know except indirectly which disinfectant substances were most effective and whether, indeed, the entire enterprise made any difference.[163] As a result, disinfections often did little to prevent the spread of cholera and, after an initial burst of enthusiasm in the 1860s, disillusionment set in. The difficulty of documenting that the procedure had made any noticeable difference in the spread or virulence of epidemics was discouraging.[164]

[161] The simple correlation between Koch's discoveries and neoquarantinist measures suggested by Evans is insufficient: Richard J. Evans, "Epidemics and Revolutions: Cholera in Nineteenth-Century Europe," *Past and Present*, 120 (August 1988), p. 145.

[162] See, for example, *Conférence 1866*, 24, annexe, appendix, pp. 1–2, 17–18.

[163] *Berichte*, Heft 1 (2nd edn.), pp. 21–25; *DVöG*, 7 (1875), p. 274; *Annales*, 2/43 (1875), p. 248; 2/41 (1874), pp. 8–13; Heine, *Die epidemische Cholera*, pp. 47–48; J. A. Gläser, *Gemeinverständliche Anticontagionistische Betrachtungen bei Gelegenheit der letzten Cholera-Epidemie in Hamburg 1892* (Hamburg, 1893), p. 46.

[164] Lotze, *Choleraepidemie von 1866*, p. 5; Wilbrand, *Die Desinfection*, p. 137; Comité, *Bericht*, pp. 28–52; Müller, *Cholera-Epidemie zu Berlin 1866*, pp. 63–65; Müller, *Cholera-Epidemie zu Berlin 1873*, p. 16; Warnatz, *Asiatische Cholera*, p. 49; Mühlhäuser, *Über Epidemieen und Cholera*, p. 87; Thomas, *Verhandlungen der Cholera-Konferenz*, pp. 36–37; Heine, *Die epidemische Cholera*, pp. 42–47; Majer, *General-Bericht*, p. 41.

The measures implemented against raftsmen, for example, had done little to hamper disease along the Prussian waterways. In the elaborate fumigations shippers underwent, as one Galician raftowner put it, "not even the lice perished."[165] Pettenkofer, at first an enthusiast of disinfecting excrement, noted how cholera spread unabated and his ardor cooled in the midseventies. At the 1874 Sanitary Conference, the British stood almost alone in their defense of disinfection against attacks from the Austrian and German delegates. At the Rome Conference in 1885, shortly after Koch had announced his discoveries but before they had become widely known or accepted, faith in disinfection reached its nadir.[166] But by the early nineties, Koch's discoveries had revived the fortunes of such flagging precautions. At the Venice Conference, delegates from nations otherwise in disagreement outdid each other in united support of this newly rejuvenated technique.[167] Chemical purification now became a cornerstone of the neoquarantinist prophylactic edifice, a measure whose effect could be directly judged by its ability to destroy the comma bacillus.[168] Disinfection was thus not a technique invented or first made possible by the discoveries of bacteriology, but in fact one that, already long in use, had become routine prevention two decades before Koch. Its fortunes were now revived with the recognition that it was supported and enhanced by the new knowledge.[169]

Provoked by Koch's discoveries and their eventual preventive implementation, the debate between localists and contagionists was put through its paces yet again at the end of the century. In Germany, Pettenkofer's focus on factors in the immediate environment was challenged by the Kochians' insistence that the comma bacillus did not require any sort of transformation by local circumstances to spark an

---

[165] *Berichte*, Heft 1 (2nd edn.), p. 46; *Medicinisches Correspondenz-Blatt des Württembergischen ärztlichen Vereins*, 47, 22 (10 August 1877), p. 171.

[166] Frank, *Cholera-Epidemie in München*, pp. 46, 54–55, 76–77, 80–81, 83, 283–84; *Conférence 1874*, pp. 67–74; *Conférence 1885*, pp. 124–35, 168.

[167] *Conférence 1892*, pp. 127–28, 175; *Recueil*, 22 (1892), p. i.

[168] This included also an end to the old miasmatist assumption that malodorous and unhealthy were synonymous. The new bacteriologically inspired admonition was that disinfection and deodorization should not be confused and that unpleasant odors alone were not necessarily harmful: A. Heidenhain, *Desinfection im Hause und in der Gemeinde* (Cöslin, [1888]), pp. 4–7. But see also Alfred Conrad Biese, *Der Sieg über die Cholera* (Berlin, 1893), p. 27. It was also now recognized that fumigations had not worked against cholera: Ernst Barth, *Die Cholera, mit Berücksichtigung der speciellen Pathologie und Therapie* (Breslau, 1893), pp. 145–47.

[169] Pace the epidemiologically whiggish approach that sees disinfection as dependent on Pasteur and Koch for more than just a boost: *Recueil*, 22 (1892), pp. i–ii; 23 (1893), pp. viii; *Annales*, 4/11 (1909), p. 323; Claire Salomon-Bayet et al., *Pasteur et la révolution pastorienne* (Paris, 1986), pp. 301–06.

epidemic. The ever mercurial Pettenkofer, though willing to accept Koch's bacillus as his factor X, was nonetheless embittered by his rival's growing influence. Their etiological antagonism culminated in 1892 during the Hamburg epidemic when Pettenkofer, seeking to demonstrate that the comma bacillus alone could not generate cholera, quaffed a large infusion of them, thus – at the expense of a mild case of diarrhea – placing himself modestly in a venerable lineage of choleraic auto-experimentation.[170] Koch and his supporters, eventually ascendant, could be more magnanimous. Many of those not immediately partisan to one warring camp or the other were able to reconcile important elements of both, narrating the story of an infectious disease whose spread, although ultimately dependent on the import of a specific cause, was determined by other predisposing factors, both local and individual.[171] Although demonstrating the transmissibility of cholera, Koch himself did not think that quarantines and cordons made practical sense, except in unusual and very particular circumstances.[172] Not even the most ardent bacteriologically informed contagionist would deny the value for the fight against cholera of improving public hygiene.[173] Temporal, local and personal factors in the spread of disease deserved full attention, as Gaffky, one of the master's preeminent students, explained in 1895 at the height of Kochianism, despite the importance of the cholera vibrio as the immediate cause of illness. The most certain protection against cholera was sanitation, especially providing clean drinking water and removing waste. Cleanliness was better than a poorly executed disinfection, as the Prussian regulations on cholera put it in 1892.[174]

[170] Kisskalt, ed., *Briefwechsel Pettenkofers: Auszüge aus sämtlichen im Archiv des Hygienischen Instituts der Universität München befindlichen Briefen* (n.p, n.d. [1935]), pp. 267ff.; Pettenkofer, *Über Cholera*, pp. 6–11.

[171] *Die Cholera in Hamburg in ihren Ursachen und Wirkungen: Eine ökonomisch-medizinische Untersuchung* (Hamburg, 1893), pt. 2, pp. 8, 24–26, 39–40; Barth, *Cholera*, pp. 88–91, 96–97; *DVöG*, 17 (1885), pp. 556–59; R. J. Petri, *Der Cholerakurs im Kaiserlichen Gesundheitsamte: Vorträge und bakteriologisches Praktikum* (Berlin, 1893), pp. 83–84; Linroth, *Om folksjukdomarnes uppkomst*, p. 76; *Deutsche Medicinische Wochenschrift*, 10, 33 (14 August 1884), p. 533; R. Kutner, ed., *Volksseuchen: Vierzehn Vorträge* (Jena, 1909), pp. 16–17; Johanna Bleker, "Die historische Pathologie, Nosologie und Epidemiologie im 19. Jahrhundert," *Medizinhistorisches Journal*, 19, 1/2 (1984), pp. 47–48.

[172] *Conférence 1885*, p. 92; PRO, FO 542/3, FO CP 7819, November 1902, p. 18; *Sanitary Record*, n.s., 14, 178 (15 February 1893), p. 394.

[173] Barth, *Cholera*, p. 98; Otto Riedel, *Die Cholera: Entstehung, Wesen und Verhütung derselben* (Berlin, 1887), p. 72; Prussia, *Stenographische Berichte, Haus der Abgeordneten*, 86 (4 July 1893), p. 2518; *SB*, 1892/93, Akst. 172, p. 923; *SB*, 1892/93, 21 April 1893, p. 1957C.

[174] *DVöG*, 27 (1895), p. 139; *Amtliche Denkschrift über die Choleraepidemie 1892* (Berlin, 1892), p. 99; *Der amtliche Erlass*, p. 25.

In Germany, disinfection continued to play the important role it had begun to assume in the 1860s. The public institutions to disinfect possessions of the poor found in London and Liverpool were held up for emulation during the seventies, although actually constructing their equivalents took another decade.[175] The first disinfection station in Berlin opened in 1886, while in Hamburg twenty were established in 1892 with appropriately elaborate procedures. As of 1887, disinfections of dwellings and possessions of cholera patients in Berlin were required.[176] In Hamburg, houses with several illnesses or deaths were disinfected, and residents evacuated and cleansed along with their effects. Objects destroyed rather than disinfected were to be compensated, lest the temptation to conceal them prevail. A novel and curious measure required wallpaper to be scoured with bread, the resulting crumbs burned.[177] According to the Contagious Disease Law of 1900, disinfection institutions were to be established throughout Germany and stricken dwellings cleansed before being reinhabited. Cholera patients and their evacuations and effects were to be purified continuously during an epidemic and meticulously detailed instructions governed the treatment of various objects. Before returning to normal life, the recuperated were to clean their bodies thoroughly, ideally taking a full bath. In 1900, strict regulations on burials and the handling of corpses were issued. Without washing or changing their clothes, the dead were to be swaddled in a shroud impregnated with disinfectants and immediately encoffinated on a layer of sawdust, leaf-mould or other absorbent material.[178] A final disinfection was to precede the casket's sealing. The

[175] *DVöG*, 5 (1873), pp. 358–64; Königliche Eisenbahn-Direction Frankfurt a.M., *Massnahmen zur Abwehr der Cholera* (Frankfurt am Main, 1884), pp. 9–23; *Deutsches Wochenblatt für Gesundheitspflege und Rettungswesen*, 1, 24 (15 December 1884), pp. 285–86; *Vierteljahrsschrift für gerichtliche Medicin und öffentliches Sanitätswesen*, 3 F., 4, Suppl. Hft. (1892), p. 161.

[176] *Annales*, 3/17 (1887), p. 184; 3/18 (1887), p. 222; *Veröffentlichungen*, 10 (1886), p. 557; Wolter, *Das Auftreten der Cholera*, p. 160; *Deutsche Militärärztliche Zeitschrift*, 22, 6 (1893), p. 243; *Stenographische Berichte über die öffentlichen Sitzungen der Stadtverordneten-Versammlung der Haupt- und Residenzstadt Berlin*, 19 (1892), 11 February 1892, p. 57; *Veröffentlichungen*, 11 (1887), p. 110; Palmberg, *Treatise on Public Health*, pp. 395–400.

[177] Hugo Borges, *Die Cholera in Hamburg im Jahre 1892* (Leipzig, n.d.), p. 87; *Der amtliche Erlass*, pp. 9, 25; Wolter, *Das Auftreten der Cholera*, p. 161; Petri, *Cholerakurs*, p. 178. Apparently this was adopted from procedures used against smallpox and scarlet fever: Carl Flügge, *Die Verbreitungsweise und Abwehr der Cholera* (Leipzig, 1893), p. 82.

[178] During this time, a dispute was ongoing whether to allow cremation, supported by Virchow as the most sanitary form of corpse disposal: Prussia, Haus der Abgeordneten, *Stenographische Berichte*, 86, 4 July 1893, pp. 2531–32.

religious ablution of corpses could occur in accord with instructions of the official physician, but only with disinfectant fluids. The coffin was to be brought at once to a mortuary, viewings were forbidden, corteges limited, burials to be prompt and only in proper cemeteries.[179]

Sequestration and the separation of sick from healthy were equally important elements of the Kochian regimen. Inhabitants of uninfected areas were advised to avoid contact with potentially contagious travelers, infected dwellings and, in general, large gatherings. Fairs, markets and other public assemblies could be prohibited, and the ill were forbidden to travel without police permission.[180] In 1884, with cholera threatening from France, the Prussians moved to hospitalize or isolate patients at home, although the possibility of evacuating the healthy from an infected dwelling was also held in reserve. In Mecklenburg the ill could be sequestered or hospitalized, if necessary against their will. In Hamburg, residents of dwellings being disinfected were moved to other quarters for a period of isolation before returning home. Cholera orphans and hospitalized children were sequestered for six days in a refuge before being brought back to their normal residence.[181] Here, apparently, there were cases of involuntary hospitalization, at least to judge from reports that many resisted and had to be removed with the aid of a constable.[182] In 1884 in Württemberg, the ill were to be brought to isolation rooms or at least sequestered at home by police guard, by notice of disease posted on their dwellings or by announcement of infection in the newspaper.[183]

In 1892 Prussian regulations expressed the desirability of, although still no direct compulsion for, having impoverished and ill-housed patients hospitalized.[184] But already the following year brought a sharpening of

---

[179] *Anweisung zur Bekämpfung der Cholera*, pp. 5, 15–16, 19; *Desinfektionsanweisung bei Cholera: Amtliche Ausgabe* (Berlin, 1907), pp. 6–11; *Reichs-Gesetzblatt*, 17 (1907), pp. 95–98.

[180] Kabierske, Jr., *Wie schützt sich ein Jeder selbst am besten vor der Cholera?* (Breslau, [1893]); *Belehrung über das Wesen der Cholera und das während der Cholerazeit zu beobachtende Verhalten* (Königsberg, 1892), p. 3; *Amtliche Denkschrift*, pp. 91ff.; *Der amtliche Erlass*, p. 5; *Veröffentlichungen*, 11 (1887), p. 591; O. Rapmund, *Polizei-Verordnung betreffend Massregeln gegen die Verbreitung ansteckender Krankheiten* (Minden i. W., 1899), pp. 1–6.

[181] Königliche Eisenbahn-Direction, *Massnahmen zur Abwehr*, pp. 9–23; G. Maas, *Schutzmassregeln gegen die Cholera* (Calbe a.S., 1892), p. 9; *SB*, 1898/1900, Akst. 690, p. 4222; Wolter, *Das Auftreten der Cholera*, p. 163; Borges, *Cholera in Hamburg*, p. 87.

[182] Evans, *Death in Hamburg*, p. 333; *Die Misserfolge der Staatsmedicin und ihre Opfer in Hamburg* (Hagen i. W., [1892]), p. 30. But for the claim that removals were voluntary, see Wolter, *Das Auftreten der Cholera*, p. 164.

[183] Guttstadt, *Deutschlands Gesundheitswesen*, v. II, p. 147; Rapmund, *Polizei-Verordnung*, p. 18.

[184] *Amtliche Denkschrift*, pp. 91ff.; *Massnahmen der Behörden für den Fall des Auftretens der asiatischen Cholera: Nebst einer Anweisung zur Ausführung der Desinfection: Nach den Berathungen der Commission im Reichsamt des Innern am 27. u. 28. August 1892* (Berlin, 1892), p. 6.

tone. Once the presence of cholera had been determined by bacteriological examination, patients were to be isolated from all but their caregivers, at home if possible, in a hospital if deemed necessary by the official physician.[185] One luckless family was forcibly sequestered in a schoolhouse, stripped, thoroughly washed with carbolic soap, issued new clothing, their dwelling disinfected, bedding and various possessions burnt. Their ample hoard of potatoes, squirreled away under the bed and therefore soiled with excrement, was thrown in a ditch, pounded to bits and drenched with undiluted carbolic acid – none of which prevented their neighbors (inspired by what the official account described as a senselessness bordering on fatalism) from seeking to steal and eat them. In certain cases, even contacts were kept in isolation under police guard. The Prussian island of Helgoland, seeking to preserve itself, cut off all communication in 1892 with the outside and, conversely, the village of Kiewo was isolated to spare the surrounding area, its inhabitants enjoined from leaving. In Meisenheim, near Koblenz, when a father who had already lost one child to the disease refused to allow another to be sequestered, it took the public prosecutor's intervention for the authorities to succeed, especially since the local population took sides against them and even the mayor criticized such actions, for which indiscretion he was duly reprimanded.[186] In 1900, with passage of the Contagious Disease Law, the compulsion to sequester the ill was formalized. The sick and those suspected of disease were to be isolated from all except family and caretakers, either at home or in a hospital.[187] Asymptomatic contacts were liable to medical surveillance up to five days unless the official physician had reason for also sequestering them and they could be subject to bacteriological examination. Isolation could be required, for example, of otherwise healthy persons who lived with a cholera patient. The official

---

[185] This was possible only in those federal states whose laws allowed compulsory hospitalization: *Ministerial-Blatt für die gesammte innere Verwaltung in den Königlich Preussischen Staaten*, 54 (1893), pp. 173–93; *Der amtliche Erlass*, p. 5. Apparently victims in Berlin were removed involuntarily: *Stenographische Berichte über die öffentlichen Sitzungen der Stadtverordneten-Versammlung der Haupt- und Residenzstadt Berlin*, 19 (1892), 8 September 1892, pp. 276–77.

[186] *Medizinischer Bericht über den Verlauf der Cholera im Weichselgebiet 1892* (Danzig, 1893), p. 11; Petri, *Cholerakurs*, p. 183; Prussia, Haus der Abgeordneten, *Anlagen zu den Stenographischen Berichten*, 1892/93, Akst. 76, p. 2069; Alexander Stollenwerk, "Die Cholera im Regierungsbezirk Koblenz," *Jahrbuch für westdeutsche Landesgeschichte*, 5 (1979), p. 266.

[187] *Anweisung zur Bekämpfung*, pp. 12–13. From debates in the Reichstag, it was evident that sequestration was considered a major intervention in personal freedom and not prescribed with a light heart. While it was made clear that the decision to isolate could not depend on consent of the patient or family, the agreement of the attending physician, in addition to the official doctor, was added as a condition to protect the patient from needless removals: *SB*, 1892/93, Akst. 172, p. 918; 1898/1900, Akst. 796, pp. 5346–47; Kirchner, *Die gesetzlichen Grundlagen*, pp. 113–14.

physician could also order the healthy inhabitants, rather than the patient, removed from infected living quarters, or, exceptionally, evacuate the entire house, marking it accordingly.[188]

Just as disinfection and isolation were the main tools of the Kochian system within the country, so too at its borders similar precautions were put into effect. In comparison to traditional quarantinism, the new variant spared public health officials at least one major agony. Since cholera was now recognized as transmitted largely by persons and only exceptionally by objects, the whole panoply of cleansings, airings and quarantines for merchandise, baggage and effects could be abandoned. Even goods earlier considered highly infectious, such as rags, were now permitted for import if they were sorted, treated and packaged for the wholesale trade.[189] In other respects, disinfection promised to render most goods harmless. For human vectors, in contrast, Koch's discoveries threw up as many problems as they solved. With the identification of an objective marker of disease, independent of clinical symptoms, the problem of the asymptomatic carrier reared its head.[190] Those who carried the bacillus without suffering symptoms could be caught only by the most oldfashioned and impracticable form of quarantine, locking up all travelers for the duration of the incubation period, and even that would be unavailing to the extent that it was possible to be a carrier without ever falling ill. Inspecting travelers and isolating the evidently diseased – the nub of the pre-bacteriological revision system – did nothing to forestall the entrance of the asymptomatic. In theory, Koch's discoveries broached the possibility of halting all potentially infectious carriers, but the practical consequences (bacteriological examination of the dejections of all travelers) promised to be only marginally less cumbersome than oldfashioned quarantine.[191]

From Koch's work a number of prophylactic possibilities were, logically

---

[188] Horror stories circulated by opponents of such measures during early discussions of the law included a case in Hamburg where a servant girl had only narrowly avoided sequestration because of her friendship with an ambulance driver: "Aus Kunst, Wissenschaft und Leben," *Tägliche Rundschau*, 59 (10 March 1893); *Anweisung zur Bekämpfung*, pp. 13–15.

[189] *Hygiea*, 55, 6 (June 1893), pp. 609–23.

[190] John Andrew Mendelsohn, "Cultures of Bacteriology: Formation and Transformation of a Science in France and Germany, 1870–1914" (Ph.D. diss., Princeton University, 1996), pp. 459–75. The problem had been recognized by Pettenkofer as early as 1855: Erwin H. Ackerknecht, "Anticontagionism Between 1821 and 1867," *BHM*, 22, 5 (September–October 1948), p. 581. For other adumbrations, see *DVöG*, 7 (1875), p. 282; C. G. Ehrenberg, *Ein Wort zur Zeit: Erfahrungen über die Pest im Orient und über verständige Vorkehrungen bei Pest-Ansteckung zur Nutzanwendung bei der Cholera* (Berlin, 1831), p. 6.

[191] Although in Egypt in 1911 in fact mass bacteriological examinations of pilgrims was undertaken: *Annales*, 4/18 (1912), pp. 72, 80.

speaking, equally possible: returning to oldfashioned quarantine of the most extended sort; bacteriological inspection of all travelers; devising some other system of keeping tabs on possibly infected voyagers until those who turned out, in fact, to be infected could be identified, isolated and treated. None of these solutions promised to be easily implementable. For nations with a constant influx across the frontiers at thousands of points, quarantining or bacteriologically inspecting every border crosser threatened logistical nightmares. But other means of surveilling travelers presupposed an equally elaborate machinery of supervision and control. Starting in the 1860s, the "English technique" of inspection and medical surveillance, still innocent of the possibility of bacteriological examination, had sought to replace quarantines with a system of retaining the symptomatic while keeping tabs on healthy travelers as they went about their business until it could be known whether they were infected or not. Koch's discoveries now lent scientific weight to this inspection or revision system. The Kochians agreed with localists that quarantines and cordons in the traditional sense were largely impossible to carry out effectively and, in any case, ruinous to commerce and communication. At the same time, unlike the Pettenkoferians, they considered it worthwhile preventing carriers from entering as yet uninfected places.[192] Their solution, focused on inspection and medical surveillance, beefed up the British revision system with new bacteriological techniques. All healthy travelers were to be admitted without quarantine, but kept under medical surveillance during an incubation period of five to six days in expectation of identifying the first cases, isolating them and thus nipping a potential epidemic in the bud.

An important issue raised by Koch's discoveries concerned the identity of those subject to surveillance, sequestration and disinfection. Quarantine in the 1830s, seeking to isolate everyone arriving from infected areas, had required a commercially intolerable blunderbuss approach, made doubly unfeasible by the beginnings of mass travel and trade. With the introduction of the revision system in the sixties, inspectors had sought instead to identify and isolate those who presented evident symptoms. When Koch's discoveries raised the problem of the asymptomatic carrier, new issues had to be confronted. The old methods of checking for symptoms (including that wonderfully French technique of having physicians at frontier railway stations mingle with the passen-

---

[192] C. K. Aird, *Die Cholera 1886 und die nach 55jährigen Erfahrungen gegen dieselbe angewandten Schutzmittel* (Berlin, 1887), pp. 54–55; *DVöG*, 17 (1885), pp. 556–59; 27 (1895), p. 162; Riedel, *Die Cholera*, pp. 62–63; R. Grassmann, *Schutzmassregeln gegen die asiatische Cholera* (Stettin, 1892), p. 1.

gers in hopes of spotting those who did not attack with requisite gusto the buffet tables awaiting them in the restaurant) no longer offered more than partial protection.[193] Before Koch, external symptoms, though only indirectly, were the sole indicators of disease; now the cholera bacillus provided an objective marker. To mangle one of the great lines from *Iolanthe*: And a disease within the nation/Shall be ascertainable by bacteriological examination. In theory, microscopic searches for the cholera bacillus might have served to narrow and delineate precisely the category of those who were now targeted.[194] But in practice, it broadened the field of those feared as infectious.

The discovery of the cholera vibrio was a double-edged sword in terms of identifying those subject to restrictive measures. On the one hand, it allowed a theoretically more accurate targeting of measures. But on the other, the fact that it was unfeasible actually to perform bacteriological examination of all possibly infected persons, combined with the focus on transmission from one person to another that was encouraged by Koch's discoveries, meant that the circle of the potentially infectious was enlarged to include also those without symptoms who were contacts of the ill. After the 1892 cholera epidemic, public health authorities began treating those suspected of cholera and asymptomatic carriers as though they were in fact stricken, subjecting them to the same sequestrations as actual patients.[195] Although such procedures were challenged in 1895 by a Supreme Court decision (based on the 1835 Prussian regulation which foresaw the isolation only of those in fact suffering from disease), the amalgamation of potential with actual victims of cholera in fear of their role as possible carriers was formalized in the Contagious Disease Law of 1900.[196] Those who, though symptomless, may have come into contact with patients or soiled objects were suspected of infectiousness and subject to surveillance and possibly sequestration.[197] The law's implementation decrees allowed apparently healthy people in whose excrement bacteriological examination had revealed the presence of cholera bacilli to be treated as though actually

---

[193] *Bulletin*, 3, 25 (1891), p. 143.

[194] *Hygiea*, 55, 6 (June 1893), pp. 611–12; *Förhandlingar*, 1895, p. 54. For background, see Mendelsohn, "Cultures of Bacteriology," chs. 9–11.

[195] *Der amtliche Erlass*, pp. 7–8; Rapmund, *Polizei-Verordnung*, pp. 163–64.

[196] GStA, 84a/11011, printed, untitled sheet sent to Bundesrat by the Geschäftsausschuss des Berliner Ärzte-Vereins-Bundes, 1 December 1895.

[197] *Anweisung zur Bekämpfung*, p. 13; *Reichs-Gesetzblatt* (1904), 9/3020, p. 69; Kirchner, *Die gesetzlichen Grundlagen*, pp. 105–06; *Centralblatt für allgemeine Gesundheitspflege*, 12 (1893), p. 77; Petri, *Cholerakurs*, p. 183.

ill. A ship with a passenger identified as a carrier would thus, for example, be treated as infected even though no single case of apparent cholera was present onboard.[198]

At the same time, the old criteria based on clinical symptoms naturally remained in force.[199] Moreover, rather than being sharpened and focused by the new bacteriological tests (to exclude diarrhea sufferers with no comma bacillus for example) the burden of proof now rested on symptomatic patients to prove that they were not, or were no longer, carrying the bacillus, thus adding new criteria to old, rather than substituting one for the other. In the Contagious Disease Law distinctions were drawn between the ill, those suspected of illness ("Krankheitsverdächtige") and those suspected of infectiousness ("Ansteckungsverdächtige"). Krankheitsverdächtige were those with symptoms who had not yet demonstrated, in two successive bacteriological examinations one day apart, that they were in fact not infected. At least three bacteriological examinations were required in cases where there was reason to suspect cholera even after two negative tests. Requiring three negative examinations to dispel the suspicion of disease naturally enhanced the potential for lengthy sequestrations and, in at least one case, a carrier of the cholera bacillus was isolated for 250 days until he had met these criteria.[200] A similar expansion in the definition of the potentially infectious brought on by bacteriology occurred also in other nations. In the measures taken on the French border with Spain in 1890, for example, all travelers suffering from gastro-enteritis were retained and treated on the spot, but those who, though without symptoms, nonetheless raised suspicions of infection could also be kept for observation. Similar measures in 1910 allowed the authorities to retain for observation contacts of the ill or suspected. In Sweden in 1915, those who were suspected of disease, even though its presence could not precisely be determined, and those suspected of being carriers, although symptomless, could also be subjected to surveillance or isolation.[201]

Measures were implemented in Germany that followed the new Kochian emphasis on examination and isolation of the potentially

[198] Schmedding and Engels, *Gesetze*, p. 57; *Reichs-Gesetzblatt* (1907), 15/3316, pp. 91–92; M. Weirauch, *Die Bekämpfung ansteckender Krankheiten* (Trier, 1905), p. 199; *Conférence 1911*, p. 415.

[199] For example, see *Amtliche Denkschrift*, p. 96.

[200] *Anweisung zur Bekämpfung*, pp. 12–13; *Reichs-Gesetzblatt* (1916), 8/5019, pp. 29–30; Kirchner, *Die gesetzlichen Grundlagen*, pp. 105–06; *Conférence 1911*, p. 544.

[201] Monod, *Le choléra*, pp. 603–05; Proust, *La défense de l'Europe*, pp. 420–23; *JO*, 42, 210 (4 August 1910), pp. 6762–63; *JO Débats*, Chambre, 19 December 1912, p. 3320; *SFS*, 1915/539; *Betänkande med förslag till hälsovårdsstadga för riket och epidemistadga*, pp. 131ff., 191–92; *SFS*, 1919/443.

infectious while not necessarily ending quarantine as a result. Inspecting traffic on the inland waterways was a precaution in effect since at least the 1850s and had not in any specific sense been inspired, but at most given a continued purchase on life, by Koch's theories. In 1873 and then again in 1892, a system of control stations for examining and sequestering vessels was elaborated, first along the Elbe, and subsequently also on the Oder, Rhine and Weichsel. Ships were to be inspected on average once daily, disinfecting their bilgewater and encouraging sailors to cease insanitary habits such as dumping excrement directly overboard. Decommissioned military physicians were put to use as inspectors, in part because it was hoped that their uniforms would command respect with the maritime population.[202] In 1892, no less than 150,000 vessels were inspected, 87,000 disinfected and 680,000 people examined, of whom 127 proved to be infected. By the turn of the century, regulations required that ships be inspected daily, stricken crew removed, the apparently healthy onboard infected vessels subject to observation quarantines of five or six days and the boats to disinfection. In 1883, quarantine was imposed at German seaports. Ships from Turkey, the Persian Gulf, Red Sea and the west coast of Africa and all with cases on board or from infected ports were to be inspected, ill or suspected travelers isolated for the duration of the incubation period or until they had recuperated, their effects disinfected or destroyed. Healthy travelers underwent an observation quarantine for six or seven days and disinfection.[203]

If such maritime measures combined the new Kochian inspection system with vestiges of oldfashioned quarantinism, a novelty of the 1880s and nineties was the intensified control of overland and especially railroad traffic. Quarantines on terrestrial traffic had by this time largely been abandoned on the continent and the brunt of prevention thus fell to inspections. As will be discussed later, the steady stream of Slavic emigrants to the new world passing in transit through Germany left an impress on the precautions adopted. Rather than quarantines, there were now medical inspections of travelers at the main border crossings with retention or turning back only of the ill. In 1884, physicians at the Prussian and Bavarian frontiers inspected passengers arriving by rail

---

[202] Mecklenburg, *Was vermag die Sanitäts-Polizei*, pp. 45–46; Prussia, Haus der Abgeordneten, *Anlagen zu den Stenographischen Berichten*, 1892/93, Akst. 76, p. 2070.

[203] Petri, *Cholerakurs*, pp. 191–94; *Conférence 1893*, pp. 255–56; *Amtliche Denkschrift*, pp. 24, 82ff.; Kaiserliches Gesundheitsamt, "Übersicht über den Verlauf der Cholera im Deutschen Reiche während des Jahres 1894" (copy in Stabi); *Anweisung zur Bekämpfung*, pp. 55–61; Weirauch, *Bekämpfung*, pp. 320–29.

from cholera-stricken France, detaining the ill and suspected and disinfecting railroad carriages. Two years later, similar measures were imposed by the Prussians and Saxons on their Austrian borders and, in 1892, the Prussian borders to Galicia and Austrian Silesia were closed except at railroad crossings, with similar controls imposed at the Alsatian frontier.[204] It quickly became apparent, nonetheless, that a medical inspection, however cursory, of all overland travelers was impossible and a more flexible system of medical surveillance was implemented. Railway personnel were instructed in 1892 to watch out for passengers suffering from choleraic symptoms, subjecting them to further examination. Symptomatic passengers could be prevented from leaving the train except at stations with a hospital to receive them, or they could be required to give their name and address if refusing treatment. In 1904, victims of the plague were banned as passengers on the railroads and those suffering from cholera, leprosy, typhus, yellow fever or smallpox were allowed to travel only with permission of the official physician at the departure station and then only in separate compartments with their own toilets. Because not all overland travelers could be retained for several days and because asymptomatic carriers would in any case slip through, the authorities also established means of keeping tabs on recent arrivals, formalized in the 1900 Contagious Disease Law. Travelers from infected areas were to report to the police, who kept them under medical surveillance for up to five days, subjecting their excrement to bacteriological examination if necessary, but more commonly simply inquiring daily as to the state of their health.[205]

In Sweden, the debate between Koch and Pettenkofer unleashed similar disputes over the best precautions against cholera. Medical opinion, having favored various forms of localism at midcentury, now swung back toward contagionism, although of course there were exceptions. Pettenkofer, earlier a strong influence, and other localists now came under attack, while Koch's star rose.[206] During the mid-1880s, the two sides appeared equally influential, but by the 1890s Koch and what

[204] *Amtliche Denkschrift*, pp. 17–18; Königliche Eisenbahn-Direction, *Massnahmen zur Abwehr*, pp. 9–23; Guttstadt, *Deutschlands Gesundheitswesen*, v. II, pp. 140–41; Ottfried Helmbach, *Die Cholera, ihr Auftreten, ihre Ursachen und die gegen sie nothwendigen Schutzmassregeln* (Brandenburg a.H., 1887), pp. 21–22; *Veröffentlichungen*, 10 (1886), p. 612.

[205] *Amtliche Denkschrift*, pp. 108, 112; *Der amtliche Erlass*, pp. 6, 11–12; *Anweisung zur Bekämpfung*, pp. 6, 65–73; *Reichs-Gesetzblatt* (1904), 4, p. 29; *Massnahmen der Behörden*, p. 5.

[206] *Förhandlingar*, 1885, pp. 174–76; Linroth, *Om folksjukdomarnes uppkomst*, pp. 21, 31, 74; E. W. Wretlind, *Koleran* (Stockholm, 1892), p. 17; G. L. Læstadius, *Om koleran samt skydds- och botemedel deremot* (Stockholm, 1884), p. 13; *Eira*, 9, 5 (1885), p. 156; *Hygienische Rundschau*, 19, 15 (1909), p. 869.

the Swedes identified as the Berlin position had won the upper hand.[207] And yet, as in Germany, the return to contagionism did not mean an outright rejection of the Pettenkoferian or sanitationist heritage. Koch might be right – so the widespread conclusion ran – that a bacillus was necessary, but various preconditions, from the social to the personal, explained why cholera spread or not.[208] Careful attention was paid to Koch's discoveries and their implications, with medical circles debating in the mideighties whether the need for quarantines followed necessarily from identification of the comma bacillus. By the 1890s, the issue had boiled down to whether Sweden should abandon oldstyle quarantinism wholly, adopting the new inspection system, or whether quarantines still had a role to play.[209]

A compromise solution similar to the German was worked out, combining a reaffirmation of quarantines with inspection and eventually adding a system of medical surveillance of travelers. In response to the 1892 epidemic the Swedes modified the revision system introduced in the mid-1870s back in a more quarantinist direction. Whereas, earlier, inspection had been allowed at any harbor, ships from infected ports and those with disease onboard were now to dock at the observation stations off the coast, quarantined for forty-eight hours and inspected. More importantly, healthy passengers on infected ships, allowed to land under the 1875 regulations, were now sequestered along with the ship for six days.[210] For railroad wagons, special instructions applied that demonstrated the intensity of the control now imposed on traffic into Sweden. As a rule, they could not be introduced from infected places. For Denmark, where only Jutland was stricken, certain exceptions were allowed whereby empty Swedish freight wagons could be ferried over from Elsinore to Helsingborg on ships which, prohibited from carrying passengers, mail or other cargo, were in return exempted from the two-day observation quarantine. Certification that the rolling stock had had no contact with infected areas was required

[207] *Förhandlingar*, 1884, pp. 265ff.; 1893, pp. 50, 73; Ernst Almquist, *Om koleran enligt Svensk erfarenhet* (Gothenburg, 1886), pp. 26–28; Ernst Almquist, *Thatsächliches und kritisches zur Ausbreitungsweise der Cholera* (Gothenburg, 1886), pp. 12–19; *Koleran. Dess uppträdande och orsaker samt de skyddsåtgärder som emot densamma böra användas: Af en Svensk läkare* (Lund, 1892), pp. 8–11; Ernst Almquist, *Om koleran, dess sätt att utbreda sig ock dess sätt att smitta* (Stockholm, 1893), pp. 5–7.

[208] *Förhandlingar*, 1892, pp. 93–94; *Koleran*, pp. 8–11; Wretlind, *Koleran*, pp. 11–13, 18–19; *Helsovännen*, 8, 8 (1893), p. 111; E. W. Wretlind, *Huru förhindras farsoters spridning* (Stockholm, 1892), p. 6.

[209] *Förhandlingar*, 1884, pp. 268–71, 281; 1895, pp. 33ff.; *Förhandlingar vid Helsovårdsföreningens i Stockholm sammankomster år 1884*, pp. 53ff., 86ff.; Richard Wawrinsky, *Om förebyggandet af epidemier genom anordning af isoleringslokaler* (Stockholm, 1901), pp. 43, 54–57.

[210] *SFS*, 1892/57, §§4–5; 1892/95, §2; 1875/21, §5; *RD prot*, FK 1895:8, pp. 44, 50.

and the wagons themselves were cleansed and disinfected under medical supervision.[211]

Internally, the Swedes also took an approach similar to the German. In 1892, special instructions dealt with cholera on the railroads. Infected coaches were to be disinfected, each longhaul train to draw a special wagon for isolating the ill, tickets were not to be sold to persons suffering from or suspected of cholera, who should instead be exhorted to seek aid at the nearest hospital, with written notice sent the authorities who could then isolate and treat them. Travelers who fell ill en route were to be isolated, or the other occupants of the compartment moved. A station master notified of a case of cholera on board was to telegraph ahead to arrange for inspection and removal. In 1893 a system of medical surveillance was introduced. Quarantines were moderated in various ways: ships underway from infected ports for more than ten days without incident were allowed to land without the two-day observation quarantine. In distinction to the liberal principles of revision adopted in 1875, however, healthy passengers on infected ships still had to undergo quarantine. In addition to the two days of observation quarantine, three days of medical surveillance were now added for passengers (five for the crew) of ships granted free pratique. Passengers informed the authorities where they intended to disembark, that locality was notified and travelers, equipped with the appropriate documents, reported to the inspector at their destination, leaving an address.[212] Voyagers were to be inspected daily during the surveillance period, reporting their new destinations if they left in the meantime and pursued by the police if they had not checked in there within twelve hours of arrival. Those who let rooms to travelers from infected or suspected places were to report this forthwith. Each locality was to establish a hospital or sickroom where ill travelers could be isolated and cared for.[213] Unusual in Sweden were the elaborate disinfection procedures imposed on imported goods. In response to cholera in Russia in 1892, used bedding and clothing other than for personal use could be imported only after extensive purification;

[211] *SFS*, 1892/67.
[212] Hæffner, *Lexikon*, pp. 38–40, 47, 77; *SFS*, 1893/60, §§2–5; 1893/73; *Förhandlingar vid sjette allmänna svenska läkaremötet*, 1893, pp. 162–63; *Hygiea*, 56, 2 (February 1894), pp. 170–86; *RD prot*, FK 1894:37, pp. 16–17.
[213] *SFS*, 1893/61; *Hygiea*, 56, 2 (February 1894), p. 179. This surveillance system provoked controversy in parliament, but mainly because of the burdens imposed by the central government on local budgets by the requirement that a hospital be provided to isolate the ill: *Bihang*, AK, 1894, Motioner, No. 111; Första Kammarens Tillfälliga Utskotts (No. 2) Utlåtande No. 6, 1894; Andra Kammarens Tillfälliga Utskotts (No. 4) Utlåtande No. 10; *Bihang*, 1894, 8 Saml., 2 Afd., 2 Band, 10 Häft, No. 10, 15 March 1894; Wawrinsky, *Om förebyggandet af epidemier*, pp. 90–91.

and rags were allowed only from certain countries and then only in bales and by limited means of transportation under restricted conditions to specific destinations, with certification of origin from Swedish or Norwegian consuls, disinfected upon arrival and stored in warehouses with double locks and separate possession of the two sets of keys.[214]

Such measures put Sweden in a more oldfashioned quarantinist position than its European neighbors. The country took elaborate precautions against imported goods, subjected all travelers from infected places to two-day observations and required even the healthy on infected ships to undergo the full duration of quarantine. While the rest of Europe was adopting the inspection system, formalized at the 1893 Dresden Conference, the Swedes retained more of their traditional quarantinist defenses.[215] Not until the turn of the century in regulations against plague did the Swedes follow the lead taken elsewhere to eliminate the two-day observation quarantine for all ships in contact with infected areas, and even then sequestration of healthy passengers on infected ships continued. In 1905, cholera and the plague were dealt with together in this spirit, with no automatic observation quarantines and various moderations that allowed healthy passengers of some infected ships to avoid isolation, subject however to medical surveillance.[216] In 1915, with the prospect of epidemics magnified by the war, however, the Swedes backpedaled once more.[217] Local prophylactic initiatives, once the bane of reformers, were again allowed. Quarantine institutions were organized by the central state, but municipalities might also establish them if they so chose – ports, for example, that wanted their own observation station against plague and cholera. Healthy passengers on infected ships were again subject to five days' observation quarantine, and elaborate procedures governed the admission to free pratique. Passengers on regular ferries (otherwise exempt from such detailed strictures) which had had contact with infected areas were inspected and quarantined if cases were found and healthy travelers were subject to five days medical surveillance, as were overland voyagers having passed through diseased areas. If Norwegian or Finnish territory was stricken, the borders could be sealed or guards posted on the main roads to instruct travelers where to go for surveillance; personnel on trains from infected areas were to pay attention to the health of passengers, isolating and treating those with symptoms. At the end of the war, a general

[214] *SFS*, 1892/57; 1892/66; 1893/72; 1905/46.

[215] *RD prot*, AK 1895:8, pp. 70–71; *Hygiea*, 56, 2 (February 1894), pp. 186–90.

[216] *SFS*, 1899/47; J. E. Bergwall, *Om pesten och dess bekämpande* (Stockholm, 1901), pp. 60–61; *SFS*, 1905/46, §§2–5; 1909/6.   [217] *SFS*, 1915/539.

epidemic disease law in 1919 dealing mainly with domestic precautions continued this Swedish quasi-quarantinist *Sonderweg*.[218] Those who could not provide for themselves at home were to be cared for in a hospital or other isolated circumstances. After removal, recuperation or death, the patient's living quarters, clothing and bedding were to be cleansed, and worthless objects destroyed. The sick could be forbidden from attending school or visiting public amusements, schools could be closed and unnecessary crowds dispersed. In dwellings of the ill gatherings without a prior cleansing were forbidden. As in the German law of 1900, asymptomatic carriers could be sequestered or suffer other restrictions of their liberty.

When cholera threatened from Spain and elsewhere in the mid-1880s and then again in the early nineties, the response in France was neoquarantinist. Invoking the law of 1822, still the fundamental text on contagious disease prevention, the authorities set up observation posts, forbidding the import of bedding, fruits and certain vegetables.[219] Travelers from Spain were to declare their destination in France, reporting to the local mayor within twenty-four hours of arrival for inspection. All who lodged visitors from infected countries were to notify the authorities, declaring suspicious cases of illness. At Lyons, passengers from the south were sprayed with carbonate of soda for fifteen minutes before being allowed to pass; elsewhere they were fumigated with sulfur heaped on live coals. In 1884, Nice forbade access to all who had not performed five days' quarantine at the city gates.[220] In the early 1890s the French finally applied the revision system largely on the British model, reducing quarantines and replacing them in most cases with inspection and medical surveillance. Ships from suspected ports had linen and other personal effects disinfected. The observation quarantines required by the 1876 regulation were reduced in 1892 to twenty-four hours.[221] In 1896, ships were divided into more nuanced categories and the conditions imposed in each ameliorated: healthy passengers from suspected

---

[218] *SFS*, 1919/443; *Betänkande med förslag till hälsovårdsstadga för riket och epidemistadga*, pp. 131ff.; *Bihang*, Prop. 1919:153; *Bihang*, 1919, Andra lagutskottets utlåtande Nr. 38; Ch. Lundberg, "Den svenska epidemilagen den 19 juni 1919," *Nordisk Hygienisk Tidsskrift*, 1, 4 (July–August 1920).

[219] *Bulletin*, 57, 3rd ser., 29 (1893), p. 586; *JO*, 22, 167 (22 June 1890), p. 2912; *Recueil*, 22 (1892), pp. 702–04; Monod, *Le choléra*, p. 609; Monod, *La santé publique*, p. 12; Humbert, *Du role de l'administration*, pp. 14–15. The precepts of the 1822 law were continued in the CSP of 1953, but then largely ended by the law of 1 July 1965: Jean-Marie Auby, *Le droit de la santé* (Paris, 1981), p. 240.

[220] Monod, *Le choléra*, pp. 606–08; *Annales*, 3/12 (1884), pp. 156, 160–61; 3/14 (1885), pp. 206–07; 3/24 (1890), pp. 110–11; *JO*, 24, 236 (31 August 1892), p. 4374; *BMJ*, 2 (4 October 1884), pp. 667; *Medical Record*, 43, 1 (1893), p. 1.

[221] *Annales*, 3/24 (1890), pp. 199, 203; *Hygiea*, 55, 6 (June 1893), pp. 609–23; *Recueil*, 21 (1891), p. 948; *Bulletin*, 57, 3rd ser., 30 (1893), p. 597.

ships were issued sanitary passports and allowed to disembark, subject to five days' surveillance at their eventual destination, while those on infected vessels continued to undergo an observation quarantine, now reduced to no more than five days for cholera. In 1908 and again two years later, observation quarantines were required of overland travelers suspected of cholera.[222]

All travelers crossing the border were medically examined in that they descended from the train, filed two abreast between barriers to be viewed by a physician. The ill and suspect, including all suffering from gastro-enteritis, were retained in special isolation rooms. Baggage was examined to prevent soiled linen from slipping by without steam disinfection.[223] Healthy travelers received sanitary passports recording their inspection and the address of their destination in France, to be presented within twenty-four hours of arrival to the local mayor (forewarned by mail), where they would be examined anew and medically surveilled for at least five days. Travelers who went elsewhere than announced were to report to the authorities within twelve hours. Rail passengers from Spain who descended before their intended destination were to be reported and medically examined. Travelers themselves apparently helped out in this regard, denouncing fellow voyagers who made suspiciously frequent use of the station lavatories. The punishments foreseen were based on the 1822 law and included jail up to a fortnight and fines.[224] During the epidemic of 1892, the two observation posts in the Pyrenees were supplemented by thirty more at the other frontiers, especially in the northeast where the border, lacking natural obstacles, was harder to guard. Travelers' soiled clothing was fumigated, washed, ironed and sent on within a few hours to their destination, and this at the simple cost of carriage.[225] In 1908, in reaction to cholera in Russia, suspected travelers

---

[222] *JO*, 28, 20 (21 January 1896), pp. 360–61, arts. 57–59; *Recueil*, 25 (1895), pp. 426–30; 32 (1902), p. 241; A. Chantemesse and F. Borel, *Hygiène internationale: Frontières et prophylaxie* (Paris, 1907), pp. 248–54; *JO*, 40, 255 (19 September 1908), pp. 6493–94, art. 3; *JO*, 40, 306 (10 November 1908), p. 7623; *JO*, 42, 210 (4 August 1910), pp. 6762–63; Humbert, *Du rôle de l'administration*, pp. 38–39.

[223] In 1890, 135,000 people crossed the border from Spain into France and were inspected. Over 8,000 disinfections of baggage were undertaken, each lasting some twenty minutes. Three or four travelers were detained after inspection, and but a single case of cholera was introduced, one traveler transmitting it to his mother, who died: *Recueil*, 22 (1892), pp. 63–64; *Annales*, 3/24 (1890), pp. 193–203; *Conférence 1892*, p. 128.

[224] Monod, *Le choléra*, pp. 603–08; Proust, *La défense de l'Europe*, pp. 420–23; *Bulletin*, 3, 25 (1891), pp. 143, 762–71; *Recueil*, 21 (1891), pp. 570–74; 22 (1892), pp. 702–04; Monod, *La santé publique*, pp. 148–49; *Annales*, 3/24 (1890), pp. 478–79.

[225] *JO*, 24, 236 (31 August 1892), p. 4374; *JO*, 24, 250 (14 September 1892), p. 4561; *Bulletin*, 57, 3rd ser., 30 (1893), p. 592; *Annales*, 3/28 (1892), pp. 335ff.; *Medical Record*, 43, 1 (1893), p. 1. There were 268,561 overland travelers subject to medical examination during a sixty-day period coming through one of the thirty-two stations, plus 81,351 arriving via ship.

from infected regions could be retained at the border and sequestered for up to five days. Those not quarantined who were headed for Paris were met at the station, inspected and medically surveilled daily at home for five days.[226]

Within the country, in contrast, measures were distinctly less detailed. In certain places, regulations required disinfection of lodgings and effects of the ill and incineration of the dust and sweepings from their dwellings, forbidding the beating of carpets from windows, in stairwells or courtyards. In the Loiret a prohibition of the ill appearing in public or using public transport was considered.[227] In 1902, after a decades-long legislative gestation, parliament finally disgorged a law on public health. Only at this late stage were public interests placed above private, did (as one observer put it) propriety take precedence over property.[228] Intended to remedy France's woeful lag in such respects (the nation of Pasteur, but the last one, as reformers ruefully admitted, to draw the practical consequences of his discoveries), the law strengthened the power of the central state to impose public health measures on individual localities. With respect to contagious diseases, extraordinary precautions could be decreed during epidemics or if local strictures proved insufficient.[229] Disinfection of infected dwellings and objects, destruction if necessary, and notification of disease were now mandated.[230] The law itself said nothing about sequestration, but such measures were spelled out the following year in a ministerial circular that outlined the regulations localities were expected to promulgate. The ill were to be isolated, at home if possible, in a hospital if necessary, with removal accomplished in special conveyances, subsequently disinfected. After recovery, patients were not to venture into public without cleansing and disinfection. The ill were prohibited from

---

[226] *JO*, 40, 255 (19 September 1908), pp. 6493–94. Travelers from Russia to Paris were thus subject to a total of at least four medical inspections: at the French border, in Paris, and two at home: *Annales*, 4/10 (1908), pp. 356–62; Mosny, *La protection de la santé publique*, p. 86.

[227] *Recueil*, 21 (1891), pp. 953–55; 22 (1892), p. 2.

[228] François Burdeau, "Propriété privée et santé publique: Etude sur la loi du 15 février 1902," in Jean-Louis Harouel, ed., *Histoire du droit social: Mélanges en hommage à Jean Imbert* (Paris, 1989), p. 125; Shapiro, "Private Rights, Public Interest," p. 5.

[229] Paul Strauss, *La croisade sanitaire* (Paris, 1902), p. 52; *JO*, 1901, Doc., Chambre, 2807, pp. 193–97; Paul Strauss and Alfred Fillassier, *Loi sur la protection de la santé publique (Loi du 15 Février 1902)* (2nd edn.; Paris, 1905), p. 301. Its article 8 in effect finally replaced the 1822 law: *Annales*, 3/49 (1903), p. 169.

[230] In 1914 the obligation to report was extended from physicians to family heads and others: Léon Bernard, *La défense de la santé publique pendant la guerre* (Paris, 1929), p. 9. This was continued by the CSP article L 11–12. On disinfection, see Evelyn Bernette Ackerman, *Health Care in the Parisian Countryside, 1800–1914* (New Brunswick, 1990), p. 101.

using public transportation and it was specifically forbidden to throw the excretions of the contagiously ill into streets, gardens or court-yards.[231]

Although Britain had been the first to implement the neoquarantin-ist revision system, the old sanitationist faith remained strong in medical and official thinking. The new bacteriological approach to cholera and other diseases was adopted only slowly. The Indian doctors remained a potent source of anticontagionism, with J. M. Cuningham, Sanitary Commissioner in India, the most prominent of those who argued against quarantinism on the basis of experience in the Orient.[232] "In India," as he put it, "so far as all experience goes, to impose quarantine or cordons in order to keep out cholera is a proceeding no more logical or effectual than it would be to post a line of sentries to stop the monsoon."[233] When, in the mid-1880s, the Mediterranean powers slapped vexatious quarantines on each other's shipping, British medical and official opinion disdainfully dismissed such efforts as unfortunate relapses into bygone epidemiological conceptions. British ships were regarded as equipped with the best sanitary precautions and hence bless-edly free of infection. "And when," as one observer superciliously put it, "at any fever-ridden port, tongs are stretched out suspiciously for their papers, it is a commonplace and trite remark that the tongs are in the wrong hands."[234] Koch's discoveries were at first contested by the British officials in charge of evaluating them, both Indian and metropolitan, who favored instead the Pettenkoferian line that some sort of transfor-mation was necessary before the bacillus could transmit disease.[235] This is perhaps unsurprising considering that in 1883 Koch had managed to accomplish, after a few weeks' stay in India, what had hitherto eluded the massed forces of British science, thereby embarrassingly challenging the foundations of Britain's anticontagionist approach with evidence

[231] A.-J. Martin and Albert Bluzet, *Commentaire administratif et technique de la loi du 15 février 1902, relative a la protection de la santé publique* (Paris, 1903), pp. 55ff.; Monod, *La santé publique*, pp. 229–31.

[232] Lambert, *John Simon*, pp. 848–55; Bellew, *Cholera in India*, pp. 4–9, 772ff.; PRO, FO 407/80, In continuation of CP No. 5003, FO, January 1888, no. 2; FO 407/84, FO CP No. 6106, June 1891, p. 221; David Arnold, *Colonizing the Body: State Medicine and Epidemic Disease in Nineteenth-Century India* (Berkeley, 1993), ch. 1 and pp. 189–93.

[233] J. M. Cuningham, *Cholera: What Can the State do to Prevent It?* (Calcutta, 1884), pp. 25, 130; Proust, *La défense de l'Europe*, p. ix.

[234] *Indian Medical Gazette*, 19 (January 1884), p. 11; John Murray, *Observations on the Pathology and Treatment of Cholera* (2nd edn.; London, 1884), Preface to the 2nd edn.; *Lancet*, 2 (14 July 1883), p. 77; *BMJ*, 2 (4 October 1884), pp. 666–67; PRO, FO 881/5155*, FO CP 5155*, p. 33; PRO 30/29/365, FO CP 5011, 2 October 1884; *BMJ* (16 September 1882), p. 521.

[235] *Cholera: Inquiry by Doctors Klein and Gibbes, and Transactions of a Committee Convened by the Secretary of State for India in Council* (n.p., 1885), pp. 4–9; *PP* 1886 (4873) xxxi, 763, p. xiii.

unearthed in its own backyard.[236] Koch's theories, even when accepted, were not regarded as any reason to bolster the old theory or practice of quarantine. Richard Thorne Thorne, Medical Officer of the Local Government Board, planted himself firmly in the epidemiological tradition of his predecessors. The comma bacillus was useful in distinguishing real cholera from attacks of mere diarrhea, he conceded, yet bacteriology in no way lessened the importance of sanitation. Thirty years ago, he declared in 1888, his predecessor John Simon had said that "excrement-sodden earth, excrement-reeking air, excrement-tainted water, these are for us the causes of cholera," and this held good now just as then.[237] In the early nineties, reputable British public health experts were still rejecting Koch's bacillus as the cause of cholera, appealing instead to atmospheric conditions or simple filth. Sanitary reform alone was still considered sufficient to prevent epidemics. The reason why Britain had not been hit by cholera, so the confident sanitationist conclusion in 1886, was that hygienic practices meant that the country did not offer "a congenial field on which [cholera] may disport itself." Indeed, germ theory as a whole was still being doubted and ridiculed down to the very end of the century.[238]

Nonetheless, such unreconstructed sanitationism was no longer representative of the mainstream of official opinion. British authorities at home walked the line between the sanitationism of the Indian officials and the revival of quarantines prompted in southern Europe by the epidemics of the mid-1880s, reaffirming their commitment to the neoquarantinist system of inspection, isolation and disinfection first elaborated in the sixties.[239] Techniques of revision were now consolidated in the

---

[236] Not to mention disproving the official British view of the 1883 cholera epidemic in Egypt, that, arising independently there, it had not been imported from India: PRO, FO 881/5155*, FO CP 5155*, p. 35; Howard-Jones, *Scientific Background*, p. 52; Mark Harrison, *Public Health in British India: Anglo-Indian Preventive Medicine 1859–1914* (Cambridge, 1994), pp. 111–12; Arnold, *Colonizing the Body*, p. 194; Robert L. Tignor, "Public Health Administration in Egypt Under British Rule, 1822–1914" (Ph.D. diss., Yale University, 1960), pp. 62–64.

[237] R. Thorne Thorne, *On the Progress of Preventive Medicine During the Victorian Era* (London, 1888), pp. 58–59; *PP* 1894 (7539) xl, 1, pp. xviii, xxix–xxxii; *BMJ*, 2 (4 October 1884), pp. 666–67; *Cholera: Inquiry by Doctors Klein and Gibbes*, pp. 4–9; Eyler, *Arthur Newsholme and State Medicine*, pp. 41–43; Steven J. Novak, "Professionalism and Bureaucracy: English Doctors and the Victorian Public Health Administration," *Journal of Social History* (Summer 1973), pp. 456–57.

[238] *Sanitary Record*, n.s., 13, 154 (15 February 1892), pp. 389–90; n.s., 14, 165 (1 August 1892), pp. 55–56; n.s., 16, 273 (23 February 1895), p. 1415; *PP* 1886 (4873) xxxi, 763, pp. viii–ix; *PP* 1894 (8215) xxxvii, 667, p. v; *Sanitary Record*, n.s., 8, 85 (15 July 1886), p. 2; 18 (9 October 1896), p. 301; Watkins, "English Revolution in Social Medicine," pp. 267–74.

[239] PRO, FO 881/4678, FO CP 4678, November 1882, pp. 18–19; FO, 407/115, FO CP 6368, July 1893, pp. 87–88; *BMJ*, 2 (13 August 1887), pp. 339–40; Harrison, *Public Health in British India*, p. 115.

mideighties. In 1885, the Public Health (Shipping) Act extended the infectious disease powers of local officials to the port sanitary authorities, allowing them to cleanse and disinfect, destroy infected bedding and hospitalize victims without proper lodging. In 1884 a system designed to detect cases of disease arriving via maritime routes was instituted that facilitated cooperation between port authorities across the country, preventing vessels from evading sanitary inspection by docking elsewhere. In 1890, the Local Government Board issued regulations based on the assumption that cholera could be spread through dejections of the ill, allowing customs officers to detain possibly stricken ships for twelve hours, to hospitalize the afflicted and to retain suspected passengers for up to two days.[240]

Within the country, the authorities also enhanced their abilities to identify, isolate and disinfect cases of contagious disease. In 1890, the provisions of the 1866 Sanitary and 1875 Public Health Acts were reinforced. Dairies suspected of distributing infected milk could be shut down and powers of disinfection were enhanced, with local authorities now permitted to cleanse houses and objects directly, and owners given only twenty-four hours to undertake it themselves. Bedding, clothing and the like could be ordered disinfected, with compensation for damages, and it was made an offense knowingly to cast infectious waste into refuse receptacles. In Grimsby and Hull, excreta were removed from cholera houses in metal pails, disinfected, taken to the nightsoil depot on the far side of the tracks, mixed with sawdust and petroleum and incinerated.[241] Corpses were still regarded as dangerous. The 1846 Nuisances Removal Act allowed the Privy Council to order speedy interment and the 1866 and 1875 acts authorized local officials to remove corpses from overcrowded dwellings. In 1890, burial was required within forty-eight hours, unless the body was kept in a mortuary or separate room and no conveyances other than hearses were to be used for their transport. During the 1892 epidemic in Grimsby and Cleethorpes, wakes were forbidden and bodies interred in quicklime; later they were wrapped in sheets soaked in carbolic acid with the Inspector of Nuisances witnessing each encoffination and burial in chloride of lime, remaining for this purpose at the cemetery until the grave had been covered.[242]

---

[240] Hardy, "Smallpox in London," pp. 127–33; Hardy, "Cholera, Quarantine"; Frazer, *History of English Public Health 1834–1939*, pp. 212–13; *Sanitary Record*, n.s., 12, 135 (15 September 1890), p. 135; *Conférence 1893*, p. 118.   [241] 53 & 54 Vict. c. 34; *PP* 1894 (7539) xl, pp. 136, 179.

[242] 9 & 10 Vict. c. 96, s. 5; 29 & 30 Vict. c. 90, s. 27; 38 & 39 Vict. c. 55, ss. 141–42; 53 & 54 Vict. c. 34, ss. 8, 11; *PP* 1894 (7539) xl, pp. 134–36; Whitelegge and Newman, *Hygiene and Public Health*, p. 521.

The Infectious Diseases (Prevention) Act of 1890 continued the powers already in the 1866 and 1875 acts to detain any infected and already hospitalized person who had no suitable lodgings to return to. In some localities the occupants of houses with a cholera death were evacuated while their dwellings were disinfected. In Rotherham, healthy inhabitants of infected dwellings who refused the offer of shelter at the hospital were visited daily at home to check on their health. After discovery of a plague case in Liverpool in 1891, contacts were sequestered and the infected dwelling carefully disinfected: the wallpaper was stripped, bedding and clothing were incinerated. All ashpits in the infected and neighboring streets were purified, drains and sewers thoroughly flushed with disinfectants. Persons associated with the ill were detained from business, their wages paid, schools attended by the children temporarily closed.[243] In 1891, the Public Health (London) Act continued the prohibition of infected persons from willfully appearing without proper precautions in public or from passing on undisinfected bedding or clothing. The ill were forbidden to milk animals, pick fruit or otherwise work with food or at other occupations in a manner likely to transmit disease. With good cause and the sanction of a Justice, local authorities could use force to execute their duties. Occupiers of insanitary premises who refused to state or willfully misstated the owner's name and address were liable to fines.[244]

THE THIRTIES REDUX

In terms of personal predisposition to cholera, increasing experience with the disease and the insights harvested by Koch served, perhaps surprisingly, to alter only marginally the recommendations familiar from the 1830s. Among the shifts was a greater emphasis on personal cleanliness, especially with respect to the oral and anal sphincters – the targeted hygiene permitted by knowledge of microbes. Smoking, drinking, eating or otherwise bringing hands in contact with the mouth in the presence of the ill were warned against. Store clerks who handled money should not also touch food; paper napkins were preferable to cloth in restaurants; postmen should wash their hands after each round. More general measures of personal hygiene, today routine childrearing practice in industrialized nations, were also formulated in response to

[243] 53 & 54 Vict. c. 34, s. 12; *PP* 1894 (7539) xl, pp. 197, 248; PRO, MH 19/247, E. W. Hope to Public Health Department, 14 November 1901.   [244] 54 & 55 Vict. c. 76, ss. 68, 69, 115, 117.

the threat of cholera and other contagious diseases: be wary of public toilets, using them only when the seats had been cleaned or furnished with paper covers; wash hands with soap and brush before each meal and after each use of the toilet; do not lick fingers when turning the pages of a book or handling writing instruments, in general, do not put fingers in the mouth and avoid kissing for the same reasons.[245] In other respects, the recommendations made for personal conduct in epidemic times remained remarkably consistent throughout the tergiversations of official policy over the course of the century, from quarantinism to anti-quarantinism to neoquarantinism: regular habits, no overexertion, moderate exercise and emotions, dry feet; avoid damp evening air, go early to bed, do not bathe in cold water, be cheerful, ventilate your rooms, avoid dangerous food and drink. Even flannel belts remained in vogue.[246]

One striking feature of the late-century recommendations and official admonitions was the oldfashioned approach to personal predisposition now reintroduced. Whereas such measures had not figured prominently at midcentury, the 1880s and nineties now saw a flourishing of advice on diet and personal habits. Overeating was still dangerous, although the rationale was no longer the vaguely moral sense that excess sapped bodily strength, exposing one to infection, but the more mundane consideration that an overly full stomach's juices were diluted and less fatal to the cholera bacillus. Chewing food thoroughly promised to spare the stomach excessive digestive efforts and spices were rejected as discouraging mastication. Drinking cold fluids while overheated remained dangerous and ripe fruit risky. Moderation, a regular lifestyle and avoidance of anxiety still lessened predisposition, but fear – no longer a disruption

---

[245] Kabierske, *Wie schützt sich*; Maas, *Schutzmassregeln*; Königliche Eisenbahn-Direction, *Massnahmen zur Abwehr*, pp. 9–23; *Anweisung zur Bekämpfung*, pp. 65–73; *Förhandlingar*, 1892, pp. 94–95, 125–28; 1893, p. 157; Grassmann, *Schutzmassregeln*, pp. 5, 15–16; Boleslaw Kapuscinski, *Was ist Cholera und wie bekämpft man sie?* (Posen, 1892), pp. 19–22; *Anweisung zur Bekämpfung gemeingefährlicher Krankheiten im Bereich der Deutschen Reichspost* (Berlin, 1931), p. 7; Barth, *Cholera*, pp. 221–24; Wretlind, *Koleran*, pp. 11–13, 18–19; Paul A. Koppel, *Die Cholera: Wesen, Vorbeugungs- und Verhaltungsmassregeln* (Mühlhausen i. Ch., 1892), pp. 14–15; Borges, *Cholera in Hamburg*, pp. 37–39; *Vierteljahrsschrift für gerichtliche Medicin und öffentliches Sanitätswesen*, 3 F., 4, Suppl. Hft. (1892), p. 168; *Koleran*, p. 15; *Amtliche Denkschrift*, Anlage 7; Gläser, *Gemeinverständliche Anticontagionistische Betrachtungen*, p. 49.

[246] Martin, *Haupt-Bericht*, pp. 840–47; Günther, *Die indische Cholera*, pp. 112–24; *Bulletin*, 14 (1848–49), pp. 619–22; *Recueil*, 3 (1874), pp. 316–28; *Annales*, 3/12 (1884), pp. 194ff.; Proust, *La défense de l'Europe*, pp. 429–36; *LMG*, 7 (1849), pp. 595–97; Longmate, *King Cholera*, p. 161; *PP* 1847–48 (917) li, pp. 66–68; *SFS*, 1874/68; 1875/21; Grassmann, *Schutzmassregeln*, p. 2; Borges, *Cholera in Hamburg*, pp. 37–39; *Koleran*, p. 15; *Moniteur universel*, 102 (12 April 1849), pp. 1331–32; 106 (16 April 1849), p. 1390; C. Hergt, *Geschichte der beiden Cholera-Epidemien des südlichen Frankreichs in den Jahren 1834 und 1835* (Koblenz, 1838), pp. 63–65; *Annales*, 2/1 (1854), p. 94; Barth, *Cholera*, p. 151.

of the psyche that undermined resistance – was now, more prosaically, merely an irrational emotion that, counteracting clear judgments, might prompt rash and unwise actions. Bad beer, bitter spirits and cheese were still to be avoided, while good red wine continued to exert its beneficent influence.[247]

<h3 style="text-align:center">ETIOLOGICAL EPISTEMOLOGY</h3>

So far, we have been looking at the development of prophylactic strategies to the extent that they were similar or gradually converged across national boundaries. The belief common in the 1830s that, contagious like the plague, cholera required strict quarantinist precautions gradually gave way in the face of experience to a recognition that it was not generally transmitted directly and that other factors also contributed to its epidemic spread. From this sprang at first a faith in sanitation and the elimination of unhygienic conditions propitious to, if not actually the cause of, epidemics. A purebred sanitationist approach was, in turn, gradually modified by the increasing evidence, culminating in Koch's discovery that cholera was in fact transmissible, that it was usually passed through water tainted by infected excrement and that neoquarantinist techniques of inspection, isolation and disinfection served to hamper its spread in the short term, while general hygienic reforms promised to make epidemics less common in the long. In the broad scope a combination of sanitationism and neoquarantinism carried the day.[248]

Traditional quarantinism eventually became a logical impossibility. The oldfashioned variety had presupposed an ability to isolate all potentially infected travelers for the duration of the incubation period. The development of mass and rapid transportation and the commercial vexations imposed by the inherited precautions helped end them. To limit its dysfunctional effects, quarantine was increasingly targeted. The authorities at first kept an eye out for travelers with suspicious symptoms, sequestering them, in turn, for ever shorter periods that corresponded to more accurate calibrations of the incubation period. With the revision system, quarantine was in effect both moderated and broadened, the entire nation turned into a lazaretto without walls. Travelers were

---

[247] Kabierske, *Wie schützt sich*; Grassmann, *Schutzmassregeln*, p. 2; Petri, *Cholerakurs*, p. 170; *Der Choleralärm in Europa 1884* (Hannover, 1884), p. 108; Maas, *Schutzmassregeln*; Koppel, *Cholera*, pp. 14–15; Helmbach, *Cholera*, pp. 27–29; Barth, *Cholera*, pp. 149–50; *Belehrung über das Wesen der Cholera*; *Amtliche Denkschrift*, Anlage 7; *Der amtliche Erlass*, pp. 26–28.
[248] Pelling, *Cholera, Fever and English Medicine*, pp. 295ff.

inspected upon arrival to isolate the obvious cases, with others then to be identified as they went about their business, if and when they succumbed. Eventually, recognition of the role played by intermediary carriers (rats and fleas for plague, mosquitoes for yellow fever) also lessened the role of quarantine, undercutting the usefulness of attempts to break direct chains of transmission between humans, while enhancing the role of pest control. For cholera the main dilemma was posed by asymptomatic human carriers, who sorely tried even the revision system. By the early twentieth century, the expectation that travelers would present symptoms during the surveillance period was undermined by the recognition that asymptomatic carriers could still transmit disease even months later.[249]

Increasing knowledge of the disease (of the immediate empirical sort amassed by customs inspectors, practicing physicians, public health officials and quarantine officers, as well as the formalized scientific variety, whether Snow's adumbrations, Pettenkofer's eclectic intellectual peregrinations or finally Koch's contribution to the bacteriological revolution) was, in the long run, the basis of change in the prophylactic strategies applied to cholera and other contagious diseases. In a general sense, there was of course an overall correlation between the development of a scientific understanding of epidemic diseases and the techniques employed to combat them. Early in the century, with little agreement on the origin and nature of cholera, convergence among nations on preventive strategies was correspondingly weak. Each struck out in its own direction and the international sanitary conferences, held regularly as of 1851 in hopes of forging common approaches, could for decades come to no consensus. Because of such divergent and sometimes contradictory beliefs, preventive measures at midcentury were determined more in terms of political than scientific consensus. The length of quarantine, for example, was decided largely by the arbitrary fiat of local administrators with little regard for incubation periods.[250] Starting with the 1866 Conference, however, the state of scientific knowledge, such as it was, began to be more accurately reflected in the precautions adopted.[251] By the 1890s, a general agreement had been wrought on the validity of Koch's discoveries and, in tandem, a large,

---

[249] Howard-Jones, *Scientific Background*, p. 90; *Conférence 1911*, pp. 22–23.

[250] *Conférence 1903*, pp. 23–24.

[251] *Conférence 1866*, 37, annexe, pp. 2–7. The amount of politicking between nations with different etiological views should not, however, be ignored. Brouardel spoke of the "Dutch auction" by means of which the ten-day incubation period of plague had been brokered among delegates at the 1897 Venice Conference: PRO, FO 542/3, FO CP 7819, November 1902, p. 32.

although by no means complete, measure of international convergence on the principles of neoquarantinism.[252] New information on incubation periods allowed cholera quarantines to be shortened, to five days at the 1893 Conference. In 1897, observation quarantine for plague was cut to ten days, in 1903 to seven. In 1911, the disturbing news that incubation periods had lost much of their significance, now that asymptomatic carriers were known to transmit disease for months, began to be dealt with.[253] Similarly, by 1897, the role of rats in the transmission of plague was recognized and, by the 1903 Conference, measures of deratization were agreed to, although the action of fleas in passing the disease among rodents was not yet sufficiently firm to be acted on.[254]

Such knowledge was, of course, not limited to any one country, although it could on occasion be resisted temporarily for reasons of national amour propre, and it is therefore not surprising that these nations – otherwise so various in their approach to different matters of equal import – should gradually have converged in their prophylactic strategies. By the late 1880s and early nineties, the preventive consensus appeared, if not unisonal, at least harmonious. Although the International Sanitary Conferences had met since 1851, it was not until the 1890s that agreement was sufficient to produce conventions signed by a majority of the attending powers. In 1892 at Venice, 1893 at Dresden and 1894 at Paris, understandings were negotiated that, taken together, implemented the tenets of neoquarantinism – the revision system first developed by the British – throughout Europe and in the Middle East.[255] By the early 1890s nations, like Greece, that had remained staunchly in the quarantinist camp were slowly being persuaded that inspection and disinfection could replace oldfashioned precautions, and the Spanish too underwent a process of liberalization after 1897.[256] The French, beginning as sanitationists, then converting to quarantinism, gradually moved back in the former direction during the last decades of the century. The Italians slowly abandoned their initially quarantinist approach, beginning to shift position after the 1865 epidemic, discovering the futility of oldfashioned restrictions during the

---

[252] *Conférence 1894*, p. 14; *Conférence 1893*, p. 32.

[253] *Conférence 1893*, p. 138; *Conférence 1897*, pp. 111–13; *Conférence 1903*, pp. 18, 88–90, 93; Howard-Jones, *Scientific Background*, p. 90; *Conférence 1911*, pp. 22–23, 44.

[254] Howard-Jones, *Scientific Background*, p. 85; *Conférence 1897*, pp. 111–13; *Conférence 1903*, pp. 18, 88–90, 93; *L'echo médical du Nord*, 7, 38 (20 September 1903), pp. 425–29.

[255] *Conférence 1885*, pp. 237–42, 299–301; *Conférence 1892*, pp. 127–28; *Comptes rendus* (1893), pp. 933–37; *Conférence 1893*, pp. 79, 99–110; PRO, FO 83/1279, George Strachey to the Earl of Rosebery, No. 6A, 19 July 1893.   [256] *Conférence 1892*, p. 175; *Conférence 1903*, p. 53; *Conférence 1911*, p. 656.

1884 epidemic and finally, by 1893, espousing principles that approximated the British.[257] By the early nineties, after the epidemics of the late 1880s and especially that of 1892, oldstyle quarantinism stood discredited by its inability to keep cholera at bay and the principles of neoquarantinism were being generally adopted.[258]

By the turn of the new century, this emerging consensus prompted expressions of satisfaction that the goal had finally been achieved. An Italian delegate gave voice to this prophylactic whiggery, claiming that the Paris Conference had brought matters sanitary into line with the requirements of political economy. The doctrines of liberalism had now been extended to public health, much to the profit of commerce and navigation, the principle of civil solidarity among nations affirmed.[259] In the most general terms, the consensus struck a balance between sanitationism and contagionism. No one would deny that, once imported, disease was encouraged to spread by insalubrious local conditions and that hygienic improvements were worth the effort. Conversely, even the most faultless surroundings could not, by reason of cleanliness alone, resist disease if its cause be introduced in sufficient quantities. Bacteriology and the scientific underpinnings it provided for contagionism coalesced with sanitationism to bring forth a unified approach to public health: salubrious surroundings combined with preventive measures, whether observation quarantines, disinfection or surveillance of possible carriers. By the prewar decade, there was widespread agreement that, by ensuring effective sanitary reform within each nation, controls imposed at the borders could be, if not abolished, at least moderated.[260] Sanitation at home meant neoquarantinism abroad.

Part of the story of the response to contagious disease is thus doubtless a gradual convergence of preventive strategies across national borders that sprang from an improving etiological understanding. At the same time, while advances in scientific knowledge accompanied prophylactic developments, they did not dictate them. Sometimes the right measures were adopted in advance of their eventual scientific justification. The revision system, first instituted by the British in the 1860s, would later be undergirded by the insights of bacteriology, but the edifice had been constructed at least two decades before its epistemological foundation was

---

[257] *Conférence 1874*, pp. 172–73; *Conférence 1885*, p. 97; *Revue d'hygiène et de police sanitaire*, 8 (1886), p. 145; PRO, FO 881/6405, FO CP 6405, p. 73; Snowden, *Naples in the Time of Cholera*, pp. 84–85.

[258] *Conférence 1893*, pp. 33–39.   [259] *Conférence 1903*, pp. 218–19.

[260] Monod, *La santé publique*, pp. 36–37; Jack D. Ellis, *The Physician-Legislators of France: Medicine and Politics in the Early Third Republic, 1870–1914* (Cambridge, 1990), p. 180; *Conférence 1903*, pp. 33–34; *Conférence 1911*, pp. 23, 575, 592–93.

poured. Sometimes the right measures were instituted for the wrong reasons, as when British sanitarians at midcentury were mistaken in their reasons for considering a pure water supply and prompt disposal of human waste protection against cholera. Conversely, the wrong measures could be rejected for the wrong reasons, as when the British attacked cordons and quarantines at midcentury on the basis of theories that were already in contradiction to the best available knowledge, considering them powerless to halt the spread of disease caused by atmospheric conditions which nothing could affect.[261] Thorne Thorne's attempt half a century later to claim that the British rejection of quarantine had been in perfect harmony with scientific principle only highlighted the extent to which epidemiological knowledge and prophylactic practice proceeded in large measure independently of each other. They now believed that cholera was transmissible between humans, he admitted, but Britain's traffic with the rest of the world was too great to permit quarantinist detentions. When it came to choosing a prophylactic course, in other words, what science prescribed mattered less than the dictates of commerce and social intercourse.[262]

Sometimes the same prophylactic technique could have different, even diametrically opposed, etiological underpinnings. Many precautions corresponded clearly and closely to various views of disease causation: isolating patients made sense only given a belief that illness was spread by direct personal contact; good ventilation promised to be an effective precaution only if it were caused miasmatically or at least transmitted through the air. But other preventive measures were adopted with quite varied justifications. Disinfection, for example, was supported both by those who considered cholera miasmatic (because it eliminated pestilential vapors) and by those who thought it transmitted fecally (because it destroyed the contagium thus transported), while observers who thought it directly conveyed from person to person were less likely to see much use for the policy.[263] Sanitary reforms, such as sewerage, made as much sense to Snowians, who thought the disease spread through excrement, as to those who saw general filth as its source.

---

[261] Howard-Jones, *Scientific Background*, p. 100; *Conférence 1851*, 9, p. 3. Do not forget, one observer admonished, that the abandonment of quarantine, however effective it may have been, was based on the erroneous and almost exploded theory that epidemics were caused by some occult atmospheric change: *Public Health*, 5 (1892–93), pp. 105–06.

[262] *Conférence 1893*, pp 49–50. Governments, as another British observer put it, "are more easily affected by the impediments to the transport of troops and merchandize in the ships they subsidize than by arguments addressed to scientific minds": PRO, FO 407/80, In continuation of CP No. 5003, FO, January 1888, no. 2.   [263] *Conférence 1874*, pp. 67–74.

Sometimes scientific knowledge offered, or at least did not discriminate between, different preventive techniques among which nations could choose for reasons other than the scientific. Asymptomatic carriers, for example, posed a stark prophylactic dilemma: either a return to strict quarantinism at the borders or an increased emphasis on local measures, both sanitationism and medical surveillance. To catch the asymptomatic meant retaining all travelers at the border, with repeated bacteriological inspections of their excrement until a sufficiently prolonged series of negative examinations had laid fears of potential transmission to rest, and isolating those who tested positive – a return, in effect, to quarantine of the most oldfashioned sort. The alternative was to abandon restrictive measures at the frontiers, relying instead on local precautions, whether improving the internal sanitary state of each nation or, through medical surveillance, targeting bacteriological examinations, isolation and care in a manageable fashion at people for whom there was reason to suspect potential infection and at places where the disease had in fact broken out. Prophylactic interventions could thus take place either at the borders or the interior of each nation, either in a quarantinist or a more sanitationist (or at least neoquarantinist) sense.[264] Neglect of one preventive arena required correspondingly greater attention to the other. Local actions to control disease lessened the necessity of imposing drastic measures to protect the frontiers from epidemic transgression. Conversely, strict border controls allowed nations greater leeway at home. It was the hope of reformers that each nation would chose to improve its internal sanitary condition, focusing efforts on stricken localities and suspected carriers rather than imposing external precautions. In prophylactic terms, however, there was nothing in the scientific knowledge of cholera's etiology that necessarily dictated this outcome rather than a strict quarantinist approach.[265] Quarantine of all travelers and bacteriological examination of their excrement until proven uncontagious was perhaps not an easy or convenient procedure – and many nations considered it unfeasible – but it was, in terms of the state of scientific knowledge, perfectly rational.[266] The choice between such alternatives therefore depended on other factors.

[264] *Conférence 1911*, pp. 30, 255, 463, 575, 592–93.
[265] Howard-Jones, *Scientific Background*, p. 100.
[266] The Spanish were being disingenuous when they later claimed that the overland quarantines they had established in 1885, for the first time since 1843, had been based on a "misunderstanding" of the new bacteriological discoveries: *Conférence 1893*, p. 52.

PARTING OF THE WAYS

Beyond the gradually emerging consensus on the principles of neoquarantinism combined with domestic sanitary reform, however, an equally significant element of the development of preventive strategies was the manner in which each nation, or bloc of nations, took its own and often divergent approach to a common challenge. Despite tendencies toward convergence, differences in approach remained more pronounced than would be expected if prophylactic strategy were to have been determined solely by the state of etiological knowledge. Such divergences were stark at midcentury, with Britain in the grip of Chadwickian sanitationism while the continental nations were being led by a recently converted France back along the path of quarantinism.[267] But in spite of tendencies toward convergence during the following decades and a broadly common implementation of the neoquarantinist revision system, differences remained. The basic division separated the British from the continent, a broadly sanitationist from a generally quarantinist inflection. But even on the continent, different approaches also emerged and developed that turned some nations (the Netherlands and later Germany, at times parts of Scandinavia, occasionally Russia) into prophylactic allies who supported Britain against the hard core of quarantinist nations around the Mediterranean.

During the 1890s – at the time that Koch's theories were becoming widely accepted, when the system of neoquarantinist revision had apparently been accepted – opinion on cholera still diverged almost as starkly as at midcentury. Throughout the 1880s and nineties, during the interminable disputes that pitted the British against most other European nations over the question of precautions to be imposed in the Middle East, the contrast was between the fundamentally sanitationist approach taken by the British and their Indian allies and the quarantinism of the major continental powers.[268] At the Venice Conference in 1892, for example, the British delegates thought that British scientific and public opinion still "differ so profoundly" from the continental on the question of quarantine that they prepared for major disagreement.[269] At the 1894 Paris Conference, the French formulated what

[267] Richardson, *Health of Nations*, v. II, p. 235.

[268] PRO, FO 407/32, E. Baring to Earl Granville, 5 November 1883, p. 10; FO 881/5197, FO CP 5197, February 1886, p. 7.

[269] PRO, FO 83/1281, pp. 37–38, FO to British Delegates, 22 January 1892; p. 100, Marquis of Salisbury to Phipps and Thorne Thorne, 17 May 1892. Because of such differences, any diagnosis

should have been the consensus: modern rational principles of prophy-laxis based on the discoveries of Pasteur and Koch that replaced oldfash-ioned quarantine with disinfection and other elements of the revision system.[270] At the same time, however, Cuningham, other representatives of British India and their prophylactic allies argued a position on cholera that remained largely miasmatic.[271] Meanwhile, the Spanish were insist-ing that, with all due respect for the tenets of the new system, neoqua-rantinism was but an adjustment to modern times of the fundamental principles of its oldfashioned variant. Although Koch's discoveries had brought advances in knowledge and practice (shortening the period of observation, effective disinfectants, the certainty that humans and their effects were the only vectors of transmission), the inherited verities of quarantinism still held true: retaining the suspected, isolating the ill and forbidding the healthy to circulate freely until assured of their harm-lessness. These, in Spanish eyes, were the timehonored principles of quarantine, of a rational and mitigated quarantine to be sure, but nonetheless of a true, consistent and basically unchanged quarantine. The previous year, the Turks had put it in much the same way: Koch's discoveries were important and useful, but not sufficient to persuade them to abandon the quarantines which had spared them cholera for half a century.[272]

In terms of the precautions adopted, differences also persisted that revealed a continuing tension between fundamentally divergent preven-tive strategies. The Turks and the Spanish insisted that, whatever the prophylactic implications of the new bacteriological discoveries, they would maintain strict quarantines.[273] But it was not just the quarantin-ist fringes that held out against an otherwise accepted consensus. At the 1893 Dresden Conference, the British had accepted the proposal that passengers on infected ships be observed for up to five days only on the condition that they could interpret this not as an observation quarantine, but to mean that travelers would be surveilled at home, as dictated by the revision system, not detained in special institutions for this

of whether cholera were present on board ships inspected in the Middle East "will depend very much upon the school in which the medical man shall have been trained and the nationality to which he belongs": FO 83/1281, p. 45; FO 83/1283, Thorne Thorne, memo, 15 January 1892.

[270] *Conférence 1894*, pp. 90–91; *Recueil*, 22 (1892), pp. i–ii; 23 (1893), pp. viii.

[271] *Conférence 1894*, pp. 189–90; *Conférence 1897*, pp. 83, 86–89; *Sanitary Record*, n.s., 13, 154 (15 February 1892), pp. 389–90; n.s., 14, 165 (1 August 1892), pp. 55–56; PRO, MH 19/244, J. M. Cuningham, "Memorandum on the Cholera in Egypt," 9 July 1883, p. 2.

[272] *Conférence 1894*, pp. 87–88; PRO, FO 83/1330, Paris Sanitary Conference, no. 9, Phipps, 1 March 1894; *Conférence 1893*, pp. 68–70.

[273] *Conférence 1893*, pp. 68–70; *Conférence 1894*, pp. 86–89.

purpose.[274] The new system of inspection, isolation and disinfection was to be understood, in the British view, in its neoquarantinist formulation, not as an excuse to reimpose quarantines of observation. This provisional agreement to read different meanings into a common formulation broached a debate between nations in support of the revision system and those which continued to rely on more oldfashioned principles by imposing observation quarantines. At the 1903 Paris Conference, dispute erupted overtly. Britain dismissed observation quarantines as obsolete, managing to enlist on its side the Netherlands, Germany and Russia.[275] The outcome of this disagreement, whether quarantines should still be permitted even vestigially, was that each country was left to choose the system it preferred, observation quarantines or medical surveillance.

At the 1911 Paris Conference this dichotomy between more and less quarantinist nations continued, now refracted through the issue of subjecting travelers to bacteriological testing. New knowledge had emerged concerning asymptomatic carriers who remained healthy but contagious for longer than what had previously been considered cholera's incubation period. Such new vectors of transmission, suspected since the epidemic of 1892 but formalized as a scientific discovery only since the 1903 Conference, meant that the usual practice of neoquarantinism could no longer guarantee security.[276] Bacteriological examination now promised to reveal all carriers, symptomatic or not. Like oldfashioned quarantines, however, bacteriological examination of all travelers in the age of mass transportation presented formidable logistical hurdles: collecting fecal samples and then either retaining all passengers in anticipation of the results or in some other way being able to locate carriers again. Most nations agreed that bacteriological examination of all travelers was impossible and that testing must be targeted: at passengers on ships with cholera cases or in bad hygienic condition, at contacts of the ill, at those using certain modes of transportation (third-class ticket holders, for example).[277] In this debate too there persisted a clear distinction between nations in favor of mass bacteriological examination at the borders and those unwilling to employ such quarantinist tactics. The two sides of the argument were (1) that the problem of asymptomatic carriers had finally and irrevocably bankrupted a quarantinist approach

[274] *Conférence 1893*, p. 121; PRO, FO 83/1277, "The British Delegates to the Dresden Sanitary Conference to the Earl of Rosebery," 18 April 1893, p. 4.

[275] *Conférence 1903*, pp. 275, 281–82; PRO, FO 83/2055, Thompson to Power, 22 October 1903.

[276] Howard-Jones, *Scientific Background*, p. 90; *Conférence 1911*, pp. 22–23, 463; *Annales*, 4/14 (1910), pp. 433–38.   [277] *Conférence 1911*, pp. 30, 156–58, 464, 596, 607, 628, 677–78.

and that improving internal sanitary conditions in hopes of increasing general resistance to epidemics was the only solution and (2) that the venerable quarantinist principle of identifying and isolating the contagious had in fact been rejuvenated by the discoveries of bacteriology, whatever the practical problems of implementation. Portugal, Austria and Hungary, Romania, Brazil and Turkey advocated bacteriological examination at the borders, with retention of passengers until the results were available, while Egypt had in fact implemented such a system. Germany favored examinations, but coupled with the surveillance system to locate infected passengers once the results were known, rather than retention at the border. France had no faith in its ability to find infected travelers again and no desire to retain them in the meantime; Italy and the Netherlands agreed. Britain thought that long journeys would have eliminated most of the danger, that testing promised to be commercially vexatious and that, in any case, the examination was a repugnant procedure, often requiring the compulsory ingestion of laxatives, unworthy of innocent passengers.[278] The outcome of this latest twist to an old antagonism was a compromise permitting authorities to require bacteriological examination of travelers, but only if they were not delayed more than the five days already allowed for either surveillance or observation quarantine.[279]

Given the continuation of basic differences in prophylactic strategy, even as scientific knowledge concerning cholera crystallized, the question arises why nations faced with the same problems nonetheless differed in these respects. At midcentury, when the divergences were most pronounced, the influence of strong personalities with vigorously argued theories played an important role: Chadwick and Southwood Smith helped guide the British in a sanitationist direction; Pettenkofer's influence in Bavaria and later the Empire served to moderate quarantinist tendencies inherited from the 1830s. But none of these reformers were more than strong voices in an otherwise clamorous field of debate, articulators of opinions that may have helped tilt a prophylactic balance in their direction, but hardly able alone or unaided by other factors to mold opinion and action to their tastes. Other causes, ones undergirding the direction indicated by such reformers, must also have been important. As experience and scientific knowledge of cholera and other contagious diseases accumulated, the centripetal force drawing prophylactic tactics

---

[278] *Conférence 1911*, pp. 30, 44–45, 255, 418–25, 421, 594–99, 600–02, 614, 625, 635, 643.
[279] *Conférence 1911*, pp. 113, 130–31, 677–78.

toward convergence increased, and yet differences remained. It is to their origins that we must now turn.

THE JOY OF QUARANTINES

One factor that slowed any movement away from quarantinism in certain nations was public opinion. While official circles, closely informed by scientific expertise, were often quick to recognize that cholera was not contagious in a pestilential sense and ready to discount oldfashioned precautions, they were often prevented from abandoning outmoded positions by popular pressure to the contrary. Numerous instances testify to the difficulties governments had eliminating or reducing quarantines against the popular will. In 1850, when Paris fired the Marseilles quarantine board for imposing overly draconian measures, it found its ability to moderate strict precautions hampered by local opinion. Because cholera had struck Tunis and Malta, but three days as the ship sails, popular fears along the Mediterranean coast had been aroused. Grudgingly accepting the impossibility of lowering their guard in epidemic times, the Paris authorities reversed themselves, once again allowing municipalities to submit ships from infected ports to an observation quarantine of three to five days, even without cholera onboard. As late as 1897, passengers from British steamships quarantined at Marseilles were prevented from landing, as much – given the pitch of public anxiety on shore – for their own safety as from any fears of plague being transmitted.[280] Similar testimony to the popularity of quarantines was given at the International Sanitary Conferences. Popular opinion did not, the Spanish delegates in 1851 complained, allow them to end maritime quarantines. Indeed, secret ballots were insisted on by the Mediterranean representatives in hopes of avoiding censure from their governments or public opinion at home for votes more liberal than was palatable for domestic consumption.[281] In 1866, the Italians repudiated the Convention of 1851 because of popular demands, fueled by fear of the epidemic that year, to tighten the prophylactic reins. During the

---

[280] Baker, *Laws Relating to Quarantine*, p. 414; *Medical Times*, 1 (1850), p. 152; *Gazette des hopitaux* (1880), p. 755; *Moniteur universel*, 209 (28 July 1850), p. 2591; 225 (13 August 1850), p. 2815; PRO, FO 881/6984, FO CP 6984, December 1898, no. 166.

[281] *Conférence 1851*, 11, p. 25. No other measures, however rigorous or thorough, would satisfy public opinion, the Spaniards lamented, while a detention, even of a few days, was what the voice of the Mediterranean people required: PRO, FO 97/211, Perrier to Addington, 25 September 1851; PC1/4533, John Sutherland and Anthony Perrier, Report of Proceedings, no. 7, 7 August 1851.

fifties, the Ionian Islands refused to relax quarantine lest public opinion be alarmed.[282] In 1893, representatives from Germany, Sweden and Italy dwelt on the difficulties of abolishing quarantines that were held in popular favor. Swedish authorities complained that attempts at reform in a neoquarantinist direction were impeded by popular opinion which took fright whenever cholera approached the coast, clamoring for the security of the old system. In Greece, the population attributed its exemption from the epidemic of 1855 to stern enforcement of quarantine, resisting any change, and as late as 1903 the authorities here claimed that they could not dispense with quarantine against the plague because of public opinion.[283]

In 1892, Germany endured the full force of popular hopes for refuge in restrictive precautions. Individual cities and localities went far beyond what was permitted in law by imposing inspections and disinfections against each other and especially in seeking to control travelers from Hamburg, the Typhoid Mary of German municipalities. In Hamburg, physicians at the main railroad stations were to prevent the patently ill from departing. In Düsseldorf and elsewhere, arriving passengers were inspected before permitted out. Disinfectors in Wittenberg sprayed travelers from Hamburg and even coaches in transit with chloride of lime and carbolic acid solution. In Berlin, all Hamburg trains stopped at a single station for inspection of passengers and disinfection of baggage.[284] Within Prussia baggage was disinfected with steam, often destroying possessions in the process; travelers were fumigated, doused with carbolic acid or had their clothing and, on occasion, even their unclothed bodies, scrubbed. All visitors from Hamburg were to report to the police within twelve hours, be observed for six days and examined if suspected of disease. All packages sent by mail from Hamburg and other infected areas were to be reported before opening, with the police determining whether they contained objects whose introduction was prohibited. In Lübeck, the import of certain goods was forbidden or restricted for the first time since the 1830s. In Wismar, nonlocals were

---

[282] *Conférence 1885*, p. 19; PRO, MH 98/1, untitled ms., signed Anthony Perrier, 5 February 1856; FO 97/216, Draft to Sir Anthony Perrier, no. 3, 14 June 1859; International Sanitary Conference, no. 29, 15 June 1859; PC1/2670, International Sanitary Convention, no. 70, 27 August 1859.

[283] *Conférence 1893*, pp. 19, 33, 53–54; *RD prot*, AK 1895:8, pp. 70–71; *Conférence 1892*, p. 175; *Conférence 1903*, p. 51; PRO, FO 83/2056, Grenfell to Chamberlain, no. 185, 9 December 1901; MH 19/238, FO CP February 1893, p. 10.

[284] Wolter, *Das Auftreten der Cholera*, p. 158; Fliescher, *Choleraepidemien in Düsseldorf*, pp. 26–27; Pagel, *Gesundheit und Hygiene*, p. 98; Ferdinand Hueppe, *Die Cholera-Epidemie in Hamburg 1892* (Berlin, 1893), pp. 46–47; *Vierteljahrsschrift für gerichtliche Medicin und öffentliches Sanitätswesen*, 3 F., 4, Suppl. Hft. (1892), p. 165.

simply forbidden to stay. A Westphalian magistrate required, on pain of fines, his subordinates to catch a certain number of flies daily in hopes of mitigating the epidemic.[285] Seeking to limit the excesses demanded by popular opinion and discourage an indiscriminate application of restrictions, the authorities often moved to specify clearly the circumstances under which certain procedures were permitted. In Germany in 1892, Berlin imposed strict regulations in hopes of avoiding the even more drastic measures otherwise being enforced helter skelter by localities. During discussion of bacteriological examinations at the 1911 Conference, the French delegates were at pains to specify precisely the conditions under which they would be allowed, lest public opinion ("so negligent of hygiene in times of sanitary peace, but so quick to panic at the first hint of disease") otherwise insist on such measures for each and every traveler.[286]

Why this influence of public opinion? Quarantinism, the most visible and tangible method of prophylaxis, was also the most popular among the broad masses who neither traded nor traveled across international borders.[287] It appeased immediate fears of contagion, satisfying the public desire for a quick and obvious fix in a way that sanitationism, the work of long decades and vast infrastructural investment, could not. But why did public opinion in favor of quarantinism matter more in some nations than others? One Swedish observer suggested that the level of general education was to blame. While central Europe had gone far in abolishing restrictive measures, the nations of the northern and southern periphery shared an affinity for quarantinism because of their similar levels of education. Sweden in this respect, according to his precise but unspecified calibrations, lay somewhat behind Denmark, but slightly ahead of Naples. But the entire north and all of the south were collectively less well developed, as measured by the appeal to popular opinion here of cordons, quarantines and restrictive measures, than the center.[288] This analysis from midcentury was to be contradicted as the

[285] Flügge, *Verbreitungsweise und Abwehr*, p. 75; Prussia, Haus der Abgeordneten, *Anlagen zu den Stenographischen Berichten*, 1892/93, Akst. 76, p. 2071; Helm, *Cholera in Lübeck*, pp. 56–57; "Sanitäts-Gesetzgebung," *National-Zeitung* (8 September 1892); Preussischer Medizinalbeamten-Verein, *Verhandlungen*, 10 (1893), p. 8. Similar excesses took place at the instigation of localities in Sweden: *RD prot*, FK 1894:37, pp. 15–16.

[286] *Amtliche Denkschrift*, pp. 21–22; Prussia, Haus der Abgeordneten, *Anlagen zu den Stenographischen Berichten*, 1892/93, Akst. 76, p. 2071; *Conférence 1911*, pp. 566–68.

[287] The hindrance quarantine threw up to commerce, as Edward Malet put it, was felt only by a few merchants, while all suffered the dread of cholera: PRO, FO 881/5197, FO CP 5197, February 1886, p. 7.

[288] Carlson, *Iakttagelser om Choleran*, p. 41. Florence Nightingale shared a similarly dismissive view

French retook a quarantinist position during the following decades and, most dramatically, as the 1892 epidemic in Hamburg sent the rest of Germany scurrying for the solace of exaggeratedly restrictive precautions. The *Kulturländer* of central Europe were not, it turned out, as immune to quarantinist temptations as it may have seemed from the periphery. And yet, the point is well taken, for it highlights the fact that, broadly speaking, quarantinist public opinion was forceful in those nations that tended in this prophylactic direction in any case, and less so, or not at all, in those whose approach was less restrictive. The question, why nations varied in their preventive strategies, cannot therefore rest content with public opinion.

COMMERCE AND QUARANTINES

Two factors played major roles in determining how any individual nation reacted to the threat of cholera and more generally to contagious disease. Neither is surprising nor subtle, yet both are crucial to understanding the divergence of national responses. The first concerns the role of trade and commerce, especially foreign, in the economies of these respective countries. At one level, the desire of trading and commercial interests to carry on unimpeded by quarantines or sanitary cordons was obvious and clearly expressed. Overly strict quarantines imposed at the Suez, for example, threatened to undermine the canal's advantage for Mediterranean ports in the first place, driving shipping from the Orient back around the Cape and to British ports as in pre-Lessepsarian days.[289] Conversely, nations, like Greece, where commerce, industry and travel were not as predominantly important as elsewhere, found quarantinism economically less damaging.[290] But commercial interests averse to quarantinism could, of course, be found in all nations and the question was the extent to which they made themselves felt. The 1835 Prussian regulation on contagious diseases, for example, restricted trade, forbidding the import of various goods from infected countries. On the other hand, it paid attention to commercial concerns in removing the decision to shut down fairs from the hands of local authorities, allowing the police to suspend or limit weekly markets, but reserving the power to close annual fairs for higher officials. The founding of the Zollverein and its ambition to promote freer trade among the German

---

of the contagionism of the "Southern and less educated parts of Europe": Rosenberg, *Explaining Epidemics*, p. 95.   [289] PRO, FO 83/1280, p. 71.
   [290] *Conférence 1893*, p. 72; *Annales*, 2/30 (1868), pp. 21–22.

states was credited in a general fashion with having moderated oldfashioned precautions here, and Hamburg and other Hanseatic cities had
long traditions of resisting quarantinism.[291]

In Sweden too attention was paid to commercial interests in developing prophylactic techniques. The quarantine inspection required in 1834
was abolished in 1840 at the behest of commercial and shipping interests. In 1847, at the same time that the movement of travelers was being
strictly controlled by requiring health attests or five-day observation quarantines, the import of goods was facilitated by classifying as infectious
only the bedding and clothing of crew and passengers of ships from
infected ports, allowing all other objects except rags to pass. During discussions at midcentury it was the Burgher Estate, formerly the most consistent supporters of quarantinism in the 1830s, which now voiced a
concern with the expense of locally varying measures and their harmful
effect on trade, commerce and foreign investment.[292] In France, a
government report in 1834 dwelt on the commercial costs of divergent
precautions applied by each nation in the Mediterranean. Plague quarantines began to be resented after the conquest of Algeria revealed that
they impeded communication with Africa. Aubert-Roche's call in the
early 1840s for a relaxation of such measures was prompted by hopes of
recapturing the commercial advantages that Britain, but also Austria,
had won by moderating quarantinism, thereby restoring to France the
advantage of proximity to the Orient.[293] The Prus report on the plague
in 1846 advocated moderating quarantines in the Mediterranean ports,
seeking to assuage fears of epidemics while not imposing useless obstacles on travel and commercial relations. It was such considerations that
eventually prompted the French to call the first International Sanitary
Conference, held in Paris in 1851, with the goal of regulating quarantines uniformly among the Mediterranean nations. Lowering the com-

---

[291] *Gesetz-Sammlung* (1835), 27/1678, pp. 239–86; H. Reinhard, *Die Verbreitung der Cholera im Königreiche Sachsen nach den Erfahrungen der Jahre 1832–1872* (Dresden, n.d.), pp. 1–3; Evans, "Epidemics and Revolutions," pp. 140–41. One of the interesting contrasts that Evans fails to pursue in his Hamburg book, although he points it out, is why neighboring Lübeck, although similar to Hamburg in being, as he puts it, bourgeois and trade-oriented, should nonetheless have been more strongly quarantinist and not have followed the same allegedly Anglophilic propensity for a hands-off approach as Hamburg.

[292] *SFS*, 1840/10; 1847/38, §§3–4; *Bihang*, 1853–54, viii, No. 85; *Borgare*, 1853–54, i, pp. 172ff., 183; *Bilagor till Borgare*, 1853–54, Memorial No. 33.

[293] Howard-Jones, *Scientific Background*, p. 11; *L'union médicale*, 7, 72 (18 June 1853), p. 285; Paul Faivre, *Prophylaxie internationale et nationale* (Paris, 1908), p. 74; *Annales*, 33 (1845), pp. 243–44, 286–88; *Moniteur universel*, 171 (20 June 1843), p. 1566; Tardieu, *Dictionnaire d'hygiène publique*, v. III, pp. 269–70; *DVöG*, 8 (1876), p. 238; *Bulletin*, 9 (1843–44), pp. 200–12.

mercial impediments thrown up by the dictates of public health promised to allow all nations to profit from the steampowered extension of travel, trade and communication that was taking off during this period.[294]

Quarantinism was not, of course, a binary decision, either for or against. Such precautions could be implemented variously in ways that were more or less burdensome to commerce. Business interests were far more likely to accept restrictions if at least they were imposed uniformly, with no localities given competitive advantages by lax enforcement.[295] How to finance such precautions was also important. Swedish business interests during the 1840s, for example, looked with envy to Britain where the state paid the costs of quarantine as a matter of national concern while, at home, expenses were defrayed by fees levied on shipping and travelers.[296] As a result, they complained, the price of public health fell heavily, unpredictably and unfairly as a business expense on ships with the misfortune to be in the wrong place at the wrong time. After sufficient prodding of this sort, some quarantine costs were split in 1847 between the state and shipping.[297] At the same time, the Swedish state was willing to go only so far to please commercial interests. The government already covered much of such costs, it noted, and there was no reason why shipping could not afford the remaining sums, or why, as one member of the Noble Estate put it, the state should assume the business expenses of prosperous merchants. In any case, the politicians reckoned, whatever the complaints of traders, the costs were ultimately borne through increased prices by all members of society.[298] The way quarantinist strictures were implemented could also mean the difference between the tolerable and the impossible. At the 1851 Paris Conference,

---

[294] *Rapport à l'Académie royale de médecine … par M. le Dr. Prus*, p. 217; *Conférence 1851*, 2, p. 3; 7, annexe; 11, pp. 5–12; Ch. Bernard, "Congrès Sanitaire Européen," *Le Siècle*, 6, 5731 (11 August 1851).

[295] *Moniteur universel*, 171 (20 June 1843), p. 1567; *Recueil*, 9 (1880), pp. 29–52. This had been a concern also during earlier plague epidemics and remained so later in the United States: Ch. Carrière et al., *Marseille ville morte: La peste de 1720* (Marseilles, 1968), p. 313; Howard Markel, *Quarantine! East European Jewish Immigrants and the New York City Epidemics of 1892* (Baltimore, 1997), pp. 171–72.

[296] *SFS*, 1847/38; 1848/36. The British rejected paying for quarantine through fees proportional to tonnage, seeing this as a tax on the northern, clean, trading nations for benefit of their southern, infected, noncommercial neighbors: PRO, FO 97/215, Board of Trade, "Report Upon Proposed Sanitary Convention"; FO 881/406, FO CP 406, p. 12; MH 98/24, "Memorandum relative to the Negotiation respecting the System of Quarantine in the Mediterranean," 11 April 1853, p. 24.

[297] *Bilagor till Borgare*, 1840–41, No. 122; *Borgare*, 1840–41, i, p. 409; vii, pp. 132–33; *Bihang*, 1840–41, 1. Saml., 2 Afdl., no. 165; *SFS*, 1847/34.

[298] *Ridderskapet och Adeln*, 1853–54, vii, p. 475; *Borgare*, 1847–48, iv, pp. 386–89; *Bihang*, 1847–48, iv, 2, no. 73; 1853–54, viii, no. 85.

for example, during proposals to moderate restrictions on ships from the Orient, a major sticking point was precisely which sorts of cargo to quarantine and disinfect. The old distinction between susceptible and safe goods, inherited from plague regulations and applied to cholera during the 1830s, was hotly debated. A new one was advocated between animal and vegetable matter, the former subject to disinfection, the latter only voluntarily. Once it became clear, however, that one of the main motives behind this new approach was the British desire to exempt cotton from restrictions, attempts to reach a consensus were scuttled.[299]

Such finetuning indicates the extent to which commercial interests were not invariably opposed to quarantines. The General Board of Health estimated that British merchants were sufficiently unconcerned by the burdens of quarantine, eventually passed on to consumers, that effective opposition to such measures would have to come from the government acting on the public's behalf.[300] Among the Mediterranean nations, business interests in the latter half of the century did not reject quarantines. In the venerable dichotomy between commercial concerns and public health they often favored the latter, reckoning in the logic of a broader self-interest that an epidemic was more costly than restrictive measures. In any case, they calculated, business tended to recoup in the increased activity following an epidemic what it had lost during it.[301] In certain cases, Marseilles and Toulon especially, ports were granted monopolies of commerce from the Levant, equipped with lazarettos and the machinery of quarantine and enjoyed more than their share of shipping funneled through such facilities.[302]

In determining the stance adopted by business interests, much depended on the approach of their trading partners, but this could work in both directions. In classic prisoner's dilemma terms, those who traded mainly with quarantinist nations had to follow suit, *mutatis mutandis* for those whose partners were antiquarantinists.[303] During the 1840s and

---

[299] *Conférence 1851*, 7, annexe, pp. 26–29; 19, 20, 21, pp. 13–18.

[300] *PP* 1849 (1070) xxiv, pp. 76–77. See also John B. Blake, "Yellow Fever in Eighteenth-Century America," *Bulletin of the New York Academy of Medicine*, 2/44, 6 (June 1968), pp. 682–83.

[301] *Conférence 1874*, pp. 118–27; *Recueil*, 5 (1876), p. 51; *Annales*, 4/11 (1909), pp. 314–15; *Revue d'hygiène et de police sanitaire*, 3 (1881), pp. 728–29; *Conférence 1866*, 24, annexe, p. 4; 29, annexe, pp. 3–5, 50–51; 37, annexe, p. 6.

[302] *Annales*, 33 (1845), pp. 288–92; *Moniteur universel*, 171 (20 June 1843), p. 1567; Daniel Panzac, *Quarantaines et lazarets: L'Europe et la peste d'orient* (Aix-en-Provence, 1986), p. 55; Françoise Hildesheimer, *Le bureau de la santé de Marseille sous l'ancien régime* (Marseilles, 1980), pp. 20–21, 203; Charles Carrière, *Négociants marseillais au XVIIIe siècle* (Marseilles, n.d.), v. I, p. 220.

[303] Already during the first epidemic, the Austrians, who quickly ended cordons against their other neighbors, were persuaded by the Italians to retain them to the south where Trieste and

fifties, French commercial interests along the Mediterranean favored quarantinist measures in hopes of avoiding retaliation from the Italians and others who feared that France was being insufficiently cautious. Portugal, though liberally inclined, was obliged to follow the quarantinist lead of the Spaniards, while Naples generally followed Spain and Rome. The Swedes, in turn, were prompted in 1879 to introduce strict new measures against the plague in fear of mercantile repercussions, lest the continental states which had forbidden imports from stricken Russia apply similar precautions to Sweden. The Greeks remained faithful to their quarantinist approach because their primary commercial ties with the Turks obliged them to mirror Ottoman prophylactic practice, and Romania and Bulgaria followed the Turkish lead for much the same reasons.[304] The British dependencies in the Mediterranean (Malta, Cyprus, Gibraltar and the Ionian Islands) demonstrated this commercially imitative effect most clearly. Despite the antiquarantinism of the metropolitan power, and often much to London's embarrassment, they imposed measures of a wholly Mediterranean ilk, lest their ships otherwise be denied free pratique.[305] No nation can act alone in questions of quarantine, as a British observer put it in explaining how Gibraltar's restrictive practices, so at odds with the official British position, were in effect imposed by the Spanish.[306] Conversely, those who dealt with antiquarantinists had to follow suit to remain competitive. The French, for

Venice feared that, the rest of the world still believing cholera to be contagious, a blockade threatened if they were not thus protected against Austria: Joseph Johann Knolz, *Darstellung der Brechruhr-Epidemie in der k.k. Haupt- und Residenzstadt Wien, wie auch auf dem flachen Lande in Oesterreich unter der Enns, in den Jahren 1831 und 1832, nebst den dagegen getroffenen Sanitäts-polizeylichen Vorkehrungen* (Vienna, 1834), pp. 230–33; W. Sander, *Die asiatische Cholera in Wien beobachtet* (Munich, 1832), p. 103.

[304] *Moniteur universel*, 209 (28 July 1850), p. 2591; 171 (20 June 1843), p. 1567; *Conférence 1851*, 2, p. 3; 7, annexe; 11, pp. 5–12; PRO, FO 97/211, Perrier to Viscount Palmerston, 23 October 1851; *Hygiea*, 41, 2 (February 1879), pp. 130–40; 41, 4 (April 1879), pp. 265–77; 41, 5 (May 1879), pp. 329–33; *Conférence 1859*, 31, pp. 3–4; *Conférence 1903*, p. 52; *Conférence 1897*, p. 69; PRO, FO 881/6405, FO CP 6405, p. 73; PC1/2670, letter to Lord J. Russell, 29 July 1859.

[305] *Conférence 1874*, pp. 172–73. Other nations did not, of course, pass up the opportunity to berate the British for this apparent inconsistency: *Conférence 1851*, 10, pp. 4–5; *Conférence 1874*, pp. 172–73; *Lancet*, 1 (9 January 1892), pp. 111–12; *BMJ*, 1 (23 January 1892), pp. 161–63; *Recueil*, 5 (1876), p. 51. For the British response, see *Conférence 1897*, p. 203; *Practitioner*, 42 (January–June 1889), pp. 399–400; PRO, FO 83/1330, British Delegates to the Earl of Kimberley, 7 April 1894; FO 97/217, International Sanitary Conference no. 70, 27 August 1859; MH 19/239, Thorne Thorne to the President [of the LGB] and Hugh Owen, 21 January 1897; MH 19/244, T. Thomson, "Intercolonial Conference as regards Plague and Cholera Regulations," 21 January 1903; MH 19/278, Armand Rüffer to Viscount Cromer, 17 May 1900.

[306] Milroy, *Quarantine as It Is*, pp. 10–12; *Transactions of the National Association for the Promotion of Social Science* (1862), p. 877; PRO, FO 83/2056, Government House, Nicosia, to Chamberlain, 5 January 1901; FO 542/3, FO CP 7819, November 1902, pp. 1–2, 18; MH 19/238, Thorne Thorne to President of LGB, 5 January 1893.

example, began to appreciate already in the 1840s that their quarantinist approach was not without opportunity costs. When Britain, followed
by Austria, changed rules to admit ships from the Levant with clean bills
of health to free pratique, commercial pressure on France to do likewise
mounted. Travelers from Constantinople or Alexandria to Paris saved
time by passing via London or Vienna. Steam boats had quickened the
pace of transportation, trading interests complained, but such gains
were being squandered in quarantine. It was no coincidence that it was
de Lesseps, builder of the Suez canal, who in 1882 caused a stir in the
French Academy of Science by arguing the case against quarantines on
behalf of commercial interests.[307]

   That country which most consistently opposed such restrictions
because of their harm to commercial relations was, not surprisingly,
Britain. Only here was the argument against quarantines formulated in
universal terms – not in those of minor comparative advantage, but as
an issue of general laws of nature and economics that could be violated
only at the cost of debilitating loss. Quarantine, as John Simon put it,
was possible only to the extent that a nation lived apart from the great
highways of commerce or was prepared to subordinate its trade to political concerns. But even those who willingly paid this price, he predicted,
would find their efforts unavailing. Against quarantines there operated
the strongest of all law-breaking influences: eager commercial interests
and the instincts of contempt for narrow self-protectiveness brought in
their train. "And thus, practically speaking, where great commercial
countries are concerned, it can scarcely be dreamt that quarantine
restrictions will be anything better than elaborate illustrations of leaki-
ness."[308] Its role as the greatest shipping power and its commercial relations with the empire, especially India, made quarantine commercially
undesirable. The beginnings of regular steampowered maritime connections with the eastern Mediterranean in the 1840s prompted hopes
of moderating restrictions. Constant communication with the continent
and, in general, the density of its intercourse with other nations made

---

[307] *Bulletin*, 9 (1843–44), pp. 237–43; *Lancet*, 1 (1844), pp. 20–23; *Conférence 1851*, 48, p. 5; *Annales*, 3, 7 (1882), pp. 565–67; *BMJ* (16 September 1882), p. 520. The same de Lesseps, as French consul in the Middle East, had protected himself along with 200 fellow nationals by isolating them in his property outside Aleppo during the cholera epidemic of the 1830s: Jacques Poulet, "Epidémiologie, sociologie et démographie de la première épidemie parisienne de choléra," *Histoire des sciences médicales*, 3–4 (July–December 1970), p. 148.

[308] *PP* 1866 (3645) xxxiii, pp. 461–62; Baly and Gull, *Reports on Epidemic Cholera*, pp. 214–32; *Conférence 1874*, pp. 145–49; Sven Lysander, *Några synpunkter och iakttagelser angående karantänsinrättningar* (Stockholm, 1902), p. 3.

quarantine unfeasible. The 5,800 people who arrived at Dover during a typical August week late in the century, for example, could not all have been sequestered. It was the British who consistently argued the case against restrictions throughout the International Sanitary Conferences, starting already in 1866 with their insistence that whatever increased chance of epidemic attended free and proliferating communication was but a minor disadvantage compared to the vast benefits conferred. In direct opposition to the business interests of quarantinist nations, the British argued that theirs was a country which suffered more in commercial terms from restrictive practices than from an epidemic.[309]

Steadfastly pursuing commercial interests and their prophylactic consequences, Britain was brought into conflict with other European powers, especially France, in the Middle East. At the 1881 Conference, the European powers agreed to establish a system of sanitary surveillance of the Red Sea, the Egyptian ports and routes followed by pilgrims to Mecca. The British occupation of Egypt the following year, however, turned matters on their ear, ending Anglo-French cooperation. The British now dominated the Alexandria Sanitary Council, nominally an international body, safeguarding their prophylactic interests through strategic alliances with the Egyptian delegates, several of whom, including the president, were in fact Britons. Since this meant largely unhindered passage of shipping between India and the homeland, the other powers accused them of neglecting the public health of Europe for their own gain.[310] After cholera hit Egypt in 1883 and British dominance of the Alexandria Council continued to rile the other European powers, the Rome Conference in 1885 sought to break the impasse. Here the British proposed to exempt ships with clean bills of health traveling from India to England without calling at ports in between from the delays of inspection or quarantine at the Suez. Although the British presented their demands in general terms (quarantinism as an affront to human liberty, the only true guarantee of public health to be found in sanitary reform), their rivals rejected this as but special pleading for Britain's shipping interests in the masquerade of universalism.[311] Britain, conversely,

---

[309] PRO, FO 83/1280, p. 136, Chamber of Shipping of the UK to Earl Granville, 5 March 1885; *Lancet*, 71, 2 (1 July 1893), pp. 50–51; *Conférence 1893*, pp. 49–50; *Sanitary Record*, n.s., 14, 175 (1 January 1893), p. 326; *Conférence 1866*, 5, p. 43; 33, p. 10; 30, p. 4.

[310] Harrison, *Public Health in British India*, pp. 125–26; PRO, FO 407/32, Memorandum by Sir E. Baring, 8 June 1884, p. 113; *Gazette médicale de Paris*, 36 (6 September 1890), pp. 430–31; *Comptes rendus* (1892), pp. 1458–62; *Annales*, 3/10 (1883), pp. 114–15; Oleg P. Schepin and Waldemar V. Yermakov, *International Quarantine* (Madison, CT, 1991), pp. 49–50.

[311] Goodman, *International Health Organizations*, p. 64; *Conférence 1885*, pp. 169–70, 176, 183.

argued that decision-making in the canal should bear some correlation to shipping in the region, justifying their preponderant say.[312] Despite defeat at Rome, British commercial muscle eventually had its way. Because of their owners' sway over the Alexandria Council and because they could threaten transit fees and the worth of shareholder's stock by sending their shipping (four-fifths of all traffic in the canal) along the old route around the Cape (with a five-day observation quarantine in the Suez, the roundabout voyage was but two days longer), British ships were in fact allowed to pass through the canal without delay as long as they avoided all contact with the shore, a procedure known as transit in quarantine.[313] In 1892 at the Venice Conference, a compromise was brokered whereby the continental powers agreed to recognize transit in quarantine as official procedure in return for a reorganization of the Alexandria Council that, by reducing the Egyptian influence, deprived the British of their monopoly.[314] When rats were eventually recognized as a vector of plague, it was of course the British who sought to avoid allowing overly cautious measures against rodents to slow the pace of trade.[315]

So consistent was the association of antiquarantinism with the nation's commercial elements that the British were repeatedly attacked by continental observers for allegedly preferring the interests of trade to those of public health – an epidemiological element, no doubt, in the foreigners' view of Britain as a nation of shopkeepers. Human life, as delegates from the Mediterranean countries eager to command the moral highground argued, was neither a form of portable property nor interest-bearing capital. Time might be money, in the English proverb, but public health was gold. The insinuation repeated by the more quarantinist nations that the only real losers from restrictive precautions were not business and commerce as such, but the much less important

[312] PRO, FO 78/2007, p. 161, No. 336, 12 September 1866; FO 83/1278, Walpole to Under Secretary of State, FO, 9 February 1893; FO 83/1281, FO to the British Delegates, No. 6, 29 January 1892; FO 83/1330, Phipps, 20 February 1894; FO 407/32, Memorandum by Mr. Lister, 18 August 1884, p. 175.

[313] *Comptes rendus* (1892), pp. 1458–62; *Conférence 1885*, pp. 367, 374; McDonald, "History of Quarantine," pp. 40–41; PRO, FO 407/32, T. Farrer to Lister, 27 August 1884, pp. 191–92; FO 881/5328, FO CP 5328, October 1886, pp. 200, 200D; 407/80, In continuation of CP No. 5003, FO, January 1888, p. 7.

[314] *Conférence 1892*, pp. 15–16, 108–09, 193; PRO, FO 407/80, In continuation of CP 5003, FO, January 1888, no. 1; FO, 407/115, FO CP 6368, July 1893, p. 30.

[315] PRO, FO 83/2055, Thomson to Power, 1 November 1903; FO 83/2056, LGB to Under Secretary of State, FO, 12 March 1903; MH 19/244, T. Thomson, "Rats and Ship-Borne Plague," 24 July 1903.

category of leisured tourists, irritably idling away their time in lazarettos, was a not so veiled swipe at the British, the indefatigable tourists of the day.[316] In riposte, British antiquarantinists attacked in kind, arguing that their nation could be proud of its immense investment in hygienic improvement, the lead it had commanded in sanitationist reform and the steadily declining level of mortality thus achieved. Public health, as Thorne Thorne put it, was an integral part of British prosperity; the two were not, as their continental opponents would have it, at odds.[317]

But Britain, of course, hardly stood alone in protecting commercial interests against overly zealous precautions. In the 1840s, steam travel up the Danube gave Austria a quick maritime connection to Constantinople and a mercantile stake in lessening restrictions and such interests continued into the 1880s.[318] Germany continued its quarantinist approach through the sixties, then changing position at the latest by the early nineties. The restrictions imposed on German ships, goods and travelers by other nations during the 1892 epidemic, not to mention the havoc wreaked at home as each locality eagerly levied sanctions against its neighbors, came as a prophylactic revelation that stoked sympathies with the British position.[319] By the early 1890s, Germany's acquisition of colonies in East Africa encouraged a common interest with the British in relaxing restrictions on traffic in the Suez. Germany's shipping industry had been developing mightily since the eighties and, through the canal, German transit resembled the British more than that of the other powers in being larger and dominated by cargo rather than passenger ships. Germany also had interests at stake in specific exports. Artificial wool or shoddy, a local specialty manufactured from old rags, was regarded with suspicion abroad as especially infectious and particular exertions were required to prevent its banning. At the Dresden Conference in 1893, the Germans won a victory in alliance with the British when the import of shoddy and rags hydraulically compressed and packaged for the wholesale trade was allowed. Thorne Thorne, the

---

[316] *Conférence 1851*, 10, pp. 8–9; 12, p. 20; 11, pp. 15–18; *Conférence 1866*, 6, pp. 6–7; *Conférence 1892*, p. 156; PRO, FO 407/32, Horace Walpole to Lister, 4 September 1884; FO 881/5424, FO CP 5424, April 1887, p. 30; *Conférence 1866*, 24, annexe, p. 4; 29, annexe, pp. 3–5, 50–51; 37, annexe, p. 6; 33, pp. 11–12; Almquist, *Om koleran, dess sätt att utbreda sig*, p. 29.

[317] *BMJ*, 2 (13 August 1887), pp. 339–40; *Conférence 1885*, p. 290.

[318] *Lancet*, 1 (1844), pp. 20–23; PRO, FO 407/80, In continuation of CP No. 5003, FO, January 1888, Inclosure in No. 1; Panzac, *Quarantaines et lazarets*, p. 110.

[319] *Conférence 1866*, 6, pp. 6–7; 26, pp. 4–6; *Conférence 1893*, p. 17. The British, for their part, had reason to cooperate more with Germany and Austria-Hungary after the occupation of Egypt in 1882 alienated the French: Harrison, *Public Health in British India*, pp. 125–26; PRO FO 881/5424, FO CP 5424, April 1887, no. 118.

quasi-sanitationist who opposed quarantines in principle, and Koch, whose discoveries showed that, although transmissible, cholera was only rarely conveyed by goods, could thus agree to moderate restrictions on imported merchandise.[320]

Koch's discoveries helped resolve the commercial dilemmas of preventing epidemics and moderated the antagonism between countries with divergent trading interests. In the mid-1880s, the continental nations had imposed vexatious restrictions on each other's trade and the same occurred again in 1892. By now, however, Koch's work was beginning to make clear the extent to which prohibiting or disinfecting merchandise might be useful, revealing that goods, other than those few in which the cholera bacillus was transmissible (mainly used and soiled clothing and foodstuffs like milk, butter and cheese), were innocuous and that regulations restricting their circulation were not only economically harmful, but useless.[321] In 1892, the Germans forbade the import of used linen, clothing and bedding, rags, fruit, vegetables and butter from Russia, France and the Netherlands. In 1893, in contrast, the export of only milk and rags was prohibited from infected areas and packages sent by mail had to have their contents noted on the wrapping. In the Contagious Disease Law of 1900, milk, used clothing, bedding and rags could not be exported from infected areas, but limitations on the mail were suppressed. In order to end the sorts of restrictive measures imposed haphazardly by local fiat in 1892, imports from infected places within Germany could no longer be prohibited.[322] Already the 1893 Dresden Conference drew lessons from the previous year's epidemic, scoring a victory for the antiquarantinist forces (Britain and Germany, supported by Austria-Hungary) in the agreement to set maximum limits on the restrictions nations might impose on each other during epidemics. At the 1903 Paris Conference, in turn, the virtues of disinfection were sung. Thanks to the insights of bacteriology, targeted and effective disinfectants promised to reconcile the age-old choice between commercial intercourse and public health by minimizing the measures necessary at frontiers. It was now agreed that no merchandise was in and of itself able to transmit cholera or plague, but only when soiled with infectious

---

[320] Harrison, *Public Health in British India*, pp. 130–31; PRO, FO 83/1282, Lowther and Mackie to the Marquis of Salisbury, No. 2, 6 January 1892; *Amtliche Denkschrift*, pp. 44, 56; *Conférence 1893*, pp. 100, 235–36.

[321] Flügge, *Verbreitungsweise und Abwehr*, pp. 76–77; Kabierske, *Wie schützt sich*, p. 3; *Amtliche Denkschrift*, pp. 32, 118–19; Petri, *Cholerakurs*, pp. 85–90.

[322] *Amtliche Denkschrift*, p. 16; *Der amtliche Erlass*, p. 7; *Anweisung zur Bekämpfung*, pp. 18–19; *SB*, 1892/93, Akst. 172, p. 919.

material. Disinfection was therefore to be limited to contaminated objects, although a few things (linen, used clothing and bedding and the like) could be disinfected or even prohibited, whether contaminated or not.[323]

THE GEOEPIDEMIOLOGY OF DISEASE

The second factor that helps explain why different nations took various approaches to these common problems concerns geography. During the 1830s, those nations geographically further down cholera's route and therefore favorably placed along the learning curve were able to profit from the hardwon experience of the epidemiological avantgarde. During the following half-century of accumulating experience with cholera, such geographical factors became institutionalized, with nations adopting longterm preventive strategies that corresponded to their position in the geoepidemiology of the disease.

At the simplest level, sheer distance from the source and pathways of epidemic advance gave nations thus blessed a sense of security and room to maneuver that those closer to the front lines found hard to emulate. In these terms, Britain was among the most favored. Although the protection of sheer distance was reduced by steam locomotion and the opening of the Suez, it was still largely spared the most direct ravages of cholera by virtue of its location. Much of Britain's insouciance in the face of cholera, its ability to insist that disease was rarely if ever imported by sea despite the steady arrival of ships from India, derived from the automatic quarantine imposed by the voyage's duration.[324] "The quarantine which protects her," as Henri Monod, Director of Public Hygiene at the French Interior Ministry, put it, "is the length of time which it takes to reach her ports."[325] Least favored were the nations in closest proximity to the sources of cholera in the Orient or, for yellow fever, the Americas. Already in 1851, with the Suez still a decade and a half away, the Two Sicilies, for example, portrayed themselves as the epidemiological navel

---

[323] *Conférence 1893*, pp. 79, 99–110, 199; *Comptes rendus* (1893), pp. 933–37; *Conférence 1903*, pp. 21–23, 159–60.

[324] A. Netter, *Vues nouvelles sur le choléra* (Paris, 1874), pp. 2, 93; *Conférence 1885*, pp. 101, 170–71, 369; *Conférence 1892*, pp. 169–70; PRO, FO 407/32, T. Farrer to Lister, 27 August 1884, pp. 190–91.

[325] *BMJ*, 1 (23 January 1892), pp. 161–63. For similar views, see *DVöG*, 12, 1 (1880), p. 13; *Transactions of the Seventh International Congress of Hygiene and Demography*, 10–17 August 1891 (London, 1892), p. 55; *Lancet*, 1 (9 January 1892), pp. 111–12; *Conférence 1892*, pp. 129–30; PRO, FO 407/84, FO CP 6106, pp. 172–73; FO 407/110, FO CP 6157, February 1892, pp. 50–51; *JO*, 16, 298 (29 October 1884), p. 5683.

of the world, located at the intersection of Europe, Asia and Africa, surrounded by the most productive countries of the world, its ports host to
thousands of ships. For the Turks, their geographical location and consequent exposure to cholera was the reason they refused to abandon strict
quarantines, whatever the scientific merits of the new moderated system.
Greece, in turn, perched – as it saw matters – on the cusp of contagion,
argued that a complacent approach to epidemic disease was not possible.
Cholera had struck only once (in 1854 when quarantines had not been
fully implemented and the capital and Piraeus occupied by French and
British troops) and hence the faith in quarantinism here remained strong.
Spain excused its quarantinist proclivities with its geography, climate and
the devastating epidemics of yellow fever early in the century.[326]

In a more general sense, the importance of geography is revealed in
the basic split between the Mediterranean countries, in close contact
with the Oriental founts of cholera, and the Atlantic nations at a further
remove. The division between Atlantic and Mediterranean Europe separated nations afraid of epidemics that threatened directly from the
Orient from those for whom the disease became a problem mainly once
it had invaded Europe itself. This was a division honored often in the
breach, one whose fronts crumbled to reform repeatedly during the
course of the century. It was also a dichotomy with many exceptions:
Germany with its few Baltic ports, starting out contagionist only to end
up in alliance with the British by the 1890s; Russia and Austria-Hungary,
with vast expanses facing both west and east, willing to lower their guard
occidentally, but more concerned to maintain precautions in the other
direction; Italy, some of whose states were quarantinist, others not.[327]
Nonetheless, this division between Mediterranean and Atlantic, north
and south, was a basic geographic dichotomy, the expression of fundamental geoepidemiological blocs that shines through with sufficient
consistency beneath many twists and tergiversations to allow its
identification as a crucial factor in the development of prophylactic
strategies.

At the 1851 Paris Conference, the main epidemiological antagonism

---

[326] *Conférence 1851*, 12, p. 20; *Conférence 1866*, 23, annexe, pp 28–29; PRO, FO 407/32, Précis of a
Paper read to Earl Granville by Count Nigra, 10 June 1884, p 127; FO 407/40, CP 5005, FO,
September 1884, no. 1; *Conférence 1893*, pp. 68–71; *Conférence 1851*, 35, p. 22; PRO, FO 97/215, Xavier
de Isturiz to Earl of Clarendon, 5 April 1853; MH 98/24, "Memorandum relative to the
Negotiation respecting the System of Quarantine in the Mediterranean," 11 April 1853, p. 27.

[327] *Deutsche Medizinal-Zeitung*, 11, 74 (15 September 1890), p. 831; Hirsch, *Über die Verhütung*, pp.
14–15; *Conférence 1874*, pp. 161–62; *Conférence 1851*, 12, pp. 4–10; *Conférence 1897*, p. 144. But see also
Conférence 1903, p. 48.

separated the British, still in the throes of Chadwickian sanitationism, from the quarantinist nations of the Mediterranean – Greece, Spain and various, but not all, of the Italian states. Between these poles, other nations ranged themselves depending on a number of factors: the Russians with their direct terrestrial borders on the east who were unwilling to reject quarantinism out of hand; the Austrians who favored the British example of hygienic measures for cholera, but had no intention of dropping their quarantinist guard against the plague; the Portuguese whose willingness to strike a compromise between the two camps may have been a result of their peculiar predicament, suspended between their interests as a Mediterranean nation and their all-important trading relations with the British; the Sardinians who were heavily influenced by the British example and whose state was among the least quarantinist of the Italian peninsula; and finally the French, whose spirit was willing to forego quarantinism, but whose national flesh, straddling both the Atlantic and the Mediterranean, remained open to the temptations of a restrictive approach.[328] The hardcore quarantinists of the Mediterranean (Tuscany, the Two Sicilies, the Papal States, Spain and Greece) successfully undercut the attempt spearheaded by Britain and France (for the moment united as the main antiquarantinists) to exclude cholera from quarantines, limiting restrictive measures to plague and yellow fever. Hygiene was all well and good, was their position, but it was obviously insufficient since all the sanitary advances achieved since the last plague epidemic had not sufficed to prevent cholera.[329]

In 1874, when the revision system was discussed as a replacement for quarantines, similar fronts reopened. Greece and Portugal now led the charge against relaxing quarantine. Hygiene might ameliorate the ravages of an epidemic, but could scarcely prevent its import. Southern Europe had its own particular prophylactic interests and, although the Atlantic nations might fear restrictive precautions more than an epidemic, that was no reason to impose their preferences on the Mediterranean. Europe was a unity neither in terms of geography nor ethnography and the same preventive strategy could not be applied everywhere. Austria-Hungary and Russia, in contrast, had by this point tempered their previously quarantinist approaches. Russia, with its far-reaching overland boundaries,

---

[328] *Conférence 1851*, 7, annexe, pp. 8–9; 5, pp. 7–8; 10, pp. 6–7, 12–13, 15–17; 5, pp. 6–7; 9, pp. 8, 12; 12, pp. 4–10, 21; 11, pp. 30–31; 18, p. 6; PRO, FO 97/210, Sutherland, 26 August 1851; FO 97/211, Perrier to Viscount Palmerston, 23 October 1851. The proportion of Portuguese exports to Britain was much higher than the equivalent for Spain throughout the latter half of the nineteenth century: B. R. Mitchell, *European Historical Statistics* (New York, 1975), F2, pp. 549, 561.

[329] *Conférence 1851*, 7, annexe, pp. 11, 18, 39; 10, pp. 4–5; 9, pp. 6–7; 10, pp. 8–9; 39, pp. 4–7.

concluded that quarantines along its Persian frontier, where contacts across the divide were dense and intimate, was impossible. Since cholera had ravaged its territory endemically for many years now, the disadvantages of quarantines were becoming apparent. Given the persistence of this fundamental geoepidemiological dichotomy, no common system could be agreed to, and instead a compromise allowed both systems, revision and quarantine, with each country deciding which to follow.[330] *Cujus regio, ejus remedium.*

The consequences of this persistent split between north and south were drawn in 1885 when a revision system was adopted that included special measures to satisfy the Mediterranean nations. Free pratique was to be accorded only after inspection of ships upon arrival, passengers and crew were housed in special quarters to permit disinfection and sequestration, vessels en route for less than ten days underwent a 24-hour observation, passengers on infected ships were quarantined for five days. Overland, all trains from stricken countries were to be changed at the border and accompanied by a physician. In 1892, the north/south divide continued in the dispute over whether to allow British ships from India transit in quarantine through the Suez.[331] At the 1893 Dresden Conference, the divide was played out over the issue of compulsory disinfection. The hardcore quarantinist countries still resisted the inspection system. France had softened its position in favor of revision, but remained concerned to assure public security, positioning itself as prophylactic broker between north and south. In this spirit, it sought to require disinfection of goods and effects, while Britain and Germany insisted on a purification only of cholera victims' clothing, with voluntary measures for other objects. It was also here that the split, mentioned earlier, between nations which insisted on observation quarantines as part of a revisionist approach and Britain, claiming the right to surveille travelers at their homes rather than quarantining them, was resolved by allowing each to impose measures as they saw fit.[332] In 1894 Spain's restatement of its faith in the principles of quarantinism, however modified and modernized, set the scene for yet another expression of this longstanding geographically determined disagreement. At the 1897 Conference on the plague, Spain and Portugal, joined now by Bulgaria and Russia,

---

[330] *Conférence 1874*, pp. 82–83, 86–87, 118–27, 172–73; *Annales*, 43 (1875), pp. 252–53; FO 881/3421, FO CP 3421, 7 January 1878, p. 2; *Recueil*, 5 (1876), p. 46.
[331] *Conférence 1885*, pp. 237–42, 254, 292–96; *Conférence 1892*, pp. 113–14, 135, 156–60; *Conférence 1893*, pp. 14–16.
[332] *Conférence 1893*, pp. 47–48, 52, 68–70, 120–21, 138, 237–40, 245–46; *Comptes rendus* (1893), pp. 933–37.

reaffirmed the case for quarantinism. As the French portrayed it here, this geoepidemiological dispute had been a constant for half a century: the nations in closest proximity to the sources of infection remained strictly quarantinist, while Britain, at a secure remove and with its perfected sanitationist reforms, did not fear disease. In between, those nations endangered only after the first line of European defense had been breached sought to mediate such extremes. In 1911, the north/south disjunction was given vent in the argument over whether bacteriological investigations could rejuvenate quarantinist tactics in the face of asymptomatic carriers or whether such obstacles rendered this approach useless.[333]

But of course the pathways of transmission were more complicated than a simple north–south movement or a percolation westward from India, and each nation often had more immediate neighbors it eyed warily. For the Germans it was Poland, Galicia and ultimately Russia; for France, Spain; for Britain, Ireland; for Sweden, Denmark and Russia. At the 1874 Conference, the British sought to deflect attention from India as the source of contagion by claiming that, with cholera now endemic in Russia for several years, the most immediate threat was posed from this quarter.[334] France found itself in a peculiar position astraddle an epidemiological fault line. With one coast on the Mediterranean, the other lapped by the Atlantic, its interests diverged. While Paris sought to position France in the antiquarantinist camp, the Mediterranean authorities, Marseilles especially, consistently pulled in the other direction.[335] In 1850, two ships from Malta were quarantined upon arriving at Marseilles. While Paris ordered that only vessels with death or illness be retained, the local authorities refused to ease restrictions. The Marseilles Quarantine Board was thereupon dismissed, the entire establishment removed from the city and Dr. Melier from the Academy of Medicine appointed to reconstitute the Board in a more liberal spirit, with regulations, for example, that limited strictures for vessels from infected ports, eliminating quarantine altogether for those without illness. And yet,

---

[333] *Conférence 1894*, pp. 87–88; *Conférence 1897*, pp. 38, 92–93, 175, 268; *Conférence 1911*, p. 463.

[334] *Conférence 1874*, pp. 299–304. The French especially had not only focused on the Indian sources of cholera, but had accused the British of increasing cholera by neglecting the upkeep of basic infrastructure in India: PRO, FO 78/2006, pp. 198, 399.

[335] *Recueil*, 5 (1876), p. 51; Goodman, *International Health Organizations*, p. 46; Panzac, *Quarantaines et lazarets*, p. 112. Not all Mediterranean cities were contagionist: Aix (not a port city, of course) in 1835, for example, tended to be anticontagionist: Daniel Panzac, "Aix-en-Provence et le choléra en 1835," *Annales du Midi*, 86, 119 (1974), pp. 435–37. This split between north and south, although not as stark, was apparent also in the eighteenth century: Françoise Hildesheimer, "La protection sanitaire des côtes françaises au XVIIIe siècle," *Revue d'histoire moderne et contemporaine*, 27 (July–September 1980), pp. 466–67.

despite decisive action from the capital, the course had changed once
again within months. Popular fears of importing cholera from Tunis and
Malta, coupled with commercial anxieties of retaliation from other
nations, brought back quarantines.[336] The agreement reached at the
1851 Paris Sanitary Conference and promulgated in 1853 institutionalized a compromise between such competing interests by allowing
different regulations for the ports of France's two coasts.[337] While for the
plague measures were similar along both, for ships with foul cholera bills
of health, quarantines could be two days shorter on the Atlantic. In 1876,
a new set of maritime sanitary measures continued such tradeoffs. The
Atlantic ports, competitors with the Low Countries and Britain, were
allowed to limit quarantines to a minimum. For suspected ships, for
example, they were set at twenty-four hours of observation and an
inspection. In the Mediterranean, in contrast, such vessels could be held
in observation quarantine for three to seven days, although a single day
was also permissible.[338] The sanitationist position adopted at midcentury
and championed in Paris proved incompatible with the geoepidemiological realities of the Mediterranean coast. During the 1860s and seventies, France's peculiar position impelled its prophylactic interests in a
quarantinist direction as fears of disease took precedence over commercial ambitions. Starting in the 1890s, it began to moderate this approach,
but its geoepidemiological split still left it sympathetic to both sides of the
argument, a force for reconciliation between the extremes of
Mediterranean quarantinism and British sanitationism.[339]

Germany straddled a similar, though inverted, division, with a quarantinist northeast and an antiquarantinist south and southwest. During the
1860s and seventies, Bavaria continued the behavior first learned during
the thirties, feeling less threatened from eastern Europe than the
Prussians and more willing to accept Pettenkoferian conclusions on the
impracticability of quarantines.[340] For its attitude, it was counted, along
with Britain, among the sanitationist nations.[341] The Prussian authorities,

---

[336] Baker, *Laws Relating to Quarantine*, p. 414; *Medical Times*, 1 (1850), p. 152; *Gazette des hopitaux*
(1880), p. 755; *Moniteur universel*, 209 (28 July 1850), p. 2591; 225 (13 August 1850), p. 2815.
  [337] Although regulations of different strictness for the two coasts had been instituted already in
the ordinance of 20 March 1822: *Annales*, 6, 2 (1831), p. 459.
  [338] Baker, *Laws Relating to Quarantine*, pp. 414–15; *Recueil*, 5 (1876), pp. 4–24, 46; 9 (1880), pp. 16–24;
Proust, *La défense de l'Europe*, pp. 395, 399–404; Monod, *Le choléra*, pp. 615–16; *Medical Record*, 43, 1
(1893), p. 1.
  [339] *Conférence 1874*, pp. 172–73; *Conférence 1893*, pp. 47–48; *Conférence 1897*, p. 268; *Conférence 1911*,
p. 23.
  [340] Its 1883 regulations, for example, recommended disinfection, but not sequestration: *DVöG*, 16
(1884), pp. 140–44.   [341] *Conférence 1866*, 37, annexe, p. 5; 38, pp. 8–11.

in contrast, although accepting Pettenkofer in certain respects, remained more firmly quarantinist. The dogmatically quarantinist line still being argued by the Prussian delegates at the 1866 Constantinople Sanitary Conference was motivated by the same geoepidemiological considerations that had concerned them in the thirties. Prussia's eastern provinces were threatened by cholera from its neighbors, especially Poland and Galicia. Although conceding the general uselessness of restrictive measures, the Prussians perched – as they saw it – perilously on an epidemiological frontier, and sought refuge behind quarantinist bulwarks. Even former hotbeds of localism along the eastern borders, Königsberg for example, had in the meantime taken a contagionist tack.[342]

Geography, however, meant not just immovable physical features, a Braudellian constant of massive, but often imponderable effect. The mountain could also come to Mohammed, and that by third-class rail carriage. The fear of contagion, prompted by proximity to its sources, that motivated much prophylactic behavior was aggravated during the last decades of the century by emigration. The stream of Slavic transmigrants passing through Germany, especially Hamburg and Bremen, on their way to Britain and the new world focused the authorities' concerns during the 1880s and nineties on this parade of potential carriers.[343] Singled out for particular attention in the controls imposed on all travelers at the border were emigrants, in particular the poor Slavic Jews on whose transport – in a classic contradiction between public health and profit – the development of German passenger lines, including the Ballin empire, was built. These were people, in the official view, who posed dangers because of their way of life, their indolence, poverty, uncleanliness and poor nutrition. At vulnerable points – the border of an infected neighboring state, say, or with groups of emigrants or travelers from infected areas – thorough medical inspections were recommended of passengers and their effects, possibly also disinfection of baggage.[344] In

[342] *Vierteljahrsschrift für gerichtliche Medizin*, n.F., 18 (1873), pp. 74–84; *Conférence 1866*, 6, pp. 6–7; 26, pp. 4–6; W. Schiefferdecker, *Die Choleraepidemie vom Jahre 1871 in Königsberg* (Königsberg, 1873), pp. 65–66; *Berichte*, Heft 6, pp. 117, 121–22.

[343] Although not as directly caught up in such concerns as the Slavic transmigrants, seasonal agricultural laborers, especially from Poland, were also part of a general current of nativist exclusionism during the 1880s and nineties and fears of cultural, rather than epidemiological, pollution: Ulrich Herbert, *A History of Foreign Labor in Germany, 1880–1980* (Ann Arbor, 1990), pp. 10–12, 18; Martin Forberg, "Foreign Labour, the State and Trade Unions in Imperial Germany, 1890–1918," in W. R. Lee and Eve Rosenhaft, eds., *The State and Social Change in Germany, 1880–1980* (New York, 1990), pp. 107–16.

[344] S. Adler-Rudel, *Ostjuden in Deutschland 1880–1940* (Tübingen, 1959), pp. 3–5; *Amtliche Denkschrift*, pp. 91ff.; Prussia, Haus der Abgeordneten, *Anlagen zu den Stenographischen Berichten*, 1892/93, Akst. 76, p. 2066.

1892, the Prussians imposed special measures on Russian transmigrants. In fear of prompting illegal border crossings, they were not forbidden to enter, but were instead medically inspected at the frontier, bathed, their clothing and effects disinfected, the sick retained. The healthy were then transported across Germany in special trains that did not stop once underway, although pausing at special feeding facilities constructed at Ruhleben outside Berlin to prevent contact with the capital. In the absence of special trains, dedicated coaches on normal trains and measures to prevent transmigrants from using the station waiting rooms, restaurants and toilets were a substitute. Depending on their origin, transmigrants were subject to different regimens: less strict for the Austro-Hungarians than the Russians, who were inspected at border stations set up by the main shipping lines under auspices of the Prussian government, bathed, disinfected and quarantined for twenty-four hours.[345] Once at one of the port cities, emigrants were housed out of contact with the locals until their departure. On the Amerika quay in Hamburg a shed was built in 1892 for this purpose, where arriving trains deposited their passengers for further bathing, medical inspection and disinfection. In 1901, new and improved facilities were constructed to house up to 1,000 emigrants at once, conveying them from railroad to ship in isolation from the city.[346] Conditions here, depending on the testimony, were either pleasant, with the emigrants cared for, fed according to their customs, entertained with music, ministered to by personnel who spoke their language and religious representatives of the various faiths. Or they were overcrowded, with bad food and dominated by the police – in short, worse than prison, for which dubious pleasure, to add injury to insult, the emigrants were charged one mark daily. In Hamburg too the Russians were subject to an especially strict regimen, isolated in the suburb of Veddel, stripped, medically examined and, if healthy, bathed and inspected daily thereafter. Transmigrants from infected areas were isolated, bathed, examined and subject to five days of quarantine, as required by the American government.[347]

The general problems posed by transmigration were, of course,

[345] *Amtliche Denkschrift*, p. 19; Chantemesse and Borel, *Hygiène internationale*, p. 284.

[346] *Die Cholera in Hamburg*, p. 37; Jack Wertheimer, *Unwelcome Strangers: East European Jews in Imperial Germany* (New York, 1987), pp. 14, 26, 50–51; B. Nocht, *Vorlesungen für Schiffsärzte der Handelsmarine über Schiffshygiene, Schiffs- und Tropenkrankheiten* (Leipzig, 1906), pp. 47–55.

[347] Lysander, *Några synpunkter*, p. 47; *JO*, 1911, Chambre, Doc., Annexe 1218, p. 1058; *BMJ*, 1 (1 April 1893), p. 715; Chantemesse and Borel, *Hygiène internationale*, pp. 285–86; René Lacaisse, *L'hygiène internationale et la Société des nations* (Paris, 1926), p. 169; Markel, *Quarantine!*, pp. 74–75; Alan M. Kraut, *Silent Travelers: Germs, Genes and the "Immigrant Menace"* (New York, 1994), pp. 50–51.

heightened during epidemics. When cholera broke out in Hamburg in 1892, Prussia refused to admit Russian emigrants with only steerage tickets or none at all. As the United States began rejecting emigrants because of the epidemic, Russians in the Low Countries and elsewhere who, unable to proceed westward, sought to return home through Germany were refused reentry.[348] Because the United States refused to admit emigrants from cholera-ridden Hamburg, the shipping companies, anxious for their lucrative trade, began quarantining passengers for six days before boarding.[349] But the port cities also faced a Hobson's choice between imposing restrictions to appease the Americans and driving emigrants, repelled by such strictures, along other routes of passage instead.[350] The Contagious Disease Law continued such measures, restricting the entrance of transmigrants from infected countries to border crossings with facilities for inspection and sequestration, transporting them in special trains or at least separate coaches and then only in compartments without upholstery, all to be disinfected after each use, limiting unavoidable overnight stays to stations with facilities for such purposes.[351]

A geographical analysis based on proximity to the origins of contagion, even when those sources appear on the doorstep as with transmigrants, does not, however, work in a straightforward manner. Sweden, for example, located safely on what (from a Mediterranean vantage at least) seemed to be the epidemiological periphery, maintained a consistently more quarantinist approach than its Scandinavian neighbors, one that, as opponents complained, put it in company with the Balkan and Mediterranean nations rather than with the more obvious countries of comparison, Denmark, Norway and Britain.[352] Both Denmark and Norway had early adopted a more moderate approach while the Swedes maintained oldfashioned tactics.[353] Part of the reason is that the Swedes, rightly or wrongly, saw themselves as menaced from several sides by contagion. The threat from Russia, where cholera was considered during

---

[348] *Amtliche Denkschrift*, p. 19. Emigrants were generally refused readmission to Russia and a Russian re-emigrant on German soil was thus a German problem: Prussia, Haus der Abgeordneten, *Anlagen zu den Stenographischen Berichten*, 1892/93, Akst. 76, p. 2103.

[349] For similar measures in Hamburg's law of 14 January 1887, see *DVöG*, 20 (1888), p. 329.

[350] GStA, 84a/11012, Kaiserliches Gesundheitsamt, Reichs-Gesundheitsrat, Ausschuss für Seuchenbekämpfung einschliesslich Desinfektion, minutes, 9 September 1905, Tjaden.

[351] *Anweisung zur Bekämpfung*, p. 7; *Reichs-Gesetzblatt*, 9/3020 (1904), p. 72.

[352] *RD prot*, FK 1895:8, p. 52.

[353] [S. J. Callerholm], *Några ord om kolera, spärrningar och krämare-intresse* (Stockholm 1853), p. 3; [Johan Carl Hellberg], *Om åtgärder till Cholerafarsotens Utestängande* (Stockholm, 1853), p. 4; *Bidrag till allmänhetens upplysning*, p. 125; *Conférence 1851*, 24, pp. 11–13.

the 1890s to have become epidemic, was judged an immediate danger on the eastern frontier, more proximate than for others in the region. When the Germans restricted the flow of transmigrants from Russia in the early nineties, the problem was exported northwards instead, with would-be emigrants now passing through Sweden. Special quarantines and other restrictive precautions were accordingly imposed on such travelers.[354] But Russia was not the only problem. Denmark too, especially when the 1892 epidemic threatened from Germany, was feared as a source of infection. When the idea of a common Scandinavian policy against cholera was broached in 1893, many Swedes resisted cooperation with the Danes, who were regarded as too proximate to Germany for comfort. Coordinating policy with its southern neighbor meant moving Sweden's epidemiological frontier closer to the infected continent. When danger threatens, no one, as one physician put it, surrenders the keys to his house without pressing cause.[355]

In France, the fear of contagion from its neighbors was also potent. As during the 1820s, Spain once again played the role of epidemiological whipping boy, prompting new measures at the Pyrenees. Italy also sparked worries, and vague anxieties over "des peuples orientaux" were voiced.[356] Given the comparative infrequency of transmigration, fears of disease importation via this route were not so prevalent as in Germany, but were heard.[357] In 1896 ships transporting emigrants, pilgrims and other large groups in poor sanitary conditions could be subjected to special precautions. The quality of transmigrants, according to an official analysis, had declined since midcentury. They now hailed especially from eastern Europe and the Orient and the threat of disease following in their train had increased proportionately.[358] Admiring the German model of isolating emigrants en route, the French attempted something similar.[359] During the First World War, such problems were raised again, but not until the 1920s, with increased immigration from nontraditional sources, in part to make up for labor

---

[354] *Förhandlingar*, 1895, pp. 33–34, 51; *Hygiea*, 56, 2 (February 1894), p. 172; *SFS*, 1893/68; 1893/95.

[355] *Upsala Läkareförening*, 28 (1892–93), p. 288; *Förhandlingar*, 1893, pp. 40–41.

[356] *JO*, 1911, Chambre, Doc., Annexe 1218, p. 1059.

[357] *Bulletin*, 57, 3rd ser., 29 (1893), pp. 592–600; 3, 55 (1906), pp. 69–71; Chantemesse and Borel, *Hygiène internationale*, pp. 269–71.

[358] *JO*, 28, 20 (21 January 1896), p. 361; *JO*, 1911, Chambre, Doc., Annexe 1218, p. 1061; *Annales*, 4/5 (1906), pp. 278–81; *Bulletin*, 3, 65 (1911), pp. 114–16; Chantemesse and Borel, *Hygiène internationale*, p. 277.

[359] *JO*, 1911, Chambre, Doc., Annexe 1218, p. 1058; *Annales*, 4/14 (1910), pp. 437–38; Humbert, *Du rôle de l'administration*, pp. 33–38; [André] Cavaillon, *L'armement antivénérien en France* (Paris, n.d. [1927]), p. 109.

shortages caused by the war, were fears of the consequences voiced more clearly.[360]

Nor, despite its sanitationist traditions, was Britain immune to the sorts of quarantinist tendencies that the British were happy to ridicule on the continent. Goods from infected territories, including the used bedding and clothing of travelers, were subject to strict measures of disinfection or destruction in 1893.[361] Immigrants too became a worry, much as in Germany.[362] Transmigrants destined for the United States, mostly Scandinavians with sufficient funds, tended (in the eyes of the authorities) to be cleanlier and less objectionable than migrants to Britain, who were largely Russians, Poles and Germans, often Jewish.[363] The precautions imposed were reminiscent of the continental. Immigrants with cholera were hospitalized, the healthy in a filthy or unwholesome condition were detained on board, reinspected after an interval and, if clean enough, "liberated." At Hartlepool, emigrants remained onboard until arrival of their train, then marched three hundred yards to special carriages reserved for such traffic. In London, all immigrants and transmigrants were inspected, had to provide names and final destinations, were crossexamined as to their intended addresses (where local authorities were alerted to their impending arrival) and, if the answers were unsatisfactory, consigned to the care of the Jewish shelter. In 1892, the requirement that migrants provide name and address of their destination before disembarking was sharpened to include not just cholera-infected ships, but also those with passengers in a filthy and unwholesome, but otherwise healthy, state – a measure aimed apparently at Russian Jewish emigrants in particular.[364] The introduction of the Cleansing of Persons Act in 1897, allowing gratis purification of those seeking such service, gave voice to anxieties over the pestilence allegedly introduced by immigrant aliens. In 1905 the Aliens Act

---

[360] Bernard, *La défense de la santé publique pendant la guerre*, ch. 4; *Revue d'hygiène*, 48 (1926), pp. 804–09; William H. Schneider, *Quality and Quantity: The Quest for Biological Regeneration in Twentieth-Century France* (Cambridge, 1990), ch. 9; Gary S. Cross, *Immigrant Workers in Industrial France: The Making of a New Laboring Class* (Philadelphia, 1983), pp. 63–68, ch. 8.

[361] *PP* 1894 (7538) xl, 363, pp. 944–46.

[362] Already the Dirigo, with a cargo of emigrants in 1854, had prompted precautions: *PP* 1854 (492) xlvi, p. 7. For similar concerns in the 1870s, see Brand, *Doctors and the State*, p. 42.

[363] Germans – national stereotypes to the contrary – had also earlier been considered especially filthy, allegedly intolerable even to the Irish, for whose hygienic habits British sanitary reformers generally had little patience: *PP* 1849 (1115) xxiv, p. 127.

[364] *PP* 1896 (137) lxvii, pp. 732–33, 736; *Sanitary Record*, n.s., 14, 168 (15 September 1892), p. 138; n.s., 14, 175 (1 January 1893), p. 326; *Conférence 1893*, p. 51; *Amtliche Denkschrift*, p. 43; PRO, FO 881/6401*, R. Thorne Thorne, "Disease Prevention in England," 7 June 1893, p. 2; MH 19/238, Thorne Thorne to President of LGB, 5 January 1893.

officially ended Britain's laissez-faire treatment of foreign arrivals, limiting immigration to selected ports where prospective inhabitants traveling steerage could be inspected and the diseased rejected.[365]

Sheer remove or proximity to the sources of infection, whether in a fundamental geoepidemiological sense or as raised by the problem of migration, was, however, only one geographical factor at work. Topography could also play a role, although it was not always clear precisely which. The Russians at the 1851 Paris Conference were impressed with the ability of peripheral regions like Sweden and Siberia to keep cholera at bay via quarantinist means. As a general rule, they concluded, quarantines were useful in certain situations (on islands or peninsulas, at seaports) while less effective in the continental interior where traffic could not be as thoroughly controlled.[366] In Sweden, two contradictory arguments were regularly advanced concerning its position vis-à-vis contagious disease. On the one hand, as a sparsely settled, farflung country with an extensive seacoast dotted by many harbors, Sweden was a difficult place to quarantine.[367] But much more frequent and apparently influential was the contrary argument, that such geographical peculiarities meant that quarantinism was custom-tailored to its predicament. Because of its location on the far periphery, with one topographical toe – the southern provinces – dipped gingerly into the epidemiological morass of Europe, while the vast, practically uninhabited regions of the north lay beyond the pale of infection, the very geography of the country encouraged contagionist views. Unlike the southern and more densely populated areas of Europe, where disease could be introduced from all points on the compass and the argument that, arising spontaneously, it was not in fact imported at all could be maintained with some plausibility, Sweden's position in the currents of transmission had made it strikingly clear from early on that cholera arrived only, leaning on its wanderer's staff, from across the borders.[368] Disease of this sort – so the reasoning – did not arise autonomously in Sweden, blessed as it was by remote location and an inhospitable climate, and was introduced only

[365] 60 & 61 Vict. c. 31; *PP* 1897 (147) vii, 441; *Hansard*, 1897, v. 50, cols. 1298–99, 1303, 1305; 1897, v. 51, col. 133; 26 Geo. 5 & 1 Edw. 8 c. 49, s. 85; Bernard Gainer, *The Alien Invasion: The Origins of the Aliens Act of 1905* (London, 1972), p. 199; Michael R. Marrus, *The Unwanted: European Refugees in the Twentieth Century* (New York, 1985), pp. 36–37; Bridget Towers, "Politics and Policy: Historical Perspectives on Screening," in Virginia Berridge and Philip Strong, eds., *AIDS and Contemporary History* (Cambridge, 1993), pp. 65–66.   [366] *Conférence 1851*, 12, pp. 4–10.

[367] [Callerholm], *Några ord om kolera*, p. 20; *Borgare*, 1853–54, iii, pp. 502–21; *Förhandlingar*, 1868, pp. 162–65; 1895, p. 51; *Conférence 1874*, pp. 130–31; *Annales*, 4/12 (1909), pp. 239–40.

[368] Rolf Bergman, "De epidemiska sjukdomarna och deras bekämpande," in Wolfram Kock, ed., *Medicinalväsendet i Sverige, 1813–1962* (Stockholm, 1963), p. 361.

through foreign shipping. When it did arrive, Sweden's sparse habitation and the vast internal distances spanned by the trails of transmission revealed clearly how, and therefore that, the disease was carried from one place to the next.[369] As for prophylaxis, its distant location and quasi-insular position, surrounded by water on its most accessible sides, meant that quarantinism was the tactic of choice. The frontier with Norway was safe because the long distances and the highland's healthy state were thought protection enough. Maritime borders were easier to protect than terrestrial ones since quarantine stations were required at only a few points to control the whole coastline and the archipelago permitted convenient isolation of possibly infectious travelers. Sweden's comparatively low level of trade, its sparsely settled circumstances and the lack of bustling internal communication thus made cordons and quarantines easier to implement than elsewhere.[370]

Such topographically informed arguments continued throughout the century. In the 1890s, the issue had boiled down to whether Sweden should abandon quarantines wholly, adopting revision instead. The arguments in favor of quarantines typically portrayed the old system as ideal for a country like Sweden, favorably surrounded by water, with a long coastline and many harbors, while the nation's vast expanse and sparse population hampered implementation of revision. The government's arguments in favor of its decision to continue observation quarantines, rather than switching entirely to inspection, also dwelt on the convenient fit between topography and prophylaxis that spoke for retaining the old. At the 1893 Dresden Conference, Sweden and Norway joined in restrictionist harmony to insist on observation quarantines, singing the praises of their peninsular topography that blessed them with the possibility of erecting barriers at the border against the import of disease.[371]

In Denmark a similar topographical influence made itself felt. Having taken a prophylactically liberal position at first, the Danes switched position, reestablishing quarantines in 1884. By the 1885 Conference, they

---

[369] *Sammandrag ur Gällande Författningar och Föreskrifter af hwad iagttagas bör till förekommande af Utrikes härjande Farsoters inträngande i Riket* (Stockholm, 1831), p. 5; *Eira*, 9, 5 (1885), pp. 150–51.

[370] [Swederus], *Till Svenska Läkaresällskapet*, p. 20; *Förhandlingar*, 1892, p. 124; 1893, pp. 40–41; *Koleran*, p. 11; *Förhandlingar vid det allmänna Svenska Läkaremötet*, 1886, p. 92; *Upsala Läkareförening*, 28 (1892–93), p. 287; Bergwall, *Om pesten*, p. 54; [Hellberg], *Om åtgärder*, pp. 9–10; von Düben, *Om karantäner*, pp. 1–2.

[371] *Förhandlingar*, 1895, pp. 33ff.; *RD prot*, AK 1895:8, pp. 70–71; FK 1895:8, pp. 43–44; *Conférence 1893*, pp. 53–54, 120. At the 1897 Venice Conference, however, Sweden and Norway played down this prophylactic *Sonderweg*, arguing that, although they had ratified neither the Dresden nor Paris conventions, they had in fact executed their dispositions: *Conférence 1897*, p. 68.

had joined the restrictive camp, arguing that neglect of precautions had exposed the country to cholera in 1853 and that, thanks to topographical circumstances (pen- and insular), it was actually in a position to implement effective quarantine. At the 1893 Dresden Conference, along with Greece, Portugal and Turkey, Denmark abstained from condemning overland and maritime quarantines. Because of its geographical position, its delegate announced, Denmark could not renounce the freedom to take all means, including quarantine, to protect itself.[372] The Norwegians too succumbed to the lure of topographical advantage. Norway's merchant fleet, at sea the globe over, gave it economic interests against restrictive measures, but the geographical features favorable to quarantinism with which the Scandinavian peninsula had been blessed could not be ignored.[373] Greece, sharing little in common with the Scandinavians other than a similarly aqueous geography, followed prophylactic suit. It was not just a matter of proximity to the sources of contagion, but also of the topographical ability to implement quarantinist precautions. When the revision system was discussed as a replacement for quarantines in 1874, the Greeks argued for the old system, convinced that in their circumstances – sparsely populated and surrounded by water – it would be effective.[374] The Portuguese also argued the case on behalf of Mediterranean nations with long coastlines for retaining quarantines. But water was not an absolute requirement for a topographical interest in quarantinism. The Swiss – no great seafarers to be sure, but able, thanks to their vertiginous landscaping, to control access better than most continental countries – also tended to be quarantinists, arguing in 1874 against the revision system and generally supporting the hard core of the restrictionist nations. In France, similar arguments were heard when, cholera striking Spain in 1890, a quarantinist approach was encouraged by the natural obstacles impeding long-distance travel across the southwestern frontier, the fact, for example, that only two rail lines crossed the Pyrenees.[375]

Geography was thus an important factor. Partly it was a matter of proximity to the sources of cholera, whether the Orient in a general sense, or less distant neighbors. Partly it was a question whether topog-

---

[372] *Conférence 1885*, p. 98; *Conférence 1893*, pp. 40, 107, 120.

[373] *Conférence 1893*, pp. 53–54; *Conférence 1897*, p. 176.

[374] *Conférence 1874*, pp. 82–83. See also *Annales*, 3/10 (1883), p. 131; Daniel Panzac, *La peste dans l'empire Ottoman, 1700–1850* (Louvain, 1985), pp. 461–63; Emile Y. Kolodny, *La population des îles de la Grèce* (Aix-en-Provence, 1974), pp. 146–47.

[375] *Conférence 1874*, pp. 118–27, 161; *Conférence 1885*, pp. 292–96; *Conférence 1893*, p. 236; Faivre, *Prophylaxie internationale*, p. 182.

raphy and location allowed quarantinism as a feasible technique. Nations set apart from their neighbors, whether by water or mountains, and able to control access had reason to consider quarantinism a viable option for longer than did the bulk of continental Europe. In thinly settled countries the pathways of transmission were more apparent than among teeming peoples, and contagionism and quarantinism were more plausible approaches to adopt. Nations favored in such respects were in much the same position that rural areas had been in vis-à-vis the cities during the 1830s: the progress of the disease could be accurately traced, not losing itself in the jumbled and indiscriminate density of the towns, where a noncontagionist approach enjoyed the benefit of the doubt.[376]

Sweden and Greece, to take the extremes, were cases of partial geographical determinism: because they were in a position to implement such precautions effectively, because they felt threatened by neighbors, the quarantinist impulse was strong. The opposite end of the spectrum of possible geographical positions vis-à-vis the epidemic stream was occupied by the Netherlands. Their trading interests gave them similar antiquarantinist motives as the British, but even if they had not, it is unclear what they could have done. Their situation as a small country of transit at the heart of Europe, across which washed an immense and unending flood of goods and travelers, prevented them from adopting quarantinist strategies, indeed of doing much of anything on their own to hold cholera at bay.[377] Even the revision system was hard to implement under such geoepidemiological circumstances. In 1903, the Dutch regretted their inability to implement in any useful fashion the medical surveillance required by revision of passengers in transit, and in 1911 a similar argument was marshaled against the possibility of implementing bacteriological examinations.[378] More generally speaking, most continental countries were in a similar position. With uncontrollable traffic across the terrestrial frontiers, overland quarantines were quickly abandoned as hopeless after the 1830s.[379] The discussion during the following decades was almost exclusively limited to maritime traffic, whose bottlenecked nature meant that quarantine, though still bothersome, was at least within the realm of the feasible. The division between Atlantic and Mediterranean Europe was thus not just a question of

---

[376] *Eira*, 9, 5 (1885), pp. 150–51; *BMJ* (4 November 1882), p. 918; (25 November 1882), pp. 1066–68; *Conférence 1874*, pp. 53–54; *Annales*, 30 (1868), p. 24; 3/12 (1884), p. 365.

[377] *Conférence 1866*, 30, pp. 14–15. Similar arguments from Belgium are in *Conférence 1874*, p. 248.

[378] *Conférence 1903*, p. 282; *Conférence 1911*, p. 48.

[379] With the exception of 1885, even Spain did not impose overland quarantines or cordons after 1843: *Conférence 1893*, p. 52.

proximity to the sources of contagion, but also one of topography. The nations of central Europe, with their overland frontiers traced largely arbitrarily in terms of natural features and their dense interconnections, found quarantine difficult to implement. The Mediterranean nations and Scandinavia, in contrast, which received much of their traffic via the more easily controllable maritime routes, found quarantinism a more tempting proposition.[380]

Britain's predicament in turn was, as always, slightly anomalous. In theory, its insular position should have provided, as in Sweden, a geographically influenced interest in quarantinism, although, on the other hand, the extent of its coastline was held up as cause why such precautions would not work.[381] And, indeed, its epidemiologically advantaged position was often appreciated, insulated from the continent as it was by "the aqueous isolating belt, which has oftentimes done us invaluable service by raising a barrier to the march of the contagious enemies with which the less fortunate Continental nations have occasionally to do battle."[382] What distinguished the British, however, was that they in fact regarded their geoepidemiological position as equivalent to the mainland neighbors. From the British perspective, given its proximity and connections to the continent, maritime quarantines were no more feasible than the terrestrial.[383] Epidemiologically speaking, Britain was a continental nation. Because it enjoyed protection in the duration of the passage from India, it did not share the Mediterranean fear of unquarantined contacts with the Orient. Because of the polymorphosity and intensity of its intercourse with the rest of the world, maritime quarantines did not find the continued welcome they enjoyed in some continental countries.

EUROPE AGAINST THE ORIENT

Geoepidemiological factors played a role not only in the various preventive strategies implemented among the European nations, but also in the approach taken by Europe as a whole to the Orient. Ultimately, the goal of prophylactic endeavor was to sanitize each nation, whether west or east, thus preventing the spread of disease. But before the happy day of this hygienic utopia had dawned much could, in European eyes, be

---

[380] *Conférence 1874*, p. 248; *Recueil*, 5 (1876), p. 51.
[381] Joseph Adams, *An Inquiry into the Laws of Different Epidemic Diseases* (London, 1809), pp. 46–47.
[382] *Sanitary Record*, n.s., 14, 167 (1 September 1892), p. 108; n.s., 14, 178 (15 February 1893), p. 395.
[383] *Conférence 1885*, p. 369; PRO, FO 78/2006, p. 401, The British Cholera Commissioners to Lord Stanley, 3 October 1866; FO 881/5328, FO CP 5328, October 1886, p. 200B; *Conférence 1874*, p. 146; *JO*, 16, 298 (29 October 1884), p. 5683.

accomplished through the judicious application of quarantinist and, later, neoquarantinist techniques to the connections between Orient and Occident. Moreover, the attempt to loosen quarantinist measures in the west, to shift from oldfashioned precautions to the revision system and more generally to neoquarantinism, depended in large part on Europe's ability to impose more drastic regulations on the Orient than it was – increasingly – willing to tolerate at home. Liberality here rested on exclusion outward and as the European nations sought to ease measures domestically, their attitude toward the Orient became less hospitable. Once again, despite a significant measure of pan-European agreement, divisions opened up between the British, broadly willing to treat the Oriental like other nations, however mercenary the motives of their apparent largesse, and the continent, more uniformly persuaded of the need for strict precautions.

Starting with Napoleon, the European nations, above all France, had brought the principles of quarantinist prophylaxis against the plague and cholera to the Middle East, gradually convincing local elites of the efficacy and desirability of such measures.[384] By midcentury, the Europeans were content with their handiwork. The 1851 Sanitary Conference was dominated by good intentions toward the nations of the Middle East, from which the threat of disease (especially plague) was posed most clearly. The French and British took the lead in welcoming the Turks and Egyptians to the table of sanitarily well-regulated nations. Ships from the Ottoman Empire were normally quarantined regardless of their hygienic state or whether their port of origin was in fact infected and whether to relax such strictures was the issue at hand. In 1847, the French had established a network of medical observers posted throughout the Middle East to report on the plague and since, in the interim, none had yet observed a case, they were prepared to conclude that the disease was not endemic and that ships from here need not automatically be quarantined in the absence of actual epidemics. The time had come, the French and British sought to persuade their warier neighbors, to acknowledge and reward the sanitary improvements accomplished in Turkey and Egypt, quarantining only those ships with foul bills of health.[385] The general tenor was thus one of benevolence vis-à-vis the

---

[384] Panzac, *La peste dans l'empire Ottoman*, ch. 16.

[385] *Conférence 1851*, 7, annexe, pp. 14–15; 29, annexe 1, pp. 1–26; 7, annexe, pp. 19–21; 35, pp. 11–12; Proust, *L'orientation nouvelle*, p. 34; *Annales*, 49 (1853), pp. 461–65. For the Ottomans were one of the French delegates, the British, one of the Sardinians; against them, the Two Sicilies, Portugal, Spain, Russia, Greece and one of the Austrian delegates – in other words largely the north/south divide: *Conférence 1851*, 35, pp. 16–22; 36, pp. 3–6.

Middle East, or at least the Turkish parts of the Ottoman Empire. For centuries, as the Ottoman delegate put it, the European quarantine system had been based on mistrust, inspired by fears of the Orient's sanitary state that were no longer justified. Sutherland, the British delegate, gave the most messianic expression of this accommodation between east and west, welcoming the new approach to the Ottomans as the outcome of sanitationist philosophy. Contagious disease had divided the human family, creating barriers between Orient and Occident. Along its frontiers, Europe kept in readiness a kind of peacetime army against diseases of the east. Once the lessons of public hygiene had been widely adopted here, however, such quarantinist exclusions could end. Europe should pass eastward the lessons of public hygiene, enriched by its experience and science, just as the west had earlier received similar instruction from the Orient.[386]

By 1866, however, the atmosphere had changed dramatically. Because of the longstanding capitulations and the privilege of extraterritoriality granted foreigners, the Ottomans were negotiating from a position of only partial sovereignty, discussing with aliens matters that would otherwise have been a concern of domestic politics.[387] After the 1865 epidemic and recognition of the Mecca pilgrims' role as carriers, the sanitationist harmonies of midcentury had evaporated, France was firmly in the quarantinist camp and the tone had become distinctly chilly. In contrast to 1851, the tenor of debate between the Turks and Persians, on the one hand, and the French on the other was acrimonious, each side accusing its opponents of neglecting sanitary concerns, with charges of bad faith and even sacrilege, spiced by sarcastic comments from both parties on the alleged defects of Asiatic logic. The French now wheeled out the martial imagery to justify their drastic proposals, comparing the need for decisive action to prevent cholera's spread out of Egypt to blockading, starving and even bombarding enemy countries in wartime.[388] Oldfashioned quarantinism had fallen out of favor in much of non-Mediterranean Europe, but the belief, still active in 1851, that hygienic reforms would soon solve the problem of epidemic disease had proven to be one of the more naive aspects of messianic sanitationism. It was now generally agreed that, while quarantines within Europe were largely impracticable, they remained useful when

---

[386] *Conférence 1851*, 35, pp. 13–16; 39, pp. 9–14.
[387] *Conférence 1866*, 10, pp. 4–12; 8, pp. 13, 21; Robert L. Tignor, *Modernization and British Colonial Rule in Egypt, 1882–1914* (Princeton, 1966), pp. 51–52.
[388] *Conférence 1866*, 4, p. 18; 5, pp. 5, 27; 33, p. 13.

shifted closer to the source of disease.[389] The goal was to seal off the Orient during epidemics, sparing Europe the vexations of similar measures at home. The French proposed that, were cholera to erupt among pilgrims at Mecca, the Ottoman authorities should suspend all maritime communication between the Arab ports and the Egyptian seaboard, thus preserving the Mediterranean and Europe. Instead, pilgrims could either remain at Mecca during the outbreak or make their way overland by caravan through the desert, a voyage whose duration and remoteness would make of it, in the words of the French delegate, "the best quarantine applicable to large numbers of people."[390] Quarantines were a nuisance, as one Frenchman put it, but they dare not abandon such ramparts thrown up "to preserve Europe from all compromises with the rude and injurious habits of the Oriental populations."[391]

The solution, therefore, was to shift quarantinist efforts closer to the initial source of contagion or, as one delegate put it in 1866, to make the Turks "the gatekeepers of public health."[392] As part of this new quarantinist displacement eastward, the attitude of welcoming the Orient to the company of sanitary nations now gave way to horrifying imagery of the east as the suppurating source of disease. Asia, as Gobineau had formulated it in a less dramatic version of Metternich's notorious geographical telescoping, began at the Suez. The east was portrayed as a natural location for quarantinist techniques that had outlived their usefulness in Europe. These nations were often sparsely populated, commercial relations were less active and natural barriers helped contain the spread of disease.[393] They were also, as a British delegate put it in 1874, countries where the populations traveled slowly, with little concept of the value of time, where – by implication – quarantines would be less vexatious than in the west.[394] Quarantinist measures were necessary in the Orient, as the French argued in 1903 in response to Egyptian pleas for European-style sanitationism. The means of communication had outstripped social developments and Egypt was as yet unprepared for the principles of modern prophylaxis. Only imprudence would propose applying the

---

[389] The European powers could more easily agree on quarantinism applied to pilgrims since international trade was only tangentially involved: W. F. Bynum, "Policing Hearts of Darkness: Aspects of the International Sanitary Conferences," *History and Philosophy of the Life Sciences*, 15 (1993), p. 430.

[390] *Conférence 1866*, 1, annexe, pp. 1–6; 29, annexe, p. 49; *Annales*, 3/13 (1885), p. 238.

[391] Girette, *La civilisation et le choléra*, p. 35.   [392] *Conférence 1866*, 10, p. 12.

[393] Bonnafont, *Le choléra et le congrès*, p. 14; André Siegfried, *Suez, Panama et les routes maritimes mondiales* (Paris, 1941), p. 126; *Conférence 1866*, 29, annexe, p. 6; 37, annexe, p. 6. One should not overemphasize the novelty of this approach in 1866, however, since similar sentiments were expressed also in 1851: *Conférence 1851*, 37 annexe, pp. 9–11.   [394] *Conférence 1874*, p. 84.

same measures to Bedouins and fellahs as to the citizens of Liverpool or London. Whether or not the Orient could yet be treated sanitarily like Europe was still being discussed at length in 1911. The Egyptians, supported in this case by the British and seconded by an array of non-western nations, pleaded for control over their own affairs in order to implement hygienic measures of a European sort, resisted having quarantinism imposed on them and generally demanded the right to be treated as the sanitary equals of the west.[395]

Geography, from the European vantage, spoke for a displacement of quarantinist efforts. While the stream of epidemic transmission to central Europe could not easily be blocked in, say, Italy and Spain, with their extensive coastlines and long land frontiers, the eastern Mediterranean, especially Egypt, was a bottleneck at which communication could effectively be throttled. Topography offered a natural defense against exotic disease in the necessity that travelers pass through the Suez and the west was justified in imposing restrictions here as part of what Proust called "Europe's sanitary charter."[396] The French viewed the Suez as "the outer gate of a European sea, at which the nations of Europe have a right to arrest the approach of Asiatic diseases."[397] The general goal was to prevent Muslim pilgrims from bringing cholera or plague from India and elsewhere to the Middle East, failing that to isolate it in the Hejaz and, finally, to take special precautions in the event that Egypt were struck, cutting communication with infected places. Measures to this end included quarantines and inspections of maritime traffic between the Orient and Europe as well as sanitary measures imposed on pilgrims who, congregating from the entire globe, turned Mecca into an epidemiological turntable. The pilgrims, as an Italian delegate put it, because of their almost professional filthiness and their misery, were exceptionally dangerous vectors of transmission.[398]

Significant in this respect was the connection between prophylaxis in east and west. The process of relaxing precautions in Europe, the transition to neoquarantinism, in effect presupposed attempts, in the form of

---

[395] *Conférence 1903*, p. 532; *Conférence 1911*, pp. 99–104, 122, 301–06.

[396] *Conférence 1866*, 39, p. 6; *Conférence 1903*, p. 471; R. Dujarric de la Rivière, *Prophylaxie nationale et internationale des maladies épidémiques* (n.p., 1948), pp. 199–200; *Recueil*, 21 (1891), p. 831; PRO, FO 78/2005, Earl Cowley to Earl Russell, 9 October 1865, No. 1092.

[397] PRO, FO 83/1281, p. 37, FO to British Delegates, 22 January 1892; FO, 407/115, FO CP 6368, July 1893, p. 30.

[398] *Conférence 1866*, 29, annexe, pp. 10–15; 37, annexe, pp. 9–10; *Conférence 1874*, pp. 107–11; *Conférence 1885*, p. 219; *MTG* (5 May 1866), pp. 480–81; *Transactions of the Seventh International Congress of Hygiene and Demography*, pp. 61ff.; *Indian Medical Gazette*, 26 (December 1891), pp. 372–74; *Conférence 1894*, p. 44.

quarantine and inspection in the Red Sea and the Suez, to prevent cholera from entering the Mediterranean and thence Europe. The counterpart to loosening measures in Europe, as Proust put it, was to ensure that the entry to disease in the Red Sea was shut tight.[399] In 1866, a surveillance and quarantine station on the island of Perim at the mouth of the Red Sea was discussed as a barrier to cholera's westward spread. At the 1874 Vienna Conference, where revision was first proposed as an alternative to oldfashioned precautions in Europe, it became clear that such reforms presupposed mounting a front line of quarantinist defense in the Middle East. In 1881 a lazaretto was built on the island of Kamaran where pilgrims were treated as though infected and quarantined for at least ten days.[400] At the 1885 Rome Conference, the new revision system was, in modified form, extended to the Middle East, but applied more strictly than in Europe. Special measures for the faithful en route to Mecca were particularly restrictive, with repeated inspections of pilgrim ships to and from the holy city and the threat of observation quarantines and disinfections if illness were found.[401] In 1892, such precautions were tightened, with infected pilgrim ships from the Hejaz or other ports on the Arab Red Sea coast heading for Suez or the Mediterranean to undergo a fortnight's quarantine at El-Tor. These vessels were to pass the canal in quarantine, accompanied by a steam-powered longboat, while guards on dromedary along the banks had orders to fire on pilgrims seeking to debark. If cholera appeared between El-Tor and Suez, the ship was sent back. After quarantine at El-Tor, Egyptian pilgrims underwent another three days of observation and an inspection, while the non-Egyptian faithful were simply forbidden to disembark in Egypt. Pilgrims were to enjoy the fruits of neither the revision system nor the bacteriological revolution. Because of their numbers, they were subject to observation quarantines, even if not infected, rather than medical inspections in the European sense. A freight ship was easy to inspect, but for a pilgrim ship with 2,000 passengers it was considered simpler to wait and see whether anyone fell sick than to examine each traveler.[402]

---

[399] *MTG* (5 May 1866), pp. 480–81; Artur Luerssen, *Die Cholera, ihre Erkennung und Bekämpfung: Ein Erfolg der modernen Naturforschung* (Berlin, [1906]), p. 25; *Conférence 1885*, pp. 171–72; *Conférence 1892*, p. 25; *Recueil*, 25 (1895), p. 404.

[400] *Conférence 1866*, 29, annexe, pp. 26–27; *Conférence 1874*, pp. 107–11, 384ff.; *Conférence 1894*, pp. 62, 129; Proust, *L'orientation nouvelle*, p. 135. For details on Kamaran, see Fréderic Borel, *Choléra et peste dans le pèlerinage musulman, 1860–1903* (Paris, 1904), ch. 5; John Baldry, "The Ottoman Quarantine Station on Kamaran Island 1882–1914," *Studies in the History of Medicine*, 2, 1/2 (March–June 1978).

[401] *Conférence 1885*, pp. 142–43, 228–34.

[402] *Conférence 1892*, pp. 218–19, 227–28, 236; Faivre, *Prophylaxie internationale*, pp. 35–44.

In 1894, an entire conference was devoted to the problem of preventing cholera's spread from central Asia, especially via the Mecca pilgrimage. Once again, at French behest, strict measures were imposed on Muslim pilgrims, extending the precautions adopted for the Red Sea now to the Persian Gulf. It was not in Europe, as the indefatigable Proust put it, hammering home his message, that one should await the arrival of cholera in order to fight it, but along the customary routes where its passage could be barred.[403] In 1897, faced with the plague, an outright ban of the Mecca pilgrimage was considered by several nations and imposed by the Romanians, but also by the British who were pressured to halt the exodus of the faithful from Bombay for several years thereafter.[404] More moderate than outright prohibition were proposals to require of the faithful proof that they had the necessary wherewithal for the arduous journey, thereby limiting it to the better-off and, it was hoped, stemming the spread of disease. The Dutch insisted on such measures for pilgrims from their Indian colonies, the French and the Austrians imposed analogous measures and others proposed something similar for British India. The British, however, motivated by a typically motley combination of concern for Muslim sensibilities and proprietary interests in the lucrative business of transporting the faithful, opposed such strictures, insisting that pilgrimage was a religious injunction that could not be reserved for the rich.[405] Such attempts to shift the brunt of prevention to the Middle East continued into the twentieth century and not until 1957 was the Mecca pilgrimage freed of special international health legislation.[406]

Although such measures pitted Europe as a whole against the Levant, western opinion was far from unanimous. France consistently took the lead in advocating strict precautions in the Middle East and it was joined, generally speaking, by the quarantinist bloc of continental nations. In 1866, its position, that cholera should be kept out of Europe by imposing restrictions in the Middle East, was put most forcefully by Portugal.[407]

---

[403] *Conférence 1894*, pp. 16–17, 27, 29–30, 120–31; *Conférence 1903*, p. 167; *Annales*, 3/28 (1892), p. 55; Proust, *L'orientation nouvelle*, p. 126; *Recueil*, 27 (1897), p. 278; PRO, FO, 407/115, FO CP 6368, July 1893, p. 10.

[404] *Conférence 1897*, pp. 23, 93–95, 96, 101, 104; PRO, MH 19/279, CP 4033 of 1902; *Recueil*, 27 (1897), pp. 319–20.

[405] *Conférence 1866*, 29, annexe, pp. 19–25; *Conférence 1894*, pp. 122–23, 158–59; PRO, FO 83/1330, British Delegates to the Earl of Kimberley, 7 April 1894, p. 2; Goodman, *International Health Organizations*, p. 57. By the 1903 Conference, attempts thus to restrict the Mecca pilgrimage had been abandoned: *Conférence 1903*, p. 105. [406] Goodman, *International Health Organizations*, p. 6.

[407] And seconded by the Prussians, Austrians, Greeks, Belgians, Spaniards, Italians, Dutch, Swedes and Norwegians: *Conférence 1866*, 2, pp. 9–10; 4, p. 21.

The Italians, who later in the century abandoned their quarantinist approach when it came to matters European, were more willing to take a hard line with the Orient, arguing that pilgrimage, however worthy, was not an indispensable social necessity like commerce, which should therefore be left unrestricted.[408] Not surprisingly, the nations of the Middle East protested such high-handed sanitary tactics. Overly strict measures threatened political instability and Muslim sovereigns suspected of collaborating with the European powers in regulating or restricting pilgrimages feared attack from the pious.[409] But more fundamentally such prophylactic partiality was simply unjust. The Turks and Persians, for example, attacked French plans for pilgrims to return overland through the desert as condemning them, in the name of public health, to hunger, misery and death.[410] Seeking to turn the Europeans' geoepidemiological reasoning back against them, a Persian delegate in 1866 argued that quarantinist techniques could, in fact, be most effectively implemented in the west where national boundaries were clearly demarcated, the requisite administrative machinery in place and the natives sedentary and obedient. The Turks, though generally quarantinist, rejected the international prophylaxis proposed in 1885 as onesided: protecting the west from Oriental infection was doubtless necessary, but the Levant had equal claims to defense against epidemics of European origin. The Egyptians protested quarantines imposed on pilgrims in the Suez in the midst of foreign circumstances, surrounded as the Muslim faithful were by Christians who rarely spoke their language. Most generally, the eastern delegates argued, often with a politesse ripe with irony, that the Orient could not, alas, afford the sorts of sanitary measures made possible in Europe by marvelous prosperity and centuries of progress and that it was accordingly unfair to demand the sacrifices under discussion.[411]

The Levantine nations were not alone, however, in their objections to proposals spearheaded by the French. The Russians in 1866, for example, still uncertain that cholera was spread by transmission, remained

---

[408] *Conférence 1894*, p. 44.

[409] *Conférence 1866*, 3, pp. 6–7; 5, p. 10; *Conférence 1894*, p. 165; PRO, FO 78/2005, Earl Cowley to Earl Russell, 9 October 1865, No. 1092; FO 78/2007, Herman Merrivale to Under Secretary of State for Foreign Affairs, 15 March 1866; letter, 2 March 1866, p. 55.

[410] Not forgetting the camel problem. With the beginning of steamer transport on the Red Sea in the 1840s, the ability to provision caravans had diminished. The 50,000 or so camels required for overland pilgrimages were simply not available: *Conférence 1866*, 5, pp. 6–8.

[411] *Conférence 1866*, 38, p. 10; *Conférence 1885*, pp. 96, 217; *Conférence 1892*, p. 142; *Conférence 1911*, p. 122; *Conférence 1903*, pp. 444–51, 455; PRO, FO 78/2006, p. 354, letter, Goodeve and Dickson, 10 September 1866; *Conférence 1894*, p. 165.

unconvinced that French-style plans would be effective. The Austrians pointed to the hypocrisy of the ban on pilgrimages discussed for Mecca in 1897 since such measures would never be countenanced for Catholics headed for Lourdes.[412] Even the Portuguese and the French, otherwise warm supporters of quarantining cholera in the Middle East, recognized on occasion that the Levant had equal claims to protection from the west.[413] But it was the British who most consistently sought to douse French enthusiasm for restrictive measures. Partly their insouciance stemmed from the security of distance, cholera rarely if ever having arrived via the longhaul maritime routes.[414] Partly it followed from their generally sanitationist approach. The Native Passenger Ships Acts, for example, were attempts through sanitation to create hygienic conditions onboard for pilgrims, thus avoiding the need for stricter quarantinist measures.[415] Partly it was a question of commercial interests. Arguing the uncontagiousness of cholera and a localist etiology meant that traffic from India, where cholera was endemic and ships inevitably treated as infected by their ports of destination, would escape restriction and the focus of preventive efforts would shift from quarantine to sanitary reform.[416] The British opposed restrictions on vessels from India and were encouraged on this point by the Indian authorities who were even more averse than they to quarantinism.[417] Imposing strict precautions in the Middle East for all shipping from the Orient, rather than individually by choice at European ports, meant allowing the Mediterranean nations to quarantine also the trade of Britain and other antiquarantinist powers, granting the southern countries protection without any of the otherwise attendant commercial disadvantages.[418] Fears were rife that the French were using sanitary precautions as an excuse to impose commercial restrictions in other respects

[412] *Conférence 1866*, 3, p. 6. The Turks threatened to apply any measures imposed on Muslims equally to all other pilgrims headed for Jerusalem: *Conférence 1897*, pp. 93–95; *Conférence 1911*, p. 444.

[413] *Conférence 1866*, 33, p. 14; *Conférence 1885*, p. 217.

[414] *Annales*, 3/10 (1883), pp. 253–58; *Conférence 1885*, pp. 101, 170–71; *Transactions of the Seventh International Congress of Hygiene and Demography*, pp. 61ff.; *Indian Medical Gazette*, 26 (December 1891), pp. 372–74.

[415] *Conférence 1866*, 29, annexe, pp. 19–24; *Conférence 1894*, pp. 51–52; Harrison, *Public Health in British India*, pp. 118–20.

[416] If cholera arose independently in unsanitary India, why not in unsanitary Damietta, as J. Mackie, surgeon to the British consulate in Alexandria asked rhetorically: PRO, FO 881/4863, FO CP 4863, October 1883, p. 43; FO 881/5155*, FO CP 5155*, p. 29.

[417] PRO, FO 83/1331, "Memorandum of the views of the Secretary of State for India regarding the attitude to be taken in behalf of India at the Paris Sanitary Conference of February 1894."

[418] PRO, FO 407/32, T. Farrer to Lister, 27 August 1884, p. 190; FO 407/40, FO CP 5005, September 1884, no. 15; FO 407/110, FO CP 6157, February 1892, pp. 120, 219; FO, 407/115, FO CP 6368, July 1893, p. 31; FO 423/13, FO CP 4814, 22 June 1883, p. 15.

as well, depriving British transport interests of the Algerian pilgrim traffic, for example.[419]

The basic disagreement between Britain and the continental powers over precautions in the Middle East allowed commercial and anticolonialist ideological motives to be harmoniously intertwined. While the French, Italians, Austrians and Germans regarded the Suez and the measures administered by the Alexandria Board of Health as a means of preserving Europe from cholera and plague, the British saw the issue in narrower terms, conceding the Egyptians the right of all states to protect themselves from epidemics, but wishing to saddle them with neither the responsibility for an epidemiological gatekeeping function on behalf of the Occident, nor the European control over their prophylactic actions thus implied.[420] The west should not, the British argued at the 1892 Venice Conference, oblige Egypt to serve as Europe's lazaretto and the Middle East deserved equal protection from European epidemics.[421] In a fortuitously happy coincidence of commercial interest and colonial consideration, British arguments in support of Egyptian sovereignty over the Suez and their objections to French hopes of internationalizing control over precautions imposed at the canal were motivated less by a principled taking of the native side than by British expectations of being able to influence the Egyptians to adopt a lenient view of prevention in a way they could not assume in a truly international council, with only one seat along with the quarantinist European powers.[422] If precautions imposed at the Suez were seen as a matter of concern directly to Europe, not just Egypt, the British admitted internally, then such measures would have to be under international control, no longer the outcome of Anglo-Egyptian decisions, and British shipping would be governed by the

[419] PRO, FO 83/1280, p. 71; FO 83/1281, telegram to Lowther, 20 January 1892 and p. 46.

[420] PRO, FO 881/5424, FO CP 5424, April 1887, p. 15; FO, 407/115, FO CP 6368, July 1893, p. 30.

[421] *Conférence 1892*, p. 105. This was an argument, in other words, analogous to the European objections put forth when the Americans imposed restrictions on the entry of diseased emigrants, thus turning, as it were, Europe into an extension of the lazarettos of New York and New Orleans: *JO*, 1911, Chambre, Doc., Annexe 1218, p. 1062; *Conférence 1894*, pp. 283–84; *Conférence 1881*, pp. 76–77; Weindling, *International Health Organisations*, p. 5.

[422] PRO, FO 83/1281, pp. 37–38, FO to British Delegates, 22 January 1892; p. 100, Marquis of Salisbury to Phipps and Thorne Thorne, 17 May 1892. The same held for British objections to French proposals during the 1850s and later of having European sanitary observers in the Middle East, rather than leaving matters to the Constantinople and Alexandria Boards of Health, in local hands: *Conférence 1859*, 29, pp. 1–2; FO 97/217, Draft to Sir Anthony Perrier, no. 6, 5 July 1859; PC1/2670, International Sanitary Conference, no. 53, 18 July 1859, no. 55, 20 July 1859; FO 407/32, E. Baring to Earl Granville, 5 November 1883, pp. 10–11; Memorandum by Dr. Buchanan, 21 November 1883, p. 16.

quarantinist nations.[423] A narrow interpretation of the Alexandria Board's role allowed British support for Egyptian prophylactic autonomy against French desires for European control in the Middle East and, at the same time, meshed happily with its shipping interests.

Finally, there remained the question of relations between the European powers and their colonial subjects. Some, like Germany, with few Muslim colonials were untroubled by the pilgrim problem and able to support the French proposals without reservation. Those with significant Islamic populations, in contrast, had to walk the line between limiting the epidemiological dangers of pilgrimage and not offending religious sensibilities. The Dutch supported the French proposals, seeking to portray the cholera problem as one limited to British India. Austria-Hungary, with its Muslim subjects in Bosnia and Herzegovina, and Russia were both concerned to prevent pilgrims returning cholera-stricken from Mecca.[424] The British, in contrast, with sixty million Muslim subjects in India, many of whom regarded the precautions sought by the French as an indignity, an inconvenience, an infringement of liberty and an unnecessary expense, faced a greater task than other European powers.[425] With both Muslims and Hindus sensitive to any regulation, sanitary or otherwise, of pilgrimages, the Indian government, fearful lest quarantinist tactics spark unrest, favored general sanitary measures instead.[426]

ADMINISTRATIVE CAPACITY

Finally, among the factors explaining the prophylactic tactics adopted by any given country, there was the question of administrative capacity, the extent to which nations had the bureaucratic, fiscal and statutory wherewithal – broadly speaking the state power – to enact the protective measures chosen. At least two elements were important: the wealth and resources commanded by society in general and the state's direct administrative capacity. Although quarantines did not come cheap, the sums involved paled in comparison to the massive infrastructural investment

[423] PRO, FO 407/32, T. Farrer to Lister, 27 August 1884, p. 190; FO 423/13, FO CP 4814, 22 June 1883, p. 15. This changed in the early twentieth century: Baldry, "Ottoman Quarantine Station," p. 85.

[424] *Conférence 1894*, pp. 56–58, 85; *Conférence 1866*, 2, pp. 13–14; 4, p. 21; *Conférence 1892*, p. 217; PRO, MH 19/239, Consul-General Freeman to the Marquess of Salisbury, 12 February 1897.

[425] The combination of commercial interests in not hampering relations between India and Britain and the need to pay attention to native sensibilities comes out in PRO, FO7/982, letters dealing with the Vienna Conference, dated September and October 1875.

[426] Harrison, *Public Health in British India*, pp. 107–08, 117–18; FO 78/2007, Herman Merrivale to Under Secretary of State for Foreign Affairs, 15 March 1866 and pp. 373, 505–07.

required to bring up to hygienic snuff the cities of nineteenth-century Europe. The costs of quarantine – topically applied to solve urgent and immediate problems – were also politically easier to justify than the slow, patient, massive and expensive increments of sanitary reform. Moreover, although even maritime quarantines required considerable personnel in the form of soldiers, sentries, inspectors and the like, the bureaucratic requirements of the neoquarantinist inspection systems were potentially greater. Quarantinism, at least in the maritime variant that had become the only realistic option after the failures of the 1830s, had the advantage of a certain bottleneck logic. Once terrestrial cordons had been abandoned (the massive deployments of manpower and materiel on the scale, most extremely, of the Austrian measures against the plague), quarantine in its maritime incarnation had the advantage of allowing administrative energies to be focused on particular people at circumscribed places during moments of threat. Quarantinism was thus not only a strategy that appealed to countries in certain geoepidemiological positions, it was also the poor country's tactic of choice. The Greeks and the Turks, for example, agreed – for once – that quarantinism held out the best hopes of epidemiological security to impoverished nations. Their cities were in substandard hygienic condition, impeding hopes of extinguishing disease once it had penetrated, and their public health administrations were not prepared to keep all travelers under surveillance, as demanded by the revision system. Quarantines were therefore the best solution.[427]

It was a leitmotif of discussions that the British were among the few nations able to afford the immense expense of hygienic improvements and that they alone had the state capacity to implement revision as an alternative to quarantine. The wealthy British, it was often noted with a mixture of admiration and envy, had been able to pay for sanitary improvements that left them more insouciant in the face of imported disease than other nations could afford to be. Could one really, as the Turkish delegate put it, compare the sanitary state of Spain, some Italian provinces, the French Midi, Greece or the Ottoman Empire with Britain, which had spent such vast sums over the last thirty years on sanitary measures that its soil, ports and habitations were practically immune to transmissible disease?[428] In terms of administrative capabilities, it was

---

[427] Snowden, *Naples in the Time of Cholera*, p. 84; *Conférence 1893*, pp. 71–72; *Conférence 1903*, pp. 94, 282; *Conférence 1894*, pp. 87–89; PRO, FO 83/1277, British Delegation to the Dresden Conference, account no. 5, 29 March 1893.

[428] *Conférence 1892*, pp. 129–30, *Transactions of the Seventh International Congress of Hygiene and Demography*, p. 55; *Conférence 1885*, p. 290; *Conférence 1892*, p. 143; *Recueil*, 27 (1897), p. 322.

also the British who held a commanding lead. Although histories of such matters in Britain tend to strike a self-depreciating pose, arguing that the central authorities had little effective public health power, the implicit comparison that informs such conclusions appears to be with conditions during the following century rather than with contemporary circumstances elsewhere.[429] At the time, the British were the envy of other European public health reformers, admired by their neighbors for dramatic and sustained investments in a sanitationist approach to city planning and urban infrastructure. No other nation, as Palmberg summed it up in his magisterial comparative study, has a sanitary code so complete and precise. Pettenkofer understandably favored British hygienic reforms which he credited with gradually conferring immunity to cholera.[430] France was still at the theoretical stage when it came to sanitary reform, Britain already at that of practice, Monod, an epidemiological Anglophile, admitted.[431] Others waxed even more enthusiastic.[432] Despite its enormous trade, sanitary reforms allowed Britain to enjoy relative immunity to cholera without the need for quarantines. Such interventions, moreover, managed to be effective and yet fully reconcilable with personal liberties and the rights of property. In the most general terms, Britain was praised as that country most consequently in pursuit of the sanitationist vision of a prophylactically united Europe, while quarantinists pitted nations against each other.[433]

But not just Britain's general sanitary example earned it praise; also the machinery of the interventions it targeted more specifically at containing transmissible disease impressed its neighbors. In France especially, the powers allocated at midcentury to the General Board of

[429] R. A. Lewis, *Edwin Chadwick and the Public Health Movement 1832–1854* (London 1952), p. 159; George Rosen, *From Medical Police to Social Medicine* (New York, 1974), pp. 176–200, Evans, *Death in Hamburg*; Morris, *Cholera 1832*, p. 54; Longmate, *King Cholera*, pp. 11, 29–30; Michael Durey, *The First Spasmodic Cholera Epidemic in York, 1832* (York, 1974), pp. 5–6; Durey, *Return of the Plague*, pp. 8–9, 88–89; Coleman, *Yellow Fever in the North*, p. 140.

[430] Palmberg, *Treatise on Public Health*, p. iii; Max von Pettenkofer, "Über die Cholera von 1892 in Hamburg und über Schutzmassregeln," *Archiv für Hygiene*, 17–18 (1893), p. 126; *BMJ*, 2 (23 August 1884), p. 380; Pettenkofer, *Choleraexplosionen*, p. 23; Pettenkofer, *Über Cholera*, p. 32.

[431] *Annales*, 3/25 (1891), pp. 134–35; 3/5 (1881), pp. 553–54; Monod, *Le choléra*, pp. 625ff.; *JO*, 1901, Sénat, Débats, 21 May 1901, p. 663; Richard Harrison Shryock, *The Development of Modern Medicine* (New York, 1947), pp. 238–39. Generally, see Lion Murard and Patrick Zylberman, *L'hygiène dans la république: La santé publique en France, ou l'utopie contrariée (1870–1918)* (Paris, 1996), ch. 5. For a modern echo, see Aquilino Morelle, *La défaite de la santé publique* (Paris, 1996), pp. 231–35.

[432] Luerssen, *Die Cholera*, p. 23; Hirsch, *Über die Verhütung*, p. 36; *Förhandlingar vid Helsovårdsföreningens i Stockholm sammankomster år 1884*, p. 79; *DVöG*, 27 (1895), p. 148; *Vierteljahrsschrift für gerichtliche und öffentliche Medicin*, 5 (1854), p. 288; *Revue d'hygiène*, 48 (1926), pp. 1152–64.

[433] *Monatsblatt für öffentliche Gesundheitspflege*, 17, 6 (1894), p. 99; Hueppe, *Cholera-Epidemie in Hamburg*, p. 12; Gähde, *Cholera in Magdeburg*, p. 34; Monod, *La santé publique*, p. 8; *DVöG*, 12, 1 (1880), p. 13.

Health during epidemics were envied by public hygienists. Later it was the Local Government Board which served, despite all British tendencies toward decentralized administration, as a model of what the French might achieve in these respects. Britain's public health administration, well staffed with its 8,000 sanitary officers and prepared for the medical surveillance of travelers and other facets of the revision system, was much admired.[434] The British applied measures like disinfection with force and energy, not, as one observer lamented, the halfhearted belatedness characteristic of the French administration. When the French finally passed a national public health law in 1902, the model they took was Britain.[435] Others were no less unstinting in their praise. Observers from Germany and Sweden admired the Boards of Health with their clearly defined nature and effective powers of interrogating inhabitants and owners of dwellings, inspecting localities, undertaking necessary works and suggesting improvements. The Nuisances Removal Act, allowing unsanitary conditions to be remedied at any time, not just under epidemic threat, was lauded, as were the disinfection institutions and the system of house-to-house visitations.[436]

In terms of overt precautions (uniformed officials requiring detailed questionnaires handed over by tongs from arriving ships, lazarettos replete with bored travelers waiting out their incubation periods and the like), Britain may have been less prophylactically interventionist than some of its continental neighbors. But the sort of measures required by its more pronouncedly sanitationist approach were in many respects, not just in terms of the funds required, more drastic than what was undertaken across the Channel.[437] The historiography of British public health intervention has tended misleadingly to focus on what the British state failed or was ill equipped to accomplish without bothering overly to inquire what its neighbors were up to at the

---

[434] *L'union médicale*, 7, 121 (11 October 1853), p. 477; *Revue médicale française et étrangère*, 2 (31 October 1853), pp. 450–54; *Annales*, 3/5 (1881), pp. 553–54; 3/49 (1903), p. 163; *Conférence 1897*, p. 450; *Recueil*, 22 (1892), p. 42; Paul Brouardel, *La profession médicale au commencement du XXe siècle* (Paris, 1903), p. 182.

[435] *Annales*, 3/1 (1879), p. 269; Strauss, *La croisade sanitaire*, pp. 53–54; *JO*, 1901, Sénat, Debat, 21 May 1901, p. 664; *Recueil*, 21 (1891), pp. 870–71.

[436] A. Liévin, *Danzig und die Cholera: Ein statistisch-topographischer Versuch* (Danzig, 1868), p. 1; *Upsala Läkareförening*, 13, 1 (1877–78), p. 18; Alfons Labisch, "Die gesundheitspolitischen Vorstellungen der deutschen Sozialdemokratie von ihrer Gründung bis zur Parteispaltung (1863–1917)," *Archiv für Sozialgeschichte*, 16 (1976), p. 337; *DVöG*, 7 (1875), pp. 276–77; Friedrich Sander, *Untersuchungen über die Cholera* (Cologne, 1872), p. 40; Cordes, *Cholera in Lübeck*, p. 62; Helm, *Cholera in Lübeck*, p. 41; Freymuth, *Giebt es ein praktisch bewährtes Schutzmittel*, p. 15; *L'union médicale*, 7, 121 (11 October 1853), p. 477.

[437] Gerard Kearns et al., "The Interaction of Political and Economic Factors in the Management of Urban Public Health," in Marie C. Nelson and John Rogers, eds., *Urbanisation and the Epidemiologic Transition* (Uppsala, 1989), pp. 33–34.

same time. Much of the story of the General Board of Health, for example, doubtless concerned the Victorian aversion to centralized administration and the localist backlash to Chadwick's Benthamite ambitions that eventually left the new Board responsible to Parliament and more dependent on local authorities.[438] It is also true that even the Chadwickian Board could not in fact accomplish what, on paper, it was capable of. Many of the Board's directives were resisted or ignored by local authorities over whom it exercised but little direct power.[439] But even though the old Board failed partly because of the dogmatism of Chadwick's sanitationist ideology and partly because of the resistance to centralization prevalent among local authorities and well spoken for in the Commons, the pertinent British officials, whether the Board in its various incarnations or the Guardians, were still able to take steps of a sort that public health enthusiasts in France could only dream of: enforcing zoning regulations, entering private dwellings to inspect for insanitary conditions and remedying them if necessary, removing nuisances and generally acting on powers that across the Channel were to be emulated only half a century later. Moreover, there were examples of sanitary reform on a local level that showed how effective even in decentralized Britain such measures could be. Under John Simon's tenure as Medical Officer of Health during the early 1850s, existing legislation was fully exploited to turn London into a showcase of sanitary improvement. Using his powers of compulsory drainage, water supply and nuisance removal and the powers of Medical Officers to order improvements within dwellings, fining recalcitrant owners, Simon managed to squeeze compulsion from even a laissez-faire system, with inspectors examining and certifying weekly the progress of work previously ordered, notices issued for negligence and, when all else failed, direct intervention by the authorities. Simon's "sanitary rotas" had inspectors examining hundreds of houses at regular intervals, thus transforming what had been envisaged as temporary visitations during epidemics into a system of permanent and periodic sanitary superintendence of the dwellings of the poor.[440]

The question of administrative capacity was thus important for the

[438] Morris, *Cholera 1832*, p. 205; *Hansard*, 1854, v. 134, col. 1417; 1854–55, v. 136, cols. 912–13; Simon, *English Sanitary Institutions*, p. 205.

[439] Lewis, *Edwin Chadwick*, pp. 188–89; *PP* 1849 (1115) xxiv, p. 22, 27–28, 35; *PP* 1850 (1273) xxi, 3, pp. 138–42; *PP* 1854–55 (1893) xlv, 69, pp. 6, 24–25, 49–50, 62–63; Jones, *Making of Social Policy*, p. 37; Durey, *Return of the Plague*, p. 211; Longmate, *King Cholera*, p. 163.

[440] Lambert, *John Simon*, pp. 185, 196–97; Christopher Hamlin, "Muddling in Bumbledom: On the Enormity of Large Sanitary Improvements in Four British Towns, 1855–1885," *Victorian Studies*,

choice of prophylactic strategy, but there was no foregone correlation between the ability to intervene and the manner in which to do so. The alleged paragon of laissez-faire, Britain, was a more drastic enforcer of public health than the land of Napoleonic centralization, to take one of the starkest contrasts. Conversely, some nations chose quarantinism as the path of least resistance because they lacked the administrative resources to do otherwise.[441] The couplets quarantinist/interventionist and sanitationist/laissez-faire, suggested by an Ackerknechtian view, do not hold. This can be seen most clearly in the odd bedfellows sometimes joined by the issue of administrative capacity. In the debate over the relative merits of surveillance and observation quarantines, the Russians sided with the British. Because of their system of internal passports, the Russians had little trouble tracking travelers from infected places and so were happy to replace observation quarantines with surveillance. At the 1911 Conference, the Germans too thought that they would have no problem locating surveilled passengers whose bacteriological examinations showed them to be infectious. The Egyptians also favored surveillance, imposing on their subjects a variant of revision that was in effect more drastic than observation quarantines. To avoid a five-day quarantine, all passengers were required to give an address and deposit a cash caution, partly returned after five days if they presented themselves daily for medical inspections.[442] In contrast to these nations, confident in their ability to locate travelers, the French allowed that surveillance might work for states able to control internal circulation or willing to impose Egyptian-style measures, but that in those with freedom of movement, such an approach was difficult to implement and observation quarantines were therefore needed as an alternative. Similar objections were voiced to proposals of bacteriologically examining all travelers and then keeping track of them until the results were in. Short of putting a police officer on the trail of each, as the French complained, there was little hope of again finding travelers who proved to be infectious. The most authoritarian and the most liberal nations could thus agree on a surveillance system, while those nations with neither the political willingness to impose the necessary controls nor the administrative muscle to locate travelers

32 (Autumn 1988); Mark Brayshay and Vivien F. T. Pointon, "Local Politics and Public Health in Mid-Nineteenth-Century Plymouth," *Medical History*, 27, 2 (April 1983), pp. 177–78.

[441] Quarantinism allowed them the easy choice of postponing needed sanitary reforms, as Thorne Thorne put it: MH 19/239, Thorne Thorne, untitled report, 23 November 1893.

[442] *Conférence 1903*, pp. 94, 283; *Conférence 1911*, p. 418.

once they had entered the country fell back on the simpler solution of imposing quarantines at the borders.[443]

A constellation of factors is thus required to explain the prophylactic strategy adopted by any particular nation. Political culture and regime, the Ackerknechtians' all-explaining single cause, was doubtless important, but alone it is insufficient and, moreover, appears to point in various directions. Strictly quarantinist during the 1830s, the Germans nonetheless quickly modified their position in a more liberal direction with no corresponding political change. They became heavily influenced by Pettenkofer during the late 1870s when, if politics dictated prophylaxis, they should have been becoming more conservative, and not until the nineties and then with the Contagious Disease Law in 1900 did they adopt a strict neoquarantinist position. The Swedes remained more consistently quarantinist throughout the century. The French, in turn, are even harder to make sense of in such respects: antiquarantinist during the Second Republic and the early authoritarian phase of the Empire, then switching back in a quarantinist direction during the later, liberal Imperial evolution and the early decades of the Third Republic. Other factors are therefore also needed to account for prophylactic inclination: position in the geoepidemiology of the disease in question, with pilgrims and migrants bringing mobility to otherwise fixed geographical considerations; the topographical possibilities of making effective use of certain techniques; the dictates of trade and commerce in pursuing or avoiding a quarantinist approach. Most important is the fact that none of these variables seems capable alone of explaining preventive choices. Even the British were wary of arguing the cause of commerce in defiance of a general interest in public health.[444] Only together, in a matrix of different causes, do they account for the path pursued by any particular nation. Britain, for example, might in theory have had topographical reasons for adopting a quarantinist approach, but commercial interests proved stronger. With respect to diseases of animals, in contrast, the British were, and remain, strict quarantinists, having no sufficiently pressing trading interests to override their topographically influenced eagerness to exclude avoidable illness. For the Swedes, the situation was the reverse of the British, with commercial concerns insufficiently pow-

---

[443] *Conférence 1903*, p. 284; *Conférence 1911*, p. 420. In "backward countries," as the British noted, surveillance would not work: PRO, FO 83/1279, Report of British Delegates, 18 April 1893; FO 542/3, FO CP 7819, November 1902, p. 20.

[444] If we had argued only the interests of shipping against quarantine, the FO snapped to the LGB, we would never have convinced other nations to follow our lead in reducing such burdens: FO 83/2056, FO to LGB, 66,436/1903, 19 May 1903.

erful to convince it to abandon the security promised by its location and topography. The French and Germans in turn balanced the respective demands of commerce and geography: strict measures for transmigrant traffic but little support for quarantines late in the century among the Germans, a geoepidemiologically influenced split between north and south and a growing concern with transmission through the Suez for the French.

CHAPTER 4

Smallpox faces the lancet

Smallpox sounded variations on the epidemiological themes first heralded with cholera. More endemic than the classic contagious diseases, smallpox was commonly regarded as among the worst of humanity's travails, an ailment that struck with blind disregard for sex or mode of life, favoring the young especially with its ravages, adding the humiliation of disfigurement for survivors of its other symptoms. That no one is spared either love or smallpox was the early modern version of our own, rather gloomier and mundane belief in the inevitability of the fiscus and the reaper.[1] It was considered the most painful and debilitating of diseases, most lethal and costliest in its economic ravages. Even the plague would seem less destructive, was the grim calculation from early in the nineteenth century, were it not that we normally count children's lives only once they have survived smallpox.[2]

While one of fate's hardest blows, however, smallpox was also the first contagious disease for which an effective, preventive medical intervention was developed and the first finally to be eradicated, a date set officially at 1979.[3] Smallpox was thus an illness that allowed humanity to test its prophylactic prowess, the only shameful illness, as Lorain put it, because the one that could best be avoided. Inoculation, or variolation, and then vaccination equipped humans with preventive powers beyond the traditional techniques of breaking chains of transmission.

---

[1] "Belehrung über ansteckende Krankheiten," *Anhang zur Gesetz-Sammlung*, 1835, Beilage B zu No. 27 gehörig, p. 23; Maria Stoiber, "Aus der bayerischen Impfgeschichte," *Münchner Medizinische Wochenschrift*, 117, 7 (14 February 1975), p. 259.

[2] Christian August Struve, *Anleitung zur Kenntniss und Impfung der Kuhpocken* (Breslau, 1802), pp. 1–2; Joh. M. Ekelund, *Barn-koppor och vaccinen: Jemförde, och såsom Identiske, samfällt afhandlade* (Nyköping, 1802), p. 168; August Hirsch, *Handbook of Geographical and Historical Pathology* (London, 1883), v. I, p. 140; Eberh. Munck af Rosenschöld, *Til Allmänheten om kokoppor, et säkert Förvaringsmedel emot Menniskokoppor* (Lund, 1801), pp. 1–2; *PP* 1813–14 (243) xii, p. 377.

[3] Donald A. Henderson, "The History of Smallpox Eradication," in Abraham M. Lilienfeld, ed., *Times, Places, and Persons: Aspects of the History of Epidemiology* (Baltimore, 1980), pp. 99–108; Jack W. Hopkins, *The Eradication of Smallpox* (Boulder, 1989).

The lancet and then later the needle allowed an unprecedented degree of control over nature, an ability to intervene into basic biological processes to tame events of otherwise horrendous effect. Inoculation and vaccination were integral parts of the Enlightenment faith in humanity's capacity to control its own destiny, the medical equivalent to Newtonianism in the physical sciences.[4] Because of this dramatic turnabout from the traditional view of smallpox as inevitably part of human existence, inoculators and vaccinators had to counter the claim that preventing it contradicted divine intentions to punish humanity for its sins, granting us instead the opportunity for ennoblement through patient acceptance of our pustulous fate. Arising at a certain historical moment, they argued, smallpox could not be an inherent part of human nature and, because imported to the west, there was no reason why it should not be eradicated. Striking especially infants with hideous suffering and disfigurement, smallpox could not, with the best of intentions, be regarded as enhancing a sense of humanity. The ability to prevent it, far from being counter to God's intentions, was in fact part of the divine plan, a tool granted mortals to fulfill their role in the larger scheme.[5] No one, after all, argued one early proponent of the lancet in a classic reductio, considered the use of food and clothing impious. God had never promised to help humans if they did not help themselves.[6]

Smallpox thus offered unusually propitious prophylactic circumstances. Because inoculation and then especially vaccination were effective preventive techniques targeted at a highly destructive ailment, the state had cause, early on, to encourage, promote and finally require their use. In nations like Sweden and Bavaria, the state threw its weight behind vaccination already early in the nineteenth century, but even in Britain several decades later and then half a century after that in France, government authorities took an unprecedented interest in matters of the lancet.

---

[4] *Annales*, 4/24 (1915), p. 27; Genevieve Miller, *The Adoption of Inoculation for Smallpox in England and France* (Philadelphia, 1957), p. 195.

[5] Bernhard Christoph Faust, *Versuch über die Pflicht der Menschen, Jeden Blatternkranken von der Gemeinschaft der Gesunden abzusondern: Und dadurch zugleich in Städten und Ländern und in Europa die Ausrottung der Blatternpest zu bewirken* (Bückeburg, 1794), pp. 3, 7–8; Struve, *Anleitung zur Kenntniss*, pp. 2, 85–87; E. Z. Munck af Rosenschöld, *Förslag till Hämmande af den på flere orter nu härjande koppfarsoten* (Lund, 1802), pp. 9–11; Johann Karl Sybel, *Erfahrungen über die Kuhpocken* (Berlin, 1801), p. 5.

[6] James Sanders, *A Comprehensive View of the Small Pox, Cow Pox, and Chicken Pox* (Edinburgh, 1813), pp. 73–74; Joseph Friedrich Thierfeld, *Prüfung einiger gangbaren Vorurtheile wider die Blatternimpfung: Eine Predigt zur Belehrung für solche Eltern, die sich bis jetzt nicht entschliessen konnten, von diesem bekannten Rettungsmittel Gebrauch zu machen* (Freyberg, 1812), pp. 9–24; David Schultz, *Berättelse om koppors ympande, öfverlämnad till högloflige Kongl. Sundhets-Commissionen* (Stockholm, 1756), pp. 92–93.

Vaccination was among the first areas in which the state's power was applied directly and tangibly, in an act of prophylactic puncturing, to the bodies of all citizens, elevating without compunction the health of the community in precedence over individual autonomy and inviolability.[7] The state's motives for wielding the lancet varied during the course of development from the first widespread use of inoculation in the late 1700s to the promulgation of compulsory vaccination laws during the following century. Early on, a mercantilist concern for the interests of the late absolutist regime held sway, with inoculation and vaccination promising to increase population and thus wealth, the argument demonstrated through sophisticated cost/benefit calculations based on the pecuniary value of each extra citizen.[8] The lancet – so ran the blithe mercantilist conceit – allowed the felicitous union of the government's interests with the happiness of the people.[9] General considerations of the public good, the need to limit the infectiveness of the individual in order to spare the community, became, in turn, the main concerns later in the nineteenth century.

PRE-INOCULATION

Before inoculation became popular in Europe during the late eighteenth century, the strategies available against smallpox did not differ from those thrown into the fray with other contagious diseases. But even thereafter, the old techniques long remained an arrow in the prophylactic quiver of possible precautions. Cordons promised little against a disease generally recognized as endemic, but sequestration and disinfection were suitable responses. Before Jenner's discovery, isolation was discussed as an alternative or complement to inoculation and this continued into the era of vaccination.[10] In Germany, Juncker proposed

---

[7] J. Rogers Hollingsworth et al., *State Intervention in Medical Care: Consequences for Britain, France, Sweden and the United States, 1890–1970* (Ithaca, 1990), pp. 117–22; Georges Vigarello, *Le sain et le malsain* (Paris, 1993), pp. 204–05.

[8] *Preste*, 1815, v. 1, pp. 521–29; *Handbok för Vaccinatörer och Vaccinations-Föreståndare: På Kongl. Maj:ts Nådigste Befallning, igenom Dess Sundhets-Collegium Författad och Utgifven År 1813* (Stockholm, 1813), p. 4; Rosenschöld, *Til Allmänheten*, p. 27; *Zeitschrift für die Staatsarzneikunde* (1821), p. 15; *DZSA*, 15 (1828), pp. 237–58; Ekelund, *Barn-koppor och vaccinen*, p. 177; Faust, *Versuch über die Pflicht*, p. 13; H. Stickl, "Zur Entwicklung der Schutzimpfung aufgezeigt an der Entwicklung der Bayerischen Landesimpfanstalt im 19. und 20. Jahrhundert," *Fortschritte der Medizin*, 95, 2 (13 January 1977), p. 76; Miller, *Adoption of Inoculation*, ch. 7; Johannes-Peter Rupp, "Die Entwicklung der Impfgesetzgebung in Hessen," *Medizinhistorisches Journal*, 10, 2 (1975), p. 104; Rolf Å. Gustafsson, *Traditionernas ok: Den svenska hälso- och sjukvårdens organisering i historie-sociologiskt perspektiv* (Stockholm, 1987), pp. 164–66.

[9] Rosenschöld, *Förslag till Hämmande*, p. 6; Sv. Hedin, *Kopporna kunna utrotas eller Vaccinationen til sina lyckligaste följder* (Stockholm, 1802), p. 22.

[10] *Annales*, 18 (1837) pp. 74–75; Pierre Darmon, *La longue traque de la variole: Les pionniers de la médecine préventive* (Paris, 1986), pp. 71–72; Jean-Pierre Peter, "Les médecins français face au problème de

a combination of isolation and widespread inoculation, intending – by sequestering all who succumbed over a period of five or ten years – to rid Europe once and for all of the disease. Others, recognizing that isolation alone did not eliminate the possibility of disease later reappearing, proposed it as a temporary precaution until all inhabitants of infected areas had been vaccinated. Examples as far afield as the Hottentots, the Kaffir and the good citizens of Rhode Island were held up as examples of sequestration's preventive abilities.[11]

The earliest regulation making vaccination compulsory, that of Piombino and Lucca from 1806, also isolated infected dwellings. In France, infected houses were marked and isolated, sometimes up to a month after recuperation; parents were forbidden to let children out in public until cured and victims to enter churches, schools or theaters until three months after recovery. The deceased were not permitted burial services in churches and guardians of patients were required to report all cases.[12] In 1807, smallpox victims were forbidden to enter Anspach in Bavaria and police prevented the contact of healthy persons with infected dwellings.[13] In Bavaria and other German states infected dwellings were to be treated as though plague-stricken, quarantined for a month, and in general all techniques used for pestilential disease were permitted against smallpox.[14] When, in the 1820s, the beneficial effects

l'inoculation variolique et sa diffusion (1750–1790)," *Annales de Bretagne et des pays de l'ouest*, 86, 2 (1979), p. 261.

[11] Faust, *Versuch über die Pflicht*, pp. 10, 13–17, 28; F. L. Augustin, *Die Königlich Preussische Medicinalverfassung* (Potsdam, 1818), v. I, pp. 169–70; Sybel, *Erfahrungen über die Kuhpocken*, pp. 5–7; *Journal der practischen Arzneykunde und Wundarzneykunst*, 19, 1 (1804), pp. 63–69; Johann Jakob Günther, *Geschichte der Vaccine und ihrer Impfung* (Cologne, 1802), pp. 34–36; Otto Lentz and H. A. Gins, eds., *Handbuch der Pockenbekämpfung und Impfung* (Berlin, 1927), pp. 495–96; Chr. H. Eimer, *Die Blatternkrankheit in pathologischer und sanitätspolizeilicher Beziehung* (Leipzig, 1853), p. 204.

[12] *Jahrbuch der Staatsarzneikunde*, 1 (1808), pp. 121–23; *Bulletin*, 3, 55 (1906), p. 112; "Circulaire du Préfet de Marengo à MM. les Maires de son département," "Arrêté de M. le Baron de Roujoux, Préfet du département de Saone-et-Loire," 8 June 1813, "Arrêté du Préfet du département de Gènes" and "Extrait de l'Arrêté du Préfet du département des Landes," in *Collection des bulletins sur la vaccine publiés par le Comité central* (Paris, 1814); G. Borne, *Vaccination et revaccinations obligatoires: En application de la loi sur La Protection de la Santé Publique* (Paris, 1902), p. 31; *Annales*, 3/50, 3 (July 1903), pp. 257–58; Franz Seraph Giel, *Die Schutzpocken-Impfung in Bayern* (Munich, 1830), pp. 390–91.

[13] John Cross, *A History of the Variolous Epidemic Which Occurred in Norwich in the Year 1819, and Destroyed 530 Individuals, with an Estimate of the Protection Afforded by Vaccination* (London, 1820), pp. 245–47.

[14] *Jahrbuch der Staatsarzneikunde*, 1 (1808), pp. 119–20; Giel, *Schutzpocken-Impfung in Bayern*, pp. 157–58; G. Cless, *Impfung und Pocken in Württemberg* (Stuttgart, 1871), p. 80; Lübeck, "Regulativ über das Verfahren beim Ausbruche der Menschenblattern," 15 October 1823, a printed version in BA, Reichskanzleramt, 14.01/999; *Magazin für die gesammte Heilkunde*, 3 (1834), p. 537; Augustin, *Preussische Medicinalverfassung*, v. I, pp. 175–76; v. II, p. 622; Yves-Marie Bercé, *Le chaudron et la lancette: Croyances populaires et médecine préventive (1798–1830)* (Paris, 1984), p. 72; Anneliese Gerbert, *Öffentliche Gesundheitspflege und staatliches Medizinalwesen in den Städten Braunschweig und Wolfenbüttel im 19. Jahrhundert* (Braunschweig, 1983), p. 14.

of the first wave of vaccination wore off and smallpox again spread, those who were unconvinced by the need for revaccination proposed quarantinist techniques instead. The epidemic of 1833 near Bautzen in Saxony was fought with a combination of efforts to promote vaccination and strict isolation. The 1835 Prussian regulation on contagious disease treated smallpox much as other transmissible ailments. Vaccination was not compulsory except in limited circumstances and victims were to be sequestered at home, or at least warning signs posted. If the disease spread, isolation facilities were to be established and other precautions reminiscent of those applied to cholera and the plague ensued.[15]

Also in Britain, during the period when vaccination was establishing itself, support for the tenets of quarantinism remained strong.[16] Victims were sequestered in the late eighteenth century, compulsorily so in the case of relief recipients, and the ill and inoculated banished from towns. Isolating the ill and marking infected dwellings were frequently proposed, as was disinfection or destruction of victims' clothing. In one case the Medical Officer of a small village sealed the garden door of an infected house, threw food and necessities over the hedge, paid the breadwinner's wages, supported the children during sequestration and, in the end, had the furniture and clothing burnt and the cottage almost pulled down.[17] In Sweden too venerable prophylactic approaches continued to do service into the era of vaccination. The 1816 law on smallpox marshaled the whole arsenal of quarantinist techniques. Victims were isolated for almost a month or hospitalized while unprotected family members were removed, if necessary by order of the mayor, and lodged with relations or at municipal expense. Burials were performed, as with other contagious diseases, quickly after sundown with no procession.[18]

---

[15] *DZSA*, NF, 20 (1862), p. 5; Dietrich Tutzke, "Blatternsterblichkeit und Schutzpockenimpfung in der Sächsischen Oberlausitz 1800–1875," *Wissenschaftliche Zeitschrift der Martin-Luther-Universität Halle-Wittenberg*, Mathematisch-Naturwissenschaftliche Reihe, 4, 6 (1954–55), p. 1102; *Gesetz-Sammlung*, 1835, 27/1678; *Zeitschrift für die Staatsarzneikunde*, 58 (1849), p. 231.

[16] Cross, *History of the Variolous Epidemic*, p. 221; *Edinburgh Journal of Medical Science*, 1 (1826), pp. 282–84; *Hansard*, 1853, v. 125, cols. 1011–12; Iconoclastis, *Pethox Parvus: Dedicated, Without Permission, to the Remnant of the Blind Priests of That Idolatry* (London, 1807), pp. 12–18; *Cobbett's*, 1806, v. 7, cols. 886–87.

[17] E. G. Thomas, "The Old Poor Law and Medicine," *Medical History*, 24, 1 (January 1980), pp. 8–9; J. R. Smith, *The Speckled Monster: Smallpox in England, 1670–1970, with Particular Reference to Essex* (Chelmsford, 1987), pp. 27, 149–50; *PP* 1808 (287) i, p. 645; *Hansard*, 1815, v. 31, cols. 1120–21; *PP* 1854–55 xlv, p. 627; *First Report of the Royal Commission Appointed to Inquire into the Subject of Vaccination* (C.-5845) (London, 1889), Q 658.

[18] Rosenschöld, *Förslag till Hämmande*, pp. 16–23; "Kongl. Maj:ts Nådiga Förordning, Om Hwad, i händelse af yppad Koppsmitta iakttagas bör," 11 December 1816, *Kongl. Förordningar*, 1816.

During the eighteenth century, inoculation served to replace such quarantinist approaches to smallpox, but never became more than a partial substitute. The new technique caught on mainly among the upper classes and was more popular in some nations than others. In Britain, it had been widely adopted already in the 1720s and thirties. At midcentury, foundlings were inoculated and, at the other end of the social spectrum, a past history of either smallpox or variolation gradually became almost a precondition for employment as a servant in aristocratic households.[19] While inoculation was also popular in Sweden, in Germany and especially in France it was often fiercely resisted up to the point when the development of vaccination rendered the issue largely superfluous.[20] By the 1830s, vaccination was effectively substituting for both traditional quarantinist techniques and inoculation. In Trier in 1826 it was still argued that, to convince recalcitrants to vaccinate, it should be pointed out that this would spare the community the trouble and expense of quarantinist measures. In Sweden, vaccination was supported with the arguments that the quarantinist alternatives were costly and that the poor could not isolate stricken children at home when they lacked sufficient room to live under normal circumstances. Compared to the trouble and vexations of quarantinist precautions, vaccination seemed a less irksome prophylactic route that promised to leave normal life largely undisturbed. By 1835, Frederick VI, ruler of Denmark and Schleswig-Holstein, was able confidently to assert that quarantinist measures could effectively be replaced by vaccination.[21]

---

[19] J. R. Smith, *Speckled Monster*, chs. 2, 3; C. W. Dixon, *Smallpox* (London, 1962), p. 239.

[20] Arnold H. Rowbotham, "The 'Philosophes' and the Propaganda for Inoculation of Smallpox in Eighteenth-Century France," *University of California Publications in Modern Philology*, 18, 4 (1935), pp. 265–74; Miller, *Adoption of Inoculation*, pp. 174, 180, 184–85, 191; Heinrich Bohn, *Handbuch der Vaccination* (Leipzig, 1875), pp. 85–87, 91; Pierre Darmon, *La variole, les nobles et les princes: La petite vérole mortelle de Louis XV* (n.p., 1989), pp. 55–68; Mary Lindemann, *Health and Healing in Eighteenth-Century Germany* (Baltimore, 1996), pp. 333–34; Andreas-Holger Maehle, "Conflicting Attitudes Towards Inoculation in Enlightenment Germany," in Roy Porter, ed., *Medicine in the Enlightenment* (Amsterdam, 1995), pp. 205–10; Peter Sköld, *The Two Faces of Smallpox: A Disease and Its Prevention in Eighteenth- and Nineteenth-Century Sweden* (Umeå, 1996), ch. 4. But see the more positive characterization of the French case in Jean-François de Raymond, *Querelle de l'inoculation* (Paris, 1982), pp. 81–102.

[21] *DZSA*, 15 (1828), p. 250; Heinrich Eichhorn, *Massregeln, welche die Regierungen Deutschlands zur gänzlichen Verhütung der Menschenblattern zu ergreifen haben, wobei die Häusersperre zu entbehren ist* (Berlin, 1829), pp. 97–104; *Bihang*, 1815, iv, 3, pp. 1338–48; *Magazin für die gesammte Heilkunde*, 3 (1834), pp. 537–40; Augustin, *Preussische Medicinalverfassung*, v. I, pp. 169–70; *Mittheilungen aus dem Gebiete der Medicin, Chirurgie und Pharmacie*, 3 (1835), pp. 81–83; *Annales*, 18 (1837) pp. 75, 132.

VACCINATION

In most European nations, vaccination was quickly adopted as the most effective means of prevention. Although inoculation (injecting a weak strain of smallpox) remained popular in Britain, vaccination (injecting cowpox) was beginning to gain a toehold by the 1820s. Public confidence in the technique was growing apace, the National Vaccine Establishment reported in 1814, and by the thirties the vast majority of children born in London were being vaccinated. The middle and upper classes adopted the lancet so eagerly that by 1857 Simon could claim that the "civilized classes" had almost forgotten what smallpox was like.[22] Compared to the homeland of vaccination, the Germans enjoyed the advantages of backwardness. Inoculation had never found the same favor here as in Britain, except perhaps for Hannover and Saxony where British influences were strong. The clergy resisted, leading physicians, like van Swieten and de Haen, were opposed and the princely patrons notable for their absence. Frederick the Great's attempt to introduce variolation to Prussia was dashed when Baylies, the English doctor to whom he confided this task, proved to be a charlatan. Germany, inoculation's supporters lamented, had not developed the benevolent institutions to encourage the practice among the lower classes found in Britain.[23] With less competition from old methods, vaccination was embraced early. Since Britain was at war with France and the Netherlands when Jenner published his discoveries, Germany was the first foreign country to which vaccine was conveyed, with parcels of dried lymph sent in 1800 to Hannover and Vienna. That year Heim established an institution in Berlin to promote the lancet on the model of the Jennerian Society and in 1801 the royal physician, a Briton named Brown, inaugurated the technique by vaccinating the daughter of a prominent financier.[24] From here, vaccination spread quickly in use and

---

[22] *PP* 1813–14 (243) xii, pp. 375–77; *PP* 1833 (753) xvi, p. 155; *PP* 1857 (sess. 2) (2239) xxxv, p. 148; Cross, *History of the Variolous Epidemic*, pp. 20–21; *PP* 1807 (14) ii, p. 66; *PP* 1852–53 (434) ci, 77, p. 21; *PP* 1856 lii, p. 487.

[23] Abraham Zadig, *Plan nach welchem die Einimpfung der Pocken in einer ganzen Provinz allgemein einge-führt, und die längst gewünschte Ausrottung der Seuche erreicht werden könnte* (Breslau, 1797), pp. 16–30; Emil Ungar, *Über Schutzimpfungen insbesondere die Schutzpocken-Impfung* (Hamburg, 1893), pp. 9–10; H. J. Parish, *A History of Immunization* (Edinburgh, 1965), p. 24; Ute Frevert, *Krankheit als politisches Problem 1770–1880* (Göttingen, 1984), p. 69; Alfons Fischer, *Geschichte des deutschen Gesundheitswesens* (Berlin, 1933), v. II, p. 266. The situation was similar in Austria: see Johannes Wimmer, *Gesundheit, Krankheit und Tod im Zeitalter der Aufklärung: Fallstudien aus den habsburgischen Erbländern* (Vienna, 1991), p. 117.

[24] James Moore, *The History and Practice of Vaccination* (London, 1817), pp. 243–45; *Journal der prac-tischen Arzneykunde und Wundarzneykunst*, 11, 1 (1800), pp. 182–87; Lentz and Gins, *Handbuch der*

popularity. Inoculation was prohibited, parents were exhorted to have their children protected, institutions for this purpose were established and vaccination offered – free of charge to the poor and sometimes to all.[25]

The Swedes, in turn, were enthusiastic adherents of the lancet, moderately so for inoculation, but with special fervor when it came to vaccination.[26] Emanuel Timoni's account of variolation in Turkey, published by the Royal Society in London in 1714, was bought the previous year by the exiled Swedish king, Charles XII, who sent it to Stockholm from Adrianople.[27] At midcentury, after David Schultz reported on British developments, inoculation was first performed here in 1754–55, with the royal family helping lead the way in 1769. Already during the summer of 1798 news of Jenner's discovery reached Sweden, and the first vaccination was performed in October 1801, by Munck af Rosenschöld in Lund.[28] The Collegium Medicum supported the new technique eagerly, the clergy was encouraged to disseminate the news and the practice spread quickly. Few objections were voiced and the lancet appears to have been widely welcomed, with the vast majority of infants vaccinated voluntarily.[29] Swedes regarded themselves as eager supporters of the technique and were soon being praised abroad as possibly the best-vaccinated

Pockenbekämpfung, p. 234; Giel, *Schutzpocken-Impfung in Bayern*, p. 25. However, some Germans, like the French, regarded the new technique suspiciously as another swindle associated with Anglomania: Ehrmann, *Über den Kuhpocken-Schwindel bei Gelegenheit der abgenöthigten Vertheidigung* (Frankfurt am Main, 1801), p. 1.

[25] K. G. Kühn, *Die Kuhpocken, ein Mittel gegen die natürlichen Blattern, und folglich ein sehr wichtiger Gegenstand für die gesamte Menschheit* (Leipzig, 1801), pp. iv–v; Günther, *Geschichte der Vaccine*, pp. 172–76; Struve, *Anleitung zur Kenntniss*, pp. 57–61; *Kuhpocken und Kuhpocken-Impfung als ein ohnfehlbares Mittel die Kinderblattern zu verhüten* (Mannheim, 1801), p. 8; Leonhard Voigt, *Das erste Jahrhundert der Schutzimpfung und die Blattern in Hamburg* (Leipzig, 1896), p. 30; Stickl, "Zur Entwicklung der Schutzimpfung," p. 76; Eimer, *Blatternkrankheit*, p. 102; Heinrich A. Gins, *Krankheit wider den Tod: Schicksal der Pockenschutzimpfung* (Stuttgart, 1963), p. 227.

[26] Günther, *Geschichte der Vaccine*, p. 44; John Rogers and Marie Clark Nelson, "Controlling Infectious Diseases in Ports: The Importance of the Military in Central–Local Relations," in Nelson and Rogers, eds., *Urbanisation and the Epidemiologic Transition* (Uppsala, 1989), pp. 95–96; Sköld, *Two Faces of Smallpox*, chs. 4, 5.

[27] Abbas M. Behbehani, *The Smallpox Story* (Lawrence, KS, 1988), pp. 11–12; Arthur M. Silverstein, *A History of Immunology* (San Diego, 1989), pp. 25–26; de Raymond, *Querelle de l'inoculation*, p. 34.

[28] David Schultz, *Berättelse om koppors ympande*; François Dezoteux and Louis Valentin, *Traité historique et pratique de l'inoculation* (Paris, L'an 8 de la Republique [1800]), pp. 98–99; *Förhandlingar vid De Skandinaviske Naturforskarnes tredje Möte, i Stockholm den 13–19 Juli 1842* (Stockholm, n.d.), p. 863; Sven-Ove Arvidsson, "Ur smittkoppornas historia i Sverige," *Nordisk medicinhistorisk årsbok* (1976), pp. 70, 73.

[29] *Hygiea*, 58, 6 (June 1896), pp. 565–90; Rosenschöld, *Förslag till Hämmande*, p. 6; RA, Skrivelser till kungl. Maj:t, Collegium Medicum, 1833, v. 60, no. 465, 28 October 1833; *Preste*, 1850–51, iii, pp. 122–24; *Bihang*, 1885, AK Tillfälliga Utskotts (No. 1) Utlåtande No. 19.

nation.[30] With its winning combination of early and widespread protection and its peerless system of national statistics, Sweden served the lancet's proponents well as a source of arguments illustrating vaccination's beneficial effect on mortality.[31] In France, the lancet got off to a slow start. Inoculation was legalized early, in 1755, but physicians who expected support for the new technique were surprised at the resistance of a nation that otherwise prided itself on embracing anything that improved humanity's lot.[32] Vaccination fared little better. A Frenchman in Stockholm, Bourgoing, may have been the first to report back to Paris on the new development, but it was vaccination's British roots and its coincidence with the Napoleonic wars that led it at first to be regarded with suspicion.[33] Once it had leaped the hurdles thrown up by the Vaccine Committee in Paris early in the century, however, it began to catch on, helped on its way by Napoleon's support and encouragement from the pulpit.[34] In 1806, prefects were instructed to encourage vaccination and during the following decade it became one of the reforms spread (more abroad than at home) in the train of Napoleonic expansion.[35]

At the beginning of the nineteenth century, most states provided their citizens with the opportunity for such protection, often gratis for the

---

[30] *Ridderskapet och Adeln*, 1815, v. 3, p. 669; *Förhandlingar*, 1908, p. 217; Charles T. Pearce, *Vital Statistics: Small-Pox and Vaccination in the United Kingdom of Great Britain and Ireland and Continental Countries and Cities* (London, 1882), pp. 63, 67–68; P. Kübler, *Geschichte der Pocken und der Impfung* (Berlin, 1901), pp. 244–45; *JO*, 1881, Chambre, Doc., p. 136; Hubert Boëns, *La vaccine au point de vue historique et scientifique* (Charleroi, 1882), p. 60; Giel, *Schutzpocken-Impfung in Bayern*, p. 38.

[31] *PP* 1857 (sess. 2) (2239) xxxv, pp. 168–69; Kaiserliches Gesundheitsamt, *Beiträge zur Beurtheilung des Nutzens der Schutzpockenimpfung* (Berlin, 1888), pp. 75ff. It was, of course, attacked for this reason by antivaccinators: William Arnold et al., *Notes on Vaccination: Dedicated to the Board of Guardians for the Union of West Bromwich* (Oldbury, 1889), pp. 38ff.; *SB*, 6 March 1874, p. 229.

[32] [Joseph] Power, *Précis historique de la nouvelle methode d'inoculer la petite verole avec une exposition abrégée de cette Methode* (Amsterdam, 1769), pp. 3–4; M. Gatti, *Réflexions sur les préjuges qui s'opposent aux progres et a la perfection de l'inoculation* (Brussels, 1764), pp. 212–17; Günther, *Geschichte der Vaccine*, p. 40; Parish, *History of Immunization*, p. 24.

[33] Carolus Zetterström, *Initia historiæ vaccinationis in Svecia* (Uppsala, 1816–21), pp. 78–80; Struve, *Anleitung zur Kenntniss*, p. 52; Robert G. Dunbar, "The Introduction of the Practice of Vaccination into Napoleonic France," *BHM*, 10, 5 (December 1941), pp. 635–50.

[34] AN F[19] 5596, "Lettre circulaire et ordonnance de M.gr l'Eveque de Valence, au sujet de la Vaccine," 27 July 1813; *Journal der practischen Arzneykunde und Wundarzneykunst*, 19, 1 (1804), p. 59; Dora B. Weiner, *The Citizen-Patient in Revolutionary and Imperial Paris* (Baltimore, 1993), pp. 293–94; Jean-François Lemaire, *Napoléon et la médecine* (Paris, 1992), pp. 242–43; Evelyn Bernette Ackerman, *Health Care in the Parisian Countryside, 1800–1914* (New Brunswick, 1990), pp. 67–75.

[35] Borne, *Vaccination et revaccinations obligatoires*, p. 29; Jacques Léonard, *La médecine entre les savoirs et les pouvoirs* (Paris, 1981), p. 64; Calixte Hudemann-Simon, *L'état et la santé: La politique de santé publique ou "police médicale" dans les quatre départements rhénans, 1794–1814* (Sigmaringen, 1995), ch. 5. At midcentury it became part of the French "civilizing mission" in Algeria: Yvonne Turin, *Affrontements culturels dans l'Algérie coloniale: Ecoles, médecines, religion, 1830–1880* (2nd edn.; Algiers, 1983), pp. 337–42.

poor, and many offered inducements for voluntary vaccination.[36] In Britain, private institutions vaccinated the poor at no charge starting in the 1790s and in 1808 a National Vaccine Establishment was set up to continue such practices. In Norwich, the city surgeons were paid to vaccinate the poor, others often did so free of charge and in 1812 each indigent who could produce a vaccination certificate was promised half a crown by the Guardians. In 1815 a bill had sought unsuccessfully to provide for the free protection of the poor who desired it, but in 1840 Guardians and overseers were directed to contract with physicians to vaccinate all residents, not just paupers, who so wished, the costs borne by the poor rates. The following year, this was extended by explicitly stating that vaccination was not to be considered parochial relief and conveyed no deprivation of rights. Vaccination stations were established to offer the procedure at appointed times and measures taken to inform the public. When such precautions proved insufficient, vaccinators might call directly at the dwellings of the poor and, if it appeared that local authorities had been neglectful, the Poor Law Board could demand clarification, urging increased efforts. By midcentury, the British had thus created a national system of free vaccination. It remained voluntary, however, and its connections to the Poor Law authorities tarnished it, despite the officially nonpauperizing nature of the service.[37]

In Germany as well, efforts to encourage voluntary vaccination were widespread. Bavarian priests, school teachers and physicians were exhorted to exert themselves on the lancet's behalf, with enthusiasts promised official support of their careers. Clergy were to supply doctors lists of those to be protected, the police with those who had not been; the practice was to be encouraged from the pulpit and offered free twice a year. Various means of informal pressure were also exerted, with parents of unvaccinated children in Saxony during an epidemic in the early 1830s, for example, summoned to the police station to explain their neglect.[38] In Sweden voluntary measures were also promoted, with

---

[36] Among such incentives, most inventive was the lottery ticket printed on the back of each Spanish vaccination certificate: Karl Süpfle, *Leitfaden der Vaccinationslehre* (Wiesbaden, 1910), p. 40.

[37] Cross, *History of the Variolous Epidemic*, pp. 20–21, 25–26; *PP* 1814–15 (439) ii, p. 835; *Hansard*, 1815, v. 31, cols. 845–46, 1120–21; 3 & 4 Vict. c. 29; 4 & 5 Vict. c. 32; 30 & 31 Vict. c. 84, s. 26; *PP* 1852–53 (434) ci, p. 85; R. J. Lambert, "A Victorian National Health Service: State Vaccination 1855–1871," *Historical Journal*, 5, 1 (1962), pp. 251–52.

[38] *Jahrbuch der Staatsarzneikunde*, 1 (1808), pp. 109–21; Giel, *Schutzpocken-Impfung in Bayern*, pp. 52–53, 96–103, 126–27; Rupp, "Die Entwicklung der Impfgesetzgebung in Hessen," pp. 111–12; Johann Michael Zimmermann, *Über Menschenpocken, die richtige Weise zu impfen, und die wahre Bedeutung der Schutzpockenimpfung* (Salzbach, 1844), p. 38; Tutzke, "Blatternsterblichkeit und Schutzpocken-impfung," p. 1104.

encouragements in the form of rewards paid to parents who vaccinated their offspring and a tax on recalcitrants considered. In 1804, district governors were to enlist enlightened and diligent citizens to work as vaccination superintendents and vicars to appoint parish clerks for the same purpose. In 1810, all heads of households were required to report annually the unprotected in their care, with the district Medical Officer seeking to have them vaccinated.[39] In France, prefects were instructed to encourage vaccination already early in the century, ensuring that the procedure was offered regularly and bestowing rewards, prizes and other honors on physicians who had been especially zealous in wielding the lancet.[40] The unvaccinated were excoriated as enemies of humanity to be expelled from the bosom of society; mayors and other local authorities were expected to exert pressure on parents by paying frequent visits to large families, reminding them that their offspring would otherwise not be matriculated and threatening to isolate their dwellings if the disease struck.[41]

COMPULSION

As confidence in the harmlessness and effectiveness of vaccination grew, public health authorities increasingly came to realize the inability of a purely voluntary effort to protect the bulk of the population.[42] As with any public good, the free-rider problem spoke in favor of compulsion, but of what sort? Were indirect forms sufficient or should the requirement be made universal? If so, was a directly enforceable obligation to vaccinate needed or merely a system of disincentives for default?

The first attempts at compulsion were generally indirect, targeting various groups as they passed through the state's hands, whether to serve

---

[39] *Ridderskapet och Adeln*, 1815, v. 3, pp. 561–63; *Preste*, 1815, v. 1, pp. 413–15, 521–29; Ekelund, *Barnkoppor och vaccinen*, pp. 201–07; *Kongl. Medicinalstyrelsens underdåniga skrifvelse den 8 Juni 1894, med förslag till förnyadt nådigt reglemente för skyddskoppympningen i riket* (Stockholm, 1894), pp. 4–5.

[40] Borne, *Vaccination et revaccinations obligatoires*, p. 29; *Moniteur universel*, 173 (21 June 1832), p. 1361; George Weisz, *The Medical Mandarins: The French Academy of Medicine in the Nineteenth and Early Twentieth Centuries* (New York, 1995), p. 91; Jean-Noël Biraben, "La diffusion de la vaccination en France au XIXe siècle," *Annales de Bretagne et des pays de l'ouest*, 86, 2 (1979), pp. 265–76; Chantal Beauchamp, *Délivrez-nous du mal: Épidémies, endémies, médecine et hygiène au XIXe siècle dans l'Indre, l'Indre-et-Loire et le Loir-et-Cher* (n.p., 1990), ch. 6; John Spears and Diane Sydenham, "The Evolution of Medical Practice in Two Marginal Areas of the Western World, 1750–1830," in Jean-Pierre Goubert, ed., *La médicalisation de la société française 1770–1830* (Waterloo, Ontario, 1982), pp. 203–04.

[41] *Bulletin sur la vaccine*, 33 (July 1813) and 3 (January 1811) in *Collection des bulletins sur la vaccine*.

[42] *Zeitschrift für die Staatsarzneikunde* (1821), pp. 17–18, 25–26.

in the military, collect public assistance, receive an education or be married. Soldiers were often among the first to be vaccinated and, later, revaccinated. In Bavaria, all recruits who had not had smallpox underwent the lancet starting in 1807, while in Prussia similar requirements followed two decades later. Bavarian children who had neither had smallpox nor been vaccinated were not permitted to immatriculate at educational or similar institutions as of 1805. Baden and Westphalia expanded similar measures in 1808 to include those accepted as apprentices or in guilds. Orphans, foundlings and others raised at the public expense were to be vaccinated, as were children of the poor who received public support. Hamburg extended compulsory vaccination from orphans to all supported by poor relief in 1819. The unvaccinated could no longer do garrison duty or serve as nightwatchmen. Physicians tending to the poor were to exhort them to protect their children; in 1821 pupils at charity schools had to be vaccinated and two years later enrollment in all public schools in the suburbs required similar protection, as did all apprenticeships.[43] Analogous measures in Prussia culminated in the 1835 regulation on contagious disease which required vaccination of all seeking admission to various public institutions or requesting different forms of aid. For schools and other educational establishments vaccination was not, however, yet required. In Frankfurt, similar arrangements were not instituted until 1841, but these were then expanded by the demand that all who sought citizenship in the citystate be vaccinated.[44]

In Britain, certain forms of indirect compulsion were introduced early, others quite late. In 1799, all soldiers not otherwise protected were to be vaccinated, while in the navy only voluntary protection was offered at first, with compulsion following in 1864.[45] In 1811 the town of Hungerford threatened the poor who, having refused vaccination, fell ill with removal to the pest house, in 1824 upping the stakes to deny relief

[43] Giel, *Schutzpocken-Impfung in Bayern*, pp. 84–86; *Gesetz-Sammlung*, 1826, 18/1039, p. 119; Zimmermann, *Über Menschenpocken*, pp. 37–38; *Annalen für die gesammte Heilkunde* (1827), pp. 13–14; Gerbert, *Öffentliche Gesundheitspflege*, p. 149; Voigt, *Jahrhundert der Schutzimpfung*, pp. 30–31.

[44] Kaiserliches Gesundheitsamt, *Beiträge zur Beurtheilung*, pp. 105–06; *Second Report of the Royal Commission Appointed to Inquire into the Subject of Vaccination* (C.-6666) (London, 1890), QQ. 1451, 1460; *Gesetz-Sammlung*, 1835, 27/1678, §56; *Anhang zur Gesetz-Sammlung*, 1835, Beilage B zu No. 27 gehörig, p. 28; *Blattern und Schutzpockenimpfung. Denkschrift zur Beurtheilung des Nutzens des Impfgesetzes vom 8. April 1874 und zur Würdigung der dagegen gerichteten Angriffe: Bearbeitet im Kaiserlichen Gesundheitsamte* (Berlin, 1896), pp. 53–54; Edward J. Edwardes, *A Concise History of Small-Pox and Vaccination in Europe* (London, 1902), pp. 74–77; *BMJ* (13 February 1904), pp. 378–79; *PP* 1852–53 (434) ci, 77, pp. 54–57.

[45] Christopher Lloyd and Jack L. S. Coulter, *Medicine and the Navy 1200–1900* (Edinburgh, 1961–63), v. III, pp. 348–52; v. IV, pp. 46–47, 210–12; Moore, *History and Practice of Vaccination*, pp. 118–19; *Hygiea*, 36, 10 (September 1874), p. 549; *Second Report into the Subject of Vaccination*, Q. 2646.

for all who spurned the lancet. Admission to educational institutions, in contrast, was a less effective portal than in Germany since compulsory and universal schooling was introduced only in the 1870s and eighties, a full century after Prussia. By the end of the century, candidates to be pupil teachers were admitted only if vaccinated, although the Education Department still had no authority to exclude children from school on this basis. Eton, Rugby, Harrow and other public schools required vaccination.[46] Although suggestions to this effect were made, poor relief recipients do not seem generally to have been required to vaccinate their children. At the turn of the century, however, workhouse inmates were won for the technique by the promise of improved rations and relief from the routine of oakum-picking and stone-breaking.[47] Various government departments required vaccination as a condition of employment. Targeted compulsion was also practiced informally in that some private contractual relations were made dependent on the lancet. Many life insurance companies, for example, refused to insure the unvaccinated (or at least to pay benefits in case of death by smallpox) and landlords to rent to them. Some employers sought to require vaccination of their workers and there were attempts to create a masters' association whose members promised not to hire unprotected servants and laborers.[48]

In France, the prolonged journey to compulsory vaccination forced the authorities to rely heavily on similar indirect requirements. Receipt of public assistance was often made contingent on the lancet and workers and apprentices had to demonstrate protection when collecting their livrets. In 1810 and again in 1834 vaccination was required of university students.[49] The military was in principle required to vaccinate at various times, in 1804 and during the thirties, forties, seventies and eighties, but practice was imperfect.[50] In 1874, the Roussel law required vac-

---

[46] Thomas, "The Old Poor Law and Medicine," p. 13; James Van Horn Melton, *Absolutism and the Eighteenth-Century Origins of Compulsory Schooling in Prussia and Austria* (Cambridge, 1988), ch. 7; *Hansard*, 1877, v. 235, cols. 749–50; 1893, v. 17, col. 100; William Tebb, *Compulsory Vaccination in England: With Incidental References to Foreign States* (London, 1884), p. 63.

[47] *Cobbett's*, 1808, v. 11, cols. 842–43; *Public Health*, 15 (1902–03), pp. 599–600.

[48] *PP* 1893–94 (412) lxxiii, p. 485; R. M. MacLeod, "Law, Medicine and Public Opinion: The Resistance to Compulsory Health Legislation 1870–1907," *Public Law* (Summer/Autumn 1967), p. 209; Tebb, *Compulsory Vaccination in England*, pp. 12, 16; *Annales*, 3/43 (1900), p. 172; *Revue d'hygiène et de police sanitaire*, 21 (1899), p. 1055; *BMJ* (1 September 1888), p. 502; *Eira*, 23, 11 (15 June 1889), p. 335.

[49] *Bulletin sur la vaccine*, 9 (July 1811); 2 (December 1810); 4 (February 1811) in *Collection des bulletins sur la vaccine*; Darmon, *La longue traque de la variole*, pp. 203–04; Borne, *Vaccination et revaccinations obligatoires*, pp. 29, 39, 48–49; *Annales*, 3/50, 3 (July 1903), p. 258.

[50] *Annales*, 3/5 (1881), p. 326; 3/50, 3 (July 1903), p. 259; *Bulletin*, 3rd ser., 23 (1890), p. 396; *La revue scientifique de la France et de l'étranger*, 47 (1891), p. 303; Henri Monod, *La santé publique* (Paris, 1904), p.

cination of women caring for infants as well as their charges. In the Liouville bill of 1881 revaccination would have been required as a condition of public assistance, enlistment, immatriculation and civil service employment. In fact, however, matters were less simple. Well into the eighties, parents' resistance prevented the vaccination of pupils and the requirement had to be nailed fast repeatedly. Individual employers began, in the absence of any parliamentary will to introduce a general compulsion, to require the lancet of their workers.[51]

The Swedes reversed matters, introducing a general compulsion, in 1816, before requiring specific groups to vaccinate. While this movement from the universal to the particular was theoretically illogical, it appears to have been ineffective enforcement of the general law that encouraged the authorities to target particular groups. In 1833, for example, the multitude of parents refusing to vaccinate prompted measures that betrayed the authorities' frustration. The 1816 law was now more firmly to seek its aim by having its precepts read aloud in church, lists of the unvaccinated were to be annotated with the measures to be taken against recalcitrants as well as testimony to the vaccinator's performance and fines could be imposed on those who had neglected their duties. In 1853, vaccination was required for enrollment in school.[52]

The next stage was to require vaccination of all children and sometimes adults as well. Although the home of vaccination, Britain was slower and more hesitant than other nations in adopting such preventive obligations. In part, the problem was that, inoculation being widespread, physicians with vested interests in the old technique worked to delay the new and had the advantages of familiarity on their side. As vaccination was increasingly being required on the continent, Jenner was still fighting for recognition that his procedure was an advantage at all. The

53; Biraben, "La diffusion de la vaccination," p. 274; Darmon, *La longue traque de la variole*, p. 368; Lemaire, *Napoléon et la médecine*, p. 243; Friedrich Prinzing, *Epidemics Resulting from Wars* (Oxford, 1916), p. 200.

[51] *JO*, 1881, Chambre, Doc., p. 137; *JO*, Chambre, Débats, 8 March 1881, p. 438; *Annales*, 3/50, 3 (July 1903), p. 259–60; Monod, *La santé publique*, p. 53; *Recueil*, 21 (1891), pp. 289–90; Paul Strauss and Alfred Fillassier, *Loi sur la protection de la santé publique (Loi du 15 Février 1902)* (2nd edn.; Paris, 1905), p. 252; *Bulletin*, 3, 25 (1891), p. 240; *Annales*, 3/26 (1891), p. 174.

[52] *Kongl. Medicinalstyrelsens underdåniga skrifvelse den 8 Juni 1894*, p. 6; *SFS*, 1853/67, §2; *Hygiea*, 56, 11 (November 1894), p. 497. The preliminary versions also required vaccination for marriage: "Kongl. Sundhets-Collegii till Kongl. Maj:t inlemnade underdåniga förslag till förnyadt Nådigt Reglemente för skyddskoppympningen i Riket," (15 April) 1852, copy in Statistiska Centralbyrån, Biblioteket, Kongl. Sundhets Collegii Samlingar, v. 1; *Förhandlingar*, 1871, p. 135, 143–45; 1872, p. 321; *Betänkande angående skyddskoppympningens ordnande enligt nådig befallning avgivet av Medicinalstyrelsen jämte särskilt tillkallade sakkunniga* (Stockholm, 1913), pp. 48–53; *Bihang*, 1915, Särskilda utskotts nr. 1 utlåtande nr. 2, p. 58; Prop. 1915:78, pp. 7–8.

lower classes in particular preferred inoculation to vaccination. Another
issue was that, as in Sweden, vaccination was at first performed by a
motley assortment of lay practitioners whose technical inadequacies
brought the procedure into more disrepute than on the continent, where
only trained medical personnel wielded the lancet.[53] Means of enlight-
ening and encouraging the public to vaccinate were the substance of
early discussions in Parliament, while compulsion was regarded as ill
suited to British traditions and sensibilities. Nonetheless, the inability of
merely voluntary measures to protect sufficiently was becoming increasingly obvious. Early in the century proposals were made to restrict and
regulate inoculation, prohibit parents from taking ill and unvaccinated
children into public and isolate inoculated patients in government-pro-
vided dwellings when private accommodation was unavailable.[54] In
1807, the Royal College of Physicians weighed in solidly behind vaccination, sought to protect the poor gratis and recommended restrictions
on the inoculated to prevent them from transmitting disease. Attempts
during the 1810s to limit the free movement of the inoculated came to
naught when it was argued that thus exposing others to danger was
already an offense in common law. A celebrated case of a mother convicted for exposing her inoculated child in public, infecting eleven and
killing eight, made it seem as though common law would in fact be used
to restrict inoculation. But, by the 1820s, this incident remained the only
use of such powers and, in any case, propagating smallpox was only a
misdemeanor and no laws directly prohibited inoculation.[55] As the gap
between British inaction and the compulsory measures gradually being
introduced elsewhere during the 1820s began to widen, the voices urging
the adoption of continental-style measures (prohibiting inoculation, regulating and eventually requiring vaccination) became more insistent. In
1838, the Provincial Medical and Surgical Association, forerunner of the
British Medical Association, petitioned Parliament to forbid untrained
personnel from inoculating and in 1840 the law on extending vaccination finally made inoculation a misdemeanor, subject to jail sentences up
to one month. In 1867, the prohibition of inoculation was reinforced by
criminalizing behavior liable to spread smallpox.[56]

---

[53] *Cobbett's*, 1806, v. 7, cols. 879, 893; Dixon, *Smallpox*, pp. 277–78; *PP* 1807 (14) ii, p. 62; *Hansard*, 1840, v. 54, cols. 1256–60; J. R. Smith, *Speckled Monster*, ch. 5.
[54] *Cobbett's*, 1806, v. 7, cols. 881–82, 886–87; *PP* 1808 (287) i, p. 645; *PP* 1813–14 (243) xii, pp. 375–76.
[55] *PP* 1807 (14) ii, pp. 57–61; *Hansard*, 1815, v. 31, cols. 183–84; Cross, *History of the Variolous Epidemic*, pp. 218–19; *Edinburgh Journal of Medical Science*, 1 (1826), pp. 282–84.
[56] Cross, *History of the Variolous Epidemic*, pp. 24–26; *Edinburgh Journal of Medical Science*, 1 (1826),

Prohibiting inoculation was a far step from requiring vaccination, however, and in this respect the government remained passive, despite increasingly insistent calls for compulsory measures by midcentury. Officers of Health were instructed in 1851 to seek out and attempt to ensure vaccination of the unprotected during epidemics. In 1859 the Epidemiological Society came out strongly in favor of requiring the lancet.[57] The state of vaccination and the corresponding smallpox mortality in Britain was deplorable compared to the continent, it argued, and compulsion the only solution.[58] The same year, Lyttleton's private member's bill in the Lords put the first measures for compulsion up for discussion, requiring parents to have children protected at public vaccination stations within three months of birth unless otherwise dealt with by a private physician. If the child was ill, a delay of two months was permitted. Certificates of vaccination were to be forwarded to the Registrar of births and deaths who, in turn, was to send notice of their obligation to act to new parents. Despite some objections in the Commons to the principle of compulsion this passed.[59]

While far-reaching in intent, the 1853 law failed to live up to its ambitions. Because the Poor Law Board remained the administrator, prejudice against the lancet was not dispelled among the lower classes who were still convinced that, official assurances to the contrary, by taking their children to public vaccinators they were receiving parish relief. Enforcement of its provisions remained lax and the recording and notification clauses were ineffective. Vaccinators, not paid to do so, often did not transmit copies of their certificates to the Registrar and, in any case, the lack of compulsory registration of births in England and Wales (unlike Scotland and Ireland) made any system of recording incidence a rough estimate at best.[60] Because of such limitations, reforms were attempted. Already the following year a bill sought unsuccessfully to shift control of vaccination to the General Board of Health, requiring it of all adults within three months and all who entered Britain to reside there, with the authorities empowered to levy fines in negligent districts. When

pp. 282–84; *British and Foreign Medical Review*, 6 (1839), pp. 189–90; *Quarterly Review*, 33 (1826), p. 550; 3 & 4 Vict. c. 29, viii; Lambert, "A Victorian National Health Service," p. 251; W. M. Frazer, *A History of English Public Health 1834–1939* (London, 1950), p. 72; 30 & 31 Vict. c. 84, s. 32.

[57] C. Fraser Brockington, *Public Health in the Nineteenth Century* (Edinburgh, 1965), pp. 178–79; *PP* 1852–53 (434) ci, pp. 77ff.

[58] The extremes were posed in the contrast between Connaught in Ireland, with a smallpox mortality of 60/1000 for the ten years ending 1841, and Lombardy, with 1.5/1000: *Hansard*, 1853, v. 125, cols. 1003–04.

[59] *PP* 1852–53 (447) vii, pp. 473ff.; *Hansard*, 1853, v. 129, cols. 473–74; 16 & 17 Vict. c. 100.

[60] *PP* 1854–55 (88) xlv, 629; *PP* 1871 (246) xiii, 1, p. v; *Hansard*, 1871, v. 204, col. 229.

John Simon arrived as Medical Officer at the Board of Health he sought to plug holes in the 1853 law with a bill in 1856 that would have obliged all children to be vaccinated, giving the Guardians power to prosecute from the rates and authorizing the Board to inspect, approve vaccinators and establish qualifications of competency. Smallpox prophylaxis, however, now ran into the beginnings of the antivaccinationist movement, while the prospect of transferring administration to the Board provoked the ire of those opposed to its centralizing ambitions. The bill was withdrawn and a Select Committee appointed to inquire into the worth of vaccination itself, thus potentially calling into question the very practice whose enforcement was sought.[61]

Despite embracing it early and eagerly, the German states approached vaccination in various ways, being both among the first and the last to introduce compulsion. Hannover took the lead, conferring the first formal scientific recognition on Jenner by electing him in 1801 to Göttingen's Royal Academy of Sciences. Hessen was the first German state to institute compulsory vaccination, on 6 August 1807. Bavaria followed at the end of the same month, requiring as one of the many facets of Montgelas's reform program the protection of all children before age three.[62] In Erfurt, integrated into the Napoleonic Empire, compulsory vaccination of all unprotected children within three weeks was demanded by the French occupiers in November 1807. By edicts of 1821 and 1839 Hannover required all subjects to have their children vaccinated and similar measures were instituted in Baden.[63] In Hamburg, in contrast, voluntary methods and limited forms of indirect compulsion held sway for decades and not until the Franco-Prussian war did the city tack in a different direction. After soldiers returning in 1871 sparked the severest epidemic of the century, a law allowing compulsory vaccination

---

[61] *PP* 1854–55 (252) vi, 349; *PP* 1854–55 (88) xlv, 629; *PP* 1856 (218) vi, p. 527; *Hansard*, 1856, v. 143, cols. 549–53; Lambert, "A Victorian National Health Service," p. 256.

[62] Charles Creighton, *Jenner and Vaccination: A Strange Chapter of Medical History* (London, 1889), pp. 205–06; Rupp, "Entwicklung der Impfgesetzgebung in Hessen," p. 110; *Jahrbuch der Staatsarzneikunde*, 1 (1808), pp. 109–21; Giel, *Schutzpocken-Impfung in Bayern*, pp. 96–103; Stickl, "Zur Entwicklung der Schutzimpfung," p. 76; M. E. v. Bulmerincq, *Das Gesetz der Schutzpocken-Impfung im Königreiche Bayern, in seinen Folgen und seiner Bedeutung für andere Staaten* (Leipzig, 1862), pp. vi–vii; M. E. von Bulmerincq, *Ergebnisse des Bayerischen Impfgesetzes* (Munich, 1867), p. 6; *JO*, Chambre, Doc., 18 Feb. 1881, p. 136.

[63] H. R. Abe, "Aus der Frühgeschichte der deutschen Impfgesetzgebung," *Zeitschrift für die gesamte Hygiene und ihre Grenzgebiete*, 26, 5 (May 1980), p. 373; H. R. Abe, "Die Einführung der ersten obligatorischen Pockenschutzimpfung auf dem Boden der heutigen DDR," in J. Antall et al., eds., *Acta Congressus Internationalis XXIV Historiae Artis Medicinae* (Budapest, 1976), v. I, pp. 343–44; *PP* 1852–53 (434) ci, 77, pp. 54–57; Francisca Loetz, *Vom Kranken zum Patienten: "Medikalisierung" und medizinische Vergesellschaftung am Beispiel Badens 1750–1850* (Stuttgart, 1993), pp. 162–63.

of all inhabitants quickly passed the following year. Similarly laissez-faire conditions prevailed in the Grand Duchy of Oldenburg where, according to an ordinance of 1819, children were to be vaccinated, but, if parents refused, no more drastic consequences were threatened than reserving the right to adopt more stringent measures. Fines followed the failure to report cases of smallpox, but not for refusing the lancet. In Saxony during the 1840s compulsion under threat of fines was allowed only in certain exceptional cases and the rule remained that vaccination was voluntary.[64]

Prussia, belying its omni-interventionist reputation, remained even more of a laggard than Hamburg. Although it had instituted various means of encouragement and indirect compulsion, obligatory vaccination was introduced only by the Imperial law of 1874.[65] Enthusiasm for the lancet was lukewarm at first, public opinion in Berlin uninspired by the new technique. Marcus Herz, a prominent local physician, lent his authority to the opponents.[66] The government did little, compared to other German states, to support or encourage the practice. In July 1801, parents in Silesia were exhorted to have their children vaccinated and medical men asked to lend their support. But later that month a circular reined in such initial enthusiasms.[67] Vaccination was to be performed only by physicians and, in any case, more information collected before commitments were undertaken. Except when faced with an epidemic, parents should not be encouraged to vaccinate their children since the effects were not yet fully understood and the consequences unclear. The following year, however, cautiously favorable information had persuaded

[64] Albert Wulff, ed., *Hamburgische Gesetze und Verordnungen* (2nd edn.; Hamburg, 1903), v. II, p. 382; Prinzing, *Epidemics Resulting from Wars*, p. 239; Voigt, *Jahrhundert der Schutzimpfung*, pp. 7, 18, 44; Richard J. Evans, *Death in Hamburg: Society and Politics in the Cholera Years 1830–1910* (Oxford, 1987), pp. 221–25; *PP* 1852–53 (434) ci, p. 130; *Blattern und Schutzpockenimpfung*, pp. 54–55; *Zeitschrift des K. Sächsischen statistischen Bureaus*, 22 (1876), p. 208.

[65] Gerard Kearns et al., "The Interaction of Political and Economic Factors in the Management of Urban Public Health," in Nelson and Rogers, *Urbanisation and the Epidemiologic Transition*, p. 30; *SB*, 1874, v. 3, Akst. 7; *Blattern und Schutzpockenimpfung*, p. 51. But see also Jürgen Stein, "Die Pockenvakzination in Preussen bis zum Reichsimpfgesetz von 1874 unter besonderer Berücksichtigung des Regierungsbezirkes Frankfurt (Oder)," *Zeitschrift für ärztliche Fortbildung*, 81 (1987), pp. 1081–83.

[66] *D. Marcus Herz an den D. Dohmeyer, Leibarzt des Prinzen August von England über die Brutalimpfung und deren Vergleichung mit der humanen* (2nd edn.; Berlin, 1801), pp. ix–xii; Ragnhild Münch, *Gesundheitswesen im 18. und 19. Jahrhundert: Das Berliner Beispiel* (Berlin, 1995), pp. 230–32. Herz, who was Jewish, allegedly considered vaccination a reprehensible Christian doctrine: Moore, *History and Practice of Vaccination*, pp. 243–45.

[67] Bohn, *Handbuch der Vaccination*, pp. 127–28; Kaiserliches Gesundheitsamt, *Beiträge zur Beurtheilung*, p. 100; Creighton, *Jenner and Vaccination*, pp. 222–23; Augustin, *Preussische Medicinalverfassung*, v. I, pp. 174–75; v. II, pp. 614–17.

the authorities to warm to the new technique. Another circular obliged physicians to recommend vaccination, persuading parents to abandon inoculation. In 1803, vaccination celebrated another incremental victory when inoculation was forbidden except when expressly requested by parents (and then only during epidemics) and when the inoculated could be fully isolated under police supervision.[68] At the beginning of 1810, when an epidemic struck Berlin, the inhabitants were exhorted to be vaccinated. Later that year, the Prussians tried a limited form of compulsion, requiring the lancet for the yet unprotected, but only when and where an epidemic struck.[69]

In 1812, when infected foreign troops passed through Germany without occasioning an epidemic and this happy outcome was attributed to the increasing prevalence of vaccination, the technique seemed firmly in the saddle of official favor. The road was clear for Prussia to join the other German states with compulsion when in 1825 the pertinent ministry held out the possibility of an administrative regulation to this effect. Two years later, the authorities of Trier accepted this invitation. The entire population was to be registered for these purposes, and a physician appointed for each 15,000 citizens to vaccinate gratis. Resisting parents would face the full force of persuasive authority, with local officials, the pastor and possibly the district magistrate seeking to change their minds. In default, fines and jail sentences of up to five days might ensue. Already in 1829, however, Berlin changed position, ending the possibility of compulsion. Matters were then arranged as definitively as they would be until unification by the contagious disease regulation of 1835. This encouraged vaccination, enlisting the support of civil servants, but did not include any legal requirement except during epidemics for the potentially infectious inhabitants of stricken dwellings and, if the disease spread, possibly for others as well. During nonepidemic times, only the parents of the unvaccinated whose children fell ill could be fined. Before 1874, in other words, there was no general legal compulsion to vaccinate in Prussia and, during healthy times, no punishments for neglect of the lancet.[70]

[68] Philipp Hunold, *Annalen der Kuhpocken-Impfung zur Verbannung der Blattern* (Fürth, 1801–02), pp. 88–95, 351–56; Augustin, *Preussische Medicinalverfassung*, v. I, pp. 174–75, 611–12, 614–17.

[69] Augustin, *Preussische Medicinalverfassung*, v. I, p. 622; v. II, pp. 622–3; *Blattern und Schutzpockenimpfung*, p. 52; Claudia Huerkamp, "The History of Smallpox Vaccination in Germany: A First Step in the Medicalization of the General Public," *Journal of Contemporary History*, 20 (1985), p. 624; Rupp, "Die Entwicklung der Impfgesetzgebung in Hessen," p. 115.

[70] Augustin, *Preussische Medicinalverfassung*, v. I, pp. 625–26; Kaiserliches Gesundheitsamt, *Beiträge zur Beurtheilung*, pp. 105–07; *DZSA*, 15 (1828), pp. 237–58; *Blattern und Schutzpockenimpfung*, pp. 52–53;

The very diversity of German approaches helped push these states in the direction of compulsion. Those (Württemberg, Bavaria and Hessen) with a general requirement weathered the disease far better than others. Already during the 1820s, calls for an all-German obligation to undergo the lancet were heard as vaccinating states found their efforts undermined by the continuous import of disease from free-riding neighbors.[71] But for Germany as a whole, as for Hamburg, it was the epidemic of 1870–72, following the Franco-Prussian war, that finally prompted new legislation. Smallpox may have been spread by French POWs, many of whom were imprisoned at Spandau, there providing (partly because 10 percent of the French army was African) curious Berliners with a goal for their Sunday perambulations, from which, after bartering with the captives, they returned with more than just exotic impressions.[72] Wartime patterns of smallpox dissemination testified to the virtues of vaccination, encouraging efforts to extend protection to the entire population. The thoroughly protected German army suffered but a tiny fraction of the deaths of the French, the military endured much less than civilians and, among the instructive comparisons adduced by proponents of the lancet, Bavaria, with its comparatively well-vaccinated population, had proportionally one-quarter the smallpox mortality of ill-vaccinated Berlin. With such examples goading it along, the Reichstag passed a general law in 1874 requiring vaccination and revaccination, free of charge at public institutions: every infant before the end of the calendar year following its birth and every schoolchild again within five years of age twelve.[73]

Following a route that reversed German developments, the Swedes passed their first compulsory law early. In 1816 all children were to be protected before age two, with fines for recalcitrant parents and a requirement subjecting all unvaccinated during epidemics to the lancet.[74] After this initial burst of activity, however, matters were left to vegetate for the

Frevert, *Krankheit als politisches Problem*, p. 73; *Gesetz-Sammlung*, 1835, 27/1678, §§54–55; *BMJ* (13 February 1904), pp. 378–79.

[71] *Zeitschrift für die Staatsarzneikunde* (1821), pp. 23–26; v. Bulmerincq, *Gesetz der Schutzpocken-Impfung*, pp. vi–vii, 2; *SB*, 18 February 1874, p. 103.

[72] Oskar Matzel, *Die Pocken im Deutsch–Französischen Krieg 1870/71* (Düsseldorf, 1977), pp. 7–8, 34–36; Prinzing, *Epidemics Resulting from Wars*, ch. 8. But see also Lentz and Gins, *Handbuch der Pockenbekämpfung*, pp. 199–200.

[73] *DVöG*, 20 (1888), p. 94; G. Jochmann, *Pocken und Vaccinationslehre* (Vienna, 1913), pp. 165–66; *SB*, 23 April 1873, p. 286; *SB*, 1874, v. 3, Akst. 7.

[74] "Kongl. Maj:ts Nådiga Reglemente För Vaccinationen i Riket," 6 March 1816, and "Kongl. Maj:ts Nådiga Förordning, Om Hwad, i händelse af yppad Koppsmitta iakttagas bör," 11 December 1816, *Kongl. Förordningar*, 1816.

better part of a century. The French, in turn, were enthusiastic vaccinators abroad, laggards at home. The first place anywhere to require vaccination of its citizens was the small Apennine principality of Piombino and Lucca, ruled by Elisa, the Imperial sister and a strong adherent of the lancet. All children unscarred by smallpox were required in 1806 to be vaccinated and all future infants within two months of birth.[75] At home, however, the French did not legislate a general compulsion until a century later. The patchwork of various indirect and local requirements satisfied the authorities that, despite the absence of a general law, vaccination was, in practical terms, widespread. The technique, in the self-satisfied conclusion of the pertinent authorities at the beginning of the nineteenth century, had made more rapid progress than elsewhere in Europe, thus gradually becoming "so to speak universal."[76] An aversion to compulsion continued throughout the smorgasbord of subsequent regimes. Whether during the Napoleonic period, the Restoration, the July Monarchy or the Second Empire, the central government did little more than exhort its prefects to encourage vaccination, continuing the usual indirect forms of compulsion. At midcentury, for example, the poor were still required to vaccinate as a condition of public assistance and they were also given pecuniary rewards for protecting their children.[77] Reform proposals tended to be of a voluntaristic bent, at best seeking to employ indirect requirements. A typical specimen would have insisted on vaccination for all hospital admissions. Others, during the late Second Empire, specifically eschewed the introduction of a general legal requirement.[78]

The lag between France's hands-off approach and the course charted by its neighbors, even the allegedly so liberalist British, became increasingly stark and lamented during the latter half of the century.[79] There was more legislation, as one report complained in 1881, dealing with the spread of animal diseases than those of humans. Nor had proposals for compulsion been absent. The Academy of Medicine had spoken in its favor in the 1840s and a deputy unsuccessfully introduced a bill to this

---

[75] *BMJ* (2 June 1906), pp. 1297–98; Gins, *Krankheit wider den Tod*, p. 23; *Jahrbuch der Staatsarzneikunde*, 1 (1808), pp. 121–23.

[76] AN, F[8] 99/1, Ministère de l'Intérieur, Société centrale de vaccine, no. 3870; Borne, *Vaccination et revaccinations obligatoires*, p. 35.

[77] *Moniteur universel*, 173 (21 June 1832), p. 1361; 125 (5 May 1842), p. 1009.

[78] *L'union médicale*, 7, 120 (8 October 1853), pp. 473–74; *Moniteur universel*, 80 (21 March 1866), p. 343; 142 (22 May 1867), p. 608; 172 (20 June 1868), p. 887; *Recueil*, 2 (1873), pp. 159–62.

[79] *Bulletin de la Société de médecine publique et d'hygiène professionnelle*, 1 (1877), pp. 234–47; 2 (1879), pp. 102–07, 150–64; Ch.-Ch. Steinbrenner, *Traité sur la vaccine* (Paris, 1846), pp. 698–719; *L'union médicale*, 7, 62 (26 May 1853), pp. 245–46; *Annales*, 3/5 (1881), pp. 33–34; 3/50, 3 (July 1903), p. 250; E. Monteils, *Histoire de la vaccination* (Paris, 1874), pp. 269–70, 277.

effect during the last years of the Second Empire.[80] As across the Rhine, the Franco-Prussian war and the disparity of the two warring armies' epidemiological fates began to concentrate French minds wonderfully. Although also vaccinated, their military had lost over 23,000 to smallpox, while the Germans suffered under 500 casualties. The unprotected state of the civilian population had apparently endangered the soldiers and the conclusion followed that it too should be subject to precautions. Compared to the prompt German response, however, the results were meager. The Third Republic's early governments saw little reason to change the hands-off approach taken by every previous administration, at least since the first Napoleon. Public health officials were issued no tools more effective than exhorting local mayors to provide citizens the opportunity to be vaccinated if they so desired.[81] With the stabilization of the Republic, however, matters changed and the Consultative Committee came out in the 1880s in favor of following the example of its neighbor. On this basis, Liouville introduced a bill that would have introduced the strictest vaccination regimen anywhere, requiring the lancet of infants before six months and revaccination every decade from ages ten to fifty. The parliamentary commission, however, reined in these prophylactic animal spirits, extending the period for vaccination to one year (six months in times of epidemic) and limiting revaccination to once before age twenty-one. Liouville's bill passed in the Chamber by a wide margin, but in the Senate the best once again proved to be the enemy of the better and it disappeared amidst calls for legislation that would deal with public hygiene in a broad sense, not just vaccination.[82]

By the tail of the century, the problem was no longer the requisite expert backing, but official lethargy. The Academy of Medicine and most medical organizations were solidly in line behind compulsion by the 1880s and early nineties. The authorities, however, were hampered by the vagaries of the French parliamentary mechanism and, while several bills were introduced, none emerged as a law.[83] Only in 1902 with

[80] *JO*, Chambre, Doc., 18 Feb. 1881, p. 136; *PP* 1852–53 (434) ci, 77, p. 52; Weisz, *Medical Mandarins*, p. 92; Monteils, *Histoire de la vaccination*, pp. 285–86.

[81] *Bulletin*, 3/23 (1890), pp. 395–97; Paul Strauss, *La croisade sanitaire* (Paris, 1902), p. 31; *JO*, Chambre, Débats, 8 March 1881, p. 439; *La revue scientifique de la France et de l'etranger*, 47 (1891), pp. 303–07; *Annales*, 3/5 (1881), p. 570.

[82] *Recueil*, 10 (1881), pp. 266–72; *Annales*, 3/2 (1879), pp. 158–59; *JO*, 1881, Chambre, Doc., pp. 136–37; Chambre, Débats, 8 March 1881, pp. 437–38; *Annales*, 3/50, 3 (July 1903), p. 259.

[83] *Bulletin* 2/10 (1881), pp. 554–70; *JO*, Chambre, Débats, 8 March 1881, pp. 441–42; *Journal d'hygiène*, 16, 15, no. 713 (22 May 1890), p. 241; *Recueil*, 21 (1891), pp. 64, 413–14; Darmon, *La longue traque de la variole*, p. 382; Paul Brouardel, *La profession médicale au commencement du XXe siècle* (Paris, 1903), p. 172; Borne, *Vaccination et revaccinations obligatoires*, p. 51; *Annales*, 3/50, 3 (July 1903), p. 260.

the passage of the law on public hygiene did compulsory vaccination make it on the books. Here, buried amidst a sprawling legislative conglomerate that sought to bring France into proximity of its more advanced neighbors along the whole gamut of public health, was a single article that required vaccination by one, followed by two rounds of revaccination at ages eleven and twenty-one.[84] Although late, vaccination in this version was among the strictest in any nation. At the same time, the practical administrative circumstances of its introduction were not propitious. The fines for default were moderate by comparison with those threatened in Germany and, earlier, in Britain.[85] Despite regulations from Paris, the machinery of vaccination remained rudimentary in many departments, with some large communes undertaking none at all. Because local mayors had been entrusted with the prosecution of recalcitrants, enforcement was often lax.[86] In response to such inadequacies, various localities took more drastic measures without thereby improving the general state of affairs across the nation. During the epidemic of 1913, for example, the authorities of Marseilles dispatched teams of lancet-wielders into working-class neighborhoods, vaccinating more than 90,000 people in the streets, in laundries, rag storehouses, the municipal heating plant, flophouses, not forgetting 263 who were punctured in cinemas. During the First World War, remedies were sought by allowing, in emergencies, the vaccination or revaccination of all who had not been protected within the last five years.[87] Not until midcentury could the system be considered well functioning.[88]

DIRECT COMPULSION AND REPEATED PROSECUTIONS

A general compulsion could be accomplished either directly or mediately; vaccination might be actually enforced or the authorities could remain content with punishing nonvaccination. In the German states, attempts were made to give fines and other punishments for defaulters

---

[84] *JO*, 34, 49 (19 February 1902), p. 1173; renewed by the CSP in 1953, art. L 5.

[85] The 1902 law foresaw fines of 1 to 5 francs, while the German law of 1874 had penalties up to 62 francs (50 Marks) and the British 1853 law's maximum fines of 5 pounds were the equivalent of 125 francs: *Annales*, 3/50, 3 (July 1903), p. 248; Monteils, *Histoire de la vaccination*, p. 277.

[86] *Bulletin*, 3/49 (1903), pp. 132, 141; 3/57 (1907), p. 411; *Annales*, 4/24 (1915), p. 28.

[87] Darmon, *La longue traque de la variole*, pp. 403–04; *JO*, 1915, p. 6321; 1918, p. 5678; *JO*, Chambre, Débats, 1915, p. 129, 843; *JO*, Sénat, Débats, 1915, p. 496; *Annales*, 4/24 (1915), pp. 192–200; Léon Bernard, *La défense de la santé publique pendant la guerre* (Paris, 1929), ch. 11. This was renewed in a decree of 12 August 1966.

[88] André Latrille, *Les difficultés d'application de la loi du 15 février 1902 relative à la protection de la santé publique* (Bordeaux, 1944), pp. 124–25.

sufficient bite to ensure eventual compliance. In Würzburg defaulting
parents were threatened with fines or jail on bread and water for those
too poor to pay. In Hessen, fines were doubled if children remained
unvaccinated longer than a year. In the Bavarian law of 1807 a graded
scale of fines, increasing for each year of default, although exempting
paupers, encouraged compliance. As of 1811, parents of unvaccinated
pupils were fined at triple the earlier rate and the children excluded from
school.[89] In the Swedish vaccination law of 1816, defaulting parents were
fined, the sums doubling if they resisted during epidemics, with jail for
those unable to pay.[90] The Napoleonic law of 1806 requiring vaccination in Piombino and Lucca foresaw fines or a fortnight in jail for defaulting parents. During the early years of the century, French prefects often
took their responsibilities with draconian seriousness, some taking coercive measures against recalcitrant heads of families and guardians, in
other cases sequestering the unvaccinated ill in their homes, requiring
them to pay the costs of such measures to boot. In Liouville's bill of 1881
an element of public shame was to add punch to enforcement: recidi-
vists risked, at their own expense, having their names posted on the town
hall door. The 1902 law invoked the penal code for neglect of vaccination.[91] The British vaccination act of 1853, though threatening fines, in
fact had little bite. There was no official specifically charged with execution or proceeding against offenders and local authorities had no means
of financing prosecutions.[92] Matters improved somewhat when the 1858
Public Health Act, shifting certain responsibilities to the Privy Council,
provided for such costs. In response to the beginnings of the antivaccination movement, more effective tools of enforcement were provided in
1861 when the Guardians or overseers were permitted to appoint an
officer to proceed against defaulting parents, defraying their expenses
from the poor rates. In 1867 Guardians were required to investigate cases
of infants remaining unvaccinated and prosecute recalcitrant parents.[93]

[89] Giel, *Schutzpocken-Impfung in Bayern*, pp. 136–38, 157–58; *Annalen für die gesammte Heilkunde* (1827),
p. 17; Rupp, "Die Entwicklung der Impfgesetzgebung in Hessen," p. 110; Bohn, *Handbuch der
Vaccination*, p. 130; *Jahrbuch der Staatsarzneikunde*, 1 (1808), pp. 109–21.

[90] "Kongl. Maj:ts Nådiga Reglemente För Vaccinationen i Riket," 6 March 1816, §14, and
"Kongl. Maj:ts Nådiga Förordning, Om Hwad, i händelse af yppad Koppsmitta iakttagas bör," 11
December 1816, *Kongl. Förordningar*, 1816; *SFS*, 1853/67, kap. 6.

[91] *Jahrbuch der Staatsarzneikunde*, 1 (1808), pp. 121–23; *Annales*, 3/50, 3 (July 1903), pp. 257–58; *JO*,
1881, Chambre, Doc., p. 137; *JO*, 34, 49 (19 February 1902), p. 1176.

[92] 16 & 17 Vict. c. 100, ix; *Hansard*, 1853, v. 125, cols. 1008–09; 1856, v. 143, cols. 549–53; *PP*
1854–55 (88) xlv, p. 629; Lambert, "A Victorian National Health Service," p. 254.

[93] 21 & 22 Vict. c. 97; *Hansard*, 1859, v. 153, col. 37; 24 & 25 Vict. c. 59; *Hansard*, 1861, v. 164, col.
674; *BMJ* (3 July 1880), p. 3; *PP* 1864 (18) l, p. 599; 30 & 31 Vict. c. 84, ss. 27, 31.

More immediately and drastically, children and others could directly be taken and forcibly vaccinated. Such an approach, though obviously effective, was used only exceptionally. In Sweden, a prominent antivaccinator claimed to have succumbed when presented with the choice of allowing his child to be vaccinated or having it done by force. Even if true, this appears to have been an isolated case without backing in the applicable legislation.[94] In Britain direct force was also not used.[95] The Select Committee of 1871 specifically rejected direct compulsion, arguing that, without the support of public opinion, allowing policemen to take children from parents to the vaccination station was out of the question. Very few Britons were willing to grant the state such powers and the authorities never seriously proposed measures of this ilk.[96] Nonetheless, vaccination was sometimes enforced in a manner that approximated direct force. In the 1870s and eighties, the Local Government Board instructed vaccination officers to visit stricken localities and, personally identifying the unprotected, to employ the utmost exertion to have them vaccinated. They were to inquire house to house and, in tenements, room to room. To the parents of unprotected children notice should be given requiring the lancet within a specified period, generally less than twenty-four hours, with the officers returning to ensure compliance.[97] Nor in France does direct compulsion appear to have been used, except under Napoleonic laws for the benefit of subject peoples. The French occupiers of Erfurt decreed in 1807 that vaccination would be carried out against defaulters compulsorily ("mit Gewalt und durch militärische Exekution") by a physician accompanied by constables. Just how seriously the French authorities took these matters may be judged by their proclamation requiring the vaccination of all minors within

[94] V. Vallberg, *Böra vi tvingas att låta vaccinera våra barn?* (Stockholm, 1910), pp. 5–6; Sköld, *Two Faces of Smallpox*, p. 459. However, during discussions of the 1897 bill on compulsory vaccination and revaccination, the requirement for school children to be vaccinated was discussed in terms that made it sound as though those who had not been vaccinated before attending school might simply be brought by suitable means to be so: *Bihang*, Prop. 1897:4, p. 23. Similarly, health authorities were instructed personally to supervise ("själv övervaka") that unvaccinated school children in fact underwent the lancet ("befordras till skyddskoppympning").

[95] John C. McVail, *Half a Century of Small-Pox and Vaccination* (Edinburgh, n.d. [1919]), p. 27; Edwardes, *Concise History of Small-Pox*, p. 134; *Hansard*, 1883, v. 280, col. 1042.

[96] *PP* 1871 (246) xiii, 1, p. iv; *Hansard*, 1872, v. 212, col. 933; 1877, v. 235, col. 738; 1878, v. 239, col. 493; *Final Report of the Royal Commission Appointed to Inquire into the Subject of Vaccination* (C.-8270) (London, 1896), sect. 510.

[97] Danby P. Fry, *The Law Relating to Vaccination* (6th edn.; London, 1875), pp. 168–71; PRO, MH 113/9, "Memorandum on the steps specially requisite to be taken in places where Small-Pox is prevalent."

fourteen days and threatening resisting parents with jail as "enemies of their children."[98]

Even in Germany such drastic intervention was not implemented with much consistency. In Hessen in 1807, children were forcibly brought before the authorities and vaccinated. In Prussia in 1826, soldiers could be vaccinated if necessary through the use of direct compulsion. The following year, the residents of Trier could be forcibly vaccinated during epidemics. In 1829, however, such direct compulsion was ended by instructions from Berlin and various other measures over the following years made it clear that a direct compulsion to vaccinate was not legal, even in times of epidemic.[99] In the 1835 Prussian regulation on contagious diseases, however, the tide changed. During epidemics, the unvaccinated were to undergo the lancet at once, if need be by means of force ("Zwangsimpfung"). In 1838 a decree determined that, in case of epidemics, defaulters could be arrested and children vaccinated even against the will of their parents and later court decisions upheld this interpretation of the 1835 regulation.[100]

The 1874 Imperial law vacillated between these various approaches to compulsion. The initial bill allowed the authorities to order the lancet for all residents of an infected area, enforcing this directly by taking to the vaccination station those who had no good cause to remain unprotected. In other cases it foresaw the usual array of fines and possible jail sentences (up to three days) for defaulting parents. During the Reichstag debates, however, objections were voiced to direct compulsion. Lasker argued that actually compelling vaccination might be possible for children, on the assumption that, their guardians having been neglectful, the state acted in loco parentis, but similar measures for adults were impossible. A special commission accepted such objections, admitting that calling vaccination compulsory had not been intended to convey more than that it was required and that enforcement would be ensured in the usual manner through fines and jail, not directly applied force. In the Reichstag, the nature of the punishments was then altered. A motion

[98] Abe, "Aus der Frühgeschichte der deutschen Impfgesetzgebung," p. 373; Abe, "Die Einführung der ersten obligatorischen Pockenschutzimpfung," pp. 343–44.

[99] Bohn, *Handbuch der Vaccination*, p. 130; *Gesetz-Sammlung*, 1826, 18/1039, p. 119; *DZSA*, 15 (1828), p. 251; Kaiserliches Gesundheitsamt, *Beiträge zur Beurtheilung*, pp. 107–08; *Blattern und Schutzpockenimpfung*, pp. 52–53.

[100] *Gesetz-Sammlung*, 1835, 27/1678, §55; Walter Lustig, *Zwangsuntersuchung und Zwangsbehandlung* (Munich, 1926), p. 26; Lentz and Gins, *Handbuch der Pockenbekämpfung*, pp. 505, 537; *DVöG*, 2 (1870), p. 416; *Blattern und Schutzpockenimpfung*, p. 84.

passed eliminating any mention of direct compulsion, instead threatening those who ignored official summons during epidemics with fines or
jail. In the third reading, attempts to limit the scope of obligation to the
young were rejected, but the entire paragraph was then eliminated by a
majority of one, removing the possibility of any particular compulsion
during times of epidemic.[101]

Finally, to bring a tortuous legislative journey to port, Windthorst's
motion that local procedure be superseded by the passage of Imperial
legislation was rejected in favor of allowing such measures to remain
in force during epidemics. Statutes like the 1835 Prussian regulation,
directly compelling vaccination during epidemics, thus continued even
though analogous provisions had been eliminated from the Imperial legislation.[102] Although Imperial law did not permit vaccinating children
with the aid of a policeman, such procedures remained legal in those
states, like Prussia and others, empowered to use force in the execution
of sanitary measures.[103] The Imperial Contagious Disease Law of 1900
did little to clarify such ambivalence, permitting local states with the requisite legislation to enforce protection against smallpox, while others were
left with the vague admonition to bring about widespread vaccination "in
an appropriate manner." Those parts of the Empire covered by the 1835
Prussian regulation were specifically instructed in 1904 to compel defaulters to vaccinate.[104] Well into the twentieth century, legal commentators
were still arguing both sides of the issue with equal fervor.[105]

---

[101] *SB*, 1874, v. 3, Akst. 7, §§14–15; *SB*, 9 March 1874, pp. 255–56, 260–61; *SB*, 14 March 1874, pp. 341, 348.

[102] *SB*, 14 March 1874, p. 357. Other states with similar provisions included ten Prussian prov-inces, Württemberg, Baden, Hessen, both Mecklenburgs, Sachsen-Weimar, Sachsen-Coburg-Gotha, Anhalt, Reuss jüngere Linie, Schaumburg Lippe, Lippe, Hamburg and Alsace-Lorraine: Kübler, *Geschichte der Pocken*, p. 327; Martin Kirchner, *Schutzpockenimpfung und Impfgesetz* (Berlin, 1911), pp. 38–39; Lentz and Gins, *Handbuch der Pockenbekämpfung*, pp. 540–43.

[103] *Blattern und Schutzpockenimpfung*, p. 84; Hermann Kastner, *Der Impfzwang und das Reichs-Impfgesetz vom 8. April 1874* (Berlin, 1909), p. 46; Schmedding and Engels, *Die Gesetze betreffend Bekämpfung über-tragbarer Krankheiten* (2nd edn.; Münster, 1929), pp. 196, 422; *SB*, 1888/89, Akst. 134, p. 863; Bernhard J. Stern, *Should We Be Vaccinated? A Survey of the Controversy in Its Historical and Scientific Aspects* (New York, 1927), p. 119.

[104] *Reichs-Gesetzblatt*, 1904, 9/3020, p. 92; Lentz and Gins, *Handbuch der Pockenbekämpfung*, p. 599.

[105] *Medizinalarchiv für das Deutsche Reich*, 2 (1911), pp. 177–79; *Über die Einführung einer Gewissensklausel in das Reichsimpfgesetz: Bericht über die Sitzung des Landesgesundheitsrats (Ausschuss für die Seuchenbekämpfung) vom 10 Oktober 1925* (Berlin, 1926), p. 106; Max von Seydel, *Bayerisches Staatsrecht* (Tübingen, 1913), v. II, p. 264; Kirchner, *Schutzpockenimpfung und Impfgesetz*, pp. 26, 34–35. The argument for the precedence of local legislation during epidemics was generally conceded, but for the legitimacy of employing direct compulsion during normal times controversy remained: H. Böing, *Schutzpocken-Impfung und Impfgesetz* (Berlin, 1911), p. 39; [Curt] Spohr, *Berichtigung der falschen Darstellung der Entstehungsgeschichte des Impfgesetzes* (Dortmund, 1911); *SB*, 1895–97, 12 March 1896, pp. 1397, 1403, 1405–06.

With exceptions, direct force was thus only sparingly applied and the leverage available to the authorities limited to the usual array of fines and possible jail sentences. Fines, however, could be employed to ensure compliance almost as effectively as direct compulsion. By prosecuting repeatedly, cumulating the fines and, in most cases, thus condemning the recalcitrant to bankruptcy and/or jail, objectors were placed before the unpleasantly Hobsonian choice of vaccinating their children or taking the drastic consequences.[106] The question of repeated prosecutions was to play a major role in most nations as the popular groundswell against vaccination began to rise and increasing numbers of parents proved willing to take up the gauntlet thrown down by the public health authorities. Whether repeated prosecutions for nonvaccination violated the principle of *ne bis in idem*, that one not be punished twice for the same crime, could be argued with equal conviction in both directions: that the delict of recalcitrance was a singular event, atoned for by payment of the requisite fine, which thus in effect became a tax on nonvaccination, or that it was a repeated offense, periodically committed anew as each deadline for vaccination passed and thereby justifying the authorities in their zeal to ensure compliance through repeated proceedings. Multiple prosecutions became the primary legal issue in the battle over compulsory vaccination. When the authorities in several nations eventually lost the opportunity to prosecute repeatedly, resistors could buy exemption from vaccination through payment of fines and the system became in effect voluntary.

In Britain in 1863 the first shots were fired in a battle that would stretch over the following decades. A parent had been convicted and fined for failure to vaccinate. When the child subsequently remained unprotected, the authorities brought renewed charges, only to be thwarted by the courts which now ruled that default was a single offense for which the father could not be twice convicted.[107] Vaccinators, however, were quick to remedy this check to their ambitions. In 1867, an act allowed the authorities to proceed against recalcitrant parents repeatedly for default, revoking the precedent set here by *Pilcher* v. *Stafford*. Parents were brought before a magistrate, who had absolute discretion whether to prosecute or

---

[106] The bitter joke among antivaccinators was that only the rich and the poor could avoid vaccinating their children, the former by paying the fines, the poor by working them off in jail, while the middle class was forced to comply: *SB*, 1895–97, 12 March 1896, p. 1406.

[107] *Pilcher* v. *Stafford*, 27 January 1864: *Final Report into the Subject of Vaccination*, sect. 96; *BMJ* (3 July 1880), p. 3; *Shaw's Manual of the Vaccination Law* (London, 1887), pp. 3–4.

not.[108] Penalties inflicted were not, however, for the failure to vaccinate, but for disobedience to the magistrate's order, which meant that punishment could include imprisonment. Moreover, a test case decided that disobedience was a criminal act and prisoners were therefore without claim to the more humane treatment accorded debtors.[109] Alternatively, when fines were not paid, defaulters' possessions could be sold to raise the necessary monies.[110] Whether recalcitrant parents were prosecuted thus depended both on the inclinations of the local magistrate and the approach taken by the Guardians of the Poor, hence varying widely. Although Guardians had been allowed since 1861 to appoint Medical Officers to enforce vaccination, few had actually done so. In 1871, the central authorities sought to end such local variation. Guardians were now obliged, not just permitted, to appoint a vaccination officer who, using information from the Registrar of births, sought out and ensured that children were vaccinated, prosecuting offenders. It was thus only in the seventies that the compulsion to vaccinate, though on the books as of 1853 and beefed up with repeated prosecutions since 1867, began to be efficiently enforced.[111]

In Germany the question of repeated prosecutions also varied locally. The Bavarian law of 1807, for example, foresaw fines repeated until vaccination had taken place, while the 1835 Prussian regulation said nothing to this effect. The Imperial law was ambiguous in making no specific provision for repeated prosecutions, but giving the authorities latitude to require vaccination within a certain time. The issue, therefore left to the courts, varied widely by locality.[112] Local magistrates had, on occasion, decided against multiple prosecutions and the Saxon supreme court of appeal in Dresden briefly, but not decisively, favored similar arguments during the late 1870s. Upon appeal or revision, such decisions were, however, overturned and, generally, the courts allowed repeated prose-

---

[108] 30 & 31 Vict. c. 84, s. 31; *Hansard*, 1866, v. 182, col. 1101. Even though repeated convictions were not spelled out explicitly in the law, their permissibility was confirmed by the Court of Queen's Bench in the case of *Allen* v. *Worthy*: *BMJ* (3 July 1880), p. 3; *Shaw's Manual of the Vaccination Law*, p. 6; *Final Report into the Subject of Vaccination*, sects. 100–01.

[109] Dixon, *Smallpox*, pp. 279–80. This meant, for example, that those thus jailed could not receive letters and slept on plank bedsteads: *Sanitary Record*, 8 (28 June 1878), p. 411.

[110] This was a new technique used in order not to gratify the wishes of antivaccinators to become jailed martyrs rather than mere debtors. Jail followed only when they had no goods left to meet the fines: *Sanitary Record*, 8 (25 January 1878), p. 59; 8 (14 June 1878), p. 380.

[111] 24 & 25 Vict. c. 59; 34 & 35 Vict. c. 98, s. 5; *First Report into the Subject of Vaccination*, QQ 322, 350, 477.

[112] Kastner, *Impfzwang und das Reichs-Impfgesetz*, p. 26; *Veröffentlichungen* (1893), pp. 647–49; *SB*, 1895–97, 12 March 1896, p. 1406; *SB*, 1909–11, Akst. 571, p. 2808; *Medizinalarchiv für das Deutsche Reich*, 2 (1911), p. 180; Kirchner, *Schutzpockenimpfung und Impfgesetz*, p. 34.

cutions.[113] In allegedly liberal Hamburg, defaulters were sentenced up to eight times. In Darmstadt, the unfortunate Herr Heyser was summoned monthly to vaccinate his children, duly convicted after each refusal. Never unambiguously decided, the issue remained one of contention and ongoing dispute.[114] In Sweden, proposals for what would become the first compulsory vaccination law, in 1816, foresaw fines for recalcitrant parents repeated for each year of neglect. The regulation itself seems to have left open the possibility of increasing and therefore repeated fines, but the language was unclear.[115] In 1828 enforcement was strengthened. Defaulting parents were reported and given another chance, but if results were still not forthcoming fines were doubled and eventually transformed into jail sentences. In 1853, repeated and increasing fines were clearly foreseen and testimony from the turn of the century indicates that resistors were multiply punished. The 1916 law on vaccination, in turn, foresaw the possibility of reporting recalcitrants to the central authorities, who could order repeated and higher fines than those foreseen in its letter.[116]

AN OPPOSITION ARISES

In each of these nations, movements opposed to compulsory vaccination, indeed sometimes to vaccination at all, arose to wrest significant concessions from the authorities. At a minimum, in those countries like Germany and France that continued to require the lancet, various technical improvements, such as using animal rather than human lymph and then glycerinating it to lessen the chances of transmitting other diseases, were introduced in the wake of resistance. At the other extreme, notably in Britain and later Sweden, compulsion was abolished altogether. Although they have largely vanished, leaving only residual traces, these antivaccination movements were vast and powerful in their heyday at

[113] *SB*, 1888/89, Akst. 134, p. 863; *SB*, 1879, Akst. 304, p. 1744; *SB*, 1881, Akst. 123, p. 709; Curt Spohr, *Impfgesetz vom 8. April 1874* (Dortmund, 1911), pp. 34–41; *Deutsche Medizinalzeitung*, 5, 10 (1884), pp. 13–15; *BMJ* (23 September 1899), p. 790; *Blattern und Schutzpockenimpfung*, p. 85; W. Born, *Amtliche Erledigung von Eingaben an Sr. Majestät den deutschen Kaiser* (Hagen i. W., 1889), p. 4; C. L. Paul Trüb et al., "Die Gegner der Pockenschutzimpfung und ihre Propaganda im 19. Jahrhundert und später," *Medizinische Monatsschrift*, 27 (1973), p. 75.

[114] *SB*, 1879, Akst. 304, p. 1732; *SB*, 1882/83, Akst. 164, p. 571; BA, R86/1205, v. 2, Petitions-Kommission, 5 December 1906, minutes, Wallenborn, von Stein; *SB*, 1908, Akst. 499, p. 2621.

[115] *Preste*, 1815, v. 1, pp. 399–400; "Kongl. Maj:ts Nådiga Reglemente För Vaccinationen i Riket," 6 March 1816, §14, *Kongl. Förordningar*, 1816.

[116] *SFS*, 1828/77, §7; *SFS*, 1853/67, §23; *Bihang*, 1903, AK, Motion 146, p. 2; *SFS* 1916/180, §21; *Bihang*, 1915, Motion AK 225; Motion AK 87, p. 7; *Bihang*, 1916, Prop. 32, pp. 27–28.

the end of the nineteenth century, serving as forerunners of more recent forms of popular resistance to technological innovation.[117] They were one of the first and most successful examples of single-issue movements, arising in response to a particular problem, only to fade once the matter at hand had been resolved. Antivaccination was one of a constellation of extraparliamentary popular movements flourishing during the middle and late nineteenth century as part of the emergence of mass political participation, before the development of organized parties had managed to incorporate such otherwise inchoate aspirations to power among the hitherto unenfranchised.

In Britain, antivaccination coincided during the 1870s with the development of other organizations and interest groups in opposition to Gladstone's first government. The Reform Act of 1867 had revolutionized the status of urban nonconformists and the Gladstonian administration was expected by many to inaugurate vast programs of social improvement. When it failed to fulfill such high hopes, protest associations arose, of which antivaccination was one. These included among their causes also temperance, antislavery, peace and antivivisection and many participants were also involved in various movements that claimed to embody an alternative to allopathic biomedical practice – homeopathy, *Naturheilkunde* and the like.[118] They were part of what the Medical Officer of Health for Leicester, fortress of antivaccination, in frustration called "the anti-everything section of the community."[119] We will meet them again in the following chapter campaigning against the regulation of prostitution and for the statutory imposition of standards of moral purity. They were found to some extent in all the nations under the glass here, but were strongest and most vociferous among the Protestant, Germany included, while weakest in France.

Opposition to vaccination was as old as the technique itself. Much of

[117] Joshua Ira Schwartz, "Smallpox Immunization: Controversial Episodes," in Dorothy Nelkin, ed., *Controversy: Politics of Technical Decisions* (2nd edn.; Beverly Hills, 1984), p. 198. As late as the 1960s, Wilson's standard text on the dangers of immunization was intended as an honest answer to antivaccinators: Graham S. Wilson, *The Hazards of Immunization* (London, 1967), pp. 2–5.

[118] D. A. Hamer, *The Politics of Electoral Pressure: A Study in the History of Victorian Reform Agitations* (Hassocks, 1977); Lloyd G. Stevenson, "Science down the Drain: On the Hostility of Certain Sanitarians to Animal Experimentation, Bacteriology and Immunology," *Bulletin of the History of Medicine*, 29, 1 (January–February 1955), pp. 14–15; Richard D. French, *Antivivisection and Medical Science in Victorian Society* (Princeton, 1975), ch. 8; Andreas-Holger Maehle, "Präventivmedizin als wissenschaftliches und gesellschaftliches Problem: Der Streit über das Reichsimpfgesetz von 1874," *Medizin, Gesellschaft und Geschichte*, 9 (1990), pp. 137–39; Kirchner, *Schutzpockenimpfung und Impfgesetz*, p. 100; Darmon, *La longue traque de la variole*, pp. 371–79; *Der Impfgegner*, 12, 11 (1894), p. 2.

[119] *Sanitary Record*, n.s., 16, 252 (29 September 1894), p. 1057.

the early resistance was motivated by the mercenary self-interest of inoculators with a vested stake in the old technique.[120] At the other extreme, antivaccination took on a theological inflection, with the lancet (as one of the first and most dramatic examples of mortals' ability to intervene beneficially in nature's processes) raising venerable questions of humanity's place in the universe and the extent to which it should trespass on divine prerogative.[121] Traditional theological arguments, useful against any human attempt to meddle with God and nature, fulfilled their purpose also against vaccination. In Sweden, old women preceded the establishment of vaccination stations in rural areas, seeking to convince locals that lancet and cross were irreconcilable. Smallpox was commonly viewed as a punishment or trial ordained from on high; avoiding it was thus to cheat divine justice or at least to shirk the ennobling effects of suffering. Vaccination was un-Christian in violating biblical prohibitions of intermixture between man and beast and of cuttings or marks on the body.[122] Regarding this not as a technical issue of medical procedure, but as one of religious conscience, antivaccinators accepted the state's claim to impose a particular solution in this instance as little as in other cases where the freedom of individual decision was guaranteed.[123]

While thus picking up steam as a moral and sometimes religious movement, antivaccination became overtly political when legislation requiring the lancet turned what had been a question of medical preferences into an issue balancing the liberties of the individual against the community's claims to protect the public wellbeing. In all nations antivaccinators portrayed themselves as part of a grassroots, populist movement fighting for the rights of individual self-determination against the hubris of official opinion and its allopathic medical allies and often,

---

[120] Friedr. Gotthilf Friese, *Versuch einer historisch-kritischen Darstellung der Verhandlungen über die Kuhpocken-Impfung in Grossbrittanien* (Breslau, 1809), pp. 3–4; *Betänkande angående skyddskoppympningens ordnande*, p. 14; *Blattern und Schutzpockenimpfung*, p. 39; Darmon, *La longue traque de la variole*, p. 169.

[121] The arguments that in our own day are put through their paces once again by genetic engineering.

[122] Thierfeld, *Prüfung einiger gangbaren Vorurtheile wider die Blatternimpfung*, pp. 9–24; *Preste*, 1815, v. 1, pp. 413–15; *Förhandlingar vid De Skandinaviske Naturforskarnes tredje Möte, 1842*, p. 864; *PP* 1856 (109) lii, pp. 512–14; Dixon, *Smallpox*, p. 234; Stern, *Should We Be Vaccinated?*, pp. 34, 43; Schultz, *Berättelse om koppors ympande*, pp. 90–91; Miller, *Adoption of Inoculation*, ch. 5; Leviticus, 19:26; Jno. Pickering, *Which? Sanitation and Sanatory Remedies, or Vaccination and the Drug Treatment?* (London, 1892), pp. 5–6.

[123] H. Martini, *Commentar zu dem Reichs-Impfgesetz vom 8. April 1874* (Leipzig, 1894), p. 147; P. A. Siljeström, *Vaccinationsfrågan: Ett bidrag till bestämmandet af de gränser, inom hvilka en vetenskaplig teori må äga rätt att göra sig gällande i lagstiftningen* (Stockholm, 1874), pp. 91–92; William White, *The Story of a Great Delusion* (London, 1885), pp. xlvii–xlviii; T. Massey Harding, *Small-Pox and Vaccination* (London, 1868), p. 44; *Hansard*, 1867, v. 187, col. 1872.

indeed, against expertise of any sort.[124] From their vantage, antivaccinators, like sanitationists faced with cholera, opposed common sense to
abstract science: was disease the result of invisible entities, whose existence had to be taken on faith in the experts, or that of the all too visible,
malodorous, unpleasant and insalubrious conditions in which most of
humanity lived? Official opinion was embodied in a triad of provaccination oppression: government bureaucrats, officially sanctioned biomedical opinion and the established church. The healthy instincts of the
resisting majority were being held in thrall to the provaccinating opinions of an ingrown, selfvalidating caste of official, bureaucratic, academic and scientific expertise.[125] The choice, in antivaccinating eyes,
was between the democratically liberal route of permitting all individuals to follow their own conscience on so intimate a corporeal matter and
the rule of dogmatic, booklearned expertise, enforced by the iron hand
of state authority, *Sachverständigen-Gutachten mit gewaltsamer Ausführung.*[126]
Vaccination was medical terrorism inflicted by fanatics who happened
to enjoy the backing of the state.[127]

Allopathic biomedical opinion, in turn, arrayed itself in largely
serried ranks behind vaccination.[128] The lancet presented it with
one of the earliest instances where medical knowledge of a trained,
scientific and specialized sort, not accessible to a commonsensical or lay
approach, allowed physicians to offer patients realistic hopes of an

[124] This being the era when the concept of professionalization, expertise and experts, medical
and otherwise, underwent significant development apace: F. M. L. Thompson, ed., *The Cambridge
Social History of Britain 1750–1950* (Cambridge, 1990), v. III, pp. 176–79; Charles E. McClelland, *The
German Experience of Professionalization* (Cambridge, 1991); Paul Weindling, *Health, Race and German
Politics Between National Unification and Nazism, 1870–1945* (Cambridge, 1989), pp. 20–25; Anne Digby,
Making a Medical Living: Doctors and Patients in the English Market for Medicine, 1720–1911 (Cambridge,
1994), pp. 24–28; Roy MacLeod, ed., *Government and Expertise: Specialists, Administrators and Professionals,
1860–1919* (Cambridge, 1988), pp. 2ff.; Logie Barrow, "Why Were Most Medical Heretics at Their
Most Confident Around the 1840s?," in Roger French and Andrew Wear, eds., *British Medicine in an
Age of Reform* (London, 1991), pp. 181–82.

[125] Vallberg, *Böra vi tvingas?*, p. 81; Ludwig Friedrich Geiger, *Die Impf-Vergiftung oder die physische und
geistige Verkrüppelung der Staatsgesellschaft* (Stuttgart, 1850), p. 28; *RD prot*, AK 1916:58, p. 52; *Petition des
Dr. H. Oidtmann in Linnich um Abschaffung des Impfzwanges* (Linnich, 1879), pp. 1–2; Born, *Amtliche
Erledigung*, p. 8; G. Fr. Kolb, *Zur Impffrage* (Leipzig, 1877), pp. 10–11.

[126] W. Brunn [W. Born], *Der Nationalliberalen politische Abdankung: No. 1. Die Impffrage* (Berlin, n.d.),
p. 23; *SB*, 1885/86, Akst. 313, p. 1691; *RD prot*, AK 1916:67, p. 64; [C. G. G.] Nittinger, *Die Impffregie
mit Blut und Eisen* (Stuttgart, 1868), p. 3; H. Oidtmann, "Bericht über den Stand der Impffrage im
März und April 1881," copy in BA, R86/1204, v. 2.

[127] V. Vallberg, *Vaccinationstyranniet: Några ord till vårt lands läkare, regering och riksdag* (Stockholm,
1912), pp. 3, 24; Geiger, *Impf-Vergiftung*, pp. 34, 46; *Hansard*, 1883, v. 280, col. 995; C. G. G. Nittinger,
Die Impfung ein Missbrauch (2nd edn.; Stuttgart, 1867), pp. 16, 45.

[128] *Betänkande angående skyddskoppympningens ordnande*, pp. 102–03; Lentz and Gins, *Handbuch der
Pockenbekämpfung*, p. 602; Frazer, *History of English Public Health*, p. 71. One prominent exception was
Vogt, head physician of the largest hospital in Bern: A. Wernher, *Zur Impffrage* (Mainz, 1883), p. 44.

effective intervention, justifying their claims to a monopoly of treatment, exalted social status and, needless to say, appropriate recompense.[129] Fighting antivaccinators was, for allopathic medicine, part of staking its claim to scientific authority and a privileged position vis-à-vis the myriad currents of what later, once its preeminence was no longer in dispute, would come to be called "alternative" forms of prevention, healing and cure. From this vantage, physicians had good reason to regard skeptically antivaccinators' demand that the public debate, discuss and participate in what, for them, were issues of a scientific, professional and technical character – claims of the sort culminating in the insistence that, on issues such as vaccination, the entire population should vote.[130] Conversely, the attempt to professionalize vaccination outraged opponents. Reserving the lancet for certified physicians was interpreted as an attempt to shroud the whole procedure in medical mystery, removing it from the arena of democratic debate to the arcane deliberations of the initiated.[131]

The fight between the two camps was thus one of gloves-off pugilism. In their more literary moments, antivaccinators favored allusions to *Gil Blas* and Lesage's parody of bloodletting physicians unwilling to abandon a technique they knew did more harm than good. Less subtly, they attacked vaccinators as arrogant all-knowers, the "tools of medical blood-poisoners and oppressors of conscientious parents," "the State-privileged manufacturers of disease" or "oppressors of the people armed with police truncheons."[132] They were perverters of common

[129] It was ironic, as one pointed out, that popular mistrust was strongest precisely for the one disease that medical science could most reliably prevent: *Liverpool Medico-Chirurgical Journal*, 19 (1899), p. 224; Huerkamp, "History of Smallpox Vaccination in Germany," pp. 620–22; Anne Marie Moulin, *Le dernier langage de la médecine: Histoire de l'immunologie de Pasteur au Sida* (Paris, 1991), p. 386; George D. Sussman, "Enlightened Health Reform, Professional Medicine and Traditional Society: The Cantonal Physicians of the Bas-Rhin, 1810–1870," *BHM*, 51 (1977), pp. 574–75.

[130] *Deutsches Archiv für Geschichte der Medicin und Medicinische Geographie*, 2 (1878), pp. 101–03; *Staatsbürger-Zeitung* (4 November 1887), copy in BA, R86/1204, v. 3; William Tebb, *The Results of Vaccination and the Inequity and Injustice of its Enforcement* (London, 1887), p. 14. But conversely, antivaccinators who did not manage to bend parliament to their will, as in Germany, were equally willing to argue that parliamentarism was incapable of bringing such issues to satisfactory resolution: Born, *Amtliche Erledigung*, p. 14.

[131] William Tebb, *Sanitation, not Vaccination, the True Protection Against Small-Pox* (London, [1881]), p. 10; V. Vallberg, *Anmärkningar till riksdagsdebatten om vaccinationsfrågan vid 1912 års riksdag* (Stockholm, 1912), pp. 40–41; *Our Legislators on the Vaccination Question: A Record of Parliamentary and Extra-Parliamentary Utterances and Opinions from 1802 to 1880* (London, 1880), pp. vii–ix; Kübler, *Geschichte der Pocken*, p. 337.

[132] *Staatsbürger-Zeitung* (4 November 1887), copy in BA, R86/1204, v. 3; William Hume-Rothery, "Advice to Anti-Vaccinators," *National Anti-Compulsory-Vaccination Reporter*, 4 (1 January 1877); 1, 5 (1 February 1877), p. 1; *Über die Einführung einer Gewissensklausel*, p. 6.

sense and enemies of the human race, medical despots and the most powerful profession in the land, with the politicians in their pocket.[133] The perennial claim of physicians' mercenary stake in their professional techniques was put through its paces also in this case.[134] As usual in such accusations, the logical tension between the interests of physicians in appearing capable of preventing or healing disease in order to justify their station and fees, on the one hand, with their presumed desire not to be so effective as actually to diminish illness and hurt business, on the other, was left unresolved.[135] Vaccinating physicians, for their part, returned such compliments in kind, dismissing their opponents with a sneer as a motley assortment of herbalists, hygienists, hydropathists, homeopaths and professors of a hybrid collection of other -isms. Many of the antivaccinating doctors (the ultimate insult) had their degrees from American universities. Many of their followers were too ignorant to know better.[136] Opponents resisted also the participation of officially sanctioned religion in vaccination, the promotion by established clergy of the lancet's virtues. In Britain, the Lord Bishop of Winchester instructed district visitors to the poor to inquire whether their children had been baptized and vaccinated. In France, the clergy, with some exceptions, strongly favored vaccination, presenting it as a gift from

[133] London Society for the Abolition of Compulsory Vaccination, *Vaccination or Sanitation? The Question of the Hour!*, copy in BA, R86/1204, v. 2; White, *Story of a Great Delusion*, p. 479; *Ridderskapet och Adeln*, 1856–58, v. 3, pp. 120–21; [Lord] Clifton, letter to the Editor of the *Chatham and Rochester News*, 23 November 1876, reprinted in *National Anti-Compulsory-Vaccination Reporter*, 4 (1 January 1877); "The Medical Profession and Vaccination," *Hackney Examiner and Shoreditch Chronicle* (18 January 1884); *Zukunft: Zeitschrift für gemeinnützige naturwissenschaftliche Heilkunde*, 11 (1887), p. 169.

[134] Although whether this implied that they were simply oblivious to the lancet's dangers or – more perverse – whether they actively favored vaccination knowing that it would help spread disease and drum up business depended on the observer: Hjalmar Helleday, *Den brännande vaccinationsfrågan: Några ord för dagen* (Östersund, 1912), pp. 13–14; J. Butterbrodt, *An den hohen deutschen Reichstag in Berlin. (Die 10te verbesserte) jetzt 24te Bitte oder: Der Kampf gegen Unnatur und Aberglauben bezw. gegen die Vernichtung der Menschheit von Seiten der sogenannten Medicinischen Wissenschaft* (n.p., n.d.), p. 15; *RD prot*, AK 1915:87, pp. 16–17; Ossian Holmqvist, *Uttalanden i Vaccinationsfrågan* (Värnamo, 1914), pp. 3–6; Darmon, *La longue traque de la variole*, p. 231; Stern, *Should We Be Vaccinated?*, pp. 34, 43; *Der Impfgegner*, 2, 3 (1 March 1877), pp. 21–22; H. Oidtmann, *Dr. H. Oidtmann als Impfgegner vor dem Polizeigericht: Weshalb ich meine Kinder nicht habe impfen lassen* (Düsseldorf, n.d. [1877]), pp. 42–44; Hugo Meyer, *Zur Aufklärung in der Impffrage* (Aachen, 1882), p. 31; *SB*, 1885/86, Akst. 313, p. 1691.

[135] Moore, *History and Practice of Vaccination*, pp. 112–14; J. Thorburn, *Vaccination: A Condensed Summary of the Evidence in Its Favour and the Objections Urged Against It* (London, 1870), pp. 38–41; *DVöG*, 30, 3 (1898), p. 564.

[136] Thorburn, *Vaccination*, p. 40; Kolb, *Zur Impffrage*, p. 10; *SB*, 1882/83, Akst. 164, pp. 567, 579. The judgment of antivaccinators' ignorance and lack of education was often based on amateur graphological analysis by MPs of the signatures appended to petitions of a sort that is possible in those continental nations where a particular style of handwriting was, and remains, taught in schools: *SB*, 1877, Akst. 176, p. 498; *SB*, 1895–97, 12 March 1896, p. 1410.

God.[137] The Napoleonic authorities invoked theological arguments in its favor and men of the cloth, both Catholic and Jewish, were often enlisted in the good fight.[138] In Prussia, clergy were also helpful in this respect. In Sweden, the church was implicated, for reasons to be discussed later, not only in the encouragement, but also the nuts and bolts of administering vaccination, a role that resistors resented for its potent mixture of theology and therapeutics. Although many antivaccinators were religiously motivated, attacks on the lancet were often combined with criticism of the established church.[139]

The antivaccination movements provoked an immense outpouring of literature, ranging from cartoons to popular pamphlets to treatises with scientific ambitions, culminating in terms of respectability in the infamous ninth edition *Britannica* article on vaccination by Creighton who shifted his position from pro to anti during its composition.[140] The controversy has been called the greatest in the history of medicine and one of the major, although largely forgotten, political disputes of the nineteenth century – third in Germany only to the Kulturkampf and unification in terms of public interest.[141] It was certainly that which prompted the most inspired feats of poetasting.[142] The dispute generated passions of a quasi-religious fervor framed in manichean dichotomies of good and evil, split families and friendships asunder and sent (especially in Britain and Germany) hundreds and thousands into the fray, willing to suffer fines and

[137] *Hansard*, 1872, v. 212, cols. 926–27; Bercé, *Le chaudron et la lancette*, ch. 5; Bercé, "Le clergé et la diffusion de la vaccination," *Revue d'histoire de l'église de France*, 69, 182 (January–June 1983); Darmon, *La longue traque de la variole*, pp. 205, 230; AN F[19] 5596, "Lettre circulaire et ordonnance de M.gr l'Evêque de Valence au sujet de la vaccine"; Biraben, "La diffusion de la vaccination en France au XIXe siècle," p. 268; Hudemann-Simon, *L'état et la santé*, pp. 442–43.

[138] "Circulaire du Préfet de Marengo à MM. les Maires de son département," "Lettre de M. l'Eveque de Chambéry aux Curés et Succursalistes de son diocèse," "Circulaire du Consistoire central des Israélites, à MM. les membres des divers Consistoires départementaux de l'Empire," in *Collection des bulletins sur la vaccine*.

[139] Edgar M. Crookshank, *History and Pathology of Vaccination* (London, 1889), v. I, p. 420; *RD prot*, AK 1885:56, p. 20; *Ridderskapet och Adeln*, 1859–60, v. 2, pp. 88–89; *Bihang*, 1859–60, v. 8, no. 158, pp. 4–5. Although provaccinators often attacked their opponents as clerical obscurantists, this was far from holding across the board: *Antivaccinator*, ed. H. Molenaar, 1 (1911), p. 93.

[140] Bibliographies include: *A Catalogue of Anti-Vaccination Literature* (London, 1882); H. Molenaar, *Impftod: Bibliographie der internationalen medizinischen Literatur über Impfschäden, Nutzlosigkeit der Impfung und Verwandtes* (Leipzig, 1912) (*Antivaccinator*, 1912). See also: H. Molenaar, *Verzeichnis 600 angesehener Impfgegner aus vielen Kulturländern aus dem Adressbuch circa 1200 tätiger Impfgegner von Dr. med. H. Oidtmann Linnich (1882) ausgewählt* (Bayreuth, n.d. [1914]); *PP* 1857 (sess. 2) (2239) xxxv, 139, p. lxxxi.

[141] Dixon, *Smallpox*, p. 282; *SB*, 14 March 1874, p. 353; Bohn, *Handbuch der Vaccination*, p. 146.

[142] *The Vaccine Phantasmagoria* (London, 1808); *Vaccinia: or, the Triumph of Beauty* (London, 1806); *Iconoclastis, Pethox Parvus: Dedicated, Without Permission, to the Remnant of the Blind Priests of That Idolatry* (London, 1807), pp. 12–18.

jail rather than obey the dictates of public health authorities.[143] The government experts sought to frame the issue as one of technical details, a matter on which science had pronounced and to which resistance was therefore evidence of irrational and delusionary thinking. For the antivaccinators, in contrast, fundamental issues of morality and liberty were at stake. Vaccination poisoned the political, moral and religious substance of the state and the issue was the key to understanding all political struggles and revolutions of the day. A people that had surrendered the fundamental right of control over its own body was still unprepared for freedom. The medieval persecutions of heretics, the anti-Catholic Kulturkampf in Germany, slavery in the United States: these were the analogies to their cause that flowed easily from antivaccinationist pens.[144] The rhetoric was kept at a frothing boil. Antivaccinators carried books of photographs with gruesome depictions of the damages allegedly wrought by the lancet to lend punch to their more abstract arguments. Both sides portrayed their position as that of reason and enlightenment, with provaccinators regarding their opponents guilty of unreasoning rejection of clearly proven scientific truth. Antivaccinators, in turn, placed themselves in a proud scientific and socially reformist tradition – Galileos and Jan Husses willing to suffer for the truth.[145] They were convinced that the future would regard vaccination as a outmoded superstition, as incomprehensible in retrospect as the witch trials and flagellants of the Middle Ages, Chinese foot binding, Indian tattooing, bleedings, astrology and phrenology.[146] Others described it as a peculiar western genuflection before Asiatic relig-

[143] A title that sums up the whole battle is William Blair, *The Vaccine Contest: Or "Mild Humanity, Reason, Religion, and Truth, Against Fierce, unfeeling Ferocity, overbearing Insolence, mortified Pride, false Faith, and Desperation"; Being An Exact Outline of the Arguments and Interesting Facts, Adduced by the Principal Combatants on Both Sides, Respecting Cow-Pox Inoculation* (London, 1806).

[144] Geiger, *Impf-Vergiftung*, p. 55; *Dr. Nittinger's Biographie: Aus dessen Nachlass vom Jahre 1871* (Stuttgart, 1874), pp. 36–37; W. Born, *Öffentliche Anfrage an die Behörden des Deutschen Reiches: Ist das Impfzwangs-Gesetz ein Mord-Gesetz oder ein Wohlfahrts-Gesetz* (Berlin, n.d.), p. 14; H. Oidtmann, "Bericht über den Stand der Impffrage im März und April 1881," copy in BA, R86/1204, v. 2; Tebb, *Sanitation, not Vaccination*, p. 10; Tebb, *Compulsory Vaccination in England*, p. 12.

[145] *Der "Segen" der Impfung* (Frankfurt, n.d.); *RD prot*, AK 1916:58, p. 18; *PP* 1807 (14) ii, pp. 57–58; Butterbrodt, *An den hohen deutschen Reichstag*, p. 2; *Der Impfgegner*, 1, 3 (1 August 1876), p. 35.

[146] *Antivaccinator*, 1912, Vorwort; Boëns, *La vaccine*, aux lecteurs; Alexander Wheeler, *Vaccination: Opposed to Science and a Disgrace to English Laws* (London, 1879); Mary C. Hume-Rothery, ed., *150 Reasons for Disobeying the Vaccination Law, by Persons Prosecuted Under It* (Cheltenham, 1878); H. F. Germann, *Historisch-kritische Studien über den jetzigen Stand der Impffrage* (Leipzig, 1875), v. I, p. 306; *Petition des Dr. H. Oidtmann*, p. 16; *Der Impfgegner*, 1, 2 (1 July 1876), pp. 17–18, 20, 25; Heinrich Oidtmann, "Der Aberglaube an die Schutzkraft der Impfung," in *Mehr Licht! Eine deutsche Wochenschrift für Literatur und Kunst*, 1, 46 (16 August 1879); *SB*, 1890/92, Akst. 541, p. 2871; Bihang, 1912, AK Motioner 235; Paul A.L. Mirus, *Die Impffrage und der Verband deutscher Impfgegner-Vereine* (Dortmund, 1910), Vorwort; Hugo Wegener, *Unerhört!! Verteidigung und Angriff eines Staatsbürgers: Gegen Kirchner!* (Frankfurt, 1911), p. 1.

ions, a tribute to pagan deities or devil worship. Vaccinators, they charged, had ceased to think scientifically, accepting vaccination's worth on faith, as dogma.[147]

Antivaccinationism was a rainbow of varying persuasions and approaches, a veritable blunderbuss of crankdom. Many, a group one may call holistic antivaccinators, drank from one of the many streams of alternative medicine, homeopathy, hydropathy, *Naturheilkunde* and the like. Rejecting allopathic medicine's faith in its ability to control, correct or otherwise improve nature, they believed in the existence of a natural harmony.[148] Corporeal balance was health, while illness indicated a disequilibrium to be righted, not a demonic, foreign and harmful something to be combated, overcome and expelled from the mortal coil. Accepting the principles of allopathic medicine and its recourse to unnatural bodily interventions and injections, fighting evil with evil, denied this self-regulating harmony to imply that the world either drifted aimlessly according to no plan or was guided by malevolent intentions in need of correction.[149] "Natural" cures should therefore substitute for the artificiality of vaccination.[150] Medical progress was, in the antivaccinating view, of

---

[147] V. Vallberg, *Västerländsk Baalsdyrkan* (Stockholm, 1911), pp. 5–9; *Hansard*, 1883, v. 280, col. 1004; Verdé-Delisle, *De la dégénérescence physique et morale de l'espèce humaine déterminée par le vaccin* (Paris, 1855), p. 2.

[148] Many, for example, rejected the very foundations of vaccination, the principle of acquired immunity, insisting instead that the unlikelihood of catching smallpox twice was but a statistical curiosity: Siljeström, *Vaccinationsfrågan*, pp. 101–02; Svenska förbundet mot vaccinationstvånget, Göteborg, *Yttrande över Medicinalstyrelsens "Betänkande angående skyddskoppsympningens ordnande"* (Gothenburg, 1914), p. 32; *Der Impfgegner*, 8, 4 (1890), p. 27; *SB*, 1884/85, Akst. 287, pp. 1268–69, 1274–75; *SB*, 1882/83, Akst. 164, p. 578; Stevenson, "Science down the Drain," p. 2; F. B. Smith, *The People's Health 1830–1910* (New York, 1979), pp. 166–68.

[149] Vallberg, *Västerländsk Baalsdyrkan*, pp. 5–9; *Dr. Nittinger's Biographie*, p. 74; *Gesundes Blut! Flugblatt für die arzneilose Heilkunde* (Leipzig, n.d. [c. 1890], copy in BA, R86/1204, v. 4; Nittinger, *Impfung ein Missbrauch*, Vorrede, p. 46; C. G. G. Nittinger, *Das falsche Dogma von der Impfung und seine Rückwirkung auf Wissenschaft und Staat* (Munich, 1857), p. 33; Vallberg, *Böra vi tvingas?*, p. 83; Spohr, *Impfgesetz*, pp. 3–4; Hjalmar Helleday, *Vaccinationstvånget* (Stockholm, 1904), p. 37; Pickering, *Which?*, pp. 4–5, 24–25; L. Belitski, *Gegen Impfung und Impfzwang* (Nordhausen, 1869), p. 4.

[150] The whole question of naturalness was, of course, hopelessly muddled. Inoculation and vaccination, far from being the creations of interventionist Enlightenment science, were in fact the formalization of "natural" folk customs practiced, in the first case in Turkey and, in the latter, by milkmaids and others in Jenner's home county of Gloucestershire. Conversely, many of the "alternative" forms of medicine were hardly "natural" in any obvious sense of the word. Homeopaths were dismissed by strict *Heilkunde* adherents as still believing in the need to inject poisons, however diluted their allopathy might be. Other forms of nonallopathic medicine were even less "natural": electric light baths, hypnosis, x-ray treatments. See *Dr. Nittinger's Biographie*, pp. 36, 75; Kübler, *Geschichte der Pocken*, p. 337. In fact, some of its opponents had objected to inoculation precisely because it was but the adoption of rude folk wisdom, one imported from the east no less: Crookshank, *History and Pathology of Vaccination*, v. I, pp. 39, 43; *Hansard*, 1883, v. 280, col. 1004; Dixon, *Smallpox*, p. 227; Vallberg, *Västerländsk Baalsdyrkan*, pp. 5–9, 50; Gatti, *Réfléxions sur les préjuges*, pp. 212–17.

minor importance in the overall balance of nature that was, at heart, perfect and could not, in any case, be much influenced by human intervention. For the religious, vaccination implied that the Creator had worked so imperfectly that his creatures were dangerous until punctured by a physician and that a healthy unvaccinated child was a threat to society, much like a mad dog or a keg of gunpowder.[151] Everything in nature served a purpose, even smallpox, which, in this view, was a necessary crisis of the body permitting the purge of dangerous substances.[152]

At the same time, other antivaccinators remained huddled under the umbrella of Enlightenment science, rejecting the lancet not because all medical intervention was bad, but because in this case, allopathy had gone astray. "A skilled bacteriologist," as George Bernard Shaw, rarely the physician's best friend, put it, "would just as soon think of cutting his child's arm and rubbing the contents of the dustpan into the wound, as vaccinating it in the same official way. The results would be exactly the same."[153] Such resistors were often firm believers in evolution, convinced that vaccination, the intimate biological contact between humans and lower forms of life, counteracted progress of the species. In Britain, Alfred Russel Wallace, the prominent evolutionist, testified at length in opposition before the Vaccination Commission and Herbert Spencer was also skeptical of the worth of compulsory vaccination.[154] Others rejected not the lancet as such, but its obligation. While accepting vaccination as of proven worth, some still denied the state's right to compel it. Rejecting the logic of public goods and the virtues of herd immunity, they regarded attempts to make the lancet compulsory as an admission

[151] Belitski, *Gegen Impfung und Impfzwang*, pp. 2–3; Mary Hume-Rothery and William Hume-Rothery, "The Vaccination Question," in *Social Notes Concerning Social Reforms, Social Requirements, Social Progress*, 7 (20 April 1878), copy in BA, R86/1204, v. 1; Mary Hume-Rothery, *150 Reasons*; *Second Report into Vaccination*, Q. 5656; Wernher, *Zur Impffrage*, p. 50; *Der Impfgegner*, 1, 2 (1 July 1876), p. 19.

[152] Verdé-Delisle, *De la dégénérescence*, pp. 31–32; C. G. G. Nittinger, *Über die 50jährige Impfvergiftung des württembergischen Volkes* (Stuttgart, 1850), p. 18; Brunn, *Nationalliberalen politische Abdankung*, p. 10; Verein zur Förderung des Volkswohls in Magdeburg, *Anweisung zur naturgemässen Behandlung von Pocken-Kranken* (n.p., n.d.), in BA, R86/1204, v. 2; *SB*, 1877, Akst. 176, p. 498; *SB*, 1885/86, Akst. 313, p. 1691; *Revue d'hygiène et de police sanitaire*, 20 (1898), p. 781; Wernher, *Zur Impffrage*, p. 5.

[153] Quoted in Stern, *Should We Be Vaccinated?*, pp. 81–82. On Shaw and vaccination, see Roger Boxill, *Shaw and the Doctors* (New York, 1969), pp. 63–71. The medical profession defended itself against his attacks in: *BMJ* (4 October 1902), pp. 1078–79; (18 October 1902), pp. 1283, 1260; (8 November 1902), pp. 1557–78; (15 November 1902), p. 1631. Lewis Carroll, his mathematical training offended by antivaccinators' misuse of statistics, held up literature's end in favor of the lancet: Lewis Carroll, *Three Letters on Anti-Vaccination (1877)* (n.p., Lewis Carroll Society, 1976).

[154] *Anti-Vaccinator*, 1 (1911), p. 30; V. Vallberg, *Vaccination och degeneration* (n.p., n.d.), pp. 1–7; Verdé-Delisle, *De la dégénérescence*, pp. v–vi; O. T. Axell, *Vaccinationen en villfarelse* (Östersund, 1905), pp. 15–18; Herbert Spencer, *Social Statics* (New York, 1886), pp. 422–23.

of bankruptcy, a bringing of the state's force to bear where persuasion had failed.[155] Others, believing that the technique had not yet been scientifically proven, sought to delay any consideration of compulsion until its merits had been demonstrated. Moderate antivaccinators of this ilk often accepted the right of the state to inflict the lancet on certain groups: men in the armed forces, children in state schools, all residents of territories menaced by epidemic.[156] The least vehement objectors accepted vaccination, arguing merely that, its protection not lasting longer than a year or two, it made little sense to require it.[157]

Something about inoculation and then vaccination set apart these supremely intimate statutory interventions into the literal body politic from other prophylactic techniques, provoking a particular form and degree of resistance even among those otherwise willing to accept the tenets of allopathic medicine. Unlike quarantine which affected only travelers or, at most, residents of infected areas during epidemics, vaccination aimed at the entire population of a certain age, whether immediately threatened or not. The tie between the intervention and the eventuality against which it protected was theoretical and often indirect, affecting many who had no immediate reason to tolerate medical interference. Unlike other public health precautions, which generally subjected only the individual's outward circumstances to community control, vaccination allowed the state to violate the integrity of a healthy body, requiring the contraction of a disease, however slight, by an otherwise fit and harmless infant. Vaccination also fell prey to the general folk rejection of bacteriology that persists down to our own day. But more than this, vaccination with its direct puncturing of the epidermal defenses, its violation of bodily integrity, was an especially galling example of the hubris of scientific medicine. Food entered the blood only after an elaborate process of digestion and refinement, the lancet's opponents argued. Vaccination, in contrast, sidestepped such safeguards, proceeding directly to the blood and delivering a "blow into the very centre thus otherwise guarded by nature in the providence of God." If God had wanted vaccine injected into the blood, as one put it with a variant on the classic appeal to the obviousness of divine intention, he would have provided a suitable

[155] *Hansard*, 1898, v. 56, col. 431; v. 62, cols. 343–48, 397; Vallberg, *Vaccinationstyranniet*, pp. 3, 24.

[156] Siljeström, *Vaccinationsfrågan*, pp. 4–5; *Journal d'hygiène*, 6, 237 (7 April 1881), pp. 155, 165; *SB*, 14 March 1874, p. 353; *Hansard*, 1898, v. 57, col. 778; 1883, v. 280, cols. 987–88; *National Anti-Compulsory-Vaccination Reporter*, 1, 5 (1 February 1877), p. 1; *Bulletin*, 3, 25 (1891), pp. 33–34; *Moniteur universel*, 172 (20 June 1868), p. 887; *JO*, Chambre, Débats, 8 March 1881, p. 438. Some accepted vaccination with human lymph, rejecting only animal lymph: *SB*, 1879, Akst. 304, p. 1732.

[157] Böing, *Schutzpocken-Impfung und Impfgesetz*, pp. 5–6.

orifice.[158] Because the lancet violated natural bodily defenses, it was thought to provoke a host of other ailments, whether tuberculosis, cholera, syphilis, nervousness, a general decline in maternal lactation or (inexplicably one of the more pressing concerns) dental decay.[159] Verdé-Delisle, perhaps the most extreme antivaccinator who attributed largely every human ailment to the lancet, was given a run for his money in the blanket-condemnation department by the Swedish pastor Liljekvist, for whom vaccination was the cause of masturbation, hysteria, sexual perversion, hemorrhoids, scrofula, humpbackedness, osteonecrosis and a groaning smorgasbord of other ailments.[160]

In a more general sense, vaccination was thought to violate laws of nature and logic. A poison could not protect against its own effects. With vaccination, an otherwise healthy person was required to undergo infection with illness, the body itself was changed in ways not the case with other forms of prophylaxis, the recipient was subject to a precaution against an eventuality that had not yet occurred.[161] Inoculation and vaccination contradicted common sense, seeking to fight disease with disease, vainly expecting to bring cleanliness out of the unclean, violating the doctrine of asepsis by introducing foreign bodies into the blood.[162] With vaccination and the introduction of cowpox rather than human smallpox, matters got worse. The sense that there was something

[158] *Vaccination Tracts*, [ed. J. J. Garth Wilkinson and William Young] (London, 1879), pp. 8–10; White, *Story of a Great Delusion*, p. 594; Geiger, *Impf-Vergiftung*, p. 54; Born, *Öffentliche Anfrage an die Behörden*, p. 10; Pickering, *Which?*, pp. 143–44; *Final Report into the Subject of Vaccination*, p. 217; *PP* 1856 (109) lii, p. 514.

[159] Vallberg, *Vaccination och degeneration*, pp. 1–7; V. Vallberg, *Ist die allgemeine Zahnfäulnis eine Folge der Kuhpockenimpfung?* (Leipzig, n.d.); Nittinger, *Impfregie mit Blut und Eisen*, p. 43; Albert Carter, *Vaccination a Cause of the Prevalent Decay of the Teeth, and a Scourge to Beauty, Digestion and Soundness: An Experience from Many Lands* (London, 1877), pp. 5–7; Oidtmann, *Oidtmann als Impfgegner*, pp. 12–13; *SB*, 1879, Akst. 304, pp. 1732, 1734–35; *SB*, 1882/83, Akst. 164, p. 562; J. Edmund Güntz, *Über die Verhütung der Syphilis* (Leipzig, 1870), pp. 96–97; Harold Whiston, *Why Vaccinate?* (2nd edn.; Macclesfield, 1906); Axell, *Vaccinationen en villfarelse*, pp. 15–18; *Anti-Vaccinator*, 1 (1911), p. 30; *Förhandlingar*, 1880, p. 215; Ernest Hart, *The Truth About Vaccination* (London, 1880), p. 13; Gideon, *Pocken-Impfung ist stets syphilitische Vergiftung* (Berlin, n.d. [1878]); Alfred Milnes, *The Theory and Practice of Vaccino-Syphilis* (London, 1891); Pierre Darmon, "Quand le vaccin faisait peur aux Anglais . . .," *L'histoire*, 68 (June 1984), p. 92. Dental decay was often interpreted as a symptom of racial degeneration: Weindling, *Health, Race and German Politics*, p. 228.

[160] Verdé-Delisle, *De la dégénérescence*, pp. 66–139; *RD prot*, AK 1915:87, p. 16.

[161] *Deutsche Zeitschrift für die Staatsarzneikunde*, 11 (1858), pp. 309–10; *SB*, 1890/92, Akst. 541, p. 2870; *Dr. Nittinger's Biographie*, p. 38; Germann, *Historisch-kritische Studien*, v. I, p. 117; v. III, p. 28; Svenska förbundet, *Yttrande*, pp. 1–2; *Bihang*, 1915, Prop. 78, pp. 23–24; *Second Report into the Subject of Vaccination*, Q 5656; Mirus, *Impffrage*, pp. 16–17.

[162] BA, R86/1204, v. 2, "II. Internationaler Congress der Impfgegner und Impfzwanggegner vom 9. bis 12. October 1881 in Cöln," p. 4; Vallberg, *Västerländsk Baalsdyrkan*, p. 29; Pickering, *Which?*, pp. 17–18; *SB*, 1877, Akst. 176, p. 498; Born, *Amtliche Erledigung*, p. 8; *Über die Einführung einer Gewissensklausel*, p. 6; *Bihang*, 1903, AK Motion 146, p. 11; Louis Duvrac, *Est-il permis de proposer*

deeply unnatural about this mixing of vital juices across the species line – brutalization in the most literal sense – began already with the British inoculators, defending their technique against vaccination with claims that humans would be bestialized by injections of animal disease.[163] Cartoonists by the score could not resist the temptation to play with this tailor-made theme of the half-man–half-beast.[164] "Vaccination is," as one put it, "the cutting, with a sharp instrument, of holes in your dear little healthy babe's arm, and putting into the holes some filthy matter from a cow – which matter has generally in addition passed through the arm of another child." Some things were more hideous than death itself, another warned, among them the injection of bestial blood into children. Vaccination infected the human race at the very fount of life with animal excrement.[165] When the Japanese scientist Noguchi in 1915 began deriving animal lymph from rabbit testicles for injection into children, some antivaccinators found reason anew for revulsion. In the most extreme formulations, the fear of species transgression led to prophecies of general decline, a countering of the laws of evolution and degeneration of the human race. Such mixture of human and beast was not only unnatural, but irreligious, going beyond pollution to abomination.[166]

l'Inoculation de la petite Vérole? Question de médecine, discutée dans les Ecoles de la Faculté de Médecine de Paris, le 30 Décembre 1723 . . . (Paris, 1755), p. iv.

[163] *Betänkande angående skyddskoppympningens ordnande*, p. 14; Wernher, *Zur Impffrage*, p. 51. Out of national amour propre, Pasteur's vaccinations were therefore seen as more akin to inoculation, employing a weakened version of the same human disease, than Jenner's technique of injecting animal ailments into humans: "Congrès de Paris," *L'ami du peuple*, 9, 40 (6 Oct 1889). Again, this is an issue with modern resonances in the objections raised to trans-species organ transplants and genetic manipulation.

[164] *PP* 1807 (14) ii, p. 60. The reactions of vaccinators to such fears were dismissive: Simon wrote "there was no more reason in this belief [of bovinization] than if vaccination had been charged with occasioning infants to cut their teeth, or with leading boys to prefer cricket to Cornelius Nepos." See *PP* 1857 (sess. 2) (2239) xxxv, p. 164; Struve, *Anleitung zur Kenntniss*, p. 78.

[165] *Vaccination Tracts*, no. 6, pp. 6–7; *Second Report into the Subject of Vaccination*, Q. 5716; *Our Legislators on the Vaccination Question*, p. 15; H. D. Dudgeon, *Compulsory Disease: An Historical Sketch of the Rise and Spread of the Vaccine Dogma* (n.p., 1881), p. 2; Helleday, *Vaccinationstvånget*, p. 36; *PP* 1856 (109) lii, p. 500. Sometimes it was the European race that was being ruined in its perfection and especially its lily-white complexion: Nittinger, *Das falsche Dogma von der Impfung*, pp. 40–41; Nittinger, *Offene Klage vor Gericht wider die Impfvergiftung in Würtemberg* (Leipzig, 1865), pp. 3–6; Benj. Jung, *Verbot der Kuhpocken-Impfung* (Stuttgart, 1864), pp. 18–19.

[166] *RD prot*, AK 1916:58, p. 30; Lentz and Gins, *Handbuch der Pockenbekämpfung*, pp. 311–12; *Anti-Vaccinator*, 1 (1911), p. 30; Vallberg, *Vaccination och degeneration*, pp. 1–7; Verdé-Delisle, *De la dégénérescence*, pp. v–vi; Geiger, *Impf-Vergiftung*, p. 47; *SB*, 18 February 1874, p. 109; *Revue d'hygiène et de police sanitaire*, 20 (1898), p. 781; Axell, *Vaccinationen en villfarelse*, pp. 15–18; *Vaccination Tracts*, no. 4, pp. 8–10; *SB*, 1885/86, Akst. 313, p. 1692. Conversely, when vaccination was introduced to India, British colonial authorities mistakenly expected that the Hindu reverence for all things bovine would facilitate its acceptance: David Arnold, "Smallpox and Colonial Medicine in Nineteenth-Century India," in Arnold, ed., *Imperial Medicine and Indigenous Societies* (Manchester, 1988), p. 53.

The dispute that had raged over cholera between sanitationists and quarantinists, the fundamental clash between seeing disease either as endemically the product of unpropitious local conditions or as imported from outside, was repeated for smallpox. Even many of the same actors returned for a reprise of their roles in the previous dispute: Proust, arch-quarantinist and now vaccinator par excellence in France; Koch who reappeared as the dark angel of the lancet, "our dictator in the doctrine that the unvaccinated are guilty of spreading smallpox," or "Professor Bazillen-Koch," in the titulations of opponents.[167] Many antivaccinators took a classically sanitationist approach to smallpox, regarding it as yet another of the ailments caused by filth.[168] More specific versions, attributing smallpox to the wearing of woolen clothing, saw the solution in other fibers. Vaccinating physicians, it was claimed, neglected the insights of the common people, that health was achieved not by mixing cowpox with the blood, but by making homes healthy and sanitary. Some in this school were even willing to draw the conclusion that smallpox was not contagious.[169]

The bacteriological revolution did little to convince confirmed doubters. Bacteriologists could argue only by analogy that a microorganism, still unidentified, of the sort responsible for cholera also caused smallpox and not until the development of virology in the early twentieth century, and the identification of wholly new forms of microorganisms responsible for some transmissible disease, was the issue clarified.[170] During the

---

[167] *Der Impfgegner*, 7, 12 (December 1889), p. 74; 8, 3 (1890), p. 18; *SB*, 1895–97, 8 May 1896, p. 2205; H. Oidtmann, "Beschwerdeschrift gegen den Geh.-Rath Dr. Koch, den Verfechter der Impfschutzlehre – aus dem Jahre 1889," *Der Impfgegner*, 8, 1 (January 1890).

[168] Tebb, *Results of Vaccination*, pp. 35–36; Tebb, *Sanitation, not Vaccination*; Jno. Pickering, *Anti-Vaccination: The Statistics of the Medical Officers to the Leeds Small-Pox Hospital Exposed and Refuted* (Leeds, 1876), pp. 32–34; *Our Legislators on the Vaccination Question*, pp. vii–ix; *DZSA*, 11 (1858), pp. 309–10; P. Spohr, *Die Folgen der Impfung in Volk und Armee* (Leipzig, 1891), p. 10; Meyer, *Zur Aufklärung in der Impffrage*, pp. 8–10; *PP* 1856 (109) lii, p. 519; "Discours de M. A. Vogt, prof. d'hygiène a Berne," *L'ami du peuple*, 9, 39 (29 September 1889); Nittinger, *Über die 50jährige Impfvergiftung*, p. 61; *Über die Einführung einer Gewissensklausel*, pp. 12–13; *Remarks on the Prevailing Epidemic of Small-Pox, Its Cause and Prevention* (London, n.d. [1871]), p. 11; *Second Report into the Subject of Vaccination*, Q. 6254–55; *First Report into the Subject of Vaccination*, Q. 901.

[169] Axel Helmstädter, "Post hoc – ergo propter hoc? Zur Geschichte der deutschen Impfgegnerbewegung," *Geschichte der Pharmazie*, 42 (1990), p. 22; London Society, *Vaccination or Sanitation?*; Tebb, *Results of Vaccination*, pp. v–vi; Hugo Martini, *Der Impfzwang in seiner moralischen und wissenschaftlichen insbesondere juristischen Unhaltbarkeit* (Leipzig, 1879), p. 125; *SB*, 3 May 1877, pp. 1025–26; *Hansard*, 1883, v. 280, col. 1027. More careful observers like Creighton walked the line, arguing that smallpox was imported, but that filth favored its spread: *Second Report into the Subject of Vaccination*, QQ. 5250–51. Conversely, provaccinators were willing to concede that sanitation was important, while insisting that it alone could not prevent such diseases: S. Wolffberg, *Die Impfung und ihr neuester Gegner* (Bonn, 1880), pp. 58–61.

[170] *SB*, 1882/83, Akst. 164, pp. 578–79; A. P. Waterson and Lise Wilkinson, *An Introduction to the History of Virology* (Cambridge, 1978), pp. 3–5, 10–11, 33–34, 154–56.

nineteenth century, the case for and against vaccination was therefore argued on the basis of largescale statistical correlations.[171] These, however, were sufficiently complex and subtle in their implications to offer little conviction in a debate in which emotions flared so readily. Most opponents did not deny the general decrease in smallpox that had blessed the nineteenth century, but disputed the hoc in the vaccinators' post and propter claim that the lancet was the cause.[172] Acclimatization to the disease or the general advance of sanitation and civilization instead lay behind the decline of smallpox and most other transmissible diseases.[173] Some sought to turn the tables, arguing that vaccination had in fact increased the incidence of smallpox which had otherwise been lessening.[174] Vaccinators argued, in contrast, that declines in the incidence of smallpox, far from being distributed evenly across the population, were specific to certain nations, areas and groups, ones that – not coincidentally – were the best vaccinated.[175]

Instead of the lancet, sanitationist antivaccinators sought the same general hygienic solutions with which Chadwickians had hoped to keep cholera at bay.[176] Totalizing ambitions, of the sort common among the early sanitationists, to cure all social ills in the process of preventing epidemics, were repeated for smallpox. If, in fact, the unvaccinated

[171] A great deal of scholarly firepower was deployed in statistical arguments. One of the great controversies concerned Keller, who used figures from Austrian railroad personnel to argue that vaccination was of no use. Having become the patron saint of countless antivaccination pamphlets, Keller's calculations were exposed as manipulated by Josef Körösi in his *Kritik der Vaccinations-Statistik und neue Beiträge zur Frage des Impfschutzes* (Berlin, 1889). See *Journal of State Medicine*, 10, 6 (June 1902), pp. 313–14; *Bihang*, 1915, Särskilda utskotts nr. 1 utlåtande nr. 2, pp. 40–41; *SB*, 1884/85, Akst. 287, p. 1279.

[172] Although some did deny that smallpox had declined, claiming instead that it had simply become transformed into less virulent forms, chickenpox above all: *Über die Einführung einer Gewissensklausel*, pp. 12–13; *A Medical Debate on Vaccination at la Société médicale des Praticiens de Paris* (London, 1904), p. 7.

[173] *Bihang*, 1915, Särskilda utskotts nr. 1 utlåtande nr. 2, pp. 40–41; 1912, AK Motion 235; *PP* 1856 (109) lii, p. 500; Siljeström, *Vaccinationsfrågan*, pp. 55–56; *Journal d'hygiène*, 6, 229 (10 Feb 1881), pp. 70–72; Alfred R. Wallace, *Forty-Five Years of Registration Statistics, Proving Vaccination to Be Both Useless and Dangerous* (London, 1889). [174] *Bihang*, 1885, AK Motion 79.

[175] BA, R86/1205, v. 2, Petitions-Kommission [of the RT], 5 December 1906; *SB*, 1909–11, Akst. 571; Prussia, Herrenhaus, *Stenographische Berichte*, 1914–15, col. 526; *Bihang*, 1903, AK Tillfälliga Utskott (No. 2) Utlåtande 30, pp. 10–11; *Hansard*, 1883, v. 280, col. 1019; *First Report into the Subject of Vaccination*, QQ. 351, 684, 749, 759; Kaiserliches Gesundheitsamt, *Beiträge zur Beurtheilung*, pp. 1ff.; *RD prot*, FK 1912:20, p. 42.

[176] *Vaccination Inquirer and Health Review*, 5, 58 (January 1884), p. 201; Tebb, *Compulsory Vaccination in England*, p. 63; *Nineteenth Century*, 11, 63 (May 1882), p. 795; *Report of the Sixth Annual Meeting of the London Society for the Abolition of Compulsory Vaccination*, 14 April 1886 (London, 1886), pp. 11–13; Dudgeon, *Compulsory Disease*, p. 7; Pickering, *Which?*; Alfred Russel Wallace, *The Wonderful Century* (London, 1898), pp. 213, 269–87; White, *Story of a Great Delusion*, p. xxxiv; W. Scott Tebb, *A Century of Vaccination and What It Teaches* (2nd edn.; London, 1899), p. 259; Geiger, *Impf-Vergiftung*, p. 47; *SB*, 3 May 1877, p. 1026; *SB*, 1882/83, Akst. 164, p. 561; *SB*, 1890/92, Akst. 541, p. 2871; *RD prot*, AK 1916:58, p. 7; *Hansard*, 1883, v. 280, col. 992; *Second Report into the Subject of Vaccination*, Q. 5214.

tended to die more than the protected, one objector argued in a concession to statistics that surrendered no ground to causality, then only because they were usually among the poorest living in the worst hygienic circumstances. Thus substituting sociology for biology implied that the solution, far from being some particular prophylactic technique, lay with a broad program of social reform to eliminate the very basis of smallpox and all other filth diseases.[177] In contrast, holistic antivaccinators tended to regard the classic sanitationists as mere tinkerers, neglectful of the big picture. Smallpox was the outcome of a poison produced by the body itself, against which little, other than perhaps a life of harmony with the cosmic forces, could be done. Hygiene, more than a mundane technical matter of plumbing, waste removal and ventilation, was an all-consuming moral and ontological issue, a question of the relationship of humanity to nature. Immunity to smallpox, indeed all disease, would come not by contaminating the blood with poison, whether vaccine or other allopathic medicines, but through vegetarianism, alternative medical doctrines promising a corporeal balance and, for some, simply by means of self-control, a healthy diet, fresh air, regular bathing, work, rest, diversion, sleep and, in general, moderation.[178]

Such antivaccinators often sought similar ends as their sanitationist colleagues (allowing even the poor the clean, comfortable, well-nourished, spacious lifestyle enjoyed by the better-off), but with an emphasis on personal and individual choices in such matters and little of the reforming vision or focus on collective action characteristic of the Chadwickians. Their concerns and recommendations were largely intended for those classes which, enjoying a choice in the matter, had, for individual reasons, not yet adopted correct habits. Disease, as one cautioned, was the outcome of indulgence, neglect or disobedience. Those who were cautious in their mode of life and surroundings, temperate, virtuous and obedient could snap their fingers at infection.[179]

---

[177] Siljeström, *Vaccinationsfrågan*, pp. 82–83; P.A. Siljeström, *Ytterligare bidrag till utredande af vaccinationsfrågan* (Stockholm, 1875), v. III, pp. 47–48; P.A. Siljeström, *A Momentous Education Question for the Consideration of Parents and Others Who Desire the Well-Being of the Rising Generation* (London, 1882), pp. 10–17; Axell, *Vaccinationen en villfarelse*, pp. 14–16; Vallberg, *Böra vi tvingas?*, pp. 12–18; *Remarks on the Prevailing Epidemic*, p. 11; Pickering, *Which?*, pp. 84–85, 143.

[178] Nittinger, *Über die 50jährige Impfvergiftung*, pp. 18, 60; Helleday, *Vaccinationstvånget*, p. 38; *Über die Einführung einer Gewissensklausel*, pp. 12–13; *Bihang*, 1903, AK, Motion 146, p. 12; 1912, AK Motion 235; Holmqvist, *Uttalanden i Vaccinationsfrågan*, pp. 3–6; Geiger, *Impf-Vergiftung*, p. 54; *SB*, 23 April 1873, p. 283; *Third Report of the Royal Commission Appointed to Inquire into the Subject of Vaccination* (C.-6192) (London, 1890), Q 7394.

[179] *SB*, 1884/85, Akst. 287, p. 1347; Verein zur Förderung des Volkswohls, *Anweisung zur naturgemässen Behandlung*; Pickering, *Which?*, p. 5.

Implicit in this more individualized approach to smallpox was a tendency to assign personal, rather than social, responsibility to the victims of illness and, more generally, to take a view of the vaccination issue that was markedly more biologistic and eugenicist than the sanitationists. That the lowest and uncleanest classes were more likely to fall ill than the strong and healthy was a common opinion among such antivaccinators. Smallpox therefore performed a kind of eugenic spring cleaning and vaccination, in turn, threatened to burden society with the young, the poor and the sick – all fetters, in this view, on the strides the community could otherwise take – who had earlier been killed off.[180] More specifically, antivaccinators of this ilk worried that the lancet pooled the blood of the entire nation, good and bad, high and low, thereby reducing its quality to the lowest common denominator and transmitting the corruptions of ancestors to coming generations. Class purity was also threatened in that nobles and commoners, middle and lower classes thus mixed their blood.[181]

Many antivaccinators drew such prophylactic contrasts in terms of grand principle: all nations faced a choice between two approaches to smallpox, the lancet or sanitationism. The two seemed irreconcilably contradictory strategies, one seeking to keep filth and disease at bay, the other to introduce them into even the intimate recesses of the body.[182] Among some resistors, quarantinist techniques (isolating the ill, for example) were regarded as equally abhorrent to vaccination and, in general, part of the same antisanitationist, restrictionist state medical mentality. Vaccination and quarantine were regarded by such opponents as similar in their attempt to swindle nature, allowing humans to persist in their insalubrious ways rather than requiring a reform of their behavior in a sanitationist direction. Quarantinism and vaccination were equally reprehensible insofar as both implied a neglect of sanitary

---

[180] Pickering, *Anti-Vaccination*, pp. 32–34; Pickering, *Which?*, p. 85; *Förhandlingar*, 1908, p. 226; Siljeström, *Ytterligare bidrag*, v. I, pp. 28–29, 38–41; Siljeström, *Momentous Education Question*, pp. 10–17.

[181] *Vaccination Tracts*, no. 4, pp. 8–10; *Über die Einführung einer Gewissensklausel*, pp. 6, 16; *Bihang*, 1915, Prop. 78, pp. 23–24; *Hansard*, 1883, v. 280, col. 986; *SB*, 1885/86, Akst. 313, p. 1692; *Hansard*, 1877, v. 235, cols. 732–33, 739. But another antivaccinator drew the opposite conclusion, arguing that the only advantage of vaccination was that at least it destroyed inherited ideas that noble blood was somehow special and distinct: Brunn, *Nationalliberalen politische Abdankung*, p. 8. In India a variant on this class-based fear of blood mixing left arm-to-arm vaccination unpopular since, with high-caste parents exempting their children from such uses, low-caste or Untouchable children were often the only vaccinifers available: David Arnold, *Colonizing the Body: State Medicine and Epidemic Disease in Nineteenth-Century India* (Berkeley, 1993), pp. 141–42.

[182] Tebb, *Results of Vaccination*, pp. 35–36; *Vaccination Inquirer and Health Review*, 7, 78 (September 1885), p. 93; Tebb, *Sanitation, not Vaccination*, p. 10; London Society, *Vaccination or Sanitation?*; *Final Report into the Subject of Vaccination*, p. 215; *Vaccination Tracts*, no. 4, pp. 8–10.

reforms.[183] But at the same time, the analogy thus suggested between vaccination and quarantinism did not hold with much consistency. The principles of the two techniques were diametrically opposed: isolation of the victim to curb transmission of the infectious agent on the one hand, spreading it in hopes of stimulating universal immunity on the other. Many antivaccinators did not share the millenarian Chadwickian belief that sanitary reform would solve all medical problems and were willing to admit that smallpox was not a simple filth disease tameable by public hygiene alone. Many – eventually most – in fact came to accept the principles of neoquarantinism, although they would have been loath to call them that, as the alternative to vaccination.[184] Measures of isolation and quarantine had been marshaled against smallpox before Jenner and many opponents of the lancet now returned to this tradition. Sanitationism in the ecumenical definition of antivaccinators included such venerable neoquarantinist techniques as notification of disease to the authorities, isolation of victims, surveillance of their contacts and disinfection of dwellings.[185] The acme of antivaccination, institutionalized in the so-called Leicester system (about which more below), was nothing but strict neoquarantinism now applied to smallpox.[186]

[183] *Third Report into the Subject of Vaccination*, QQ 9662–70; *BMJ* (13 February 1904), pp. 378–79; White, *Story of a Great Delusion*, p. 595; Siljeström, *Vaccinationsfrågan*, p. 10; Boëns, *La vaccine*, pp. 162–63. A leaflet, "John Bull in Medical Fetters," shows him tied by the doctors with various ropes marked Pharmaceutical poisons, Vaccine Poison, Medical despotism, Fees, Fees, Fees, The Blood Poisoner and finally, Quarantine Laws, thus associating vaccination and quarantine: copy in Countway Library, Harvard Medical School, RC 183 A3 S70. The really consequent advocates of this approach also rejected procedures that might otherwise seem sanitationist, like baths, as mere attempts to undo the consequences of bad living: *Der Impfgegner*, 12, 11 (1894), pp. 2–3.

[184] *Final Report into the Subject of Vaccination*, sect. 452; Duvrac, *Est-il permis de proposer l'Inoculation de la petite Vérole?*, p. 40; Garth Wilkinson, *On the Cure, Arrest, and Isolation of Smallpox by a New Method* (London, 1864), p. xvii; Dorothy Porter and Roy Porter, "The Politics of Prevention: Anti-Vaccinationism and Public Health in Nineteenth-Century England," *Medical History*, 32 (1988), pp. 236–37; Dixon, *Smallpox*, p. 291.

[185] C. Killick Millard, *The Vaccination Question in the Light of Modern Experience* (London, 1914), p. 7; *SB*, 1878, Akst. 224, p. 1439; *SB*, 1884/85, Akst. 287, p. 1344; *Bihang*, 1903, Motion AK 146; 1915, Prop. 78, pp. 23–24; Motion AK 213, pp. 1–3; Motion AK 225; Motion FK 87; *RD prot*, AK 1915:87, p. 7; *Final Report into the Subject of Vaccination*, p. 215; Helleday, *Den brännande vaccinationsfrågan*, pp. 8–9; Svenska förbundet, *Yttrande*, pp. 1–2, 62–63; *Bulletin*, 3, 25 (1891), p. 33; J. J. Garth Wilkinson, *The Infectious Nature of the Vaccine Disease, and the Necessity of Excluding the Vaccinated and Revaccinated, During That Disease, from Intercourse with Healthy Persons* (London, 1877), pp. 3, 15–16; Meyer, *Zur Aufklärung in der Impffrage*, p. 29; *Über die Einführung einer Gewissensklausel*, p. 6; Crookshank, *History and Pathology of Vaccination*, v. I, p. 465; *Hansard*, 1898, v. 56, cols. 456–57; Wilkinson, *Cure, Arrest, and Isolation*, pp. xxi–xxii; Porter and Porter, "Politics of Prevention," p. 245.

[186] J. T. Biggs, *Leicester: Sanitation versus Vaccination* (London, n.d. [1912]), p. 461; Stuart M. F. Fraser, "Leicester and Smallpox: The Leicester Method," *Medical History*, 24, 3 (July 1980). Leicester was one of the first towns to introduce the compulsory notification of disease by means of a private bill: *Hansard*, 1898, v. 57, col. 761.

As one would expect from any populist movement that sought to counterpose folk beliefs to the precepts of academic medicine and the doctrines of distant professional and political elites, antivaccination recruited heavily from the working and urban artisanal classes. Inoculation and then vaccination had long been adopted voluntarily by the middle and upper ranks of society while the popular classes had tended to view such techniques with distrust and suspicion.[187] Because of such differing prophylactic habits, requiring vaccination affected lower more than upper classes, provoking most ire from below.[188] In Germany, the movement recruited primarily from the lower and working classes. In Britain, where both middle and lower classes were well represented, those who rejected vaccination altogether tended to be workers or artisans while their social superiors in the movement often opposed not the technique as such, but merely its compulsion. In Sweden, resistance was found among workers, while railway personnel in Småland constituted one of the movement's kernels.[189] However, because the issue affected humans as biological as much as social animals, provoking strong sentiments of conscience and conviction, individuals from all walks of life could be found among the lancet's opponents. The professions of antivaccination petitioners to the Reichstag, for example, varied from master joiner up to squire and in Sweden resistance spread up the social scale, including at least one hydropathically interested noble. In Britain, the movement attracted also wealthy supporters and was sufficiently well bankrolled to pay the fines imposed on poor resistors.[190] It was also possible for largely biological criteria, cutting across those of class or status, to be the basis of resistance. In Germany, for example, women presented themselves as especially concerned by vaccination, first as

[187] Académie de médecine, Paris, V15 d2B(a), Le Comité central de vaccine à M. le C. d'E, Prefet du departement de la Seine, 11 September 1809, no. 348; Ekelund, *Barn-koppor och vaccinen*, pp. 210–12; Zetterström, *Initia historiæ vaccinationis*, p. 85; *Preste*, 1815, v. 1, pp. 521–29; Moore, *History and Practice of Vaccination*, pp. 118–19; Cross, *History of the Variolous Epidemic*, pp. 20–21, 24; *Zeitschrift des K. Sächsischen statistischen Bureaus*, 22 (1876), p. 206; *Nineteenth Century*, 11, 63 (May 1882), p. 802. In Britain, however, the lower classes had favored variolation, while resisting vaccination: J. R. Smith, *Speckled Monster*, ch. 5.
[188] Eimer, *Blatternkrankheit*, pp. 146–47; Mich. Reiter, *Würdigung der grossen Vortheile der Kuhpocken-impfung für das Menschengeschlecht* (Munich, 1852), pp. 48–49.
[189] Matzel, *Pocken im Deutsch–Französischen Krieg*, p. 13; Bohn, *Handbuch der Vaccination*, p. 145; Fraser, "Leicester and Smallpox," p. 327; *BMJ* (4 April 1896), p. 862; *Hansard*, 1815, v. 31, cols. 845–46; 1866, v. 182, col. 1103; 1872, v. 212, cols. 926–27; *RD prot*, AK 1916:58, p. 35.
[190] *SB*, 1882/83, Akst. 164; *Hygiea*, 36, 9 (September 1874), pp. 459–60; *Ridderskapet och Adeln*, 1859–60, ii, pp. 88–89; *Bihang*, 1859–60, viii, Allmänna Besvärs- och Ekonomi-Utskottets Betänkande 158, pp. 4–5; 1862–63, xi, 1, Motioner hos Ridderskapet och Adeln 240, pp. 595–96; viii, Allmänna Besvärs- och Ekonomi-Utskottets Betänkande 35, pp. 3–5; *BMJ* (5 July 1902), p. 50.

natural advocates of the infants subject to the technique, but equally as creatures whose mammary glands were thought to be particularly harmed by cowpox.[191]

In religious terms, antivaccination was associated with nonestablished Protestant sects, while Catholic regions tended to have less powerful movements: France less than Britain, Sweden or Germany; within Germany, Bavaria less than Prussia.[192] Indeed, in France the peculiarly obstinate quality of antivaccination was explained as a characteristic of Protestant sectarianism. Conversely, Protestants linked acceptance of the lancet to Catholics' unquestioning belief in dogma, with vaccinating physicians analogous to high priests of the medieval church.[193] In the Protestant nations, free-church movements in opposition to established religion were the carriers of resistance: in Sweden Baptists, in Württemberg Pietists, Calvinists in the Netherlands, with nonconformists of every stripe in Britain and Quakers especially well represented.[194] At the same time, the role of the Catholic Center Party in Germany, among the most fervent opponents, helped undercut any simple or invariable religious correlations.[195]

[191] Cowpox was considered a disease of the udders with analogous effects when transferred to the human female: *SB*, 1879, Akst. 304, pp. 1733–35; Nittinger, *Impfregie mit Blut und Eisen*, p. 4.

[192] Although in Montreal, French-Canadians were heavily opposed before the smallpox epidemic of 1885 and, in Milwaukee, Wisconsin, Germans and Poles were the main antivaccinators. Apparently the new world did something to the religious divide: William Osler, *The Principles and Practice of Medicine* (8th edn.; New York, 1919), pp. 316, 330; Judith Walzer Leavitt, "Politics and Public Health: Smallpox in Milwaukee, 1894–1895," in Leavitt and Ronald L. Numbers, eds., *Sickness and Health in America* (2nd edn.; Madison, 1985), p. 373.

[193] *Revue d'hygiène et de police sanitaire*, 20 (1898), p. 780; Vallberg, *Anmärkningar till riksdagsdebatten*, pp. 40–41; Born, *Öffentliche Anfrage an die Behörden*, p. 19; *Fraya: Zeitung für Volks-Aufklärung*, 1, 1 (10 November 1882), pp. 1–6; *SB*, 1872, Akst. 56; *SB*, 23 April 1873, p. 283; *SB*, 1895–97, 12 March 1896, p. 1409; BA, R86/1204, v. 2, "II. Internationaler Congress der Impfgegner und Impfzwanggegner vom 9. bis 12. October 1881 in Cöln," p. 2; "Die Berechtigung des Impfzwanges," *Konstitutionelle Vorstadt-Zeitung*, Vienna, 24, 140 (23 May 1878); Martini, *Commentar zu dem Reichs-Impfgesetz*, pp. 146–47; L. Belitski, *Die Kuhpockenimpfung ein medizinisches Unfehlbarkeitsdogma* (Nordhausen, 1872); Germann, *Historisch-kritische Studien*, v. III, p. 28; Dudgeon, *Compulsory Disease*, p. 7; Boëns, *La vaccine*, aux lecteurs; Belitski, *Gegen Impfung und Impfzwang*, pp. 2–3.

[194] *Förhandlingar*, 1908, p. 223; *RD prot*, AK 1916:58, pp. 35–37; Wernher, *Zur Impffrage*, pp. 50, 184; Kübler, *Geschichte der Pocken*, p. 239; Cless, *Impfung und Pocken in Württemberg*, p. 18; MacLeod, "Law, Medicine and Public Opinion," pp. 114, 196; Fraser, "Leicester and Smallpox," pp. 331–32; Jack Simmons, *Leicester: Past and Present* (London, 1974), v. I, p. 17; R. A. McKinley, ed., *A History of the County of Leicester* (London, 1958), v. IV, p. 282; *Hansard*, 1872, v. 212, col. 929; Sköld, *Two Faces of Smallpox*, p. 439. In the Netherlands, however, the situation was muddied by the low uptake of vaccination among Catholics as well: Willibrord Rutten, *"De vreselijkste aller harpijen": Pokkenepidemieën en pokkenbestrijding in Nederland in de achttiende en negentiende eeuw* (Wageningen, 1997), pp. 337–47.

[195] Kolb, *Zur Impffrage*, p. 10; BA, R86/1204, v. 2, "II. Internationaler Congress der Impfgegner und Impfzwanggegner vom 9. bis 12. October 1881 in Cöln," p. 6; Bohn, *Handbuch der Vaccination*, p. 146; *DVöG*, 20 (1888), p. 95.

THE PARTICULARITIES OF ANTIVACCINATION

At its peak, in the late nineteenth century, antivaccination became an international movement. In 1879 Hubert Boëns, a Belgian, founded the Ligue internationale des antivaccinateurs which claimed some success in its campaign against the Liouville bill in France.[196] The eventual abolition of compulsion in some nations was not only the result of the strength of such opposition. Vaccination was to some extent a victim of its own success. As the practice spread and smallpox epidemics became less virulent, the need for enforcing the lancet became diminishingly obvious and antivaccinators found more willing ears for their position.[197] But such common factors cannot explain the differences among the movements and their relative success or failure, except insofar as the best-vaccinated nations should, by this logic, have had the most vociferous protest. Despite features shared across antivaccinationism in all European nations, the movements differed in their organizational prowess, levels of mass participation and ability to influence official decisions. Britain and Germany had the strongest, able in the first case to wrest concessions that eventually made the lancet voluntary, unsuccessful for such aims in the latter. Sweden, with its early choice of compulsion, remained comparatively untroubled by resistance until the twentieth century, when significant changes were finally demanded and won. France, which did not seek to impose compulsion until 1902, remained correspondingly unperturbed by protest.

Antivaccination was strongest, most vociferous and crowned with greatest success in Britain.[198] The movement began in earnest after passage of the 1853 law required the lancet of all infants. In 1854, a measure aiming to improve enforcement encountered the first protests in Parliament and was withdrawn, while three years later a bill proposed to repeal compulsion altogether.[199] Prompted by such incipient rumbling in the ranks, the government, spoken for by Simon, issued a confident

---

[196] BA, R86/1204, v. 2., H. Oidtmann, "Bericht über den Stand der Impffrage im März und April 1881"; "II. Internationaler Congress der Impfgegner und Impfzwanggegner vom 9. bis 12. October 1881 in Cöln," p. 5; Boëns, *La vaccine*, aux lecteurs and pp. 46–47; Tebb, *Sanitation, not Vaccination*, p. 1.

[197] Many antivaccinators – so ran a favorite charge leveled by their opponents – had never seen a case and many were confusing chickenpox or other minor ailments with the disease: BA, R86/1204, v. 5, "Bericht über den Kongress der Impfgegner zu Berlin am 24. und 25. September 1899."

[198] Logie Barrow, of the University of Bremen, is at work on a study of British antivaccinationism.

[199] Creighton, *Jenner and Vaccination*, pp. 349–50; J. R. Smith, *Speckled Monster*, pp. 121–33; Lambert, "A Victorian National Health Service," p. 254; *PP* 1857 (sess. 2) (59) iv, p. 675.

defense of the technique, attacking resistance as a marginal and tran-
sient phenomenon and objections to the lancet as minor issues to be
addressed by technical remedies. During the following decade, as protestors became a major player in British politics, the authorities and their
provaccinating allies continued to portray them as a fringe of medical
eccentrics motivated by ignorance and prejudice.[200] Such official cavali-
erness became, however, increasingly difficult to sustain. Even friends of
the lancet advised the authorities not to underestimate the many respectable citizens whose reasonable concerns brought them into the ambit of
protest, recommending, in lieu of official contempt, positive campaigns
to carry information on the benefits of protection and the follies of resistance into the homes of the poor.[201] When the Vaccination Acts of 1867
and 1871 demonstrated the government's intent to enforce the lancet,
resistance took off. Antivaccination became a mass political movement,
in certain areas especially, during the following quarter century, subsid-
ing only once it had accomplished its primary task of making the procedure a matter of individual choice.

Antivaccination was a geographically localized movement, strong in
the Midlands and the north where local leaders and persecuted martyrs
whipped agitation into a froth, and differed regionally in its social
makeup and character.[202] In the north, antivaccinators tended to
belong to the lower middle class, artisans or shopkeepers, while in
London and the south, they were middle- to upper middle-class people
devoted to social reform. The movement also evolved in tactics and
focus. The National Anti-Compulsory Vaccination League, established
during the mid-1870s in Cheltenham by the couple Hume-Rothery, was
intended as a middle-class organization, independent of the working-
class movement in the north and London.[203] Its tactics consisted largely
of letterwriting and local initiatives, aiming to influence Boards of
Guardians. The Guardians were the authorities most immediately
responsible for enforcing vaccination, but their willingness as elected
bodies to comply depended heavily on grassroots opinion. Some were
enthusiastic in their fervor, prosecuting resistors with tireless application, nine, ten, on occasion nineteen and in the case of the stubborn and
luckless John Abel of Farringdon, no less than thirty-four consecutive

---

[200]   *PP* 1857 (sess. 2) (2239) xxxv, pp. 165, 197, 227 and passim; *PP* 1852–53 (434) ci, 77, p. 21;
Hansard, 1867, v. 188, col. 651; 1870, v. 202, cols. 1588–89.
[201]   *Hansard*, 1871, v. 204, cols. 227–28; 1877, v. 235, cols. 732–33.
[202]   *Final Report into the Subject of Vaccination*, sect. 517; *Hansard*, 1898, v. 57, cols. 775–78.
[203]   MacLeod, "Law, Medicine and Public Opinion" pp. 114–15, 123.

times.[204] Others, in contrast, had been elected on the condition that they refuse to prosecute defaulters. In London's East End, Mile End especially, candidates for the Board at the turn of the century were unelectable, regardless of party affiliation, unless they opposed the lancet and approximately an eighth of all Boards did not enforce the acts.[205] In a few such cases, the central authorities sought to compel them, most notably in that of the Keighley Union, whose members were jailed in York Castle after refusing a mandamus from the Court of Queen's Bench.[206] But unless London was hankering for a major showdown, such solutions clearly had their limits when the Guardians represented widespread local opinion.[207]

An effective tactic of resistance was to encourage martyrs for the cause, parents who willingly endured repeated fines and jail sentences, ultimately having their possessions seized and auctioned off. Associations were formed to pay the fines of the poor. Although later leaders questioned the effectiveness of the martyrs strategy, in fact it presented the government with one of its main stumbling blocks. Even though the vast majority of the British accepted vaccination, the hard kernel of those with moral, medical or religious objections threatened to hobble the entire system of compulsion. No law, short of direct physical force – uniformly regarded as unworkable – could oblige true objectors to vaccinate. They, in turn, with their strife and suffering rallied the support of others who, in less confrontational circumstances, would have been content to submit. A vicious cycle followed that could best be broken by allowing principled objectors an egress in the form of a conscience clause.[208] Because of this self-reinforcing relationship of martyrdom and protest, even provaccinators, like the British Medical Association, were eventually willing to concede such a clause, often in the hope that ultimately the numbers of those vaccinated would actually increase once the fanatics had been assuaged.[209]

---

[204] *Hansard*, 1881, v. 260, cols. 1309–10; 1877, v. 235, col. 737; *PP* 1871 (69) lviii, p. 849; *BMJ* (7 November 1896), pp. 1397–98; Naomi Williams, "The Implementation of Compulsory Health Legislation: Infant Smallpox Vaccination in England and Wales, 1840–1890," *Journal of Historical Geography*, 20, 4 (1994), pp. 403–05.

[205] *Hansard*, 1898, v. 56, cols. 428, 455; *Final Report into the Subject of Vaccination*, sect. 513.

[206] Although not before being freed by an angry mob during the first attempt to transport them to jail: *Sanitary Record*, 5 (26 August 1876), pp. 135–36.

[207] *Final Report into the Subject of Vaccination*, sect. 512.

[208] *Hansard*, 1878, v. 239, col. 478; *BMJ* (5 July 1902), p. 51; *Hansard*, 1870, v. 202, cols. 1584–85; 1878, v. 239, col. 493; 1898, v. 56, col. 431; 1898, v. 62, col. 345; *PP* 1871 (246) xiii, 1, pp. iii–v; *PP* 1876 (110) lxi, p. 304; *Final Report into the Subject of Vaccination*, sect. 517.

[209] *BMJ* (7 November 1896), pp. 1397–98; *Hansard*, 1898, v. 62, cols. 369–70.

At the local level, antivaccination won its most dramatic successes in Leicester.[210] The municipal authorities here had been reasonably diligent in enforcing the lancet during the late 1860s and early seventies.[211] When they decided to prosecute defaulting parents starting in 1869, however, resistance and fierce struggle ensued. During the following two decades, some 6,000 defaulters were prosecuted, with the usual penalty being 10 shillings' fine or seven days in prison. So heated were emotions that nearly two-thirds of the police force was needed to keep order at auctions of goods seized to pay the recalcitrants' fines. In the end no auctioneer would undertake to sell such property and a magistrate, a former mayor, declined to hear the prosecutions.[212] The issue soon percolated into local politics. After 1882 most of the Corporation opposed the lancet and the following year, in the triennial elections to the Board of Guardians, antivaccinating candidates won a majority. Their triumph was shortlived, however, since the Board, with the vote of the chairman deciding the issue, narrowly reintroduced a policy of prosecuting, issuing 2,274 summons over the next three years. Resistors now changed tactics, taking to the streets. When a protest was organized in March 1885 amidst such combustible circumstances, the result was largest antivaccination demonstration ever, with some 20,000 participants. The Leicester Guardians, in the absence of any guidance from the Local Government Board, thereupon voted to cease all prosecutions. At the subsequent elections antivaccinators once again won a majority and the new Board of Guardians pledged not to comply with the law. The triumph of the movement in Leicester was reflected in the incidence of vaccination, as it dropped from rates similar to those elsewhere during the seventies to some 60 percent of infants in the early 1880s, finally ending at a low of only 4 percent in 1889, after antivaccinationists had seized the city in their grip like latterday Anabaptists their Münster and the vast majority of parents defied the law.[213]

With Leicester revealing both the strength of the movement in certain

[210] Banbury and Keighley were other centers of the movement: Barrie Trinder, *Victorian Banbury* (Shopwyke Hall, 1982), pp. 150–51.

[211] Although there was some dispute on this point: *Hansard*, 1898, v. 57, col. 761; Fraser, "Leicester and Smallpox," p. 329; Simmons, *Leicester*, v. I, p. 17; McVail, *Half a Century of Small-Pox*, p. 70; Dales-L. Ross, "Leicester and the Anti-Vaccination Movement 1853–1889," Leicestershire Archaeological and Historical Society, *Transactions*, 43 (1967–68), p. 35.

[212] Stanley Williamson, "Anti-Vaccination Leagues," *Archives of Disease in Childhood*, 59, 12 (December 1984), p. 1195; Simmons, *Leicester*, v. I, p. 18; *Hansard*, 1898, v. 57, col. 762.

[213] Christopher Charlton, "The Fight Against Vaccination: The Leicester Demonstration of 1885," *Local Population Studies*, 30 (Spring 1983), pp. 60–64; Fraser, "Leicester and Smallpox," pp. 329–30; Simmons, *Leicester*, v. I, p. 19.

areas, but also its impotence in national politics, antivaccinators now increasingly refocused their attention from local authorities to Parliament. In 1880 the London Society for the Abolition of Compulsory Vaccination was founded with the goal of going for the administrative jugular, whipping up sufficient support to sustain a government inquiry into the entire issue and eventually abolishing or at least reforming the acts. This meant winning over a critical mass of physicians, administrators and parliamentarians and, to this end, avoiding the excesses and behavior that had served to brand antivaccination an eccentric and extravagant movement. Helpful in this respect was the adherence of several prominent and otherwise well-regarded followers. Compared to the other nations, where cranks and Grub Street intellectuals spoke for the cause, personages such as Wallace, Shaw and Spencer here added their luster.[214] The curious story of the article on vaccination in the ninth edition of the *Britannica* (1888) illustrates the propitious influence of such prominence.[215] The editors asked Edgar Crookshank, provaccinating professor of comparative pathology and bacteriology at Kings College, London, for the article. When he switched positions after studying the matter, however, and his manuscript was rejected, Charles Creighton was the next choice. When he too changed horses in middraft, the editors resigned themselves to the inevitable, lending the imprimatur of their standard reference work to the cause.

Pressure on Parliament had long been a common tactic, but one as yet uncrowned by much success. Candidates for public office were targeted according to their stance on the issue and voters urged to sign pledges to vote only for opponents of compulsion.[216] Incensed during the late 1860s at the government's intent to prosecute violators repeatedly, antivaccinators pressed Parliament to appoint a Royal Commission to investigate all aspects of the matter. In 1870 a bill sought to limit to

---

[214] MacLeod, "Law, Medicine and Public Opinion," pp. 189–91. Wallace self-destructed in his testimony before the Royal Commission, when he was caught doctoring his statistics and forced to back down on his claim that the incidence of smallpox increased in tandem with that of vaccination: *Third Report into the Subject of Vaccination*, QQ 7394ff. His attack on vaccination was included in the first edition (1898) of his *Wonderful Century*, but silently omitted from the second: F. B. Smith, *People's Health*, pp. 166–67. Provaccinators, of course, remained resolutely unimpressed by the intellectual pedigree of such opponents. High intellectual attainment, one sniffed, was obviously no guarantee of being able to weigh evidence and thus no bar to antivaccinationist attitudes: *Hansard*, 1898, v. 56, cols. 445–46. Viennese antivaccinationism also enjoyed an intellectually distinguished following: Josef Körösi, *Die Wiener impfgegnerische Schule und die Vaccinationsstatistik* (Braunschweig, 1887), p. 1. [215] Arnold, *Notes on Vaccination*, p. 111.

[216] *Hansard*, 1877, v. 235, cols. 732–33; *Report of the Sixth Annual Meeting*, p. 10; "The Medical Profession and Vaccination," *Hackney Examiner and Shoreditch Chronicle* (18 January 1884); *National Anti-Compulsory-Vaccination Reporter*, 1, 5 (1 February 1877), p. 1.

two the number of prosecutions for vaccination default. Here was introduced the concept that would eventually, after long battle, resolve the issue: a conscience clause to exempt the hard core of principled objectors after payment of a certain number of fines.[217] The authorities and their supporters remained unmoved. Limiting prosecutions, they argued, amounted to selling indulgences for nonvaccination to those able to afford the requisite fines. Various actions deemed harmful to the public weal (from entering railroad coaches in motion to suicide) were forbidden and it would be peculiar to exempt the guilty of consequences after a certain number of transgressions. Once the unvaccinated had been exempted, another argued with a rhetorical appeal to consistency, previously convicted inebriates could pursue their interests in drunk and disorderly conduct undeterred by any legal consequences for the rest of their lives.[218]

The government made significant concessions, however, in appointing a Select Committee which, in turn, walked a Solomonic line between the two sides. Over the virtues of the lancet it did not quibble: vaccination afforded a safe and great, if not absolute, protection against smallpox and the state accordingly had the duty to protect the entire population. But the sensibilities of convinced resistors also deserved consideration. Although the committee agreed that parents had no right to expose their children or neighbors to the risk of disease, the aim of the law, to vaccinate the entire population, was not necessarily furthered by a fruitless contest of wills with determined objectors pursued with multiple penalties. It therefore recommended that whenever parents had been successfully prosecuted twice, no further penalties be imposed with respect to the same child. Although, in fear of vitiating the law altogether by allowing also parents who were merely apathetic or neglectful to shirk their responsibilities, it did not include an explicit conscience clause exempting objectors in principle, it did accept the main point of the 1870 antivaccinating bill, that multiple prosecutions be capped.[219] In 1871, a bill incorporating many of the committee's recommendations was put forth. Its original intent had been to limit multiple prosecutions, relieving parents of further liability who had either paid the full penalty of 20 shillings or been charged two penalties for default. While this clause survived objections in the Commons, in the Lords it was struck out by a majority of one, and the Commons subsequently agreed, for

[217] *PP* 1867 (276) lix, p. 177; *PP* 1870 (126) iv, p. 751; *Hansard*, 1870, v. 202, cols. 1584–85.

[218] *Hansard*, 1870, v. 202, cols. 1585–90; 1872, v. 212, col. 930; *BMJ* (3 July 1880), pp. 5–6; (31 July 1880), p. 178; *Hansard*, 1883, v. 280, cols. 1042–43.   [219] *PP* 1871 (246) xiii, 1, pp. iii–v.

fear of passing nothing at all, to the amended version. Hopes of appeasing resistors were thus not only spurned, the bill's other provisions revealed the government's determination to ensure widespread vaccination. Guardians were now required to appoint Vaccination Officers who, using information from the Registrar of births, sought out and ensured that infants had been vaccinated, prosecuting defaulting parents.[220]

In subsequent years, objectors attempted, unsuccessfully as yet, to reintroduce the limit on prosecutions that had been so narrowly denied them.[221] The government in the meantime aimed to ensure as widespread vaccination as possible in the face of objections and to strike a balance between wielding the lancet and alienating protestors. In 1871, the Poor Law Board's vaccination duties were transferred to the Local Government Board (LGB), which now became the central authority for public health. Shortly thereafter the LGB instructed Vaccination Officers, unless specifically authorized to act independently, to submit all cases of default to the Guardians and to be guided by their instructions, in effect granting these discretion whether to prosecute or not. The problem, as in Leicester, was that certain Guardians were refusing to instruct their officers to proceed against defaulters. An act in 1874 now remedied this situation, granting the LGB powers to prescribe the duties of Guardians and their Officers in enforcing vaccination, thus in theory ending the anomaly that local authorities had been able to set themselves against the law by refusing to prosecute.[222] But having taken with one hand, the central government now gave with the other. A year later, in a policy formulated most explicitly in a letter to the Guardians of the Evesham Union, the LGB took two, somewhat contradictory, decisions. On the one hand Guardians were reminded of their duty to prosecute defaulters, but at the same time, they were granted discretion to determine appropriate measures in individual circumstances. Vaccination Officers were not to prosecute repeatedly except with the Guardians' blessing.[223] The Guardians were thus both obliged to prosecute for

---

[220] *PP* 1871 (191) vi, p. 559; *Hansard*, 1871, v. 208, cols. 1709, 1711, 1882–83; 34 & 35 Vict. c. 98, s. 5; *First Report into the Subject of Vaccination*, Q. 322.

[221] *PP* 1872 (91) vi, 471; *PP* 1877 (97) vii, 333; *PP* 1878 (74) ix, 41; *PP* 1880 (222) vii, 595; *Hansard*, 1881, v. 260, cols. 1309–10.

[222] *BMJ* (5 July 1902), p. 31; 37 & 38 Vict. c. 75; Fry, *Law Relating to Vaccination*, pp. 23–27, 79–84; *Hansard*, 1874, v. 221, col. 836; 1874, v. 220, cols. 1614–16; Christine Bellamy, *Administering Central–Local Relations, 1871–1919: The Local Government Board in Its Fiscal and Cultural Context* (Manchester, 1988), p. 127.

[223] *PP* 1876 (110) lxi, pp. 303–04; *Practitioner*, 56 (1896), pp. 503–04; *Final Report into the Subject of Vaccination*, sect. 113; *Hansard*, 1883, v. 280, col. 1013; 1898, v. 62, col. 323; MacLeod, "Law, Medicine and Public Opinion," pp. 122–23.

default, but also granted discretion whether to do so repeatedly for the same violation. With a few exceptions, like the jailing of the Keighley Guardians, the tacit agreement was thus that, in areas where antivaccinating opinion was strong, the Guardians were permitted to decide whether to prosecute repeatedly for default.[224]

During the early 1880s, parliamentary antivaccinators escalated their tactics, seeking to abolish compulsion altogether, not just repeated prosecutions. The government, in turn, stuck to its guns, insisting that, despite mishaps, vaccination was safe and effective.[225] At the same time, it was becoming increasingly clear that the compulsion to undergo an unpopular procedure, especially as enforced through multiple prosecutions, was provoking widespread resistance. After the Leicester demonstration had revealed the extent of objection in at least one major city, the government appointed a Royal Commission in 1889 to investigate the matter. Its reports, issuing with massive regularity over the next seven years, set the stage for a final resolution of the issue. On the one hand, the commission reaffirmed the value of vaccination, refusing to follow opponents in attributing the decline of smallpox merely to sanitary improvements. It did not want to make vaccination voluntary, but also thought that multiple prosecutions and other attempts at strict enforcement had prompted more resistance than otherwise necessary, thus defeating the overall aim of widely disseminating the lancet's benefits. Over the objections of medical and public health authorities, it recommended ending multiple prosecutions and providing some form of conscience clause to exempt fervent objectors.[226]

The legislative response came in 1898 with the new Vaccination Act.[227] Its evolution through Parliament demonstrated the slippery-slope nature of concessions to antivaccinators. The government had initially refused to follow the Royal Commission's recommendation of a conscience clause, fearing that a simple declaration of objection without prosecutions for default would tempt parents who would otherwise have vaccinated to heed the call of exemption. Instead it offered the compromise of no longer prosecuting parents after two penalties. From the antivaccinating vantage, this did little to mitigate the inherent problem of

[224] *Hansard*, 1878, v. 239, cols. 479–80; 1898, v. 62, cols. 313–14.
[225] *PP* 1882 (25) vi, p. 681; *PP* 1884 vii, p. 621; *PP* 1888 (77) vii, 627; *PP* 1894 (22) ii, p. 647; *PP* 1882 (385) lviii, p. 613.
[226] *Hansard*, 1883, v. 280, col. 1039; *Final Report into the Subject of Vaccination*, sects. 78–83, 151–54, 509, 511, 515, 521, 524–25; *BMJ* (7 November 1896), pp. 1397–98; (5 July 1902), p. 30.
[227] 61 & 62 Vict. c. 49.

compulsion, merely relieving of the law's onus those able to afford the requisite fines.[228] And indeed the government's legislative logic was now precarious: having thus sold exemptions to the wealthy, what was the reasoning, much less the equity, behind requiring the lancet only of those unable to afford the penalties? The official slide down the slope contin ued. In the standing committee, a declaration of objection was intro-duced, to be made by parents once they had been fined for default. In the third reading an amendment sought to allow exemption altogether, after no penalties, in return for a declaration of conscientious objection. This garnered support not just from antivaccinators, but also from many friends of the lancet who agreed that compulsion had led to more dissent and less vaccination than would otherwise have been the case.[229] In the Lords, strong voices spoke out for ignoring public opinion to insist on compulsion, but the Commons was able to override such sentiments to insert a conscience clause in the act.[230] In the meantime, the government was becoming aware of the political costs of bucking the current of resistance. In July 1898, the National Anti-Vaccination League swung an election in Reading from a Tory to a Liberal antivaccinator and Conservatives began to treat the lancet's opponents with greater respect. Balfour now came with a proposal that bowed to protesting sentiment, with a version of the amendment to allow conscientious objection without any preliminary penalties, although for the moment only as a four-year trial, thus in effect granting antivaccinators all they sought short of complete repeal. Parents were allowed to exempt their new-borns if, within four months, they satisfied two justices of their conscien-tious fears that vaccination would cause harm. Defaulters were not to be prosecuted more than once (at least until the child was four) and those imprisoned were to be treated as first-class misdemeanants.[231]

Despite such concessions, the battle was not yet over. Since the deter-mination of objection had been left to local authorities, the vagaries of regional variation once again played a role. Where resistance was strong, procedures were facilitated: mothers, not just fathers, were allowed to file for objector status and hearings were held at special hours to accommo-date busy parents. But where magistrates favored vaccination, parents were crossexamined or bullied, their motives questioned and certificates

---

[228] *Hansard*, 1898, v. 56, col. 469; v. 54, cols. 1677–78; *PP* 1898 (135) vii, p. 595; *Hansard*, 1898, v. 56, cols. 428–30; 1898, v. 62, col. 303.

[229] *PP* 1898 (285) vii, 599, ss. 2–3; *Hansard*, 1898, v. 62, cols. 329, 369–70, 384, 397.

[230] *Hansard*, 1898, v. 64, cols. 28–30, 42–43, 55–56, 403–05, 457ff.

[231] *Hansard*, 1898, v. 62, cols. 405–13, 462–63, 478–80; 61 & 62 Vict. c. 49, ss. 2–5.

refused when strict standards remained unsatisfied.[232] Because of such discrepancies and since the lancet was still theoretically required, anti-vaccinationists pressed on. Bills to remove compulsion altogether were introduced to no result. More promising was the attempt to ease the conditions of conscientious objection, removing what few hurdles still existed to exemption. In 1907, after the landslide Liberal election the previous year had brought 100 opponents of compulsion into Parliament, the government once again responded to the force of protest, introducing a bill to replace the certificate of objection with a simple statutory declaration, free of stamp duties to boot. Provaccination magistrates attempting to frustrate protesters' hopes for exemption were provoking needless opposition, the government argued, and a statutory declaration promised to sidestep the problem. Despite MPs who saw here evidence of yet another lamentable caving in to the most ignorant faction of popular opinion, the measure passed by a large majority.[233]

The effects of the 1898 and 1907 acts together were, not surprisingly, to reduce the overall percentages of children vaccinated. Although some 200,000 infants were exempted during the first four months after the 1898 act alone, the immediate overall effect was actually to increase the numbers being protected. The 1907 act, however, was followed by a considerable increase in the children exempted by statutory declaration and in 1909 the proportion of infants vaccinated had declined from a high of 78 percent in 1906 to barely 60 percent.[234] On the basis of such dwindling results, antivaccinationist MPs began a series of annual motions to repeal the acts altogether, but not until after the Second World War were they successful. In 1946, with the National Health Service Act, vaccination was no longer compulsory. By this point, so many parents were invoking the conscience clause that in many places fewer than half of all infants were vaccinated. With compulsion eliminated, the number of protected infants sank from 41 percent in 1946 to 27 percent, although it tended to climb when epidemics struck. In the 1970s, routine vaccination of infants was discontinued and by this point, the danger of small-pox had declined such that what had by now become the needle posed greater dangers than the disease itself.[235]

[232] *BMJ* (5 July 1902), p. 35; *Hansard*, 1907, v. 174, cols. 1276–80; J. R. Smith, *Speckled Monster*, pp. 136–37.
[233] *PP* 1905 (105) i, 341; 7 Edw. 7 c. 31; *Hansard*, 1907, v. 174, cols. 1276–80, 1271–74; v. 179, cols. 1182–83.
[234] *PP* 1899 (89) lxxxiii, pt. 1, p. 291; *Hansard*, 1904, v. 136, col. 254; *PP* 1911 (5939) xxxii, 1, p. 65; *Hansard*, 1907, v. 179, cols. 1182–83; Lambert, "A Victorian National Health Service," p. 14.
[235] *PP* 1911 (204) v, 891; *PP* 1912–13 (127) v, 653; *PP* 1913 (69) v, 959; *PP* 1914 (107) vi, 583; *PP* 1926

CONTINENTAL OBJECTIONS

In Germany, the forces of antivaccination were also powerful, although ultimately unable to end compulsion. The movement flourished after the 1874 law required the lancet throughout the Empire. It was also given a lift by the decision taken around the time of unification, first in the trade law of the North German Confederation in 1869, to allow freedom of medical cure, *Kurierfreiheit*, permitting anyone, whether academically trained physician or not, to treat patients. The ranks of so-called alternative practitioners were thereby boosted, among which vaccination and allopathic medicine in general were regarded suspiciously, and with them resistance.[236] Although it is hard to measure comparative strengths, German antivaccinationism appears to have been similar in scope and organization to the British. Some observers thought that, while the German movement relied heavily on the efforts of few heroic leaders, the British was more adept at enlisting ordinary citizens. Nonetheless, the signatures amassed by the Germans on petitions to the Reichstag were impressive: some 30,000 in the years immediately following 1874, tripling by the end of the century. The most prominent adherent to the cause was none other than the Emperor himself who, after 1882 and the birth of the crown prince, was persuaded by a certain Dr. Hübner to violate the law by leaving his children unvaccinated.[237] The German, and more generally the continental, movement was often judged more radical than the British, inclined to reject the very technique, not just its imposition.[238] On the other hand, opposition to the lancet here appears to have been impelled less by a desire to challenge the state's public health prerogatives than by fears of the individual risk posed by vaccination and indignation at the perceived hubris of academic medicine's support of the technique

(125) iv, 465; *PP* 1927 (139) iii, 961; *PP* 1930–31 (118) iv, 631; B. Semple, "Pockenschutzimpfung in Grossbritannien: Früher und Heute," *Das öffentliche Gesundheitswesen*, 37 (1975), pp. 574–75; Michael O'Brien, "Legal Implications of the Use of Vaccines," *Medico-Legal Journal*, 47 (1979), p. 153; J. R. Smith, *Speckled Monster*, p. 147.

[236] Geoffrey Cocks and Konrad H. Jarausch, eds., *German Professions, 1800–1950* (New York, 1990), p. 81; Bohn, *Handbuch der Vaccination*, p. 145; Kübler, *Geschichte der Pocken*, pp. 334–37; *Über die Einführung einer Gewissensklausel*, pp. 87–90; Cless, *Impfung und Pocken in Württemberg*, p. 19. The British Medical Act of 1858 also did not prohibit the practice of healing by non-registered doctors: Roy Porter, *Disease, Medicine and Society in England 1550–1860* (London, 1987), p. 51.

[237] "Ein Urtheil aus dem eigenen Lager in Paris über den deutschen Impfkampf," *Der Impfzwanggegner*, 7, 8/9 (August–September 1889); *SB*, 1877, Akst. 176, p. 498; *SB*, 1890/92, Akst. 541; *Eira*, 16, 12 (30 June 1892), p. 389.

[238] Kirchner, *Schutzpockenimpfung und Impfgesetz*, p. 100; Jochmann, *Pocken und Vaccinationslehre*, p. 263; *Über die Einführung einer Gewissensklausel*, p. 40; *Vaccination Inquirer and Health Review*, 7, 78 (September 1885), pp. 89, 94.

– a resistance, in other words, fired by medical rather than political motives.[239]

Strong and eventually crowned with success, the British movement naturally provided the example to be emulated. After the British conscience clause showed what could be accomplished, many German resistors also shifted from seeking to end vaccination altogether to a similar form of exemption.[240] One obvious difference was that the German movement, unable to achieve its goals, lasted longer than the British, persisting well into the present century. In the late 1880s the international movement focused its energies on Berlin, now, after victory in Britain, regarded as the stronghold of official provaccinationism. By the end of the century, international resistance was dominated by Germans.[241] During the Weimar years antivaccinators tried out novel approaches, appealing to the new democratic spirit as cause to end compulsion. Disputes in 1925 in the Prussian Landtag over a conscience clause on the British model revealed that half a century of debate had done little to advance the arguments on either side of the issue.[242]

As in Britain, the strength and nature of antivaccinationism varied regionally. In Bavaria, one of the first states to require vaccination, little resistance was to be found and only rarely did anyone refuse to submit. In Prussia, isolated movements arose, in Magdeburg for example, but protest

[239] Maehle, "Präventivmedizin als wissenschaftliches und gesellschaftliches Problem," pp. 129, 136–37; Eberhard Wolff, "Medizinkritik der Impfgegner im Spannungsfeld zwischen Lebenswelt- und Wissenschaftsorientierung," in Martin Dinges, ed., *Medizinkritische Bewegungen im Deutschen Reich (c. 1870–c. 1933)* (Stuttgart, 1996), pp. 81–82; Eberhard Wolff, "Medikalkultur und Modernisierung: Über die Industrialisierung des Gesundheitsverhaltens durch die Pockenschutzimpfung und deren Grenzen im 19. Jahrhundert," in Michael Dauskardt and Helge Gerndt, eds., *Der industrialisierte Mensch* (Hagen, 1993), p. 195; Loetz, *Vom Kranken zum Patienten*, pp. 291–92.

[240] [C. G. G. Nittinger], *Der Kampf wider die Impfung im Volk und Parlament von England* (Stuttgart, 1867), pp. 40–44; *Über die Einführung einer Gewissensklausel*, p. 86; Max v. Niessen, *Das Rätselraten in der Impffrage* (Berlin, 1929), p. 40; *SB*, 1882/83, Akst. 164, pp. 564–66; *SB*, 1909–11, Akst. 571, p. 2806; *Medizinalarchiv für das Deutsche Reich*, 2 (1911), p. 177.

[241] *International Correspondence of the Antivaccinators edited in English and French by Dr. med. H. Oidtmann*, February 1888, in BA, R86/1204, v. 3; R86/1204, v. 5, "Bericht über den Kongress der Impfgegner zu Berlin am 24. und 25. September 1899."

[242] GStA, 84a/3669, Deutscher Reichsverband zur Bekämpfung der Impfung, Ortsgruppe Hagen i. W., to Deutsche Reichsregierung, n.d. [c. 12 April 1919]; Georg Schreiber, *Deutsches Reich und Deutsche Medizin: Studien zur Medizinalpolitik des Reiches in der Nachkriegszeit (1918–1926)* (Leipzig, 1926), p. 47; *Über die Einführung einer Gewissensklausel*; Stern, *Should We Be Vaccinated?*, p. 119. During this period, colonial physicians in German East Africa, welcomed by the natives as bearers of the lancet's blessings, shook their heads in wonder that, in the distant homeland, disputes over the worth of vaccination still raged: Otto Peiper, *Pocken und Pockenbekämpfung in Deutsch–Ostafrika* (Berlin, 1935), pp. 3, 8, 19.

was not widespread.[243] Active movements were, in contrast, found in Hessen, Württemberg and Saxony. Württemberg may be regarded as the fortress of German antivaccinationism, in large measure thanks to the efforts of the preternaturally energetic C. G. G. Nittinger.[244] A medical student caught up by the liberal movement in Heidelberg during the aftermath of the July Revolution, he cast himself into biological research with the sort of polymathic exuberance possible only in the heady days before the onset of professionalization and specialization. At midcentury, he sought to correlate typhus with atmospheric conditions, then claiming to have identified cyanogen as the cause of smallpox. From here he became more generally interested in poisons, abandoned academic medicine, including vaccination which he had earlier practiced, to devote himself to "nature's cosmic remedies." His untiring efforts helped make Stuttgart the German equivalent of Leicester, where parents refused to vaccinate their children in large and increasing numbers and whence dissent spread to neighboring territories, Baden especially.[245] While resistance in southern Germany tended to reject the lancet altogether, favoring "natural" approaches to smallpox, opposition in the cities of the north, in Berlin, Hamburg and Dresden, was prompted less by opposition to the technique as such than by the fear that it spread other diseases, and antivaccination here was especially prominent in Social Democratic circles. Saxony was also a center of resistance, whether because of the Social Democratic influence, as in some accounts, or because, as others claimed, alternative medicine was especially influential here. After the turn of the century Frankfurt became one of the movement's strongholds.[246]

One means used by German resistors to jam sticks into the spokes of the 1874 law was to exploit the right of postponing for three to five years the vaccination of sickly children. Physicians sympathetic to the cause were willing to issue the necessary certificates for reasons not among those originally intended by the authorities, arguing, for example, that

[243] *Über die Einführung einer Gewissensklausel*, p. 40; von Bulmerincq, *Ergebnisse des Bayerischen Impfgesetzes*, p. 65; *PP* 1852–53 (434) ci, 77, pp. 54–57; *SB*, 1879, Akst. 304, pp. 1742–43; *Ärztliches Vereinsblatt für Deutschland*, 51 (July 1876), pp. 87–88; *Zeitschrift des Königl. Preussischen Statistischen Bureaus*, 30 (1890), p. 3; *Medicinische Zeitung*, 2, 26 (29 June 1859), pp. 125–26.

[244] Matzel, *Pocken im Deutsch–Französischen Krieg*, p. 13; *SB*, 6 March 1874, p. 230; *SB*, 1884/85, Akst. 287, pp. 1339, 1346. A list of his many works on the subject can be found in Germann, *Historisch-kritische Studien*, v. II, pp. xiv–xvi. See also Nittinger, *Über die 50jährige Impfvergiftung*, p. 16; Nittinger, *Das falsche Dogma*. [245] *Dr. Nittinger's Biographie*, pp. 35–36; Kübler, *Geschichte der Pocken*, p. 241.

[246] *SB*, 1878, Akst. 224, pp. 1438–40; *SB*, 6 March 1874, p. 227; *SB*, 1879, Akst. 304, p. 1744; *SB*, 1888/89, Akst. 134, p. 862; *Hansard*, 1883, v. 280, col. 1023; *Zeitschrift für Medizinalbeamte*, 25, 18 (20 September 1912), p. 669.

vaccination posed a danger because the lymph injected was equivalent to syphilitic poison. In Frankfurt, five antivaccinating physicians issued almost as many exemption certificates as the city's other 400 doctors together. Oidtmann, one of the most active antivaccinators, issued certificates that were widely accepted, except in Chemnitz where they were rejected because he had not actually inspected the children in question. So successful was such resistance that, by the early 1890s in cities such as Dresden, Zwickau and Leipzig, around a fifth of infants had their vaccinations postponed.[247] Another way of partially circumventing compulsion was to employ diluted potions of serum, as did one Saxon physician whose patients thereby hoped to be spared the worst of the lancet's consequences. In Dresden, a certain Dr. Engelmann, known to vaccinate with few pustules, enjoyed a brisk business among dissident parents. In 1892 he vaccinated 2,500 children, more than all the city's other private physicians combined. The authorities eventually clamped down, fining him and requiring children with few lancet marks to be inspected and revaccinated if the first instance proved to have been insufficient.[248] In Saxony, the Interior Ministry ordered district prefects in areas with unusually many postponement certificates or where vaccinations by private physicians were uncharacteristically unsuccessful to investigate why. The vaccinator was to inspect children to determine the gravity of the reasons for postponement and, if unconvincing, to wield the lancet.[249]

As in Britain, antivaccinationism became a political movement in its own right, only loosely and somewhat contradictorily associated with the established parties. Many from the Catholic Center and large elements of the Social Democrats opposed compulsion, but many antivaccinators were unhappy to be associated with either of these camps. The liberals, both National and Progressives, supported the lancet, thus reaping the ire of resistors.[250] Candidates were tested for their

---

[247] Albert Guttstadt, *Deutschlands Gesundheitswesen*, (Leipzig, 1891) v. II, pp. 286–87; *Zeitschrift für Medizinalbeamte*, 25, 18 (20 September 1912), pp. 671–72; *Der Impfgegner*, 8, 7 (1890), p. 39; *Korrespondenzblatt der ärztlichen Kreis- und Bezirks-Vereine im Königreich Sachsen*, 59, 6 (15 Sept 1895), p. 73.

[248] *Korrespondenzblatt der ärztlichen Kreis- und Bezirks-Vereine im Königreich Sachsen*, 59, 8 (15 October 1895), p. 21; 55, 8 (15 October 1893), p. 126; 56, 6 (15 March 1894), pp. 101–02.

[249] BA, R86/1220, "Ministerium der geistlichen, Unterrichts- und Medizinalangelegenheiten, M.d.g.A.-M. No: 394I.U.I., M.d. In. II. No: 6480," 22 May 1895; *Korrespondenzblatt der ärztlichen Kreis- und Bezirks-Vereine im Königreich Sachsen*, 59, 6 (15 September 1895), p. 73.

[250] Born, *Öffentliche Anfrage an die Behörden*, p. 14; *Ärztliches Vereinsblatt für Deutschland*, 51 (July 1876), p. 88; Brunn, *Der Nationalliberalen politische Abdankung*, pp. 3–4, 8; H. Oidtmann, *November-Flugblatt der Impfgegner, 1879*, p. 3, in BA, R86/1204, v. 2. As good populists, antivaccinators raged against the usual heady concoction of liberal–socialist–Jewish support for vaccination: R. Crüwell, "Die

position on the issue and supported accordingly. By the early 1890s, the number of Reichstag delegates pledged against compulsion had tripled from approximately thirty to ninety.[251] Within the Reichstag, antivaccination made inroads while ultimately unable to overcome the government's determination to stay the course. In 1879, the coreporter of the committee responsible for such petitions was converted to the cause, demanding that the government examine anew the whole issue while suspending compulsion in the meantime. When his provaccinating colleague agreed a few years later, the stage was set for an official inquiry.[252] In 1884, a Vaccination Commission was established, including delegates of the federal states and not forgetting three resistors. Unlike its British counterpart four years later, the German commission did not bow in an antivaccinationist direction, dealing with the issue as a largely technical matter. That vaccination, when poorly performed, occasionally caused harm, especially by spreading other diseases, was not denied. At question was not whether vaccination was good or bad, but the more limited topic of how to lessen the inherent risks of what, in sum, was clearly a beneficial operation, improving rather than abandoning the lancet.[253]

In 1888, the Office of Public Health provided a statistical defense of the technique, demonstrating both the need felt by authorities to respond to protests, but also a determination to stick to their guns. The following year the government thought it detected a flagging of the movement, but the early nineties revealed this to have been but a temporary lull. After the turn of the century antivaccinating petitions arrived in increasing numbers and with ever growing confidence.[254] In 1908, the Reichstag committee coreporter was once again converted to the cause. In 1914, objectors came closer to achieving their goals when petitions were, for the first time, sent on by the Reichstag to the government for consideration,

Verwüstung der Volkskraft: Ein ernstes Wort in ernster Zeit," *Zukunft*, 11 (1887), in BA, R86/1204, v. 3, p. 169.   [251] *Der Impfgegner*, 8, 3 (1890), p. 19; 11, 11 (1893), pp. 1–3.

[252] *SB*, 1879, Akst. 304, pp. 1742–43; *SB*, 1881, Akst. 123, pp. 706–09; *SB*, 1882/83, Akst. 164, pp. 569, 571–76.

[253] BA, R86/1205, v. 1, "Petition des Comités des internationalen Verbandes der Impfgegner, – Abtheilung Deutschland, – eingereicht durch den Dr. med. H. Oidtmann in Linnich um: Einsetzung einer wirklichen Sachverständigen-Commission zur Revision des Impfgesetzes und seiner ursprünglichen Unterlagen," 28 January 1886; *SB*, 1885/86, Akst. 313, pp. 1692–93; *SB*, 1882/83, Akst. 164, p. 579; *SB*, 1884/85, Akst. 287, p. 1257.

[254] Kaiserliches Gesundheitsamt, *Beiträge zur Beurtheilung*; *SB*, 1888/89, Akst. 134, p. 862; *SB*, 1890/92, Akst. 541, p. 2875; Prussia, Herrenhaus, *Stenographische Berichte*, 28 May 1914, p. 526; Eberhard Wolff, "'Triumph! Getilget ist des Scheusals lange Wuth': Die Pocken und der hindernisreiche Weg ihrer Verdrängung durch die Pockenschutzimpfung," in Hans Wilderotter and Michael Dorrmann, eds., *Das grosse Sterben: Seuchen machen Geschichte* (Berlin, 1995), pp. 183–84.

rather than just being passed over, and when a motion in favor of appointing a commission with equal representation of both sides to investigate the issue was defeated only in a tie vote.[255] The authorities, however, remained steadfast and the 1874 law continued in effect into the postwar period, both in east and west Germany, eventually replaced in the Federal Republic in 1976, with compulsion finally ended in 1982. The result was, not surprisingly, that the Germans remained more thoroughly protected than the British, with some 70 percent of the former vaccinated in the mid-1970s, while 90 percent of the latter were not.[256]

Although Sweden had introduced universal vaccination already in 1816, resistance did not assume noteworthy dimensions until midcentury. Compulsion had not been singlemindedly enforced and it was not until the law of 1853 lent some teeth to the authorities' bark that widespread objections were heard. Vaccination was popular and widely practiced during the first decades of the century. Early resistors in fact argued that precisely this acceptance of the lancet allowed compulsion to be dispensed with.[257] Nonetheless, protest was unlikely to have been sparked merely because a precaution was superfluous and there is evidence that, at midcentury, doubt was beginning to gnaw at the previously so untroubled Swedish faith in the lancet. In parliament, the first objections came in 1856 in the Burgher Estate with a motion to eliminate compulsion.[258] Three years later a similar proposal surfaced among the Nobles, but thereafter matters quieted until the early 1870s, when an epidemic following the Franco-Prussian war called forth agitation and articulate leaders like Melander, Siljeström and, later, Israel Holmgren, a professor at the Karolinska institution, were prepared to lead it. Toward the turn of the century, the movement was strong enough to prompt physicians' complaints that the authorities in Stockholm were apparently no longer enforcing vaccination.[259] As elsewhere, antivaccination varied by

---

[255] *SB*, 1908, Akst. 499, p. 2621; *SB*, 29 April 1914, pp. 8346–47; Prussia, Herrenhaus, *Stenographische Berichte*, 28 May 1914, pp. 524–25.

[256] Hans Stengel, "Nützliche Krankheitserreger: 100 Jahre gesetzliche Pockenschutzimpfung in Deutschland," *Zeitschrift für Allgemeinmedizin*, 50, 31 (10 November 1974), p. 1396; Wolfgang Schumacher and Egon Meyn, *Bundes-Seuchengesetz* (4th edn.; Cologne, 1992), p. 61; H. Spiess and C. E. Pilars de Pilar, "Die Impfpflicht gegen Pocken in der Bundesrepublik Deutschland," *Das öffentliche Gesundheitswesen*, 37 (1975), p. 577.

[257] *Förhandlingar*, 1908, pp. 222–24; *Borgare*, 1856–58, Bilagor, pp. 371–73, Memorial 165.

[258] *Ridderskapet och Adeln*, 1856–58, iii, pp. 120–21; *Borgare*, 1856–58, Bilagor, pp. 371–73, Memorial 165; *Bihang*, 1856–58, viii, no. 14, pp. 10–11; *Borgare*, 1856–58, ii, pp. 94–95.

[259] *Förhandlingar*, 1908, pp. 222–24; *Hygiea*, 36, 9 (September 1874), pp. 459–60; *Bihang*, 1915, Prop. 78, pp. 36–37; *Förhandlingar vid sjunde allmänna Svenska Läkaremötet*, 1895, pp. 168, 170. For similar complaints earlier, see *Förhandlingar*, 1871, pp. 133–34; *Förhandlingar vid det allmänna Svenska Läkaremötet*, 1886, p. 76.

region, springing up under the influence of local resistors, languishing elsewhere. Flashpoints included Kalmar, Örebro and Närke and, more broadly, the north. In certain areas protest was so widespread that local authorities felt unable to enforce the law. The percentage of infants vaccinated sank into the 1800s in some places and in Skellefeå, a hotbed of recalcitrance, it was scarcely 15 percent.[260] Antivaccination was often represented as a struggle between the countryside and the bureaucrats of Stockholm. Socially, supporters could be found among civil servants in Småland and free-church groups. As elsewhere, the movement was linked with currents of alternative medicine, hydropathy and homeopathy especially.[261]

Ignoring incipient resistance, the authorities decided in the mid-1890s that, although Sweden had been among the first to require vaccination, it had been prophylactically surpassed by other nations, too many children remained unprotected and enforcement had proven sufficiently lackluster that reform was in order. Stricter enforcement of the lancet and compulsory revaccination for the civilian population were their solutions. The proposals here resembled the German law of 1874 and in general Germany was held up as the model to emulate in such matters. Fines for default were to be increased and the authorities permitted to raise them until compliance had been assured. The bill that emerged in 1897 followed suit.[262] In parliament, however, committee was unimpressed by the need for change. Compulsory revaccination struck it as unnecessary since the nation's smallpox mortality was better than most. In 1898, the government conceded defeat, proposing instead a new law that left revaccination voluntary except for the military. Once again, however, parliament saw no need to fix the unbroken and rejected even this scaled-back bill.[263] Frustrated by its futile attempts to improve vaccination, the authorities appointed a commission which, unlike its British and German predecessors, deliberately excluded antivaccinators, regarded as incompetent and prejudiced. In the usual Swedish

---

[260] *Bihang*, 1912, AK andra tillfälliga utskotts utlåtande 6, pp. 3–4; *RD prot*, AK 1912:23, p. 28.

[261] *RD prot*, AK 1916:58, p. 35; AK 1916:67, p. 64; FK 1897:13, pp. 7–9; *Bihang*, 1898, Prop. 2, p. 20; 1916, Motion, AK 227; *Ridderskapet och Adeln*, 1859–60, ii, pp. 88–89; *Bihang*, 1859–60, viii, No. 158, pp. 4–5; 1862–63, xi, 1, No. 240, pp. 595–96; 1862–63, viii, no. 35, pp. 3–5; *RD prot*, FK 1912:20, pp. 57–59.

[262] *Förhandlingar vid sjunde allmänna Svenska Läkaremötet*, p. 158; *Bihang*, 1897, Prop. 4, pp. 19–21; *Betänkande angående skyddskoppympningens ordnande*, p. 17; *Kongl. Medicinalstyrelsens underdåniga skrifvelse den 8 Juni 1894*, pp. 9, 27; *Hygiea*, 56, 11 (November 1894), pp. 485–525.

[263] *Bihang*, 1897, Sammansatta Stats- och Lagutskottets Utlåtande 4; *RD prot*, FK 1897:13, pp. 7–9, 59–60; AK 1897:17, p. 18; *Bihang*, 1897, Riksdagens skrifvelser till Konungen m.m., no. 68, pp. 8–9; *Bihang*, 1898, Prop. 2; *Bihang*, 1898, Lagutskottets Utlåtande 67; Riksdagens Skrifvelse 135; *RD prot*, FK 1898:26, pp. 38–49.

manner, the stately pace of its labors delayed a report until 1913. On the eve of its publication, in 1912, the parliamentary committee responsible for antivaccination motions appeared to be making concessions to the cause, considering ways of appeasing objectors that would have, in effect, ended compulsion. When the commission report finally emerged, however, it offered a fulldress defense of the government's concern to strengthen vaccination. Noncompliance was punishable with fines, raised in cases of default during epidemics, and in exceptional cases the central authorities could impose even higher sums.[264]

Once again, parliament thwarted the government's desires. Although the upper chamber supported such plans, many in the lower house insisted on some form of conscience clause on the British model and the bill failed. In 1915, antivaccination mounted to a fever pitch, with some 40,000 petitioners seeking to be freed of compulsion, an extraordinary number compared per capita to similar compilations in Britain and Germany. Despite fears that the eventual end of the First World War threatened an epidemic, the authorities reluctantly concluded that a conscience clause was unavoidable.[265] The following year, the government grudgingly yielded to the will of the majority. Although making it perfectly clear that it regarded objections as irrational and incomprehensible, it was willing, in order to achieve the practical goal of improving vaccination, to consider a conscience clause if that was what it took to pass the law. Its proposal made exemption dependent on the guardian's belief that vaccination threatened the child's health. Hoping to avoid the consequences of a loosely formulated exemption, as in the British law of 1907, the Swedes sought to impose strict qualifications. A belief in the perils of the lancet had to be anchored in personal experience, not just derived from a perusal of antivaccination literature or other indirect sources of information, thus deterring all but the most convinced resistors.[266] Objectors were to appear before the authorities to testify, bringing witnesses or testimony if necessary to strengthen their case, with minutes of the hearing attached to their formal written application. Antivaccinators, under no illusions as to the government's intentions, rejected a conscience clause of this stripe, supported on this point

---

[264] *RD prot*, FK 1912:20, p. 40; *Bihang*, 1912, AK andra tillfälliga utskotts utlåtande 6; *RD prot*, AK 1912:23, p. 24; *Betänkande angående skyddskoppympningens ordnande*, pp. 48–53, 121; *Bihang*, 1915, Prop. 78, pp. 7–8.   [265] *RD prot*, FK 1915:75, pp. 79, 81.
[266] *Bihang*, 1916, Prop. 32, pp. 3, 8; *RD prot*, AK 1916:58, pp. 34–35. A related bill, also intended to tackle the antivaccination problem head on, dealt with objectors in the army, making it a violation of martial law for soldiers to refuse the lancet: Prop. 1916:33.

by the parliamentary committee.[267] Once again, upper and lower chambers parted ways over vaccination. Some moderations to the conscience clause were introduced in committee, while the insistence on personal experience was retained, and in this form did the bill finally pass into law.[268] While still shying away from the liberality of the British approach, the 1916 text thus punctured the 1853 law's theoretically absolute compulsion to vaccinate children in two respects: a one-year moratorium for sickly children with medical certification and the empirically based conscience clause. The age of vaccination was raised from two to six, thus moderating compulsion, but in return revaccination was required for certain groups: the military, foreign seasonal workers, inmates of forced labor institutions, medical personnel and all residents of an epidemically stricken area.[269]

In France, little resistance arose to a measure that was required only belatedly. Until 1902, smallpox prophylaxis remained at best indirectly enforced and there were few reasons to object. Stronger, as so often, in theory than practice, the French may have had the weakest antivaccination movement, but they could boast the most extreme exponent of the cause – Verdé-Delisle, for whom the lancet was the origin of largely every weakness and evil known to civilized humankind. Individual detractors could be found in France, but an organized movement of the sort familiar elsewhere never flourished.[270] That which did arise varied regionally as in other countries, with Brittany, for example, known as a fount of obstreperance.[271] The ideology of foreign antivaccinationism was met in France with undisguised contempt. When the international antivaccination league presumed to bring its cause to the land of reason and enlightenment, holding a congress in Paris in 1880, it was greeted with a screech of disdainful hilarity. The authorities were not, however, wholly unconcerned by potential public resistance. They worried that

---

[267] Especially the sparsely settled rural areas of northern Sweden, it was argued, would find it difficult to fulfill the conditions of the clause: *Bihang*, 1916, Motion AK 227; Motion AK 228; 1916, Lagutskottets utlåtande 22, pp. 31–35.

[268] *RD prot*, FK 1916:56; AK 1916:58; *Bihang*, 1916, Lagutskottets memorial 33; *RD prot*, FK 1916:64; AK 1916:67; *SFS* 1916/180.

[269] Alfred Petrén, *Den nya vaccinationslagen med kommentar* (Stockholm, 1916), pp. 3–10.

[270] Verdé-Delisle, *De la dégénérescence*; *Annales*, 3/50, 3 (July 1903), p. 235; Borne, *Vaccination et revaccinations obligatoires*, pp. 149; *Recueil*, 10 (1881), p. 262; *JO*, 1881, Chambre, Doc., p. 136; *JO*, Senat, Débats, 30 January 1902, p. 83; Biraben, "La diffusion de la vaccination en France," p. 268; Olivier Faure, "La vaccination dans la région lyonnaise au début du XIXe siècle: Résistances ou revendications populaires," *Cahiers d'histoire*, 29, 2/3 (1984), p. 192.

[271] *Revue d'hygiène et de police sanitaire*, 20 (1898), pp. 769–88; AN F[19] 5596, Minister of the Interior to the Ministre des Cultes, 30 September 1809; Darmon, *La longue traque de la variole*, pp. 208–09, 229.

submerging so dramatic an initiative as compulsory vaccination in the enveloping embrace of an omnibus measure like the 1902 law might undercut support and feared that opinion in the official bureaucracy had outstripped that on the street.[272] Compulsion lasted here until 1979.[273]

THE OUTCOME OF OPPOSITION

These nations thus took divergent paths in response to a common epidemiological problem. Although vaccination was broadly accepted in orthodox medical circles, differing social, political and administrative circumstances in each nation made it only variously possible to enforce the technique. In Britain compulsion was eventually abandoned after widespread protest, while similar resistance in Germany failed to persuade the authorities to dispense with such useful measures. In Sweden, home to an early form of compulsion, objections eventually forced the authorities to open loopholes, however constricted by the bureaucracy's sphincteral exertions, for conscientious dissenters. France, long the laggard of the pack, sprinted to the front in 1902 by adopting the most draconian measures, although their enforcement doubtless left much to be desired. To see the issue solely in terms of the compulsion to vaccinate or its absence would, however, be misleading. Misgivings of the sort expressed most dramatically in the antivaccination movements could be assuaged in other ways as well and the influence of protest did not exhaust itself solely in terms of whether the lancet was required or not.

Resistance focused the authorities' attention more resolutely than otherwise on various technical improvements that promised to make vaccination less dangerous and objectionable. In the early days, for example, there were few, if any, limitations on who could wield the lancet and the resulting haphazard standards of performance helped fuel protest. Already in 1811 resistance in the Bavarian countryside was attributed to incompetence among vaccinators. A few years later, Swedish legislators were concerned to spell out their duties in hopes of avoiding such problems. In France resistance was often prompted by the inadequacies of vaccinators, who in many departments were mainly midwives and old women. Even with the lancet reserved for trained physicians, as in Germany after 1874, problems arose when certain local authorities, contracting out public vaccination to the lowest bidders, managed to

[272] *Revue d'hygiène et de police sanitaire*, 20 (1898), p. 780; *JO*, Chambre, Doc., 18 Feb. 1881, p. 136; Borne, *Vaccination et revaccinations obligatoires*, pp. 135–36; *Bulletin*, 3, 49 (1903), p. 132; 3, 57 (1907), p. 410.   [273] Jacques Moreau and Didier Truchet, *Droit de la santé publique* (Paris, 1981), p. 104.

secure the services of only young and inexperienced doctors.[274] Most nations therefore sought to improve the competence of vaccinators. In Britain the 1840 and 1853 acts limited the practice to legally qualified medical practitioners, but this still left some two dozen professions in the running, including clergymen, druggists and midwives, many of whom were less than proficient. In response, the 1858 Public Health Act allowed the Privy Council to determine the qualifications of official vaccinators and the following year they were obliged to demonstrate adequate training.[275] The Germans went further. The 1835 Prussian regulation limited vaccination to trained physicians and surgeons and then only on the condition that they follow official procedures precisely (§51). The 1874 law threatened heavy fines and jail sentences for unauthorized vaccination and for physicians who violated the compact by which, in return for a monopoly on the lancet, they took care to wield it with competence and care.[276] When this proved insufficient to assuage resistors' fears, recommendations were made for a more thorough oversight of physicians' abilities, along with other technical improvements (forbidding the procedure during epidemics of other diseases, ensuring adequate waiting rooms at the vaccination stations, specifying disinfection procedures for the instruments and so forth). Training was improved and, as of 1887, all newly minted MDs had to demonstrate proficiency in vaccination.[277] In Sweden too, where technical prerequisites were less strictly controlled, the authorities sought to temper fears by threatening stiff penalties for vaccinators who performed their tasks improperly, although the measures were not formalized until 1916.[278]

The question of what sort of vaccine lymph to employ was another issue that, going to the heart of many objections, also spoke to the

[274] *PP* 1857 (sess. 2) (2239) xxxv, p. 228; Giel, *Schutzpocken-Impfung in Bayern*, p. 140; *Ridderskapet och Adeln*, 1815, v. 3, pp. 352–53; Bohn, *Handbuch der Vaccination*, p. 135; *SB*, 1884/85, Akst. 287, p. 1414.

[275] *Bihang*, 1915, Särskilda utskotts nr. 1 utlåtande 2, p. 47; 3 & 4 Vict. c. 29; 16 & 17 Vict. c. 100; *PP* 1857 (sess. 2) (2239) xxxv, pp. 229–30; John Simon, *English Sanitary Institutions* (London, 1890), pp. 281–82; Frazer, *History of English Public Health*, p. 73; 21 & 22 Vict. c. 97, ii; 30 & 31 Vict. c. 84, s. 4; *Hygiea*, 56, 11 (November 1894), p. 508.

[276] *Reichs-Gesetzblatt*, 1874, 11/996, §§15–17; *SB*, 9 March 1874, p. 267; Güntz, *Über die Verhütung der Syphilis*, p. 136. British observers admired the Germans for punishing physicians who vaccinated incompetently with severe penalties, thus undercutting antivaccinating complaints: *Lancet* (20 August 1898), p. 469.

[277] *SB*, 1881, Akst. 123, p. 712; *SB*, 1884/85, Akst. 287, pp. 1261–62; *Veröffentlichungen*, 9, 2 (4 August 1885), p. 48; Huerkamp, "History of Smallpox Vaccination in Germany," pp. 629–30; *Hygiea*, 56, 11 (November 1894), p. 508.

[278] *RD prot*, FK 1897:13, pp. 2–5; *Bihang*, 1897, Prop. 4; *Betänkande angående skyddskoppympningens ordnande*, pp. 117–18; *SFS* 1916/180, §23.

authorities' ability to tailor measures either to aggravate or soothe protest. Vaccination had initially used human lymph, produced by arm-to-arm techniques, but various disadvantages ensued. Vaccination had to proceed regularly and constantly throughout the year to maintain a steady supply of lymph and the more ample quantities required by epidemics were hard to assure. The vaccinated had to be seen twice (first to be punctured, then as lymph donors in the epidemiological chain letter of arm-to-arm) and strictures were required to ensure that they did not neglect their duties as sources of lymph.[279] Alternatively, certain groups of children were used as a lymph reservoir: the motherless waifs, for example, of the Stockholm orphanage or the children of garrisoned soldiers.[280] Most distressing, because the safety of human lymph depended on the health of previous donors, other diseases were sometimes spread from one child to another and fears of transmission were a pressing concern of antivaccinators. The better-off worried that the lancet brought their children into intimate proximity with epidemiologically suspect classes, souring the enthusiasm of those social groups otherwise among the most ardent supporters of vaccination. Would members of the House, one English MP asked rhetorically, care to take their children to "some low vaccination station like Bethnal Green or the purlieus of Westminster, where they could make no inquiry as to the antecedents of the children from whom the vaccine matter was taken?"[281]

As of midcentury, techniques were developed that avoided such problems. First, lymph began to be produced by transmission between calves rather than humans. Pioneered by the Italians, starting in Naples in 1848, this technique then passed to France during the sixties. In 1866 Pissin brought animal lymph from Paris to Berlin and during the following decade the procedure was perfected by Ludwig Pfeiffer and Leonhard Voigt, allowing institutions for the production of calf lymph to be established throughout Germany. Animal lymph was safer since the health of the calves could be better supervised and they were not subject to certain diseases, above all syphilis, that could otherwise be

---

[279] 30 & 31 Vict. c. 84, s. 17; 34 & 35 Vict. c. 98, s. 10; *SFS*, 1853/67, §§16, 23; *Kongl. Medicinalstyrelsens underdåniga skrifvelse den 8 Juni 1894*, p. 25; *Bihang*, 1897, Prop. 4.

[280] *Preste*, 1850–51, iii, pp. 122–24; *Bihang*, 1850–51, viii, Allmänna Besvärs- och Ekonomi-Utskottets Betänkande 14; RA, Skrivelser till Kungl. Maj:t, Collegium Medicum, 1803–05, v. 22, no. 1494.

[281] *Hansard*, 1877, v. 235, col. 739; *Preste*, 1850–51, iii, pp. 122–24; *Kongl. Medicinalstyrelsens underdåniga skrifvelse den 8 Juni 1894*, p. 25; *Hygiea*, 56, 11 (November 1894), p. 509; *Förhandlingar vid sjunde allmänna Svenska Läkaremötet*, pp. 168, 170; *SB*, 1884/85, Akst. 287, p. 1261; Güntz, *Über die Verhütung der Syphilis*, p. 116.

transmitted. Moreover, it allowed production of the quantities of lymph necessary for the full implementation of universal vaccination and for meeting fluctuations in demand. It was also discovered, starting in the 1860s, but not perfected and widely adopted until the nineties, that adding glycerin to lymph killed off bacteria while sparing the virus, thus improving safety.[282]

Despite this commonly accessible knowledge of techniques that would have served the interests of authorities everywhere in widely disseminating the lancet's benefits, the point at which calf lymph was put into general use varied widely among nations. The French, with no compulsion and therefore few pressing motives, took no particular initiatives in this regard until 1902, by which point animal lymph was standard operating procedure.[283] The British also lagged. In the late 1860s, word was only slowly filtering through that a new technique was being tried out on the continent. A decade or so later nothing more than further information on animal lymph was being demanded and only by the late seventies were bills dealing with the issue finally put forth. Not until the turn of the century did a measure more or less requiring animal lymph make the books, ironically in the same bill that ended compulsion.[284] In Sweden, too, the spirit was willing, but the flesh feeble. Although there were motions in parliament to prohibit the use of any but animal lymph already during the 1850s, half a century later the authorities still had to admit their inability to produce the quantities required to replace the human variety.[285] It was the Germans, in contrast, who sought to introduce such improvements in hopes of calming objectors' fears, lessening the pressure to vitiate vaccination's effectiveness by easing compulsion. Hopes of universally requiring the lancet, the authorities acknowledged, brought in their train the responsibility to guarantee its harmlessness. In the late 1870s, animal lymph was proposed to meet objectors' concerns.

---

[282] M. Depaul, *Expériences faites a l'Académie impériale de médecine avec le cow-pox ou vaccin animal* (Paris, 1867), pp. 51–54; Borne, *Vaccination et revaccinations obligatoires*, p. 43; Darmon, *La longue traque de la variole*, pp. 350ff.; Lentz and Gins, *Handbuch der Pockenbekämpfung*, pp. 302–06, 264–65.

[283] *Recueil*, 32 (1902), pp. 3–4; *Annales*, 2/35 (1871), p. 214; 3/49 (1903), p. 67. They did introduce glycerinated animal lymph and various other technical improvements for military vaccinations in the hope of calming the opposition of those few souls who, "blinded by false theories or unconsidered objections," resisted the benefits of vaccination: *Recueil*, 27 (1897), p. 256.

[284] *PP* 1868–69 xxxii, p. 9; *Hansard*, 1877, v. 235, col. 735; *PP* 1878–79 (131) i, 35; *PP* 1880 (9) vii, 591; 61 & 62 Vict. c. 49; *Hansard*, 1898, v. 54, col. 1676; Stevenson, "Science down the Drain," p. 17; MacLeod, "Law, Medicine and Public Opinion," pp. 192–93; Porter and Porter, "Politics of Prevention," p. 234.

[285] *Ridderskapet och Adeln*, 1850–51, ii, pp. 239–40; *Bihang*, 1850–51, viii, Allmänna Besvärs- och Ekonomi-Utskottets Betänkande 14, pp. 10–11; *Kongl. Medicinalstyrelsens underdåniga skrifvelse den 8 Juni 1894*, pp. 20–21; *Hygiea*, 56, 11 (November 1894), pp. 485–525; *RD prot*, 1897, Prop. 4, pp. 25–26.

By the early eighties, its use had increased dramatically and at the time of the Vaccination Commission in 1884, the technique had been sufficiently perfected that its exclusive use could be recommended. The following year, it was decided to use only animal lymph and by the nineties twenty-five state institutions were producing the substance, now used in 97 percent of all vaccinations.[286] In tandem, the authorities were delightedly reporting that antivaccination agitation, in this case in Berlin and Erfurt, had apparently been calmed by the introduction of animal lymph. They could now argue persuasively that the very few documented cases of syphilis transmission demonstrated the success of the new technique.[287]

REVACCINATION

Revaccination was another technical issue that spoke to broader questions of enforcing the lancet in different national contexts. Taking his cue from Sydenham's belief that disease produced permanent changes in the body, Jenner had been convinced that one round protected for a lifetime. As experience with the first cohort of vaccinees began to trickle in during the 1820s and thirties, however, it became clear that its effectiveness diminished with the years and that repetition was required. To vaccinate but once was thus, in effect, to stop short of making the lancet effective and to provide resistors with good reason to believe that the whole enterprise was useless, if not actually harmful.[288]

The necessity of revaccination was most easily accepted on the continent where no sentiments of national amour propre hindered what, in Britain, was often regarded as an attempt to besmirch the reputation of a local luminary and where the advantages of backwardness could be reaped. From the lancet's earliest days questions of whether its protection lasted a lifetime were posed in Germany. During the Württemberg epidemic of 1814–17, Elsässer in Stuttgart was among the first to argue that vaccination's effect was temporary. During the 1820s and thirties, it became increasingly clear that Jenner had overestimated the duration of

---

[286] *DVöG*, 11, 4/2 (1879), p. 711; *SB*, 1878, Akst. 224, p. 1446; *Ärztliches Intelligenz-Blatt*, 26, 29 (22 July 1879), p. 311; *Zeitschrift des k. sächsischen statistischen Bureaus*, 30, 1/2 (1884), p. 3; *SB*, 1884/85, Akst. 287, p. 1257; *SB*, 1882/83, Akst. 164, p. 580; *Veröffentlichungen*, 9, 2 (4 August 1885), p. 46; Süpfle, *Leitfaden der Vaccinationslehre*, p. 37; *Kongl. Medicinalstyrelsens underdåniga skrifvelse den 8 Juni 1894*, p. 28.

[287] *Zeitschrift des Königl. Preussischen Statistischen Bureaus*, 30 (1890), p. 3; *SB*, 1909–11, Akst. 571, p. 2805.

[288] *Tidskrift i militär helsovård*, 16, 1-2 (1891), pp. 24–27; *PP* 1857 (sess. 2) (2239) xxxv, pp. 172–73; Dixon, *Smallpox*, p. 288.

his method.[289] In 1829, the army of Württemberg demonstrated the virtues of repetition when local garrisons (where soldiers were now vaccinated upon recruitment regardless of their previous smallpox status and thus often revaccinated) were spared during an epidemic. Soldiers here became in 1833 the first group to be subject to formal revaccination. The Prussians followed suit a year later, with the Bavarians, the Hannoverians and the Badenese falling into line during the late 1830s and early forties.[290] By the forties, the tide was flowing strongly and revaccination being discussed as a measure also for the general population.[291] Württemberg also took the lead in this respect, requiring revaccination of civilians already in 1829. Except for Sachsen-Meinigen in the late 1850s and a few other minor states, however, no other such measures were passed until the Imperial vaccination law of 1874 made Germany the first country to require a second encounter with the lancet, in this case at age twelve.[292]

Prompted by their Jennerian faith, the British, in contrast, resisted revaccination for a longer period. Cases in which the vaccinated had nonetheless come down with smallpox were blamed on degenerated lymph in a hermetically unfalsifiable argument that, in its most extreme version, appeared to claim that the only perfect vaccination was one not followed by smallpox.[293] For the military, however, prudence took precedence over even Jenner's reputation and the army was revaccinated starting in 1840, the navy in 1871.[294] For civilians, in contrast, revaccination

---

[289] McVail, *Half a Century of Small-Pox*, p. 28; Eimer, *Blatternkrankheit*, p. 102; *DVöG*, 20 (1888), p. 91; Lentz and Gins, *Handbuch der Pockenbekämpfung*, p. 238; Eichhorn, *Massregeln, welche die Regierungen Deutschlands zu ergreifen haben*, pp. 105–44; Kongl. Sundhets-Collegii, "Circulaire till samtlige Läkare i Riket," 1839, copy in Riksdagsbiblioteket, Stockholm; *Annales*, 18 (1837) p. 77; Heinz Bohn, *Bedeutung und Werth der Schutzpockenimpfung* (Berlin, 1867), p. 17; *Deutsches Archiv für Geschichte der Medicin und Medicinische Geographie*, 2 (1878), p. 119.

[290] *Blattern und Schutzpockenimpfung*, p. 47; *Gesetz-Sammlung*, 1834, 16/1544; Friedrich Ring, *Zur Geschichte der Militärmedizin in Deutschland* (Berlin, 1962), p. 124; *Anhang zur Gesetz-Sammlung*, 1835, Beilage B zu No. 27 gehörig, p. 28; *DVöG*, 20 (1888), pp. 87–88; Kübler, *Geschichte der Pocken*, pp. 228–29; Kastner, *Impfzwang und das Reichs-Impfgesetz*, p. 13; Matzel, *Pocken im Deutsch–Französischen Krieg*, p. 11; Münch, *Gesundheitswesen im 18. und 19. Jahrhundert*, p. 236.

[291] *Annalen der Staats-Arzneikunde*, 9, 1 (1844), pp. 89–117; Zimmermann, *Über Menschenpocken*, pp. 92–93; Aug. Fr. Zöhrer, *Der Vaccinprocess und seine Crisen* (2nd edn.; Vienna, 1846), pp. 14–20; *Zeitschrift für die Staatsarzneikunde*, 58 (1849), p. 231.

[292] Franz Heim, *Historisch-kritische Darstellung der Pockenseuchen, des gesammten Impf- und Revaccinations-wesens im Königreiche Württemberg innerhalb der fünf Jahre Juli 1831 bis Juni 1836* (Stuttgart, 1838), pp. 580–81; *DVöG*, 20 (1888), p. 93; Kastner, *Impfzwang und das Reichs-Impfgesetz*, p. 13; *SB*, 6 March 1874, p. 238; *Gesetz-Sammlung*, 1835, 27/1678, §56.

[293] Charles Creighton, *A History of Epidemics in Britain* (Cambridge, 1894), v. II, pp. 611–12; R. Thorne Thorne, *On the Progress of Preventive Medicine During the Victorian Era* (London, 1888), pp. 9–10; Dixon, *Smallpox*, pp. 285–88; *Hansard*, 1883, v. 280, col. 1019.

[294] *Second Report into the Subject of Vaccination*, Q. 2659; Lloyd and Coulter, *Medicine and the Navy*, v. IV, p. 211.

was never required. In the late 1850s, Simon was persuaded of revaccination's benefits by the German military experience. During the sixties, recognizing the importance of revaccination, the authorities provided public access to the procedure gratis but despaired at being able to enforce it compulsorily.[295] The Royal Commission, likewise favoring revaccination in theory, considered it administratively impossible to enforce on a mobile adult population. Once protests against vaccination began to be voiced, the authorities were understandably leery of the prospect of extending their demands to include its repetition. In 1898, the government's promise in the Lords to put forth a bill on revaccination, subject of course (as was the first encounter with the lancet by this point) to the conscience clause, helped bring the upper house around in support, despite strong misgivings there about ending compulsion. When it failed to live up to its assurances, private bills sought to introduce revaccination at age twelve, but, bereft of the government's backing, these amounted to naught.[296]

Sweden, in turn, followed the British course in not adopting compulsory revaccination. The army was revaccinated starting in 1849.[297] For civilians, it was encouraged in the 1850s, but two decades later nothing more ambitious than proposals to make confirmation dependent on two rounds of the lancet were being broached.[298] By the nineties, revaccination was again being demanded by reformers and the authorities were holding up Germany as a model of what could be accomplished, Britain of what was to be feared. Nothing came of matters, however, until the First World War and then only to require revaccination of certain especially exposed groups, including again the military.[299] In France, without

[295] *PP* 1857 (sess. 2) (2239) xxxv, pp. 184–90, 194–95; Anne Hardy, *The Epidemic Streets: Infectious Disease and the Rise of Preventive Medicine, 1856–1900* (Oxford, 1993), pp. 111, 116; *First Report into the Subject of Vaccination*, QQ. 101, 152; *Hansard*, 1883, v. 280, cols. 1020–21; *PP* 1871 (246) xiii, 1, p. iii; 30 & 31 Vict. c. 84, s. 8; 34 & 35 Vict. c. 98, s. 9; E. P. Hennock, "Vaccination Policy Against Smallpox, 1835–1914: A Comparison of England with Prussia and Imperial Germany," *Social History of Medicine*, 11, 1 (April 1998), p. 59.

[296] *Final Report into the Subject of Vaccination*, sect. 533; *BMJ* (5 July 1902), p. 30; *Hansard*, 1898, v. 64, cols. 36, 38; *PP* 1904 (18) iv, 173; *Hansard*, 1904, v. 136, cols. 249, 254; *Practitioner*, 56 (1896), pp. 506–07.

[297] *SFS* 1849/8; *Kongl. Medicinalstyrelsens underdåniga skrifvelse den 8 Juni 1894*, p. 7; *Hygiea*, 56, 11 (November 1894), p. 497; Sköld, *Two Faces of Smallpox*, pp. 479–96.

[298] *SFS*, 1853/67; *Förhandlingar*, 1872, p. 321; Marie Clark Nelson and John Rogers, "The Right to Die? Anti-Vaccination Activity and the 1874 Smallpox Epidemic in Stockholm," *Social History of Medicine*, 5, 3 (December 1992), p. 374.

[299] *Tidsskrift i militär helsovård*, 16, 1-2 (1891), pp. 24–27; *Kongl. Medicinalstyrelsens underdåniga skrifvelse den 17 Januari 1896, i anledning af inkomna yttranden öfver styrelsens förslag till förnyadt nådigt reglemente för skyddskoppympningen i riket* (Stockholm, 1896), p. 44; *Bihang*, 1915, Prop. 78, pp. 45–46; Petrén, *Den nya vaccinationslagen*, pp. 3–10.

compulsory vaccination, revaccination was scarcely an issue. For longer than elsewhere on the continent, official medical opinion held fast to the Jennerian faith of lifelong protection, blaming examples to the contrary on degenerated lymph. In 1840, the Academy of Medicine still rejected the need for revaccination.[300] But opinion was hardly unanimous and others invoked the successes of revaccination in northern Europe. During the late forties, the tide began to change. At the Academy of Science in 1840, Serres acknowledged that the lancet protected only temporarily and recommended repetition, at least during epidemics, and later that decade the Academy of Medicine was won over.[301] As elsewhere, the example of the German military proved tempting and in 1857 revaccination began to be practiced in the army.[302] In the seventies, the authorities were recommending revaccination to employers and reformers calling for indirect means of compelling it; in 1881, the Liouville bill sought vainly to make it obligatory. As of 1883, revaccination was required of pupils in lycées and colleges and starting in 1888 all children over ten had to be revaccinated to remain at public school. In 1891, students of medicine and pharmacy were to be revaccinated before immatriculation at the university. By the nineties, the French were solidly in line on revaccination and, in 1902, two rounds – unparalleled elsewhere – were introduced.[303]

NEOQUARANTINISM AND THE LANCET

Whether to loosen or tighten the reins of vaccination was only one set of choices posed to authorities facing resistance. While rejecting (compulsory) vaccination, protestors only seldom denied that something had to be undertaken against smallpox.[304] Their preferred course of action,

[300] Lentz and Gins, *Handbuch der Pockenbekämpfung*, p. 238; *Mémoires*, 8 (1840), pp. 568–673; *Bulletin*, 5 (1840), p. 362.

[301] *Moniteur universel*, 287 (14 October 1825), p. 1412; *Bulletin*, 3 (1838–39), p. 6; 5 (1840), p. 10; *Annales*, 30 (1843), pp. 213–17; *Bulletin*, 13 (1847–48), pp. 721–22; Kübler, *Geschichte der Pocken*, pp. 247–48; Borne, *Vaccination et revaccinations obligatoires*, pp. 40–41; Weisz, *Medical Mandarins*, p. 92.

[302] Steinbrenner, *Traité sur la vaccine*, pp. 698–719; *L'union médicale*, 7, 62 (26 May 1853), pp. 245–46; *Annales*, 3/5 (1881), p. 326; 3/19 (1888), p. 348; 3/50, 3 (July 1903), p. 259; *Revue d'hygiène*, 48 (1926), pp. 373–75.

[303] *Recueil*, 2 (1873), pp. 159–62; *Annales*, 3/1 (1879), p. 445; 3/24 (1890), pp. 171–72; *JO*, 1881, Chambre, Doc., p. 136; 13, 16 (17 January 1881), pp. 267–68; Borne, *Vaccination et revaccinations obligatoires*, p. 49; *Revue d'hygiène et de police sanitaire*, 20 (1898), pp. 769–88; *JO*, 34, 49 (19 February 1902), p. 1174, sect. 6; *Bulletin*, 2/10 (1881), p. 570.

[304] *Journal der practischen Arzneykunde und Wundarzneykunst*, 19, 1 (1804), p. 61; *Ridderskapet och Adeln*, 1815, v. 3, pp. 659–72; Munck af Rosenschöld, *Förslag till Hämmande*, p. 16; *Hygiea*, 36, 10 (September 1874), pp. 547–48.

except for the rare radical who believed that clean living and sanitary surroundings sufficed, corresponded to the neoquarantinist precautions that the authorities had by this point, during the 1870s and eighties, long been implementing to stave off other contagious diseases.[305] They were, in other words, familiar prophylactic refrains firmly in the official repertoire, not – as earlier in the century when the Chadwickians had advocated their totalizing sanitationist solution to cholera – one element of an unfulfillably expansive vision of social reform. Antivaccinators in all nations demanded some variety of neoquarantinism applied to smallpox. Seen from the perspective of the sum total of precautions taken against the disease, the question posed by the protesting movements was therefore less whether vaccination should be compulsory or not, but rather should neoquarantinism face smallpox alone as the sole prophylactic intervention (except insofar as individuals chose to vaccinate voluntarily), or should it and compulsory vaccination be sent into the epidemiological fray in tandem. No government relied on the lancet exclusively; at issue was the relative balance between the two techniques.

From the vaccinators' point of view, isolation, disinfection and, generally, the neoquarantinist approach to smallpox were unrealistic if applied alone. Isolation of smallpox cases would work only when the mass of the population had already, thanks to the lancet, been rendered unreceptive. Otherwise, the length of the incubation period and the facility with which the contagion spread raised the same sorts of problems as asymptomatic cholera carriers, allowing the disease easily to be imported and transmitted before anyone was aware of it.[306] Isolation was also a more expensive and cumbersome technique than compulsory vaccination, demoralizing to the quarantined, tempting to circumvent, difficult to ask of the poor who lived in crowded circumstances, hard to implement in sparsely settled rural areas and dependent on the construction of costly and unpopular special hospitals, replete during epidemics, but otherwise vacant.[307] Finally, provaccinators argued that, given the state's right to restrict indi-

---

[305] *Cobbett's*, 1806, v. 7, cols. 886–87; *SB*, 1882/83, Akst. 164, p. 572; *Annales*, 3/50, 3 (July 1903), p. 242; *Hansard*, 1861, v. 164, cols. 678–79; *Die Cholera. Ihre Verhütung und Heilung: Von einem erfahrenen Arzte* (Hannover, 1885), pp. iv–vii; Nittinger, *Das falsche Dogma*, p. 23. The only doubts on the legitimacy of neoquarantinist techniques came from France where observers feared that removals and isolation would not be accepted: *Bulletin de la Société de médecine publique et d'hygiène professionnelle*, 2 (1879), pp. 328–34.

[306] Wernher, *Zur Impffrage*, p. 20; *Betänkande angående skyddskoppympningens ordnande*, pp. 48–50; *Bihang*, 1915, Särskilda utskotts nr. 1 utlåtande 2, p. 43; *RD prot*, FK 1912:20, pp. 41–42, 56.

[307] *Bihang*, 1815, iv, 3, pp. 1338–48; *Hansard*, 1904, v. 136, cols. 249–52; *Annales*, 3/50, 3 (July 1903), p. 242; *DZSA*, NF, 20 (1862), p. 9; Cless, *Impfung und Pocken in Württemberg*, p. 80.

vidual liberties for the common good, vaccination (a quick jab twice a life-time) was a less intrusive imposition than neoquarantinism (reporting cases to the authorities, removal and sequestration of the ill and their families, surveillance of contacts, disinfection, sometimes destruction, of belongings and dwellings).[308] From the antivaccinators' perspective, neo quarantinism – no longer the evil that had earlier been combated by strict sanitarians when it came to cholera – was now a reasonable alternative to the lancet. Their ambitions were to persuade the authorities to abandon vaccination in favor of neoquarantinist techniques, and in certain cases they were successful. In no nation, however, did the authorities not include neoquarantinism as part of their prophylactic strategy.

In Britain, the Leicester system, developed in the Mecca of antivaccinationism, was simply the application of neoquarantinist principles to smallpox. Once the Leicester Guardians refused to enforce the vaccination acts in 1886, the sanitary authorities, with little choice but to bow to local orthodoxy, began applying neoquarantinist methods. The Leicester system, based on powers granted under the Public Health Act of 1875, had been developed in the mid-1870s at the behest of the Medical Officer of Health, William Johnston, who had intended it to supplement, not replace, vaccination.[309] Physicians were required to report smallpox cases within twelve hours; the victims and their families were compulsorily isolated in hospitals for two weeks, their homes disinfected, clothing and bedding burnt or purified. Contacts of the victims were kept under surveillance and sometimes also quarantined.[310] They

---

[308] *Bihang*, 1903, AK Tillfälliga Utskott (No. 2) Utlåtande 30, p. 11; 1915, Särskilda utskotts nr. 1 utlåtande 2, p. 43; *Betänkande angående skyddskoppympningens ordnande*, pp. 48–53; *Hygiea*, 36, 10 (September 1874), pp. 547–48; *Hansard*, 1898, v. 57, cols. 770, 785; *Bulletin*, 3, 25 (1891), p. 109; Tebb, *Century of Vaccination*, pp. 88–89; *SB*, 23 April 1873, pp. 284–86; *SB*, 1884/85, Akst. 287, pp. 1346–47. Some antivaccinators agreed: see Martini, *Commentar zu dem Reichs-Impfgesetz*, p. 148; *SB*, 23 April 1873, p. 286; *SB*, 1884/85, Akst. 287, p. 1347; *Annales*, 18 (1837) pp. 162–63; 3/50, 3 (July 1903), p. 242.

[309] *Lancet* (17 October 1885), p. 737; *Final Report into the Subject of Vaccination*, sect. 482; Fraser, "Leicester and Smallpox," pp. 315, 331–32; MacLeod, "Law, Medicine and Public Opinion," pp. 195–96.

[310] Patients could apparently be compulsorily removed, but only persuasion by the medical authorities was allowed for their contacts. If persons liable to infection refused to be quarantined, they were visited daily by the inspector, warned against going to work or undue exposure, but were not confined to the house, although they had to remain at home until the sanitary staff had attended them. They were also prohibited from entering the homes of the uninfected, public institutions or meetings, under penalty of forfeiting their monetary allowance to cover food and rent: *Final Report into the Subject of Vaccination*, sects. 480, 482; Millard, *Vaccination Question*, p. 128; Biggs, *Leicester*, pp. 474–76; *Appendix VI to the Final Report of the Royal Commission on Vaccination* (C.-8612) (London, 1897), pp. 2–3; J. T. Biggs, "How Leicester Deals with Smallpox," *Vaccination Inquirer* (1 November 1892); W. McC. Wanklyn, *The Administrative Control of Smallpox* (London, 1913), p. 41.

were in practice prevented from working by threats of informing their employers of their condition. If willing, they were given a disinfectant bath at the hospital, if not, provided with antiseptics at home. The infectiously ill were forbidden to work in occupations likely to facilitate transmission, especially dealing with food, and were not allowed to return library books without first disinfecting them. Quarantined patients were compensated for loss of working time and contacts who stayed away from work were also generally provided with half-pay.[311]

But Leicester was only the most dramatic example of a technique that in fact had also been applied earlier and elsewhere in Britain. Indeed, in the twentieth century, the system became known as the English method, much as with neoquarantinism applied to cholera. Until the 1860s, British authorities had regarded vaccination as the truest arrow in their quiver, but the cholera and cattle plague epidemics of 1866 had served to concentrate their minds on more traditional remedies. In 1868, James Young Simpson recommended extending neoquarantinist techniques (the "stamping-out system") used to control rinderpest also to smallpox.[312] In London during the early 1870s, prophylactic emphasis shifted from the lancet to tracing victims and their contacts, isolating or removing them, disinfecting dwellings, clothes and bedding. The powers granted by the Public Health Act of 1875 to require notification, hospitalization, surveillance of contacts and disinfection and to visit lodging houses to inspect vagrants and others allowed the authorities, employing the tenets of neoquarantinism, to develop an enforceable alternative to vaccination.[313] Public health officials were specifically instructed to remove smallpox victims whose domestic accommodation could not guarantee their isolation. In Scotland in the mid-1880s, convalescent patients were treated much like cholera victims half a century earlier, instructed to keep to the center of the street when venturing into public,

[311] Thomas Windley, *Leicester and Smallpox* (Leicester, 1902), p. 9; *Sanitary Record*, n.s., 16, 252 (29 September 1894), p. 1058; *Appendix VI to the Final Report*, pp. 9–10; 60 & 61 Vict. c. 218 (priv. act), clauses 49, 53, 55; McKinley, *History of Leicester*, v. IV, p. 283; Millard, *Vaccination Question*, p. 128; *Hygienische Rundschau*, 14, 17 (1904), pp. 817–21.

[312] J. R. Smith, *Speckled Monster*, p. 143; *MTG*, 1 (1868), pp. 5, 32. Stamping out involved destroying, in the case of infected animals, and isolating, in that of humans, victims to prevent transmission: McVail, *Half a Century of Small-Pox*, pp. 56–57; Dixon, *Smallpox*, p. 291.

[313] Hardy, *Epidemic Streets*, pp. 123–24; Anne Hardy, "Smallpox in London: Factors in the Decline of the Disease in the Nineteenth Century," *Medical History*, 27, 2 (April 1993), pp. 111–12; *Final Report into the Subject of Vaccination*, sects. 495–503; *Hansard*, 1898, v. 62, col. 403; Millard, *Vaccination Question*, pp. 19–21; Biggs, *Leicester*, p. 72. Similar techniques were also employed in Australia, heavily influenced here by the metropolitan example: Alan Mayne, "'The Dreadful Scourge': Responses to Smallpox in Sydney and Melbourne, 1881–1882," in Roy Macleod and Milton Lewis, eds., *Disease, Medicine and Empire* (London, 1988), pp. 227–30.

encouraged to identify themselves with distinguishing marks. In 1888, the Local Government Board ordered the application of neoquarantinist techniques to smallpox.[314] At the turn of the century, vagrants and other itinerants were often isolated if stricken, although there was no direct legal mandate for such actions and substantial payments were on occasion required in lieu of claims for damages. Once compulsory vaccination was wholly abolished in 1948, Britain switched entirely to the neoquarantinist principle of isolating victims, although seeking, when possible, also to vaccinate their contacts.[315]

In Germany, the principles of neoquarantinism also became part of preventive practice, although here they ran in strict tandem to vaccination. Although antivaccinators had not persuaded the authorities to abandon compulsion, the movement's strength and insistence meant that concessions were in order. In theory, repeated vaccination should have provided sufficient protection against smallpox, replacing other neoquarantinist measures. But in fact the authorities were never willing to abandon the full array of precautions in their arsenal, especially given the resistors' ability to spread mistrust and suspicion of the lancet. In the 1870s arguments circulated to the effect that, insufficient alone, vaccination needed to be complemented by disinfection and isolation. In the eighties, both the Bavarian authorities and Krupp's factories in Essen tried isolating smallpox patients rather than relying wholly on vaccination. In 1886, an ordinance in Hamburg required removal of smallpox victims to hospitals.[316] Then, in the Imperial Contagious Disease Law, the neoquarantinist tenets advocated by antivaccinators were implemented, giving the Germans the benefits of a dual-track approach covering every epidemiological eventuality. While the 1874 law enforced the lancet as a means of individual prophylaxis, the whole gamut of neoquarantinist precautions was now targeted also at smallpox.[317] Victims were to be isolated, their houses marked. Contacts, whether colleagues or even just the postman, as well as residents of stricken houses and workers who

---

[314] PRO, MH 113/6, "Memorandum on the Duties of Sanitary Authorities in Reference to Epidemics of Small-Pox," January 1877; repeated in 1888: MH 113/9, "Memorandum on the steps specially requisite to be taken in places where Small-Pox is prevalent"; Ian Levitt, ed., *Government and Social Conditions in Scotland 1845–1919* (Edinburgh, 1988), pp. 133–34; *Second Report into the Subject of Vaccination*, pp. 246–47; *Appendix VI to the Final Report*, p. 2.

[315] *Journal of State Medicine*, 11 (1903), pp. 654–55; *Public Health*, 15 (1902–03), pp. 599–600; Semple, "Pockenschutzimpfung in Grossbritannien," p. 574.

[316] *Berliner klinische Wochenschrift*, 9 (5 February 1872), p. 75; *SB*, 1884/85, Akst. 287, pp. 1295, 1344; Voigt, *Das erste Jahrhundert der Schutzimpfung*, p. 9.

[317] *Reichs-Gesetzblatt*, 1904, 9/3020; H. A. Gins, *Der Pockenschutz des deutschen Volkes* (Berlin, 1917), p. 48.

handled possibly dangerous objects, were considered suspected of infectiousness ("Ansteckungsverdächtig") and subject to surveillance up to two weeks. Generally, this meant nothing more alarming than a doctor inquiring periodically about their health, but if the official physician decided that such people should not frequent public (including work-) places or be subject to other limitations on their freedom of movement and, if they proved unwilling to abide, they too could be isolated. Public assemblies could be prohibited, as could economic activity in infected houses. Disinfection of used clothing and sickrooms could be ordered, as well as special treatment of corpses. Arriving foreigners and locals who had visited infected areas were liable to surveillance. For certain categories of outsiders (the homeless and itinerant, emigrants, seasonal laborers, gypsies, tinkers, vagrants, peddlers and the like) an especially restrictive form of surveillance was possible that included limiting their choice of residence and work, requiring them to appear personally before the health authorities and prohibiting their presence in certain places. If a foreign country were infected, transmigrants were allowed to cross the border only where they could be medically inspected, the ill and contagious isolated. The mass transportation of transmigrants by railway was allowed only in special wagons and in compartments without upholstering. Foreign workers from infected areas were to be vaccinated within three days of arrival unless already protected.

In France as well, despite its legislative lag, a neoquarantinist approach was long discussed.[318] In 1870, the Comité consultatif recommended disinfecting the homes of smallpox victims, sequestering them in special wards, and later in the decade it became normal to hospitalize poor patients with few opportunities to take precautions at home. In 1870 a special commission in Paris recommended isolation hospitals for smallpox on the "English model." Small villages in the Loire-Inférieure were isolated when smallpox struck in the late 1880s and early nineties and in Nancy and elsewhere patients were sequestered and their lodgings and effects disinfected. Bordeaux's public health authorities consciously paired an encouragement of vaccination with isolation and disinfection, but at the same time others lamented the absence of effective means to compel isolation of recalcitrants.[319] The 1902 public

---

[318] *Bulletin de la Société de médecine publique et d'hygiène professionnelle*, 2 (1879), pp. 102–07, 150–64; 1 (1877), pp. 234–47; *Rapport sur les travaux du conseil central d'hygiene publique et de salubrité de la ville de Nantes et du département de la Loire-Inférieure*, 1880, pp. 101–03; *JO*, Débats, Chambre, 9 March 1907, p. 603.

[319] *Recueil*, 2 (1873), pp. 159–62; Darmon, *La longue traque de la variole*, p. 398; *Annales*, 2/35 (1871), p. 222; 3/15 (1886), pp. 219–29; *Recueil*, 21 (1891), pp. 544–46, 959; *Annales*, 3/18 (1887), pp. 225–29; 3/16 (1886), p. 468.

hygiene law took a similarly dual-track approach, requiring the lancet as well as notification, disinfection and, if need be, destruction of objects of transmission. Sequestration of the ill, though not provided for in the law itself, was spelled out in ministerial circular the following year. The ill were to be isolated (at home if possible, in a hospital if necessary) with removal accomplished in special transports; after recovery, they were not to venture into public before cleansing and disinfection. During the 1910 smallpox epidemic in Paris, isolation, disinfection and vaccination of immediate contacts were practiced all together.[320] Only in Sweden, where the tenets of neoquarantinism were slow to be adopted also for other diseases, did vaccination continue to be treated largely independently of any broader prophylactic approach.

THE CAUSES OF VARIATION

Once again, though a biologically common problem faced all nations, a range of divergent strategies was pursued: Britain with its early embrace of compulsion, switching then, under impetus of antivaccinationism, to allow for exemptions; Germany with its patchy and various local approaches, coordinated finally after unification to require vaccination and revaccination of all citizens without exception; early compulsion in Sweden, with its halfhearted and grudging willingness later to follow the British example on conscience clauses; and finally France with its century of inertia capped by a thunderclap conversion to a form of compulsion that, in theory at least, was stricter than the German. Why?

An Ackerknechtian posing of the problem suggests a connection between political regime and prophylactic approach. Although such consistent relationships were hard to discern in the case of cholera, with smallpox similar correlations seem more plausible. At the least, the issue of individual rights and their violation by the lancet arose frequently and insistently. Cholera was at first pursued with timehonored and tested methods earlier developed for plague and other diseases and thus did not pose novel dilemmas in these terms. For smallpox, in contrast, new preventive techniques had to be assimilated by the varying political traditions of each nation. Moreover, the lancet broached a new dimension of potential civil liberties' transgressions: not just the quasi-incarceration of quarantine, but direct and immediate violation of bodily integrity, the injection of "foreign" and "unnatural" substances

---

[320] Monod, *La santé publique*, pp. 229–31; *Annales*, 4/15 (1911), p. 107.

into the blood, the inducement of disease, however mild, in a still healthy subject.

Vaccination was consistently debated in broad terms of political ideology, the relations between state and individual and the community's right to trespass on personal autonomy by invoking a higher common purpose to justify a biologically intimate and (in the early days at least) not always harmless intervention. Proponents portrayed vaccination as a public good: since the lancet was not infallible, the protection afforded each individual increased as more of the community was covered. As one French observer put it, the danger of a fire is measured not by the intensity of the initial spark, but the combustibility of the material on which it falls.[321] Objectors were free riders who, reaping the benefits of herd immunity, themselves posed a threat to the community. Compulsion was therefore justified to ensure that all shared this common burden.[322] Opponents, in turn, to the extent that they did not consider vaccination intrinsically objectionable, regarded it as a private good, whose fruits anyone so desiring could enjoy, but which remained an act the state should not compel. Downplaying the risk of spreading disease to others and elevating the autonomy of the individual to an absolute, antivaccinators portrayed personal health, including the lancet, as a matter for each person alone to decide.[323] "I stand," as one put it, "for the right of every citizen . . . to maintain the purity and integrity of his person as against all theory or practice of unsettled and unsought defilement – his right to resist even state-authorized invasion of the fountain of life to the debasement of the current coin of its realm."[324]

Provaccinators argued their position in similar terms across national boundaries: because potentially contagious individuals not only harmed themselves, but posed threats to their fellow citizens, the state had the obligation to render them harmless. It was not the benefit to the individ-

---

[321] *Annales*, 3/25 (1891), p. 351; *SB*, 1884/85, Akst. 287, pp. 1257, 1260; W. McConnel Wanklyn, *A Survey of the Present Position of Smallpox and Vaccination as Affecting This Country* (London, 1922), p. 21.

[322] Kastner, *Impfzwang und das Reichs-Impfgesetz*, p. 10; *SB*, 1884/85, Akst. 287, p. 1260; *SB*, 1909–11, Akst. 571; *Blattern und Schutzpockenimpfung*, pp. 97–98; *DZSA*, 15 (1828), pp. 238–39; Eimer, *Blatternkrankheit*, pp. 146–47; Giel, *Schutzpockenimpfung in Bayern*, pp. 386–88.

[323] Wegener, *Unerhört!!*, p. vi; Vallberg, *Vaccinationstyranniet*, pp. 3, 24; *Nineteenth Century*, 11, 63 (May 1882), p. 785; *Hansard*, 1898, v. 62, col. 316; Creighton, *Jenner and Vaccination*, pp. 350–51; Vallberg, *Böra vi twingas?*, p. 80; Butterbrodt, *An den hohen deutschen Reichstag in Berlin*, p. 9; *SB*, 1879, Akst. 304, p. 1736; *SB*, 1882/83, Akst. 164, p. 560; *SB*, 1895–97, 12 March 1896, p. 1405; Brunn, *Nationalliberalen politische Abdankung*, p. 8; *Recueil*, 11 (1883), p. 327; *Hansard*, 1856, v. 141, col. 23; *PP* 1856 (109) lii, p. 500; F. B. Smith, *People's Health*, p. 168.   [324] Arnold, *Notes on Vaccination*, p. 111.

ual, but the threat posed by the unprotected to others that anchored the community's right to insist on vaccination. "Each French citizen," as one put it lapidarily, "has the right to die of smallpox, but not the right of infecting his fellow citizens."[325] Even though vaccination might, on rare occasions, prove harmful, no one had the right to exempt themselves from a precaution that served the common good. Smallpox, like all contagious ailments, was not a victimless disease. The lancet's risks, though real, were small and decreasing with technical advances and in any case paled in comparison to its benefits. Equivalent risks adhered to other undeniable goods, whether school gymnastics, railroads or chloroform, whose virtues no one would, for that reason alone, dream of rejecting.[326] Antivaccinators saw the lancet as an individual matter, a personal choice made within the sphere of privacy that insulated the individual and the family from the community's predations.[327] Conversely, provaccinators assigned to the state a role as defender of dependent children with the misfortune of having neglectful parents. Vaccination did not so much limit the liberties of adults as ensure those of infants.[328] As with any argument using principle to plug holes in the leaky dyke of reality, slippery slope analogies did yeoman service. Admitting its infringement of personal liberties, proponents argued that compulsory vaccination was no more a violation than other laws against which objections were no

[325] *Annales*, 3/1 (1879), p. 445; *DVöG*, 20 (1888), p. 104; Bohn, *Handbuch der Vaccination*, pp. 345–47; Ungar, *Über Schutzimpfungen*, pp. 17–18; *Medizinalarchiv für das Deutsche Reich*, 2 (1911), p. 181; Jochmann, *Pocken und Vaccinationslehre*, pp. 264–65; *Jahrbuch der Staatsarzneikunde*, 1 (1808), pp. 99–105; Wernher, *Zur Impffrage*, p. 46; *Hansard*, 1856, v. 143, cols. 549–53; 1861, v. 164, col. 676; *PP* 1852–53 (434) ci, 77, p. 4.

[326] *Bihang*, 1815, iv, 3, pp. 1338–48; 1903, AK Tillfälliga Utskott (No. 2) Utlåtande 30, p. 11; *RD prot*, AK 1915:87, p. 43; *Anhang zur Gesetz-Sammlung*, 1835, Beilage B zu No. 27 gehörig, pp. 26–27; *DZSA*, 15 (1828), pp. 238–39; Reiter, *Würdigung der grossen Vortheile der Kuhpockenimpfung*, pp. 48–49; *SB*, 1882/83, Akst. 164, p. 569; *SB*, 1909–11, Akst. 571, p. 2809; *Über die Einführung einer Gewissensklausel*, pp. 107–08; *Hansard*, 1883, v. 280, col. 1026; *PP* 1852–53 (434) ci, 77, p. 52; *JO*, 1881, Chambre, Doc., p. 136; Strauss and Fillassier, *Loi sur la protection de la santé publique*, p. 253; *RD prot*, AK 1915:87, p. 14; *Hansard*, 1870, v. 202, col. 1589; *Blattern und Schutzpockenimpfung*, p. 123.

[327] The liberty defended was therefore often not that of the individual as such, but of the parents to control their families against statutory encroachment: *Moniteur universel*, 172 (20 June 1868), p. 887; *Bulletin*, 3, 25 (1891), p. 271; *Hansard*, 1861, v. 164, col. 680; Mary Hume-Rothery, *150 Reasons*; *PP* 1856 (109) lii, p. 500; *Cobbett's*, 1806, v. 7, cols. 881–82; *Lancet* (20 August 1898), p. 469; *Bihang*, 1856–58, viii, Allmänna Besvärs- och Ekonomi-Utskottets Betänkande 14, pp. 10–11; *Ridderskapet och Adeln*, 1815, v. 3, pp. 659–72; Wernher, *Zur Impffrage*, p. 2; Jeanne L. Brand, *Doctors and the State: The British Medical Profession and Government Action in Public Health, 1870–1912* (Baltimore, 1965), p. 47.

[328] *Hygiea*, 36, 10 (September 1874), pp. 547–48; *PP* 1857 (sess. 2) (2239) xxxv, p. 224; *Hansard*, 1856, v. 143, cols. 549–53; 1898, v. 62, col. 367; Strauss, *La croisade sanitaire*, p. 27; Abe, "Aus der Frühgeschichte der deutschen Impfgesetzgebung," pp. 373–74; Jochmann, *Pocken und Vaccinationslehre*, pp. 264–65; Reiter, *Würdigung der grossen Vortheile der Kuhpockenimpfung*, pp. 48–49; Wernher, *Zur Impffrage*, p. 46; Monteils, *Histoire de la vaccination*, pp. 280–86, 295.

longer raised: compulsory schooling, military service, registration of births and deaths, nuisance abatement. A line drawn in the sand at vaccination was therefore, from this view, arbitrary and capricious.[329] Objectors, in turn, warned of an ever encroaching degree of medical intervention. Once the state's right to wield the lancet had been admitted, one wondered, where would things end: "Are we to be leeched, bled, blistered, burned, douched, frozen, pilled, potioned, lotioned, salivated, not only *secundum artem*, but by Act of Parliament?"[330]

Despite such common issues of principle raised in all nations, differences in preventive approach were pronounced. More so than for cholera, precautions against smallpox do seem to have followed a rough Ackerknechtian correlation between politics and prophylaxis. Germany after 1874 required the lancet of its citizens, brushing aside the objections of numerous and well-organized antivaccinators. Liberal Britain, in contrast, although preceding Prussia in making the procedure obligatory, was persuaded of the error of its ways by grassroots protest and, abandoning this step away from its otherwise more sanitationist inclination to public health, allowed vaccination once again to become a matter of individual choice. Sweden, embracing compulsion in the first days of the constitutional monarchy, became increasingly willing to consider a voluntary approach as the public voice raised the decibels of its protest. Only France, belatedly but fiercely provaccinationist, is hard to place in such an accounting, although a convinced Ackerknechtian might dwell on the extent to which its bark (the insistence after 1902 not only on compulsion, but two rounds of revaccination) was worse than its bite (the infelicities and inefficacies of actually wielding the lancet), thus preserving its reputation as a liberal polity despite this otherwise uncharacteristic dalliance with rigorous intervention.

Without question, there were clear differences among the approaches taken by different nations, the assumptions the authorities could make unchallenged, the sorts of attitudes they could take for granted. The Swedes prided themselves on being among the first nations to act on the principle that the state ought to spread the lancet's benefits by imposing it.[331] They were also among the few willing to argue that the state had

[329] *Hansard*, 1853, v. 125, col. 1013; 1872, v. 212, col. 930; 1878, v. 239, col. 493; 1883, v. 280, cols. 1026, 1042–43; 1898, v. 62, col. 368; Monteils, *Histoire de la vaccination*, pp. 269–70; Borne, *Vaccination et revaccinations obligatoires*, pp. 152–53; *SB*, 1882/83, Akst. 164, p. 577; *Annales*, 3/50, 3 (July 1903), pp. 237–38; *Borgare*, 1856–58, ii, pp. 94–95. [330] *PP* 1856 (109) lii, p. 514.
[331] "Kongl. Sundhets-Collegii till Kongl. Maj:t inlemnade underdåniga förslag till förnyadt Nådigt Reglemente för skyddskoppympningen i Riket" (15 April) 1852, copy in Statistiska Centralbyrån, Stockholm, Kongl. Sundhets Collegii Samlingar, v. 1, p. 12.

the right to require vaccination even of protestors because its duties included helping also those too ignorant to know their own good.[332] More generally, it was Germany which, especially after 1874, was seen as the enforcer of drastic interventions, the classic land of sanitary and preventive requirement, as one Frenchman put it.[333] A degree of compulsion was employed here that even provaccinators abroad often found excessive. Allusions to the German system as an example of the despotism to be rejected was, not surprisingly, a staple of antivaccinationist rhetoric, both domestic and foreign. One would think that Germans had sufficient occasion to be imprisoned, one protestor complained during debates over whether recalcitrants should be jailed, without adding yet another incarcerational possibility.[334] German discipline and obedience to authority did frequent duty in explaining this approach. Accepting compulsion, German resistors sneered at their compatriots, showed that the nation had swallowed its loss of personal freedom, remaining unprepared for liberty.[335] The French, in turn, were happy to portray their own passive approach as the outcome of enlightenment. In the Napoleonic era, before the sense of slipping behind their well-vaccinated neighbors took hold, the French regarded their voluntary tack as a sign of the greater liberality distinguishing them from the more authoritarian methods adopted in northern Europe.[336] During the final years of the Second Empire, when suffrage reform, parliamentarism and other issues of heady importance were on the table, Monteils's proposal for compulsory vaccination was rejected with appeals to classic small-state liberalism and a desire, after two decades of Bonapartist rule, to resist any incursions, however well intended, on personal liberty. When the issue came up again during the Third Republic, liberal sentiments now had

[332] That is, that the state had the right to impose a private good, not just the public good of preventing citizens from being infectious: *RD prot*, AK 1915:87, p. 18. This was precisely the claim that Munck af Rosenschöld had earlier rejected: *Ridderskapet och Adeln*, 1815, v. 3, pp. 659–72. See also Gerd Göckenjan, *Kurieren und Staat machen: Gesundheit und Medizin in der bürgerlichen Welt* (Frankfurt, 1985), p. 100.

[333] Strauss, *La croisade sanitaire*, p. 30; Siljeström, *Vaccinationsfrågan*, p. 92.

[334] *SB*, 6 March 1874, p. 234; *SB*, 14 March 1874, p. 354; PRO, MH 80/2, Vaccination Bill 1898, Parliamentary Committee, 21 June 1898, p. 147, reverse, Johnson-Ferguson; *Hansard*, 1898, v. 62, col. 402; *RD prot*, AK 1916:58, p. 32; *National Anti-Compulsory-Vaccination Reporter*, 1, 5 (1 February 1877), p. 2.

[335] McVail, *Half a Century of Small-Pox*, p. 30; *JO*, Senat, Débats, 30 January 1902, p. 82; Conrad Schenck, *Die Blattern in allen ihren Beziehungen* (Quedlinburg, 1844), p. 108; Mirus, *Impffrage*, Vorwort; *Vaccination Inquirer and Health Review*, 7, 78 (September 1885), p. 94; *Die Misserfolge der Staatsmedicin und ihre Opfer in Hamburg* (Hagen i. W., [1892]), p. 18; *Dr. Nittinger's Biographie*, p. 36.

[336] "Circulaire de M. le Préfet du département du Calvados à MM. les Sous-préfets et Maires, relative à l'inoculation de la Vaccine," in *Collection des bulletins sur la vaccine*.

the field to themselves. State education, so ran the complaints, had already brought with it state geometry and state religion; now state vaccination threatened to usher in state pathology and state hygiene. Compulsory vaccination, Benjamin Raspail lamented, contradicted republican principles. Soon, as the Comte de Maillé put it, dusting off a rhetorical perennial, everything would be obligatory, even liberty. Whatever the Prussians might find acceptable, compulsion violated French political instinct.[337]

But it was, of course, in Britain, the land of liberty and civil rights, that the true foil to Teutonic interventionism was thought to be found. A resistance to continental compulsion in favor instead of voluntarism had long been a debating point here.[338] Obligatory vaccination was seen as but another example of the limitless statutory meddling characteristic of the continent.[339] Even observers who otherwise envied the ability of the "despotic" and "paternal" nations to implement effective legislation in such matters knew only too well that in a "free nation" like Britain a law with little public support would be either neglected or badly executed. Others, who did not wish to emulate the continent, thought they knew even better that compulsion would be "too little in accordance with the spirit of our government, and too repulsive to the feelings of Englishmen."[340] Even the prohibition of inoculation, elsewhere a strictly technical consequence of introducing vaccination, was an issue here phrased in terms of personal liberty.[341] When the British at first required vaccination, foreign observers marveled at this apparent contradiction of their concern for the claims of the individual. If the British could reconcile compulsion with personal liberty, held a common opinion, then

---

[337] *Moniteur universel*, 172 (20 June 1868), p. 887; 80 (21 March 1866), p. 343; *La médecine contemporaine*, 21 (1880), p. 148; *JO*, Chambre, Débats, 8 March 1881, pp. 441, 437–38; *Bulletin*, 3, 25 (1891), pp. 65, 69.

[338] *Cobbett's*, 1806, v. 7, cols. 881–82, 890–91; 1808, v. 11, cols. 842–43; T. M. Greenhow, *An Estimate of the True Value of Vaccination as a Security Against Small Pox* (London, 1825), pp. x–xi, 69–70; *Hansard*, 1840, v. 52, cols. 1109–11; 1853, v. 129, col. 474.

[339] "Let us leave compulsion to countries like Austria, where the number of hens a man may keep in his yard, or the number of bakers or butchers in a town, are alike regulated by law, and where the subject may be forcibly seized by the police, and carried off and vaccinated; or, like Sweden, where prayers out of church, or out of canonical hours, are illegal; and where childen are forcibly torn from their nurses' or parents' arms, and triumphantly borne away to church and baptized": *PP* 1856 (109) lii, p. 519; *National Anti-Compulsory-Vaccination Reporter*, 5 (1 February 1877), pp. 1–2.

[340] Cross, *History of the Variolous Epidemic*, p. 220; *Hansard*, 1898, v. 57, col. 783; Greenhow, *Estimate of the True Value of Vaccination*, p. 70; *Hansard*, 1898, v. 64, col. 55; 1861, v. 164, cols. 673, 680; 1898, v. 56, col. 431.

[341] *Hansard*, 1840, v. 52, cols. 1109–11; v. 54, cols. 1256–60; Joseph Adams, *An Inquiry into the Laws of Different Epidemic Diseases* (London, 1809), p. 3.

so could the Germans or the French.[342] When the acts were subsequently repealed, things appeared to have returned to normal. The British respect for personal freedom, their natural intolerance for compulsion in any shape, was thought to lie behind the strength of antivaccinationism here and hence repeal.[343]

This spectrum of approaches could, however, equally well be viewed from the opposite angle. German provaccinators were pleased at being, for once, leaders of public health innovation, envied and emulated among the likeminded abroad.[344] Conversely, the British in their unwillingness to impose the lancet with determination or consistency were regarded less as a beacon of liberty than an example of incompetence and mismanagement. The veneration of personal liberty, however admirable in general, had in this case been exaggerated, undermining the common good.[345] The conscience clause was wholly rejected by the Germans and regarded with bemused skepticism by the French.[346] Within Britain, there was of course agreement with such opinion, moderates recognizing that the inability to compel even benevolent measures like vaccination was a regrettable consequence of venerating personal liberty, the less temperate simply envying the decisive interventions possible and practiced on the continent. "The facility of controlling evils, and of punishing knaves, in arbitrary governments," one observer grudgingly admitted, "is some compensation for the loss of the blessings of liberty."[347]

Whether positively or negatively, the correlation between political

[342] Nittinger, *Impfregie mit Blut und Eisen*, p. 3; *Moniteur universel*, 172 (20 June 1868), p. 887; *JO*, Senat, Débats, 30 January 1902, p. 87; *Revue d'hygiène et de police sanitaire*, 2 (1880), p. 268; Bohn, *Bedeutung und Werth der Schutzpockenimpfung*, p. 19; *SB*, 1872, Akst. 56, p. 215; von Bulmerincq, *Ergebnisse des Bayerischen Impfgesetzes*, p. 9; *Annales*, 2/35 (1871), p. 219.

[343] *Lancet* (20 August 1898), p. 469; Biggs, *Leicester*, p. 80; *Hansard*, 1898, v. 56, col. 431; *Revue d'hygiène et de police sanitaire*, 20 (1898), p. 779; *SB*, 1909–11, Akst. 571, pp. 2807–08.

[344] Eimer, *Blatternkrankheit*, pp. 101–02; Wernher, *Zur Impffrage*, pp. 266–67; Süpfle, *Leitfaden der Vaccinationslehre*, p. 38; *L'echo médical du Nord*, 7, 8 (22 February 1903), p. 91.

[345] Friese, *Versuch einer historisch-kritischen Darstellung*, pp. 130–31; *Hygienische Rundschau*, 9 (1899), p. 116; "Kongl. Sundhets-Collegii till Kongl. Maj:t inlemnade underdåniga förslag till förnyadt Nådigt Reglemente för skyddskoppympningen i Riket," p. 13; Eimer, *Blatternkrankheit*, pp. 101–02; v. Bulmerincq, *Gesetz der Schutzpocken-Impfung*, p. 139; *Edinburgh Journal of Medical Science*, 1 (1826), p. 285; *Recueil*, 11 (1883), p. 327.

[346] *Revue d'hygiène et de police sanitaire*, 20 (1898), pp. 769–88; *Recueil*, 23 (1893), pp. 45–46. The Swedish authorities, although eventually conceding their own version, also initially rejected the idea: *RD prot*, AK 1915:87, p. 18; *Bihang*, 1915, Särskilda utskotts nr. 1 utlåtande 2, pp. 45–46.

[347] Moore, *History and Practice of Vaccination*, p. 115; Cross, *History of the Variolous Epidemic*, pp. 240–43; *British and Foreign Medical Review*, 6 (1839), pp. 189–90; *Hansard*, 1898, v. 57, col. 783; v. 56, col. 446; v. 62, col. 368; Edwardes, *Concise History of Small-Pox*, p. 114; *Liverpool Medico-Chirurgical Journal*, 19 (1899), p. 225; *BMJ* (2 June 1906), p. 1298; Wilkinson, *On the Cure, Arrest, and Isolation of Smallpox*, p. xxiii.

regime and prophylactic strategy was thus often drawn by contemporaries. More specifically, an Ackerknechtian approach is bolstered by the apparently snug fit between the degree to which popular opinion was given expression in these respective political systems and the willingness of the authorities to take grassroots antivaccinating sentiment into consideration. In Britain, the state did not of its own accord make vaccination an issue by seeking to put compulsion on the books. Much of the initiative, both for and against, fell to private member's bills and the debate was one carried out largely between different factions of civil society rather than, as on the continent, between the state and antivaccinators. Britain was a more constitutional system, as a German observer pointed out, the government more representative of the parliamentary constellation than in Germany, and when resistance was strong in the Commons the authorities had to follow suit.[348] Antivaccination was but one aspect of the broader growth of popular politics, strengthened by the introduction of votes for the working class following the 1867 and 1884 Reform Acts. In Germany, with its weak representative institutions prior to unification, there was little debate concerning vaccination before proposal of the 1874 law. In Britain, as well as Sweden, in contrast, the authorities paid more attention to antivaccinating sentiments than was the case in Germany and, later, France. Laws could not, so an oft-expressed concern in Britain, run contrary to widespread sentiment. The common argument here that, compulsion provoking resistance which would not otherwise exist, making the lancet voluntary would in practice bring about more vaccination conceded the need to tailor prophylaxis to local political instinct.[349] In those nations where debate was lively, it was invariably the lower chambers, most proximate to antivaccinationist agitations, where resistance to compulsion was felt, while the upper were more willing to heed the overarching interests of the state.[350] In both Sweden and Britain, the upper houses of parliament supported compulsion and it was, of course, elected local authorities, the Boards of Guardians, which provided the most stiffnecked resistance in Britain.

Nonetheless, despite the undeniable existence of a roughhewn Acker-

[348] *Hansard*, 1864, v. 175, cols. 779–80, 1640–41; 1864, v. 173, cols. 1908–09; *Über die Einführung einer Gewissensklausel*, pp. 102–03.
[349] J. R. Smith, *Speckled Monster*, p. 176; *Hansard*, 1878, v. 239, col. 493; 1898, v. 64, col. 414; 1898, v. 62, cols. 405–09; *Final Report into the Subject of Vaccination*, sects. 521, 527; *Cobbett's*, 1806, v. 7, cols. 890–91; Bohn, *Bedeutung und Werth der Schutzpockenimpfung*, p. 19; *Hansard*, 1867, v. 188, col. 651; 1883, v. 280, col. 1013; 1898, v. 56, col. 431; 1898, v. 62, cols. 325, 343–48, 397; *Shaw's Manual of the Vaccination Law*, pp. 190–91.   [350] *Hansard*, 1898, v. 64, cols. 28–57.

knechtian correlation, once we move from the concerns of the logger to those of the cabinetmaker, political regime in any simple sense fails to explain the variation in prophylactic approach among nations. The anomalies are too numerous and prickly to allow such easy solutions. Those countries which eventually ended or at least loosened compulsion had also been among the earliest to require the lancet in the first place: Sweden above all, but Britain too had preceded Prussia and the German Empire, not to mention France, along the path to compulsion. France, allegedly a liberal and therefore long a non- and only late-vaccinating nation, followed a meandering prophylactic path that correlates only spottily with political regime: eagerly vaccinationist under the first Napoleon, it took a laissez-faire stance during the authoritarian reign of the Second Empire, only to adopt draconian measures during the liberal Third Republic.[351] Variations within nations are equally troublesome: in Germany, it was not conservative Prussia that first implemented compulsion, but Bavaria, Württemberg and other states along the more liberal southwestern fringe. Among the British Isles, local anomalies also threaten an Ackerknechtian with intellectual indigestion. While England and Wales abandoned vaccination in the face of protest, the technique never raised problems of a similar magnitude in Scotland and Ireland where, with all due respect to indigenous variation, political regime and general ideology did not starkly diverge from the metropolis.[352]

Such anomalies were recognized sporadically by contemporaries. Since recruits to the British navy, one observer pointed out, had long been compulsorily vaccinated, it was not just in the "military" states that, as some antivaccinators argued, such practices held sway. Before the conscience clause, Britain had subjected its citizens to compulsion, thus falling, in the eyes of French antivaccinators, into the same camp as Germany. Similarly, Britain and Württemberg during this period were, from the vantage of a German protestor, alike in their embrace of compulsion. France, as Swedish observers pointed out, though highly

---

[351] *Journal d'hygiène*, 6, 239 (21 April 1881), p. 181.

[352] Although, it must be admitted, the Scots are often portrayed as being more willing to accept statutory intervention than the English. Given the traditionally close intellectual connections between the continent and Scotland, the continental concept of medical police with its emphasis on state action to protect public health was more popular there than in England: *Supplement to the EMSJ* (February 1832), p. cclx; Lindsay Paterson, *The Autonomy of Modern Scotland* (Edinburgh, 1994), pp. 58–59; John M. Eyler, *Victorian Social Medicine: The Ideas and Methods of William Farr* (Baltimore, 1979), p. 30; Roy M. MacLeod, "The Anatomy of State Medicine: Concept and Application," in F. N. L. Poynter, ed., *Medicine and Science in the 1860s* (London, 1968), p. 202; Brenda M. White, "Medical Police, Politics and Police: The Fate of John Roberton," *Medical History*, 27 (1983), p. 409.

democratic and with a well-developed concept of freedom, had none-theless in 1902 introduced very strict measures. Provaccinators in the House of Lords could appeal both to the example of Austria (usually considered the height of despotism by antivaccinators) and the United States (surely the other end of almost any political spectrum one would care to imagine) as places where compulsion was imposed.[353] In an observation similarly fluid in its political promiscuity, one antivaccina-tor argued that the English aristocracy had embraced Jenner's discov-ery in 1798, hoping thereby to avoid the fate of their French brethren by demonstrating the monarchy's concern for the nation's wellbeing, while democratic America, seeking the best of both worlds, had annex-ed the cowpox to the republic.[354]

It is also hard to orient a political compass by the usual poles in this dispute. Left could mean a championing of the liberties of the individ-ual against the claims of the state, but might also indicate support for the community's interests over those of the lone shirker. The right could seek to strengthen the powers of the nation through public health, but could equally advocate a vindication of individual prerogatives against the statist moloch. As a result, the political alliances forged for or against the lancet were motley indeed. In the French Third Republic, during debates over the Liouville bill, opposition to the state's ambition to compel vaccination came from the right while the left supported the pro-posal as an eminently social measure.[355] In Britain, on the other hand, Tories were more willing than Liberals and Radicals to favor compul-sion, while a conscience clause found disproportional backing in the latter camps. At the same time many Conservatives opposed throwing the state's weight behind the lancet and the National Anti-Vaccination League estimated its following as approximately one-third Tory.[356] At the other end of the spectrum, some Liberals favored compulsion, prompting the hard core of Radical opponents to doubt the consistency of their laissez-faire approach. The issue did not, it was observed, follow

---

[353] _Hygiea_, 36, 10 (September 1874), p. 549; _Moniteur universel_, 172 (20 June 1868), p. 887; _JO_, Senat, Débats, 30 January 1902, p. 87; _JO_, 1881, Chambre, Doc., p. 136; [Nittinger], _Kampf wider die Impfung_, pp. 40–44; _RD prot_, AK 1916:58, pp. 17, 47; _Hansard_, 1898, v. 64, col. 28. From Scottish MPs, the com-parison was between Germany and Chicago (together at last!), both places where children had to be vaccinated to attend school: _Hansard_, 1898, v. 62, col. 368; 1898, v. 56, cols. 440–42; _PP_ 1856 (109) lii, p. 515.

[354] Dudgeon, _Compulsory Disease_, pp. 4–5. See also Lion Murard and Patrick Zylberman, _L'hygiène dans la république: La santé publique en France, ou l'utopie contrariée (1870–1918)_ (Paris, 1996), pp. 376–77.

[355] _JO_, Chambre, Débats, 8 March 1881, pp. 437–40.

[356] _Hansard_, 1898, v. 56, col. 468; v. 57, col. 762; 1898, v. 62, col. 316; MacLeod, "Law, Medicine and Public Opinion," pp. 202–05; Malcolm Elliott, _Victorian Leicester_ (London, 1979), p. 96.

standard party-political lines.[357] The Oldham Guardians, for example, although split evenly along party lines, were all fervent antivaccinators. In Mile End, candidates for the Board could stand as Liberals or Tories as they liked but had no chance of election unless they opposed compulsion. And indeed, given the political polymorphosity of the issue, opportunists had an open field, allowing one MP to assure a deputation of antivaccinators the day before a general election: "Gentlemen, if you will only vote for me tomorrow, you can all get the small-pox the day after."[358]

In Sweden, equally multiplicious alliances were brokered. Provaccinators were, in their opponents' eyes, a curious mixture of paternalist right and authoritarian left, both, in this case, united by their faith in rule by the government bureaucracy. Resistors, for their part, were no less checkered an assortment: on the right were a group of worthy farmers with firm ideas about nature and medicine and the extent to which the latter should meddle with the former. The left wing, in contrast, were radicals, including many (but far from all) socialists, tending to embrace the more anarchic types who resisted all forms of authority, medical included. In the center were found various free-church members, especially Baptists, suspicious of all science. Party-wise it was all but impossible to identify antivaccinators as of one coloring or another.[359] In Germany, the lancet also forged peculiar combinations of groups with little else in common. Support for compulsion tended to come from the liberals, both National and Progressives, allied in this case with conservatives, although there were differences of opinion in both camps.[360] The opposition, in turn, was mounted by equally unholy alliances: in Württemberg by democrats and Pietists; in the Empire as a whole, socialists and Catholics. Prussian medical authorities complained that they had to counter resistance from both aristocratic conservatives and Social Democrats. In the debates over the 1874 law, coming as they did at the beginning of the Kulturkampf, the Catholic Center provided the most consistent opposition to the demands of a centralizing state against

[357] *National Anti-Compulsory-Vaccination Reporter*, 1, 5 (1 February 1877), p. 1; 2, 8 (1 May 1878), p. 145; *Der Impfgegner*, 2, 3 (1 March 1877), p. 1; *Hansard*, 1898, v. 62, col. 392.

[358] *Hansard*, 1898, v. 57, col. 780; 1898, v. 56, col. 455; 1898, v. 64, col. 29.

[359] *RD prot*, AK 1916:67, p. 64; AK 1916:58, pp. 36–37, 40.

[360] For attacks by resistors on liberals for this reason, see Oidtmann, *November-Flugblatt der Impfgegner*, p. 3; Rud. Crüwelt, "Die polizeilichen Zwangsmassregeln zur Verhütung der Volksseuchen," *Der Volksarzt für Leib und Seele: Eine Monatsschrift für gesunde Lebensanschauung*, 2, 1 (January 1887), Beilage; *Staatsbürger-Zeitung* (4 November 1887), copy in BA, R86/1204, v. 3. For conservatives opposed to vaccination, see *SB*, 1895–97, 8 May 1896, p. 2217; *SB*, 9 March 1874, p. 264.

the claims of the individual and the family to determine their own epidemiological fates.[361]

The socialists, in their (at best) vacillating opposition, are an interesting example of the lancet's political ambiguity. Socialists could be found on both sides of the issue. It was an obvious leftist position to take a sanitationist approach to questions of public health, insisting that not vaccination but an improvement of miserable living conditions promised to end epidemic disease.[362] In the 1890s, the Social Democratic Party was rife with antivaccinators, with 88 percent of its Reichstag delegates pledged to vote against compulsion in 1893, the highest proportion by far (comparable only to the Süddeutsche Volkspartei) of any party.[363] This position did not, however, necessarily endear the socialists to other antivaccinators, many of whom were aghast to find themselves caught in political flagrante with the left. Socialist opposition was just tactical posturing, some accused, while others – faced with friends like these – considered enemies superfluous.[364] Moreover, the socialist position was far from unanimous. The left generally conceded the state's prerogative to intervene for the public weal and vaccination struck many as an excellent example of the principle. Compulsion, as one put it, was not usually a naughty word in their vernacular.[365] One of its most fervent supporters was Bebel, who regarded vaccination as an example of benign statutory intervention for the general good.[366] When the issue was discussed in 1894 such ambiguities were apparent. A delegate from Bremerhaven argued that there were votes to be found among objectors and that, in any case, socialists were generally against compulsion. Others in contrast considered vaccination a scientific issue on which the party should take no official position. A motion from Hamburg against compulsion was defeated, but only narrowly. The following year, Reisshaus supported an antivaccinating motion in the Reichstag, cheered from the left for his support of sanitary reforms to prevent epidemics. In parliamentary dis-

---

[361] Kübler, *Geschichte der Pocken*, p. 239; Bohn, *Handbuch der Vaccination*, p. 146; *DVöG*, 20 (1888), p. 95; Gins, *Krankheit wider den Tod*, p. 254; *SB*, 14 March 1874, p. 337.

[362] *SB*, 18 February 1874, p. 108; *SB*, 6 March 1874, p. 243; *SB*, 3 May 1877, p. 1026; *SB*, 1895–97, 12 March 1896, p. 1409; Wernher, *Zur Impffrage*, p. 48; *DVöG*, 6 (1874), p. 355.

[363] The percentages of antivaccinators in other parties' delegations were as follows: Conservatives, 4.5 percent; Center, 14 percent; National Liberals, 5.8 percent; Süddeutsche Volkspartei, 82 percent; Social Democrats, 88.5 percent (*Der Impfgegner*, 11, 11 [1893], p. 3).

[364] Born, *Öffentliche Anfrage an die Behörden*, p. 14; *Der Impfgegner*, 8, 3 (1890), p. 19.

[365] *SB*, 1895–97, 12 March 1896, p. 1416.

[366] *RD prot*, AK 1915:87, p. 41. Such support so outraged at least one antivaccinator that he was moved to verse to attack Bebel's position: Arno Erich Elmhain, "Till 'Frihetslejonet'," in [V. T. Vallberg], *In Tyrannos* (Stockholm, 1912).

cussion in 1896, socialist MPs were found on both sides.[367] In October 1899 a similar dispute flared up at the party convention (where minds were otherwise occupied by the heady battle between Bebel and Bernstein), with an antivaccinating proposal rejected by the reporter, who considered the matter a strictly medical issue and the position advocated at variance with the party's principles.[368]

The Swedish Social Democrats presented a similar study in tergiversation. Branting, their leader, accepted the authority of the medical experts in favor of compulsion. He was willing to allow a certain consideration for conscientious objectors, as with conscription, but otherwise society had a claim on the allegiance of its citizens in the face of threats, whether military or epidemiological. The agitation against vaccination (dismissed as "Saxon-kultur") he attacked as leading to an "unreasonable popular opinion" and he came close to the paternalist view that considered it the state's task to require of citizens acts they did not realize were in their own best interest. Other Social Democrats, in contrast, saw antivaccination as an important movement that the party should not ignore and compulsion as an example of authoritarian inclinations of a Germanic bent.[369]

In a more general sense, the political ambiguity of compulsory vaccination is revealed also by the multiplicity of traditions in which it could be situated. Some, for example, counted it among the blessings of the French Revolution, another of the liberating interventions that, in this case, freed humanity from the epidemiological old regime.[370] Pope Leo XII (1823–29), in contrast, agreed that vaccination was part of the revolutionary heritage, only to draw the opposite conclusion and banish it from the Papal States. Still others regarded the first attempts to compel vaccination as indications of absolutist leanings incompatible with a

---

[367] *Protokoll über die Verhandlungen des Parteitages der Sozialdemokratischen Partei Deutschlands* (1894), pp. 93–94; *SB*, 1895–97, 12 March 1896, pp. 1405–09; Wilhelm Schröder, ed., *Handbuch der sozialdemokratischen Parteitagen von 1863 bis 1909* (Munich, 1910), pp. 204–05.

[368] *Berliner Ärzte-Korrespondenz*, 42 (21 October 1899); *Protokoll über die Verhandlungen des Parteitages der SPD* (1899), pp. 87, 91.

[369] *RD prot*, AK 1912:23, pp. 24–25, 29; AK 1915:87, pp. 50–52, 58; AK 1916:58, pp. 32, 51–53. Others, outside the party, attacked the Social Democrats as having sold out to the interests of a bureaucratically ruled state: *RD prot*, AK 1916:67, p. 64.

[370] In the GDR, the compulsion imposed by the Napoleonic armies was seen as part of the liberation from the old regime and as an adumbration of the socialist concern for the welfare of common people – part, in other words, of the grand Enlightenment project stretching from Voltaire to Honnecker: Abe, "Aus der Frühgeschichte der deutschen Impfgesetzgebung," pp. 373–74; Abe, "Die Einführung der ersten obligatorischen Pockenschutzimpfung auf dem Boden der heutigen DDR," pp. 343–44. See also Bohn, *Handbuch der Vaccination*, p. 134; Rowbotham, "Philosophes and the Propaganda for Inoculation," pp. 274–84.

democratic age.[371] In 1848, antivaccinators could see the revolution both as the lamentable outcome of the poisoning of the body politic brought in the lancet's train and as a welcome occasion to affirm democratic rights not to be subjected to such obligations: vaccination as the cause of democracy and democracy as the opportunity to defeat vaccination.[372] Antivaccinators could be antidemocratic and eugenicist, but they could also be social radicals who welcomed, as the lancet's only advantage, that it deprived the aristocracy of its absurd claim to the blueness of its blood, or who attacked vaccinators as seeking primarily to provide serviceable cannon fodder for the war machine.[373] Because of such political indeterminacy, the international antivaccinationist movement agreed to ignore party-political considerations, focusing its attack exclusively on the question of compulsion.[374] We therefore need either a more subtle sense of political ideology and practice that will allow us to distinguish "liberal" England from "paternalist" Scotland and "liberal" Prussia from "paternalist" Württemberg, one that will explain why Britain repealed compulsory vaccination while France introduced a drastic version, one that can generally account for the anomalies thrown up by a simple linking of political regime to prophylactic technique. Or we must recognize that an Ackerknechtian approach, whatever its appeal at first glance, does not have the endurance required for the long haul.

GEOEPIDEMIOLOGY

If political regime explains more of the variation in prophylactic approaches to smallpox than to cholera, geoepidemiological considerations account for less. Smallpox had, like all contagious disease, been imported from some place of origin, but unlike cholera this had occurred much earlier and the ailment was, during the evolution of modern preventive strategies, already long endemic. It was not an illness against which the hope of effectively shutting it out, of remaining safe and dry on the banks of the stream of contagion, could offer much solace. Various nations nonetheless regarded themselves, and were seen by others, as standing in different positions vis-à-vis the flow of transmis-

---

[371] Von Bulmerincq, *Ergebnisse des Bayerischen Impfgesetzes*, p. 8; *Revue d'hygiène et de police sanitaire*, 20 (1898), p. 781; *Dr. Nittinger's Biographie*, p. 38.

[372] Geiger, *Impf-Vergiftung*, pp. 55–58, 64; Eimer, *Blatternkrankheit*, p. 146.

[373] Brunn, *Nationalliberalen politische Abdankung*, p. 8; *RD prot*, AK 1915:87, p. 57.

[374] BA, R86/1204, v. 2, "Einladung zu dem 2. internationalen Congress der Impfgegner und Impfzwanggegner im Laufe des Monats October 1881 zu Cöln"; "II. Internationaler Congress der Impfgegner und Impfzwanggegner vom 9. bis 12. October 1881 in Cöln," p. 6.

sion, some therefore investing considerable efforts in lessening the incidence of epidemics through stricter controls at the frontier.

Much as with cholera, Germany was regarded as epidemiologically beleaguered from many sides because of its location (having pitched their tent on Fifth Avenue, as Stravinsky once remarked disparagingly of the Poles, they should not wonder at the traffic) at the center of the continent. Already during the Napoleonic invasions, vaccination's worth had been demonstrated as smallpox did less damage than feared, despite the German states' exposed position as the tramping ground of peregrinating armies. East Prussians at midcentury were thought to be especially convinced of the lancet's virtues because, living on the epidemiological frontier, they had a tangible sense of the protection thus afforded against contagion imported from Poland.[375] The authorities consistently argued the case for compulsion from Germany's geoepidemiological position, surrounded as it was by ill-vaccinated neighbors.[376] Because of its exposed predicament, with terrestrial frontiers on most sides and masses of travelers, transmigrants and foreign seasonal workers, quarantinism was no more of a solution for smallpox than it had been for cholera. Only universal and consistent application of the lancet promised to curb the potential for epidemic transmission that threatened from across the borders in all directions. In the late nineteenth century, the danger was seen as emanating from France, the Netherlands, Belgium, the Tirol, Switzerland, Austria, Bohemia, Poland and Russia. After the turn of the century, one of the main fears remained Russia, but other suspects included now also the Mediterranean countries and Britain. Different parts of Germany of course had regionally specific fears: Bavaria and Saxony of Austria, Baden and Württemberg of France and Switzerland.[377] When epidemics did arise, it was almost invariably in border regions or port cities, with almost two-thirds of cases occurring in such areas. One-third to one-half of all instances of smallpox struck foreigners, especially seasonal agricultural laborers from Russia, Poland and

[375] Augustin, *Preussische Medicinalverfassung*, v. II, pp. 625–26; *Medicinische Zeitung*, 2, 26 (29 June 1859), p. 126.

[376] And foreign observers agreed: *Kongl. Medicinalstyrelsens underdåniga skrifvelse den 17 Januari 1896*, pp. 42–44; *Bihang*, 1897, Prop. 4, pp. 17–18; Sammansatta Stats- och Lagutskottets Utlåtande 4, pp. 25–26; *Sanitary Record*, 19 (12 February 1897), p. 122.

[377] Süpfle, *Leitfaden der Vaccinationslehre*, p. 38; *DZSA*, NF, 20 (1862), pp. 10–16; Prussia, Herrenhaus, *Stenographische Berichte*, 1914–15, 28 May 1914, cols. 525–26; BA, R86/1205, v. 2, Petitions-Kommission [of the RT], 5 December 1906, minutes, Breger; *Über die Einführung einer Gewissensklausel*, p. 39; Wernher, *Zur Impffrage*, pp. 31–32; Kaiserliches Gesundheitsamt, *Beiträge zur Beurtheilung*, pp. 51–53; *SB*, 1884/85, Akst. 287, pp. 1272, 1295, 1345; *Zeitschrift des k. sächsischen statistischen Bureaus*, 30, 1/2 (1884), p. 2.

Galicia, but also temporary workers in the coal mines of Upper Silesia, the Ruhr and the Saar from the east as well as from Belgium and Italy.[378] Peddlers, beggars, rag smugglers for the paper industry, re-immigrants from the new world and other itinerants were also regarded fearfully as potential vectors of transmission. The very fact that the German population was well vaccinated meant that, whatever role geoepidemiology alone might play, attention would tend to focus on (unprotected) foreigners as among the especially susceptible. The authorities tailored their measures accordingly, with Prussia beginning at the turn of the century to require vaccination of foreign workers and others from the east who were not otherwise protected.[379]

Although matters were more ambiguous in Sweden, the influence of geography remained palpable. The role of geoepidemiological considerations depended in large measure on what was thought about vaccination to begin with. Sometimes, Sweden's situation was presented as one of happy isolation, at least in comparison to nations like Germany and Britain.[380] Antivaccinators were delighted to seize on its cold climate and choice position, remote from the main epidemiological currents, as reasons for its favorable smallpox mortality rates and grounds enough to shun compulsion. Since smallpox was invariably imported, isolating the infected was sufficient protection. Its wide distances and sparse population hampered transmission, allowing Sweden an enviable degree of prophylactic insouciance.[381] Proponents of vaccination, in contrast, portrayed it as menaced from abroad, especially by Russia and Galicia, sometimes Finland, othertimes Denmark and Germany. Long distances and an uncrowded population spoke for vaccination since other solutions, such as isolation, required excessive expenses for hospitals and

---

[378] Kaiserliches Gesundheitsamt, *Beiträge zur Beurtheilung*, p. iii; Wernher, *Zur Impffrage*, pp. 135–36; *SB*, 1909–11, Akst. 571, p. 2806. But in another earlier source from the 1880s, although foreigners are mentioned as a significant source of smallpox, the number of cases among those not born in Germany was only 25 out of 202: Kaiserliches Gesundheitsamt, *Beiträge zur Beurtheilung*, pp. 53–54; Jochmann, *Pocken und Vaccinationslehre*, p. 171.

[379] O. Rapmund, *Polizei-Verordnung betreffend Massregeln gegen die Verbreitung ansteckender Krankheiten* (Minden i. W., 1899), pp. 42–43, 179–80; Gins, *Krankheit wider den Tod*, p. 250; *SB*, 1884/85, Akst. 287, p. 1345; *Deutsches Archiv für Geschichte der Medicin und Medicinische Geographie*, 2 (1878), p. 122; Jochmann, *Pocken und Vaccinationslehre*, p. 172; Gins, *Pockenschutz des deutschen Volkes*, p. 56; Lentz and Gins, *Handbuch der Pockenbekämpfung*, p. 513; M. Weirauch, *Die Bekämpfung ansteckender Krankheiten* (Trier, 1905), pp. 285–87.

[380] *Kongl. Medicinalstyrelsens underdåniga skrifvelse den 17 Januari 1896*, pp. 42–43; *Bihang*, 1915, Prop. 78, pp. 33–34, 40; Motion AK 214, pp. 5–6; *RD prot*, AK 1915:87, p. 27; FK 1915:76, p. 3.

[381] *Bihang*, 1897, Sammansatta Stats- och Lagutskottets Utlåtande 4, pp. 25–26; *RD prot*, AK 1916:58, p. 24; Zetterström, *Initia historiæ vaccinationis in Svecia*, p. 85; *Bihang*, 1915, Prop. 78, p. 40; Wernher, *Zur Impffrage*, pp. 256–57.

unreasonably long journeys of the rural population.[382] The First World War roused fears that large movements of personnel and materiel, especially at its eventual conclusion, would sweep epidemics in their train, overwhelming neoquarantinist strategies.[383] Both views left a legislative imprint. On the one hand, Sweden's geoepidemiologically favored position and its consequently low smallpox rates explain the reluctance of parliament on several occasions to impose the stricter measures of vaccination and revaccination urged on it by public health authorities.[384] On the other, the dangers of certain vectors were sufficiently worrisome to prompt precautions. As elsewhere, beggars, gypsies, foreign sailors and seasonal agricultural workers from the east, the so-called Galizier-importen, were feared as carriers. Such groups were accordingly subject to compulsory vaccination and revaccination, even as similar requirements were eased for the native and sedentary population.[385]

In France, likewise, the import of smallpox from abroad was a concern. Marseilles with its farflung connections and resident foreigners was feared as a major source of disease. Because Bordeaux considered itself one of the most exposed regions, thanks to its port and the constant influx of outsiders, it established a system of vaccination stations in 1882 to encourage the practice. The end of compulsory vaccination in Britain was regarded ominously since the British, cosmopolites that they were, were certain to spread contamination and requiring the lancet at the borders was discussed in the Academy of Medicine.[386] Before the 1902 law, there had been hopes of requiring vaccination of at least foreigners residing in France, but in fact they were not subject to the same measures as natives until 1903.[387] As elsewhere, the fear of transmission by itinerants was keen, given expression in proposals to

---

[382] *Bihang*, 1915, Särskilda utskotts nr. 1 utlåtande 2, pp. 43–44; Motion AK 216, p. 14; *RD prot*, AK 1915:87, pp. 15, 23, 31; *Bihang*, 1908, AK Tillfälliga Utskott (No. 2) Utlåtande 30; *RD prot*, FK 1915:76, p. 10; Sköld, *Two Faces of Smallpox*, p. 145. Even vaccination was difficult in such sparse circumstances: RA, Ecklesiastikdepartementet, Konseljakter, 3 December 1897, No. 31, Förste provinsialläkaren i Upsala län, 30 September 1894, "Till Konungens Befallningshafvande i Upsala län."

[383] *Bihang*, 1915, Prop. 78, pp. 33–34, 40; *RD prot*, AK 1915:87, pp. 23, 37, 43; FK 1916:56, pp. 17, 25.

[384] *Bihang*, 1897, Sammansatta Stats- och Lagutskottets Utlåtande 4, p. 25.

[385] "Kongl. Maj:ts Nådiga Förordning, Om Hwad, i händelse af yppad Koppsmitta iakttagas bör," 11 December 1816, §3, *Kongl. Förordningar*, 1816; *Förhandlingar vid De Skandinaviske Naturforskarnes tredje Möte*, p. 863; *RD prot*, FK 1912:20, p. 56; *Bihang*, 1915, Motion AK 216, p. 14; *Betänkande angående skyddskoppympningens ordnande*, pp. 52, 112; Petrén, *Den nya vaccinationslagen*, pp. 3–10.

[386] *JO*, 1912, Chambre, Doc., sess. extra., annexe 2220, p. 20; *Annales*, 3/18 (1887), pp. 225–28; Borne, *Vaccination et revaccinations obligatoires*, pp. 53–54, 145; *Bulletin*, 3, 57 (1907), p. 415.

[387] *Recueil*, 28 (1898), pp. 99–100; *JO*, 35, 205 (31 July 1903), p. 4915; *JO*, 1910, Sénat, Doc., annexe 134, p. 890; Sénat, Débats, p. 869.

restrict the movements of the footloose, requiring the lancet of vagabonds and foreign workers.[388] Britain, in turn, was regarded in various
ways, usually as a projection of foreign observers' own preoccupations.
The Germans, at the eye of the epidemiological storm, considered the
British protected by their insularity, apart from the main thoroughfares
of European mass peregrination. The Swedes, in contrast, securely
ensconced in their corner of the continent, regarded them as exposed to
infection through commercial contacts with the rest of the world.[389] The
British themselves seem to have agreed with the Germans, at least to
judge from the paucity of concern attached to the problem of smallpox
transmission from abroad.[390] The Irish were regarded, much like seasonal workers in Germany and Sweden, as vectors and native itinerants
were, as elsewhere, feared for similar reasons, but few practical consequences followed such concerns.[391]

Topography also played a role, although once again less pronounced
than with cholera. In Sweden, the nation's sparse population and
farflung open spaces had prophylactic consequences. The rise of antivaccinationism here, and its eventual success, owed much to a general
distrust of the lancet that was encouraged by the informality and incompetence with which it was applied and the consequent lapses of protection. Among its more densely settled neighbors, the tendency was
to strengthen the formal technical requirements for vaccinators. In
Sweden, in contrast, the vast distances separating many of its citizens
and the gulf between the availability of medical care in town and countryside did not permit the luxury of expert attention to each vaccination.[392] Well into the nineteenth century, a much broader group of
persons remained authorized to wield the lancet than elsewhere and
parish clerks, midwives and school teachers long remained the usual vac-

[388] *JO*, Chambre, Débats, 9 March 1907, p. 603; *JO*, 1911, Sénat, Débats, p. 460; 1911, session
extra., p. 1678; *Annales*, 3/29 (1893), p. 568; 3/17 (1887), p. 304; Cavaillon, *L'armement antivénérien en
France* (Paris, n.d. [1927]), p. 58; Ackerman, *Health Care in the Parisian Countryside*, p. 73.
[389] *SB*, 1909–11, Akst. 571, p. 2806; Kirchner, *Schutzpockenimpfung und Impfgesetz*, p. 94; *RD prot*, FK
1912:20, p. 62; AK 1915:87, p. 27; FK 1915:76, p. 3; *Bihang*, 1915, Prop. 78, pp. 33–34, 40; Motion AK
214, pp. 5–6.
[390] One of the few observers who was worried was *Edinburgh Journal of Medical Science*, 1 (1826),
pp. 282–84.
[391] *PP* 1854–55 (88) xlv, p. 631; *Hansard*, 1853, v. 125, cols. 1011–12; 1883, v. 280, col. 1009; *Journal
of State Medicine*, 11 (1903), pp. 654–57; McVail, *Half a Century of Small-Pox*, pp. 47–48; *Sanitary Record*,
20 (29 October 1897), p. 470.
[392] *Ridderskapet och Adeln*, 1850–51, iii, pp. 205–19; *Bihang*, 1915, Särskilda utskotts nr. 1 utlåtande
2, p. 43; Ole Berg, "The Modernisation of Medical Care in Sweden and Norway," in Arnold J.
Heidenheimer and Nils Elvander, eds., *The Shaping of the Swedish Health System* (New York, 1980), p.
23.

cinators in many rural areas. In 1828, vaccinators were required to have their abilities certified, but this narrowed the field only slightly. In the 1853 legislation, parish clerks were considered the main vaccinators in the countryside and, indeed, they were not allowed to refuse this duty if chosen to fulfill it.[393] During the latter half of the century, the divergence between Sweden and other nations in this respect widened. In Britain as of 1853, only medical practitioners (although admittedly a broad category) could vaccinate and the Germans were even more restrictive. In Sweden, in contrast, although complaints of inexpert vaccination were common into the twentieth century, the demand that physicians be given a monopoly on the lancet was rejected as impossible in a sparsely inhabited nation with comparatively few doctors. In the failed 1897 bill, vaccination was to have been limited to physicians and other trained personnel, but even here, in the frontier regions of the Lappmark, others were also permitted take lymph if necessary to continue the epidemiological chain of arm-to-arm vaccination.[394] Vaccinators, whether of the highly skilled or seat-of-the-pants variety, also continued to wield the lancet not as professionals, but as largely unpaid volunteers, for longer in Sweden than elsewhere. At first they were rewarded for their efforts only with prizes and medals for the especially zealous. Later they were paid for each operation, either by the vaccinated or the poor box, but the sums involved were inadequate and bonuses for the diligent remained an important feature of the system.[395]

Another aspect of this only quasi-medicalized system was the important role assigned the clergy – not surprising perhaps considering that there were many more of them than physicians.[396] During epidemics early in the century, clergy announced infected homes from the pulpit, helped find refuge for evacuees and generally served as a source of example and exhortation of the lancet's benefits for their parishioners.

---

[393] *SFS*, 1828/77; 1853/67, §67; Sköld, *Two Faces of Smallpox*, pp. 401–12.

[394] *Kongl. Medicinalstyrelsens underdäniga skrifvelse den 8 Juni 1894*, pp. 18–19; *Hygiea*, 56, 11 (November 1894), pp. 485–525; *Betänkande angående skyddskoppympningens ordnande*, pp. 90–91, 121; *Bihang*, 1903, AK, Motion 146, p. 4; *RD prot*, FK 1912:20, pp. 44, 48; *Bihang*, 1897, Prop. 4. There were similar complaints from the German countryside, whether east Elbian Posen or Alpine Bavaria, that sparsely settled populations would have a hard time complying with vaccination regulations: *SB*, 9 March 1874, p. 264.

[395] "Kongl. Maj:ts Nådiga Reglemente För Vaccinationen i Riket," 6 March 1816, *Kongl. Förordningar*, 1816; *SFS*, 1853/67, §§9, 20–22. Only by the late nineteenth century was it proposed to have the state pay vaccinators according to schedules and the distances traveled: *Bihang*, 1897, Prop. 4, §12; *Betänkande angående skyddskoppympningens ordnande*, p. 98.

[396] Ragnar Norrman, "Prästerna och vaccinationen: En regionalundersökning avseende Uppsala län 1811–1820," *Kyrkohistorisk årsskrift* (1979), pp. 105–07; Otto E. A. Hjelt, *Svenska och Finska medicinalverkets historia 1633–1812* (Helsingfors, 1892), v. II, pp. 215–23.

More technically, the church's role as registrar of demographically pertinent events was extended to include also vaccination, continuing
undiminished throughout the century especially in rural areas. Clergy
compiled lists of the already- and not-yet-protected and issued certificates of compliance.[397] The vestry approved measures taken against
the unvaccinated and punished incompetent vaccinators. Clergy were
to check the certificates of recent arrivals to their parishes, notifying
vaccinators of newly baptized infants and schools of pupils who
remained unprotected. Because of the nation's topography, its sparse
population and vast spaces, the Swedish strategy thus relied on non-
professional vaccinators and an administration exercised by the
churches.[398] In comparison to other systems, it was this informality that
stuck out. Worse, it also helped provoke resistance, permitting the
lancet to be wielded inexpertly and entrusting the clergy, servants in
this case of both God and the state, with administrative tasks performed only indifferently – often, for example, registering as vaccinated, on the basis of information only from their parents, children
who were not.[399]

ADMINISTERING PROPHYLAXIS

A political interpretation thus allows only a rough orientation among the
force fields of prevention, while geoepidemiology played a role, although
less important than for cholera. To explain the variations in national
approaches to smallpox, and especially the anomaly of Britain's prophylactic volteface, we must turn to other factors, especially a consideration
of the way in which the British state implemented vaccination. Its
precise execution and administration explains much of the variation in
the strength and effectiveness of resisting movements and the authori-

[397] *Kongl. Medicinalstyrelsens underdåniga skrifvelse den 17 Januari 1896*, p. 75; "Kongl. Maj:ts Nådiga
Förordning, Om Hwad, i händelse af yppad Koppsmitta iakttagas bör," 11 December 1816, *Kongl.
Förordningar*, 1816; Ekelund, *Barn-koppor och vaccinen*, p. 204; *Ridderskapet och Adeln*, 1815, v. 3, pp.
561–64; *Bihang*, 1815, iv, 3, pp. 1338–48; "Kongl. Maj:ts Nådiga Reglemente För Vaccinationen i
Riket," 6 March 1816, *Kongl. Förordningar*, 1816; Sköld, *Two Faces of Smallpox*, pp. 394–95.

[398] *Kongl. Medicinalstyrelsens underdåniga skrifvelse den 8 Juni 1894*, pp. 6, 23; *SFS*, 1853/67, §13;
1874/16; *Bihang*, 1897, Prop. 4, p. 13; 1915 Prop. 78, §§14–15. At first only clergy of the state church,
but later also Jewish and other Christian clergy, were entrusted with such tasks.

[399] Schenck, *Blattern in allen ihren Beziehungen*, p. 107; Kübler, *Geschichte der Pocken*, pp. 244–45; Preste,
1850–51, iii, pp. 122–24; *Ridderskapet och Adeln*, 1815, v. 3, pp. 352–53; 1850–51, iii, pp. 205–19; *Hygiea*,
36, 10 (September 1874), p. 550; 56, 11 (November 1894), p. 502; *Bihang*, 1912, AK andra tillfälliga
utskotts utlåtande nr. 6; *Kongl. Medicinalstyrelsens underdåniga skrifvelse den 8 Juni 1894*, pp. 10–11.

ties' ability to enforce their ambitions. Much, though perhaps not the devil himself, lay in the details.

In certain ways, the British faced a more pressing problem than the continent. The disadvantages of precocity played a role in the persistence of inoculation and competition from this side added to other forms of protest. Since conscription for the military had lapsed after the Napoleonic wars and compulsory schooling was not introduced until the late nineteenth century, fewer British citizens passed through such portals of indirect compulsion that, on the continent, served to snag at least most males. In Germany and Sweden, with longer traditions of compulsory schooling, the use of immatriculation to enforce vaccination indirectly was largely uncontroversial.[400] In Britain and France, where compulsory schooling came only at the end of the century, largely coinciding with the vaccination issue rather than preceding it, the two questions were often discussed in terms of each other. In Britain, provaccinators used compulsory schooling as an analogy for vaccination, while protestors in Leicester resisted the 1902 Education Act (establishing a machinery of local administration) much as they had the lancet. In France, objections to compulsory schooling dovetailed with opposition to vaccination.[401]

The British also complicated matters in the specifics of implementing their system.[402] British vaccinators, paid only for successful attempts, had a mercenary motive for nonetheless registering failed operations, thus helping to bring the procedure into disrepute. Infants were vaccinated at the tender age of three months, rather than later as in most other nations (Ireland and Scotland, six months; Sweden, two years; Denmark, seven; Germany, up to two years; France, within the first year).[403] Besides raising the squeamish issue of puncturing the freshly baked, the result was that skeptical parents, fortified with the ironclad conviction of

[400] *Kongl. Medicinalstyrelsens underdåniga skrifvelse den 17 Januari 1896*, pp. 9, 53; *Zeitschrift des k. sächsischen statistischen Bureaus*, 30, 1/2 (1884), p. 1. A similar point was made for France: see *Annales*, 3/50, 3 (July 1903), p. 258. In Prussia, compulsory schooling dated from 1763, in Sweden 1842, but in Germany, vaccination of all school children was not actually required until the 1870s: *Blattern und Schutzpockenimpfung*, p. 54; *Reichs-Gesetzblatt*, 1874, 11/996, §13.

[401] *Hansard*, 1898, v. 62, cols. 405–06; 1883, v. 280, cols. 1042–43; Simmons, *Leicester*, v. I, pp. 58–59; *Moniteur universel*, 172 (20 June 1868), p. 887; *La médecine contemporaine*, 21 (1880), pp. 147–52.

[402] This is the general theme also of Graham Mooney, "'A Tissue of the Most Flagrant Anomalies': Smallpox Vaccination and the Centralization of Sanitary Administration in Nineteenth-Century London," *Medical History*, 41, 3 (1997).

[403] 3 & 4 Vict. c. 29, i; 30 & 31 Vict. c. 84, s. 6, 16; *Hygienische Rundschau*, 9 (1899), p. 110; 16 & 17 Vict. c. 100, ii. In the workhouses, infants were vaccinated when only a few days old, something, as resistors argued, the rich would never tolerate: *Hansard*, 1883, v. 280, col. 991.

post hoc–propter hoc logic, could blame vaccination for every garden-variety childhood ailment suffered during the following years.[404] Since infants also, unless attended by their private physician, underwent the lancet at public vaccination stations, those who had been careless in the timing of their conception had to endure a foray into winter weather and the discomfort of draughty waiting rooms, repeating the whole rigmarole eight days later to ensure success.[405]

Perhaps most important among the mechanical details of vaccination, the central British state put itself at the mercy of local officials. When vaccination first went on the books at midcentury, the Poor Law authorities (in the absence of any other department with an organized local machinery) were entrusted with its enforcement and administration. This meant that vaccination, for reasons of largely arbitrary administrative juxtaposition, was run by officials with neither the expertise nor the interest to deal with such public health measures and, worse, that the lancet was tainted with the stigma of the Poor Law. Since vaccination lay in the hands of the Guardians (elected, unsalaried and therefore largely beyond the control of the central authorities), compulsion could not be upheld where recalcitrant sentiments predominated.[406] The complicated relations between the Boards and Vaccination Officers (on the Guardians' payroll, but taking their instructions from the LGB), the attempt with the Evesham doctrine to avoid more conflict than necessary with local officials and finally the direct disobedience in Keighley, Leicester and other hotbeds of protest: all were stages in the gradual process by which the central authorities lost their ability to compel vaccination against determined resistance. The central powers in effect had no reliable means of forcing obstreperous local authorities to bend to their will. In Leicester distress and commitment warrants issued to terrify defaulters rested harmlessly in the pigeonholes of the police station. With resistance on the scale mounted in Leicester, the authorities would have had to prosecute thousands of cases annually. How, one resister taunted, did they intend to jail the majority of the city's 200,000 inhabitants who rejected the lancet? Imposing compul-

---

[404] Hence Medical Officers often recommended raising the vaccination age: Richard Griffin, *Statement of the Grievances of the Poor Law Medical Officers, with Remarks on Sanitary Measures and Vaccination* (Weymouth, 1857), p. 21; *Dublin Medical Press* (5 November 1862), p. 458. Similar arguments were also heard in Sweden: *Betänkande angående skyddskoppympningens ordnande*, p. 104.

[405] *Dublin Medical Press* (5 November 1862), p. 458.

[406] Lambert, "Victorian National Health Service," p. 2; *Hansard*, 1853, v. 125, col. 1008; *PP* 1854–55 (88) xlv, pp. 631–32; *BMJ* (3 July 1880), p. 2; F. B. Smith, *People's Health*, pp. 161–62; *Sanitary Record*, 20 (13 August 1897), pp. 173–74; Edwardes, *Concise History of Small-Pox*, p. 114.

sion by a decree from Whitehall would have required support of a quality not to be found in Parliament. Without the overwhelming backing of the Commons, no government could have forced the lancet on local authorities.[407] Vaccination thus touched on the neuralgenic point of central–local relations and, because of the way it had initially been implemented, anticentralizers could whip up fervent opposition by invoking the lancet as a particularly dastardly example of the moloch's ambitions.[408] Cities like Leicester and Keighley were long-standing nests of localism, self-government and opposition to London's designs, and the vaccination question was but one issue through which this was expressed.[409]

Illustrative of the importance of administrative detail are the differing fates of vaccination in England, on the one hand, and Scotland and Ireland on the other. The Scottish and Irish accepted the lancet much more readily than the English and resistance played only a minor role. That the Scottish and the Irish shared the advantages of prophylactic backwardness with the continent was not the case, since inoculation had enjoyed even greater favor here than in England and rejection of vacci-nation as an unnecessary substitute was pronounced early in the century. Antivaccination nonetheless never took hold as in England, leaving Scotland and Ireland to be celebrated as places where, their having secured complete compliance, smallpox had been reduced to a minimum.[410] Perhaps it was, as Irish MPs were wont to claim, that their countrymen were simply more sensible than the unreasonable English and hence immune to such delusions. Perhaps Catholicism played a role in Ireland in reducing resistance. Or perhaps the Scottish and Irish were more likely to favor a paternal government on the continental model, promising to save the ignorant from themselves (although plenty of similar sentiments were expressed on behalf of the English in the

[407] Biggs, *Leicester*, pp. 348–54; *Hansard*, 1898, v. 57, col. 762; v. 62, col. 372; v. 64, col. 457, 414–16; 1864, v. 175, cols. 1640–41; *Final Report into the Subject of Vaccination*, sect. 515.

[408] German provaccinators, in contrast, were pleased that, for once, the much criticized police powers that could here be brought to bear allowed an effective implementation of a beneficial tech-nique while the British impotently relied on local authorities: *Hygienische Rundschau*, 9 (1899), p. 116. British provaccinators, not surprisingly, sought to have enforcement entrusted to more willing authorities: *Hansard*, 1883, v. 280, col. 1042; 1898, v. 56, col. 444.

[409] *Hansard*, 1898, v. 57, cols. 761, 780, 799–800; Biggs, *Leicester*, p. 348; F. B. Smith, *People's Health*, pp. 167–68.

[410] *PP* 1807 (14) ii, p. 62; *Cobbett's*, 1806, v. 7, col. 896; *Hansard*, 1870, v. 202, cols. 1587–88; 1871, v. 204, col. 222. In 1868–70, while there were only two convictions for default in Scotland, England and Wales had 1,419, with thirteen multiple convictions for the same child, Ireland 2,850 and thir-teen, respectively. The main contrast may therefore have been between Scotland and the rest: *PP* 1871 (69) lviii, pp. 849–51; *Hansard*, 1878, v. 239, col. 485.

Lords).[411] Equally plausible, the Scottish and Irish were simply more adept at implementing legislation in a manner that did not provoke resistance, soothing that which did arise. Physicians played a large role in shaping the law on this matter. The authorities here were more flexible than their English counterparts, with multiple prosecutions, for example, generally not pursued and only one penalty enforced for non-vaccination. Home visits by the official vaccinator, of a sort not practiced in England, allowed the authorities to distinguish between parents who failed to protect their children on principle and the simply neglectful. As in Germany, the visiting physician sought to vaccinate children unless the parents specifically refused. Whereas in England the next step after a refusal was prosecution, in Scotland this domiciliary visit allowed officials a degree of flexibility and persuasion absent from the repertoire of their English colleagues.[412] In 1898, the English flattered by imitation when they sought to introduce home visits, raise the age of vaccination to six months and in other ways follow the Scottish approach.[413] In Scotland, far more vaccinations were undertaken by private family physicians than in England, where official public vaccinators bore the brunt and were supposed to inspect even those carried out privately. When the family physician visited in Scotland in his guise as public vaccinator, the likelihood that he could persuade hesitant parents was greater than for the anonymous official entrusted with this task across the border. Scottish authorities were also willing to calm objections by paying lost wages to those who were incapacitated by the lancet for a day or two.[414]

The English also worked themselves into a tactical impasse in a more general sense. From the individual's point of view, vaccination could be a private good: better to be protected than not, regardless of what anyone else did. From that of society as a whole, however, it was a public good: as long as pockets of the unprotected remained, epidemics could

---

[411] *Hansard*, 1898, v. 57, cols. 783, 787; 1898, v. 62, cols. 368, 518.

[412] *PP* 1871 (246) xiii, 1, p. iv; *Hansard*, 1878, v. 239, cols. 483, 493, 496, 504; *Final Report into the Subject of Vaccination*, sects. 518, 529; Deborah Brunton, "Practitioners Versus Legislators: The Shaping of the Scottish Vaccination Act," *Proceedings of the Royal College of Physicians of Edinburgh*, 23 (1993), p. 200.

[413] *Hansard*, 1898, v. 56, col. 470; 1898, v. 57, col. 765, 781; *Lancet* (2 May 1896), p. 1211; 61 & 62 Vict. c. 49, s. 1. Such visits were not, however, much of a success in England. Partly the problem was that resistance, once roused from its lair, could not be domesticated by such technical finetuning. The public regarded the official vaccinators on their doorsteps more as bailiffs than as doctors, often inviting them to go vaccinate the cat: *Hansard*, 1898, v. 57, cols. 774, 782.

[414] *Revue d'hygiène et de police sanitaire*, 20 (1898), pp. 771–72; *Hansard*, 1898, v. 57, col. 788; *Recueil*, 23 (1893), pp. 47–48.

take hold and spread, endangering the vaccinated despite their relative individual immunity.[415] In terms of public hygiene, vaccination was thus, *grosso modo*, an all-or-nothing choice. If not every member of society was to be vaccinated, then it was hard to justify any lesser degree of compulsion. Absolute and universal compulsion, on the one hand, and voluntary protection, on the other, were the alternatives. How precisely to enforce the lancet was thus a crucial decision. The English relied exclusively on fines, multiple if necessary, with jail for those who could not pay. This meant that in effect exemptions were permitted – ones based in large measure on resistors' net worth. When the law imposed fines for noncompliance without seeking to enforce any more direct form of compulsion, the issue could be and was phrased by its opponents in terms of a tax on the right not to vaccinate. The rich paid the fines, while the poor had to suffer jail for the privilege of exemption.

That compulsion affected primarily the lower classes was no secret. The problem with the vaccination acts, the President of the Board of Health complained in 1864, was the reluctance to prosecute the poor for disobedience. The cardinal principle of public hygiene, that no one be allowed exemption from rules applicable to all, was thus not only being violated, but along plutocratic lines at that.[416] One of the consequent peculiarities of the British debate was the extent to which compulsion was portrayed as class legislation under which the lower orders especially suffered, a leitmotif of the debate here.[417] In Germany, by comparison, the issue was much less irksome. When class distinctions came up, the argument was not that the rich could buy exemption, but the less pressing consideration that they enjoyed the convenience of private physicians while the poor had to endure vaccination stations.[418] When the 1874 law itself allowed only fines (and jail) to enforce the lancet, some objectors were willing explicitly to draw the conclusion that, in order to prevent such penalties from becoming a plutocratic tax on nonvaccination, the possibility of direct compulsion, allowed in some federal states

[415] *Annales*, 3/18 (1887), p. 32; *SB*, 1884/85, Akst. 287, p. 1260.

[416] *Hansard*, 1864, v. 173, cols. 1908–09; *Final Report into the Subject of Vaccination*, sect. 523.

[417] Tebb, *Results of Vaccination*, pp. 19–24; William Hume-Rothery, "Advice to Anti-Vaccinators," *National Anti-Compulsory-Vaccination Reporter*, 4 (1 January 1877); *Vaccination Tracts*, no. 6, pp. 7–8; Mary Hume-Rothery, *150 Reasons*; White, *Story of a Great Delusion*, p. 484; *Hansard*, 1853, v. 129, col. 474; 1872, v. 212, cols. 926–27, 929–32; 1877, v. 235, col. 738; 1878, v. 239, col. 504; 1883, v. 280, col. 991; 1898, v. 56, col. 457; 1898, v. 57, cols. 773, 779; *PP* 1882 (25) vi, 681; *Second Report into the Subject of Vaccination*, Q 6662; *Speech of Alfred Milnes, MA (Lond.) at the Leicester Demonstration Against Compulsory Vaccination* (London, 1886), p. 3.

[418] *SB*, 18 February 1874, p. 108. It was, however, of course observed that the poor who could not afford fines often ended in jail: *SB*, 9 March 1874, p. 259.

through local statute, was implicitly assumed in the legislation.[419] The conscience clause was the final drawing of consequences from the British authorities' only halfhearted attempts to enforce vaccination. Imitated backhandedly in Sweden, ridiculed and rejected in France and Germany, such exemption from a thereby eviscerated requirement was the grudging recognition that, given principled resistance, a public good had to be enforced strictly or not at all.[420] "If they were not prepared," as the record of one MP's opinion put it, "to enforce vaccination in this country as they did in Germany, even at the point of the bayonet, it seemed to him that it was their duty to find some method by which those who conscientiously objected might have their objections met without becoming law breakers."[421]

The Germans, in contrast, although not ruling out multiple prosecutions, tended instead to rely on direct physical compulsion on an ad hoc and occasional basis, as permitted by local statute. All citizens were thus subject to the same laws with no, or few, exceptions permitted: *hart aber gerecht*.[422] This led, on occasion, to cases that made civil libertarians cringe. One of the most notorious occurred in Hildesheim, where, entering the home of the unfortunate and obstinate Herr Butterbrodt, the police arrested him and vaccinated his children while his wife lay ill in bed. In another case from 1912, three policemen in full uniform accompanied by a female colleague broke down the front door of Ernst and Pauline Todtenhagen in Heepen, forced their way into the parlor with the aid of a crowbar, pried mother and child apart, forcibly restraining her, while taking the latter off to be vaccinated.[423]

But the authorities were equally capable of more flexible and efficacious, less heavy-handed behavior. In Plettenberg, near Düsseldorf, resistance spread in 1912. During the summer vaccinations, most parents avoided their obligations by presenting postponement certificates from

[419] *Die Grenzboten*, 47 (1888), pp. 226–27; *Ärztliches Vereinsblatt für Deutschland*, 51 (July 1876), p. 92; *SB*, 1881, Akst. 123, p. 701.

[420] Jochmann, *Pocken und Vaccinationslehre*, p. 174; Kirchner, *Schutzpockenimpfung und Impfgesetz*, pp. 148–49; Süpfle, *Leitfaden der Vaccinationslehre*, p. 39; *Annales*, 3/41 (1899), p. 269.

[421] PRO, MH 80/2, Parliamentary Committee, 21 June 1898, Vaccination Bill 1898, p. 147, reverse, Johnson-Ferguson.

[422] Hence the antivaccinators, prominent and committed enough to publish on the subject, who had to admit that, much to their regret, their children had ultimately been vaccinated against their will: *Protest beim hohen Königlich Preussischen Justiz-Ministerium bezw. beim deutschen Volke*, 17 April 1887, in GStA, 84a/3667; Born, *Öffentliche Anfrage an die Behörden*, p. 10. But there were exceptions, including Heinrich Rühlemann who went to prison at least thirteen times, thereby apparently sparing his daughter: Born, *Amtliche Erledigung*, p. 3.

[423] *SB*, 1895–97, pp. 1404, 2218; BA, R86/1218, "Der Minister des Innern. M.10660," 26 April 1913. For a similar case, see *Staatsbürger-Zeitung* (4 November 1887), copy in BA, R86/1204, v. 3.

a sympathetic physician. The district administrator instructed the local authorities to proceed against parents only of older children, leaving the younger ones for the moment to see whether they would be protected voluntarily before the end of the year. Older children were inspected to determine whether in fact their health would be endangered, and the parents only then summoned to produce proof of vaccination. Resisting parents, in turn, filed a complaint with the local police. The district administrator decided that children should be brought in for inspection, but not vaccination, while the complaint was being considered. A summons sent out to fifty-seven parents produced only five at the appointed hour. Of these, no health reasons spoke against vaccinating one, two sets of parents were prepared to vaccinate privately, while the last two infants, being ill, were exempt for the moment. For the parents who had not appeared, compulsory inspections were now possible, but the police decided to be flexible and patient. The medical officer along with a police assistant and a secretary from the mayor's office now traveled to their homes. While waiting in the wagon, the physician had the policeman request permission for the inspection, intending to seek entrance only in cases of continued refusal. In fact, no one resisted, but this troupe of peripatetic enforcers also found only fifteen children at home. The parents of children with no health problems were now issued a new summons to produce certificates by a certain date or risk compulsion. Those houses with no one at home received a similar summons and many of these parents complained to the Interior Ministry. But in fact, the police's actions prompted most parents of unexamined children now to have their offspring vaccinated by a certain Dr. Lackmann in Finnetrop. The result was that only four children in all had neither been examined nor vaccinated. Two of these had really been absent, one was going to be vaccinated and the other parents also promised to follow suit.[424]

Another example of the Germans' ability to combine tactical finesse with a purposeful insistence on their preventive agenda came with the question of damages caused by vaccination. Unlike the British who, inspired by faith in Jenner, were reluctant to admit that the lancet could do harm, the German authorities suffered no such hesitations. One of the motives for appointing the 1884 Vaccination Commission was to investigate officially the claims of such damages, seeking to lay to rest

---

[424] BA, R86/1218, "Der Königliche Landrat des Kreises Altena i.W., Tageb. Nr. A.9465, Betrifft: Impfgeschäft in Stadt und Amt Plettenburg," 4 December 1912.

any objections they had sparked.[425] But the corollary of such official frankness was that the German authorities were also resolute in their prosecution of false claims of damage.[426] Libel and slander law was used to counter unsubstantiated allegations against vaccinators in a way that seems to have had been without parallel in other nations.[427] Through a combination of resolute prophylactic saber-rattling, personal attention and enough administrative *Fingerspitzengefühl* to know when to postpone and give in, the authorities thus managed to accomplish their goal without provoking widespread resistance inflamed by the martyrdom of repeated prosecution.[428]

To see the issue in Ackerknechtian terms as a matter of political traditions and their prophylactic corollaries (authoritarianism or liberalism; compulsory or voluntary vaccination) is thus to paint the picture with an instrument intended for graffiti rather than calligraphy. It is true that the German antivaccination movement was unable to convince the authorities to end compulsion while the British succeeded. In addition to the difficulties of fitting the lackadaisical but ultimately draconian French and the initially interventionist and later moderate Swedes into a simple Ackerknechtian schema, however, there are other reasons to seek a more nuanced coloration. First, regarding the issue as one of compulsion or not forces what was a more subtle decision into a binary mold, a stark black-or-white choice that did not, in fact, confront reformers at the time. The British came close to not abolishing compulsion; the Germans nearly never passed it. Antivaccination in Germany was not without its effects on the authorities. Most immediately, it was out of fear of provoking even more resistance that plans to include an element of direct

[425] *SB*, 1882/83, Akst. 164, pp. 568–69, 579; *SB*, 1884/85, Akst. 287, pp. 1269, 1274–75, 1348; Huerkamp, "History of Smallpox Vaccination in Germany," p. 629; Gideon, *Pocken-Impfung*, p. 4; *Veröffentlichungen*, 9, 2 (15 December 1885), p. 272; 9, 2 (4 August 1885), p. 45.

[426] BA, R86/1220, "Ministerium der geistlichen, Unterrichts- und Medizinalangelegenheiten, M.d.g.A.-M. No: 394I.U.I., M.d. In. II. No: 6480," 22 May 1895; *Korrespondenzblatt der ärztlichen Kreis- und Bezirks-Vereine im Königreich Sachsen*, lix, 6 (15 Sept 1895), p. 73.

[427] Born, *Öffentliche Anfrage an die Behörden*, p. 14; *Der Impfzwanggegner*, 6, 9 and 10 (September–October 1888), p. 57; *SB*, 1895/97, p. 1404; *SB*, 1882/83, Akst. 164, p. 567; *SB*, 1877, Akst. 176, p. 497. Such tactics were common in other respects as well, with lèse majesté, for example, used to prosecute for even indirect criticisms of the monarch: R. J. V. Lenman, "Art, Society, and the Law in Wilhelmine Germany: The Lex Heinze," *Oxford German Studies*, 8 (1973), p 98; Eric A. Johnson, *Urbanization and Crime: Germany 1871–1914* (Cambridge, 1995), p. 26.

[428] Confidence in the effectiveness of such informal persuasion dated back to the early nineteenth century when, in Koblenz in 1816 for example, the authorities were certain that resistant parents would be persuaded by the combined eloquence and reason of the local authorities – medical, governmental and religious – who were all in unison to pay a personal visit to this effect, joined if distance permitted by the Kreiscommissar: Augustin, *Preussische Medicinalverfassung*, v. II, pp. 642–43.

compulsion in the 1874 law were shelved by the Reichstag.[429] More generally, major concessions were made to antivaccinators in the form of technical improvements that helped fulfill the authorities' end of a tacit bargain with resistors by which, if the state insisted on the lancet, then it was also obliged to assure the effectiveness and safety of the procedure. To focus only on the question of compulsion, or its absence, is thus to draw a fairly arbitrary line separating into two starkly opposing camps what in fact was a continuum of responses to smallpox ranging from the eventually voluntary approach in England through the Swedish system of compulsion reluctantly tempered with the possibility of escape and France's combination of a loud bark with a somewhat less sharply fanged bite to end finally with the Germans' less (on paper) draconian, but (in practice) more effective requirement that all be vaccinated and revaccinated. All nations eventually employed some combination of vaccination, voluntary or compulsory, with neoquarantinist techniques of the sort applied also to other contagious diseases.

But within this spectrum, although not as stark as a simple focus on compulsion would suggest, there remained important differences. For this there were both longterm and proximate, both general and specific causes. Among the latter were the tactical infelicities that characterized British legislation, compared, above all, to the German. The German authorities were more flexible in their rigor than the British. They were more willing and earlier able to admit that the lancet had its defects, moving adeptly to correct them, whether through revaccination, the use of animal lymph or tightening the qualifications of vaccinators. They developed a system of implementation that, although ultimately enforced by penal sanctions, was applied in a flexible and individualizing manner so as to limit resistance to those who were firm in their convictions rather than just negligent or indifferent. Though strict and rigorous, enforcement applied equally to all without exacerbating class differences, as did the British practice of repeated prosecutions and fines.

In a more general sense, the British suffered from the precocious success of variolation, the burden of precedence that, having hitched their wagons to a technically inferior technique, impeded the transition to vaccination. The accumulating effect of prophylactic tradition building was becoming increasingly important. The preventive *Sonderweg*

---

[429] *SB*, 18 February 1874, p. 104. To the already existing oppositions of Catholics and Socialists, one feared, would now be added a *Pockenopposition*: *SB*, 9 March 1874, p. 257.

adumbrated already early in the eighteenth century when the British, having imposed strict quarantinism against the plague threatening from Marseilles, now suddenly reversed course, the sanitationist reaction to cholera that (again with an initial flourish of quarantinism then rapidly abandoned) followed a century later – this was the pattern of prophylactic response that, slowly becoming institutionalized, was repeated when it came to smallpox. Because of the power and influence of an environmentalist approach, vaccination here faced a stronger presumption than on the continent that it was unnecessary since general public hygiene would serve to limit the force of epidemics. Such faith in sanitationism, while not absent across the Channel, was strongest in Britain where provaccinators had to counter, time and again, the idea that the decline in smallpox had been due mainly to general hygienic improvements and that further provision of potable water, clean air and effective sewerage would render the lancet superfluous.[430] Continental techniques of prevention were adopted only to be cast off. Once we have seen the same pattern of behavior put through its paces again for venereal disease, it will become clear that this tendency (first to play it safe by adopting strict measures, then to decide that they do not suit British circumstances) had itself become part of the explanation of prophylactic variation, had itself become an institutional habit and a cause in its own right. The different prophylactic approaches adopted for cholera (sanitarily inclined in Britain, more quarantinist in their inflection on the continent) were becoming more firmly entrenched through the experience with smallpox vaccination, were becoming learned institutional behavior.

---

[430] *PP* 1854–55 (88) xlv, p. 629; *Hansard*, 1867, v. 187, col. 1870; 1898, v. 57, col. 784; 1883, v. 280, col. 1020; 1907, v. 174, col. 1273; *Final Report into the Subject of Vaccination*, sects. 51–52, 78–83; *First Report into the Subject of Vaccination*, QQ. 749, 759; *BMJ* (5 July 1902), p. 69.

CHAPTER 5

Syphilis between prostitution and promiscuity

Venereal disease (for the purposes here primarily syphilis) complicated the problems of prophylaxis. Cholera and smallpox were acute epidemic diseases that quickly ran their course with evident external symptoms and a disabling effect on the victim. Identifying the stricken was therefore simple: they were usually in no position to object to precautions imposed and, indeed, had reason to seek the care that usually accompanied them. Syphilis, in contrast, whatever its origins, spread widely in the sixteenth century and by the nineteenth was endemic, afflicting a large (circa a tenth of adult urban males) fraction of the population. Its nature, with a surreptitious, protracted development and often painless symptoms, meant that it could be dissimulated and hidden by its sufferers, many of whom did not in fact realize they were ill, and the afflicted accordingly had ample opportunities to act as vectors of transmission. Symptoms neither necessarily drove the stricken to seek care nor prevented them from living life as usual. In fact, in the days before salvarsan and then penicillin, the protracted and unpleasant treatments that medicine had to offer were more inconvenient and debilitating than the disease.[1] Because transmission generally required direct contact with permeable membranes, syphilis was in theory more easily preventable than diseases with more diffuse and multiple pathways of contagion. Because instinct nonetheless brought such membranes into frequent contact, in fact syphilis became among the most widely disseminated of transmissible ailments, spreading eventually the world over. Because it was most often passed through sex, especially of an extramarital and illicit variety, strong moral opprobrium attended its infection. Elaborate rituals of avoidance and euphemism governed even the mere mention of such disease in all nations throughout the nineteenth century and well

---

[1] Johann Friedrich Fritze, *Handbuch über die venerischen Krankheiten* (new edn.; Berlin, 1797), p. 2; E. Finger et al., eds., *Handbuch der Geschlechtskrankheiten* (Vienna, 1910), v. III, p. 2694; *Mitteilungen*, 8 (1910), p. 73.

into the twentieth. Given such stigma, victims often avoided the prophylaxis and even the treatment that tacitly testified to their transgression. For both biological and social reasons, syphilis's victims often sought to sidestep organized attempts at prevention and cure.[2]

Because of the moral clouds hanging over VD, it was an oft-debated issue whether in fact there should be any attempt to prevent the disease at all. The plague had long been seen as punishment for human sins; cholera was initially regarded in similar terms; smallpox was sometimes viewed as the outcome of modern life's evils. By the middle of the nineteenth century at the latest, however, such mixture of the medical and the moral was largely confined to theologians of a particular stripe or peculiarly principled adherents of allegedly alternative forms of healing. With syphilis, in contrast, moral questions persisted well into the twentieth century, only to flare up again in our own time in response to the AIDS epidemic. If VD was the just dessert of illicit sex – such was the reasoning – why should society mobilize against it?[3] Its spread was voluntary in the sense that victims, assumed able to control their sex drives, exposed themselves by choice to risk and should therefore bear the consequences.[4] Indeed, attempting to prevent (or for that matter to cure) the consequences of sin would be tantamount to encouraging vice; prophylaxis underwrote fornication.

But even when authorities could be persuaded that – moral qualms aside – VD was a public problem of consequence to all, not just the wretches who had put themselves in harm's way, only a limited number of weapons remained in their prophylactic armamentarium. The nature of the disease ruled out many of the precautions marshaled against other ailments. Because VD was largely endemic, controls at the borders to keep out carriers promised little. Because of its many victims, long duration and intermittent appearance, and since the ill did not present an indiscriminate threat to their surroundings as with other more easily transmitted diseases, traditional methods of quarantine and isolation were either unnecessary, impracticable or both. The paucity of debili-

---

[2] *Annales*, 16 (1836), p. 266; Alain Corbin, "Présentation," in A. Parent-Duchâtelet, *La prostitution à Paris au XIXe siècle* (Paris, 1981), p. 24; *ZBGK*, 4, 1 (1905), p. 5; R. Ledermann, *Zur Verhütung und Bekämpfung der Syphilis* (Berlin, 1903), pp. 3–4; *Mitteilungen*, 17, 1 (1919), p. 2; Braus, *Die Syphilis und ihre steigende soziale Gefahr* (Düsseldorf, n.d. [c. 1890]), p. 40.

[3] Samuel Solly, a Victorian surgeon, has been immortalized for his remark in 1868 that syphilis was "intended as a punishment for our sins and we should not interfere in the matter": J. D. Oriel, *The Scars of Venus: A History of Venereology* (London, 1994), p. 175.

[4] Louis Deck, *Syphilis et réglementation de la prostitution en Angleterre et aux Indes: Etude de statistique médicale de 1866 à 1896* (Paris, 1898), p. 12; Charles J. Macalister, *Inaugural Address on the Dangers of the Venereal Diseases* (Edinburgh, 1914), p. 22.

tating symptoms made it hard to convince the stricken that they should be cured, much less isolated, in hospitals. The sex drive, needless to say, perversely counteracted whatever otherwise innate tendency keeps humans at bay from infection, thus hampering attempts to break chains of transmission. Because the contagion survived only briefly outside the human body in any case, the whole panoply of sanitationist and disinfective measures was largely irrelevant.[5] More generally, because VD could be concealed (at least before the age of serological testing), the authorities wielded the heavy stick of compulsory precautions only at the risk of driving victims into hiding, thus defeating their purposes from the outset.

THE LOGIC OF REGULATION

VD prophylaxis did not necessarily involve a focus on, much less the regulation of, prostitution, but during the nineteenth century regulationism bore the brunt of the most heated debates. Because of the difficulties of applying traditional preventive techniques to venereal diseases, other methods were required. Rather than hinging precautions against syphilis on symptoms, regulation took an occupational marker, the sale of sex, to guide its attempts to interrupt transmission at crucial nodal points. Prostitutes were an obvious target on which to train the preventive cannons. In an era when much extramarital sex involved whores, when they remained a comparatively clearly defined occupational group and a ubiquitous feature of urban life, measures aimed in this direction promised a solution that left the rest of society untouched. Acting as an epidemiological interface, prostitutes facilitated (in direct proportion to the number of their clients and the carelessness of their commerce) the transmission of disease. Besides being likely carriers, they were identifiable and therefore potentially subject to precautions. By curing, isolating or otherwise taking infected vendors of copulation out of circulation, more chains of transmission would be broken for less effort than in targeting other groups. Clean up the sidewalks, as one observer put it, and you will have spared the rest of the city.[6]

---

[5] Friedrich August Walch, *Ausführliche Darstellung des Ursprungs, der Erkenntniss, Heilung und Vorbauung der venerischen Krankheit* (Jena, 1811), pp. 235–37; *ZBGK*, 14, 4 (1912), p. 137; *Underdånigt betänkande angående åtgärder för motarbetande af de smittosamma könssjukdomarnas spridning* (Stockholm, 1910), v. I, pp. 272–73; Theodor Rosebury, *Microbes and Morals* (New York, 1971), p. 250.

[6] *DVöG*, 36 (1904), p. 416; Robert Hessen, *Die Prostitution in Deutschland* (Munich, 1910), pp. 170–72; *Huitième congrès international d'hygiène et de démographie, 1894: Comptes-rendus et mémoires* (Budapest, 1895), v. V, p. 522.

Attempts to regulate prostitution (establishing official brothels, registering whores and requiring their specific dress, behavior and residence)
dated back to at least the ancient Greeks and were undertaken in all
European nations during the Middle Ages. While the wide spread of
syphilis starting in the late fifteenth century had instead prompted
attempts to suppress prostitution outright, by the eighteenth century a
modern version of regulation was being elaborated. Mandeville argued
the case for state-regulated whorehouses in 1724 and such ideas were
carried on half a century later by Restif de la Bretonne who sketched out
plans for a fully rationalized system of prostitution – a kind of copulative
Cartesianism based on official brothels, with inhabitants classified by age
and beauty and priced accordingly, priests ministering to their spiritual
needs, arrangements made for the children who issued and for retirement
of the superannuated.[7] Old regime regulations were temporarily abolished during the Revolution in 1791 and prostitutes, enjoying the freedom
of occupation extended to all, unfolded their activities in a burst of what,
from a neoclassical point of view, was healthy free market competition,
but from a moralist's perspective seemed a riot of open solicitation and
public licentiousness. Two years later the backlash set in. Prostitutes, forbidden to appear in public, were inscribed on police registers and medically inspected. During the Napoleonic era the regulationist system
evolved of housing prostitutes in official brothels, registering them if they
lived elsewhere, periodically inspecting them and hospitalizing or otherwise treating the ill.[8] From France, it spread the world over, implemented
at one time or another, in various guises, in all western nations and
remaining in effect, although often in attenuated form, in many today.[9]

Regulationism presupposed that, with much illicit sex taking place in
consort with prostitutes, targeting them gave access to many of the most
dangerous liaisons so that sanitizing commercial copulation prevented
VD transmission in general. Prostitutes were the main and most accessible link in the chain of transmission, what the rat was for the plague,
and the mosquito for yellow fever.[10] Every regulationist had a favorite

---

[7] Erica-Marie Benabou, *La prostitution et la police des mœurs au XVIIIe siècle* (Paris, 1987), ch. 10.
[8] A.-J.-B. Parent-Duchatelet, *De la prostitution dans la ville de Paris* (2nd edn.; Paris, 1837), v. II, pp.
53–55, 480–81, 487–88; J. Jeannel, *De la prostitution dans les grandes villes au dix-neuvième siècle et de l'ex-
tinction des maladies vénériennes* (Paris, 1868), p. 167; Jill Harsin, *Policing Prostitution in Nineteenth-Century
Paris* (Princeton, 1985), pp. xvi–xvii; Susan P. Conner, "Politics, Prostitution and the Pox in
Revolutionary Paris, 1789–1799," *Journal of Social History*, 22, 4 (1989).
[9] Théodore de Félice, "Situation abolitionniste mondiale," *International Review of Criminal Policy*,
13 (October 1958), p. 4; Jürgen Kahmann and Hubert Lanzerath, *Weibliche Prostitution in Hamburg*
(Heidelberg, 1981), pp. 45–46; Cecilie Højgård and Liv Finstad, *Backstreets: Prostitution, Money and Love*
(Cambridge, 1992), ch. 7.
[10] Fernand Mignot, *Le péril vénérien et la prophylaxie des maladies vénériennes* (Paris, 1905), pp. 41, 75;

example of the havoc potentially wreaked by infected prostitutes. Among the most striking was the happily innocent account of a whore from Bordeaux who, upon retiring and seeking to be struck from the register, recounted the details of her career: three decades without ever having been reported ill, relations with an estimated 36,000 men, most notably one day, on the occasion of a choral society contest, when she had slept with sixty-three. Imagine, ran this account, what would have happened had she ever been infected.[11] This was every regulationist's nightmare, the happy hooker as typhoid Mary.

Regulationists considered prostitution a necessary evil, required by the contradiction, most generally, between what they regarded as the imperious demands of (at least male) sexuality and the social and moral impossibility of general promiscuity. More specifically, the troublesome disparity separated the age of sexual maturity and that of marriage. The only means, short of widespread continence, of reconciling such contradictions were (1) lowering the age of marriage, (2) raising – through an insistence on chastity – the age at which sexual activity became regular or (3) loosening the tie between sex and marriage altogether, which in turn, lest a wave of illegitimacy result, assumed the use of contraception. All three routes, though advocated by one reformer or another, were generally dismissed by regulationists as unrealistic, undesirable or both. Were men to achieve fulfillment of their sexual needs (and this in a day when copulatory orgasm at regular intervals was regarded not merely as pleasure, but a biological necessity for both mental and physical health and when masturbation was feared as more dangerous than commercial sex, surpassed in peril perhaps only by the temptations of pederasty) and were most (at least middle-class) women to remain chaste if unmarried and monogamous if wedded, then prostitution was required to square the circle.[12] Prostitution was a necessity for middle-class society, the safety vulva that allowed its men to amass the education and property

---

ZBGK, 4, 2 (1905), p. 76; Filipp Josef Pick, *Die internationale Prophylaxis der venerischen Krankheiten und der Bericht des internationalen Congresses zu Paris 1867* (Prague, 1870), p. 4; *La syphilis* (1904), p. 641.

[11] Louis Lande, *Les affections vénériennes et leur prophylaxie générale a Bordeaux* (Paris, 1873), p. 10.

[12] Joseph Kornig, *Medicinischpolitischer Vorschlag der Lustseuche in grossen Städten, vorzüglich in Wien Einhalt zu thun* (n.p., 1786), pp. 31–32; *Wochenschrift für die gesammte Heilkunde*, 31 (3 August 1850), p. 523; *Zeitschrift für die Staatsarzneikunde*, 42 (1841), p. 72; *New Orleans Medical and Surgical Journal*, 11, 1 (July 1854), p. 703; Michael Mason, *The Making of Victorian Sexuality* (Oxford, 1994), pp. 205–15; Tommie Lundquist, *Den disciplinerade dubbelmoralen: Studier i den reglementerade prostitutionens historia i Sverige 1859–1918* (Gothenburg, 1982), p. 66; Roy Porter and Lesley Hall, *The Facts of Life: The Creation of Sexual Knowledge in Britain, 1650–1950* (New Haven, 1995), chs. 4, 5, 6; Lesley A. Hall, "Forbidden by God, Despised by Men: Masturbation, Medical Warnings, Moral Panic, and Manhood in Great Britain, 1850–1950," in John C. Fout, ed., *Forbidden History* (Chicago, 1992); Jean Stengers and Anne Van Neck, *Histoire d'une grande peur: La masturbation* (Brussels, 1984).

required to provide their families with the appropriate status while neither having to renounce sex, nor defile women from the class of their nuptial ambitions. Prostitution was society's seminal drain, channeling off excess libido just as waste water was safely disposed of.[13]

Prostitution, in the eyes of nineteenth-century regulationists, was therefore a given. The law could not make humans virtuous and prostitution could be suppressed as little as sin declared illegal. Attempts to prohibit it were misguided and fruitless: misguided because they violated the individual's right to bodily autonomy, including the sale of its sexual potential;[14] fruitless because, the demand for prostitution being a constant, if suppressed at one spot, it was certain to reappear elsewhere, or – worse – disappear underground to wreak uncontrolled damage. On the other hand, ignoring prostitution to allow it free rein was equally untenable as an invitation to public license and epidemiological havoc. Leaving prostitution unrestricted granted the individual unwarranted precedence over the health of the community. Freedom of prostitution, as the regulationist credo summed it up, was the liberty to poison and infect – free syphilis in a free state, in the Italians' taunt.[15] With both strict suppression and laissez-faire eliminated as possibilities, regulation to curb the worst excesses of prostitution, limiting its danger as a vector, was the solution.[16]

[13] Lecky put this most memorably when he described the prostitute as "the most efficient guardian of virtue," without whom "the unchallenged purity of countless happy homes would be polluted": William E. H. Lecky, *History of European Morals* (New York, 1869), v. I, p. 299. See also *Mémoires de M. Gisquet, ancien préfet de police* (Paris, 1840), v. IV, p. 365; Keith Thomas, "The Double Standard," *Journal of the History of Ideas*, 20, 2 (April 1959), p. 197; Sheldon Amos, *A Comparative Survey of Laws in Force for the Prohibition, Regulation and Licensing of Vice in England and in Other Countries* (London, 1877), p. 517; Parent-Duchatelet, *De la prostitution*, v. I, p. 7; Jeannel, *De la prostitution*, pp. 168–70. The idea of the seminal drain was not, of course, invented by the Victorians, but stretches back at least to Augustin as the source of the view of prostitutes as a necessity, however loathsome, without which society would be convulsed by its sexual passions: anon., *The Greatest of Our Social Evils: Prostitution* (London, 1857), p. 337; Alain Corbin, "Commercial Sexuality in Nineteenth-Century France: A System of Images and Regulations," *Representations*, 14 (Spring 1986), p. 213.

[14] Parent-Duchatelet, *De la prostitution*, v. II, p. 41; Edvard Welander, *Blad ur prostitutionsfrågans historia i Sverige* (Stockholm, 1904), pp. 94–97; *Schmidts Jahrbücher der In- und Ausländischen Gesammten Medicin* (1853), p. 249; *DVöG*, 1 (1869), p. 379; Karl Åkermark, *Prostitutionen och polisreglementet* (Stockholm, 1903), p. 14; Dubois-Havenith, ed., *Conférence internationale pour la prophylaxie de la syphilis et des maladies vénériennes: Enquêtes sur l'état de la prostitution et la fréquence de la syphilis et des maladies vénériennes dans les différents pays* (Brussels, 1899), v. I/2, p. 165; Louis Fiaux, *La police des moeurs devant la Commission extra-parlementaire du régime des moeurs* (Paris, 1907), v. I, pp. 7–9, 13.

[15] *ZBGK*, 16, 8 (1915), pp. 257–61; Dubois-Havenith, ed., *Conférence internationale pour la prophylaxie de la syphilis et des maladies vénériennes: Rapports préliminaires* (Brussels, 1899), v. I/1, quest. 1, pp. 21–22; Dubois-Havenith, *Conférence internationale: Enquêtes*, v. I/2, p. 165; Mary Gibson, *Prostitution and the State in Italy, 1860–1915* (New Brunswick, 1986), p. 65.

[16] Hermann Eulenberg, ed., *Handbuch des öffentlichen Gesundheitswesens* (Berlin, 1881), v. I, p. 455; L. Pappenheim, *Handbuch der Sanitäts-Polizei* (2nd edn.; Berlin, 1870), v. I, p. 238.

Regulationism in effect imposed the traditional prophylactic solution of breaking chains of transmission through identification and, when necessary, isolation on an epidemiologically crucial, limited and potentially manageable group, thereby sparing the rest of society similar, and unfeasible, measures. That prostitutes were a despised and outcast category facilitated their subjection to such strictures, but from the regulationist view this was a largely coincidental advantage. Regulationists argued two justifications for imposing precautions on prostitutes. First, such measures were not appreciably different from those required of the victims of other contagious diseases or the medical inspections and attendant consequences visited on military recruits and sometimes members of the merchant marine. Quarantining travelers from places stricken by cholera, plague or yellow fever, isolating the victims of leprosy, scarlet fever or diphtheria, banishing smallpox sufferers from public: such precautions sparked no protest on behalf of the unfortunate. Why, then, should not prostitutes be subject to similar sanitary stricture? The Contagious Disease Acts, as Acton put it for Britain, simply extended to VD the same principles applied to other preventable afflictions.[17] Secondly, prostitution was a dangerous occupation and should, like any other insalubrious industry, be subject to public health measures.[18] Prostitution, in the extreme regulationist position, was the active commercial exploitation of men's helpless thralldom to their sexual instincts – much, in this logic, as restaurants are the cruel oppressors of gluttons.[19] Its practitioners were public women and regulation was the public health measure appropriate to their situation. Prostitutes were to be controlled like butchers or bakers; their bodies were analogous, from this vantage, to any other perishable good and, when infected, should be seized just like spoiled foodstuffs. Inspecting them for disease was

---

[17] L. Reuss, *La prostitution au point de vue de l'hygiène et de l'administration en France et a l'étranger* (Paris, 1889), p. 287; *ZBGK*, 15, 8/9 (1914), pp. 272–73; *Förhandlingar*, 1881, p. 70; Welander, *Blad ur prostitutionsfrågans historia*, p. 99; Macalister, *Inaugural Address*, p. 30; Georg Mackensen, *Die Bekämpfung der Geschlechtskrankheiten und der gleichnam. Reichsgesetzentwurf* (Lüneburg, 1919), p. 17; Félix Regnault, *L'évolution de la prostitution* (Paris, n.d. [1906?]), pp. 241–42; *Annales des maladies vénériennes*, 1 (1906), p. 126; Eugen Miller, *Die Prostitution: Ansichten und Vorschläge auf dem Gebiete des Prostitutionswesens* (Munich, 1892), p. 27; William Acton, *Prostitution, Considered in Its Moral, Social, and Sanitary Aspects, in London and Other Large Cities and Garrison Towns* (2nd edn.; London, 1870), p. vii.

[18] Reuss, *La prostitution*, p. 290; *ZBGK*, 15, 8/9 (1914), p. 274; Dubois-Havenith, *Conférence internationale: Enquêtes*, v. I/2, p. 164; Fiaux, *Police des moeurs*, v. I, p. 380; *La syphilis* (1904), p. 712; A. Blaschko, *Syphilis und Prostitution vom Standpunkte der öffentlichen Gesundheitspflege* (Berlin, 1893), p. 146; *PP* 1867–68 (4031) xxxvii, 425, Q. 314.

[19] Nils Stjernberg, *Kriminalpoliti: Studier till den svenska strafflagsreformen* (Uppsala, 1918), p. 116. See also Carol Smart, *Women, Crime and Criminology: A Feminist Critique* (London, 1976), pp. 89–91.

no more degrading than checking the calibration of a bartender's glasses.[20]

Treating prostitution as a matter of public health and its dangers as those posed by a particularly insalubrious occupation, regulationists were unimpressed by the argument, leveled with increasing frequency over the century, that their system punished one sex for the benefit of the other. It was not women as such who were targeted, but prostitutes. That the demand for commercial intercourse came from males while the supply was primarily female was a matter of nature, incidental to the functioning of the system.[21] Men simply did not solicit or prostitute themselves.[22] To argue that targeting prostitutes was an injustice to women, in this reasoning, was as logical as saying that statutes on vagrancy were unfair to men because most vagabonds were male or laws against theft unjust to the poor: true, but trivial. Regulation did not necessarily assume that women were the cause of VD's spread; it simply drew consequences from the fact that prostitutes, who happened to be women, were the epidemiological bottleneck that could most easily be controlled, while their customers, who happened to be male, were much more difficult to contain. Had supply and demand been reversed, or at least balanced from both sexes, many regulationists would have been equally happy to subject male purveyors of commercial copulation to the same regimen.[23]

Regulationists thus regarded their position as the expression of modern, rational, hygienic principles, the application of enlightened public health measures to a devastating scourge. Rather than bowing to moralizing notions that prostitution could be repressed or should be ignored, regulationism – in its own view – unflinchingly accepted it as a

[20] *SFPSM: Bulletin mensuel* (1902), p. 221; O. Commenge, *La prostitution clandestine à Paris* (Paris, 1897), pp. 477–78; Dubois-Havenith, *Conférence internationale: Rapports préliminaires*, v. I/1, quest. 1, pp. 21–22; quest. 3, p. 13; *DVöG*, 41 (1909), p. 734; Acton, *Prostitution*, p. 219; *ZBGK*, 5, 6 (1906), pp. 220–21; Corbin, "Présentation," p. 16.

[21] *DVöG*, 41 (1909), p. 734; *PP* 1882 (340) ix, 1, p. xxi; *Sanitary Record*, n.s., 14, 164 (15 July 1892), p. 29; *SFPSM: Bulletin mensuel* (1902), p. 419; *PP* 1878–79 (323) viii, QQ 3144–46; *Hansard*, 1883, v. 278, col. 792; *Glasgow Medical Journal*, 19, 3 (March 1883), p. 173; *Förhandlingar*, 1881, p. 29; Regnault, *L'évolution de la prostitution*, pp. 243.

[22] When male prostitution was discussed at all, and this was seldom, it was almost without exception homosexual: Fiaux, *Police des moeurs*, v. I, pp. 452, 529–30, 668; *Vierteljahrsschrift für gerichtliche Medicin und öffentliches Sanitätswesen*, 31 (1906), p. 133; Abraham Flexner, *Prostitution in Europe* (New York, 1914), p. 31; *Annales*, 2/9 (1858), pp. 142–52; *Förhandlingar*, 1911, p. 519–20; Welander, *Blad ur prostitutionsfrågans historia*, p. 3; Harsin, *Policing Prostitution*, p. 302. For exceptions, see *Archiv für Syphilis und Hautkrankheiten*, 1 (1846), p. 284; Iwan Bloch, *Die Prostitution* (Berlin, 1925), p. 216; Iwan Bloch, *Das Sexualleben unserer Zeit* (4th–6th edns.; Berlin, 1908), pp. 350–51.

[23] *Underdånigt betänkande angående könssjukdomarnas spridning*, v. I, p. 194; Welander, *Blad ur prostitutionsfrågans historia*, pp. 178ff., 184; *Hygiea*, 51, 3 (March 1889), p. 152; Dubois-Havenith, *Conférence internationale: Rapports préliminaires*, v. I/1, quest. 4, p. 48; *Hansard*, 1870, v. 203, col. 605; 1872, v. 209, col. 341.

necessary evil, seeking instead to control it and thus to stem the spread of VD with the same strategies applied to other diseases, as yet another aspect of the public's health. As an unfortunate requirement, much like cesspools, drains, abattoirs and dumps, prostitution was impossible to forbid, necessary to tolerate.[24] Regulationism was not the handmaiden of vice, but the facilitator of unavoidable seminal release. Official brothels, far from being temples to the delights of Venus, replete with the pleasures of debauch, were to be efficient purveyors of sexual relief for incontinent men in as simple, unostentatious, regimented and unerotic a form as possible.[25] Hence the myriad of regulations restricting sartorial excess, limiting opening hours, forbidding alcohol, dance music, card playing and anything else that might divert attention from the essential socially therapeutic function of officially sanctioned copulation.

Although regulationism was considered advanced, rational, efficient and public-minded, it rested on improvised legal foundations. Nineteenth-century legal codes sought to be modern in separating sin and crime, ending the old regime's attempts to regulate morality through law by prohibiting, for example, extramarital sex.[26] They generally did not criminalize the act of prostitution itself for those of legal age, although many of its ancillary and associated activities (soliciting, brothel keeping, procuring) were prohibited. In the (eventually) nonregulationist nations, Britain especially, prostitution itself was not illegal and no limitations, other than those requiring citizens to conduct themselves decently in public, were imposed on its practitioners. In the regulationist systems, prostitution was not illegal (with the exception, in France, of bursts of revolutionary moralism in 1793 and again during the Commune; with the exception in the German lands of Saxony during the 1830s and forties, Württemberg, Bavaria and a few others), but those who sold sex without being registered were liable to punishment.[27] Prostitution, in the logic of regulationism, could not successfully be suppressed or criminalized and

[24] Parent-Duchatelet, *De la prostitution*, v. II, pp. 52–53; *Förhandlingar*, 1881, p. 28; Pick, *Prophylaxis der venerische Krankheiten*, pp. 4–5; *Annales*, 16 (1836), pp. 279–80; *Vierteljahrsschrift für gerichtliche Medicin und öffentliches Sanitätswesen*, 31 (1906), p. 133; Corbin, "Commercial Sexuality," pp. 213–14; anon., *Greatest of Our Social Evils*, p. 301; *Zeitschrift für die Staatsarzneikunde*, 58 (1849), pp. 385–88.

[25] *Zeitschrift für die Staatsarzneikunde*, 58 (1849), p. 450.

[26] With some oldfashioned remnants: in Sweden, for example, extramarital sex remained illegal until the penal code of 1864; indeed, intercourse where one or both were married, but not to each other, continued to be regarded as "hor" and punishable, although seldom prosecuted, up to 1942. See Ingemar Folke, "Anteckningar om prostitutionen och lagen," in Gunilla Fredelius, ed., *Ett onödigt ont: En antologi mot porr och prostitution* (Stockholm, 1978), p. 45; Tomas Söderblom, *Horan och batongen: Prostitution och repression i folkhemmet* (Stockholm, 1992), p. 176.

[27] *Jahrbuch für Gesetzgebung, Verwaltung und Volkswirtschaft*, 21 (1897), p. 845; Carl Wilhelm Streubel, *Wie hat der Staat der Prostitution gegenüber sich zu verhalten?* (Leipzig, 1862), pp. 6–7; Maïté Albistur and Daniel Armogathe, *Histoire du féminisme français du moyen âge à nos jours* (n.p., n.d.), p. 328.

attempting to accomplish the impossible would only expose the law to ridicule and contempt.[28] Ignoring it altogether, on the other hand, meant abandoning hopes of controlling commercial sex, encouraging public licentiousness.[29] Seeking a middle way between these two extremes in the form of laws that, admitting the inevitability of sex at the cash nexus, sought to define its limits and set penalties for their transgression, meant, however, in effect legally recognizing prostitution, however backhandedly, and treating it like any other profession. Legislation that sought to regulate the profession in all its seamy detail threatened to provoke a scandal.[30] Dealing with prostitution in law was also hampered by the difficulties of defining the act in a legally usable fashion. If it were identified with respect to its commercial element, then should it be in terms of cash only or any exchange of value? If the latter, then how could the mistress be distinguished from the high-class prostitute, the woman who occasionally traded sexual favors for luxuries from the one who insisted on hard currency, the prostitute from the concubine, the kept woman or, for that matter, as radical critics argued, females who married for money or, indeed, any married woman in bourgeois society? If the commercial element were sidestepped, then how could legislation avoid prohibiting all extramarital sex? How could the difference between prostitution and libertinage be defined in legal terms? Even if, as reformers often suggested, not prostitution as such, but only solicitation and public hawking be punishable, how could the law discriminate between an offer of venal sex and a friendly glance, vulgar sartorial tastes and the prostitute's professional plumage, and so on?[31]

Tarnishing the law by complicity with sin was what the regulationists sought to avoid by entrusting instead the elaboration of the conditions under which prostitutes plied their trade not to normal legislation but to more informal and supple means in the shape of local ordinances and the implicit and discretionary powers of the police. Seeking to control

[28] J. K. Proksch, *Die Vorbauung der venerischen Krankheiten vom sanitäts-polizeilichen, pädagogischen und ärztlichen Standpunkte aus betrachtet* (Vienna, 1872), p. 30.

[29] London, with its public debauch, was generally held up in the late nineteenth century as the example to avoid: Acton, *Prostitution*, pp. 100, 112; anon., *Greatest of Our Social Evils*, p. 192; *Zeitschrift für die Staatsarzneikunde*, 42 (1841), p. 69; *Hygiea*, 51, 3 (March 1889), pp. 135–36; *Annales*, 2/41 (1874), pp. 102–03; 2/43 (1875), p. 309; Jeannel, *De la prostitution*, p. 146; Reuss, *La prostitution*, pp. 481–82; Welander, *Blad ur prostitutionsfrågans historia*, p. 92; Regnault, *L'évolution de la prostitution*, p. 105; Dubois-Havenith, *Conférence internationale: Rapports préliminaires*, v. I/1, quest. 4, p. 77; Mason, *Making of Victorian Sexuality*, pp. 92–93.

[30] Reuss, *La prostitution*, pp. 348–50; C. J. Lecour, *La prostitution à Paris et à Londres 1789–1871* (2nd edn.; Paris, 1872), p. 40; *Annales des maladies vénériennes*, 1 (1906), p. 202; Amos, *Comparative Survey of Laws*, p. 17.

[31] Edouard Dolléans, *La police des mœurs* (Paris, 1903), p. 68; *Bulletin*, 3, 19 (1888), p. 255.

prostitution, while not locked fast in the detailed provision of normal law, continental regulationism was therefore often based on an improvised, ad hoc series of local police decrees and administrative measures that were alleged, when challenged as to their legality, to rest on vague and general powers of ensuring public order assigned the police by various, often ancient, statutes. When questioned in 1876 in the Parisian Municipal Council as to the source of his authority in these respects, Voisin, the prefect of police, responded by pounding the table and invoking the capitularies of Charlemagne.[32]

Police powers over prostitution in France were derived from a smorgasbord of ordinances, decrees and local laws dealing with various aspects of public order and health. The penal codes of 1791, 1795 and 1810 were silent on prostitution, but article 484 of the latter sanctioned the pertinent regulations by leaving them in place for all matters not otherwise addressed. The law of 5 April 1884, granting municipal police powers to prevent epidemics, was seized on by regulationists to include the sanitary surveillance of prostitutes. In the fullness of time, some 570 local measures eventually regulated prostitution, with approximately half giving as their motive the need to maintain order and security, the other half invoking the needs of public health as well.[33] In Germany, the legal situation was only slightly more regular. The Prussian Allgemeines Landrecht from 1794 specified the conditions under which prostitution was permitted, while the Prussian and, later, Imperial criminal codes forbade it, except in accord with local police regulations, thus providing at least the rudiments of a legal framework. The 1835 contagious disease regulation was on occasion invoked as authority for the control of prostitution. The Prussian Contagious Disease Law of 1905, unlike the Imperial equivalent of 1900 which made no mention of such matters, spelled out the procedures (compulsory inspection, testing and hospitalization) allowed on prostitutes.[34] In Sweden, prostitution, except that conducted in brothels, was no longer forbidden after the 1864 criminal code ended the prohibition of extramarital sex in general. Vagrancy

---

[32] Jeannel, *De la prostitution*, pp. 168–70; Amos, *Comparative Survey of Laws*, p. 67; Yves Guyot, *Prostitution Under the Regulation System* (London, 1884), pp. 10, 161.

[33] Parent-Duchatelet, *De la prostitution*, v. II, pp. 491, 503–04, 509; Fiaux, *Police des moeurs*, v. I, p. 29; Flexner, *Prostitution in Europe*, pp. 133–34; Lecour, *La prostitution à Paris*, pp. 34–35, 38–39; Harsin, *Policing Prostitution*, pp. 64–65; *SFPSM: Bulletin mensuel* (1902), p. 319.

[34] Robert Schmölder, *Die Bestrafung und polizeiliche Behandlung der gewerbsmässigen Unzucht* (Berlin, 1917), p. 6; *ZBGK*, I, 3 (1903), pp. 177–80; *Gesetz-Sammlung*, 1905, 38/10649, §8; *Allgemeine Ausführungsbestimmungen zu dem Gesetze, betreffend die Bekämpfung übertragbarer Krankheiten, vom 28. August 1905: Amtliche Ausgabe* (Berlin, 1906), pp. 16, 24–25.

laws were therefore invoked to allow the prosecution (with up to three years of hard labor at Landskrona) of prostitutes who refused to submit to regulation in those municipalities with such measures in place.[35] The British Contagious Disease Acts, in turn, as instruments of national law, were the exception to this rule of regulation through local statute.[36]

Because the system entrusted such powers to the police and its administrative fiat, one of the most criticized aspects of regulation was its tendency to place prostitutes outside the law, stripped of the protections against arbitrary arrest and imprisonment guaranteed other citizens. Women in Paris, for example, were registered as prostitutes before a police tribunal on the basis of a vice squad patrolman's complaint, without a normal court hearing and the right to defend themselves with legal counsel and witnesses.[37] In Germany, the situation was marginally better, with Prussian reforms in 1907 guaranteeing prostitutes a semblance of due process.[38] Britain was again the exception in that a formal judicial process in court was required, with a judge pronouncing on the validity of the police's claim that an arrested woman who refused to register voluntarily was in fact a common prostitute.[39] Thanks to this localist, ad hoc nature of regulationism, peculiar contradictions and circumstances were common. In many cases, regulation was practiced only in contravention of existing law. In Sweden, inscription exempted prostitutes from prosecution that they would otherwise have been subject to as vagrants.[40] In Germany, the most general contradiction was between the Prussian ALR,

---

[35] Carl Malmroth, "Om de smittosamma könssjukdomarnas bekämpande i Sverige," in *Underdånigt betänkande angående könssjukdomarnas spridning*, v. IV, pp. 46–51; Söderblom, *Horan och batongen*, p. 206; Britt-Inger Lind and Torsten Fredriksson, *Kärlek för pengar? En bok om prostitutionsprojektet i Malmö 1976–1980* (Stockholm, 1980), p. 14.

[36] Although the distinction between the British rule of law in this respect and the continental rule by administrative statute was not as clearcut as the British sometimes liked to portray. For one thing, the CD Acts, by not defining the term "prostitute," left the police with much discretionary power. And conversely, nations other than Britain also regulated prostitution in the form of regular laws, such as Hungary, Italy and Belgium: see *Transactions of the Medico-Legal Society*, 9 (1911–12), p. 103; Benjamin Scott, *A State Iniquity* (London, 1890), p. 11; F. B. Smith, "Ethics and Disease in the Later Nineteenth Century: The Contagious Diseases Acts," *Historical Studies* (Australia), 15, 57 (October 1971), p. 129; Dolléans, *Police des moeurs*, p. 80; Dubois-Havenith, *Conférence internationale: Rapports préliminaires*, v. I/1, quest. 1, p. 74; Flexner, *Prostitution in Europe*, p. 136; Guyot, *Prostitution Under the Regulation System*, p. 54; [André] Cavaillon, *Les législations antivénériennes dans le monde* ([Paris], 1931), p. 44; Gibson, *Prostitution and the State*, p. 30.

[37] *Bulletin*, 3, 19 (1888), pp. 193–94; Flexner, *Prostitution in Europe*, pp. 133–34; Alain Corbin, *Women for Hire: Prostitution and Sexuality in France after 1850* (Cambridge, MA, 1990), p. 32; Harsin, *Policing Prostitution*, pp. xvi–xvii, 94–95.

[38] *Ministerial-Blatt für die Preussische innere Verwaltung*, 1908, p. 15; *ZBGK*, 16, 8 (1915), p. 258. For similar reforms, see *DVöG*, 1 (1869), pp. 386ff.; Eulenberg, *Handbuch des öffentlichen Gesundheitswesens*, v. I, p. 455.　　[39] Amos, *Comparative Survey of Laws*, p. 72; *PP* 1871 (c. 408-1) xix, 29, p. vi.

[40] Flexner, *Prostitution in Europe*, p. 137; *Underdånigt betänkande angående könssjukdomarnas spridning*, v. I, p. 104; *Bihang*, 1889, FK, Motion 27, p. 3.

which specified in detail the conditions under which prostitution could be exercised, and the Prussian, and then later Imperial, penal codes which, in principle, outlawed commercial sex.[41] Brothels, though theoretically forbidden by §180 of the Imperial penal code were, thanks to legalistic legerdemain, in fact still required in cities like Hamburg and Mainz and flourished less officially in scores of other towns. Criminal law contradicted administrative practice when a broad definition of procuring, including the mere fact of renting to prostitutes, meant that both landlords as well as the vice squad, which registered prostitutes and their place of residence, were technically guilty of pimping.[42] More specific examples included the unfortunate case of a prostitute in Halle who had married her pimp. As husband, he was legally expected (BGB §1353) to live with her, but as pimp he was forbidden by local regulation to do so. The court ruled that because she had married her pimp in hopes of circumventing regulations, not as the foundation of a normal marital existence, she was in fact prohibited from living with her husband.[43]

THE REGULATIONIST IDEAL TYPE

Although regulationism differed not only between nations, but also from city to city, certain characteristics were common to most forms. Prostitutes were inscribed on the police's registers, required to carry a card to that effect. Those who otherwise engaged in commercial sex could be punished and/or registered. Inscribed prostitutes were medically inspected at regular intervals, sometimes at their dwellings, most often at stations run by the police. Examinations took place, with or without the use of a speculum, at intervals that varied from fortnightly under the British CD Acts and in Frankfurt, to weekly in Berlin and Stockholm, twice weekly in Paris, Belgium, Italy, Spain and Gothenburg and four times a week in Hannover.[44] The infected were hospitalized and

[41] BA, 15.01, RmdI, 11866, p. 26, Reichs-Gesundheitsrat, 1908, Kirchner "Massnahmen zur Bekämpfung der Geschlechtskrankheiten im Deutschen Reich"; Dubois-Havenith, *Conférence internationale: Enquêtes*, v. I/2, p. 662; Stephan Leonhard, *Die Prostitution, ihre hygienische, sanitäre, sittenpoliziliche und gesetzliche Bekämpfung* (Munich, 1912), p. 29.

[42] Alfred Urban, *Staat und Prostitution in Hamburg vom Beginn der Reglementierung bis zur Aufhebung der Kasernierung (1807–1922)* (Hamburg, 1925), pp. 85–93; *ZBGK*, 17 (1916), p. 183; Flexner, *Prostitution in Europe*, p. 140; Wilhelm Haldy, *Die Wohnungsfrage der Prostituierten (Kuppeleiparagraph und Bordellwirt)* (Hannover, 1914). [43] *ZBGK*, 10, 8 (1909/10), pp. 283–84.

[44] Emile Richard, *La prostitution à Paris* (Paris, 1890), pp. 120–21; Amos, *Comparative Survey of Laws*, p. 44; Lundquist, *Den disciplinerade dubbelmoralen*, p. 92; Max Silber, *Womit sind die ansteckenden Geschlechtskrankheiten als Volksseuche im Deutschen Reiche wirksam zu bekämpfen?* (Leipzig, 1902), pp. 42–43; *New Orleans Medical and Surgical Journal*, 11, 1 (July 1854), pp. 675, 679; Chéry, *Syphilis, maladies vénériennes et prostitution* (Toulouse, n.d. [1911]), p. 93; Albert Guttstadt, *Deutschlands Gesundheitswesen* (Leipzig, 1891), v. II, pp. 366–68.

prostitutes who failed to appear for inspections were liable to incarceration. In certain cities, like Paris early in the nineteenth century, some lived and worked in official closed brothels; later open bordellos, where only the business of sex was conducted, became common. Elsewhere, as in Berlin after midcentury and in Sweden generally, bordellos were not tolerated and prostitutes worked from their own lodgings.

A welter of restrictions, with transgressions punishable by fines and jail, governed the actions, behavior and dress of registered prostitutes. If they were allowed to live by themselves, rules determined the neighborhoods they could call home. In some cities (Bremen, Dortmund, Essen) a few streets were set aside for such purposes, in what was known as the barracks system. Prostitutes were generally forbidden to show themselves at their windows, which usually had to be frosted or curtained. They were allowed on the streets only at certain hours and required to dress unostentatiously. In Berlin, male garments were restricted to indoor masquerade balls; in Paris prostitutes were forbidden to appear in public without a hat. They were not allowed to hawk their wares in an annoying or insistent fashion; in Paris they were forbidden entirely to address men accompanied by women or children.[45] They were generally prohibited from the vicinity of churches, military barracks, schools, royal and public buildings and each city had particular forbidden places. In Berlin public theaters were off limits; in Gothenburg and Oslo it was only the front rows thereof; in Nantes the museums and library were; in Leipzig the Gewandhaus concerts and the race track; in Bremen public swimming pools; in Stockholm the royal palace; in Hamburg the zoo.[46]

Regulating prostitutes was generally entrusted to a special division of the police, the vice squad, police des moeurs or Sittenpolizei. In England special elements of the Metropolitan Police, London's force, took enforcement of the CD Acts from local authorities, and in Oxford after 1826 a special university corps applied the old rules at night, according to which prostitutes could be arrested as such, while during daytime the normal city police applied the new Vagrancy Act, holding them liable

---

[45] Fiaux, *Police des moeurs*, v. I, pp. 714–15; *Zeitschrift für die Staatsarzneikunde*, 58 (1849), pp. 428–54; *Bihang*, 1903, AK, Motion 88, p. 3; *New Orleans Medical and Surgical Journal*, 11, 1 (July 1854), p. 690; Regnault, *L'évolution de la prostitution*, p. 106; Guttstadt, *Deutschlands Gesundheitswesen*, v. II, pp. 368–71.

[46] *Zeitschrift für die Staatsarzneikunde*, 58 (1849), pp. 428–54; Mignot, *Le péril vénérien*, pp. 135–36; *DVöG*, 1 (1869), pp. 387; Lundquist, *Den disciplinerade dubbelmoralen*, p. 82; Blaschko, *Syphilis und Prostitution*, pp. 182–84; *ZBGK*, 14, 3 (1912), p. 95; Carl Malmroth, "Om de smittosamma könssjukdomarnas bekämpande," p. 56; Kari Melby, "Prostitution og kontroll," in Anne-Marit Gotaas et al., eds., *Det kriminelle kjønn* (Oslo, 1980), p. 87.

only if behaving in a riotous or indecent manner.[47] The vice squad's first duty was to register prostitutes, ferreting out informal practitioners and keeping the ranks of those targeted for precautions as replete as possible. By registering ladies of the night, clandestine prostitution (the German term, *Winkelhurerei*, the whoring in nooks, has the advantage of vivid imagery) was to be contained. Britain under the CD Acts was slightly anomalous in this respect since prostitutes, not being registered in the continental sense, were not divided into the official and the clandestine. Instead, the Metropolitan Police sought to bring under sanitary surveillance all women who in fact acted as prostitutes. In addition, the vice squad ensured that registered prostitutes conducted themselves according to regulations and appeared for their appointed examinations.

IMAGES IN THE CAVE

The ideal form of regulationism was French.[48] In other nations that followed this example, variations were practiced on these basic themes. In Germany, as always, matters fluctuated by locality. Generally speaking, inscription was voluntary in the south, compulsory in the north.[49] Bavaria abandoned regulation altogether in 1861, forbidding prostitution of any variety, then had a system of voluntary inscription with no brothels, but by the early twentieth century stood in vociferous support of the old regulationist system against attempts to abolish it. At the other end of the spectrum, preunification Hamburg had a well-organized system of official brothels and found ways to continue it in practice (up until 1922) even after bordellos had been officially outlawed in the 1870s.[50] In Prussia, the ALR from 1794 permitted whores to work only in official brothels and the Prussian penal code of 1851 (§146) forbade prostitution except in accord with police regulations.[51] Even when regulation was

---

[47] Paul McHugh, *Prostitution and Victorian Social Reform* (London, 1980), pp. 43–44; Scott, *State Iniquity*, p. 30; Amos, *Comparative Survey of Laws*, p. 190; Arthur J. Engel, "'Immoral Intentions': The University of Oxford and the Problem of Prostitution, 1827–1914," *Victorian Studies*, 23, 1 (Autumn 1979), pp. 79–83.

[48] Although the French admired the Belgians for the perfection of their practice in such matters.

[49] Willi Bauer, *Geschichte und Wesen der Prostitution* (2nd edn.; Stuttgart, 1956), p. 100; *PP* 1916 (8189) xvi, 1, p. 183; Dubois-Havenith, *Conférence internationale: Enquêtes*, v. I/2, p. 668; Michael Bargon, *Prostitution und Zuhälterei* (Lübeck, 1982), p. 73. However, Bremen also had only a voluntary system of inscription: *ZBGK*, 17, 1/2 (1916), p. 25.

[50] *Underdånigt betänkande angående könssjukdomarnas spridning*, v. II, pp. 174–78; Schmölder, *Bestrafung und polizeiliche Behandlung*, p. 10; Urban, *Staat und Prostitution in Hamburg*, pp. 140–45.

[51] ALR, II 20, §§999–1027; *Zeitschrift für die Staatsarzneikunde*, 42 (1841), pp. 91–92; F. L. Augustin, *Die königlich Preussische Medicinalverfassung* (Potsdam, 1818), v. I, p. 191.

allowed, the brothel question provoked long debate. In Berlin, bordellos were forbidden at the turn of the century following the extensive spread of VD in the train of the Napoleonic wars, but then permitted once again at the behest of the commanding French general. When the Prussian king sought to close them again some years later, the police had in the meantime warmed to their advantages and sought to evade his demands. In 1836 brothels were concentrated in the Königsmauer, provoking protests from the neighbors. At midcentury, the bordello battle flared up anew, with a middle-class campaign led by a spirits manufacturer against them, and they were shut down in 1845. In 1851 they reopened at the insistence, among others, of the army commander, with new regulations issued in 1853. This experiment ended already in 1856 when the Prussian superior court ruled that, whatever the intentions of lawmakers in permitting brothels under police regulation, in fact §147 of the penal code on procuring outlawed them and official bordellos were closed down once again, this time for good. This interpretation of the Prussian penal code to rule out official brothels continued when taken over verbatim (§180) into the new Imperial code.[52]

In the Empire, therefore, a form of attenuated regulationism held sway, with brothels forbidden, but prostitutes registered and controlled by the police in those localities that so chose. Despite their prohibition, brothels flourished in many German cities. Hannover closed its in 1866 and Frankfurt the following year, Dortmund in 1873 and Cologne in 1880, while Erfurt and Leipzig held out a few years longer. But many municipal authorities enforced the law only laxly. Hamburg, indeed, had a de facto system of compulsory brothels in that regulations forbade prostitutes from working in houses other than those designated by the police.[53] Not until the early 1920s were Hamburg's bordellos shut down, only to be – by virtue of their central placement – promptly converted (confirming the first principle of real estate on the paramount importance of location) into prime office space. Dresden and Bremen avoided the precepts of the criminal code for years by having the police deal not

[52] *Archiv für Syphilis und Hautkrankheiten*, 1 (1846), pp. 276–77; *Wochenschrift für die gesammte Heilkunde*, 31 (3 August 1850), pp. 481ff.; *Schmidts Jahrbücher der In- und Ausländischen Gesammten Medicin* (1853), p. 249; *Maanedsblad udgivet af Foreningen imod Lovbeskyttelse for Usædlighed*, 3 (1881), pp. 36–40; Chéry, *Syphilis*, p. 90; *Annales*, 46 (1851), p. 85; Dubois-Havenith, *Conférence internationale: Enquêtes*, v. I/2, p. 662; Blaschko, *Syphilis und Prostitution*, pp. 63–64.
[53] Waldvogel, *Die Gefahren der Geschlechtskrankheiten und ihre Verhütung* (Stuttgart, 1905), pp. 76–77; Dubois-Havenith, *Conférence internationale: Enquêtes*, v. I/2, p. 667; Blaschko, *Syphilis und Prostitution*, pp. 63–64; Richard J. Evans, *The Feminist Movement in Germany 1894–1933* (London, 1976), pp. 53–54; Margot D. Kreuzer, *Prostitution: Eine sozialgeschichtliche Untersuchung in Frankfurt a.M.* (Stuttgart, 1988), pp. 37–39.

with brothel owners, as earlier, but directly with the prostitutes, thus officially ignoring the fact that they lived and worked in bordellos. In Bremen prostitutes could live and work in the Helenenstrasse, a bordello block near the center of town, as part of that municipality's much studied and admired barracks system.[54] In Frankfurt, police ambitions to concentrate prostitution around the central railroad station foundered in the face of early forms of NIMBYism. Local neighborhood residents protested and were supported by the railroad administration, which, with hopes of housing its personnel conveniently nearby, feared that ticket punchers would balk at hanging their caps in a redlight district. After the First World War, the French brought the issue to a boil once again by forcing the Germans to establish official brothels in the occupied territories, adding insult to injury by making them foot the bill as an occupation cost and insisting that they be womanned only by Germans.[55]

In Sweden, though brothels were outlawed in the criminal code, the Stockholm police sought to establish official ones in the late 1830s. When attacked and stoned by local residents, however, these had to be closed and bordellos never became part of the regulationist system here. In other respects, regulation was established in thirteen Swedish cities starting at midcentury and continuing until the system was abolished in 1918, by which point most municipalities had abandoned it voluntarily. Control of prostitutes was based on the leverage vagrancy laws permitted police over those with no other means of support. Tackling prostitution indirectly, in terms of having no livelihood, allowed the authorities wide latitude in defining who fell under such strictures, but the disadvantage was that women could avoid the law's consequences by having, on paper at least, regular employment.[56]

It was Britain that, from a continental perspective, was the odd land out. The closest it came to regulationism were the Contagious Disease Acts, in effect from 1864 until the mid-1880s and notorious in the British literature, although far from exceptional compared to continental measures. Before the CD Acts, prostitution and solicitation had largely been

[54] *Mitteilungen*, 22 (1924) p. 7; *ZBGK*, 17, 1/2 (1916), pp. 11–20; Elisabeth Meyer-Renschhausen, *Weibliche Kultur und soziale Arbeit: Eine Geschichte der Frauenbewegung am Beispiel Bremens 1810–1927* (Cologne, 1989), pp. 307–16.

[55] *Mitteilungen*, 10 (1912), pp. 94–95; *Münchener medizinische Wochenschrift*, 56, 23 (1909), p. 1164; BA, 15.01, RmdI, 11890, Der Preussische Minister des Innern an Herrn Reichsminister für die besetzten Gebiete, 11 May 1926, pp. 311, 313.

[56] Lundquist, *Den disciplinerade dubbelmoralen*, pp. 66, 72; Edvard Welander, *Om de veneriska sjukdomarnes historia i Sverige* (Stockholm, 1898), p. 194; *Hygiea*, 51, 3 (March 1889), p. 144; Dubois-Havenith, *Conférence internationale: Enquêtes*, v. I/2, pp. 460–64; Fredelius, *Ett onödigt ont*, p. 14.

ignored except as they occasioned public disturbance or offense to morals. Prostitution was a question of sin and morality – as common opinion would have it – not the province of humanmade law.[57] The Disorderly Houses Acts of 1752 and 1818 licensed institutions offering music and dancing. Complaints against those which also served as brothels were possible, but complicated.[58] In 1744 the authorities were given the means to arrest prostitutes, along with rogues, vagabonds and other itinerants. The 1824 Vagrancy Act then, unlike the earlier version, included prostitutes among vagrants, allowing the authorities to pursue them for behaving publicly in a riotous and indecent manner. This in fact restricted the ability to arrest women, who could earlier have been apprehended merely for being on the streets unable to give a satisfactory account of themselves, while now they had to be behaving indecorously to boot. The 1839 Metropolitan Police Act, the 1847 Town Police Clauses Act and, eventually, the 1875 Public Health Act strengthened the police's ability to act against prostitutes, granting them powers to arrest and fine those who solicited to the annoyance of inhabitants or passersby, and remained their basic weapons in these respects for over a century.[59]

With the first of the CD Acts in 1864, however, the British went beyond merely suppressing publicly flagrant prostitution. The concern was first and foremost with the venereal state of the army. The incidence of VD in the Crimea had been appalling and during the early 1860s attention was again focused on the issue by an outbreak of disease among troops returning from India. VD was in general a major problem in the British army, ravaging the ranks far worse than the forces of any continental nation.[60] Prostitution in various garrison towns was now regulated. If the police or physicians informed a Justice of the Peace that a prostitute was infected, she could be instructed to appear for medical examination and, if diseased, hospitalized up to three months. Women who refused examination or treatment, leaving the hospital early for example, could be imprisoned, as could brothel owners who allowed infected prostitutes to ply their trade. Two years later, in 1866, things

---

[57] *Hansard*, 1844, v. 74, col. 1232; v. 75, col. 878; 1847, v. 93, col. 811; 1849, v. 107, col. 954.

[58] 25 Geo. 2 c. 36; 28 Geo. 2 c. 19; Stefan Petrow, *Policing Morals: The Metropolitan Police and the Home Office 1870–1914* (Oxford, 1994), p. 148; Edward J. Bristow, *Vice and Vigilance: Purity Movements in Britain Since 1700* (Dublin, 1977), pp. 54–55.

[59] 17 Geo. 2 c. 5; 3 Geo. 4 c. 40; 5 Geo. 4 c. 83, s. 3; T. E. James, *Prostitution and the Law* (n.p., 1951), pp. 32–33; Engel, "Immoral Intentions," p. 80; 2 & 3 Vict. c. 47; Bristow, *Vice and Vigilance*, p. 54; 10 & 11 Vict. c. 89, cl. 28; Susan M. Edwards, *Female Sexuality and the Law* (Oxford, 1981), pp. 56–57.

[60] John Gill Gamble, "The Origins, Administration, and Impact of the Contagious Diseases Act from a Military Perspective" (Ph.D. diss., University of Southern Mississippi, 1983), ch. 2; Alan Ramsay Skelley, *The Victorian Army at Home* (London, 1977), pp. 53–54.

were tightened up. Not just prostitutes suspected of disease could be examined, but all prostitutes resident in or near the affected districts. It was no longer because of their suspected epidemiological state, but purely their profession, that they were to be inspected. This deprived the police of some discretion and possible abuse of power, but at the cost of subjecting all prostitutes in scheduled districts to inspection. British practice thus approximated more closely continental norms, while still avoiding the registration of prostitutes and official brothels in order to sidestep objections to fullscale regulationism.[61] Medical examinations could now be required at regular intervals for up to a year. If infected, prostitutes were liable to be detained in a hospital, arrested if they refused to come voluntarily, and kept until discharged or up to six months. In 1869, a few further loopholes were plugged: the acts were extended to more garrison towns, applicable to all prostitutes living within an extended geographical radius, inspections were conducted more frequently, the maximum time prostitutes could be hospitalized was prolonged by another three months and women who were menstruating were prevented from avoiding inspections for that reason, detained for five days before examination.[62]

During the late 1860s, enthusiasts proposed extending the CD Acts not only to all of Britain, but also to include the civilian population, thereby introducing, in effect, regulationism on a continental scale.[63] Though a Select Committee of the Lords supported extension, a committee in 1868 shied away from such far-reaching reform at short notice

---

[61]   27 & 28 Vict. c. 85; 29 Vict. c. 35, ss. 15–16, 20–24; *Transactions of the Medico-Legal Society*, 9 (1911–12), p. 101; *PP* 1867–68 (4031) xxxvii, 425, QQ 7030–31.

[62]   32 & 33 Vict. c. 96. The British system was thus not technically regulation on the continental model in that prostitutes were not registered as such, although they were encouraged by the strictures otherwise imposed to submit "voluntarily" to periodical inspection. The acts spoke only of prostitutes' liability to submit to examination, thus emphasizing the purely sanitary aspect of surveillance, avoiding association with the other ways that the lives of continental prostitutes were controlled. The CD Acts in fact introduced a variety of what, from a continental perspective, should be called reformed or neoregulationism. Control of prostitution was spelled out in a national law, not left to the vagaries of local ordinance; examination could be decreed only by a court, not by the arbitrary fiat of the police; the primary intention was sanitary surveillance of a public health threat, not regulation as such of prostitution as an occupation or, indeed, a way of life: Amos, *Comparative Survey of Laws*, p. 212. This was part of the reason why French observers found the CD Acts a model of improvements that should be implemented at home: *Annales*, 2/41 (1874), pp. 122–23.

[63]   Harveian Medical Society of London, *Report of the Committee for the Prevention of Venereal Diseases, Read Before, and Adopted by, the Society, July 1st, 1867* (London, 1867), p. 13; *PP* 1867–68 (266) lv, 421; *PP* 1883 (316) lv, 71; William Acton, *The Contagious Diseases Act: Shall the Contagious Diseases Act be Applied to the Civil Population?* (London, 1870); Acton, *Prostitution*, p. xi; *Medical Press and Circular*, 6 (26 August 1868), p. 180; *BMJ*, 2 (27 November 1869), pp. 581–83.

and Simon's consideration of the question in his annual report for that year advised against it.[64] Regulating prostitution in the military was a legitimate state concern, he argued, since, by insisting on celibacy, society was obliged to face its consequences. But to argue by analogy for extension to the civilian population was another matter. To care for all infected prostitutes in London alone would require doubling the number of existing hospitals and expenditure on such a scale to alleviate the medical effects of sin promised to be a hard sell for the average taxpayer. VD prophylaxis should instead remain a private matter: caveat emptor. Gladstone's administration paid attention to such notes of hesitation, deciding to seek further investigation before any expansion.[65] Proposals to extend the acts provoked a countermovement to abolish them altogether which, by leading eventually to the end of even limited regulationism in Britain, proved once again that the best is often the foe of the better.

THE DECLINE OF REGULATION

Although widely adopted, by century's end regulationism was under attack from without while being hollowed out internally. Even by its own standards it was failing. Part of the problem lay with inadequate medical technique. Being registered and inspected was no guarantee that official prostitutes were less infectious than clandestines. In the era before serological tests for syphilis or microscopic ones for gonorrhea, a simple examination for symptoms could not promise more than the catch of an occasional infected person. Prostitutes, who had no incentive to be found diseased, hospitalized and deprived of their livelihood, dissimulated to hide symptoms. Given the numbers to be inspected daily, each examination was so cursory, usually no more than a minute or two, as to be of little use. Since disinfection came into use only late in the century, it is likely, indeed, that as much disease was transmitted during examinations as discovered.

With Neisser's identification in 1879 of the gonorrhea microbe, new problems arose. Estimates of the numbers of inspected prostitutes who, while asymptomatic, were infected with the gonococcus climbed stead-

---

[64] *PP* 1868–69 (306) vii, 1, p. iii; *Transactions of the National Association for the Promotion of Social Science* (1869), pp. 436–51; Thomas Beggs, *The Proposed Extension of the Contagious Diseases Act in Its Moral and Economical Aspects* (London, 1870), p. 3.

[65] *PP* 1868–69 (4127) xxxii, 1, pp. 11; McHugh, *Prostitution and Victorian Social Reform*, p. 48; Judith R. Walkowitz, *Prostitution and Victorian Society: Women, Class and the State* (Cambridge, 1980), pp. 86–87.

ily, from Neisser's own calculation of 20 percent in 1888 to the conclusion by the turn of the century that half of the registered were afflicted. With the development of the Wassermann test for syphilis in 1905, the problem of the asymptomatic carrier confirmed the unreliability of examinations for purely clinical manifestations. Compounding the problem were a number of other issues: the indeterminacy of both the Wassermann and gonorrhea tests, where a single negative finding was not conclusive proof that the patient was uninfectious, the vast numbers who were now being identified as stricken by these new and powerful diagnostic tools and, most discouraging, the absence of any effective cure even when cases were found. As with cholera, the bacteriological revolution made diagnosis potentially more certain, but its practical application less realistic. The exactness of microscopic inspections, as one observer put it for gonorrhea, became almost a burden.[66] Unable to exclude the possibility of disease through cursory clinical examinations of registered prostitutes, the system was doubly dangerous, in the eyes of its detractors, in encouraging a deceptive sense of security. Mistakenly believing that regulation was a guarantee of disease-free commercial sex, some disappointed men had gone so far as to sue municipal authorities for damages resulting from illness contracted in official brothels.[67] A veritable battle of the venereologists raged over the question whether VD was more prevalent among registered or clandestine prostitutes, whether – in other words – the system worked at all, with little sense of closure to what was a statistically indeterminable dispute.[68]

More generally, unless a significant fraction of those who engaged in potentially dangerous sex could be identified, inscribed and cured, or at least isolated, there was little justification for the system. Various developments, however, were hampering regulationism's ability to be effective. Among those who sold sex, ever fewer were officially registered and subject to the examinations, whatever their worth. At the same time, changing mores were making extramarital sex decreasingly the exclusive preserve of transactions between prostitutes, of whatever stripe, and

[66] Hammer, quoted in Magnus Möller, "Undersökningar i vissa frågor rörande de smittosamma könssjukdomarna," in *Underdånigt betänkande angående smittosamma könssjukdomarnas spridning*, v. IV, p. 57.
[67] Ph. Ricord, *Lettres sur la syphilis* (3rd edn.; Paris, 1863), p. 287; *Medical Enquirer*, 3 (15 November 1877), p. 153; Åkermark, *Prostitutionen och polisreglementet*, pp. 23–25.
[68] *ZBGK*, 3, 7 (1904–05), pp. 273–75; Blaschko, *Syphilis und Prostitution*, pp. 75–83; *La syphilis* (1904), p. 684; Charles Mauriac, *Syphilis primitive et syphilis secondaire* (Paris, 1890), pp. 108–09; *Annales*, 2/36 (1871), pp. 292–94; Dubois-Havenith, *Conférence internationale: Rapports préliminaires*, v. I/1, Verchère, pp. 16–17; quest. 1, p. 108; Lande, *Les affections vénériennes*, p. 16; Deck, *Syphilis et réglementation*, pp. 15–62 and passim; *ZBGK*, 8, 1 (1908), p. 14.

their clients. If not earlier, then certainly by the First World War, the problem of VD transmission had become more one of promiscuity than of prostitution. As sexual relations before and outside marriage between men and unmercenary partners grew as a proportion of illicit sex among the urban middle classes, as casual liaisons gradually became the normal course of prenuptial experimentation for young women and not just their brothers, regulationism failed to keep up. Once the system no longer could claim to provide prophylactic access to a significant percentage of illicit intercourse, its justification was undercut. Changing sexual tastes, a desire for at least the illusion of seduction and romance even in commercial relations and a shift away from the production-line sex of oldfashioned brothels, led to a decline in official bordellos, a proliferation of informal institutions, often themed or specialized in exotic erotic practices, and an increase in registered prostitutes working and living alone. More disturbing from the regulationist view was the accompanying massive increase in the numbers of clandestine prostitutes, some fulltime practitioners, but many who sold sex only as a sideline – both varieties sprouting up, as one observer grumbled, like poisonous mushrooms.[69] The numbers are naturally unreliable, but by general agreement registered prostitutes made up no more than a small and diminishing fraction of all who pursued mercenary sex during the last decades of the nineteenth century.[70] Many prostitutes appear also to have treated commercial copulation as a transitional phase between other jobs, before marriage and, in general, as but one element of a longer work cycle, undermining regulationism's assumption that they were a clearly defined professional group of fulltime career workers.[71] These potential sources of infection among parttime, intermittent and otherwise clandestine prostitutes were, of course, much harder to control. As their ranks swelled to dwarf those of their official sisters, the vice squad could not pretend to be doing more than inexpertly checking the symptoms of a few selected prostitutes and regulationism's claim to help hinder the spread of disease diminished in plausibility.

With the rise of irregular prostitution, one of regulationism's inherent dilemmas was aggravated. As the ranks of the unregistered swelled

[69] Corbin, *Women for Hire*, pp. 115–26, 186–89; Harsin, *Policing Prostitution*, pp. 51, 345–46; Mason, *Making of Victorian Sexuality*, pp. 81–88; *ZBGK*, 17, 1/2 (1916), p. 25; *SFPSM: Bulletin mensuel* (1902), p. 414.

[70] Estimates varying from 1 percent to 20 percent: *BJVD*, 2, 5 (January 1926), p. 71; Flexner, *Prostitution in Europe*, pp. 142–45, 150; Corbin, *Women for Hire*, pp. 37–38, 130.

[71] *ZBGK*, 15, 6 (1914), p. 200; *Mitteilungen*, 15, 3/4 (1917), p. 43; XVIIth International Congress of Medicine, London 1913, Section XIII, *Dermatology and Syphilography* (London, 1913), pp. 41–43.

and the vice squad's energies were increasingly consumed with the apprehension and inspection of clandestine and therefore often merely alleged prostitutes, the potential for mis- and abuse of police powers, the cases of mistaken accusation and the corresponding outrage as the daughters, sisters and wives of prominent men, chancing to be in the wrong place at an unfortunate time, were occasionally swept along in overeager police razzias all grew, helping to undermine the system. Not surprisingly, major battles over regulation were often sparked by scandals, as women with neither mercenary nor sexual intent were apprehended: the Forissier scandal in Paris where the vice squad had the misfortune of roughing up and arresting a journalist, his sister and his fiancée, in the process bringing upon themselves the appointment of an extraparliamentary commission in 1903; the Cass affair in London when a dressmaker who insisted on her innocence was arrested for solicitation in 1887; the case of Marie Köppen in Berlin, daughter of a jockey, apprehended in 1897 while waiting for her fiancé. The mass arrests or *rafles* carried out in Paris when the density of prostitution provoked neighborhood objections inevitably caught up both professionals and passersby in their net.[72]

As prostitution became ever more informal, regulationism's means of identifying the object of its attentions followed suit. In an increasingly desperate attempt to adapt, the definition of prostitution – always lax and subject to police interpretation in any case – was extended to the breaking point. In Anhalt, for example, women were registered as prostitutes who were infected and had had sex with more than one man, even though no money had changed hands.[73] In Britain, the CD Acts, for all their formal legality in other respects, granted the police broad latitude in defining their target. The concept "common prostitute," not being spelled out in the law, was generally interpreted to mean a woman who openly solicited men or frequented brothels, music halls and the like, and it was not necessary to prove that she had performed sexual acts or received payment. Even women whose crime was having occasional sexual relations with more than one man were sometimes considered

[72] Fiaux, *La police des moeurs*, v. I, pp. iv–v; Theresa Wobbe, *Gleichheit und Differenz: Politische Strategien von Frauenrechtlerinnen um die Jahrhundertwende* (Frankfurt, 1989), p. 47; A. de Morsier, *La police des moeurs en France et la campagne abolitionniste* (Paris, n.d. [1901]), p. 34; Commenge, *La prostitution clandestine*, pp. 115–16. In Norway, Christian Krohg's *Albertine* (1887) portrayed an innocent woman thrust into regulation's maw.

[73] Dubois-Havenith, *Conférence internationale: Enquêtes*, v. I/2, pp. 668–69; Chéry, *Syphilis*, pp. 92–93; Marion A. Kaplan, *The Jewish Feminist Movement in Germany: The Campaigns of the Jüdischer Frauenbund, 1904–1938* (Westport, 1979), p. 122.

prostitutes.[74] In a similar way, measures aimed at prostitutes were gradually extended to encompass also otherwise respectable professions believed to serve primarily as fronts for illicit sex. Women were not, in some proposals, to be hired as waitresses, for example. In Copenhagen, a police regulation of 1883 forbade bar owners from employing women other than family members to serve.[75] Attacking the issue from the other direction, female waitresses were on occasion subjected to inspections much like prostitutes.[76]

Able at best to deal with the minority of officially inscribed prostitutes, regulationism thus failed to come to grips with the greater problem of clandestines, even more so with the general issue of promiscuous intercourse of a noncommercial nature. As the century progressed, its claims to have an effect on the incidence of VD worthy of its machinery, cost and complication were ever more stridently questioned.

THE ABOLITIONIST CHALLENGE

Not only was regulationism hollowed out from within, by its own internal failings and by developments in sexual practices that it failed to accommodate, it also faced a massive frontal assault from without. Its sworn enemy came in the form of abolitionism, the movement that arose first in Britain to repeal the CD Acts, subsequently jumping to the regulationist nations of the continent.

Narrowly speaking, abolition sought to end regulation, but many abolitionists hoped also to solve the problem of prostitution altogether. Some believed that, through criminalization, commercial fornication could be driven underground and at least minimized. Others, accepting the ubiquity of the demand for market sex, sought instead to remove the

---

[74] Abraham A. Sion, *Prostitution and the Law* (London, 1977), p. 75; F. B. Smith, "Ethics and Disease," pp. 119–21; Amos, *Comparative Survey of Laws*, p. 66.

[75] Germund Michanek, *Studenter och hetärer: Kulturhistoriska bilder från gamla tiders Upsala* (n.p., 1971), p. 92; Germund Michanek, *En morgondröm: Studier kring Frödings ariska dikt* (Uppsala, 1962), p. 43; Lundquist, *Den disciplinerade dubbelmoralen*, p. 351; *Underdånigt betänkande angående könssjukdomarnas spridning*, v. II, p. 76; *DVöG*, 26 (1894), pp. 224–25; Bloch, *Die Prostitution*, v. II/1, p. 401.

[76] Dubois-Havenith, *Conférence internationale: Enquêtes*, v. I/2, pp. 668–69; Dubois-Havenith, ed., *Conférence internationale pour la prophylaxie de la syphilis et des maladies vénériennes: Compte rendu des séances* (Brussels, 1900), v. II, p. 162; Chéry, *Syphilis*, pp. 92–93; Herbert Reinke, "Die Polizei und die 'Reinhaltung der Gegend': Prostitution und Sittenpolizei im Wuppertal im 19. und im frühen 20. Jahrhundert," in Jürgen Reulecke and Adelheid G. z. C. Rüdenhausen, eds., *Stadt und Gesundheit: Zum Wandel von "Volksgesundheit" und kommunaler Gesundheitspolitik im 19. und frühen 20. Jahrhundert* (Stuttgart, 1991), p. 137. But in Bavaria, female service personnel were common and not generally suspected of prostitution: *DVöG*, 26 (1894), pp. 224–25; Regina Schulte, *Sperrbezirke: Tugendhaftigkeit und Prostitution in der bürgerlichen Welt* (Frankfurt am Main, 1979), p. 103.

fundamental causes of prostitution. Such an approach could and did take different forms. The most exalted and ambitious came from the socialists and other radical critics who saw prostitution as a problem of capitalist property relations extended to the affective realm of the family and therefore as but one of the many conundrums eventually to be resolved through dramatic reform if not actual revolution. The bourgeois family, with its premium on female virginity and fidelity, its concern with amassing property and achieving social station, shifted the age of marriage ever more gerontocratically and fired the engines of debauch that drove middle-class males in sexual assault on the otherwise virtuous women of the working classes, who, in turn, were forced by necessity and tempted by the possibility of easy money for their favors. Come the revolution, when women would have meaningful work at reasonable wages and men would no longer regard their spouses as a form of property whose virginity and subsequent fidelity were worth a nuptial premium, both the supply of and demand for prostitutes would dry up. Proletarian virtue, which came in both puritanical and free-love variants, would solve the VD problem. As in the classic sanitationist vision, broad social reform promised an answer to epidemiological issues. The fight against prostitution and VD, as a member of the Independent Social Democratic Party during the Weimar Republic put it, is the same as the fight for the liberation of the working class.[77]

One notch below this all-or-nothing approach came reformers who believed that prostitution could at least be reduced by social changes implementable within bourgeois capitalist society. Above all, the condition of women needed improvement, both economically and legally, bringing them to parity with men and removing the impetus for prostitution. With the social and economic circumstances of the sexes equalized, both men and women would (depending on the ethical ambitions of the visionary in question) either be chaste and pure or both indulge their instincts with abandon, the double standard having been unified through a race either to the top or into the gutter.[78] Legal equality included reforms as basic as the vote, expected to raise society's moral tone, as well as more specialized concerns with the position of women and wives. Stricter rules of guardianship promised to protect girls from

---

[77] Werner Thönnessen, *The Emancipation of Women: The Rise and Decline of the Women's Movement in German Social Democracy 1863–1933* (London, 1973), pp. 22, 37; *Sitzungsberichte der verfassunggebenden Preussischen Landesversammlung*, 1919/21, 25 February 1920, cols. 9946–47; Mignot, *Le péril vénérien*, p. 145.

[78] Ricord, *Lettres sur la syphilis*, p. 289; Ernst Kromayer, *Zur Austilgung der Syphilis: Abolitionistische Betrachtungen über Prostitution, Geschlechtskrankheiten und Volksgesundheit* (Berlin, 1898), pp. 2–4.

abusive and exploitative parents. Tightened laws on seduction would force men to bear the legal and economic consequences of illegitimate children, reducing the likelihood of impregnated and abandoned women resorting to prostitution.[79] In France, for example, this meant proposals to end the prohibition of paternity suits on behalf of illegitimate children, adopted by the Napoleonic Code (art. 340) in hopes of protecting the family.[80] Monetary damages were sought for seduction, since loss of virginity reduced a woman's nuptial capital, and for default on promises of marriage, while easier access to divorce for infidelity or transmission of VD promised to put husbands on shorter leashes. More radically, the German Mutterschutz movement advocating having the state assume the economic obligations of fatherhood. Legal prohibitions on sexual harassment by employers and others in positions of authority, though they did not originate in the abolitionist movement, found its favor.[81] Economic equality, in turn, meant improving access for women to education and providing those who worked with better wages and wider occupational choices. Housing reforms were necessary to lessen overcrowding, which, many believed, fostered the incest, promiscuity and early seduction by which girls were first propelled down the slippery slope toward prostitution.[82] Conversely, for men, if property were more equally apportioned, the material hurdles to marriage would be lowered, more would be earlier wedded and the bachelors who remained would have less disposable income to squander on commercial copulation.[83]

---

[79] Mary C. Hume-Rothery, *A Letter Addressed to the Right Hon. W. E. Gladstone . . . Touching the Contagious Diseases' Acts of 1866 and 1869 and Their Proposed Extension to the Civil Population of This Kingdom* (Manchester, 1870), p. 11; *BMJ* (8 August 1914), pp. 283–85; Acton, *Prostitution*, p. ix; *ZBGK*, 16, 12 (1915/16), p. 370; Dubois-Havenith, *Conférence internationale: Rapports préliminaires*, v. I/1, quest. 5, p. 10.

[80] Jack D. Ellis, *The Physician-Legislators of France: Medicine and Politics in the Early Third Republic, 1870–1914* (Cambridge, 1990), p. 236; Louis Fiaux, *La police des mœurs en France et dans les principaux pays de l'Europe* (Paris, 1888), p. 854. Not until the concern with depopulation during the late nineteenth century spurred an interest in improving the legal position of children born out of wedlock did this end, in 1912: Robert A. Nye, *Masculinity and Male Codes of Honor in Modern France* (New York, 1993), p. 81; *Annales des maladies vénériennes*, 1 (1906), pp. 125–26; Theresa Mcbride, "Divorce and the Republican Family," in Elinor A. Accampo et al., eds., *Gender and the Politics of Social Reform in France, 1870–1914* (Baltimore, 1995), p. 75.

[81] *Annales*, 4/20 (1913), pp. 418–19; 4/28 (1917), pp. 27–28; Acton, *Prostitution*, p. ix; Gibson, *Prostitution and the State*, p. 54; Dubois-Havenith, *Conférence internationale: Rapports préliminaires*, v. I/1, quest. 5, pp. 10–11, 32; *PP* 1871 (c. 408-1) xix, 29, p. xxxiv; Lecour, *La prostitution à Paris*, p. 251; Hume-Rothery, *Letter Addressed to Gladstone*, p. 10; Commenge, *La prostitution clandestine*, p. 17.

[82] Lecour, *La prostitution à Paris*, p. 251; *ZBGK*, 3, 8/9 (1904–05), p. 308; Lundquist, *Den disciplinerade dubbelmoralen*, p. 322; *SB*, 20 June 1925, p. 2492D; Acton, *Prostitution*, p. 182; Leonhard, *Prostitution*, p. 12; Françoise Barret-Ducrocq, *Love in the Time of Victoria* (London, 1991), pp. 15–27. But see also Mason, *Making of Victorian Sexuality*, pp. 139–43.

[83] Amos, *Comparative Survey of Laws*, pp. 9–10, 28–30; Reuss, *La prostitution*, pp. 483–84; Deborah

At this level of reform, whether among socialists or the moderates willing to tinker with the existing system, the utopianism that dogged all environmentalist approaches to disease was apparent.[84] Such reforms might well limit prostitution in the long term, but in the short run they were unlikely to have much effect. What could be done while waiting for the Messiah? It was here that abolitionism in the strict sense found its role.

Abolitionism was a broad church, a mongrel pack uniting Christians of various stripes with spiritualists and free-thinkers, physicians, lawyers and sociologists, liberals, libertarians and socialists, clergy, moralists and trade union members. That it became an international movement starting already in the 1870s did not help contain its diversity. Adherents to the general cause of repeal ranged from those with strict moral objections to extramarital sex of any sort, paid for or not, for whom the fight against regulation was the thin edge of a broader campaign against immorality *tout court*, to those who objected not to fornication or prostitution as such, but to the state's attempt to meddle in such private matters and, more particularly, to the injustice of making prostitutes alone bear the brunt of precautions. Abolition was thus approached from both a moral vantage and from one that emphasized civil rights, to take just the two farthest extremes, as well as any number of perspectives in between.[85] Despite this breadth, certain themes were common to most abolitionist arguments.

Most generally, abolitionists refused to distinguish between public health and morality. Regulationists did not generally assert the desirability of prostitution as such, although many regarded it as a necessary evil that fulfilled functions whose absence society would have regretted. Instead they separated moral objections to commercial sex and its statutory regulation from the inevitability of mercenary copulation and the consequent need to have the state ensure its harmlessness. Whatever its moral implications, regulation served a public health function.

Gorham, "The 'Maiden Tribute of Modern Babylon' Re-Examined: Child Prostitution and the Idea of Childhood in Late-Victorian England," *Victorian Studies*, 21, 3 (Spring 1978), p. 355.

[84] For example, the insistence that to combat prostitution the solution was to improve the economic conditions of the proletariat, suppress alcoholism, raise living standards, aid single mothers and illegitimate children, ennoble the tone of public morality and enhance the respect for women – all in a day's work: *ZBGK*, 8, 2 (1908), p. 56.

[85] On the varieties of abolitionism, see Blaschko, *Syphilis und Prostitution*, pp. 143–44; *La syphilis* (1904), pp. 695–96; *ZBGK*, 15, 6 (1914), p. 207; Ed. Jeanselme, *Traité de la syphilis* (Paris, 1931), v. I, p. 378; Gibson, *Prostitution and the State*, p. 5; Mary Gibson, "The State and Prostitution: Prohibition, Regulation, or Decriminalization?," in James A. Inciardi and Charles E. Faupel, eds., *History and Crime* (Beverly Hills, 1980), p. 200; Corbin, *Women for Hire*, p. 234.

Abolitionists, in contrast, refused to categorize so neatly. Social utility and morality could not be easily divorced. Because VD (ignoring for the moment the so-called syphilis of the innocents) was generally acquired through voluntary and sinful acts, there was an inherently moral element to its spread that distinguished it from other contagious ailments, caught by the misfortunate through chance and circumstance.[86] Attempting to mitigate the consequences and spread of VD in effect meant smoothing the path of vice. What was morally wrong could not be hygienically right.[87] More particularly, abolitionists objected to having the state sullied by its association with immorality. Regulating prostitution was tantamount to recognizing it as a legitimate occupation. A state that represented law and justice could not also validate vice; it could not sanctify marriage on the one hand, whoring on the other.[88] Regulating prostitution meant that, by providing uninfected female bodies for the delectation of libertines, the state sought to make vice safe for the sinner. Abolitionists thus agreed with their enemies that the state should not be too directly implicated in the regulation of vice, but drew diametrically opposed conclusions. Where the regulationists saw this as an argument for arranging controls through ad hoc, local and administrative measures, not making them part of the legal code, abolitionists wanted the state out of the business of prostitution altogether. Ultimately the difference between regulationists and abolitionists came down to the evil they sought to eradicate: VD in the former case; prostitution, illicit sex, immorality *tout court* in the latter. Regulationists were willing to put up with prostitution if they could limit VD; many abolitionists preferred even an increase in VD to tolerating prostitution. Even if VD were eliminated, as a German put it, we would still be against prostitution. Our object, as a British colleague agreed, must not be to make prostitution healthy, but to prevent the making of prostitutes.[89]

But how to bring morality and authority into harmony? The civil lib-

[86] Amos, *Comparative Survey of Laws*, p. 156; Åkermark, *Prostitutionen och polisreglementet*, p. 14; *RD prot*, FK 1889:19, p. 39; Constance Rover, *Love, Morals and the Feminists* (London, 1970), p. 78.

[87] A contrast neatly embodied in a dispute betwen J. Holroyde and Josephine Butler in 1891: *Transactions of the Seventh International Congress of Hygiene and Demography*, 9 (1891), p. 234–36; Scott, *State Iniquity*, p. 103; D. W. Bebbington, *The Nonconformist Conscience: Chapel and Politics, 1870–1914* (London, 1982), p. 40.

[88] *PP* 1871 (c. 408) xix, 1, p. 13; Miller, *Prostitution*, p. 34; *Glasgow Medical Journal*, 4, 19 (1883), p. 128; *PP* 1882 (340) ix, 1, p. xviii; *ZBGK*, 16, 7 (1915), p. 231; Amos, *Comparative Survey of Laws*, p. 224; *Bihang*, 1889, FK, Motion 27, p. 2.

[89] Hume-Rothery, *Letter Addressed to Gladstone*, p. 4; BA, R86/1065, "Fünfter Bericht des Deutschen Frauenvereins zur Hebung der Sittlichkeit," Soest, Neukirchen, May 1897; Scott, *State Iniquity*, pp. 277–78; *ZBGK*, 16, 12 (1915/16), p. 364; XVIIth International Congress of Medicine, *Dermatology and Syphilography*, pt. 2, p. 214.

erties abolitionists thought that eliminating regulation and treating prostitutes no differently than other citizens, punishing them only insofar as their behavior violated standards of public conduct and decency, would allow morality to become once again a private matter, ending the iniquitous treatment of one social group.[90] The moral question was solved by ignoring it. Prostitution as such should not be a concern of the state since otherwise the fundamental civil right of bodily autonomy, possessed even by prostitutes, would be violated and public authority illegitimately drawn into the realm of private morality.[91] Such abolitionists rejected the regulationist claim that, where public health was at stake, individual liberties must yield, focusing instead on the violation of prostitutes' rights as citizens. Whatever dangers she might pose, as one put it, a syphilitic prostitute was not the equivalent of a trichinous porkchop.[92] Objections to regulationism from this vantage were, quite simply, that it violated the rights otherwise enjoyed by all citizens. Regardless of the sanitary benefits of the system, women caught in it were being deprived of their claim to equal treatment before the law.[93] More specifically, regulation violated all manner of civil rights in the name of public health. In the fullfledged systems with their submission of prostitutes to police fiat, this was evident. But even in Britain, the CD Acts put the burden of proof on the accused, involving neither trial nor committal procedures and therefore no provision for release by habeas corpus.[94] One of the main concerns of such abolitionists, spurred on by regulationism's tenuous legal underpinnings, was that no greater legislative edifice than necessary be

[90] Otto M. Westerberg, *Reglementeringsfrågan* (Stockholm, 1903), p. 36; Louis Fiaux, *La prostitution réglementée et les pouvoirs publics dans les principaux états des deux-mondes* (Paris, 1902), pp. xxviii; Dubois-Havenith, *Conférence internationale: Rapports préliminaires*, v. I/1, quest. 2, Fiaux, pp. 61–62.

[91] Hence the uninspiring slogan of French abolitionists – "A free woman on a free sidewalk": *Journal of the American Medical Association*, 47, 16 (1906), p. 1249; *Friedrichs Blätter für Gerichtliche Medicin und Sanitätspolizei*, 29 (1878), p. 54; *Centralblatt für allgemeine Gesundheitspflege*, 4 (1885), p. 190; Fiaux, *Police des moeurs*, v. I, p. xxxvii; Dubois-Havenith, *Conférence internationale: Enquêtes*, v. I/2, p. 164; *ZBGK*, 6, 5 (1907), pp. 165–74.

[92] Fiaux, *Police des moeurs*, v. I, pp. 29, 86; Dubois-Havenith, *Conférence internationale: Rapports préliminaires*, v. I/1, quest. 2, Fiaux, p. 111.

[93] J. Birbeck Nevins, *Statement of the Grounds upon Which the Contagious Diseases Acts Are Opposed* (3rd edn.; Liverpool, 1875), p. 28; *The Constitution Violated* (Edinburgh, 1871), pp. 26–27; Westerberg, *Reglementeringsfrågan*, pp. 15–16; S. Dahlbäck, *I Prostitutionsfrågan* (Stockholm, 1903), p. 3; Dubois-Havenith, *Conférence internationale: Rapports préliminaires*, v. I/1, quest. 2, Fiaux, p. 2; *Hansard*, 1870, v. 203, cols. 576–79; Frida Stéenhoff (Harald Gote), *Den reglementerade prostitution ur feministisk synpunkt* (Stockholm, 1904), pp. 12–14, 27; *Förhandlingar*, 1889, p. 54; *Bihang*, 1889, FK, Motion 27, p. 2.

[94] *Transactions of the National Association for the Promotion of Social Science* (1869), p. 442; Amos, *Comparative Survey of Laws*, p. 75; Deck, *Syphilis et réglementation*, pp. 11–12; *PP* 1871 (c. 408) xix, 1, p. 13; *PP* 1882 (340) ix, 1, p. xviii; F. B. Smith, "The Contagious Diseases Acts Reconsidered," *Social History of Medicine*, 3, 2 (August 1990), p. 197; F. B. Smith, "Ethics and Disease," p. 121.

erected on such spindly foundations. Police intervention, in this view, ought to be limited to maintaining circulation on public thoroughfares, preventing congregations of prostitutes and, in general, upholding public decorum and order. In 1886, this position – that prostitution as such not be a crime and the state limit itself to prosecuting only marginal aspects of commercial sex (the involvement of minors, acts committed with fraud or violence, public indecency and the like) – won the imprimatur of the International Abolitionist Federation.[95]

For the moralist abolitionists, in contrast, more was at stake. Above all, their objections concerned the double standard of morality by which male sexual license was condoned while similar behavior among females, whether for fun or profit, remained abhorred. Regulation was based on the premise that, since male sexual activity could not be confined to marriage, prostitution was a necessary and normal aspect of society. Encouraging women to act like men, indulging whatever tastes they might have for sexual license, though theoretically a way of ending the double standard, was rejected out of hand by most moralist abolitionists. Putting the sexes in such a position of only apparent equality, they feared, with no special protections for women, would in fact allow men to dominate their mates sexually by virtue of their greater social power.[96] Instead, moralist abolitionists tended to put the issue the other way around: what means were available to bring men up to the same high standards of chastity, restraint and morality as women? Male lust was not a force of nature, in their analysis, but an artifact of social mores and customs. With a very modern, Eliasian sense of social constructionism (applied deftly to male behavior, but not to female, which was regarded as the same sort of baseline standard assigned by the regulationist vision to men's conduct), moralist abolitionists refused to accept male lust as a natural given, insisting that sexual behavior, determined by social forces, could change. The goal was not to accept male license but to rein it in.[97]

Since the sex drive was mutable, the force behind the spread of VD

[95] Guyot, *Prostitution Under the Regulation System*, pp. 345–46; de Félice, "Situation abolitionniste mondiale," pp. 4–5.

[96] Hilda Sachs, *Den svarta domen: Männens skuld och kvinnornas straff* (Stockholm, 1912), pp. 11–12; Amos, *Comparative Survey of Laws*, p. 40; Brennecke, *Wie ist der Kampf gegen die Geschlechts-Krankheiten zu führen? Referat erstattet am 2. Oktober 1905 in der 17. Allgemeinen Konferenz der deutschen Sittlichkeitsvereine zu Magdeburg* (Berlin, 1905), p. 5.

[97] Susan Kingsley Kent, *Sex and Suffrage in Britain, 1860–1914* (Princeton, 1987), pp. 67, 70–71; Sheila Jeffreys, "'Free From All Uninvited Touch of Man': Women's Campaigns Around Sexuality, 1880–1914," *Women's Studies International Forum*, 5, 6 (1982), pp. 629–32; Wobbe, *Gleichheit und Differenz*, p. 40; Amos, *Comparative Survey of Laws*, p. 11; C. Ströhmberg, *Die Bekämpfung der ansteckenden Geschlechtskrankheiten im Deutschen Reich* (Stuttgart, 1903), p. 34; Waldvogel, *Gefahren der Geschlechtskrankheiten*, p. 54.

could also be influenced. Rather than attacking the incidental dangers of nonmonogamous sex, as did the regulationists, abolitionists focused on the impulse behind it, seeking to break the chain of transmission at the act which conveyed disease rather than at the infection itself. The law, as Josephine Butler put it, should aim at vice, not its physical effects.[98] Because sex was not a necessary act (a blind spasm of instinct in whose grip men committed acts that might, as the regulationists argued, be reprehensible but, because largely involuntary, not sinful), but a learned and therefore controllable behavior, moral responsibility attached to illicit pursuits and their consequences. Because of this moral element inherent in the transmission of VD, the state should not take precautions as with other communicable diseases and, in any case, it was certainly under no obligation to ensure the epidemiological unobjectionability of public women. In fact, for some abolitionists, the consideration that regulation might hamper the spread of VD, thus tempering the penalties of sin and promoting immorality, was reason enough to object.[99] The most extreme statement of this position came from Katarina Scheven, who was often quoted with horror by regulationists to the effect that, if science ever invented a way of avoiding VD, the effect would be a moral syphilization of society with consequences worse than the merely corporeal.[100]

Instead, the solution to the spread of VD through prostitution was threefold: first, regulation had to go. Prostitution was only one part of the larger issue of licentiousness and immorality. The supply of commercial sex being dependent on the demand and the demand, in turn, stimulated by measures that appeared to guarantee its harmlessness, ending regulation would by itself help reduce the incidence of extramarital sex.[101] Secondly, shut down the supply side of mercenary sex more generally by repressing and – in the opinion of many, although not all, moralist abolitionists – criminalizing commercial copulation or at least its public manifestations, clearing the streets of prostitutes and closing brothels, prosecuting pimps and procurers, raising the age of consent.[102]

[98] *PP* 1871 (c. 408-I) xix, 29, p. xxxiv.

[99] Mauriac, *Syphilis primitive*, p. 103; *Hansard*, 1883, v. 278, col. 789; 1866, v. 182, col. 815; *PP* 1871 (c. 408-I) xix, 29, pp. xxxiii, xlviii; *PP* 1871 (c. 408) xix, 1, p. 13; *Sanitary Record*, n.s., 14, 164 (15 July 1892), p. 29; Hume-Rothery, *Letter Addressed to Gladstone*, p. 4. Even as civil libertarian an abolitionist as J. S. Mill employed such arguments: *PP* 1871 (c. 408-I) xix, 29, p. lx.

[100] Jeanselme, *Traité de la syphilis*, v. I, p. 378.

[101] *Hansard*, 1883, v. 278, col. 762; *PP* 1882 (340) ix, 1, p. xviii.

[102] Dubois-Havenith, *Conférence internationale: Rapports préliminaires*, v. I/1, quest. 6, pp. 31–33; *SB*, 21 January 1927, pp. 8705A–C; Wobbe, *Gleichheit und Differenz*, pp. 41–42; *RD prot*, FK 1889:20, pp. 3–4, 11; *Bihang*, 1903, AK, Motion 88, p. 7; Anita Ulrich, *Bordelle, Strassendirnen und bürgerliche Sittlichkeit in der Belle Epoque* (Zurich, 1985), pp. 133–36.

Thirdly, close down the demand side by insisting on chastity before marriage, restraint thereafter, encouraging earlier weddings for the middle classes and combating pornography and other forms of indecency widely believed to foster a taste for illicit sex.[103] If all else failed, masturbation could be encouraged for men to keep them satisfied if not pure. The German abolitionist Hanna Bieber-Böhm was emblematic of this wing of the movement in holding up as an ideal the marriage of two virgins at age twenty-five, followed by complete fidelity thereafter. In fact, it would be better if humans had mating periods like other animals, setting aside certain times of the year for rutting, able to spend the rest untroubled by such vexatious urges.[104]

Depending on whether they were more concerned with morality or civil rights, abolitionists' attitude toward prostitutes varied. The very term "abolitionism," borrowed from the antislavery movement, suggested a concern with their rights as citizens whose innate liberties were being violated.[105] To the extent that prostitutes, the objects of male sexual aggression, were hampered from following a more righteous path by an economic structure that denied them decent jobs and a hypocritical moral codex that held females to disproportionate standards, they were seen as the largely innocent victims of a system established to satisfy the desires of middle- and upper-class men at the expense of the innocence, health and dignity of poor women. Prostitution, as Avril de Sainte-Croix put it, was not an occupation freely chosen, but a necessity forced upon the unwilling by cruel circumstance.[106] At the same time, however much the system might stack the odds against prostitutes, clearly an element of free will was involved. Only a tiny minority of women exposed to similar influences in fact followed this path, while most led lives of virtue.[107] While condemning men as the first corrupters, those abolitionists con-

---

[103] Amos, *Comparative Survey of Laws*, pp. 29–30; Mignot, *Le péril vénérien*, p. 109; *Transactions of the National Association for the Promotion of Social Science* (1870) p. 231; Arthur Newsholme, *Health Problems in Organized Society* (London, 1927), pp. 107–09.

[104] Lucy Bland, *Banishing the Beast: English Feminism and Sexual Morality 1885–1914* (London, 1995), pp. 278–79; Hjördis Levin, *Testiklarnas herravälde: Sexualmoralens historia* (n.p., 1986), p. 89; Dubois-Havenith, *Conférence internationale: Rapports préliminaires*, v. I/1, quest. 5, p. 30; Hume-Rothery, *Letter Addressed to Gladstone*, p. 16.

[105] Some were content portraying regulation as equally loathsome as slavery. Others went further, regarding regulated prostitution as "a bondage so hideous as to find no parallel in the worst atrocities of negro slavery": Otto Münsterberg, *Prostitution und Staat* (Leipzig, 1908), p. 26; Hume-Rothery, *Letter Addressed to Gladstone*, p. 5; Sachs, *Den svarta domen*, p. 8.

[106] *ZBGK*, 1, 3 (1903), pp. 165–66; Dolléans, *Police des moeurs*, pp. 15–16; Fiaux, *Police des moeurs*, v. I, p. 359.

[107] One of the few novelties in the debate over the motive forces behind prostitution has been the attempt to apply rational choice theory to the decision to sell sex, portraying prostitutes as not

cerned especially with social morality often regarded prostitutes as their willing accomplices, implicated by acquisitiveness, laziness, hypertrophied sensuality or any number of motives other than hardship and suffering in the system that rewarded licentiousness with lucre. Bieber-Böhm, for example, agreed with regulationists that prostitutes were the main source of VD transmission, entertained no sentimental notions of gender solidarity between respectable and fallen women in the face of male lust and sought to condemn recalcitrant prostitutes to reformatories or even forced labor colonies. Some abolitionists saw prostitution not just as the imposition of male desire on unwilling females, but also as a form of competition among women themselves. Anna Pappritz, another prominent German abolitionist, argued that prostitution was reprehensible, not just as sin, but because whores, able to live without working in the usual sense, threatened to undermine the efforts of women in the conventional labor force. Offering easy access to sex without responsibility, it also undercut the willingness of men to shoulder the burdens of marriage and family, following the logic of the old saw about buying milk rather than owning cows.[108] Upright women who worked for a living and sought a husband thus saw both their professional and matrimonial aspirations threatened by prostitutes.

All abolitionists, whatever their differences, agreed that regulation was above all a gender issue. The system was profoundly unfair to women in subjecting them alone to the regimen, sparing their customers. Infected men might not be the most efficient vectors of transmission but they (those walking lancets, in Fiaux's imagery, tipped with noxious vaccine) were the ultimate source of disease. Regulation was thus not seen as

determined wholly by their gender or class background, but as rational interest maximizers working within certain constraints and making the conscious, economically motivated decision to rent their bodies: Walkowitz, *Prostitution and Victorian Society*, pp. 19–21; Söderblom, *Horan och batongen*, pp. 32, 138–43; Luise White, *The Comforts of Home: Prostitution in Colonial Nairobi* (Chicago, 1990), pp. 10–21; Marilynn Wood Hill, *Their Sisters' Keepers: Prostitution in New York City, 1830–1870* (Berkeley, 1993), ch. 3; Margaretha Järvinen, *Prostitution i Helsingfors: En studie i kvinnokontroll* (Åbo, 1990), pp. 17–18; Sabine Kienitz, *Sexualität, Macht und Moral: Prostitution und Geschlechtererziehungen Anfang des 19. Jahrhunderts in Württemberg* (Berlin, 1995), pp. 81–91; Gail Pheterson, *The Prostitution Prism* (Amsterdam, 1996), pp. 17–18; Nickie Roberts, *Whores in History* (Hammersmith, 1992), pp. 235–36. On the other hand, economic motives have also been downplayed to the extent that the rise of the welfare state has removed the Hobsonian choice between destitution and prostitution: Leif G. W. Persson, *Horor, hallickar och torskar: En bok om prostitutionen i Sverige* (Stockholm, 1981), pp. 187–89.

[108] Dubois-Havenith, *Conférence internationale: Rapports préliminaires*, v. I/1, quest. 5, pp. 29–30; *Mitteilungen*, 8 (1910), p. 51; Richard J. Evans, *Feminist Movement*, pp. 42–43; Charles Bernheimer, *Figures of Ill Repute: Representing Prostitution in Nineteenth-Century France* (Cambridge, MA, 1989), pp. 211–12; *ZBGK*, 16, 12 (1915/16), p. 364; Petra Schmackpfeffer, *Frauenbewegung und Prostitution* (Oldenburg, 1989), pp. 32–37.

targeted at prostitutes who happened to be women (a system trained on carriers regardless of their gender), but as a form of punishment reserved exclusively for females. Since the client acted as immorally as the prostitute (in fact more so, since he was prompted by lust alone while she might also be moved by economic necessity), fairness dictated that either both should be subject to precautions or neither.[109] From the regulationist view, prostitutes were the epidemiological fulcrum of illicit sex, each having many more contacts than her male customers. Since women were, for reasons that the Germans liked to call *fortpflanzungstechnisch*, able to have more frequent sex than men and prostitutes put this venereal advantage to work, efficiency spoke for aiming measures at them, not the johns. Abolitionists countered that the number of men who had illicit sexual relations was much larger than their partners in vice and that, at any given time, many more males were infected than females. When looking therefore to assign responsibility for the spread of VD, rather than just weighing technical issues of public health efficiency, the argument for targeting prostitutes alone was less clearcut.[110]

Regulation was also a class issue. Because the middle-class male could neither marry until long after sexual maturity, nor engage in illicit liaisons with women of the class into which he hoped to wed, he had, if not chaste, recourse to the sexual favors either of working-class mistresses or prostitutes recruited in large measure from the same milieu. It was therefore widely believed that prostitutes' customers came disproportionately from the middle and upper classes.[111] That prostitutes were recruited especially from the lower classes was, of course, as trivially true as for any other unskilled profession. The class nature of prostitution became one of the flash points in the debate.[112] Abolitionists attacked the sexual egotism of bourgeois males who, unable to be con-

---

[109] BA, R86/1065, Vorstand des rheinisch-westfälischen Frauen-Vereins zur Hebung der Sittlichkeit, "Einem hohen Reichstag . . .," Bonn, 29 November 1890; Dubois-Havenith, *Conférence internationale: Rapports préliminaires*, v. I/1, quest. 2, Fiaux, p. 58; *Hansard*, 1883, v. 278, col. 819; 1873, v. 216, col. 232; *PP* 1871 (c. 408) xix, 1, p. 13.

[110] Möller, "Undersökningar i vissa frågor rörande de smittosamma könssjukdomarna," p. 68; *Underdånigt betänkande angående könssjukdomarnas spridning*, v. I, pp. 69–70; Macalister, *Inaugural Address*, p. 23; Stéenhoff, *Den reglementerade prostitution*, p. 25; Heinz Dreuw, *Die Völkervernichtung: Vorschläge zu ihrer Verhütung und Bekämpfung* (Berlin, 1926), v. I, p. 51.

[111] A. Theod. Stamm, *Die Verhütung der erblich-giftigen, verbreitetsten Ansteckungen* (Zürich, 1883), pp. 66–67; *Hansard*, 1870, v. 203, cols. 580–81; Dubois-Havenith, *Conférence internationale: Rapports préliminaires*, v. I/1, quest. 5, pp. 7–8; Silber, *Womit sind die ansteckenden Geschlechtskrankheiten zu bekämpfen?*, p. 34; A. Blaschko, *Die Geschlechtskrankheiten* (Berlin, 1900), p. 9; Corbin, *Women for Hire*, pp. 186–200.

[112] Conveniently ignoring the extent to which prostitutes catered to a working-class clientele as well: Frances Finnegan, *Poverty and Prostitution: A Study of Victorian Prostitutes in York* (Cambridge, 1979), pp. 114–15, 134; Mason, *Making of Victorian Sexuality*, pp. 102–03; Walkowitz, *Prostitution and Victorian*

tinent yet unwilling to allow the women of their own station similar freedoms, sought mercenary satisfaction among their social inferiors. The parties of the left worked this vein of attack with particular vigor, arguing that prostitution was the exploitation of lower-class women by middle-class men. Working-class girls, employed as servants, often became prostitutes after having been seduced, impregnated and abandoned by men of the family.[113] Aristocratic rakes and libertines, to put things in more salacious terms, were often portrayed in the British debate as the customers for specialized forms of debauchery of the sort requiring dedicated implements and athletic agility. Abolition in its moralist variety was here often the expression of a strain of middle-class sexual respectability, seeking to contain upper-class excesses, and joined with a provincial radical distrust of the cosmopolitan, worldly London elites.[114]

Strengthening this sense of sociosexual hypocrisy came the somewhat contradictory argument that regulationism threatened primarily the prostitutes who catered to the lower classes – streetwalkers, brothel whores and the like – leaving untouched courtesans and others of the venereal elite. During the Restoration, there had been desultory attempts to submit French courtesans to inspections, but these had been abandoned after protest from their influential protectors and, generally speaking, such high-class or "private" prostitutes were left alone.[115] From the regulationist vantage, besides the obvious fact that special consideration was granted upper-class prostitutes and their elite clientele, the logic was that such women – amply rewarded for their services, fastidiously maintained and available to only few customers – were simply, in terms of public health, less efficient and destructive vectors. Prostitutes arrayed in velvet, as one put it, are not as dangerous as those in calico.[116]

Society, p. 23; Lundquist, *Den disciplinerade dubbelmoralen*, p. 217; *RD prot*, FK 1889:20, p. 22; Welander, *Blad ur prostitutionsfrågans historia*, p. 84.

[113] *Annales*, 4/20 (1913), pp. 419–20; Vera Konieczka, "Arten zu sprechen, Arten zu schweigen: Sozialdemokratie und Prostitution im deutschen Kaiserreich," in Johanna Geyer-Kordesch and Annette Kuhn, eds., *Frauenkörper, Medizin, Sexualität* (Düsseldorf, 1986), p. 109; *RD prot*, FK 1889:20, p. 12.

[114] *Hansard*, 1873, v. 216, col. 251; 1876, v. 230, cols. 1556, 1563; *PP* 1871 (c. 408-1) xix, 29, p. xxxv; McHugh, *Prostitution and Victorian Social Reform*, p. 26; Roy Porter and Hall, *Facts of Life*, pp. 126–27.

[115] *Hansard*, 1878, v. 240, col. 485; *Constitution Violated*, p. 38; Harsin, *Policing Prostitution*, p. 17; Kathryn Norberg, "From Courtesan to Prostitute: Mercenary Sex and Venereal Disease, 1730–1802," in Linda E. Merians, ed., *The Secret Malady: Venereal Disease in Eighteenth-Century Britain and France* (Lexington, 1996), p. 43.

[116] Pappenheim, *Handbuch der Sanitäts-Polizei*, v. II, p. 237. Some abolitionists also agreed with this view: Dubois-Havenith, *Conférence internationale: Rapports préliminaires*, v. I/1, quest. 4, p. 80.

NATIONAL VARIATIONS

Despite common themes and, eventually, an international organization, the abolitionist movement varied among nations. While the British branch, fountainhead of the cause, tended to be pious and libertarian, the continental varieties were more secular, less concerned with moral issues and more willing to allow the state to intervene (in ways other than regulation) against prostitution and VD.

In Britain, the dual nature of abolitionism was on radiant display, with the movement both highly moralist and religious, on the one hand, and strongly concerned with individual rights on the other. From a continental perspective, British abolitionism appeared mesmerized by the problems of immorality and indecency, curiously indifferent to the ravages of VD. Opposition to state interference in such matters and resistance to the prospect of granting the authorities greater powers over the private lives of citizens, prostitutes or not, were leitmotifs of debate here – ones formulated most prominently by J. S. Mill.[117] As a result, while the movement for repeal was strong, there was little desire to put anything in place of the CD Acts. Having once gotten the state out of the business of vice, most British abolitionists were happy to leave the problem of prophylaxis to voluntary efforts. Swedish abolitionism was also moralistic, but less laissez-faire. The movement was heavily influenced by Christian and moral concerns, advocating chastity before marriage, self-control thereafter and statutory powers over anything that might encourage public salacity.[118] That the state should wield a firm hand against prostitution was accepted by all Swedish abolitionists, few of whom favored what were considered to be anarchic British conditions. Abolitionism that sought to have the state actively combat prostitution and VD was regarded as modern and scientific, compared to the oldfashioned variety, satisfied with a mere end to regulation. Unlike the British, the Swedes were also strongly suppressionist, refusing to allow the state to ignore prostitution and insisting that, if commercial sex were not to be outlawed altogether, at least the laws on public order should be enforced to end solicitation.[119]

---

[117] *Underdånigt betänkande angående könssjukdomarnas spridning*, v. I, p. 100; v. II, pp. 159–60; Corbin, *Women for Hire*, pp. 216–17; McHugh, *Prostitution and Victorian Social Reform*, pp. 25–26; *SFPSM: Bulletin mensuel* (1902), p. 280; *Bulletin*, 3, 19 (1888), p. 187.

[118] *Underdånigt betänkande angående könssjukdomarnas spridning*, v. I, p. 102; *Förhandlingar*, 1881, pp. 13–17; Ulf Boëthius, *Strindberg och kvinnofrågan* (Stockholm, 1969), pp. 63–65; Lundquist, *Den disciplinerade dubbelmoralen*, pp. 68, 322.

[119] *RD prot*, FK 1889:20, p. 16; Dubois-Havenith, *Conférence internationale: Compte rendu*, v. II, p. 346;

In Germany opinion ran the gamut of the abolitionist spectrum, from those, like Blaschko and von Düring, who rejected the system out of hand, to others whose ambitions for reform would have been satisfied by a bit of deft tinkering. Abolitionists could be politically radical, as in Bremen and Hamburg, or quite conservative, as in Hannover.[120] As in Sweden, there was little patience for the idea that ending regulation was the final goal. Many were appalled by the post-repeal conditions of prostitution in London, indicative of the inadequacies of a laissez-faire approach, and were willing to grant the state wide latitude in intervening against VD.[121] Suppressing public solicitation and compulsorily treating the infected were popular positions and some favored criminalizing prostitution. Even those who most vehemently rejected regulation, preferring (if that were the choice) to leave prostitution untouched, took for granted that the police should have the authority to inspect those arrested for solicitation and that fellow abolitionists who refused to concede such powers were being unrealistic.[122] The French movement, by far the weakest, was also the least moralizing and most secular. Abolitionists here also tended to grant the state a more important role in combating VD than the Butlerite wing. Few objected to strict enforcement of public order and the suppression of solicitation, many fearing otherwise the import of unacceptable London conditions, where the sidewalks had become bazaars of venereal commerce. Most viewed with patronizing distaste the moralizing common in Protestant nations and belonged instead to the civil libertarian wing of the movement, rejecting regulation and, indeed, all state meddling in sexual relations in the name of individual liberty and equality before the law.[123]

Much of this variation among abolitionist movements was based on

Malmroth, "Om de smittosamma könssjukdomarnas bekämpande," pp. 175–76; *Förhandlingar*, 1881, pp. 16–23; 1889, pp. 53–54; Westerberg, *Reglementeringsfrågan*, pp. 19–20, 35; *Bihang*, 1889, FK, Motion 27, p. 7.

[120] Münsterberg, *Prostitution und Staat*, p. 19; E. von Düring, *Prostitution und Geschlechtskrankheiten* (Leipzig, 1905); Nancy R. Reagin, *A German Women's Movement: Class and Gender in Hannover, 1880–1933* (Chapel Hill, 1995), ch. 7.

[121] Dubois-Havenith, *Conférence internationale: Rapports préliminaires*, v. I/1, quest. 4, p. 77; *ZBGK*, 17, 7 (1916), p. 197; 1, 1 (1903), p. 1; Richard J. Evans, *Feminist Movement*, pp. 164–65.

[122] *ZBGK*, 16, 12 (1915/16), pp. 365–67; Dubois-Havenith, *Conférence internationale: Rapports préliminaires*, v. I/1, quest. 4, p. 78; XVIIth International Congress of Medicine, *Dermatology and Syphilography*, pp. 47ff.; Brennecke, *Wie ist der Kampf zu führen?*, p. 22; *ZBGK*, 3, 8/9 (1904–05), p. 307.

[123] Regnault, *L'évolution de la prostitution*, pp. 105–07; Molléans, *La police des moeurs*, pp. 165–70; Corbin, *Women for Hire*, p. 225. A general account can be found in Elisabeth Anne Weston, "Prostitution in Paris in the Later Nineteenth Century: A Study of Political and Social Ideology" (Ph.D. diss., SUNY, Buffalo, 1979), chs. 3, 4.

religion, with the primary distinction separating Protestant from Catholic nations. Abolition was a Protestant and especially a nonconformist, free-church issue. The Reformation, sanctioning sex within marriage while rejecting both extramarital dalliances and fornication for the unwed, had closed down official brothels and in general helped end the church's more tolerant attitude toward mercenary sex.[124] The medieval church's views of human nature (the inherent quality of evil, the inevitability of sin) were more congruent with the tenets of regulation (that, male sexuality being uncontainable within marriage, it was better to render illicit sex safe than condemn or ignore it) than was Protestantism (individuals are responsible for their behavior, continence can be demanded of men, sex is an inherent biological drive and not evil, at least when directed to higher purposes through marriage, but extramarital intercourse is therefore especially lamentable).[125] That regulationism met greatest resistance in Protestant nations, while being maintained, well into the twentieth century, in Catholic ones was no coincidence.

Although many clergy opposed the CD Acts in Britain, the Church of England never committed to repealing them, many Anglicans supported them and most abolitionists among men of the cloth were nonconformists. In Sweden, the movement was founded by Alfred Testuz, pastor at the reformed church of Stockholm, in 1878 and a decade later the leaders of the established Lutheran church came out in support of his position.[126] In Germany, abolitionism in its different varieties was largely Protestant.[127] In France, Protestants were a marked feature of abolitionist membership, helping brand the movement here as one of peculiarly principled outsiders.[128] Conversely, French regulationists

---

[124] Bloch, *Die Prostitution*, v. II/1, pp. 44–58; Lyndal Roper, *The Holy Household: Women and Morals in Reformation Augsburg* (Oxford, 1989), pp. 102ff.; Leah Lydia Otis, *Prostitution in Medieval Society: The History of an Urban Institution in Languedoc* (Chicago, 1985), pp. 43–45; Peter Schuster, *Das Frauenhaus: Städtische Bordelle in Deutschland (1350–1600)* (Paderborn, 1992), ch. 6.

[125] Jean Delumeau, *Sin and Fear: The Emergence of a Western Guilt Culture, 13th–18th Centuries* (New York, 1990), pp. 431–36; Jacques Rossiaud, *La prostitution médiévale* (n.p., 1988), pp. 90–92, 164–68.

[126] Scott, *State Iniquity*, pp. 183–84; F. B. Smith, "Ethics and Disease," p. 127; F. B. Smith, "Contagious Diseases Acts Reconsidered," p. 203; *PP* 1871 (184) lvi, 625, p. 627; *PP* 1878 (306) lxi, 97; *PP* 1878–79 (20) lviii, 385; Bebbington, *Nonconformist Conscience*, pp. 38–39; E. R. Norman, *Church and Society in England 1770–1970* (Oxford, 1976), pp. 151–52; Lundquist, *Den disciplinerade dubbelmoralen*, pp. 68, 322, 340.

[127] Ursula Baumann, *Protestantismus und Frauenemanzipation in Deutschland* (Frankfurt, 1992), ch. 3/3.

[128] Corbin, *Women for Hire*, pp. 215–16; *Annales*, 3/9 (1883), pp. 278–79; Josephine E. Butler, *Personal Reminiscences of a Great Crusade* (London, 1911), pp. 70, 81; Glen Petrie, *A Singular Iniquity: The Campaigns of Josephine Butler* (London, 1971), pp. 163–66. Even in Japan, Protestants led the abolitionist movement: Sheldon Garon, *Molding Japanese Minds: The State in Everyday Life* (Princeton, 1997), p. 98.

scored easy rhetorical points by tarring their opponents with accusations of puritanism, more interested in a holy war against sin than concerned to curb VD, and French abolitionists were forced to riposte that
they too could be secular and worldly.[129] Abolitionism was part of the
broad current of nonconformist, free-church radicalism that in the
middle and late nineteenth century was expressed in a variety of reform
movements: abolition of slavery, temperance, antivivisection, disestablishment, education, eugenics, suffrage and, last but certainly not least,
antivaccination. The radicals who made up the backbone of abolitionism, especially in Britain, were a new breed of activists, insistent on
applying moral, ethical and religious absolutes to political issues, impa-
tient with the niceties of parliamentary procedure, fiercely individualistic and jealously protective of civil liberties, suspicious of authority,
including that of medical men.[130] For such instinctive libertarians, the
religious tyranny of the pope was easily analogous to the medical despotism of vaccinating physicians or the illegitimate claims to power of
the authorities whose ambition it was to inspect prostitutes, register
births, compel children to be educated and peddlers to be licensed, or
who backed any of the myriad other incursions onto turf that should
rightly remain the individual's alone.[131] Appeals to personal autonomy
in the face of state medicine's ambitions to sacrifice individual conscience to the common weal worked as well for abolition as they had for

---

[129] Dolléans, *La police des moeurs*, p. 161; Fiaux, *Police des moeurs*, v. I, pp. 335, 359–60; Deck, *Syphilis et réglementation*, pp. 14; *La syphilis* (1904), pp. 665–70; Louis Fiaux, *L'intégrité intersexuelle des peuples et les gouvernements* (Paris, 1910), p. 335; *SFPSM: Bulletin mensuel* (1902), p. 273; Dubois-Havenith, *Conférence internationale: Rapports préliminaires*, v. I/1, quest. 2, Fiaux, pp. 39–41; Mignot, *Le péril vénérien*, p. 143; *Annales*, 46 (1851), p. 85.

[130] F. B. Smith, "Contagious Diseases Acts Reconsidered," p. 200; F. B. Smith, *The People's Health 1830–1910* (New York, 1979), pp. 166–68; McHugh, *Prostitution and Victorian Social Reform*, pp. 25–26, 70–94, 234–52; Lyndsay Andrew Farrall, "The Origins and Growth of the English Eugenics Movement, 1865–1925" (Ph.D. diss., Indiana University, 1969), pp. 290–95; Richard D. French, *Antivivisection and Medical Science in Victorian Society* (Princeton, 1975), ch. 8; James S. Roberts, *Drink, Temperance and the Working Class in Nineteenth-Century Germany* (Boston, 1984), pp. 23–24, 64; Coral Lansbury, "Gynaecology, Pornography and the Antivivisection Movement," *Victorian Studies*, 28, 3 (Spring 1985); Brian Harrison, *Drink and the Victorians: The Temperance Question in England 1815–1872* (London, 1971), pp. 26–28.

[131] Mary C. Hume-Rothery, *Women and Doctors or Medical Despotism in England* (Manchester, 1871), pp. 1–2; Chas. Bell Taylor, *A Speech Delivered at Exeter in Reference to the Proposed Extension of the Contagious Diseases Acts to that City* (London, 1880), p. 4. Garth Wilkinson (homeopath, Swedenborgian and writer) united repeal and antivaccination, and his description of the horrors of speculum examinations, with their graphic accounts of flesh violated by steel, made them sound as though but one step removed from vivisection: James John Garth Wilkinson, *The Forcible Introspection of Women for the Army and Navy by the Oligarchy, Considered Physically* (London, 1870), pp. 3, 18. For similar arguments, see *Deutsches Archiv für Geschichte der Medicin und Medicinische Geographie*, 2 (1878), p. 116; *SB*, 24 January 1927, p. 8716B.

antivaccination.[132] Where such currents were strong, in Britain above all, but also in Scandinavia and, less so, in Germany, abolitionism won a following; where they were weak or nonexistent, in the Catholic nations, so too was the movement to end regulation.

Another factor in the variety of abolitionism was the timing of the respective national movements. In the Protestant nations, abolition and the host of social purity movements that sprang up in the last third of the century interacted variously. Social purity advocates sought to counteract not just prostitution, but also immorality in a more general sense, public indecency, pornography, lascivious etchings, suggestive plays, procuring and the white slave trade. In Britain, abolitionism in the strict sense had triumphed by the mid-1880s, before the social purity crusades marched off. Social purity was a movement, even in Britain, that sought to enlist the force of legislation on behalf of morality, to give the state a greater role in shaping ethics. In the British case, because of the staggered timing of the two, they have tended to remain distinct in the eyes of historians who have preferred to save abolition for the cause of liberal democracy, while dismissing social purity as an overly enthusiastic, meddling, uncharacteristically persecuting and puritanical affair.[133] In other nations, with abolitionism developing later and more inextricably intertwined with the social purity movements, such neat typological surgery has proven trickier to perform. Much, for example, of the portrayal of German abolitionism as conservative and illiberal rests on its close connections with social purity during the 1880s and nineties, its consequent unwillingness to remain content with repeal, but instead seeking also to have the state criminalize prostitution and in other ways take up cudgels on behalf of morality.[134] Swedish abolitionism's support for the criminalization of prostitution can also be seen as a legacy of its close associations with social purity.

[132] William Arnold et al., *Notes on Vaccination: Dedicated to the Board of Guardians for the Union of West Bromwich* (Oldbury, 1889), pp. 79–82; Hume-Rothery, *Letter Addressed to Gladstone*, p. 16; Hume-Rothery, *Women and Doctors*, pp. 1–2; Walter Dünnwald, "Sind volksfeindliche Zwangsgesetze von der Art des Reichsimpgesetzes und des Geschlechtskrankengesetzes als rechtsgültig (für jedermann verbindlich) anzusehen?," *Deutsche Gesundheits-Zentrale*, 3, 1 (January 1926).

[133] McHugh, *Prostitution and Victorian Social Reform*, pp. 18, 28, 180; Judith R. Walkowitz, "Male Vice and Feminist Virtue: Feminism and the Politics of Prostitution in Nineteenth-Century Britain," *History Workshop*, 13 (Spring 1982), pp. 84–88.

[134] Blaschko, *Syphilis und Prostitution*, pp. 143–44; *ZBGK*, 15, 6 (1914), p. 207; Richard J. Evans, *Feminist Movement*, pp. 49–50; Richard J. Evans, "Prostitution, State and Society in Imperial Germany," *Past and Present*, 70 (February 1976), p. 121; Lutz Sauerteig, "Frauenemanzipation und Sittlichkeit: Die Rezeption des englischen Abolitionismus in Deutschland," in Rudolf Muhs et al., eds., *Aneignung und Abwehr: Interkultureller Transfer zwischen Deutschland und Grossbritannien im 19. Jahrhundert* (Bodenheim, 1998), pp. 170–73.

RESULTS OF ABOLITIONISM

The movement won its aim directly during the nineteenth century only in Britain and parts of Scandinavia.[135] In Britain, abolitionism arose when regulationists proposed to extend the CD Acts also to civilians. In 1870 a Royal Commission was established, weighing in two years later with an attempt to be Solomonic. The majority report favored retaining a variant of the old system while stripping it of its most objectionable aspects. The periodic examination of prostitutes was effective, but offensive to public opinion and impossible to extend to the entire country. Its recommendation was therefore to return to the voluntary measures of the 1864 act, abandoning the examination of prostitutes and instead focusing efforts on hospital cure. Prostitutes suspected of disease were to be inspected, with the infected hospitalized (unlike the 1864 act) until cured, although not more than three months. VD hospitals, treating prostitutes free of charge, were to be established in any willing city, no longer limited to garrison towns and the army, and the administration of the acts shifted from the military to the Home Office. Alas for the majority, both its flanks were savaged by vociferous minorities: regulationists who saw no reason to abandon medical examinations and abolitionists seeking to throw out the entire system. With such divided advice, the government's willingness to act decisively was hampered.[136]

In 1872, Home Secretary Bruce put forth a bill that gave legislative incarnation to the commission's attempt at a compromise. He agreed that whatever system was chosen had to apply to the entire nation, not just garrison towns and the military, and that periodic examinations could not be extended. The bill offered to repeal the CD Acts, seeking in their stead to knit together a patchwork of alternative measures. Women were to be protected by raising the age of consent and strengthening punishments for indecent assault, procuring and brothel owning. Instead of regulation as such, the police were to receive wideranging powers over suspected prostitutes, allowing them to be arrested for mere solicitation, for example, rather than requiring riotous or indecent behavior. Convicted prostitutes who remained infected at the expiration of their prison sentence were to be retained in a hospital until cured,

---

[135] In Italy, regulation was partially repealed through the Crispi reforms of 1888, but in 1891 the Nicotera Regulation largely returned Italy to the regulationist camp: Gibson, *Prostitution and the State*, pp. 42–85.

[136] *PP* 1871 (c. 408) xix, 1, pp. 8–11; McHugh, *Prostitution and Victorian Social Reform*, pp. 65–68.

although no longer than another nine months. Repealers, though appreciating the end of the acts, were concerned that the bill did not go far enough and the government, motivated largely by hopes of appeasing them and therefore uninterested in an unsatisfying measure, allowed the bill to die. The following year the abolitionist position gained support and the government no longer defended the CD Acts collectively, with Gladstone and Childers, among others, abstaining. The government was now split and the Bruce bill no longer official policy.[137] In 1879 a Select Committee was appointed to examine the acts, including repealers and taking extensive evidence from their side, reconstituted after Liberal victory in the general elections of 1880 and reporting two years later. Its conclusions in favor of a variant of the existing system passed only by a narrow majority (eight to six) over an abolitionist alternative, formulated by Stansfeld. Stansfeld had his comeuppance, however, in the Commons in April 1883, when his motion condemning periodical examinations won.[138] Since inspections were the cornerstone of the system, the acts had in effect been vitiated, although they lingered on in a twilight existence for another three years. One final defense of regulation followed before the government threw in the towel. In 1883 it vainly put forth bills that, while repealing the acts, sought to encourage more infected prostitutes voluntarily to make use of hospital care, allowing the authorities to retain women until cured and hospitalize the infected.[139] In 1886, with the return of Liberals to power, having lost it briefly the previous year, Stansfeld's bill to end the acts passed by large majority.[140]

With the acts repealed, the authorities had at their disposal only the venerable tools of repressing open solicitation and their motivations in this respect were ambiguous at best.[141] They were willing to crack down on unseemly public behavior and on the criminality and exploitation associated with prostitution, but preferred to leave commercial sex as such untouched, convinced that, suppressed in one spot, it would merely

---

[137] _Hansard_, 1872, v. 209, cols. 334–35; _PP_ 1872 (42) i, 261; McHugh, _Prostitution and Victorian Social Reform_, pp. 77–78, 96; F. B. Smith, "Ethics and Disease," p. 133; _PP_ 1873 (29) i, 22; _Hansard_, 1873, v. 216, cols. 218ff.   [138] _PP_ 1882 (340) ix, 1; _Hansard_, 1883, v. 278, cols. 749, 853.

[139] The analogy employed here was the 1867 Poor Law Amendment Act that allowed workhouse authorities to detain inmates with contagious disease: _PP_ 1883 (259) ii, 369; _Transactions of the National Association for the Promotion of Social Science_ (1869), p. 436; _Hansard_, 1883, v. 280, cols. 1834–36; Scott, _State Iniquity_, p. 224; J. L. Hammond and Barbara Hammond, _James Stansfeld_ (London, 1932), ch. 17.

[140] 49 Vict. c. 10.

[141] In Glasgow, this approach had been taken from the outset, with stronger powers entrusted to the police after 1870 to suppress brothels, solicitation and prostitution itself chosen as an alternative to any form of regulation: Linda Mahood, _The Magdalenes: Prostitution in the Nineteenth Century_ (London, 1990), pp. 119ff.

arise in another and, more generally, shunning the job of enforcing public morality. Many of the various social purity organizations, like the National Vigilance Association, that sprang from the abolitionist cause to flourish during the white slavery agitations following repeal, in contrast, sought to have prostitution repressed outright and wanted the police to clear thoroughfares of streetwalkers, raising the tone of public perambulation. To complicate matters, magistrates were often unwilling to convict women on police testimony alone, requiring corroboration from witnesses that not only had solicitation taken place, but that it had been unruly or annoying to passersby. When women were arrested, the press often criticized the police for overzealous enforcement and cases of mistaken identity – the Cass, d'Angely and others – became infamous, discouraging further crackdowns. Whether prostitutes could be and were arrested and convicted in significant numbers depended therefore in large measure on the vagaries of public opinion. Only when social purity movements had aroused common sentiment against solicitation were the police and the courts pressured to arrest and convict streetwalkers by ignoring the annoyance clause.[142]

In 1881, the House of Lords report on the white slave trade proposed that solicitation as such, with or without annoyance, be criminalized, along with stronger police powers to shut down brothels, thereby taking a step toward cracking down on prostitution itself. The Criminal Law Amendment Bill in 1884 incorporated this solicitation clause, proposing as a novelty to make it a crime not only for prostitutes to hawk their wares, but also for men to importune women. Although passing in the Lords, the bill faltered in the Commons on hesitations at investing the Metropolitan Police with powers similar to those taken from them by repeal. In 1885, the bill passed after power had in the meantime returned to a Conservative government, but now without the contentious solicitation clause.[143] The Criminal Law Amendment Act (following public outrage at the exposure by W. T. Stead in the *Pall Mall Gazette*'s Maiden Tribute scandal of the ease with which British women might be procured for continental brothels and played out against the

---

[142] Petrow, *Policing Morals*, p. 117, 122–39; Robert D. Storch, "Police Control of Street Prostitution in Victorian London: A Study in the Contexts of Police Action," in David H. Bayley, ed., *Police and Society* (Beverly Hills, 1977), pp. 51–55; Bland, *Banishing the Beast*, p. 109; Bristow, *Vice and Vigilance*, p. 115.

[143] Petrow, *Policing Morals*, pp. 131–33; *PP* 1884 (271) ii, 395; Sion, *Prostitution and the Law*, p. 92; *Hansard*, 1883, v. 279, col. 1294; 1885, v. 299, cols. 199–200; 48 & 49 Vict. c. 69; Frank Mort, "Purity, Feminism and the State: Sexuality and Moral Politics, 1880–1914," in Mary Langan and Bill Schwarz, eds., *Crises in the British State 1880–1930* (London, 1985), pp. 213–15.

new universal household franchise and the belief widespread among workers that prostitution was an issue of class exploitation for the benefit of randy toffs) raised the age of consent to sixteen, extending that at which procuring was a crime to twenty-one.[144] Brothels, which had been treated as a nuisance on par with gaming houses and other places likely to attract an unruly crowd, were now also outlawed in their own right for the first time. Various measures regulating and licensing establishments of public refreshment and amusement sought to hamper what were otherwise disguised bordellos.[145] In 1898 the Vagrancy Law Amendment Act cracked down on pimps, allowing them to be flogged, and in 1912 (in what was perhaps the highpoint of the social purity movement's influence) men convicted a second time of soliciting were also subject to such direct application of the state's will. In 1905, the Aliens Act allowed foreign prostitutes to be deported. This focus on suppressing public manifestations of prostitution continued with the forbidding, in the 1959 Street Offences Act, of solicitation under any circumstances, with prostitutes convictable on police testimony alone.[146]

In Scandinavia, abolition was also successful in ending regulation, although what replaced it here, as will be seen, was almost diametrically opposed to the outcome in Britain. Norway took the lead, ending regulation in 1888, Denmark followed in 1906, while the thoroughness of Swedish legislative habits slowed developments here. The Swedish branch of the abolitionist movement having been founded in 1878, motions in this spirit followed during the late 1880s and early nineties. These were rejected by the government on the authority of the Swedish Medical Association, which still considered regulation indispensable. At the dawn of the new century, social purity movements in Stockholm began to agitate against the system and more parliamentary motions in favor of repeal followed.[147] Finally in 1903, the Regulation Commission

---

[144] Bristow, *Vice and Vigilance*, pp. 110, 198; Frank Mort, *Dangerous Sexualities: Medico-Moral Politics in England since 1830* (London, 1987), sect. 3; *Hansard*, 1884–85, v. 298, col. 1181.

[145] Rover, *Love, Morals and the Feminists*, p. 69; Flexner, *Prostitution in Europe*, p. 294; Amos, *Comparative Survey of Laws*, pp. 128–29; 10 Edw. 7 and 1 Geo. 5 c. 24, clauses 76–77.

[146] 61 & 62 Vict. c. 39; 5 Geo. 4 c. 83, s. 10; 2 & 3 Geo. 5 c. 20, s. 3, 7(5); 5 Edw. 7 c. 13; Sion, *Prostitution and the Law*, pp. 74ff.; John F. Decker, *Prostitution: Regulation and Control* (Littleton, CO, 1979), pp. 116–17; Leon Radzinowicz and Roger Hood, *A History of English Criminal Law and Its Administration from 1750* (London, 1986), v. V, p. 696.

[147] *Bihang*, 1889, FK, Motion 27; 1889, FK Tilfälliga Utskott (No. 2) Utlåtande 6; Edvard Welander, *Bidrag till de veneriska sjukdomarnes historia i Sverige* (2nd edn.; Stockholm, 1905), pp. 253–56; *Underdånigt betänkande angående könssjukdomarnas spridning*, v. I, pp. 104–07; *Bihang*, 1903, AK, Motion 88.

was appointed to examine the matter. It pondered the issue for several years before disgorging a multivolume report in 1910 and another demi-decade of deliberation passed until regulation was finally ended in 1918. The system had in the meantime been fading, ended already by the late nineteenth century in Malmö, Uppsala, Lund, Eskilstuna, Jönköping and Falun, so that only Stockholm and Gothenburg still maintained full-blown systems at the time of final abolition.[148]

In other nations, abolition had less of an effect, at least for the moment. In Germany, the movement was precocious but insufficiently powerful. Some of the earliest disputes over regulation anywhere were fought in Berlin during the 1840s and fifties. The positions advanced here rehearsed many arguments that would later become standards in the abolitionist canon: that official bordellos were schools for sin rather than social necessities, that they did nothing to curb clandestine prostitution, that male lust and female pecuniary gain being equally reprehensible, singling out whores for punishment was unjust and that, in any case, the state should not sully itself by tolerating vice.[149] For the moment, victory was with these midcentury abolitionists *avant la lettre* as official brothels were outlawed, first in Prussia, later in the Empire as well. While winning the bordello battle, however, the war of regulation remained lost. Beyond these early triumphs, abolitionism achieved little before the Weimar years. In France, there was a flurry of abolitionist organizing in the mid- and late 1870s, with a movement officially founded in 1878, partly prompted by Butler's mission to this, the citadel of regulation. Instigated by Yves Guyot's attacks on the *police des moeurs*, commissions were appointed to investigate and various scandals led to the demission of the implicated officials in 1879. The battle against regulation in Paris during the seventies was led by radical republicans, who saw the vice squad as a remnant of the Second Empire's authoritarianism, backed by hostility among Parisians against the government that, after the Commune, remained in Versailles. The authorities responded by obstructing the foundation of a French branch of the international Abolitionist Federation. In the early and mid-1880s, minor victories were scored when the Parisian municipal council sought, with only tangential success, to abolish the vice squad and a commission investigating regulation changed tack to oppose the

---

[148] *Bihang*, 1918, Prop. 154; *SFS*, 1918/460; *Underdånigt betänkande angående könssjukdomarnas spridning*, v. I, p. 348.

[149] *Archiv für Syphilis und Hautkrankheiten*, 1 (1846), pp. 277–78; *Wochenschrift für die gesammte Heilkunde*, 31 (3 August 1850), p. 486; S. Neumann, *Die Berliner Syphilisfrage: Ein Beitrag zur öffentlichen Gesundheitspflege Berlins herausgegeben in Vertretung des ärztlichen Comités des Berliner Gesundheitspflege-Vereins* (Berlin, 1852), pp. 37–38.

system.[150] In practical terms, however, little resulted and support for regulation remained firm. When the Société française de prophylaxie sanitaire et morale (SFPSM), established to ponder such matters, polled its
constituent organizations on the system, only fifty-one were for freeing
prostitution altogether, while 410 favored at least some form of medical
surveillance. There was no strong movement and when abolition ever
arrived, as one supporter gloomily prognosticated, it would be in the form
of a decree from on high, not, as in Britain, the result of grassroots pressure. Well into the twentieth century, the debate between the two sides,
largely resolved elsewhere, continued to be fought, with arguments familiar for over half a century wearily batted back and forth.[151]

THE SCANDINAVIAN *SONDERWEG*

While all nations underwent abolitionist attack, not all responded alike.
Britain bowed to the insistence that the state exit the business of regulating vice. In Scandinavia, abolition also triumphed, but the results
were very different. There developed here a system that was, by the early
twentieth century, to become the model for reformers in the regulationist nations who, seeking to end inherited methods, nonetheless considered it irresponsible to have the state abandon such matters to venereal
anarchy. This Scandinavian system of universal citizen regulation, or
sanitary statism as it was called by French observers, was the outcome of
an evolution that stretched over most of the nineteenth century, being
adopted at different rates in the Nordic nations.[152]

Sanitary statism's basic principle was that all infected citizens were
obliged to be treated and, in return, the state would provide all with
free medical care, at least for VD. Because VD was fraught with few
acute symptoms, because there was little impetus from nature's side for
victims to seek care, much from society's to avoid it, a requirement to be
treated (unnecessary for other contagious ailments) had to be clearly stipulated. As corollaries to this basic duty imposed on all diseased citizens
were measures (some enforced through the penal code) that prohibited
and sought to contain potentially transmitting behavior: obligatory
notification to the authorities of all cases, medical inspections and
certification of the suspected, isolation and, if necessary, hospitalization

[150] *ZBGK*, 8, 1 (1908), pp. 10–14; Corbin, *Women for Hire*, pp. 215–20; Fiaux, *L'intégrité intersexuelle*, p. viii; Guyot, *Prostitution Under the Regulation System*, p. 309; Fiaux, *Police des moeurs*, v. I, p. 231; Harsin, *Policing Prostitution*, pp. 336–38.

[151] *La syphilis* (1905), p. 131; Fiaux, *La prostitution réglementée*, pp. xiv–xv, xxxv; Louis Spillmann, *L'évolution de la lutte contre la syphilis* (Paris, n.d. [1932?]), pp. 16–19.

[152] Cavaillon, *Les législations antivénériennes*, p. 48.

of the afflicted, contact tracing, criminalization of endangerment and transmission. Sanitary statism thus treated all infected citizens alike, regardless of their sex, status or profession, and it attacked VD with measures similar to those martialed against other contagious ailments. Traditional public health attempts to break chains of transmission were now applied not just to prostitutes, but – in an expanded form – to all carriers. Rather than sweeping VD under the rug of regulationism, it was to be brought into the clear prophylactic light of precautions that applied to everyone.

Although culminating in Sweden during the early twentieth century, sanitary statism had been evolving for well over a century. In the late eighteenth century, general medical inspections had been undertaken in the countryside, sometimes of all inhabitants in an area hard hit by syphilis, sometimes of various categories considered especially liable to infection: sailors, herring drivers, itinerant artisans, loose women and the like. At first, in the absence of government instructions to this effect, physicians themselves had taken the initiative for such inspections. Then, in 1774, a royal instruction for provincial physicians required measures to avert epidemics and, in this connection, syphilis inspections were carried out, often of hundreds of people, whether infected or not, occasionally entire municipalities.[153] In 1787, the Collegium Medicum recommended inspections of various occupations thought likely to be infected. All were to be exhorted from the pulpit to seek timely treatment and in return promised free medical care. In 1810, prompted by the ideas set forth in 1803 by C. F. von Schulzenheim on the occasion of relinquishing his presidency of the Royal Academy of Science, parliament asked the king to limit the spread of VD by restricting the circulation of itinerant professions, except after medical examination with the results noted in their internal passports. A variety of traveling coffee houses and pubs, run largely by women in the countryside and feared as centers of prostitution, were to be forbidden altogether.[154] With the Collegium Medicum's imprimatur, a royal circular from 1812 codified this practice of general

---

[153] Welander, *Om de veneriska sjukdomarnes historia*, pp. 85–89; *Hygiea*, 63, 6 (June 1901), p. 679; Welander, *Bidrag till de veneriska sjukdomarnes historia*, p. 116; Lundquist, *Den disciplinerade dubbelmoralen*, pp. 54–55; Welander, *Blad ur prostitutionsfrågans historia*, p. 9; Dubois-Havenith, *Conférence internationale: Enquêtes*, v. I/2, pp. 495–96.

[154] Malmroth, "Om de smittosamma könssjukdomarnas bekämpande," pp. 6–7; Otto E. A. Hjelt, *Svenska och Finska medicinalverkets historia 1633–1812* (Helsingfors, 1892), v. II, pp. 320–21; Nils Thyresson, *Från Fransoser till AIDS: Kapitel ur de veneriska sjukdomarnas historia i Sverige* (n.p., 1991), pp. 79–80; *Ridderskapet och Adeln*, Besvärs- och Economie-Utskotts Betänkande, 1 September 1809, pp. 69–74; *Ridderskapet och Adeln*, 21 April 1810, pp. 911–12; *Borgare*, 21 April 1810, v. 6, pp. xliii–xliv. On the connection between coffee and commercial copulation, see Bloch, *Die Prostitution*, v. II/1, pp. 400–04.

medical inspections. The basic principle was to require examination of all whose profession or mode of life made them possible carriers. Particular attention was directed at inns, while loose women and vagrants were to be kept away from fairs and other public gatherings. Large groups of the general population now also found their mobility restricted in the interests of VD prevention.[155] Canteen keepers, coffee boilers, costermongers and hawkers, especially those from port cities and other places likely to be infected, were obliged to carry health attests, as were house-to-house peddlers, apprentices, wandering Jews and similar itinerants who needed one, renewable every three months, in order to be issued an internal passport.

Not surprisingly for proposals that sought to examine all members of various groups for a stigmatized disease, objections were raised: first, that limiting the mobility of entire occupations threatened economic damage and, secondly, that honorable members of inspected categories found repugnant the implication of likely infection. The effect of such protests was to exempt for the moment itinerant peddlers who were homesteaders or married from examination and certification, requiring nonetheless that the declaration from their local clergy required for internal passports state that VD was not present in their homes. This system of general inspections, while thus less far-reaching than its movers had foreseen, nonetheless nailed fast the principle that the authorities could require examination of large groups of the popular classes, both men and women, that were not limited to, nor even necessarily included, prostitutes.[156]

The 1812 royal circular and its attendant regulations codified a novel method of identifying the infected, but said little about how and where to cure them. In 1809, concerns during the Napoleonic wars with improving Sweden's military preparedness and promoting population growth prompted proposals to establish medical institutions in the countryside to treat VD patients, including even the well-to-do. Once the general inspection system began after 1812, the costs of treating the resulting cases increased dramatically. Local clinics – intended to provide for the poor – had in effect been turned into lock hospitals, now housing twice as many venereal patients as victims of all other ailments

---

[155] RA, Skrivelser till Kungl. Maj:t, Collegium Medicum, 1812, v. 26, no. 226, "Collegium Medicum on Veneriske Smittans förekommande och hotande"; A. Hilarion Wistrand, ed., *Författningar angående medicinal-väsendet i Sverige* (Stockholm, 1860), pp. 107–09.

[156] *Borgare*, 11 November 1809, v. 3/2, pp. 107–08; *Ridderskapet och Adeln*, 3 April 1810, pp. 82–85; Malmroth, "Om de smittosamma könssjukdomarnas bekämpande," pp. 8, 10–11.

combined.[157] Some localities had established special venereal hospitals, but since they had proven insufficient, the government asked the Estates in 1815 to consider the use of general revenues to pay for such treatment. The Estates countered with a tax of three skilling for each registered person to finance new VD hospitals. Two years later, the government turned most hospitals over to local administration, stipulated that each contain special venereal wards and allowed free treatment for the needy in those provinces which had taxed themselves for such purposes.[158] To avoid local variations, a tax of three skilling per capita was then accepted by the Estates for the entire nation.[159] Thus was introduced, first among nations, the principle of free hospital care for VD. All VD patients were given the right to hospitalization, but since they were also permitted to leave as they pleased, before whatever final resolution medicine of the day might offer, the requirement that the infected be cured was not compulsory in any watertight sense.[160]

This system of general inspections of broad segments of the population with free and quasi-compulsory medical care was adopted at first without major controversy. Proposals were advanced to make the inspections of those who worked in inns, pubs and bars a regular, twice-yearly event and, more drastically, to incarcerate in special institutions the unfortunates who could not be cured, lest they otherwise spread disease after returning to their families.[161] In 1817, the principles of this approach were debated anew when some sought to extend and enhance its provisions. A proposal in the Burgher Estate would have required inspections of soldiers and sailors, asked employers to examine servants and workers, noting their state of health on their papers when they left, and demanded prenuptial health certificates from such social groups. The pertinent committees warmed to the idea, suggesting in turn that employers be required to report suspected infection among workers and

---

[157] *Ridderskapet och Adeln*, 15 July 1809, pp. 258–59; 29 March 1815, v. 1, p. 187; *Bihang*, 1815, v. 3, pp. 596–98.

[158] *Bihang*, 1815, v. 1, pp. 504–07; 1815, v. 3, p. 598; *Ridderskapet och Adeln*, 15 July 1809, p. 259; 5 January 1810, pp. 146–47; 18 January 1810, p. 869; "Kongl. Maj:ts Nådiga Instruction, hwarefter Directionerne öfwer Läns Lazaretterne i Riket och öfwer Cur-anstalterne till Veneriska smittans hämmande, hafwa sig att rätta," 17 December 1817, *Kongl. Förordningar*, 1817; *Kongl. Maj:ts Förnyade Nådiga Instruction för Provincial-läkarne i Riket*, 13 June 1822 (Stockholm, 1822), §11.

[159] *Bihang*, 1817–18, 1. saml., pp. 48–53; Stats- och Bevillnings-Utsk., Betänk. 157, v. 4/2, pp. 688–90; Stats- och Besvärs-Utskottens Betänk. 294 1/2, v. 4/4, pp. 1755–56, 1954–55; Underdäniga Skrifvelser 228, v. 10, pp. 591–92.

[160] Welander, *Bidrag till de veneriska sjukdomarnes historia*, p. 143; *ZBGK*, 11, 11 (1911), p. 403; XVIIth International Congress of Medicine, *Dermatology and Syphilography*, p. 77.

[161] *Ridderskapet och Adeln*, 29 March 1815, v. 1, p. 192; *Preste*, 11 May 1815, v. 1, pp. 464–68.

allowing the clergy and vestry to decide, when VD spread, whether to inspect only the afflicted or the entire congregation.[162] Others, in contrast, were less willing to accept such restrictions on personal liberty, even in the service of noble prophylactic goals. Inspecting all members of a congregation because a few were infected was insulting to the honor of the healthy and the modesty of women, and generally violated the protections each individual deserved in society, while examining only the servant classes was socially unjust. Visions of the Inquisition come to Sweden danced in the heads of objectors.[163] Yet fortune favored inspections and the system was elaborated and extended. In 1822 royal instructions for provincial physicians added new aspects. During general inspections the name, age and residence of the diseased were to be reported to the clergy, who in turn were to ensure hospitalization of the most contagious. Physicians were to investigate the source of infection (contact tracing) of their patients, reporting the results to allow examination of such carriers. If contacts refused even after attempts at persuasion, the authorities could take appropriate measures, performing inspections compulsorily.[164]

This system of general medical inspections, with health certificates as a prerequisite for internal passports, lasted in its fullblown version until midcentury when it was first supplemented and eventually replaced by regulationism. In the course of development, sanitary statism increasingly narrowed its focus, so that by the time regulation began to gain ground, the transition from one approach to the other was not jarring. Initially, medical examinations had been carried out of all in an infected area. The 1812 circular, in turn, foresaw inspections that, while still quite general, focused on specific groups believed to be particularly at risk. A royal circular the following year then allowed inspections of women employed in inns, pubs and restaurants and this was extended to include loose women caught out at night or who otherwise could be suspected of infection. During the early decades of the century, the Stockholm police subjected women believed to be prostitutes (employees of bars

---

[162] *Borgare*, 30 December 1817, v. 1, pp. 436–39; *Bihang*, 1817–18, 8. Saml., no. 76, pp. 373–78; Besvärs- och Ekonomi-Utskotts Betänk. 123, p. 818.

[163] *Ridderskapet och Adeln*, 1817–18, v. 5/1, 4 April 1818, pp. 233–35; 9 January 1818, v. 1, pp. 767–70; *Bihang*, 1817–18, 8. Saml., no. 76, pp. 373–78; *Borgare*, 4 April 1818, v. 1, p. 1596; *Preste*, 1817–18, 4 April 1818, v. 3, pp. 410–11; *Bihang*, 1817–18, Besvärs- och Ekonomi-Utskotts Betänk. 123, p. 821.

[164] *Kongl. Maj:ts Förnyade Nådiga Instruction för Provincial-läkarne i Riket*, §10; *Underdånigt betänkande angående könssjukdomarnas spridning*, v. I, pp. 265–66; Welander, *Bidrag till de veneriska sjukdomarnes historia*, p. 120.

and restaurants above all) to inspection on a discretionary basis.[165] The 1822 instructions for physicians in the provinces ordered them to inspect and report not just certain groups, but also individuals named as possible sources of infection. In 1824 health attests could be required of vagrants and married persons from the working classes with no fixed abode who hailed from infected areas. By the late 1830s, the governor of Stockholm and the health ministry, while still rejecting fullblown regulationism as incompatible with Swedish morals, agreed that loose women were the main problem and sought a system of regular weekly inspections of females (but also men) whose occupations gave reason to suspect disease, as well as of women with no visible means of support.[166] In 1837, the commander of the Stockholm garrison, worried at the increasing incidence of VD in the ranks, began to press for stronger measures. Weekly inspections of soldiers followed and sailors arriving from abroad were now to be questioned as to their venereal status before landing.[167]

The focus on potentially prostituted women also narrowed. A few tolerated brothels, otherwise forbidden in law, were established in Stockholm, but closed after popular protest a few months later. A form of clandestine bordello was then improvised, whereby coffeehouse proprietors were permitted to employ more servants than necessary on the condition that they submitted to police supervision and regular inspections. As a class of fulltime professional prostitutes arose during the course of urbanization to replace traditional forms of casually mercenary sex in the countryside, it became increasingly plausible to target measures at such women.[168] In 1847, the practical basis for a regulationist system in Stockholm was laid. The municipal authorities approved a proposal to require, by force if necessary, weekly medical inspections of loose women without abode or employment, those who worked in bars and the like and especially ones who had already been hospitalized for VD. For various technical reasons, however, it was not until 1859 that regulationism came to Stockholm in fulldress regalia. Prostitutes were now to be examined weekly, either for free at the inspection stations or elsewhere at their expense, and failure to comply was punishable by a

---

[165] *Hygiea*, 9, 3 (March 1847), p. 180; Nils Staf, *Polisväsendet i Stockholm 1776–1850* (Uppsala, 1950), p. 417; Welander, *Om de veneriska sjukdomarnes historia*, p. 183.

[166] *Kongl. Maj:ts Förnyade Nådiga Instruction för Provincial-läkarne i Riket*, §10; Wistrand, *Författningar*, p. 250; *Hygiea*, 9, 3 (March 1847), pp. 178–89.

[167] Dubois-Havenith, *Conférence internationale: Enquêtes*, v. I/2, p. 458; *SFS*, 1839/11; 1843/18; Welander, *Blad ur prostitutionsfrågans historia*, p. 16.

[168] Staf, *Polisväsendet i Stockholm*, p. 421; Lundquist, *Den disciplinerade dubbelmoralen*, p. 65; *Underdånigt betänkande angående könssjukdomarnas spridning*, v. I, p. 343.

year's hard labor. Unlike the French system, but like the German, official brothels were not a feature.[169]

In 1864, with reform of the penal code, regulationism was retrofitted with a legal foundation. The criminalization of extramarital sex ended, but sex for hire (except that conducted in brothels) was not outlawed. Instead, regulation was grounded in the laws on vagrancy, with prostitutes who did not follow police regulations prosecuted as vagabonds. In 1875, new decrees on contagious disease allowed municipalities to introduce regulation, thus formalizing the system.[170] Regulation in Sweden was introduced to supplement across-the-board inspections of broad categories of everyday citizens. Despite the shift, with regulation, from a class focus (on the popular strata) to one on gender, the two systems continued to run in parallel. In 1864 and again in 1873, the principle of free hospital care for all VD sufferers paid for by special taxes was reaffirmed. General inspections lessened in extent without wholly disappearing. In 1860 the abolition of internal passports reduced the leverage authorities could apply under those who resisted examinations.[171] The instructions for provincial physicians of 1890, while somewhat diminishing their force, nonetheless retained such inspections. Physicians discovering VD patients who refused care were to report them, thus ensuring that they would be hospitalized and treated. Though recalcitrants could still be compulsorily inspected and treated, contacts were no longer necessarily examined and those traced by physicians did not have to be reported. General inspections of all in an infected area were still possible, although decreasingly common.[172]

Given this long and never wholly vanquished tradition of general inspections, the Regulation Commission, reporting in 1910 on its search for alternatives to the control of prostitutes, in fact went back to the future. First, it rejected regulation. Although starting out favorably inclined, the commission made a volteface during the course of its deliberations, largely accepting the abolitionists' arguments and rejecting

[169] Welander, *Om de veneriska sjukdomarnes historia*, pp. 190–94; *Underdånigt betänkande angående könssjukdomarnas spridning*, v. I, pp. 346–47; Dubois-Havenith, *Conférence internationale: Enquêtes*, v. I/2, pp. 459–60.

[170] Welander, *Blad ur prostitutionsfrågans historia*, p. 29; Dubois-Havenith, *Conférence internationale: Enquêtes*, v 1/2, pp. 460–61; Westerberg, *Reglementeringsfrågan*, pp. 10–11; Lind and Fredriksson, *Kärlek för pengar?*, p. 14; *Hygiea*, 37, 11 (November 1875), p. 651.

[171] Dubois-Havenith, *Conférence internationale: Enquêtes*, v. I/2, pp. 497, 514; *SFS*, 1873/48; Malmroth, "Om de smittosamma könssjukdomarnas bekämpande," p. 11; Lundquist, *Den disciplinerade dubbelmoralen*, p. 221.

[172] *SFS*, 1890/58, §28; *Underdånigt betänkande angående könssjukdomarnas spridning*, v. I, pp. 270–71; *Transactions of the Seventh International Congress of Hygiene and Demography*, 9 (1891), pp. 208–09.

even the sort of neoregulationist tinkering under consideration else-where. Regulation as such was to be ended, but, rather than abandon-ing all control over prostitutes, they were to be subsumed into larger categories of epidemiologically dangerous persons to whom a new system of sanitary surveillance extended. The committee did not want to forbid prostitution as such, nor target women who worked mainly at respectable occupations in addition to their venereally mercenary pur-suits, but those who sold sex fulltime were still to be prosecuted accord-ing to the vagrancy laws. In addition sanitary measures (examination and treatment, voluntary if possible, compulsory if necessary, with the police bringing recalcitrants to the hospital) were to be taken against three groups of persons: those who had been arrested or warned for prostitution, those accused of certain sexual crimes (transmitting or endangering others with VD, soliciting, child abuse) and those reported by physicians as sources of infection. This meant that for fulltime pros-titutes, a form of backdoor regulation would have remained in that their occupation was outlawed and its practitioners liable to compulsory medical examination at regular intervals. When abolitionists therefore objected, the government changed tack, ending the medical surveillance of those in violation of the vagrancy statutes, thus removing any partic-ular focus on prostitutes. The attempt to single out fulltime prostitutes as defined in terms of vagrancy – retailers of sex without a day job – would have had as its main result, in the words of one observer, a proliferation of manicurists.[173]

Although ending regulation, the commission foresaw a broad front of statutory intervention to control prostitution and the spread of VD. It disavowed specific aspects of the old system of general inspections in afflicted areas, a technique it sniffily rejected as perhaps possible in soci-eties of low cultural development like Finland and Russia, but no longer tenable for Sweden.[174] And yet, its recommendations and the Lex Veneris that eventually emerged in 1918 cast off regulation to return to the basic principles of the inherited system that had first been codified almost precisely a century earlier: requiring all infected, regardless of sex

[173] *ZBGK*, 19, 2 (1919), pp. 34; *Reformer och skenreformer: Ett uttalande med anledning af Reglementerings-kommitténs betänkande* (Stockholm, 1912), p. 7; *Svenska Läkaresällskapets Handlingar*, 41 (1915), p. 3; *Bihang*, 1918, Prop. 154, p. 59; *RD prot*, FK, 1918:39, p. 49; Thyresson, *Från Fransoser till AIDS*, ch. 17; *Svensk Tidsskrift*, 8 (1918), p. 201.
[174] *Underdånigt betänkande angående könssjukdomarnas spridning*, v. I, pp. 275, 309–10. This was, perhaps, a cultural cringe before Neisser's condemnation of such inspections as the outcome of primitive Nordic cultural conditions and hence inapplicable to Germany's more sophisticated social relations: Blaschko, *Syphilis und Prostitution*, pp. 119, 126–30.

or status, to be treated; providing them with free medical care to remove
any excuse not to be; modernizing the attempt to identify cases of infection that had once been accomplished through general inspections and
putting teeth in the obligation to be treated by requiring that the infected
be reported, that sexual contacts be traced, inspected and cured and that
epidemiologically dangerous behavior be punished.[175] A vestige of
general inspections remained in the provision (§7) of special medical
efforts for rural localities where VD had become widespread. Marriage
was forbidden for the contagious, dissolvable in cases where infidelity
had left one partner infected; the state was granted custody of children
raised in a manner likely to encourage prostitution, and transmission
and endangerment with VD were punishable offenses. Providing,
indeed enforcing, medical care, on the one hand, and punishing those
who might or did spread infection, on the other, were the carrot and
the stick of this new, modernized version of the venerable Swedish
system.[176] It was no longer a moral offense, prostitution, which sparked
the state's intervention, but transmission, a violation of the canons of
health. VD in this approach was to be treated much like other contagious diseases, subjecting all infected – whether male or female, hooker
or respectable burgher – to similar measures. The originality of the
Scandinavian system, as a French observer put it, was that it ignored distinctions between the sexes, social groups and diseases. The driving principles were the equality of all before the law and the individual's
subordination to the collectivity.[177]

WHENCE THE SCANDINAVIAN *SONDERWEG*?

Why was this system of sanitary statism implemented earlier in Sweden
(and, with variations in detail and timing, also in the other Scandinavian
nations), preceding by decades similar reforms elsewhere? An answer lies
with socioepidemiological peculiarities of the Nordic regions. The wide
spread of VD in the countryside of this still predominantly rural nation

[175] *ZBGK*, 19, 2 (1919), pp. 34; *Förhandlingar*, 1912, p. 478; *Bihang*, 1918, Prop. 154, p. 15; *SFS*,
1918/460; *Nordisk Hygienisk Tidsskrift*, 2, 6 (November–December 1921), p. 311; *Förhandlingar*, 1920, p.
219.   [176] *SFS*, 1918/459; *Bihang*, 1918, Prop. 154, p. 15.
[177] Regnault, *L'évolution de la prostitution*, p. 262; Dolléans, *La police des moeurs*, p. 175; *Annales*, 4/34
(1920), p. 367; Sydney M. Laird, *Venereal Disease in Britain* (Harmondsworth, 1943), p. 45. The one
exception to the general equality of the Swedish system was that the wealthy who could afford
the private medical care that kept them out of hospitals were also exempt from the other requirements that the state imposed on those who took advantage of its offer of free care: *DVöG*, 26 (1894),
p. 237.

and the perception of syphilis as largely nonsexual in its transmission meant that general inspections were possible and necessary, while regulation with its focus on an urbanized class of quasiprofessional prostitutes remained largely irrelevant here until later in the century, Scandinavia appears to have been more widely afflicted with syphilis during the late eighteenth and early nineteenth centuries than its neighbors to the south. The Seven Years War and the Finnish War of 1790, followed by the Napoleonic campaigns, brought epidemics in the wake of returning troops to Sweden and Norway, leading to such a thorough contamination of the countryside that syphilis became a "true folk illness."[178] VD, one cleric complained, was so widespread that public communions threatened to transmit it even further.[179] Not only was VD broadly strewn in general, but it seems to have been especially so in the countryside. Early in the century (the figures start in 1822), syphilis was not nearly as prevalent in Stockholm as it was to become later in the century, but much more so in rural areas than was to be true in subsequent decades, although with gonorrhea and soft chancre such disparities between town and countryside were less glaring.[180]

---

[178] *Hygiea*, 63, 6 (June 1901), pp. 678–79; Blaschko, *Syphilis und Prostitution*, pp. 94, 114; *ZBGK*, 5, 7 (1906), p. 256; 15, 3 (1914), pp. 82–83; Friedrich Laupheimer, *Der strafrechtliche Schutz gegen geschlechtliche Infektion* (Berlin, 1913), p. 86; *Mitteilungen*, 16, 5/6 (1918), p. 83; Malmroth, "Om de smittosamma könssjukdomarnas bekämpande," pp. 2, 15; August Hirsch, *Handbook of Geographical and Historical Pathology* (London, 1885), v. II, p. 69.

[179] *Preste*, 1817–18, v. 3, 4 April 1818, p. 422. The problem of transmission via the chalice provoked concern already in the late eighteenth century, later convincing certain Protestant churches to introduce individual cups and sparking an entire government report in Denmark: L. Duncan Bulkley, *Syphilis in the Innocent* (New York, 1894), p. 145; Macalister, *Inaugural Address*, p. 31; Gustave Metzger and Charles Muller, *La coupe de communion et les maladies contagieuses* (2nd edn.; Geneva, 1905), pp. 13–14; *Betænkning angående Forandringer i Reglerne for Uddelingen af Nadverens Sakramente, afgiven af den af Ministeriet for Kirke- og Undervisningsvæsenet den 18. September 1903 nedsatte Kommission* (Copenhagen, 1904). For similar fears with AIDS, see House of Commons, 1986–87, Social Services Committee, *Problems Associated with AIDS* (13 May 1987), v. III, p. 337; Margaret Brazier and Maureen Mulholland, "Droit et Sida: Le Royaume-uni," in Jacques Foyer and Lucette Khaïat, *Droit et Sida: Comparaison internationale* (Paris, 1994), p. 364. In Tuscany faced with cholera in 1835, long spoons were recommended for such purposes: Michael Stolberg, *Die Cholera im Grossherzogtum Toskana* (Landsberg, 1995), p. 27.

[180] *Underdånigt betänkande angående könssjukdomarnas spridning*, v. III, pp. 11–12. The incidence of syphilis in Stockholm was still thrice what it was in the rest of the country. Nor should one exaggerate the prevalence of VD in the countryside. The Farmers' Estate objected, for example, to the imposition of a three-skilling tax to pay for treatment because it thought more funds than necessary would thus be collected in the countryside: *Bihang*, 1817–18, v. 4/2, Stats- och Bevillnings-Utsk. Betänk. 157, pp. 688–90; Stats- och Besvärs-Utskottens Betänk. 294 1/2, pp. 1755–56; *Bonde*, 23 May 1818, v. 5, pp. 156–58. So vehement were their objections that in 1823 they managed to impose a system of geographically variable taxes, dependent on the urgency of the problem: *Bihang*, 1823, v. 4/4, "Riksens Höglofl. Ständers Stats- och Bevillnings Utskotts Betänkande, angående en af hvarje mantalskrifven Person årligen intill nästa Riksdag utgående afgift till Veneriska smittans hämmande"; *SFS*, 1830/43.

Another issue seems to have been the relative mobility of the population, both in- and externally. The seafaring nature of the Scandinavian
economies, the coming and going of fishermen, meant that fresh sources
of infection were ever available, helping prompt early precautions aimed
at sailors.[181] Peculiarities of the fishing trade also encouraged the wide
spread of VD in the countryside. In the 1790s, record herring catches in
Bohuslän, in western Sweden, stoked the local economy, attracting thousands of fishermen and other workers from every corner of the realm
who consorted merrily, returning home during the winter with more
than just the fruits of their labors. At the beginning of the new century,
however, the herring catch began to diminish and fishermen decreased
in importance as carriers, although not so quickly that they could avoid
a mention in the 1812 royal circular as a special group subject to medical
inspections, and hospitalization if infected.[182]

The countryside colored the Swedish approach to VD also in the
sense that rural habits and customs tipped the prophylactic balance in
the direction of sanitary statism. As elsewhere before the nineteenth
century, syphilis was not regarded as an exclusively venereal disease. A
commission in 1804 concluded that it could afflict the entire body, thus
spreading through everyday contacts as well as sexually, and such views
were maintained late into the century. Rural customs only made matters
worse. The problem was not just a wide spread of disease in the hinterland, but also the fear that, because of uncouth rustic habits, syphilis was
transmitted through quotidian interactions, not just sexually, thus again
requiring broadly focused precautions. Customs common in the countryside were often held up for reprobation: inadequate diets, ignorance
of the pathways of transmission, poor hygienic habits (the shared use
and negligent cleanliness of every conceivable household implement,
spitting in or licking the eye to remove sties), polymorphous sleeping
arrangements (including the indiscriminate bunking of travelers with
the family), earthy child-minding practices (sucking the penises of infants to calm them, licking clean their runny noses, maternal premasti-
cation of their food). Figures from early in the century show that, while
syphilis was generally a sexually transmitted disease in Stockholm, in the
countryside it was much more likely to be spread through simple cohab-

[181] Welander, *Bidrag till de veneriska sjukdomarnes historia*, pp. 94–100; Stig Cronberg, "The Rise and
Fall of Sexually Transmitted Diseases in Sweden," *Genitourinary Medicine*, 69 (1993), p. 184.
[182] Wistrand, *Författningar*, pp. 107–09; Sven Hellerström and Malcolm Tottie, "De veneriska
sjukdomarna," in Wolfram Kock, ed., *Medicinalväsendet i Sverige, 1813–1962* (Stockholm, 1963), p. 407;
Dubois-Havenith, *Conférence internationale: Enquêtes*, v. I/2, pp. 495–97; Malmroth, "Om de smittosamma könssjukdomarnas bekämpande," p. 2.

itation. Peasant sexual customs, with premarital sex a commonplace, also meant that the venereal routes of transmission were well paved in the countryside.[183]

None of these problems were exclusively Scandinavian, of course. With the suppression of brothels starting in the sixteenth century, prostitutes had been forced out of cities across Europe to join the itinerant population of the countryside. Peasant indifference to prenuptial continence was common in other regions as well, with high illegitimacy rates in parts of German-speaking central Europe.[184] Views of commercial sex varied much by social class, with the tradeoff between moral purity and venereal profit evaluated differently according to the observer's economic position.[185] Nor were these exclusively issues of the early nineteenth century. The adoption of personal hygiene was a protracted development whose speed varied much among nations and geographically within them, resisted especially in the countryside where filth was long considered normal, indeed wholesome, with water and washing feared as enervating and debilitating.[186] During the sixteenth and seventeenth centuries, syphilis was not yet regarded as an exclusively venereal disease.[187] Only slowly, with the adoption of habits of personal hygiene, was its spread increasingly restricted to sexual contacts. The nonsexual dissemination of VD has hence long been

[183] Friedrich J. Behrend, ed., *Syphilidologie*, 2 (1840), pp. 449–50; *Hygiea*, 37, 11 (November 1875), p. 650; Thyresson, *Från Fransoser till AIDS*, pp. 63, 66–67; Jonas Frykman and Orvar Löfgren, *Culture Builders: A Historical Anthropology of Middle-Class Life* (New Brunswick, 1987), pp. 174, 203; *Underdånigt betänkande angående könssjukdomarnas spridning*, v. III, pp. 15–17; Malmroth, "Om de smittosamma könssjukdomarnas bekämpande," p. 2; Fredelius, *Ett onödigt ont*, p. 51; *MTG* (24 July 1869), pp. 96–97; (28 August 1869), p. 246.

[184] Michael Mitterauer, *Ledige Mütter: Zur Geschichte unehelicher Geburten in Europa* (Munich, 1983), pp. 23–27; G. R. Quaife, *Wanton Wenches and Wayward Wives: Peasants and Illicit Sex in Early Seventeenth-Century England* (London, 1979), chs. 2, 3; W. R. Lee, *Population Growth, Economic Development and Social Change in Bavaria 1750–1850* (New York, 1977), pp. 307–08.

[185] Kienitz, *Sexualität, Macht und Moral*, pp. 81–88.

[186] Among the themes of Jean-Pierre Goubert, *The Conquest of Water: The Advent of Health in the Industrial Age* (Cambridge, 1989), chs. 2–4, 9; Georges Vigarello, *Concepts of Cleanliness: Changing Attitudes in France Since the Middle Ages* (Cambridge, 1988); Richard L. Schoenwald, "Training Urban Man: A Hypothesis About the Sanitary Movement," in H. J. Dyos and Michael Wolff, eds., *The Victorian City* (London 1973), v. II, p. 675; Jacques Léonard, *Archives du corps: La santé au XIXe siècle* (n.p., 1986), pp. 115–35; Geneviève Heller, "Ideologie et rituels de la propreté aux XIXe and XXe siècles," in Arthur E. Imhof, ed., *Leib und Leben in der Geschichte der Neuzeit* (Berlin, 1983).

[187] Annemarie Kinzelbach, "'Böse Blattern' oder 'Franzosenkrankheit': Syphiliskonzept, Kranke und die Genese des Krankenhauses in oberdeutschen Reichsstädten der frühen Neuzeit," in Martin Dinges and Thomas Schlich, eds., *Neue Wege in der Seuchengeschichte* (Stuttgart, 1995); Jon Arrizabalaga et al., *The Great Pox: The French Disease in Renaissance Europe* (New Haven, 1997), p. 35; Schuster, *Das Frauenhaus*, p. 185; Georges Vigarello, *Le sain et le malsain* (Paris, 1993), p. 55; J. M. Eager, *The Early History of Quarantine: Origin of Sanitary Measures Directed Against Yellow Fever* (Washington, DC, 1903), p. 13.

considered a sign of primitive customs and low cultural development, an indication that the basic hygienic habits of middle-class life (the sanitized interface we present to each other, except – although increasingly even there, depilated, deodorized, belatexed – in sex) have not yet been achieved.[188] Sex is the primary means of syphilitic transmission only in civilized, or at least hygienic, societies. Various forms of nonvenereal syphilis (bejel in the Arab world, sibbens in Scotland, radesyge in Norway, saltfluss in Sweden, skerljevo in the Balkans) may have been etiological variants on their sexual cousin.[189] In rural nineteenth-century Russia (continuing into twentieth-century Soviet Buryatiya) syphilis was equally regarded as a disease of noxious living conditions and filthy habits. Bulkley, writing his standard work on syphilis insontium in the 1890s, thought that transmission through shared use of utensils was still common among the rural and poorer classes of Europe.[190] By the twentieth century, the fear had shifted to infection through the communal use of various items, whether eating utensils or toilet seats, in a way that in our own day has been largely eradicated by the massive application of disinfection and disposability. In the twentieth century, nonvenereal syphilis is regarded as a common childhood ailment in some Middle Eastern, Asian and African nations with poor socioeconomic conditions and primitive sanitary arrangements, spread largely through direct contact with infectious skin lesions.[191] Sexually transmitted diseases were thus created as a separate and especially stig-

---

[188] Even so, VD spreads in ways that are hard to classify as either sexual or not: consider the story of a Hussar who fell from his horse, suffering a wound to the forehead, was subsequently infected through a prostitute's kiss to the same spot and sought compensation for his injuries as work-related (rejected, since he had neglected to have the wound expertly treated). Or that of the French cavalier who, following digital hankypanky with women of indifferent morals, took some snuff and eventually lost part of his nose to a chancre. Sexual or not?: J. Jadassohn, ed., *Handbuch der Haut- und Geschlechtskrankheiten* (Berlin, 1931), v. XXIII, pp. 105–26; *Annales de dermatologie et de syphiligraphie*, 4, 9 (1908), p. 601.

[189] *ZBGK*, 20, 5/6/7 (1922), p. 100; Kenneth F. Kiple, ed., *The Cambridge World History of Human Disease* (Cambridge, 1993), p. 1034; P. Frederick Sparling, "Natural History of Syphilis," in King K. Holmes et al., eds. *Sexually Transmitted Diseases* (New York, 1984), p. 298; Ellis H. Hudson, *Treponematosis* (New York, 1946), pp. 92ff.; Charlotte Roberts and Keith Manchester, *The Archaeology of Disease* (2nd edn.; Ithaca, 1995), pp. 150–59.

[190] Laura Engelstein, *The Keys to Happiness: Sex and the Search for Modernity in Fin-de-Siècle Russia* (Ithaca, 1992), ch. 5; Susan Gross Solomon, "The Soviet–German Syphilis Expedition to Buriat Mongolia, 1928: Scientific Research on National Minorities," *Slavic Review*, 52, 2 (Summer 1993), pp. 221–23; Karl Wilmanns, *Lues, Lamas, Leninisten: Tagebuch einer Reise durch Russland in die Burjatische Republik im Sommer 1926* (Pfaffenweiler, 1995), pp. 284, 296; Edward B. Vedder, *Syphilis and Public Health* (Philadelphia, 1918), pp. 29–30; Bulkley, *Syphilis in the Innocent*, p. 143; Bloch, *Das Sexualleben unserer Zeit*, pp. 403, 440.

[191] A. Ravogli, *Syphilis in Its Medical, Medico-Legal and Sociological Aspects* (New York, 1907), p. 441; *La prophylaxie antivénérienne*, 1, 1 (1929), pp. 589–93; Elizabeth Fee, "Sin Versus Science: Venereal

matized class of illness not only by a sense of the sinfulness of sex, but equally by the triumph of personal hygiene that eventually left venereal contact as their predominant mode of transmission. Erasmus, for example, that alleged purveyor of civilized habits, dismissed the effectiveness of castrating syphilitics to curb the spread of disease with the consideration that kissing, touching and sharing drinking cups were equally dangerous.[192] Nature, to put it bluntly, knows no sexually transmitted diseases.

Nor was it only in Scandinavia that measures approximating general inspections were found. Indeed, looking backwards from the first half of the nineteenth century, the Scandinavian approach was not unusual. Analogous precautions had been common or at least considered across Europe. The principle of applying similar strictures to VD as other contagious diseases and of subjecting all infected citizens, not just prostitutes and other narrowly selected categories, to the same measures was an approach systematized first by the Scandinavians, but hardly one they had invented. Initial precautions against VD in the late fifteenth and early sixteenth centuries throughout Europe had often aimed not at prostitutes, but larger groups of infected, sometimes all. From 1496 some Swiss cantons isolated all syphilitics, forbidding them from appearing in public. Two years earlier, the Parlement of Paris had banished all stricken foreigners, sequestering others in their homes, housing the homeless in special institutions. In Troyes all infected were driven from the city and elsewhere (Bern, Prague, Würzburg, Bamberg) they were isolated much like lepers. In Scotland, quarantine and isolation were employed against syphilitics early in the sixteenth century.[193] In France proposals were advanced early in the nineteenth century that struck most of the themes characteristic of the Scandinavian approach: treating VD like other diseases, isolating and requiring treatment of the infected, criminalizing transmission, tracing contacts, improving access to medical care. During the eighteenth century, various categories of men, not just the women they frequented, had been kept under police

---

Disease in Twentieth-Century Baltimore," in Fee and Daniel M. Fox, eds., *AIDS: The Burdens of History* (Berkeley, 1988), p. 122; Abram S. Benenson, ed., *Control of Communicable Diseases in Man* (15th edn.; Washington DC, 1990), p. 426.

[192] Ellis Herndon Hudson, *Non-Venereal Syphilis: A Sociological and Medical Study of Bejel* (Edinburgh, 1958), pp. 4, 9; Rolf Winau, "Amors vergiftete Pfeile: Die Lektionen der Syphilis," *Kursbuch*, 94 (1988), p. 115.

[193] Finger et al., *Handbuch der Geschlechtskrankheiten*, v. I, p. 122; v. III, p. 2672; Parent-Duchatelet, *De la prostitution*, v. II, p. 49; Oriel, *Scars of Venus*, p. 11; Georg Sticker, *Abhandlungen aus der Seuchengeschichte und Seuchenlehre* (Giessen, 1908), v. I/1, p. 87; Mahood, *Magdalenes*, pp. 20–21.

surveillance: foreigners, notorious libertines, debauched priests. In Brest during the 1830s, not just prostitutes, but also soldiers, sailors and workers in the arsenal were inspected monthly.[194] In Germany, clients, not only prostitutes, had long been the object of precautions. Regulations from Hamburg during the 1760s held men equally liable for committing crimes of the flesh. The Berlin brothel regulations of 1792 punished prostitutes for infecting their customers, but if they could identify the source of their disease among the johns, he was fined or jailed and made to bear medical costs. Both the ALR and the 1835 Prussian regulation punished those, male or female, who knowingly transmitted VD.[195] Solutions reminiscent of the Swedish were also tried in Prussia early in the nineteenth century. The wide dissemination of syphilis following the Napoleonic wars prompted a crackdown on urban brothels and special techniques in the countryside of surveilling and reporting VD focused on all diseased, prostitutes or otherwise, requiring treatment. In Berlin, infected men as well as women arriving at the Charité were interrogated as to the source of their disease, with the police inspecting both stricken prostitutes and the men of the laboring classes who were the origin of their ailments.[196]

Nonetheless, all nuances aside, VD was still, during the early nineteenth century, regarded differently in Scandinavia than elsewhere in Europe, seen more in the nonvenereal fashion that had in the meantime faded in other latitudes. To the south, syphilis, because more concentrated in cities, not as widespread and less transmitted through nonsexual contacts, was considered a more exclusively venereal disease, fraught with its attendant stigma, and the possibility of imposing the universal

---

[194] *Annales*, 2/5 (1856), pp. 23–51, 59; Benabou, *La prostitution et la police des moeurs au XVIIIe siècle*, pp. 112–25; Louis Fiaux, *L'armée et la police des moeurs* (Paris, n.d. [1918?]), p. 211; Jeannel, *De la prostitution*, p. 359.

[195] William W. Sanger, *The History of Prostitution* (New York, 1859), p. 191; Augustin, *Preussische Medicinalverfassung*, v. I, pp. 188–89; ALR II 20, §1013–15, 1026; *Gesetz-Sammlung*, 1835, 27/1678, §71; Fr. J. Behrend, *Die Prostitution in Berlin und die gegen sie und die Syphilis zu nehmenden Massregeln* (Erlangen, 1850), pp. 29–30.

[196] *Archiv für Syphilis und Hautkrankheiten*, 1 (1846), pp. 276–77; Augustin, *Preussische Medicinalverfassung*, v. I, pp. 761–65; Jadassohn, *Handbuch der Haut- und Geschlechtskrankheiten*, v. XXIII, p. 37; *Zeitschrift für die Staatsarzneikunde*, 42 (1841), pp. 93–94. For similar approaches, see *Wochenschrift für die gesammte Heilkunde*, 31 (3 August 1850), pp. 486–87; *Zeitschrift für die Staatsarzneikunde*, 58 (1849), pp. 468–71; Acton, *Prostitution*, p. 138; Gerd Göckenjahn, "Syphilisangst und Politik mit Krankheit," *Sozialwissenschaftliche Sexualforschung*, 2 (1989), pp. 53–54. Such early sexual egalitarianism was the result of an indifference to gender and a preoccupation with class and status. The authorities were less interested in the sex of those reported than their station. If the source was of high rank, including officers in the military, they were left alone on the assumption that they would seek treatment on their own. But on the other hand, gender was important in that sources of infection were often left alone if male, since men, for anatomical reasons, were thought to have little desire for more sex until cured.

measures instituted in Scandinavia was ruled out here. In Germany early in the century, for example, although syphilis was seen as a primarily venereal disease, the fear of transmission through everyday contacts was much more urgent than would later be the case. Besides sex, there remained an impressive catalogue of common, but risky interactions: birth, wetnursing, circumcision and, above all, the common use of potentially transmitting objects, trousers, towels, sponges, syringes, glasses, spoons, pipes and wind instruments. The solution, other than avoiding sex with the stricken, was therefore also to exercise care in general social intercourse with potentially infectious persons.[197] In France during the late eighteenth century, to take another step toward a more singularly venereal approach, syphilis was regarded as a disease transmitted foremost through sex and primarily an urban ailment, only now being spread also to the countryside by metropolitan infants placed with wetnurses and brought home by rural seasonal workers in the cities.[198]

The peculiarities of VD epidemiology in Scandinavia thus gave rise to sanitary statism. Since syphilis was thought to be a widespread, endemic disease in the countryside, passed in large measure through everyday contacts, only secondarily a venereal illness and certainly not one transmitted primarily via a professional urban class of prostitutes, general inspections made sense in a predominantly rural nation like Sweden of the early nineteenth century. However little you might like them, as one observer put it, once VD was endemic the only means of eradication were such blanket examinations.[199] Because VD was regarded as an endemic and only incidentally venereal disease in the countryside, the stigma of sexual transmission was not yet felt here with the full force it would later assume. Mass and general inspections, though not treated with insouciance, were therefore not as embarrassing, discomforting or likely to be resisted as would have been the case later and elsewhere when and where syphilis was seen as essentially venereal.[200]

---

[197] Finger et al., *Handbuch der Geschlechtskrankheiten*, v. III, p. 2707; "Belehrung über ansteckende Krankheiten," *Anhang zur Gesetz-Sammlung*, 1835, Beilage B zu No. 27 gehörig, p. 38; Alfons Fischer, *Geschichte des deutschen Gesundheitswesens* (Berlin, 1933), v. II, p. 574.

[198] Claude Quétel, "Syphilis et politiques de santé a l'époque moderne," *Histoire, économie et société*, 3, 4 (1984), pp. 554–55; Claude Quétel, *History of Syphilis* (Baltimore, 1990), p. 105. In contrast, in Germany, it was still possible a century later to regard syphilis as a threat emanating from the countryside with the mass immigration to cities of people with raw customs and habits: Ströhmberg, *Bekämpfung der ansteckenden Geschlechtskrankheiten*, pp. 40–41.

[199] *Preste*, 1817–18, v. 3, 4 April 1818, p. 418.

[200] The endemic spread of syphilis, as Corbin observes, deculpabilizes the victim: Alain Corbin, "La grande peur de la syphilis," in Jean-Pierre Bardet et al., eds., *Peurs et terreurs face à la contagion* (Paris, 1988), p. 335.

What sort of honor was at stake, the parliamentary committee considering objections against general inspections to the effect that they violated the dignity of worthy citizens asked skeptically in 1818, if it had to be bought at the cost of health and wellbeing of those who would otherwise be infected? VD was considered more like a normal contagious disease in the Swedish countryside than elsewhere and tactics like those used against other ailments were therefore possible.[201] Another factor in the willingness to accept general inspections of all citizens arose from the communal mentality of agrarian society. In 1817, a proposal was debated to allow the local clergy to decide, when faced with an epidemic of VD, whether to inspect only those suspected of infection or the entire community. The arguments in favor of investing them with powers of universal compulsory genital inspection suggested that it would provoke more resentment to have individual examinations of the suspected (in the unlikely event that they would even be reported by their fellow villagers) than to subject all to an unpleasant but necessary precaution.[202] Once again, the universalism of Scandinavian political instinct turns out to have a peasantist basis.

Not until the century was well along, as the nation began to urbanize, as rural folk adopted the hygienic habits of their city cousins, thereby restricting transmission to sexual contacts, and as a class of professional metropolitan prostitutes found the clientele for fulltime work, did mass examinations cease being the strategy of choice, did regulation gain in plausibility. Early in the nineteenth century, prostitutes did not exist as a separate class in the countryside, where commercial sex was purveyed by women who otherwise worked in (sometimes peripatetic) establishments of amusement and refreshment.[203] But by the 1830s at the latest, VD was becoming identified as an issue especially in Stockholm, where many unemployed persons drifted, leading in the official analysis to increased immorality and its attendant venereological consequences. In 1841, recognizing that VD was a particular problem here, the tax underwriting hospitalization was raised to twelve skilling for Stockholm, while limited elsewhere to a maximum of five. By the early twentieth century, the Swedes were proudly and chauvinistically including themselves among the cultured nations of central and western Europe where VD was primarily an urban problem, not widespread in the countryside, while in

---

[201] *Bihang*, 1817–18, Besvärs- och Ekonomi-Utskotts Betänk. 123, p. 818; Finger et al., *Handbuch der Geschlechtskrankheiten*, v. III, p. 2706.   [202] *Preste*, 1817–18, v. 3, 4 April 1818, pp. 413, 419–20.

[203] "Whore" was the term then used to refer to unmarried mothers, who were distinguished in peasant custom by various articles of dress and subject to ostracization: Jonas Frykman, *Horan i bondesamhället* (Lund, 1977), p. 9 and passim; *Underdånigt betänkande angående könssjukdomarnas spridning*, v. I, pp. 184, 343.

more backward areas, Russia and the Balkans, the reverse remained true.[204]

Scandinavia was thus unusual not only in the development of a general inspection system early in the nineteenth century. While such techniques had been employed on an ad hoc basis elsewhere as well, the Swedes were the first to systematize them. More striking, however, was the manner in which, once the era of regulation and its narrow focus on prostitution had passed, the Swedes returned to the fundamentals of this earlier strategy in the new system of sanitary statism. The Scandinavians knew well that their approach was unusual and pathbreaking. Such reforms, especially in latecomer Sweden, were passed at the dawn of the era when Scandinavia in general, Sweden in particular, began to be viewed by much self-consciously progressive opinion elsewhere in Europe and North America as a social laboratory for experiments in a third way between the extremes of capitalism and communism.[205] The Scandinavians themselves trumpeted their achievements in these respects and foreign observers joined in this chorus of exultation.[206] The perfection of the Nordic approach was a common theme, for here the state had been willing to intervene decisively in protection of the community from disease, here matters (in the loftiest of accounts) had been taken to the endpoint of historical development.[207] Similar strategies were advocated at home and German reformers in particular followed Nordic developments with emulative interest.[208] Abolitionists, needless to say, approved of this

---

[204] *Hygiea*, 9, 3 (March 1847), pp. 178–89; *SFS*, 1841/35; *Underdånigt betänkande angående könssjukdomarnas spridning*, v. I, pp. 50, 88, 91; *ZBGK*, 5, 7 (1906), p. 256. This was the case even though, by the early twentieth century, Sweden, Finland and Russia were among the only nations still to allow VD inspections of all inhabitants of a specific area and examinations of certain, usually itinerant, occupations suspected of being vectors.

[205] Arne Ruth, "The Second New Nation: The Mythology of Modern Sweden," in Stephen R. Graubard, ed., *Norden: The Passion for Equality* (Oslo, 1986).

[206] *Förhandlingar*, 1912, p. 478; Hilding Bergstrand, *Svenska Läkaresällskapet 150 år: Dess tillkomst och utveckling* (Lund, 1958), p. 294; Erik Pontoppidan, *What Venereal Diseases Mean and How to Prevent Them: Five Lectures Given at the University of Copenhagen* (London, n.d. [1903?]), pp. 53–54; *ZBGK*, 18, 1 (1917), p. 12; 18, 9 (1917/18), p. 230; Albert Neisser, *Die Geschlechtskrankheiten und ihre Bekämpfung* (Berlin, 1916), p. 61; *Mitteilungen*, 15, 3/4 (1917), p. 51; Sybil Neville-Rolfe, *Social Biology and Welfare* (London, 1949), p. 175; Louis Fiaux, *Le délit pénal de contamination intersexuelle* (Paris, 1907), p. 18.

[207] Laupheimer, *Der strafrechtliche Schutz*, p. 70; Hans Haustein, *Geschlechtskrankheiten und Prostitution in Skandinavien* (Berlin, 1925), p. 2; Thomas Parran, *Shadow on the Land: Syphilis* (New York, 1937), ch. 5; Abraham Flexner, *An Autobiography* (New York, 1960), pp. 122–23; *Annales*, 4/20 (1913), p. 386; *La prophylaxie antivénérienne*, 1, 1 (1929), pp. 604–06; Vigarello, *Le sain et le malsain*, p. 228.

[208] [F. Germann], *Vorschläge zur Abwehr der Syphilis und zur Milderung ihrer Folgen* (Leipzig, 1872), pp. 24–29; Kromayer, *Zur Austilgung der Syphilis*, pp. 70–76; *ZBGK*, 19, 3 (1919), pp. 69, 83; 6, 4 (1907), p. 113; 15, 6 (1914), p. 212; 18, 2/3 (1917), p. 48; Dolléans, *La police des moeurs*, pp. 136, 148–50; *Annales*, 4/34 (1920), p. 369; Allan M. Brandt, *No Magic Bullet: A Social History of Venereal Disease in the United States Since 1880* (expanded edn.; New York, 1987), p. 140.

end to regulation and the shift to new preventive techniques.[209] But others pointed out that Scandinavian measures went far beyond the strictures of regulationism, at least for those who were not prostitutes. Even abolitionists, one warned, should consider whether they preferred the fire of the Scandinavian system to the frying pan of regulationism.[210] One French observer described the Scandinavian approach as the ultimate extension of regulationism, a system which brought all citizens, not just prostitutes, under its wing. Many recognized full well that sanitary statism was possible only in a polity informed by a consensus granting the state unprecedented powers to enforce common interests even at the expense of individual rights, an approach occasionally described as absolutist.[211] Nor did such compulsion seem to lower the incidence of disease, compared at least to voluntarist Britain.[212]

In a way that would become increasingly familiar during the subsequent decades, the Scandinavians had thus struck out in their own social policy direction, bringing in this case a novel prophylactic strategy to bear on an old foe. They agreed with abolitionists that regulation was unfair and ineffective in its focus on one particular occupational group, however commandeeringly it may at one time have straddled the pathways of transmission. But they equally disagreed with the Butlerites, for whom abolition was satisfied with repeal. Bringing regulation to a close, far from ending the state's role in the fight against VD, was to extend it. The state in the Scandinavian system was to take up the cause with greater powers and more intimate interventions than regulationists had ever dared propose. All citizens who might pose epidemiological risks were now subject to measures much like those which had earlier governed the actions of prostitutes alone.

<hr />

[209] BA, 15.01, RmdI, 11892, p. 28, Württembergischer Landesausschuss zur Bekämpfung sittlicher Not an den Deutschen Reichstag, April 1922.

[210] BA, 15.01, RmdI, 11866, p. 31, Reichs-Gesundheitsrat, 1908, Kirchner "Massnahmen zur Bekämpfung der Geschlechtskrankheiten im Deutschen Reiche"; Neisser, *Geschlechtskrankheiten und ihre Bekämpfung*, p. 244; Finger et al., *Handbuch der Geschlechtskrankheiten*, v. III, p. 2709; *ZBGK*, 6, 3 (1907), p. 86.

[211] Dolléans, *La police des moeurs*, p. 137; Fiaux, *L'intégrité intersexuelle*, p. 112; Fiaux, *La police des moeurs en France*, v. I, pp. cv–cvi; Regnault, *L'évolution de la prostitution*, p. 273; Hans Carlheinz Sennhenn, "Die Bekämpfung der Geschlechtskrankheiten in Skandinavien, England, Frankreich, Italien u. USA unter besonderer Berücksichtigung der neueren Ergebnisse und Bestrebungen" (diss., Munich, 1939), pp. 18–19; *Annales*, 4/34 (1920), pp. 367–69; 4/20 (1913), pp. 386, 415–16.

[212] L. W. Harrison et al., *Report on Anti-Venereal Measures in Certain Scandinavian Countries and Holland* (London, 1938), p. 120.

NEOREGULATIONISM

Abolitionism left an imprint even in those nations which did not repeal regulation. The success of the movement, combined with the increasingly evident shortcomings of the old system, prompted reconsideration in all countries. Although reform had been mooted for decades, it was only toward the end of the century that regulationists began to adapt to new circumstances. Organizations were founded to channel the debate on reform, the SFPSM in 1901, the Deutsche Gesellschaft zur Bekämpfung der Geschlechtskrankheiten the following year.[213] Those willing to accept reform of the inherited system, the neoregulationists, conceded the justice of many abolitionist criticisms: that it was unnecessarily harsh and concerned to punish prostitutes at the expense of assuring their health; that its targets were largely arbitrary; that, creating a pariah class of official whores, it hampered the return of registered women to normal life; that, failing to encompass more than a fraction of all prostitutes or risky sexual activity, it could not possibly achieve its own goals. Regulation, though not perfect, deserved reform rather than the scrapheap. Neoregulationists were willing to recognize that VD was a contagious disease like others whose prevention, divested of moral opprobrium, should employ similar techniques. Although prostitutes were still to be regulated, the focus of intervention should be hygienic, not moral or punitive. Microbes, not sin, were the enemy. Regulation was to become primarily a sanitary and only secondarily a police measure.[214]

The system was to be legally normalized so that, no longer the province of administrative fiat, it received a clearly defined basis in law. This necessarily raised the question of prostitution's legal standing.[215] A central tenet of the old system was that prostitution should be controlled, but not prohibited. Many neoregulationists now sought instead to criminalize acts associated with prostitution, both in hopes of limiting its public manifestations, but equally in order to regularize its legal situation.

[213] *Annales*, 2/4 (1855), pp. 309–12; 2/5 (1856), pp. 23–269; Parent-Duchatelet, *De la prostitution*, v. II, pp. 491–93; *Annales des maladies vénériennes*, 1 (1906), pp. 201–02; Silber, *Womit sind die ansteckenden Geschlechtskrankheiten zu bekämpfen?*, p. 50; Siegfried Borelli et al., eds., *Geschichte der Deutschen Gesellschaft zur Bekämpfung der Geschlechtskrankheiten* (Berlin, 1992); Lutz Sauerteig, *Krankheit, Sexualität, Gesellschaft: Geschlechtskrankheiten und Gesundheitspolitik in Deutschland im 19. und frühen 20. Jahrhundert* (Stuttgart, 1998), ch. 3.
[214] Mignot, *Péril vénérien*, p. 153; *Bulletin*, 2, 17 (1887), p. 597; Neisser, *Geschlechtskrankheiten und ihre Bekämpfung*, p. 62; *ZBGK*, 5, 6 (1906), p. 222; *Deutsche medicinische Wochenschrift*, 16 (1893), pp. 385–86.
[215] Corbin, *Women for Hire*, pp. 100ff., 253; *ZBGK*, 1, 3 (1903), pp. 322–24; Blaschko, *Syphilis und Prostitution*, pp. 152–53.

Tolerated and dealt with only incidentally in law, regulated prostitution was at the mercy of the vice squad's informal and potentially arbitrary decisions. Neoregulationist attempts to criminalize behavior associated with prostitution were motivated by hopes of establishing in law the nature of the crime and the consequences of its pursuit. In France, proposals by Fournier in the Academy of Medicine in 1888, and subsequent attempts at legal implementation at the hands of Berry, Bérenger and others, sought to outlaw solicitation, aiming thereby to target the (neo)regulationist mechanism at those women who actually sold their favors, whether registered or not in the old sense, and to assure public order and propriety by suppressing overt manifestations of the sex trade. Prohibiting solicitation criminalized the action and not the person; it meant making behavior that could be defined in law, rather than the ad hoc judgments of the vice squad, the basis for prosecution and promised to restrict police interventions to the residual function of ensuring public decency.[216]

Beyond this largely unobjectionable level of reform, neoregulationism sparked controversy. Since the vendors of sex were not the only carriers, since the number of infected men was vast and since they were more likely to spread VD beyond the realm of whoredom, some neoregulationists proposed shifting the focus from prostitutes exclusively, paying equal attention to all who might transmit illness. All who were tempted by potentially risky sexual behavior – male or female, gaudy streetcorner hooker and bespectacled family father – should be subject to sanitary precautions. As a preliminary step, it was proposed to extend medical inspections from prostitutes also to their clients and, more generally, to promiscuous men.[217] Such ideas, long advanced, were now given a serious hearing. Medical examinations of johns as well as prostitutes had been advocated at least since the eighteenth century. In 1850 Diday had proposed inspecting all brothel clients, issuing a dated card noting some physical peculiarity so that prostitutes might check that bearer and holder of the card were one and the same.[218] Later in the

---

[216] *Bulletin*, 3, 19 (1888), pp. 297, 415–44; 2, 17 (1887), pp. 592–637; Fiaux, *La prostitution réglementée*, pp. 142–43, 149, 323–26, 336–39; Fiaux, *Police des moeurs*, v. I, pp. 235–36; Corbin, *Women for Hire*, pp. 255–56, 317–18; Jean-Pierre Machelon, *La république contre les libertés? Les restrictions aux libertés publiques de 1879 à 1914* (Paris, 1976), p. 195.
[217] *Underdånigt betänkande angående könssjukdomarnas spridning*, v. I, pp. 69–70; *ZBGK*, 2, 8 (1903/04), pp. 322ff.; 1, 3 (1903), pp. 176, 322–24; 4, 1 (1905), p. 58; Dolléans, *La police des moeurs*, pp. 108–16.
[218] Johann Valentin Müller, *Praktisches Handbuch der medicinischen Galanteriekrankheiten* (Marburg, 1788), p. 66; *DVöG*, 1 (1869), pp. 379–80; *ZBGK*, 2, 1 (1903), p. 19; *Annales*, 2/4 (1855), pp. 309–13; *PP* 1866 (200) xi, 523, p. v.

century inspections of potentially infectious men were advocated, with (in one case) brothel clients caught in flagrante who refused to appear for examination to be humiliated by posting their photograph at the scene of their transgression. In 1902 Neisser proposed controlling and issuing cards to clients as well as prostitutes.[219] John Stuart Mill considered genital inspections less degrading for men than women and eminently doable. Others, in contrast, feared that imposing the military's genital-parade techniques on civilians would shame brothel customers, while in Italy inspection techniques involving curtains (in Germany little holes) that revealed only the organs at issue were proposed to avoid any unnecessary affront to modesty.[220]

That all men of certain categories should be subject to VD inspections was an idea long in circulation. Soldiers and sailors, both naval and merchant, were obvious candidates for attention, but other groups were also envisioned: prisoners and vagabonds, recipients of public assistance, workers in large factories, government employees, prospective civil servants, applicants for admission to universities or certain professions.[221] Health certificates testifying to the absence of syphilis should, in certain proposals, be required for a variety of endeavors: marriage, inheritance, action in a court of law, savings accounts, voting as an elector and application for passports and hunting licenses.[222] Although such recommendations had occasionally and sporadically been instituted early in the century, outside Scandinavia generalized inspections did not take root. Examinations of broad categories of civilians having disappeared, they were rejected later in the century as violating the rights of citizens who presented no particular venereal threat. The common conclusion was that, whatever theoretical reasons spoke for subjecting johns and other men also to inspections, in practice the results were unpromising. The average male would refuse precoital genital

---

[219] Wilhelm Rudeck, *Syphilis und Gonorrhoe vor Gericht: Die sexuellen Krankheiten in ihrer juristischen Tragweite nach der Rechtsprechung Deutschlands, Österreichs und der Schweiz* (2nd edn.; Berlin, 1902), p. 88; *PP* 1871 (c. 408-1) xix, 29, p. liii; *ZBGK*, 1, 4 (1903), p. 359; Lundquist, *Den disciplinerade dubbelmoralen*, p. 85.

[220] *PP* 1871 (c. 408-1) xix, 29, p. lx; Max von Niessen, *Womit sind die ansteckenden Geschlechtskrankheiten als Volksseuche im Deutschen Reiche wirksam zu bekämpfen?* (Hamburg, 1903), p. 30; Gibson, *Prostitution and the State*, p. 176; Stamm, *Verhütung der Ansteckungen*, p. 71.

[221] Lande, *Les affections vénériennes*, pp. 93–94; Pappenheim, *Handbuch der Sanitäts-Polizei*, v. II, pp. 239–49; Eulenberg, *Handbuch des öffentlichen Gesundheitswesens*, v. I, p. 458; [Germann], *Vorschläge zur Abwehr der Syphilis*, p. 29; Jeannel, *De la prostitution*, p. 358; Gibson, *Prostitution and the State*, p. 176; F. Oppert, *Visceral and Hereditary Syphilis with Special Reference to Measures of Public Hygiene* (London, 1868), pp. 96–98; H. Mireur, *La syphilis et la prostitution* (2nd edn.; Paris, 1888), pp. 73ff.

[222] *Annales*, 2/4 (1855), p. 313; 2/5 (1856), pp. 56–61; Alfred N. Baer, *Die Hygiene der Syphilis, ihre Prophylaxe und Behandlung* (Berlin, 1891), pp. 32–37.

inspections in brothels, seeking gratification elsewhere. The inspections, like those of prostitutes, would at best be cursory and no competent physician would undertake the work of venereal doorkeeper in a brothel, a *Schankerspion*.[223]

Although neoregulationism in its most heroic formulations was tempted by the generalized sanitary surveillance of the Scandinavian systems, its heart never strayed from a preoccupation with prostitutes. Neoregulationists held fast to the cardinal tenet of the old system, that whores were the epidemiological bottleneck at which transmission could most effectively be throttled. Whatever other reforms may have diffused the exclusive focus on prostitutes, female merchants of sex still remained the main object of statutory concern. Far from easing the state's control of commercial copulation, the aim was to make it more effective, ensuring that more prostitutes were brought under a reformed version of surveillance. Criminalizing solicitation, for instance, promised to expand the ranks of those liable to arrest. The ambition was to extend sanitary surveillance from the formally registered to all who sold sex even on an occasional basis and the hope that, by making such measures less onerous than earlier, fewer would seek to exempt themselves.[224] Prostitutes of one variety or another remained at the center of even neoregulationist endeavors.

Though they could be found in all European nations, neoregulationists were naturally best represented where the old system remained in effect. In France such ideas, formulated by Alfred Fournier and Léon Le Fort, came to first fruition in a major and protracted debate in the Academy of Medicine in 1887–88, whose outcome put the physicians on record in favor of a moderate form of neoregulationism.[225] In the standard French manner, however, the ideological wrangles were interminable, the practical results meager. Stiffnecked resistance from the old guard continued in subsequent decades to block change before the First World War and regulation enjoyed a continued existence largely untroubled by reform well into the twentieth century. The only immediate result of the Academy's ruminations was to have vice squad medical personnel recruited competitively, no longer at the prefect's discretion.

[223] Blaschko, *Syphilis und Prostitution*, pp. 127–30; *SFPSM: Bulletin mensuel* (1902), p. 153; Proksch, *Vorbauung der venerischen Krankheiten*, p. 31; Walch, *Ausführliche Darstellung*, pp. 239–41; Dubois-Havenith, *Conférence internationale: Rapports préliminaires*, v. I/1, quest. 6, p. 12; Oppert, *Visceral and Hereditary Syphilis*, pp. 96–98; Dolléans, *La police des moeurs*, p. 109.

[224] *ZBGK*, 1, 3 (1903), pp. 163–64; Dubois-Havenith, *Conférence internationale: Rapports préliminaires*, v. I/1, quest. 2, Fiaux, p. 18; *La syphilis* (1904), p. 700; *Bulletin*, 3, 19 (1888), pp. 291–92; Neisser, *Geschlechtskrankheiten und ihre Bekämpfung*, p. 240.　　　[225] *Bulletin*, 3/19 (1888).

Attempts at reform during the 1890s died in both the Paris Municipal Council and the Assembly.[226] In 1894 Bérenger pressed the Senate to outlaw solicitation, limiting venereal transactions in public. The following year, a version passed here, truncated by regulationists, that remained satisfied with punishing pimps, procurers, bar owners and others in the prostitutive helping professions, dealt with minors and outlawed various forms of public obscenity. Never debated, the bill was condemned by opposition to a Sisyphean cycle of roundtrips to the Chamber over the following decades, while only those parts dealing with obscene drawings and writings became part of a revision of the law of 2 August 1882 on such matters. The elaborate reforms proposed by the extraparliamentary commission appointed by Combes in 1903 found their only fruit in a 1908 law limiting the inscription of minors, while other attempts at change during the prewar period came to naught.[227]

FASTIGIUM

Nineteenth-century Europe was the locus classicus of prostitution. Social conditions conspired to increase both demand and supply, making commercial sex an everyday feature of metropolitan life. The reduction of the overall need for female labor in the early phases of the industrial revolution, migrations from the countryside, the overabundance of women in retail, the needle trades and domestic service, the demographic surplus left behind by emigration to the new world: such factors left too many women chasing too few economic and nuptial prospects, swelling the supply of prostitution.[228] Social custom and sexual habits conspired to strengthen the demand. The disparity between social convention and biological imperative was particularly marked during this period, the more so the higher the social class. The advanced age of marriage, as middle-class men underwent prolonged educations and accumulated the capital required to spare future wives the need to work, combined with the double standard and the pedestalization of women,

---

[226] *La syphilis* (1904), p. 693; *Annales des maladies vénériennes*, 1 (1906), pp. 201–02; Harsin, *Policing Prostitution*, pp. 338–39; Fiaux, *Police des moeurs*, v. I, p. 701; Corbin, *Women for Hire*, p. 317.

[227] Fiaux, *La prostitution réglementée*, pp. 142–43, 323–26, 336–39; Corbin, *Women for Hire*, pp. 313–19; Fiaux, *Police des moeurs*, v. I, p. 236; Harsin, *Policing Prostitution*, pp. 330–33, 348; Cavaillon, *Les législations antivénériennes*, pp. 338–40; Machelon, *La république contre les libertés?*, pp. 195–96.

[228] Finnegan, *Poverty and Prostitution*, p. 24; Storch, "Police Control of Street Prostitution," p. 53; Richard J. Evans, "Prostitution, State and Society in Imperial Germany," pp. 106–07; Gibson, *Prostitution and the State*, p. 16; Lynn Abrams, "Prostitutes in Imperial Germany, 1870–1918: Working Girls or Social Outcasts?," in Richard J. Evans, ed., *The German Underworld: Deviants and Outcasts in German History* (London, 1988), pp. 189ff.

meant that many bachelors, seeking sex, could not find it in the class of their nubile ambitions, while the married, often frustrated by the longueurs of bourgeois domesticity, were happy to shop the venereal market for alternatives.[229] The lack of trustworthy contraception kept the ties between sex, reproduction and marriage firmly cemented. Lowering the age of marriage, insisting on continence or abandoning the double standard and permitting women to sow their wild oats – all three possibilities for narrowing the gap between social and instinctual demands were rejected as immoral, impractical or both. The belief that the reproductive drive could be suppressed only at the expense of (at least) male health, along with the conviction that almost any other form of sex was better than masturbation, combined to render prostitution one of the few traversable avenues of male sexual release.[230] At the same time, the VD problem could no longer be linked exclusively to prostitution, at least not in the official sense of regulation. Changes in sexual habits and mores meant that the old system no longer gave access to an epidemiologically significant amount of transmission.[231] Nonmarital relations – whether commercial or nonprofit – became increasingly commonplace for both men and women. In the years spanning the turn of the century, public health authorities were forced to confront a moral evolution that was changing their dilemma from one of prostitution to that of promiscuity.

The problem of VD assumed proportions perceived to be critical at the turn of the century. The first reliable statistical soundings, undertaken during this period, began to reveal its unsuspected dimensions. In Prussia, a census of all in treatment on 30 April 1900 uncovered some 100,000 VD patients, many more than expected. Eight percent of workers in Germany were estimated to be infected each year, 16 percent of shopkeepers and commercial employees and up to a quarter of all

[229] The classic example of this tension between nubility and sex was the "Belgravian Lament," an exchange of letters in the London *Times* of 1861 ostensibly between, on the one hand, the mothers of daughters with difficulties finding men willing to marry them because (such was their accusation) of the increasing competition from "pretty horsebreakers," who were sexually available without making the demands of marriage and, on the other, the eligible bachelors who replied that, in fact, the material expectations for marriage in their class had escalated to the point where wedded life was unaffordable and that their dalliances with women they had no intention of marrying was the result not the cause of these daughters' inability to become engaged: Trevor Fisher, *Prostitution and the Victorians* (Phoenix Mill, 1997), ch. 5; E. M. Sigsworth and T. J. Wyke, "A Study of Victorian Prostitution and Venereal Disease," in Martha Vicinus, ed., *Suffer and Be Still: Women in the Victorian Age* (Bloomington, 1972), p. 85.
[230] Sheldon Watts, *Epidemics and History: Disease, Power and Imperialism* (New Haven, 1997), pp. 139–40.   [231] *Annales*, 2/36 (1871), pp. 292–94; Braus, *Syphilis und ihre steigende soziale Gefahr*, p. 38.

students. In large cities, 10–12 percent of adult males at any given time had syphilis and each man could expect to have gonorrhea at least once in his life. Fournier estimated in 1899 that 17 percent of adult Parisian males were syphilitic. The Royal Commission's report in 1916 startled Britain by revealing that at least a tenth of the urban population was infected with syphilis, many more with gonorrhea.[232] Whether this revealed a worrisome increase or just the continuation of an already severe problem was hard to determine, but clearly such figures provided no basis for relief and insouciance.[233] A widespread belief in the possibility of casual transmission added worrisome emphasis to such figures. Neisser's identification of the gonorrhea microbe in 1879 meant that many instances could now be diagnosed even in the absence of symptoms. The Wassermann test in 1906 held out the promise of a potentially objective marker of disease only to reveal the unexpected extent of syphilis's ravages, with many other ailments now unmasked as ultimately the outcome of its tertiary phases. While Herbert Spencer had been able to oppose the CD Acts forty years previous, convinced that the issue was not sufficiently grave to warrant drastic intervention, Blaschko told the International Congress of Medicine in London in 1913, now more accurate statistics revealed the disturbing dimensions of the problem.[234]

During the last decades of the nineteenth century all European nations heard vigorous debates on a whole constellation of issues, among which prostitution and VD were important, but only partial elements: others included the social relations of the sexes; the nature of the family; the purpose and function of sex in general; the morality of contraception; indecency, cultural degeneration and eugenic decline. Sexuality was endlessly debated: normal and perverse, homo- and

[232] BA, 15.01, RmdI, 11866, p 26, Reichs-Gesundheitsrat, 1908, Kirchner "Massnahmen zur Bekämpfung der Geschlechtskrankheiten im Deutschen Reiche"; Blaschko, *Geschlechtskrankheiten*, pp. 8–11; Silber, *Womit sind die ansteckenden Geschlechtskrankheiten zu bekämpfen?*, p. 33; Borelli et al., *Geschichte der DGBG*, p. 24; XVIIth International Congress of Medicine, *Dermatology and Syphilography*, p. 94; Malcolm Morris, *The Story of English Public Health* (London, 1919), p. 135; *Nineteenth Century*, 82 (July–December 1917), p. 582; Sauerteig, *Krankheit, Sexualität, Gesellschaft*, ch. 2/7.

[233] Ulrich Linse, "Über den Prozess der Syphilisation: Körper und Sexualität um 1900 aus ärztlicher Sicht," in Alexander Schuller and Nikolaus Heim, eds., *Vermessene Sexualität* (Berlin, 1987), p. 166; Dubois-Havenith, *Conférence internationale: Compte rendu*, pp. 27–28.

[234] Allan M. Brandt, "AIDS in Historical Perspective: Four Lessons from the History of Sexually Transmitted Diseases," *American Journal of Public Health*, 78, 4 (April 1988), p. 367; *Mitteilungen*, 8 (1910), p. 73; *ZBGK*, 12, 6 (1911), pp. 202–05; John M. Eyler, *Sir Arthur Newsholme and State Medicine, 1885–1935* (Cambridge, 1997), p. 279; XVIIth International Congress of Medicine, *Dermatology and Syphilography*, pp. 37–38, 94; Herbert Spencer, *The Study of Sociology* (New York, 1884), pp. 84–90.

hetero-, pro- or recreational, irrepressible animal instinct or sublimat-
able cultural construct, and so forth.[235] Prostitution became linked
not just with sex and disease, but with more general issues of crime
and social decline. The development of criminology, in the hands of
Tarnowsky, Lombroso, Ferrero and their colleagues, as an intellectual
enterprise with pretensions to scientific rigor and academic respectability focused attention on the prostitute as the female counterpart to male
deviants. Bourgeois fears of the criminal underworld and dangerous
classes came to a boil in debates during the 1890s over the Lex Heinze
in Germany and the light it shed on Wilhelmine Berlin's seamy under-
belly, in the Maiden Tribute scandal of the mid-1880s in London, in the
anxieties over the urban mob provoked in France by Le Bon's work.[236]
The white slave trade issue, endlessly debated in all nations at the turn
of the century, made prostitution, perversion and indecency matters of
international diplomacy, cooperation and legislation. Eugenics, depopulation and contraception were a triad of closely related issues fought
out in terms of each other. The general preoccupation with declining
birthrates (common to all European nations, although especially pronounced among the French) granted the effects of VD in causing ster-
ility and limiting family size particular importance.[237] The popularity
of eugenic ideas made the allegedly degenerative effect of syphilis a
matter of concern.[238] This potent stew of supercharged subjects, com-

[235] A sampling of this groaning intellectual buffet table can be found in Linse, "Über den Prozess
der Syphilisation"; Nye, *Masculinity and Male Codes of Honor*; Elias Bredsdorff, *Den store nordiske krig om
seksualmoralen* ([Copenhagen], 1973); Mason, *Making of Victorian Sexuality*.

[236] Lee H. Bowker, *Women, Crime and the Criminal Justice System* (Lexington, 1978), ch. 2; Ann-Louise
Shapiro, *Breaking the Codes: Female Criminality in Fin-de-Siècle Paris* (Stanford, 1996); Daniel Pick, *Faces
of Degeneration* (Cambridge, 1989).

[237] *Bulletin*, 2, 17 (1887), p. 592; Dubois-Havenith, *Conférence internationale: Rapports préliminaires*, v. I/1,
Fournier, pp. 12–44; *La syphilis* (1904), pp. 659–61; Spillmann, *L'évolution de la lutte*, pp. 78–79; *Hansard*,
1876, v. 230, cols. 1602–03; *PP* 1867–68 (4031) xxxvii, 425, Q 6359; *ZBGK*, 14, 11 (1913), pp. 383–407;
12, 12 (1911/12), p. 421; Max Homburger, *Die strafrechtliche Bedeutung der Geschlechtskrankheiten* (Leipzig,
1910), p. 7; *Vierteljahrsschrift für gerichtliche Medicin und öffentliches Sanitätswesen*, 31 (1906), p. 136. Generally,
see Richard A. Soloway, *Demography and Degeneration: Eugenics and the Declining Birthrate in Twentieth-
Century Britain* (Chapel Hill, 1990); Paul Weindling, *Health, Race and German Politics Between National
Unification and Nazism, 1870–1945* (Cambridge, 1989), pp. 241–48; J. M. Winter, "The Fear of
Population Decline in Western Europe, 1870–1940," in R. W. Hiorns, ed., *Demographic Patterns in
Developed Societies* (London, 1980); J. M. Winter and M. S. Teitelbaum, *The Fear of Population Decline*
(New York, 1985); Richard Wall and Jay Winter, eds., *The Upheaval of War* (Cambridge, 1988), sect.
4; Simon Szreter, *Fertility, Class and Gender in Britain, 1860–1940* (Cambridge, 1996); William H.
Schneider, *Quality and Quantity: The Quest for Biological Regeneration in Twentieth-Century France*
(Cambridge, 1990).

[238] XVIIth International Congress of Medicine, *Dermatology and Syphilography*, p. 38; Robert A.
Nye, *Crime, Madness and Politics in Modern France: The Medical Concept of National Decline* (Princeton,

bining and recombining in volatile compounds, at times brewing into an overarching sense of cultural crisis – an anxious coming to terms with urbanism, technology and modernity in general – obviously extends far beyond the limits of this study. Suffice it to say that such factors helped add urgency and import to the debate over VD and prostitution.

Spicing this already piquant discussion was the question of disease among those who had not engaged in sexual irregularities, syphilis insontium, of the innocent. The regulationist focus on prostitutes as the primary vector had obscured the damage inflicted on the spouses and children of their clients. Ibsen's *Ghosts* and Brieux's *Damaged Goods*, both plays scandalous and popular at the turn of the century, brought the punch of *belles lettres* to the expertise of an otherwise heavily medicalized debate, focusing attention on the suffering families of errant husbands. To counter both the insistence of moralists that VD, as a disease voluntarily risked by fornicators, should not be the focus of precautions at all and regulationism's exclusive focus on prostitutes as the main carriers, reformers sought instead to present syphilis as a public problem that (however reprehensible any individual act of transmission might be) potentially threatened all, even the chaste, monogamous and newly born, one that therefore had consequences for the health and strength of the entire nation. They dwelt at length on nonsexual, or innocently sexual, forms of transmission: as a workplace accident in professions where the oral orifice served as a working member (paperhangers, shoemakers, saddlers, needleworkers and especially glassblowers); as the result of vaccination or tattooing; as something passed between careless barber and client, neglectful physician and patient, unsuspecting spouse and unfaithful partner, infected parent and sinless babe, wetnurse and infant.[239] Up to a fifth of syphilis cases, Bulkley's influential book argued in 1894, were wives infected by misbehaving husbands. Such "innocent" instances helped shift attention away from prostitutes

1984), p. 161; Peter Weingart et al., *Rasse, Blut und Gene: Geschichte der Eugenik und Rassenhygiene in Deutschland* (Frankfurt, 1988), p. 124.

[239] Braus, *Syphilis und ihre steigende soziale Gefahr*, pp. 4–5; Jeannel, *De la prostitution*, pp. 143–44; Baer, *Hygiene der Syphilis*, p. 32; Proksch, *Vorbauung der venerischen Krankheiten*, p. 14; Corbin, "La grande peur de la syphilis," p. 332; *Bulletin*, 3, 56 (1906), p. 190; Neisser, *Geschlechtskrankheiten und ihre Bekämpfung*, p. 4; Homburger, *Die strafrechtliche Bedeutung der Geschlechtskrankheiten*, pp. 10–11; *ZBGK*, 15, 8/9 (1914), p. 280; Lande, *Les affections vénériennes*, p. 12; Dubois-Havenith, ed., *IIe Conférence internationale pour la prophylaxie de la syphilis et des maladies vénériennes: Rapports préliminaires* (Brussels, 1902), v. I, reports by Castelo, Petrini de Galatz, Ramazzotti and Rona.

to the more general problem of VD's dissemination in the population at large.[240]

As the weaknesses of regulation became increasingly obvious and as abolitionism's fervor elevated in pitch, reform was everywhere on the agenda. The Scandinavian nations blazed the trail toward new techniques of fighting old scourges. Neoregulationists strove to change the inherited system in a similar direction, abandoning the exclusive focus on inscribed prostitutes and subjecting more of those who were infected or engaged in risky practices to the same precautions applicable to other ailments. On the continent neoregulationists were increasingly met halfway by a new brand of abolitionists who, rejecting the hyperliberalism of the movement's Butlerite wing and its hands-off approach, were willing to grant the state an important role in the fight. This second generation of abolitionism, which often styled itself scientific, arose at around the turn of the century.[241]

In contrast both to the libertarian arguments that regarded abolitionism's task accomplished with repeal, as well as to the moralists who combined the battle against prostitution with one against extramarital sex and indecency in general, this neoabolitionist wing of the movement advocated firm sanitary, but not moral, intervention by the authorities. The state should not leave matters of sex and disease to individual conscience, nor, however, should it concern itself unduly with ethical issues beyond such bedrock necessities as protecting the young from predation and preserving a modicum of public decency. In Scandinavia, Germany and France this new style of abolition edged out the oldfashioned variety that lingered longer in other nations, Britain, Switzerland and the Netherlands especially.[242] Neoabolitionists often approximated the position of neoregulationists, willing as they were to accept certain statutory interventions to control commercial sex.[243] Thanks to this emerging consensus between neos of both camps, the old system was increasingly seen by many as a lost cause and debate shifted to a new array of prophylac-

[240] Bulkley, *Syphilis in the Innocent*, pp. 28, 109, 202; Quétel, *History of Syphilis*, p. 137; *ZBGK*, 1, 1 (1903), p. 5; 2, 1 (1903), p. 19; Ravogli, *Syphilis*, p. 440; XVIIth International Congress of Medicine, *Dermatology and Syphilography*, p. 95; Dubois-Havenith, *Conférence internationale: Rapports préliminaires*, v. I/1, Fournier, p. 44.

[241] *ZBGK*, 2, 8 (1903/04), pp. 322ff.; 4, 1 (1905), pp. 45–47; Neisser, *Geschlechtskrankheiten und ihre Bekämpfung*, p. 240; Max Flesch and Ludwig Wertheimer, *Geschlechtskrankheiten und Rechtsschutz* (Jena, 1903), pp. 75–76; Malmroth, "Om de smittosamma könssjukdomarnas bekämpande," pp. 175–76; *Journal des maladies cutanées et syphilitiques*, 14, 10 (October 1902), pp. 723–24.

[242] *ZBGK*, 17, 7 (1916), pp. 193–97; Jeanselme, *Traité de la syphilis*, v. I, p. 378; Meyer-Renschhausen, *Weibliche Kultur und soziale Arbeit*, p. 279; *Underdånigt betänkande angående könssjukdomarnas spridning*, v. I, pp. 99–102.   [243] *ZBGK*, 15, 8/9 (1914), pp. 272–75; Dolléans, *La police des moeurs*, p. 184.

tic techniques applicable not just to prostitutes, but to all infected. Up for discussion was a smorgasbord of possibilities that (besides the overarching sorts of reforms – ethical, economic and sanitary – aiming to decrease both demand for and supply of commercial sex) included also more narrowly focused public health interventions: making medical treatment widely and sometimes freely available and in return demanding treatment of the infected; requiring notification of VD and modifying the strictures of physician–patient confidentiality to coopt doctors into the reporting process; tracing and treating contacts; taking precautions against patients whose behavior threatened others with infection; criminalizing the transmission of VD. For a sense of the broad array of strategies now up for discussion and, increasingly, implementation, we may take the most important seriatim.

Least controversial was the proposal that education on the perils of VD be disseminated widely, especially to the young.[244] Attempts were to be made to defuse the stigma and shame of VD, allowing a more detached approach to genital ailments in general. Closely related were efforts to include the study of VD as a standard facet of medical education and to endow chairs of venereology. More disputed, in contrast, was the question whether such enlightenment should extend also to the means of avoiding disease – feared as potentially an encouragement to libertinage – or whether exhortations to chastity and selfcontrol ought to suffice.[245]

CRIMINALIZING TRANSMISSION

One of the techniques considered for its ability to extend the range of sanitary intervention from prostitutes to all citizens who posed epidemiological risks was the criminalization of transmission. Because VD was usually spread through voluntary (however instinctually overdetermined) acts, attaching penalties to its knowing spread made more sense than for diseases like cholera, where individuals had little control over the harm they could wreak, and followed the precedent already set with

---

[244] *Bulletin*, 2, 17 (1887), pp. 635ff.; Fiaux, *Police des mœurs*, v. I, p. cxvi; Spillmann, *L'évolution de la lutte*, ch. 4; G. Archdall Reid, *Prevention of Venereal Disease* (London, 1920), pp. 116–17. Skeptics of the effectiveness of such measures pointed out that physicians, who presumably knew most about VD, were also among the categories with the highest incidence: *Annales des maladies vénériennes*, 1 (1906), p. 126; *Bihang*, 1903, AK, Motion 88, p. 7.

[245] Pappenheim, *Handbuch der Sanitäts-Polizei*, v. II, p. 236; *ZBGK*, 3, 8/9 (1904–05), p. 317; Dubois-Havenith, *Conférence internationale: Rapports préliminaires*, v. I/1, quest. 6, pp. 34–35; *Journal des maladies cutanées et syphilitiques*, 14, 10 (October 1902), p. 803.

smallpox, whose victims were sometimes forbidden to appear in public. Nonetheless, criminalizing transmission of VD could not, it was widely realized, be more than a partial measure and invoking penal sanctions against moral transgressions raised concerns, especially the possibility of blackmail.[246] In practical terms, punishing transmission was more a matter of raising a banner than throwing up an effective palisade against VD's encroachments. Given the stigma of such disease, accusations of infection (and thereby admissions of being afflicted oneself) were rare. With the practical problems of proving cause, knowledge and intent on the part of the perpetrator, convictions were infrequent.[247] Nonetheless, it was argued, if criminal law could not by itself raise the moral tone of society, if punishment did not necessarily breed virtue, at least it would draw a legal line at the limits of acceptable behavior, encourage the sick to be treated (lest they otherwise have the insult of criminal or civil pros-ecution added to the injury of disease) and give the authorities leverage of last resort under recalcitrants who persisted in risky actions.[248] In certain instances (the various German texts, for example, that held pros-titutes liable for infecting their clients) criminalizing transmission was part of regulationism and did not expand the focus of precautions.[249] Moreover, even where criminalization did not aim only at prostitutes, it was clear that, in practice, those most vulnerable to charges were likely to be sexual merchants of one variety or another.[250] Nonetheless, crim-inalizing transmission, as proposed in the context of reforming regula-tionism, was intended to go beyond the narrow focus of the old system, drawing the average citizen, and in particular males, into the ambit of statutory intervention.[251] Abolitionists favored the technique since it

---

[246] *ZBGK*, 1, 1 (1903), pp. 73–74; Lecour, *La prostitution à Paris*, p. 251; *Vorentwurf zu einem Deutschen Strafgesetzbuch* (Berlin, 1909), p. 665.

[247] *ZBGK*, 19, 3 (1919), p. 63; Reid, *Prevention of Venereal Disease*, pp. 17–18; *PP* 1916 (8189) xvi, 1, p. 182; Welander, *Blad ur prostitutionsfrågans historia*, pp. 160–61; *ZBGK*, 15, 1 (1914), pp. 29–30; 1, 1 (1903), p. 5; Laupheimer, *Der strafrechtliche Schutz*, p. 89; Rudeck, *Syphilis und Gonorrhoe vor Gericht*, p. 43; Jadassohn, *Handbuch der Haut- und Geschlechtskrankheiten*, v. XXIII, p. 116; *ZBGK*, 2, 10 (1903/04), pp. 408–09; *Annales*, 4/20 (1913), pp. 418–19.

[248] *ZBGK*, 15, 1 (1914), p. 25. An exemplary case of the sort foreseen by reformers was that of a Swedish cattle trader who, acquiring syphilis in Stockholm, spread it widely back home. Despite being warned by his physician, he continued having sex and was sentenced to jail: *Mitteilungen*, 25, 1 (1927), p. 8.

[249] Blaschko, *Syphilis und Prostitution*, p. 133; *Archiv für Syphilis und Hautkrankheiten*, 1 (1846), p. 274; Behrend, *Prostitution in Berlin*, pp. 20–21; *Zeitschrift für die Staatsarzneikunde*, 58 (1849), pp. 428–54; Augustin, *Preussische Medicinalverfassung*, v. I, pp. 188–89; *Mitteilungen*, 27, 3 (1929), pp. 74–75.

[250] Wobbe, *Gleichheit und Differenz*, pp. 77–78; *Mitteilungen*, 25, 11/12 (1927), p. 129.

[251] Albert Hellwig, *Gesetz zur Bekämpfung der Geschlechtskrankheiten vom 18. Februar 1927* (Munich, 1928), p. 140; *ZBGK*, 1, 1 (1903), pp. 16–18, 74; 3, 8/9 (1904–05), p. 305; Finger et al., *Handbuch der Geschlechtskrankheiten*, v. III, p. 2703; Amos, *Comparative Survey of Laws*, p. 232.

focused on the act, not persons, their gender or profession, and more generally because it formed part of an alternative to regulationism. If nothing else, it promised to punish the results of the old, but stubbornly persistent idea that sleeping with a virgin cured syphilis.[252]

Most nations had legal codes that already allowed both civil and criminal action for bodily harm and VD infection was often accepted as one form this could take. The French penal code, for example, spoke (§§309–11, 319–20) only of blows and wounds as actionable damages, but these concepts had been extended in practice during the century to include disease transmission.[253] In Germany (penal code §§223–31), similar practice had been the case since the late eighteenth century.[254] In conjunction with the Lex Veneris, comparable measures were included in chapter 14 of the Swedish penal code. British law foresaw punishment only for assault occasioning actual bodily harm and this required intention; whether VD transmission could be pursued accordingly was therefore unclear.[255] The German civil code (BGB §823) allowed restitution for damages to body or health, including transmission of VD, and the French equivalent (§§1382–83) had provisions that were eventually interpreted similarly.[256] Discussion now therefore tended to concern, first, whether a prohibition of transmission should be formulated specifically in terms of VD and, more importantly, whether to criminalize not just actual infection, but also mere endangerment. Should the sheer fact of having sex, whether disease resulted or not, implicate infectious lovers who had not informed their partners? One advantage of focusing on endangerment was to sidestep the ticklish problem of having to prove

---

[252] Dolléans, *La police des moeurs*, p. 17; Dubois-Havenith, *Conférence internationale: Enquêtes*, v. I/2, pp. 14–15; *ZBGK*, 17 (1916), pp. 100–01; Brennecke, *Wie ist der Kampf zu führen?*, p. 22; *ZBGK*, 16, 12 (1915/16), p. 370; Hume-Rothery, *Letter Addressed to Gladstone*, p. 11; Stéenhoff, *Den reglementerade prostitution*, p. 27; Laupheimer, *Der strafrechtliche Schutz*, pp. 40–41; Neisser, *Geschlechtskrankheiten und ihre Bekämpfung*, p. 129; *ZBGK*, 11, 2 (1910), p. 64.

[253] *ZBGK*, 1, 1 (1903), p. 4; 11 (1910), p. 29; Laupheimer, *Der strafrechtliche Schutz*, pp. 70–72; Fiaux, *Police des moeurs*, v. I, p. ccxi; Homburger, *Die strafrechtliche Bedeutung der Geschlechtskrankheiten*, pp. 16ff.; *Deutsche medicinische Presse*, 6, 22 (1902), pp. 174–76; Ravogli, *Syphilis*, p. 446.

[254] In Prussia, the ALR (II 20, §§691, 1026) threatened all not living in brothels who had sex knowing that they were infected with jail. The 1835 Prussian regulation emphasized (§71) that the prohibition on transmitting disease applied equally to men and women. Precautions during the Napoleonic wars threatened to punish those who wantonly spread the disease, holding them liable for the costs of cure. The Oldenburg criminal code of 1814 (art. 387) made it illegal to transmit VD: Augustin, *Preussische Medicinalverfassung*, v. I, pp. 762–63; Finger et al., *Handbuch der Geschlechtskrankheiten*, v. III, p. 2703.

[255] Cases of transmission were tried in civil court: *Simpson and Wife* v. *Davey* (1874). See George Vivian Poore, *A Treatise on Medical Jurisprudence* (London, 1901), pp. 47–48.

[256] *ZBGK*, 1, 1 (1903), pp. 28, 91; 2, 1 (1903), p. 28; *Journal de médecine de Paris* (1903), pp. 281–82.

not only that infection had occurred, but that X was the cause of Y's illness. This was often difficult for an ailment with a long incubation period and few symptoms. Moreover, it was hard to avoid probing the details of Y's sexual habits and activities if X's culpability as the source of infection was to be demonstrated and there remained the problem of proving that X knew he was ill at the time of intercourse. On the other hand, endangerment raised the more general issue of the nature of the injury sustained if, in fact, no infection had occurred. How often indeed would the "victim" even be aware of having been trespassed against? With what likelihood would the endangered person brave the stigma of VD to file charges in the absence of actual transmission? By criminalizing every act of sex by the infected, so skeptics worried, the floodgates of denunciation and blackmail would be opened.[257] Despite such hesitations, however, the advantages of endangerment seemed to outweigh the negatives and the ambition of abolitionist and neoregulationist reformers was to punish the act of sex while infected, rather than the fact of infection.

The British lacked specific legislation outlawing transmission. The Act Relating to Offences Against the Person of 1861 dealt with wounds and harm inflicted with or without weapons or other instruments, but, sandwiched between clauses dealing with shooting and strangling, this part did not seem to have foreseen transmission.[258] Proposals to legislate specifically on the matter were heard sporadically, but with little result.[259] When criminalization finally reached the point of serious consideration – forced upon the British at the insistence of their allies during the First

---

[257] *ZBGK*, 11 (1910), p. 205; *Vorentwurf zu einem Deutschen Strafgesetzbuch*, p. 665; Rudeck, *Syphilis und Gonorrhoe vor Gericht*, p. 58; *ZBGK*, 3, 8/9 (1904–05), p. 306; *Deutsche medicinische Wochenschrift*, 16 (1893), pp. 385–86; Neisser, *Geschlechtskrankheiten und ihre Bekämpfung*, p. 134; *Förhandlingar*, 1912, p. 394; *Ärztliche Sachverständigen-Zeitung*, 21, 9 (1 May 1915), p. 99; Fiaux, *Police des moeurs*, v. I, p. 393.

[258] 24 & 25 Vict. c. 100, cl. 20. In *R. v. Clarence* (1886–90) a man who transmitted gonorrhea to his wife was found not guilty of assault under this statute because his wife had (unknowingly) consented to sexual relations, thus overturning the conclusions of an earlier case, *R. v. Bennet* (1866). Alistair Orr, "Legal AIDS: Implications of AIDS and HIV for British and American Law," *Journal of Medical Ethics*, 15 (1989), p. 65; Martha A. Field and Kathleen M. Sullivan, "AIDS and the Criminal Law," *Law, Medicine and Health Care*, 15, 1–2 (Summer 1987), p. 49; Gerald Forlin and Piers Wauchope, "AIDS and the Criminal Law," *Law Society's Gazette*, 84, 12 (25 March 1987), p. 884; Angus Hamilton, "The Criminal Law and HIV Infection," in Richard Haigh and Dai Harris, eds., *AIDS: A Guide to the Law* (2nd edn.; London, 1995), p. 28. The 1861 act did not apply in Scotland.

[259] *Hansard*, 1878, v. 240, col. 475; 1883, v. 280, col. 1837; *PP* 1871 (c. 408) xix, 1, p. 18; *PP* 1875 (97) lxi, 337, p. 343; Malcolm Morris, *The Nation's Health: The Stamping Out of Venereal Disease* (London, 1917), p. 121; *Förhandlingar*, 1912, p. 394; *Journal des maladies cutanées et syphilitiques*, 14, 10 (October 1902), p. 796; McHugh, *Prostitution and Victorian Social Reform*, p. 37; Amos, *Comparative Survey of Laws*, p. 424.

World War – the opposite extreme prevailed and proposals now went far beyond what was in effect elsewhere, undercutting their own prospects by overweening ambition. The Criminal Law Amendment Bill of 1917 (cl. 5) foresaw punishment not only for intercourse while infected but also the very act of soliciting or inviting others to sex, potentially increasing the number of cases immeasurably. Beauchamp's sexual offenses bill the following year would have defined transmission as actual bodily harm, punishable by five years of penal servitude, and allowed compulsory medical examination of those suspected of sex while infected.[260] Neither measure made it to the books, although a variant of the principle did find a temporary and emasculated wartime expression in Defence of the Realm Act (DORA), Regulation 40d, now applicable only to infected women who solicited or had sex with members of the armed forces.

In Germany, reformers had long sought to make endangerment a crime, but results were forthcoming only in the twentieth century.[261] During the protracted Lex Heinze debates of the 1890s, proposals to outlaw extramarital sex by the infected were approved in the pertinent committee, only to be dropped by the Reichstag in the face of objections. In the First World War infectedly having sex was punishable in military regulations, first for prostitutes, later all women and eventually also men.[262] Formalizing the criminalization of endangerment was advocated during the war, not least by the DGBG, and in the following years. The fruits were finally borne first in the 11 December 1918 ordinance (§3) which punished sex while infected for both men and women and then in the 1927 VD law which (§5) continued this principle.[263] Sweden followed

---

[260] Suzann Buckley, "The Failure to Resolve the Problem of Venereal Disease Among the Troops in Britain During World War I," in Brian Bond and Ian Roy, eds., *War and Society: A Yearbook of Military History*, 2 (1977), pp. 70–71; *Mitteilungen*, 27, 3 (1929), p. 80; Lucy Bland, "'Cleansing the Portals of Life': The Venereal Disease Campaign in the Early Twentieth Century," in Langan and Schwarz, *Crises in the British State*, p. 204; Roy Porter and Hall, *Facts of Life*, p. 234.

[261] *Mitteilungen*, 27, 3 (1929), p. 81; *Vorentwurf zu einem Deutschen Strafgesetzbuch*, p. 665. There were isolated instances of endangerment being criminalized early: in the Oldenburg penal code of 1814 (art. 387), the Altenburg Landsrecht of 1814 and the Saxon penal code of 1838, only sex, not infection, was required of a diseased prostitute for punishment. Jadassohn, *Handbuch der Haut- und Geschlechtskrankheiten*, v. XXIII, p. 37; Laupheimer, *Der strafrechtliche Schutz*, p. 25; *ZBGK*, 1, 1 (1903), p. 8; Streubel, *Wie hat der Staat der Prostitution gegenüber sich zu verhalten?*, p. 11.

[262] Rudeck, *Syphilis und Gonorrhoe vor Gericht*, pp. 56–57; Dubois-Havenith, *Conférence internationale: Enquêtes*, v. I/2, p. 702; *ZBGK*, 1, 1 (1903), pp. 13–15; 11 (1910), pp. 208–10; *Deutsche Juristen-Zeitung*, 20, 17/18 (1 September 1915), p. 890; *Mitteilungen*, 15, 1/2 (1917), p. 35; 27, 3 (1929), p. 82.

[263] *Reichsgesetzblatt*, 1918/184, p. 1431; *ZBGK*, 17 (1916), p. 142; Neisser, *Geschlechtskrankheiten und ihre Bekämpfung*, p. 128; *Sammlung der Drucksachen der verfassunggebenden Preussischen Landesversammlung*, 1919/21, Drcksch. 1823; *Mitteilungen*, 15, 5/6 (1917), p. 101; Cornelie Usborne, *The Politics of the Body in Weimar Germany* (Houndsmills, 1992), p. 21; *ZBGK*, 19, 3 (1919), p. 64: *Mitteilungen*, 27, 3 (1929), p. 82.

the lead of Denmark and Norway, reforming its penal code in connection with the Lex Veneris of 1918 to criminalize endangerment. In distinction to practice elsewhere, accusations did not have to be leveled by the victim, except between spouses, but could also be brought by the state.[264] In France, in contrast, little happened. The civil code's strictures on bodily harm were, by the late nineteenth century, used to hold men liable for transmission, even unintentionally. The penal code, however, was employed in these respects only later than elsewhere.[265] Proposals formally and specifically to prohibit transmission were advanced in the early twentieth century. Combes's extraparliamentary commission sought to replace regulation with a system that held all criminally accountable for such actions.[266] Nothing came of this, however, and, though similar measures were still being debated in the 1920s, transmission was not criminalized until 1960.[267]

While the French did little with respect to general transmission, they did take the lead in a subbranch of such concerns, attempting to prevent passage between wetnurses and their charges. Wetnursing continued to be common in France later and was a more widespread custom than elsewhere. In tandem, the problems of lactational transmission remained pressing, prompting a widespread literature on the subject already in the late eighteenth century and the establishment of an office in Paris to check the health of wetnurses arriving from the provinces.[268] In 1775, the Paris medical faculty proposed identifying syphilitic infants by a note attached to their arms before dispatching them for care and a

[264] *Underdånigt betänkande angående könssjukdomarnas spridning*, v. I, pp. 161–67; *American Journal of Public Health*, 26 (April 1936), p. 357; *Bihang*, 1918, Prop. 154, p. 26; *Svensk juristtidning*, 5 (1919), pp. 108–09.

[265] Laure Biardeau, *Le certificat prénuptial: Etude de droit comparé de le législation* (Paris, 1931), pp. 321–23; Mignot, *Péril vénérien*, pp. 179–80; *L'echo médical du Nord*, 7, 12 (22 March 1903), pp. 141–43; Claire Salomon-Bayet et al., *Pasteur et la révolution pastorienne* (Paris, 1986), p. 235; *Recueil*, 21 (1891), p. 365; Alfred Fillassier, *De la détermination des pouvoirs publics en matière d'hygiène* (2nd edn.; Paris, 1902), p. 170.

[266] Dolléans, *La police des moeurs*, p. 232; *La prophylaxie antivénérienne*, 1, 1 (1929), p. 293; *Annales des maladies vénériennes*, 1 (1906), p. 125; *La syphilis* (1903), pp. 69–71; *Annales*, 4/20 (1913), pp. 388–89; Fiaux, *Le délit pénal de contamination intersexuelle*; *SFPSM: Bulletin mensuel* (1902), p. 268; de Morsier, *La police des moeurs en France*, p. 177; Lion Murard and Patrick Zylberman, "Evolution historique des MST et de leurs représentations: De la maladie comme crime," in Nadine Job-Spira et al., eds., *Santé publique et maladies à transmission sexuelle* (Montrouge, 1990), p. 85; Fiaux, *Police des moeurs*, v. I, pp. cxvi, cxcviii.

[267] At least indirectly in that the CSP in 1960 threatened the infected who refused treatment with fines or jail: CSP, L 285; Cavaillon, *Les législations antivénériennes*, pp. 35–37; Cavaillon, *L'armement antivénérien en France* (Paris, n.d. [1927]), p. 153; Quétel, *History of Syphilis*, pp. 210, 268.

[268] George D. Sussman, *Selling Mother's Milk: The Wet-Nursing Business in France, 1715–1914* (Urbana, 1982), pp. 6–7; Susan P. Conner, "The Pox in Eighteenth-Century France," in Merians, *Secret Malady*, p. 26.

few years later wetnurses were forbidden to tend to the children of soldiers without prior inspection. In 1780, a hospice was opened in Paris to allow care of stricken infants by infected wetnurses.[269] Damages against parents who had permitted their child to infect its wetnurse and vice versa had been upheld already in the early nineteenth century and the French continued to legislate on such matters well into the second half of the twentieth.[270]

Similar measures were also on occasion tried elsewhere.[271] Influenced by Hunter's mistaken conclusion that secondary syphilis was not transmissible, the belief that infants did not endanger their caretakers may explain why, although most cases of lactational transmission passed from children and court cases usually involved nurses demanding damages from parents, the first legislative step generally reversed cart and horse, forbidding infected women from offering their services. Only later did measures follow to protect wetnurses from their charges: in the Danish law of 20 March 1906 and in the 1912 Austrian penal code (§304).[272] The obvious solution, holding both partners to their end of the bargain, was also implemented: in the Danish law of 10 April 1874 (§2), the Norwegian penal code (§358) and the German VD law of 1927 (§§14–15).[273] The importance attached to such measures varied with the customariness of wetnursing in the first place. The British, less enthusiastic consumers of commercial lactation than the French, may therefore have seen no need to criminalize such transmission. The same argument cannot, however, explain why the Swedes, though also abstemious wetnursers, nonetheless extensively regulated the profession.[274] An office to inspect prospective nurses was established in Stockholm already in 1757. The 1812 circular on VD, in turn, ended the requirement that they be examined, but punished

---

[269] *Annales*, 2/5 (1856), pp. 268–69; 2/4 (1855), p. 306; Quétel, *History of Syphilis*, p. 104.

[270] *Annales*, 2/5 (1856), p. 24; 2/21 (1864), pp. 99–152; Ravogli, *Syphilis*, p. 445; Fiaux, *Police des moeurs*, v. I, pp. cci, ccxi; Corbin, "La grande peur de la syphilis," pp. 333–34; Salomon-Bayet, *Pasteur et la révolution pastorienne*, pp. 234–35; Alfred Fournier, *Nourrices et nourrissons syphilitiques* (Paris, 1878), pp. 28–29; Valerie Fildes, *Wet Nursing: A History from Antiquity to the Present* (Oxford, 1988), pp. 238–39; CSP, art. L 169–75.

[271] *ZBGK*, 8, 4 (1908), p. 151; Dubois-Havenith, *Conférence internationale: Rapports préliminaires*, v. I/1, quest. 6, p. 11; *La syphilis* (1905), pp. 705ff.

[272] Camille Appay, *De la transmission de la syphilis entre nourrices et nourrissons* (Paris, 1875), pp. 5–12, 67, 83; XVIIth International Congress of Medicine, *Dermatology and Syphilography*, p. 63; Finger et al., *Handbuch der Geschlechtskrankheiten*, v. III, pp. 2689–90; Mauriac, *Syphilis primitive*, pp. 252–53.

[273] Continued in the German VD law of 1953 (§8), which also forbade (§7) syphilitic women from nursing other children and afflicted infants from being nursed by others than their mothers.

[274] *Mitteilungen*, 23, 2 (1925), pp. 9–10; *Underdånigt betänkande angående könssjukdomarnas spridning*, v. I, p. 314; Ulla-Britt Lithell, *Breast-Feeding and Reproduction: Studies in Marital Fertility and Infant Mortality in 19th-Century Finland and Sweden* (Uppsala, 1981), pp. 20–21; Viking Mattsson, "Ammor och barnafödande i Malmö 1750–1850," *Scandia*, 46, 2 (1980), p. 175.

those without health certificates who proved to be infectious, as well as parents who sent out syphilitic infants for care.[275]

NOTIFIABILITY

One of the problems with legislation on transmission lay with the requirement that the objectionable act be committed by perpetrators in the knowledge that they were infected.[276] Since the fact that X knew of his infectiousness at the time of transmission had to be proven in court, conviction was generally possible only when it could be shown that he had been warned of his condition by a physician, ideally one acting in some official capacity.[277] Criminalizing transmission was therefore closely related to another technique included in the bouquet of tactics proffered to replace regulation, making VD notifiable.

The requirement that contagious diseases be reported to the authorities by physicians, and sometimes also by family members, guardians or others in a position to know, had long been in effect for ailments other than VD. Notification had also, of course, long been a cornerstone of regulation, with the finding and curing of infectious prostitutes the aim. When, however, reporting was to be extended from the acute contagious diseases to VD and from prostitutes to the entire sexually active population, new problems arose to hamper an application of such venerable control techniques. Unlike the acute illnesses, syphilis (with its comparative paucity of obvious symptoms, its unpleasant treatments and its stigma) did not motivate patients to seek out medical aid or to reveal themselves to the authorities, encouraging, if anything, concealment. Moreover, since VD was – barring epidemics – more prevalent than other diseases and its duration prolonged, it was unclear what the authorities could or should do with the thousands of notifications they might expect to receive. Certainly, quarantining or isolating so many for so long was out of the question.[278] Nature and society conspired to

---

[275] Welander, *Bidrag till de veneriska sjukdomarnes historia*, p. 187; Lundquist, *Den disciplinerade dubbelmoralen*, p. 56; Wistrand, *Författningar*, pp. 107–09, 467; Thyresson, *Från Fransoser till AIDS*, ch. 11.

[276] In hopes of easing the burden of proof, the Danish, Norwegian and eventually Swedish laws made it actionable to have sex not just knowing, but suspecting, that one was infected. The German VD law of 1927 punished those who knew or should have known.

[277] *BJVD*, 2, 5 (1926), p. 44; *ZBGK*, 11 (1910), p. 66.

[278] Max Hodann, *History of Modern Morals* (London, 1937), pp. 106–07; Morris, *Nation's Health*, pp. 92–97; Finger et al., *Handbuch der Geschlechtskrankheiten*, v. III, pp. 2715–16; *ZBGK*, 14, 3/4 (1916), pp. 42–48; 19, 7/8 (1919/20), pp. 181–82; Neisser, *Geschlechtskrankheiten und ihre Bekämpfung*, p. 123; *Sitzungsberichte der verfassunggebenden Preussischen Landesversammlung*, 1919/21, 25 February 1920, pp. 9927–28.

hinder the free revelation and treatment of syphilis. In such circumstances, statutory interventions seeking to flush it into the open threatened in fact to undermine their intended effect. On the other hand, because VD was transmitted in large measure through particular, purposive and voluntary sexual acts (unlike other diseases where a simple sneeze could be an epidemiological offense), it would, in theory, be easier to hold individuals accountable for their infectious conduct and thus, in fact, make sense to bring to the authorities' attention behavior that should be restrained. Such were the arguments vying for consideration in the question of notification.

One (weak) version of notifiability that raised few hackles required only a reporting of the fact of infection, without naming names, as the basis of reliable statistics. The stronger, nominative variant, reporting the identities of patients, sought to ensure that precautions were applied to the infected, allowing, in extreme cases, the arrest and isolation of carriers who persisted in risky behavior. On this, opinions divided. Some held that nominative reporting had proven its mettle against other diseases and that equity demanded including VD as well. Others feared that such requirements would discourage syphilitics from seeking treatment, worsening the problem.[279] Abolitionists split between those who rejected notifiability as inappropriate for VD and those welcoming it as part of the prophylactic armamentarium needed to replace regulation. Women's organizations especially saw reporting as an important element of reform.[280]

Notification by doctors threatened to weaken the strictures of physician–patient confidentiality and practitioners often resisted such attempts to harness them in service to the state's epidemiological information-gathering efforts, undercutting the trust and goodwill of the clients on whom, in this period, the medical profession still depended directly for the bulk of its remuneration. It was the promise of confidentiality that lured the infected to their consulting rooms in the

---

[279] XVIIth International Congress of Medicine, *Dermatology and Syphilography*, p. 93; Fiaux, *Police des moeurs*, v. I, p. 389; *Mitteilungen*, 22, 6 (1924); Pontoppidan, *What Venereal Diseases Mean*, pp. 53–54; *ZBGK*, 2, 11/12 (1903/04), pp. 433–34; Waldvogel, *Gefahren der Geschlechtskrankheiten*, p. 84.

[280] Blaschko, *Syphilis und Prostitution*, p. 125; *ZBGK*, 16, 12 (1915/16), pp. 364–65; 4, 1 (1905), pp. 61, 70; 17, 9 (1916/17), pp. 256–57, 269; 18, 11 (1917/18/19), pp. 277–78; Möller, "Undersökningar i vissa frågor rörande de smittosamma könssjukdomarna," p. 5; Brennecke, *Wie ist der Kampf zu führen?*, p. 22; Dubois-Havenith, *Conférence internationale: Enquêtes*, v. I/2, pp. 14–15; Stéenhoff, *Den reglementerade prostitution*, p. 27; *Mitteilungen*, 18, 5/6 (1920), p. 116; 18, 3 (1920), p. 74; David J. Evans, "Tackling the 'Hideous Scourge': The Creation of the Venereal Disease Treatment Centres in Early Twentieth-Century Britain," *Social History of Medicine*, 5, 3 (December 1992), p. 429.

first place and physicians known to report VD would soon find, was the dire prediction, that their patients had gone elsewhere. Reporting their patients, as one put it, was tantamount to chasing them out the door.[281] In small communities, notification, however confidential in theory, would in practice expose the ill to public discrimination. Those who could not avoid such strictures by consulting a physician of their choice would be particularly affected, leaving the poor and especially those dependent on public health insurance vulnerable to being reported. One means of lessening this dilemma for physicians was to require reporting also by others, family members, heads of households, sometimes even landlords. In addition to doctors, the Bolton Improvement Act of 1877, for example, required notification of those in control of the patient's dwelling.[282] In various local versions of the British Infectious Diseases (Notification) Act of 1889 laypersons, in particular householders, were also drawn into the circle of those liable to notify. Such attempts at lay reporting were not, however, very effective, the main problem being that they presupposed a degree of medical expertise that could hardly be expected in any legally enforceable manner of the population at large.[283]

As in other aspects of this prophylactic battle, the Scandinavians took the lead in making VD reportable. The Swedes had introduced notification early on, only to allow it to languish at midcentury. The 1822 royal instructions to provincial physicians required reporting by name of the infected identified during general inspections and this was reaffirmed for recalcitrants in the corresponding instructions of 1890. Denmark, in the law of 1906, and then Sweden in the Lex Veneris of 1918 required general anonymous reporting for statistical purposes, with

---

[281] *ZBGK*, 5, 7 (1906), p. 253; *Ärztliche Sachverständigen-Zeitung*, 21, 9 (1 May 1915), p. 99; *Deutsche medicinische Wochenschrift*, 16 (1893), pp. 385–86; Blaschko, *Syphilis und Prostitution*, p. 125; Otto Better, *Die Geschlechtskrankheiten: Ihre Überwindung und Verhütung* (Berlin, 1921), p. 69; Claudia Huerkamp, *Der Aufstieg der Ärzte im 19. Jahrhundert* (Göttingen, 1985), p. 257; Bridget Towers, "Politics and Policy: Historical Perspectives on Screening," in Virginia Berridge and Philip Strong, eds., *AIDS and Contemporary History* (Cambridge, 1993), p. 67.

[282] *Mitteilungen*, 15, 3/4 (1917), pp. 47, 53; *Sanitary Record*, 7 (2 November 1877), pp. 287–88.

[283] *PP* 1916 (8189) xvi, 1, p. 49; *Transactions of the Seventh International Congress of Hygiene and Demography* (1891), v. 9, pp. 166–67. Instead, "dual systems" of notification were tried out, with notification either by lay persons or practitioners: *Sanitary Record*, n.s., 8, 90 (15 December 1886), p. 277. In France a similar system of notification, not adopted in the 1902 law, was provisionally introduced in 1914 and then formally in 1935: Mosny, *La protection de la santé publique* (Paris, 1904), pp. 21–23; *Annales*, 3/16 (1886), p. 468; Léon Bernard, *La défense de la santé publique pendant la guerre* (Paris, 1929), p. 9; Lion Murard and Patrick Zylberman, *L'hygiène dans la république: La santé publique en France, ou l'utopie contrariée (1870–1918)* (Paris, 1996), p. 318. This was continued by the CSP art. L 11–12.

nominative notification of recalcitrants who failed to follow their physician's instructions or continued infectedly to have sex.[284]

Parts of Germany had also implemented measures early, only to enforce them laxly. The 1835 Prussian regulation required notification of syphilis only when harm otherwise threatened patient or society. With unification, complications ensued. The penal code forbade breaches of medical confidentiality, thus apparently prohibiting reporting. At the same time §327 punished those who hampered precautions to prevent the spread of VD, which might, in Prussia's old provinces where the 1835 regulation still held sway, have required reporting. In fact, however, matters were rarely enforced on this point and no general requirement to report thereby upheld.[285] To the extent that notification was supported at all within the DGBG, only a limited form (following the Swedish example), of recalcitrants alone, won favor.[286] Yet many feared that even such a restricted version required more information about patients' personal circumstances than big-city physicians were likely to possess. Such hesitations explain the unceleric pace of reform on this point. After lengthy debate, with heated opposition from physicians, VD was not included among notifiable ailments in the 1900 Contagious Disease Law. Similarly, long discussion whether to include VD in the Prussian implementation statute of the Imperial law at first limited notification to prostitutes, only then to eliminate it altogether after physicians testified that otherwise syphilitics would resort to quacks, defeating the purpose of reform.[287]

During the war, notification became a more commonly accepted procedure in that all soldiers were obliged to report themselves when infected and, if found diseased at periodic examinations, were compulsorily treated. At the demobilization in 1918, some military authorities

---

[284] *Kongl. Maj:ts Förnyade Nådiga Instruction för Provincial-läkarne i Riket*, §10; *SFS*, 1890/58, §28; *SFS*, 1918/460, §§9–11; *Nordisk Hygienisk Tidsskrift*, 2, 6 (November–December 1921), p. 311; *ZBGK*, 5, 7 (1906), p. 253.

[285] *Gesetz-Sammlung*, 1835, 27/1678, §65, pp. 259–60; *Berliner klinische Wochenschrift*, 35 (1898), pp. 134–35; Rudeck, *Syphilis und Gonorrhoe vor Gericht*, p. 90.

[286] *ZBGK*, 15, 8/9 (1914), p. 283; 19, 4 (1919), p. 100; 3, 8/9 (1904–05), p. 315; Dubois-Havenith, *Conférence internationale: Enquêtes*, v. I/2, pp. 701–02; Waldvogel, *Gefahren der Geschlechtskrankheiten*, p. 84; Laupheimer, *Der strafrechtliche Schutz*, pp. 60–61; Neisser, *Geschlechtskrankheiten und ihre Bekämpfung*, pp. 117–20.

[287] *ZBGK*, 19, 3 (1919), p. 70; 2, 11/12 (1903/04), p. 435; 4, 1 (1905), pp. 32–33; Jadassohn, *Handbuch der Haut- und Geschlechtskrankheiten*, v. XXIII, p. 38; *Mitteilungen*, 18, 5/6 (1920), p. 116; 18, 3 (1920), pp. 74; BA, 15.01, RmdI, 11869, "Präsident der Kaiserlichen Gesundheitsamtes Dr. Bumm," pp. 196ff.; "Sitzungsbericht der am 8. Okt. 1915 auf Einladung des General-Gouvernements in Belgien zu Brüssel abgehaltenen Besprechung über die Massnahmen zur Bekämpfung der Geschlechtskrankheiten," pp. 218–19; Neisser, *Geschlechtskrankheiten und ihre Bekämpfung*, p. 250; Laupheimer, *Der strafrechtliche Schutz*, p. 62.

sought to extend such precautions into civilian life. The initial ambition had been to retain all infected personnel until cured, but defeat and subsequent revolution proved such hopes unrealistic. Instead, demobilized soldiers were to be reported by name to their local social insurance office for further treatment. The traditional arguments against notification (that confidentiality would be undermined and the ill driven to quacks) were assuaged for the moment by appeals to the necessities of immediate circumstance and to the logic that passing information from one set of (military) medical authorities to another (the insurance bureaucracy) did not violate confidentiality.[288] The issue resurfaced during the interwar years in suggestions to harness the power of notification to the goal of VD prophylaxis. Heinrich Dreuw, inexhaustible and rhetorically flamboyant abolitionist, was the tireless advocate of a system of general compulsory notification for all infected and his ideas were formulated in legislative terms by Alfred Beyer in the Prussian Landesversammlung and Käthe Schirmacher, the radical feminist turned conservative nationalist, in the Reichstag.[289] The authorities, many physicians and the DGBG, however, remained skeptical about universal notification and the 1927 VD law (§9) mirrored such hesitations, emulating the Swedish Lex Veneris in requiring reporting only of recalcitrants whose behavior threatened to spread disease.[290]

In Britain, after objections from physicians, VD was not included in the 1889 Notification of Diseases Act. The Royal Commission on VD, debating the issue once again against a background of resistance from medical circles, concluded in 1916 that the advantages of notification were outweighed by the need for strict confidentiality.[291] France, in turn, did not make VD notifiable until 1960 when, subjected to the unfortunate precedent of a Vichy decree, the infected who refused treatment

---

[288] *Reichsgesetzblatt*, 1918/185, p. 1433; Paul Posener, *Die Bekämpfung der Geschlechtskrankheiten* (Berlin, 1927), pp. 53–54; *Mitteilungen*, 15, 5/6 (1917), p. 100; BA, 15.01, RmdI, 11881, "Aktenvermerk über die Besprechung am 7. Dezember 1918," p. 14; [Paul] Kaufmann, *Krieg, Geschlechtskrankheiten und Arbeiterversicherung* (Berlin, 1916), pp. 21–24; Sauerteig, *Krankheit, Sexualität, Gesellschaft*, ch. 4/3.1.

[289] BA, 15.01, RmdI, 11886, pp. 126ff., meeting in the RmdI, 16 December 1919; *Mitteilungen*, 18, 3 (1920), pp. 72–73; Käthe Schirmacher, *Flammen* (Leipzig, 1921), pp. 43–48; Heinz Dreuw, *Allgemeine, gleiche, diskrete Anzeige- und Behandlungspflicht* (Berlin, 1919); Dreuw, *Völkervernichtung*; Dreuw, *Die Sexual-Revolution: Der Kampf um die staatliche Bekämpfung der Geschlechtskrankheiten* (2nd edn.; Bern, 1921).

[290] BA, 15.01, RmdI, 11875, Breger, Reichsgesundheitsamt an den Herrn Reichsminister des Innern, II 818/20, 20 February 1920, p. 334; *ZBGK*, 19, 4 (1919), pp. 96–103; *Sammlung der Drucksachen der Preussischen Landesversammlung*, 1919/21, Drcksch. 1823; *Sitzungsberichte der Preussischen Landesversammlung*, 1919/21, 25 February 1920, cols. 9926–27; *Mitteilungen*, 18, 1/2 (1920), p. 35; 18, 5/6 (1920), pp. 112, 116.

[291] Oriel, *Scars of Venus*, p. 194; *PP* 1916 (8189) xvi, 1, pp. 48–50; Morris, *Nation's Health*, pp. 92–97; *Mitteilungen*, 15, 1/2 (1917), p. 11; Dorothy Porter and Roy Porter, "The Enforcement of Health: The British Debate," in Fee and Fox, *AIDS*, p. 114; Eyler, *Arthur Newsholme and State Medicine*, p. 292.

were to be reported.[292] While Britain and France thus shied away from making syphilis and gonorrhea reportable in adults, they were willing to extend the principle to ophthalmia neonatorum, gonococcal conjunctivitis, a disease treatable by a simple application of silver nitrate, thus preventing thousands of cases of blindness. This was made notifiable in France already in 1892 and in Britain in 1914.[293]

Tracing sexual contacts in search of the source of contagion was another technique variously employed. VD was unlike less discriminating ailments in that it was often (although, with prostitutes and their frequently drunken clients, far from always) the case that the infected could identify the origin of disease. In Berlin during the early nineteenth century, those who were reported as the source by the ill seeking treatment at the Charité, whether prostitutes or men of the lower classes, were apprehended and treated as well. Measures in 1810 and then the Prussian 1835 regulation formalized this approach, requiring physicians to identify the sexual partners of poor patients, reporting them to the police for treatment. During the 1870s, Würzburg established a procedure allowing prostitutes as well as men to report the suspected origin of infection and in Hamburg a system of tracing contacts had been in effect long before similar measures were introduced for the rest of the nation.[294] In France, inspections of soldiers, sailors, prostitutes and workers in the arsenal and elsewhere were introduced in Brest as of 1830, with the infected expected to identify the source of their affliction. Infected naval sailors were required to report their contacts as of 1888, as soldiers eventually were as well, but similar measures for civilians were not implemented.[295] The Swedish Lex Veneris required physicians to trace contacts, reporting names and addresses of the sources, who were subject to exhortations and, if necessary, compulsion to report for examinations and treatment.[296] The German VD law of 1927 followed this example in requiring treatment of those suspected of infection (§4).

---

[292] CSP, art. L 257–60.

[293] XVIIth International Congress of Medicine, *Dermatology and Syphilography*, p. 96; L. W. Harrison, *The Diagnosis and Treatment of Venereal Diseases in General Practice* (3rd edn.; London, 1921), p. 465; Paul Brouardel, *La profession médicale au commencement du XXe siècle* (Paris, 1903), p. 184.

[294] *Annales*, 16 (1836), p. 285; *Zeitschrift für die Staatsarzneikunde*, 42 (1841), pp. 93–94; Augustin, *Preussische Medicinalverfassung*, v. II, pp. 761–62; *Gesetz-Sammlung*, 1835, 27/1678, §69, pp. 259–60; *Mitteilungen*, 15, 3/4 (1917), p. 51; *ZBGK*, 15, 8/9 (1914), p. 275; *Underdånigt betänkande angående könssjukdomarnas spridning*, v. I, p. 283; v. II, pp. 115–16.

[295] Fiaux, *L'armée et la police des moeurs*, p. 211; *Bulletin*, 2, 17 (1887), p. 650; *SFPSM: Bulletin mensuel* (1902), pp. 59–60; G. Thibierge, *La syphilis et l'armée* (Paris, 1917), p. 189; Cavaillon, *Les législations antivénériennes*, pp. 32–33.

[296] *SFS*, 1918/460 §§11–15, 21; *Förhandlingar*, 1920, p. 219; *American Journal of Public Health*, 26 (April 1936), p. 359.

Closely related to the question of notifiability was the confidentiality of the physician–patient relationship. Did doctors owe allegiance foremost to their patients or did the community's public health concerns, in particular those of innocent but endangered third parties, take precedence? Even if society's interests tempered the inviolability of the medical relationship and situations arose in which a physician might justifiably notify the authorities or warn third parties of potential dangers, would the ultimate effect be dysfunctional if the infected therefore avoided treatment and remained infectious? Such were the issues of debate. How strictly medical confidentiality was interpreted varied among nations according to a rule of thumb by which the greater the state's role in matters of public health, the less sacrosanct could be the private relation between doctor and patient. In Sweden and (increasingly) Germany, confidentiality ceded priority to the preventive interests of the community, while in Britain and especially France less changed, at least not until well into the twentieth century. More generally, in all nations the development of public hygiene as an accepted state concern and the growth of health insurance systems chipped away at the exclusivity of the relationship between the ill and their caregivers.[297]

During the latter half of the nineteenth century, the requirements of professional secrecy were still interpreted strictly. The Prussian ALR made medical confidentiality a legal obligation and the Imperial penal code (§300) punished unauthorized disclosure of such secrets, resting on legal foundations that reached back into the early eighteenth century.[298] In France, medical secrecy sported a venerable pedigree, having been included among the statutes of the Parisian faculty of medicine in 1598. The Napoleonic penal code (art. 378) of 1810 punished violations of confidentiality and, during the nineteenth century, an absolute conception of professional secrecy was rigorously enforced, especially after a celebrated court case in 1885.[299] Physicians here could not breach confidence even in court, as expert witnesses, or with their patients' permission, although such strictures began to loosen in the twentieth century.[300] Other

---

[297] Dominique Thouvenin, *Le secret médical et l'information du malade* (Lyons, 1982), pp. 137–42; Mirko D. Grmek, "L'origine et les vicissitudes du secret médical," *Cahiers Laennec*, 29 (1969), pp. 28–31.   [298] ALR II 20, §505; *ZBGK*, 4, 1 (1905), p. 53.

[299] Raymond Villey, *Histoire du secret médical* (Paris, 1986), p. 42; L. Stévenard, *Le secret médical* (Paris, 1905), ch. 7; Murard and Zylberman, *L'hygiène dans la république*, pp. 304–07.

[300] *La syphilis* (1904), p. 76; Villey, *Histoire du secret médical*, pp. 63–67, 103, 135; *BJVD*, 2, 5 (1926), p. 52; Jean-Marie Auby, *Le droit de la santé* (Paris, 1981), p. 329; Thouvenin, *Le secret médical*, pp. 74–76, 90–99; René Savatier et al., *Traité de droit médical* (Paris, 1956), pp. 279–81, 283–85. In Germany too

nations, including Sweden, which had formulated their practices later in the nineteenth century, tended to take a less absolute approach. The Swedish Royal Instruction for Physicians of 1890 required secrecy in general, but allowed exceptions determined by specific legislation and instructions that might require its breach. Anglo-Saxon common law privileged communication between attorney and client, but not between physician and patient, and the British had no specific legal texts dealing with the issue, although medical secrecy was commonly practiced nonetheless. Neither the Swedes nor the British foresaw punishments for violations of professional confidentiality.[301]

Exceptions to confidentiality were often conceded in cases where physicians were called on to testify in court or when required to by other laws.[302] In England, the Duchess of Kingston case of 1776 had established the precedent that a physician could be required to testify to matters otherwise covered by his obligation to confidentiality. In Prussia exceptions to medical secrecy dated back to the Prussian ALR which, though legislating confidentiality, also obliged those with knowledge of serious crimes to speak. In Germany, law with precedence over medical secrecy included the penal code's requirement of giving warning in cases of serious crime (§§138–39) and the Contagious Disease Law of 1900. In France, although the demands of certain laws that disease be reported were exempt from the strictures of confidentiality, it was not until the twentieth century, especially during the Vichy regime, that more significant exceptions were made to the comparatively absolute understanding of medical secrecy here.[303]

Toward the turn of the century, new attention to the blameless victims of syphilis also shifted focus to the problem of medical confidentiality. Ibsen's *Ghosts* and Brieux's *Damaged Goods* underlined the irrationality, from the victim's perspective, of forbidding physicians from warning an unsuspecting wife of the dangers to which her husband exposed her.[304]

there were instances when, even after the patient's death, physicians refused to testify in court since they had not been released from their obligations: *ZBGK*, 11 (1910), pp. 220–22.

[301] *SFS*, 1890/58, §60; Möller, "Undersökningar i vissa frågor rörande de smittosamma könssjukdomarna," p. 9; Ravogli, *Syphilis*, p. 334; Finger et al., *Handbuch der Geschlechtskrankheiten*, v. III, p. 2713; Earl Jowitt, ed., *The Dictionary of English Law* (London 1959), p. 450; *ZBGK*, 5, 7 (1906), p. 247; *BJVD*, 2, 5 (1926), p. 46.   [302] *ZBGK*, 4, 1 (1905), pp. 9ff.; 2, 11/12 (1903/04), pp. 464–65.

[303] *BJVD*, 2, 5 (1926), pp. 48, 52; Stévenard, *Le secret médical*, pp. 76–77; Poore, *Treatise on Medical Jurisprudence*, p. 12; ALR, II 20, §506; *ZBGK*, 11 (1910), p. 223; Villey, *Histoire du secret médical*, p. 75; Quétel, *History of Syphilis*, p. 208; Jacques Moreau and Didier Truchet, *Droit de la santé publique* (Paris, 1981), p. 126.

[304] In F. Ottmer's *Schweigen* (1902), a physician in love with a woman who wishes to marry a syphilitic suitor wonders whether to tell her parents about the fiancé in hopes of sparing his beloved, but finally, allowing his professional instincts to prevail over his amorous inclinations, says nothing.

In cases where husband and wife consulted the same physician, he was in theory enjoined from telling the woman what she herself was suffering for fear of disclosing the spouse's affliction, nor even allowed to counsel her to cease sexual relations in hopes of breaking the cycle of continuous reinfection. The same held for wetnurses who consulted their employers' physician for syphilis acquired from their charges.[305] Reformers could point to numerous cases where a narrow interpretation of confidentiality had harmed innocent victims and serious disagreements over whether physicians were entitled to warn third parties were fought out in the medical literature.[306] In one celebrated case, a Parisian physician avoided the obstacles that a strict understanding of secrecy put in the way of warning his infected patient's fiancée by threatening the suitor with a public slap in the face in his opera box that evening had he not in the interim broken off the engagement. More pragmatically minded fathers were counseled to require life insurance policies of prospective sons-in-law, thereby forcing them to divulge information about current health and past ailments.[307]

Reformers who sought to ease the strictures of confidentiality argued that the development of public health necessarily whittled down the absolute claims of individual inviolability.[308] The loosening of medical secrecy was a gradual process, with some of the exceptions made to the sanctity of the physician–patient relationship sporting a long history. In France, an edict as early as in 1666 required a report from physicians treating those wounded in fights.[309] In situations of

[305] *Annales*, 4/20 (1913), pp. 389–93; *ZBGK*, 4, 1 (1905); Rudeck, *Syphilis und Gonorrhoe vor Gericht*, p. 73; Baer, *Hygiene der Syphilis*, p. 48; Fournier, *Nourrices et nourrissons syphilitiques*, pp. 28–29. Many of the problems raised in such cases stemmed not so much from the strictures of medical confidentiality as from the institution of the family physician. The contradiction was that the physician was at one and the same time the family doctor and yet committed to upholding the absolute rights of one individual. Had the wife simply consulted another physician, presumably such situations would never have arisen in the first place. The typical case, as one observer caustically put it, that is always discussed by medical casuists is that Dr. A is consulted by syphilitic Major B who is going to marry Miss C. A is a lifelong friend of C's father. In real life syphilitic Major Bs don't consult the family doctor of their fiancée: *BJVD*, 2, 5 (1926), p. 46.

[306] *ZBGK*, 4, 1 (1905), pp. 38–40; 1, 1 (1903), pp. 38–39; *Mitteilungen*, 23, 5 (1925), p. 24; Fillassier, *De la détermination des pouvoirs publics*, p. 170; *La syphilis* (1903), p. 223; *BJVD*, 2, 5 (1926), pp. 46, 53; Morris, *Nation's Health*, p. 132.

[307] If he refused, suspicions were in order: Rudeck, *Syphilis und Gonorrhoe vor Gericht*, pp. 67–68; *ZBGK*, 2, 10 (1903/04), p. 400; *Journal des maladies cutanées et syphilitiques*, 14, 10 (October 1902), p. 782. Part of the problem was the tradition of the husband's prerogative of sexual access to his wife which, in canon law, was not waived even in cases of his being afflicted with contagious disease: Jean Imbert, *Histoire du droit privé* (Paris, 1950), pp. 58–60.

[308] *ZBGK*, 4, 1 (1905), pp. 32–40.

[309] Fillassier, *De la détermination des pouvoirs publics*, p. 171. Ironically, precisely such exceptions, with their political overtones, may have encouraged an insistence on secrecy in France. Confidentiality

national emergency – treason or plots against the public weal, for example – exceptions to medical secrecy were in legal place.[310] Life and health insurance companies began during the nineteenth century to insist on information from physicians that in a simpler age would have remained confidential. Legislation requiring the causes of death to be reported necessarily eased any rigid understanding of secrecy and the issue now was whether similar exceptions should also be made for VD infection. Once notification of other contagious diseases was a fact in most nations, major inroads had been made onto the territory of strict confidentiality.[311] No one, as one observer put it, would dream of allowing a physician to keep secret a case of diphtheria or typhus in a baker or a restauranteur.[312]

Although most nations had some form of secrecy requirement, the obstacle it threw up to notification varied. Some were willing to abandon confidentiality as the necessity of notification demanded; others avoided or postponed notification, using secrecy as an excuse for inaction.[313] Not surprisingly, those nations that required reporting and contact tracing of VD were also most likely to interpret professional confidentiality loosely. The obligation to report cases of VD that, in Sweden for example, began already early in the century and the contact tracing embodied in the Lex Veneris meant that medical secrecy in any narrow sense had long been compromised.[314] In Germany, suggestions were made early in the twentieth century to loosen the penal code's strictures on such matters and in 1905 a supreme court decision reassured physicians not to fear punishment for reporting notifiable diseases, including VD. The 1911 Reichsversicher-ungsordnung (§141) held employees of health insurance institutions to

was taken seriously here partly because it had been caught up in political purposes in 1832, when Gisquet had ordered physicians to report names of insurgents wounded in the June uprising and none did. Such requirements were attempted again by the Germans and the Vichy government in 1944 for wounded members of the resistance: Villey, *Histoire du secret médical*, pp. 67, 161; J. Ruffié and J.-C. Sournia, *Les épidémies dans l'histoire de l'homme* (Paris, 1984), p. 138; Jacques Léonard, *La France médicale: Médecins et malades au XIXe siècle* (n.p., 1978), p. 246; Savatier et al., *Traité de droit médical*, p. 283.

[310] Swedish penal code, ch. 8, §22; German penal code, §§138–39.

[311] The German Contagious Disease Law of 1900, the French law on the exercise of medicine of 1892 and the public health law of 1902, the Notification of Disease Act of 1889 in Britain.

[312] *ZBGK*, 5, 7 (1906), p. 244; 4, 1 (1905), p. 34.

[313] *Annales*, 4/20 (1913), p. 388; Fiaux, *Police des moeurs*, v. I, p. 497.

[314] *ZBGK*, 19, 2 (1919), pp. 30–31. The Swedish secrecy law of 1980 continued this approach by requiring medical confidentiality except in cases where a breach is demanded by government authority: Lotta Westerhäll and Ake Saldeen, "Réflexions sur le Sida et le droit suédois," in Foyer and Khaïat, *Droit et Sida*, pp. 400–03.

the same standards of secrecy as physicians, thus theoretically preventing a report to them from breaching confidence.[315] During the First
World War, however, the issue remained debated and demands were
heard in parliament to clarify the matter once and for all.[316] In France,
laws during the postwar period explicitly held others than purely
medical personnel to the standards of professional confidentiality,
allowing doctors to pass along without qualms information concerning
patients.[317]

QUACKS

Since statutory interventions broached the possibility that the infected
might avoid physicians who could report them, initiate contact tracing,
start compulsory treatment and so forth, it followed that many victims
were likely to seek unorthodox and unofficial forms of cure, thus
hurting, from the view of official academic medicine, their own interests.[318] One solution lay in maintaining and even strengthening the
principle of confidentiality, to which doctors were liable but quacks not,
although that, of course, blocked hopes of enlisting private physicians
in the service of public health. Alternatively, treatment of VD by
anyone other than officially trained and licensed physicians could be
prohibited.

The simplest solution, adopted in many nations, was to forbid those
without medical licenses from treatment. In Scandinavia this was
accomplished first in Norway (1889), followed by Denmark (1906) and
Sweden (1915). In Britain, the Venereal Diseases Act of 1917 excluded
unofficial treatment.[319] In France, although there had long been proposals to this effect, little followed. Article 405 of the penal code on
defrauding and cheating was occasionally leveled against charlatans, but
this was, at best, an exceptional and inadequate tool.[320] In Germany,
there were complications. Early measures forbade unlicensed medical
personnel to treat VD and this principle was continued in the 1835

---

[315] Neisser, *Die Geschlechtskrankheiten und ihre Bekämpfung*, p. 249; BA, 15.01, RmdI, 11866, pp. 72ff.,
"Aufzeichnung über die am 4. und 5. März 1908 abgehaltene Sitzung des Reichs-Gesundheitsrats
(Ausschuss für Seuchenbekämpfung), betreffend die Bekämpfung der Geschlechtskrankheiten," p.
81; Borelli et al., *Geschichte der DGBG*, p. 36; Sauerteig, *Krankheit, Sexualität, Gesellschaft*, ch. 4/3.1.

[316] *ZBGK*, 18, 1 (1917), p. 3; 17, 9 (1916/17), p. 255; *Mitteilungen*, 15, 5/6 (1917), pp. 97–99; 23, 5
(1925), p. 24; Neisser, *Geschlechtskrankheiten und ihre Bekämpfung*, pp. 321–22.

[317] *JO*, 14 April 1946, p. 3138, art. 6; *JO*, 25 April 1946, p. 3422, art. 5; CSP, L 293, art. 4.

[318] Leonhard, *Prostitution*, p. 245; *DVöG*, 36 (1904), p. 432; 41 (1909), p. 731; Fiaux, *Police des moeurs*,
v. I, p. 496.   [319] 7 & 8 Geo. 5 c. 21.

[320] *Annales*, 16 (1836), p. 279; Cavaillon, *L'armement antivénérien*, p. 51.

Prussian regulation.[321] The issue was vexed later in the century, however, by the peculiar tradition of *Kurierfreiheit*, whereby citizens were granted in 1869 the right to be treated by the charlatan of their choice.[322] Either the requirement to report had to be extended to all practitioners, raising the problem of how those without any formal professional training (who might indeed reject the most basic tenets of academic medicine) could be held legally accountable for diagnosing and reporting, or the freedom of cure would have to be restricted, allowing only licensed physicians to treat notifiable diseases.[323] Because of the right to seek cures of any stripe, the German discussion remained fraught with controversy. Proposals early in the twentieth century to prohibit quacks were frequent but fruitless.[324] During and immediately following the war, quacks were forbidden to treat VD, but in 1919 and 1920 bills for a more general prohibition fell to the new Weimar assembly's unwillingness to restrict the freedom of cure.[325] Only in 1927 with the VD law was *Kurierfreiheit* finally ended for genital diseases, requiring as it did that only licensed physicians treat such ailments, although not insisting necessarily that allopathic methods be used.[326]

A corollary to clamping down on quacks were measures to prevent

[321] Augustin, *Preussische Medicinalverfassung*, v. II, pp. 764–65; *Gesetz-Sammlung*, 1835, 27/1678, pp. 259–60.

[322] On contrasting systems of medical regulation in France and England, see Jean-Charles Sournia, *La médecine révolutionnaire (1789–1799)* (Paris, 1989), pp. 124–26; M. Jeanne Peterson, *The Medical Profession in Mid-Victorian London* (Berkeley, 1978), p. 36; Anne Digby, *Making a Medical Living: Doctors and Patients in the English Market for Medicine, 1720–1911* (Cambridge, 1994), p. 31; Matthew Ramsey, "The Politics of Professional Monopoly in Nineteenth-Century Medicine: The French Model and Its Rivals," in Gerald L. Geison, ed., *Professions and the French State, 1700–1900* (Philadelphia, 1984).

[323] In the Contagious Disease Law of 1900, practitioners were required to report notifiable diseases not just when they knew they were present, but also when they merely suspected it, in theory making it easier to implicate quacks in reporting: *Reichs-Gesetzblatt*, 1900, 24/2686, §1; Walter Lustig, *Die Bekämpfung des Kurpfuschertums* (2nd edn.; Berlin, 1927), p. 48.

[324] Chrzelitzer, *Der Kampf gegen die Geschlechtskrankheiten* (Berlin, 1903), pp. 7–9; Segger-Bethmann, *Die Geschlechtskrankheiten, ihre Entstehung, Verhütung, Behandlung und Heilung* (Berlin, n.d. [1903]), pp. 5–6; von Niessen, *Womit sind die Geschlechtskrankheiten wirksam zu bekämpfen?*, pp. 4–6, 33; Dubois-Havenith, *Conférence internationale: Rapports préliminaires*, v. I/1, quest. 6, p. 11; Finger et al., *Handbuch der Geschlechtskrankheiten*, v. III, pp. 2710–11.

[325] Hellwig, *Gesetz zur Bekämpfung der Geschlechtskrankheiten*, p. 5; *Mitteilungen*, 18, 1/2 (1920), pp. 38–39; *ZBGK*, 19, 4 (1919), pp. 99–100; *Sammlung der Drucksachen der Preussischen Landesversammlung*, 1919/21, Drcksch. 1823; *Sitzungsberichte der Preussischen Landesversammlung*, 1919/21, 25 February 1920, cols. 9928, 9951–52.

[326] Schmedding and Engels, *Die Gesetze betreffend Bekämpfung übertragbarer Krankheiten* (2nd edn.; Münster, 1929), pp. 327–28; *Mitteilungen*, 25, 11/12 (1927), p. 138; Cornelie Usborne, "Die Stellung der Empfängnisverhütung in der Weimarer Gesundheits- und Bevölkerungspolitik," in Reulecke and Rüdenhausen, *Stadt und Gesundheit*, p. 284; *Die Auswirkungen des Gesetzes zur Bekämpfung der Geschlechtskrankheiten* (Berlin, n.d. [1928]), p. 11.

self-medication. In Britain, the 1889 Indecent Advertisements Act prohibited publicity relating to complaints or infirmities arising from sexual intercourse and the 1917 VD Act banned advertising cures for such ailments.[327] Though advertising cures was banned from periodicals in Germany during the early interwar years, in fact such notices flourished to the extent that the DGBG began to counter them with warnings of fraud and proposals for a more effective ban were heard.[328] The 1927 VD law (§11) resolved the issue by punishing public dissemination of such material. In France, similar proposals were put forth in the extraparliamentary commission at the turn of the century and again in the early 1930s, but to no avail.[329]

An important factor in the question of unlicensed treatment was the degree to which nonallopathic methods and theories commanded a following. This varied much among nations, slight in France, somewhat in Britain and Scandinavia, strong in Germany, the land of Hahnemann and homeopathy and a hundred other medical -isms, all marshaled in glorious cacophony under the general rubric *Naturheilkunde*. The claims of *Naturheilkündler* to a say in the treatment of VD here continued undeterred well into the twentieth century.[330] Many Social Democrats and Communists favored alternative therapies, opposing the 1927 VD law's concession of a monopoly to licensed physicians.[331] With the development of salvarsan by Paul Ehrlich, *Naturheilkündler* were spurred to new heights of indignation. Here was another product of the medico-chemical industrial lobby that, while earning the handmaidens of sexual capitalism fortunes, cost misguided syphilitics not only money but their health.[332] The champions of such

[327] 52 & 53 Vict. c. 18; 7 & 8 Geo. 5 c. 21.

[328] *Mitteilungen*, 18, 1/2 (1920), pp. 38–39; 17, 6 (1919), p. 107; *Sammlung der Drucksachen der Preussischen Landesversammlung*, 1919/21, Drcksch. 1823.

[329] Fiaux, *Police des moeurs*, v. I, pp. 460–61; Cavaillon, *Les législations antivénériennes*, pp. 56–57.

[330] Weindling, *Health, Race and German Politics*, pp. 21–25; BA, 15.01, RmdI, 11892, pp. 54ff., Eingabe des Zentralverband für Parität der Heilmethoden, 15 April 1922; *Korrespondenzblatt für Abgeordnete, Regierung und Behörden betr. den Entwurf eines Gesetzes zur Bekämpfung der Geschlechtskrankheiten*, 1 (1 May 1922). There are similar protests in BA, 15.01, RmdI, 11891.

[331] Because many in the Socialist Party base were for *Naturheilkunde*, although leaders like Hilferding were not, voting on the 1927 law's §7 was left free to individual choice: *SB*, 1924/26, Anlage 2714, pp. 13–15; *SB*, 21 January 1927, pp. 8676B, 8686B; 24 January 1927, pp. 8722–24; 26 January 1927, pp. 8756A–8758C; *Sitzungsberichte der Preussischen Landesversammlung*, 1919/21, 25 February 1920, cols. 9951–52.

[332] "Schulmedizin und Gesetzentwurf zur 'angeblichen' Bekämpfung der Geschlechtskrankheiten," *Der Volksarzt*, 3, 6 (15 June 1922); [Rudolf Spuhl], *Gesetzgeberische Sexualdiktatur* (n.p., [Berlin], n.d. [1922]), pp. 3–7; Dreuw, *Völkervernichtung*, v. I, pp. 2, 55–70; Kafemann, *Syphilis-Vorbeugung oder Salvarsan?* (Munich, 1915), p. 23; Lutz Sauerteig, "Salvarsan und der 'ärztliche Polizeistaat': Syphilistherapie im Streit zwischen Ärzten, pharmazeutischer Industrie, Gesundheitsverwaltung

public health populism claimed tirelessly that the salvarsan industry reaped unconscionable profits, that the Weimar government, taking its cut in the form of higher taxes, was in cahoots with the chemical concerns, that the Jews too were involved in such sinister machinations, that the authorities sought to conceal deaths caused by the new treat ment, that salvarsan turned Europeans into blacks and a long litany of similar imbecilities.[333] Thanks to such efforts, the Reichstag was persuaded to debate the virtues of salvarsan in March 1914 and, although it concluded in his favor, Ehrlich was humiliated by the process. In the 1927 VD law, such concerns were given their due in the provision that potentially dangerous treatments, including salvarsan and mercury, could be undertaken only with patient permission.[334]

MARRIAGE

Marriage also interested public health reformers as an epidemiological bottleneck at which the infectious could be identified and cured. Proposals abounded, starting already late in the eighteenth century, seeking to require a VD examination as a nuptial prerequisite. Since military recruits were inspected – such was the logic sometimes advanced – why not matrimonially inclined couples?[335] Those opposed

und Naturheilverbänden (1910–1927)," in Martin Dinges, ed., *Medizinkritische Bewegungen im Deutschen Reich (c. 1870–c. 1933)* (Stuttgart, 1996).

[333] Dreuw, *Völkervernichtung*, v. I, pp. 76–77; Dreuw, *Spanische Stiefel: Ein Einblick in die moderne Kultursklaverei zur Dressur des Geistes* (Berlin, 1923); Dreuw, *Kultur-Korruption: Erlebtes und Erstrebtes im Kampf für Wissenschaft und Wahrheit* (Berlin, 1923), pp. 196–200; Dreuw, *Menschenopfer: Offener Brief an die Medizinalverwaltung* (Berlin, n.d. [1922]), pp. 2–6; Ludwig, *Heilung der Syphilis durch erprobtes ungiftiges, naturgemässes Verfahren ohne Einspritzungen, ohne Quecksilber, ohne Salvarsan* (Berlin, n.d. [1922]), pp. 11–14; Erwin Silber, *Salvarsan? Quecksilber? Naturheilbehandlung?* (Berlin, 1927); H. Lemke, *Die Syphilis und ihre Heilung auf naturgemässer Grundlage ohne Quecksilber und Salvarsan* (Berlin, 1925), pp. 6–7, 38–43; *Mitteilungen*, 27, 2 (1929), p. 62; *SB*, 21 January 1927, p. 8687B; 24 January 1927, p. 8715B–C; BA, 15.01, RmdI, 11875, "Abschrift aus Nr. 163 der Westfälischen Allgemeinen Volkszeitung Dortmund vom 16. 7. 1919," pp. 346ff.; "Hat der Kampf gegen das Salvarsan eine antisemitische Tendenz?" *Kölnische Volkszeitung* (2 April 1914); "Eine Regierungserklärung betr. Salvarsan," *Kölnische Volkszeitung* (20 April 1914); "Die Preisgestaltung des Salvarsans," *Frankfurter Zeitung* (24 June 1914); "Ehrlich über den Preis des Salvarsan," *Hamburgischer Correspondent* (27 June 1914), copies in the BA, 15.01, RmdI, 11882, pp. 55, 70, 99, 101, respectively.

[334] Oriel, *Scars of Venus*, p. 93; *Auswirkungen des Gesetzes zur Bekämpfung der Geschlechtskrankheiten*, pp. 7, 11; Jadassohn, *Handbuch der Haut- und Geschlechtskrankheiten*, v. XXIII, p. 62. It was a curious combination of many socialists, all Communists and the völkisch parliamentary fractions which supported this concession: Silber, *Salvarsan?*, p. 114; [Spuhl], *Gesetzgeberische Sexualdiktatur*, p. 6.

[335] Kornig, *Medicinischpolitischer Vorschlag*, pp. 26–27; *Preste*, 1817–18, 4 April 1818, v. 3, p. 422; *Annales*, 2/5 (1856), pp. 64–66; Ströhmberg, *Bekämpfung der ansteckenden Geschlechtskrankheiten*, pp. 53–54; *ZBGK*, 2, 10 (1903/04), p. 396; 17 (1916), p. 100; von Niessen, *Womit sind Geschlechtskrankheiten zu bekämpfen?*, p. 34; Neisser, *Geschlechtskrankheiten und ihre Bekämpfung*, pp. 144–56, 168; *La syphilis* (1904), p. 224; *Annales*, 3/43 (1900), pp. 191, 466–67.

objected that such limitations restricted an inalienable human right, that they threatened to decrease the already low level of fertility and that, rather than preventing transmission, they would merely confine it to illegitimate unions. With such a law on the books, a Berlin neurology professor warned, the fathers of Schiller and Beethoven, the mothers of Zola and de Maupassant and both Kleist's parents could not have married.[336] Such inspections involved an invasion of privacy that many found objectionable. As one British observer put it, "I do not imagine that any of the few British matrons left would willingly take their young daughters before marriage to a venereal disease specialist for a cervical swabbing, and I rather fancy that if they did the result would be, in some cases, more surprising than satisfactory to the parties concerned."[337] Abolitionists, in contrast, liked the idea, as did the women's movement more generally. A club of the uninfected was proposed, among whom nuptial possibilities could be chosen.[338]

In Sweden such measures had long been in effect for diseases other than VD and proposals to extend them were afoot. By 1918 marriage of the infected was restricted and in 1920 prenuptial certificates were required. Marriage was allowed for the afflicted so long as both partners had informed the other, but forbidden, except with royal dispensation, if the disease was still in its contagious stages.[339] In France, bills to similar effect peppered the late 1920s, but not until 1942, under the Vichy Regime, was the civil code (art. 63) amended to require prenuptial certificates.[340] In Britain, in contrast, nothing prevented the infected from marrying. Nor did the Germans (before the Nazi era) require pre-nuptial certificates as such, although a law in 1920 encouraged the

[336] BA, 15.01, RmdI, 11874, Ministerium des Innern, M. 10167, 14 February 1919, p. 29; *Annales*, 3/3 (1880), pp. 435–37; *La syphilis* (1903), p. 223; *ZBGK*, 12, 12 (1911/12), pp. 421–22, 429–30; *Underdånigt betänkande angående könssjukdomarnas spridning*, v. I, pp. 145–48.

[337] *BJVD*, 2, 5 (1926), p. 45.

[338] *ZBGK*, 16, 12 (1915/16), pp. 373–74; Kristine von Soden, *Die Sexualberatungsstellen der Weimarer Republik 1919–1933* (Berlin, 1988), pp. 21–22; *ZBGK*, 17 (1916), p. 106. This was the converse of the official brothels, proposed by Sperck, to be reserved for syphilitics, *les avariés*, as it were, *chez soi*: *Annales*, 4/20 (1913), p. 403.

[339] Wistrand, *Författningar*, p. 24; *Underdånigt betänkande angående könssjukdomarnas spridning*, v. I, p. 139; *Borgare*, 1817, v. 1, pp. 436–39; *ZBGK*, 12, 12 (1911/12), p. 429; *SFS*, 1918/460, §8; Sennhenn, "Bekämpfung der Geschlechtskrankheiten," p. 14; Cavaillon, *Les législations antivénériennes*, p. 550; Jean Sutter, *L'eugénique* (Paris, 1950), p. 76.

[340] Biardeau, *Le certificat prénuptial*, pp. 265–79; Spillmann, *L'évolution de la lutte*, pp. 229–31; Cavaillon, *L'armement antivénérien*, pp. 31, 158; Cavaillon, *Les législations antivénériennes*, pp. 42–43; Mireur, *La syphilis et la prostitution*, pp. 59ff.; Paul Smith, *Feminism in the Third Republic: Women's Political and Civil Rights in France 1918–1945* (Oxford, 1996), p. 223; Schneider, *Quality and Quantity*, ch. 6; CSP, L 155–58. Art. L 158 was then abrogated by the law of 18 December 1989 (art. 3).

betrothed to be examined. The German civil code in theory required informing the spouse-to-be of infection and the 1927 law reinforced this by forbidding marriage without such disclosure (§6).[341]

Finally, among the measures considered by venereal reformers, comes the question of personal hygiene. Although this remains, of course, a matter largely beyond the bounds of legislation, in at least one case, circumcision, it fell within the ambit of public health. Many observers, as early as Fallopia, attributed to this ritual practice a certain degree of hygienic and perhaps also prophylactic virtue. Both the Egyptians and Jews, it was often believed, had adopted it as a specific precaution against VD.[342] It was a common observation that, for this reason, Jews were less afflicted with VD than gentiles, Muslims in India less than Hindus.[343] Conclusions drawn from the experience of Jews and Muslim colonials convinced many European reformers, especially the British and Dutch, of circumcision's worth.[344] While many thought that simple genital hygiene promised similar advantages, others advocated the widespread adoption of circumcision, although recognizing that, given the objections to compulsory vaccination, wielding the knife in such tender circumstances was unlikely to find broad support.[345] On the other hand, however hygienically admirable circumcision might be, it (and especially the circumstances of its ritual performance) could be a nexus of transmission, as the mohel sucked the infant's fresh wound (metsitsah) to stanch the bleeding and disease was transmitted in one direction or the

[341] *Mitteilungen*, 23, 2 (1925), p. 9; 27, 3 (1929), p. 67; Biardeau, *Le certificat prénuptial*, pp. 213–18; Weindling, *Health, Race and German Politics*, pp. 294–94, 361–64; Usborne, *Politics of the Body*, pp. 142–44; Weingart et al., *Rasse, Blut und Gene*, pp. 274–76, 513–18; Rudeck, *Syphilis und Gonorrhoe vor Gericht*, pp. 107–13, 121–27; *ZBGK*, 12, 12 (1911/12), pp. 422–23; *Sammlung der Drucksachen der Preussischen Landesversammlung*, 1919/21, Drcksch. 1823. This was continued in the 1953 VD law (§6).

[342] Quétel, *History of Syphilis*, p. 56; Dreuw, *Völkervernichtung*, v. I, p. 30; Mignot, *Péril vénérien*, p. 25; Proksch, *Vorbauung der venerischen Krankheiten*, pp. 21–22; *ZBGK*, 2, 6 (1903/04), pp. 248–55. It is equally clear, however, that, while some Hebraic law has sanitary justification in the light of modern medicine, much does not and that to attribute its motivation to hygienic ambitions alone is largely speculative: Robert P. Hudson, *Disease and Its Control* (Westport, 1983), pp. 63–65.

[343] Müller, *Praktisches Handbuch*, p. 27; *PP* 1867–68 (4031) xxxvii, 425, QQ. 2669–70, 2749, 5405; Mignot, *Péril vénérien*, p. 25. The proverbial sobriety of the Jews was also considered a factor here: *Glasgow Medical Journal*, 4, 19 (1883), p. 111.

[344] *Annales*, 4/34 (1920), p. 136; XVIIth International Congress of Medicine, *Dermatology and Syphilography*, p. 100; *DVöG*, 41 (1909), p. 744; *BMJ* (31 December 1910), p. 1767; *Lancet*, 2, 2 (29 December 1900), pp. 1869–1871; Bloch, *Das Sexualleben unserer Zeit*, pp. 421–22. Such beliefs continue into the AIDS era: *AIDS*, 3 (1989), pp. 373–77; 11 (1997), pp. 73–80.

[345] Ricord, *Lettres sur la syphilis*, p. 293; Mireur, *La syphilis et la prostitution*, pp. 171–75; Friedrich Weinbrenner, *Wie schützt man sich vor Ansteckung?* (Bonn, 1908), pp. 5–6; Stamm, *Verhütung der Ansteckungen*, pp. 62–64.

other.[346] From the middle of the nineteenth century, therefore, hygienic reformers sought to convince Jewish communities to abandon the practice of irrumation, the first convert being the Paris consistoire, won over by Ricord.[347]

REFORMS

While Scandinavia blazed new directions and public health authorities in Britain responded for the moment largely by withdrawing from the prophylactic arena, the regulationist nations began a long and arduous process of reform. Neoregulationists and neoabolitionists alike sought to shift the focus from registered prostitutes to a larger proportion of those engaged in risky sexual activity, hoping to couple a promise of easy, and sometimes free, access to medical care together with measures of the sort outlined here that subjected the VD-infected to precautions much like those used against other contagious disease.

In France, hopes for reform, though starting auspiciously, amounted to naught until after the Second World War. In 1903, prompted by the Forissier affair, Combes appointed an extraparliamentary commission to investigate the vice squad. Starting out firmly regulationist, the commission was persuaded by the arguments of its abolitionists, especially Yves Guyot and Avril de Sainte-Croix, to perform a volteface, proposing a wholly new system that would have gone beyond the ambitions of moderate neoregulationism. The commission agreed not to outlaw prostitution as such, accepting instead the neoregulationist approach of bringing it into the ambit of criminal law by prohibiting certain forms of public solicitation, display and pimping. Unlike neoregulationism, however, it went further to propose ending the old system once and for all. Instead of targeting only prostitutes, all VD victims were now, in principle at least, to be the object of precautions. All arrested for solicitation who were infected but not under treatment were to be hospitalized, every citizen held responsible for transmitting VD, free medical

---

[346] Or simply from the act of cutting, without the sucking, as the Prussian regulation of 1835 warned: "Belehrung über ansteckende Krankheiten," *Anhang zur Gesetz-Sammlung*, 1835, Beilage B zu No. 27 gehörig, p. 38. See also Sander L. Gilman, "Plague in Germany, 1939/1989: Cultural Images of Race, Space, and Disease," in Andrew Porter et al., eds., *Nationalisms and Sexualities* (New York, 1992), pp. 179–81.

[347] *Annales*, 33 (1845), p. 229; 2/21 (1864), p. 364; 3/6 (1881), p. 157; 3/44 (1900), pp. 262–63; 4/20 (1913), p. 392; Jeannel, *De la prostitution*, pp. 339–42; Pappenheim, *Handbuch der Sanitäts-Polizei*, v. I, pp. 301–03; Stamm, *Verhütung der Ansteckungen*, pp. 62–64; *Friedrichs Blätter für Gerichtliche Medicin und Sanitätspolizei*, 29 (1878), pp. 103–04; Bulkley, *Syphilis in the Innocent*, pp. 179–80; Jadassohn, *Handbuch der Haut- und Geschlechtskrankheiten*, v. XXIII, p. 8.

care to be provided for the poor. Heavily indebted to the sanitarily statist vision of Scandinavian reformers, the commission's overweening ambitions managed to unite the opposition of both regulationists and neos, leading to nothing other than a limited law of 11 April 1908 on the protection of minors.[348]

In Germany, change in the direction indicated by the Scandinavians proved more promising. Reformers, still convinced that prostitutes were the primary source of infection, proposed modifications to the old system. To lure clandestines out of the shadows, the stick of regulationism's strictures was to be made less cudgelsome, the carrot of free medical care now proffered.[349] In 1905, the Prussian version of the Contagious Disease Law struck out in new directions by subjecting also VD to the precautions (examination, testing, isolation, compulsory treatment of the infected and surveillance of the suspected) allowed in the Imperial law for other contagious ailments, although in this case only if contracted by a prostitute. Prostitutes were subject to regular medical inspection and treatment. The obligation to be cured could be satisfied by certification from a physician and only in its absence, or if it was feared that they were still selling their favors despite infection, could prostitutes be hospitalized. The definition of prostitute (those engaged in professional fornication) was broadened to encompass others than just the inscribed, thereby allowing authorities greater leverage over clandestines. VD in Prussia was thus dealt with like other transmissible ailments, prostitutes were subject to a largely medical surveillance of the sort favored by neoregulationists and the authority over them now spelled out in law. Nonetheless, while for other contagious diseases strictures implicated all victims, for VD the target remained prostitutes, however expanded the official concept thereof.[350]

It was again in Prussia that further steps were taken in a Scandinavian

---

[348] Fiaux, *Police des moeurs*, v. I, pp. xxxiv–xxxvii, cxvi, cxcviii, ccl, 457–58, 462–64; *La syphilis* (1904), p. 80; *ZBGK*, 8, 1 (1908), p. 20; *Annales*, 4/20 (1913), pp. 405–06; Corbin, *Women for Hire*, pp. 313–14; Harsin, *Policing Prostitution*, pp. 330–33, 348; Cavaillon, *Les législations antivénériennes*, pp. 338–40.

[349] *ZBGK*, 15, 6 (1914), p. 212; BA, 15.01, RmdI, 11866, p. 26, Reichs-Gesundheitsrat, 1908, Kirchner "Massnahmen zur Bekämpfung der Geschlechtskrankheiten im Deutschen Reiche," pp. 72ff.; "Aufzeichnung über die am 4. und 5. März 1908 abgehaltene Sitzung des Reichs-Gesundheitsrats (Ausschuss für Seuchenbekämpfung), betreffend die Bekämpfung der Geschlechtskrankheiten," Koch, pp. 311ff.; Der Reichskanzler, 25 February 1909, III B 211.

[350] *Allgemeine Ausführungsbestimmungen zu dem Gesetze vom 28. August 1905*, pp. 16, 24–25; Neisser, *Geschlechtskrankheiten und ihre Bekämpfung*, pp. 250–51; Martin Kirchner, *Die gesetzlichen Grundlagen der Seuchenbekämpfung im Deutschen Reiche unter besonderer Berücksichtigung Preussens* (Jena, 1907), p. 185; Walter Lustig, *Zwangsuntersuchung und Zwangsbehandlung* (Munich, 1926), p. 13; *DVöG*, 41 (1909), p. 728; *ZBGK*, 6, 3 (1907), p. 77.

direction with the Interior Ministry's decree of 11 December 1907, continuing the trend toward a more purely medical surveillance of prostitutes. Medical consultations were now made freely available to all who
sold sex, whether inscribed or not, and as long as they attended them,
the police refrained from official registration. Inscription, in any case,
could occur only after a court decision, not just at the vice squad's discretion. If prostitutes continued selling sex during treatment, however,
they risked being hospitalized. The hope was thus to bring all prostitutes,
clandestine and registered, out of the woodwork by offering them
medical care in return for being spared the maw of regulationism per
se.[351] Undercutting the ambitions of this new approach, however, were
a number of factors. Most obviously, both the 1905 Prussian Contagious
Disease Law and the 1907 decree violated the letter of the criminal code.
The police could not legally have knowledge of unregistered prostitutes,
much less arrange for their medical care, without either apprehending
them or themselves being guilty of procuring. Some police, backed by
their allies among regulationist physicians, were also unhappy at losing
their powers of control over prostitutes, often insisting that those who
were spared inscription while undergoing medical treatment nonetheless report regularly, thus obscuring the difference between the old and
reformed systems. More technically, it was unclear how prostitutes'
medical treatment was to be paid for. In Berlin, municipal funds were
used to reimburse physicians, but in other cities prostitutes had to pay
themselves, thus lessening the appeal of the carrot that was to entice
clandestines.[352]

Since the clash between the old style of regulation and ambitions to
moderate its bite thus remained enshrined in law, reformers turned their
attention to the legal codes. The DGBG proposed two changes to the
criminal code during the general overhaul of such matters broached
early in the new century: first, that not the sheer fact of unregulated
prostitution be punishable, but only that conducted so as to endanger
public order, health or decency, thereby moderating the force of the law

---

[351] *Ministerial-Blatt für die Preussische innere Verwaltung* (1908), pp. 14–16; *SB*, 1924/25, Anlage 975,
p. 11; *ZBGK*, 16, 8 (1915), p. 258; *Deutsche Juristen-Zeitung*, 13, 5 (1 March 1908), cols. 279–83; BA,
15.01, RmdI, 11866, p. 30, Reichs-Gesundheitsrat, 1908, Kirchner "Massnahmen zur
Bekämpfung der Geschlechtskrankheiten im Deutschen Reiche"; "Aufzeichnung über die am 4.
und 5. März 1908 abgehaltene Sitzung . . .," pp. 78–79; Der Reichskanzler, 25 February 1909, III
B 211, pp. 311ff.

[352] *Mitteilungen*, 8 (1910), p. 46; Borelli et al., *Geschichte der DGBG*, p. 35; Neisser, *Geschlechtskrankheiten
und ihre Bekämpfung*, p. 245; XVIIth International Congress of Medicine, *Dermatology and
Syphilography*, p. 51; *ZBGK*, 15, 6 (1914), p. 212; 8, 12 (1908/09), p. 416; DGBG, *Bericht über die Tätigkeit
in den Jahren 1902–1912* (Berlin, n.d. [1912]), p. 5; Chéry, *Syphilis*, p. 213.

over clandestines; secondly, to amend the clause prohibiting all forms of procuring, including the mere renting to prostitutes, thus (without real-lowing brothels) acknowledging the reality that prostitutes had to live somewhere and ending the theoretical liability for pimping of author-ities who sought to exercise medical survelllance over whores without registering them. The overall goal, as with previous reforms, was to shift the emphasis away from police control and toward sanitary surveillance, allowing medical interventions that did not necessarily bring with them the full force of regulation, scaring off prostitutes and swelling the ranks of the clandestine.[353]

THE FIRST WORLD WAR

The First World War marked an important break with basic regulation-ist assumptions. With the mass global peregrination of troops, the sexual fraternization of mobilized life, the disruption of domestic rou-tines and other appurtenances of war encouraging the spread of disease in general, the venereal sort in particular, VD became one of the many problems accentuated by the conflict that clamored for new solu-tions. With the wide dissemination of illness, earlier fears of eugenic decline were now amplified.[354] As VD rates in the countryside rose to urban levels, regulation's preoccupation with metropolitan circum-stances became less pertinent. As distinctions between the military and home fronts, soldiers and civilians, blurred, precautions initially tar-geted at the military often ended up equally applicable to those in mufti.[355] Many inherited prophylactic assumptions dissolved in the acid bath of wartime conditions. Primary – from the vantage here – among such casualties was the idea that big-city prostitutes alone could or should be the exclusive concern. The war's encouragement of a loos-ening of morals both at home and the front; new freedoms enjoyed by women economically as they filled the jobs of the mobilized that spurred concurrent changes in traditional notions of female sexual

[353] *Mitteilungen*, 8 (1910), pp. 46–47; *ZBGK*, 17 (1916), p. 183; *Vorentwurf zu einem Deutschen Strafgesetzbuch*, pp. 694, 850–53; Neisser, *Geschlechtskrankheiten und ihre Bekämpfung*, pp. 258, 317–19.

[354] H. C. Fischer and E. X. Dubois, *Sexual Life During the World War* (London, 1937); *Mitteilungen*, 13, 2 (1915), p. 22; 12 (1914), p. 112; Macalister, *Inaugural Address*, pp. 15–16; J. M. Winter, *The Great War and the British People* (London, 1985), pp. 10–18; Schneider, *Quality and Quantity*, ch. 5; Lutz Sauerteig, "Militär, Medizin und Moral: Sexualität im Ersten Weltkrieg," in Wolfgang U. Eckart and Christoph Gradmann, eds., *Die Medizin und der Erste Weltkrieg* (Pfaffenweiler, 1996), pp. 197–201.

[355] Friedrich Hampel, *Die Ausbreitung der Geschlechtskrankheiten durch den Krieg und ihre Bekämpfung* (Greifswald, 1919), pp. 5–6, 16; Robert Weldon Whalen, *Bitter Wounds: German Victims of the Great War, 1914–1939* (Ithaca, 1984), p. 67; *Bulletin*, 3, 75 (1916), p. 678.

behavior; the spread of VD among soldiers and subsequently to their families when on leave; the realization that, with the death of millions of husbands and nubile men and the difficulties of founding families in war-ravaged circumstances, extramarital sex and disease transmission were likely to be rampant after the end of hostilities: such factors conspired to make VD prophylaxis increasingly a problem of all adults, not just prostitutes.[356]

The double standard was collapsing, not (as social purity crusaders had hoped) by raising men to the virtuously chaste level of women, but by lowering females to the tawdry male denominator of promiscuity. In Saxony at war's end, to take but one example, most women reported as infected were not prostitutes – registered, clandestine or amateur – but simply female workers who had sex not for money, but motivated by what the authorities recorded as youthful frivolity and the search for pleasure. The gradations between amorous extramarital sex and cash-up-front prostitution had become so fine that regulationism's thumbnail categorizations (to the extent they ever had) no longer held true.[357] Such developments encouraged an acceptance of measures that went far beyond narrow regulation, aiming instead at sanitary surveillance not just of certain groups, but encompassing the entire population of potentially VD-threatened citizens.[358] Wartime circumstances in which individuals had learned to subordinate their interests to the community's eased the imposition of interventions that earlier would have been rejected.[359]

Most directly, during the war more men than ever had undergone the stringent prophylactic controls customary in the military, their position approximating that of inscribed prostitutes. Soldiers had long been subject to medical inspection as a condition of service, but specific vene-

[356] Thibierge, *La syphilis et l'armée*, pp. 21–23; Cate Haste, *Rules of Desire. Sex in Britain: World War I to the Present* (London, 1992), p. 56; Bristow, *Vice and Vigilance*, p. 146; *Mitteilungen*, 15, 3/4 (1917), p. 43; Kafemann, *Syphilis-Vorbeugung oder Salvarsan?*, p. 5.

[357] BA, 15.01, RmdI, 11881, "Übersicht über die in den Einzelstaaten mit der Verordnung der Reichsregierung zur Bekämpfung der Geschlechtskrankheiten, vom 11. Dezember 1918 . . . gemachten Erfahrungen," p. 288; *ZBGK*, 18, 1 (1917), p. 6; 15, 6 (1914), p. 200.

[358] "Die Auswirkungen des Reichsgesetzes zur Bekämpfung der Geschlechtskrankheiten vom 18. February 1927. (Auf Grund von Äusserungen der Landesregierungen). Denkschrift d. Reichsmin. d. Innern von Jan. 1930." Zu II A 1604/3.12, copy in Stabi, 4/Kd 5237; *Mitteilungen*, 13, 5/6 (1915), pp. 94–95; *ZBGK*, 17 (1916), p. 183; 18, 1 (1917), p. 2; 19, 5/6 (1919/1920), pp. 141–42.

[359] *ZBGK*, 16, 12 (1915/16), p. 383; Kaufmann, *Krieg, Geschlechtskrankheiten und Arbeiterversicherung*, pp. 36–37. A venereal version of Titmuss's explanation why solidaristic social policy was accepted as one of the lessons of mutual interdependence taught by the Second World War: Richard Titmuss, *Problems of Social Policy* (London, 1950), pp. 506–07; Richard Titmuss, "War and Social Policy," in his *Essays on "The Welfare State"* (2nd edn.; London, 1963).

real examinations were a more controversial matter. In the continental armies, little debate was wasted over the propriety of inspecting recruits and such precautions as existed were tightened up. In France, the Academy of Medicine recommended examinations every two weeks, as well as at furlough and return, and the authorities followed suit in 1916.[360] Britain, with its volunteer army, in contrast, had long regarded genital examinations as humiliating and likely to discourage recruitment. Its commonwealth allies, in contrast, with few such qualms, enforced frequent inspections of soldiers, the New Zealanders notorious for their "dangle parades." During the war they pressured the British to take a more active role in preserving the health of soldiers. The Americans, Canadians and Australians exhorted the British to follow their lead, insisting on compulsory inspection of prostitutes, examinations of soldiers, mandatory cure of the infected, emergency treatment centers in all cities, records to be kept of the afflicted, stricken personnel docked half pay, packets of disinfectants issued all men and special hospitals and mobile clinics to treat the diseased – a system, in other words, that for soldiers combined continental regulation with the Scandinavian method of universal compulsory treatment. Not all of these recommendations were adopted, but the British did move, however belatedly and reluctantly, toward a more active strategy. In 1916 venereal ablution rooms were established in barracks and soldiers who had risked infection were directed to attend for treatment within twenty-four hours: washing of the genitals, irrigation of the urethra with potassium permanganate solution ("pinky panky"), followed by applications of calomel ointment. In 1917, the packet system, of postcoital disinfectants, was finally authorized for British troops.[361]

The regulation of prostitution was also tightened, with public health authorities agreeing that a period of hostilities, mobilization and widespread disease was not the moment to abandon the tried and true for brave new experiments, and even the British were impelled to go along.

[360] *Bulletin*, 3, 75 (1916), pp. 679–81; *Annales*, 4/26 (1916), pp. 175–76; Thibierge, *La syphilis et l'armée*, p. 166; Fiaux, *L'armée et la police des moeurs*, pp. 263–64; Magnus Hirschfeld, *The Sexual History of the World War* (New York, 1934), pp. 96–97.

[361] Edward H. Beardsley, "Allied Against Sin: American and British Responses to Venereal Disease in World War I," *Medical History*, 20, 2 (April 1976), pp. 189–98; Bridget A. Towers, "Health Education Policy 1916–1926: Venereal Disease and the Prophylaxis Dilemma," *Medical History*, 24, 1 (January 1980), p. 76; Oriel, *Scars of Venus*, pp. 199–201; Reid, *Prevention of Venereal Disease*, p. 8; *History of the Great War* (London, 1923), v. II, pp. 125–29; Brandt, *No Magic Bullet*, ch. 3; Jay Cassel, *The Secret Plague: Venereal Disease in Canada 1838–1939* (Toronto, 1987), pp. 127–39; Mark Harrison, "The British Army and the Problem of Venereal Disease in France and Egypt During the First World War," *Medical History*, 39 (1995), pp. 146–49.

Over half of infections in the ranks, the German authorities calculated, stemmed from prostitutes at home, so stricter domestic precautions were necessary. Calls were heard in the regulationist nations for expanded control over clandestines and amateurs.[362] Most directly, prostitutes available for the troops were strictly regulated. Even the British army command accepted the necessity of such strictures for its soldiers on the continent, at least until March 1918 when official brothels were placed out of bounds to crown forces. Contact tracing was implemented for British soldiers in France, with women identified as sources examined and removed from the area if diseased. In France, the Academy of Medicine recommended tightening the system, with daily inspections of brothel prostitutes, outlawing of solicitation, rigorous surveillance of public places and banishment of whores from military areas, and the authorities agreed. Women apprehended for soliciting were inscribed on special lists and other measures taken to identify clandestines who would earlier have escaped official notice. Prostitutes were once again explicitly banished from the vicinity of schools, military barracks and churches, hotel keepers forbidden to lodge the inscribed in default on their medical inspections. It being impossible in current circumstances, the French Ministry of Interior noted in 1919, to abolish regulation, the aim was to consolidate and make it more effective.[363]

In Britain, where regulation was no more, attempts continued to repress prostitution and, more particularly, to prevent the paths of soldiers and harlots from crossing. While the government feared anything that might smack of restoring the CD Acts, potentially reigniting protest, the military authorities, both domestic and especially those of the Dominion allies, sought measures that, while preserving soldiers from infection, would not cut off access to commercial sex, considered a normal aspect of life in the ranks and necessary for morale. Caught between feminists at home and the Dominions abroad, and divided internally as well, the British authorities reluctantly and lethargically cobbled together a system of controlling mercenary sex in the military. In 1914, the commander of Cardiff imposed evening curfews, prohibiting all women from licensed premises and those of ill repute from appearing anywhere in public. Other proposals early in the war to exclude prosti-

---

[362] *ZBGK*, 20, 1/2 (1921), pp. 15–17; BA, 15.01, RmdI, 11869, "Begründung zu dem Antrage auf Änderung der §§ 180 und 361,6 Str.G.B.," pp. 393–94; *Mitteilungen*, 16, 5/6 (1918), p. 83; Thibierge, *La syphilis et l'armée*, pp. 21–23, 188–89.

[363] Oriel, *Scars of Venus*, p. 201; *History of the Great War*, v. II, pp. 123–24; *Bulletin*, 3, 75 (1916), p. 681; *Annales*, 4/26 (1916), pp. 175–76; 4/27 (1917), pp. 209–10; 4/28 (1917), pp. 8, 247–48; 4/29 (1918), pp. 10–12; Fiaux, *L'armée et la police des moeurs*, pp. 263–64; Cavaillon, *L'armement antivénérien*, p. 87.

tutes from military areas were at first rejected in fear that soldiers' sexual demands would be met instead by amateurs or promiscuous women, doing little to curb the incidence of VD. In 1916, DORA, Regulation 13a, allowed military authorities to ban anyone (changed from any woman in order to avoid the appearance – whatever the reality – of targeting females only) convicted of prostitution or vagrancy from the vicinity of military camps. Two years later, after continued pressure from their allies for more drastic measures, the British reluctantly issued DORA, Regulation 40d, which sought to plug holes by encompassing also the as-yet-unconvicted amateur, making it an offense for any infected woman to have sex with or solicit soldiers. The concern with sex between soldiers and women (whether prostitutes, amateurs or those just happy to see the troops) also inspired a system of semiformal control, with patrols womanned by volunteers set up to befriend and discourage young females in public places considered likely to have relations with soldiers.[364]

Another wartime change in attitude was the increased willingness to treat civilians akin to soldiers, subjecting them to similar precautions and helping erase regulation's sharp distinction between controlled groups and others. Most directly, army regulations affected also the civilian population. Though aiming primarily at clandestine prostitutes, the focus of such measures on all potential carriers continued the general prewar prophylactic trend toward an ever more expansive embrace. In Altona in 1916 the commander of the Ninth Army Corps issued instructions reminding civilians that the penal code punished transmission, requiring all infected to report the fact to the police and ordering medical inspection and potential hospitalization of anyone suspected of illness. All who indulged infectedly in extramarital sex in Posen risked punishment by special wartime regulations.[365] In France, contact tracing was mandated for the infected, regardless of gender, and the Academy of Medicine recommended regular fortnightly inspections, as for soldiers, of the Africans brought over to work in war factories.[366] Suggestions

[364] Lucy Bland, "In the Name of Protection: The Policing of Women in the First World War," in Julia Brophy and Carol Smart, eds., *Women-in-Law: Explorations in Law, Family and Sexuality* (London, 1985), pp. 28, 33–38; Buckley, "Failure to Resolve the Problem of Venereal Disease," pp. 66–68, 80; Bland, "Cleansing the Portals of Life," pp. 193, 202–03; Joan Lock, *The British Policewoman* (London, 1979), p. 26; Haste, *Rules of Desire*, pp. 32–33. The recruitment of women to the police was also an outcome: Philippa Levine, "'Walking the Streets in a Way No Decent Woman Should': Women Police in World War I," *Journal of Modern History*, 66, 1 (March 1994).

[365] *ZBGK*, 14, 3/4 (1916), pp. 46–47; *Mitteilungen*, 15, 1/2 (1917), p. 35; Meyer-Renschhausen, *Weibliche Kultur und soziale Arbeit*, p. 356.

[366] *Annales*, 4/27 (1917), p. 211; *Bulletin*, 3, 75 (1916), pp. 679–81; 3, 77 (1917), p. 386; *Annales*, 4/26 (1916), pp. 175–76.

were heard, especially in Germany, that wartime conditions now allowed
the regular inspection of all citizens, combatants or not, on the analogy
of examinations undergone by soldiers. To advocate, as did Dreuw and
others, that measures like surveillance, notification and isolation should
be applied not just to prostitutes, but to all infected citizens, no longer
seemed wholly fanciful. Neither did calls for an end to regulation and the
imposition, in its stead, of an obligation for all brothel clients to be
inspected beforehand, buy a condom and be disinfected postcoitally.
Nor, as a final example of this altered approach from the early Weimar
years, was it venereally utopian to argue that, by subjecting all citizens,
even respectable burghers, to regular Wassermann tests (serological
soundings that, requiring no genital inspection, were bereft of immediate sexual connotations) and issuing certificates to be treated like any
other official document, the stigma of syphilis and its treatment would
be diminished.[367]

The ambitions of the German military authorities for measures to
smooth the epidemiological transition from hostilities to peace, even
though most fell by the way after the collapse of the Kaiserreich, demonstrated the change in attitude. They wished to be able to report by
name all infected recruits to the health insurance carriers, retaining
them for compulsory treatment before demobilization. The trend was to
assimilate VD to other contagious diseases, much as reformers had long
sought. Retaining only the VD-infected, it was feared, would in effect
expose the husbands among them as luckless philanderers, potentially
adding needless marital dissent to the already imposing list of postwar
problems, and the solution was therefore to require treatment for victims
of all contagious diseases before discharge. Most generally, when the
military authorities discussed measures like reporting and compulsory
treatment to ensure that soldiers were not returned infected to civilian
life, they argued that such tactics would not be temporary ones, nor
limited only to active participants, but that, through inspections for the
reserves, the entire adult male population would pass through the hands
of military physicians, with precautions for all VD victims eventually

---

[367] *ZBGK*, 18, 7 (1917/18), pp. 177–81; Dreuw, *Allgemeine, gleiche, diskrete Anzeige- und Behandlungspflicht*,
pp. 1–2; Dreuw, *Völkervernichtung*; Dreuw, *Kultur-Korruption*; *ZBGK*, 15, 8/9 (1914), pp. 280–84; 16, 7
(1915), pp. 217, 226–28; 20, 5/6/7 (1922), pp. 100–01. The wide incidence of VD during the war may
have helped reduce its stigma. In Germany, reformers sought to encourage this normalization of VD
by having medical consultation centers womanned so that female patients would approach them
with less trepidation: BA, 15.01, RmdI, 11874, Katharina Scheven, Deutscher Zweig der
Internationalen Abolitionistischen Föderation to the Reichsamt des Innern, 7 June 1919, p. 142.

evolving out of such techniques.[368] Who would have thought before the war, as a participant in army discussions on how to combat VD put it, that the state would be telling civilians what bread to eat, materials to wear and foodstuffs to feed their cattle? Now such interventions were taken for granted. Precautions such as making VD notifiable could be discussed anew since the majority of adult men, serving as soldiers, accepted reporting and inspections as perfectly normal.[369] The near-universal experience of military service and its rigors during the war made increasingly palatable the treatment of men much as regulated prostitutes, while the necessities of war allowed an extension of measures formerly reserved for prostitutes to the civilian population as well.

PERSONAL PROPHYLAXIS

The wide spread of VD in wartime circumstances meant that regulation, however reformed, however inclusive of new groups, would not suffice. Other means of hampering disease dissemination were necessary and, among the debates, the most intense concerned personal prophylaxis. Personal means of prevention, whether in the form of condoms or the still popular use of post- and sometimes precoital antisepsis, raised the hoary ethical issue of the wages of sin. Such techniques, as indeed any attempt to mitigate, avert, reduce or heal the physical results of VD, were seen as immoral because, removing the consequences, they threatened to encourage illicit sex.[370] Public health was set in direct competition with morality.

Such dilemmas were far from new. During the reign of Charles II in the late seventeenth century, as one version of the story goes, the luckless Dr. Condom or Conton invented the device that was to bear his name and was forced by the ensuing outrage to change both that and his address. The French showed that the British had not cornered the market on moral fulmination when, in 1772, Guilbert de Préval was

---

[368] BA, 15.01, RmdI, 11869, "Niederschrift über die Verhandlungen der Vollversammlung der Vorstände der Landesversicherungsanstalten und Sonderanstalten im Reichsversicherungsamt am 14. Dezember 1915," pp. 123–24; "Aufzeichnung über die kommissarische Beratung im Reichsamt des Innern vom 29. Mai 1916, bereffend die Zurückhaltung der mit ansteckenden Krankheiten behafteten Heeresangehörigen nach Überführung des Heeres auf den Friedensfuss," pp. 282–84; *Mitteilungen*, 15, 5/6 (1917), p. 100; 16, 5/6 (1918), pp. 81–83, 102.

[369] BA, 15.01, RmdI, 11869, Fornet, "Anzeigepflicht bei Geschlechtskrankheiten," pp. 196ff.; "Sitzungsbericht der am 8. Okt. 1915 auf Einladung des General-Gouvernements in Belgien zu Brüssel abgehaltenen Besprechung über die Massnahmen zur Bekämpfung der Geschlechtskrankheiten," pp. 208–18.   [370] C. Levaditi, *Prophylaxie de la syphilis* (Paris, 1936), pp. 18–19.

expelled from the medical faculty of the University of Paris for claiming to have discovered a means of preventing syphilis and thus, in the eyes of his detractors, giving libertinage free rein.[371] It is not our task, a German physician sniffed half a century later, to give advice to the lewd who seek to commit excess without suffering the consequences. The pope's pastoral letter of 1826 condemned prophylactics as deflecting the punishments providence had in store for sinners, wisely if perhaps a bit predictably intending to punish them in the member with which they had erred. Conversely, arguments that a moral approach was misplaced in respect to a biological and epidemiological problem and that prevention was a higher good than whatever venereal excesses it might encourage were of equally venerable stock.[372]

By the First World War, the violent debates of the late nineteenth century over the morality of contraception were still fresh in memory and nowhere, the Catholic countries especially, had the dispute subsided. Neomalthusianism, expounded in Britain already during the 1820s by Francis Place and then anonymously by George Drysdale at midcentury, identified the root of many social problems in overpopulation, seeking a solution not, as had Malthus, in chastity, but in contraception that permitted a divorce between sex and the responsibilities of procreation and family. Contraception, was the argument, would permit early marriages, postponing childbearing rather than the wedding, and thus help undercut the demand for prostitution. Au contraire, the scandalized opponents claimed: the result would be a moral decline as sex came to be regarded re- rather than procreationally and the point of marriage as pleasure rather than parenthood. Nature's intentions would be subverted and, indeed, sex without the possibility of fertilization was little short of murder. Rather than undermining whoring, marriage itself would become prostituted, as Swedish abolitionists insisted, ironically finding themselves in agreement with Bebel, Nordau and others who argued that bourgeois society had already, without much assistance from the condom, managed to produce this unhappy result.[373]

The proponents of personal prophylaxis now continued their argu-

---

[371] Walch, *Ausführliche Darstellung*, pp. 251–52; *ZBGK*, 12, 1 (1911), pp. 35–37; Norman E. Himes, *Medical History of Contraception* (New York, 1970), ch. 8; Parent-Duchatelet, *De la prostitution*, v. II, pp. 534–37; Benabou, *La prostitution et la police des moeurs*, p. 426; Jacques Donzelot, *The Policing of Families* (New York, 1979), p. 172.

[372] Finger et al., *Handbuch der Geschlechtskrankheiten*, v. I, p. 124; Owsei Temkin, *The Double Face of Janus* (Baltimore, 1977), p. 482; August Friederich Hecker, *Deutliche Anweisung die venerischen Krankheiten genau zu erkennen und richtig zu behandeln* (2nd edn.; Erfurt, 1801), pp. 39–40.

[373] Boëthius, *Strindberg och kvinnofrågan*, p. 72.

ments that, whatever their effects in reducing the risks of extramarital sex, no other means of controlling VD held out such promise. Measures of public hygiene affected only a small part of the population; regulated prostitution was of increasingly doubtful effectivity; appeals to abstinence, however noble and well intentioned, were likely to be ignored. Personal prevention, in contrast, harnessed the instincts of reproduction and self-preservation together in a mutually virtuous circle. The condom, in the words of one unabashed admirer, had spared millions from infection and its inventor deserved a place next to Jenner in the pantheon of public hygiene. Personal prophylaxis, much like vaccination, shifted the preventive emphasis from public and necessarily collective measures that, violating civil rights, isolated victims in hopes of breaking chains of transmission, to actions and behavior expected of individuals to limit their own potential contagiousness. Precisely because VD spread through voluntary and discrete acts, rather than indiscriminate exhalation, expectoration or excretion, interrupting transmission by encouraging individual prophylaxis was crucial.[374]

The search for a personal solution to VD infectiousness had long been underway. Early attempts to counteract venereal poison included postcoitally tying ligaments around the penis, applying dismembered but still living pigeons, chickens or frogs to the glans and having the penis irrumated by members of the lower classes. Substances were sought to toughen the skin of the genitals, lessening their receptivity to infection.[375] Compared to such ideas (over which modern observers, blessed with 20/20 hindsight from the smug vantage of the antibiotical age, may be permitted a brief and thoroughly unhistoricist chuckle) the condom – however fragile the thin barrier (linen, bestial ceca, vulcanized rubber, latex) protecting the genitals from the virulently suppurating world of malevolent microorganisms – represented a real advance. Early in the twentieth century, disinfections and ablutions alone had still held their own vis-à-vis the condom, although their disadvantage in not offering women much protection was well recognized.[376] Elaborate procedures

---

[374] Ferdinand Thugut, *Syphilis: Ihr biologischer Ursprung und der Weg zu ihrer Ausrottung* (Stuttgart, 1931), pp. 97–99; *ZBGK*, 14, 4 (1912), pp. 138–39; Lande, *Les affections vénériennes*, p. 92.

[375] Walch, *Ausführliche Darstellung*, pp. 243–44, 248; Christoph Girtanner, *Abhandlung über die Venerische Krankheit* (Göttingen, 1788), v. I, pp. 414–15; Boyveau Laffecteur, *Traité des maladies vénériennes, anciennes, récentes, occultes et dégénérées* (Paris, 1807), pp. 49ff.; Proksch, *Vorbauung der venerischen Krankheiten*, p. 42; Hecker, *Deutliche Anweisung*, pp. 41–42.

[376] Levaditi, *Prophylaxie de la syphilis*, p. 114; Cavaillon, *Les législations antivénériennes*, p. 16; Reid, *Prevention of Venereal Disease*, p. 15; Müller, *Praktisches Handbuch*, pp. 67–68. Madame de Sévigné's immortal line about condoms being "as strong as gossamer, as sensual as armor" also did yeoman service.

of disinfection were spelled out, paying careful attention to each body part, gargling with alcohol after kissing, disinfectants dispensed in automats in public toilets, worked by foot levers to minimize the risk of contamination.[377] Metchnikoff–Roux and Neisser–Siebert salves, calomel and other lotions were developed during the first decade of the new century to be applied postcoitally in hopes of preventing an infection from taking hold. The condom grew in popularity over the nineteenth century, however, and already early on observers were recommending a combination of their use along with disinfectant ablutions, striking a modern note that would not change appreciably over the following years.[378]

Complicating the otherwise broad support among public health reformers for personal prophylaxis, however, was the fact that some means, especially the condom, also had contraceptive effects. In addition to the objections that sidestepping conception defeated the intentions of nature or providence, the argument against such devices focused on their alleged eugenic effects: lowering fertility rates and the quality of successive cohorts. Inspired by fears of demographic decline, most nations had sought to restrict the sale or at least the advertisement and display of contraception, often including in their sweep also those devices that were equally useful in curbing the spread of VD.[379] Thanks to the Lex Heinze, the German penal code after 1900 (§184/3) forbade the display and advertisement, but not sale, of objects intended for lewd purposes. Whether this included condoms was a matter of dispute, with certain lower courts ruling that it did not. In 1903, however, the supreme court decided that condoms (useful in, and therefore an encouragement to, extramarital sex) were meretricious. To the dismay of venereal reformers, the court extended the reach of §184, ruling in 1910 to prohibit catalogues of contraceptive devices mailed to wedded couples since, despite vows of fidelity, the articles might still serve the purposes of extramarital dalliance.[380] The battlelines on contraception were complicated and

[377] Weinbrenner, *Wie schützt man sich vor Ansteckung?*, pp. 29, 37. Regulations for the personal hygiene and cleansing of prostitutes had been elaborated since the early nineteenth century at least: *Zeitschrift für die Staatsarzneikunde*, 58 (1849), pp. 428–54; *New Orleans Medical and Surgical Journal*, 11, 1 (July 1854), p. 679; *DVöG*, 1 (1869), pp. 386ff.; *ZBGK*, 1, 3 (1903), p. 180.

[378] Touton and Fendt, *Der Umschwung in der Syphilisbehandlung im ersten Jahrzehnt des XX. Jahrhunderts und die jetzige Lage* (Wiesbaden, 1911), pp. 3–7; Paul Maisonneuve, *The Experimental Prophylaxis of Syphilis* (New York, 1908), pp. 55ff.; Reid, *Prevention of Venereal Disease*, pp. 2–4; Walch, *Ausführliche Darstellung*, pp. 248–52; Girtanner, *Abhandlung über die Venerische Krankheit*, v. I, p. 269.

[379] Girtanner, *Abhandlung über die Venerische Krankheit*, v. I, p. 280; XVIIth International Congress of Medicine, *Dermatology and Syphilography*, p. 60.

[380] *ZBGK*, 13 (1911), p. 162; 11 (1910), pp. 227–28; 16, 7 (1915), p. 222; 3 (1911), pp. 167–70; 14, 4

often ran at crosspurposes. Many abolitionists, especially the conservative wing of the women's movement, who might otherwise have welcomed a means of lessening the necessity of regulation, opposed such devices as encouraging sin.[381] Even the Socialists were divided on the issue, with some adopting a neomalthusian line (that smaller families promised to improve the lot of individual workers), while others, like Kautsky, Zetkin and Luxemburg, rejected family planning as a conservative attempt to blame working-class sexual mores for social problems, regarding the problem instead as that of a misdistribution of resources, not too many consumers.[382] Thanks to such crosscutting, even during the interwar period when much changed in other respects, the authorities shied away from attempts to untangle the contraceptive effects from the antivenereal virtues of many birth control devices, lifting the prohibition on promotion and display. Not until the middle Weimar years, with penal code reform and the 1927 VD law, was §184 interpreted such that only indecent or offensive advertisement was punishable.[383]

Britain was unusual in this respect in that birth control propaganda was not hindered by law after 1877, but Sweden, responding in 1910 to what was perceived as ever more immoral publicity for contraceptive devices (love without children) and the general fears of depopulation familiar from other nations, passed a law emulating the German Lex Heinze in outlawing the advertisement, but not sale, of prophylactic means.[384] In France, the church's position on contraception added

---

(1912), p. 135; 14, 11 (1913), p. 406; *Mitteilungen*, 11 (1913), pp. 23–24; James Woycke, *Birth Control in Germany 1871–1933* (London, 1988), pp. 49–50; Finger et al., *Handbuch der Geschlechtskrankheiten*, v. III, p. 2686; Laupheimer, *Der strafrechtliche Schutz*, pp. 44–45.

[381] *ZBGK*, 16, 12 (1915/16), p. 369; Waldvogel, *Gefahren der Geschlechtskrankheiten*, p. 78; Brennecke, *Wie ist der Kampf zu führen?*, p. 24.

[382] Jean H. Quataert, *Reluctant Feminists in German Social Democracy, 1885–1917* (Princeton, 1979), pp. 97–98; Usborne, "Die Stellung der Empfängnisverhütung," pp. 279–83; Usborne, *Politics of the Body*, pp. 112–18; Woycke, *Birth Control in Germany*, p. 55; Weindling, *Health, Race and German Politics*, p. 251; R. P. Neuman, "The Sexual Question and Social Democracy in Imperial Germany," *Journal of Social History*, 7, 3 (Spring 1974), pp. 277–79; Christiane Dienel, *Kinderzahl und Staatsräson: Empfängnisverhütung und Bevölkerungspolitik in Deutschland und Frankreich bis 1918* (Münster, 1995), ch. 7. In Britain, the working-class movement was generally hostile to contraception until the end of the nineteenth century: Angus McLaren, *Birth Control in Nineteenth-Century England* (London, 1978), chs. 3, 9, 10; Richard Allen Soloway, *Birth Control and the Population Question in England, 1877–1930* (Chapel Hill, 1982), ch. 4.

[383] BA, 15.01, RmdI, 11886, p. 13, meeting in the RmdI, 15 April 1919; Der Minister des Innern, M. 11908, 10 June 1919, Arbeitsausschuss zur Bekämpfung der Geschlechtskrankheiten, 24 April 1919; Schmedding and Engels, *Gesetze betreffend Bekämpfung übertragbarer Krankheiten*, p. 337; *Mitteilungen*, 23, 5 (1925), p. 23; Usborne, *Politics of the Body*, pp. 109–12.

[384] *ZBGK*, 12, 9 (1911), pp. 326–28; *Förhandlingar*, 1911, p. 513; 1912, p. 255; Eva Palmblad, *Medicinen som samhällslära* (Gothenburg, 1989), pp. 133–35; Jeffrey Weeks, *Sex, Politics and Society: The Regulation of Sexuality Since 1800* (2nd edn.; London, 1989), pp. 46–47.

weight to the belief that prophylactics encouraged sexual license. Proposals had long been made to forbid publicity and sale of such devices, finally passing in 1920, and popular habit resisted the use of condoms more than elsewhere.[385] The sale of condoms was allowed after 1967, but advertisement not permitted until 1987 (and then only without mention of their contraceptive effects) when the AIDS epidemic put the issue on the table once again.[386]

By the early twentieth century, however, the tradeoffs among VD, contraception and fertility were being weighed more carefully. Arguments were now heard that, restricting the reproduction also of the least worthy, contraception's eugenic effects did not necessarily favor decline and that, in any case, since VD too hampered fertility, condoms were preferable to the clap.[387] The war especially served to soften up inherited battlelines, with the spread of VD among military and civilians alike demonstrating the folly of ignoring effective prevention and soldiers serving as guinea pigs for new techniques. Such lessons were drawn in almost all nations, although with markedly different degrees of alacrity: quickly among the continental nations and the colonial powers among the Allies, with greater reservations and hesitations among the British.

In Germany, the war shunted fears of declining birthrates to second place, now ceding priority to hopes of curtailing VD. The navy had long issued prophylactics to sailors and this was now extended to terrestrial combatants as well. Since the demands of war production limited the supplies of rubber available for condoms, the authorities drew on the experience of the American army to recommend postcoital ablution as well. Soldiers were given access to disinfectants and automats dispensing the substances installed in barracks.[388] In 1916, the DGBG petitioned the

---

[385] Ann F. La Berge, *Mission and Method: The Early Nineteenth-Century French Public Health Movement* (Cambridge, 1992), p. 265; *Annales*, 46 (1851), p. 75; Corbin, "La grande peur de la syphilis," p. 331; Schneider, *Quality and Quantity*, p. 120; Mary Louise Roberts, *Civilization Without Sexes: Reconstructing Gender in Postwar France, 1917–1927* (Chicago, 1994), p. 95; Martine Sevegrand, *Les enfants du bon dieu: Les catholiques français et la procréation au XXe siècle* (Paris, 1995), pp. 45–46.

[386] CSP, L 282; Claude Got, *Rapport sur le SIDA* (Paris, 1989), p. 109; Michel Setbon, *Pouvoirs contre SIDA: De la transfusion sanguine au dépistage: Decisions et pratiques en France, Grande-Bretagne et Suède* (Paris, 1993), p. 173; Foyer and Khaïat, *Droit et Sida*, p. 11; Jeanne Pagès, *Le contrôle des naissances en France et à l'étranger* (Paris, 1971), pp. 159–62, 211–26.

[387] *ZBGK*, 14, 11 (1913), pp. 404–05; August Forel, *Die sexuelle Frage* (5th edn.; Munich, 1906), pp. 503–05; Neisser, *Geschlechtskrankheiten und ihre Bekämpfung*, pp. 94–95; *Mitteilungen*, 12 (1914), pp. 37–39; 13, 5/6 (1915), pp. 99–103; BA, 15.01, RmdI, 11887, p. 87, Der Präsident des Reichsgesundheitsamts, II 1671/21, 28 April 1921; Nye, *Masculinity and Male Codes of Honor*, p. 82; Usborne, *Politics of the Body*, ch. 3.

[388] *ZBGK*, 16, 10 (1915/16), pp. 301–03; *Mitteilungen*, 17, 2/3 (1919), p. 28; BA, 15.01, RmdI, 11875,

government not to hamper the dissemination of prophylactic devices. With the surplus of women and the difficulties of founding families in ravaged circumstances, the incidence of extramarital sex, one high-level government committee was told, was likely to increase after the war and fertility to drop. Therefore condoms would do no additional damage to population levels and a great deal of good to those of VD, and disinfective techniques should also be encouraged. For civilians, disinfection stations were established after the war in major cities, with advertisements posted in public toilets.[389] In France, the Academy of Medicine roused itself to recommend that men frequent prostitutes only armed with a condom and mayors were advised to set up cleansing cabinets in brothels. Disinfection stations were established for soldiers modeled on the American example and the French were permitted to ablute with the Yankees if their own were closed.[390] Personal prophylaxis came to be regarded as an effective tool during the postwar period in Sweden and the Lex Veneris now contradicted earlier law in holding forth the possibility of public education in the techniques thereof.[391]

In Britain, the Royal Commission on VD ignored the entire matter, whether condoms or the packet system (of disinfectants), making a brief allusion to mercury treatments and Metchnikoff and Roux's work on calomel salve in the midst of its report, but otherwise refusing to recommend the extension to civilians of measures that were eventually, however reluctantly, to be adopted in the military.[392] Personal prophylaxis was, however, too effective to be brushed aside by the fear of encouraging vice and subsequent debates revealed an almost ludicrous willingness to split terminological hairs in hopes of avoiding allegedly moral consequences. The National Council for Combatting Venereal

"Aufzeichung über die am Donnerstag, den 10. und Freitag, den 11. Juli 1919, im Reichsgesundheitsamt abgehaltene Sitzung des Reichs-Gesundheitsrats . . .," p. 162; Lutz Sauerteig, "Moralismus versus Pragmatismus: Die Kontroverse um Schutzmittel gegen Geschlechtskrankheiten zu Beginn des 20. Jahrhunderts im deutsch–englischen Vergleich," in Dinges and Schlich, *Neue Wege in der Seuchengeschichte*, p. 217; Woycke, *Birth Control in Germany*, pp. 51, 112.

[389] *ZBGK*, 17 (1916), p. 143; 18, 8 (1917/18), p. 199; BA, 15.01, RmdI, 11875, v. Gruber, "Referats-Zusammenfassung für die Sitzung des Reichs-Gesundheitsrats am 11. Juli 1919," pp. 7–10; Neisser, *Geschlechtskrankheiten und ihre Bekämpfung*, p. 93; *Mitteilungen*, 13, 5/6 (1915), p. 102; 17, 2/3 (1919), p. 28; 24, 9 (1926), p. 101.

[390] *Bulletin*, 3, 77 (1917), p. 386; *Annales*, 4/27 (1917), p. 209; 4/29 (1918), pp. 294–303.

[391] *SFS*, 1918/460, §27; *Betänkande angående åtgärder för spridande av kunskap om könssjukdomarnas natur och smittfarlighet m.m.* (Stockholm, 1921), pp. 168–75.

[392] Richard Davenport-Hines, *Sex, Death and Punishment: Attitudes to Sex and Sexuality in Britain Since the Renaissance* (London, 1990), pp. 223–24; *Nineteenth Century*, 82 (July–December 1917), pp. 583–84, 1046.

Diseases (NCCVD) rejected the packet system because of the moral implication that those who equipped themselves with disinfectants intended to sin, hoping avoid the consequences. Because the element of intention and therefore moral culpability was less pronounced, it was, however, willing to accept "early preventive treatment" (centers where those coming from possibly infectious sex could repair to be disinfected), even though the inevitable delay made this less effective than packets. Army doctors favored extending the packet system that had finally been authorized for soldiers in 1917 also to civilians. During the final war years and early in the peace, packets were sold to civilians, but this was curtailed after 1917 when the Venereal Diseases Act, forbidding quacks from treating VD, also prevented pharmacists from recommending disinfectants to customers. In 1919 the Astor Committee on diseases and demobilization rejected extending the packet system to civilians, so irritating some members of the NCCVD that the organization split, with the Society for the Prevention of Venereal Disease (SPVD) forming to promote the widespread use of packets and personal disinfection in general. Two ablution stations were established in Manchester in 1919–20 in public toilets, but closed again shortly following protest from social purity and feminist organizations.[393]

During and immediately after the war, the two sides on the issue were thus gradually reconciled in northern Europe, while in Britain and France personal prophylaxis remained contentious. Conservatives came to see that VD was as great a threat as immorality or depopulation; the left moderated its opposition to neomalthusianism. By the early interwar years, the debate between the morality and the efficiency of personal prophylaxis, though not over, had largely been settled in the official mind in favor of the pragmatic stance that such techniques were too important to be sidetracked by worries of increased illicit sex.[394]

MEDICAL CURE

That VD was best tackled by ensuring the broadest possible cure of the ill, providing widespread access to treatment, ideally free for at least the

---

[393] Towers, "Health Education Policy 1916–1926," pp. 80–86; *Nineteenth Century*, 84 (July–December 1918), p. 171; Reid, *Prevention of Venereal Disease*, pp. x–xiii, 5, 169; *Mitteilungen*, 17, 1 (1919), pp. 2–4; Levaditi, *Prophylaxie de la syphilis*, p. 24; Oriel, *Scars of Venus*, p. 200; Davenport-Hines, *Sex, Death and Punishment*, pp. 229, 237; *Mitteilungen*, 23, 2 (1925), p. 11; Bristow, *Vice and Vigilance*, p. 152.

[394] Usborne, "Stellung der Empfängnisverhütung," pp. 271–83; Usborne, *Politics of the Body*, pp. 102–06; Sauerteig, "Moralismus versus Pragmatismus," p. 220.

poor, was an idea with a long and nationally ecumenical pedigree.[395] Free hospital treatment was a cornerstone of the Scandinavian approach and various laws in Germany and France promised the poor similar care.[396] The problem, of course, was that until an actual cure was possible, intention and outcome bore little relation to each other. In the long run, the possibility of curing VD would help undermine regulation and all other forms of drastically interventionist prevention, treatment substituting effectively for prophylaxis, post for ante facto approaches. When cure was first held out, however, as a realistic eventuality, with salvarsan after 1910, it raised many of the same issues as personal prophylaxis. With a disease like syphilis (prolonged and significantly symptomless) cure played a different prophylactic role than for acute epidemic diseases. With ailments like cholera and smallpox – short and violent, the fastigium closely following infection – curing individual victims, if at all possible, was largely inconsequential from the vantage of public health. Isolating patients (to the extent that the disease itself did not take them out of circulation) promised to prevent further transmission, but whether they were cured was largely irrelevant since the disease would, in any case, shortly have run its course for better or worse. With syphilis, in contrast, patients remained infectious, able to go about life normally and in undiminished thrall to the instincts that had gotten them into trouble in the first place, thus continuously a potential source of disease. Curing syphilitics therefore became a crucial part of prevention, an element of breaking chains of transmission; cure was important not only for the individual, but also for society. Wrapping the penis in dead frogs or lathering it up with Metchnikoff and Roux's salve after a possibly infectious coitus were acts of cure from the vantage of the member's owner, of prophylaxis from that of his next sexual partner. The Scandinavian system of requiring treatment of the stricken was a recognition that, epidemiologically speaking, the crucial aspect of regulation had been not registration and inspection, but medical attention

---

[395] Kornig, *Medicinischpolitischer Vorschlag*, pp. 25–26; Müller, *Praktisches Handbuch*, pp. 64–65; Stamm, *Verhütung der Ansteckungen*, p. 68; Fiaux, *Police des moeurs*, v. I, pp. 495–97; *ZBGK*, 3, 8/9 (1904–05), p. 312; 8, 1 (1908), pp. 12–13; Guyot, *Prostitution Under the Regulation System*, p. 309; *Journal of Cutaneous Diseases*, 23 (1904), p. 278; Jeanselme, *Traité de la syphilis*, v. I, pp. 422–23; *Annales des maladies vénériennes*, 1 (1906), p. 125; Anne Marie Moulin, "L'ancien et le nouveau: La réponse médicale à l'épidémie de 1493," in Neithart Bulst and Robert Delort, eds., *Maladies et société (XIIe–XVIIIe siècles)* (Paris, 1989), pp. 126–29.

[396] Augustin, *Preussische Medicinalverfassung*, v. II, pp. 762–63; Cavaillon, *L'armement antivénérien*, pp. 25–26; Pappenheim, *Handbuch der Sanitäts–Polizei*, v. II, p. 247.

for infected prostitutes and that a more effective solution was thus – cutting to the chase – to cure all who were ill.[397]

The distinction between prophylaxis and cure remained important, however, from the viewpoint of morality. Seen from an unwavering ethical stance, any attempt to circumvent the infirmities foreseen by nature and divine calculation as punishment for sexual transgression, whether through prophylaxis before the fact or cure afterwards, threatened to undermine the disincentives to fornication provided by VD. Cure could thus, especially if painless, be as conducive to immorality as prophylaxis. On the other hand, charity, altruism and common decency spoke for an attempt to alleviate the sufferings of syphilitics.[398] If imposed in suitably unpleasant circumstances, cures could even be part of the disincentive to sin. When, after 1614, VD victims were first admitted to the Hôtel-Dieu in Paris for whatever treatment was then possible, they were flogged upon entry and discharge to remind them that care did not imply condoning the results of sin.[399] Throughout the nineteenth century a more subtle disincentive approach was continued. Hospitals were sometimes reserved for VD patients exclusively and many that maintained separate wards for the infected offered them only substandard treatment and harsh conditions (no visitors, censored mail, special uniforms, worse food). The mercury treatments common through the end of the nineteenth century, with their unpleasant and dangerous side effects, were in many respects their own best punishment, as were attempts to starve syphilis out, not to mention the cures that involved ingesting live a certain Guatemalan lizard daily for a month.[400] It was perhaps in the face of these toe-curling alternatives that the popular imagination seized with such eagerness on the idea that sleeping with a virgin held out a solution.[401] When penicillin brought the

---

[397] Rosebury, *Microbes and Morals*, p. 251; *Underdånigt betänkande angående könssjukdomarnas spridning*, v. I, p. 376.

[398] Parent-Duchatelet recommended a clear distinction between cure and prophylaxis, the one an act of charity extended to the ill, even sinners, the other a temptation to transgression: Parent-Duchatelet, *De la prostitution*, v. II, pp. 538, 541.

[399] In Germany similar chastisement added insult to injury by being called *Willkommen und Abschied*: Parent-Duchatelet, *De la prostitution*, v. II, p. 171; *Annales*, 16 (1836), p. 271; *Zeitschrift für die Staatsarzneikunde*, 58 (1849), pp. 428–54.

[400] Girtanner, *Abhandlung über die Venerische Krankheit*, v. I, pp. 414–15; Ziegelroth, *Die physikalisch-diätetische Therapie der Syphilis* (Berlin, 1900), pp. 120–21. Indeed, during the Middle Ages, mercury cures were reserved for the poor, intended to have a deterrent effect, while the aristocracy experimented with the altogether more pleasant, though not effective, remedy of guaiacum: Temkin, *Double Face of Janus*, pp. 472–84; Finger et al., *Handbuch der Geschlechtskrankheiten*, v. I, p. 118; Rudolf Weil, *Verhaltungsmassregeln bei ansteckenden Geschlechtskrankheiten* (Berlin, n.d. [1902]), pp. 4–7.

[401] Proksch, *Vorbauung der venerischen Krankheiten*, p. 42; Fiaux, *Police des mœurs*, v. I, p. 391; *ZBGK*,

promise of an effective and largely painless cure, it was attacked precisely because, supplanting long, arduous and unpleasant treatments, antibiotics threatened to encourage sexual insouciance. Early treatments, of American GIs during the Second World War, often tended to be rougher and more unpleasant than strictly necessary so as not to forego the disincentive of earlier procedures.[402] The regulations of various health insurance systems, excluding victims of VD and other allegedly self-inflicted ailments from benefit, were a continuation of the same disincentive approach.

During the era of the First World War, such attitudes changed. Most generally, for the first time in modern memory, the possibility of a medical cure was seriously entertained, potentially allowing a post facto solution to the VD problem to supplement and perhaps replace prevention. With Ehrlich and Hata's discovery of salvarsan and its apparently effective cure of syphilis in 1909, the answer to an age-old issue seemed at hand. Even though it quickly became apparent that salvarsan was neither infallible nor without its unpleasant side effects, the advantages were notable. No longer did largely symptomless patients have to be persuaded to enter hospitals for lengthy and unpleasant mercury cures. Shorter treatment times on an outpatient basis held out the hope of deflecting the resistance of the stricken to medical attention.[403] In Britain especially, salvarsan's possibilities had a major influence on prophylactic strategizing.[404] The conclusions drawn by the Royal Commission on VD in 1916 were based on its promise of an effective cure that allowed the authorities to sidestep the moral quagmire of personal prophylaxis, attacking the problem after the fact and thereby ignoring the issue of intention that separated active and reprehensible fornication from an all-too-human and therefore forgivable succumbing

---

16, 12 (1915/16), p. 371; Hellwig, *Gesetz zur Bekämpfung der Geschlechtskrankheiten*, p. 144; *Mitteilungen*, 27, 3 (1929), p. 70; Reid, *Prevention of Venereal Disease*, p. 72; Davenport-Hines, *Sex, Death and Punishment*, p. 263; Rudeck, *Syphilis und Gonorrhoe vor Gericht*, pp. 6–9, 16; Ambroise Tardieu, *Dictionnaire d'hygiène publique et de salubrité* (Paris, 1854), v. III, p. 213; Lesley A. Hall, *Hidden Anxieties: Male Sexuality, 1900–1950* (Cambridge, 1991), p. 44. Sometimes women slept with boys or "decent" men with the same intentions: Jadassohn, *Handbuch der Haut- und Geschlechtskrankheiten*, v. XXIII, pp. 24–25; *ZBGK*, 19, 1 (1919), p. 22. A similar belief appears to have continued with AIDS: Jean-Pierre Baud, "Les maladies exotiques," in Eric Heilmann, ed., *Sida et libertés: La régulation d'une épidemie dans un état de droit* (n.p., 1991), p. 22.   [402] Rosebury, *Microbes and Morals*, pp. 131–32.

[403] Touton and Fendt, *Umschwung in der Syphilisbehandlung*, pp. 86–87; Rosebury, *Microbes and Morals*, pp. 213–15; *Mitteilungen*, 8 (1910), pp. 71–72; *ZBGK*, 12, 6 (1911), pp. 202–05.

[404] In fact, medical technique had played a special role for VD in Britain for a long time, this being one of the rare occasions when the British preferred cure to prevention. The increasing effectiveness of treatment for VD was one of the reasons Simon opposed extending the CD Acts to civilians: *PP* 1868–69 xxxii, 1, pp. 13–16.

to temptation. The commission recommended as the nub of its solution providing broad and free access to medical care and the 1916 Public Health (Venereal Diseases) Regulations foresaw hospital treatment for VD patients, free diagnostic tests for physicians attending the ill and gratis supplies of salvarsan equivalents. This new emphasis on treating rather than preventing VD continued the following year in the Venereal Diseases Act which excluded all but qualified medical practitioners, thus in effect upping the stakes of the curing game.[405] If cures were thought possible and the solution of choice, then the government had to demonstrate its purposefulness by excluding the ineffective nostrums proffered by quacks.

The wartime period also saw major changes in the scope of hospital care in most nations. Where inpatient treatment, if it had existed at all, was grossly inadequate, reformers called for expanded provision. Where the demeaning treatment of VD patients in hospitals had discouraged admission, changes were proposed to integrate the stricken among others in regular wards under normal conditions.[406] Increased and mainstreamed facilities were now instituted as part of the focus on cure as an ever more important facet of the solution to VD. Before the war, Britain had been a laggard in such hospital provision. Medical treatment for civilians was available only in the scarce voluntary institutions which handled these diseases or through private practitioners. Although from the repeal of the CD Acts until the war, the state had paid little attention to VD, the report of the Royal Commission in 1916 spurred changes. In 1917, a new system of VD treatment centers was created, largely funded by the central government, operated by voluntary hospitals on behalf of local authorities and offering what was in effect Britain's first universal free health service, without means or residence tests. By the 1920s, there were some two hundred VD treatment centers in England and Wales, with 75 percent of the costs paid by the central authorities, the rest by localities.[407]

[405] *BJVD*, 1, 1 (January 1925), p. 12; *History of the Great War*, v. II, p. 145; W. M. Frazer, *A History of English Public Health 1834–1939* (London, 1950), pp. 339–41; Arthur Newsholme, *Health Problems in Organized Society* (London, 1927), p. 167; Eyler, *Arthur Newsholme and State Medicine*, p. 289; David Evans, "Tackling the Hideous Scourge," p. 428.

[406] *Annales*, 16 (1836), pp. 271–72; Dubois-Havenith, *Conférence internationale: Rapports préliminaires*, v. I/1, quest. 6, pp. 6–11; *Bulletin*, 2, 17 (1887), p. 609; Fiaux, *Police des moeurs*, v. I, pp. 460–61, 575; Blaschko, *Syphilis und Prostitution*, p. 118; Guyot, *Prostitution Under the Regulation System*, p. 345.

[407] *PP* 1867–68 (4031) xxxvii, 425, Q 3062; Harveian Medical Society, *Report of the Committee for*

In other nations, hospital provision that had been expanded during the war for the military continued into the peace. In France, centers for dermatological and venereal diseases, established for the troops starting in 1916, were continued after the armistice. VD clinics were set up in large towns, some 395 in total, welcoming all patients, especially workers in the war factories, but also infected civilians, offering them anonymous and free (though informally means-tested) treatment.[408] In Germany, with its precocious health insurance system, the problem was less providing accessible treatment than ensuring that the insurance carriers did not exclude coverage for VD, an issue to be discussed later. In December 1918, the Minister of War conceded the impossibility of retaining all infected soldiers until cured. Instead, the solution was to provide widespread medical care for the stricken, free of cost to demobilized combatants and their dependants who could not afford it or whose care was not covered by health insurance. Such special provisions for soldiers and their families, however, were but temporary measures that ended in 1919 and the longterm solution here was to expand insurance coverage to a larger fraction of the population, providing care for the poor who were not members through public assistance.[409] In addition, consultation centers were established during the early Weimar years, some four hundred in all, with forty in Berlin alone. Motivated by a variety of impulses (eugenic, social Darwinist, some aiming to improve the situation of workers), these dispensed advice and information on disease, contraception, family planning and sexuality in general. Unlike the clinics in Britain and France, they explicitly did not – lest they compete with physicians whose services were already underwritten for the bulk of

---

the Prevention of Venereal Diseases, p. 7; Davenport-Hines, *Sex, Death and Punishment*, pp. 186–88; Jeanne L. Brand, *Doctors and the State: The British Medical Profession and Government Action in Public Health, 1870–1912* (Baltimore, 1965), p. 64; David Evans, "Tackling the Hideous Scourge," pp. 413–14, 428, 433; *BJVD*, 1, 1 (January 1925), p. 14; *History of the Great War*, v. II, p. 130. The British accomplishment here was much like what the Swedes had done a century earlier: free, universal medical care for a particular set of diseases.

[408] Jean-Baptiste Brunet, "Evolution de la législation française sur les maladies sexuellement transmissibles," in Job-Spira et al., *Santé publique et maladies à transmission sexuelle*, p. 116; Murard and Zylberman, *L'hygiène dans la république*, pp. 573–75; Cavaillon, *L'armement antivénérien*, pp. 1–11; *Annales*, 4/32 (1919), p. 246; 4/27 (1917), p. 195; Jeanselme, *Traité de la syphilis*, v. I, p. 424; Léon Bernard, *La défense de la santé publique pendant la guerre* (Paris, 1929), ch. 22; Quétel, *History of Syphilis*, pp. 176–77; CSP, L 295–305. This clinic system was then continued after the Second World War: *JO*, 19 August 1948, pp. 8150–51.

[409] *Mitteilungen*, 17, 1 (1919), pp. 7–12; *SB*, 1924/25, Anlage 975, p. 5; Georg Schreiber, *Deutsches Reich und Deutsche Medizin: Studien zur Medizinalpolitik des Reiches in der Nachkriegszeit (1918–1926)* (Leipzig, 1926), pp. 24–25; *Mitteilungen*, 17, 4/5 (1919), p. 87; 18, 3 (1920), pp. 72–73.

German workers through the insurance system – offer medical treatment.[410]

THE NEW APPROACH

One result of the war was thus to make it clear that neither regulation nor inaction were sufficient responses to a problem becoming more urgent. The Scandinavian nations had been prompted to take a sanitarily statist approach already in the nineteenth century and others now found this system of extending measures to the entire population increasingly attractive. The ever widening spread of disease conspired with the general regimentation of life under wartime conditions to make the citizen-as-potential-patient approach already familiar in the north acceptable elsewhere as well. Because of the war, one French observer noted, they now lived under a regime analogous to that of Scandinavia, where the ill, men or women, must be cured.[411] And yet, although all nations were under similar pressures to pursue more interventionist tactics, in fact the choices made among possible strategies diverged considerably. As throughout the history of prophylaxis, similar problems did not necessarily mean similar solutions. Scandinavia led the way, Germany sought to emulate the Swedes, Britain pursued a divergently voluntary approach, while in France reforming ambition outstripped its legislative reach and, despite many suggestions for change, little was undertaken.

Prompted by public fears of epidemics and pressure from the military, the British authorities halfheartedly proposed measures more draconian than they would have preferred. The Criminal Law Amendment Act, debated from 1917 through the early 1920s, would have repressed prostitution vigorously, criminalizing endangerment of VD, but never made it to the books. DORA, Regulation 40d, sparked protest from women's organizations which saw in it, at best, an unfair shifting of the burden of

---

[410] *Mitteilungen*, 24, 9 (1926), p. 99; Kristine von Soden, "Auf dem Weg zur 'neuen Sexualmoral' – die Sexualberatungsstellen der Weimarer Republik," in Geyer-Kordesch and Kuhn, *Frauenkörper, Medizin, Sexualität*, pp. 237–62; von Soden, *Sexualberatungsstellen der Weimarer Republik*; Hodann, *History of Modern Morals*, p. 104. Only after the Second World War in the Soviet Zone were VD clinics established: Stefan Kirchberger, "Public-Health Policy in Germany, 1945–1949," in Donald W. Light and Alexander Schuller, eds., *Political Values and Health Care: The German Experience* (Cambridge, 1986), pp. 204–05. British and Swedish venereologists also complained of the competition: Roy Porter and Hall, *Facts of Life*, p. 240; *American Journal of Public Health*, 26 (April 1936), p. 360; Lesley A. Hall, "'The Cinderella of Medicine': Sexually-Transmitted Diseases in Britain in the Nineteenth and Twentieth Centuries," *Genitourinary Medicine*, 69 (1993), p. 317.

[411] Fiaux, *L'armée et la police des moeurs*, p. xi.

proof to females, or – worse – an attempt to resuscitate regulationism. Given the first general elections with female (over thirty) suffrage looming in the summer of 1918, this was a worrisome prospect. The War Office largely ignored the act and after the armistice it was withdrawn. Although efforts had been made to repress prostitution during the war, any return to the CD Acts was ruled out. Because of moral objections, personal prophylaxis was only reluctantly and ineffectually pursued. Measures in effect elsewhere were also rejected. Making VD notifiable continued to be resisted as likely to discourage medical care, at least of the licensed sort, and similar objections held for compulsory treatment.[412]

Instead, the British trained their efforts on education and making treatment free, or inexpensive, and widely available. Rejecting both regulation and other forms of broad statutory intervention, they cobbled together a response that avoided coercion and treated all diseased, men or women, alike – a system of freely available medical care like the Scandinavian, but on a strictly voluntary basis and without the Nordic hankering for compulsion and its attendant machinery: notification, mandatory treatment, punishment of the recalcitrant.[413] Even in the army, where control and discipline were strictest and compulsion most plausibly successful, the British took a more voluntary tack than other nations. They had learned early from experience in 1873 with Lord Cardwell's order docking the pay of soldiers under treatment for VD that the result was not, as it appeared in the official statistics, less disease, only less illness reported, as the men sought to avoid the economic as well as the corporeal consequences of their misfortune.[414] During the First World War, the lessons drawn here were continued, with punishments imposed for concealing, but not suffering, disease. British soldiers were required to pay hospital stoppages for all illness not due to service in the field, not just VD, while their Commonwealth colleagues were

---

[412] David Evans, "Tackling the Hideous Scourge," pp. 428–30; Buckley, "Failure to Resolve the Problem of Venereal Disease," pp. 70–71; Davenport-Hines, *Sex, Death and Punishment*, p. 228; *Mitteilungen*, 16, 5/6 (1918), p. 103; Haste, *Rules of Desire*, p. 54; *PP* 1914 (7474) xlix, 109, p. 2; *PP* 1916 (8189) xvi, 1, pp. 48–51; Morris, *Nation's Health*, pp. 92–97.

[413] *PP* 1916 (8189) xvi, 1, pp. 50, 65; *BJVD*, 2, 5 (January 1926), p. 72.

[414] *PP* 1882 (340) ix, 1, p. x; Deck, *Syphilis*, p. 30; Myna Trustram, *Women of the Regiment: Marriage and the Victorian Army* (Cambridge, 1984), pp. 128–30. Other nations also learned from this example: *Bulletin*, 2, 17 (1887), p. 651; Fiaux, *L'armée et la police des moeurs*, p. 261; Malmroth, "Om de smittosamma könssjukdomarnas bekämpande," p. 38; *Annales de dermatologie et de syphiligraphie*, 4, 9 (1908), p. 607. In the British navy, the lesson had been learned already in the late eighteenth century: Christopher Lloyd and Jack L. S. Coulter, *Medicine and the Navy 1200–1900* (Edinburgh, 1961), v. III, pp. 357–58.

specifically fined for venereal afflictions.[415] The main principles behind the British approach were that chains of transmission, usually forged in circumstances of intimacy largely beyond the state's ken, could not be severed except by voluntary compliance, that treatment and cure should be made convenient and accessible and that anything likely to discourage patients from seeking or continuing medical care should be avoided, whether cost, compulsion, reporting or contact tracing.[416] Patients were not subject to the strictures common in other nations, Scandinavia and eventually Germany especially, and the authorities were correspondingly limited in their ability to intervene actively against the spread of disease.

In Germany, in contrast, the lesson drawn from similar wartime experiences was the need to broaden the state's narrow focus on official prostitutes. Local authorities, aghast at the increase of VD during the immediate postwar years, urgently requested the Imperial health office to introduce compulsory medical examinations for all, regardless of gender or occupation. By the early interwar period, the rapprochement between neoregulationists and neoabolitionists was proceeding apace, laying the groundwork for consensus on a form of sanitary statism, although without the Scandinavians' most drastic means of compulsion, and the government was ready for reform.[417] Early in 1918, a bill broadened the terms of the prophylactic battle.[418] Prostitutes, inscribed or not, were no longer to be liable under the penal code, but remained regulated in a sanitary sense, subject to medical surveillance, inspection and hospitalization. Other neoregulationist demands were met in punishing endangerment and forbidding engagements by infected wet-nurses or the parents of diseased infants. Quacks were targeted by prohibiting treatment at a distance and by unlicensed medical practitioners; advertising and display of alleged remedies were forbidden except in professional periodicals. Most importantly, the shift in focus from prostitutes to all citizens continued in full force. In committee, it

---

[415] Although during the war all sickness except VD and alcoholism were admitted as contracted through service, so VD was treated differently, but only in the fact of losing a privilege accorded to other ailments: _History of the Great War_, v. II, p. 122–23; Towers, "Health Education Policy 1916–1926," p. 76.

[416] Paul Adams, _Health of the State_ (New York, 1982), p. 116; Laird, _Venereal Disease in Britain_, p. 45; Eyler, _Arthur Newsholme and State Medicine_, p. 281.

[417] BA, 15.01, RmdI, 11886, the Stadtrat, Zella-Mehlis, to the President of the Reichsgesundheitsamt, 29 January 1920, p. 200; _Mitteilungen_, 22, 6 (1924), pp. 33–34; _Mitteilungen_, 25, 3 (1927), pp. 21–22; Flesch and Wertheimer, _Geschlechtskrankheiten und Rechtsschutz_, pp. 75–76.

[418] _SB_, 1914/18, Drcksch. 1287; _ZBGK_, 18, 8 (1917/18), p. 197; _Mitteilungen_, 16, 1/2 (1918), pp. 10ff.; Hellwig, _Gesetz zur Bekämpfung der Geschlechtskrankheiten_, p. 10.

was proposed to require all infected, not just prostitutes, to be treated on pain of punishment. The government objected, fearful that denunciations would ensue and the ill be driven to quacks. A moderated version, however, found its favor that required medical care, though with no threats of drastic consequences in default, and foresaw hospitalization of those who refused or broke off treatment, much as the victims of other transmissible illnesses could be isolated under the Contagious Disease Law.[419]

The collapse of the Kaiserreich halted the progress of this particular bill, but its gist was improvised by a decree in December that criminalized endangerment and required medical care, if necessary by force, for all infected who might otherwise spread disease, although also insisting on the patient's approval for therapeutic interventions that threatened life or health. While the police in fact did not often enforce compulsory treatment, fearing that it might drive the infected underground, they welcomed the legal leverage thus provided as helpful in concentrating the minds of the infected on voluntarily seeking aid. More significantly, with all citizens now liable for transmitting disease and obliged to be treated, the focus of precautions had definitively shifted from prostitutes alone to the venereally infected in general.[420] Though a breakthrough in theory, this did not, of course, mean that, in practice, respectable family fathers infected through dalliances were now treated on the same footing as streetcorner tarts. The most immediate effect of the new measures was to give the authorities purchase over women who were neither registered nor even prostitutes in any professional sense at all. But it also meant that they now had powers over men who transmitted disease of much the same sort that earlier had applied only to women.[421] Male vagabonds and drifters could be compulsorily treated, for example, and in some localities (Baden for one) the authorities took matters further, subjecting all suspected of transmission to mandatory medical attention, including those who had had relations with more than one person or with the diseased. In

---

[419] BA, 15.01, RmdI, 11873, Der Präsident des Kaiserlichen Gesundheitsamts, II 2331/18, 18 September 1918, pp. 485–86.

[420] *Reichsgesetzblatt*, 1918/184, p. 1431; Posener, *Bekämpfung der Geschlechtskrankheiten*, pp. 53–54; BA, 15.01, RmdI, 11881, "Übersicht über die in den Einzelstaaten mit der Verordnung der Reichsregierung zur Bekämpfung der Geschlechtskrankheiten, vom 11. Dezember 1918 . . . gemachten Erfahrungen," pp. 283–85; *ZBGK*, 19, 3 (1919), p. 68; Hellwig, *Gesetz zur Bekämpfung der Geschlechtskrankheiten*, p. 370.

[421] The desire of the authorities to treat men on the same footing as earlier only prostitutes is made evident in BA, 15.01, RmdI, 11881, "Der Präsident des Reichs-Gesundheitsamts an den Herren Staatssekretär des Innern," 7 December 1918, p. 20.

Frankfurt, men were hospitalized who refused or broke off treatment, who had been caught in police razzias or who had been identified as contacts. The double standard had thus finally been fused in measures that strictly, but at least equitably, held all who infectedly engaged in extramarital sex, whatever their status or gender, to the same rules, threatening them with compulsory treatment and penal consequences if they endangered others.[422]

Concurrent with this expansion of prophylactic strictures ran the debate over regulation properly speaking – whether finally to end it. Powerful forces still backed the system, even if of a reformed variety: the police and the Justice Ministry, the health insurance carriers who feared a wider dissemination of VD, Catholic bishops, but also some Protestant organizations, several of the individual states in the Reichsrat – Hessen, Württemberg, Bavaria.[423] Foreign policy considerations also played a role, since, the French having established official brothels in their occupation zone, the Land governments here (Hessen for example) supported the system.[424] Nonetheless, despite inaction by the first parliament elected with female suffrage immediately following the Kaiserreich's fall, the political winds during the early Weimar years were clearly blowing against regulation. Concerns were strong that the class elements of the old system not be perpetuated in new legislation. Equally important, the majority in parliament was, in the words of an Interior Ministry memo, hopelessly in thrall to abolitionism and the government dared not propose anything short of repeal.[425]

The broadening of measures to include all potential carriers, begun in 1918, continued in the protracted negotiations that culminated at long last in the VD law of 1927. Initial drafts followed the earlier precedent in requiring all suspected of VD to provide health certification or face

---

[422] *Mitteilungen*, 25, 1 (1927), pp. 3, 8; 25, 11/12 (1927), p. 128.

[423] *Die Polizei*, 17, 11 (19 August 1920), p. 229; BA, 15.01, RmdI, 11887, Der Reichsminister der Justiz, II a 1523 Schä, 1 October 1920; Verband deutscher Landesversicherungsanstalten, 7 January 1921, p. 51; Bemerkungen und Anträge Bayerns, 29 March 1921, p. 74; 15.01, RmdI, 11892, Württembergischer Landesausschuss zur Bekämpfung sittlicher Not an den Deutschen Reichstag, April 1922, p. 28. Among Protestants opinions were divided: compare *Evang.-Kirchliche Nachrichten*, 1, 3 (27 December 1920), with BA, 15.01, RmdI, 11891, p. 80, Evang. Volksbund für Württemberg an das Reichsministerium des Innern, 29 September 1920.

[424] BA, 15.01, RmdI, 11887, RmdI meeting, 9 November 1920, pp. 33ff., Koch.

[425] *Mitteilungen*, 17, 6 (1919), pp. 116–17; BA, 15.01, RmdI, 11886, pp. 186ff., meeting in the RmdI, 21 January 1920, Kraus; pp. 126ff., meeting in the RmdI, 16 December 1919, Gottstein; 15.01, RmdI, 11887, Aufzeichung für die Genfer Konferenz, p. 59; RmdI meeting, 9 November 1920, pp. 33ff.; Der Reichsminister des Innern, II A 76, 24 January 1921; 15.01, RmdI, 11891, p. 80, Evang. Volksbund für Württemberg an das Reichsministerium des Innern, 29 September 1920; *ZBGK*, 19, 4 (1919), p. 94.

medical inspection, with the ill who were likely to spread disease subject to treatment. Prompted by the Left Liberals in 1919, the Prussian parliament asked the national government to adopt reforms that would shift VD prophylaxis from regulation to a system of sanitary surveillance and with the 1927 VD law they were finally in place.[426] Regulation was ended and prostitution decriminalized, with the penal code no longer forbidding all unregulated whoring, but only public solicitation in general and commercial sex as such near churches and schools and in dwellings inhabited by children, although allowing an exception for small communities that chose to forbid it across the board.[427] Procuring was redefined to prohibit brothels absolutely, with or without police permission, but at the same time permitting landlords to rent to prostitutes so long as they did not charge exploitative rates. Concentrating prostitution in certain parts of the city was also ruled out.[428] The role of the police was much diminished from the glory days of the *Sittenpolizei*, called on now primarily to keep order, apprehend violators of public decency, report those suspected of spreading VD, bring recalcitrants to examinations or the hospital and in general acting only on behalf and behest of the health authorities.[429]

These, in turn, now focused not on prostitutes per se, but anyone suspected of spreading VD: the citizen as carrier. Of such – whether male or female, fulltime, amateur or not in the sex business at all – they could require medical examination and certification of either health or continuing treatment from a physician, if necessary on a regular basis. They could be obliged to undergo treatment with a physician of their choice and, if necessary because of the likelihood of transmission, be

---

[426] BA, 15.01, RmdI, 11886, pp. 123ff., "Vorläufiger Entwurf eines Reichsgesetzes zur Bekämpfung der Geschlechtskrankheiten"; *ZBGK*, 19, 7/8 (1919/20), pp. 173–85; *Mitteilungen*, 25, 11/12 (1927), p. 128; Bauer, *Geschichte und Wesen der Prostitution*, p. 103; *SB*, 1924/25, Anlage 975; *Reichsgesetzblatt*, 1927/1/9, pp. 61–64.

[427] Social Democrats worried lest the clause prohibiting prostitution near churches and schools, insisted on by the Center, be used as a backdoor to reintroduce regulation, since in large cities there was scarcely a spot not near such institutions. Some jurists claimed that, in theory at least, regulation of a certain sort could have continued on the basis of Land law. But such fears were incidental to the main decision to end regulation in the old sense: A. V. Knack and Max Quarck, *Das Reichsgesetz zur Bekämpfung der Geschlechtskrankheiten und seine praktische Durchführung* (Berlin, 1928), p. 23; *Mitteilungen*, 25, 8 (1927), p. 74.

[428] Although, as earlier, various localities knew how to circumvent such theoretical prohibitions: Karl Linser, *Die Geschlechtskrankheiten* (Dresden, 1941), p. 101.

[429] Although there were grey areas dealing with such matters as police razzias in search of the potentially infectious: "Die Auswirkungen des Reichsgesetzes"; *Mitteilungen*, 27, 1 (1929), p. 28; 25, 11/12 (1927), p. 141; Schmedding and Engels, *Gesetze betreffend Bekämpfung übertragbarer Krankheiten*, pp. 328–29; Hellwig, *Gesetz zur Bekämpfung der Geschlechtskrankheiten*, p. 395; Christoph Sachsse and Florian Tennstedt, *Geschichte der Armenfürsorge in Deutschland* (Stuttgart, 1988), v. II, pp. 129–30.

compulsorily hospitalized.[430] Contact tracing was undertaken of the diseased.[431] Those who knowingly endangered others by infectedly having intercourse, not just actually transmitting as in the criminal code, could be jailed (§5). Notifiability was introduced in a limited form in order not to discourage the ill from seeking treatment, with physicians to report only patients who interrupted their cures or endangered others, whether by the circumstances of their work (as barbers, wet-nurses etc.) or irresponsible conduct. The law obliged all who knew, or should know, that they were infected to be treated by a licensed physician, although, in fear of blackmail, no punishment for neglect was foreseen. The corollary to this theoretically compulsory treatment was free medical care. The implementation decrees in each federal state were to ensure that those unable to afford their own physician, who were not covered by health insurance or for whom there was some disadvantage in being treated for VD through the system (risking termination if their employer found out, for example) would be dealt with at the public expense.

Prostitutes were thus no longer the exclusive focus of prevention: they were not inscribed, they were no longer targeted alone among potential carriers and the hygienic regulations to which they were subject did not dictate the terms of their lives in other respects, as in the old system.[432] Regulation, in other words, had ended, but those who violated rules of public morality or were suspected of transmission were liable to inspection and treatment. At the heart of this shift in prophylactic focus lay the question how to identify those within a vast group of carriers on whom to target measures. Precautions had either to be wholly generalized in an impractical fashion (regular Wassermann tests for all citizens) or they had to single out certain groups for reasons other than the purely epidemiological. Under regulation, the pertinent category had been occu-

---

[430] Hellwig, *Gesetz zur Bekämpfung der Geschlechtskrankheiten*, pp. 386–89; *Mitteilungen*, 25, 11/12 (1927), p. 148. Authorization to use direct force was explicitly stated to avoid the problem of local variation: *SB*, 1924/25, Anlage 975, p. 7; *Reichsgesetzblatt*, 1927/1/9, §4. For the variations of allowable force in the various states: see BA, 15.01, RmdI, 11876, "Zusammenstellungen der Äusserungen auf das Rundschreiben des Herrn Reichsministers des Innern, vom 6 August 1920," pp. 235–38; RmdI, 15.01/11887, Der Reichsminister des Innern, II A 76, 24 January 1921; *Mitteilungen*, 25, 11/12 (1927), pp. 161–62.

[431] §4 of the law did not explicitly require contact tracing, but Prussian and Bavarian implementation decrees did: Ernst Steinke, *Erfahrungen über Ermittlungen und Meldungen von Ansteckungsquellen vor der Einführung des Reichsgesetzes zur Bekämpfung der Geschlechtskrankheiten* (Greifswald, 1927), p. 6.

[432] *Mitteilungen*, 18, 5/6 (1920), p. 112. The targeting of those who offered sex for sale in public, whatever their gender, and permitting the same treatment of others who spread VD as for prostitutes were also features of reforms of the penal code during this period: *Mitteilungen*, 23, 5 (1925), pp. 23–24.

pationally defined. If this system was to end, targeting would have to be accomplished by some other criteria, most likely ones based on the sexual habits of the persons in question. Obviously, prostitutes, whom the authorities could with some plausibility assume to be both infected and likely to transmit, would be more liable to medical surveillance than other citizens.[433] That they would be as subject to the new form of medical surveillance as they had been to the old form of control was the hope that bought the support of neoregulationists for reform and the fear (that regulation would be indirectly reintroduced) that repelled some abolitionists. The new measures thus in no way exempted prostitutes from control, but they did expand beyond this core constituency the group of those who would receive equal attention. In the Prussian regulations specifying the law's details, for example, the suspected included not only prostitutes, but also those who had sex while infected, who had been reported as contacts by the diseased or who had multiple sexual partners. In Bavaria the same group was identified more lapidarily as prostitutes and the promiscuous.[434] Regulation as a system targeted at prostitutes thus ended, but venereal control was not abandoned. Rather than have medical inspection dependent on the largely arbitrary fact of registration, it was now to be based on epidemiologically more significant criteria, rendering surveillance if anything more inclusive and more effective.[435]

In France, similar reforms were attempted, but for a long time amounted to naught. A commission at the Ministry of Hygiene sought to draw on the wartime experience at least to modify regulationism, introducing some of the principles of sanitary statism. In 1926 it formulated a bill subjecting both sexes to the same precautions, no longer targeting prostitutes except through a regular law and only insofar as they solicited in certain public places. Instead, all acts of transmission and endangerment were to be punishable and the ill were to be required, by

---

[433] BA, RmdI, 15.01/11887, p. 87, Der Präsident des Reichsgesundheitsamts, II 1671/21, 28 April 1921; *Mitteilungen*, 24, 11 (1926), p. 120; 27, 1 (1929), p. 29. In Frankfurt, when authorities sought to inspect all prostitutes, they objected that the new law required examination only of the ill who refused medical treatment: *Mitteilungen*, 26, 1 (1928), pp. 4–5.

[434] *SB*, 24 January 1927, p. 8725C–D; Hellwig, *Gesetz zur Bekämpfung der Geschlechtskrankheiten*, pp. 384, 400; Kreuzer, *Prostitution*, p. 12.

[435] *ZBGK*, 19, 5/6 (1919/1920), pp. 135–53. The attempt of the 1927 law to follow Scandinavian precedents was then, after a resurgence of regulation and repression of prostitution during the Nazi regime, followed by the Federal Republic's VD law of 1953. This required all infected to be treated, prohibiting in the interim sex of any sort, and allowed authorities to hospitalize recalcitrants. It required health certificates and inspections of the infected and those suspected of being infectious or of transmitting VD.

threat of fines, jail or hospitalization, to follow their prescribed treatment. Attempts to bring this and similar proposals to legislative fruition, however, failed.[436] In 1939, a decree in the last days of the Third Republic allowed physicians to report the infected believed to be endangering others and punished those who refused treatment. Soliciting was prohibited. During the occupation, in 1942, physicians were obliged to report VD patients, tracing contacts, and the sick, in turn, to be treated, compulsorily in hospitals if necessary.[437] No general law on the matter ensued, however, as in Germany or Scandinavia. Prostitutes remained regulated and official brothels died only a slow and protracted death. In the late 1920s, it was decided no longer to license new bordellos, with current authorizations allowed to lapse. During the occupation, however, in 1941, brothels were recognized as establishments of public entertainment and taxed accordingly, giving municipalities every interest in their proliferation.[438] Only after the Second World War, in 1946, were official brothels (compromised by their collaboration with the Germans) and registration abolished by the Marthe Richard law, with soliciting and procuring made offenses.[439] At the same time, what was given with one hand was withdrawn with the other. A law two weeks later replaced the registration system with a centralized national sanitary index, tracking prostitutes for the purposes of contact tracing and medical treatment.[440] Under the 8 July 1948 law, anyone inscribed on this register and all arrested for solicitation, even before charges had been proven, were subject to periodic examination.[441] Under the guise of a purely sanitary regime, the old system had thus reappeared, indeed been rendered more efficient. Not until 1960, with an end to the register, was regulation and its exclusive targeting of prostitutes finally over. In return, with well over

[436] James F. McMillan, *Housewife or Harlot: The Place of Women in French Society 1870–1940* (Brighton, 1981), pp. 174–77; Cavaillon, *L'armement antivénérien*, pp. 25, 151, 154–58; Gustav Scherber, *Die Bekämpfung der Geschlechtskrankheiten und der Prostitution* (2nd edn.; Vienna, 1939), p. 98; Cavaillon, *Les législations antivénériennes*, p. 51; *Centenaire d'Alfred Fournier: Conférence internationale de défense sociale contre la syphilis: Rapports* (Paris, 1932), pp. 215–25; N.-M. Boiron, *La prostitution dans l'histoire, devant le droit, devant l'opinion* (Nancy, 1926), pp. 244ff.

[437] Laws of 29 November 1939, 31 December 1942: Quétel, *History of Syphilis*, pp. 207–08.

[438] *BJVD*, 2, 5 (January 1926), p. 73; Cavaillon, *L'armement antivénérien*, p. 151; Corbin, *Women for Hire*, pp. 344–45.

[439] 13 April 1946 law: *JO*, 14 April 1946, p. 3138; Dominique Dallayrac, *Dossier Prostitution* (Paris, 1966), pp. 280–83; Félicien Davray, *Les maisons closes* (Paris, 1980), pp. 167–68; Alphonse Boudard, *La fermeture* (Paris, 1986); Max Chaleil, *Le corps prostitué* (Paris, 1981), ch. 11. Richard's own motivation for closing brothels seems to have been strictly sanitary, that the prostitutes there were the most infectious: Marthe Richard, *Mon destin de femme* (Paris, 1974), pp. 327–28.

[440] Law of 24 April 1946: *JO*, 25 April 1946, p. 3422; Dallayrac, *Dossier Prostitution*, pp. 283–84; Jacques Robert and Jean Duffar, *Libertés publiques* (3rd edn.; Paris, 1982), pp. 216–17.

[441] *JO*, 9 July 1948, p. 6642, art. 2.

half a century's delay, France formally adopted the basic features of the Scandinavian system, requiring the infected to be treated, physicians to report patients, contacts to be traced, the recalcitrant to be hospitalized, forbidding the infected to pursue certain professions and indirectly holding them liable for transmission.[442]

In the regulationist nations, especially Germany, valiant attempts were thus made to emulate the Scandinavian model. The main principle implemented was to require treatment of all infected citizens, providing them, in return, with free or at least accessible medical care. As corollaries to this overall ambition, various measures (notification, contact tracing and criminalizing transmission) sought to discourage risky behavior and to ensure that the infected in fact received treatment.

VARIATIONS ON A PROPHYLACTIC THEME

With VD we have yet again a common epidemiological problem that was approached with markedly different strategies in various nations. Indeed, the tactics adopted here varied, if anything, more starkly than for other transmissible diseases. The typologies are, as always, less than hermetic, but at least three different approaches can be distinguished among the nations under the glass here: regulationism, tempered by its eventual reform, in France and Germany; abolition and a strictly voluntary approach in Britain; sanitary statism in Scandinavia, emulated after 1927 in Germany as well.[443] Among these, one may distinguish again between an interventionist and a voluntary approach. In the first case, regulationism attempted to clamp down on the epidemiological fulcrum of transmission located at prostitution. When this eventually proved inadequate, sanitary statism extended similar interventions to the entire population. The primary difference between the two tactics was the scope of the intervention, with sanitary statism applying broadly regulationist techniques to the entire sexually active population. While the Scandinavian nations may, from one perspective, have emulated the

---

[442] CSP, L 255–85. These measures, like the 1948 law, traced their parentage back to a Vichy law of 31 December 1942, which in turn picked up many of the themes broached by Henri Sellier, Minister of Health in the Popular Front government, in his bill of November 1936, as well as various wartime measures: Auby, *Le droit de la santé*, p. 392; Brunet, "Evolution de la législation française," pp. 116–17.

[443] There are variants and permutations on such typologies, which often also include a fourth possibility, prohibitionism, as in most of the United States: Cavaillon, *Les législations antivénériennes*, pp. 25, 54–55; Gibson, "State and Prostitution," p. 195; Decker, *Prostitution: Regulation and Control*, p. 74; Dolléans, *La police des moeurs*, pp. 175–76; Jeanselme, *Traité de la syphilis*, v. I, p. 426; Amos, *Comparative Survey of Laws*, pp. 246–47; de Félice, "Situation abolitionniste mondiale," p. 4.

British example in abolishing regulation, what they put in its place made them, if anything, more interventionist than the regulationists.

In contrast, the voluntary approach, pursued paradigmatically in Britain, rested on the logic that, because of its moral implications, the volitional aspect of its transmission and its nonacute symptomology, VD could not be dealt with like other contagious diseases. Compulsion and repression threatened to drive its victims out of the light and further into the recesses of society, aggravating the problem. Lord Cardwell's attempt to dock the pay of infected soldiers, rewarding dissimulation, was the classic example of such dysfunctional results. A voluntary strategy – encouraging sufferers to undergo treatment and removing whatever obstacles might discourage them – was, in this reasoning, likely to be as effective, and certainly much less noxious, than a compulsory one. *On soignera plus de malades par la liberté que par la force.*[444] In the long run, the development of medical technology and its growing ability to treat VD tipped the balance in favor of a voluntary solution. The possibility of a cure undercut the need for the old administrative techniques of isolating the infectious, whether prostitutes or any contagious citizen. As treatment and punishment gradually were disassociated, victims had diminishing reason not to submit to medical care. As larger numbers of patients were able, courtesy of national and other forms of health insurance, to consult physicians and as medicine could better deliver relief, the plausibility of a voluntary solution grew, the need for coercion fading. Medical care, as one observer put it, was more effective against VD than the penal code.[445]

For cholera, the tendency had been for a gradual, though never complete, approximation of different national strategies. For smallpox, the prophylactic contrasts remained starker, varying from compulsion to freedom of vaccination. For VD, the divergence was dramatic, at least until well into the latter half of the twentieth century and the antibiotic age. During the interwar era the extremes were represented at one end by Scandinavia and Germany (after 1927), where all infected citizens were subject to sanitary surveillance, and at the other by Britain, where the state had largely abandoned any form of coercion. The balance between individual rights and those of the collectivity could hardly, one

---

[444] Dubois-Havenith, *Conférence internationale: Rapports préliminaires*, v. I/1, quest. 2, Fiaux, p. 110; Beggs, *Proposed Extension of the Contagious Diseases Act*, p. 3; Proksch, *Vorbauung der venerischen Krankheiten*, p. 34.
[445] *ZBGK*, 18, 9 (1917/18), p. 230; E. Leredde, *Domaine, traitement et prophylaxie de la syphilis* (Paris, 1917), pp. 444–45; Ströhmberg, *Bekämpfung der ansteckenden Geschlechtskrankheiten*, p. 54; Braus, *Syphilis und ihre steigende soziale Gefahr*, p. 40.

French observer pointed out, have been more differently inclined.[446] Most generally, the Swedish and German laws requiring treatment of the infected encroached on the right of bodily self-determination, while the British voluntarist approach assumed individual corporeal autonomy as its fundamental principle. Other nations, observing this refusal to intervene against VD, were aghast. Their concern for civil rights might be exemplary, but prophylactically the British were ineffective and backward. The preventive vacuum left by the repeal of the CD Acts horrified polities more vigorous in their pursuit of disease.[447] In the case of contagious illness, they charged, much as in the earlier debates over quarantinism, no nation could stand alone. As a major seafaring power, venereally unprotected Britain served as a reservoir of infection continually reexported abroad. Absolute respect for individual liberty, a French observer admonished the British, tolerating even behavior that contradicted public morality, was an abuse of freedom, an act of complicity with evil.[448]

Attempts to reform regulationism, of the sort undertaken in France and Germany, are not difficult to understand and have been dealt with extensively in the literature. Similarly, an attempt has been made here to explain Scandinavia's shift from regulation to sanitary statism, a revival and modernization of an approach initially spearheaded early in the century when syphilis was perceived to be endemic and largely nonvenereal, confinable therefore only through general inspections and treatment. More challenging, in contrast, is the hope of accounting for the British *Sonderweg* in matters venereal. What was the reason for this dramatic juxtaposition between the interventionism, whether regulationist or sanitarily statist, of the continent and Britain's laissez-faire approach?

The British approach was not the result of an inability or unwillingness to face the venereal issue.[449] Although eventually repealing regulation, the British equipped their police with formidable powers of

---

[446] *Annales*, 4/34 (1920), p. 369.

[447] *Mitteilungen*, 25, 11/12 (1927), p. 129; 15, 1/2 (1917), p. 12; 23, 2 (1925), p. 9; Dubois-Havenith, *Conférence internationale: Rapports préliminaires*, v. I/1, quest. 4, pp. 14–15, 77; Verchère, p. 23; Miller, *Prostitution*, pp. 49–55; *Underdånigt betänkande angående könssjukdomarnas spridning*, v. II, p. 50; *Förhandlingar*, 1881, pp. 44–45; *ZBGK*, 4, 2 (1905), p. 74; 2, 11 (November 1905), p. 426; *Hygiea*, 51, 3 (March 1889), p. 136; *Annales*, 2/41 (1874), pp. 102–03; 3/15 (1886), p. 517; Regnault, *L'évolution de la prostitution*, p. 105; Reuss, *La prostitution*, pp. 481–82, 500–01; Jeannel, *De la prostitution*, p. 146.

[448] Jeannel, *De la prostitution*, pp. 141, 134, 156; Amos, *Comparative Survey of Laws*, p. 2; *Friedrichs Blätter für Gerichtliche Medicin und Sanitätspolizei*, 29 (1878), p. 54; Pick, *Prophylaxis der venerischen Krankheiten*, pp. 6–10; *Annales*, 2/41 (1874), pp. 106–07.

[449] *Förhandlingar*, 1912, p. 64; *Medical Magazine*, 19 (1910), p. 653; *Underdånigt betänkande angående könssjukdomarnas spridning*, v. II, p. 50.

repressing prostitution. By the twentieth century, prostitutes could be arrested for soliciting, whether they annoyed anyone in the process or not. After 1885, brothels were outlawed and suppressed; pimps were prosecuted vigorously as of 1898, and flogged if incautious enough to be caught twice. When obliged to take more drastic actions by force of circumstances, above all during the two world wars, the British were also able and willing, after prodding, to reach deep into the prophylactic armamentarium. Precautions during the First World War have already been touched upon. During the interwar years, prostitutes consorting with the troops occupying Germany were subject to a form of regulation.[450] During the Second, strict measures were once again implemented at home. In the northeast, local authorities introduced the Tyneside scheme of contact tracing in 1943, with the infected interviewed by specially trained staff, their contacts visited at home and persuaded to undergo treatment. Defence Regulation 33b of November 1942 required anyone named as a source of infection by two patients to undergo examination and compulsory treatment if ill.[451]

Nor was it a matter of some allegedly British liberalist fear, reinforced by puritanical qualms, of having the state legislate on matters sexual. With repeal behind them in the mid-1880s, the attentions of many abolitionists, feminists and moral reformers now embraced state action to raise the tone of public life. The social purity crusades following the Maiden Tribute scandal, unlike the more laissez-faire moral reform movements of the preceding decades, sought to achieve their goals through statutory intervention. The Criminal Law Amendment Act of 1885, one of its notable successes, had the state actively work to repress prostitution, procuring, incest, brothels, homosexuality and other alleged blemishes on the nation's moral complexion. Stead's revelations had provoked, as one contemporary French observer noted, a reaction against the otherwise liberalist British approach.[452] On the other hand, the British not only repealed regulation, but (thanks to their voluntary

[450] BA, 15.01, RmdI, 11880, "Regulations Made by the General Officer Commanding-In-Chief, the British Army of the Rhine for the Prevention of Prostitution and Venereal Disease, Pursuant to Article 1 of Ordinance 83," 21 October 1926, p. 76; Inter-Allied Rhineland High Commission, Aide Memoire, 6 January 1927, p. 101.

[451] *BJVD*, 19, 1 (March 1943), pp. 22–23; 21, 1 (March 1945), pp. 18–21, 26–32; Laird, *Venereal Disease in Britain*, p. 49; Frederick F. Cartwright, *A Social History of Medicine* (London, 1977), p. 120.

[452] *Annales*, 3/15 (1886), p. 517; Petrow, *Policing Morals*, pp. 122–24; McHugh, *Prostitution and Victorian Social Reform*, p. 263; Mort, "Purity, Feminism and the State," pp. 209–11; Walkowitz, "Male Vice and Feminist Virtue," p. 85; Brian Harrison, "State Intervention and Moral Reform in Nineteenth-Century England," in Patricia Hollis, ed., *Pressure from Without in Early Victorian England* (London, 1974), pp. 304ff.

approach) never adopted many of the legal constraints on the infected that were considered commonplace elsewhere. They did not criminalize transmission or endangerment, nor make VD reportable, although for other contagious diseases such precautions were in fact put to especially draconian effect.[453] They did not require that the infected be examined, treated or help identify sexual contacts, nor did they prohibit or hamper them from marrying.[454] Almost the only limitation on the perfect freedom to suffer and spread VD in Britain (with the exception of provisional wartime measures) were potential nuptial consequences: that marriages could be nullified if one partner was ill, that women infected by their husbands could (eventually) sue for divorce and maintenance.[455]

Why, then, was this voluntary approach taken in Britain, contrasting so starkly with the belief elsewhere in Europe that only vigorous statutory intervention would serve to rein in such evil? Readers who have persisted this far will not be surprised by the frequently proffered explanation that frames the issue in the classically Ackerknechtian terms of political regime and culture. From an Olympian perspective, there was a general tendency for conservatives to favor regulation, liberals its abolition. Abolitionists portrayed their struggle in strictly Ackerknechtian terms, as a battle between the forces of democracy, enlightenment and morality, arrayed in serried ranks against absolutism, autocracy, paternalism and sin.[456] From the other side, regulationists were on occasion willing to concede that theirs was a system that discounted individual rights, while defending it as necessary to preserve broader social interests. Their opponents were

---

[453] England had set early standards in this respect, forbidding in 1604 those with plague sores from appearing outside their homes on pain of hanging. It was a common law misdemeanor to expose the contagiously infected in public. In 1867 behavior was criminalized that might spread smallpox. In the 1936 Public Health Act, penalties were imposed on those who, infected with a notifiable disease (which did not include VD), exposed others to infection in public (including checking books out of libraries) or engaged in occupations with a risk for transmission: Paul Slack, *The Impact of Plague in Tudor and Stuart England* (London, 1985), p. 211; Jowitt, *Dictionary of English Law*, p. 966; 30 & 31 Vict. c. 84, s. 32; 26 Geo. 5 & 1 Edw. 8 c. 49, ss. 148–49, 155.

[454] Although, as with vaccination, there was, during the 1930s, a Scottish anomaly with strong sentiments here favoring a Scandinavian approach, placing more faith in the state's decisive intervention: Parran, *Shadow on the Land*, p. 116.

[455] Laird, *Venereal Disease in Britain*, p. 49; Morris, *Nation's Health*, p. 127; A. James Hammerton, *Cruelty and Companionship: Conflict in Nineteenth-Century Married Life* (London, 1992), pp. 109–10, 120; Gail Savage, "'The Wilful Communication of a Loathsome Disease': Marital Conflict and Venereal Disease in Victorian England," *Victorian Studies*, 34, 1 (1990), pp. 38–42.

[456] Münsterberg, *Prostitution und Staat*, p. 26; *ZBGK*, 15, 6 (1914), pp. 216–17; Fiaux, *Police des moeurs*, v. I, pp. cccxcv–cccxcvi; *Förhandlingar*, 1912, p. 64; *Hansard*, 1883, v. 278, col. 763; Petrie, *Singular Iniquity*, pp. 95, 127; Sandra Stanley Holton, "State Pandering, Medical Policing and Prostitution: The Controversy Within the Medical Profession Concerning the Contagious Diseases Legislation 1864–1886," *Research in Law, Deviance and Social Control*, 9 (1988), pp. 166–67.

dismissed as ultrarevolutionaries, Mazzinians and other unreasonably liberal souls who preferred endangering the public health to endowing the police with necessary powers.[457]

And yet, any hopes of invoking an alembicated Ackerknechtianism to explain adequately the differing fates of regulation and repeal must prepare for disappointment. Conservatism and regulation, liberalism and abolition do not pair up as neatly as they must to carry conviction – not within any nation, even less among them. The fact that abolitionism, to start with the opponents, was of at least two broadly different varieties, civil libertarian and moralist, meant that crosscutting alliances were unavoidable: the former with the left, the latter with the right. Moralist abolitionists and social conservatives often shared principles and personnel. In the Swedish parliamentary debates of 1889, on the other hand, liberals and Christian conservatives were united in abolition, opposed in this case to the more secular right. Conversely, the fact that regulationists could both be authoritarians (persuaded of the state's right to assure public order, individual liberties be damned) as well – especially in their neo-varieties – as progressive reformers, convinced that theirs were the principles of enlightened public hygiene, meant that political polarities on such issues were rarely binary.[458] The same preventive technique could be supported for quite divergent ideological motives. Left and right in Germany united during the interwar period, for example, in support of making VD notifiable, the conservatives because they favored stronger state control in such matters, the Independent Socialists because they hoped thus to achieve a degree of prophylactic equality by subjecting all citizens to the same precautions. In France, numerous were the instances where successive mayors of widely divergent political affiliation – moderate, radical, republican, Bonapartist – all unfailingly maintained the institutions of regulation.[459] In Britain, while it was broadly true that Conservatives supported the CD Acts, Liberals were

[457] *ZBGK*, 16, 8 (1915), pp. 257–61; *Hansard*, 1883, v. 278, col. 827.

[458] Lundquist, *Den disciplinerade dubbelmoralen*, p. 349; *ZBGK*, 8, 1 (1908), p. 29; Fiaux, *La prostitution réglementée*, pp. 282–83. State-run brothels started out as the regulationist idea par excellence and, having been defeated at midcentury, were then proposed again in Sweden of the 1960s and seventies, now by liberals and Social Democrats, as a way of ministering to the needs of the sexually outcast. The handicapped and others unable to fulfill their erotic needs on the free affective market were to be assured through the state of a provider of last resort. But this idea was then trounced once again in the following decades once feminism began to exert an influence on the left, the interests of marginal men no match for those of women: Lars Ullerstam, *The Erotic Minorities* (New York, 1966), pp. 150–53; Lind and Fredriksson, *Kärlek för pengar?*, p. 200.

[459] *Sitzungsberichte der Preussischen Landesversammlung*, 1919/21, 25 February 1920, cols. 9935–50; de Morsier, *La police des moeurs en France*, p. 149.

badly split on the issue. The acts had been first implemented by a Liberal government, but it was also from Liberals that repealers expected their end. The Liberal Party, especially its leadership, did not embrace abolition as a cause in some sense naturally its own, but had it forced down its maw by abolitionists, who threatened to, and did, support Tory candidates unless the repeal line was toed. By the mid-1870s, abolition was gradually, but tepidly, becoming a Liberal issue. Gladstone, Bright and Childers had voted for repeal and the hope was persuading them to include it in the party program. Gladstone may personally have found the acts distasteful, but they were not sufficiently compelling as practical politics to motivate stronger condemnation. By the eighties, repealers had managed to make the cause enough of a Liberal position that they no longer sought to split the party, now shifting tactics to back Liberal candidates. In April 1883, the party managers came out in support. In 1886, when repeal was made official, many Tories also voted against the acts. Repeal was not clearly a party political issue separating Liberals from Tories. Both parties largely ignored the struggle until its final phases, the Liberals' support was grudgingly won, the Conservatives' opposition far from unanimous.[460]

The position of the left on matters venereal illustrates such ambiguities. While sharing numerous assumptions, socialists and abolitionists differed on at least as many again. The abolitionist analysis, that prostitution was caused largely by poor social conditions and inequalities under which women suffered and that regulation was a form of class oppression, put them in proximity to the socialist position on such issues. Hume-Rothery's exposé of marriage in capitalist society, for example, with women as the chattel of their husbands, sounded themes of appeal to the left.[461] On the other hand, the abolitionist solution was less welcome here. Hume-Rothery's conclusion, that women be given the vote and thereby the opportunity to exert a purifying influence on social morals, implied that bourgeois respectability was the inherent appurtenance of one sex and that, in any case, the vote was sufficient to solve

---

[460] Fiaux, *L'intégrité intersexuelle*, pp. 18, 64; Scott, *State Iniquity*, pp. 99–100, 167–68, 170–71, 220–22; Walkowitz, *Prostitution and Victorian Society*, p. 99; Petrie, *Singular Iniquity*, pp. 145–46; McHugh, *Prostitution and Victorian Social Reform*, pp. 109, 140–41, 206–08, 222; *Hansard*, 1886, v. 304, col. 1152. Repeal was in this sense like many of the other moral reform movements that, while appealing perhaps most particularly to Liberals, cut across party allegiances: Brian Harrison, "State Intervention and Moral Reform," pp. 294–96.

[461] Dolléans, *La police des moeurs*, p. 172; Hume-Rothery, *Letter Addressed to Gladstone*, p. 11. The British Communist Party adopted Butler as a heroine: Marian Ramelson, "The Fight Against the Contagious Diseases Act," *Marxism Today*, 8, 6 (June 1964), p. 184.

such problems, both assumptions unlikely to impress socialists of any but the most reformist stripe. Though socialists usually remained unsatisfied by mere repeal, Bebel in Germany and Branting in Sweden favored abolition. The German Social Democrats condemned regulation and the vice squads, the British Trades Union Congress was won for the cause and a Working Men's National League was established in Britain as the proletarian division of repeal.[462] But even then, Swedish, French and other socialists did not pay much attention to what were considered women's issues at the turn of the century. Most generally, the objection to abolition was that its ambitions were too limited. Socialists criticized the bourgeois feminist movement for believing that the answer to prostitution was a modification of personal morality rather than a fundamental change in society.[463] Male chastity was no substitute for social reform. Kollontai and other socialist feminists rejected abolitionism for not seeing the big picture, that prostitution would disappear only with the end of capitalism. In the Parisian Municipal Council, for example, neoregulationist reforms proposed in 1890 were rejected by right and left alike, the former because they threatened to limit police powers, the latter because the solution was socialist revolution, not neoregulationist tinkering.[464] As always with utopians, the best was the enemy of the good.

On the other hand, a socialist concern for equality can be detected in the left's support of Scandinavian-style measures. Although such an approach had been first tried early in the century, thus not sparked by socialists, once it reappeared on the agenda a century later, the left discovered ideological affinities. In Sweden during discussions of the Lex Veneris, Social Democrats fought the right in support of provisions that subjected all citizens to compulsory measures, not targeting prostitutes. In Germany during similar debates preceding the 1927 VD law, the left was especially concerned that notification and compulsory treatment not affect only the poorer who belonged to social insurance, but all citizens. The Communists went so far as to favor periodic inspections of entire groups (students, soldiers, pregnant women) in

---

[462] Richard J. Evans, "Prostitution, State and Society in Imperial Germany," p. 124; Scott, *State Iniquity*, p. 382; McHugh, *Prostitution and Victorian Social Reform*, pp. 112–13, 119; Fiaux, *La prostitution réglementée et les pouvoirs publics*, pp. 282–83. Generally, see Karen Hunt, *Equivocal Feminists: The Social Democratic Federation and the Woman Question 1884–1911* (Cambridge, 1996).

[463] Lundquist, *Den disciplinerade dubbelmoralen*, pp. 369–70; Corbin, *Women for Hire*, pp. 238–39; Charles Sowerwine, *Sisters or Citizens? Women and Socialism in France Since 1876* (Cambridge, 1982), ch. 1; Gunilla Johansson, "Motståndet mot reglementeringen," in Fredelius, *Ett onödigt ont*, p. 22; Weston, "Prostitution in Paris in the Later Nineteenth Century," p. 118.

[464] Hjördis Levin, "Alexandra Kollontay och prostitutionen," in Fredelius, *Ett onödigt ont*, pp. 24ff.; Fiaux, *Police des moeurs*, v. I, pp. 233–34; Fiaux, *L'intégrité intersexuelle*, p. 79.

order to avoid the problem of physicians reporting only members of certain classes.[465]

More generally, the same difficulties of finding consistent Ackerknechtian correlations between political regime and prophylactic strategy held across countries as well and taxonomic constants were hard to identify. A politically motley assortment of nations had either never introduced, or subsequently abolished, regulation, ranging from liberal Britain and the United States through the proto-social democratic nations of Scandinavia to Bolshevik Russia. Conversely, nations of similar political disposition varied much in prophylactic terms. Britain allowed freedom of prostitution and no regulation; the United States, in contrast, also had only sporadic regulation, but many states forbade and actively suppressed commercial sex and took a lead in implementing preventive techniques rejected in Britain, such as prenuptial certificates.[466] Britain was pressured by its presumably equally liberal Commonwealth allies during the First World War to take precautions safeguarding the health of the military. At the other end of the spectrum, Prussia outlawed official brothels and implemented at best a fairly haphazard variant of regulationism, while allegedly liberal Hamburg ran the tightest system of venereal control in Germany, including official brothels that flew in the face of Imperial law, and inspections of all sailors.[467] When Italy (temporarily) followed Britain's lead in abolishing regulation, observers struck about, with little success, in search of what it might have been in their political regimes that thus united them.[468] Attempts to classify nations across the globe according to their prophylactic approach to VD served up what were, in terms of political regime, very mixed salads.[469]

[465] Lundquist, *Den disciplinerade dubbelmoralen*, p. 418; *Sitzungsberichte der Preussischen Landesversammlung*, 1919/21, 25 February 1920, cols. 9935–36, 9948–50; *SB*, 21 January 1927, p. 8689; Knack and Quarck, *Reichsgesetz zur Bekämpfung der Geschlechtskrankheiten*, p. 4.

[466] *Mitteilungen*, 24, 11 (1926), p. 120; Hodann, *History of Modern Morals*, p. 82; Cavaillon, *Les législations antivénériennes*, pp. 28–29; *Annales*, 3/23 (1890), p. 395.

[467] *Underdånigt betänkande angående könssjukdomarnas spridning*, v. I, p. 283; *Förhandlingar*, 1912, p. 60; *Mitteilungen*, 21, 4 (1924), p. 18; 23, 3 (1925), p. 15; Sanger, *History of Prostitution*, ch. 16.

[468] Fiaux, *La prostitution réglementée*, p. xxxv; Fiaux, *L'intégrité intersexuelle*, p. vii. Similarly, Pappritz could find nothing better than their similarly advanced state to explain why Denmark, Norway and Italy had all, at the time she was writing, managed to abolish regulation: Ann Taylor Allen, "Feminism, Venereal Diseases, and the State in Germany, 1890–1918," *Journal of the History of Sexuality*, 4, 1 (July 1993), p. 33.

[469] Regulationist nations were the Mediterranean countries, some Latin American and Japan; Britain, the Netherlands and Switzerland were abolitionist, while the Scandinavian countries, Australia, Canada and the United States were sanitarily statist: Jeanselme, *Traité de la syphilis*, v. I, pp. 426–27; Regnault, *L'évolution de la prostitution*, pp. 174–76; J.-G. Mancini, *Prostitutes and Their Parasites* (London, 1963), pp. 29–30. Or consider Sigerist's grudging wartime respect for the strict but effective measures imposed in that odd triplet of countries, Germany, Denmark and the Soviet Union: Henry E. Sigerist, *Civilization and Disease* (Ithaca, 1944), p. 78.

Nonetheless, an Ackerknechtian approach, if suitably modified, does explain much of the British *Sonderweg*. There is little doubt that the strength, tactics and persistence of abolitionism here, compared to its relative weakness elsewhere, goes far in accounting for repeal. The government finally succumbed to such pressure in what one regulationist disgustedly called its "shirk and surrender" policy.[470] The gradual enfranchisement of the working class after 1867 meant that opposition among the middle and lower classes had an effect. Repealers warned ominously of the popular unrest that might follow a misstep under the acts or their continued enforcement. Butler and her followers consciously portrayed their cause as one of interest to the working class, winning allies in a way that, where the labor movement was still weak or unconcerned with such matters, would have been unlikely.[471] In terms of numbers, influence and effect, British abolitionism found its equal only in the Scandinavian movements. In France abolition never became more than a fringe cause, at home in the distant suburbs of mainstream politics with an appeal mainly to radicals, socialists, anticlericals and Protestants. In Germany, though stronger, the movement was never comparable to the British. Abolitionism came late here: the Allgemeine Konferenz der deutschen Sittlichkeitsvereine was founded in 1888, the German branch of the International Abolitionist Federation only in 1898, twenty years after the Swedish equivalent, and the Federation never counted more than about 1,000 members. The lament of German abolitionists, that there was no movement worth the mention, was not just self-indulgent autoflagellation.[472]

Abolitionism across the Channel must be seen, however, not just in a narrow Ackerknechtian sense as the expression of British democracy, an example of grassroots organizing and mobilization not (yet) the case in other nations, but also as the result of a particularly Protestant moralizing approach to politics, as well as the outcome of a certain strain of feminism prominently represented in the Victorian women's movement. Two other factors, religion and sex, must be added to the political equation.

The grassroots, democratic nature of repeal agitation and its Protestant, puritan aspect were inseparably joined features. In Britain,

---

[470] *Hansard*, 1886, v. 303, col. 1911.

[471] Walkowitz, *Prostitution and Victorian Society*, p. 91; *PP* 1871 (c. 408-1) xix, 29, p. xvii, xxxv; Gibson, *Prostitution and the State*, p. 47.

[472] Richard J. Evans, "Prostitution, State and Society in Imperial Germany," pp. 121–22; Richard J. Evans, *Feminist Movement*, pp. 53–54, 61; Blaschko, *Syphilis und Prostitution*, p. 143; *DVöG*, 26 (1894), p. 196; Sauerteig, "Frauenemanzipation und Sittlichkeit," pp. 175–77.

abolition was one of the numerous issues forced on the established parties by narrowly focused, vehemently motivated and persistent reform movements of a radical and nonconformist tenor, often emanating from the northern counties – an array of worthy causes that stretched from disestablishment and education to more general moral and political issues such as slavery, vivisection, temperance, pacifism, women's suffrage, not forgetting antivaccination. Such movements applied moral criteria to political issues, were generally unwilling to brook compromise with opponents, regarded as in thrall to sin itself, and often phrased demands in all-or-nothing terms. In the case of the CD Acts, much as with vaccination, the most radical opponents saw the issue as one of ethics, not public health, concluding that it was better for the government to take no action at all against VD, thereby not conspiring with immorality, than to seek reform of a system that was thoroughly rotten at its core. Reform movements of a rainbow palette arose on such single issues, seeking to bend the established parties, and especially the Liberals, to their will. Staffed by principled "faddists" usually from the lower middle classes and upper, skilled working classes, such reform agitations marked an important step in the evolution of the political parties from representing elites and notables to an accounting of ideological currents and social interests within a broader cross-section of the population.[473]

Such reform movements were, of course, not unique to Britain. In Scandinavia, where temperance was powerful and closely associated with religious reform, analogous connections held between abolition and popular mobilization in general. In Germany, similar forms of grassroots protest against the established parties of *Honoratioren* arose in a broad variety of movements, ranging from the Pan-German, Navy and other colonialist and imperialist leagues, through antisemitic, eugenic and racialist organizations to the riotous multiplicity of *Heilkunde* and *Lebensreform*.[474] Such organizations differed from the British in several

---

[473] Walkowitz, *Prostitution and Victorian Society*, p. 99; Olive Banks, *Faces of Feminism* (Oxford, 1981), ch. 2; Bebbington, *Nonconformist Conscience*, p. 40; D.A. Hamer, *The Politics of Electoral Pressure: A Study in the History of Victorian Reform Agitations* (Hassocks, 1977); Hollis, *Pressure from Without in Early Victorian England*, p. 22.

[474] Lydia Svärd, *Väckelserörelsernas folk i Andra kammaren 1867–1911* (Stockholm, 1954); Geoff Eley, *Reshaping the German Right: Radical Nationalism and Political Change After Bismarck* (New Haven, 1980); Weindling, *Health, Race and German Politics*, chs. 1, 2; Paul Lawrence Rose, *Revolutionary Antisemitism in Germany* (Princeton, 1990); James F. Harris, *The People Speak! Anti-Semitism and Emancipation in Nineteenth-Century Bavaria* (Ann Arbor, 1994), p. 5; Wolfgang R. Krabbe, *Gesellschaftsveränderung durch Lebensreform: Strukturmerkmale einer sozialreformerischen Bewegung im Deutschland der Industrialisierungsperiode* (Göttingen, 1974); Karl E. Rothschuh, *Naturheilbewegung, Reformbewegung, Alternativbewegung* (Stuttgart, 1983), chs. 8, 9.

respects. They did not share the messianic, moralistic, quasi-religious aura that such movements often took on in the Anglo-Saxon realm. Antivivisection, with its insistence on a single moral standard extending also to animals, was unique to Britain; German temperance did not generally go so far as to advocate teetotalism or prohibitionism; continental abolition did not insist on sexual morality in as strict a sense. Many of these movements did not enter the political realm as directly as in the English-speaking world, bereft as they were during the first half of the century of viable electoral and parliamentary fora. The German temperance movement avoided it, the abolitionist movement found little support among Liberals in the Reichstag and the discounting of demands for the vote in the continental women's movement has long been noted and pondered.[475]

Secondly, the coincidence of such movements with unification and their preoccupation with national development and improvement allowed them to appreciate statutory interventions of a kind that in Britain were rejected. In looking to the state to promote their various plans for enhancing the nation (whether through acquiring colonies, ameliorating the racial stock or turning all citizens into vegetarians) rather than, as in Britain, seeking to protect local autonomy from central control, the German movements were more likely to welcome statutory initiatives, both in public health and other respects, than their cross-Channel counterparts. Antivaccination in both nations had managed to phrase its arguments in terms of degeneration and decline, those opposed claiming that the lancet caused illness, however much the authorities insisted on its benefits. Though objectors did not manage in Germany to end compulsion, antivaccination here was comparably strong to the British movement. For abolitionism, in contrast, the argument against the system could not rely on similar logic. Regulationists had a much easier time portraying their controls as the last bulwark against a dangerous scourge; abolitionists often had to phrase their case in terms of the importance of personal liberties, despite the public consequences of not controlling prostitutes. The concern with national strength in this case spoke for regulation and abolition in Germany was weakened accordingly. In comparison to the Protestant nations, such movements of multifarious reform, though present, were weaker in France and other Catholic countries and abolitionism, like antivaccination, was correspondingly hobbled.[476]

---

[475] James S. Roberts, *Drink, Temperance and the Working Class*, p. 7; Sauerteig, "Frauenemanzipation und Sittlichkeit," pp. 190–91.

[476] Steven C. Hause with Anne R. Kenney, *Women's Suffrage and Social Politics in the French Third*

Political and moral motives were seamlessly fused in such movements, in none more so than repeal. The CD Acts were attacked as a statutory guarantee of aristocratic libertinage. Regulated prostitution sacrificed the morals and health of working-class women to the extravagances and perversions of upper-class randiness.[477] In opposition to the alleged amorality of aristocratic behavior, faithfulness, a conjunction of sex with affection, moderation in matters venereal – such were the norms of middle- and upper working-class respectability by which repeal was demanded. Abolition was phrased in terms of a middle- and working-class assault on aristocratic privilege and license and equally in those of morality against sin. Sex and class were inextricably intertwined. It has, of course, long been claimed that Victorian Britain was unusually puritanical, dominated by middle-class standards of restrictive respectability. The British were allegedly more moral in sexual terms, prudish indeed, than their continental neighbors, hesitant to discuss sex and its attendant issues openly and more willing to insist on male continence. They were a steadier race than the French, ran one typical categorization of national characteristics, able to control their passions and inclinations and more likely to condemn sexual transgression than excuse it as a foible.[478] On the continent, in contrast, the aristocratic double standard held sway for longer, women and the bourgeoisie equally its victims.[479]

Within each nation, similar contrasts have been drawn in social terms among bourgeois standards of propriety, the libertinage of the aristocracy and the dissolution or virtue (depending on the value put on the disjunctions between sex, love and marriage allegedly characteristic of life at the lower margin) of proletarian mores. The aristocracy espoused the double standard as its birthright, custom and culture fostered sensual libertinage, an inherited sense of privilege combined with sufficient wherewithal

Republic (Princeton, 1984), pp. 257f.; Patrick Kay Bidelman, *Pariahs Stand Up! The Founding of the Liberal Feminist Movement in France, 1858–1889* (Westport, 1982), pp. 58–62; Anne Cova, "French Feminism and Maternity: Theories and Policies 1890–1918," in Gisela Bock and Pat Thane, eds., *Maternity and Gender Policies* (London, 1991), p. 127.

[477] James E. Mennell, "The Politics of Frustration: 'The Maiden Tribute of Modern Baylon' and the Morality Movement of 1885," *North Dakota Quarterly* (Winter 1981), pp. 69, 74–75; Roy Porter and Hall, *Facts of Life*, p. 276.

[478] Mort, *Dangerous Sexualities*, pp. 88, 112–14; *Annales*, 3/15 (1886), pp. 416–18; anon., *Greatest of Our Social Evils*, p. 171; Lecky, *History of European Morals*, v. II, pp. 301–02; Flexner, *Prostitution in Europe*, pp. 41–42; *PP* 1916 (8189) xvi, 1, p. 181; *PP* 1878–79 (323) viii, QQ. 1898–1901. The Swedes drew a similar contrast between northern Europe and the Latins: *Underdånigt betänkande angående könssjukdomarnas spridning*, v. II, p. 194.

[479] Meyer-Renschhausen, *Weibliche Kultur und soziale Arbeit*, p. 370; Norbert Elias, *The Civilizing Process* (Oxford, 1994), pp. 325–27, 504.

allowed nobles to take what pleased them. The bourgeoisie sought to end such immorality and inequality between the sexes by insisting on continence, chastity and fidelity, holding all to the same standard of conduct. The proletariat, finally, was virtuous, although not necessarily chaste in the bourgeois sense. Bloch, the prolific sexologist, distinguished between free proletarian sexuality and the reproachable promiscuity of the upper classes.[480] Sex and emotion were allegedly more closely combined in working-class families than in the property-driven unions of the bourgeoisie. Unwed mothers were not shunned, marriages were often formalized only after impregnation, prenuptial sex accepted more indulgently.[481] Recent work has shifted these neat sociosexual parallels, demonstrating, for example, that the middle classes were not irremediably "Victorian" in their sexual attitudes, that bourgeois respectability was also characteristic of attitudes among the higher reaches of the laboring classes and that workingmen had not, in fact, been inoculated against the temptations of commercial sex by the supposedly easy availability of the nonmarket variety in their circles.[482] Whatever the shift in nuance brought by revision, however, the basic parallel between middle-class morality and aristocratic libertinage helps explain the British peculiarity on regulation, tying class, politics and ethics together. British political development, the rise in influence of the lower middle classes during the latter half of the nineteenth century and the moralizing approach taken here to the statutory control of commercial sex: these were all part of a whole. Ending regulation and imposing respectable sexual morality were aspects of democratization, the triumph of middle-class mores, while the continuation of the system on the continent reflected the persistence of the old regime, political, social and sexual.

FEMINISM

To this particularly fervent mixture of class and moral reform that informed the British repeal movement came the feminist element. Since

---

[480] Bloch, *Das Sexualleben unserer Zeit*, pp. 264–65, 313–16.

[481] Flexner, *Prostitution in Europe*, pp. 17–27; Dubois-Havenith, *Conférence internationale: Rapports préliminaires*, v. I/1, quest.5, pp. 7–8; Schulte, *Sperrbezirke*, p. 94; Levin, "Alexandra Kollontay och prostitutionen," pp. 33, 52.

[482] Roy Porter and Hall, *Facts of Life*, pp. 126–27 and passim; Finnegan, *Poverty and Prostitution*, pp. 114–15, 134; Mason, *Making of Victorian Sexuality*, pp. 102–03, 117–18, 133ff.; Lundquist, *Den disciplinerade dubbelmoralen*, p. 217; M. Jeanne Peterson, "Dr. Acton's Enemy: Medicine, Sex and Society in Victorian England," in Patrick Brantlinger, ed., *Energy and Entropy: Science and Culture in Victorian Britain* (Bloomington, 1989); Eric Trudgill, *Madonnas and Magdalens: The Origins and Development of Victorian Sexual Attitudes* (New York, 1976), ch. 8.

the supply of mercenary sex in the nineteenth century involved primarily females, the position of women in each of the societies in vitro here was a factor in dealing with the problem. The role of women and relations between the sexes were reflected variously in different strategies of coping with prostitution. Regulationism presupposed a double double standard, assuming (gender-wise) that men could not contain their instincts while respectable women should be chaste and then (in terms of class) that prostitutes were necessary as a special category of fallen women from the poorer strata to reconcile the sexual contradictions of upper-class life. Abolition, in turn, was compatible with a broad spectrum of social attitudes toward women, ranging from acceptance of the necessity of prostitution to an insistence that males be as continent as females, but it generally sought to avoid having the state enforce any particular one. Finally, sanitary statism rested on a belief that men and women would or should act similarly and therefore be treated alike.

Since regulation was based on the double standard, accepting the sacrifice of certain women to the sexual needs of all men, while abolition wished to bar the state from the business of upholding such disparities, one might well expect to find an end to officially sanctioned mercenary copulation in those nations where women had most to say about the matter. And, indeed, a rough correlation holds between the strength and organization of the women's movement (including its male allies) and the fate of regulation across the nations considered here. One of the first causes around which women organized to press for interests particular to their sex – preceding and in many ways serving as dress rehearsal for the vote – was the end of regulation.[483] Although they could not yet generally vote during the heyday of repeal, women exerted considerable power through their participation in such movements of moral and social reform.

Repeal in Britain marked the first exercise of power by women in their own sex-specific interests. When, in 1870, the Liberal but unrepealing candidate Henry Stork was defeated after abolitionists threw their support to his opponent, Gladstone's government was aghast, not yet realizing, as a prominent abolitionist put it, that a new force had appeared in the political firmament and that, with women fighting for

---

[483] Walkowitz, *Prostitution and Victorian Society*, pp. 6, 94; Lundquist, *Den disciplinerade dubbelmoralen*, pp. 227, 322, 417. Indeed, the vote for women was more firmly opposed by some men because they feared, on the evidence of the repeal campaign, that enfranchised women would insist on impossibly strict moral standards: Rover, *Love, Morals and the Feminists*, p. 1; F. B. Smith, "Ethics and Disease in the Later Nineteenth Century," p. 134.

their own gendered concerns, the niceties of party allegiance counted
for little. One of Butler's many contributions to abolition was insisting
on a specifically female vantage around which women could be mobilized in support of their fallen sisters, with whom, in terms of the usual
nongendered categories of class and status, they shared little.[484] The CD
Acts, by allowing any female to be arrested on suspicion of prostitution,
created common interests among all women. Educated women, as
Annie Besant put it, now identified with prostitutes, their own flesh and
blood, uniting to protect them against male passions. Simply because she
was a woman, Butler said, she would believe the testimony of the worst
prostitute (in this case that speculum examinations were painful) even
if all the physicians in the world insisted otherwise.[485] From among
women, and their male supporters, came arguments against regulation
of an elemental biological sort. Vaginal examinations were rejected as
an intervention of the most intimate and intrusive sort, as instrumental
rape. Violation of the body, not to cure disease, but merely to determine
whether a woman was fit for fornication, was intrinsically wicked. The
use of the speculum raised the pitch of protest, women portrayed as laid
out like carcasses for dissection, turned upside down on the infernal
machine, warm flesh violated by cold steel, "police in the very bowels,"
women "split open by the State," as Garth Wilkinson put it.[486] United
by their shared revulsion to so intimate an act of state intervention,
women formed the natural opposition to the CD Acts.[487] Christabel
Pankhurst's infamous claim that, the majority of men being infected
with gonorrhea, sex and marriage threatened women with epidemiological damage was an analogous argument that sought to mobilize females
on the basis of common biological interests.[488]

[484] Scott, *State Iniquity*, p. 124; *Report of the Ladies' National Association for the Repeal of the Contagious Diseases Act, for the Year Ending November 14, 1871* (Liverpool, 1871), p. 5; McHugh, *Prostitution and Victorian Social Reform*, p. 20.

[485] *PP* 1871 (c. 408-1) xix, 29, p. lix; *Transactions of the Seventh International Congress of Hygiene and Demography*, 9 (1891), p. 237; Wilkinson, *Forcible Introspection of Women*, p. 22. Similar arguments could also be found elsewhere: Sachs, *Den svarta domen*, p. 7; Meyer-Renschhausen, *Weibliche Kultur und soziale Arbeit*, pp. 364–65.

[486] Wilkinson, *Forcible Introspection of Women*, pp. 3–10; Taylor, *Speech at Exeter*, pp. 5–7; Ornella Moscucci, *The Science of Woman: Gynaecology and Gender in England, 1800–1929* (Cambridge, 1990), pp. 112–27; *PP* 1871 (c. 408-1) xix, 29, pp. xxxiii, 835; Nevins, *Statement of the Grounds*, p. 24; Corbin, *Women for Hire*, p. 227; Bristow, *Vice and Vigilance*, pp. 82–83.

[487] Kent, *Sex and Suffrage in Britain*, pp. 119–24; Corbin, *Women for Hire*, p. 105. Objections to genital examinations were part of a more general rejection of male midwifery and gynaecology: Hume-Rothery, *Letter Addressed to Gladstone*, p. 11; Hume-Rothery, *Women and Doctors*, p. 6.

[488] Bland, "Cleansing the Portals of Life," pp. 194–96; Bland, *Banishing the Beast*, pp. 244–45. From protest against such statutory corporeal intrusion, women, it has been argued, were led nat-

In a direct fashion, there was thus a general correlation between the strength and influence of the women's movement and repeal. Abolition, much like abortion later, was an obvious issue around which women from different classes and backgrounds could unite behind common interests. Without abolitionism and women's action on behalf of their gendered concerns, repeal would not have succeeded. In Britain, the United States, and the Scandinavian nations – all with strong feminist movements – regulationism was either never (or only marginally) in effect or repeal came early.[489] Conversely, where feminism trod a more conservative path, as in Germany, or where it remained barely ambulatory, as in France, only tepid challenges were mounted and regulationism survived well into the twentieth century.

The story is not, however, exhausted by such a straightforward account. Abolition was not merely an example of women exercising newfound organizational and political muscle to defend their kind against the intrusions of public health authorities. It was in particular a certain variety of feminism – one which, long in disfavor, has only recently begun to enjoy the fruits of historiographical rehabilitation – that inscribed repeal on its banner. From the perspective of Anglo-American political development, it has been customary to see early feminism as an outgrowth of liberalism, an attempt to extend to women the same inalienable rights won already by men and thereby to achieve equal treatment for both sexes. In contrast, feminism on the continent, especially in Germany but with similar currents also in Scandinavia, tended to argue a separate spheres position: that, although perhaps equal in some theoretical and ultimate sense, in practice the sexes were different and that women should pursue not an abstract and inapplicable form of equality, but rather seek fulfillment in their own particular realm, whether that be defined narrowly as motherhood, more broadly as the nurturing professions or in some heroically lofty sense as carriers of the nation's ethical ideal.[490] Seen

urally to the antivivisection movement: Coral Lansbury, *The Old Brown Dog: Women, Workers and Vivisection in Edwardian England* (Madison, 1985), p. x and ch. 5; Andreas-Holger Maehle, "Präventivmedizin als wissenschaftliches und gesellschaftliches Problem: Der Streit über das Reichsimpfgesetz von 1874," *Medizin, Gesellschaft und Geschichte*, 9 (1990), p. 139.

[489] Margaret Hamilton, "Opposition to the Contagious Diseases Acts, 1864–1886," *Albion*, 10, 1 (Spring 1978), p. 15; Scott, *State Iniquity*, pp. 99–100; Richard J. Evans, *The Feminists: Women's Emancipation Movements in Europe, America and Australasia 1840–1920* (London, 1977), pp. 68–71.

[490] Although Mona Ozouf has sought to argue that the strict universalism of French political ideology, including its feminism, was what kept women out of politics (their difference not being up to the demands of egality) while in the Anglo-Saxon world women gained admission precisely as women, not as abstract human beings, because of their difference: Mona Ozouf, *Les mots des femmes: Essai sur la singularité française* (Paris, 1995), pp. 376–81.

from the separate spheres approach, equal rights feminism forced women
to conform to an ideal that, although claiming gender universality, had in
fact been developed by and for men. The other way around, separate
spheres was, at best, a conservative ideology, accepting the basic tenet of
traditional relations between the sexes, that biology determined gender,
although claiming to evaluate women's particular role more positively
than was usually true.[491]

   In tandem, sexual rights were viewed on the analogy of civil and political liberties. Sexual freedom and its attendant personal pleasure
together were a corollary of individual autonomy and inviolability, while
repression and puritanism were aspects of a conservative social view that
emphasized the interests of the community. Among turn-of-the-century
reformers and sexologists such venereal whiggery was systematized.
Pleasure, in this view, was a human right, facilitating its pursuit one of
the goals of a well-ordered polity. Abstinence and other attempts to
hamper or channel individual delight for the benefit of society, conversely, were politically conservative. The Marxist belief that, come the
revolution, natural sexual relations uncorrupted by capitalist property
concerns would allow a regularization of behavior between the sexes,
was part of this tradition. Most extreme in this respect were the views of
Wilhelm Reich, for whom regular orgasm was a precondition of health,
both biological and political, and sexual repression the instinctual basis
of fascism.[492] This whiggish approach to sexual emancipation naturally
assumed that men and women were alike in terms of instinctual
response. It made little sense, after all, for a doctrine that believed in
development and progress in such matters to have one gender striving
for betterment while the other played by different and possibly antithet-
ical rules. Traditionally acknowledged differences in the behavior of the
sexes were therefore viewed as a function of social conditioning, which
would end as soon as women were treated like men. Once released from
the fear of unwanted pregnancy by foolproof contraception and from
inherited moral restrictions by enlightened mores, women could and
would act sexually in much the same fashion as men, which is to say, with
the same embrace of promiscuity, the same premium put on venereal
variety, the same discount on monogamy. Freeing humans sexually from
the bonds of reproduction and social convention thus meant permitting

[491]   Richard J. Evans, *Feminist Movement in Germany*, pp. 3, 30; Quataert, *Reluctant Feminists in German
Social Democracy*, pp. 9–10; Kaplan, *Jewish Feminist Movement in Germany*, p. 6.
[492]   *ZBGK*, 11, 3 (1910), p. 82; Hirschfeld, *Sexual History of the World War*, ch. 20; Paul A. Robinson,
The Freudian Left (New York, 1969).

them to be promiscuous, it meant allowing women to act in the ways that historically men had called their own. Writers in many nations, from Léon Blum (*Du Mariage*) through Edvard Brandes (*Et besøg*) in Denmark to Charles Reade (*Hard Cash*) in Britain, proposed that women sow wild oats just like their future husbands and managed for their pains to provoke storms.[493]

The inherited orthodoxy has tended to see a movement from a "conservative" separate spheres feminism to a "progressive" equal rights approach and from a repressive view of sexuality to a more liberatory instinctual inclination. Progress has been toward increased individual rights, both political, social and sexual, with a corresponding decrease in the claims enforceable by an oldfashioned sense of community. The problem with such tidy teleologies is the quantity of empirical dust they leave under the carpet. Most simply, the national classifications between "progressive" Anglo-American feminism and the "conservative" continental variety are hard to maintain. British feminists, though politically radical, were sexually conservative. On the continent, a reversed conundrum held true. Saint-Simonian feminists believed both in the ennobling potential of motherhood and in free love. German feminists like Helene Stöcker who advocated the use of contraception and championed the cause of unmarried mothers, insisting that the state fulfill the obligations of paternity, may have believed in separate sexual realms, but it is hard to classify them as more conservative than equal rights feminists whose ambitions were largely exhausted by the achievement of suffrage. Similarly, the separatist ideology of notable Scandinavians, Ellen Key for example, was hardly incompatible with victory for feminist reforms earlier than most elsewhere. Conversely, and most pertinent here, there was also a long and hardy strand of separate spheres ideology in British feminism.[494] This moralizing and allegedly conservative approach lay behind the social purity feminism that was crucial to the repeal movement. Central to the social purity approach was the belief that, while the sexes acted differently in instinctual and ethical terms, women could and should set the moral standard for society, elevating even men to restraint and moderation. Prudery and progress were complements in a view

[493] XVIIth International Congress of Medicine, *Dermatology and Syphilography*, p. 55; Kromayer, *Zur Austilgung der Syphilis*, p. 4; Nye, *Masculinity and Male Codes of Honor*, p. 83; Bredsdorff, *Den store nordiske krig om seksualmoralen*, pp. 38–39; Petrie, *Singular Iniquity*, p. 140.

[494] Nancy F. Cott, *The Grounding of Modern Feminism* (New Haven, 1987), pp. 46–50; Kathryn Gleadle, *The Early Feminists: Radical Unitarians and the Emergence of the Women's Rights Movement, 1831–1851* (Houndmills, 1995), pp. 183–85; Martin Pugh, *Women and the Women's Movement in Britain 1914–1959* (New York, 1993), pp. 236–49.

whose most lapidary formulation was Christabel Pankhurst's slogan, votes for women, chastity for men.

Feminist movements of the late nineteenth century involved important elements of sexual repression and a "puritanical" approach in general that has made it increasingly difficult to tie them uncomplicatedly to liberalism, allowing instead a recognition of their close alliances also with socially conservative movements. Repealing regulation, repressing prostitution, outlawing immoral art and literature, shutting down lewd music halls and so forth were means to the more general end of reforming male sexual behavior. The National Vigilance Association, for example, combined feminists and social conservatives in their ambitions to enlist the state and its coercive powers on behalf of changing male behavior through the repression of vice and public immorality.[495] The demand that women should act sexually like men was rejected by most early feminists as only an apparent form of egalitarianism that in fact threatened to deprive women of their last remaining defenses against male lust, subjecting relations between the sexes to the naked play of power.[496] The reluctance of feminists to embrace contraception was emblematic of this approach. Many male sexual reformers in the late nineteenth century, Karl Pearson for example, held that contraception allowed women to approach sex as a source of pleasure rather than a fount of anxiety over unwanted pregnancy. But many early feminists feared contraception as removing the last barrier to unbridled male lust, leaving women fully exposed to the allegedly limitless wants of their partners, and the right to refuse intercourse in marriage was a central feminist claim.[497] The demand for contraception did not, thanks to such hesitations, become an explicit feminist demand until after the turn of the century.[498] The close connections between feminism and eugenicism

---

[495] Bristow, *Vice and Vigilance*, pp. 102ff.; Petrow, *Policing Morals*, pp. 122–25. For parallel developments in the United States, see David J. Pivar, *Purity Crusade, Sexual Morality and Social Control, 1868–1900* (Westport, 1973).

[496] Brennecke, *Wie ist der Kampf zu führen?*, p. 5; Margaret Jackson, *The Real Facts of Life: Feminism and the Politics of Sexuality c. 1850–1940* (London, 1994), p. 103; Sheila Jeffreys, *The Spinster and Her Enemies: Feminism and Sexuality 1880–1930* (London, 1985), p. 98; Brian Harrison, *Prudent Revolutionaries: Portraits of British Feminists Between the Wars* (Oxford, 1987), p. 313; Wobbe, *Gleichheit und Differenz*, p. 107; Doris Kaufmann, *Frauen zwischen Aufbruch und Reaktion: Protestantische Frauenbewegung in der ersten Hälfte des 20. Jahrhunderts* (Munich, 1988), pp. 33–34.

[497] Although all feminists tended to agree that contraception was desirable in granting women control over pregnancy: McLaren, *Birth Control in Nineteenth-Century England*, ch. 11; Angus McLaren, *A History of Contraception* (Oxford, 1990), pp. 196–97; Philippa Levine, *Victorian Feminism 1850–1900* (Gainesville, 1994), pp. 149–50; Carol Dyhouse, *Feminism and the Family in England 1880–1939* (Oxford, 1989), pp. 169–74.

[498] Bland, *Banishing the Beast*, ch. 5; Davenport-Hines, *Sex, Death and Punishment*, pp. 220–21; Kent,

are another example of the – from a twentieth-century vantage – "conservative" inflection of the early women's movement that is hard to reconcile with a portrayal of feminism as essentially an offshoot of liberalism.[499] Seen from the classic approach, the moralist abolitionists and social purity feminists were conservative and prudish and their stance anomalous considered from the view that expects feminism to have advocated increased individual liberties and been part of the development of ever greater sexual freedom, as measured at least in the ease and unrestrictedness of promiscuous copulation.[500] At best they represent a bastard heritage for the modern women's movement, victims, as they were, of sexual false consciousness. When not rejecting these conservative strands as only inauthentically feminist, traditional accounts have tended to puzzle over the apparent contradictions between the radical and reactionary elements combined in the movements.[501]

It is this sexual whiggery which, like so many teleologies, has been crumbling. As part of the prolonged morning after of the self-proclaimed sexual revolution of the 1960s and the current inflection of the sex wars, it has become increasingly clear to many feminists that the assumption that men and women act alike in matters reproductive was bought on overly easy intellectual credit.[502] The belief of the early

---

Sex and Suffrage in Britain, pp. 104–05, 112; Paul Smith, *Feminism in the Third Republic*, p. 220; J. A. Banks and Olive Banks, *Feminism and Family Planning in Victorian England* (Liverpool, 1964), pp. 97–103, 120; Johanna Alberti, *Beyond Suffrage: Feminists in War and Peace, 1914–1928* (Houndsmill, 1989), pp. 72–73, 120–25; Dienel, *Kinderzahl und Staatsräson*, ch. 9.

[499] Bland, *Banishing the Beast*, ch. 6; Bristow, *Vice and Vigilance*, p. 140; Mort, "Purity, Feminism and the State," pp. 212, 218; Mort, *Dangerous Sexualities*, pp. 92–95; Anna Bergmann, *Die verhütete Sexualität: Die Anfänge der modernen Geburtenkontrolle* (Hamburg, 1992), p. 87; Christl Wickert, *Helene Stöcker* (Bonn, 1991), pp. 68, 79–80.

[500] Rover, *Love, Morals and the Feminists*, pp. 2, 45, 97; Bristow, *Vice and Vigilance*, p. 77.

[501] Walkowitz, for example, sought to make sense of the apparently contradictory melange of liberatory and repressive ideas in abolitionism by arguing that the original impulse was emancipatory, but that repeal was then turned to repressive goals by the male-dominated social purity movements. Her basic position remains that repeal and social purity were at odds: Walkowitz, "Male Vice and Feminist Virtue," pp. 86–89; Judith R. Walkowitz, "The Politics of Prostitution," *Signs*, 6, 1 (1980), pp. 123ff.; Walkowitz, *Prostitution and Victorian Society*, pp. 7, 117, 246–48; Allen, "Feminism, Venereal Diseases, and the State in Germany," p. 29; Haste, *Rules of Desire*, pp. 15–16; Michanek, *En morgondröm*, p. 65; Mary Spongberg, *Feminizing Venereal Disease: The Body of the Prostitute in Nineteenth-Century Medical Discourse* (New York, 1997), p. 85; Christoph Sachsse, *Mütterlichkeit als Beruf: Sozialarbeit, Sozialreform und Frauenbewegung 1871–1929* (2nd edn.; Opladen, 1994), pp. 98–107; Weeks, *Sex, Politics and Society*, pp. 87–88. Others have solved the problem by dividing feminism into two camps, separate spheres and equal rights, whose twain never meets: Banks, *Faces of Feminism*, ch. 5; Bärbel Clemens, *"Menschenrechte haben kein Geschlecht!" Zum Politikverständnis der bürgerlichen Frauenbewegung* (Pfaffenweiler, 1988).

[502] Sheila Jeffreys, *Anticlimax: A Feminist Perspective on the Sexual Revolution* (London, 1990); Deirdre English, "The Fear that Feminism Will Free Men First," in Ann Snitow et al., eds., *Powers of Desire* (New York, 1983), pp. 477–83.

abolitionists that the sexes are instinctually different and their insistence
that male behavior adjust to women's expectations now appear in a more
positive light, less as puritanism and more as the justified vindication of
specifically female demands. Current antipornography campaigns have
traced their pedigree back to Victorian repeal.[503] Thanks to this political and historiographical seachange, the most recent accounts of abolitionism no longer take these early feminists to task for having been
allegedly misled by puritanical ideas and reactionary male allies, seeking
to contain and control sexuality rather than set it free. The conservative
side of British feminism, aiming to hold all humans to a high standard
of sexual conduct, and its egalitarian aspect, wishing to treat men and
women equally, were not, these revisionists have argued, in contradiction, but in fact part and parcel of the same ambition.[504] In the late nineteenth century, one recent account concludes, the demand for a single
moral standard to which also men should be held was central to British
feminism. The assertion of female moral superiority is now seen as a
claim to status and the right to criticize male domination in a realm
where women would not be condemned to inferiority.[505] Early feminists
have been defended as being not prudes, but women who refused sexual
interaction with men, seeking to protect themselves from transgression.
These "prudish" feminists are, indeed, now portrayed as the most
radical of the movement, aiming to enlist the state in the task of alter-
ing male behavior and granting women complete control over sexual
access.[506]

Such revision has been most extensive in the Anglo-American realm
since here separate spheres feminism appeared to be a creature apart
from the mainstream of the equal rights approach. But in other nations,

[503] Walkowitz, "Male Vice and Feminist Virtue," pp. 79–93. Perhaps because pornography was
legalized earlier in Scandinavia than elsewhere, parallels between antipornography and antiprosti-
tution feminism were quickly drawn here: Fredelius, *Ett onödigt ont*, p. 7 and passim; Levin, *Testiklarnas
herravälde*, pp. 10–11, 27, 306.

[504] Kent, *Sex and Suffrage in Britain*, pp. 205–06; Spongberg, *Feminizing Venereal Disease*, pp. 108–09;
Lucy Bland, "Feminist Vigilantes of Late-Victorian England," in Carol Smart, ed., *Regulating
Womanhood* (London, 1992), pp. 47–52; Lucia Zedner, *Women, Crime, and Custody in Victorian England*
(Oxford, 1991), p. 18; Philippa Levine, *Feminist Lives in Victorian England* (Oxford, 1990), pp. 86–88,
97–98.

[505] Bland, *Banishing the Beast*, p. xiii and ch. 7; Brian Harrison, "Women's Health and the
Women's Movement in Britain: 1840–1940," in Charles Webster, ed., *Biology, Medicine and Society
1840–1940* (Cambridge, 1981), p. 66; Levine, *Victorian Feminism 1850–1900*, pp. 148–49; Alberti, *Beyond
Suffrage*, pp. 116–20; Barbara Caine, *Victorian Feminists* (Oxford, 1992), p. 41; Mort, "Purity, Feminism
and the State," p. 211; Walkowitz, "Male Vice and Feminist Virtue," p. 86.

[506] Jeffreys, "Free From All Uninvited Touch of Man," pp. 629–31, 635; Jeffreys, *Spinster and Her
Enemies*, pp. 1–2; Jackson, *Real Facts of Life*, pp. 2–3; Sheila Jeffreys, ed., *The Sexuality Debates* (New
York, 1987).

where it has long been recognized as part of a conservative variant, revision has also been busy. In Germany, for example, the social purity feminists, formerly castigated as an irremediably reactionary inflection of the movement, are now being vindicated in their own right. They were not, it is claimed, misled by conservatives in their insistence on male restraint, but acted on the principle central not only to the bourgeois, but also large elements of the socialist feminist movement, that men and women be held accountable to the same moral criteria. Attacking the double standard was here too a way of criticizing male dominance, not – as seen from the anachronistic retrospection of the late twentieth century – an attempt to suppress incipient strivings for sexual liberation.[507] In France, any singular historiography of the women's movement has also been giving way to a plurality of feminisms, a major strain of which was Catholic and familialist in orientation, advocating equivalence rather than equality. Maternalist feminism, runs the revisionist argument, was the savvy and best strategy that could be hoped for in a situation where the allegedly natural allies on the left feared female suffrage as aiding the right, but where all, including conservatives, could be won for profamilialist policies in the face of widespread fears of national infertility and decline. Here, too, a single standard of sexual morality was a self-consciously radical feminist demand.[508]

Such historiographical revision focuses attention on a hitherto neglected and misunderstood aspect of British feminism, its social purity wing. For equal rights feminists, repeal was necessary in order to treat

[507] Wobbe, *Gleichheit und Differenz*, pp. 24–29, 102; Allen, "Feminism, Venereal Diseases, and the State in Germany," p. 29; Ann Taylor Allen, *Feminism and Motherhood in Germany, 1800–1914* (New Brunswick, 1991), pp. 1–7; Meyer-Renschhausen, *Weibliche Kultur und soziale Arbeit*, pp. 6–11, 271–73; Barbara Greven-Aschoff, *Die bürgerliche Frauenbewegung in Deutschland 1894–1933* (Göttingen, 1981), pp. 103–06; Irene Stoehr, *Emanzipation zum Staat? Der Allgemeine Deutsche Frauenverein – Deutscher Staatsbürgerinnenverband (1893–1933)* (Pfaffenweiler, 1990), pp. 39–40; Irene Stoehr, "'Organisierte Mütterlichkeit': Zur Politik der deutschen Frauenbewegung um 1900," in Karin Hausen, ed., *Frauen suchen ihre Geschichte* (Munich, 1983); Renate Bridenthal et al., eds., *When Biology Became Destiny: Women in Weimar and Nazi Germany* (New York, 1984), chs. by Meyer-Renschhausen and Hackett; Dienel, *Kinderzahl und Staatsräson*, pp. 217–20; Christiana Hilpert-Fröhlich, *"Auf zum Kampfe wider die Unzucht": Prostitution und Sittlichkeitsbewegung in Essen 1890–1914* (Bochum, 1991), pp. 42–43. But see also the tack back in the direction of traditional political classifications in Reagin, *A German Women's Movement*, pp. 2–6, 253–57 and, for Britain, Susan Kingsley Kent, *Making Peace: The Reconstruction of Gender in Interwar Britain* (Princeton, 1993), ch. 6.

[508] Paul Smith, *Feminism in the Third Republic*, pp. 5, 43–62; Bidelman, *Pariahs Stand Up!*, pp. xviii–xix; Karen Offen, "Depopulation, Nationalism, and Feminism in Fin-de-Siècle France," *American Historical Review*, 89, 3 (June 1984), pp. 671–76; Karen Offen, "Defining Feminism: A Comparative Historical Approach," *Signs*, 14, 1 (1988), pp. 134–50; Claire Goldberg Moses, *French Feminism in the Nineteenth Century* (Albany, 1984), p. 231; Christine Bard, *Les filles de Marianne: Histoire des féminismes 1914–1940* (n.p., 1995), pp. 66–69, 219–23, 382.

the sexes alike in the eyes of the law. For their social purity colleagues, in contrast, repeal was but one element in a larger endeavor of refashioning male sexuality and overall social mores. Abolition lay close to the core of the purity feminists' morally reforming vision whereas for their comrades in feminism, it was necessary perhaps, but largely peripheral to more important concerns. The fervor and strength of the British repeal movement must therefore be seen in terms of the important role played in this cohort of feminists by the ideology of moral rejuvenation. Social purity and its fervent insistence on ethical reform was not a brake on the feminist movement as a whole, not a diversion by conservatives of efforts along irrelevant tangents. Quite the contrary, purity feminism represented a radical phalanx of the movement, much as all the fads and reform causes of this era of protodemocratic upheaval, whether horrified by cruelty against animals or loath to see the sabbath desecrated by work, were the cutting edge of populist politics, however peculiar, fanatical and misguided they may have appeared to patricians of the established parties or, today, to retrospecting contemporaries.

Social purity was, of course, pursued also by continental feminisms. Movements aiming to combine morality with public hygiene had existed in France already in the 1830s when the Société de la morale chrétienne petitioned the Parisian police to suppress prostitution. During the first years of the following century, the SFPSM sought to encourage chastity and early marriage, combating vice and immorality, and all French feminist organizations by this point opposed regulation in favor of a single standard of morality for both sexes.[509] In Germany, social purity was given expression during the 1880s in the *Sittlichkeitsvereine*, which (founded in both male and female variants) combined attempts to change male sexual behavior with hopes of preserving traditional female roles. The mainstream feminist movements, including the Jewish, also inscribed an end to the double standard on their banners.[510] The endless debates over the Lex Heinze brought to a boil many of the same concerns over public immorality given expression in Britain during the Maiden Tribute

---

[509] Parent-Duchatelet, *De la prostitution*, v. I, pp. 559–60; Corbin, *Women for Hire*, pp. 231–32, 265–67; Hause with Kenney, *Women's Suffrage and Social Politics*, p. 39; Jean Rabaut, *Histoire des féminismes français* (Paris, 1978), pp. 224–25, 277–78.

[510] John C. Fout, "The Moral Purity Movement in Wilhelmine Germany and the Attempt to Regulate Male Behavior," *Journal of Men's Studies*, 1, 1 (August 1992), pp. 5, 8, 24–25; Marion Kaplan, "Prostitution, Morality Crusades and Feminism: German-Jewish Feminists and the Campaign Against White Slavery," *Women's Studies International Forum*, 5, 6 (1982), p. 622; Sauerteig, "Frauenemanzipation und Sittlichkeit."

scandal. Ending regulation was sometimes the least of social purity's endeavors, which could also include, as in the proposals of one Berlin organization, a veritable smorgasbord of interventions: taxing bachelors, those notorious rakes, to pay for medical care of the VD-infected, imposing military-style prophylactic controls on the unmarried, ruthlessly suppressing public solicitation, monitoring dance halls, bringing single women living alone under female supervision and, last but certainly not least, flogging all voluntary emigrants, assumed to consist mainly of pimps, white slave traders and criminals. The fight against VD, as another put it, involved a battle against extramarital sex as well.[511]

And yet, despite the presence of social purity concerns also on the continent, British feminism appears to have been unique in its close alliance with such endeavors. Anglo-Saxon feminism was often portrayed as being more concerned than other movements with respectable morality and chastity, or at least becoming so during the last decades of the nineteenth century as social purity won the upper hand. The separate spheres feminism of Helene Stöcker, for example, was at one and the same time conservative (compared to an equal rights approach) in its maternalist focus and yet also startlingly unabashed in its frank insistence that female chastity was as socially conditioned as male promiscuity and could be changed, that women be free to seek sexual fulfillment outside marriage and that the state relieve them of the externalities of reproduction. Stöcker was, of course, radical also within the context of German feminism, but her Mutterschutz movement and the "new ethics" associated with it received wider support from advanced opinion here than did equivalent advocates of contraception and free love in Britain (Besant, Stopes).[512] Seen from the continent, the British movement, its attack on the CD Acts and its "puritanical" moral vantage thus represented a unique and effective tying together of gender, politics and morality: a concern with equal civil rights, an obsession with the single moral standard, the organizational wherewithal to put

---

[511] Adalbert Wahl, *Deutsche Geschichte* (Stuttgart, 1932), v. III, pp. 636–39; R. J. V. Lenman, "Art, Society, and the Law in Wilhelmine Germany: The Lex Heinze," *Oxford German Studies*, 8 (1973); BA, R86/1065, Der volkswirtschaftliche Verband, Berlin, "Praktische Vorschläge zur Bekämpfung der Prostitution vom Gesundheitsstandpunkt"; Brennecke, *Wie ist der Kampf zu führen?*, p. 7.

[512] Rover, *Love, Morals and the Feminists*, p. 12; Gibson, *Prostitution and the State*, p. 92; Bergmann, *Die verhütete Sexualität*, p. 87; Allen, "Feminism, Venereal Diseases, and the State in Germany," p. 48; Weindling, *Health, Race and German Politics*, pp. 252–57; Greven-Aschoff, *Die bürgerliche Frauenbewegung in Deutschland 1894–1933*, pp. 66–67, 95; Richard J. Evans, *Feminist Movement in Germany*, pp. 116–38; Levin, *Testiklarnas herravälde*, pp. 10–11, 91, 128, 143, 158.

punch behind program.[513] While the continental movements were more willing to accept differential behavior between the sexes, British feminists insisted on a single moral standard for both. British feminism was thus unusual in two respects. Not only was it precocious and strong, but the moralizing nature of its ideology made repeal more central to its mission of changing sexual roles and ethical standards than on the continent.

The nonconformist reform movements applied ethical precepts to various causes, whether the unity of moral standards common to blacks and whites, animals and humans or males and females. These movements were associated with Protestantism and found in Germany and Scandinavia as well as Britain, though less so in France. They were also linked to the development of democratic politics, the first untutored and unfiltered expression of grassroots opinion. In Britain and, less, in Scandinavia, these movements focused on such ethical issues. In Germany, the emphasis was on national, more than individual, health and regeneration and such movements, though a protest against the established parties and political system, welcomed the state's active participation in pursuit of their goals. Feminism was one aspect of this broader current of grassroots politics and its social purity wing sought to improve the lot of women by taming male conduct, much as temperance aimed to halt the domestic violence, uncouth behavior and squandering of family resources that followed abuse of the bottle. To the extent that "bourgeois" propriety expressed the moral concerns of particular social strata (primarily the lower middle and upper working class), British moralism and puritanism were connected to the nation's political evolution – the expression in ethical terms of its democratic development and the particular inflection of its feminist movement. The continued willingness to accept the double standard, characteristic of continental morality, reflected a persistence of aristocratic and antifeminist traditions. In this general sense, then, a modified and expanded Ackerknechtian approach explains much of the reason why the British repealed regulation early, and other nations only later. The early development of Protestant-based democratic feminist politics and grassroots opinion, for which regulation smacked of aristocratic male privilege, would not tolerate the system.

[513] Johanna Geyer-Kordesch, "Sozialhygiene und Sexualreform: Die Kritik der 'Feministinnen' in England im 19. Jahrhundert," in Reulecke and Rüdenhausen, *Stadt und Gesundheit*, pp. 257–60. This split between Anglo-American and continental feminism, much of which rests on a continued acceptance of what, from the former perspective, appears a double standard, persists down to the present day: Amy Guttman, "The Challenge of Multiculturalism in Political Ethics," *Philosophy and Public Affairs*, 22, 3 (1993), pp. 205–06; Ozouf, *Les mots des femmes*, pp. 384–92.

Slaves (as historians are) of overdetermination, tillers in the vineyard of multicausality, they will not be relieved by such a single, general origin of the divergence between British and continental prophylactic strategies of the obligation to point out some of the more immediate and concrete factors behind such differences. Among these was the foreign nature of regulation to British traditions and law. During the Middle Ages, Britain had had official brothels, much like the continent, but only in three cities.[514] When regulation was attempted anew in the 1860s, it was a foreign import that invested a national police force with unprecedented powers, holding up the specter of centralization to friends of local control. Prostitutes were treated as members of a special class, not as individuals, in a way that, though perhaps a snug fit with continental traditions of corporatism, contradicted the freer, more individualistic British notions of socioeconomic organization.[515] Indeed, abolitionists everywhere, not just in Britain, objected precisely to the corporatism of regulation, however modernized, which treated prostitutes as members of a guild rather than individuals.[516] To compound such injury, regulation was introduced late to Britain, at a time when its disadvantages were becoming ever more evident elsewhere. Broached at midcentury, long after the wildfire of VD associated with the Napoleonic wars, and having been abolished before the panic over syphilis that gripped Europe at the end of the century, regulation in Britain neatly managed to sidestep pressing motives on its own behalf that might have been presented by such epidemics.[517] The acts were abolished more easily than on the continent also because they were a single set of national laws, passed by Parliament and thus repealable in like manner, rather than (as in France) a welter of local regulations and decrees, each claiming to rest inviolably on venerable precedent and hence as difficult to uproot as weeds.[518]

---

[514] Ruth Mazo Karras, *Common Women: Prostitution and Sexuality in Medieval England* (New York, 1996), ch. 2.

[515] Hammond and Hammond, *James Stansfeld*, p. 118; Scott, *State Iniquity*, p. 141; Taylor, *Speech at Exeter*, pp. 7–8; McHugh, *Prostitution and Victorian Social Reform*, pp. 43–44; *Hansard*, 1876, v. 230, cols. 1559, 1565.

[516] Flexner, *Prostitution in Europe*, p. 150; Scott, *State Iniquity*, pp. 1–4; Fiaux, *Police des moeurs*, v. I, pp. xvii–viii, 29, 91; Dolléans, *La police des moeurs*, p. 5; *SFPSM: Bulletin mensuel* (1902), p. 220; XVIIth International Congress of Medicine, *Dermatology and Syphilography*, p. 55; Dubois-Havenith, *Conférence internationale: Rapports préliminaires*, v. I/1, quest. 1, p. 74.

[517] Dubois-Havenith, *Conférence internationale: Enquêtes*, v. I/2, p. 8; *Hansard*, 1870, v. 203, col. 577; 1876, v. 230, col. 1599; 1873, v. 216, cols. 229–30; *PP* 1868–69 xxxii, 1, pp. 13–16.

[518] Harsin, *Policing Prostitution*, p. 325; Bristow, *Vice and Vigilance*, p. 78; Amos, *Comparative Survey of Laws*, pp. 183–84.

WAR AND THE MILITARY

More generally among the other factors behind prophylactic variation was the nature of the military system in each nation. War, the epidemic spread of VD and attempts to combat it were closely associated: during the Napoleonic wars in Sweden, France and Prussia, during the First World War among all combatant nations. In both cases, returning soldiers acted as carriers. Being spared such a major influx of contagion in the early nineteenth century and again a hundred years later, when infected soldiers were kept in France until cured, may have deprived the British of at least one stimulus to more drastic intervention. Whatever the case in such particular instances, the conditions of armed service and their variation among nations were an important factor. Prostitution and the military were intimately connected. Massings of young, generally unmarried and enforcedly celibate males stoked the market for commercial sex, regardless of the national colors under which they rallied, but different kinds of military organization prompted varying degrees of demand.

Though regulation had often been initiated by military authorities in hopes of limiting the spread of VD in the ranks, the continental systems were not as particularly tied to the military as were the British CD Acts. Continental regulation aimed not just at prostitutes consorting with soldiers, but applied just as much to those with a civilian client base and a broader focus was naturally also true for the Scandinavian systems of general inspections. The CD Acts, in contrast, were prompted by and concerned with the extremely high incidence of disease in the armed forces. From focusing on the military, British regulationism then sought (unsuccessfully in the event) extension to civilians, whereas on the continent the movement, if any direction, took the opposite course.

The British military was notorious for having by far the worst VD rates of any European force.[519] Regulationists naturally liked to argue that the absence of their system here allowed a wide spread, but in fact there is – although statistics are notoriously nonexistent – no particular reason to think that the high military incidence of VD was paralleled by similar rates in the civilian population.[520] It was the British military,

[519] The incidence of VD in the British army in 1860 was 369/1000, compared to 70 in the French and 34 in the Prussian forces: Skelley, *Victoran Army at Home*, p. 54; Fiaux, *L'armée et la police des moeurs*, p. 246.
[520] In fact most observers made the opposite assumption: *PP* 1916 (8189) xvi, 1, pp. 181–82; *Underdånigt betänkande angående könssjukdomarnas spridning*, v. I, p. 52.

not the absence of regulation, that was peculiar.[521] The basic distinction was between Britain's volunteer military and the conscript armies of the continent. On the one hand, Britain had a voluntary, professional army, recruited for lengthy periods of service largely from the poorer members of society, and soldiers were, with exceptions, required to live in conditions of celibacy while being paid a wage sufficient to allow them to traffic in mercenary sex.[522] Because service times were long and voluntary, the routine was less intense, leave time lengthier, the liberties permitted the men more expansive than in the conscript armies with shorter service times (two years in Germany, one or three years in France) and discipline was less strict than on the continent where the military was a national obligation, not an occupational choice. A strong demand for commercial sex and correspondingly high infection rates were the outcome in Britain. Long service in distant colonies, where only a few soldiers were permitted wives and families, served to accentuate such characteristics.[523] The continental armies, in contrast, with their universal conscription and abbreviated service allowed soldiers and sailors to remain more firmly anchored in civilian society, retaining ties to family, wives, lovers, companions.[524] Their merely token pay, shorter leave times and stricter discipline also hampered whatever ambitions they may have entertained as consumers of commercial venery.[525]

As a captive population, subject to a strict regimen, with the good of the group taking obvious precedence over individual rights and preferences, soldiers were especially vulnerable to public health interventions. Living under conditions ideally suited to the spread of contagious

[521] Kromayer, *Zur Austilgung der Syphilis*, p. 26; *Underdånigt betänkande angående könssjukdomarnas spridning*, v. I, p. 355; *Hansard*, 1873, v. 216, col. 260.

[522] Acton, *Prostitution*, p. 176; *PP* 1878–79 (323) viii, QQ. 3008, 3020; F. B. Smith, "Contagious Diseases Acts Reconsidered," pp. 206–07; *Förhandlingar*, 1912, p. 280; Dubois-Havenith, *Conférence internationale: Enquêtes*, v. I/2, pp. 681–82. British soldiers were paid the equivalent of a daily wage, after expenses, of 60–80 centimes, while the French received 5: Deck, *Syphilis et réglementation*, p. 81.

[523] *Underdånigt betänkande angående könssjukdomarnas spridning*, v. I, pp. 355–57; Deck, *Syphilis et réglementation de la prostitution*, pp. 81–82; *PP* 1867–68 (4031) xxxvii, 425, Q. 6383; Kenneth Ballhatchet, *Race, Sex and Class Under the Raj* (London, 1980), p. 66.

[524] In contrast, the remoteness of the Victorian army from British society has often been noted: Gwyn Harries-Jenkins, *The Army in Victorian Society* (London, 1977), pp. 4–5.

[525] Dubois-Havenith, *Conférence internationale: Enquêtes*, v. I/2, p. 14; *Hansard*, 1873, v. 216, col. 260; *Bulletin*, 3, 57 (1907), p. 465; *SFPSM: Bulletin mensuel* (1902), p. 13; Corbin, *Women for Hire*, pp. 199–205. On the other hand, universal conscription may have hampered the ability to marry early, since men were called up at precisely the age when they could have been tying the knot and the military authorities were granted certain controls over their nuptiality: Flesch and Wertheimer, *Geschlechtskrankheiten und Rechtsschutz*, p. 2; Mignot, *Péril vénérien*, p. 109; Winter, *The Great War and the British People*, pp. 7–8.

disease (this was particularly the case among sailors), the armed forces bore the brunt of special precautions. The basic requirement was that military personnel report themselves when infected. Also common were inspections upon enlistment and in conjunction with furloughs, leaves and discharges. In France, soldiers had been inspected for disease already before the revolution and, in 1781, all hapless enough to have been thrice treated found their service prolonged by two years. Inspections continued throughout the nineteenth century. In 1887, the Academy of Medicine recommended that mass monthly genital examinations be discontinued as discouraging soldiers from revealing their illness, replaced by individual inspections in private, and in 1902 this was put into effect. In 1912 monthly VD musterings were required of all soldiers.[526] Already early in the century, all Swedish military recruits were inspected at enlistment and then monthly thereafter, later weekly, often on Sundays just before church – and that regardless, as one observer put it, of how virtuous a life they lived. Starting in the thirties, garrisoned troops were examined regularly and, as of 1858, all were inspected before and after furloughs, marches and other transports.[527] In Germany, similar measures dated back at least to the Napoleonic campaigns. The Prussian 1835 regulation required civilian physicians treating syphilitic soldiers to report them to their commanding officers and all were to be inspected for VD at recruitment, marching out and discharge, with the infected retained until cured, even if this lasted longer than their time of service. The German army after unification inspected soldiers upon discharge; in the navy all personnel were examined monthly and sometimes denied shore leave in ports reputed to be heavily infected.[528] In Britain, by contrast, inspections were the exception and resisted by the military authorities, lest they discourage recruitment.[529] Genital inspections had

[526] Lecour, *La prostitution à Paris*, pp. 89–90; Mireur, *La syphilis et la prostitution*, p. 83; Fiaux, *L'armée et la police des moeurs*, pp. 211, 261; Jeannel, *De la prostitution*, pp. 361–62; *Annales*, 46 (1851), p. 73; *PP* 1867–68 (4031) xxxvii, 425, Q. 5259; *SFPSM: Bulletin mensuel* (1902), pp. 58–59; *Bulletin*, 2, 17 (1887), p. 652; 3, 57 (1907), pp. 463–64; Thibierge, *La syphilis et l'armée*, p. 166.

[527] *Hygiea*, 51, 3 (March 1889), p. 153; *Förhandlingar*, 1881, p. 29; *Borgare*, 1817, v. 1, pp. 436–39; Malmroth, "Om de smittosamma könssjukdomarnas bekämpande," p. 38; Thyresson, *Från Fransoser till AIDS*, p. 83; Welander, *Blad ur prostitutionsfrågans historia*, pp. 10, 16; *Hygiea*, 9, 3 (March 1847), p. 185; *Underdånigt betänkande angående könssjukdomarnas spridning*, v. I, p. 323; Wistrand, *Författningar*, pp. 633ff.

[528] Augustin, *Preussische Medicinalverfassung*, v. II, pp. 763–65; *Gesetz-Sammlung*, 1835, 27/1678, §§65, 73; Silber, *Womit sind die ansteckenden Geschlechtskrankheiten zu bekämpfen?*, p. 54; Dubois-Havenith, *Conférence internationale: Enquêtes*, v. I/2, pp. 669–70; O. Rapmund, *Polizei-Verordnung betreffend Massregeln gegen die Verbreitung ansteckender Krankheiten* (Minden i. W., 1899), p. 56; Rudeck, *Syphilis und Gonorrhoe vor Gericht*, p. 85; *Underdånigt betänkande angående könssjukdomarnas spridning*, v. I, p. 326.

[529] Such inspections threatened the army's ambitions of recruiting from higher up the social

been common until 1859, when they were ended on recommendation of a Royal Commission. Only certain regiments continued the procedure. The Coldstream Guards carried out weekly inspections, with five to six hundred soldiers (the married excepted) examined in half an hour – in line, penis displayed, prepuce retracted.[530] Although many reformers favored examining soldiers as the obvious complement to control of prostitutes, inspections were unpopular and considered demeaning, degrading and insulting to the respectable and the married.[531]

The consequences for the VD debates of this basic contrast between recruited and volunteer armies were twofold. With the military loath to extend inspections to soldiers, statutory attempts to control transmission in Britain remained narrowly focused on prostitutes. The abolitionists could therefore with justice claim that women were being unfairly singled out while the other half of the epidemiological equation remained unfactored.[532] Moreover, because of the close tie between British regulation and the military, radicals who opposed standing armies could combine this dislike with that of the CD Acts in a self-reinforcing vituperative circle.[533] Conversely, among the universally conscripting nations where military inspections were standard-issue procedure, the arguments against regulation were deprived of much of their moral outrage. Since soldiers were subject to compulsory notification, treatment and periodic inspection as part of their involuntary service to the nation, why – such was the logic – was it unreasonable to require similar procedures of prostitutes? Regulation was no more a deprivation of liberty than conscription.[534] From this angle, abolitionist arguments, that VD examinations unfairly singled out women, appeared in a new light. While, for example, some 700 to 800 Swedish

scale: *PP* 1868–69 (306) vii, 1, Q. 1284; *PP* 1871 (c. 408-1) xix, 29, p. xliii. Similar worries that too draconian conditions of service might hinder recruitment also lay behind resistance to the packet system in 1914: Reid, *Prevention of Venereal Disease*, pp. 118–20. In much the same fashion, the government abandoned compulsory vaccination for the military in the midst of the First World War in fear of losing volunteers: J. R. Smith, *The Speckled Monster: Smallpox in England, 1670–1970, with Particular Reference to Essex* (Chelmsford, 1987), pp. 142–43. Conversely, rampant VD could hardly have been an inducement to enlist and in fact the Canadians worried in 1916 that recruitment would be hampered if effective precautions were not taken: Buckley, "Failure to Resolve the Problem of Venereal Disease," p. 75.   [530] *PP* 1867–68 (4031) xxxvii, 425, QQ. 5658–68.

[531] *PP* 1867–68 (4031) xxxvii, 425, pp. xxxi, xliii–xliv, QQ. 7045, 2433–34; *PP* 1868–69 (306) vii, 1, p. iv; *PP* 1871 (c. 408) xix, 1, p. 17.

[532] Indeed, the logic of the matter was that, since inspecting soldiers was not feasible, the focus had to be on prostitutes instead: *PP* 1867–68 (4031) xxxvii, 425, Q. 6380.

[533] *Transactions of the National Association for the Promotion of Social Science* (1870), p. 233; *Hansard*, 1870, v. 203, col. 585; Wilkinson, *Forcible Introspection of Women*, p. 18.

[534] *La syphilis* (1904), p. 713; Lecour, *La prostitution à Paris*, pp. 40–41.

prostitutes were inspected annually, fifty to sixty thousand men were subject as soldiers to similar examinations.[535] Moreover, in Britain medical inspections and regulation remained narrowly focused on one particular outcast group and, even had they been extended to soldiers and sailors, in the absence of national conscription, they would have remained a measure for the marginal. On the continent, in contrast, since universal conscription meant that practically all males had undergone such examinations, they were perhaps more sympathetic to their purpose and ambition. At the least, the logical pull of argument here was not to hinder an extension of VD inspections to the civilian population, as in Britain, but on the contrary to extend it. Women and the armed forces, observers in France grumbled, bore the brunt of inspections while civilian males were equally implicated in spreading disease. They too should be subject to such precautions, thus extending examinations to all.[536]

In Scandinavia this line of argument could be advanced with even greater conviction. One reason why the debates over abolition were less impassioned and controversial in Sweden than in Britain was the nature of the alternative. The CD Acts could be portrayed as especially unfair because of the extent to which prostitutes alone were targeted. In Sweden, in contrast, regulation aimed at prostitutes, of course, but it was far from being the only precaution invoked against VD. The tradition of general inspections lived on even during the reign of regulation. When regulationists defended their system, arguments in its favor came more readily than was possible in Britain. Medical inspections for VD did not concern just loose women, as one put it; they had existed for broad groups since 1812. Soldiers and sailors were also liable to such examinations and, if it was true that they did not have to display their genitals as often or regularly as prostitutes, that was because men did not in the same way offer their bodies on Venus's auction block, not because prostitutes as such were being singled out. As soon as there was a reason to suspect VD, then men as much as women were subject to inspections.[537] To understand the continental approach, one must therefore keep in mind that it included not only measures aimed at prostitutes, but that soldiers, which meant in the long run most males, were liable to similar control. In Scandinavia with its early universal focus, the contrast with the British situation was even starker. The tenor of the British discus-

---

[535] *Förhandlingar*, 1881, p. 29; Welander, *Blad ur prostitutionsfrågans historia*, p. 185.
[536] *SFPSM: Bulletin mensuel* (1902), pp. 71, 153; Regnault, *L'évolution de la prostitution*, pp. 262–63.
[537] *RD prot*, FK 1889:19, p. 54.

sions, not to mention the ensuing historiography of the movement, with abolitionist charges of a discriminatory focus on prostitutes and women, did not apply without qualification to the continental situation, where statutory intervention of one form or another already affected close to half the population.[538]

Looked at the other way around, the British inability to impose outright preventive measures on soldiers forced them to cast about for other precautions. Shortening the period of recruitment and widening the possibilities of marriage were proposals that aimed to make prostitution a less drearily predictable part of life in uniform.[539] Giving soldiers diversions in their free time other than drink and debauchery, improving recreational (especially sports) facilities: such were changes advocated in hopes that, if they could not sublimate baser instincts, at least they might distract or exhaust them, providing diversion from the idleness that, as Osler put it, was the mother of lechery.[540] The British were admired among continental reformers for their emphasis on sports and other wholesome pursuits, both in the army and out.[541] From the military such proposals spilled into civilian life, in the form of Boy Scouts and other organizations designed to punctuate the otherwise sedentary habits of the middle classes with bouts of vigorous physical activity of a nonvenereal nature. Limiting access to alcohol through licensing restrictions and the like was also part of such campaigns.

INSURANCE

The nature of the social insurance system, if any, also helped incline nations prophylactically in one direction or the other. The basic contrast was between those nations, above all Sweden and then Germany after 1883, that provided health care for the bulk of citizens in some prepaid form or another, and those (Britain and France) that through the early

[538] Finger et al., *Handbuch der Geschlechtskrankheiten*, v. III, p. 2672.

[539] Dubois-Havenith, *Conférence internationale: Compte rendu*, pp. 351–53; *Conférence internationale: Enquêtes*, v. I/2, pp. 14–15; Trustram, *Women of the Regiment*, ch. 3.

[540] William Osler, *The Principles and Practice of Medicine* (8th edn.; New York, 1919), p. 278; Buckley, "Failure to Resolve the Problem of Venereal Disease," p. 68.

[541] *Mitteilungen*, 23, 2 (1925), p. 12; Johannes Breger, *Die Geschlechtskrankheiten in ihrer Bedeutung für Familie und Staat* (Berlin, 1926), p. 28; *Annales*, 4/28 (1917), pp. 27–28. Although in their organized and institutionalized form as gymnastics and the like, the British had adopted the Swedish and German models: George Newman, *The Building of a Nation's Health* (London, 1939), ch. 8; Bruce Haley, *The Healthy Body and Victorian Culture* (Cambridge, MA, 1978), ch. 6; Vincent-Pierre Comiti, *Histoire du droit sanitaire en France* (Paris, 1994), pp. 90–103; Nye, *Crime, Madness and Politics in Modern France*, ch. 9.

years of the twentieth century did not. In Germany the principles of social insurance had been applied to VD even before Bismarck. The Berlin brothel regulations of 1792 established a mutual aid fund financed by the owners to pay the costs of treating infected prostitutes, lessening the financial incentives to conceal disease. Similar insurance arrangements for prostitutes were continued later in the century, in 1868 in Leipzig for example.[542] From 1883, however, the problem achieved a more general resolution, for the johns at least, with the health insurance system. Although it included at first only manual workers, demographic and economic developments and a gradual broadening of its membership had conspired to put much of the population on its rosters by the early twentieth century, with only the best-paid salaried employees and most prosperously self-employed still fending for themselves. While Sweden had long treated VD patients at the public expense, in neither France nor Britain, during the debates of the late nineteenth century, was there a national health insurance system.

The consequences for VD prophylaxis of such contrasts were various. Thanks to their uncluttered social policy landscape, British reformers trod terra nova, both needing and able to establish novel institutions. Measures came late, but when they finally did arrive, they struck out in new directions. The policlinics and ambulatory VD treatment centers set up during the First World War as the first form of free national health provision for a particular set of diseases were necessary because there were few other venues of cure, but they were also possible for much the same reason. In Germany, in contrast, fewer motives spoke for introducing such direct and targeted state-paid care for the infected, most of whom had insurance coverage. Although health insurance encompassed an ever expanding majority of the population, while the poorest were treated courtesy of public assistance, there did remain groups for whom access to medical care continued to be a problem: domestics and lower

---

[542] Augustin, *Preussische Medicinalverfassung*, v. I, pp. 189–90; *Zeitschrift für die Staatsarzneikunde*, 58 (1849), pp. 428–54; *DVöG*, 1 (1869), pp. 386–92. In this way, by making the cure of infected prostitutes a business expense borne by venereal entrepreneurs, the Germans also avoided the debate over public goods raised in Britain slightly later in the century. Curing prostitutes at the public expense, Simon warned in 1868, meant implausibly asking taxpayers to foot the cost of making indulgence safe for the morally marginal: *PP* 1868–69 xxxii, 1, p. 12. For similar views, see *Lancet*, 64, 1 (1853), p. 137. These were the same sorts of arguments raised when insurance against industrial accidents had first been proposed: should their cost be borne as a business expense or by the general public? See Hans-Peter Ullmann, "Industrielle Interessen und die Entstehung der deutschen Sozialversicherung 1880–1889," *Historische Zeitschrift*, 229, 3 (December 1979), pp. 584–88; Monika Breger, *Die Haltung der industriellen Unternehmer zur staatlichen Sozialpolitik in den Jahren 1878–1891* (Frankfurt, 1982), pp. 79ff.

civil servants who, not members, could not necessarily afford private care, and the unemployed who had exited the system.[543] After the end of hostilities in 1918, problems inherent in the patchwork coverage of the German system became acute. Dependants of insurance members, for example, were still not covered which, in the case of VD, meant that a man who had been cured might be continuously reinfected by his untreated wife. Reformers used such dysfunctional examples to press for changes: free treatment for all citizens, an extension of health insurance to dependants or, at the least, providing care for the poor without the consequences of poor relief.[544] German reformers often admired the free treatment provided in Britain and Scandinavia, but the authorities saw no reason to duplicate what was largely in place already through the health insurance system. In the 1927 VD law, despite the call of Socialists, Communists and Left Liberals for free medical care to complement the new requirement of compulsory treatment, the authorities felt no need to hold out such promises precisely because prepaid care already existed in broad practice.[545] To patch up holes in an otherwise wideflung net of social provision, however, the law did allow the poor, nonmembers and others who, though participants, might suffer disadvantage from being dealt with through the health insurance system to be treated at the public expense.[546]

The British situation thus stood in distinction to Germany where free medical treatment clinics were discussed at war's end only for demobilized soldiers, not for wider groups of the population, and the interwar consultation centers were allowed to dispense only contraceptive and medical advice, not to treat patients.[547] In France, similar policlinics specializing in VD, established during and after the First World War, aimed

[543] BA, 15.01, RmdI, 11866, pp. 72ff., "Aufzeichnung über die am 4. und 5. März 1908 abgehaltene Sitzung des Reichs-Gesundheitsrats (Ausschuss für Seuchenbekämpfung), betreffend die Bekämpfung der Geschlechtskrankheiten," pp. 78–80; *ZBGK*, 19, 4 (1919), pp. 123–26; Blaschko, *Syphilis und Prostitution*, p. 118; Silber, *Womit sind die ansteckenden Geschlechtskrankheiten zu bekämpfen?*, p. 53; Dubois-Havenith, *Conférence internationale: Enquêtes*, v. I/2, p. 698.

[544] *Mitteilungen*, 17, 1 (1919), pp. 7–11; Neisser, *Geschlechtskrankheiten und ihre Bekämpfung*, p. 228; Dreuw, *Allgemeine, gleiche, diskrete Anzeige- und Behandlungspflicht*, p. 1; *Sammlung der Drucksachen der Preussischen Landesversammlung*, 1919/21, Drcksch. 1823; *ZBGK*, 19, 5/6 (1919/1920), p. 169; *Mitteilungen*, 16, 5/6 (1918), p. 81.

[545] *Mitteilungen*, 15, 1/2 (1917), p. 11; Scherber, *Bekämpfung der Geschlechtskrankheiten*, p. 99; *SB*, 21 January 1927, pp. 8678B, 8685C, 8694A; 26 January 1927, pp. 8756A–B, 8758A, 8708B–C; 24 January 1927, p. 8717B.

[546] Hellwig, *Gesetz zur Bekämpfung der Geschlechtskrankheiten*, p. 389. Earlier discussions to this effect are in BA, 15.01, RmdI, 11866, "Denkschrift, betreffend Massnahmen zur Bekämpfung der Geschlechtskrankheiten: Bearbeitet im Kaiserlichen Gesundheitsamte," p. 331.

[547] Hodann, *History of Modern Morals*, p. 104; *Mitteilungen*, 26, 1 (1928), p. 6; *Reichs-Gesundheitsblatt*, 6, 3 (21 January 1931), p. 52.

more pointedly at the poor than in Britain, with the rest of the population considered able to pay its own way. Conversely, in Sweden, where
the state had long financed hospital treatment of VD patients, ambulatory clinics were superfluous.[548] The presence of a fullfledged social
insurance system thus precluded certain options that institutionally less
endowed nations still had available.

Broadly speaking, German health insurance covered most cases of
VD, and during the early twentieth century the authorities remained
content with tinkering rather than radical reform. Instead, the issues
broached here concerned finetuning the system, by ending, for example,
the right of carriers to exclude from full benefit diseases acquired willfully or through sexual excess.[549] Similar issues arose later also in Britain,
where insurance members could be denied sickness or disablement
benefit up to a year if the problem had been caused by their own mis-
conduct. Since the system here, at the beginning of the twentieth
century, still covered only a small proportion of the population, however, the disincentive effect was less pronounced.[550] France's mutual aid
societies caused similar problems.[551] In Germany other laws added to
this disincentive effect. The Prussian regulations on servants of 1810, still
in effect at the end of the century, allowed employers to fire those who
had contracted VD through immoral behavior, thereby propelling many
a domestic on a trajectory whose downward slope ended in a brothel.
Similar measures were possible for sailors through the end of the century
and, among white-collar employees, shop clerks could be fired without
the customary six weeks' notice if incapacitated by contagious disease.[552]
Ending the exclusion of VD from benefit was a drawn-out process,
moved along by a gradual recognition among insurance carriers that
they were being penny-wise and pound-foolish, saddling themselves with

[548] Cavaillon, *L'armement antivénérien*, pp. 124, 130; Dubois-Havenith, *Conférence internationale: Enquêtes*, v. I/2, p. 515.

[549] Blaschko, *Geschlechtskrankheiten*, pp. 15–21; Blaschko, *Syphilis und Prostitution*, p. 117; *DVöG*, 36 (1904), pp. 423–24; Rudeck, *Syphilis und Gonorrhoe vor Gericht*, pp. 94–96; Silber, *Womit sind die ansteckenden Geschlechtskrankheiten zu bekämpfen?*, p. 52.

[550] L. W. Harrison, *Diagnosis and Treatment of Venereal Diseases*, p. 440; Morris, *Nation's Health*, pp. 81–82; David Evans, "Tackling the Hideous Scourge," p. 418. In Sweden, most health insurance carriers excluded VD from benefit, but here the disincentive effects were negligible since patients were entitled to medical care from the state: Dubois-Havenith, *Conférence internationale: Enquêtes*, v. I/2, p. 516.

[551] *Annales*, 16 (1836), p. 265; *ZBGK*, 8, 1 (1908), pp. 12–13; Fiaux, *Police des moeurs*, v. I, pp. 460–61; *SFPSM: Bulletin mensuel* (1902), pp. 346–47; Cavaillon, *L'armement antivénérien*, p. 19.

[552] Jadassohn, *Handbuch der Haut- und Geschlechtskrankheiten*, v. XXIII, p. 89; Blaschko, *Syphilis und Prostitution*, p. 105; Dubois-Havenith, *Conférence internationale: Enquêtes*, v. I/2, p. 698; Kaufmann, *Krieg, Geschlechtskrankheiten und Arbeiterversicherung*, p. 12.

the longterm effects of syphilis rather than treating it at once. Finally, in 1903 reforms ended the exception for VD patients who were now to be treated like those with any other illness.[553]

Medical confidentiality was another issue affected by the nature of the insurance system. The general rule was that, the more generous and embracing the coverage offered through public means, the less disease could remain the exclusive province of private communication between patient and physician. In nations with extensive social insurance, third-party payers naturally demanded to know the diagnosis before reimbursing physicians. The premium on confidentiality was of necessity discounted in the era of social insurance. Discussion shifted instead to other means of preserving some modicum of privacy, whether and how, for example, to extend the obligations of professional secrecy also to the bureaucrats of the insurance carriers. Since privacy and protection from exposure bore directly on the inclination of patients to seek treatment, a fine line had to be walked between third-party payers' right to know and the disincentives of publicity. In Germany, for example, the poor not covered by health insurance could, if their families were unable to reimburse costs, be treated courtesy of public assistance in their home communities. For those who hailed from small villages, however far they may have moved in the interim, this often meant having their ailments exposed to common knowledge. Reformers therefore sought to have costs born instead by the community of current residence, the *Ortsgemeinde*, rather than the *Heimatsgemeinde*. This change, however desirable from a public health point of view, was resisted by the large cities thereby threatened with disproportionate burdens.[554]

Notifiability also implicated the insurance system, the issue being differential treatment between average citizens, who as insurance members were liable to have their ailments reported, and those who, in consulting private physicians, avoided such strictures. Reformers in favor of making VD notifiable thus sought to balance the general desirability of reporting with hopes of avoiding preferential treatment for the wealthy. Since insurance members were already in effect reported when

---

[553] *DVöG*, 36 (1904), p. 425; *ZBGK*, 8, 8 (1908), p. 295; Blaschko, *Syphilis und Prostitution*, pp. 105–06; Rudeck, *Syphilis und Gonorrhoe vor Gericht*, p. 96. In Sweden, the law on health insurance carriers, 4 July 1910, forbade such exclusions: *Underdånigt betänkande angående könssjukdomarnas spridning*, v. I, p. 87.

[554] Finger et al., *Handbuch der Geschlechtskrankheiten*, v. III, p. 2696; Dubois-Havenith, *Conférence internationale: Enquêtes*, v. II/2, p. 699; XVIIth International Congress of Medicine, *Dermatology and Syphilography*, pp. 69–71; Blaschko, *Syphilis und Prostitution*, p. 119; Waldvogel, *Gefahren der Geschlechtskrankheiten*, p. 82; *Mitteilungen*, 4, 9 (1926), p. 98.

their ailments were identified by physicians seeking reimbursement, justice demanded that also private patients be treated similarly. In Germany, Socialists and their allies opposed the DGBG's interwar proposals that physicians be allowed, but not obliged, to report patients indulging in potentially risky behavior since this threatened to affect primarily the lower classes.[555] Reporting, in other words, should be for all or not at all.[556] Their opponents pointed out that, even with a general requirement, private patients willing to consult physicians under assumed names could avoid being reported and that, however benign the intentions, general notification would be only apparently democratic.[557] Such concerns were prevalent during discussions in the early Weimar years and the authorities, anxious to avoid the impression that class considerations were influencing prophylactic strategies, dropped for the moment hopes of making VD generally notifiable.[558] Only in the VD law of 1927 was notification finally required in all cases where the attending physician feared that the patient's behavior might transmit. In Sweden as well, notifiability was a prominent feature of the Lex Veneris, while in France and Britain, with their less-developed insurance systems, reporting was not required.[559] The existence of a well-developed health insurance system thus spoke in favor of making VD notifiable and the logic of reporting, in turn, necessitated a universal requirement in order to avoid a differential, class-based treatment of the infected.

In a general sense, the presence of social insurance helped tip the balance between a voluntary and more interventionist approach. The

[555] *Sitzungsberichte der Preussischen Landesversammlung*, 1919/21, 25 February 1920, cols. 9926–27, 9935; *ZBGK*, 4, 1 (1905), p. 61; 18, 11 (1917/18/19), p. 283; 18, 1 (1917), p. 2.

[556] This was also the gist of Dreuw's reform proposals on universal notifiability: *Sitzungsberichte der Preussischen Landesversammlung*, 1919/21, 25 February 1920, cols. 9949–50, 9956; *ZBGK*, 14, 3/4 (1916), pp. 44–46; 19, 4 (1919), p. 96; *Mitteilungen*, 18, 5/6 (1920), pp. 114–16. Members of the German Communist Party opposed compulsory notifiability because of this unfairness, instead favoring periodical inspections of entire groups. Their example was taken from the contemporary Soviet Union, but could just as well have come from nineteenth-century Sweden: *SB*, 21 January 1927, p. 8689C; "Rapport présenté par M. le professeur Neisser," in Dubois-Havenith, *IIe Conférence internationale: Rapports préliminaires*, v. I, pp. 22–23; Ulrich Linse, "Alfred Blaschko: Der Menschenfreund als Überwacher," *Zeitschrift für Sexualforschung*, 2, 4 (1989), pp. 311–12.

[557] Hellwig, *Gesetz zur Bekämpfung der Geschlechtskrankheiten*, p. 217; *Mitteilungen*, 15, 3/4 (1917), pp. 47–53; *ZBGK*, 2, 11/12 (1903/04), pp. 452–53; *PP* 1916 (8189) xvi, 1, p. 182; XVIIth International Congress of Medicine, *Dermatology and Syphilography*, p. 49.

[558] BA, RmdI, 15.01/11886, pp. 126ff., meeting in the RmdI, 16 December 1919.

[559] But even in Scandinavia, class issues had not entirely disappeared. Those patients who could afford it and preferred not to take advantage of the offer of free medical care for VD were also not subject to notification: Möller, "Undersökningar i vissa frågor rörande de smittosamma könssjukdomarna," pp. 12–13; *ZBGK*, 15, 6 (1914), p. 210; 19, 2 (1919), p. 41; XVIIth International Congress of Medicine, *Dermatology and Syphilography*, p. 49; *American Journal of Public Health*, 26 (April 1936), p. 360.

quid of easy access to treatment in those nations with extensive insurance
or similar provision found its recompense in the quo of the obligations
that could reasonably be demanded in return in the form of compulsory
treatment, notification, isolation of recalcitrants and contact tracing.[560]
In Britain and France, in contrast, the logic of reciprocity dictated that
less could be and was asked of potentially infectious citizens. The late
development of national health insurance in Britain fit hand-in-glove the
voluntary prophylactic strategy adopted. Since little was offered the
victims, little could be demanded of them. However, once health insurance was in place for at least some fraction of the population, reformers here too began worrying about the tradeoff between providing
benefits to the syphilitic and being allowed to demand in return that they
be held to certain standards of behavior.[561] In contrast, Scandinavia and
then Germany offered victims cure at the public expense and, in turn,
could demand precautions with greater justification. Early reformers in
Prussia advocated a system that, offering the infected free care, would in
turn require contact tracing. By the time health insurance had been
changed in 1903 to remove the exclusion of "self-inflicted" diseases,
observers could argue that, since the hospitals were now willing to treat
patients and insurance to pay, the state could reasonably deal with VD as
with other contagious ailments, requiring reporting, isolation and the
like. *Behandlungsrecht* implied *Behandlungspflicht*.[562]

The European nations thus took markedly different approaches to the
problem of VD, ranging (once regulation had been ended) from Britain's
completely voluntary attempts to encourage medical care of the ill to the
broad requirements imposed first in Scandinavia, then Germany and
finally in France that the infected be cured, the infectious traced and
treated. In both Scandinavia and Germany, regulation was abandoned
because it was not accomplishing what it claimed to. VD had become
endemic, prostitutes were only a small minority of those infected and
infecting, changing sexual mores were, in any case, sidestepping them (or
at least the diminishing band of the registered) altogether. In Sweden the

---

[560] In a similar sense, the German disability insurance system made it easier to contemplate compulsory treatment than in either Britain or France where no similar quid pro quo was yet offered.
The Reichsversicherungsordnung §§1269–72 allowed insurance carriers to require treatment in
order to prevent permanent disability. Those who refused without cause could be denied benefits
for eventually resulting invalidity that might otherwise have been prevented.

[561] *Mitteilungen*, 22, 6 (1924), pp. 33–34; XVIIth International Congress of Medicine, *Dermatology
and Syphilography*, p. 93.

[562] *Zeitschrift für die Staatsarzneikunde*, 58 (1849), pp. 468–71; *ZBGK*, 4, 1 (1905), p. 36; Neisser,
Geschlechtskrankheiten und ihre Bekämpfung, pp. 229–31; *ZBGK*, 19, 5/6 (1919/20), p. 169.

wide and apparently nonsexual spread of VD during the late eighteenth century combined with the rural peculiarities of this still agrarian nation to encourage a nonregulationist solution early on; in Germany, similar fears (that disease had become so pervasive that new precautions were required) arrived with the First World War.

Regulation in its classic form was eventually rejected everywhere, in Britain already in the 1880s, in Sweden and Germany during the early interwar years, in the land of its invention not until the 1960s. Seen from a comparative perspective, the indignation that often informs the historiography of the British CD Acts seems myopic. They were a moderate, limited, reformed version of regulation. Their eventual rejection was due not only to the manner in which they imported to Britain a system perceived to be alien and out of step with domestic political habit. Equally a problem were the technical and institutional infelicities of their implementation: the control only, in a nation without universal conscription, of women; the localized nature of their enforcement that made strictures easy to avoid; their bringing of the heavy guns of regulation to bear on the narrow problem of VD in the military, rather than a broader concern with infection in society at large – a disproportion, in other words, of problem and solution. In any case, Britain was early, but not alone, in rejecting regulation. What needs to be explained is thus not only why repeal was successful in Britain, but why, having eventually all rejected regulation, the nations under the glass here adopted such divergent strategies thereafter.

With VD, as a stigmatizing and concealable disease, a certain logic spoke for a voluntary solution as the best prophylactic strategy in a way not the case for more acute contagious ailments. The afflicted were to be encouraged to seek aid rather than having imposed the machinery of notification and hospitalization that especially the British were otherwise happy to train on smallpox or cholera. For VD, the preventive choice was thus binary. Once ambitions to deal with the problem by focusing only on prostitutes had proven untenable, the solution was either a completely voluntary approach (providing but not mandating treatment) or a generalized compulsory one (requiring it of all infected). Given such either/or alternatives posed for VD, combined with the institutional lag in terms of medical care and social insurance characteristic of turn-of-the-century Britain, the choice here of a voluntary solution appears less mysterious, and also less exclusively due to the allegedly inherent liberalism of British political instinct. For the Swedes, Germans and eventually French, in contrast, with their concern for VD in the population at large, not just among soldiers, with their hankering to involve the state in such matters and the institutional machinery to do so, the choice was for the other fork in the path. Both the British and the continental nations adopted (divergent) strategies that continued and elaborated the approaches they had taken to the other diseases investigated here. Because VD presented the issue in stark black-or-white terms, either voluntary or compulsory tactics with little of the middle ground elaborated with neoquarantinism, the two prophylactic camps that had been developing, for all the various reasons examined here, since at least the first cholera epidemics, separating the British from the continent, were now framed in the contrasting hues of voluntarism or statutory intervention.

CHAPTER 6

The politics of prevention

To each nation its own preventive strategy: that could be the motto drawn from the evolution of the public health response to contagious disease during the century from the first European cholera epidemics to the cusp of the antibiotical era. Why? Given that, in epidemiological and biological terms, the problem faced by each country has been much the same, why have they responded in markedly different ways? Is there an Archimedian point from which to pry an account of why nations have reacted with such different preventive tactics? That each has learned from epidemiological experience how better to counter the next onslaught is an observation on the historical evolution of public health so commonplace that, if anything, the historiographical temptation has been rather to caution against whiggish assumptions of an ever improving mastery of preventive techniques.[1] What is at stake here, in contrast, are not such common learning experiences through which all nations eventually pass, arriving presumably at similar goals, but rather the different strategies they have adopted despite being faced with common problems.

Differences in scientific knowledge among nations that might have prompted varied responses cannot provide an explanation for at least two reasons. First, for the purposes of prevention, the state of the art in the nineteenth century was comparable, if not identical, across all. Sanitationist etiologies enjoyed greater credence in Britain than on the continent, outside France at least; knowledge of inoculation and vaccination varied slightly among countries; the antagonism between Koch

---

[1] Martin Dinges, "Pest und Staat: Von der Institutionengeschichte zur sozialen Konstruktion," in Martin Dinges and Thomas Schlich, eds., *Neue Wege in der Seuchengeschichte* (Stuttgart, 1995), pp. 80–85; Per-Gunnar Ottosson, "Fighting the Plague in 17th- and 18th-Century Sweden: A Survey," in Anders Brändström and Lars-Göran Tedebrand, eds., *Society, Health and Population During the Demographic Transition* (Stockholm, 1988), p. 318; Ann G. Carmichael, *Plague and the Poor in Renaissance Florence* (Cambridge, 1986), p. 128; Michael Durey, *The Return of the Plague: British Society and the Cholera 1831–1832* (Dublin, 1979), p. 119.

and Pasteur caused minor etiological distortions like a lag in the adoption of plate culture methods in France; salvarsan was invented and first employed on a large scale in Germany.[2] In no case, however, was the difference sufficiently important by itself to explain, and not just justify, such significant variation in preventive strategies.[3]

Secondly, even the presence of variation in etiological knowledge among nations would not necessarily, by itself, have caused prophylactic difference. The link between knowledge and action was flexible and indeterminate.[4] Chadwickian sanitarians would clearly have been more concerned with improving the noxious environmental conditions at the root of disease while contagionists worried instead about breaking transmissive chains. Between these two outlying positions, however, stretched a broad middle range where etiological conceptions and preventive tactics coexisted in polymorphous perversity. Sanitarians could advocate disinfection of dwellings, removal and even isolation of the ill; contagionists were no enemy of hygienic improvements, especially as they promised to make life inhospitable for the specific microorganisms of their concern. Whitewashing and fumigation could be marshaled either in hopes of destroying contagion or quelling the source of miasmatic putrefaction. Bacteriological analysis was used both to identify victims for isolation and, applied to water moulds or food, to serve the purposes of improving environmental conditions.[5] Whether they thought the plague stemmed from noxious air or contagion, the advice of Florentine authorities in the fifteenth century was to avoid throngs in public places.[6] Reformers concerned with domestic hygiene moved easily from a concern with sewer gas to germs during the nineteenth century, employing much the same tactics to cleanse homes regardless of the noxious

[2] Thomas D. Brock, *Robert Koch: A Life in Medicine and Bacteriology* (Madison, 1988), p. 177.

[3] Mendelsohn's argument that there were at least two kinds of bacteriology, Pasteurian and Kochian, with radically different conceptions of microbes and their role, might be an example of opposing etiologies with varying prophylactic consequences, although his distinction clearly replicates the traditional contagionist/sanitationist polarity, now transposed to the realm of bacteriology itself: John Andrew Mendelsohn, "Cultures of Bacteriology: Formation and Transformation of a Science in France and Germany, 1870–1914" (PhD diss., Princeton University, 1996); W. F. Bynum, *Science and the Practice of Medicine in the Nineteenth Century* (Cambridge, 1994), p. 160.

[4] One of the themes of Christopher Hamlin, *Public Health and Social Justice in the Age of Chadwick: Britain, 1800–1854* (Cambridge, 1998).

[5] Dorothy E. Watkins, "The English Revolution in Social Medicine, 1889–1911" (Ph.D. diss., University of London, 1984), p. 313.

[6] John Henderson, "Epidemics in Renaissance Florence: Medical Theory and Government Response," in Neithart Bulst and Robert Delort, eds., *Maladies et société (XIIe–XVIIIe siècles)* (Paris, 1989), p. 182.

influence, whether miasma or microbe.[7] The question of predisposition united contagionists and sanitarians behind certain tactics, even though they explained the outcomes differently. Southwood Smith, archsanitarian, was the director of the London fever hospital where patients were isolated; the hyperquarantinist Koch advocated water purification as the solution to Hamburg's cholera problem. The connection between etiological position and prophylactic consequence was not invariant and consistent. Florence Nightingale, as so often, was being overly dogmatic when she insisted that "Quarantine follows logically and inevitably on 'contagion' – as Sanitary measures on 'non-contagion.'"[8]

Indeed, rather than knowledge determining action in any but the broadest sense, etiological conceptions were highly influenced by factors external to narrow epistemological considerations. Especially (but not exclusively) before the bacteriological revolution, etiological knowledge was inextricably bound up with other factors, political, administrative, economic, geographic. Etiological theories have been used selectively not to determine, but to justify sanitary policies adopted for largely different reasons.[9] Scientific insight did not bring with it automatically the measures taken; there was no one-to-one correspondence between knowledge and action, no knowledge unmediated by political, cultural and other considerations. Such portentous conclusions should, however, occasion no surprise. Anyone who has dipped into recent history of science, indeed history of any stripe, will know that legions of gleeful skeptics are afoot, upending heroic teleologies and slaying time and again the long putrefied dragons of naive empiricism. It has not for a long time been an interesting or novel conclusion to point to the chronological specificity and historical construction of knowledge, the scientific variety not excluded.

Such skepticism, rather than the end of scholarly inquiry, should be but the prod behind searches for better answers. The issue is no longer whether these various approaches to contagious disease were historically constructed and determined by considerations other than the internally scientific, but rather, given that they were permeable to other influences, identifying these and seeking to account for their relative importance.

---

[7] Nancy Tomes, "The Private Side of Public Health: Sanitary Science, Domestic Hygiene and the Germ Theory, 1870–1900," *BHM*, 64, 4 (1990), pp. 509–15.

[8] John M. Eyler, *Victorian Social Medicine: The Ideas and Methods of William Farr* (Baltimore, 1979), p. 188.

[9] Mark Harrison, *Public Health in British India: Anglo-Indian Preventive Medicine 1859–1914* (Cambridge, 1994), pp. 109, 113–14; Richard J. Evans, *Death in Hamburg: Society and Politics in the Cholera Years 1830–1910* (Oxford, 1987), pp. 268–69.

Because one foundation has turned to sand does not mean that there are no underpinnings whatsoever. With the crumbling of the Führerbunker, are we (to stick with the architectural analogies that drive discussion of these matters) consigned to live in an epistemological trailer park? Knowledge of disease etiology, whether scientific in the modern sense or not, was no more than the background against which prophylactic strategies were decided upon. It provided an overall map to guide broadly the authorities in their preventive ambitions, but it did not determine in any precise sense the measures chosen. Although for cholera and the other classic contagious diseases there was a gradual and general convergence on the principles of neoquarantinism, sharp variations in prophylactic approach still distinguished nations even into the twentieth century. For smallpox and VD, preventive strategies varied even more dramatically.

If not etiology, then perhaps politics, the overarching theme of the investigation here, explain such variation? Seeking to determine why nations diverged so starkly in strategy, it is tempting to ascribe an important role to their different political traditions and systems. The political implications of measures that sought, in direct and immediate terms, to define the respective spheres of individual and community were obvious and unavoidable. The power and persistence of a linking together of political ideology and prophylactic strategy, of the sort exemplified by Ackerknecht, derives from a search for an answer to this question of variation. But here too few simple correlations hold in the face of comparative historical scrutiny. Even contemporaries recognized the ill fit of such expectations. The French especially were chagrined at the extent to which the British, proud of their individual liberties and decentralized government, could nonetheless impose precautions of a stringency only dreamt of by Gallic reformers. During the first cholera epidemic, it was the British who, in French eyes, imposed the more drastic precautions, surpassing even those of the autocracies. Never, Moreau de Jonnès confided to Pym, would he have been able to propose quarantinist measures of the sort initially implemented in Britain at home.[10] The British, despite their laissez-faire reputation, in fact turned out to be great interveners of a certain stripe. They had few

[10] PRO, PC1/108, Moreau de Jonnès to Pym, 28 February 1832, 19 March 1832; M. J. Mavidal and M. E. Laurent, eds., *Archives parlementaires de 1787 a 1860*, v. II/69, pp. 455–56; *Archives générales de medecine*, 27 (1831), p. 137; Roderick E. McGrew, *Russia and the Cholera 1823–1832* (Madison, 1965), p. 14. For similar comparisons with the Germans, see *Bulletin*, 3, 55 (1906), p. 68; *Centralblatt für allgemeine Gesundheitspflege*, 12 (1893), p. 76; J. C. Albers, et al., eds., *Cholera-Archiv mit Benutzung amtlicher Quellen*, 2 (1832), pp. 378–80.

compunctions of the sort entertained on the continent at making the ill legally liable for endangering others or transmitting disease; they were happy to remove the afflicted without adequate domestic circumstances to hospitals, by force if necessary. Though the British were more protective of their individual liberties than any other nation, Palmberg concluded, they also cheerfully submitted to sanitary regulations that encroached on such rights.[11] A concern with liberty did not necessarily imply quiescence in terms of public health.

The fundamental implication of a political interpretation of public health is that prophylactic strategy and ideology are correlated. The actions taken to curb the spread of contagious disease directly impinge on the rights of the citizen, subordinating the diseased or at-risk individual to the claims of the community. Approaches to prevention may be expected to reflect common assumptions held in a society as to where group and individual interests diverge, how much autonomy citizens can rightfully claim, the power of the community over its members. In a general sense, public health reformers have sought to portray any simple zero-sum tradeoff between the concerns of the individual and those of the community as misleading. The right to be spared prophylactic imposition was not the only measure of liberty; there was also the freedom from disease. Traditional conservative quarantinists argued this line, claiming that the community's concern for the general health took precedence in such matters over the individual's right to infect others. Conversely, liberals objected to many such interventions when they impinged on personal liberties too drastically or for insufficiently redeeming purpose. There was, however, also an understanding of public health that transcended such sterile oppositions between community and individual. Much like Roosevelt's Four Freedoms and T. H. Marshall's social rights, society's concern with public health was a positive freedom that, while limiting absolute individual autonomy, returned to each a higher measure of liberation from affliction. Public health was a public good that justified limitations on individual freedom.

And yet, were matters that simple, divergences would be inexplicable. In a broad sense, transcending national peculiarities, the higher good of public health might require individual limitations, but there remained various ways of accomplishing such aims, some more considerate of personal liberties than others. Even within the ambit of the common goal of protecting the community from epidemic disease, political inflections could plausibly be read into different strategies. Quarantinism, vaccination and regulation, alike in their readiness to sacrifice individual liberties to the communal good, were often seen as conservative. In contrast, sanitationism and the voluntary approaches taken in some nations with respect to smallpox and VD were judged liberal in their concern for the civil rights of even the infectious and socially reformist, perhaps even socialist, in their search for solutions through broad reform of the environment and society. A focus on the environmental and social factors behind disease and a willingness to leave specific interventions to the free choice of the afflicted has been, in this view, the position of the left, while the right embraced contagionism and later its modernization in the guise of bacteriology, finding here justification of its belief that disease prophylaxis and social reform were two distinct matters with few mutual inflections and that specific, targeted interventions (whether isolating cholera victims, vaccinating children or inscribing prostitutes) were the means to lower morbidity even in the absence of other change.[12]

Such assumptions of a correspondence between politics and prophylaxis do not, however, hold with much consistency. First, it is clear that the pertinent distinction is not that between conservative interventionism and liberal laissez-faire, but rather between different sorts of intervention. Too often a misleading contrast has been drawn between the decisive interpositions of conservative quarantinist regimes and liberal sanitationism, happy to leave citizens in peace and therefore acting only in ways that did not involve a frontal assault on personal liberties. Liberty and inaction have been confused.[13] Contagionism is seen as a "ruling-class doctrine," the strategy of "bureaucratic interventionism," the policy of strong government that allowed more decisive interventions than possible with an environmental approach and more than would be tolerable under liberal ideology.[14] While an effective autocracy

---

[12] John Duffy, *The Sanitarians: A History of American Public Health* (Urbana, 1990), p. 206.

[13] Evans's claim that Pettenkoferian sanitationism involved less statutory intervention than Kochian bacteriology, for example, ignores the extent to which the massive infrastructural investment and regulation of the former approach demanded statutory efforts at least as drastic as, if different from, the fairly precisely targeted interventions necessary to break chains of transmission: Evans, *Death in Hamburg*, p. 242. Similar claims are made for India in David Arnold, *Colonizing the Body: State Medicine and Epidemic Disease in Nineteenth-Century India* (Berkeley, 1993), p. 195.

[14] R. J. Morris, *Cholera 1832: The Social Response to an Epidemic* (New York, 1976), pp. 183–84; Evans, *Death in Hamburg*, pp. 262, 264, 476; Martha L. Hildreth, *Doctors, Bureaucrats, and Public Health in France, 1888–1902* (New York, 1987), p. 111; Paul Weindling, *Health, Race and German Politics Between National Unification and Nazism, 1870–1945* (Cambridge, 1989), p. 163.

can mandate public health, concludes a recent observer, democratic regimes can do little more than educate their citizens.[15]

The very question has been *mal posée*, resting on the dubious assumption that the decentralized laissez-faire approach, supposedly characteristic above all of the British, permitted only few and, at best, liberal public health interventions, while the centralized continental administrations, beholden to the ideology of medical police, were ready and able to act more broadly and effectively. The received historiography has tended until recently to exaggerate the allegedly decentralized impotence of British public health initiatives, neglecting the extent to which local administrations were in fact active and effective or to which reforms under Simon's auspices achieved much of Chadwick's ambition to vest strong sanitary powers in the national state.[16] Correspondingly, there has been a tendency to overemphasize the effectiveness of the continental powers: fragmented and then federalized Germany where control over the machinery of public health was vested at the national level only after 1880, but even centralized France where, in fact, authority in such matters was entrusted to the usually ineffective mercies of local mayors.[17] Even in despotic Prussia, one observer of the early cholera epidemics mocked, Berlin quickly shifted initiative to the local communities, where the business of *Gemeinden* and *Landkreise* was managed by an elected magistracy.[18]

The choice of the British for a differently interventionist solution from those pursued on the continent was not, after all, in hopes of doing nothing, but of being equally, if not more, effective than the drastic alter-

---

[15] Kenneth F. Kiple, ed., *The Cambridge World History of Human Disease* (Cambridge, 1993), p. 205.

[16] Correctives can be found in: F. M. L. Thompson, ed., *The Cambridge Social History of Britain 1750–1950* (Cambridge, 1990), v. III, pp. 193–94; Christopher Hamlin, "Muddling in Bumbledom: On the Enormity of Large Sanitary Improvements in Four British Towns, 1855–1885," *Victorian Studies*, 32 (Autumn 1988); Mark Brayshay and Vivien F. T. Pointon, "Local Politics and Public Health in Mid-Nineteenth-Century Plymouth," *Medical History*, 27, 2 (April 1983), pp. 177–78; John Prest, *Liberty and Locality: Parliament, Permissive Legislation, and Ratepayers' Democracies in the Nineteenth Century* (Oxford, 1990), pp. 166–70; Elliott A. Krause, *Death of the Guilds: Professions, States, and the Advance of Capitalism, 1930 to the Present* (New Haven, 1996), p. 81; Hamlin, *Public Health and Social Justice*, pp. 257–64; Simon Szreter, *Fertility, Class and Gender in Britain, 1860–1940* (Cambridge, 1996), ch. 4.

[17] A.-J. Martin, *Des épidémies et des maladies transmissibles dans leurs rapports avec les lois et réglements* (Lyons, 1889), pp. 16–18; Lion Murard and Patrick Zylberman, *L'hygiène dans la république: La santé publique en France, ou l'utopie contrariée (1870–1918)* (Paris, 1996), pp. 123–28; Dorothy Porter, "Introduction," in Dorothy Porter, ed., *The History of Public Health and the Modern State* (Amsterdam, 1994), pp. 12–13; Allan Mitchell, *The Divided Path: The German Influence on Social Reform in France After 1870* (Chapel Hill, 1991), pp. 17–19; Richard S. Ross, "The Prussian Administrative Response to the First Cholera Epidemic in Prussia in 1831" (Ph.D. diss, Boston College, 1991), pp. 36–39, 177–80. Similarly, for an earlier period, absolutist regimes, with their reliance on directives from distant centers, were often ineffective responders to plague: Dinges, "Pest und Staat," p. 83.

[18] F. W. Becker, *Letters on the Cholera in Prussia: Letter I to John Thomson, MD, FRS* (London, 1832), p. 48.

natives. The logic of voluntary and environmentalist measures was that, in the long run, they achieved more than the harsh but punctual compulsion of quarantinist approaches. Already during the first cholera epidemic, Gilbert Blane (otherwise a contagionist) argued that the best protection was afforded not through compulsory precautions of the sort imposed initially by the Board of Health, but through preventive measures applied prior to epidemic arrival and adopted through peaceful persuasion.[19] What was the likelihood, Thorne Thorne later scoffed, that the British would abandon the protection afforded by their system of massive sanitary investment for the illusion of security offered by five days' quarantine?[20] Such reliance on sanitationist reform and voluntary compliance became increasingly important with the development of public health through the end of the century. The argument in favor of abandoning the lancet's compulsion was that the result would be, in fact, a more broadly effective vaccination. By the time syphilis was tackled again after the debacle of the Contagious Disease Acts, voluntary compliance had become a crucial element of the prophylactic strategies adopted in Britain, a means of avoiding the stigma and likelihood of concealment that threatened to follow in the train of compulsion. A noncompulsory approach was, in this reasoning, ultimately more efficient in preventing disease, reaching greater numbers of victims and driving fewer into the epidemiological underground than heavyhanded tactics. In fact, seen from a longer historical perspective, the British solution to each of these epidemiological problems has proven to be the one eventually adopted by most other nations, however different their starting points. Neoquarantinism for cholera and other classic contagious diseases was originally the "English system," eventually adopted by all other western nations. Voluntary vaccination and some variant of the Leicester system (surveillance to detect initial cases along with vigorous containment measures) have together become the method broadly employed in other countries and by international organizations.[21] Prostitution has become deregulated almost everywhere and provision

---

[19] Gilbert Blane, *Warning to the British Public Against the Alarming Approach of the Indian Cholera* (London, October 1831), pp. 2–3.

[20] R. Thorne Thorne, *On the Progress of Preventive Medicine During the Victorian Era* (London, 1888), p. 60.

[21] Thomas McKeown, *The Modern Rise of Population* (London, 1976), p. 108; E. P. Hennock, "Vaccination Policy Against Smallpox, 1835–1914: A Comparison of England with Prussia and Imperial Germany," *Social History of Medicine*, 11, 1 (April 1998), pp. 69–70. However, containment could, and did, involve violently compulsory methods during the international smallpox eradication campaign: Paul Greenough, "Intimidation, Coercion and Resistance in the Final Stages of the South Asian Smallpox Eradication Campaign, 1973–1975," *Social Science and Medicine*, 41, 5 (September 1995), pp. 633ff.

of medical care for the infected combined with public education is now
broadly the strategy of choice.

Quarantinism was, of course, drastically interventionist in its suspen-
sion of individual rights for the public good. But at the same time, as a
specifically targeted technique, it sought to limit the scope of statutory
intervention to crucial nodal points of transmission. The role of quarantinism as the poor and administratively underdeveloped nation's tactic
of choice, as became clear during the late nineteenth century when the
Mediterranean nations felt unable to match the massive infrastructural
investment required by sanitationism on the British model, indicates the
extent to which it in fact was a technique that asked less of the state.
There is much to be said for Moreau de Jonnès's argument during the
first cholera epidemic that quarantinism was the response of weak and
unstable regimes, able at best to concentrate efforts at certain points, but
hampered in sustaining any massive intervention into the lives of their
subjects by fears of possible unrest. During the 1830s the French July
Monarchy quickly discovered that, while external cordons were popular,
demonstrating the government's concern while affecting at most a few
travelers, similar measures imposed internally were much more likely
to provoke unrest.[22] An unpopular regime was expected to rattle its
prophylactic sabers along the borders, but could not demand heavy
sacrifices of its citizens at home.

For the other allied techniques under consideration here, much the
same holds. In each case, the fundamental logic was that of the bottleneck, the decisive action at a certain crucial spot (or in the case of vaccination, time) that spared the need for more broadly focused precautions.
Vaccination was arguably a less drastic intervention than the neoquarantinist techniques of notification, isolation and disinfection applied to
smallpox, certainly for those unfortunate enough to fall ill. Consider how
many people, Koch argued, would have to be sequestered and for how
long and vaccination began to seem benign in comparison.[23] While with
cholera the issue could still be posed in terms of individual freedom
against statutory intervention, in the case of vaccination it was more
clearly a question of two different sorts of intervention, equally draconian in their limitation of personal liberties: either the lancet or the quarantine flag. In limiting controls to prostitutes, regulation was also a less
drastic measure than sanitary statism applied to the entire adult popu-

---

[22] *Observations sur le choléra-morbus, recueilliés et publiées par l'ambassade de France en Russie* (Paris, 1831), pp. 7–17.   [23] *SB*, 1884/85, Akst. 287, p. 1347; *Cobbett's*, 1806, v. 7, cols. 886–87.

lation, not to mention the ambitions entertained by moral reformers of persuading all of the virtues of chastity and fidelity, changing their behavior to end the scourge of VD.

The other way around, sanitationism could be no less draconian in its imposition on the individual, its reliance on massive statutory ingress.[24] John Roberton, introducer of the concept of medical police to Scotland and convinced miasmaticist, was not above advocating "the entire destruction of many houses" to prevent disease.[25] Carl Barriés, a Hamburg physician persuaded that cleanliness was the core of the problem and that cholera afflicted mainly the insalubrious dwellings of the poor, hoped that, by removing the etiological tinder, epidemics could be prevented altogether. To this effect, he proposed that large cities extend "purification chains" ten to twenty miles out from their centers. A sort of sanitary SWAT team, each would be equipped with thirty to sixty purification machines of his invention to steamclean filthy dwellings, clothing and possessions. Investigatory commissions, sent in as a sanitary avantgarde, would scout an area for filth, removing the inhabitants of noxious houses, changing their clothes and bathing them in vinegar. The doors and windows of objectionable dwellings sealed and the front doors punctured with holes, steam would then be pumped in for six to eight hours.[26] Some miasmatists, fearing the spread of contaminated atmospheres, recommended measures as strict as any contagionist: identifying and marking infected dwellings, sequestering patients. Others advocated preemptive removals of the most crowded populations to avoid miasmatic buildup, with much the same result, although motivated for different reasons, as their contagionist opponents.[27]

Similarly, the house-to-house visitations undertaken by the British to check for cholera's premonitory symptoms required an administrative machinery as effective as that necessary to impose quarantine at border

---

[24] Christopher Hamlin, "Predisposing Causes and Public Health in Early Nineteenth-Century Medical Thought," *Social History of Medicine*, 5, 1 (April 1992), p. 49; Gerry Kearns, "Zivilis or Hygaeia: Urban Public Health and the Epidemiological Transition," in Richard Lawton, ed., *The Rise and Fall of Great Cities* (London, 1989), pp. 120–22.

[25] Brenda M. White, "Medical Police, Politics and Police: The Fate of John Roberton," *Medical History*, 27 (1983), p. 411.

[26] Carl Barriés, *Wodurch kann die Weiterverbreitung der Cholera in Deutschland verhindert und der Stoff zu dieser Krankheit in der Wurzel vernichtet werden?* (Leipzig, 1831).

[27] D. A. Gebel, *Aphorismen über die Brechruhr, nebst Angabe ihrer Heilung, Vorbeugung und sonstigen polizeilichen Maassregeln* (Liegnitz, 1831), pp. 34–40; T. M. Greenhow, *Cholera: Its Non-Contagious Nature and the Best Means of Arresting its Progress* (Newcastle, 1831), pp. 11–13; Tilesius v. T., *Über die Cholera und die kräftigsten Mittel dagegen, nebst Vorschlag eines grossen Ableitungsmittels, um die Krankheit in der Geburt zu ersticken* (Nürnberg, 1830), pp. 129–31; *Supplement to the EMSJ* (February 1832), p. cclxxxiii.

crossings. The ability to track and keep under surveillance passengers from infected origins of the sort that only the British and Russians felt up to was as great an intervention as inspections and detainment at the frontiers. Reporting contagious disease and removing victims, cornerstones of the British neoquarantinist system, were interventions comparable in their footprint to quarantine. Building the isolation hospitals needed to apply the Leicester system required investment on a scale at least equal to that necessary for compulsory vaccination.[28] Universal vaccination, though a broader intervention than imposing quarantines at the borders, was cheaper and more cost-effective than the alternative. Nations with effective public health systems (able to detect, diagnose and report early cases of smallpox, effectively isolate patients, vaccinate and surveille contacts and impose rigorous disinfections) might dispense with universal application of the lancet, but others could not.[29] Quarantinism, vaccination and regulation were the poor nation's prophylactic strategies, while sanitationism, neoquarantinism and sanitary statism cost more resources and administrative muscle than many could muster. In a more general sense, the vast outlays required to build the basic elements of urban sanitary infrastructure required massive statutory activity and intervention, although this obvious point does not always register on the false dichotomies that contrast the decisive interventionism of nations applying quarantinist policies with the allegedly laissez-faire approach of sanitationism.[30] Far from being drastic interjections, quarantinism, vaccination and regulation were, from this vantage, limited and targeted ones that presupposed the severe application of force and control at certain crucial nodes precisely to atone for an inability to exert similar precautions across the entire nation or against all citizens.

In a broader sense, there has been an Eliasian tradeoff between points at which the pressure needed to bring about hygienically satisfactory behavior was applied: outside or within the individual. Quarantine and isolation assumed an inability to predict who would and would not obey strictures not to transmit disease. Criminalizing transmission, in contrast, presupposed a basic willingness to forego risky behavior, with only occasional transgressions. To the extent that a nation was sufficiently homogeneous to assume common and acceptable standards of behav-

---

[28] The isolation hospital system rivaled in size the old voluntary system by the First World War: John M. Eyler, *Sir Arthur Newsholme and State Medicine, 1885–1935* (Cambridge, 1997), p. 86.
[29] "Smallpox Vaccination: A Survey of Recent Legislation," *International Digest of Health Legislation*, 5, 2 (1954), p. 224.   [30] Kearns, "Zivilis or Hygaeia," pp. 112–20.

ior, it might get by with less external control.[31] Conversely, a broad spectrum of social differentiation, especially the presence of a (in bourgeois eyes) suspect urban lower class early in the nineteenth century, meant that stronger external controls were necessary. Similarly, stark differentiation between town and countryside (as on the continent, Sweden especially) aggravated the problem of what habits could be taken as customary and immigration, with its import of foreign proclivities, prompted the application of external controls. It was a common complaint of observers from the Mediterranean that the nations of northern Europe had an easier time of such matters since, education levels being higher, customs less barbaric, morals more refined and the habit of obeying laws more common, certain impositions by the authorities (in particular the regulation of prostitution) could be dispensed with.[32] As distinctions between urban and rural and among classes have moderated during the course of the past century, the development of public health can increasingly be described in terms of the gradual internalization of controls, a growing emphasis on the responsibility of individuals for their own conduct, safety and health. Dealing with the danger of contagious disease has helped promote "civilized" behavior in the Eliasian sense, habits of personal hygiene.[33] Foreigners remain the main public health "other" in the twentieth century, although vestiges of an older class-based approach persist in the social differentiation of tobacco habits and the consumption of supposedly unhealthy foodstuffs.

The issue was thus not one of interventionism vs. laissez-faire, action vs. inaction, authoritarianism vs. liberalism, but of different forms of intervention, some more drastic and apparent, others more subtle, but nonetheless effective for that. The same nation, to take just one example from the first cholera epidemic, that professed an inability to martial the necessary troops to cordon off Sunderland when the disease struck was nonetheless able, once the epidemic hit York, to roust the required personnel to visit every single house during the third week of November

[31] Donald C. Bross, "Legal Aspects of STD Control," in King K. Holmes et al., eds., *Sexually Transmitted Diseases* (New York, 1984), p. 925; Deborah Jones Merritt, "The Constitutional Balance Between Health and Liberty," *Hastings Center Report*, 16, 6 (December 1986), suppl., p. 5.

[32] PRO, FO 542/3, FO CP 7819, November 1902, p. 21; Félix Regnault, *L'Evolution de la prostitution* (Paris, n.d. [1906?]), pp. 250–57; *Annales*, 4/12 (1909), pp. 239–43; Yves-Marie Bercé, *Le chaudron et la lancette: Croyances populaires et médecine préventive (1798–1830)* (Paris, 1984), p. 302.

[33] Johan Goudsblom, "Zivilisation, Ansteckungsangst und Hygiene: Betrachtungen über ein Aspekt des europäischen Zivilisationsprozesses," in Peter Gleichmann et al., eds., *Materialen zu Norbert Elias' Zivilisationstheorie* (Frankfurt, 1977), pp. 216–18; Michael Stolberg, "Gottesstrafe oder Diätssünde: Zur Mentalitätsgeschichte der Cholera," *Medizin, Gesellschaft und Geschichte*, 8 (1989), p. 18.

1832, inspecting for victims and filthy circumstances, cleansing and fumi-gating as they went.[34]

GUI BONO?

A second issue in the contrast drawn between quarantinism and envi-ronmentalism in a political interpretation of public health concerns the interests for which these various tactics spoke. Ackerknecht and his more recent followers portray quarantinism as the doctrine of autocratic elites unconcerned with the plight of the poorest in their squalid circum-stances, opposed by free-trading liberals and social reformers. But who in fact was pressing for quarantinist precautions? True, cordons and quarantines often provoked popular resistance and rebellion, as in Königsberg in 1831. But, equally, the authorities felt the pressure of public opinion in favor of a quick, obvious and, it was hoped, effective solution. In certain cases the common people rejected contagionist the-ories as but a rationalization of excuses to oppress them with vexatious precautions. But contagionism was just as much the commonsense eti-ology of the average person while environmentalism in its various incar-nations, with its vague attribution of disease to unseen and untestable atmospheric influences and its modern bourgeois insistence on salubrity and personal hygiene, was learned behavior, at first unfamiliar to the popular imagination.[35] Public opinion in uninfected Swedish provinces in 1834 clamored for the right to impose quarantines. In Tuscany, the local citizenry, fed up with the authorities' inaction, massed on the Genoese border in the summer of 1835 to turn back all travelers and goods.[36] In the Mediterranean nations especially, quarantinism had, since the plague epidemics of the fifteenth century, been the demand of the common people for statutory action on their behalf.[37] Quarantines

---

[34] *Hansard*, 1831, v. 9, cols. 310–14; *EMSJ*, 109 (October 1831), p. 415; Michael Durey, *The First Spasmodic Cholera Epidemic in York, 1832* (York, 1974), p. 4; Margaret C. Barnet, "The 1832 Cholera Epidemic in York," *Medical History*, 16, 1 (January 1972), pp. 27–31, 38.

[35] Claudine Herzlich and Janine Pierret, *Malades d'hier, malades d'aujourd'hui* (Paris, 1984), p. 35; Roger Cooter, "Anticontagionism and History's Medical Record," in Peter Wright and Andrew Treacher, eds., *The Problem of Medical Knowledge* (Edinburgh, 1982), pp. 96–99; Christian Barthel, *Medizinische Polizey und medizinische Aufklärung: Aspekte des öffentlichen Gesundheitsdiskurses im 18. Jahrhundert* (Frankfurt, 1989), pp. 131–44; Charles Rosenberg, *The Cholera Years* (Chicago, 1962), p. 37. As Vigarello points out, however, bacteriology and the emphasis on personal cleanliness that it encour-aged (although far from inventing) was also part of this middle-class learned behavior: Georges Vigarello, *Le sain et le malsain* (Paris, 1993), p. 259.

[36] Michael Stolberg, *Die Cholera im Grossherzogtum Toskana* (Landsberg, 1995), p. 21.

[37] Henderson, "Epidemics in Renaissance Florence," pp. 169–71. Similar demands were made in the United States, faced with cholera and yellow fever: David F. Musto, "Quarantine and the Problem of AIDS," *Milbank Quarterly*, 64, suppl. 1 (1986), pp. 102–05.

imposed at the borders, affecting largely merchants and travelers, did not in the early nineteenth century much concern the average person, although similar measures imposed domestically were less popular. The same popular attraction of the most drastically and obviously interventionist measures can be seen in our own day, where contagionist fears of easy AIDS transmission and the resulting insistence on precautions such as isolating the afflicted and banishing infected children from classroom attendance has been the popular demand, expressed clearest where the common voice is heard most directly, while tolerant attitudes have been the position of the informed medical elite and its allies in the government bureaucracies.

The implication that elites imposed quarantinist measures on an unwilling populace is misleading in another sense as well. Choices among preventive strategies split elites themselves. Traders suffered in a general sense the aversion to quarantines and other restrictions on free movement attributed to them by Ackerknecht, but their interests depended in equal measure on other factors. Some derived profits from the monopolies of transit granted them by systems of quarantine. Importers might be hurt by such strictures, but exporters sought preemptive precautions lest other nations impose even more draconian measures. Locked into an epidemiological pas de deux by mutual desires for security, even trading interests in quarantinist nations could live with such precautions so long as all abided by the same rules. More generally, commercial and propertied interests divided in prophylactic terms. Property, aware that it stood to bear the fiscal burdens of sanitary infrastructural reform, had quite different ambitions than commerce.[38] Manufacturers, limited by new zoning regulations, purveyors of night soil, slumlords and others with a financial stake in the hygienic old regime had reasons to oppose reform of a Chadwickian bent.[39] In Paris, rag pickers precipitated riots during the 1832 cholera epidemic when threatened with destitution by the unimpeachably sanitationist measure of more frequent garbage removals.[40] Environmentalism may have treated the rights of the individual with more respect than did quarantinism, but it curbed those of the property owner, an equally

---

[38] Gerry Kearns, "Cholera, Nuisances and Environmental Management in Islington, 1830–1855," in W. F. Bynum and Roy Porter, eds., *Living and Dying in London* (London, 1991), pp. 96, 118–22; Kearns, "Zivilis or Hygaeia," pp. 121–22; Gerry Kearns, "Private Property and Public Health Reform in England 1830–1870," *Social Science and Medicine*, 26, 1 (1988), pp. 188, 191–94.

[39] Lesley Doyal with Imogen Pennell, *The Political Economy of Health* (London, 1979), p. 147.

[40] *Moniteur universel*, 94 (3 April 1832), p. 953; 96 (5 April 1832), p. 973; Jacques Poulet, "Épidémiologie, sociologie et démographie de la première épidemie parisienne de choléra," *Histoire des sciences médicales*, 3–4 (July–December 1970), pp. 155–56.

important constituency in the eyes of nineteenth-century liberal ideology.[41]

Social readings of prophylactic tactics are also muddied when accounting for the question of individual predisposition. A socially reformist version of sanitation, seeking to provide basic hygienic infrastructure for all urban denizens and to bring the poorest up to minimum levels of nutrition, space, ventilation and light, clearly offered broad change as the solution to diseases seen as arising from impoverished and squalid circumstances. Improving social conditions to eliminate cholera, ameliorate smallpox, remove the circumstances that bred prostitution and spread VD: such was the environmentalist vision. In contrast, contagionist etiologies, culminating in bacteriology, and their attribution of disease to specific microorganisms, ravaging in large measure independently of social circumstance, tended to be conservative in shifting the focus of prevention from ameliorable environmental conditions to narrower interventions that sought to break chains of transmission. Vaccination imposed unwelcome intrusions on the poor rather than removing the general causes of smallpox, while regulation controlled working-class women for the pleasure of their male superiors.

The social focus of these two prophylactic inclinations was not, in fact, quite so obvious. Quarantinist precautions often afflicted the poor most. Removals to hospitals concerned those who could not be isolated in their squalid and cramped dwellings.[42] Not just the merchant, but especially his workers who lived from their wages day to day were hurt by any limitation on commercial activity.[43] On the other hand, quarantinism was socially indiscriminate in affecting not only itinerant peddlers, journeymen and the streams of poor emigrants traveling third-class rail and steerage, but also wealthy tourists, entrepreneurs, traders and their merchandise.[44] Quarantinism, in the eyes of its defenders, was thus egalitar-

[41]   Gerard Kearns et al., "The Interaction of Political and Economic Factors in the Management of Urban Public Health," in Marie C. Nelson and John Rogers, eds., *Urbanisation and the Epidemiologic Transition* (Uppsala, 1989), p. 34; Watkins, "English Revolution in Social Medicine," pp. 295–96.

[42]   *Förhandlingar*, 1866, pp. 170–71; *Stenographische Berichte über die öffentlichen Sitzungen der Stadtverordneten-Versammlung der Haupt- und Residenzstadt Berlin*, 19 (1892), 8 September 1892, p. 278; Richard Wawrinsky, *Om förebyggandet af epidemier genom anordning af isoleringslokaler* (Stockholm, 1901), pp. 54–57; Paul Slack, *The Impact of Plague in Tudor and Stuart England* (London, 1985), p. 232.

[43]   Joseph Ayre, *A Letter Addressed to the Right Honourable Lord John Russell . . . on the Evil Policy of those Measures of Quarantine and Restrictive Police, Which Are Employed for Arresting the Progress of the Asiatic Cholera* (London, 1837), pp. 3–7, 24–25.

[44]   Although the focus of many quarantinist and neoquarantinist measures on poor travelers, in third-class carriages and steerage, in the mass transport of emigration or pilgrimage, belied this impartiality and betrayed a sanitationist preoccupation with filth as a precondition of disease: *Conférence 1885*, pp. 299–301; *Conférence 1911*, pp. 156–57, 596, 607–08, 628; *Anweisung zur Bekämpfung der Cholera. (Festgestellt in der Sitzung des Bundesrats vom 28. Januar 1904): Amtliche Ausgabe* (Berlin, 1905),

ian in its impartial subjection of all travelers to its strictures.[45] Their opponents were the wealthy mercantile interests, quarantinists argued, while they spoke for the concerns of the little people.[46] Whereas the rich could insulate themselves by staying at home during epidemics, the poor had no choice but to venture out and therefore deserved the protection afforded by such measures.[47] The poor, especially devastated by disease, were the ones who gained most from strict precautions; quarantinism was, as Proust argued, a democratic doctrine.[48] Most directly, the poor often enjoyed a higher standard of living when sequestered or quarantined, or at least were supported at public expense.

To the extent that hygienic reform moved beyond public goods (draining swamps, laying on potable water and sewerage) of benefit to all to take in hand conditions that afflicted especially the poor (through food inspections, housing and zoning regulations), its benefits trickled down the social ladder.[49] Since the rich did not live in circumstances that required correction, the focus of the state's sanitationist energies, whether welcome or not, were the poor.[50] The house-to-house visitations, undertaken both in Bavaria and Britain, and inspections of dwellings in France called primarily on the lower classes.[51] Sanitationists of

pp. 65–73; Sven Lysander, *Några synpunkter och iakttagelser angående karantänsinrättningar* (Stockholm, 1902), pp. 13–14.

[45] *Bulletin*, 57, 3/29 (1893), pp. 592–600. In the same way, applying Gerhard Oestreich's idea that absolutism's leveling of differences paved the way for subsequent democratization, it has been argued that measures against the plague in the seventeenth and eighteenth centuries imposed willy nilly the principle of equality before the law, regardless of status and station: Dinges, "Pest und Staat," p. 78.

[46] David Eversley, "L'Angleterre," in Louis Chevalier, ed., *Le choléra* (La Roche-sur-Yon, 1958), p. 185; *Recueil*, 5 (1876), pp. 46–50; Sherston Baker, *The Laws Relating to Quarantine* (London, 1879), p. ix.

[47] *Staats-Zeitung*, 283 (12 October 1831), p. 1548.

[48] *JO*, 16, 298 (29 October 1884), p. 5683; *Conférence 1866*, 26, pp. 4–6.

[49] Carl Barriés, *Relation über die Natur der asiatischen Cholera* (Hamburg, 1832), p. 51; Carl Barriés, *Die Cholera morbus* (Hamburg, 1831), pp. 68–69 and Anhang following p. 238; G. Hirsch, *Über die Contagiosität der Cholera: Bemerkungen zu dem Sendschreiben des Herrn Präsidenten Dr. Rust an A. v. Humboldt* (Königsberg, 1832) p. 54. During the first cholera epidemics, however, it was apparently soldiers and prisoners, whose circumstances could be and were most easily improved, who benefited most: AN, F[16] 521, Minister of Commerce and Public Works to the Prefects of those Departments with central houses of detention, Paris, 6 April 1832; Préfecture de la Moselle to the Minister of Commerce and Public Works, Metz, 17 April 1832; Trolliet, Polinière et Bottex, *Rapport sur le Choléra-Morbus* (Lyons, 1832), p. 49; *Moniteur universel*, 91 (31 March 1832), p. 928; *Berliner Cholera Zeitung* (1831), pp. 131–33, 142.

[50] *Annales*, 6 (1831), p. 433. The development of germ theory, however, focused attention also on sanitary improvements to be made in the dwellings of the rich: neat, perhaps, but unhygienic: Tomes, "Private Side of Public Health," p. 510.

[51] *PP* 1850 (1273) xxi, 3, pp. 103, 138–39; *PP* 1854–55 (1893) xlv, 69, pp. 62–64; Aloys Martin, ed., *Haupt-Bericht über die Cholera-Epidemie des Jahres 1854 im Königreiche Bayern* (Munich, 1857), p. 857; Franz Xaver Kopp, *Generalbericht über die Cholera-Epidemie in München einschlüssig der Vorstadt Au im Jahre 1836/37* (Munich, 1837), pp. 67–68; *L'union médicale*, 7, 121 (11 October 1853), p. 477; A. Dominique, *Le choléra à Toulon* (Toulon, 1885), pp. 8–10.

the day considered the benefits of personal and public cleanliness so obvious that the lower classes would intuitively back reforms.[52] On the other hand, many sanitationist recommendations, however well intentioned, mocked the plight of the poorest in the absence of broader reform. Advice on diet, dress and living conditions intended to reduce personal predisposition made little sense for those classes happy to eat at all and unable to follow finetuned culinary and other exhortations. "All these," as Louis Blanc remarked, "were doubtless very sage prescriptions, but they were a farce when addressed to that portion of the people to whom an unjust civilization so grudgingly doles out bread, lodging, clothes, and rest."[53] The question of personal predisposition and individually dependent factors in the spread of disease loosened the links between benevolent social reform and sanitationism. Although a focus on predisposing habits and other personal factors was not unique to sanitationists (contagionists also needed to explain why not all exposed to disease succumbed), a preoccupation with environmental causes was more likely to include in its scope not only broad, naturally and socially determined circumstances of urban life, but also more individualized factors.[54]

Personal hygiene was preeminent here. The extent to which the habits of individual cleanliness, now routine behavior among all classes in the industrialized world, are learned behavior (however much we may think that the involuntary shudder of disgust at their absence is nature speaking) has of course long been revealed by historians.[55] We have been inoculated by historical and cultural constructivism against

---

[52] W. Rimpau, *Die Entstehung von Pettenkofers Bodentheorie und die Münchner Choleraepidemie vom Jahre 1854* (Berlin, 1935), pp. 82–83, 91.

[53] Louis Blanc, *The History of Ten Years, 1830–1840* (London, 1844), v. I, p. 615; *Ansprache ans Publicum, zunächst der Herzogthümer Schleswig und Holstein über die epidemische Cholera vom königl. Schleswig-Holsteinischen Sanitätscollegium zu Kiel* (Kiel, 1831), p. 6; *Berliner Cholera Zeitung* (1831), p. 132; Rudolf Virchow, *Collected Essays on Public Health and Epidemiology* (Canton, 1985), v. I, pp. 23–24.

[54] Barbara Dettke, *Die asiatische Hydra: Die Cholera von 1830/31 in Berlin und den preussischen Provinzen Posen, Preussen und Schlesien* (Berlin, 1995), p. 301.

[55] Georges Vigarello, *Concepts of Cleanliness: Changing Attitudes in France Since the Middle Ages* (Cambridge, 1988); Jean-Pierre Goubert, *The Conquest of Water: The Advent of Health in the Industrial Age* (Cambridge, 1989); Richard L. Schoenwald, "Training Urban Man: A Hypothesis About the Sanitary Movement," in H. J. Dyos and Michael Wolff, eds., *The Victorian City* (London 1973), v. II, p. 675; Jacques Léonard, *Archives du corps: La santé au XIXe siècle* (n.p., 1986), pp. 115–35; Geneviève Heller, "Idéologie et rituels de la propreté aux XIXe et XXe siècles," in Arthur E. Imhof, ed., *Leib und Leben in der Geschichte der Neuzeit* (Berlin, 1983); Peter Reinhart Gleichmann, "Städte reinigen und geruchlos machen: Menschliche Körperentleerungen, ihre Geräte und ihre Verhäuslichung," in Hermann Sturm, ed., *Ästhetik und Umwelt: Wahrnehmung, ästhetische Aktivität und ästhetisches Urteil als Momente des Umgangs mit Umwelt* (Tübingen, 1979); Jonas Frykman and Orvar Löfgren, *Culture Builders: A Historical Anthropology of Middle-Class Life* (New Brunswick, 1987), ch. 5.

the anachronism of assuming that hygiene, deodorization, disinfection and all other means of holding back the vermiculating, festering, malodorous reality of human biomass in dense urban proximity were in some sense natural behaviors. An entire school of thought has sought to counter the sanitarians' own whiggish Eliasian account of the march of civilization spreading hygienic habits before it, instead indicting sanitationist attempts to inculcate habits of personal cleanliness among the lower classes as an example of middle-class hegemony, a form of social control.[56] In its most general incarnation, this approach condemns the allegedly repressive and disciplinary aspects of social policy, seeking to turn on its ear the Marshallian triumphant teleology of the welfare state.[57] It is certainly true that sanitationists during the early nineteenth century regarded habits supposedly prevalent among both the lower classes and foreign immigrants not only as revolting, but as posing direct epidemic risks.[58] Seen from environmentalism's socially reformist mode, these were people who had not yet been provided with the appurtenances of middle-class, hygienic life, but who would, once that had been corrected, adapt naturally to improved circumstances. Seen from the less tolerant inflection, the problem was less their external surroundings and more the appalling habits they persisted in continuing.

A concern with environmental factors easily slipped into one that included also personal predisposing causes, thus harnessing also morality to an explanation of disease incidence. Morality in a broad religious sense had long been part of the explanation of illness. Plague had been understood as God's punishment for transgression and atonement and penance remained part of the strategy for ending and avoiding

[56] An extreme example that views sanitationism as a middle-class attempt to control allegedly insanitary and immoral proletarian behavior, thus unifying both the environmentalist approach to cholera and the moralist approach to syphilis as part of one totalizing sanitationist practice of social control can be found in Frank Mort, *Dangerous Sexualities: Medico-Moral Politics in England Since 1830* (London, 1987), pp. 29, 70 and ch. 1. For a more sophisticated version, see Reinhard Spree, *Soziale Ungleichheit vor Krankheit und Tod* (Göttingen, 1981), pp. 156–62.

[57] Following the inspiration, of course, of Foucault and Donzelot: Peter Squires, *Anti-Social Policy: Welfare, Ideology and the Disciplinary State* (Hemel Hempstead, 1990); Linda Mahood, *Policing Gender, Class and Family: Britain, 1850–1940* (London, 1995).

[58] E. L. Jourdain, *Conseils hygiéniques pour se préserver du choléra-morbus* (Colarm, 1832); J. R. L. de Kerckhove dit de Kirckhoff, *Considérations sur la nature et le traitement du choléra-morbus* (Anvers, 1833), p. 202; *Gazette médicale de Paris*, 3, 49 (1832), p. 500; *Die morgenländische Brechruhr (Cholera morbus), von der Sanitäts-Commission in Lübeck bekannt gemacht* (Lübeck, 1831), pp. 4–5, 7; Morris, *Cholera 1832*, pp. 85–86, 93, 120; Alain Corbin, *The Foul and the Fragrant* (Cambridge, MA, 1986), pp. 143–45; Vijay Prashad, "Native Dirt/Imperial Ordure: The Cholera of 1832 and the Morbid Resolutions of Modernity," *Journal of Historical Sociology*, 7, 3 (September 1994), pp. 248–49.

epidemics up through the early eighteenth century.[59] By the time of cholera a religious approach had faded, although still persisting in such acts as the prayer ordered by the British king in 1831 or the national day of fasting proposed by President Taylor in response to the 1849 epidemic in the United States.[60] By the time cholera threatened in 1853, however, when the Presbytery of Edinburgh suggested a national fast, Palmerston replied that what was needed was purification of towns rather than humiliation.[61] Neither religion nor morality was the solution any longer.

For those who focused on issues of morality with cholera, it was now individual lapses of personal control, no longer the broad question of society's religious shortcomings. Concentrating on the environmental aspects of disease, the elision between physical and moral factors became a slippery slope. Dirt, sexual excess and alcohol were the three pathological habits of the underclass identified by sanitary reformers to explain their proclivity to disease.[62] Cholera, as one observer put it, spread especially among those in poor living conditions who suffered from drunkenness, debauchery, bad food and cold: an indistinguishable melange of objective environmental and subjective moral circumstances.[63] If most diseases, as one antivaccinator pursued this logic, were the result of deprivation and destitution, then the solution was to give all classes the chance to live in healthy circumstances, urging them to be sober, industrious, temperate and cleanly. Encouraging salubrious and provident habits among the lower classes promised to make them respectable, healthy and moral.[64] The highpoint of this mixing of morality and hygiene was the hope, expressed by one German reformer, that the same inculcated habits of cleanliness and germ avoidance that disinclined children to touch the seats of public toilets and kiss strangers would also

---

[59] Slack, *Impact of Plague*, p. 327; Jean-Noël Biraben, *Les hommes et la peste en France et dans les pays européens et méditerranéens* (Mouton, 1976), v. II, p. 63.

[60] John Simon, *English Sanitary Institutions* (London, 1890), p. 171; Rosenberg, *Cholera Years*, pp. 121–22; Arthur Newsholme, *Health Problems in Organized Society* (London, 1927), p. 3.

[61] Arthur Newsholme, *Evolution of Preventive Medicine* (Baltimore, 1927), p. 10; David Hamilton, *The Healers: A History of Medicine in Scotland* (Edinburgh, 1981), p. 188. Theological views were nonetheless expressed in France and Italy during the 1884 epidemic: Frank M. Snowden, *Naples in the Time of Cholera, 1884–1911* (Cambridge, 1995), pp. 73–74.

[62] Ute Frevert, *Krankheit als politisches Problem 1770–1880* (Göttingen, 1984), p. 139.

[63] [Carl Trafvenfelt], *Sammandrag af Läkares åsigter och erfarenhet af den Epidemiska Choleran uti Asien och Europa* (Stockholm, 1831), v. I, pp. 32–33; Morris, *Cholera 1832*, pp. 84–85; Olivier Faure, *Histoire sociale de la médecine* (Paris, 1994), p. 113.

[64] Jno. Pickering, *Which? Sanitation and Sanatory Remedies, or Vaccination and the Drug Treatment?* (London, 1892), pp. 84–85, 143; Alfons Labisch, *Homo Hygienicus: Gesundheit und Medizin in der Neuzeit* (Frankfurt, 1992), pp. 111–20.

override the sexual urge, making the idea of intercourse with a public woman hygienically revolting.[65]

Such slippage from environmental to moral factors became especially treacherous when attention shifted to VD. Some observers have argued that a sanitationist approach to VD encouraged a view of women's bodies as the source of disease; the belief, common at midcentury, that an uninfected woman's secretions could spontaneously contaminate her partner in effect transferred the tenets of an environmental understanding to these ailments.[66] In a less extreme fashion, it is certainly the case that a focus on the environmental factors of VD allowed moral questions to command the highground. High living densities did not automatically promote the spread of VD (in the way that would be the case with tuberculosis or smallpox) without the further factor of promiscuous, or at least unhygienic, relations. Middle-class reformers were convinced that the indiscriminate sleeping habits of the lower classes were an element in disease dissemination, not to mention the seduction and incest that often propelled girls along a prostitutive career path.[67] As recent work has shown, the working classes were also attuned to such concerns, often deliberately seeking to separate density from promiscuity, the men and women arising, dressing and exiting, for example, in separate shifts.[68] Similar elision was possible when factoring in the contribution of alcoholic intemperance to venereal indulgence.[69] The line here between environmental (the density that followed in poverty's train) and moral (the promiscuity that did not by itself result from proximity) elements was a fine one indeed.

With the debate over regulation, at the latest, whatever inherent alliances existed between sanitationism and the left, quarantinism and the right had broken up. With the moral concerns evoked by VD a focus on the social context of prostitution and syphilis did not always indicate a hope of improving the lot of women or reforming society. It could

---

[65] Friedrich Weinbrenner, *Wie schützt man sich vor Ansteckung?* (Bonn, 1908), pp. 7–9.

[66] Mary Spongberg, *Feminizing Venereal Disease: The Body of the Prostitute in Nineteenth-Century Medical Discourse* (New York, 1997), pp. 34–36; Sandra Stanley Holton, "State Pandering, Medical Policing and Prostitution: The Controversy Within the Medical Profession Concerning the Contagious Diseases Legislation 1864–1886," *Research in Law, Deviance and Social Control*, 9 (1988), pp. 153–54. This belief in the spontaneous generation of gonorrhea faded after the discovery in the 1870s of dormant gonococcal infections that, though symptomless, could pass on disease: Harry F. Dowling, *Fighting Infection: Conquests of the Twentieth Century* (Cambridge, MA, 1977), p. 87.

[67] Ulrich Linse, "Über den Prozess der Syphilisation: Körper und Sexualität um 1900 aus ärztlicher Sicht," in Alexander Schuller and Nikolaus Heim, eds., *Vermessene Sexualität* (Berlin, 1987), p. 181.   [68] Michael Mason, *The Making of Victorian Sexuality* (Oxford, 1994), pp. 139–44.

[69] *PP* 1916 (8189) xvi, 1, p. 65.

equally involve an insistence on chastity and self-restraint, advocated by both left and right, both proletarian and patriarchal virtue, and it often included a willingness to blame the individual for a style of living that brought with it disease of a voluntarily acquired nature. Attention to the social context of illness did not always mean a concern for the poor or downtrodden whose conditions were to be ameliorated as part of a unified epidemiological and social reform program. A focus on filth could encourage improvements in the urban environment, but it could also cause alarm over immigrants not yet up to hygienic snuff, prompting calls for cleansings or even exclusion, as in Germany during the mass waves of transmigration of the late nineteenth century, in Britain during the same period, or a century earlier in the United States during yellow fever epidemics.[70] Nor did it even mean an exclusively class-centered concern with the poor, but often extended its scope to include national and ethnic rivalries. What the bourgeoisie thought of the working classes was equally the opinion of the English for the Irish, the Germans for Poles, Europeans for Indians, the Anglo-Americans for continental Europeans and many gentiles for the Jews of Slavic Europe.[71] More importantly, the habits of the upper classes, especially sexual and dietary excess, were often equally the object of condemnation. It was not just poverty, the objective misery of abject social circumstance, but the individual conduct in such conditions that predisposed. Because of this disjunction between the personal and the social, predisposing factors could also implicate those classes whose living conditions were not hygienically objectionable. Sexual excess, though often identified as a proclivity of the lower orders, could be equally a problem among the upper classes in the eyes of bourgeois reformers. Gluttony and other culinary indulgence were also habits for which the better-off ("drunk as a lord") could be duly castigated. Following from Rousseau's ideas, it was thought (before Villermé empirically demonstrated the opposite during the 1820s and thirties) that the rich, indulgent and lax were the ones most at risk from disease.[72] An important school of thought during the first cholera epi-

---

[70] Martin S. Pernick, "Poltics, Parties and Pestilence: Epidemic Yellow Fever in Philadelphia and the Rise of the First Party System," in Judith Walzer Leavitt and Ronald L. Numbers, eds., *Sickness and Health in America* (2nd edn.; Madison, 1985), p. 357; Howard Markel, "Cholera, Quarantines, and Immigration Restriction: The View from Johns Hopkins, 1892," *BHM*, 67, 4 (1993), pp. 692–93; Howard Markel, *Quarantine! East European Jewish Immigrants and the New York City Epidemics of 1892* (Baltimore, 1997), chs. 4, 5.

[71] Mary Poovey, *Making a Social Body: British Cultural Formation 1830–1864* (Chicago, 1995), ch. 3.

[72] William Coleman, *Death Is a Social Disease: Public Health and Political Economy in Early Industrial France* (Madison, 1982), p. 149.

demics held that the disease struck equally the wealthy and that certain lifestyle factors peculiar to the better-off explained this social equalization of incidence.[73]

Susan Sontag's famous plea not to attribute illness to lifestyle, with its attendant blaming of the patient, updated the observation made during the first cholera epidemic that contagious diseases struck without moral intent, often sparing drunkards and gluttons, carrying off virgins and the abstemious.[74] She advocated a return to a purely biological view of illness of the sort once encouraged by the bacteriological revolution, but often regarded by reformers as willfully oblivious to the environmental context of disease. Opinion that fancied itself progressive was now suggesting that perhaps the social and environmental background of illness had been exaggerated. Sometimes a disease is just a disease. Germ theory, while perhaps discouraging major social and environmental reform in favor of targeted biomedical interventions, at least had the advantage of relieving much of the moral stigma that might otherwise attach to disease, explaining it not as the result of immoral habits, but of an unfortunate encounter with malevolent microorganisms.[75] With AIDS, the inherited correlations have been turned on their head. Conservatives have in this case focused on lifestyle, blaming the promiscuity of high-risk groups and the insanitary habits of drug addicts for their particular susceptibility, while most progressives have explained the disease as but the morally neutral result of a specific infectious organism which for largely fortuitous reasons has struck certain groups with special devastation.[76] In France, for example, the strategy of those who

[73] L. A. Gosse, *Rapport sur l'épidémie de choléra en Prusse, en Russie et en Pologne* (Geneva, 1833), p. 328; A. N. Gendrin, *Monographie du choléra-morbus epidémique de Paris* (Paris, 1832), pp. 11, 287–88; *Årsberättelse om Svenska Läkare-Sällskapets arbeten* (1830), p. 140; M. F. Magendie, *Leçons sur le choléra-morbus, faites au Collège de France* (Paris, 1832), p. 241; Charles Creighton, *A History of Epidemics in Britain* (Cambridge, 1894), v. II, pp. 830–31; PRO, PC1/108, A. Moreau de Jonnès to W. Pym, 13 April 1832; *Staats-Zeitung*, Beilage zu No. 285 (14 October 1831), pp. 1557–59; Charles C. F. Greville, *The Greville Memoirs* (2nd edn.; London, 1874), v. II, pp. 287–88; François Delaporte, *Disease and Civilization: The Cholera in Paris, 1832* (Cambridge, MA, 1986), pp. 107–13.

[74] *Geschichte der Cholera in Danzig im Jahre 1831* (n.p., n.d.), p. 38; Susan Sontag, *Illness as Metaphor* (New York, 1978), pp. 46–55, 60–61.

[75] Labisch, *Homo Hygienicus*, pp. 143–44, 255. Moral factors were, however, still invoked to explain differentials in susceptibility and predisposition: Charles Rosenberg, "Banishing Risk: Continuity and Change in the Moral Management of Disease," in Allan M. Brandt and Paul Rozin, eds., *Morality and Health* (New York, 1997), pp. 39–41.

[76] Dennis Altman, *AIDS and the New Puritanism* (London, 1986), p. 183; Paul R. Gross and Norman Levitt, *Higher Superstition: The Academic Left and Its Quarrels with Science* (Baltimore, 1994), p. 185; Jane Lewis, "Public Health Doctors and AIDS as a Public Health Issue," in Virginia Berridge and Philip Strong, eds., *AIDS and Contemporary History* (Cambridge, 1993), p. 39; Peter H. Duesberg, *Infectious AIDS: Have We Been Misled?* (Berkeley, 1995), pp. 333, 515.

sought to calm hysteria, avoid panic, prevent stigmatization of the infected and seek solutions through voluntary precautions has been to emphasize the specific cause of the disease and the difficulties of its practical transmission, while the extreme right has underlined the possibility of multifactoral etiologies and cofactors that allegedly broaden the scope of danger, potentially exposing ordinary citizens to risk and thus justifying draconian precautions.[77]

The political implications of prophylactic positions have thus been neither unambiguous nor invariant. The left had obvious reasons to favor a sanitationist approach that promised to improve living conditions for the poorest.[78] But political and social radicals could also be contagionists and quarantinists, not to mention vaccinationists and regulationists, accepting that etiology, prophylaxis and reformist good intentions did not, in this case, coincide.[79] If in fact disease were contagiously spread, then representatives of the worst-off, realizing that their followers would be among the most affected, often sought to have the state take effective precautions, even if that meant quarantinist measures. In France, for example, workers' associations in Marseilles demanded that the fight against smallpox, a disease so devastating to the working class, be carried out vigorously and that vaccinations be available at workers' clinics.[80] More generally, what are the political valences of a doctrine that subordinates the individual to the community in such terms? The position of traditional conservatives?[81] That of the left?[82] That of the extreme right, the Nazis, for example, whose slogan in these matters was "Gemeinnutz geht vor Eigennutz"?[83]

Conversely, quarantinism and political conservatism also do not go hand in hand in simple harmony. The most historically specified instance of this putative correlation is the supposed coincidence of

[77] Michael Pollak, *Les homosexuels et le sida: Sociologie d'une épidémie* (Paris, 1988), p. 164.

[78] *SB*, 18 February 1874, p. 108; Alfons Labisch, "Die gesundheitspolitischen Vorstellungen der deutschen Sozialdemokratie von ihrer Gründung bis zur Parteispaltung (1863–1917)," *Archiv für Sozialgeschichte.* 16 (1976), pp. 337–38, 360–66.

[79] Durey, *Return of the Plague*, pp. 108–09; Anne Hardy, "Lyon Playfair and the Idea of Progress," in Dorothy Porter and Roy Porter, eds., *Doctors, Politics and Society: Historical Essays* (Amsterdam, 1993), pp. 88–91.

[80] Jean Humbert, *Du role de l'administration en matière de prophylaxie des maladies épidémiques* (Paris, 1911), p. 152.

[81] K. F. H. Marx, *Die Erkenntnis, Verhütung und Heilung der ansteckenden Cholera* (Karlsruhe, 1831), pp. 271–72.

[82] Jack D. Ellis, *The Physician-Legislators of France: Medicine and Politics in the Early Third Republic, 1870–1914* (Cambridge, 1990), p. 180.

[83] Gerhard Venzmer, *Kampf den Bazillen* (Munich, 1936), pp. 96–97, 225.

Koch's discoveries, the implementation of neoquarantinism and the strengthening of conservatism in Germany. Koch's work and its legislative percolation can not, however, be attributed to the political rise of conservatism after 1879 in any simple sense. First of all, his discoveries were hardly accepted overnight or even wholeheartedly by German officialdom and, to the extent that they were, certainly not until well into the 1890s, long after the political shift of which they were allegedly part. As late as the early nineties, Koch himself was skeptical that his ideas would be embraced by the authorities. Well into the decade much opinion of an anti-Kochian sort could be found and there was no one theory on cholera accepted by all.[84] Moreover, the Social Democrats, who should, in such a straightforward political accounting, have been most resistant to Kochianism, were far from uniformly opposed to his ideas or their prophylactic implications. Bebel was a particular admirer of Koch.[85] Socialists in Berlin accepted the need for disinfection, isolation and reporting of contagious diseases, insisting only that the costs of such measures be assumed by the state.[86] During discussion of the Contagious Disease Law at the end of the century, it was not the left, but the Center Party which objected to its powers of isolating the ill against their will, seeing this as a measure that most affected society's weakest members and a violation of the rights of the family. Socialists, in contrast, claimed that workers suffered heavily the consequences of disease, that, if anything, the law did not intervene vigorously enough and that,

---

[84] *Zeitschrift für Hygiene und Infektionskrankheiten*, 15 (1893), pp. 162–63; Ernst Barth, *Die Cholera, mit Berücksichtigung der speciellen Pathologie und Therapie* (Breslau, 1893), p. 85; Otto Riedel, *Die Cholera: Entstehung, Wesen und Verhütung derselben* (Berlin, 1887), pp. 58–59; *Deutsche Vierteljahrsschrift für Gesundheitspflege*, 17 (1885), p. 554; Carl Flügge, *Die Verbreitungsweise und Abwehr der Cholera* (Leipzig, 1893), p. 83; R. Telschow, *Zur Entstehung der Cholera und ein Rat zur Verhütung derselben* (Berlin, 1893), pp. 2–7; *Die Misserfolge der Staatsmedicin und ihre Opfer in Hamburg* (Hagen i. W., [1892]), pp. 3–4; C. Sturm, *Der allein sichere Schutz vor Cholera* (Berlin, 1893), pp. 20–24; Ferdinand Hueppe, *Die Cholera-Epidemie in Hamburg 1892* (Berlin, 1893), p. 98; J. A. Gläser, *Gemeinverständliche Anticontagionistische Betrachtungen bei Gelegenheit der letzten Cholera-Epidemie in Hamburg 1892* (Hamburg, 1893), pp. 49–50; *Monatsblatt für öffentliche Gesundheitspflege*, 17, 6 (1894), pp. 112–13; *Bulletin de l'Académie de médecine*, 3, 28 (1892), pp. 527–43.

[85] *Die Misserfolge der Staatsmedicin und ihre Opfer in Hamburg* (Hagen i. W., [1892]), p. 28; Gerd Göckenjan, *Kurieren und Staat machen: Gesundheit und Medizin in der bürgerlichen Welt* (Frankfurt, 1985), pp. 331–34.

[86] *Stenographische Berichte über die öffentlichen Sitzungen der Stadtverordneten-Versammlung der Haupt- und Residenzstadt Berlin*, 19 (1892), 11 February 1892, pp. 56ff.; 19 (1892), 8 September 1892, p. 278. Because of the Social Democratic Party's acceptance of quarantinist measures, Evans is obliged to argue that, when the party joined with the Hamburg authorities to man disinfection stations and the like, this was but tactical cooperation with the state, much like voting for war credits in 1914: Richard J. Evans, "Die Cholera und die Sozialdemokratie," in Arno Herzig et al., eds., *Arbeiter in Hamburg* (Hamburg, 1983), pp. 203–12.

illness and death being the ultimate violations of individual liberty, the state had reason, in such respects, to sacrifice civil rights to the needs of the community.[87] A similar situation held for vaccination, where the most vigorous opposition came not from the left, but from various marginal subcultural movements that, if they can be situated politically at all, tended toward the other end of the spectrum.

Searches for the political bases of prophylactic strategies have thus borne little fruit. The Germans were quarantinist when it came to cholera in the 1830s, but both quickly revised their position during the course of that epidemic and then switched tacks to side with the British during the course of the century in a manner that does not seem explicable in terms of any continuing autocratic tradition here. The French, in turn, flip-flopped on prophylactic issues in a fashion that cannot easily be paired with their various changes of regime: antiquarantinist during the late Restoration, the brief Second Republic and the early, autocratic phase of the Empire; increasingly quarantinist during the later, liberal era of Napoleon III's reign and the Third Republic. For smallpox, the situation is similar. The Germans were enthusiastic vaccinators, but so were the Swedes, for a long while at least. The French in turn followed a meandering prophylactic path that correlates only spottily with political regime: eagerly wannabe vaccinationist during the rule of the first Napoleon, they took a decidedly hands-off approach under the reign of his nephew and then left it to the liberal and in many respects allergically antistatist Third Republic to introduce some of the most draconian legislation anywhere. For syphilis, the problem is similar. Regulationism, which in the Ackerknechtian-inspired accounts is the conservative system, was in fact in place in a bewildering assortment of places: the Mediterranean nations, some Latin American and Asian ones, several European. Conversely, those countries which had either never adopted regulation or repealed it spanned an equally diverse political smorgasbord, ranging from liberal Britain and the United States through proto-social democratic Scandinavia to Bolshevik Russia. Analyzed more closely, things become even more complicated. Liberal Britain allowed freedom of prostitution and no regulation; the liberal United States, in contrast, also had no regulation,

---

[87] *SB*, 1892/93, 21 April 1893, pp. 1959D–1960A, 1964D–1965D. In later discussions, however, the emphasis switched in a more Pettenkoferian and sanitationist direction: *SB*, 1898/1900, 24 April 1900, pp. 5069D–5070B. But in the final reading most Socialists supported the law despite its violation of individual rights because the government had agreed to compensate those who were isolated and provide disinfections free of charge. Party members were permitted to vote their conscience on this issue: *SB*, 1900, 12 June 1900, pp. 6014D, 6016B.

but forbade and actively suppressed prostitution, taking the lead in introducing interventions rejected in Britain, such as prenuptial certificates.[88] Sweden abolished regulation only to impose instead a system of control extended to all citizens, followed then not only by Germany during the late Weimar republic, but also belatedly by France in 1960. Ackerknechtian correlations between politics and prophylaxis, in other words, are hard to line up with any consistency beyond isolated and fairly fortuitous groupings.

Such a decoupling of the link between prophylaxis and politics stands in the tradition of recent work that has increasingly shorn science of its political implications, turning the tide of the relentless reduction of knowledge to power characteristic of much historiography of the 1970s and eighties. It has been has shown, for example, that eugenic thought was not a monopoly of the right nor necessarily and inherently conservative.[89] Much the same has also been claimed for holistic thought in German-speaking central Europe and for geopolitics.[90] More dramatic has been the depoliticization of women's history, at least in any simple fashion, to the point where left and right, conservative and progressive, no longer make much sense of the multiplicity of possible positions.[91]

A MULTIPLICITY OF ORIGINS

As a caricatured rule, sociologists are good at elucidating necessary causes, but stumble in believing them sufficient in any given circumstance.

---

[88] *Mitteilungen*, 24, 11 (1926), p. 120; [André] Cavaillon, *Les législations antivénériennes dans le monde* ([Paris], 1931), pp. 28–29.

[89] Weindling, *Health, Race and German Politics*, pp. 91–101, 111; William H. Schneider, *Quality and Quantity: The Quest for Biological Regeneration in Twentieth-Century France* (Cambridge, 1990), p. 11; Michael Burleigh and Wolfgang Wippermann, *The Racial State: Germany 1933–1945* (Cambridge, 1991), p. 28; Gunnar Broberg and Matthias Tydén, *Oönskade i folkhemmet* (Stockholm, 1991), pp. 178–79; G. R. Searle, *Eugenics and Politics in Britain 1900–1914* (Leyden, 1976), pp. 38–41; Peter Weingart et al., *Rasse, Blut und Gene: Geschichte der Eugenik und Rassenhygiene in Deutschland* (Frankfurt, 1988), pp. 105–14; Atina Grossmann, *Reforming Sex: The German Movement for Birth Control and Abortion Reform, 1920–1950* (New York, 1995); Cornelie Usborne, *The Politics of the Body in Weimar Germany* (Houndsmills, 1992), pp. 133–42; Nils Roll-Hansen, "Geneticists and the Eugenics Movement in Scandinavia," *British Journal for the History of Science*, 22/3, 74 (September 1989); Gunnar Broberg and Nils Roll-Hansen, eds., *Eugenics and the Welfare State: Sterilization Policy in Denmark, Sweden, Norway and Finland* (East Lansing, 1996), pp. 260–61; R. P. Neuman, "The Sexual Question and Social Democracy in Imperial Germany," *Journal of Social History*, 7, 3 (Spring 1974), p. 277; Michael Freeden, "Eugenics and Progressive Thought: A Study in Ideological Affinity," *Historical Journal*, 22, 3 (1979); Richard J. Evans, "In Search of German Social Darwinism," in Manfred Berg and Geoffrey Cocks, eds., *Medicine and Modernity* (Cambridge, 1997), pp. 60–63.

[90] Anne Harrington, *Reenchanted Science: Holism in German Culture from Wilhelm II to Hitler* (Princeton, 1996); David Thomas Murphy, *The Heroic Earth: Geopolitical Thought in Weimar Germany, 1918–1933* (Kent, OH, 1997), pp. 23–26. [91] See the literature cited in ch. 5, nn. 494–513.

Historians, in contrast, spend their time excavating proximate causes, either oblivious to the necessary ones or convinced that they are trivially obvious, requiring no further attention. It falls to comparativists to juggle a concern with identifying and demonstrating empirically the pertinence of necessary causes, without losing sight of the sufficient ones that are equally part of any given historical story in its chronological specificity.

Though politics were certainly part of the story, a simple Acker-knechtian reading of prophylactic strategies cannot explain the poly-morphous divergence of the precautions imposed across nations. As supplement and replacement, other factors have been adduced here: geoepidemiological location, both in terms of positioning vis-à-vis the epidemic currents of contagious disease and in those of the topography required to make certain preventive strategies work; and commercial interest and administrative capacity, both of which had implications for various tactics. No one of these factors suffices alone to explain why nations adopted such divergent preventive strategies to common prob-lems. Only in various combinations, differently calculated for different diseases at different times, does an answer to that question emerge. Such factors were the general conditions within whose ambit prophylactic decisions were taken, but only a historical accounting of the precise steps behind every such choice can explain any specific outcome. Each nation's preventive strategy depended on a permutation of these factors that was peculiar to it.

Only as a very general concern did commerce, for example, encour-age nations to abandon quarantinism. It was, after all, the preeminent trading interests of the time, Venice, Ragusa, Marseilles, that had first and most thoroughly imposed quarantine. In Marseilles of the eight-eenth century, many of the sanitary intendants, responsible for such strictures, were commercial men themselves. Partly this mutual cohabi-tation of commerce and quarantines was the result of a weighing of two evils, with prevention taking precedence over profit. Partly, noncommer-cial considerations still played a more important role than would later be the case. In Marseilles during the plague of 1720, the epidemic was seen as divine wrath against the sins of the city, and commerce, its especial vocation, was all but condemned as a maleficent force.[92] Religion and its imperatives still outweighed trade. Only thereafter, with the rise of the

---

[92] Françoise Hildesheimer, *Le bureau de la santé de Marseille sous l'ancien régime* (Marseilles, 1980), p. 200; Carlo M. Cipolla, *Public Health and the Medical Profession in the Renaissance* (Cambridge, 1976), pp. 39–40; Ch. Carrière et al., *Marseille ville morte: La peste de 1720* (Marseilles, 1968), pp. 310–13; Laurence Brockliss and Colin Jones, *The Medical World of Early Modern France* (Oxford, 1997), p. 349.

more removed nations, Britain and the Netherlands, as mercantile powers, did quarantinism gradually cease being the preventive strategy of choice for commercial interests.

Commercial considerations influenced prophylactic strategies, but not in any consistent fashion. Merchants in Marseilles during the plague epidemic of 1720 argued that the disease arose from within the city, not imported by their ships, when threatened with quarantine and then, conversely, that it came from without, not from their storehouses, when these were subject to disinfection.[93] British trading interests helped shift policies away from quarantinism already with the threat of plague in the early eighteenth century and continued to press in this direction a century later in the cholera era and during the interminable wranglings with other European powers over the appropriate measures to take in the Middle East. In Germany, similar interests, including the Hanseatic shipping lines, resisted attempts to impose restrictions on the free movement of goods and passengers, whether the hopes of public health authorities to limit the flux of Slavic transmigrants or the precautions marshaled abroad in the wake of Hamburg's cholera epidemic in 1892. In the Mediterranean nations, in contrast, facing the more immediate prospect of contagion, commercial interests were not uniformly adverse to quarantinist measures, realizing that they could not contradict public opinion on so delicate and important an issue. In certain cases, Marseilles especially, they reaped benefits from the monopolies of transit thereby granted. That Britain became the greatest commercial power of the time, trading heavily with the very fount of cholera, doubtless aggravated its allergies to quarantinism. But for the Mediterranean nations, the hopes of certain business interests to remain unrestricted in their movements were not sufficient to outweigh the threat of contagion. Nations generally took prophylactic cues from their partners in commerce to avoid penalties to their competitive ambitions, with trading blocs locked into preventive prisoner's dilemmas. The decision whether to be quarantinist or not was taken for reasons that may have included commerce, but cannot be limited to it.

Nor did geography, though an important and too often neglected factor in determining public health strategies, point unambiguously in any one direction. It clearly played a larger role the less endemic the

---

[93] Georg Sticker, *Abhandlungen aus der Seuchengeschichte und Seuchenlehre* (Giessen, 1912), v. I/1, pp. 227–28.

disease. For plague and cholera, the geoepidemiological positioning of a country vis-à-vis the sources of contagion was important. For smallpox geography was less crucial, but still a consideration. Even with syphilis, the most homegrown of the ailments here, port cities and seafaring nations faced particular problems, while disparities between town and countryside remained important. And yet, beyond this level, geography meant different things.

In a general sense, those nations closest to the sources, perceived or real, of infection were more inclined to be quarantinist than those, especially Britain, whose greater remove allowed a degree of insouciance. But exceptions were as common as the rule, often determined by topographical ability to impose quarantinism effectively. Though hardly a nation exposed on the front line of epidemiological attack from the Orient, Sweden joined the Mediterranean powers in holding fast to quarantinist principles longer than others in northern Europe, partly because it feared its Russian neighbors, but equally because its peninsular position allowed it to impose effective border controls. Conversely, Britain's insular position, which – topographically speaking – should, in theory, have favored a quarantinist approach (and which did, and continues to, permit this with respect to epizooties), was not a sufficiently compelling motive compared to its commercial stake in unrestricted trade. The Mediterranean nations were by and large more quarantinist in inclination than the Atlantic, but among them other factors could hold sway. The individual Italian states, for example, varied in their quarantinist proclivities despite a shared geoepidemiological predicament. After unification, Italy changed direction to move out of the Mediterranean camp of quarantinist nations (Spain, Portugal, Greece) and toward a more Atlantic perspective.

Equally important, what counted as a source of contagion was only partly an epidemiological given, but equally a matter of historically and culturally conditioned fears and anxieties. Each nation had its favorite epidemiological whipping boy: Poles and Galicians for the Germans, Russians for the Swedes, Irish for the English, Spanish for the French, Catholics for Protestants, while (to paraphrase Tom Lehrer) everybody feared the Orient. Just how malleable and indeterminate such anxieties were can be seen in the contradictory epidemiological views of Jews: criticized by some as poor, filthy and infectious, lauded by others as sober, provident and clean.[94]

[94] For a smattering of such contradictory views, see Dettke, *Die asiatische Hydra*, p. 265; James Kerr, "National Health," in William Harbutt Dawson, ed., *After-War Problems* (London, 1917), p. 266;

For the topographical factor, similar vacillations held true. Generally speaking, nations that were sparsely populated, liminally positioned and (quasi-) insular could see with clarity that certain diseases were imported and, because able with some expectation of success to exclude them, were more likely than those positioned in the thick of territorial interconnections to be quarantinist. This is a more general formulation of the rule that contagionism was a doctrine of the countryside, sanitationism of cities.[95] The Swedes were the obvious case, far removed from the Oriental sources of certain diseases, but inclined nonetheless (because they could) to apply quarantinist tactics. Then again, the argument could go both ways. The Portuguese thought that their nation with its long coastline required quarantine while the Norwegians argued that, precisely because of their extensive coasts and numerous ports, they could not possibly isolate all travelers.[96] Most obviously, the British case – strongly antiquarantinist despite its famously insular position – demonstrated that topography was not destiny.[97] The Italians illustrated the ambiguity starkly, arguing at the 1903 International Sanitary Conference on the plague that their impressive coastline and exposed position as the first port of call for ships from the Middle East put them in a highly vulnerable position. But precisely this precarious epidemiological perch, they continued, allowed them painful insights into the hopelessness of attempts to halt disease at the borders and the need instead to focus preventive measures on infected localities, snuffing out outbreaks before they could spread.[98]

Administrative wherewithal was also not a factor that unambiguously pointed in any one particular direction. In certain matters of detail, administration did influence prophylaxis. The lack of a national system of birth registration impeded ambitions in nineteenth-century Britain for an effective accounting of vaccination. The absence of universal conscription and the lateness of widespread primary schooling meant that indirect methods of requiring the lancet were less easily available

Verhandlungen, 1 (1832), pp. 429–30; Barth, *Die Cholera*, p. 26; *Berliner Cholera Zeitung* (1831), p. 157; *Berlinische Nachrichten von Staats- und gelehrten Sachen*, 213 (12 September 1831); Franz Freiherr von Hallberg zu Broich, *Einige Erfahrungen bei ansteckenden Krankheiten, zur Bekämpfung der Cholera* (Jülich, 1831), p. 4; Nancy Tomes, "Moralizing the Microbe: The Germ Theory and the Moral Construction of Behavior in the Late-Nineteenth-Century Antituberculosis Movement," in Brandt and Rozin, *Morality and Health*, p. 286; *Verhandlungen* (1831), p. 102; [Trafvenfelt], *Sammandrag af Läkares åsigter*, v. I, pp. 177–78. [95] See ch. 2, n. 90.
[96] *Conférence 1874*, pp. 118–27, 130–31, 238–39; *Conférence 1885*, p. 98.
[97] Either that, or it showed that the Channel was not sufficient protection for the British to think of themselves, epidemiologically speaking, in insular terms, at least not for humans.
[98] *Conférence 1903*, pp. 30–34; *Conférence 1893*, pp. 33–39.

here than on the continent. In a broader sense, quarantinism was seen as a cheaper and less administratively demanding prophylactic solution compared to sanitationist reform, the poor and ill-equipped nation's tactic of choice. Two so otherwise different political systems as Russia and Britain both agreed for administrative reasons on the medical surveillance of travelers.

On the other hand, consistent patterns correlating with administrative capacity or practice are hard to determine. The British, for all their vaunted laissez-faire and minimal state, could both take a hands-off approach and be drastically interventionist. In all cases, they initially tried out, but did not sustain, measures as quarantinist, vaccinationist and regulationist as the continental polities. In other respects (the criminalization of exposure by the infected, for example, or removals of the ill to hospitals) they set the standard for other nations, showing that, if they so desired, strict interventions that swept aside niceties of civil rights were in their repertoire. The flesh was capable, whatever doubts might have gnawed at the spirit. About the Swedes' ability to intervene few questions have been entertained. The French, though great theoretical believers in the firm guidance of a strong central state, were often chronic laggards in practice. With the exceptions of regulating prostitution and insisting on quarantinist precautions in the Middle East, where they set the pace, in other respects they trailed the lead taken in northern Europe and Britain. Even in these last two nations, with arguably the most centralized administrations among those under the glass here, resistance from the provinces played a major role in prophylactic strategy, whether Marseilles rejecting Parisian sanitationism early in the century or uninfected localities in the Swedish hinterland standing stubbornly on their right to cut off access for the rest of the world. Finally, about the Germans it is hard to say anything across the board. The range of preventive strategy was great and inconsistent. Hamburg was liberal when it came to cholera, draconian on prostitution, Bavaria was laissez-faire on both counts, but an eager enforcer of the lancet, while Prussia tended to belie as often as it confirmed its interventionist reputation.

None of these factors alone can explain why a particular nation chose a specific prophylactic course. Various combinations of hues chosen from a palette of factors determined the final tint in each individual case. The closest approximation to an underlying primary factor was knowledge, both scientific and practical. Etiological advances obviously put pressure on all nations, however insistently other considerations may have favored quarantinism, to abandon oldfashioned precautions. Similarly, practical experiences with disease, often largely independent of formal scientific knowledge, also influenced prophylactic behavior, as with the Italians' move away from quarantinism in the 1870s and eighties. In other respects, the factors considered here intertwined in various ways to push nations in one direction or the other. For Britain, commerce and geography far outweighed topography to undercut quarantinism. For Sweden, a combination of topography (the ability to quarantine) and geography (fear of infection from Russia) took precedence over commercial interests pointing away from quarantinism. For the Germans, geoepidemiological concerns remained important, whether the fear of contagion from the east in the 1830s or later the stream of transmigrants, but they were counterbalanced by increasingly important commercial considerations brought to the fore by the shock of having quarantinism imposed in full force in 1892 and the hopes of shipping interests not to be excluded from the traffic in emigrants. The French vacillated, hamstrung by their peculiar geoepidemiological position, perched on the faultline between Mediterranean and Atlantic. The approach of the Mediterranean nations was generally determined by a combination of geography and topography, but could be tempered and altered by experience, as in the Italian case. To say that each of these factors could have different effects depending on the context (insularity, for example, in certain cases allowing an appreciation of quarantines, othertimes not) does not mean that they did not themselves exert an influence, only that precisely which it was can be determined only in conjunction with others in their historical specificity.

In summation, consider the case of Hamburg: antiquarantinist when it came to cholera, regulationist on prostitution, whereas Prussia reversed these positions, strictly quarantinist on cholera, yet lax on the prostitution question, indeed at times abolitionist. Political traditions, whether Teutonic strictness in the case of brothels, or liberal Anglophilic, anti-Prussian liberalism of the sort adduced by Evans in that of cholera, cannot account for Hamburg's prophylactic stances as elegantly as does its geoepidemiological position. As a port city, it was allergic to quarantines and other restrictions on trade, but equally it was a hotbed of prostitution among sailors and hence favored strict intervention in this case as readily as it loathed it in the former. In other respects, Hamburg may have had divergent prophylactic interests that cannot be reduced in simple fashion to political traditions. Although opposing quarantines, it was also concerned to ensure that its ships were not infected and therefore not barred from foreign ports, which spoke for some form of precautions. Its concern to preserve a generous share of the lucrative emigrant transport business meant that it had to toe the line dictated by the receiving nations, above all the United States, which again meant accepting strict measures that belied any general laissez-faire approach.

TRADITIONS ARE LEARNED

Nations adopted quite divergent preventive strategies during the nineteenth century, ones that continue in many respects down to our own day. The vaccillations and inconsistencies within the policies of a given country should not be underestimated. Britain relented on vaccination and regulation, but insisted on isolating the infectious. Sweden abandoned compulsion for smallpox and freed prostitutes from control, yet subjected all citizens to similar measures in return. France was draconian on vaccination and regulation, but in many other respects inactive. Germany joined the British camp of neoquarantinist nations, but toed the line of the lancet. The way in which a specific historical accounting, in full national context, is required to explain any particular decision has been examined in detail here. Nonetheless, smoothing over obvious anomalies, it is fair to say that, broadly speaking, different national styles may be discerned. At one extreme, the British consistently adopted tactics that impinged less obviously and immediately on the rights of individuals than did the measures imposed, at the other end of the spectrum, in Germany. British strategies were not less interventionist, but differently so. Applying environmentalist rather than quarantinist measures, they controlled property, in Kearns's lapidary summation, rather than people.[99] Conversely, the Germans tended to take an approach that gave more consideration to the needs of the community than the claims of the individual. France and Sweden fell somewhere between these two outliers.

It will not have escaped even the inattentive reader that such a dichotomy fits snugly with accepted conceptions of political traditions in these nations during the broad sweep of the period in question, liberal and authoritarian for lack of more sophisticated terms. To draw from this that British liberal instincts were reflected in its public health strategies, with a German penchant for control from above similarly mirrored

---

[99] Kearns, "Private Property and Public Health Reform," p. 188. For Britain's control of places rather than persons, see Szreter, *Fertility, Class and Gender in Britain*, p. 187.

would be, however, a thoroughly unremarkable conclusion. This is, after all, largely the level of analysis at which Ackerknecht and those articulating political interpretations of prophylaxis have been content to rest and, as we have seen, such a correspondence is inadequate. Nonetheless, although differences in political systems did not cause prophylactic variations, they are roughly correlated with them.

If so, the question arises whether the broad correspondence of political tradition with prophylactic strategy has not been approached from the wrong direction. Rather than political traditions determining prevention, may it not be that prophylactic imperatives helped shape these traditions in the first place? Traditions cannot, after all, be irreducible first causes in historical explanation, but are themselves learned behavior – reinforced, diverted or undermined by accumulated experience. Although they may incline certain decisions in one direction or another, political traditions too are formed and shaped by other factors that, in this context, are more proximate to first causes. At so basic a level of explanation, the pertinent factors sound obvious, indeed trivial. Much of what historians do, alas, is showing that what one-half of all sociologists know to be obviously true (while disagreeing with the others) was in fact also the case. Britain's liberal approach to public health, indeed its liberalism *tout court*, may in some measure have been the result of its insular placement toward the end of certain formative epidemiological events of the eighteenth and early nineteenth centuries. Prussia's stricter tactics, in contrast, were to a historically interesting degree determined by its position on the epidemiological front lines of the battle against cholera. To the extent that the coformation of prophylactic behavior through such basic determining factors as have been identified here can be demonstrated over a long span of time, then perhaps the roots of political traditions in the interaction of such factors as geo- and topography, economic interest and administrative machinery can be elevated from the realm of a plausible, but amorphous generality to that of a fruitful historical conclusion.

Take the question of geoepidemiology, the interplay of disease and geography. The marriage of geography and history, though apparently foreordained, has not on the whole been a happy one. Geographers at first insisted on a shotgun wedding, tying history in wifely subordination to nature. Not until Lucien Febvre, speaking for historians, took up the issue was some measure of equality and mutually respectful relations between the spouses introduced. The connections between politics and landscape have not been easy to discern. Ellen Semple, disciple of

Ratzel, argued invariant laws of geographical determination. Mountain dwellers, according to one of her most infamous maxims, their horizons bounded from birth by the surrounding peaks, are inherently conservative. Nonsense, was Febvre's return, there is no lockstep by which landscape determines mentality; mountaineers come in all temperaments and inclinations.[100] To make it historical, in other words, he had to argue that in fact geography is not that important, at least not as significant as the determinists, crushing Clio lifeless in their embrace, had sought to make it.[101] Nonetheless, when Braudel took up similar issues, he veered back in the direction of Semple and her ilk once again. He encouraged a generation of historians to think of geography as fundamental to historical evolution, but his conclusion with respect to the political implications of vertiginous topography was that, distant and inaccessible to government control, mountains were the seat of liberty: a conclusion, in other words, that, although it stood Semple on her dogmatic head, agreed with her in seeing a direct and largely invariant connection between landscape and temperament.[102] The sorry uses to which the otherwise interesting field of geopolitics was put at the hands of prewar powermongers and in service to imperialist ambition, then suffering worse at the hands of the Nazis, did not help. Nor did the close ties between geographical speculation and colonialist attitude.[103] Tying together geography and ideology, world and worldview, has not been an easy task. In the case treated here, however, the suggestion that a nation's placement in the flux of an important epidemic, its geoepidemiological positioning, may influence its preventive strategy, from here its views of the respective claims of community and individual and ultimately its political instincts, is a comparatively precise, verifiable and potentially fruitful result. It does not insist on an invariant and particular outcome of geographical or topographical positioning, since geoepidemiology is but one of several causal factors. It does suggest that an element as basic and crucial as epidemiologically relevant location has played an impor-

[100] Ellen Churchill Semple, *Influences of Geographic Environment* (New York, 1911), pp. 600–01; Lucien Febvre, *A Geographical Introduction to History* (New York, 1925), p. 200.

[101] Geographers must not change themselves into historians, Brunhes warned, but must insist on the "essential facts" that were the touchstones of true geography: Jean Brunhes, *Human Geography* (Chicago, 1920), p. 552.

[102] Fernand Braudel, *The Mediterranean and the Mediterranean World in the Age of Philip II* (New York, 1972), v. I, pp. 38–41; Paola Sereno, "A l'origine d'un pays: Le rôle de la montagne dans la géographie politique et culturelle de la Sardaigne à l'époque romaine," in Jean-François Bergier, ed., *Montagnes, fleuves, forêts dans l'histoire: Barrières ou lignes de convergence?* (St. Katharinen, 1989), pp. 46–47.

[103] Robin A. Butlin, *Historical Geography: Through the Gates of Space and Time* (London, 1993), pp. 20–22.

tant role in how the inhabitants of a particular territory have evaluated their position – precarious or protected – in the onslaught of disease and that how they have reacted to their predicament in these respects may have had an influence in broader political terms as well.

As we have seen here, national divergences in prophylactic strategy began in a serious sense with the first cholera epidemics of the 1830s, then continued through the vaccination issue and into the tactics applied to syphilis toward the end of the century. In real measure, similar national variations have extended into our own day concerning AIDS. Britain has been notable for its voluntary approach, following from the policies adopted for syphilis early in the century; Sweden has continued the sanitarily statist strategy it pioneered for VD; France has vacillated between inaction and voluntariness; in Germany, where the lessons of the Nazi regime have in the interim occasioned a major shift in emphasis at the federal level, only the Bavarians have sought to continue the old habits of quarantinist prevention applied to this new epidemic. Strong traditions of prophylactic response were developed during the first cholera epidemics, continuing to evolve during the course of the nineteenth century to the point where, by the time the tactics applied to syphilis were brought to provisional conclusion a hundred years later, such learned behavior had itself become part of the explanation for why these nations reacted so variously. Different traditions of prevention began, developed and matured during the course of the evolution traced here, arising in response to the fundamental factors that have been analyzed, finally to become a cause in their own right.

One of the classic historical fallacies is the abrupt start, the assumption that a development picked up by the scholar only in midstream in fact originates with the attention now devoted to it. Risking such chronological myopia, it seems nonetheless fair to hazard the suggestion that significant national divergence in prophylactic terms can be dated at the earliest from the eighteenth century and the last plague epidemics, then picking up steam in the 1830s with cholera. Against the plague, European nations established varying elaborations of public health machinery. The Mediterranean cities in close connection with the Levant were the first to develop maritime trentine and then quarantine: Ragusa in 1377, Genoa and Venice soon thereafter. The Austrians were protected epidemiologically as a benefit of their defense policies, with the military frontier, erected across the Balkans starting in the sixteenth century, also serving as a sanitary cordon in times of plague. By the late seventeenth century, France was in the forefront of international developments in prevention.

A permanent health board had been established at Marseilles in 1640, with a massive lazaretto a few decades later. In 1720 a plague wall, one hundred kilometers in length, was erected near Avignon. Travelers were quarantined, goods and possessions disinfected and fumigated, cities isolated, bills of health issued. Special measures for burials and on cleanliness in public places were promulgated, domestic animals driven out or killed. Infected houses were marked, patients required to wear distinguishing clothing and sometimes banished, dwellings and possessions purified or destroyed, entire neighborhoods on occasion razed.

Not until the seventeenth century did the more (from the vantage of this disease) removed northern epidemiological hinterlands also institutionalize similar measures.[104] Precautions taken in Britain followed the example set on the continent, with the authorities exhorted to keep cities clean, prevent transmission, identify and isolate the ill. Although tardy compared to Italy and France, by the sixteenth century Britain had become a dutiful prophylactic pupil, making isolation of the infected official policy throughout the kingdom in 1578, establishing pesthouses and appointing plague doctors, identifying and isolating the ill, controlling shipping after the epidemic of 1665. British regulations were, in fact, especially strict in the rigor with which household quarantine was imposed, with sanctions added in 1604 that allowed the whipping or even hanging of those exiting. The Quarantine Act of 1721 empowered the authorities to draw sanitary cordons around infected towns, compelling removal of the infected to plague hospitals and executing resistors.[105]

Up through the eighteenth century, except for the general emphasis on preventive measures that one would expect earlier and more elaborately in those countries most proximate to the sources of this particular contagion, the approach taken in all nations to the plague (and yellow fever) was thus broadly similar.[106] Nor, in terms of domestic preventive ambitions, did these polities diverge as significantly during the late eighteenth and early nineteenth centuries as they would over the following hundred years. The Austrian J. P. Frank elaborated his influential theory of medical police during the 1780s. His vision of an all-encompassing

---

[104] Dinges, "Pest und Staat," pp. 80–85; Ottosson, "Fighting the Plague in 17th- and 18th-Century Sweden," pp. 311–15.

[105] Slack, *Impact of Plague*, pp. 45–47, 201–11, 277–78, 324, 327; George Clark, *A History of the Royal College of Physicians of London* (Oxford, 1966), v. II, p. 524.

[106] J. M. Eager, *The Early History of Quarantine: Origin of Sanitary Measures Directed Against Yellow Fever* (Washington DC, 1903), pp. 23–24.

statutory responsibility for public health has been viewed as emblematic of absolutist ambitions for broad central control and, perhaps predictably, as an adumbration of twentieth-century totalitarianism.[107] Similar plans for medical police were developed by the Enlightenment *philosophes* and set in motion during the revolutionary and Napoleonic period in France.[108] Here, indeed, the inventor of the guillotine headed a committee to plan a fully developed national public health system, mischievously intertwining ambitions for total control and firm statutory power with hopes of social improvement and progress.[109] In Britain, similar proposals had been formulated by William Petty, Nehemiah Grew and John Bellers during the eighteenth century, despite the lack of an absolute monarchy willing to formulate at least ambitions to put such intentions into effect.[110] Bentham drew up plans for strong centralized hygienic intervention while Andrew Duncan and John Roberton introduced German concepts of medical police to Scotland.[111]

While such visions of rational, centrally coordinated, total systems of public health were formulated on paper, their realization left much to be desired even on the continent. Napoleonic public health administration, though centralized, shied away from many of the consequences of practical implementation, and such matters during the Third Republic were entrusted to municipalities. The defeat by the forces of local self-government in Britain of Chadwick's plans for a centralized sanitary system is well known.[112] Even in the German states theoretical reach outstripped practical grasp and Frankian ambitions proved difficult and expensive to implement, remaining largely unaccomplished. Russia, with its highly centralized system, came perhaps closest to the

[107] George Rosen, *From Medical Police to Social Medicine* (New York, 1974), p. 143; Frevert, *Krankheit als politisches Problem*, p. 66; Göckenjan, *Kurieren und Staat machen*, pp. 98–99.

[108] George D. Sussman, "Enlightened Health Reform, Professional Medicine and Traditional Society: The Cantonal Physicians of the Bas-Rhin, 1810–1870," *BHM*, 51 (1977), pp. 566–67; Dora B. Weiner, *The Citizen-Patient in Revolutionary and Imperial Paris* (Baltimore, 1993), p. 22; Susan P. Conner, "The Pox in Eighteenth-Century France," in Linda E. Merians, ed., *The Secret Malady: Venereal Disease in Eighteenth-Century Britain and France* (Lexington, 1996), p. 28; Brockliss and Jones, *Medical World of Early Modern France*, pp. 734–38; L. J. Jordanova, "Policing Public Health in France 1780–1815," in Teizo Ogawa, ed., *Public Health* (Tokyo, 1981), pp. 16–17.

[109] Jean-Charles Sournia, "L'idée de police sanitaire pendant la révolution," *Histoire des sciences médicales*, 22, 3–4 (1988), pp. 271–73; Jean-Charles Sournia, *La médecine révolutionnaire (1789–1799)* (Paris, 1989), pp. 196–97; Matthew Ramsey, "Public Health in France," in Dorothy Porter, *History of Public Health*, pp. 48–49.

[110] Howard Freeman et al., eds., *Handbook of Medical Sociology* (Englewood Cliffs, 1963), p. 21; Richard Harrison Shryock, *The Development of Modern Medicine* (New York, 1947), pp. 77, 98–100.

[111] White, "Medical Police, Politics and Police."

[112] Anthony Brundage, *England's "Prussian Minister": Edwin Chadwick and the Politics of Government Growth, 1832–1854* (University Park, 1988), pp. 9–10.

Enlightenment–absolutist vision of medical police, while the Swedes, prompted by severe population problems of great concern to mercantilist bureaucrats, were among the first to implement such reforms.[113] In the core of major western European states, however, divergences in terms of public health during this period were less pronounced than they were to become over the following century.

The European nations under the glass here were thus largely comparable in their approach to contagious disease up through the end of the seventeenth century. It was then during the plague epidemic of the 1720s, the last major such incident before cholera swept through a century later, that adumbrations appeared of the divergence in prophylactic strategies that was increasingly to separate Britain from the continent. The year after the harsh Quarantine Act of 1721, a reaction sounding Ackerknechtian themes arose and measures were reformed. Isolations and cordons, of the sort imposed at Marseilles, were attacked as perhaps suitable for arbitrary governments, but intolerable to "English liberty." Ships continued to be quarantined, but cordons around infected cities, forced removals of the ill and death penalties for transgression were ended. Opposition to harshly quarantinist measures came from merchants, especially trading partners of Turkey, but much of the charge was mounted by the political opponents of Walpole (trying to establish himself as chief minister) who were happy, now that it was clear that the epidemic in Provence had spared Britain, to use the Quarantine Act tactically to brand their foe as indebted to despotic and foreign precedents.[114]

Once cholera hit a century later, the preventive scissors opened wider, with Germany, France and Sweden more inclined to retain quarantinist measures that were increasingly being abandoned in Britain. Such basic prophylactic postures, separating (as the outliers) the more liberal stance struck by the British from the more draconianly interventionist position of the Germans, with the French and the Swedes tending in one direction or the other for reasons that are best explicable in the specific historical context of any given measure, then continued and were amplified for the other diseases under consideration here. Prophylactic traditions developed gradually under the impress of geographic, economic, administrative and political factors that put these various nations in different positions vis-à-vis the disease in question.

[113] Dorothy Porter, "Introduction," pp. 6–7, 12–13.
[114] Alfred James Henderson, *London and the National Government, 1721–1742* (Durham, NC, 1945), pp. 35–39, 53–54; Slack, *Impact of Plague*, pp. 331–33.

The British increasingly nailed fast their environmentalist and voluntary approach, moving from sanitation through neoquarantinism for cholera, ending compulsory vaccination and abolishing regulation. The Germans, though following the British lead in terms of neoquarantinism, nonetheless implemented measures, above all in the Contagious Disease Law of 1900, that were less considerate of individual rights than their British equivalents. They required vaccination into the latter part of the twentieth century and abolished regulation only to adopt a variant of sanitary statism. The Swedes recognized the advantages of quarantinism for their particular situation, did grudgingly forsake vaccination, but extended a form of strict VD prophylaxis to the entire civilian population. The French, in turn, abandoned whatever environmentalist inclinations they had shared with the British early in the nineteenth century to become increasingly quarantinist, imposed (on paper at least) a strict form of vaccination and then finally and belatedly abolished regulation, but took up the tenets of sanitary statism.

Preventive strategies against contagious disease go to the heart of the social contract, requiring a determination of where the line runs between the interests of the individual and those of the community. The continental approach tended to treat the public weal as preeminent, while the concerns of affected individuals (whether travelers in quarantine, the sequestered infected, vaccinees or prostitutes) ceded priority. The British generally reversed these priorities. It is this close connection between politics and prophylaxis that explains the attractions of an Ackerknechtian approach. Such political interpretations of preventive strategies appear, however, to have inverted matters. It was not British liberalism or German interventionism (to take again the outliers) that, by themselves, determined prophylactic strategies, but the imperatives of geoepidemiology, and the associated factors identified here, that helped shape not only the preventive precautions they encouraged, but indeed the very political traditions of these nations.

Index

Note: In the absence of a bibliography, short titles of books cited more than once in the footnotes are indexed with a reference to a page on which a full citation appears.